A User's Guide to Pa

Other titles in the 'A User's Guide' series:

A User's Guide to Copyright
Seventh Edition—February 2016
9781847666857
£100

A User's Guide to Data Protection
Second Edition—July 2016
9781784512491
£110

A User's Guide to Trademarks and Passing Off
Fourth Edition—May 2015
9781780436852
£110

www.bloomsburyprofessional.com/usersguide

A User's Guide to Patents

Fourth edition

Trevor Cook, Solicitor
Partner, Wilmer Cutler Pickering
Hale and Dorr LLP

Bloomsbury Professional

Bloomsbury Professional Limited, Maxwelton House, 41–43 Boltro Road, Haywards Heath, West Sussex, RH16 1BJ

© Bloomsbury Professional Limited 2015

Bloomsbury Professional, an imprint of Bloomsbury Publishing Plc

A CIP Catalogue record for this book is available from the British Library.

ISBN 978 1 78043 489 6

Typeset by Phoenix Photosetting, Chatham, Kent.
Printed and bound in Great Britain by CPI Group (UK) Ltd, Croydon, CR0 4YY

Contents

Contents

Preface and acknowledgements

This fourth edition of this book is the first in its thirteen-year history to have been published by the same publisher as the previous edition, so my thanks are owed to Bloomsbury Professional for the continuity that they have been able to provide. As with previous new editions the vast amount of rewriting occasioned by new case law is a remarkable reflection of the pace of development and refinement of the case law when the underlying legal framework has remained essentially unchanged.

As before, I am only too well aware that there is so much more that could be written, and that I have chosen to omit much that others might consider should properly be included. My excuse remains that *A User's Guide to Patents* is a book not intended to be a textbook on patent law and practice for experts in the subject, especially as there are many other books which fulfil that role admirably. Instead the aim of the book is to give to 'users' in the most general sense – those who have an interest, for whatever reason in such matters, including I hope those without a legal background, but who want to know more about what is involved in patent law and practice – a sense of the issues that one meets in patents, how they are dealt with, and how they can go about finding out more about them.

I have retained the same structure as in previous editions. Thus the first section of the book, consisting of the first six chapters, deals with the generalities of patent law and practice, and the second section, of three chapters, tries to give an idea of how such law addresses the different needs of those particular sectors of industry which have presented specific challenges to the patent system of one sort or another. The perspective of the book is in the main that of English law, which in large part implements European norms in this area, although where there are especial or instructive differences from the law in some other jurisdictions I have sought to identify these and Chapter 4, on procedural issues, now includes some discussion of the forthcoming Unified Patent Court. I have set out my understanding of the law as at 31 August 2015.

Preface and acknowledgements

A particular feature of the various Appendices is an exhaustive listing and analysis of English decisions on infringement and validity that now goes back nearly 20 years.

As ever, where I have expressed opinions these are mine alone, as are any errors, and I would be grateful if readers would bring them, and the inevitable omissions, to my attention at: trevor.cook@wilmerhale.com.

Trevor Cook
September 2015

Abbreviations

CA	English Court of Appeal (from which appeal lies to the UK Supreme Court, and formerly to the UK House of Lords)
CAFC	Court of Appeals for the Federal Circuit (US appellate court that hears all patent appeals and from which appeal lies to the US Supreme Court)
CJEU	Court of Justice of the EU (formerly European Court of Justice (ECJ))
CPC	Community Patent Convention (*not in force*)
CPR	Civil Procedure Rules (rules that govern civil litigation procedure in England and Wales)
EEA	European Economic Area (consisting of the EU plus Iceland, Liechtenstein and Norway)
EFTA	European Free Trade Area (Iceland, Liechtenstein, Norway and Switzerland)
EPC 73	Original version of European Patent Convention 1973 (*in force before 13 December 2007*)
EPC	Current, amended, version of European Patent Convention (*in force as from 13 December 2007*). An updated jubilee fifteenth edition of the EPC was published in October 2013. The EPC remains the foundation stone of European cooperation in the patent field
EPO	European Patent Office
ETSI	European Telecommunications Standards Institute
EU	European Union (formerly the European Community)
HL	UK House of Lords (replaced by UK Supreme Court)
IPC	International Patent Classification
PA 77	Patents Act 1977 (main UK patent statute)

Abbreviations

PCT	Patent Cooperation Treaty – administered by the WIPO
PLT	Patent Law Treaty (concerned with procedural matters)
SPC	Supplementary Protection Certificate
TRIPs	Trade-Related Aspects of Intellectual Property Rights – administered by the WTO
USPTO	United States Patent and Trade Mark Office
WIPO	World Intellectual Property Organization – administers the PCT
WTO	World Trade Organization – administers TRIPs

Table of statutes

Table of statutes

Table of statutory instruments

Table of European material

Table of European material

Table of European material

Table of international legislation

Table of cases

Table of cases

Table of cases

Table of cases

Table of cases

Table of cases

L

M

Table of cases

Table of cases

Table of cases

Table of cases

Table of cases

Table of cases

Table of cases

Table of cases

Part 1
Patents generally

Chapter 1

Introduction to the patent system

3

Introduction

What are patents?

1.01   Article 27(1) of the Agreement on Trade-Related Aspects of Intellectual Property (TRIPS) to which most countries of the world are party[1] imposes on these countries an obligation by which 'patents shall be available for any inventions, whether products or processes, in all fields of technology, provided that they are new, involve an inventive step (ie are non-obvious) and are capable of industrial application (ie are useful).' It then goes on to set various minimum criteria with which such patent systems must comply, for example, as to term (which must be at least 20 years from application) and as to those activities of third parties against which patents can be asserted.

In this way the term 'patent' can now be said to have a clear and well-accepted meaning. In a more general sense, however, a patent is a right granted by the state, and of specific duration to stop third parties from undertaking within that state, certain defined activities as are nowadays delineated by the 'claims' of the patent. The principle behind the patent system is that of a bargain, in that in exchange for the patentee using it to tell the world how to perform his or her invention (so that the public can freely use it on expiry of the patent term) the state grants the patentee a limited monopoly for a certain period over the activities that are the subject of the claims. However, the state will only grant such a monopoly where the claimed invention is new, manifests some real advance over what has been done before, and is generally of a technical nature. Such was not always the case, which makes a consideration of the history of, and justification for the patent system relevant, especially as the justification for the patent system is currently being challenged in some quarters. In parallel with the development of the patent system other types of right, eg copyright, have developed, and an appreciation of the nature of patents can also be gleaned from a comparison with such other forms of intellectual property (IP).

1   See **Appendix 1** for a list of TRIPS members.

The value of patents, and their limitations

1.02   A patent can, in principle, be used to prevent third parties from making patented articles, or using a patented process, irrespective of whether the third party has copied from the patentee, or has undertaken independent design or research work that is in total ignorance of the patent. A granted patent has a number of statements at the end called the 'claims'; which define the area of the monopoly. If a competitor's product or process falls within the scope of any of these claims then – on the face of it – this is an infringement of the patent, and the competitor's activity can be stopped by an action brought in the courts and damages awarded for past infringements. The nature of the activities that infringe patents, and the remedies for such infringement, are discussed in **Chapter 6**. The procedures adopted in the context of such infringement actions are discussed in **Chapter 4**.

Patents are not, in general, available simply 'on demand'. Instead it can take time and expense to negotiate with the relevant patent office to get one granted: a process called 'prosecution' – that is discussed next in **Chapter 2**. Even after a patent has been granted, there is no guarantee that it will be of any real value. Not only may the invention that it protects prove not to be of any real commercial interest, but even if it is of commercial value; such that others wish to use it, its value may be limited. For example, it may force a competitor to look for an alternative non-infringing process or product, that can indeed put such a competitor to both expense and cause time delay; however, the alternative solution may prove a superior solution. However, if a competitor decides to use the patented invention without the licence of the patentee, and to go ahead and infringe the patent, then the only way to enforce the rights given by the patent is to commence a law suit against the rival. Policing of the patent is the responsibility of the patentee – neither the patent office nor usually the state[1] – does this for the patentee. The procedures involved in so doing are amongst those discussed later in **Chapter 4**, and the natures of the activities that can constitute such infringement, and the defences to them, are discussed in **Chapter 6**. However, such patent litigation, in any country, can be both lengthy and expensive, and is not ultimately assured of success. In large part this is because the possession of a granted patent, duly examined and granted by a patent office, does not guarantee that it is valid, because such examination can only act as a 'coarse sieve' in checking for the validity of the patent. It is always open to third parties, for example, in responding to such litigation, to challenge such validity on one of the grounds discussed in **Chapter 5**, despite the fact that in the course of the prosecution of the application the patent office may well have considered, and been satisfied as to, the very same matters.

Related to their value against the activities of competitors, patents can confer a measure of security which serves to encourage the wider exploitation of the invention that the patent protects. There are many ways in which patents can be so exploited. A large worldwide operation might itself exploit in all territories the inventions protected by its patents. Smaller enterprises, or individuals, might choose to exploit their patents in their home territory but to licence such exploitation to third parties abroad, thereby obtaining royalty income from the licensees. Such considerations, and the issues that arise as to such licences, are discussed in more detail in **Chapter 3**, in relation to transactions in patents.

Patents can also be regarded as assets, although they are rarely valued as such on company balance sheets, unless they have been acquired from a third party, or this is the only way in which the company owning them can show a net asset value. Despite this, the existence of patents or patent applications, even if of dubious, or uncertain scope or validity, is of considerable interest to potential financial backers, and will in general make them more sympathetic to financing a new company, particularly in an area in which patents are perceived as being important, eg biotechnology.

Although an inventor is under no obligation to patent an invention in order to exploit it; and it can sometimes be better to keep the invention as a trade secret, such an inventor risks others independently making the same invention, themselves patenting it, and thereby limiting the scope of the original inventor to use the invention. If this is a concern, and the inventor, though not wanting to patent the invention, wishes to prevent others who independently make the same invention from patenting it, such an inventor should undertake a 'defensive publication' of the invention, so as to destroy the 'novelty' of any subsequent patent application for it.[2] However, the existence of a granted patent does not give its owner any right to use the invention. The owner must still, for example, comply with any regulatory constraints, or the practice of the owner's particular invention may still infringe the patent of another to a different invention: as many different patents can cover a particular article or process in different ways.

1   In some countries (but not the UK or the USA) patent infringement may also be a criminal offence, but proceedings alleging patent infringement will generally still be brought at the behest of the patentee.
2   No especial formality is required for making a 'defensive publication,' but one mechanism that is widely used for so doing is that of publication in Research Disclosure – see http://www.researchdisclosure.com/. The benefit of using this particular route is that the Research Disclosure archive is listed in the shortlist of PCT Minimum Documentation which patent examiners must consult by virtue of the Patent Cooperation Treaty (PCT) (see **Chapter 2** at para 2.19).

'Dramatis personae' involved with patents

1.03   Many different types of people are involved in the patenting process. Patent offices (in the UK – the UK Intellectual Property Office, which was formerly called the UK Patent Office) are run by the state, or by groupings of countries, and are staffed by patent examiners, who generally have a technical background that enables them to understand the particular technology that is the subject of a particular patent application.

The intricacies of the process of drafting a patent application and prosecuting it through to grant (discussed only in general terms in **Chapter 2**) are best left to the specialist professions of patent agents or patent attorneys, who must normally themselves have a technical background. They will also argue matters which arise in the course of such patent prosecution, and which cannot be resolved by negotiation with the examiner, in patent office tribunals. Although in the USA patent attorneys must also qualify as lawyers, the specialist patent attorney professions in the UK (the Chartered Institute of Patent Attorneys (CIPA) whose members are automatically treated as entitled to practice as 'registered patent agents' under the Copyright, Designs and Patents Act 1988) and elsewhere in Western Europe, need not be, and are generally not, also members of the legal profession. This can limit their scope to act in court in, eg patent infringement legal proceedings, although in the UK such restrictions have been considerably eased, and patent attorneys are entitled also to perform, in relation to patent matters, many of the roles that lawyers (namely solicitors and barristers) normally undertake in court. Despite this, major patent litigation in the UK almost invariably also involves the use of barristers and solicitors, who may also in some circumstances, become involved in proceedings before patent office tribunals.

Relationship of patents to other intellectual property rights

Introduction

1.04   Patents are only one type of intellectual property right (IPR) a term given to a number of quite different legal rights, each concerned with the safeguarding of intangibles, such as concepts, technology and goodwill. In the field of technology, the most relevant intellectual property rights are trade secrets (a form of confidential information) and patents. The other major IPRs, viz. copyright and trade marks, do not directly protect concepts and technology as such, although copyright has been pressed into service to protect computer programs, with consequences in terms of its limitations in so doing, discussed in **Chapter 9**, and trade marks can provide a valuable adjunct to the protection of a technology which can survive long after the relevant patents have expired.

One approach to categorizing such protection is by its aim. In the most general sense, what people are seeking to protect by means of IPRs can be categorized into three broad classes – ideas and inventions, information and data, or names and reputations. Of these, patents and trade secrets are best suited to the protection of ideas and inventions, although patents provide little if any protection for mere ideas that cannot readily be put into practice. Alternatively, one can try to categorize IPRs by how and when they come into being, which leads to a broad split between those that protect some creative or innovative activity, such as patents, trade secrets, copyright, and rights in designs, and those that arise out of a trading activity of some type, eg trade marks. However, one classifies them, it should be recognized that different IPRs can be used to protect different things in different, sometimes overlapping, ways, and there is often little straightforward connection between what one is seeking to protect, and the IPR best suited to doing so.

The value of all IPRs lies in the fact that they are effective against all persons and organizations in the particular country in which they subsist. This is in contrast with an agreement, or contract, whereby a person or organization agrees not to do something (eg a restrictive covenant) which is only effective against the person or organization with whom the contract is made.[1] Another benefit is that most IPRs are regarded as 'property' which can be valued and transferred or licensed, rather like a piece of land, thus constituting something identifiable for potential financial backers, and of benefit to purchasers or licensees.

Patents and other IPRs generally only provide a right to stop most others doing something. They do not give their owners a positive right to do something that they could not otherwise do. Intellectual Property Rights are thus in a sense 'negative' rights. However, the extent to which any particular IPR can be used to stop third parties doing certain things will largely depend on whether or not official registration of the IPR is required. If, as with patents, registration is necessary, the law tends to confer a limited monopoly on the owner of the right by which no one else is entitled to exploit the subject matter of the right, not even someone who develops the same thing independently of the registered owner of the right. In other cases, such as copyright, registration is not necessary, and then the only protection is generally against derivation from the material protected by the IPR. In such other cases, establishing the existence of a chain of derivation from the subject matter of the right, to the party accused of infringing the right becomes important. It is, however, irrelevant for establishing patent infringement, and indeed one English judge felt obliged in one case to observe in this context that 'there is no tort of non-infringement'.[2]

Although a variety of other IPRs can act as adjuncts to, or fill the lacunae in, patent protection, two of the most closely associated rights are trade secrets and plant variety rights. Mention should also be made of 'utility models', which exist in many countries (albeit not the UK or the US) and which have many of the features of patents.

1   And can also only be for a rather more limited term than the duration of most IPRs under competition law legislation – eg three years maximum (except in exceptional circumstances) under EU competition law. – See for example, the Commission Notice on restrictions directly related, and necessary to concentrations ((2001/C 188/03) – OJ C 188/5) at para 15.
2   Jacob J in *Beloit v Valmet* [1995] RPC 705 (Patents Court).

Utility models

1.05   Although TRIPS is strict about defining the requirements for a patent, Article 2 of the Patent Cooperation Treaty (PCT) states that for the purposes of the PCT: 'Reference to a "patent" shall be construed as references to patents for inventions, inventor's certificates, utility certificates, utility models, patent or certificates of addition, inventors certificates of addition, and utility certificates of addition'.

This loose definition, for the procedural purposes of the PCT, reflects the fact that many countries of the world, in addition to what might be termed a 'full' patent system complying with the requirements of TRIPS, have a 'cut-down' (sometimes termed 'petty') patent system, providing some of the benefits of the full system, but at generally lower cost, and which also provide a route into (and sometimes a route out of) the full patent system. Such systems, as to which the most generally accepted term seems to be that of 'utility model', provide protection similar to, but generally more limited in one way or another, than that conferred by patents. Typically, they are unexamined (and so generally need to be examined before they can be asserted against a third party[1]) and are available for certain types of invention that may lack the degree of the inventive step necessary for a patent.

In the European Union (EU) utility models are available in most countries – notable exceptions are the UK, Luxembourg and Sweden, although in the UK the speed with which a patent granted via the national route that has also been examined can be secured means that utility models would not fulfil any useful purpose. The extent of protection that utility models confer varies considerably from one national system to another. An invention which qualifies for protection as a utility model in one EU Member State may not qualify, at least not on the same terms, in another. Thus some Member States, eg Belgium and France, require the same inventive step for a utility model as for a patent – while others, eg Greece, Italy and Spain, accept a lesser inventive step. Similarly, novelty is determined in some Member States on a domestic basis, but on an international basis in others. Other differences for example, concern the term of protection[2] or the application procedure.

Late in 1997, the European Commission proposed a Directive on Utility Models[3] that would have obliged those few Member States that lack such a system to introduce one, and would moreover have harmonized certain features of such existing systems throughout the EU. However, work on this proposal was suspended in March 2000, and it was formally withdrawn in September 2005.[4] The European Commission also issued a *Commission Staff Working Paper* in July 2001[5] – inviting comment on the possibility of introducing a Community Utility Model, that would have been a unitary right having effect throughout the EU, but no further action has been taken as a result of this.

1   However, not all patents are necessarily examined before grant, eg in the EU patents prosecuted nationally in Belgium, Italy and the Netherlands – although this must in general be done when one comes to seek to enforce them. In Spain examination of national patents is optional, and in France they are examined only for novelty.
2   This is reflected for example in their name of 'short-term patent' in Ireland.

3   Proposal for a European Parliament and Council Directive Approximating the Legal
    Arrangements for the Protection of Inventions by Utility Model (COM (97) 691)
    ([1998] OJ C 36/98). Amended version presented on 28 June 1999 (COM (1999)
    309).
4   *Communication from the Commission* – outcome of the screening of legislative
    proposals pending before the Legislator (COM (2005) 462).
5   26 July 2001, SEC (2001) 1307.

Trade secrets

1.06   The aim of the patent system in encouraging inventors to
disclose their discoveries to the public can be contrasted with attempting
to protect such inventions by trying to keep them secret, although only
certain types of invention, eg manufacturing processes that cannot be
reverse-engineered, lend themselves to being kept secret. Although the
UK, similarly to many other countries, has for a long time protected
such trade secrets under its own law of confidential information (that
in the UK is entirely judge made, and can be used to prevent the use,
or further dissemination of information which is confidential in nature,
and which has been communicated in circumstances importing an
obligation of confidence) TRIPS, Articles 39(1)–(2) have provided the
first international obligation to protect undisclosed information. TRIPS,
Article 39(3) mandates the protection of certain types of data supplied
to regulatory authorities.[1] The law of trade secrets varies considerably
as between different countries, and is one of the few areas of intellectual
property not yet to have been the subject of any harmonization within
the EU – although this situation is now set to change.[2]

1   See below: para 1.10, fn 27.
2   See Proposal for a Directive of the European Parliament and of the Council on the
    protection of undisclosed know-how and business Information (trade secrets) against
    their unlawful acquisition, use and disclosure (COM (2013) 813).

Plant variety protection

1.07   Although TRIPS, by Article 27(3)(b) permits exclusions from
patentability for 'plants and animals other than microorganisms,
and essentially biological processes for the production of plants and
animals, other than non-biological and microbiological processes', it
does mandate 'the protection of plant varieties either by patents or by
an effective *sui generis* system or by any combination thereof'. The
European Patent Convention (EPC) has such an exclusion, but countries
in Europe comply with this requirement of TRIPS by their adherence to
the most widely recognized system of *sui generis* protection for plant
varieties, namely that established under the International Convention for
the Protection of New Varieties of Plants (the 'UPOV Convention') and
which was most recently revised in 1991. The European Union also has
its own system for granting a unitary plant variety right having effect

throughout the EU under Council Regulation 2100/94 on Community plant variety rights[1] that coexists with national systems such as that established in the UK, and which is now the subject of the Plant Varieties Act 1997. The exclusion from patentability of plant (and animal) varieties in the EPC has caused particular problems in relation to the patenting of transgenic plants and animals, and these are discussed later in **Chapter 8**.

1   [1994] OJ L227/1.

A brief history of the patent system

Early days

1.08   As with other important historical developments, many contend for the honour of having invented the patent system. As always with such controversies, the answer rather depends on what one means by a patent system, as governments have for long granted 'patents', in the sense of monopolies, to specific traders. However, such a grant was often a way in which the government could raise money without directly levying taxes, or to reward friends and supporters. The Republic of Venice is generally recognized as having the earliest systematic system for granting patents for inventions, although Florence has been credited with one of the earliest patent grants, viz. of that to the architect Brunelleschi in 1421 for a new kind of boat which could carry heavy loads. The Venetian Statute 1474 prohibited the manufacture of any 'new and ingenious device' in Venice other than by its originator, so that more would 'apply their genius, discover and build devices of great utility and benefit'.[1]

The establishment of a formal and systematic linkage between the grant of such limited term exclusive rights, and a technical advance of public benefit is also to be found in the English Statute of Monopolies 1623, imposed by Parliament on a reluctant but weak King who, as had his predecessors, used the grant of patents conferring monopolies to raise revenue for the Crown in response to Parliament having previously limited the scope for the Crown to impose taxes of other sorts without its consent. The English law courts had already, in 1601, held such a patent, where it was not for an invention, to be bad in *Darcy v Allan*, a case concerning a monopoly in playing cards and, in which, counsel for those challenging the patent defined the principle as follows:

'Where any man by his own charge and industry or by his wit or invention doth bring any new trade into the Realm, or any engine tending to the furtherance of trade that never was used before; and that, for the good of the Realm; that in such cases the King may grant to him a monopoly patent for some reasonable time until the subjects may learn the same in consideration of the good he doth bring by his invention to the Commonwealth, otherwise not'.

The Statute of Monopolies outlawed the grant of patents subject to the following exception that formed the basis for the UK patent system (and indeed remained in force in the UK[2] – until replaced by principles set out in the EPC by the Patents Act 1977):

'Any letters patent and grants of privilege for the term of 14 years or under hereafter to be made of the sole making or working of any manner of new manufacture within this realm to the true and first inventor and inventors … as also they be not contrary to the law nor injurious to the state…'.

Later in the following century, patents (as well as copyright) were enshrined in the US Constitution, Article 1, s 8, which gave to Congress the power: 'to promote the progress of science and useful arts by securing for limited times to authors and inventors the exclusive right to their respective writings and discoveries'.

Shortly afterwards, the French law of 1791 declared: 'All new discoveries are the property of the author; to assure the inventor the property and temporary enjoyment of his discovery, there shall be delivered to him a patent for five, ten or fifteen years'. Such a fine declaration of principle, almost treating a patent as a natural human right, has a resonance in the next century in the writings of the Victorian engineer, Charles Babbage, inventor of the analytical engine and the difference engine, the earliest (albeit mechanical) form of stored program computer, and much more recently, the inventor James Dyson. Thus, Babbage in 1829 criticized the British patent system as 'vicious and fraudulent legislation, which … deprives the possessor of his natural rights to the fruits of his genius'. James Dyson in 1997, in criticizing the need to pay renewal fees to keep patents in force, wrote that 'an invention is piece of creative art, like a book or a song, and those don't require fees'.[3] However, the subsequent spread of patent laws has been based on a perception of their economic benefit to society, rather than of their being a human right, although as discussed below the economic arguments have been the subject of controversy.

1   Mandich, Giulio, *Venetian Patents (1450–1550) – Journal of the Patent Office Society*, (1948) vol 3, 166 and 176–77.
2   It has survived to this day in some Commonwealth countries, eg Australia, in which the law, in its definition of 'patentable inventions' expressly incorporates reference to the Statute of Monopolies, and to the concept of 'manner of new manufacture' which, with its inherent flexibilities (that it might be suggested allow it to reflect the current needs of commerce somewhat better than more recent formulations of patentability) still governs the law, and where patents have, even in recent times, been held invalid (at least at first instance) on the grounds of being 'generally inconvenient', an objection which originated in the old English cases under the Statute of Monopolies. Australia has on occasion considered abandoning such reference – see *Patentable Subject Matter* (Australian Government Advisory Council on Intellectual Property, December 2010). However, it still remains part of its law.
3   Dyson, James, *Against the Odds* (Orion, 1997).

Modern patent history

1.09   Many developed countries had patent systems by the latter half of the nineteenth century, and to impose some structure on the welter of bilateral agreements that had built up between such countries, the Paris Convention for the Protection of Industrial Property of 1883 established a world intellectual property order. Under this Convention its member countries agreed, broadly stated amongst other things, on certain minimum standards as to most IPRs, but especially as to patents, not to discriminate against each others' nationals in the granting of patents, and, critically, to treat patent applications filed in one contracting country as having been filed on the same date in a second contracting country provided that, within one year of the first filing (the 'priority filing', establishing a 'priority date') the application was filed in that second contracting country (the 'national filing' or 'convention filing').[1] The Paris Convention has been revised on several occasions, the last major revision being at Stockholm in 1967.

On a regional basis, much of the current law in Europe can be traced back to work undertaken under the aegis of the Council of Europe in the 1950s and 1960s, starting with a plan submitted by a French senator in 1949. A Committee of Experts was established who met in Strasbourg in 1955, and based their further work on plans submitted in 1953–54. Their continuing work led to the Convention on the Unification of Certain Points of Substantive Law on Patents for Inventions, signed in Strasbourg in 1963 (and known as the 'Strasbourg Convention'). By then, the European Economic Community (EEC) – as the EU was then termed – was also undertaking work in this field and had, by 1962, produced a draft European Patent Convention for a unitary patent system which would have operated in parallel with existing national patent systems. Work on this was abandoned in 1965, as it failed adequately to address the needs of European countries that were not members of the EEC, but recommenced in 1968, this time along a 'two convention' approach that overcame the problems faced by the 1962 original draft.

In the 'two convention' approach, one convention would have centralized patent examination and grant, and be open to any country that wanted to join. This would result in the grant of what in effect would be a 'bundle of national patents' each having effect in those of the Member States of the convention that had been designated by the applicant. The other convention would address the specific needs of the EEC, and result in a single patent having effect throughout it. Drafting of these two conventions, which were in due course to become the European Patent Convention (EPC) and the Community Patent Convention (CPC) respectively, then proceeded in parallel, basing the substantive law for each system on that established under the Strasbourg Convention 1963. The EPC was signed in 1973 by the governments of 14 European countries, including the UK, which was not at the time a member of the EEC.[2] The EPC came into effect in 1978, and was amended in 2000, that amendment coming into effect on 13 December 2007. The EPC provides the basis for substantive patent law throughout Europe, and the system it also established of prosecuting patents via the European Patent Office (EPO) to secure a bundle of national patents, as discussed further in **Chapter 2**, has now to a significant extent supplanted the prosecution of patent applications in national patent offices in Europe.

The Community Patent Convention had a much more troubled history, and although the first version of this was agreed in 1975 at Luxembourg it never entered into force. Revisions made in 1985 and 1989 fared no better, and in 2000 the European Commission made a further effort to move forward with it, by proposing a Regulation on the Community Patent.[3] This incorporated the principles of the CPC, and adopted much of its language. Although a substantial degree of progress was made with this proposal, it foundered in its original form on questions of language and judicial arrangements. The last 15 years have seen a number of initiatives from the Commission aimed at overcoming these objections.

Its latest initiative, that appears likely at last to succeed, and is likely to come into effect in 2017, would provide the option of a unitary right, to be available once a patent has been granted by the EPO, that would cover most, but not necessarily all, of the EU. The legal basis for this approach lies in the 'enhanced cooperation' mechanism introduced by the Treaty of Lisbon. The system providing for such option of a 'European patent with unitary effect' will come into force, once a separate international treaty as between most EU Member States, the Agreement on a Unified Patent Court, has entered into force. Such European patent with unitary effect will have effect in all countries that have ratified the Agreement when it is granted. The Unified Patent Court established by the Agreement will have jurisdiction not only over European patents with unitary effect, but also (subject to transitional provisions) over traditional European patents with national effect for those EU Member States that have ratified the Agreement.[4]

On a more international basis, the Patent Cooperation Treaty (PCT) 1970 (which did not however come into force until 1978) provided for a common national filing, and for a single search (an 'International Search Report') of the prior art, after which 'International Phase' the application then proceeded in national offices (the 'National Phase'). Optionally, one can request that a common, non-binding, examination report be prepared (an 'International Preliminary Report on Patentability'). The Patent Cooperation Treaty 1970 addresses matters of its own procedure, and neither establishes any standards as to substantive law, nor as to national procedural laws, except insofar as such laws interact with applications proceeding by that route. The Patent Cooperation Treaty

1970 is administered by the World Intellectual Property Organisation (WIPO), and is discussed further in **Chapter 2**.

Although attempts were subsequently made by WIPO to move forward with a Patent Law Treaty, to address matters both of substantive and procedural law internationally, the Patent Law Treaty 2000 concerns only procedural issues, and no further progress has been made. The major international development of the 1990s for patents, and for the substantive law of intellectual property generally – came from another direction entirely – negotiations in the context of a new trade round in the GATT which culminated in the establishment of the World Trade Organisation (WTO) and the Agreement on TRIPS in 1994 which set new, and higher, minimum standards of substantive law for patents (and for other IPRs) and to which WTO members were obliged (subject to certain transitional provisions) to adhere.[5] Moreover, and for the first time, through its dispute resolution mechanism, this provided an international tribunal which could adjudicate as to the meaning of expressions found in international patent, and other intellectual property law treaties, to most of which it mandates adherence. It seems unlikely that higher minimum standards of patentability than those at present mandated by TRIPS will be agreed in further WTO rounds, and such developments are now taking place in the context of bilateral trade negotiations, with the result that recent bilateral or regional trade agreements to which the EU or USA are party have incorporated a chapter which mandates a number of 'TRIPS Plus' norms as minimum standards of substantive law for IPRs, including those as to patents.[6]

1   For the significance of these terms see: **Chapter 2** at paras 2.10–2.18.
2   See Van Empel, Martijn, The *Granting of European Patents* (AW Sijthof-Leyden, 1975).
3   *Proposal for a Council Regulation on the Community patent* (COM (2000) 412 of 1 August 2000, [2000] OJEC C337/E/278) and the *Commission Staff Working Paper: A Community policy for the realisation of the Community patent in the context of a revision of the European Patent Convention (Common Approach)* (SEC (2001) of 7 May 2001) and the *Common Political Approach on the Community Patent* of 3 March 2003 (Council Document 6843/1/03), the Communication from the Commission to the European Parliament and the Council – *Enhancing the Patent System in Europe* (COM (2007) 29 March 2007). A Commission Proposal for a common court system for litigation not only as to unitary Community patents but also national patents granted via the EPO route was held by the Court of Justice of the European Union (CJEU) to be inconsistent with the European Union Treaties in Opinion 1/09 of 8 March 2011. In response to this the Commission supported a litigation regime for the unitary patents that would be granted for most of the EU to be established by a separate international treaty amongst those EU Member States that wish to participate in the unitary patent – see the draft Agreement on a Unified Patent Court, and draft Statute – Revised Presidency text (Document 15539/11 PI 133 COUR 59, 19 October 2011).
4   As to the European Patent with unitary effect see Council Decision of 10 March 2011 authorizing enhanced cooperation in the area of the creation of unitary patent protection [2011] OJEU L76/53, Regulation (EU) No. 1257/2012 of the European Parliament

and of the Council of 17 December 2012 implementing enhanced cooperation in the area of the creation of unitary patent protection [2012] OJEU L361/1 and Council Regulation (EU) No. 1260/2012 of 17 December 2012 implementing enhanced cooperation in the area of the creation of unitary patent protection with regard to the applicable translation arrangements [2012] OJEU L361/89. Italy and Spain objected to the language regime that is proposed for the European Patent with unitary effect, and indeed unsuccessfully brought proceedings before the Court of Justice of the European Union to challenge the Regulation authorizing the use of the enhanced cooperation approach for this purpose – see Joined Cases C-274/11 *Kingdom of Spain v Council of the European Union* and C-295/11 *Italian Republic v Council of the European Union* (CJEU, 16 April 2013). The implementing Regulations were themselves also unsuccessfully challenged in Cases C-146/13 and C-147/13 *Kingdom of Spain v European Parliament and Council of the European Union* (CJEU 5 May 2015). The implementing Regulations cannot however take effect until the Agreement on the Unified Patent Court [2013] OJEU C175/1 has entered into force. This Agreement is a separate international treaty between most EU Member States (excluding at present Croatia, Poland and Spain) that will come into force once ratified by France, Germany and the UK, as well as ten other EU Member States. The litigation arrangements established by the Agreement on the Unified Patent Court are discussed in **Chapter 4** at para 4.31 et seq.

5   This has given rise to particular controversy in the context of 'access to medicines', with waivers agreed to certain TRIPS provisions, as discussed further in **Chapter 7**, para 7.02, fn 1.

6   See for example, Chapter 10 of the EU – Korea Free Trade Agreement ([2011] OJEU L 127 of 14 May 2011) and, as to patents specifically, section B, sub-section F, Article 10.35 of which mandates patent term extension for pharmaceutical and plant protection products.

Rationale for the patent system

1.10   It has become traditional to justify intellectual property, and in particular patents, as some sort of bargain between the state and the individual:[1] 'The overall objectives of intellectual property laws are to protect and reward, and thus provide an incentive to, innovation and creation, while ensuring that the resulting rights and obligations strike a fair balance between the originator, his competitors and the users'.

The economic literature, whilst accepting this 'reward theory', provides an additional justification in terms of the 'contract theory':[2]

'According to the economic literature, there are two main ways patent rights promote the progress of technology, innovation and social welfare.[3] The first reflects the private reward granted for innovation in the form of the inventor's exclusive right to use or sell the patented invention ("reward theory").

The need to introduce some ex ante incentive mechanism follows from the acknowledgement that the ultimate result of the innovation process is the production of new knowledge which rival firms could exploit, at little or no cost, and ultimately reduce the innovator's rewards to a point at which it is no longer worthwhile to conduct innovative activity at all. Exclusive legal rights to inventions in the form of patents help limit this risk by providing adequate incentives to engage in innovative activity.

The "contract theory" describes the second main way in which patents can promote innovation,[4] namely by giving exclusive rights to the inventor in exchange for the disclosure of information about the underlying technical solution. The public availability of patent documents in national and international patent offices facilitates the dissemination of technical information that can then be used by others to develop other novel solutions, creating additional gains for society.'

Even so, it is hard to avoid the impression that much innovation and creation, at least in some sectors, would still take place without patents or other forms of intellectual property, and it can be hard to find objective (or even for that matter subjective) evidence to support the proposition that patents encourage innovation. By way of example it is remarkable that most books on innovation or economic history make little reference to patents, except insofar as they provide a convenient history of innovation in certain sectors or provide some arguably spurious statistical data. For example, Jewkes et al observed, in a comment that could also be fairly made today:[5]

'The Patent Office of every industrial country contains in its files of specifications the story of industrial originality, unique in its completeness, in its detail, in its accessibility. Yet the frustrating and exasperating fact remains that these monumental heaps of documents cannot be reduced to any form which gives a sharp picture. Of course, patent statistics are not without relevance for some purposes. But unfortunately, although every patent presumably involves an invention, not every invention involves a patent. The patent has a legal meaning but, as a unit, its economic meaning ... remains tantalisingly obscure. Unfortunately, the relevance of patent statistics to what is really happening in the field of invention is very obscure. Indeed, were it not for the fact that no other statistical material exists the patent statistics would properly be ruled out of court as useless. But, because there is no other quantitative material, and especially because the patent statistics reveal a marked trend, it is natural enough to suppose that 'some figures are better than no figures.'

Inventors, as might be expected, have strong opinions about the patent system, and of its failings. What is perhaps more surprising is that many of them, at least in history, opposed it. Thus, one of England's greatest engineers, Isambard Kingdom Brunel, considered the patent system of his day to be an irrelevance worthy of abolition and believed innovation to driven by need:[6]

'Some experts in the nineteenth century were even prepared to argue that invention had already become "a social process" in which the contribution of no one individual could be crucial. Engineers such as I K Brunel and Sir William Armstrong made this their chief argument for the abolition of the patent system; all inventions, they claimed, were merely improvements or adaptations of existing knowledge. And, in developing their case, they employed arguments that modern writers have employed about the twentieth century; that most inventions were made simultaneously by several people; that inventions are called for by the existence of a need and that, since so much knowledge was already available, the need would always be met and probably by more than one person.'

However, such scepticism may in part have been attributable to a failing on the part of the patent system which exists to this day:[7]

'The contrast between the relative cheapness of inventing and the heavy costs of perfecting and developing was frequently remarked upon in the nineteenth century.... The views of Sir William Armstrong are typical. He told the Royal Commission in 1865 that "mere conception of primary ideas in invention is not a matter involving much labour, and it is not ... a thing demanding a large reward; it is rather the subsequent labour which a man bestows in perfecting the invention, a thing which the patent laws at present scarcely recognize.'

Even today inventions are often patented long before they can be practically exploited. This is a problem that is not solely limited to high technology or highly regulated areas such as pharmaceuticals which require regulatory approvals before they can be commercialized.[8] By way of a low technology example the simple zip-fastener, the first patents for which were granted in 1893, 'took about 20 years to evolve to its familiar and mature form, and it took about 30 years to become a commercial success'.[9] Today, one needs only to look to discoveries in recent decades such as the particular form of carbon called graphene[10] or in the ceramics exhibiting high temperature superconductivity, neither of which despite their promise have yet to be commercialized, to see the time that it can take to get further inventions based on the original discoveries to market. If and when they do so, the earliest of the patents in those areas of technology will have long expired, and the most important patents will be those relating to some refinement in the product or its use.

Equally, the history of famous inventions where patents have had the opportunity to play a significant role, can show such patents being invalidated, or men ruined by litigating them, on grounds totally unconnected with the technical merit of the invention.[11] Indeed the apparently arbitrary and hence unfair nature of the patent system was sometimes mitigated in Victorian times by special grants to inventors, from Parliament in the UK and by state legislatures in the USA.

Such references in books on innovation or economic history as there are to patents come to few by way of clear conclusions as to the relationship between patents and technological or economic advance. As observed by Mokyr[12] (citing Kaufer[13]): 'Economic theory and contemporary empirical research suggests that the effect of a patent system on the rate of technological progress is ambiguous and differs from industry to industry'.

Similar views were expressed by Jewkes et al:[14]

'Since the Statute of Monopolies, 1624, laid down for "the first and true inventor" rewards in the form of grants of conditional and limited monopolies, industrial societies have shown themselves peculiarly reluctant to experiment with, or to do much serious thinking about, new methods of fostering the exercise of inventive powers and of exploiting these powers for economic progress ... In the nineteenth century there were long public wrangles, which came to very little, about the merits and demerits of the patent system; a few instances of public prizes offered for desirable inventions; some cases of ex gratia payments to inventors whose lot seemed to be exceptionally unfortunate. The emphasis usually was upon ways of increasing the incentive of the individual inventor or of making his position more secure.'

Neither does a historical comparison of countries with and without patent laws assist, for there are so many extraneous factors at work. Even in an era when patent laws were themselves something of a novelty, such comparisons produced no conclusion, as noted by Prager:[15] 'for centuries before the American and French Revolutions of 1787 and 1789, France had a patent law, at least as well developed as the parallel English law, although industrially, England was much more successful than France'.

Indeed, the very relationship between innovation and industrial success seems not to be well understood. For example, an article in 1994 in the *Economist*[16] having opened with the proposition that 'in rich countries, innovation is the principle engine of economic growth' and observing that 'understanding innovation is one of the most important tasks in economics' then comments that 'it has also been one of the most neglected'. Against such a background to try to trace the relationship between patents and innovation would seem optimistic, but recent decades have seen an ever-increasing amount of work done in this area that seeks to do so.

Despite such work one is however left with the impression that we are little further forward in our understanding of these issues than in the 1950s when Penrose and Machlup made the following observations in 1951 and 1958 respectively:[17]

'If national patent laws did not exist, it would be difficult to make a conclusive case for introducing them; but the fact that they do exist shifts the burden of proof and it is equally difficult to make a really conclusive case for abolishing them.

If we did not have a patent system, it would be irresponsible, on the basis of our present knowledge of its economic consequences, to recommend instituting one. But since we have had a patent system for a long time, it would be irresponsible, on the basis of our present knowledge, to recommend abolishing it.'

In 1986, Mansfield[18] reported an empirical investigation as to the extent to which firms made use of the patent system, the differences which existed between firms and industries, and, over time, in their propensity to patent. Of particular interest was his summary over 12 industries, of the proportion of developed or commercially introduced inventions that would not have been developed or commercially introduced if patent protection had not been available. This was a refinement of previous work which had also shown differences between various sectors – that of Taylor and Silberston in 1973,[19] finding that 60 per cent of research and development in pharmaceuticals, 15 per cent of that in chemicals, and 5 per cent of that in mechanical engineering, and a negligible amount of that in electronics, were dependant on patent protection, and Mansfield et al in 1981[20] finding that 90 per cent of pharmaceutical innovation and 20 per cent of those in the chemicals, electronics and machinery sectors would not have been introduced without patents:[21]

PERCENTAGE OF INVENTIONS THAT WOULD NOT HAVE BEEN DEVELOPED OR COMMERCIALLY INTRODUCED WITHOUT PATENT PROTECTION ACROSS 12 INDUSTRIES: 1981–1983

Industry	Not introduced	Not developed
Pharmaceuticals	65	60
Chemicals	30	35
Petroleum	18	25
Machinery	15	17
Fabricated metal products	12	12
Primary metals	8	1
Electrical equipment	4	11
Instruments	1	1
Office equipment	0	0
Motor vehicles	0	0
Rubber	0	0
Textiles	0	0

One of the merits of such work, as opposed to that which simplistically looks at numbers of patents granted to the nationals of a particular country, or in a particular sector, is that it is not prey to the differences in patenting practices between different national cultures and between different industries. It is well known that the same amount of research and development expenditure in the information and communication technologies (ICT) sector results in many more patents in that sector than it would in the pharmaceuticals and biotechnology sectors. Figures of patent applications filed can also favour some countries over others – in the case of German applications because the German employee inventor law to an extent encourages companies to file patent applications which they might not otherwise choose to file, and in Japan because there is a tendency under Japanese practice, particularly in the area of chemistry, to file applications on inventions of narrower scope and with less exemplification than those in Europe or the US. With such approaches, the same degree of 'inventive activity' will tend to give rise to the filing of more patent applications. Likewise, even within a sector, numbers of patents granted can also be deceptive as they may reflect nothing more than differences of patent office practice. Thus, whereas the invention of a new group of pharmaceutical compounds will typically provide the basis for three granted patents in the USA – one with claims to the compounds themselves, one with claims to processes for their manufacture, and one with claims to novel intermediates in such manufacture, the same invention in Europe will typically be the subject of one granted patent, with claims to all three.

Another problem of trying to draw any conclusions on the basis of looking simply at numbers of patents is well demonstrated by the following comment by Jewkes et al:[22]

'When we turn to the information about patents, another enigma presents itself. Over long periods in the [twentieth] century, the annual number of patents issued has not been increasing or, where increasing, has not grown nearly so rapidly as expenditure on research and development or as the employment of R & D workers. For example, the annual number of patents issued in the United States was less in the middle of [the twentieth] century than it had been forty years earlier. And although the number of patents has been growing in recent years, the rate of increase bears no relation to expenditure or employment. So that, for each one thousand of the populations or of scientific and technical workers or for each dollar expended on research and development, the number of patents has been falling sharply.'

The extension of patent protection into new sectors has encouraged more recent research into the economics of patents which seeks to answer questions such as 'how could such industries as software, semiconductors, and computers have been so innovative despite historically weak patent protection?'[23] Against this background there has been commentary that is highly critical of the patent system and of its effect on innovation, at least in some sectors.[24] Other work has moved on from the issues associated with patenting into studying the effect of patent litigation on innovation.[25]

However, even were patents to be demonstrated to be of little, if any, benefit to innovation in some sectors of industry there would still be an economic pressure to keep them in those countries which had them, or to introduce them into those countries which lacked them (even were there to be an option not to do so under TRIPS, which there is not). This is because countries with lower standards of patent protection would, in an increasingly globalized economy, be at a disadvantage from the point of view of local investment, especially in research and development, as against those countries that had higher standards. Thus, it tends to be the less efficient local companies, looking for protection against foreign competition, which have been the most vociferous opponents of increasing local patent protection to accepted international standards.

In the same way as patents may be thought to confer more protection than is needed as an incentive to innovation in some sectors, they may still confer protection that is inadequate to meet the current needs of certain other sectors. Thus recent years have seen the development of other sorts of IPRs created to fill perceived lacunae in the patent laws, some of which creations have been more successful than others – thus in addition to the well-known example of copyright protection for computer programs one can identify entirely new rights such as those in semiconductor chip topography in the electronics sector,[26] and in regulatory data in the pharmaceutical and agrochemical sectors.[27] Such other forms of intellectual property seem to fill in these gaps almost as matter of natural selection, and to show that in intellectual property, as with the laws of physics, nature abhors a vacuum.

1 'Intellectual Property and Innovation' (UK Government White Paper, 1986).
2 *Intellectual property rights intensive industries: contribution to economic performance and employment in the European Union Industry-Level Analysis Report*, September 2013 (A joint project between the European Patent Office and the Office for Harmonization in the Internal Market) – available at – http://ec.europa.eu/internal_market/intellectual-property/docs/joint-report-epo-ohim-final-version_en.pdf.
3 [Footnote [20] in original] See, for example, [Menell, P., Scotchmer, S. (2007), *Intellectual Property Law*, in Polinsky, M.A., Shavell, S. (eds.) *Handbook of Law and Economics*, Elsevier] and [Rockett, K. (2010), *Property rights and invention*, in Hall, B.H., Rosenberg, N. (Eds.) *Handbook of The Economics of Innovation*, Vol. 1, Elsevier.]
4 [Footnote [21] in original] [Rockett, K. (2010), 'Property rights and invention', in Hall, B.H., Rosenberg, N. (Eds.) *Handbook of The Economics of Innovation*, Vol. 1, Elsevier]; [Denicolo & Franzoni (2004), *'The Contract Theory of Patents'*, *International Review of Law and Economics*, 23 (2004) 365–380.]
5 Jewkes, Sawers and Stillerman, *The Sources of Invention* (2nd edn, Macmillan, 1969) 39 and 89.
6 Jewkes et al, *The Sources of Invention*, 39.
7 Jewkes et al, *The Sources of Invention*, 154.
8 But for which there are patent extension regimes to try to compensate for this – see **Chapter 7** at para 7.24.
9 Petrowski, Henry, *On Dating Inventions* (1993) 81 (July–August) American Scientist, 314.
10 See *Graphene – The worldwide patent landscape in 2013* (UK Intellectual Property Office, 2013) – https://www.gov.uk/government/uploads/system/uploads/attachment_data/file/312676/informatics-graphene-2013.pdf – noting that the earliest mention of graphene in a patent is in one with a priority date in 1991, with a slow take-off of patenting related to graphene in the early 2000s followed by "an almost exponential increase" in worldwide patent publications since 2006.
11 Mokyr, Joel, *The Lever of Riches–Technological Creativity and Economic Progress* (Oxford, 1990), 248, recounts how the likes of Arkwright (cotton processing

machinery), Hargreave, (spinning jenny), Dunlop (pneumatic tyres), and Tennant (bleaching liquid) lost patent protection for their most famous inventions. Many of these were because of obscure prior publications which deprived the patents of novelty, but the case of *Arkwright's patent* provides an early example of insufficiency as an attack on validity as discussed in **Chapter 5** at para 5.18 'Insufficiency'. Mokyr also lists other famous inventors ruined by patent litigation – John Kay, (flying shuttle), Charles Goodyear (rubber vulcanisation), Eli Whitney (cotton gin), and the Fourdrinier Brothers (automated papermaking).

12   Mokyr, Joel, *The Lever of Riches,* which was until not that long ago one of the very few books on the history of technology to try to address in any detail (at 247–55) the effect of patent laws on inventive activity. See also Mokyr, Joel, *The Gifts of Athena: Historical Origins of the Knowledge Economy* (Princeton University Press, 2002). Other books to discuss the relationship between patent policy and innovation are Kingston, William, *Innovation* (2nd edn) (The Leonard R Sugerman Press, Washington, 2003), the first edition of which was in 1977, and Guellec, Dominique and van Pottelsberghe, Bruno, *The Economics of the European Patent System: IP Policy for Innovation and Competition* (Oxford University Press, 2007). For a recent article discussing such relationship showing the sophistication of some of the work now being done in this area, and which also contains a useful review of the literature, see Chu, Angus C. et al, *Does Intellectual Monopoly Stimulate or Stifle Innovation?* (*European Economic Review,* (2012) vol 56, 727–46).

13   Kaufer, Erich, *The Economics of the Patent System* (Harwood, 1989).

14   Jewkes et al, *The Sources of Invention,* 78.

15   Prager, Frank D, 'A History of Intellectual Property from 1545 to 1787', [1944] *Journal of the Patent Office Society,* 711.

16   *The Economist,* 18 June 1994. The article also provides a number of examples of the slow and uncertain dissemination of many technologies which have become critical to us and the failure on the part of the various inventors of these technologies to appreciate their true potential.

17   Penrose, Edith, *The Economics of the International Patent System,* (Johns Hopkins Press, 1951) and Machlup, Fritz, *An Economic Review of the Patent System,* (Study No.15 of Committee on Judiciary, Subcommittee on Patents, Trademarks, and Copyrights, 85th Cong., 2d Sess. (Comm. Print 1958)).

18   Mansfield, Edwin, *Patents and Innovation: An Empirical Study* 32(2) Management Science, 173–81. For a later, more detailed, such study, see Cohen, Nelson and Walsh, *Protecting Their Intellectual Assets: Appropriability Conditions and Why US Manufacturing Firms Patent (or Not)* National Bureau for Economic Research – Working Paper No 7552, 2000.

19   Taylor, C T and Silberston, Z A, *The Economic Impact of the Patent System* (Cambridge University Press, 1973).

20   Mansfield, Schwartz and Wagner, 'Imitation Costs and Patents – An Empirical Study', *Economic J,* (1981) vol 91 (Dec), 907–18.

21   Mansfield, Edwin, 'Patents and Innovation: An Empirical Study', 32(2) *Management Science* 173–81 at 175.

22   Jewkes et al, *The Sources of Invention,* 198.

23   Bessen, James and Maskin, Eric, *'Sequential Innovation, Patents and Imitation' Massachusetts Institute of Technology* – Working Paper (Department of Economics, 2000).

24   Jaffe, Adam and Lerner, Josh, *Innovation and Its Discontents: How Our Broken Patent System is Endangering Innovation and Progress, and What To Do About It* (Princeton University Press, 2004) and Bessen, James and Meurer, Michael, *Patent Failure – How Judges, Bureaucrats, and Lawyers Put Innovators at Risk* (Princeton University Press, 2008). The second book argues that the US patent system fails to provide predictable property rights and that in only a few sectors, most notably pharmaceuticals, do the benefits of patents outweigh their related costs.

25 See for example, Lanjouw, Jenny and Schankerman, Mark, *Patent Suits: Do They Distort Research Incentives?*', Centre for Economic Policy Research – Discussion Paper No 2042, 1998.

26 Such protection, first introduced in the 1980s, is now mandated by TRIPS, Articles 35–38 although it is of little or no relevance to integrated circuits today nor has it been for many years. Patents remain as the main protection for integrated circuits.

27 Regulatory data protection, or data exclusivity, as mandated by TRIPS, Article 39(3), has become an increasingly important form of protection in practice in the regulated sectors such as pharmaceuticals and agrochemicals. See Chapters 17–19 of Cook, Trevor, *Pharmaceuticals, Biotechnology and the Law* (LexisNexis, 2009, 2015).

Importance of patents to different sectors of industry

1.11   One clear conclusion that can be drawn from the work discussed above on the importance of patents is that their commercial value can vary considerably from sector to sector. **Chapters 7–9** seek to discuss the factors prevalent in certain industry sectors that inform the approach that tends to be adopted towards patents in those different sectors. Also, as there discussed, certain particular technologies have produced their own peculiar challenges to the patent system, sometimes as a result of attempts to exclude certain areas of activity from patentability, exclusions which are made express in the EPC.

However, and despite such differences, patent law is not generally expressed in terms that are technology specific. However, certain matters are expressly excluded from patentability and in certain sectors there is a specific 'gloss' on general patent law. Examples of the latter now exist in the area of biotechnology, where, as a result of the Biotechnology Directive[1] there are in the European Union special provisions as to 'biotechnological inventions' as to which see **Chapter 8**, and medicinal products and plant protection products, where as a result of the Supplementary Protection Certificate Regulations[2] there are in the European Union specific provisions extending the effective patent term of inventions in such fields, as to which see **Chapter 7**.

Although from the point of view of the patent prosecution practitioner, patent practice tends to be divided into chemical (with subspecialisations in pharmaceuticals and biotechnology), electronics (with subspecialisations in communications and computing) and the rest, which is primarily mechanical, the EPO divides matters in a different way, adopting the nomenclature of the IPC classes. Although the dangers of looking at numbers alone have been already identified, it is still interesting to see the most popular areas of technology in terms of patenting. Thus, in 2013 the top ten technical fields accounted for just over one-half of all applications filed in the EPO.[3]

Technical Field	Rank 2013	Numbers 2013	% Total 2013	% Change 2012–13
Medical technology	1	10,668	7.2	+2
Electric machinery, apparatus, energy	2	10.307	7.0	+4
Digital communication	3	9.101	6.1	−7
Computer technology	4	9,059	6.1	+5
Transport	5	7,244	4.9	+5
Measurement	6	6,640	4.5	+0
Organic fine chemistry	7	6,131	4.1	−7
Engines, pumps, turbines	8	5,411	3.7	−8
Pharmaceuticals	9	5,396	3.6	−14
Biotechnology	10	5,381	3.6	−4
Sub-total		75,338	50.9	−0
Others		72,531	49.1	+0
Total		**147,869**	**100**	**−0**

The second part of the book, **Chapters 7–9**, concentrates on those sectors that, though not necessarily the most important industrially, have produced legal issues that provide especial challenges to the patent system. One sector not specifically discussed in the second part of the book is that of mechanical patents. The patent system has its origins in mechanical patents, and although when licensed they do not tend to secure such high royalties as certain other types of patent they still remain an important area of patent prosecution and of litigation. Such patents can be found in all sectors of industry, including aerospace, automotive, engineering, medical devices and toys. The issues in such patent litigation tend to revolve around claim construction and obviousness. Because the claims of mechanical patents by their nature tend to be drafted using words which have ordinary English meanings, rather than special technical meanings, the issue of construction looms heavy in litigation over such patents, and as explained in **Chapter 6**, much UK and German law on the issue of patent claim construction has been developed in litigation over mechanical patents.

1   Directive of the European Parliament and of the Council 98/44 of 6 July 1998 on the legal protection of biotechnological inventions [1998] OJEU L 213/13.

2   Regulation (EC) No 469/2009 of the European Parliament and of the Council of 6 May 2009 concerning the supplementary protection certificate for medicinal products (codified version) [2009] OJEU L152/1 and Regulation (EC) No 1610/96 of 23 July 1996 concerning the creation of supplementary protection certificate for plant protection products [1996] OJEU L198/30.

3   Source: *Annual Report 2013* European Patent Office. The published statistics overstate the number of patent applications that are in fact prosecuted before the EPO because in addition to direct filings at the EPO in 2013 they include all PCT applications entering the European phase in 2013, even though such process is automatic and not all of such applications are then prosecuted in the EPO.

Sources of the current patent law in the United Kingdom

International and regional sources

1.12   It will be appreciated from the discussion earlier in this chapter that there is a hierarchy of materials that form the patent law in the UK. At the top of the hierarchy are the international treaties, namely the Paris Convention, the PCT and the Agreement on TRIPS, together with the determinations of the Dispute Settlement Body under the latter.[1] Although unlike some other countries, the UK does not have a 'self-executing' constitution, and so such treaties do not automatically form part of its law, it is inconceivable that any UK court would disregard them.

Next are the regional treaties, namely the EPC of 1973 and the various protocols to this, as amended by the Act Revising the Convention on the Grant of European Patents of 2000, which amendments came into force on 13 December 2007.[2] To this can be added, once it enters into force, the Agreement on the Unified Patent Court. The EPO has produced a substantial body of case law and commentary,[3] which though not strictly binding on courts in England & Wales and the rest of the UK is regarded, especially if it originates from the Boards of Appeal and in particular the Enlarged Board of Appeal, as being of considerable authority.[4]

Overlapping to some extent with such regional treaties in Europe, because of their high degree of membership in common, are the European Union measures, which arise out of another set of regional treaties, and in particular the Treaty on the Functioning of the European Union (TFEU). Unlike most other areas of intellectual property, effective European Union involvement in patent law has to date been limited, and so its relevance lies in the direct application of some of the TFEU provisions, and especially Articles 34, 36, 101 and 102,[5] the first two of which deal with free movement of goods and the latter two with competition law respectively.[6] Delegated European Union legislation in the latter area, but in particular Commission Regulation (EU) No 316/2014 on the application of Article 101(3) of the Treaty on the Functioning of the European Union to categories of technology transfer agreements[7] has an impact on contractual arrangements involving patents. In addition, there has been some sector-specific European Union legislation in the patents field, namely, Regulations 469/2009 and 1610/96 concerning the Supplementary Protection Certificates (SPC) for medicinal products and for plant protection products respectively,[8] and Directive 98/44 on the legal protection of biotechnological inventions.[9] The rulings of the Court of Justice of the European Union (CJEU) on the interpretation of these various European Union instruments, and on the TFEU itself, effectively bind UK courts, which must refer issues in such areas to the CJEU for a ruling on interpretation when the approach to be adopted is not *acte claire* (which can include those matters which are entirely clear to the UK court but are not clear on a European Union basis as other courts in it have come to other views). However, because there has been no harmonisation of patent law under European Union measures (other than as to certain aspects of biotechnology patenting), the scope for patent matters to be referred to the CJEU is at present very much less than in other areas of intellectual property, and most such references have concerned SPCs. Mention as a source of the law must also be made of the CPC in its various manifestations over the years[10] – certain aspects of the earliest, 1975, version of which, even though these never came into effect, form the basis for certain provisions of UK law.

1   In the field of patents, and apart from its determinations in relation to certain transitional provisions, the only determination of the Dispute Settlement Body to date has been the adoption of Panel Report WT/DS114/R of 17 March 2000 in 'Canada-Patent Protection of Pharmaceutical Products'.

2   Namely, two years after 13 December 2005, when Greece became the 15th EPC state to deposit its instrument of ratification.

3 Including the Guidelines for Examination in the EPO (which is regularly updated) and Case Law of the Boards of Appeal of the European Patent Office (the latest version of which is the 7th edn, 2013). These are also available on the EPO website at: http://www.epo.org/law-practice.html. These serve also to identify the most authoritative of the numerous decisions emanating from the EPO Boards of Appeal.

4 In *Actavis UK Ltd v Merck Ltd* [2008] EWCA 444 the English Court of Appeal held (at para 107) as a further limited ground on which it was free to depart from its own precedents that it was 'free but not bound to depart from the *ratio decidendi* of its own earlier decision if it is satisfied that the EPO Boards of Appeal have formed a settled view of European Patent law which is inconsistent with that earlier decision' and observed that in such a case it would usually follow such settled view.

5 Previously numbered as Articles 30, 36, 85 and 86 respectively of the Treaty of Rome, which established the European Economic Community, and Articles 28, 30, 81 and 82 respectively of its successor the European Community Treaty, which has been replaced by the TFEU as from 1 December 2009.

6 Discussed further in **Chapter 6** at paras 6.14–6.15.

7 See **Appendix 6**. Discussed further in **Chapter 3** at para 3.13.

8 See **Appendix 6**. Discussed further in **Chapter 7** at paras 7.24ff.

9 See **Appendix 6**. Discussed further in **Chapter 8** at paras 8.02, 8.06, 8.10, 8.12, 8.17 and 8.19.

10 See para 1.09, fn 3 above.

National sources

1.13 National measures are set out for the UK in the Patents Act 1977 ('PA 1977'), as amended, and in the Copyright Designs and Patents Act 1988, Pts V and VI. By PA 1977, s 130(7) certain provisions of the Act are 'so framed as to have, as nearly as practicable, the same effects in the UK as the corresponding provisions of the EPC, the CPC and the PCT in those territories to which those Conventions apply'. The CPC even though it never came into force, is (together with the EPC) an important part of UK law because these two conventions provide the basis for most patent law in Europe, including the national patent laws, which have been largely amended to accord with them. Thus in the UK the PA 1977 was enacted, amongst other things, to enable the UK to ratify the CPC, EPC and PCT. The PA 1977, s 91 requires judicial notice to be taken of the CPC, the EPC and the PCT and decisions in respect of them. In general the EPC forms the basis of UK law as to the validity of patents (whether obtained via the UK route or the EPO route), and the CPC the law as to their infringement. The most recent major amendment to the PA 1977 was that made by the Patents Act 2004. Most of these amendments came into force at the start of 2005, but those which needed to be made to allow the UK to ratify the Act revising the Convention on the Grant of European Patents of 2000 only came into force once the Revising Act itself did so on 13 December 2007.[1]

In addition, in the UK, there is delegated legislation under the Patents Act 1977 (or, where it implements European Union measures, made under the European Communities Act 1972) but which tends to be more procedural in nature, and which includes at the time of writing the Patents Rules 2007[2] and the Patents (Fees) Rules 2007.[3] The UK Intellectual Property Office (UKIPO) also publishes its own *Manual of Patent Practice*.[4]

Finally there is the case law of the UK, but mainly in practice in English courts. Although most of this from the last decade is now available on the Internet,[5] earlier case law, along with the most important subsequent case law is conveniently collected, and accompanied by abstracts in head notes, in various series of law reports specialising in intellectual property. These include the Reports of Patent Cases (RPC), Fleet Street Reports (FSR), and Intellectual Property and Technology Reports (IP&TR). Important patent case law from other jurisdictions is occasionally included in such reports. In addition there are a number of publications that summarize developments in such case law, some of which are listed in **Appendix 4**.

Much such treaty and statutory material, with the exception of those measures that are of a primarily procedural nature[6] is set out in **Appendix 6**.

1   See para 1.12, fn 2 above.
2   SI 2007/3291, as amended most recently by the Patents (Amendment) (No. 2) Rules 2014 (SI 2014/2401).
3   SI 2007/3292, as amended most recently by the Patents and Patents and Trade Marks (Fees) (Amendment) Rules 2010 (SI 2010/33).
4   This is available at: http://www.gov.uk/government/publications/patents-manual-of-patent-practice. It lacks the force of law, but provides a thorough and regularly updated summary of the UKIPO interpretation of each section of the PA 1977 in the light of the most recent case law.
5   British and Irish Legal Information Institute at: http://www.bailii.org.
6   Such procedural material is available, as for the UK, at: http://www.gov.uk/intellectual-property/law-practice, as for the EPO at: http://www.epo.org/law-practice/legal-texts. html and, as for the PCT, from WIPO at: http://www.wipo.int/pct/en/.

Patents and patent applications as sources of information

Introduction

1.14   The ever increasing profile of and emphasis on patents as assets in themselves or as tools to be used to secure competitive advantage can sometimes lead one to forget that a primary aspect of the justification for the patent system is in encouraging the publication of and wider dissemination of new technology.[1] The following discussion provides only a brief introduction to and overview of this aspect of patents.[2]

There are various online databases enabling patents to be searched by a number of fields, such as applicant, inventor, country or subject matter. The EPO's *espacenet* database is one of the largest such databases and is free of charge.[3] There are also various private sector databases, with extra functionality, requiring subscription. Such databases can also be used to track down related patents and patent applications, sharing a common application at some point, which can be useful if one knows of a particular patent or application and wants to know the status of its equivalents in other countries.

Classifications of patents by subject matter exist and assist in searching. On an international basis there is the International Patent Classification[4] that is administered by WIPO and is printed on the front of all patent applications and patents. The EPO and the United States Patent and Trade Mark Office (USPTO), that previously had their own more detailed classification systems now use in addition, the Cooperative Patent Classification.[5] Patent searching by classification in an attempt for example to track down potential prior art against a patent (a prior art search), or to establish whether one can use a certain technology without infringing third party patent rights (a 'right to use' search), is an activity best undertaken by specialist patent searchers, some of who are employed by firms of patent attorneys. However, all such searches have inevitable elements of subjectivity and can never be entirely thorough. Neither can patent searching assist in tracking down potential prior art that lies outside the patent literature. Moreover, such searches can only act as a coarse sieve for potentially relevant material, and once such material has been located it must then be subjected to much more detailed analysis to establish its real relevance.

1   For a fuller discussion see Van Dulken, Stephen, *Introduction to Patents Information* (4th edn, British Library, 2002) and Adams, Stephen, *Information Sources in Patents* (2nd edn, KG Saur, Munich, 2006). For more timely information, the EPO publishes *Patent Information News* quarterly, available at: http://www.epo.org/service-support/publications.html?id=105.
2   See: http://www.espacenet.com.
3   It is commonly said, apparently based on the *Eighth Technology Assessment and Forecast Report*' (USPTO, 1977) that '80% of the information in patents is never published anywhere else'. This observation is discussed in the patinformatics blog http://www.patinformatics.com/blog/revisiting-an-old-standard-80-of-technical-information-is-found-only-in-patents/ that also notes that the Chemical Abstracts Service (CAS) reports that more than 70 per cent of the new substances added to the CAS Registry come from the literature come from patents, but calculates that in fact, for chemistry at least, the actual figure is closer to 95 per cent.
4   http://www.wipo.int/export/sites/ and www/classifications/ipc/en/guide/guide_ipc.pdf.
5   http://www.cooperativepatentclassification.org/index.html.

When does information about patent applications become available?

1.15   Dissemination of new technology by means of patent applications is not immediate. Nowadays patent applications in most countries of the world are published 18 months after the priority date (the date of the first filing of an application for the patent anywhere in the world[1]). Until relatively recently one notable exception to this had been the USA, which did not publish patent applications (unless prosecuted via the PCT route, which provides for publication at the 18-month stage) and instead only published granted patents. The USA now also publishes patent applications, unless the inventor is a small- or medium-sized enterprise and certifies that there will be no corresponding foreign filing. The UK has only published patent applications since the coming into force of the PA 1977 in 1978.

As a result of the 18-month delay in publishing, the picture that patent applications can give of a technology is inevitably slightly out of date. However, in many areas they provide the earliest evidence of technical advances and of areas of research activity. In those areas in which scientific and technical publishing is not the norm, they may provide the only such evidence. However, even in areas where such publishing is common, patent applications tend to provide a fuller, and often earlier, picture of inventive activity than is provided by technical publications. What is more, because a patentee's scope to secure further protection for developments of its invention can be compromised if it publishes in technical journals before the corresponding patent application publishes (even though such publication takes place after the priority date of the patent[2]) patent publications are normally the first published disclosure of a technical advance.

1 See **Chapter 2** at paras 2.10–2.18 for the significance of the priority date.
2 See **Chapter 2** at para 2.21 for an explanation.

Where can one obtain information about patents?

1.16 Copies of patent applications and of granted patents are available in the first instance from the national or regional patent offices that publish them and most are available on the Internet, either direct from such offices or, in most cases and for a wide range of different jurisdictions, via espacenet.[1]

In addition to patents and patent applications themselves, in many jurisdictions the correspondence between the patentee or his agent and the patent office examiner (once the patent application has been published) is also available and can be inspected by any member of the public, or copies provided for a fee. Thus the files for patent applications filed at the EPO, or those filed in the UK since 1 July 1978, can be inspected and copied – indeed most in the EPO are now available online on the EPO website.[2] In the USA, the files of published patents are referred to as 'file wrappers'.[3]

1 worldwide.espacenet.com. A user-friendly source for the major jurisdictions is Google Patents – http://www.google.com/patents.
2 data.epo.org/publication-server/?lg=en.
3 Hence giving rise to the term 'file wrapper estoppel' or 'prosecution history estoppel' – a principle much more important in the USA than in Europe (and not one which has any formal application in the UK), whereby a patentee who tells the patent office one thing cannot then assert anything inconsistent with this when it comes to enforce the patent so secured – see **Chapter 6** at para 6.09, fn 6. Files of more recent US patent applications can be accessed at: portal.uspto.gov/external/portal/pair.

What do patent applications disclose about the technology?

1.17 Patent applications ought to disclose how to practise the claimed technology, and this will typically include a number of worked examples, showing how this is done. Failure to disclose how to practise the claimed technology may itself (if such means is not in itself obvious to the 'skilled person'), give rise to an attack on the patent on the ground of insufficiency.[1] In Europe it is not necessary to disclose in the patent specification the best method of practising the invention although this used to be necessary in the UK before PA 1977. However, in some other countries, and in particular the USA and Australia, there is an obligation to disclose the best method (or 'best mode') of practising the invention and a failure so to do is itself a ground on which a patent's validity can be challenged in Australia.

From the point of view of many scientists, patent specifications can often seem bloated by comparison with a scientific paper reporting on the same work. This is a consequence of patent draughtsmen erring on the side of incorporating too much disclosure rather than risking insufficient disclosure, and of seeking to include material which might provide a basis for narrower and more defendable claims than those originally sought, but ones that are still wider than the specific examples in the patent. Moreover as patent specifications, unlike many scientific papers, are not peer reviewed (at least from the point of scientific disclosure) or published in third-party journals, little premium is placed on being concise, although given the need for translations their length comes at a cost.

1   See **Chapter 5** at para 5.18 'Insufficiency'.

What do patent applications disclose about commercial intentions?

1.18 Patentees will file in areas of most commercial interest to them but they may also file in related areas in which they are also conducting research, either in an attempt to prevent competitors encroaching on their core area of interest rather than because they actually intend to operate in such related areas, or because they envisage scope for licensing such technology. Moreover some companies, attempting to hide the nature of the work that they are undertaking but still seeking to patent it, will assign rights to apparently unrelated companies which in fact they control. Thus the scope for using the patent literature to track research has its limitations, especially as much 'analysis' to assess the respective strength of different companies' portfolios often takes little more than the form of counting patents, rather than assessing their quality in terms of issues such relevance, scope and strength. Moreover, it can be hard to discern trends in a company's patenting unless the review of the relevant portfolio is extensive, and this is put into context alongside the work of such company's competitors.[1]

1   An example of what can be done along such lines, is provided by the articles in the
monthly publication, *Expert Opinion in Therapeutic Patents*, (Informa Healthcare,
ISSN 1354–3776). Indeed the very existence of such a publication illustrates clearly
the importance of patents as a source of information in the pharmaceuticals sector.

*What do patent applications disclose about the likely scope of any patent
eventually obtained?*

1.19   Patent applications as published not only consist of the
disclosure in the specification itself but are accompanied by claims and
a search report prepared by a patent office acting as a search authority.
The claims found in a patent application are however only a very rough
guide to the sort of claims, if any, likely to be granted, and it is the claims
as granted which determine the scope of the monopoly conferred by a
patent. Although in most patent systems matter cannot be added to the
specification itself after filing[1] (by which is meant the disclosure cannot
be supplemented), the claims can and will normally change in the course
of prosecution, either to be broadened (provided there is basis for that in
the specification) or, as is more likely, to be narrowed, either in response
to otherwise invalidating prior art or because the patent office examiner
considers the claims have insufficient support in the specification.

If an assessment of likely claim scope is important (for example if
one is trying to form a view as to whether any patent ultimately granted
on an application might restrict one's freedom to practice in an area of
commercial interest), copies of application files ought also be reviewed
to determine the scope of the claims most recently filed as well as the
attitude, the examiner to these. It should, however, also be recognized
that most patent systems permit, albeit sometimes only in certain
circumstances and up to a certain point of time, further 'divisional
applications' to be 'spun out' of the 'parent case' before the parent case
is granted. These are based on the same disclosure in the specification,
and so can keep open the prospect of securing claims, based on such
disclosure, but differing from those already granted on the parent case,
and often of broader scope than those initially granted. The existence
of such 'divisionals' can usually be determined from the published file.
However, in the days, now gone, when the USA waited until patent grant
to publish, and when its patent term ran from the date of grant rather
than that of filing, there was no way to determine the existence of such
applications until they were granted, giving rise to the term 'submarine
patents'.

1   See **Chapter 5** at para 5.23, 'Added matter'– as to the consequences of so doing.

How are patents and patent applications identified?

1.20   Each patent or patent application is given a separate number
by the national or regional patent office in which such application

proceeds or which is responsible for the grant of such patent. Different national authorities adopt different numbering systems although these tend to have some common features. Thus they tend to have application numbers, which start afresh each year, and publication numbers, which are sequential and do not depend on or reflect the year, but are commonly suffixed with a letter – A, B, etc – to distinguish between various stages in the progress of an application, such as publication and grant. As most patent applications are published this means that the A version will be the publication of the application, and for those systems which publish patent applications only once, the B version will be the granted version. These letters are in turn sometimes suffixed with further numbers – 1, 2, etc – which can either indicate the nature of the publication – for example in the EPO whether an application is published with a search report annexed or without, when the search report is published separately, or whether the granted patent is as first published or after amendment in the course of centralized opposition or limitation at the EPO. An outline of the numbering systems for each of the more common patents and patent applications is set out below.

European patents and patent applications – European patent applications and patents have publication numbers running from 0,000,001 since their first publication back in 1979 and reached 1,000,000 in the latter half of the 1990s; and application numbers of the format XXYYYYYY.Z, where XX is the year, YYYYYY the serial number in the year and Z a check digit.

EXAMPLE:
Title: 'Apparatus for hair removal'
Publication Number (of specification of Granted Patent) – EP 0 101 656 B1
Publication Number (of specification of Application) – EP 0 101 656 A1
Application Number (showing filed in the EPO in 1983) – 83401574.5

PCT applications – Applications proceeding via the PCT route have an application number in the format PCT/QQXXXX/YYYYYY where QQ is the patent office (eg EP or US) in which the application was initially filed, XXXX is the year and YYYYYY the serial number in the year. They are published with a WO XXXX/YYYYYY number (the WO standing for World), where XXXX is the year and YYYYYY the serial number in the year. Because the PCT is only an application route, and the applications which proceed through it become granted patents only on a national or regional basis, no granted patents are published under the PCT and so the issue of how these are numbered does not arise. Many national authorities do not themselves reprint PCT applications but instead give them a publication and application number cross referencing to the PCT application.

UK patents and patent applications – The consequence of the UK adherence to the EPC and the entry into force of PA 1977 in 1978 was that until 1998 there were three different sorts of patents effective in the UK. There were the 'old Act' patents granted under the provisions of the previous law (the Patents Act 1949), the validity of which still fell to be determined under that Act. These were not published as applications but only when grant was imminent. Such patents, which have by now all expired, can be identified from their number, which just reached 1,600,000 before being replaced by the 'new Act' patents granted under the PA 1977, either by the UK Patent Office (now the UK Intellectual Property Office), or by the EPO designating the United Kingdom. Those 'new Act' patents granted by the UK Patent Office and applied for since 1 July 1978 have publication numbers running from 2,000,000 and application numbers of the format XX/YYYYY.Z, where XX is the year, YYYYY the serial number in the year and Z a check digit. Those patents granted by the EPO but designating the UK are numbered in the EPO way, namely starting at zero. They are not reprinted (unless the national version of the EP patent is amended in proceedings in the UK, in which case they are given a C suffix, in the same way as a UK patent which has proceeded via the national route in the UK and been amended after grant), but are distinguished in for example proceedings brought on them, from other designations of the European Patent by the suffix in brackets 'GB' or 'UK'.

US patents – As the USPTO did not publish or make available applications for US patents, these used to be first published as granted patents with no suffix (although in third-party search reports referring to such US patents they are identified with an A suffix, as the first publication). Now that applications are in general published, the USPTO has adopted the system of suffixes used elsewhere, so that granted patents now have the suffix B2. As PCT applications have been able to designate the USA for many years, PCT publication of such applications has however taken place in the usual way. Granted US patents have sequential publication numbers, which are at present in the 8,000,000s. US Applications have sequential publication numbers in each year, in the format US XXXX/YYYYYYY A1 where XXXX is the year and YYYYYYY the serial number in the year.

Chapter 2

Applying for and securing the grant of a patent

Structure

Ownership

Who can apply for and be granted a patent?

2.01   On the face of matters it is the person who makes an invention, or the successor in title who is entitled to apply for a patent in respect of that invention. However, in practice, a patent application must often be filed before one has determined quite who is entitled to do so. Accordingly, under UK law, even though the Patents Act 1977 (PA 1977), s 7 specifies to whom a patent can be granted, it imposes no restriction on who can actually file an application, although if no statement of inventorship, and of right to grant of a patent is made on the request for grant of patent, such a statement must be filed within a certain specified period after filing the application. This provides the applicant with time to sort out issues of title, eg by having a suitable assignment[1] executed in its favour.

By the European Patent Convention (EPC), Article 60 the right to a European patent belongs to the inventor or his or her successor in title. The EPO, however, has no competence in matters of entitlement, and so disputes over the entitlement to a pending European patent application must be brought in national patent offices or courts, in accordance with the provisions of the Protocol on Jurisdiction, and the Recognition of Decisions in Respect of the Right to the Grant of a European Patent[2] whereupon the EPO will generally suspend prosecution of the application in issue until the matter is resolved. After grant, entitlement proceedings must be brought separately for each national designation of the patent in the relevant national patent office or court. As a result there are greater differences between different countries within Europe to the approach taken to such matters than there are to issues of validity or infringement.

In the UK, PA 1977, s 7 says much the same as EPC, Article 60, but in more detail. Thus the inventor is usually the person entitled to obtain a patent, although in, eg the context of collaborations, difficult issues can arise as to who actually *is* the inventor. In the UK the fact-intensive investigations that this type of issue can entail are generally dealt with by the UK Intellectual Property Office (UKIPO)[3] and it can be difficult to extract much by way of general legal principle from its decisions, which have all too often had the flavour of the judgments of Solomon. However, in recent years appeals in such matters to the Patents Court, and subsequently the Court of Appeal have become more common, with the result that such principles are now being articulated in those courts.

The approach to be adopted in the UK in determining the identity of the inventor was stated in *Yeda v Rhone Poulenc Rorer*[4] (the only such case to reach the UK's House of Lords) in the following terms:

'20. The inventor is defined in section 7(3) as "the actual deviser of the invention". The word "actual" denotes a contrast with a deemed or pretended deviser of the invention; it means, as Laddie J said in *University of Southampton's Applications* [2005] RPC 220, 234, the natural person who "came up with the inventive concept". It is not enough that someone contributed to the claims, because they may include non-patentable integers derived from prior art: see *Henry Brothers (Magherafelt) Ltd v Ministry of Defence* [1997] RPC 693, 706; [1999] RPC 442. As Laddie J said in the *University of Southampton* case, the "contribution must be to the formulation of the inventive concept". Deciding upon inventorship will therefore involve assessing the evidence adduced by the parties as to the nature of the inventive concept and who contributed to it. In some cases this may be quite complex because the inventive concept is a relationship of discontinuity between the claimed invention and the prior art. Inventors themselves will often not know exactly where it lies.'

Thus it is unlikely that simply contributing to a pre-characterizing (and thus typically prior art) feature of a claim is enough to make one a co-inventor. One must instead contribute to an inventive concept, although of course, different claims may reflect subtly different inventive concepts, and so one may be a co-inventor as to some claims, and not to others. The UK Intellectual Property Office and courts have a wide discretion in such cases, eg not only to put the patent in both names, but to split a patent as between the parties into two patents each owned by one party, or to leave to ownership with one party, but to impose a licence in favour of the other.[5] The inventive concept may sometimes lie in a combination, as was the case in *Henry Bros (Magherafelt) v The Ministry of Defence*.[6] In *IDA v University of Southampton's Applications*[7] the Court of Appeal (that also warned against: 'being over-elaborate … dividing the information into a myriad of sub-concepts, each of which is considered separately', and noting that by PA 1977, s 14(5)(d) there was supposed to be only one inventive concept in a patent) observed:

'39. In the context of entitlement to a patent a mere, *non-enabling* idea, is probably not enough to give the patent for it to solely [to] the devisor. Those who contribute enough information by way of *necessary* enablement to make the idea patentable would count as "actual devisors", having turned what was "airy-fairy" into that which is practical … . On the other hand those who contribute no more than essentially unnecessary detail cannot on any view count as "actual devisors" ….'

Entitlement proceedings can be brought at any time whilst a patent application is pending, or, in the UK, up to two years post-grant.[8]

Many inventions are made by inventors as part of their normal employment, and whilst their names will appear on the patent specifications as the inventors they will not usually own the patent. The European Patent Convention, Article 60 provides that where the inventor is an employee the issue of entitlement is determined under 'the law of the state in which the employee is mainly employed'. This recognizes the fact that in this area of the law there is considerable variation as between EPC contracting states, especially as to employee inventions.[9]

1   See **Chapter 3** at para 3.05.

2   See **Appendix 6**. The Protocol was considered when determining that the English court was also an appropriate forum in which to determine a trade secrets dispute that underlay a global patent entitlement dispute in *Innovia Films Limited v Frito-Lay North America, Inc.* [2012] EWHC 790 (Pat) (Patents Court) at [52]–[76]. For a similar such case, see *Conductive Inkjet Technology Ltd v Uni-Pixel Displays Inc* [2013] EWHC 2968 (Patents Court).

3   Under the procedures set out in PA 1977, s 8–10 for UK applications; s 12 for foreign and international applications claiming priority from the UK one; and s 37 for granted UK patents. See **Chapter 4** at para 4.03.

4   *Yeda Research and Development Company Limited v Rhone-Poulenc Rorer International Holdings Inc* [2007] UKHL 43 (House of Lords). Apart from reversing the decision of the Court of Appeal in this case, this judgment also had the effect of overruling the decision in *Markem Corp v Zipher Ltd* [2005] EWCA 267; [2005] RPC 31 (Court of Appeal) that had held that a person (A) who claims to be entitled to a patent that has been granted to someone else (B) could not succeed merely by proving that he or she had been the inventor, and B had not, and that instead: '[A] must be able to show that in some way B was not entitled to apply for the patent, either at all or alone' and that: 'A must invoke some other rule of law [such as allegations of breach of contract or a duty of confidence] to establish his entitlement – that which gives him title, wholly or in part, to B's application'. Such an analysis is no longer required. For a comparative review of UK, US, and Australian law in this area see: *Polwood Pty Ltd v Foxworth Pty Ltd* [2008] FCAFC 9, an Australian case.

5   See PA 1977, s 11 as to UK applications, and s 38 as to granted UK patents.

6   *Henry Bros (Magherafelt) Ltd v The Ministry of Defence* [1997] RPC 693 (Patents Court) at p. 706; [1999] RPC 442 (Court of Appeal) at p. 449.

7   *IDA v University of Southampton's Applications* [2004] EWHC 2107 (Patents Court); [2005] RPC 11 (Patents Court); [2006] EWCA Civ 145 (Court of Appeal).

8   PA 1977, s 37(9) also considered in *Yeda Research & Development Co Ltd v Rhone-Poulenc Rorer International Holdings Inc* [2007] UKHL 43 (House of Lords). Different EPO contracting states have different limitation periods as to how long after grant an entitlement proceeding can be brought.

9   As was recognized by the European Commission also, for that subset of EPC contracting states that are EU Member States in the Commission's 'Green Paper on the Community patent and the patent system in Europe' – COM (97) 314 Final, 24 June 1997.

Employee inventions in the UK

2.02 If the inventor is employed and the making of the invention is part of the inventor's employment then, under most legal systems, including that in the UK, the inventor's employers are automatically entitled to the invention, and themselves to apply to patent the invention. However, in the UK employees who are not employed to invent, or who are working well outside of their normal remit, may well own the invention themselves irrespective of any provision in their contracts of employment to the contrary. The Patents Act 1977, s 39(1) provides that:

'(1)   Notwithstanding anything in any rule of law, an invention made by an employee shall, as between him and his employer, be taken to belong to the employer for the purposes of this Act and all other purposes if –

(a)   it was made in the course of the normal duties of the employee or in the course of duties falling outside his normal duties, but specifically assigned to him, and the circumstances in either case were such that an invention might reasonably be expected to result from the carrying out of his duties; or

(b)   the invention was made in the course of the duties of the employee and, at the time of making the invention, because of the nature of his duties and the particular responsibilities arising from the nature of his duties he had a special obligation to further the interests of the employer's undertaking.'

Otherwise, by s 39(2), 'any other invention made by the employee shall, as between him and his employer, be taken for those purposes to belong to the employee'. Thus for those employees who do not have 'a special obligation to further the interests of the employer's undertaking' the invention belongs to the employer where the invention 'was made in the course of the normal duties of the employee or in the course of [specifically assigned] duties falling outside his normal duties' provided that 'an invention might reasonably be expected to result from the carrying out of his duties'. What is meant in this section by the expressions 'in the course of normal duties', 'specifically assigned', and 'reasonably be expected' was reviewed in *LIFFE Administration and Management v Pinkava*[1] where as to the first of these it observed:

'As between the employer and employee the primary source of a duty are the terms of the contract. What is it that he is employed to do must be the key question. That is not the same thing as ... what is his day-to-day work? Take for instance a research chemist working on a cancer cure for the last 10 years. Suppose he came up with a cure for arthritis. He could not seriously contend that he owned the invention because he was day-to-day working on a cancer cure. His duty as a research chemist is clearly wider than his day-to-day work.'

Section 42 prevents employees contracting out of this by providing that any term in an employee's contract of employment 'which diminishes the employees' rights in inventions of any description made by him ... shall be unenforceable against him to the extent that it diminishes his rights ...'. Neither can this restriction be side-stepped by broadly defining the 'normal duties' of the employee as the courts will look to what those duties actually are.

In practice one can distinguish between two extreme types of employee invention. For example, in the first a research scientist who is employed by a pharmaceutical company to invent does so and invents a new pharmaceutical; that invention will normally belong to the company. At the other end of the scale is another employee of the same company, who is employed as a car park attendant. He makes an invention in relation to his hobby that is model railway engines; in that case the invention will belong to the inventor himself. The difficult cases are those in which the invention does have application to the company's business, or where it is not clear whether the employee is employed to make the invention which in fact he did make. For example in *Greater Glasgow Health Board's Application*[2] a Hospital Registrar employed in the Department of Ophthalmology made an invention relating to an optical spacing device for use with an indirect ophthalmoscope, a medical instrument. The Patents Court, reversing the UK Patent Office Hearing Officer, held that the invention belonged to the employee, as his job was treating patients, not devising new ways of diagnosing and treating them, and although the invention might be a useful accessory to the work that he was employed to do, it was not really part of it.

By the Patents Act 1977, s 40 if the patent is later determined to be of 'outstanding benefit' such employee may claim compensation calculated in accordance with s 41. Although many such applications will have been made and many compromised on subsequently agreed terms, as yet the only award made by a court under this provision has been in *Kelly v GE Healthcare*[3] in which the benefit of the patents in issue was held to be of the order of £50 million, of which fair shares for the two employees who had applied were 3 per cent of this, being £1 million and £500,000 respectively.

Section 40 was amended by the Patents Act 2004 in an attempt to make it easier for an employee to mount such claims.[4] The effect of the patent in issue being assigned for nominal consideration within a group of companies on the approach adopted under s 41 was considered in *Unilever v Shanks*.[5] It was held that the 'benefit derived or expected to be derived' by the employer from the assignment of a patent was deemed to be the amount the employer could reasonably be expected to have derived if the assignee had not been connected, knowing what benefit was in fact obtained from the patent by the actual assignee. However, when it came subsequently to determining whether or not the 'invention or the patent for it (or the combination of both)' in this case was indeed of outstanding benefit to the employer, it was held on the facts that a total net benefit of £17 million over the life of the patent in issue was not, even though this represented a much higher rate of return for the employer than it made on its normal manufacturing activities.[6] Many other countries in Europe also have special, and again very different, systems for the remuneration of employee inventors.[7]

The position of employees should be contrasted with the role of directors and external consultants. Thus a director is not necessarily an employee of his or her company, although the director may as a matter of English law hold any patent, or other IPR that ensues on trust for the company, and so can be subsequently compelled by court action to assign legal title in it to the company.

Although most countries also treat the inventor and the inventor's successors in title as the applicants, there can be fine, but sometimes critical, differences in the detailed approach associated with this in practice. Moreover, although the UK treats the grant of a patent to someone not entitled to it, as a ground of invalidity, such a challenge can only be mounted by a person claiming to have the better title.[8] Moreover, in the UK and most other systems there is no particular adverse consequence of wrongly identifying the inventors. In contrast in the USA, questions not only of entitlement, but also those of inventorship can be critical to the validity of patents. Thus a US patent can be held invalid for no other reason than that the inventors have been wrongly identified. Given the complexity of much research these days, and the increasingly large number of people involved in much of it, such correct identification may not be straightforward.

1   *LIFFE Administration and Management v Pinkava* [2006] EWHC 595 (Pat) (Patents Court); [2007] EWCA Civ 217 (Court of Appeal).
2   *Greater Glasgow Health Board's Application* [1996] RPC 207 (Patents Court).
3   *Kelly v GE Healthcare* [2009] EWHC 181 (Pat) (Patents Court).
4   The amendment, in force as from 1 January 2005, seeks to make it clear that the benefit that can be taken into account includes the benefit flowing from the patented invention, rather than from the patent itself.
5   *Unilever v Shanks* [2010] EWCA Civ 1283 (Court of Appeal).
6   *Unilever v Shanks* [2014] EWHC 1647 (Pat) (Patents Court).
7   See Sanna Wolk, *'Remuneration of Employee Inventors – Is There a Common European Ground? A Comparison of National Laws on Compensation of Inventors in Germany, France, Spain, Sweden and the United Kingdom'* (*IIC*, 2011, vol. 42, 272–98). Indeed it has been suggested that the law in Germany has the effect of encouraging companies to file patent applications when they would not otherwise have done so, but which are subsequently abandoned.
8   See **Chapter 5** at para 5.03 for the position in the UK, where such a challenge can only be made by someone with a better title. Such person is, however, likely to seek in the alternative the transfer of the patent to it.

Commissioned work

2.03   A problem area as to ownership can arise as to work done not by employees, but commissioned from independent contractors. As, in the absence of express contractual provision to the contrary, the legal title to the invention will vest in the contractor, it is important, before such work is done, to agree in a written contract that all intellectual property rights (IPRs) in any invention arising out of that work will vest in the party paying for the work to be done. Otherwise, the person funding the work may have to claim that it is beneficially entitled to the invention, and establishing this may require legal proceedings. Indeed, depending, absent contractual provision, on the relationship between the parties, and how much was paid, the commissioning party may have no more than a licence to practice the invention.

It will be apparent from this that when a company involves outside personnel in activities which lead to patentable inventions, the position is very much less clear unless the legal relationship between the company and the outside body has been set up from the outset in such a way that the company owns the rights to the patents and other intellectual property that emerge. If there are specific rules that exist as to the types of contracts which have to be concluded with third-party helpers, this will reduce (but not necessarily avoid) problems arising at a later stage. The position becomes even more difficult when one engages outside/external bodies who themselves, and in turn, involve personnel who may, or may not be, employees.

When contracting with a company which may itself contract out some of the work it is not in general sufficient simply to provide for all patents, and other IPRs arising out of it, to be assigned to the company commissioning the research. Instead the commissioned party should also be under an obligation to so conduct its business as to be able to deliver those rights. Particular regard should be paid to the following:

— **Outside consultants** – who are not employed by the contractor, and who may have been brought in on a temporary basis because of their particular expertise.
— **Academic staff** – where the contractor is a university or research institution, professors and/or students will undertake work on the project. Professors and other academic staff, although employed by such an institution, are arguably employed to teach, and not to invent. Students (unless perhaps, research students) are not employed.
— **Staff of foreign contractors** – the rules under English law as to ownership would not necessarily apply, and the status of their inventions would require review on a case-by-case basis in accordance with local legal advice.

A warranty that all such people working on the project must have entered into a written contract with their respective employer will provide some protection. However, a warranty provides only a right to claim damages for its breach, and does not of itself deliver the patents, and other IPRs. Clearly, it is not practical to review the contractual arrangements of each, and every individual researcher of the contractor, but the agreement could entitle the commissioning party to inspect all such contracts if it so requires and, in practice, the arrangements for any specific key personnel should be reviewed prior to entering into the agreement.

Where work is commissioned from academic institutions, or work with such institutions is funded by third parties, particular problems of ownership can arise. It is necessary to look rather carefully at who in fact employs the academic, and the scope of this employment, in order to discover whether the institution where he or she works will have any rights to the work which it can then pass on to others. Academics may also take their work with them when moving between academic institutions. In addition, work which has been wholly or partly funded by third parties (including research councils or charitable trusts) requires special consideration as the terms of the funding may be such that certain rights accrue to these funding bodies, and not to the employing institution, or to the researchers themselves. In each case, it is better to examine these matters before the work is commenced so that the question of rights has been decided and dealt with before they arise. Otherwise if it is left until an apparently useful invention has been made it can be much more difficult, particularly as the various contenders by that stage have had their appetites whetted for some, if not all, of the rights.

One case in which the ownership of inventions made in academic institutions was in dispute was that of *Kakkar v Szelke*.[1] Quoting from the head note of the case report:

'The plaintiffs were three members of a research unit at a school of medicine in England together with the trustees of an English charitable trust which supported the work of the unit. The defendants were three members of a research unit at another medical school in England, together with two Swedish companies. The two research units had collaborated in a joint research project on anticoagulant materials. The fourth defendant, one of the Swedish companies, had provided funds for the project pursuant to separate agreements with the two medical schools. It was an express term of each of the agreements that any patentable invention made during the course of the project should belong to the fourth defendant.

The first three defendants filed an application for a United Kingdom patent and then European and international applications claiming priority from it. Subsequently they assigned their interest in the invention and in the patent applications to the fifth defendant on the fourth defendant's direction. The assignment was notified to the European Patent Office whereupon the fifth defendant was recorded as applicant for the European patents.

The plaintiffs alleged that the invention, the subject of the applications, was made jointly by the first three plaintiffs and the first three defendants and that the work had been partly funded by the charitable trust. Accordingly the plaintiffs claimed a declaration that the fifth defendant held the applications on constructive trust for itself and for the charitable trust in shares to be determined by the court.'

In this particular case there were agreements already in place, so these do not provide a panacea against these problems, but without any agreements the situation might have been even more confused and uncertain. It emphasizes the desirability of those proposing to fund such research undertaking 'due diligence' investigations as to any potentially conflicting rights of third parties.

Competition law considerations may also need to be taken account of in any contract for commissioned development. Such arrangements commonly incorporate certain restrictions on the contractor, in particular that products designed, and produced under the contract should only be supplied to the party commissioning the work. This in effect restricts the right of the contractor to select its own customers, and ostensibly is a classic restriction caught by TFEU, Article 101(1).[2] In their Notice on Subcontracting[3] the European Commission have stated that they do not regard most such arrangements as falling within what is now Article 101(1). This is because it recognizes the legitimate desire of the commissioning party to protect the economic value of its own technology, and because the subcontractor is not viewed as an independent supplier in the marketplace. Where the subcontractor's potential for independently exploiting its own developments is restricted by the arrangement, the position is more difficult. The Notice expresses the Commission's view that Article 101 does not apply to clauses restricting use of the technology to the purposes of the particular agreement, and preventing the technology and the goods, services or work resulting from its use being made available, or supplied to third parties. Certain ancillary restrictions giving reasonable protection to the technology are also regarded as not giving grounds for objection. However, in contrast, the Commission Notice setting out *Guidelines on Vertical Restraints*[4] makes it clear that vertical agreements (of which a subcontract is one) under which the buyer (the commissioner) provides only specifications to the supplier (the subcontractor) which describe the goods or services to be supplied are potentially subject to Article 101(1) and so should be analysed by reference to the Vertical Agreements Block Exemption Regulation[5] (always assuming that the parties are not able to take advantage of the Commission Notice on *Agreements of Minor Importance*).[6] Compliance in such respects with EU competition law confers a 'parallel exemption' in the UK under its national competition law, namely the Competition Act 1998.

1   *Kakkar v Szelke* [1989] FSR 225 (Ch. D).
2   Formerly EC, Article 81, and before that EEC, Article 85. This is discussed in more detail, in the context of licensing, in **Chapter 3** at para 3.11.
3   OJ C1, 1979, 2, that despite its age still remains in force – see Commission Guidelines: *Application of Article 101 of the Treaty on the Functioning of the European Union to Technology Transfer Agreements* – OJ C89 2014, 3, para 64.
4   *Guidelines on Vertical Restraints* – OJ C130 2010, 1, paras 22 and 34.
5   Commission Regulation (EU) No. 330/2010 of 20 April 2010 on the application of Article 101(3) of the Treaty … to categories of vertical agreements and concerted practices – OJEC L102 2010, 1.
6   Commission Notice – *Agreements of Minor Importance which do not appreciably restrict competition under Article 101(1) of the Treaty on the Functioning of the*

European Union – OJ C291 2014, 1. See also Commission Notice – *Guidance on restrictions of competition 'by object' for the purpose of defining which agreements may benefit from the De Minimis Notice* (C(2014) 4136 final; SWD(2014) 198 final, 25 June 2014).

Co-ownership

2.04   Where two or more parties are jointly entitled to apply for a patent (eg where there are joint employee inventors who are not both employed by the same company, and there is no agreement between the companies vesting all rights in one or other of them), local laws (in the UK PA 1977, s 36) govern their relationship as between the co-owners, in the absence of a contractual agreement between them to the contrary.

It is sometimes suggested that the mechanism of joint ownership provides the natural answer to providing the institution (or other contractor in a similar position) with a share of the success in the invention. It is also often suggested as a natural way of protecting the fruits of collaborative research. Co-ownership of patents, and other IPRs is, however, in practice rarely desirable, except perhaps in very special circumstances. This is in part because in the UK, PA 1977, s 36 only allows the co-owners to exploit the jointly held rights themselves or by their agents, and will not permit them to assign or to grant licences without the consent of the other party. Moreover inherent differences between the nature of different IPRs, and between their differing rules as to co-ownership produce different consequences for the same relationship for different IPRs, and the rules for the same IPR can vary considerably as between different countries of the world.[1]

The practical effect of PA 1977, s 36 as between co-owners who do not both manufacture, is to restrict the scope for the more active co-owner commercially to exploit the invention, and entirely frustrate it for the co-owner which lacks the capacity to exploit the invention itself.[2] It can also favour a manufacturer who co-owns a patent with an individual or an academic institution as against such co-owner. Thus it is best to have a contract which regulates the rights and obligations of the parties, either as co-owners, or in the context of an assignment to one of the parties with a sole licence back to the other (which latter course allows each party itself to exploit, even if it does not without further provision, permit sublicensing).

1   Thus the US has rules that provide greater freedom to co-owners to (eg to license without the consent of the other) rather than in the UK, and in general, than in the rest of Europe as well.
2   See *Hughes v Paxman* [2005] EWHC 2240 (Pat) (Patents Court); [2006] EWCA Civ 818 (Court of Appeal) for an example of the problems which can arise when co-owners fall out, and in which it was confirmed that the UK Patent Office had jurisdiction under PA 1977, s 37 to waive the requirements of s 36; so as to allow one co-owner to license the patent without the consent of the other co-owner.

The structure of a patent specification and its claims

Introduction

2.05   Patents and published patent applications, in whatever country they are being prosecuted, or by whatever patent office they are granted, adopt a standard structure. Thus the first page is a summary of various types of information about the patent or application, such as the various dates associated with its prosecution through the patent office, the names of the inventors and of the applicant, the classification of the technical area in which the invention is concerned, an abstract of the invention, and a list of prior art references. This is then followed by the patent specification itself, which describes the technical problem addressed by the invention, the prior art, and how to perform the invention, and sets out examples of how the invention is to be performed, and experimental results that demonstrate the qualities of the invention. It may include diagrams and drawings. The specification may be a couple of pages long in the case of some simple inventions, but can run to many pages, particularly in the fields of computing, and biotechnology.

Finally there are the claims, which are numbered and which define the precise scope of the monopoly conferred by the patent. The claims of a granted patent are all-important in patent law; as it is they which define the boundaries of the monopoly that the applicant is claiming.[1] The drafting of the claims is, therefore, a matter of considerable skill, since what the draftsman hopes to capture in the claims is the essence of what has been invented, but not too narrowly expressed. Once the patent has been granted any third party can look at the claims, and in theory at least, understand what is the 'forbidden territory' of this patent. This may, however, be difficult, because often the draftsman will often have used relatively vague, and deliberately non-limiting terms (eg 'means' for doing things) which may or may not cover a proposed activity, depending upon how wide an ambit one gives to such language. Whilst the draftsman is usually trying to obtain claims of as wide a scope as possible, the examiner on the other hand will normally try to ensure that the scope of the claims is commensurate with what the examiner thinks the inventor has invented, and that usually means narrowing the claims in the course of prosecution.

The separation between the claims and the description was a natural development in patent law, arising from the conflict between the need to delimit the monopoly, and the duty to disclose to the public detailed information on how to carry out the invention. This background was explained by the House of Lords in *British United Shoe Machinery v A Fussell & Sons*:[2]

> 'Correct delimitation was of the greatest possible importance to the inventor, because if his patent covered something which was old the patent was wholly

bad. At the same time there was the danger of confining himself to a mere outline which gave delimitation but did not tell the public the best way within those limits of performing his invention. The one duty required him to state his invention in its most general form and the other duty required him to state it in its best and therefore in a very special form. Out of that has arisen the practice, which originally was perfectly optional, of having a separate part of the specification primarily designed for delimitation.'

The function of the claims was also discussed in the subsequent decision of the House of Lords in *Electric Musical Industries v Lissen*:[3]

'The function of the claims is to define clearly and with precision the monopoly claimed, so that others may know the exact boundaries of the area within which they will be trespassers. Their primary object is to limit, and not to extend, the monopoly. What is not claimed is disclaimed. The claims must undoubtedly be read as part of the entire document, and not as a separate document. Nevertheless, the forbidden field must be found in the language of the claims, and not elsewhere.'

The expression 'what is not claimed is disclaimed' that was coined in this judgment has become widely used as a summary of the function of claims.

1   In contrast the claims of a published application may be broadened in prosecution, assuming there is basis for this in the specification, although in such a case a third party may have a limited defence to a claim for back damages as from the date of publication to the date of grant – if it operates outside the scope of the claims in the published application – but within the claims as granted.

2   *British United Shoe Machinery Co Ltd v A Fussell & Sons Ltd* [1908] 25 RPC 631 (House of Lords) at p 650.

3   *Electric Musical Industries v Lissen Limited* [1939] 56 RPC 23 (House of Lords).

Cascading claims

2.06   Those who draft patents rarely content themselves with one claim. More usually they employ a whole series of claims, each of which is numbered, and many of which refer back to one or more earlier claims. Claims that do not refer back to other claims are 'independent' claims, and, taken together, will describe the broadest scope of protection conferred by a patent. Additional limiting features introduced in the 'dependent' claims (the ones which refer back to an independent claim) make these claims narrower in scope, and they confer only a subset of the protection conferred by the independent claim on which they depend.

One reason for having dependent claims, rather than a set of independent claims, is the risk of securing the grant of a patent with claims that prove to be too wide in the light of prior art which subsequently comes to light post-grant. It is advantageous to have narrower claims present so that if the broadest claim has to be abandoned the patentee may nevertheless be able to rely on a narrower claim which does not suffer from the same defect. This practice also reflects the fact that once a patent has been granted, the form of the specification can to a large extent be regarded as being set in stone. Although there is scope in some countries, such as the UK, to amend patent claims post-grant, and patents granted by the EPO can now be made the subject of a centralized 'limitation' procedure, the scope for amending can vary from country to country, and if it can be done it is often easier to delete than to rewrite, because for example in the UK and the rest of Europe, the claims cannot be widened but only narrowed.[1] Thus, if the patentee can show that one of the dependent claims is valid, and has been infringed, then this will still leave it with an enforceable right despite any problems with the broader claims.

One consequence of such an approach is that if a particular limiting feature is found only in a dependent claim, this suggests that such feature should not be implied into the claim on which it depends. Hence, such an additional narrower feature reflects back on the scope of the independent claim on which it is dependent in that it supports the broader construction in that respect of such independent claim.

1   See below at para 2.28.

Categories of claim

2.07   Claims may either be to a physical article (eg a product or an apparatus) or to a physical activity (eg a method, a process, or a use). However, the Enlarged Board of Appeal of the EPO in its decision in G 2/88 *Friction Reducing Additive/MOBIL OIL III*[1] observed:

'Within the above two basic types of claims various sub-classes are possible (eg a compound, a composition, a machine; or a manufacturing method, a process of producing a compound, a method of testing, etc). Furthermore, claims including both features relating to physical activities and features relating to physical entities are also possible. There are no rigid lines of demarcation between the various possible forms of claim.'

Within one patent or application one may find both types of claims, and thus a patent for a novel chemical entity will typically have both product claims to the compound itself (and perhaps to compositions containing it) and also process claims to its synthesis (and perhaps to the preparation of compositions containing it, and to its use). Although a type of use is an example of a process, there are also product claims limited by use, namely the application to which the product is intended to be put, and sometimes termed 'use bound claims'. Claims to new uses have given rise to a considerable body of law in relation to patents for chemicals and pharmaceuticals, attributable to certain restrictions on the nature of the use claims that can be secured for the latter.[2] Sometimes a product can only be defined by the process by which it is made, resulting in a type of product claim termed a 'product by process' claim.[3]

1   Decision G 2/88, *Friction Reducing Additive/MOBIL OIL III* OJEPO [1990] at p. 93.

2   Such claims are discussed further in **Chapter 7** at paras 7.07–7.12.
3   Such claims give rise to certain problems that are discussed further in **Chapter 7** at para 7.04, as it is only in practice in the context of patents to chemical entities, in which such claims arise.

Two part claims

2.08 In patent practice in Europe, claims often contain a sort of preamble which 'sets the scene' for the invention, and then the word 'characterized' followed by other features. The intention behind this form of claim, also known as the 'two part claim' is that all the features up to the word 'characterized' are old, and that everything that follows the word is what differentiates the claimed invention from it. This sort of claim can be confusing to the layperson, who may concentrate on the wording before the word 'characterized' (which the layperson may find alarmingly all-encompassing) and then lose interest by the time the critical, limiting, wording is reached. However, for some inventions this approach to claim drafting is helpful in facilitating comparison of the inventive features claimed with the closest prior art, and enabling one to identify the novel feature of the invention. The European Patent Office regards a claim in two-part form as being appropriate if there exists a clearly defined state of the art from which the claimed subject matter distinguishes itself, by further technical features.

   The English courts now take the view that the two-part claim form should be so well-known that it should be taken account of in construing patent claims, which must be done from the perspective of the notionally (technically) skilled person or team.[1]

1   See *Virgin v Premium* [2009] EWCA 1062 at paras 18–22, also discussed in **Chapter 6** at para 6.09.

Example of a patent specification and claims

2.09   One of the more notorious patent specifications within Europe, because of the conflicting decisions given in the late 1980s on whether or not a particular article infringed its various national designations, was EP 0 101 656 B, innocuously entitled 'Apparatus for hair removal'. Such national designations were the subject of litigation brought by Improver Corporation against Remington in numerous European countries.[1]

   The embodiment set out in the patent, and that which was commercialized, used a rapidly rotating bent helical spring, the convex side of which was pressed against the skin where the hairs were to be removed. As the spring rotated, that part of the spring at the convex side opened up, and then as it then continued its rotation around to the concave side closed on any hairs which had slid into the space between the windings of the spring, and then pulled such hairs round to the concave side, thereby plucking them out. The alleged infringement, instead of having a bent helical spring, had a bent rubber rod with slits in it. The issue was the simply stated, although evidently not at all simply determined, one of whether the alleged infringement fell within claim 1 of the patent, which was a product claim to:

> '1 An electricity powered depilatory device comprising: a hand held portable housing (2): motor means (4,4') disposed in said housing; and a *helical spring* (24) comprising a plurality of adjacent *windings* arranged to be driven by said motor means in rotational sliding motion relative to skin bearing hair to be removed, said *helical spring* (24) including an arcuate hair engaging portion arranged to define a convex side whereat the *windings* are spread apart and a concave side corresponding thereto whereat the windings are pressed together, the rotational motion of the *helical spring* (24) producing continuous motion of the *windings* from a spread apart orientation at the convex side to a pressed together orientation on the concave side and for the engagement and plucking of hair from the skin of the subject, whereby the surface velocities of the *windings* relative to the skin greatly exceed the surface velocity of the housing relative thereto.' [*emphasis added*]

Had the draftsperson used more general terms than 'helical spring' and 'windings' (although this is more easily said than done) the defendants would not have had much of a non-infringement argument.[2] As it was, the defendants prevailed in some countries, such as England, in their assertion that even though their device might be mechanically equivalent to the claimed device it had a rubber rod with slits in it, and not a helical spring (or for that matter windings), and so did not fall with the words of the claim.

The specification had a further 19 product claims, all of which were dependent on claim 1, and which narrowed down the scope of the invention further in one respect or another. By way of example, claim 1 could cover a helical spring which is bent through any angle, whereas claim 2 limited this is to a helical spring bent through an angle of at least 90 degrees:

> '2 An electricity powered depilatory device according to claim 1 and further characterised in that said helical spring (24) arcuate hair engaging portion extends along an arc subtending more than 90 degrees whereby the surface velocities of windings of the helical spring (24) simultaneously include components extending in mutually perpendicular directions, for significantly enhanced hair removal efficiency.'

Another potential distinction over any prior art is the use of stiffening wire inside the helical spring as expressed in claim 16:

> '16 The depilatory device according to any of the preceding claims further characterised in that it further comprises a stiffening wire (28) inside said spring, said wire being substantially stationery relative to said spring.'

Thus, claim 16 can be said to be dependent on all preceding claims, including claim 1 and claim 2. The specification in this case had no process claims, nor any claims expressed in two-part form.

1   See **Chapter 6** at paras 6.05–6.07 for the English case in which these issues arose.
2   Although they may, had they done so, have run into patentability objections based on attacks of lack of novelty or inventive step (unlikely, as matters turned out) or possibly, as to sufficiency or enablement.

Applying for a patent in one country

Priority date

2.10   One of the most important concepts in patent law, such that it dominates any assessment of patentability, and yet is a consequence of a purely procedural act undertaken in the ordinary course of applying for a patent, is that of the priority date. This is the date when the first application for the patent is filed, and is in most cases the date on which the novelty, and inventive step of the invention are judged.

One consequence is that the inventor can file the patent application on one day, and the day after announce the invention in the scientific press, or sell an actual embodiment of the invention without fear of thereby invalidating any patent granted pursuant to such application, although there are very good reasons not to do so, as this limits the inventor's options in terms of withdrawing the application or developing the invention further.[1] The resulting patent is not invalidated by such action because when the patent office comes to search the 'prior art', to establish the 'state of the art', the cut-off date for such search will be the priority date, and nothing that is published afterwards, whether by the applicant or by a third party, will be of any relevance, always assuming that any resulting patent can indeed rely on that priority date. The priority date is of especial importance for seeking patent protection in more than one country, as discussed below.[2]

Different countries adopt different approaches to what prior art can be taken account of in assessing the state of the art as at the priority date. The EPC (and thus the UK and other EPC contracting states) takes the broadest approach, and thus by EPC, Article 54(2):

> 'The state of the art shall be held to comprise everything made available to the public by means of a written or oral description, by use, or in any other way, before the date of filing of the European patent application.'

This approach, which does not distinguish between material available locally, and that available abroad as at the priority date, when applied to the issue of novelty is known as 'absolute novelty'. However, some countries' laws still only regard material that is accessible locally as at the priority date as relevant (as indeed did the UK until 1978). Such an approach when applied to novelty is known as 'relative novelty'. Moreover some legal systems distinguish for such purposes between material made available by way of publication or by way of use.

The priority date can also be critical, where the same invention has been made independently at much the same time by different teams, in determining which of the patent applications resulting from such work proceeds to grant.[3]

1   See below at para 2.21, in relation to: 'When to publish or otherwise disclose material the subject of a patent application'.
2   See below at para 2.17, in relation to: 'Applying for a patent internationally'.
3   See below at para 2.23, in relation to: 'Prior unpublished applications'.

Procedural outline

2.11   In order to obtain a patent it is necessary to file an application for a patent with a patent office, and normally with the patent office of the country in which the inventor is resident. The grant of a patent is not automatic, and in practice an inventor is not entitled to a patent as of right. Thus to talk of 'registering a patent' grossly oversimplifies what is involved. Different patent offices have different procedures for granting patents. Some national offices in Europe (but not in the UK) involve mere registration once formal requirements have been met,[1] but most offices, eg the German and UK ones, the EPO and the USPTO, involve substantive examination in order to establish that the claims sought appear to be novel and inventive, and that they are not unduly broad.

The practice in the UKIPO, outlined below, is a fairly typical patent prosecution procedure.[2] Many of the stages are associated with the payment of a fee, but this is subject to wide variation as between different systems. A number of the stages listed may take place together, or can take place earlier. An application can be withdrawn at any time, and failure, for example, to request search or preliminary examination, or to file claims, abstracts and details of chain of title, all within the specified periods laid down by local laws, will itself constitute a deemed withdrawal.

The process of prosecuting a patent through to grant can take up to several years if, as in the UK or with the EPO the patent office examines them, although with the UK and some other national patent offices, particularly if special procedures are followed at the outset, a granted and examined patent can be obtained in as little as a year or so.

Time	Applicant	Patent Office	Third Parties	Comment
Date of first filing	Files an initial application ('priority filing') at the patent office.			This establishes the 'priority date'. This application may lack claims and an abstract, and consist of little more than a full description of the invention, and of how to carry it out, and details of the applicant.
Within one year of first filing	Files claims and abstract, if not already filed, and may re-file application, containing more detail than priority filing, or perhaps combining two or more closely related priority filings less than one-year-old.			Not all countries provide for refiling the application in this way to provide 'internal priority'.
Within one year of first filing	Files application (convention filing) also in, or designating, other countries in which protection is sought. Such application may contain more detail than priority filing, or perhaps combine two or more closely related priority filings less than one-year-old, and be accompanied by claims, and an abstract.			The term 'convention filing' reflects the fact that being able to rely for a priority date on an application filed within the previous year in another convention country is mandated by the Paris Convention – see para 2.17 ff, 'Applying for a patent internationally'.

– (cont)

Time	Applicant	Patent Office	Third Parties	Comment
Within 1 year of first filing (as to request)	Requests patent office to carry out 'preliminary examination' and search.	Undertakes 'preliminary examination' as to formalities, undertakes search, and prepares search report.		In the UK 'preliminary examination' is only as to formalities and not to substantive matters of patentability. The applicant can decide in the light of the search report whether or not to withdraw the application. The report also forms the basis for subsequent examination.
18 months after first filing		Publishes the application with abstract and claims, normally together with the search report.		It is not known at this stage that any patent will be granted. Such early publication effectively precludes any option of withdrawing an application and filing a new application, and so a decision as to whether to withdraw should be taken before publication. Publication may confer a right to claim damages from a third party which uses the claimed invention as from that date.
Specific period after publication (as to request)	Requests substantive examination.	Undertakes substantive examination and reports on this.		This starts the process of examination, which concludes with grant, withdrawal, or rejection.

– (cont)

Time	Applicant	Patent Office	Third Parties	Comment
Post-publication			May send the examiner observations on the application, and draw examiner's attention to 'prior art'; of which the examiner was previously unaware.	The patent office examiner is not obliged to take account of such observations, or to give reasons as to why he does not do so.
Post-publication	May notify patent office of further potential 'prior art' coming to its attention.	Considers any new citations which arise during prosecution.		Many patent offices require notification of all prior art cited in the prosecution of equivalent patent applications, and it is prudent to do so in any event.
Post-publication	Responses to initial examination report, and to subsequent office actions.	Considers applicants' responses, and responds to these.		This can be an iterative process of negotiation between the applicant and the patent office examiner. Responses normally take the form of filing proposed amended claims to take account of some of the examiner's objections but trying to meet other objections by argument, until a set of allowable claims are submitted.
Post-publication		Refuses patent (appealable) or grants patent, and publishes it in form as granted.		Any divisional applications (allowing further claims to be sought on the basis of the material in the original specification) must be filed before grant of the application from which they are divided.

The time taken and expense involved in obtaining a patent provides no guarantee that the granted patent is valid. With any patent office one can regard the examination as being in the nature of a 'coarse sieve', and the validity (or invalidity) of a patent to be a matter that is ultimately only determinable by the courts. Whilst the courts are usually the ultimate arbiters of validity, some systems provide for challenges (termed 'oppositions' in the EPO) before the appropriate patent office, sometimes within a certain period post-grant, in which third parties may seek the revocation, or amendment of the patent on the grounds that it ought not to have been granted, or not in its then existing form. Such proceedings have in general the benefit of being cheaper than court proceedings. In the UK however, there is no special opposition procedure, but a third party can always mount a revocation action against a granted patent either with the UKIPO or in the courts. Patent invalidity can arise in a number of ways, as discussed in **Chapter 5**. One reason for a patent that has been granted after search and examination to be found invalid is that no search of the prior art can ever be perfect, and there may be other more relevant items of prior art which the examiner did not find. Moreover, the examiner normally only looks at published material, and the examiner has no knowledge of commercial operations which could amount to a prior use of the invention. Finally, no examiner will have the resources, or the motivation of a commercial competitor whose freedom of action is constrained by a granted patent.

The draftsperson of the patent claims may have slavishly followed the precise embodiments worked out by the inventor. If the draftsperson has done this (as inventors who try to do their own patent drafting often do) then the claims might well have a better chance of being granted in that form, and of being valid; but would be unlikely to be of any use against competitors who, by making small modifications from what is claimed, could say that they were operating outside their scope, even though they might still benefit from the principles behind the invention. On the other hand, if the claims as granted have been drafted very broadly, and in very general terms, it should be easier to catch would-be potential infringers. However, at the same time, such claims run a greater risk of covering something which is old or obvious, or something which the specification does not enable, and as to which accordingly the claim is insufficient.[3] Any of these failings will render the broader claims invalid, which is why in practice one also has narrower claims dependent on the broader ones to provide for such an eventuality. The extent to which such invalidity in the claims of a granted patent taints the whole patent, and the possibilities of amending the claims of a granted patent to save what is good rather than just abandoning the broader ones, can vary from country to country, although within Europe a measure of harmonization is being achieved through countries aligning their previously widely differing practices with the EPO limitation procedure.[4]

1   See **Chapter 1** at para 1.05, fn 1.
2   Such details are set out in the Patents Rules 2007, SI 2007/3291, as amended.
3   See the discussion in **Chapter 5** at paras 5.18–5.21, 'Insufficiency'.
4   See below at para 2.28 in relation to 'Amendment and limitation'.

Drafting the application

2.12   An application for a patent must include a detailed 'specification' describing the invention and explaining to a person 'skilled in the art' how it can be carried out. It is also accompanied by the claims (although these can usually be filed within a specified time later) the purpose of which is to define the scope of the monopoly sought. The drafting of such a specification, and the claims to it is a specialized task calling both for technical, and legal ability if one is to secure claims of useful scope. If one is prepared to spend money on obtaining patents, then it is pointless to compromise their validity at the outset by failing to recognize this. This means that it is essential to use a skilled professional, eg in the UK a chartered patent attorney, or (and elsewhere in Europe) a member of the European Patent Institute (EPI) to do the drafting and filing, and then to carry out the subsequent prosecution of the patent application to grant, which is also a skilled and specialized process.

Most patent systems have specific requirements that must be met by an application and the claims. Under the EPC (and thus in the UK and other EPC contracting states) in addition to complying with matters of substantive patent law (eg the invention being novel and inventive) the application must, by EPC, Article 82, relate to one invention only, or to a group of inventions so linked as to form a single inventive concept, and by EPC, Article 83, disclose the invention in a manner sufficiently clear, and complete for it to be carried out by a person skilled in the art. EPC, Article 84 requires that the claims, defining the matter for which protection is sought, shall be clear and concise, and supported by the description.

In order that the patent specification serve its purpose in advancing knowledge by being usable by third parties after the patent has expired, the application must contain sufficient detail to allow another skilled worker in the technology in question to be able to repeat the invention. The precise burden of this obligation varies somewhat from country to country, and in some countries, such as Australia, the inventor must also disclose in the specification the best method that the inventor has devised for carrying out the invention in practice. This reflects the view that it is unfair for an inventor to obtain a monopoly by only giving to the public second-best methods of using the invention. This also used to be the law in the UK until 1978 but since then, and as elsewhere in Europe, this higher standard is no longer a requirement. The specification must simply be sufficient to enable the practice of the invention across the whole scope of the claims. The obligation to disclose the 'best mode' has also long been a part of US law, although under recent changes to the law a failure so to do would appear no longer to compromise a patent's validity.

Filing the application

2.13   The inventor will normally first file the patent application for the invention in the inventor's home country. In some countries the inventor is indeed obliged (unless the inventor obtains an exemption from the local patent office in the form of an 'export licence') first to file in the inventor's home country. This allows sensitive inventions (eg those relating to defence) to be dealt with specially. In the UK this obligation used to apply to all inventions, but the Patents Act 2004 limited the obligation to applications containing certain types of information only, such as that relating to military technology.[1] For such inventions failure first to file in the UK, or to obtain an export licence is an offence. In the US such failure can adversely affect the validity of US patents based on material so exported.

Most patent systems require as a minimum a request for grant on the appropriate form, the identification of the applicant (ie a full name and address), a description of the invention (ie the specification), and the requisite fee. Without these the application cannot be given a filing date, which is vital for establishing 'priority', the critical date at which 'the state of the art' for the purposes of determining novelty and inventive step, is assessed.

In most countries an application can be based on an earlier application made either in the same country, or abroad within the previous year, and priority claimed from such earlier application, as discussed below in relation to 'Applying for a Patent Internationally'. This is mandated by the Paris Convention for an application claiming priority from one filed in a different country. In contrast, claiming priority from an application filed earlier within the same country, a facility known as 'internal priority', is not mandated by the Paris Convention. However the UK, and most countries provide for internal priority, allowing one to re-file an application within a year in the same national patent office in which one first filed it, and still preserve one's original filing date as a priority date for the new filing. Otherwise, assuming that a patent subsists for a fixed-term of 20 years from filing, the patent in the country in which the priority filing had been made would expire up to a year before the equivalent patents based on Convention filings in other countries. Such internal priority also allows additional refinements developed during the priority year to be incorporated, not only in Convention filings abroad, but also in the initial, priority filing.

Most patent systems provide for applications filed to be checked for compliance with formal requirements. In the UK this stage, called 'preliminary examination', to contrast it with 'substantive examination', may be deferred for up to a year if the priority filing is in the UK, and so such a request will typically accompany a convention filing, or a filing claiming internal priority.

1   In the UK, PA 1977, s 22 makes provision for prohibiting, or restricting publication, or communication of patent applications containing information would be prejudicial to national security, or the safety of the public, and PA 1977, s 23 restricts the scope for UK residents to first to file applications outside the UK, contravention of which is a criminal offence. The Patents Act 2004 limited the scope of s 23 to applications containing information of the type set out in s 23(1A), namely those containing information which relates to military technology, or would be prejudicial to national security, or the safety of the general UK public.

Search report

2.14   The next stage in patent prosecution is for the relevant patent office to have a search undertaken to find out what has been published before the priority date of the application in the same technical area, and which might deprive the application of novelty or inventive step. This material forms part of the 'prior art', and allows the patent office to make an assessment of the 'state of the art' as at the priority date. Some patent offices, including the UKIPO, offer a fast track service, which allows one to have search results before the one-year period from filing has expired.

Search reports list the prior art references of interest, sometimes identifying the specific passage of interest, and the claims of the application to which they are relevant. Most use a code to explain the significance of the reference. The EPC and PCT systems use the following codes:

Code	Meaning	Comment
X	Particularly relevant if taken alone.	A reference which the applicant is likely to have to overcome on examination, either by argument, claim amendment, or both.
Y	Particularly relevant if combined with another document of the same category.	A reference which the applicant is likely to have to overcome on examination, either by argument, claim amendment, or both.
A	Technological background.	Rarely a problem for the applicant on examination.
0	Non-written disclosure.	Rare in search reports.
P	Intermediate document.	A document published after the priority date, but before the application date, and thus only relevant to the extent that the claim to priority can be challenged.[1]

Code	Meaning	Comment
T	Theory or principle underlying the invention.	Rare, and rarely a problem for the applicant on examination.
E	Earlier patent document, but published on, or after, the filing date.	The relevance of such a document depends on the approach that the local legal system takes to prior unpublished applications. (See below at para 2.23.)
D	Document cited in the application.	
L	Document cited for other reasons.	

Although in, for example, the EPO, the UK and other EPC contracting states it does not matter where in the world such prior proposals were published, or what they were published in, for convenience the search is usually limited to earlier granted patents, and to published patent applications in the major countries because patents are classified in a convenient way which facilitates such search. As a consequence, the quality of search can vary as between different technical areas, and can be poorer in a field in which there is less potential prior art in the patent literature, a particular problem in the early days of the patenting of computer-implemented inventions of the sort discussed later in **Chapter 9**.

1   See **Chapter 5** at para 5.05, 'Priority date'.

Publication of the application

2.15   The UK (since 1978) as with most systems, publishes patent applications (unless they have already been withdrawn by then) around 18 months after the first claimed priority date, so that even though the patent has not yet been granted (and indeed may never be granted) the public is aware of what is in the pipeline.[1]

The rights conferred by a patent application after it has been published, but before it has been granted, vary from country to country. In the UK, PA 1977, s 69 permits damages to be awarded for infringement in respect of this period, provided that the alleged infringement of the application would also be an infringement of the granted patent.

In the US there was until relatively recently no early publication, and a patent application remained secret until it was granted, at which point the resultant patent was published. As prosecution can sometimes be slow, or divisional applications (known in the USA as 'continuations' or 'continuations in part') spun-out without this being evident from the already granted patents, this practice caused some uncertainty as to what actually was in the US pipeline. The long submerged patent applications which suddenly surfaced were known as 'submarines', and could cause havoc in an industry. Since the US adhered to the PCT system (discussed below) this has been less of a problem as many applications originating in the US were prosecuted internationally via the PCT route, and PCT applications are published in the same way as most other applications. More recent changes in the law in the US have meant that even national US applications are published at the 18-month stage, unless the applicant certifies that it is below a certain size, and will not be prosecuting equivalent applications outside the US.

1   Some patent offices, eg the UKIPO, will also allow early publication, as part of the process for accelerating patent examination and grant.

Examination of the application

2.16   Once the patent office examiner has the search results, the examiner then considers whether any of the claims of the application currently on file should be allowed, having regard to the state of the art, and the contribution made by the application to the art. In the UK, to distinguish this from 'preliminary examination', this is called 'substantive examination'. Naturally the examiner should have some knowledge of the general technical area in which the examiner is examining: so as to be able to make a reasonably informed assessment. Increasingly in most patent offices the examiner who prepares the search report is also responsible for preparing the first, and subsequent examination reports.

Frequently the precise form of the claims is the subject of much argument between the applicant, or the agents, and the examiner. Thus the examination phase is in effect an iterative one, in which the examiner may object to the application on a number of grounds, and the applicant or agent responds by arguing against that view in correspondence, and/ or amending the claims, and sometimes inserting into the specification a discussion of the prior art, in response to such objections. The examiner may then repeat the objections – if the examiner does not feel that previous objections have been overcome – or perhaps raise further ones, sometimes occasioned by the very amendments suggested in response to the examiner's earlier objections.

However, in practice, it is possible in the vast majority of cases to secure the allowance of claims of some scope, albeit perhaps so narrow as to be commercially valueless, at the end of this process, and the application with such claims can then proceed through to grant as a patent, whereupon it is published in such form. However, some patent applications are refused in their entirety, although any such refusal will be subject to appeal – in the UK to a UKIPO 'hearing officer' (a senior UKIPO official) and thence to the Patents Court.

Sometimes the applicant may be keen to secure allowance of at least some claims at an early stage, but does not wish finally to abandon claims which the examiner is minded to reject, but where arguing as to this will delay grant. Alternatively the applicant may wish in effect to split the application into more than one patent, perhaps because one aspect of it protects the commercially important embodiment which it is exploiting, and the value of the rest of it lies more in its potential use against competitors. If however, the two are in the same granted patent, the downside risk associated with an adverse finding on validity, when trying to enforce this, is more serious for the patentee than if they were split into two different patents. In such cases it may be possible for a certain period, depending on the practice of the patent office in issue, to divide out another application from the application proceeding to grant, and then to continue separately the prosecution of such 'divisional application'.[1]

Whilst the draftsperson is usually intent on trying to secure claims of as broad a scope as possible, the examiner will, on the other hand, normally try to ensure that the scope of the claims is commensurate with what the examiner thinks the inventor has invented,[2] and that will usually mean in practice narrowing the claims, even though there is no legal restriction under the system in the UK, the EPO, or in other EPC contracting states on totally recasting the claims, or even broadening them, during the prosecution process, and before grant. Such narrowing must be done on the basis of material already in the specification as of its filing date, and of which there should be plenty in a well-drafted specification, and some of which will, for example, will already have found its way into dependent claims. Where, however, such narrowing is done in a way for which there is no basis in the specification, such claims may, despite conferring narrower protection, involve the impermissible addition of matter in the sense that the application in consequence discloses to the skilled person something which differs from what it did originally. This can be a dangerous trap for an applicant as, if claims are granted on such a basis, they cannot then be corrected post-grant by excising the additional, but narrowing, matter, as this would, paradoxically, have the effect of extending the protection conferred by such claims, which is itself a ground of invalidity where such extension takes place post-grant.[3]

A somewhat different philosophy applies to the prosecution of patent applications in the US before the US Patent and Trade Mark Office (USPTO) to that applying to prosecution in the patent offices of other countries. In the EPO, the UK, and indeed most countries, once the patent is granted the way in which the prosecution was carried out is largely irrelevant, except perhaps when the patentee seeks to do something in enforcing the patent which is inconsistent with the representations which were made to the patent office during prosecution.[4] In the US, the applicant must be scrupulously careful in dealings with the examiner: the applicant must not to mislead the examiner, or fail to draw to the examiner's attention to potentially relevant prior art, of which the applicant is aware. This 'duty of candour' is taken seriously, and failure to discharge it can constitute what is known as a 'fraud on the patent office': that can have the effect of making unenforceable a patent that appears perfectly sound on its face.

1   The reason for filing divisional applications was summarized as follows in *Napp Pharmaceutical Holding Ltd v ratiopharm GmbH* [2009] EWCA Civ 252 –
     '[11] Sometimes [a patent office] will say to a patentee that he has got too much in a single application (an application can only cover a single invention or group of inventive concepts …) and he must divide out or cut down. But a divisional can be sought by a patentee even if the Office does not require it. Then the patentee's purpose is to break up his/her original application into a cluster of sister patents – each having the same basic disclosure but with different claims. Much the same could be achieved by just adding these claims to the original application, but there are both real and perceived advantages in using divisionals. Firstly each patent will stand or fall on its own merits whereas otherwise there is a risk of the complications of a partially valid patent – complications with potentially different results in different member states. Secondly a possible infringer can be sued on just the divisional(s) relevant to what he does. Thirdly if the patentee is having trouble with the examination process in respect of part of his invention, he may divide out the portion which the Office accepts is all right so that it gets early grant of that, and meanwhile he can pursue his argument with the Office in respect of the remainder.'
2   Therefore, generally speaking, an application which discloses a completely new technology may be able to support very wide claims, however, as such technology develops the allowable scope of claims will tend to become increasingly narrow.
3   See **Chapter 5** at paras 5.22–5.25. In Decisions G-1/03 *PPG/Disclaimer* and G-2/03 *Genetic Systems/Disclaimer* ([2004] EPOR, p. 331) the EPO Enlarged Board of Appeal held that a disclaimer having no basis in the application as filed, did not involve an impermissible addition of subject-matter provided that its purpose was only to restore novelty in certain circumstances, or to disclaim subject-matter which was excluded from patentability for non-technical reasons.
4   See the discussion of 'file wrapper estoppel' in **Chapter 6** at fn 6 to para 6.09.

Applying for a patent internationally

Convention filings

2.17   There is no such thing as a 'world patent' or an 'international patent' and patents are national, or at most regional, monopolies, effective only in the country or region of grant. A patent granted in one country has effect only in that country, and there are differences in the legal regimes to which they are subject. As a consequence, most courts are reluctant to express views as to validity, and infringement in relation to a patent granted in another country, no matter how similar their legal systems.[1] If the patentee wants protection in a number of countries then, in general, a separate application has to be made in each country in which protection is sought. It is hardly practical to file patent applications simultaneously in all countries in which patents are sought. Yet on the face of matters, were an inventor not to do so, and were to disclose the invention after filing a patent application for it in one country; the inventor would risk invalidating any patent granted on a subsequent application made to patent the same invention in any other country. This would certainly be the case in other countries, eg the EPO, the UK, and other EPC contracting states, which adopt the 'absolute novelty' approach under which one looks to all material made available to the public anywhere in the world: as forming part of the state of the art against which novelty and obviousness can be assessed. It would also apply to other countries operating a 'relative novelty' system (which looks only to local disclosures), where details of the disclosure became known locally, before filing the equivalent application.

To avoid this problem, the Paris Convention[2] to which most countries adhere,[3] permits an inventor when filing a patent application in another Convention country to claim as the priority date the date of first filing in his home country, rather than the date of actual filing in the foreign country. This facility is subject to the proviso that the filing in the Convention country be made within one year of such priority date. Within that period the applicant can do further work on the invention, and decide whether to proceed further, and, if so, in which countries. Provided the Convention applications are on file within a period of one year of the original priority filing, then any disclosures after such priority filing will not count against material in the priority document, because the original filing date will provide the priority date.[4]

However, the one year deadline provided by the Paris Convention means on its face that to obtain fullest protection, a considerable investment in terms of filing, and translation fees has still to be made at a very early stage of an invention, before the prior art has been properly explored, and the actual commercial potential of the invention established. In consequence, most companies seek to make, at an early stage, an assessment as to the commercial value of their patents on the basis of which they determine the filing policy for a particular patent application.

1   See **Chapter 4** at paras 4.24–4.28 for a discussion of the attempts that have been made to do this within Europe, and the constraints that apply to such attempts.
2   See **Appendix 6**. Moreover the Paris Convention provisions also apply by virtue of TRIPS, as between WTO member states (see also **Appendix 6**).
3   See **Appendix 1**.
4   Although as discussed below at para 2.21 in: 'When to publish or otherwise disclose material the subject of a patent application' it is best not to make any disclosures (other than in confidence) during that 'priority year', or indeed until publication of the application.

Easing the path of international patenting

2.18   Although there is no such thing as an 'international patent', many steps have been taken to simplify the task of obtaining protection in a number of countries: namely the PCT and the EPC, which each provide common international routes (which are nowadays frequently mixed) to obtaining a number of separate national patents.[1]

The process of obtaining a patent can be broken into separate stages. Previously, apart from the initial priority filing, one had to go through all stages in each country where protection was desired. The idea behind the PCT and the EPC is to minimize unnecessary duplication by having a single body to undertake several of these procedures. The PCT provides for a common search, and a common preliminary indication as to patentability, after which the applicant must proceed in national or regional (eg the EPO) patent offices, whereas the EPC also provides for common continued, substantive examination and grant, as summarized below:

Common Activity	PCT	EPC
Convention filing	Yes	Yes
Search	Yes	Yes
Written opinion on patentability	Yes	—
Publication	Yes	Yes
International preliminary report on patentability (optional)	Yes	—
[Continued] substantive examination	No	Yes
Grant	No	Yes
Opposition	No	Yes

1   These are not the only international routes. For example, the Eurasian Patent Convention, that established the Eurasian Patent Office (EAPO), and has been ratified by the Russian Federation, Kazakhstan, Azerbaijan, the Kyrgyz Republic, Moldova, and Armenia, and has, since 1995, offered in respect of these countries procedures similar to those established under the EPC.

Patent Cooperation Treaty

2.19   There is no reason why a separate prior art search needs to be done in each country, as all countries will have access to the same databases. Provided that an adequately comprehensive search is done, once should be enough. This was the original idea behind the PCT system, to which 148 countries had become parties by the beginning of 2015, including the EPO and its contracting states, China, Japan, Korea, and the USA.

Under the PCT, the applicant files a single convention application, in one of the permitted languages, which has the effect of designating the various countries within the PCT in which protection is sought. There is a single publication, and a single search is carried out on this, by an internationally recognized searching organization (a designated national or regional patent office) which in addition to the international search report (ISR) provides a written opinion on patentability, which can in turn form the basis for the optional international preliminary report on patentability (IPRP, Chapter II). The applicant also has the option of requesting a supplementary international search report (ISIR) during this 'international phase'.

An applicant must then, if wishing to proceed, and generally within 30 months of the priority date, enter the 'national phase', and identify those countries or regions in which it wishes to seek a patent; where the various national, and/or regional examiners undertake substantive examination with the benefit of the reports, and opinions produced in the international phase. Thus the WIPO, which administers the PCT system (and which benefits from it considerably in the subsidies that the PCT fees provide for many of its other activities) does not itself grant patents as a result of this system – instead it facilitates the initial stages of the granting process by avoiding the duplication inherent in a multiplicity of procedures.

The PCT system has not only the merit of reducing the number of searches that need to be done, and paid for, but also of delaying the decision point at which national fees must be paid, and a choice made as to those countries or regions in which to proceed. It allows usually 18 months more, compared with not using the PCT, before one must fulfil national requirements, giving one more time, for example, to investigate the commercial possibilities of the invention. Use of the PCT system also enables the applicant to avoid a number of local formalities, and confers fee reductions throughout the international and national phases of the procedure.

The drawbacks of the PCT are that not all countries belong to it (although most countries of interest now do so) and the rules which govern the PCT are complex, although this is much less of a problem than it was, and has to be contrasted with the complexity inherent in dealing with a number of different systems. The PCT system has been an enormous success since its establishment in 1978, having seen continuous growth over time, with 205,300 applications filed through it in 2013, an increase of 5.1 per cent over the previous year.[1]

Complementing the PCT system a relatively recent development has been that of the 'Patent Prosecution Highway.' This is a network of bilateral agreements between various national, and regional patent offices aimed at promoting work-sharing between such offices, and enabling patent applicants to request accelerated processing in the national phase, by which patent examiners can make use of the work products from the other offices. The decision about whether to grant a patent, however, remains under the control of the national or regional offices.[2]

1   See http://www.wipo.int/pct/en/ for PCT statistics, as well as details of the PCT
    procedure.
2   For the EPO pilot of such programme see: http://www.epo.org/law-practice/legal-
    texts/official-journal/information-epo/archive/20131218.html.

European Patent Convention and the European Patent Office

2.20 The European Patent Convention provides a route by which a
'bundle of national patents' (including a UK patent) can be obtained in
response to a single application filed at the EPO that is based in Munich.
It thus goes further than the PCT in centralizing the remainder of the
substantive examination process right through to grant.

This is possible because the EPC, having now been in existence
for more than 30 years, not only provides a common examination and
granting procedure, but also to a very considerable degree harmonizes
the substantive patent laws of EPC contracting states. A single
application is filed at the EPO, which has the effect of designating those
countries of the EPC,[1] and also those 'extension states'[2] in which one
can secure protection on the basis of a single application prosecuted
through to grant. There is a single common search of the prior art, but in
addition there is a common examination procedure all the way through
to grant. The European Patent Convention examination is conducted by
one examiner, with an appeal to the Examining Division, and then on to
an EPO (generally Technical) Board of Appeal. The initial stages can
alternatively be undertaken within the PCT system.

Assuming that translations are filed and fees paid in a timely manner,
wherever and whenever these are required, patents granted via the EPO
route confer the same rights, and are subject to the same laws as those
granted by the national systems of the EPC contracting states (as well
as the extension states that are not members of the EPC) except that
a single opposition to patents granted by the EPO can be initiated in
the EPO within nine months of grant, and a single limitation procedure
can be initiated in the EPO by the proprietor at any time post-grant.
Enforcement of such patents takes place in national courts, and such
patents can also be invalidated on a national basis, but in contrast to
centralized opposition the invalidation of a patent granted by means of
the EPO route in one national court does not invalidate that patent in the
other designated countries.

The European Patent Convention is declared in its preamble to be
a 'special agreement' within the meaning of Article 19 of the Paris
Convention, that provides for members of the Paris Convention to
make agreements between themselves for the protection of IP, so long
as those agreements do not contravene the provisions of the Paris
Convention. Thus applications filed at the EPO can claim priority under
the Paris Convention in the same way as applications filed nationally.[3]
All members of the EPC are also contracting states to the PCT. The

European Patent Convention, Articles 150–153 deal with the position of international applications filed at the EPO pursuant to the PCT, and as to which the PCT prevails over the EPC in the event of conflict with the EPC.

The European Patent Office has proved adept at developing substantive patent law, notwithstanding apparent constraints written into the EPC, to keep up with advances in technology, as in the case of patents for pharmaceutical uses, biotechnology, or for computer software. Moreover, national courts throughout Europe have increasingly tended to adhere to the legal principles established at the EPO, even though its decisions in individual cases are not binding on them, except, of course, in a *de facto* sense if it rejects a patent in prosecution or on opposition. The first major revisions to the EPC were agreed in 2000, and these entered into force on 13 December 2007.[4]

One drawback to patentees of the EPO system in comparison with national systems is that an adverse decision in prosecution, or on opposition can result in the opportunity of patent protection in all the designated countries being lost. However, this has not stopped people using the EPO system in preference to national ones, and if one seeks protection in more than a few EPC countries then there are clear, cost-advantages in using the EPO, over the national route, in addition to the obvious avoidance of much duplication of work, and the greater simplicity of dealing with one patent office. Moreover, unless provisional protection is required as from publication of the application, at which point translations may be required for some jurisdictions, it permits an applicant to avoid the expense of translation costs until the applicant knows that a patent is to be obtained.

In the case of some important inventions, some patentees may adopt a 'belt and braces' approach, and will prosecute an application simultaneously in the EPO, and in the national patent offices of certain designated countries (eg that of the UK or Germany). There is nothing against the practice, except cost, although there are provisions under many national laws directed against 'double patenting' which ensure that if at the end of the day both applications proceed to grant with identical claims, one patent is revoked.[5] A further consideration, given the relatively long time to grant in the EPO, is that if one wants a rapidly granted patent in Europe (eg in relation to a product such as a game, or a novelty item where there is a low barrier to market entry, but a short effective product life) it is generally better to take the national route, and the UK offers the scope to secure an examined patent relatively quickly.

The Community Patent Convention (CPC) a separate convention to both the EPC, and the EU Treaties, but which however never entered into force, envisaged a more sophisticated European system for patents than the EPC. Under this system, instead of a bundle of national patents being granted, an applicant would have been able to opt for one single unitary patent to be granted (by the EPO) but having effect throughout all of the EU. This single patent could then have been enforced throughout the EU by means of a single court action, rather than, as at present, having to proceed separately in each EU Member State in respect of each national patent, even if such national patent has been granted by the EPO, and is thus identical, in terms of wording, to its equivalents for other designated states.

Although the first version of the CPC was agreed upon in 1975 at Luxembourg, it never entered into force, although certain of its provisions on infringement provided the basis for many national such laws. Revisions made to it in 1985 and 1989 fared no better, but the Commission persisted, and a system for unitary patent protection within much of the EU, by which an applicant at the EPO will be able to opt at grant for such unitary protection, has now been agreed, and is likely to enter into force in 2017.[6]

1   All EU Member States are also EPC contracting states. However, the EPC is a wholly separate international treaty not restricted to EU Member States, and has no direct linkage to the EU Treaties. Thus Austria, Sweden, and (Switzerland) were parties to the EPC long before all the former two joined the EU, as were a number of the countries that joined the EU in 2004. As at the end of 2014, apart from all 28 Member States of the EU: Albania, Iceland, Liechtenstein, Macedonia, Monaco, Norway, San Marino, Serbia, Switzerland, and Turkey were also contracting states of the EPC.

2   As at the end of 2014, Bosnia and Herzegovina, and Montenegro were 'extension states' of the EPC. As from 1 March 2015 it has also been possible to validate patents granted by the EPO in Morocco, making it the first country outside Europe to provide for this.

3   This can provide benefits in terms of the speed of processing, but for UK residents, permission from the UK Intellectual Property Office first to file outside the UK may still be required – see para 2.13, fn 1 above.

4   See **Appendix 6**.

5   In the UK, see PA 1977, s 73(2)–(4) as to double patenting between a UK, and an EP(UK) patent. As between UK patents, double patenting is not a ground of revocation, but PA 1977, s 18(5) precludes double patenting in prosecution, and was discussed, as a potential basis for refusing a proposed post-grant amendment, in *Koninklijke Philips Electronics NV v Nintendo Of Europe Gmbh* [2014] EWHC 1959 (Patents Court) at [290] in which the practice of the EPO as to double-patenting as between EPO applications was also considered. As to the EPO, see T-1423/07 *Cyclic Amine derivative/BOEHRINGER INGELHEIM VETMEDICA GmbH* (EPO Technical Board of Appeal 3.3.02, 19 April 2010), which emphasizes the limited nature of the legal basis under the EPC for the EPO to object to it.

6   See **Chapter 1** at para 1.09 and fns 3–4 to that paragraph.

Issues met in relation to patent applications

When to publish or otherwise disclose material the subject of a patent application

2.21   Any disclosure of the invention (other than under conditions of confidentiality) before a patent application is first filed is potentially fatal to the patentability of that application. However, this does not mean that it is wise to publish details of an invention immediately after the patent application has been filed. One can identify the following decision points in relation to whether to publish:

Date	Decision point	Comment on effect of publication before such date
Priority date	Priority filing	Precludes securing a valid patent in the UK, and the rest of the EPC for the invention, that is the subject of the priority filing, and in most other countries. (However, see below at para 2.22 for some other countries.)
Priority date + up to 12 months	Convention filing	Precludes the option of withdrawing the priority filing, and of refiling later with any prospect of securing a valid patent for the invention the subject of the priority filing. Also, to the extent that any new material in the convention filing (and of any non- convention filing claiming internal priority) which is not present in the priority filing, cannot claim priority – from the priority filing, and, therefore, must take as its priority date that of the convention, etc, filing – precludes securing a valid patent in the UK, and the rest of the EPC for any invention the subject of such new material.
Priority date + about 18 months	Publication of application	Precludes the option of withdrawing the convention filing (and of any non-convention filing claiming internal priority) and of refiling later with any prospect of securing a valid patent for the invention the subject of the convention filing. Such publication may also constitute prior art for all purposes against further, related applications that ought accordingly be filed before publication of the application takes place, in order to take advantage of the more limited effect in, for example, the UK and the rest of the EPC, in patentability terms of a prior, but unpublished, application. (See below at para 2.23.)

Accordingly, the 'counsel of perfection' is to disclose nothing of the invention in public until publication of the application has taken place, and then to disclose no more than is in the application. This, however, can prove unsatisfactory in an academic environment. Publication may be used as a measure of academic productivity, and accordingly academics will wish the freedom to publish material about the research they undertake. Precipitate publication prejudices the scope for securing patents, and any publication at all will destroy any scope for trade secret protection in respect of the material published. Accordingly, academic inventors and those collaborating with them ought to take account of these issues, for example, in agreements under which academic research is commissioned, or where academic research forms part of a collaboration. Such agreements ought to provide a mechanism under which this issue can be addressed in a manner fair to both sides. A common such mechanism is a notice scheme under which the academic will give adequate notice to the commissioning party, or collaborators, who can then at least file a patent application, or provide an explanation as to why this would be premature, and the disclosure should be delayed.

Non-prejudicial disclosures

2.22   Under the EPC, and in the UK and other EPC contracting states, there are certain limited exceptions which remove from the 'state of the art' material which would otherwise form part of it. Those exceptions applying in the UK are set out in PA 1977, s 2(4) that excludes from the 'state of the art' matter disclosed during the six months prior to filing in the following two specific types of cases only:

— various disclosures made unlawfully or in breach of confidence of material derived from the inventor (s 2(4)(a)–(b)); and
— subject to certain conditions, disclosures made by displaying the invention at a designated 'international exhibition' (s 2(4)(c)).

The European Patent Convention, Article 55 is in similar terms, although it expresses the first concept rather more elegantly than PA 1977, s 2(4)(a)–(b), as 'an evident abuse in relation to the applicant or his legal successor'.

However, these exceptions provide no generalized relief against the consequences of disclosures by the inventor himself. The consequential invalidity of such a premature disclosure can come as a considerable, and unpleasant shock to inventors who feel instinctively that such disclosures ought not to count against their own later patent application, although the contrary view is that to relieve inventors from such consequences increases the uncertainty for third parties. There is a markedly different situation in the US in relation to an inventor's own prior disclosure, which in general will not invalidate the inventor's US patent provided it is made no earlier than one year before the date of filing in the US. This provision however (which is often known as the 'grace period') only operates in the US, which means that if an inventor makes such a disclosure this will still count against the inventor in most countries outside the US. There is from time-to-time pressure to introduce grace periods in Europe, similar to those in the US, and in the 1990s the

European Commission held a hearing on the matter, although it did not feature in the its 'Green Paper on the Community patent and the patent system in Europe'.[1]

1   COM (97) 314 Final 24 June 1997.

Prior unpublished applications

2.23   It is often the case that two separate research teams working independently of each other make much the same invention, at much the same time. Say that the first files an application in January, and the second files one in February. Neither applicant knows anything about the other's application but each, in effect, will be trying to monopolize the same ground. The first has not been published, before the second is filed, so does not form part of the state of the art, as against the second. One can understand that it is undesirable to have two patents claiming essentially the same invention. What is the solution?

The basic principle is that it is the 'first to file' that prevails. However, there are various ways to apply this principle. For example, in practice although there may be large areas of overlap between the two applications there will be some material which is not common to them. Various different approaches have been used in different countries to try to solve this problem with concurrent and conflicting applications.

One approach, that can be called the 'prior claiming' approach, and which used to be the law in the UK before PA 1977, forbids granting overlapping monopolies. This is difficult to apply in practice, as it depends on being able to map out effectively the scope of each proposed claim. Indeed because of the different approaches or terminologies used by the two applicants it may not be easy to see whether there is a potential overlap between the two different claims and, if there is, what the overlap extent is. Application of this approach can in practice involve the extensive rewriting, and restructuring of claims.

Another approach, called 'the whole contents' approach, treats the first application (provided that it has subsequently been published in the ordinary course) as if it had been published at its effective filing date (namely its priority date assuming priority can properly be claimed) as a prior art reference against the second application. In most implementations of the whole contents approach (as in the EPO, the UK, and other EPC countries) the rigour of this rather artificial doctrine is limited by providing that the earlier application is only deemed to be prior art for the purposes of novelty, and not for that of inventive step. This means in practice that if the two inventions are precisely the same then the second application will be wholly deprived of novelty, and thus refused. However, if the inventions are not precisely the same then something may be salvaged from the wreck of the second application, although painful surgery may well be necessary to cut away the area disclosed by the first application.

In UK law this principle is set out in PA 1977, s 2(3) and in EPC, Article 54(3). However, unlike national EPC jurisdictions such as the UK, the EPO only looks at earlier filed EPO applications, and so does not take into account applications of earlier date being prosecuted in national patent offices (which thus can only be used to mount a challenge locally to a national designation of a patent granted via the EPO route, and not in an EPO opposition).[1]

1   Under EPC 1973, Article 54(4) provided that Article 54(3) applied only insofar as a
     state designated in respect of the later application was also designated in respect of
     the earlier application as published. This provision was deleted by EPC 2000, as from
     13 December 2007.

First to file v first to invent

2.24   As explained above, the priority date is normally the date of first filing in a patent office, and in most countries of the world this determines who is entitled to a patent: as between two inventors who have independently made the same invention, and filed patent applications on it around the same time. Thus, this is known as the 'first to file' approach, although it would be more accurate to describe it as a 'first inventor to file' approach.

A similar approach is now adopted in the US (although until recently the US had a 'first to invent' approach, which in principle used to permit an inventor who had reduced the invention to practice, to prevail over the first inventor to file an application, where such first inventor to file had not been the first to reduce the invention to practice).

Costs

2.25   Obtaining patents is not cheap, but there are ways of managing the costs involved. Looking at it from a UK perspective the initial filing of an application in the UK involves no translation costs, and if the applicant has a search done quickly then it should be in a position to decide whether to go ahead within the one-year period. If the prior art is a very close – one may decide to drop the case completely – although it is rare that a patent, even one with claims of very narrow scope, is totally without commercial value. On the assumption that the prior art does not look too damaging to the prospects of securing a patent of useful scope, the applicant must then decide whether to proceed only in the UK, or if foreign protection is contemplated, in which countries and via what route. There is no generally applicable list of countries to use. However, in most areas of industry one would be most interested in: the US, China, Japan, Korea, and the major European countries (albeit that the choice as to which European ones can be deferred till grant, if one prosecutes via the EPO). Translations, the professional fees of patent attorneys, and the official fees charged by national patent offices are all sources of cost.

Europe can be relatively cheap, at least to begin with, for an English language applicant, as the need for translations, the major source of additional expense in the EPO system, is limited at the outset. The European Patent Office will accept the specification in English, and prosecution will take place in English. Only once the EPO have agreed to grant the specification is it then necessary to validate the patent nationally by filing translations at the national patent offices of the designated countries (although to preserve rights in relation to a published application it is generally necessary also to file translations of that on publication, although this is rarely done). One must in all cases provide a translation of the claims into both French and German. Subsequently for those countries with different languages that require them further translations of the full specification as granted will be needed although the 'London Agreement' has limited considerably the need for filing translations in many of the countries of the EPC.[1] However, the applicant is not obliged to incur the expense of translation costs, even for those EPC member states requiring translations, until it knows that a patent is being granted. However, and unlike many other patent offices which charge renewal fees only post-grant, the EPO by EPC, Article 86(1) requires the payment of renewal fees in respect of pending European patent applications as from the third year, from the original date of filing.

Another point to bear in mind from the point of view of the costs of translations is the technology involved, which can affect the length of the specification. The costs of a patent application for a simple mechanical device, which may only involve a relatively short specification (say up to ten pages, and half-a-dozen claims) and a few sheets of drawings may well be relatively modest. At the other end of the scale an application in biotechnology can often involve a very lengthy specification (say over 100 pages, with possibly 40 to 60 claims) together with 20 sheets of drawings, and a lengthy sequence listing (of amino acids and/or of the nucleotide bases involved). The time and level of technical skill involved in the two cases will obviously be very different, as will any translation costs.

In 2011 the European Commission, in the context of formulating an impact assessment for the unitary patent as then proposed, published some statistics as to the costs associated with patenting in Europe.[2] This showed that the total validation costs at the time were as follows:

— equal the translation costs of the claims to French and English, ie EUR 680; if the patent proprietor wishes protection in only Germany, France, and the UK (which are parties to the London Agreement);

— are approximately EUR 12,500 when protection is sought in the 13 Member States in which most validations take place; and

— are over EUR 32,000 if a patent is validated in the whole of the EU.

In view of this, and the relative size of differing Member States, it is hardly surprising, as also noted in the same study:

'It is important to note that only around 1 000 patents out of approx. 50 000 annually validated patents (2%) are validated in all 27 Member States. Around 4 000 patents (8%) are validated in 13 Member States and 20 000 patents per year are validated in the largest 5 EU markets (40%). Approximately half of these patents are only validated in 3 Member States – an estimated 25 000 patents per year (50%).'

In fact in some areas of technology, such as telecommunications, it may in practice suffice only to validate a patent in Germany, as the largest national market in Europe, and forego protection in all other countries.

1   The London Agreement 2000 (on the application of EPC, Article 65) that entered into force on 1 May 2008, has reduced the translation costs associated with patents prosecuted via the EPO by limiting the required language translation in the countries (21 EPC member states as at 1 January 2015, including France, Germany, and the UK) that adhere to the Agreement, for a patent prosecuted via the EPO route to be validated nationally. Thus, until it comes to enforcing such patents, they need only (in those countries) be in one of the main working languages of the EPO, namely English, French, or German, that will not accordingly involve any further translation.

2   See section 4.2, Commission Staff Working Paper: *Impact Assessment – Accompanying document to the proposal for a regulation of the European Parliament and the Council implementing enhanced cooperation in the area of the creation of unitary patent protection and the Proposal for a Council Regulation implementing enhanced cooperation in the area of the creation of unitary patent protection with regard to the applicable translation arrangements* (SEC (2011) 482 final – 13 April 2011).

Matters occurring after grant

Patent term and renewal fees

2.26   The date from which the term of the patent is calculated is the filing date – that of the convention filing, or of any filing claiming internal priority, but if there has been no further filing claiming internal priority the priority date itself. The TRIPS Agreement mandates a minimum patent term (subject to payment of renewal fees) of 20 years after the date of filing. However, because of the time taken for examination to proceed to grant of the patent the effective term of the actual monopoly can be very much less. Over the years, there have been schemes to extend patent term in certain cases, and for example, under UK patent law before the PA 1977 it used to be possible to secure an extension of a patent term on grounds of 'inadequate remuneration'. Nowadays it is more common to limit extension of effective patent term to those industry sectors where there are regulatory delays in getting to market, eg in Europe the pharmaceuticals and plant protection (agrochemicals) sectors, and to link the extension of effective protection to the regulatory delay.[1]

In most countries after grant the patentee has to keep paying fees (renewal fees or annuities) to the patent office to keep the patent in force, and typically these become progressively higher as one gets towards the twentieth year. The aim of increasing the fee is to discourage patentees from maintaining in force patents which are really of no use to them, and so it is an important part of patent management to keep granted patents under review, and to assess whether they really are of continuing value to the business. Within Europe the renewal fees for a patent prosecuted by the EPO route are no longer payable to the EPO once the patent is granted, but are payable to those national patent offices where the patent is validated, and which share those fees with the EPO; there is, however, a considerable variation in the level of such fees as between different national patent offices.[2]

1   See **Chapter 7** at paras 7.24ff.
2   See section 4.3, Commission Staff Working Paper: *Impact Assessment – Accompanying document to the proposal for a regulation of the European Parliament and the Council implementing enhanced cooperation in the area of the creation of unitary patent protection and the Proposal for a Council Regulation implementing enhanced cooperation in the area of the creation of unitary patent protection with regard to the applicable translation arrangements* (SEC (2011) 482 final – 13 April 2011).

Oppositions

2.27   Once granted, European patents may be opposed at the EPO within nine months of grant, or if an opposition is already on foot, by a party to infringement proceedings under the opposed patent, provided that such party intervenes within three months of the institution of such proceedings. Otherwise, European patents can only be revoked in separate proceedings brought in national courts to revoke the resultant national patents in the states in which they have been validated. The only grounds of revocation which can be relied on in opposition proceedings are those set out in EPC, Article 100, namely that:

(a)   the subject-matter of the European patent is not patentable within the terms of EPC, Articles 52–57 (ie is in the class of unpatentable subject matter, or lacks novelty or inventive step);
(b)   the European patent does not disclose the invention in a manner sufficiently clear, and complete for it to be carried out by a person skilled in the art (equivalent to EPC, Article 83); and
(c)   the subject-matter of the European patent extends beyond the content of the application as originally filed.

Each of these grounds, and the others also available in the UK, is discussed further in **Chapter 5**, and the procedures involved are outlined in **Chapter 4**.

Some other jurisdictions, including now the US, also provide for third parties to initiate the post-grant review of granted patents by the patent office, without the need for full revocation proceedings in court.

Amendment and limitation

2.28   Once a patent has been granted, new prior art may be discovered which has the effect of invalidating some or all of the claims of that patent. Had such prior art been identified in the original search report so that it was known when the patent was being prosecuted, the claims could in some cases have been drawn in a manner that would have defined an invention which would have been novel, over such prior art. The United Kingdom (and most other common law jurisdictions) has for a long time provided for this eventuality, by expressly permitting the amendment of granted patents.[1]

Although no provision was made for it in the EPC 1973, since the coming into force of EPC 2000 such a process, which is termed 'limitation' has been available.[2] What one cannot do, however, on amendment in the UK, or limitation under the EPC is to extend the scope of the claims (which patentees are sometimes tempted to do in an effort to catch infringers) or to try to cure insufficiency by adding new matter – if such attempts are superficially successful these in themselves provide other grounds of invalidity, as discussed in **Chapter 5**. Moreover, it can be much more difficult in the context of such post-grant procedure to redraft claims to overcome an attack of lack of inventive step, as opposed to one of lack of novelty.

1   Amendment often occurs in the course of patent litigation, as to which see **Chapter 4** at para 4.20.
2   See EPC 2000, Article 105(a)–(c) in **Appendix 6**.

Chapter 3

Transactions with patents and with patent applications

Types of transaction

Introduction

3.01   As with other property rights, a patent or a patent application may be transferred or assigned to third parties, or third parties may be allowed under certain conditions to exploit it, and it is with such transactions, as well as the more complex arrangements which involve such transactions, that this chapter is concerned. As national property rights, patents (even when these have been prosecuted via the EPO) and patent applications are very much the subject of national property laws[1], and in Europe these are much less harmonized than the substantive laws relating to the validity, and infringement of these, and most other intellectual property rights (IPRs). Accordingly, this chapter will focus on this issue from the perspective of English law, although from one particular perspective, that of competition law, it is EU law rather than national law, that dominates any analysis.

Naturally, the most straightforward way for a patentee to commercialize a patented technology is itself to put it into practice, and to sell articles, or to carry out a process which makes use of the technology, and to be prepared to prevent competitors from so doing by enforcing its patent rights. The goal however is to maximize the return. If the patentee considers it can best achieve this through its own exploitation it should do so. Alternatively it will look to involving another party in one or more aspects of the exploitation. There are a number of different ways in which this can be done. It may allow others to undertake various activities protected by patents in various territories including, for example, manufacture, and so grant such parties a licence. In those cases in which a product is protected in some way by a patent, it may reserve manufacture to itself, and involve others in the marketing to a greater or lesser extent. Although in a sense these can be regarded as licences under the patent to sell the patented article, they are not usually considered to be licences as such, and are instead generally regarded to be distribution agreements, although the line between the two is sometimes not easy to draw.

1 Even the new European patent with unitary effect will, as an object of property, be treated as a national patent, but of only one of the participating Member States, as determined in accordance with the provisions of Article 7 of Regulation (EU) No 1257/2012 of 17 December 2012, implementing enhanced cooperation in the area of the creation of unitary patent protection (OJEU L361, 31 December 2012, 1).

Assignments and licences contrasted

3.02 A licence is a well-established type of transaction by which the owner of a patent or an application shares the risks and benefits by allowing one or more other parties to work the patent or application in return for payments, usually based on a percentage of income. Neither a developed product nor any regulatory approval for it are required, as the licensee may be able to undertake the work that will lead to this, but the extent to which these are available will clearly influence the nature of the deal that is struck and in particular the level of royalty that can be obtained. Such an arrangement may in the early days of a technology be preceded by some sort of preliminary agreement allowing the technology the subject of the proposed licence to be evaluated.

Alternatively, a patent or application can be the subject of an outright sale, namely an assignment. Unlike licences, assignments rarely provide for the assignor to participate in the benefits of exploitation. From the point of view of the rights owner, the advantage of a licence over an assignment is that the rights owner has the security of retaining the rights; and if the licence provides for continuing payments (royalties) then if the person exploiting the technology fails to pay these, the rights owner will normally be able to terminate the licence and still have its rights available for further licensing. Seen from the point of view of the person exploiting the technology, a licence is not ideal as its long-term right to practice under the licensed patent or application may not be totally secure, and such licensee may then have little or no right to bring proceedings in its own name against infringers, although in many countries certain types of licensees can do so.[1]

Continuing payments (royalties), which are typically geared to the use made of the invention, are not always associated with licences just as upfront payments are not always associated with assignments. A licence may be expressed to be 'paid up' which will usually mean that no further sum is payable to practice under it. A licence will often combine upfront payments, sometimes keyed to various 'milestones', with running royalties.

Very much less common is an assignment of a patent or application associated with geared payments. The seller (assignor) has no security if payment stops or the purchaser (assignee) goes into liquidation. Provisions in such agreements for the assignee to reassign the assigned patent or application back to the assignor in such circumstances may prove hard to enforce, especially in the case of assignees that go into liquidation. Moreover, provisions against further assignment of the patent or application, and thereby moving the security of such right out of the scope of the assignor's right to a reassignment, are not effective against third parties who acquire rights in the patents without notice of the situation.

1   In the UK an 'exclusive licensee' of a patent has a statutory right to bring proceedings in its own name, but the proprietor must also be joined to them – see PA 1977, s 67.

Options and rights of first refusal

3.03 A common arrangement is for an evaluation period coupled with an option to take a licence at the end of that period. For an option to be legally binding beyond all doubt, all the terms that are to apply once the option is exercised ought to be set out in the option document. Then the person to whom the option is granted has only to exercise the option to create a binding contract. If significant points of the licence remain to be negotiated, the option may be worthless because the party granting the option may refuse to conclude an agreement on the outstanding points. In practice, therefore, all the terms and conditions attaching to the rights, and benefits to be granted under the option should be negotiated at the outset, and clearly identified in the option document. An alternative, if there are areas which can be already defined at the outset but where terms remain to be resolved, would be a provision for binding expert adjudication within certain defined parameters.

In contrast to an option, a right of first refusal or pre-emption could be used to prohibit the patentee from granting a licence to a third party without giving the beneficiary of such right the opportunity to take up the right. From the potential licensor's standpoint such a right, unless expressed to be of very short duration, can severely hamper its freedom as to potential exploitation. From the licensee's viewpoint, care must be taken to ensure that the right is effective in practical terms.

More complex arrangements – collaborative agreements, joint ventures and mortgages

3.04 In many sectors, much invention, development and commercialization is a collaborative effort, and no sole organization finds itself able to undertake every aspect of the work by itself. Many such activities are contracted out. For example, universities may do fundamental research, and contract research organizations may undertake more development-oriented work. Another option is that of collaboration between two companies in the development of a new product, with a view to its subsequent exploitation by each of the collaborators. Patents are naturally one of the primary means by which the fruits of all this research are protected.

It will, however, often happen that the research in the course of which those rights are generated will be undertaken by one of these other organizations, and the question then arises, once one moves beyond the question of who owns any patents resulting from that research (namely, is it the person who does the work, or the person who pays for it[1]) how are the benefits from exploitation to be shared? Particularly in collaborative research or development, this further question involves determining who should exploit the property so created, and whether there are to be any, and if so what, restrictions on such exploitation. Attention should also be directed to whether any rights already held by either party (namely 'background', as opposed to the 'foreground' which emerges from the collaboration) are required for such exploitation. Agreements as to research and development must accordingly not only address the fundamental issues of *who* owns the technology, but also *what use* the respective parties can make of that, and also of any other necessary technology.[2]

Once one moves beyond simple subcontracted research in this way, such arrangements, even where termed joint ventures or collaborations, and even though they can take a wide variety of forms, almost always involve an element of licensing, or more rarely assignment. Similarly legal mortgages of patents and patent applications are best effected by means of an assignment, with a right of redemption, and a licence back.[3]

1   As to which see **Chapter 2** at para 2.03.
2   See, for example, Cook, Trevor & Horton, Audrey, *Practical Intellectual Property Precedents* (Sweet & Maxwell, 1998 to date) at Section B.
3   See, for example, Cook, Trevor & Horton, Audrey *Practical Intellectual Property Precedents* (Sweet & Maxwell, 1998 to date) at Section E5.

Formalities of such transactions

The legal framework

3.05 As already observed, patents (even when these have been prosecuted via the EPO) and patent applications are national rights the subject of national property laws, and in this sense they, and thus the laws governing transactions in them, are little harmonized in Europe.[1] In the UK, the regime which governs transactions in them is set out in PA 1977, ss 30–38. The Patent Act 1977, s 30 provides that patents and applications are 'personal property (without being a thing in action)' and so, except as set out in PA 1977, ss 30–38, English law as to such types of property will apply.

However, European patent applications, because they have the potential to have effect in a number of designated states, but are not before grant a bundle of separate national patents subject only to national laws, also have their own provisions under the European Patent Convention (EPC). Thus, EPC, Article 71 provides that European patent applications may be transferred, or give rise to rights in one or more of the designated states, and EPC, Article 72 requires that assignments of European patent applications be in writing, and signed by the parties to the transaction. The European Patent Convention, Article 73 provides that European patent applications may be licensed in whole, or in part, for the whole or part of the territories of the designated contracting states, but does not set out any formalities for so doing. EPC, Article 74 provides that unless otherwise specified in the EPC the European patent application, as an object of property, shall in each designated contracting state, and with effect for that state be subject to the law applicable in that state for national patent applications; therefore such licence must comply with local laws of the states covered by such licence. No express provisions are necessary in the EPC as to patents granted by the European Patent Office (EPO) route as items of property, because these have, by EPC, Article 2(2) the effect of and are subject to the same conditions as national patents.

1   Even the new European patent with unitary effect will, as an object of property, be treated as a national patent – see para 3.01, fn 1.

The transaction itself

3.06 Assignments of patents in the UK need not be signed by both parties, consistent with the usual approach in England that only the assignor or licensor of a right need sign, unless the assignee or licensee is also assuming obligations under the agreement.[1] Thus, by PA 1977, s 30(6) as amended, an assignment of a patent or patent application 'shall be void unless it is in writing and signed by or on behalf of the assignor' and by PA 1977, s 30(6A) references to 'such a transaction being signed by or on behalf of a body corporate' include references to its being under the seal of that body. Although licences need not in theory be in writing they ought to be so in practice, in order to confer certainty as to their terms, and to enable the parties to secure the benefits of registration, as explained below. The English courts will, however, imply licences in certain cases.

Especial care needs to be taken as to assignments of patent applications undertaken during the priority year as an incorrect or deficient assignment of the right to claim priority, even on the part of only one inventor, can result in a complete loss of priority, thereby potentially expanding the state of the art as against a patent which loses such priority.[2]

Even though assignments of patents and patent applications which are expressed to be 'with full title guarantee' are, because patents and patent applications are personal property, treated in England by the Law of Property (Miscellaneous Provisions) Act 1994 as implying a covenant on the part of the assignor that the assignor 'will, at his own cost, do all he reasonably can to pass title to such property', it is usual to include in any patent assignment an express such covenant, for further assurance.

Patent licences usually include a provision by which the parties will, if required by the other, execute a short formal licence for local registration purposes. The benefit of having a separate such document is to make it easier to keep confidential financial terms off any public registers. Patent assignments should also include an assignment of the right to bring proceedings for previous infringements (enforceable by PA 1977, s 30(7)) and this benefit can also be conferred on an exclusive licensee, although this is not usually done in an arm's-length exclusive licence.

1   However, this has given rise to an inconsistency with the EPC, which by Article 72 requires an assignment of a European patent application to be signed by both parties to the contract. Thus in practice it is prudent to continue to provide for signature by both, unless one is sure that only granted UK patents are in issue.

2   See *Edwards Life Sciences AG v Cook Biotech Inc.* [2009] EWHC 1304 (Patents Court) for a case in which priority was lost for this reason, and *KCI Licensing Inc v Smith & Nephew plc* [2010] EWHC 1487 (Patents Court); *HTC v Gemalto* [2013] EWHC 1876 (Patents Court), (not in issue on appeal at [2014] EWCA 1335); and *Idenix Pharmaceuticals, Inc. v Gilead Sciences, Inc. & ors* [2014] EWHC 3916 Patents Court) for subsequent cases in which such a challenge to priority failed. In the last of these cases the challenge was not to the validity of the claim to priority of the patent in suit itself, but instead to the validity of the claim to priority of a potentially prior art patent application which did not form part of the extended state of the art for the purposes of novelty, as explained in **Chapter 5** at para 5.06, unless it preserved priority. See also Bremi, Tobias – *Traps when transferring priority rights, or When in Rome do as the Romans do: A discussion of some recent European and national case law and its practical implications*, EPI Information, vol 1/2010, 17–24.

Registering transactions

3.07 Assignments and licences ought to be registered with the appropriate national patent offices as soon as possible after execution. The benefits in the UK of so doing are twofold. First, by PA 1977, s 33 registration of such transactions provides notice to third parties, who are otherwise, unless they actually knew of the transaction, not bound by it. Thus, a person who has failed to register such a transaction may lose priority to a holder of – under a subsequent inconsistent transaction. Second, by PA 1977, s 68 as amended, the assignee or exclusive licensee of a patent who does not register the transaction under which it acquires such right within six months of its taking place cannot claim costs in an action for infringements which takes place before such registration.[1]

One particular problem that can arise with transactions in European patent applications is that although an assignment submitted to the EPO (if signed by both parties) is effective, resulting in patents granted on such European patent applications being granted in the assignee's name, and appearing so on the national patent office registers of designated states, EPO practice as to licences would appear to be somewhat haphazard. Thus, these do not always appear on the national patent office registers of designated states. The counsel of perfection, which appears only to be rarely followed in practice (perhaps because of the additional formalities, costs, and fuss associated with so doing, compared with the ease of submitting such documents to the EPO) is to register such transactions locally as well.

1   Before the amendment of PA 1977, s 68 in 2006 the penalty was more severe, precluding the recovery of damages or an account of profits – see *Finecard International Ltd (T/A The Ninja Corpn) v Urquhart Dykes & Lord (a firm)* [2005] EWHC 2481 (Ch D) (Patents Court) for an example of an unsuccessful attempt to avoid such sanction in a case in which an earlier licence had been registered but a new one had not. The amended section has also been the subject of controversy, as to which see *H. Lundbeck A/S v Norpharma SpA* [2011] EWHC 907 (Patents Court) where a notification to the EPO too late to be reflected in the UK patent office register did not count as a registration under PA 1977, s 68, and *Schutz (UK) Ltd v Werit UK Ltd* [2011] EWCA Civ 927, [2011] EWCA 1337, [2013] UKSC 16, where the scope of the costs sanction, on the complex facts of that case, elicited considerable judicial comment, little of which was in agreement, except as to the poor drafting of the section, but which proved to be *obiter*, and is thus not binding as precedent.

Patent licensing generalities

Reasons for granting a licence

3.08 If a patentee considers that others can expand the use (or indeed make better use) of it, the patentee can make available the patented technology to others for a return which reflects the opportunity which the value of that technology will provide the patentee, by allowing others to manufacture. This provides the patentee with the scope to participate in the manufacturing returns without investing directly in production or marketing. This is typically done by the grant of a licence by the patentee, the licensor, to the person exploiting the technology, the licensee. There are a number of reasons for a patentee to consider that others can make better use of the technology than it can. These are explored in the following paragraphs.

Size, goals or resources – A common reason for the smaller patentee to make its technology available is lack of resources. For example, academic institutions are not established to commercially manufacture and market. Start-up biotechnology companies can be in the same position, and can lack the resources required to fund all the clinical trials needed, and to secure the necessary marketing authorizations. The expertise of others may be critical and, notwithstanding that the patentee may have developed a good idea, specialist expertise in a different type of organization may be required to fulfil the patentee's technical ambitions.

Nature of the product or process – Certain products are best manufactured in, or near to the sales territory. This may be because of some tariff or import obstruction, or because of regulatory constraints. The problem may simply relate to the cost of transportation, or to the risk of the product deteriorating during transit. Alternatively it may be a consequence of government policy to encourage local manufacture in the licensed territory.

Surplus types of product – Research targeted in a specific field may well result in a variety of potential competing products only one of which the patentee wishes to pursue. Choosing the most promising of these, and licensing the other products to others, enables some element of the research expenditure to be recovered.

Differing presentations – It may be necessary to vary presentations of the product to suit different markets. These variations may be the result of differences in consumer preference or in technical, trading, or regulatory standards. This can be costly, and it is sometimes something best left to a locally-based producer in tune with local requirements.

Differing applications – Technology developed for one type of business may have applications in other areas in which its inventor has no commercial ambitions. For example, a new chemical entity developed in the course of agrochemical research may, irrespective of agrochemical activity, also have value as a pharmaceutical. Licensing outside its area of interest provides potential revenue in a field in which the patentee could not, or lacks commercial ambition, to enter itself.

Second sourcing – A licence may be required where the demand for a particular product exceeds the patentee's ability to supply it or, where the industry requires second sourcing if it is to accept the product in view of the perils of long-term commitment to a single source.

Establishing a standard – Patenting a standard and licensing this to third parties may be the only way of establishing and policing a standard in the electronics, communications, and computing sectors. The issues associated with this are discussed in **Chapter 9**.

Settlement of proceedings – Granting a licence avoids confrontation with potential infringers, and challengers as to the scope, and validity of the licensed patents. This is important where the patentee lacks the resources to undertake litigation, which is inevitably uncertain to at least some degree in outcome. Care should, however, be taken about licensing at low royalty rates in such circumstances as the English courts have held that this can adversely effect a patentee's ability to recover damages for infringement of such patent at a higher rate later.[1] Cross-licensing is a frequent means of settling proceedings between two parties who have independently made inventions in the same technical field, and have patents, or patent applications the scope of which overlaps.

In practice it is likely that a combination of several of the above factors will be at work, and for any given patentee the balance between these factors may well differ in different territories. Thus, licensing can have the advantage of permitting the licensor both to exploit the technology directly autonomously, and at the same time have licensees who are also exploiting it in other territories, and paying the licensor royalties. It is often the case that a licensor will work the patent in the licensor's home country, and equivalents in certain other countries where the licensor has a strong local presence, but will license others under equivalent patents in other foreign countries.

1   See *General Tire & Rubber Co v Firestone Tyre & Rubber Co Ltd* [1975] 1 WLR 819; [1975] 2 All ER 173; [1975] FSR 273; [1976] RPC 197 (House of Lords). The German courts have taken a different view, regularly applying a reasonable uplift to the royalty rate as would be agreed under a comparable 'arms' length' licence between a willing licensor and a willing licensee when awarding damages for infringement. This takes account of the different circumstances which would apply to a hypothetical licence negotiated after the activity in issue has been held to infringe. – See Kuhnen, Thomas, *Patent Litigation Proceedings in Germany* (Carl Heymanns Verlag 2013) at para [2253] observing that the Munich District Court has endorsed a 66 per cent increase. The consistency of this practice with Article 13 of Directive 2004/48/EC on the infringement of IP is the subject of a current reference to the CJEU in Cases C-481/14 *Jorn Hansson* and C-367/15 *Stowarzyszenie Oławska Telewizja Kablowa*, concerning plant variety rights and copyright repectively.

Reasons for taking a licence

3.09   In contrast, the licensee's motives for taking a licence will include the following:

Access to new products – Heavy research and development (R&D) expenditure does not guarantee finding a new product, and most companies target their research into certain areas only. Therefore they will have a need to complete their product line, and to introduce new products, a need that can only be met by buying in, or licensing in, new products.

Insufficient research and development facilities – Many potential licensees lack the capacity to undertake all the necessary R&D themselves. This is particularly the case in areas such as pharmaceuticals, where even the largest companies cannot research in every therapeutic area. If the potential licensee has marketing ambitions that require technological innovation which inhouse technology cannot sustain, licensed-in technology provides an alternative. This allows the manufacturer to better manage the cost of R&D, and to limit the adverse consequences of the inherent risk that it may not come to fruition. There are obvious time-savings too, allowing the licensee to keep more closely in step with often fast-moving market trends.

Access to improvements – Every manufacturer should keep in touch with the needs of its customers and potential customers. This requires updating products, and introducing new ones – which, in turn, results in the need to enhance access to technology, which may be best achieved by taking out a licence.

Saving time and cost – For the licensee in a highly competitive market, limiting capital investment reduces costs and, by extension, prices which, in turn, improves the competitive position. The licensee is under less pressure from a cost and time perspective to develop newly discovered leads into marketable products.

Access to proven technology – In more developed economies, the licensee may see the licence as a fast track to increased market share, and market prominence generally. In emerging economies this may not be the primary concern and technology disclosures can be viewed as a platform for future developments and production.

Extending product life – A manufacturer may take a licence to enhance its existing technology. For example, a pharmaceutical manufacturer may take a licence for an advanced method of drug delivery with a view to extending the effective life of an established pharmaceutical.

Licensing may be a two-way business. For example, a company in the pharmaceutical industry, which is involved in licensing others in respect of a new chemical entity (licensing-out) may at the same time itself be a licensee of, for example, drug delivery means to enable the new chemical entity to be suitably administered (licensing-in). In some cases the two-way aspect may involve only the two parties, for example if there are two complementary technologies in separate ownership which leads to a 'cross-licence' between the owners so that each is authorized to use the other's technology. Cross-licences are also useful for avoiding litigation between the owners of directly competing technologies, but need especial analysis under competition laws (as can 'patent pools' as discussed in **Chapter 9**) as it has generally been in the electronics, communications, and computing sectors that patent pools have been established in recent years.

Licensing policy and approach

3.10 A prudent licensor will formulate its licensing policy for all potential territories before embarking on the search for licensees, and the grant of licences. The licensor should consider the potential impact of the licence on the market, on the licensor's own activities, and on those of the licensor's other licensees. The licensor should also consider the commercial bargain that could be made (or rather can no longer be made) by other means, for example, by some distribution arrangement. In theory the licensor can dictate the terms on which it will license; although if the licensee is powerful the theory can break down, as in many cases the licensee may, for example, be able to design around the patent. However, in deciding terms for licensing it is important to know exactly what patents are available to be licensed; one can then decide on ancillary matters (eg territories, licensed goods, and royalties). One purpose of the licence agreement is as a vehicle for collecting payments. However, it is of equal importance that the licence transfer, regulate, and control the use of the technology package. It is only in its simplest form that a licence is a bare permission to exploit the protected rights; over and above this the licence must set out the duties of the parties to protect the licensor's return, and the licensee's access to the licensed technology.

Mixed patent and know-how licences tend to be more common than 'pure' patent licences. Mixed licenses can have advantages if the strength of the patent protection obtainable is doubtful, which will often be the case early in the life of a patented technology. This type of licence must in addition include the necessary secrecy provisions to protect confidential know-how as trade secrets. The know-how element is usually necessary where the licensee is contemplating production, but has not achieved it because it needs to be told how to do it. This can be contrasted with cases where the prospective licensee takes a licence in consequence of settlement of patent infringement proceedings: in that case clearly it knows how to do it, but needs a licence under the infringed patents.

From a legal perspective three types of licence may be granted, although precisely what is meant by such terms if used in a licence should always be defined:

— **Exclusive**: means that the licensee alone can operate under the licenced rights (ie so that even the licensor is excluded from doing so).
— **Sole**: means that the licensor will grant no further licences so that no-one other than the licensee and the licensor can operate under the licensed rights.
— **Non-exclusive**: means whereby the licensor can itself operate under the licensed right, and can also grant as many further non-exclusive licences as it wishes.

From a commercial perspective, three main types of licensing situation can be distinguished as follows:

— the licence covers the same products or processes as those made or used by the licensor, but perhaps in a different territory;
— the licence is for different fields of use, and thus for different products or processes, than those exploited by the licensor; and
— the licence is part of a broader technical co-operation agreement between the licensor and the licensee, which may for example, involve cross-licensing.

In addition there are two main types of licence that are responses by licensors to certain situations forced upon them, rather than part of an active and voluntary licensing policy:

— the licence is granted as part of the settlement of infringement proceedings; or
— the licence is a compulsory one imposed by local laws or a licence 'voluntarily' granted under threat of such compulsion.

The type of licensing situation can, to a large extent, dictate the type of agreement, and thus for example, a compulsory licence will always be non-exclusive, as usually will be one in settlement of litigation.

The decision as to what type of licence to offer is primarily a commercial one, which is likely to have formed part of the overall licensing strategy. The most appropriate type of licence may vary from country to country. For example a UK-based company that does not itself exploit the invention might well decide to grant non-exclusive licences (with no power to sublicense) in the UK where it is very familiar with the market, and where it knows what royalty rates the market would tolerate. However, where it grants a licence for a country such as Japan, it may prefer a 'master' exclusive licensee, preferably a large company (which can be expected to accept the responsibilities inherent in such an operation) and which would then do its own sublicensing, and additionally deal with the legwork of policing such sublicensees.

The type of licence to be offered will also vary depending on the nature of the licensee. Will that licensee have sufficient resources to support the marketing operation required of it? Does it have the necessary marketing outlets, and sales and support staff? Does it have an established manufacturing facility? Does it have the technical back-up to provide after-sales service, and could it in any way be distracted in its sales efforts by its involvement with any competing or related products? If so, should it be restricted from dealing in such products?

However in a very new field, particularly if large capital investment, and/or much development work is needed, a licensee may be unwilling to take a licence unless it is exclusive. It needs such security for long enough to recoup its outlay. However, the licensor must recognize that it is shutting itself out of the market, and so may require a substantial payment on signature, in addition to royalties geared to turnover. If the licensee proves inept or indolent the licensor can find itself in an impossible position of being unable to use the technology itself, and yet receiving no benefit from the licensee. Thus, an exclusive licence must contain appropriate provisions addressing this risk – for example, for termination in such a case, for minimum royalties (which help to encourage performance) and also provisions to permit, at the option of the licensor, removal of exclusivity.

However, if a patentee is looking to licence as a way of seeking actively to promote the use of the patented invention, no agreement, however well drafted, can compensate for the selection of a poor licensee, although it can and should limit the damage that can be done by such a mistake. A poor licensee will almost inevitably undermine the eventual successful exploitation of the technology under the licence. One critical factor is the licensee's technical proficiency. It is clearly pointless licensing sophisticated technology to licensees without adequate technical skills. The licensor should assess the training which will be required. Delays in start-up may prevent the product ever entering that particular market. Moreover what may be suitable for manufacture in one country may not be so in another because, for example, of the local business environment. The licensor should carry out an in-depth technical appraisal before commitment to the licensee. As equally important, however, as the licensee's technical proficiency is its marketing proficiency.

The stage of development of the particular product is also critical. The prototype stage is not the end of development. New techniques require ongoing support. Incomplete development coupled with lack of support will lead to product failure. The practical reality in such cases is that it will be up to the licensor to 'see its licensee right'. Unless the licensor carries out regular checks to ensure quality control, the reputation of the licensed product in the local market will suffer. Exclusion and limitation of liability clauses may not suffice to protect the licensor especially where trade marks are also licensed, as in some jurisdictions loss or injury caused to third parties may result in liability on the part of the trade mark owner.

The risk of the licensee (or third parties) exporting the licensed products to territories in which it is not licensed cannot be ignored. The licensor, and its other licensees, may thus encounter competition in such territories.

In conclusion a well-structured licensing network will bring high rewards to the licensor especially for mature products requiring little support. However, the down-side risks cannot be disregarded; ultimately these can only be protected against by payments made at the outset, failing which adequate termination rights for failure to meet objectively defined targets can achieve some damage control.

Competition law considerations associated with patent licensing

Relevance of competition law

3.11   Competition law considerations impose major constraint on any patent licence. This is especially so in Europe, where EU competition law, under the Treaty on the Functioning of the European Union (TFEU) combines not only traditional competition law concerns as encountered in other jurisdictions but also concerns as to the integrity of the internal market, and accordingly seeks to limit the extent to which one can partition the market territorially, notwithstanding that the rights being licensed are territorial in nature. Control under EU law arises under TFEU, Article 101 (formerly Article 81 and before that Article 85 of its predecessor treaties). This has been held by the Court of Justice of the EU (CJEU) to apply to certain terms in patent licences, although the case law as to this is now effectively contained in the Technology Transfer Block Exemption[1] and its associated Guidelines, that are updated every ten years or so. The latter not only elaborate on specific provisions of the Block Exemption but also discuss those such agreements, and the provisions met in them which, although perhaps not falling within the Block Exemption are, in the view of the European Commission, unlikely to breach Article 101, and identifies those provisions which it can be expected will breach it.[2] Compliance with the Technology Transfer Block Exemption provides a 'safe-harbour' from the provisions of Article 101, breach of which can render the agreement void, and expose the parties to the risk of fines.

The full text of Article 101 provides:

'1.   The following shall be prohibited as incompatible with the common market: all agreements between undertakings, decisions by associations of undertakings and concerted practices which may affect trade between Member States and which have as their object or effect the prevention, restriction or distortion of competition within the common market, and in particular those which:

(a)   directly or indirectly fix purchase or selling prices or any other trading conditions;

(b)   limit or control production, markets, technical development, or investment;

(c)   share markets or sources of supply;

(d)   apply dissimilar conditions to equivalent transactions with other trading parties, thereby placing them at a competitive disadvantage;

(e)   make the conclusion of contracts subject to acceptance by the other parties of supplementary obligations which, by their nature or according to commercial usage, have no connection with the subject of such contracts.

2. Any agreements or decisions prohibited pursuant to this Article shall be automatically void.
3. The provisions of para 1 may, however, be declared inapplicable in the case of:
    —   any agreement or category of agreements between undertakings;
    —   any decision or category of decisions by associations of undertakings;
    —   any concerted practice or category of concerted practices;
    which contributes to improving the production of distribution of goods or to promoting technical or economic progress, while allowing consumers a fair share of the resulting benefit, and which does not:
    (a)   impose on the undertakings concerned restrictions which are not indispensable to the attainment of these objectives;
    (b)   afford such undertakings the possibility of eliminating competition in respect of a substantial part of the products in question.'

Although 'only appreciable effects on trade between Member States' are relevant under Article 101(1), what constitutes an 'appreciable effect' is inevitably subjective, and where the Commission, in its role as enforcing the TFEU and its predecessor treaties, has wished to exert control over an agreement it has been all too willing to find such an effect is proven. The inter-Member State element has also been interpreted quite widely, and the Commission has needed little convincing of such effects once restrictions on competition affecting trade within a substantial part of the EU, which could be only one Member State, are established. Indeed, the fact that the parties to an agreement are all from the same Member State, or are based outside the EU does not mean that there can be no effect on inter-state trade. Such effect must be appreciable, although no single criterion has been laid down as the test for such appreciability, which depends upon the commercial context, and the economic circumstances.[3] As a result many patent licence agreements with an element of exclusivity, or of territorial protection, risk falling within Article 101(1).

However, before considering the position under the *Technology Transfer Guidelines* one should consider whether the licence avoids the application of Article 101 by virtue of the Commission Notice on Agreements of Minor Importance.[4] This sets thresholds of a 10 per cent aggregate market share for vertical agreements, and a 15 per cent aggregate market share for horizontal agreements, irrespective of turnover, below which an agreement is not generally regarded as having an appreciable effect on competition, and so falls outside Article 101(1), unless such agreement has as its object the prevention, restriction, or distortion of competition within the internal market. Moreover, agreements between small- and medium-sized enterprises (SMEs) (terms which are themselves defined in the annex to a Commission Recommendation[5]) irrespective of market share, are regarded in the same light. The Commission has also adopted a Notice setting out guidelines concerning the parameters used for determining the relevant market[6] thereby enabling market share to be better assessed.

The Commission is particularly suspicious of exclusive terms in licences that compartmentalize the single European market, and diminish competition. The Commission is also concerned that within Europe a licensee not be given protection against sales of the licensed goods in its own 'exclusive' territory where such goods were originally released on the market by the licensor, or other licensees in their own particular territories. This would frustrate the application of the 'exhaustion' doctrine which has been built up, in the context of the free movement of goods throughout the EU, through application of TFEU, Articles 34 and 36 (formerly Articles 28 and 30, and before that Articles 30 and 36 respectively of its predecessor treaties) and which is discussed in **Chapter 6**, as it generally arises in the context of a defence to an action for patent infringement.

1 Currently Commission Regulation (EC) No 316/2014 of 21 March 2014 on the application of Article 101(3) of the TFEU to categories of technology transfer agreements [2014] OJ L 93/17 – see **Appendix 6**.

2 Currently Communication from the Commission – *Guidelines on the application of Article 101 of the TFEU to technology transfer agreements* (2014/C 89/3) [2014] OJ C 89/03.

3 Some guidance is provided by Commission Notice – *Guidelines on the effect on trade concept contained in Articles 81 and 82 of the Treaty* ([2004] OJ C 101/81).

4 Currently Communication from the Commission – *Notice on agreements of minor importance which do not appreciably restrict competition under Article 101(1) of the TFEU (De Minimis Notice)* (2014/C 291/01)) [2014] OJ C 291/1. See also the accompanying Commission Staff Working Document – *Guidance on the restrictions of competition 'by object' for the purpose of defining which agreements may benefit from the De Minimis Notice* (SWD (2014) 198 final, 25 June 2014).

5 Commission Recommendation 2003/361/EC of 6 May 2003 concerning the definition of micro-, small- and medium-sized enterprises (C(2003) 1422) [2003] OJ L124/36.

6 Commission Notice – *On the definition of relevant market for the purposes of Community competition law* (97/C 372/03) [1997] OJ C372/05.

Notification, exemption, and block exemptions

3.12 A patent licence that falls within TFEU, Article 101(1) is automatically void and unenforceable in all EU Member States by virtue of Article 101(2) – unless saved by Article 101(3). Parties operating such an agreement risk fines of up to 10 per cent of the annual group turnover. Article 101(3) (which until 1 May 2004 only the Commission, and not national courts, had the power to apply) saves transactions which would otherwise be prohibited under Article 101(1) if they contribute to 'improving the production or distribution of goods or to promoting technical or economic progress, while allowing consumers a fair share of the resulting benefit'. Originally such exemption could only be secured by means of a 'specific' exemption from the Commission in response to a notification made by the parties, and granted on the individual merits of the agreement in question. Such notification also had the benefit of excusing the parties from liability to fines even if the agreement was eventually found to breach Article 101(1) but was not saved by Article 101(3). However, the notification procedure was time-consuming and onerous, and in practice rarely elicited any response from the Commission, other than a formal acknowledgment or at most, and after some time, a 'comfort letter' if the Commission had no objection to the arrangement. However, at the time of negotiating and executing it there was no certainty as to the enforceability of the particular agreement.

Thus, a system of Commission Regulations setting out 'block' or 'group' exemptions, summarizing the experience of the Commission in applying both Articles 101(1) and 101(3) in dealing with individual applications for specific exemptions in certain fields, was developed. If an agreement fell within the defined parameters of a block exemption for the particular type of agreement, there was no longer any need to apply for a 'specific' exemption. It was, therefore, a 'do-it-yourself' procedure enabling the contracting parties to put a degree of certainty into their arrangements. The unique advantage conferred by compliance with a block exemption was that of certainty at the outset that an agreement was effective. Block exemptions now cover a variety of transactions that affect patents; namely R&D agreements, and specialization agreements, technology transfer agreements and vertical agreements such as those concerned with exclusive distribution. Since 1 May 2004 there has been no scope to seek a specific exemption from the Commission, and national courts have been able to apply Article 101(3) themselves (referring matters that are not *acte claire* to the Court of Justice of the EU, which also, via its lower chamber, the General Court, hears appeals from Commission decisions as to whether or not Article 101 is infringed). However, the role of block exemptions promulgated by the Commission in providing a 'safe harbour' from the provisions of Article 101 remains, although the uncertainties attributable to the market share thresholds that these all contain has increased the importance of the various Guidelines that accompany these block exemptions.

The other block exemptions of relevance to transactions involving patents, in addition to the Technology Transfer Block Exemption are:

— Commission Regulation (EU) No. 330/2010 of 20 April 2010 on the application of Article 101(3) (TFEU) to categories of vertical agreements and concerted practices[1] (Vertical Agreements Block Exemption).

— Commission Regulation (EU) No. 1218/2010 of 14 December 2010 on the application of Article 101(3) (TFEU) to certain categories of specialization agreements[2] (Specialization Agreements Block Exemption).

— Commission Regulation (EU) No. 1217/2010 of 14 December 2010 on the application of Article 101(3) (TFEU) to certain categories of R&D agreements[3] (Research and Development Agreements Block Exemption).

Moreover, as with the Technology Transfer Block Exemption, the Commission has issued guidelines that discuss the application of these:

— *Guidelines on Vertical Restraints* (2010/C 130/01).[4]
— Communication from the Commission – *Guidelines on the applicability of [TFEU] Article 101 to horizontal cooperation agreements* (2011/C 11/01).[5]

The Vertical Agreements Block Exemption (which is mutually exclusive with the Technology Transfer Block Exemption) and as explained in the *Guidelines on Vertical Restraints*, applies to vertical agreements (eg distribution agreements) which also contain certain provisions as to the assignment of IPRs to, or use of IPRs by the buyer, and may thus be of relevance in some agreements relating to patents which do not fit within the Technology Transfer Block Exemption. The Technology Transfer Block Exemption is also mutually exclusive with the Research and Development Agreements Block Exemption and the Specialization Agreements Block Exemption, both of which are discussed in the *Guidelines on Horizontal Cooperation Agreements*. The former may be of application in collaborative R&D agreements, and will apply instead of the Technology Transfer Block Exemption to any patent, and/or know how licences entered into the context of the collaboration.

1   [2010] OJ L102/01.
2   [2010] OJ L335/43.
3   [2010] OJ L335/36.
4   [2010] OJ C130/01.
5   [2011] OJ C11/01.

The Technology Transfer Block Exemption

3.13   The Technology Transfer Block Exemption (in the rest of this chapter 'the Block Exemption') applies to both patent and know-how licences, whether pure licences of each IPR or mixed licences of both.[1] Although certain specific provisions are discussed below in the context of terms commonly met in patent licences, it is convenient here briefly to outline the scope and structure of the Block Exemption. The Block Exemption can only apply where the total market share of the undertakings party to the agreement fall below certain thresholds, depending on whether the parties are competitors (20 per cent market share) or not (30 per cent market share).

For technology transfer agreements which cannot, for example, because of the market share involved, take advantage of the Block Exemption, the accompanying *Guidelines* (in the rest of this chapter 'the *Guidelines*') provide guidance as to the attitude of the Commission to various provisions found in such agreements, and also elaborate on some of the provisions of the Block Exemption. The relationship between the *Guidelines*, the Block Exemption, and the Minor Agreements Notice can therefore be summarized as follows:

	Competitors	**Non-competitors**
Minor Agreements Notice (Article 101(1))	Joint market share below 10%	Joint market share below 15%
Block Exemption (Article 101(1) and (3))	Joint market share below 20%	Joint market share below 30%
Guidelines (Article101(1) and (3))	Joint market share 20% and above	Joint market share 30% or above

Article 2 of the Block Exemption declares, pursuant to Article 101(3), that subject to the other provisions of the Block Exemption, Article 101(1) 'shall not apply to technology transfer agreements' which expression is by Article 1(c) defined as 'a technology rights licensing agreement entered into between two undertakings for the purpose of the production of contract products by the licensee and/or its sub-contractor(s)' or 'an assignment of technology rights between two undertakings for the purpose of the production of contract products where part of the risk associated with the exploitation of the technology remains with the assignor.' By Article 2(2) the exemption thereby conferred shall apply for as long as the licensed technology rights remain in effect, or, as to know-how, remains secret, unless it has become publicly known through the actions of the licensee, in which case it applies for the duration of the agreement. Article 2(3) extends its application to certain ancillary provisions in such agreements. Article 3 sets out the market share thresholds to which the Article 2 exemption is subject, depending on whether the parties are competitors or not, and Article 8 clarifies the application of such thresholds.

Article 4 sets out two 'blacklists' of 'hardcore restrictions' which the Commission regards as restrictive by their very object, and the presence of which in a licence will prevent the Block Exemption applying to it, one applicable to competing undertakings and the other to non-competing undertakings:

'4(1) Where the undertakings party to the agreement are competing undertakings, the exemption provided for in Article 2 shall not apply to agreements which, directly or indirectly, in isolation or in combination with other factors under the control of the parties, have as their object any of the following:

(a)   the restriction of a party's ability to determine its prices when selling products to third parties;

(b)   the limitation of output, except limitations on the output of contract products imposed on the licensee in a non-reciprocal agreement or imposed on only one of the licensees in a reciprocal agreement;

(c)   the allocation of markets or customers, except ...

(d)   the restriction of the licensee's ability to exploit its own technology rights or the restriction of the ability of any of the parties to the agreement to carry out research and development, unless such latter restriction is indispensable to prevent the disclosure of the licensed know-how to third parties.

4(2)   Where the undertakings party to the agreement are not competing undertakings, the exemption provided for in Article 2 shall not apply to agreements which, directly or indirectly, in isolation or in combination with other factors under the control of the parties, have as their object any of the following:

(a)   the restriction of a party's ability to determine its prices when selling products to third parties, without prejudice to the possibility of imposing a maximum sale price or recommending a sale price, provided that it does not amount to fixed or minimum sale price as a result of pressure from, or incentives offered by, any of the parties;

(b)   the restriction of the territory into which, or of the customers to whom, the licensee may passively sell the contract products, except ...

(c)   the restriction of active or passive sales to end-users by a licensee which is a member of a selective distribution system and which operates at the retail level, without prejudice to the possibility of prohibiting a member of the system from operating out of an unauthorised place of establishment.'

Article 4(1)(c) and (2)(b) are each subject to a number of exceptions, discussed more fully below, in the context of territorial and customer limitations. Article 4(3) addresses the situation where the parties are not competing undertakings when the licence is entered into, but become so later. In such a case, and provided that the agreement is not 'subsequently amended in any material respect', they are still treated for the purposes of determining which 'blacklist' of 'hardcore restrictions' applies under Article 4 as if they were not competing undertakings. Article 5 sets out some 'excluded restrictions' to which the exemption does not apply, but the presence of which in a licence will not prevent the exemption applying to the rest of it. One of these, at Article 5(2), is the restriction listed in Article 4(1)(d) for competing undertakings, but here applied to non-competing undertakings. The other 'excluded restrictions' in Article 5 are discussed in more detail below, in the context of 'Improvements' and 'Early termination'.

Article 6 allows the Commission to withdraw the benefit of the Block Exemption in individual cases, and Article 7 allows the Commission to withdraw its benefit from certain specified types of licence.

The Block Exemption is silent as to a number of restrictions commonly found in patent licences but which are not generally considered, irrespective of issues such as market share, to fall within TFEU Article 101 in the first place, and so do not preclude the application of the Block Exemption. Such restrictions are conveniently listed at para [183] of the *Guidelines*, which states:

'[183]   This section does not deal with obligations in licence agreements that are generally not restrictive of competition within the meaning of Article 101(1) of the Treaty. These obligations include but are not limited to:

(a)   confidentiality obligations;

(b)   obligations on licensees not to sub-license;

(c)   obligations not to use the licensed technology rights after the expiry of the agreement, provided that the licensed technology rights remain valid and in force;

(d)   obligations to assist the licensor in enforcing the licensed intellectual property rights;

(e)   obligations to pay minimum royalties or to produce a minimum quantity of products incorporating the licensed technology; and

(f)   obligations to use the licensor's trade mark or indicate the name of the licensor on the product.'

Certain of these restrictions were also specifically recognized as in earlier versions of the Block Exemption as not precluding its application.

National competition laws

3.14   Domestic UK competition law also imposes constraints on patent licensing. Thus, in the UK patent licences that do not fall within the Block Exemption may fall within the scope of the Competition Act 1998. However, provided that they fall within the scope of an EU block exemption, they are automatically excluded from the Article 101-like scope of the 'Chapter I prohibition' under the Competition Act 1998, s 2 by virtue of the 'parallel exemption' provisions of the Competition Act 1998, s 10. There are no domestic block exemptions under the 1998 Act relevant to patent licensing, and although the Office of Fair Trading (OFT) which administers UK competition law, did issue draft competition law guidelines on IPRs in November 2001, it took these no further.

Certain provisions of PA 1977 as originally enacted used to prohibit certain tie-in clauses in patent licences, and expressly gave either party to a patent licence agreement the right to terminate it once the last of the original licensed patents had expired. However, these provisions were repealed by the Competition Act 1998.

Specific patent licence terms – grant and scope of licence

Introduction

3.15   This section and the remaining sections of this chapter discuss in detail many of the specific provisions often found in patent licences. Of these, however, the most critical provisions, and the ones that have to be tailored most towards any particular situation, are those concerned with the grant, and the scope of the licence. It is these that determine what activities are permitted, and what activities are not permitted, under the licence.

The scope of the licence, in terms of manufacture and/or sale, or exclusively own use, should be made clear, but in most cases it will be to both manufacture and sale. The licence should be specified as being exclusive, sole or non-exclusive, and definitions given setting out what is meant by these terms as there can be some confusion in different countries as to the difference between exclusive (which precludes the licensor itself from exploiting) and sole (which does not preclude the licensor from exploiting). These terms can be applied differently to different aspects of the licensed activities, and thus it is possible for example, to grant an exclusive manufacturing licence in one European country, but a non-exclusive licence to sell in that and other European countries.

The duration of the licence should be specified, which will usually be from the date of the licence, or a relatively recent starting date chosen for accounting convenience. There are three basic choices as to duration:

(i)   life of the patents;
(ii) fixed-term; or
(iii) ongoing licence with periodic termination rights.

A fixed term is likely to be appropriate where know-how is a significant aspect of the licensed rights. It should be recognized that following termination or expiry of the agreement the licensee has no contractual duty to pay any royalty. The term of the agreement, therefore, should be as long as possible within the constraints imposed by the applicable competition law, which will in general preclude paying a royalty in respect of rights that have expired.

Identification of the licensed patents and know-how

3.16   Because a patent licence is an authority or permission from the owner of a patent to do something which such owner could otherwise prohibit, and a right to do something which is otherwise restricted by the very nature of the right itself, it is important when drafting a patent licence to appreciate the scope of such restrictions in relation to a patents as discussed later in **Chapter 6**. A licence will authorize all, or certain only of such rights, subject to such conditions as the licensor may choose to impose, within the constraints of competition law. Competition law issues can arise where the licence purports to limit the freedom of the licensee to do things that it would otherwise anyway be free to do.

The parties should ensure that the licence agreement states unambiguously the rights in respect of which the licence is to be granted. Where registered rights such as patents and patent applications are licensed[1] the registration numbers should be identified, perhaps in a schedule, unless, as is often the case in licencing in the information computing and technology (ICT) sector, they are too numerous, when a 'capture period' identifying them by reference probably to a period within which their priority dates fall may be appropriate. Because patents are essentially of a national nature, reference to the appropriate foreign rights corresponding to domestic rights should be made where the licensed territory extends beyond the domestic territory. However, if for example, patents have not yet been granted there will be uncertainty inherent in any such definition, as the scope of the claims eventually likely to be obtained, and thus the ultimate scope of the licensed rights, cannot be predicted with any certainty.[2] In such cases it may be also be important to have a clear definition of the licensed product, as to which see below.

Know-how, if this is also being licensed, presents especial problems of description. Any know-how to be disclosed should, as far as possible, be in documentary form and described in as much detail as possible. Indeed to the extent that it is not possible so to identify such material, it will not be regarded as know-how for the purposes of the Block Exemption as by Article 1(1)(i):

'"know-how" means a package of practical information, resulting from experience and testing, which is:
(i)   secret, that is to say, not generally known or easily accessible,
(ii)   substantial, that is to say, significant and useful for the production of the contract products, and
(iii) identified, that is to say, described in a sufficiently comprehensive manner so as to make it possible to verify that it fulfils the criteria of secrecy and substantiality;
These requirements are further discussed in the *Guidelines* at para [45].'

1   The expression 'technology rights' by Article 1(1)(b) of the Block Exemption means 'know-how and the following rights, or a combination thereof, including applications for or applications for registration of those rights' namely patents, utility models, design rights, semiconductor chip topographies, supplementary protection certificates, plant breeders certificates and software copyrights'.
2   For an example of the difficulties that can arise when a licence is expressed simply by reference to patent applications and/or granted patents without defining the licensed products see: *Oxonica Energy Ltd v Neuftec Ltd* [2009] EWHC 2127 (Patents Court), [2009] EWCA Civ 668 (Court of Appeal).

Identification of the licensed product

3.17   The precise nature of the licensed product, and not just the licensed rights, should also be identified. For example, with novel chemical entities a licensed patent is likely to cover a family of compounds, and if only one compound in this family is to be licensed this limitation should be stated. This approach also enables a patentee to split rights as between different licensees. Careful identification of the licensed product may also help if for some reason there are problems in adequately defining the patents and know-how that are licensed, and in ensuring that there is some meaningful royalty base that is not keyed to the precise scope of any patents eventually obtained, always subject to the competition law concerns of basing a royalty on something that is not protected by any patent or know-how.[1]

1   An example of litigation over a licence agreement over which the English courts had jurisdiction, but which turned on the question of whether or not, under different national laws, a certain product fell within the scope of a patent licence was the three actions (each under a different patent, two US ones and one German one, but all in respect of the same product) reported as: *Celltech (Adair's) US Patent* [2002] EWHC 2167; [2003] FSR 25 (Patents Court); [2003] EWCA Civ 1008; [2004] FSR 3 (Court of Appeal); *Celltech R&D Ltd v Medimmune Inc.* [2004] EWHC 1124; and *Celltech R&D Ltd v Medimmune Inc.* [2004] EWHC 22 (Patents Court); [2004] EWCA Civ 1331; [2005] FSR 21 (Court of Appeal).

Territorial limitations

3.18   It is usual, except in the ICT sector, where licences are often expressed to be worldwide in scope, for licences to be granted by reference to a specific territory or territories. In the absence of clear territorial definition the licensee may (depending on how the licensed rights are defined) be entitled to exploit on a worldwide basis. The territory or territories the subject of licence should be specified, country by country, – as inherently imprecise terminology should be avoided (eg 'Europe' or 'Asia', or terms which by their nature are likely to change during the term of the licence, eg 'the European Union'). The corollary of defining a licensed sales territory might be thought to be an appropriate export ban ensuring that licensed goods do not stray outside the agreed area. However in the EU export restrictions as between Member States are prima facie unlawful under TFEU, Article 101 given that such provisions inevitably involve some degree of partitioning of the internal market. The Block Exemption provides a limited safe harbour for licences with certain types of export restriction, depending on whether or not the parties to the licence are 'competing undertakings' as defined in Article 1(1)(n) and where they are, whether or not the agreement is a 'reciprocal', or a 'non-reciprocal' one as defined in Article 1(1)(d)–(e). Thus, for an agreement between competing undertakings the following degree of territorial market allocation can be included without losing the benefit of the Block Exemption from it:

'4(1)(c) ...

(i)   the obligation on the licensor and/or the licensee, in a non-reciprocal agreement, not to produce with the licensed technology rights within the exclusive territory reserved for the other party and/or not to sell actively and/or passively into the exclusive territory ... reserved for the other party,

(ii)   the restriction, in a non-reciprocal agreement, of active sales by the licensee into the exclusive territory ... allocated by the licensor to another licensee provided the latter was not a competing undertaking of the licensor at the time of the conclusion of its own licence,'

Contractual restrictions supporting territorial market allocation in reciprocal agreements between competing undertakings cannot so benefit. The situation is different as between non-competing undertakings, as to which restrictions as to the territory into which the licensee may actively sell the contract products, as well as certain types of territorial market allocation can be included without losing the benefit of the Block Exemption, namely: '4(2)(b) ... (i) the restriction of passive sales into an exclusive territory ... reserved for the licensor'.

The territorial right to carry out licensed manufacture need not be co-extensive with the right to sell. Thus the marketing territory can be granted in broader terms than the manufacturing territory. Thus, a patent licence could grant the licensee an exclusive right to manufacture in, say one country, but the scope of the license as to sales could be non-exclusive in all countries where patents subsist. Whilst that offers export possibilities to the licensee, it will not have such sales market to itself, as its fellow licensees manufacturing elsewhere can compete for sales in such markets. Hence before entering into such licences consideration should be given to the likelihood of parallel trade; and in general to the likelihood of competition between, or from licensees particularly from other EU countries.

Product market and field of use limitations

3.19 A patent, or a single product, can often have application to quite different product markets or fields of use. Thus, a licensor with a patent for a new chemical entity with potential utility as a pharmaceutical could license this to one company for veterinary, and another for human, applications. This may also be backed up by a contractual obligation on the part of the licensee not to operate in the other fields. The current version of the Block Exemption is silent as to this although the version that preceded it made express reference to it as an exception to the 'hardcore' restriction on 'the allocation of markets or customers'. However, the *Guidelines* at paras [208]–[215] make it clear that field of use restrictions are in general block exempted below the relevant market share thresholds.

Customer limitations

3.20   Although limitations as to the sort of customer that the licensee can supply are not a common feature of patent licence agreements they do arise in certain special cases, and the Block Exemption expressly provides a safe harbour for some of these. In the same way as for territorial limitations, in an agreement between competing undertakings the following degree of customer group allocation can be included without losing the benefit of the Block Exemption:

'4(1)(c) ...
(i)   the obligation on the licensor and/or the licensee, in a non-reciprocal agreement, ... not to sell actively and/or passively ... to the exclusive customer group reserved for the other party,
(ii)   the restriction, in a non-reciprocal agreement, of active sales by the licensee ... to the exclusive customer group allocated by the licensor to another licensee provided the latter was not a competing undertaking of the licensor at the time of the conclusion of its own licence'

As with territorial limitations, contractual restrictions supporting customer group allocation in reciprocal agreements between competing undertakings cannot benefit from the safe harbour of the Block Exemption. The situation is different as between non-competing undertakings, as to which restrictions as to the customers to which the licensee may actively sell the contract products, as well as certain other contractual restrictions supporting customer group allocation can be included, and the licence still benefit from the Block Exemption as follows: '4(2)(b) ... (i) the restriction of passive sales ... to an exclusive customer group reserved for the licensor'.

In addition there are two special situations, that of a licence to manufacture for one's own use, (a 'captive use restriction') as to which see *Guidelines* para [216]–[220]) and a second source licence, where customer allocation is also permitted. Thus, as to competing undertakings the following obligations on the licensee benefit from the safe harbour:

'4(1)(c) ...
(iii)   the obligation on the licensee to produce the contract products only for its own use provided that the licensee is not restricted in selling the contract products actively and passively as spare parts for its own products,
(iv)   the obligation on the licensee, in a non-reciprocal agreement, to produce the contract products only for a particular customer, where the licence was granted in order to create an alternative source of supply for that customer'

Identically expressed obligations for non-competing undertakings by Article 4(2)(b)(ii)–(iii) also benefit from the safe harbour, except that for second sourcing the licence can also be reciprocal. Also, as between non-competing undertakings the following further types of customer restriction on a licensee benefit from the Block Exemption:

'4(2)(b) … (v) the restriction of sales to end-users by a licensee operating at the wholesale level of trade; (vi) the restriction of sales to unauthorised distributors by the members of a selective distribution system'.

Article 4(2)(c) also excludes from the application of the Block Exemption a restriction on active or passive sales to end-users by a licensee which is a member of a selective distribution systems, and which operates at a the retail level.

Other 'hardcore restrictions'

3.21 Article 4(1) (as to competing undertakings) and Article 4(2) (as to non-competing undertakings) also set out certain other 'hardcore restrictions' that prevent an agreement which contains them from benefitting from the Block Exemption, namely price restrictions (Article 4(1)(a) and 4(2)(a) and *Guidelines* para [118]) and in a licence as between competing undertakings, output restrictions (Article 4(1)(b) and *Guidelines* paras [204]–[207]) and restrictions on a licensee's ability to exploit its own technology (Article 4(1)(d)). Certain of these restrictions are themselves qualified (as set out in para 3.13 above).

Right to sub-license

3.22 As a matter of English law a licence does not automatically confer on the licensee (even if a sole or exclusive licensee) a right to sub-license, and the right to do so must be made express if it is to apply. Sub-contracting is treated like sub-licensing; thus a right 'to manufacture' does not automatically provide a right 'to have manufactured', and if this is intended it should be so stated.

The licensor will encounter enforcement problems against sub-licensees and sub-contractors because of the English law rules on privity of contract. Where sub-licensing and sub-contracting is permitted the licensor should make the licensee responsible for the default of the sub-licensee or sub-contractor, and either expressly state that all sub-licences will cease on termination of the main licence (thus all income will cease) or require that all sub-licences be assigned to the licensor (but the licensor may then be faced with contracts with parties, which for one reason or another, it would not itself have selected). The licensor who insists on approval of each sub-licensee, and the terms of each sub-licence mitigates this risk.

In theory there is no limit to the length of a chain of sub-licensees. However, the sub-licensee will want to ensure that it will actually get the rights for which it bargained. Furthermore a sub-licensee wants to be sure that its sub-licence will continue in force, notwithstanding problems higher up the chain.

Specific patent licence terms – structuring payments for the rights granted

Royalties and other provisions as to payment

3.23   It is normal for an entire section of the licence to be devoted to the payment of royalties, and the various features attendant thereon. In addition to the provision which actually sets out the details of how the royalty is calculated there will be a provision setting out when it is payable (eg monthly, quarterly, bi-annually, or annually) and specifying a payment procedure (eg destination and currency conversion). The calculation will depend on the approach adopted (viz. sales turnover, units of production, or share of net profits from licensee's selling operation) but if the most conventional approach, that of a royalty calculated as a percentage of sales turnover, is adopted, provision ought also be made for deeming a sales turnover in the case of non-arm's length sales by the licensee, products that are hired or leased, and products sold as part of a larger piece of equipment. This can be done as part of the definition of the term 'net sales price' that will typically have been defined as the basis for the calculation of royalties, and be subject to deductions from the gross sale price for delivery charges, and so on. This can also be done by defining the term 'supply' to include products which the licensee may dispose of otherwise than by way of sale. These issues are discussed further below in relation to the royalty base.

The royalty clause will also normally provide for reporting obligations on the part of the licensee, whereby the licensee is obliged to provide, usually at the same time as it makes the royalty payment, details of how the royalty has been calculated, including sales figures broken down appropriately. It may also be required to provide an annual statement of sales certified by auditors, and a set of annual audited accounts. A licence should always include a right on the part of the licensor to inspect the relevant records of the licensee, a right which a prudent licensor should avail itself of as matter of course at least once, and generally towards the end of the life of licence, even if it has no suspicion of any underpayment, as studies have demonstrated that underpayment, albeit often inadvertent, tends to be the norm. There will also be provision for interest on overdue payments.

Lump sum payments

3.24 Although most licences have a running royalty geared in some way to the use to which the licensed patents and any licensed know how is put, if the know-how is the most important of a mixed know-how and patent licence (eg where no patents have yet been granted and there is uncertainty as to whether patents of useful scope will be secured) then it should be borne in mind that once any know-how or other trade secrets have been disclosed the clock cannot be turned back. The mere fact of the disclosure should be viewed as devaluing the trade secret itself, as the licensor is no longer the only person to know it. One way for a licensor to try to protect against this is by an upfront payment. At the time of disclosure there is no certainty that the licensee will proceed to exploit the product, and generate royalties on sales. The disclosure may provide a 'springboard effect' enabling exploitation of products not contemplated at the outset; nor easily identifiable as stemming from the original disclosure. Equally, what is confidential today may become public knowledge tomorrow. The licensee will not be keen to continue paying royalties on a technology that its competitors can freely exploit. Such an approach may also be appropriate where the commercial life of the technology may be limited, or it risks suffering early competition from rival technologies.

Even if the licence is a bare patent licence, with no know-how disclosed, the licensor might consider seeking an upfront payment particularly where the licence is exclusive, and the licensor precluded from parallel exploitation. In this case it may be reasonable to allow such a payment as an advance against the future royalties which would otherwise be payable during an agreed initial period.

Royalty base

3.25 Whilst it is contractually possible to grant licences in return for no more than a one-off payment (a 'paid up' licence) this means that the licensor takes the risk that the technology will be a huge success, and fails to share in the benefits of this. It is, therefore, generally preferable, and indeed usual, for payment to be assessed as a function of licensee's exploitation, by means of running royalties, which can be combined with milestone payments. What, however, is the best way of gearing royalties to exploitation? A fixed royalty per unit or quantity (linked to inflation) will discourage price-cutting on the part of the licensee, and limit its ability to react in the market place. It is accordingly unlikely to be attractive to a licensee. A more attractive balance between the licensor's interests and those of the licensee is to gear royalties as a percentage of selling price. Selling price as identified by an invoice is an objective test that can be substantiated.

Assessing royalties on the licensee's profits or the licensee's costs has attraction in theory to the licensee but can prove difficult to construe, and risks providing a future source of dispute. For example, if royalty is assessed on:

— *Cost of manufacture* – How this will be calculated will be rife with uncertainty. A detailed definition must be agreed to apply regardless of the actual practice of the licensee. Failure to agree such a definition will lead to uncertainty if accounting practices change throughout the agreement or if different practices apply from site to site.

— *Profits* – Then the same accounting problem arises as profits are essentially the difference between the selling price and manufacturing price.

Either way the licensor is penalized, in the first case if the licensee is efficient, and in the second case if the licensee is not. In neither case is this related to the value of the technology.

The classic structure for running royalties which avoids these problems is to charge a percentage on the 'net selling price' of each product 'made and sold' by the licensee. This can be analyzed as follows:

— *Percentage rate* – A percentage protects the licensee from the ravages of inflation, although the licensor may also seek to protect itself by imposing a minimum unit royalty in order to guard against the consequences of price wars or deflation. (The size of the percentage (the royalty rate) is discussed separately below.)

— *Net selling price (NSP)* – It is usual to deduct tax, insurance, and freight from the licensee's actual selling price of the licensed product. The licensor should also consider whether in the particular industry the product will be sold at a discount, and if so, whether such trade discounts should be allowable against the NSP or whether the list price for an arm's length transaction should apply. Often the licensed product is not itself sold – for example, it may be an intermediate used in the synthesis of a pharmaceutical compound. In such a case the licensor should attempt to define the end product, and levy royalties on its sales.

— *Made and sold* – The cash flow advantages of levying royalty on a product which is 'manufactured' but not yet sold are tempting but should be resisted, to avoid the accounting difficulty of assessing the ultimate selling price when this is not known at the time of manufacture. However, the licensor should also then consider the position at the end of the licence, to ensure that there is provision for royalty to be paid on the product manufactured during the course of the licence, and disposed of after it, assuming, of course, that this is permitted. The licence agreement should ensure that royalty is payable on sale, invoicing, first use, or other disposal. The licensor's right to collect royalty should be independent of the receipt of the purchase price by the licensee. It chooses its own customers and the licensor should not suffer because of bad debts owed to the licensee.

It is important to gear the overall term of a licence agreement to the rights that are being licensed. For example, a licence only of patents should not continue after the last extant patent expires (for there is nothing then left to license, and to justify payment of royalties) or, if know-how is an important feature of the transaction, and the prospect of patent protection is uncertain, some fixed date in the future at around the same time as any patents, were they to be secured, might be expected to expire. Nor should the licensor require the licensee to buy some other product from the licensor or its nominees. Such 'tying' is regarded as objectionable under most competition laws except in very special circumstances (see, eg the *Guidelines* at paras [221]–[225]).

In a mixed patent and know-how licence, when it comes to stipulating royalties, it can be unwise to have a single flat percentage rate irrespective of whether the article:

— is patented but uses none of the know-how;
— uses know-how but does not fall within the patent; or
— is both patented and uses know-how.

There may also be attractions in having a multiple tier royalty structure where the scope of the patents likely ultimately to be obtained is in doubt, or to provide for certain of those patents expiring, or being invalidated during the life of the agreement. If different rates are used for these various different situations it may also be necessary to scale the targets used as a basis for the minimum royalties to reflect the rates in question. One advantage of such mixed licences is that they provide some know-how remains, this can serve to keep a licence in place even if none of the patents proceed to grant; in which case such rate-scaling has much to recommend it.

A degree of rate-scaling may also be appropriate where, in order to exploit a technology a licensee requires separate patent licences from several different parties, a situation common in biotechnology. In such a case the total royalty payable may render such exploitation uneconomic, and one way to address this is with a 'royalty stacking' clause, that allows for the royalty payable to each licensor to be reduced. Such clauses require careful drafting to ensure that different licensors are fairly treated, and that it is clear what other sorts of licence are covered by such a provision. An example of a dispute over the proper construction of a royalty stacking clause is provided by *Cambridge Antibody Technology v Abbott Biotechnology*.[1]

1 *Cambridge Antibody Technology Ltd v Abbott Biotechnology Ltd* [2004] EWHC 2974, [2005] FSR 27.

Royalty rates

3.26 Royalty rates in licences are notoriously a matter of confidentiality. However, some figures do emerge in some press releases and other documents, and sometimes in the course of reported litigation.[1] There are a number of different theories as to how royalty rates are to be determined, and this will depend on a range of factors such the degree of exclusivity conferred, the sector concerned, the stage of development of the licenced technology, the likely profitability of the licenced product, including a consideration of what other royalties must be paid in order to sell the licenced product.[2] Broadly speaking, however, one can identify two types of approach as providing a starting point for any such negotiation.

The first is based on comparable licences, where these exist and the data as to them is available. The other licences need not be under the same patent, but such an approach is clearly the most appropriate in the case of a non-exclusive licence where other licences have already been granted, as there can be little that is more 'comparable' than a licence under the same patent, although there is no obligation on a licensor to grant a licence at the same royalty as it has agreed with other licensees, under the same patent, unless the licence also includes a 'most favoured nation' clause.

The second approach, the 'profit sharing' approach, is one which probably has more application to exclusive licences, especially where these relate to an untested technology, and looks to the likely profitability of the licensed technology in the hands of the licensee, and splits such likely profit as between the licensor, and the licensee in an appropriate way, taking account of matters such as the risk the parties are assuming, and the amount of investment that the licensee must make to bring the licensed product to market. The approach evidently lacks precision, given that 'profit' can be a somewhat flexible accounting concept, and the uncertainty as to the nature of the split, but in some cases it may provide the only guidance available. Thus the split depends typically on the degree to which risk is shared between the parties, so that for an early-stage licence, as to which the majority of the risk generally lies with the licensee, a split of 25 per cent to the licensor and 75 per cent to the licensee may be considered appropriate (hence giving rise to the expression 'the 25 per cent rule of thumb', and which has some basis in reported royalty rates) whereas for a later negotiated licence a more even split between the parties, or even one that favours the licensor, may be deemed appropriate.[3]

---

1   One up-to-date source of information, directed however more to merchandising and trade mark licensing than to patent licensing, is Battersby, Gregory and Grimes, Charles, *Licensing Royalty Rates* published annually by Wolters Kluwer. One reported dispute in the English courts over a patent licence in which meaningful

figures emerged was *Cambridge Antibody Technology v Abbott Biotechnology* (see para 3.25, fn 1 above) and that provided, under its 'royalty stacking' clause, for a royalty of between 2 per cent and 6 per cent, depending on whether or not certain other royalties payable by the licensee to third parties could be set-off against it. It was held on construing the clause that the licensee could not set off the particular royalties that it sought to set-off, and thus the correct royalty rate was 6 per cent. See also the discussion as to damages awards in **Chapter 6** at para 6.22, 'Damages'.

2   See for example, Razgaitis, R – *Pricing the Intellectual Property of Early Stage Technologies: A Primer of Basic Valuation Tools and Considerations*, in *Intellectual Property Management in Health and Agricultural Innovation: A Handbook of Best Practices* (eds Krattiger, A, Mahoney, RT, Nelsen, L, et al) MIHR, Oxford UK, and PIPRA, Davis USA. (Available online at: http://www.iphandbook.org) and which provides a number of examples of royalty rate ranges for different technologies.

3   See Goldscheider, R, Jarosz, J and Mulhern, C – *Use of the 25 per cent Rule in Valuing IP* – [2002] *Les Nouvelles*, 123, and that tests its factual underpinnings by reference to actual royalty rate data. The '25 per cent rule' has more recently been considered in *Profitability and royalty rates across industries: Some preliminary evidence* – KPMG, 2012, which concludes that reported royalty rates 'tend to fall between 25% of gross margins and 25% of operating margins' and also lists a number of other sources in the literature. The '25 per cent rule of thumb' used also commonly to be applied in damages calculations in patent litigation in the USA. However, in *Uniloc USA Inc and Uniloc Singapore Private Ltd v Microsoft Corp,* (Federal Circuit, 4 January 2011) the Court criticized it as 'a fundamentally flawed tool' because it did not differentiate between different industries, technologies, or parties, but rather assumed the same 25/75 royalty split regardless of the size of the patent portfolio in question, or the value of the patented technology.

Taxation

3.27   Taxation on royalties should also be addressed, and in addition to providing that the licensee is responsible in addition for any VAT chargeable on the royalty a grossing-up clause should be included, by which the licensee bears the risk of withholding taxes, and other deductions, paying to the licensor such sum as after such deductions would come to such sum as would be payable under the licence but for such withholding, with provision for the licensor to credit the licensee with any corresponding tax credits that it receives. Grossing-up clauses are not effective in all countries so local advice is needed on this aspect. In addition the licence should include an obligation on the parties to cooperate in seeking to secure double taxation relief, on the assumption that this is available between the relevant countries.

The licensor should establish whether, in certain circumstances, the receipts derived from the commercialization will be taxed in its hands as income or capital. Naturally the position will depend on the taxation regime to which it is subject. The licensee will also wish to be sure that whatever payments are made will confer upon it some form of tax relief, whether by way of an allowable deduction from profits or income, or some other specified tax allowance, eg capital allowances. Both the licensor and licensee should establish whether tax should be deducted at source, and paid over to the tax authorities in respect of any payment made under the licence, and both should take account of the impact of VAT or other similar legislation in each case.

In the UK, except in relation to payments between UK resident companies, royalties under a patent licence are subject to the deduction of income tax at the basic rate, irrespective of where the recipient is based, unless permission has been obtained from the Inland Revenue under the terms of a double taxation agreement allowing such payments to be made without deduction of tax. The paying party must account for the tax so deducted, but may retain it. Moreover, the provision of IP is regarded as the supply of a service, and so VAT will generally be chargeable on such payments.

Taxation considerations may also be taken account of in structuring the transaction in the first place, and in providing, for example, for royalties to be routed through entities based in tax favourable jurisdictions, although the value and applicability of such mechanism will depend on the circumstances of the licensor, and the benefits should in general be considerable to compensate for the extra complexity that such structures may entail.

Specific patent licence terms – other obligations on licensee

Introduction

3.28 In addition to the limitations as to territory, product market or field of use, and customers, often backed up by contractual limitations as discussed above, and obligations as to payment, a licence agreement (especially if exclusive or sole) will normally impose various other obligations on a licensee. Those as to minimum performance obligations and as to quality standards, are discussed in further detail below, but several others are also met.

A 'no challenge restriction' is an 'excluded restriction' under Article 5(1)(b) of the Block Exemption, and so does not benefit from it. An alternative approach that does however benefit from the Block Exemption, but which is only available for exclusive licences, is that for termination on challenge (discussed below under 'Early termination').

An obligation not to solicit the licensor's employees, consultants or agents during the term of the licence can be included. A licensee may be required to mark the licensed product with an indication of the licensor's name, or of the licensed patent. A licensor may wish to include restrictions preventing the licensee manufacturing or dealing in any other products the subject of the patent, or being engaged in any business that deals in competing products.

Minimum performance obligations

3.29 Since it is merely a permission to do something, a licence implies no positive duty on the part of the licensee to exploit the licensed technology. For exclusive licences, especially of fully developed and proven products the licensee should be committed to make minimum periodic payments (coupled perhaps with provision for upward adjustment by reference to the appropriate retail price index (RPI)) irrespective of the actual degree of exploitation. Such minimum return not only protects the licensor's expectation of an income stream but can also, if triggered and the licence so provides, establish an objective test for terminating the licence. Where seed technologies are disclosed, and licensed and require future substantial investment for development prior to production there will be resistance to any such minimum performance obligations. In such a case, whilst minimum performance obligations should be retained (and their application deferred as necessary to provide for the anticipated development period) their relevance could perhaps be limited to criteria for conversion of the licence from exclusive to non-exclusive.

Often as an alternative to objective criteria such as minimum periodic payments and minimum sales, the licensor may impose on a licensee an obligation to use its 'best endeavours'[1] to exploit the technology. Whilst under English law this is an onerous obligation upon the licensee which requires it to do all in its power to perform the obligation, it is not an objective criteria, and it can therefore be difficult for the licensor to show its breach on the part of the licensee. Even so, most prospective licensees will normally try in negotiations to replace such an obligation with the somewhat less onerous 'reasonable endeavours' or some variation on this.[2]

1 The meaning of the term was considered in the context of a patent licence in *Terrell v Mabie Todd & Co* (1952) 69 RPC 234, and also in *IBM United Kingdom v Rockware Glass Ltd* [1980] FSR 335.
2 This sort of terminology has not been considered by the English courts in the context of patent licences but a variation of it was considered, in a real property context, in *CPC Group Ltd v Qatari Diar Real Estate Investment Company* [2010] EWHC 1535, where previous cases considering other variations were also reviewed. However, and also in another context than patent licences 'all reasonable endeavours' was agreed, on the special circumstances of the case, to mean the same as 'best endeavours' in *Jet2.com Ltd v Blackpool Airport Ltd* [2011] EWHC 1529, [2012] EWCA 417.

Quality standards

3.30 A licensee can be required to ensure that the licensed products are of good and merchantable quality, comply with local regulations, or meet licensor's specifications, although such a provision must not have an anti-competitive aim. Thus, obligations that could be considered from a quality control (QC) perspective would include an obligation to comply with the licensor's testing, and QC procedures, to submit items to be used in the manufacturing process for the licensor's prior approval, to provide samples of products, and to permit the licensor access to the licensee's plants to inspect production. A licensor may also wish to oblige a licensee to give guarantees to its customers, and provide service and repair facilities.

Although, absent trade mark considerations, there is little scope, at least in Europe, for a licensor to be held liable in strict liability for the actions of its patent licensee it is prudent to impose an indemnity from the licensee in favour of the licensor in respect of product liability claims which might be made against the licensor arising out of the licensee's manufacture and sale of the licensed products, and to impose an obligation on the licensee to insure against claims. As with other agreements, the licensor will usually impose an obligation on the licensee not to purport to act as licensor's agent.

Specific patent licence terms – obligations on licensor

Introduction

3.31 Apart from mutual obligations, such as confidentiality and perhaps disclosing and making licences available for improvements, discussed below, a patent licensor will usually assume relatively few obligations, the most common of which is to maintain the licensed patents in force. Three other obligations that are sometimes found: as to technical assistance and training, warranties, and as to most favoured licensee, are discussed below.

Technical assistance and training

3.32 A licence with an element of know-how licensing about it will have provision as to the delivery of the know-how. However, over and above such disclosure of know-how in documentary form the licensee may, in certain circumstances, require training for the purposes of starting up, and ongoing assistance on specific problems. Typically, the training for starting up will be provided as part of the overall deal, and therefore the licensor will be careful to limit the number of work days to be provided to a finite amount. Ongoing training is usually provided at a daily consultancy rate at times to be mutually agreed. If the licensor has to go into the licensee's premises to sort out a technical difficulty this should be at the cost of the licensee. The licensor should also be careful not to guarantee performance, or to warrant that the licensee's personnel will be brought up-to-speed for an agreed cost, or within an agreed time. Differences in skills and work practices, especially in different countries may make any such commitment impossible.

Warranties

3.33 It is rare for a patent licensor to give much by way of warranties, and especially rare (and foolish) for a licensor to give that warranty which would be of most value to a licensee, namely that operating within the scope of the licence will not infringe any third-party patents or other IPRs. Neither ought a licensor warrant that a licensed patent is valid, as patents may always be invalidated on the basis of prior art unknown to the patentee, or to those responsible for undertaking a prior art search in the course of patent prosecution. Indeed, many licensors will expressly exclude such warranties, out of fear that they may be implied, and licences will often also include 'entire agreement' clauses excluding reliance on any representations made by the parties but not incorporated in the licence.

A licensor may well be prepared to warrant that it is proprietor of a patent, and that the patent is in force, although in reality this is of little value as the licensee can, and should undertake its own searches of such matters on public registers. The licensee can also reasonably insist that the licensor discloses any claims known to the licensor that have been made against the activities the subject of the licence, or that would challenge the validity of the licensed patents. In certain circumstances it may be reasonable to provide for a reduction in royalty to the extent that the licensee is obliged to pay third parties for the right to practice the licence under such third parties' patents, always assuming that the third party is prepared to accept a royalty. In the event of a third-party claim, the licensor will need in any case to take appropriate action to maintain the integrity of its licensing network even if the licence agreement does not provide for any obligation so to do on its part.

If any warranties are to be given, careful thought should be given as to the appropriate consequences of their breach, and what if anything the licensor should be obllged to do, for example, by assisting in a redesign, or in trying to secure a licence from the third party, to assist in sorting matters out. From the point of view of the licensor, it may be best to specify that the sole and exclusive remedy of the licensee in such a case is to terminate the licence, although an exclusive licensee which will be investing in the technology will not accept such a provision.

Most favoured licensee

3.34 Where the licensee takes a non-exclusive licence for a marketing territory there is always the potential for future licensees to obtain licences on more favourable conditions. Similar considerations may apply to licensees who are exclusive in one territory but may be subject to competition from parallel imports from another. The licensee will therefore try to protect itself against the potential for others to compete in its territory, perhaps at a lower price or otherwise subject to less control or restraint from the licensor, by appropriate provisions in the licence agreement. An absolute obligation upon the licensor not to grant licences on more favourable conditions other than those granted to the particular licensee is onerous on the licensor (as every licence agreement will be negotiated and have its own nuances). Clearly, however, it is reasonable that the licensee should be protected, and one solution is to offer the particular licensee the option to replace the terms of its licence agreement with those terms offered to any other licensee in their entirety. From the licensor's viewpoint care must be taken to ensure the licensee is not entitled to 'cherry pick' from other licensees' terms.

Specific patent licence terms – other aspects

Improvements

3.35   Transactions in patents, especially licences, commonly include provisions as to 'improvements'. The term has been considered in both English and Scottish case law. This has tended to give it a wide interpretation, as for example in *Buchanan v Alba Diagnostics*.[1] Here it was held that an 'improvement' was something that made a device cheaper or more effective, or more useful or valuable, or which made a device preferable as a commercial item, and so achieved the same purpose as the original device but in a better way. The mere fact that a patent could be obtained for a new development did not preclude its being an 'improvement' over the prior art patent, and so here it was held to have been assigned at the same time as the prior art patent by an assignment assigning the prior art patent, and all improvements to it.

Considerable care should be taken not to draft improvement clauses so widely as to embrace products that fall outside the scope of the original licensed inventions. Indeed, if there is a disparity between the R&D resources of the parties, and the licensee is unlikely to be able to further the technology with its own resources, consideration should be given to whether such a provision is appropriate at all. The licensor in such a case may be better served by retaining its freedom to exploit its own improvements outside the existing licence arrangement. As an alternative the agreement may give the licensee an option to take a licence of certain such improvements. Access to future developments may however be one of the main reasons for the licensee entering into the agreement, or at least to make ongoing payments. Nevertheless the licensor should never promise to the licensee to make or develop improvements. The licensor will not be able to foresee with certainty (particularly where the licence is long-term) its technical and/or commercial ambitions in the future, and in particular must maintain its freedom to shut down, or redirect, its own R&D. Therefore, the most the licensor should undertake is to agree to make available those improvements which it reduces to commercial practice.

The licensee may also make useful improvements which the licensor will wish to be able to use by at least a royalty free non-exclusive grant back licence. Failure to do so would provide the opportunity for the licensee to move ahead of the licensor in staying at the forefront of the art. However, before using this as a reason for including a mutual improvements provision giving its licensee the unfettered right to use the licensor's improvements on the existing terms, the licensor should consider how likely such an eventuality actually is. Where provision is to be made for a grant back of rights to improvements the scope for negotiating the terms of this are restricted by competition law, as discussed in the *Guidelines* at paras [129]–[132]. Thus the Block Exemption does not, by Article 5(1)(a), apply to:

'(a) any direct or indirect obligation on the licensee to grant an exclusive licence or to assign rights, in whole or in part, to the licensor or to a third party designated by the licensor in respect of its own improvements to, or its own new applications of, the licensed technology;'

As 'excluded restrictions' such 'grant back' provisions do not themselves benefit from the safe harbour that the Block Exemption affords their inclusion but this does not prevent its applying to the rest of the licence. The intent of such restrictions on 'grant back' provisions favouring the licensor is to ensure that in the longer term a technology is more widely disseminated, that licensees have an incentive to develop it, and that the licensor does not maintain its control over it, beyond the lifetime of its own patents but purely on the basis of developments made by others. Given such constraints a licensor may not wish to incorporate any provision as to improvements, although a licensee will normally wish so to do. A compromise may be possible, whereby such improvements are disclosed, subject to provisions as to confidentiality, but where a licence under them is not automatic, and which then enables a further licence to the improvement, or a modification to the old one to cover it, to be negotiated should the parties so wish.

1   *Buchanan v Alba Diagnostics* [2000] RPC 367; [2001] RPC 43; [2004] RPC 34 (House of Lords). This was a Scottish case; see also *Johnston Pump General Valve Inc v Tyco Valves Ltd* (Evans-Lombe J, 19 December 2001, unreported) for an English case that also gave the term a broad definition.

Confidentiality

3.36   In the absence of a confidentiality obligation imposed upon the licensee, the original know-how and all improvements may fall into the public domain, devaluing their worth, and allowing others to use such information free of charge. Accordingly, any agreement other than a bare patent licence, with no provision of know-how or other reason for maintaining confidentiality, should include some provision as to confidentiality. This is usually a standard reciprocal obligation in respect of confidential information provided by either party to the other, with the usual exceptions for information already in the possession of the recipient, or which comes into the public domain other than through the fault of the recipient.

The obligation of confidentiality may be general and unrestricted, or it may be limited in some way, for example, in time or to documents clearly marked as confidential. Moreover, it may be expressed automatically to apply to improvements disclosed to one party by the other, in order not to compromise the novelty of any application for a patent in relation to these. Such a clause may also provide for steps to be taken by the recipient of confidential information to prevent it falling into the public domain, for example, as to ensuring its security and limiting access on a 'need to know' basis or to people who have signed undertakings of confidentiality with the recipient, and which the recipient undertakes to enforce against such people at the request of the party providing the information.

Assignment

3.37   Although a licence is personal to a licensee, there is an element of uncertainty under English law as to whether this necessarily prevents a licensee assigning its rights under a licence. Thus, it is common to make express provision preventing the licensee from assigning its rights under the licence, at least without the written consent of the licensor. A licensor that wishes to be able to refuse consent in its discretion should impose an absolute prohibition: wording ostensibly clarifying the issue by providing that consent is in the sole discretion of licensor only invites insistence from the other side that it should be 'reasonable', whatever that means, and opens up scope for recourse to the courts. A licensee who does assign the licence should, however, recognize that it will continue to be responsible, by virtue of privity of contract, for the acts and defaults of its assignee (unless the licensee secures a release from the licensor).

Infringement by third parties

3.38   The licence will usually require that the licensee notify the licensor of infringement of the licensed rights by third parties, but there are then a wide variety of consequences that can flow from this. Much time can be taken in licence negotiations on such provisions, which in practice can rarely cover adequately the various eventualities that can arise. Provisions which go beyond an obligation merely to consult in order to decide what to do are likely to be inappropriate in anything other than an exclusive licence. In an exclusive licence such provisions might retain to the licensor the initial right to institute proceedings at its cost and risk, with the licensee having the right to conduct proceedings at its cost and risk, if the licensor declines so to do. In such a case the licence will normally also provide for the party bringing proceedings to require the assistance of the other, and may also provide for the party bringing the proceedings to retain any damages without accounting to the other. Another approach, where the licensee is given no right to bring proceedings, is to commute royalties, or to pay them into an escrow account, during the period of the infringement. In either case the licensor should ensure that such provision only applies if the infringement is significant, setting out a clear and objective test as to what this means. In the escrow option the licensor, though not be obliged to sue even a significant third party for infringement, would have the commercial incentive to do so, if royalties were accruing to which it could only obtain access on bringing the infringement to an end. Whatever the provision that is negotiated, it should be made clear that it exhaustively sets out, and excludes the application of any statutory right conferred on the licensee to bring such proceedings without the consent of the licensor, as many countries confer such rights on exclusive licensees.[1]

1   As indeed does the UK by PA 1977, s 67.

Early termination

3.39   Most patent licences are expressed to last for the life of the licensed patents, but they should also make provision for early termination in certain circumstances. Provisions for termination other than for cause are rare, and a licensee, especially an exclusive licensee, will certainly wish to resist the scope for termination without cause given the investment which it will have made in commercializing the licensed technology.

In addition to those generalized termination provisions of the type standard in most commercial agreements, by which either party can terminate for breach (which must usually be 'material' and be subject to remedy where the breach is remediable) or on insolvency, it is common to list certain specific instances giving rise to a right on the part of the licensor to terminate such as failure on the part of the licensee to pay royalties when due, or to achieve minimum sales or royalties either on a year-by-year basis, or after some particular breakpoint some way into the term of the licence. Another specific instance giving rise to a right on the part of the licensor to terminate could be a change of control of the licensee, which type of provision assumes enormous significance in the event of company reorganizations or acquisitions, and so is often the main focus of any due diligence undertaken in such cases.[1]

By Article 5(1)(b) of the Block Exemption a provision can be included in the licence that will benefit from the Block Exemption by which the licensor can terminate the licence in the event of a challenge by an exclusive licensee to the validity of the licensed IPRs. A more extensive 'no-challenge' provision, for example, providing for termination on challenge by a non-exclusive licensee, or precluding any type of licensee from making such a challenge, or indeed challenging any of the licensor's IPRs in the EU, does not so benefit, but its inclusion does not prevent the application of the Block Exemption to the rest of the licence). The *Guidelines* discuss 'no-challenge clauses' at paras [133]–[140] and note at [para 140] that a termination on challenge clause concerning solely know-how is not excluded from the Block Exemption. It also notes at para [134] that in the context of a free licence a no-challenge clause is generally considered to fall outside TFEU, Article 101(1) reflecting the view taken by the Court of Justice in Case 65/86 *Bayer v Sullhofer*[2] in holding that:

> 'A no-challenge clause in a patent licensing agreement may, depending on the legal and economic context, restrict competition within the meaning of [TFEU] Article [101(1)]. Such a clause does not, however, restrict competition when the agreement in which it is contained granted a free licence and the licensee does not, therefore, suffer the competitive disadvantage involved in the payment of royalties or when the licence was granted subject to payment of royalties but relates to a technically outdated process which the undertaking accepting the no-challenge agreement did not use.'

1   In such a case the meaning of the term 'control' should be defined, for which purpose the definition in the Corporation Taxes Act 2010, s 1124 is convenient.
2   Case 65/86 *Bayer v Sullhofer* [1990] 4 CMLR 182; [1988] ECR 5249; [1990] FSR 300.

Consequences of termination

3.40   The consequences of termination other than on expiry of the underlying right should be addressed. Such consequences can include those as to the survival of certain provisions (such as those as to auditing, and as to not disclosing confidential information), assistance with amendment of registration details, the return to the licensor of all information provided by it, the return or certified destruction of samples, and advertising materials, and what is to be done with unsold products, which could for example either be sale for a limited period post-termination by the licensee, subject to payment of royalties, or an option for the licensor to purchase unsold stock at a pre-agreed price. Consideration should also be given to what is to happen to any sublicences – should they automatically terminate or (and especially if their terms have received its prior approval) be assigned to the licensor?

In more complex licences the precise nature of the consequences may be determined by the nature of the ground of termination. Continuing provisions obliging the licensee post-termination not to use or to divulge any know-how, and other confidential information communicated by the licensor for so long as it remains secret should be included, and one obliging the licensee not to exploit the licensed patents for so long as they are still in force, has value to the licensor as it may be easier to enforce as a contractual obligation than in the context of an infringement action.

Dispute resolution

3.41 Arbitration clauses (which should specify the arbitration institute whose rules are to be chosen, and follow the form of wording recommended by the nominated institution, covering matters such as the number of arbitrators, the language, and the place of the arbitration) are common in licence agreements. Although not necessarily cheaper or faster than litigation in a single country with a good court system they can under certain arbitral rules (eg those of WIPO) confer the advantage of automatic confidentiality and of a specialist tribunal. Their major practical advantage in contracts between companies in different countries is the relative ease with which arbitration awards can be enforced in many foreign jurisdictions, which would not readily enforce the order of a court – no matter how neutral.

'Boilerplate'

3.42 As with other agreements, licence agreements will also include 'boilerplate' clauses, such as provisions as to there being no partnership, a covenant for further assurance, limitations of liability, *force majeure*, severance or renegotiation in the event of partial illegality, mechanisms for giving notice, precluding indulgence from constituting waiver, providing that the licence represents the entire agreement between the parties, and specifying the governing law as well as the courts that have jurisdiction in the event that no provision is made for arbitration. These are common to all forms of international commercial agreements, and there are no considerations that are special to licences.

Chapter 4

Procedures in disputes concerning patents

Types of dispute concerning patents

Introduction

4.01   Patent prosecution procedure discussed in **Chapter 2** involves a dialogue between the applicant for the patent and the patent office, sometimes described as an *ex parte* procedure, whereas disputes between the owner of a granted patent (or occasionally a patent application) with third parties, over such patents or applications, and which are sometimes by way of contrast referred to as *inter partes*, form the subject of this chapter. Such litigation may still take place in a patent office, but much of it takes place in the courts, and some of it can only take place in the courts.

In the UK, although patent infringement litigation is the most high profile of such proceedings, there are many other proceedings involving patents which come before the courts. Some of these are proceedings which can be brought against patentees, such as proceedings seeking revocation of a patent or a declaration that one does not infringe it, or 'threats' actions which relate to unjustified threats by a patentee to people other than manufacturers or importers (namely customers and potential customers) to bring patent infringement proceedings against them. There is also scope to seek a compulsory licence under the general power to seek such licences under the Patents Act 1977 (PA 1977), ss 48–54 in respect of a patent which is not being exploited in the UK, although few such applications have, however, ever been made in any area of technology.

In addition, there are entitlement proceedings and proceedings concerning employee inventions, which because they tend by their nature to be very fact-specific, and to give rise to few legal principles of general application, tend only rarely to find their way into the higher courts and the law reports.

However, the two most common types of proceedings are those in which the validity of a patent is attacked after grant, and those in which a patentee seeks to enforce a patent, and these are discussed separately below.

This chapter primarily focuses on proceedings in the English courts, which is where the vast majority of disputes concerning UK patents, whether granted nationally or by the EPO, are heard. As explained below at paras 4.24–4.28 courts in other EU Member States have limited scope to make orders in respect of certain types of proceedings relating to UK patents, although little or no use has been made of this option. In the same way, courts in the UK have limited scope to make orders in respect of certain types of proceedings relating to patents elsewhere in the EU (and the rest of the EEA) and the English courts have done so in one case, holding that they had jurisdiction to make (and at first instance making) a declaration of non-infringement not only in respect of the UK designation of a patent granted by the EPO, but also in respect of the corresponding French, Italian, and Spanish designations of the patent.[1] Moreover, as discussed below at para 4.30, once the Unified Patent Court Agreement comes into force, as may take place in 2017, various divisions of the new Unified Patent Court, including those based outside the UK, will be able to hear proceedings not only in respect of the new European Patent with Unitary effect[2], but also in relation to UK patents granted by the EPO, subject in the latter case to transitional provisions that permit certain opt-outs from its provisions.

1   *Actavis UK Ltd & ors v Eli Lilly & Company* [2014] EWHC 1511 (Pat) [2015] EWCA Civ 555 – see below at para 4.24, and in **Chapter 6** at paras 6.05–6.06. The Court of Appeal accepted the approach to jurisdictional issues and on direct infringement adopted in the Patents Court at first instance but set aside the declaration of non-infringement made at first instance as it disagreed with its reasoning on the issue of contributory infringement, and remitted the matter back to the Patents Court to address this issue in the light of its judgment.
2   See para 4.02 fn 2.

English Courts

4.02   In England most such proceedings (including patent infringement proceedings) must be brought either in the Patents Court (part of the High Court) or in the Intellectual Property Enterprise Court (formerly named the Patents County Court) either of which is meant by references to 'the court' below, except where otherwise stated. Certain proceedings can also be brought before the Comptroller (ie in the UK Intellectual Property Office (UKIPO), as the UK Patent Office is now known, in the name of whose head, the Comptroller, decisions are made by hearing officers), and indeed some applications, such as those for compulsory licences, and in matters of entitlement, have to be, although appeal or transfer will lie to the Patents Court.

Although an increasing amount of UK patent litigation is being attracted to the Intellectual Property Enterprise Court most of it still takes place in the Patents Court, which is part of the Chancery Division of the

High Court of England and Wales, and in which a handful of specialist judges designated to hear patent matters sit. Sometimes a hearing in such courts can take place before a deputy judge (generally a senior Queen's Counsel practising at the Patent Bar). The procedure followed in both the Patents Court and the Intellectual Property Enterprise Court is that set out in the Civil Procedure Rules (CPR), and specifically Part 63 of the CPR, supplemented by the Practice Direction – Patents and Other Intellectual Property Claims.[1] The procedure in the Patents Court is further elaborated in the Chancery Guide and the Patents Court Guide.[2]

The Intellectual Property Enterprise Court, which as the Patents County Court,[3] opened in 1990, has a co-extensive jurisdiction with the Patents Court in patent matters, although its procedures and its costs recovery regime now differ from that in the Patents Court, and since 2011 it has been subject to a limit on the damages that it can award. Its procedure is further elaborated in the Intellectual Property Enterprise Court Guide.[4] It was established in an effort to provide a more cost-effective, simple, and flexible alternative to the Patents Court. Its original procedures were intended to place more emphasis on written presentation of the parties' cases, to allow for early identification of the issues in dispute, and to place less reliance on documentary discovery than was at the time in each area the practice of the Patents Court; in effect, a move towards the practices of the courts of the civil law countries elsewhere in Europe. This differentiation was lost when the Civil Procedure Rules were introduced in 1999, but there was a return to these aims with the rule changes made in 2010, as discussed below. Separate courts in Scotland (the Court of Session), and Northern Ireland, which each have a different legal system from that in England and Wales, also have jurisdiction in patent matters, but such actions before these courts are rare.[5] Although in respect of patents the Scottish and Northern Ireland courts apply the same substantive law under the PA 1977 as the courts in England and Wales, the procedural differences, for example, in relation to securing interim injunctions ('interim interdicts' in Scotland) may be important in specific cases.

The Intellectual Property Enterprise Court is available as an alternative forum to the Patents Court for cases falling within its special jurisdiction. The special jurisdiction of the Intellectual Property Enterprise Court covers actions or matters relating to patents or designs together with any claims or matters ancillary to or arising from these. Thus the Intellectual Property Enterprise Court can, in the same way as the Patents Court, hear infringement actions, and applications for declarations of non-infringement, and determine the validity of a patent. It also has special jurisdiction over other IP rights, and indeed these at present provide most of its caseload. There is a £500,000 financial limit on the exercise of the Intellectual Property Enterprise Court's special jurisdiction (which limit can however be waived if all parties agree) and its jurisdiction covers the whole of England and Wales.[6] Proceedings may be transferred to, or retained in the Intellectual Property Enterprise Court, even if the proceedings are likely to raise an important question of fact or law. In deciding whether or not to order a transfer of a case as between the Patents Court and the Intellectual Property Enterprise Court the financial position of the parties may be relevant, in that the latter was set up to allow small- and medium-sized businesses to have patent actions determined as quickly and cheaply as possible. Its early days saw many attempts by defendants to transfer proceedings from it, which attempts were generally unsuccessful. A new body of case law has been established as to the considerations to be taken account of in determining whether or not to order a transfer.[7] However, it has also heard patent disputes as between substantial companies.[8] As the Patents County Court, the Intellectual Property Enterprise introduced a number of what were, when it started, special features of procedure and practice to patent litigation in England and Wales, although many of these were subsequently adopted by the Patents Court, and then incorporated in the CPR. In consequence of this and an unfortunate appeal record in its early years, the Patents County Court came to be much less often used by the late 1990s, and when in 1999 the original procedural differences between the two courts disappeared, the main distinction between them lay in the fact that litigation in the Patents County Court could also be conducted, irrespective of the special litigation rights that they require for the Patents Court, by registered patent attorneys. Unlike the High Court (of which the Patents Court forms part) members of both the solicitors and patent attorney professions also have rights of audience before the Intellectual Property Enterprise Court, irrespective of whether they have any special advocacy rights, although all solicitors have rights of audience before the Patents Court in relation to interim applications. Barristers have rights of audience in both courts. With the introduction of new procedures in 2010, and costs recovery restrictions in the Patents County Court, that have been preserved in the Intellectual Property Enterprise Court, significant procedural differences as between the two jurisdictions have now been introduced, as discussed further below, although the case law to date under the new regime in the Intellectual Property Enterprise Court has primarily been in other areas of IP than patents.

1   The Civil Procedure Rules (CPR) together with commentary, are set out in *Civil Procedure* (Sweet & Maxwell) or *The Civil Court Practice* (Butterworths) both of which are updated at least annually. They can also be found at http://www.justice. gov.uk/courts/procedure-rules/civil/rules. Part 63 of the CPR: 'Patents and Other Intellectual Property Claims' – modifies the CPR to make specific provision for proceedings, and in particular those concerned with patents, registered designs, and registered trade marks (see http://www.justice.gov.uk/courts/procedure-rules/civil/rules/part63) and is supplemented by the *Practice Direction – Patents and Other Intellectual Property Claims* (see http://www.justice.gov.uk/courts/procedure-rules/civil/rules/part63/pd_part63).

2   The current versions are dated October 2013 and December 2012 respectively – see
     http://www.justice.gov.uk/downloads/courts/chancery-court/chancery-guide.doc and
     http://www.justice.gov.uk/downloads/courts/patents-court/patent-court-guide.pdf
     respectively.
3   Introduced by the Copyright Designs and Patents Act 1988, ss 287–292.
4   The current version is dated April 2014 – see http://www.justice.gov.uk/downloads/
     courts/patents-court/intellectual-property-enterprise-court-guide.pdf. The Intellectual
     Property Enterprise Court provides for two types of proceeding, referred to as 'tracks'
     – a multi-track and a small claims track, but patent disputes are not eligible for the
     latter. For full review of the practice and procedure in the court see Fox, Angela –
     Intellectual Property Enterprise Court: Practice and Procedure (Sweet & Maxwell,
     2014), and for a review of its recent performance see Helmers, Christian, et al,
     Evaluation of the Reforms of the Intellectual Property Enterprise Court 2010–2013
     (22 June 2015).
5   For an outline of procedure in Scots patent cases see: Grassie, Gill, *IP and Patent
     Happenings in the North* (CIPA, March 2007) 139, and for a discussion of the
     application of *forum non conveniens* issues to related actions brought in Scotland,
     and in England see: *Vetco Gray UK Ltd v FMC Technologies Inc* [2007] EWHC 540
     (Patents Court).
6   The Patents County Court (Financial Limits) Order 2011, SI 2011/1402.
7   These cases were heard whilst it was still called the Patents County Court. The first
     such case under the new regime in which these issues were considered was *ALK-
     Abello Ltd v Meridian Medical Technologies* [2011] EWPCC 14, in which the court
     took account of the value of the claim, the financial position of the parties, and the
     fact that small- and medium-sized enterprises should not be deterred by the potential
     cost of litigation from safeguarding their rights. This decision was cited in *Caljan
     Rite-Hite Ltd v Sovex Ltd* [2011] EWHC 669, a trade mark case in the High Court,
     in which a request to transfer the case to the Patents County Court (which also has
     jurisdiction over trade marks) was refused. These issues have also been considered in
     A.S. Watson v The Boots Company [2011] EWPCC 26, *Liversidge v Owen Mumford*
     [2011] EWPCC 34, *Comic Enterprises v Twentieth Century Fox* [2012] EWPCC 13,
     Environmental Recycling v Stillwell [2012] EWHC 2097 (Pat) and *Destra v Comada*
     [2012] EWPCC 39.
8   See *Unilever Plc v S. C. Johnson & Son Inc* [2012] EWPCC 19, a proceeding for the
     revocation of two patents.

Entitlement and employee invention proceedings

4.03   By the Patent Act 1997, s 8 the Comptroller has jurisdiction to
determine the question of entitlement to a patent application before grant,
which by PA 1997, s 9 is unaffected by the grant of a patent on such
application before such determination has been made. The Comptroller
has wide powers under PA 1997, s 8, and so for example can order not
only that an application proceed in different names to those in which it
was filed, but can order an application to be amended so as to exclude
any of the matter in respect of which the question was referred to it, and
allow the person who referred the question to file a new application for
the material excluded on amendment which can benefit from the filing
date of the application in relation to which the referral was made. The
Comptroller may also order the transfer, or grant of a licence under the
application, and fix the terms of such licence.[1] The Patents Act 1977, s 12
extends many of these powers to the determination of questions about

entitlement as to applications filed under a foreign national law, a treaty, or an international convention. The Patents Act 1977, s 12 also gives the Comptroller power to determine how an application in the names of joint applicants should proceed if there is a dispute as to this, and a request is made by one of the applicants, and s 13 gives the Comptroller power to determine who should properly be named as an inventor. The Comptroller can decline to deal with any of these matters, and refer them to the Patents Court.

The EPO has no mechanism for dealing with entitlement disputes, which are matters of national law, and so the Protocol on jurisdiction, and recognition of decisions in respect of the right to the grant of a European Patent[2] sets out in which national courts (or patent offices where they have the right to determine entitlement disputes under national law), entitlement disputes in relation to European patent applications are to be determined, as between the member states of the EPC. Under this the primary jurisdiction is the residence or principal place of business of the applicant, provided that this is within one of the contracting states. The effect of notifying such disputes to the EPO before grant is to suspend prosecution of the European patent application in issue, even if it is about to proceed to grant.

Similar considerations will apply to the new 'European patent with unitary effect' that is likely to be available as from 2017, and which by Regulation 1257/2012,[3] Article 7(1) is to be treated:

'... as an object of property ... in its entirety and in all the participating Member States as a national patent of the participating Member State in which that patent has unitary effect and in which, according to the European Patent Register:
(a)   the applicant had his residence or principal place of business on the date of filing of the application for the European patent; or
(b)   where point (a) does not apply, the applicant had a place of business on the date of filing of the application for the European patent.'

Articles 7(2) and 7(3) deal respectively with the situations of joint applicants (where the Article 7(1) criteria are applied to the applicants in the order in which they are listed until one applicant is found which meets such criteria) and those in which the sole applicant, or none of the joint applicants, meet such criteria, in which case the law of Germany, as host country to the EPO, applies.

In the UK, PA 1977, s 37 gives the Comptroller powers similar to those under PA 1977, s 9 in relation to references made after grant of a UK patent or an EP (UK) patent, provided that the reference is made within two years of grant, unless it can be shown that the registered proprietor knew at the time of grant that it was not entitled to the patent.[4] As with questions of entitlement on pre-grant applications, the Comptroller can decline to deal with any of these matters, and refer them to the Patents

Court. In relation to employee inventions, applications for compensation for 'patents of outstanding benefit to the employer'[5] can be made either to the Comptroller or to the Patents Court.

1   For example, in *Elliot and BSP International Foundations Ltd v Expotech Ltd* (BL O/132/05) the Comptroller, under an equivalent post-grant power under s 37, settled the terms of a cross licence between the claimants and the defendants, having previously found that the claimants were entitled to one of the inventions in the patent but the defendants to the other, and ordered the patent put in their joint names.

2   See **Appendix 6**.

3   As to the 'European Patent with unitary effect', see Council Decision of 10 March 2011 authorizing enhanced cooperation in the area of the creation of unitary patent protection [2011] OJEU L76/53, Regulation (EU) No 1257/2012 of the European Parliament and of the Council of 17 December 2012 implementing enhanced cooperation in the area of the creation of unitary patent protection [2012] OJEU L361/1, and Council Regulation (EU) No 1260/2012 of 17 December 2012 implementing enhanced cooperation in the area of the creation of unitary patent protection with regard to the applicable translation arrangements [2012] OJEU L361/89. The countries that the European Patent with unitary effect would not cover are Spain, and any other EU Member State which has not, at the date when the patent is so registered, ratified the Agreement on the Unified Patent Court [2013] OJEU C175/1. Italy and Spain objected to the language regime that is proposed for the European Patent with unitary effect, and indeed unsuccessfully brought proceedings before the Court of Justice of the EU to challenge the Regulation authorizing use of the enhanced cooperation approach for this purpose – see Joined Cases C-274/11 *Kingdom of Spain v Council of the European Union* and C-295/11 *Italian Republic v Council of the European Union* (CJEU 16 April 2013). The implementing Regulations were themselves also unsuccessfully challenged in Cases C-146/13, and C-147/13 *Kingdom of Spain v European Parliament and Council of the European Union* (CJEU 5 May 2015) but cannot, however, take effect until the Agreement on the Unified Patent Court [2013] OJEU C175/1 has entered into force. This Agreement is discussed below at para 4.30.

4   See *Yeda Research & Development Co Ltd v Rhone-Poulenc Rorer International Holdings Inc* [2007] UKHL 43 (House of Lords) where an amendment was allowed after the two-year period to plead sole entitlement where joint entitlement had originally been sought. Note also that not all countries in Europe apply a two-year limitation period, and in some this can be longer.

5   See **Chapter 2** at para 2.02.

Declaratory proceedings

4.04   The Patents Act 1977, s 71 gives the court, or the Comptroller, the power to declare that an act or a proposed act does not infringe a patent, but requires that the applicant for the declaration has first requested an acknowledgement to such effect from the patentee, has furnished the patentee with 'full particulars in writing of the act in question', and that the patentee has refused or failed to give such acknowledgement.[1] In practice the patentee faced with such a request will often call for more detail of the proposed act, and request more time to consider a response than the applicant has given it, although some applicants, anticipating this, give only a short time for response, and initiate proceedings very soon after making such a request, and without awaiting a response. Moreover, and assuming there to be a basis, as there sometimes is in such cases, for bringing an action for infringement, even if such a request does not itself elicit an infringement action in response, once an action requesting such a declaration has been brought the patentee will in all likelihood bring its own infringement action against the applicant. Thus whilst such a procedure does serve to bring matters to a head at the time of the applicant's choosing rather than that of the patentee, and so enable the applicant, for example, to assure itself of the position before it starts to market the product, or to use the process in issue, it does not of itself provide the applicant with much by way of procedural benefit.

An action seeking such a declaration may also be brought based on the inherent jurisdiction of the court, where the patentee has asserted that an act infringes an identifiable patent. However, in *Unilever v Procter & Gamble*,[2] it was held that one could not for such purpose rely on a threat uttered in the context of 'without prejudice' negotiations to found an action for such a declaration. The scope of the jurisdiction to seek declarations based on the inherent jurisdiction of the Court was extensively reviewed in *Nokia v Interdigital*[3] in which the Court of Appeal regarded the jurisdiction as allowing, in principle, a declaration to be sought that a patent was not essential to a standard to which it had been declared.

The Comptroller also has jurisdiction under PA 1977, ss 74A–74B to provide, for the price of a small fee (currently £200) non-binding reasoned opinions, that are published, on infringement and on most aspects of patent validity on an *ex parte* basis at the request of anyone, although others can file observations, and a patentee, or its exclusive licensee can challenge such an opinion in certain circumstances.[4]

1   It was argued in *Omnipharm Ltd v Merial* [2010] EWHC 3059 (Patents Court) that this procedure was not in, and of itself, sufficient to establish standing to bring an action for such a declaration, and that a genuine intention to do the act in question must also be established, but the issue was left over to trial rather than ordered to be dealt with as a preliminary point, or treated as a basis on which to refuse an amendment to the existing revocation proceeding to introduce such a claim.
2   *Unilever v Procter & Gamble* [1999] FSR 849; [2000] FSR 344; [1999] IP & T 171.
3   *Nokia Corp v Interdigital Corp* [2006] EWHC 802 (Patents Court); [2006] EWCA Civ 1618 (Court of Appeal) further discussed in **Chapter 9** at para 9.03.
4   Thirty or so requests for opinions have been filed each year since the service was introduced in 2005. The opinions are generally issued in some three months, and are published – see http://www.gov.uk/government/collections/requests-for-opinions for recent requests – that also links to the National Archives website – that archives earlier such requests.

Threats proceedings

4.05   The Patents Act 1977, s 70 gives to a 'person aggrieved by the threats' the right to bring proceedings in the court for groundless threats of infringement proceedings. A person aggrieved by groundless threats (who need not be the person against whom the threats are made) has a right to bring proceedings to enjoin such threats, and to seek damages for them. The aim of this provision is to prevent patentees bringing pressure on, for example, retailers, or potential customers of an allegedly infringing product when their real argument is with the manufacturer of the product.[1]

Thus the provision does not apply where the threat is made against the infringer for acts of primary infringement – namely manufacturing or importing the patented product or using a patented process. Neither, as amended by PA 2004, does it apply to a threat made to such a primary infringer for other acts, such as sale, keeping or distribution. In *FNM Corporation Ltd v Drammock International Ltd*,[2] the first case in which the provision as amended was considered, this amendment did not save a letter before action from being considered a threat even though it referred only to manufacture and import, but the form of undertakings that accompanied it referred also to sale, and the recipient of the letter was in fact neither a manufacturer nor importer. However, the letter before action was saved from being regarded as an actionable threat by virtue of another amendment, that which introduced the new provision PA 1977, s 70(2A), as the patentee had no reason to suspect that the patent was invalid, and but for such invalidity the patent would have been valid and infringed, and thus the threat would have been justified.[3]

One does not avoid the provision by labelling such a threat 'without prejudice' where there is in fact, as was the case in *Kooltrade Ltd v XTS Ltd*[4] no genuine dispute or negotiation.

What constitutes a threat is objectively tested. The court will consider whether the language of the statement conveys a threat to a reasonable recipient. It does not matter what the particular recipient or the maker of the statement thinks. The reasonable recipient is taken to have knowledge of all the surrounding circumstances, and to have the commercial background of the type of person to whom such a statement was made. In *Bowden Controls Ltd v Acco Cable Controls Ltd*[5] this was understood to mean that the reasonable recipient would:

> '... read the letter carefully realising that it was meant to convey to him information which the first defendant considered important. He would realise that it contained a threat of patent proceedings. He would realise that there is nothing in the letter which explicitly excluded him from the threat .... He would conclude that the purpose of the letter was to give him information and a warning. That requires the answer: a warning as to what?'

Thus, it can be seen that both express and implied threats to commence patent infringement actions will be caught by PA 1977, s 70. However, this also provides that merely providing factual information about a patent, making enquiries for the sole purpose of discovering the identity of the primary infringer, or making an assertion about the patent for the purpose of such enquires do not constitute actionable threats. The last two of these three exceptions were added by the PA 2004, and their scope remains to be tested, as does one that allows the person alleged to have made an actionable threat to rely on the fact that he unsuccessfully used his best endeavours to identify the primary infringer. Care is also needed when taking advantage of the first exception, that for providing factual information about a patent, that an implied threat is not made, so one should not go any further, when seeking to rely on it, than sending a copy of the patent, and a covering letter drawing the recipient's attention to the registration. This renders the exception of limited value as this, for example, does not expressly permit the patentee to identify to the recipient of the letter the allegedly infringing article.

The person who successfully brings an action for unjustified threats may be awarded a declaration that the threats are unjustifiable, and an injunction to restrain the continued making of such threats and damages. However, threats actions may be countered by a counterclaim for infringement, as by succeeding in this the patentee will establish that although the threat was made it was justified, even if the patent is also found to be invalid, as long as the patentee had no reason to suspect this.

The threats provisions for patent and other IP rights have given rise to much satellite litigation since they were first introduced for patents in the late nineteenth century, and many have urged their repeal. The UK Law Commission has recently reviewed and consulted on these provisions but has however recommended their retention, proposing yet further amendments to PA 1977, s 70 – including the repeal of PA 1977, s 70(2A), as added by PA 2004, and the introduction of an exception by which a lawyer or registered patent attorney would not be liable for making threats where they have acted in their professional capacity, and on instructions from their client.[6]

1   As in *Zeno Corporation v BSM-Bionic Solutions Management GmbH*, [2009] EWHC 1829 (Pat), and *SDL Hair Ltd v Next Row Ltd* [2013] EWPCC 31, in which case a director of the company was held personally to be liable for the threats in issue.
2   *FNM Corporation Ltd v Drammock International Ltd* [2009] EWHC 1294.
3   Such a defence failed in *Sundarshan v Clariant* [2013] EWCA 919, but was allowed to stand in *Global Flood Defence Systems Ltd v Van Den Noort Innovations BV* [2015] EWHC 153 (IPEC) in respect of a patent application on the basis that it might have proceeded to grant by the time the matter came to trial.
4   *Kooltrade Ltd v XTS Ltd* [2001] IP & T 116. See *Best Buy Co Inc v Worldwide Sales Corporation Espana SL* [2011] EWCA 2018, a case concerning a corresponding provision in the legislation for registered trade marks, in which it was held that an offer to settle made in a letter making a threat but which made no concession or admission did not amount 'to the sort of settlement proposal which should, on the grounds of ... public policy ... be treated as privileged from use in court'.
5   *Bowden Controls Ltd v Acco Cable Controls Ltd* [1990] RPC 427. See also *Grimme Landsmaschinfabrik GmbH v Scott* [2009] EWHC 2691, in which a letter that expressly stated that the claimant was not bringing proceedings against the recipient, was nevertheless held to constitute an implied threat that it would do so once it was

successful in its action against another, and *FH Brundle v Perry and another* [2014] EWHC 475 (IPEC) in which an argument that because the threat had been addressed to a 'worldly wise' company chairman it would not have been taken seriously, was rejected as if a reasonable person in the shoes of the chairman understood the communication to be a threat, the extent to which it was taken seriously was irrelevant.

6   The Law Commission (Law Com No 346) *Patents, Trade Marks and Design Rights: Groundless Threats* (April 2014, Cm 8851) – http://lawcommission.justice.gov.uk/docs/lc346_patents_groundless_threats.pdf.

Attacking the validity of a patent after grant

Introduction

4.06   As one can in the UK counterclaim for invalidity in any patent infringement proceedings, it might be asked why one should seek to attack the validity of a patent once it has been granted except as such a counterclaim. There are several motives for attacking the validity of a patent other than in the context of infringement proceedings, and such actions are remarkably common in the English courts. One motive is to improve one's confidence at being free to operate without risk. This is particularly important in technologies where there is a long time to market, and which require considerable investment. Such a proceeding may also be effective in forcing the patentee to grant one a licence, or at least to do so on more favourable terms than would otherwise have been available. Moreover, prospective generic market entrants in the pharmaceuticals sector are at an especial risk of successful applications for interim injunctions being made against them, unless they have 'cleared the path' of patents that are likely to be asserted against them, either by revocation proceedings or by seeking declarations of non-infringement, or both, as appropriate.[1]

Another motive for challenging validity in the English courts is to try to secure, more rapidly than would normally be possible in the courts of most other EPO Member States, a favourable judgment that by being fully reasoned will carry weight with the courts of other EPO Member States, and especially the German infringement courts. Unlike the courts that hear patent infringement disputes in most countries those in Germany cannot themselves revoke patents, but will stay infringement proceedings before them where they are persuaded that there is a strong challenge to validity, which can only in the German litigation system (as to patents granted by the EPO) be mounted in an EPO opposition, or absent this or on its conclusion, in the German Federal Patent Court, the proceedings in which typically take much longer than those in the infringement courts.

1   See below at para 4.17: 'Interim injunctions in patent infringement matters'.

In the UK

4.07   Revocation proceedings, whether in respect of a UK or an EP (UK) patent, can be filed at any time after grant, and are brought before the court or Comptroller. The jurisdiction allowing this and the grounds for doing so are set out in PA 1977, s 72.[1] The UK designation of a patent granted via the EPO route can also be opposed as part of a central opposition filed at the EPO within nine months of grant, as discussed below. Moreover, as noted above, the Comptroller has a jurisdiction under PA 1977, ss 74A–74B whereby the Comptroller can be requested to provide non-binding opinions on most aspects of validity (and infringement) on an *ex parte* basis.[2]

1   The grounds are discussed in further detail in **Chapter 5**. It is not necessary to have an interest in the outcome of the proceedings and a 'straw man' may apply, although if without resources it must usually provide security, as in *Cairnstones v AB Hassle* [2002] FSR 35.
2   See above at para 4.04: 'Declaratory proceedings'.

In the EPO

4.08   For patents granted via the EPO route there is a period of nine months after grant during which the EPO can entertain the filing of third party 'oppositions' to the grant of the patent. The opposition proceeding is widely used in the EPO, nearly 3,000 being filed each year, which corresponds to a little under 5 per cent of the 65,000 or so patents granted each year by the EPO.[1] The first stage of the proceedings is before an Opposition Division, which consists of three examiners, and will often include the examiner who was part of the Examining Division responsible for the grant of the patent, an aspect of the procedure which has been criticized as it is felt that such examiner will be reluctant to conclude that the patent ought not have been granted in the first place. After the opposition period has expired, and oppositions have been filed, the patentee is given time to respond in writing to the oppositions, whereupon one member of the Opposition Division considers the arguments advanced and issues a preliminary, non-binding opinion. If, as is almost invariably the case, any of the opponents or the patentee have requested oral proceedings the Opposition Division will appoint a date for the hearing of the oral proceedings, and until then the patentee and opponents may file further submissions, although submissions filed too late may be excluded from consideration.

The oral proceedings are relatively informal but follow a common procedure, with each ground of attack being advanced, responded to, and adjudicated on (but without reasons being given at that time) in turn. The usual order of things is to take added matter first, then sufficiency, then novelty, and finally inventive step. At each stage the patentee is usually given an opportunity to meet any adverse ruling by the Opposition Division by filing amended claims – either a new Main Request, which is an unconditional offer to amend, or an Auxiliary Request, which is in effect an offer to amend under sufferance, and from which the patentee can resile on appeal. The new claims are then examined to see whether they have support in the specification, and do not themselves extend protection or add matter (which itself constitutes a ground of invalidity) and then the procedure continues on the basis of these new claims as before. A stage is then reached at which either all objections have been exhausted, and there are still claims on file, or where the patentee is not allowed to file any more amended claims, and the patent is revoked. At some later stage a written decision outlining the reasoning followed by the Opposition Division is circulated. About one-third of opposition cases result in patent revocation; one-third in the opposition being rejected; and the final third with the patent maintained in amended form.

The effect of a decision revoking the patent or maintaining it on amended claims (unless these were a new Main Request) can be suspended by the patentee filing an appeal within the due period after the written decision is given. An opponent can also appeal a decision to maintain the patent either amended or not. The appeal is heard by a Technical Board of Appeal, (again of three people, typically two of whom are technically, and the other legally, qualified) which follows a similar procedure to that adopted by the Opposition Division, but which may also, in the light of the amended claims filed, and the decisions that it makes on such requests, remit matters to the Opposition Division or, and generally only in the case of there being prior conflicting authority, refer a point of law to the Enlarged Board of Appeal. The Enlarged Board, which typically will have five legally qualified members (sometimes including national judges designated for that purpose) and two technically qualified members, also gives opinions on points of law referred to it by the President of the EPO. A decision of the Technical Board of Appeal revoking the patent, or upholding its validity as filed, or on amended claims, is final and there is no further appeal from this, although a petition for review by the Enlarged Board can be filed on the very limited grounds of procedural irregularity set out in the EPC, Article 112a, that can reopen proceedings by remitting matters to a Technical Board of Appeal.

1   This represents approximately 45 per cent of the total of direct European applications and of PCT applications entering the European regional phase.

The action for patent infringement in England

Introduction

4.09   The enforcement of patents, in common with other IPRs, is usually dependant on the owner of the rights taking action. No action will normally be taken by other authorities, such as the government or a patent office, to enforce IPRs on behalf of their owners, although in the UK, and as mandated by TRIPS, Article 61, certain forms of copyright and trade mark infringement are also criminal offences.[1] Although the Customs authorities have, by virtue of certain EU legislation[2] certain powers which they can use to prevent the import of pirated and counterfeit goods, and which extend also to patents, in order to make use of these a patentee must first file an appropriate application with the Customs authorities, and must then commit itself to bring an action in respect of any goods seized in response to such request.

The mere commencement of an infringement action is unlikely to result in the alleged infringer immediately stopping activity. The alleged infringer can, if so inclined (and unless the patentee applies for and is successful in obtaining an interim injunction to prevent infringement through to trial, as explained below) continue activities until after the full trial. This can typically take at least a year to take place. If infringement is established at trial then further infringement will be prevented by a permanent injunction, although the defendant may be able to suspend the effect of this pending the outcome of any appeal. The patentee will also, in addition to recovering a substantial proportion of its legal costs, be entitled to seek damages (or an account of the defendants profits) to compensate for the past infringement, for the period of up to six years before the commencement of proceedings until the infringement ceases.

Patent infringement actions are almost always met by two defences: First, that what the defendant is doing is not an infringement (in the sense that for some reason or other the product or process in issue does not fall within the scope of any of the claims of the patent asserted against it) and second, that the patent is invalid. Other more specific defences, such as those relating to personal prior use[3] may also be raised. Thus patent infringement actions involve two broad types of issue – validity[4] and infringement[5] and in the UK, almost invariably both are in issue at the same time in any infringement action. This is the same in most countries although in some, notably Germany, the infringement and invalidity jurisdictions are different, and these matters are heard in different courts at different times, with the infringement action generally coming on for trial before the revocation proceedings, unless the infringement action is stayed pending the outcome of the latter in the light of a strong *prima facie* attack on validity.

In order to decide a patent infringement action the judge (who in the English courts will generally have some technical background) has first to decide what the claims of the patent actually cover. Usually the drafting of the claims will have been done in such a way as to try to capture the essence of what has been invented rather than tying the inventor down to the precise ways of carrying out the invention that the inventor has described. Deciding the scope of the claims is often not straightforward, and the judge is likely to require expert evidence to assist in deciding what certain technical terms in the claims might mean, or be understood in context, to mean. Once the judge has decided the scope of the claims that have been asserted, the judge has to then decide whether the product or process that is alleged to infringe, compared to the meaning which the judge has decided for such claims, does in fact do so. The judge has then to consider the question of the validity of the claims in issue, in which the judge will also be assisted by expert evidence. If certain dependant claims have been stated by the patentee to have 'independent validity' the judge must consider their validity separately from the claims on which they are dependant. Unless all these hurdles are successfully negotiated by the patentee, its action will fail. However, to prevail a patentee need not succeed on all the patent claims that it asserts – all that it needs to show is that at least one claim is valid and infringed.

1   This attitude is not shared by all other countries in the EU, many of which also provide for criminal liability for patent infringement, although this is rarely used in practice. The European Commission did at one stage propose EU legislation which would have mandated criminal sanctions in the case of infringement of IPRs in certain situations, and which as originally drafted would not have distinguished between patents and other types of IPR – see *Commission Press Release IP/05/906*, 12 July 2005. This proposal was, however, dropped and the Commission has not as yet sought to reintroduce it, even though the subsequent amendments made to the EU Treaties by the Lisbon Treaty have given it a sounder legal basis on which to do so, than it had previously.
2   Regulation (EU) No 608/2013 of 12 June 2013, concerning customs enforcement of intellectual property rights, and repealing Council Regulation (EC) No 1383/2003 (OJEU L181, 29 June 2013, 15) and Commission Implementing Regulation (EU) No 1352/2013 of 4 December 2013 establishing the forms provided for in Regulation (EU) No 608/2013 concerning customs enforcement of IP rights (OJEU L 341 18 December 2013, 10). For the manner in which this is implemented in the UK, and the procedure to be followed in order to make use of it, see: http://www.gov.uk/government/publications/notice-34-intellectual-property-rights/notice-34-intellectual-property-rights.
3   See **Chapter 6** at para 6.16, 'Personal prior use'.
4   Discussed in **Chapter 5**.
5   Discussed in **Chapter 6**.

Procedural overview

4.10   Unlike most actions in the English courts, patent actions proceed by way of a 'split trial'; the procedure being directed so as to establish first, and at a separate trial, whether the defendant is liable to the patentee for its actions. Only if liability is established will proceedings move on to consider the question of remedies, and to determine in a separate trial, on further evidence, the amount of financial compensation that should be paid to the patentee. This ensures that time and money is not wasted in considering damages type issues, when in fact the patent may prove to be invalid or not infringed. In practice, the key issues in a patent infringement dispute tend to relate to liability, so that if there is a ruling resolving this in favour of the patentee, the amount of damages is often settled without the need for a further hearing.

In the liability phase the parties initially (through the statements of case) identify the details of the patentee's case, and then the basis of the defendant's defence (at which point the defendant will usually counterclaim for revocation of the patent). The statements of case also serve to establish what issues stand between the parties that need to be dealt with at, or before, trial. If the court considers that the statements of case do not fully set out the issues in dispute, it can give directions to clarify the issues. Additionally, a party may at any time make an application to the court for the provision of further information by the other party for the same purpose. In exercising its case management powers, the court will scrutinize the parties' statements of case with a view to making directions aimed at disposing of these issues, or at least narrowing them. There are a number of procedures that may usefully be employed, by either party or the court, for this purpose in the remaining stages prior to trial. The main procedures here include use of Notices to Admit Facts, Disclosure[1] and Notices of Experiments.

All issues that remain need to be dealt with at trial, by evidence, and the benefit therefore of resolving as many issues as possible prior to trial is considerable as otherwise the time needed to prepare for trial becomes extended, the length of the trial itself is increased, and ultimately the overall costs of the action are increased. A number of efforts have been made over the years to increase the speed of, and to reduce the costs of patent litigation[2] including in the Patents Court, the introduction of the 'streamlined procedure' that involves restrictions on the scope for cross-examination of witnesses, disclosure, and experiments, and envisages trial duration of no more than a day. The parties' legal advisers have a duty to draw their clients' attention to the availability of such procedure, and the court will order it where the parties agree or, in the absence of agreement, where in particular: in view of proportionality, the financial position of each of the parties, the degree of complexity, and the importance of the case it is appropriate so to do. In practice it has not, however, been much used in the Patents Court, because the default procedure in the Intellectual Property Enterprise Court is now in effect the streamlined procedure of the Patents Court.[3]

Evidence put before the court is of two sorts: evidence of fact and expert evidence (much of which is directed to matters of opinion). Witness statements and experts' reports setting out such evidence are exchanged prior to trial, and at trial, witnesses are questioned on the content of their statements. The need generally for technical expert evidence in English patent litigation means that there is little scope to seek summary judgment (that is to say, judgment on the merits and without evidence) although where the only issue between the parties is one of claim construction this may be appropriate.[4]

The following is a brief outline of the main procedural features of such a patent action in the Patents Court, although to the extent that the court so orders in the case of streamlined procedure some of the steps after the case management conference (CMC) may be omitted. Matters common to other High Court proceedings, such as those relating to costs estimates, are omitted from the outline. Typically various other applications will be made to the court in the course of the proceedings, statements of case will be amended, and so in practice the procedure is likely to be more complicated. Whilst the time limits are set down by the CPR, in most cases these can be extended by agreement, or with the permission of the court. However, the CPR places great importance on the court's management powers, and so extensions of time cannot be taken for granted.

1   Known in England & Wales before the CPR, and still known in other common law jurisdictions, as 'Discovery'.

2   Although English patent litigation is by and large no more expensive than other litigation of similar importance in the English courts, it tends to be more expensive than litigation in the courts of countries elsewhere in Europe which have a civil law system, and is thus exposed to competitive pressures, and costs comparisons from such other jurisdictions in a way that most other litigation in the English courts is not. English patent litigation is, however, quicker than that in most other jurisdictions. The cost of English patent litigation, however, remains a constant source of complaint, although the increasing trend towards transparency of awards of legal costs in other European jurisdictions shows that the actual differences are not so great as has often been suggested, and the very high level of court fees in high value cases in some European jurisdictions, such as Germany, also limit the effective costs differential.

3   See the various materials referenced at para 4.02 above, for the specifics of both Patents Court and Intellectual Property Enterprise Court procedure.

4   See for example *Abbott v Ranbaxy* [2004] EWHC 2723 (Pat) where written evidence had been filed in an application by the patentee for an interim injunction, but summary judgment was entered against it. Such an order was also made in favour of the patentee, rejecting an attack of obviousness in *Eli Lilly & Co Ltd v Neopharma* [2011] EWHC 1852 (Pat) where the same argument had been run unsuccessfully against the same patent by other defendants, despite the defendant in this one saying that it proposed to adduce different evidence. However, the court declined to make such an order favour of the patentee in *Resolution Chemicals Limited v H. Lundbeck A/S* [2013] EWHC 739 (Pat) where the Dutch court, disagreeing with the English court in an earlier case on the same patent, had held that the corresponding Dutch designation of the patent was obvious. The English court also declined in this case to

find that the defendant was precluded, whether by reason of cause of action estoppel, issue estoppel, or abuse of process, from challenging the validity where it had been related at some point to a company that had been a party to the earlier English case. See *Nampak Plastics Europe Ltd v Alpla UK Limited* [2014] EWCA Civ 1293 for an example of an appellate decision upholding summary judgment granting a declaration of non-infringement, in contrast to some earlier cases as discussed by the Court of Appeal in this case, such as *Virgin Atlantic Airways Ltd v Delta Airways Ltd* [2011] EWCA Civ 162, where the Court of Appeal reversed a decision at first instance, that had struck out the patentee's action on the basis that the acts complained of did not infringe.

Starting the action and exchange of statements of case

4.11 Although in most disputes it is usual, before starting proceedings, for the party intending to bring the proceedings to give some preliminary warning of this, in the event that a settlement can be achieved before proceedings need be brought, care must be taken in doing so in the case of patent infringement actions for two reasons. The first is that such a warning may constitute a 'groundless threat' giving rise to liability on the part of the patentee (and those making the threat on its behalf) under PA 1977, s 70.[1] The second is that it may provide the potential defendant with a basis for immediately bringing an action for a declaration of non-infringement under the inherent jurisdiction of the court,[2] without having to rely on the procedure for seeking a declaration of non-infringement as set out in PA 1977, s 71, which procedure inevitably takes time before one can start the action. It can, for jurisdictional reasons, be important to bring such a declaration procedure quickly. One reason is that it may give a potential defendant to an action under the UK designation of a EP which is under opposition at the EPO, but to which opposition the potential defendant is not a party a basis for intervening in that opposition.[3] It may also be important in trying to preserve the jurisdiction of the English court to make such a declaration, and so undermining any attempt to bring an action to secure pan-European relief, which might preclude this, in another European jurisdiction.[4]

An action for infringement of a patent in the Patents Court is commenced by the issue of a Claim Form[5] by the court at the request of the patentee on payment of the requisite court fee. The Claim Form is simply a short form on which appears the name of the claimant (namely the patentee and any exclusive licensee in a patent infringement action) and the defendant, the value of the claim, and very brief details of the claim. The document usually claims an injunction (an order that the defendants stop infringing the patent) and asks for damages (or an account of profits) and costs. The Claim Form must also be verified by a 'statement of truth' signed either by the claimant or its legal representative. Particulars of Claim, if not set out on the Claim Form, must be served (ie formally delivered) with the Claim Form or within 14 days of service of the Claim Form. The Particulars of Claim must set out in more detail all that is claimed together with an instance or instances of infringement, giving, where possible, dates, places, facts and figures, which instances are usually set out in separate Particulars of Infringement served with the Particulars of Claim. The Claim Form and Particulars of Claim must be served on all defendants within four months of issue of the Claim Form. However, this period may for good reason be extended on application made to the court before it expires.

In certain circumstances, the court may, if so requested, order pre-action disclosure, namely that a potential defendant provide certain specified documents to the claimant even before a Claim Form is issued. To secure such pre-action disclosure a potential claimant must show that it is reasonably necessary to allow it to prove its case, that the disclosure may lead to saving costs, or that it may lead to settlement. This procedure may be particularly useful to a claimant in order to clarify details of an infringing process, but this is not in practice widely used as the court will not allow it to turn into a 'fishing expedition'.

Leave of the court may be required to serve proceedings out of the jurisdiction on foreign defendants who, for example, are alleged to have committed an infringing act within the UK. However, by virtue of the Brussels I Regulation[6] and similar measures it is much easier to initiate, and to serve proceedings directly on defendants who are resident in other Member States of the EU, or by virtue of the parallel Lugano Convention, the rest of the EEA, and Switzerland. Similarly, this Regulation and these treaties enables ready enforcement of judgments obtained in the UK against defendants whose assets are based in these countries. It also provides in part the legal basis for the courts of one country in the EU to make an order in relation to matters relating to infringement (but not validity) in another country in the EU.[7]

Procedural steps in patent infringement actions in the Patents Court

STEP – open to, or responsibility of, either party unless stated	COMMENT – see also fuller discussion below	TIMING – except as stated all time limits may be extended, either by agreement between the parties, or with the permission of the court
Pre-action disclosure sought by patentee and given by potential defendant	Orders for this are rarely sought in patent actions	
Patentee issues Claim Form and serves together with Particulars of Claim and Particulars of Infringement		Serve within four months after issue (claimant can apply for an extension of time for service)
Defendant serves Acknowledgement of Service		Within 14 days of service of the Claim Form
Defendant serves Defence and Counterclaim plus Grounds of Invalidity		Within 42 days after service of the Claim Form (parties can only agree an extension up to 28 days)
Application for first case CMC		Within 14 days of filing of Acknowledgement of Service or Defence, whichever is the earlier
Patentee serves Reply and Defence to Counterclaim		21 days after service of the Defence and Counterclaim
Case management conference (CMC)		As set by the court (independent of, and does not affect timing of, other steps unless they have not already been completed and an order is made at it doing so)
Notice to Admit Facts served		21 days after service of the Reply and Defence to Counterclaim
Admissions served		21 days after service of Notice to Admit Facts
Disclosure given		As set by the court at first CMC

Further Directions Hearing	If required – may depend on how advanced matters are at the first CMC	As set by the court at first CMC (this date may not be varied except with the leave of the court)
Notice of Facts to be proved by Experiment served		21 days after service of application for Further Directions (or as set by the court at the first CMC or at the Further Directions Hearing)
Admissions (of facts to which Experiments relate)		Within 21 days of the Notice of Experiments
Performance of Repeat Experiments		As set by the court at first CMC or at Further Directions Hearing
Further Disclosure Orders		As set by the court at first CMC or at Further Directions Hearing
Meetings of Experts	Rare in patent actions	As set by the court at first CMC or at Further Directions Hearing
Exchange of Experts' Reports, Witness Statements and Civil Evidence Act Notices		As set by the court at first CMC or at Further Directions Hearing
Written questions on Experts' Reports and Replies	Rare in patent actions	As set by the court at first CMC or at Further Directions Hearing
Trial		As set by the court at first CMC or at Further Directions Hearing or (more usually) by the court after consultation with the parties
Judgment		A couple of weeks to a couple of months after trial
Further procedure depends on Order made, but may include Inquiry as to Damages or an Account of Profits, Assessment of Costs and Appeal		

Within 14 days of service of the Claim Form, the defendant may either file and serve an admission to the claim, or acknowledge service of the Claim Form. This acknowledgment is a formal document that merely gives notice of intention to defend the action, and prevents the claimant from obtaining judgment in default. It does however also constitute a submission to the jurisdiction of the English courts, unless the contrary is indicated on it, in which case an application to challenge such jurisdiction must also be mounted.

As the losing side will usually be required to make a contribution towards the winning side's costs, it is clearly of some concern to a defendant, faced with a Claim Form for patent infringement, that it should be able to recover its costs in the event that it succeeds in defending the action. In circumstances where all the claimants are resident outside of the jurisdiction, or only have assets outside the EEA, and Switzerland or where the claimant is a company which clearly could not satisfy any award for costs made against it, the defendant's concern may be well founded.[8] In such circumstances, the defendant may ask for some form of security (eg a bank guarantee or payment into a holding account) for these costs before proceeding with the preparation of a Defence, and the amount of any security is determined by the court if not agreed. Often, an initial amount will be ordered to be given as security for the first stages of the action, and as the action progresses, the question of increasing the amount of security given will then be reviewed. This procedure is available only to defendants and not claimants (unless the likely costs of the action are greatly outweighed by the costs of a counterclaim) as defendants have no (direct) control over whether proceedings are brought or not. Claimants on the other hand are able to take into account the real prospects of recovering any costs they may be awarded from the defendants when considering whether to commence an action.

The defendant must normally serve a Defence to the Particulars of Claim within 42 days of the receipt of the Particulars of Claim. This period can be extended by agreement (by up to 28 days) or by the court, which will grant reasonable extensions of time on being satisfied that the defendant is diligently proceeding with the preparation of a Defence. The Defence must also be verified by a statement of truth.

Should, as is common, the defendant counterclaim for revocation of the patent, the revocation proceedings will usually be heard concurrently with the infringement action. The defendants must give particulars of the grounds on which they are attacking the patent in a document called the Grounds of Invalidity,[9] which is served with the Defence and/or Counterclaim. Such Grounds of Invalidity will include a listing of the prior art on which the defendant relies for its attacks of anticipation and/ or obviousness.[10]

On receipt of the Defence and Counterclaim for revocation of the patent, the claimants then have 21 days in which to serve a Reply to the Defence, and a Defence to the Counterclaim. This document is usually very short and does little more than amount to a denial of the statements made by the defendants in their Defence and Counterclaim. If, however, the claimants wish to counter an allegation of invalidity on the grounds of obviousness with evidence of the commercial success of the invention, the intention so to do should be set out in the Defence to Counterclaim together with particulars in support.

1   See above at para 4.05: 'Threats proceedings'.
2   See above at para 4.04: 'Declaratory proceedings'.
3   Under EPC, Article 105.
4   See below at para 4.24: 'Attempts to secure relief in patent disputes throughout Europe based in on an action in one country'.
5   Known before the CPR as 'Writs'.
6   Regulation (EU) 1215/2012 of 12 December 2012 on jurisdiction and enforcement of judgments in civil and commercial matters – OJEU L 351, 20 December 2012, 1 (known as the 'Brussels I Regulation'). For the non-EU EEA countries (namely Iceland, Norway and Liechtenstein) and also for Switzerland, a similar regime applies by virtue of the Lugano Convention. These provisions are implemented in the UK by the Civil Jurisdiction and Judgments Acts 1982 and 1991. See below at para 4.24 for a discussion of these measures in the context of applications for 'pan-European' relief in relation to patent disputes.
7   Discussed below at para 4.24: 'Attempts to secure relief in patent disputes throughout Europe based in on an action in one country'.
8   Security for costs was ordered in *Eli Lilly & Co Ltd v Neopharma Ltd* [2011] EWHC 1852 (Pat), but not in *Resolution Chemicals Limited v H. Lundbeck A/S* [2013] EWHC 739 (Pat) where the principles applicable are set out at para [155].
9   Previously called 'Particulars of Objections'.
10 The Grounds of Invalidity, as with the other Statements of Case, can be amended either with consent of the other party or with leave of the court at any time up to the conclusion of the trial (although not in general after such conclusion – see *Vringo v ZTE* [2015] EWHC 214). This will generally involve an order that the party making the amendment meet the legal costs of the other party consequential on such amendment. Where adding a new item of prior art or a new attack on validity, it used to be the case that the defendant was at risk, where it could have done this at the outset, of the court making an order giving the patentee the option to abandon its patent with in such event the defendant paying the legal costs of the patentee between the date the document was originally filed and the date of the amendment – termed an 'Earth Closet' order after the subject matter of an early case in which it was ordered, or a *'See v Scott-Paine'* order after the subsequent case of *See v Scott-Paine* (1933) 50 RPC 56. However this practice, unique to patent litigation, was roundly condemned in *Fresenius Kabi Deutschland Gmbh and ors v Carefusion 303, Inc* [2013] EWCA Civ 1288 and so no longer applies.

Admissions, disclosure, and notices of experiments

4.12   Within a further 21 days of service of the Reply, each party may serve on the other Notices to Admit Facts, to which a response should be served within 21 days. In such a Notice, the claimant will typically seek admissions from the defendant aimed at narrowing down the issues on infringement so that it does not need to gather unnecessary evidence. The defendant will typically seek admissions from the claimant, for example, as to publication of cited prior art documents, or as to whether certain claim integers are present in a given item of prior art.[1] If a fact, included in a party's Notice to Admit Facts is not admitted by the other party, but is proved at the trial, the party who refused to admit that fact is at risk of being penalized on the costs incurred in having to prove that fact, regardless of whether or not that party was successful in the action as a whole or not.

Within 14 days of the filing of the Defence, the claimant ought to apply to the court to fix a date for a case management conference (CMC) at which directions for the future conduct of the case will be given. This will include considering whether the streamlined procedure, or any elements of it, is appropriate, fixing a trial date or trial window[2] and setting a date by which the claimant must apply for any further directions. The defendant may make the application for the first CMC if the claimant fails to do so by this date. At this first directions hearing, the court may also give directions on various matters including disclosure of documents, the number of experts (which is often only one on each side, but depends on the nature of the technology) the provision of further information or the particularization of a case, and the provision of security for costs. It will often also set out the timetable for service of witness statements and expert reports, and any expert reports in reply. However, in some cases, and given the early stage of the proceedings at which the first such hearing will take place, those directions relating to expert evidence, and the conduct of experiments (and repetitions thereof) may be left to be dealt with at a further directions hearing.

As set by the timetable, and unless ordered otherwise in the context of a streamlined procedure, the parties should provide disclosure of documents by exchanging lists of documents in their control relevant to the matters in issue in the action, and permit the inspection of such documents by the other party. Relevant documents are now defined as those on which a party relies, or that adversely affect the party's own case, and those documents that either support or adversely affect another party's case. This stage is preceded by the Notice to Admit and admissions procedure as some issues may be resolved as a result of those steps, making disclosure of documents relevant to those issues unnecessary. In practice, whilst inspection of the original documents is available to establish the authenticity of disclosed documents should this become an issue, copies are generally provided to the other side. The extent of disclosure varies from case to case depending on the matters raised in the Statements of Case, but in order to reduce the scope of disclosure in patent actions, even where a streamlined procedure has not been ordered, the following classes of documents are exempt from production unless the court specifically orders otherwise:

— documents relating to the issue of validity of the patent which either pre-date or post-date the earliest claimed priority date of the patent by more than two years;[3]
— documents relating to the issue of infringement where the defendant has chosen to serve either a product or process description which sets out the salient features of the alleged infringing product or process which is the subject of the action;[4] and
— documents relating to the issue of commercial success of the invention. However, if commercial success is pleaded by the claimant (as can happen as part of a response to a challenge to validity based on lack of inventive step) it is required to serve a schedule of commercial success which should set out details of such things as the sales of the patented product, sales of any previous equivalent product, and the amount spent on marketing and advertising. Equivalent details must be provided in the case of a patented process.

Only parties to the action must give disclosure as a matter of course. Documents which though relevant, are 'privileged' (eg in general correspondence with solicitors or patent attorneys[5]) are identified in general terms but are not disclosed to the other side. If any of the disclosure, the product/process description or the schedule of commercial success is inadequate, the court can order specific disclosure of certain classes of documents.

Documents provided on disclosure can by virtue of CPR 31.22 only be used for the purposes of the action in which such disclosure is given, and so cannot, at least whilst proceedings are ongoing,[6] be deployed in other proceedings without the leave of the court, which is only rarely given.[7] However, this 'implied undertaking' may be regarded by the parties as providing insufficient protection for confidential technical or commercial information and the parties can agree, or the court direct, that disclosure of certain types of documents be limited to, say, lawyers, patent attorneys and independent experts.[8] Although most other common law judicial systems also have a compelled disclosure procedure (usually termed 'discovery' as it used to be in English proceedings), it is not generally part of the procedure in most countries, including the civil law countries in the EU.[9]

Neither party may rely on evidence at trial or on any experiments which they may have carried out to support their case unless the procedure laid down in the rules has been followed. Under such rules a party wishing to adduce experimental evidence must serve on the other a Notice of Experiments on which they wish to rely. The Notice must set out the experiments in detail and the facts that it seeks to establish by those experiments. After the Notice has been served, the other party has to state within a given period whether or not they admit the facts sought to be established. If the facts are not admitted, the party wishing to rely on the experiments must apply for directions enabling them to rely on any such experiments. If the court orders the experiments to be repeated, then arrangements are made for the experiments to be performed in the presence of the experts, and the representatives of the other party. Evidence of the experiments may then be given at the trial.

1   *Vringo v ZTE* [2015] EWHC 214 at para [6].
2   The trial date is usually fixed for the convenience of the parties although the court will endeavour to ensure that an action comes to trial within a year of being started. An expedited trial (that comes on in a matter of months can be ordered) and often accompanies an order for an interim injunction, which is discussed in para 4.17. For a discussion of the principles applied in determining whether to make such an order see: *Warner Lambert Company LLC v Teva UK Ltd* [2011] EWHC 2018 (Pat).
3   An order by the Patents Court dispensing with such disclosure in the context of an attack on validity based on obviousness, essentially on the basis that evidence as to what the inventor actually did can be of no relevance to the artificial question of what the notional skilled person would have done in the light of the cited prior art, was reversed in *Nichia Corporation v Argos Limited* [2007] EWCA Civ 741 (Court of Appeal). See also *Hospira v Amgen* [2010] EWHC 176 (Pat).
4   There has been a tendency for product and process descriptions to become the norm, but they can be troublesome properly to draft, and are a common source of controversy, as for example discussed in *Starsight Telecast Inc & Anor v Virgin Media Ltd &Ors* [2014] EWHC 828 at paras [6]–[8], so it is well worth considering whether or not it is practicable to deal with this obligation by means of disclosure of documents in the traditional manner.
5   By virtue of the Copyright Designs and Patents Act 1988, s 280 for the purposes of proceedings in the UK privilege attaches to communications in relation to patent and other IP matters with registered patent attorneys, and European patent attorneys as if they were solicitors, privilege in whose communications is established by common law. However, the wording of this provision is probably inadequate to extend such privilege to communications with foreign patent agents, unless they are also lawyers (as US patent attorneys are) as privilege also extends under the common law to communications with foreign lawyers.
6   See below at para 4.14 for the position after trial and as to the scope for seeking an order after judgment to continue to preserve the protection provided by CPR 31.22 for disclosed documents.
7   See *Dupont Nutrition Biosciences Aps (formerly Danisco A/S) v Novozymes A/S* [2013] EWHC 155 for an example of a case in which such an order was made, albeit in rather special circumstances.
8   See Cook, Trevor 'Protection of Confidential Information in Patent Litigation in the UK' in Hansen & Shussler-Lagerheine (eds), *Patent Practice in Japan and Europe*, (Kluwer Law International, 2011), 289–301.
9   Discovery tends to be considerably more extensive in US proceedings, and extends also to taking depositions (pre-trial oral evidence). Discovery under compulsion in civil law countries in Europe is almost non-existent despite its being permitted by Article 6 of Directive 2004/48/EC of 29 April 2004 on the enforcement of IPRs, although it is common instead in certain of those countries to use 'seizure' type procedures at the start of a dispute in an effort to secure evidence.

Evidence and trial

4.13   Evidence of fact may include, for example, depending upon the particular issues in the case, how the inventor came by the invention (even though, strictly speaking, this should be of little relevance to the objective enquiry called for by an attack based on lack of inventive step) whether particular documents were published and if so when, details of any alleged prior use of the invention, and details of sales figures of articles made according to the invention if commercial success is in issue. Parties must serve witness statements setting out the evidence of facts upon which they intend to rely, and Civil Evidence Act Notices in respect of matters they seek to establish other than by evidence from a testifying witness. However, it is rare that there is much dispute in patent actions as to issues of fact, and matters instead generally revolve around expert evidence. Expert evidence is given by experts from the relevant field of technology although in practice the level of their expertise, and the nature of the 'relevant' field can be controversial. Their evidence will be set out in experts' reports.[1] The purpose of these is to give evidence on the technical issues in dispute, and offer the court guidance on matters such as:

— the meaning of scientific or technical terms (including terms of art) used in the patent, or other documents before the court;
— to present the state of the art and common general knowledge in the field at various dates, as would be perceived by those to whom the patent's teaching was addressed; and
— to explain what the patent and prior art would have taught those skilled in the art who might have considered attempting to put such teaching into effect.

The aim of such expert evidence is to help clarify technical aspects of the case so that the judge can be in the best position to make a decision on the matters in issue, having read (and seen tested in cross-examination) the independent expert's (hopefully) unbiased opinions on technical matters within his or her expertise. It is not the role of an expert to construe the patent's claims or assess validity, and infringement in the light of such a construction – that is, strictly speaking, something for the judge, although expert evidence can often stray into such areas in practice, especially under cross-examination. Neither is their job to argue the case, and an expert who appears to be overly partisan is likely to have his or her evidence discounted. The judge may order a meeting of the experts in order to identify the disputed issues, and to seek agreement as to any issues so far as possible, or order that experts prepare a statement setting out the issues upon which they agree, and disagree and the reasons for their agreement/disagreement, but such orders are rare in patent matters.

The use of written statements setting out the evidence in chief of experts and of witnesses of fact, which are exchanged a certain period of time before trial, is now an invariable aspect of the procedure, but the individuals must still be available to attend at court so that they can (if called on by the other side to do so) verify their statements on oath, and then expand on, and be cross-examined as to, their content. Each witness of fact or expert witness is first examined by counsel for the party relying on the evidence of such witness, but normally this should not amount to much more than confirming the truth of the witness statement or expert report, sometimes clarifying or revising a statement in it, and commenting on any issues which have arisen since exchange of evidence, and in particular during the trial. The witness is then cross-examined by counsel for the other side, after which an opportunity to put further questions arising out of the cross-examination is given to counsel for the party relying on the witness' evidence.

The usual order of proceedings at the trial is that counsel for the claimant makes an introductory speech that 'opens' the case, and calls its witnesses for examination and cross-examination. Counsel for the defendant then calls its witnesses, and when the evidence is finished, makes a final speech to the court. Counsel for the claimants then makes a final speech. Both speeches will elaborate on written closing arguments which are prepared both during, and immediately after the hearing, and will often be amended up versions of the 'skeleton arguments' submitted by counsel for each side shortly before the hearing, but which are in effect fully-argued briefs. The defendants' counsel has no right of reply after the claimants' counsel's final speech, unless a new point of law has been introduced in the claimants' counsel's closing speech, when the right of reply is restricted to dealing solely with the new point of law.

1   Expert's Reports in patent actions should comply not only with the CPR 1998, Part 35, the Practice Direction which supplements this, and the Protocol for the Instruction of Experts to Give Evidence in Civil Claims, but should also, because the degree of consultation between experts and lawyers tends to be greater in patent actions than in many other areas, be prepared to be mindful of the guidance set out in *Medimmune Limited v Novartis Pharmaceuticals Limited* [2011] EWHC 1669 (Patents Court) at paras [104]–[114] and which also sets out pertinent extracts from the CPR, the Practice Direction and the Protocol at paras [100]–[113]. This involves setting out how what material was provided to the expert and when, which can be important in seeking to minimize the risk of hindsight analysis. However, the judge in *Koninklijke Philips Electronics N.V. v Nintendo of Europe Gmbh* [2014] EWHC 1959 (Pat) observed at para [26] that: 'I do not accept that the way the witness was instructed has any real bearing on the weight on which I may or may not place on his evidence. Patent cases are necessarily conducted *ex post facto* and I refer to what I said in *HTC v Gemalto* [2013] EWHC 1876 (Pat) at paragraphs 271–275.'.

Judgment and its consequences

4.14   The judge may give judgment at once after the trial but is more likely to reserve judgment. The time taken before judgment is given, varies and could be a few days, but is unlikely to be more than a couple of months. In the judgment, the judge gives the reasons for the conclusions on validity and infringement. Thereafter the precise form of order (including provisions as to costs) is discussed in a separate hearing insofar as it cannot be agreed. This order is then drawn up and formally entered by the court.

A party has a right to appeal to the Court of Appeal if permission to appeal is requested, and obtained from the first instance judge. The time for initiating an appeal (four weeks) runs from pronouncement of the judgment, rather than from the entry of the order. The judge must state the reasons for allowing, or refusing permission to appeal. However, if the judge refuses permission, an application may be made to the Court of Appeal for permission to appeal, initially to a single Court of Appeal judge, who will deal with the matter on the papers, but a refusal by which can be challenged in a hearing before at least two such judges.[1] However, the Court of Appeal will usually be reluctant to interfere with the trial judge's assessment of the facts and the evidence, although this does not prevent its taking a different view on claim construction and issues that depend on it, such as infringement, anticipation and added matter. An appeal to the UK Supreme Court[2] is similarly only available with the permission of the Court of Appeal or the Supreme Court itself, and must involve a point of law of general public importance. In practice, the Court of Appeal does not grant such leave, and the Supreme Court must be petitioned to do so. Only a handful of patent disputes have succeeded in getting that far each decade.[3]

If the patentee claimant is successful the normal order would be:

— a permanent injunction against the defendant preventing infringement in the manner set out in the Particulars of Claim and Grounds of Infringement, but which unless otherwise stated will cease on expiry or lapse of the patent on which it is based (in certain cases it may be possible to suspend this pending appeal);

— an order for an inquiry as to damages suffered by the claimant or an account of the defendant's profits (this takes into account only the six-year period immediately prior to issue of the Claim Form – damages are not normally recoverable prior to this period);

— an order for delivery up (to the claimant) or destruction (confirmed by witness statement) of all infringing articles, dies, or tools;

— costs in favour of the claimant, as discussed further below; and

— a certificate of contested validity, putting the claimant in a more favourable position on costs recovery in the event that another party challenges the validity of the patent on the same grounds.

The precise nature of the remedy available under the first three heads is more fully discussed elsewhere,[4] in relation to the substantive law of patent infringement.

If however the claimant fails (because the patent has been found invalid, or not infringed, or both) the normal order would be:

— if the patent has been found invalid, an order for its revocation (this can be suspended pending appeal);

— costs in favour of the defendant, as discussed further below (although if the claimant has been successful on either validity or infringement, the costs liability will often be split accordingly).

And also, if the claimant fails and an interim injunction had previously been granted:

— lifting of the interim injunction;
— an order for an inquiry on the cross-undertaking in damages given to the defendant by the claimant as a precondition for obtaining an interim injunction (an unsuccessful claimant is not otherwise liable to a defendant in damages).[5]

If the judge finds in favour of the claimant, directions for the conduct of the subsequent damages inquiry or account will be given when making the order following judgment. Such directions may include the provision of information and/or disclosure[6] in order to enable the claimant to make an informed choice as to whether to elect for an inquiry as to damages (which is an assessment of the losses that it has suffered as a result of the defendant's infringement) or an account of profits (which is an assessment of the profits that the defendant has made as a result of its infringement). Following such disclosure the claimant must make its election, and further directions may then be given for the inquiry or account procedure. Failing agreement between the parties on a figure, the judge will determine this in separate proceedings (which can, on the rare occasions that they proceed to a full hearing, prove to be lengthier and more expensive than the initial proceedings, on liability) initiated after judgment on liability.[7]

Filing a notice of appeal does not automatically have the effect that damages or account proceedings or proceedings relating to recovery of costs are stayed pending determination of the appeal. However, the judge will, in making the order following judgment, carefully consider whether an injunction against the defendant should be stayed pending the appeal, in much the same way as if considering whether an interim injunction should be granted. In the event that a final injunction is granted, and the defendant intends to appeal, the claimant will usually be required to give a cross-undertaking as to damages, so that the defendant is able to recover damages from the claimant arising from the imposition of the injunction if the defendant's appeal succeeds. Similarly, in the event that the claimant intends to appeal a finding that the patent is invalid, the order revoking the patent will be suspended until the appeal is determined.

Irrespective of the nature of the judgment the parties should also seek an order from the trial judge as to preserving the protection for documents which were disclosed in the action, and which were relied on in open court, and as to which the parties wish to preserve confidentiality.

This is because the default position under CPR Rule 31 is that absent an order preserving the protection afforded by CPR 31.22, documents that have been relied on at trial (including documents referred to in experts' reports and witness statements) lose such protection, and so for example, can be deployed in other proceedings. The trial judge will scrutinize any such application carefully, and because of the principle of open justice it should not be assumed that just because the parties are in agreement as to it, the judge will be as well.[8]

1   It has been suggested that a failure to grant leave to appeal against a decision to revoke a patent would be contrary to TRIPS, Article 32, which states that: 'An opportunity for judicial review of any decision to revoke or forfeit a patent shall be available'. However, the contrary view is that the scope to seek leave to appeal from the Court of Appeal meets this requirement, as was held in *Pozzoli SPA v BDMO SA* [2007] EWCA Civ 588 (Court of Appeal). In practice it is very rare for the first instance court not to grant leave to appeal against its final decision in a patent infringement or revocation matter.

2   The UK Supreme Court has assumed the appellate jurisdiction from the English Court of Appeal previously exercised by the Judicial Committee of the House of Lords.

3   See below at para 4.21: 'English patent litigation in practice'.

4   See **Chapter 6** at para 6.19 et seq.

5   See below at fn 3 to para 4.17: 'Interim injunctions in patent infringement matters', as to how such calculation is approached.

6   *Island Records Ltd v Tring International PLC* [1995] FSR 560, a copyright case in which the defendant was ordered to disclose certain documents relating to the profitability of its infringing activities to enable the claimant to make an informed choice between electing for damages or an account.

7   See **Chapter 6** at para 6.21 et seq for a discussion of the principles applied in so doing.

8   See *Smith & Nephew Plc v Convatec Technologies Inc.* [2014] EWHC 146 (Pat) for an example of the limited degree to which the court will make such an order as to documents that have been relied on at trial. See also *Hospira UK Ltd v Genentech Inc* [2014] EWHC 3248 (Pat) (22 July 2014), in which the relevant principles are summarized.

Costs awards

4.15   An important feature of all English litigation is its rules on legal costs. If a party commences an action it will incur legal costs, and will cause the other side to incur legal costs too. Normally a party which wins at the trial of the action will also be awarded its 'costs' which means that the loser will have to contribute to the winner's legal costs. In practice the winner does not obtain reimbursement of all its legal costs – it will typically (unless in the Intellectual Property Enterprise Court, which, as discussed below, has a costs recovery cap) recover about one-half to two-thirds of its legal costs.[1] These legal costs include the professional fees and expenses of its solicitors, barristers, patent attorneys and experts, as well as court fees, although these are not (even with the considerable recent increases in these) so high in the UK as in some other countries. If the quantum of such costs cannot be agreed between the parties, the successful party can apply to a costs judge to determine this, and the costs of this proceeding will ultimately be paid by the unsuccessful party. Thus, any party to litigation in the English courts (other than the Intellectual Property Enterprise Court) is risking not only its own costs but also risks making a substantial contribution to the costs of its opponent. The practice has developed of the trial judge making 'interim costs awards' when making the order following judgment (including judgments both on applications made during the course of proceedings and after trial). Such awards are payable within a short period, and can sometimes reflect a substantial proportion of the legal costs the winning party might expect to recover after a full determination before a costs judge, thus making it easier to reach agreement as to the balance without such full determination.

It is often found that the parties incur roughly the same order of costs. On this basis, the claimant risks being out of pocket (disregarding any sums payable as damages) to the extent of one-third or one-half of its costs if it wins, and to the extent of about one-and-a-half to one- and two-thirds of its own costs if it loses. The trial judge can also take the conduct both before, and after the start of proceedings of both parties into account when assessing costs.

Another consequence of this approach to costs is that although once an action has been commenced, a claimant can withdraw the infringement proceedings at any time (prior to receiving judgment) it has a potential costs penalty in that unless agreed with the defendant to the contrary, the claimant will be liable for its costs, to be assessed by a costs judge if not agreed. Withdrawing the infringement proceedings does not necessarily affect a counterclaim for invalidity, however, since this is brought by the defendant, and so the claimant's patent will remain at risk. However, if no longer faced with an infringement claim, the defendant is unlikely to be so concerned with contesting the validity of the patent, and will have no such interest at all where it receives as a term of settlement a non-suit undertaking or a royalty free licence, and so it is common for the parties to agree to abandon both the claim, and the counterclaim together.

There are exceptions to the 'rule' as to the winner recovering its costs, for example, when a judge awards the claimant no more than the defendant has previously formally (though at the time of the trial unknown to the judge) offered to settle the matter by means of an offer expressed to be 'without prejudice except as to costs'. In this instance although the claimant has technically won, it should have accepted the offer. In these cases the winner will not usually get an award of costs, as this is always at the discretion of the judge, and may depend on the nature of the claim, and the way in which it is has been prosecuted. In the case of an offer that should have been accepted, it is usual that the claimant recover its costs up to the date of the offer, but must pay the costs of the defendant after that date.

Patent litigation can be complicated and costly, especially in a difficult area of technology. It may be possible to obtain 'before the event' insurance to cover the costs of instituting, or defending a patent action, and this can be a worthwhile investment for a young or smaller company at the same time as it applies for patents, even though only few UK businesses have litigation insurance for their IP. However, as with all insurance policies, the small print needs careful review, as does the level of cover, as that generally available can be unrealistically low for complex patent litigation when one factors in the risk of having to pay the other side's costs. A party may be able to enter into a conditional fee agreement (CFA) with its solicitors by which they agree to forego their fees if it loses, in exchange for an uplift in costs of up to 100 per cent if it wins, although such uplift is not recoverable from the other side. It may be possible to insure against the risk of the other side's costs under 'after the event' insurance, although the premiums for such insurance tend to be a very high percentage of the costs at risk.

In the Intellectual Property Enterprise Court, a different costs regime applies under which, with limited exceptions, the court will not order a party to pay total costs of the other side of more than £50,000 on the final determination of a claim in relation to liability, or £25,000 on an inquiry as to damages, or account of profits, and within those overall limits also restricts the amount recoverable at each stage of the proceedings.[2]

1   Another exception is proceedings before the Comptroller in which the 'costs' awarded to the successful party are capped at about £5,000 by virtue of scale fees as set out in the UK Intellectual Property Office Tribunal Practice Notice (TPN 4/2007) but are in practice considerably less.

2   See CPR, Pt 45, s IV entitled 'Scale Costs for Claims in the Intellectual Property Enterprise Court' and in particular CPR 45.31 which sets out the usual scale that applies. The background to these was discussed in *Westwood v Knight* [2011] EWPCC 011, in which the first fully reasoned award of such costs was made, albeit in the context of an action for trade mark and copyright infringement. However, the costs cap does not, by CPR 45.30, apply where: '(a) the court considers that a party has behaved in a manner which amounts to an abuse of the court's process; or (b) the claim concerns the infringement or revocation of a patent or registered design or registered trade mark the validity of which has been certified by a court or by the [Comptroller] in earlier proceedings'. Where, short of abuse of the court's process, a party has behaved unreasonably, CPR 63.26(2) allows that the court may make an order for costs at the conclusion of the hearing, rather than reserving the costs according to the usual practice (CPR 63.26(1)) and CPR 45.32 provides that costs awarded under rule 63.26(2) are in addition to the total costs awarded under CPR 45.31, as discussed in *Kemal Akhtar v Bhopal Productions (UK) Limited* [2015] EWHC 154 (IPEC) (a copyright case) and in which the earlier case law is reviewed.

Other aspects of English patent infringement litigation

Interaction between English courts and Patent Office jurisdictions

4.16   The UK Intellectual Property Office (UKIPO) (formerly the UK Patent Office) in the form of the Comptroller (although decisions are in fact made by officials in the IPO, acting as hearing officers) has a continuing jurisdiction in respect of UK patents once they have been granted, as well as a jurisdiction in respect of UK designations of European patents once granted. Thus, a revocation action can be instituted in the IPO. The Comptroller's jurisdiction is one that can in general be ousted by UK court proceedings, as unless the court stays its own proceedings the Comptroller will invariably stay those before him. It is only in the rarest, and most special circumstances in which the court will stay its own proceedings because of parallel ones before the Comptroller. The same considerations also apply to applications for declarations of non-infringement. The Comptroller also has a jurisdiction as to infringement actions but only with the active consent of both parties.[1]

The situation in respect of parallel oppositions at the European Patent Office (EPO) where there is a granted European patent validated in the UK is rather different. For patents granted via the EPO there is a period of nine months during which the EPO can entertain third-party oppositions to the grant of the patent. A determination as to this by its Opposition Division can be appealed to a Technical Board of Appeal. There is no equivalent opposition (as opposed to revocation) procedure in the IPO in respect of the UK patents that it grants. The EPO is thus competent to determine the validity of the patent it has granted, in the sense it can either revoke the patent, maintain it subject to amendments, or maintain it unamended. As a successful opposition in the EPO will have the effect of revoking the European patent in all designated states, the jurisdiction of the EPO to this extent in practice overrides that of national courts, such as those in the UK if it has been validated there.[2] However, a finding by the EPO on opposition that a patent is valid does not bind national courts, and the English courts have on occasion revoked the UK designation of a patent, the validity of which has been upheld in the EPO by a Technical Board of Appeal after opposition. However, the EPO has no jurisdiction to deal with matters of infringement, or to entertain revocation proceedings after the nine-month opposition period has expired (although under EPC, Article 105 if an opposition procedure is ongoing, further opponents can join the opposition if they become a party to infringement proceedings in respect of a national designation of the patent under opposition).

The English courts used originally to take the view that where there were parallel opposition proceedings in the EPO and in England on the UK designation of a patent granted by the EPO, an English infringement action on that UK designation ought not be stayed pending the outcome of the EPO opposition, even where the defendant undertook to be bound by the outcome in the EPO. Courts in some other EPO contracting states, and especially those lacking specialized patent courts, were more prepared to await the outcome of EPO proceedings. The view of the English courts then mellowed, in part in recognition of the unsatisfactory nature of adjudicating on issues concerning a patent the claims of which might well take a very different form at the conclusion of an EPO opposition. The position has to some extent swung back, given the overall time taken for an EPO opposition and its appeal,[3] so that it will in general be difficult to secure from the English Courts a stay of revocation or infringement proceedings pending the outcome of an EPO opposition, as although the default option is to grant a stay, the discretionary factors to be taken account of in determining whether or not to grant such a stay as enumerated by the Court of Appeal in *IPCom GmbH v HTC Europe Co Ltd*[4] will in practice only rarely favour it.

A stay of infringement proceedings in such cases would not necessarily preclude the success of an application for interim relief, which as observed in *Kimberly Clark v Procter & Gamble*[5] might be an appropriate way of proceeding in some cases as this recognizes that if a patent survives an EPO opposition, it will do so half the time on claims that have been amended.

Where in an infringement action on an EP(UK) patent there has been no stay of the UK action (pending the outcome of a parallel EPO opposition) and the EP(UK) patent is found valid and infringed, even beyond all prospect of appeal, the subsequent revocation of the patent in the EPO opposition, or its amendment so that the defendant no longer infringes, is now a basis for setting aside the order already made by the English court against such a defendant, provided that damages and costs have not already been paid under it.[6]

1   Patent Act 1977, s 61(3).
2   It was held in *R v Comptroller General; ex parte Lenzing AG* [1997] RPC 245 that the English court could not judicially review a decision of an EPO Board of Appeal to revoke a patent, and in *Virgin Atlantic Airways v Jet Airways (India)* [2012] EWHC 2153, [2013] EWCA 1713 that an English court had no jurisdiction in respect of administrative acts by the EPO.
3   This can take several years in total, even where the Technical Board of Appeal does not, as sometimes happens, remit the case to the Opposition Division for further consideration – as observed by a Technical Board of Appeal in Case T-0612/09 (11 April 2013): 'While it gives the board no pleasure to say so, four years is currently the average time taken to dispose of appeals in its list of pending cases'.
4   See *IPCom GmbH v HTC Europe Co Ltd* [2013] EWCA Civ 1496, at [68], and in which a stay was refused, which guidance slightly modified that given in *Glaxo Group Limited v Genentech Inc* [2008] EWCA Civ 23 (Court of Appeal) at paras [79]–[88] in the light of criticism made of that in the *Glaxo* case by the UK Supreme Court in *Virgin Atlantic Airways v Zodiac Seats UK* [2013] UKSC 46. In *Actavis Group Ptc Ehf v Pharmacia LLC* [2014] EWHC 2265 (Pat), [2014] EWHC 2611 (Pat) a stay was initially refused, even though the patentee had offered undertakings: (a) to seek expedition of the EPO proceedings; (b) not to seek an injunction against the defendant or its customers until the determination of the EPO proceedings; and (c) only to seek damages of 1 per cent of the defendants' net sales during the period from launch until the determination of the EPO proceedings (if the patent was held valid both by the EPO and by the English courts). However, a stay was subsequently ordered once the patentee had also offered: (i) not to seek an injunction in the UK against the defendant or its customers under the patent during its life; and (ii) only to seek damages of 1 per

cent of the defendants' net sales in the UK during the life of the patent, if the patent was ultimately held valid by the EPO, and valid and infringed by the English courts. See however *Samsung Electronics Co Ltd v Apple Retail UK Ltd and Another* [2014] EWCA Civ 250, in which English appeal proceedings were adjourned pending an application by the patentee centrally to limit the patent in suit in the European Patent Office (EPO). Limitation proceedings take only a matter of months, as opposed to the years taken by opposition proceedings and their appeals.

5   *Kimberly Clark v Procter & Gamble* [2000] FSR 235; [2000] RPC 422.

6   *Virgin Atlantic Airways v Zodiac Seats UK* [2013] UKSC 46, reversing the judgment of the Court of Appeal at [2011] EWCA Civ 163, disagreeing with *Unilin Beheer BV v Berry Floor* [2007] EWCA Civ 364 (Court of Appeal) and overruling *Poulton v Adjustable Cover and Boiler Block Co* [1908] 2 Ch 430 and *Coflexip v Stolt (No 2)* [2004] EWCA Civ 213; [2004] FSR 34 (Court of Appeal). The latter two cases did not have an EPO aspect to them but had been authority for the proposition, which the UK Supreme Court decided should no longer be followed, that when in one action a patent is found valid and infringed, beyond all prospect of appeal, but the same patent is revoked in subsequent proceedings, the defendant to the first action was still bound by the order against it for damages and costs. The subsequent proceedings would have generally to have involved a different defendant, because as observed in *Adaptive Spectrum And Signal Alignment Inc v British Telecommunications Plc* [2014] EWHC 4194 (Pat) at [87]: 'in general once a party has attacked the validity of a patent and the patent has been found valid, they cannot normally come back and attack validity again, even on new grounds'.

Interim injunctions in patent infringement matters

4.17   The main aim of the patentee in most patent infringement actions is to stop the infringer, and to preserve its monopoly. Thus the most important remedy sought at the full trial of an action is usually an injunction against continued infringement. The patentee is often not willing to permit the alleged infringer to continue its activities until trial, even though the patentee will be compensated in damages for the continued infringement if it succeeds. What it would like is an immediate injunction to prevent further infringement up to trial. However such an 'interim injunction'[1] can only be obtained where the court considers that it would otherwise be impossible to do full justice to the patentee after the trial of the action; the patentee must show that an award of damages at trial in respect of the continued infringement in the period up to trial would not be an adequate remedy.

This makes it difficult to obtain such injunctions in cases of patent infringement in the English courts. This is because, provided the scale of the defendant's continued infringement is ascertainable (which can usually be achieved by the keeping of accounts) the damage done to the patentee can relatively easily be calculated post-trial. This is especially the case, absent special circumstances (some examples of which are discussed below) given that in England the time to trial for a full hearing on the merits in a patent action is typically about a year, and where this is so ordered, rather less. Interim injunctions are intended for emergencies, and thus speed is of the essence when seeking them. Usually an application for an interim injunction must be brought within a matter of weeks, or the court will conclude that the infringement cannot really be damaging the patentee sufficiently to warrant such drastic relief.

In deciding whether or not to grant an interim injunction the judge will see written evidence from both sides, unless in cases of real urgency, or for special reasons (as explained later) evidence is only provided from the patentee. However, in deciding the matter the judge does not hear the full facts surrounding the action, or see witnesses cross-examined, and so is not in a position to resolve contradictory evidence of fact. Instead, the judge must first decide whether there is a serious case to be tried. This is a very low threshold and so is often conceded by the defendant. Assuming that there is a serious case to be tried, the judge's task is then to decide whether damages in respect of this period to the trial of the action are going to be an adequate remedy to the patentee by the time that the action is brought to trial. If damages are not an adequate remedy then the judge goes on to balance the interests of the patentee (on the assumption that an interim injunction is not granted but it succeeds at trial) against the interests of the defendant (on the assumption that an interim injunction is granted but it succeeds at trial). This is known as 'the balance of convenience'. However, the grant of an interim injunction is always within the judge's discretion, and will depend very much upon the particular commercial situation presented. This approach has its basis in the decision of the House of Lords in *American Cyanamid v Ethicon*.[2]

The position as to interim injunctions in Scotland (there referred to as 'interim interdicts') is in practice somewhat different to that in England and Wales. In Scotland whilst the 'balance of convenience' arguments still apply in theory, one may never get as far as reviewing them in practice as it is more common than in England and Wales to obtain an interim interdict on an *ex parte* basis without the prior knowledge of the defendant. If this happens, then the real argument takes place when, and if, the defendant then applies to set the interdict aside, as a condition of which it must often lodge substantial financial security, known as a 'caution'.

As interim injunctions are granted on a superficial view of the case, it is always possible that one may prove later to have been wrongly granted. In recognition of this, an interim injunction always carries with it what is called a 'cross-undertaking in damages'. The effect of this is that if the patentee obtains an interim injunction and then fails at the trial of the action, the defendant has a claim against the patentee for the damage (eg loss of profits during that interim period) that it has suffered as a result of the grant of the interim injunction.[3]

The defendant will often be able to argue that if an interim injunction is wrongly granted it can never be properly compensated under the cross-undertaking as it will never really be able to determine the market share it would otherwise have achieved, and the loss of profit it has thereby sustained. The balance between the damage suffered by the patentee by continued infringement pending trial, and that suffered by the defendant as a result of being subject to an injunction pending trial tends to be more even in most patent actions than in those on other types of IP. Thus the defendant's argument that if an interim injunction is granted it will never be able properly to calculate its loss tends to carry more weight in an action where the IP is not itself endangered by the actions of the defendant. Therefore, this argument by the defendant is more persuasive in a patent infringement action than in an action where the IP concerned is, for example, confidential information or a trade mark. To meet this approach, patentees in infringement actions, apart from providing commercial evidence (eg as to the unquantifiable effect of their being unable to establish themselves in a new market, or of the price-cutting which may ensue if the defendant is not enjoined) will attempt to provide evidence as to additional special factors favouring the grant of an interim injunction.

An example of particular application in the pharmaceuticals field, advanced in *American Cyanamid* (which concerned surgical sutures) is that with a relatively small specialized market (eg doctors) if the infringing product were to become established in the period through to trial of the action it might well be commercially impracticable to deprive the market of that product after trial owing to the damaging effect on the patentee's goodwill. Another argument met in the pharmaceuticals field concerns the dramatic, and in practice irrecoverable nature of price erosion immediately on generic entry. So powerful has this latter argument become that there is now, in effect, an obligation on prospective generic market entrants to the pharmaceuticals market to 'clear the path' before their intended launch by bringing revocation proceedings, and/or proceedings for a declaration of non-infringement (or possibly providing the patentee with the necessary wherewithal to bring infringement proceedings) as appropriate, in relation to any patents of potential concern, sufficient time in advance of market launch to secure a decision on the full merits before such launch.[4]

One instance where an interim injunction may be appropriate is where the defendant is a 'man of straw' who may not be able to meet an award of damages if the patentee prevails. The defendant may however be able to answer such an argument by undertaking to set aside a royalty on sales in a jointly-held bank account as security for any award of damages. Another argument in favour of an interim injunction, which can be used towards the end of the life of a patent, is that the full trial of the action will not take place until after expiry of the patent, at which stage no injunction can be granted. Failure to grant an interim injunction in these circumstances would have in practical terms the effect of shortening the period of monopoly provided by the patent. This argument has been run in circumstances where the pre-expiry infringement consisted of alleged 'experimentation' undertaken with a view to moving to full commercialization immediately upon expiry of the patent, as in *Monsanto v Stauffer*.[5]

It is important that a patentee be fully aware of the possible risks of obtaining an interim injunction, but failing in the full action, before deciding to apply for one. The grant of an interim injunction can also have the effect of imposing on the patentee the need to advance the action even more quickly than would otherwise be normal or the patentee might wish. This is because if there is a serious risk of having to recompense the defendant under the cross-undertaking in damages, then the patentee will want to keep the period of risk (from grant of the injunction to trial) as short as possible.

A further ground for securing an interim injunction that has been suggested, but has not yet formed the basis for the grant of one in any reported case, is where an infringement action has been stayed, pending the outcome an EPO opposition.[6] However, given the long delay before the final outcome an EPO opposition is known, such a patentee would have to be prepared to give a cross-undertaking in damages for a period of possibly several years, over the length of which period they would have little or no control.

1   Known before the CPR as 'Interlocutory injunctions'.
2   *American Cyanamid v Ethicon* [1975] 1 All ER 504; [1975] RPC 513. It has been suggested however that *American Cyanamid* is not in practice properly applied; in not considering the strength of case once the 'serious case to be tried' threshold has been reached. Thus in *Series 5 Software Ltd v Philip Clarke* [1996] 1 All ER 853; [1996] FSR 273 (Patents Court) concerning an application for an interim injunction preventing the use of confidential information, the judge analysed in detail the history of the grant of interim injunctions before *American Cyanamid*, and re-examined the House of Lord's judgment in that case. He concluded that *American Cyanamid* was not intended to represent a change in the law; it had not been the intention to exclude the consideration of the strength of the case, and it had merely advocated a flexible approach. The judge set out four principles which he derived from this analysis, and that the court should bear in mind before granting an interim injunction: (i) the facts of the case; (ii) relief must be kept flexible; (iii) the court should rarely attempt to resolve complex issues of disputed fact or law; and (iv) major factors to bear in mind are: (a) the extent to which damages are likely to be an adequate remedy for each party and the ability of the other party to pay; (b) the balance of convenience; (c) the maintenance of the *status quo;* and (d) any clear view the court may reach as to the relative strength of the parties' cases. Subsequent cases have not, however, taken account of this final point, namely the relative strength of the parties' cases.
3   Such enquiries are rare, but for a dispute as to the scope of such a cross-undertaking see *SmithKline Beecham plc v Apotex Europe Ltd* [2006] EWCA Civ 658, in the light of which in, for example, *Wake Forest v Smith & Nephew* [2009] EWHC 45 (Pat) a cross-undertaking in damages was expressed so as to allow customers although not parties to the proceedings to recover under it. For determinations as to quantum under a cross-undertaking in damages see *Les Laboratoires Servier v Apotex Inc* [2008] EWHC 2347 (Patents Court) and *AstraZeneca AB & anr v KRKA d d Novo Mesto & anr* [2014] EWHC 84 (Pat), [2015] EWCA Civ 484 (Court of Appeal). An attempt in

'This idea [of common design] does not ... call for any finding that the secondary party has explicitly mapped out a plan with the primary offender. Their tacit agreement will be sufficient. Nor ... is there any need for a common design to infringe. It is enough if the parties combine to secure the doing of acts which in the event prove to be infringements.'

The patentee here sought to join the US parent of a defendant UK company, supplied by its US parent with an ingredient which it then incorporated into an allegedly infringing deodorant product. It was assumed for the purposes of the application that the supply of the ingredient took place outside the UK, so that the parent undertook no activity in the UK. It was not suggested that the US company told the UK company to use the ingredient, or that the UK company used the ingredient other than on their own initiative. The patentee conceded that its only aim in seeking to join the parent was to secure disclosure as to the precise formulation and manner of manufacture of the ingredient, because the UK company had no such information in its possession. It was held that the patentee had 'a good arguable case' which it ought to be allowed to develop and to present at final hearing, that there was: 'a meeting of minds between [the parent] and [the subsidiary] with a view to furthering the sale of products containing [the ingredient] in the UK in whatever manner and to whatever degree [the subsidiary] might decide.'. Accordingly, the parent was ordered to be joined as co-defendant (although under the broader powers now available under the CPR to order disclosure against non-parties, such a course might no longer be necessary).

Merely being a foreign parent of a UK company which is a defendant to patent infringement proceedings is not, however, enough in itself to establish a 'common design'[3] although by also giving the customers of its UK subsidiary a lifetime warranty, and providing financial support to the subsidiary, an assertion of common design between the two was allowed to stand.[4] Neither is the supply abroad of a product, knowing the use to which it will be put in the UK, enough in itself to establish a 'common design'[5] although going further, and installing and testing such machinery in the UK, and training staff in its use has been held sufficient to do so.[6] In any event, it would not be realistic for a foreign supplier or parent to proceed with activities relating to a product with a large market in the UK in the belief that it could entirely shield itself from any consequential litigation in the UK. Thus, in the event of such proceedings against a UK company for patent infringement its foreign supplier, or parent, could not be sure of being able successfully to challenge its joinder as a co-defendant on a 'common design' theory unless it had been scrupulous in the nature of its dealings. Even were a foreign supplier to be successful in such a challenge then, depending on the contractual and commercial situation between it and its customer, it might have to fund and otherwise support such litigation for the UK company, especially if it wished the action to be defended.

Company directors may also be properly joined as co-defendants with their company, and found jointly liable for its infringement if they are personally involved in the commission of the tort to a sufficient extent, and which can thus be an especial risk for managing directors of small companies.[7]

An innocent party within the jurisdiction can also be made the subject of proceedings (eg customs authorities and/or shippers) as happened in *Norwich Pharmacal Co v Commissioners of Customs and Excise*[8] purely for the purposes of enabling information as to infringers to be secured when their identity is known to such party. In *Smith Kline & French v Global Pharmaceutics*[9] an order made in interim proceedings obliged the defendant to disclose the identity of the foreign source of the infringing product notwithstanding that there was no suggestion that the source had done anything wrong in the UK. All these, however, related to the issue of infringement or to the identity of those involved in infringement. However, the powers of the court are not limited to this, and they now have more latitude to order disclosure from non-parties under the CPR without joining them as parties to an infringement action. In *American Home Products v Novartis*[10] an order was made to secure disclosure from a non-party to the proceedings of documents potentially relevant to the issues of novelty and obviousness.

It is for obvious reasons rare in patent litigation to sue one's own potential customers, but in some circumstances, a patentee may wish to do so in order to maximize the commercial pressure that it can impose, and the court has on occasion, relying on the *Norwich Pharmacal* jurisdiction, been prepared, even before establishing that there was liability on the part of the defendant that had supplied such customers, or those customers that had already been identified, to assist the patentee in identifying other customers by ordering that the supplier identify them.[11]

1   *Resolution Chemicals Limited v H. Lundbeck A/S* [2013] EWHC 739 (Pat) at para [101].
2   *Unilever v Gillette* [1989] RPC 583 (Court of Appeal).
3   *Unilever v Chefaro Proprietaries* [1994] FSR 135 (Court of Appeal) and *The Mead Corpn v Riverwood Multiple Packaging Division of Riverwood International Corpn* [1997] FSR 484 (Patents Court).
4   *Warheit & Applied Concepts v Olympia Tools* (2 February 2001, unreported) Pumfrey J (Patents Court).
5   *SABAF v MFI and Meneghetti* [2003] RPC 14 (Court of Appeal). The issue of common design was not the subject of the subsequent appeal to the House of Lords [2005] RPC 10, but an alternative submission, that by arranging the transport for the goods the supplier had itself imported and so infringed in its own right, was advanced and was rejected. See also *Generics (UK) Ltd v H Lundbeck A/S* [2006] EWCA Civ 1261 (Court of Appeal) where the Court of Appeal upheld a judgment refusing to allow a foreign supplier to be joined on the basis of an allegation that it was a joint tortfeasor.
6   *Fabio Perini sPA v LPC Group PLC* [2010] EWCA Civ 525 (Court of Appeal).
7   *MCA v Charley Records* [2001] EWCA 1441 at paras [49]–[53]. This was a copyright infringement case.

8   *Norwich Pharmacal Co v Commissioners of Customs and Excise* [1973] 2 All ER
    943; [1973] FSR 365, [1974] RPC 101, HL. See *Mitsui & Co Ltd v Nexen Petroleum
    UK Ltd* [2005] EWHC 625; [2005] 3 All ER 511 (Ch D) for a review of some of the
    current constraints on the jurisdiction to make such orders.
9   *Smith Kline & French v Global Pharmaceutics* [1986] RPC 394.
10 *American Home Products v Novartis* [2001] FSR 784 (Court of Appeal).
11 Such an order was made in *Wobben Properties GmbH v Siemens Public Limited
    Company* [2014 EWHC 3173. The specifics are not clear from the judgment, but
    the defendant had supplied wind turbines which it appears it was alleged could be
    activated by the customers in such a way as to infringe the patent, and that because
    the patent was near the end of its life the patentee wished to join such customers
    to the proceedings before judgment against the defendant supplier, and those of its
    customers, that the patentee had been able to identify.

Patent amendment in the course of litigation

4.20   Often in the course of a patent infringement action, prior art
is unearthed by the defendant which was either not known to, or its
significance not appreciated by, the patentee when first the patent was
prosecuted through to grant, but which the patentee considers presents
a serious challenge to validity. In the UK, PA 1977, s 27 provides the
power to amend patents after grant, which allows such situations to be
addressed, and, although where there are no proceedings pending, this
can be done before the Comptroller, by PA 1977, s 75 applications to make
such amendments can (and indeed ought to[1]) take place in infringement
or revocation proceedings.[2] Amendment used to be regarded as
discretionary, and dependent on the behaviour of the patentee. However,
PA 2004, s 2 amended PA 1977, s 27 so that the principles to be applied
are those applicable under the EPC. The EPO does not take account of
behaviour in determining whether to allow patent claims to be amended
in the context of opposition proceedings, and takes a similar approach
in the context of centralized post-grant 'limitation' proceedings brought
by patentees under EPC 2000, Articles 105a–105b, and which PA 1977,
s 27 as amended is to some degree intended to track.[3]

However, the principles established in the earlier English cases on
amendment will still apply to the determination of damages, or an award
of an account of profits for the infringement of a patent that has been
amended in the course of the proceedings, or been found to be partially
valid, as PA 1977, ss 62(3)–63(2) have been amended to require the
court to take account of whether the proceedings were 'brought in good
faith'. Thus, for example, in *Smith Kline & French Laboratories v Evans
Medical*[4] the amendment was not allowed as the patentee had known of
the problems which it sought to overcome by amendment for several
years before applying to amend. Now in such a case the amendment
would be allowed, but damages or an account of profits most likely
disallowed. The Patent Act 1977, s 62(3) and s 63(2) as amended also
require the court to take into account the knowledge of the defendant

at the date of infringement, and whether 'the specification of the patent as published was framed in good faith and with reasonable skill and knowledge', which latter expression is found in earlier versions of these sections and as to which the case law under those should continue to apply.[5]

1   As in *Nikken Kosakusho Works v Pioneer* [2005] EWCA Civ 906; [2006] FSR 4 (Court of Appeal) where the patentee was not allowed to seek a post-trial amendment where this would in effect involve a second trial on validity. See also *Nokia GmbH v IPCom GmbH & Co KG* [2011] EWCA Civ 6 (Court of Appeal) in which another attempt to make a post-trial amendment was rejected. However in *Samsung Electronics Co Ltd v Apple Retail UK Ltd & anr* [2014] EWCA Civ 250 the Court of Appeal stayed a pending appeal by the patentee to allow it to proceed with a centralized limitation in the EPO, initiated after trial, and observed that it was not an abuse of process to make, and to pursue such an application.

2   See also PA 1977, s 76, which makes it clear that any such amendment must neither add matter, nor extend protection (which concepts are discussed in **Chapter 5**) as they would constitute grounds of invalidity as to a patent wrongly so amended. Moreover, as held in *Koninklijke Philips Electronics N.V. v Nintendo of Europe Gmbh* [2014] EWHC 1959 as discussed at [291]–[310] a 'double patenting' objection (see **Chapter 2**, para 2.20, fn 5) may be a ground of objection to an amendment in the circumstances as set out at [310].

3   Limitation procedure in the EPO is *ex parte*, and so third parties have no formal standing enabling them to challenge it, whereas amendment in the UK is open to third party challenge, even when other than in the context of existing litigation.

4   *Smith Kline & French Laboratories v Evans Medical* [1989] FSR 561.

5   Discussed in *Kirin Amgen's Patent* [2002] EWHC 471; [2002] RPC 43 (Patents Court); [2002] EWCA Civ 1096; [2005] RPC 9 (Court of Appeal); and *Unilin Beheer BV v Berry Floor NV* [2005] EWCA Civ 1292.

English patent litigation in practice

4.21   Appendices 2 and **3** provide a flavour of patent litigation in the Patents Court and the English Court of Appeal.[1] **Appendix 2** sets out, in a variety of different ways, the statistics of patent disputes initiated and appealed since 1981, and **Appendix 3**, for each year since 1987, summarizes each of the decided cases in which validity and/or infringement was in issue, both at first instance (namely the Patents Court (some ten to twenty each year) the Patents County Court and the Intellectual Property Enterprise Court) and in the Court of Appeal. In most of these cases the main issues have been the old stalwarts of claim construction, and scope[2] and obviousness.[3] The Court of Appeal has in general been supportive of first instance judgments, and on those occasions where it has reversed the trial judge this has tended to be on the basis of differences as to claim construction.

The UK Supreme Court has assumed the jurisdiction of the House of Lords for appeals from the Court of Appeal, and continues its tradition of taking very few patent cases.[4] For several years after its decisions in *Merrell Dow v Norton*[5] and *Biogen v Medeva*[6] in 1995 and 1996 respectively, there were no House of Lord decisions in the field of substantive patent law except one, in 2000, on the single and rather special point as to the scope of the implied defence of repair – the subject of *United Wire v Screen Repair*.[7] However, the period from 2004 to 2008 saw six patent cases argued before the House of Lords.[8]

1   See also Christian Helmers & Luke McDonagh – *Patent Litigation in the UK* – LSE Law, Society and Economy Working Papers 12/2012 at: http://ssrn.com/ abstract=2154939.
2   Discussed in **Chapter 6** at paras 6.04ff.
3   Discussed in **Chapter 5** at paras 5.09ff, 'Lack of inventive step (obviousness)'.
4   So far, only *Human Genome Sciences v Lilly* (see **Chapter 8** at para 8.07); *Schütz (UK) Ltd v Werit (UK) Ltd* [2013] UKSC 16 (see **Chapter 6** at para 6.02); *Virgin Atlantic Airways v Zodiac Seats UK* [2013] UKSC 46 (see above at para 4.16, fn 6); and *Les Laboratoires Servier v Apotex Inc* [2014] UKSC 55 (see above at para 4.17, fn 3).
5   *Merrell Dow v Norton* [1996] RPC 76 (House of Lords).
6   *Biogen v Medeva* [1997] RPC 1 (House of Lords).
7   *United Wire v Screen Repair* [2000] 4 All ER 353; [2001] RPC 24 (House of Lords).
8   *Sabaf v MFI* [2005] RPC [2004] UKHL 45; 10 (House of Lords), *Kirin-Amgen v Hoechst Marion Roussel Ltd* [2004] UKHL 46; [2005] 1 All ER 667; [2005] RPC 9 (House of Lords). *SKB v Synthon* [2005] UKHL 59; [2005] 86 BMLR 130; [2006] RPC 10 (House of Lords) *Yeda Research and Development v Rhone-Poulenc Rorer and others* [2007] UKHL 43 (House of Lords) *Conor Medsystems Inc v Angiotech Pharmaceuticals Inc* [2008] UKHL 49 (House of Lords); and *Generics (UK) Ltd v H Lundbeck A/S* [2009] UKHL 12 (House of Lords).

Patent litigation in other European countries

Introduction

4.22   The way in which patent infringement actions are conducted varies greatly between common law countries (such as the USA, England and Australia) and civil law countries (such as France, Germany and Japan) because of the underlying differences in the legal systems.

Civil law legal systems have traditionally relied much more on written submissions, and much less on oral argument than the English courts. However, in this respect English practice changed under the CPR (although the Patents Court had already modified its procedure in this direction) with increasing emphasis on fuller Statements of Case, and so-called 'Skeleton Arguments'[1] submitted before any hearing. Even so, English hearings are still normally longer than those elsewhere in Europe, although for trials this is in large part because they involve the detailed cross-examination of witnesses. This is because another difference is the approach to evidence, with little or no provision for cross-examination of witnesses in civil law systems. Another difference relates to the compelled disclosure of documents, as discussed below. It can thus be seen that the procedure in the Intellectual Property Enterprise Court, as outlined above, represents a further move towards the procedure of civil law systems elsewhere in Europe.

In the context of patent litigation further distinctions arise as a consequence of the structure of the court system in differing countries. Thus in the UK there is for patent matters *de facto* only one first instance court for major patent actions, in the Netherlands there is only one first instance court for patent matters (that in the Hague) as is the case also now in France (in Paris), although in Germany there are several first instance courts that hear patent infringement matters (even though most of these are heard in Dusseldorf). In contrast, in most other European countries[2] there has traditionally, although this is now changing, been less specialization amongst courts, with the result that many courts can hear patent matters, and some courts which get occasionally presented with them have little experience of them. Not only can this result in less predictable judgments, and a greater reliance on the fact that a patent office has granted a patent in the first place, but it also has procedural consequences. Thus, such courts tend to be more prepared to stay actions pending, for example, the outcome of parallel EPO oppositions (or even parallel actions) and are more dependent on referring matters to court appointed experts, or to remitting matters for further rounds of written argument. This in turn can lead to delays that can sometimes be reflected in greater pressures to grant interim relief pending a final decision.

There are also differences attributable to the fact that patent infringement disputes almost invariably involve issues both of validity and infringement. In most countries (eg the UK) the questions of whether the patent is valid or not, and of whether it is infringed or not, are tried by the same court. In a few countries (eg Germany) the courts in which infringement proceedings are conducted have no jurisdiction over the validity of patents, which have to be dealt with by different courts, which deal with matters at different speeds. Not only is the German Federal Patents Court, that hears nullity challenges, slower than the German infringement courts, but it is precluded from considering the German designation of European patents that are under opposition at the EPO, until the EPO opposition procedure, and its appeals have been exhausted, a process which typically takes several years, and can sometimes take much longer. This has significant consequences given the importance of Germany as a forum for patent litigation, and the reluctance of its infringement courts to stay their proceedings to await the outcome of validity proceedings, which they will only do so in the most clear cut of cases, and typically only when a newly located, apparently novelty destroying item of prior art, is cited.

1   Which have long since ceased, at least in the courts hearing patent matters, to be skeletal, and now adopt the form of fully argued briefs.
2   For an overview of national patent litigation systems in each member of the EPC see: *Patent Litigation in Europe* (3rd edn, 2013) European Patent Office at: http://www.epo.org/learning-events/materials/litigation.html. For further comparative discussions see Graham, Stuart and van Zeebroke, Nicolas – *Comparing Patent*

Litigation across Europe: A First Look, (2011) at: http://papers.ssrn.com/sol3/papers. cfm?abstract_id=1924124 and Cremers, Katrin, et al – *Patent Litigation in Europe* – ZEW Discussion Paper 13-072 (2013) at: http://ftp.zew.de/pub/zew-docs/dp/ dp13072.pdf.

Proving infringement

4.23   One major difference between civil law and common law systems is that in common law countries it is normally possible to get disclosure of documents from other parties to the litigation. Thus each party has an obligation to disclose any relevant documents in its possession, which in the case of an infringement action includes those which identify the necessary details of what the defendant is doing. Therefore, if the alleged infringer is selling something the manufacture of which is alleged to infringe a process claim, it is vital to find out exactly how such material is made, and disclosure may be essential on that issue.

In civil law countries (as are all the EU Member States – other than the UK, Cyprus, Malta and The Republic of Ireland) disclosure is not readily available, and systems have been developed to meet this, one of which is use of procedural techniques (eg the *'saisie contrefacon'* in France). Similar procedures have also long been available in Italy and Belgium, but not for example in Germany, which can cause problems there when seeking to enforce process patents. The *'saisie'* is a 'dawn raid' on the intended defendants premises by court appointed officials under a court order, without warning, under which it is possible to demand to see the alleged infringement (or to see the allegedly infringing process) and to take samples or secure documentation to give the basis for a subsequent infringement action. Such procedures are becoming more widely available as a consequence of the national implementation throughout the EU of the Enforcement Directive,[1] Article 7 of which mandates the availability of prompt, and effective provisional measures to preserve relevant evidence in respect of alleged infringement, even though Article 6, mandating the availability of orders to present evidence in the possession of a party, and specified by the other side, where such other side has itself presented 'reasonably available evidence sufficient to support its claim', seems to have had little practical effect in civil law jurisdictions.

Some civil law countries also seek to address the difficulty of establishing what the other party is doing, in the case of the alleged infringement of process claims, by establishing appropriate legal presumptions, although these are limited in scope. One common approach to the problem is the reversal of the burden of proof of infringement of process patents. The CPC expresses this principle in Article 35, and this has also been incorporated into UK law by PA 1977, s 100 that states:

'(1)   If the invention for which a patent is granted is a process for obtaining a new product, the same product when produced by [an unauthorised person] shall, unless the contrary is proved be taken in any proceedings to have been obtained by that process.

(2)   In considering whether a party has been discharged the burden imposed upon him by this section, the court shall not require him to disclose any manufacturing or commercial secrets if it appears to the court that it would be unreasonable to do so.'

The same principle was incorporated into TRIPS as Article 34. To some extent, however, it reflects a response to a problem which was met when product claims, for example for pharmaceuticals, could not be secured in some countries. Subject to what is meant by a 'new product' in this context such a provision would now seem to provide little practical benefit if it were to be limited in scope to products for which one could, by virtue of their novelty, now secure product claims.

1   Directive 2004/48 of 29 April 2004 on the enforcement of intellectual property rights
     – OJEC L 195, 2 June 2004, 16.

Attempts to secure relief in patent disputes throughout Europe based on an action in one country

4.24   As many activities which may be alleged to infringe patents take place not only in one country but throughout several, the typical patentee will be interested in securing remedies effective throughout all those countries. Ideally a patentee would prefer to secure this through an action brought in a single (reliable) jurisdiction, rather than having to bring actions in several countries, although it is rare in practice that actions need be brought in more than even a couple of jurisdictions, even against a really determined defendant.

Judgments from one court may influence, but do not in any sense bind, the courts of other jurisdictions where a prospective defendant is engaged in the same alleged infringing activities, and where the claimant has an equivalent patent. The competent courts in those jurisdictions will want to be seen to be examining the whole matter again for themselves. However, courts in different jurisdictions cannot necessarily be relied on to reach the same conclusions on similar fact situations, even when applying much the same substantive law, especially as subtly different arguments will be advanced by different legal teams. Recognizing this, in patent disputes, English judges, on those rare occasions when they differ from their colleagues elsewhere in Europe, will now always explain the reasoning which leads them to come to a different conclusion.

Even if one overcomes the reluctance of most courts to adjudicate on what, almost by definition given the territorial nature of patents, is a foreign right, enforcement abroad generally proves difficult as there are few Conventions which provide for the almost automatic enforcement of a judgment granted by a foreign court, and few members of those few

Conventions that do so. Within Europe, however, matters are different. One of the effects of the Brussels I Regulation, and its associated measures in Europe[1] is to enable a judgment given in one contracting country readily to be enforced in another contracting country, and to restrict considerably the grounds on which that other country can refuse so to do. This provides the attractive prospect of 'one stop shopping', where one can bring an action in just one jurisdiction, but having effect throughout Europe.

Such 'one stop shopping' in enforcement was in part the intent behind the development of unitary IPRs having effect throughout the EU such as, for trade marks and designs, the Community Trade Mark, and Designs Regulations respectively.[2] However, in the absence in the past of a unitary patent, or a single court in which national patents granted via the EPO with identical claims in all designated countries can be enforced with effect in all designated countries – the scope has been explored for enforcing such national patents granted via the EPO in the courts of one of the countries, but with effect in all.

As discussed more fully below, the Dutch courts were at the forefront of such developments in the early 1990s, using the Brussels Convention, the predecessor of the Brussels I Regulation, to develop such a facility, that of the 'pan-European injunction'. Subsequently this jurisdiction on the part of the Dutch courts was considerably restricted, and also resulted in attempts pre-emptively to preclude the seizure of such patent infringement jurisdiction on the part of the Dutch courts, by means of so-called 'torpedoes', which however, also proved of value in redressing some of the asymmetries of German patent litigation consequent on its split jurisdiction for infringement and validity. Two decisions in 2006 on references to what is now the Court of Justice of the EU in Case C-4/03 *GAT v LuK*[3] and Case C-539/03 *Roche v Primus*[4] considerably reduced the scope for pan-European relief to be granted in patent infringement actions in full proceedings on the merits, although the Court of Justice has in Case C-616/10 *Solvay v Honeywell*[5] confirmed that this does not prevent applications for preliminary relief being brought on a pan-European basis, and has also made it clear that its decision in Case C-539/03 *Roche v Primus* is of limited application.

None of these decisions addressed the situation in which a potential defendant to patent infringement actions in several European jurisdictions seeks a declaration of non-infringement in respect of the designations of a European patent in those different jurisdictions, but does not in the same proceedings seek to challenge the validity of the patents so designated. The first such case in which this was considered was *Actavis UK Ltd & Ors v Eli Lilly & Company*[6] in which the English Patents Court considered whether not only the UK, but also the French, Italian, and Spanish designations of a European patent would be infringed by certain products, founding its jurisdiction so to do on the basis of the Brussels I Regulation, and deciding that although the applicable law relating to the issue of infringement was that of each of the four respective countries, it was English law which applied to the procedural issue of whether or not there was a basis for bringing such a proceeding, which is significant given that it is generally easier in English proceedings than those elsewhere in Europe to establish locus to seek a declaration of non-infringement.

1   Regulation (EU) 1215/2012 of 12 December 2012 on jurisdiction and enforcement of judgments in civil and commercial matters – OJEU L 351, 20 December 2012, 1 (known as the 'Brussels I Regulation'). For the non-EU EEA countries (namely Iceland, Norway and Liechtenstein) and also for Switzerland, a similar regime applies by virtue of the Lugano Convention. These provisions are implemented in the UK by the Civil Jurisdiction and Judgments Acts 1982 and 1991. The discussion here is not affected by the amendments to the Brussels I Regulation to formalize the status of the new Unified Patent Court under the Brussels I Regulation, namely Regulation (EU) No 524/2014 amending Regulation (EU) No 1215/2012 as regards the rules to be applied with respect to the Unified Patent Court, and the Benelux Court of Justice (OJEU L 163, 29 May 2014, 1) and inserting Articles 71a–71d into the Brussels I Regulation, as to which see below para 4.34, fn 3.

2   Council Regulation 207/2009 and 6/2002, which each provide for an injunction of potentially pan-European effect when a defendant is sued in its country of domicile, but for an injunction of only national effect (despite the pan-European nature of the rights themselves) where the jurisdiction is instead based only on infringement in that country.

3   Case C-4/03 *Gesellschaft für Antriebstechnik mbH & Co KG (GAT) v Lamellen und Kupplungsbau Beteiligungs KG (LuK)* (ECJ, 13 July 2006) on a reference from the Higher Regional Court of Dusseldorf.

4   Case C-539/03 *Roche Nederland BV v Drs Primus and Goldbenberg* (ECJ, 13 July 2006) on a reference from the Dutch Supreme Court.

5   Case C-616/10 *Solvay v Honeywell* (CJEU, 12 July 2012).

6   *Actavis UK Ltd & Ors v Eli Lilly & Company* [2012] EWHC 3316 (Pat); [2013] EWCA Civ 517; [2013] EWHC 3749 (Pat); [2014] EWHC 1511 (Pat); and [2015] EWCA Civ 555. The Court of Appeal set aside the declaration of non-infringement granted by the Patents Court and remitted the matter to it for further consideration as to the issue of contributory infringement, but otherwise accepted the approach of the Patents Court.

The relevant provisions of the Brussels I Regulation

4.25   The relevant provisions of the Brussels I Regulation (which by and large correspond with those of the Brussels and Lugano Conventions, and the earlier version of the Brussels I Regulation in effect at the time of the judgments of the Court of Justice referred to above, although the numbering of the articles differs) are those concerned with jurisdiction, the stay of parallel proceedings, and with enforcement as set out below.

Jurisdiction

4.26   The main provisions of the Brussels I Regulation relevant to the issue of jurisdiction as applied to patent actions are the following:

'4(1) Subject to this Regulation, persons domiciled in a Member State shall, whatever their nationality, be sued in the courts of that Member State.

(2) Persons who are not nationals of the Member State in which they are domiciled shall be governed by the rules of jurisdiction applicable to nationals of that Member State.

....

6(1) If the defendant is not domiciled in a Member State, the jurisdiction of the courts of each Member State shall, subject to ... Articles 24 ... be determined by the law of that Member State.

....

7 A person domiciled in a Member State may be sued in another Member State:

....

(2) In matters relating to tort, delict or quasi-delict, in the courts for the place where the harmful event occurred or may occur.

8 A person domiciled in a Member State may also be sued:

(1) Where he is one of a number of defendants, in the courts for the place where any one of them is domiciled, provided the claims are so closely connected that it is expedient to hear and determine them together to avoid the risk of irreconcilable judgments resulting from separate proceedings.

...

24 The following courts shall have exclusive jurisdiction, regardless of the domicile of the parties:

...

(4) In proceedings concerned with the registration or validity of patents, trade marks, designs, or other similar rights required to be deposited or registered, irrespective of whether the issue is raised by way of an action or a defence, the courts of the Member State in which the deposit or registration has been applied for, has taken place or is under the terms of an instrument of the Union or an international convention deemed to have taken place.

Without prejudice to the jurisdiction of the European Patent Office under the Convention on the Grant of European Patents, signed at Munich on 5 October 1973, the courts of each Member State shall have exclusive jurisdiction, regardless of domicile, in proceedings concerned with the registration or validity of any European patent granted for that Member State.'

Thus, although by Article 4(1), a natural or legal person domiciled in an EU Member State must in general be sued in that person's country of domicile, Article 7(2) allows the person also to be sued in matters relating to tort (eg patent infringement) in the courts for the place where the harmful act occurred, and Article 8(1) allows the person also to be sued, where that person is one of a number of properly joined defendants, in the courts for the place where any one of them is domiciled. All this, however, is subject to Article 24(4), by which the courts of the state in which the registration of the right (eg a patent) has been applied for, or has taken place, have exclusive jurisdiction in proceedings which have as their object the registration or validity of that right.

Related actions and enforcement

4.27 The main provisions of the Brussels I Regulation relevant to the stay of related proceedings are Articles 29–30, although Article 35 suspends their application for provisional measures:

'29 ...

(1) ... where proceedings involving the same cause of action and between the same parties are brought in the courts of different Member States, any court other than the court first seised shall of its own motion stay its proceedings until such time as the jurisdiction of the court first seised is established.

....

(3) Where the jurisdiction of the court first seised is established, any court other than the court first seised shall decline jurisdiction in favour of that court.

30

(1) Where related actions are brought in the courts of different Member States, any court other than the court first seised may stay its proceedings.

(2) Where the action in the court first seised is pending at first instance, any other court may also, on the application of one of the parties, decline jurisdiction if the court first seised has jurisdiction over the actions in question and its law permits the consolidation thereof.

(3) For the purposes of this Article, actions are deemed to be related where they are so closely connected that it is expedient to hear and determine them together to avoid the risk of irreconcilable judgments resulting from separate proceedings.

....

35 Application may be made to the courts of a Member State for such provisional, including protective, measures as may be available under the law of that Member State, even if the courts of another Member State have jurisdiction as to the substance of the matter.'

Thus by Article 29, where proceedings involve the *same* cause of action and the *same* parties, any court other than the first one seized of the matter *shall* decline jurisdiction, whereas in contrast, by Article 30, where proceedings are sufficiently closely *related,* any court other than the court first seised *may* stay its proceedings. However by Article 35, application may be made to the courts of any contracting state for provisional measures even if the courts of another contracting state already have jurisdiction.

As to enforcement, by Article 36 a judgment given in one contracting state shall be recognized in another contracting state without any special procedure being required, although by Article 45, insofar as relevant to patent disputes, recognition of a judgment shall be refused, broadly speaking if:

(a) such recognition is manifestly contrary to public policy in the Member State addressed;

(b) it was given in default of appearance in cases of non-service;

(c) it is irreconcilable with an earlier judgment in a dispute between the same parties in another Member State or in a non-contracting state involving the same cause of action and between the same parties; or

(d) it conflicts with Article 24.

Application of the Brussels I Regulation to applications for pan-European patent infringement relief

4.28 The situations in which the Dutch courts were originally willing to seize cross-border, or pan-European jurisdiction normally involved allegations of acts of infringement of a bundle of national designations of a European patent, committed by various members of a group of Dutch and non-Dutch companies. The legal basis for the Dutch courts seizing pan-European jurisdiction was what are now Articles 4(1) and 8(1) of the current version of the Brussels I Regulation, providing that a defendant must be sued in the Member State in which the defendant is domiciled, and that in the case of several co-defendants with sufficiently closely related claims against them, they may be sued in the Member State in which any one of them is domiciled.

The high point of the Dutch pan-European action was in 1994, with the Hague Court of Appeal's decision in *Chiron v Organon Teknika*.[1] Here the court reasoned that it was justified in assuming jurisdiction on a pan-European basis over the alleged infringement of a bundle of national designations of a European patent, committed by various members of a group of Dutch, and non-Dutch companies provided that there was a Dutch defendant alleged to be infringing the Dutch designation of a European patent, and there was a sufficient connection between the allegedly infringing acts of the non-Dutch, and the Dutch defendants. The Dutch courts were willing to assume jurisdiction in these circumstances in spite of the fact that the courts of other Member States had exclusive jurisdiction for proceedings relating to the validity of non-Dutch designations of the European patent in issue, by virtue of what is now Article 24(4) of the Brussels I Regulation. In doing so the Dutch courts based their views on the underlying assumption that it was possible to separate the issues of infringement and validity. They also assumed that a finding of infringement on the Dutch designation of a European patent was equally applicable to the determination of the issue of infringement of the corresponding non-Dutch designations of a European patent. The basis for this assumption was that, even though the grant of a European patent resulted in the registration of a bundle of national European patents, the law on the interpretation of the claims of a European patent had, under the protocol to EPC, Article 69[2] been harmonized throughout Europe.

The English courts took a different view of cross-border injunctions in patent infringement matters.[3] In *Coin Controls v Suzo International*[4] the issues of infringement, and validity of patents were held to be so closely interrelated that they should be treated as one, and the same issue for jurisdictional purposes. Thus once the validity of a non-UK designation of European patent had been put in issue elsewhere in Europe, the obligation to decline jurisdiction in relation to issues principally concerned with validity under what is now Article 24(4) of the Brussels I Regulation required that the English court decline jurisdiction over the claim for infringement of the non-UK designations of the European patent. The English court was not prepared to divorce the issues of infringement and validity. This reasoning was subsequently approved by the English Court of Appeal in *Fort Dodge v Akzo*[5] which concerned an application for an anti-suit injunction by a defendant to a patent infringement action before the Dutch courts. Although the court declined to grant the anti-suit relief requested it referred several questions to the Court of Justice concerning the interpretation of the Brussels Convention, and the justification for the grant of cross-border injunctions in European patent actions. However, this case was settled before the reference was heard, and the issues that it raised, therefore, remained unresolved until the rulings of the Court of Justice in 2006 in Case C-4/03 *GAT v LuK*[6] and Case C-539/03 *Roche v Primus*.[7]

The contrary view expressed by courts in other jurisdictions, and the adverse effect on locally headquartered businesses, caused second thoughts on the part of the Dutch courts, reflected four years later in two Hague Court of Appeal decisions in 1998[8] holding that the power of the Dutch courts to seize pan-European jurisdiction was qualified in two respects:

(i)   it was not necessarily possible to divorce the issues of infringement and validity nor, therefore, to assume that a finding on the Dutch designation of the European patent was equally applicable to the non-Dutch designations of the European patent. Accordingly, where the validity of the non-Dutch designation of the European patent had been put in issue in proceedings in other countries, the Dutch courts were obliged to stay the proceedings before them in respect of those non-Dutch designations of European patents, pending a determination of those foreign proceedings;

(ii) where the co-defendants were part of the same group of companies (as was usually the case), the Dutch courts could only seize pan-European jurisdiction if the Dutch defendant was the so-called 'spider in the web' of that group of defendant companies.[9]

Meanwhile the earlier, and more robust, approach of the Dutch courts had already induced a practical counter-response in other jurisdictions in the 'torpedo' strategy, although this seems in practice to have found most application in preventing infringement litigation proceeding in German courts. Instead of a patentee seeking pan-European patent infringement relief in one country, this involved a potential defendant to such proceeding seeking a pan-European declaration of non-infringement in a court which dealt with patent matters slowly. Thus, such a potential defendant would commence proceedings in such a jurisdiction for both:

— a declaration of non-infringement and invalidity in respect of the European patent designating that Member State; and
— declarations of non-infringement in respect of the designations in other Member States of the European patent.

The 'torpedo' started life (in theory and in practice) in Italy, where at the time over 200 first instance courts had jurisdiction over patent matters, some of which courts were happy to let such actions drift. However, largely because of the procedural formalities involved in Italian litigation, the torpedo flourished instead for a while in another jurisdiction with fewer procedural formalities – Belgium – the courts of which did not however appreciate their being so used. The legal rationale for the 'torpedo' is similar to that for the cross-border injunction but with an opposite effect. The argument runs that commencement of proceedings for a declaration of non-infringement in the courts of a Member State, claiming such relief on a pan-European basis should, by virtue of what are now Articles 29–30 of the Brussels I Regulation, prevent the courts of any other Member State in relation to which such jurisdiction has been claimed from assuming jurisdiction over proceedings for infringement. Thus a torpedo launched in a slow jurisdiction should slow down resolution of the issue of infringement in another Member State for sufficiently long enough for the defendant either:

— to successfully oppose the European patent centrally at the EPO; and/or
— to successfully revoke some or all of the designations of the European patent before the courts of the relevant Member States.

Since, by virtue of what is now Article 24(4) of the Brussels I Regulation the torpedo can only slow down the infringement aspect of a dispute, the strategy was of most use where the defendant's invalidity arguments were better than its non-infringement ones, or where, as in Germany, the invalidity ones cannot be run in the same proceedings but only in separate, slower ones.

Torpedoes granted by other courts were respected by first instance courts in Germany[10] but not in France, where they were held, amongst other things, to be an abuse of procedure.[11] In addition the two most favoured 'torpedo' jurisdictions have undermined their legitimacy. In *Glaxo-Wellcome v Hoffman La Roche*[12] the Brussels Court of Appeal upheld the dismissal of the cross-border element of a claim on the basis that the Belgian courts lacked proper jurisdiction under what are now Articles 4(1) and 8(1) of the Brussels I Regulation. In *BL Macheen Automatische v Windmolle*[13] the Italian Supreme Court held that the Italian courts lacked proper jurisdiction to make declarations as to foreign designations of a European patent. These various decisions reflected a turn in the judicial tide in the late 1990s, and early 2000s against the use of the torpedo as a procedural device to pre-empt the Dutch, or other European courts from seizing pan-European jurisdiction, and granting a cross-border European injunction. Moreover there remained ways to limit the effect of the torpedo, such as applications for preliminary relief, which by what is now Article 35 of the Brussels I Regulation, are an exception to what are now Articles 29–30.

There has been less use of the torpedo in the light of the decisions of the Court of Justice in 2006 in Case C-4/03 *GAT v LuK*[14] and Case C-539/03 *Roche v Primus*.[15] These considerably reduced the scope for pan-European relief to be granted in patent actions in full proceedings on the merits. Case C-4/03 *GAT v LuK* concerned what is now Article 24(4) of the Brussels I Regulation (which at the time lacked the 'irrespective of whether the issue is raised by way of an action or a defence' language that was subsequently added as a result of the decision of the Court of Justice) and took the broader English, rather than the narrower German or Dutch approach, to the relevance of a validity challenge in infringement proceedings, holding that it was to be interpreted 'as meaning that the rule of exclusive jurisdiction laid down therein concerns all proceedings relating to the registration or validity of a patent, irrespective of whether the issue is raised by way of an action or a plea in objection'. Case C-593/03 *Roche v Primus* concerned what is now Article 8(1) of the Brussels I Regulation and took a narrow view of its application, at least for patent infringement proceedings, holding that it was to be interpreted:

'… as meaning that it does not apply in European patent infringement proceedings involving a number of companies established in various Contracting States in respect of acts committed in one or more of those States even where those companies, which belong to the same group, may have acted in an identical or similar manner in accordance with a common policy elaborated by one of them.'

The combined effect of these rulings was effectively to sound the death-knell for pan-European patent infringement actions on the merits. These Court of Justice decisions only related, however, to those articles of the Brussels I Regulation concerned with full proceedings on the merits, and in Case C-616/10 *Solvay v Honeywell*[16] the Court of Justice, in holding that what is now Article 24(4) of the Brussels I Regulation 'must be interpreted as not precluding, in circumstances such as those at issue in the main proceedings, the application of' what is now Article 35 of the Brussels I Regulation confirmed that its decision in Case C-4/03 *GAT v LuK* had no bearing on applications for preliminary relief, such as interim injunctions, even though validity might be in issue. The Court of Justice also held that:

> 'Article [8(1)] of [the Brussels I Regulation] must be interpreted as meaning that a situation where two or more companies established in different Member States, in proceedings pending before a court of one of those Member States, are each separately accused of committing an infringement of the same national part of a European patent which is in force in yet another Member State by virtue of their performance of reserved actions with regard to the same product, is capable of leading to "irreconcilable judgments" resulting from separate proceedings as referred to in that provision. It is for the referring court to assess whether such a risk exists, taking into account all the relevant information in the file.'

In coming to this ruling the Court of Justice explained that the particular relationship between the various defendants in Case C-593/03 *Roche v Primus*, where there was a different defendant (albeit that all were subsidiaries of the same parent) for each Member State had been such that irreconcilable judgments were not possible, whereas in other cases such as this, where there were some common defendants, such a risk did arise. However, the practical effect of this aspect of the ruling is limited in view of the ruling in Case C-4/03 *GAT v LuK*, as now reflected in the wording of Article 24(4) of the Brussels I Regulation, which limits the scope for seeking pan-European relief for patent infringement in an action on the merits as it is always open to a defendant, in one way or another, to challenge the validity of the national designations of the European patent.

1   1 December 1994, IER 1995/5.
2   As to which see **Chapter 6** at para 6.05.
3   Note however that the English Courts have no problem in assuming cross-border jurisdiction in respect of rights, such as copyright, as to which, because they are not registered, raise no issue under what is now Article 24(4) of the Brussels I Regulation – see *Pearce v Ove Arup* [1999] 1 All ER 769; [1999] FSR 525; [2000] Ch 403; [2000] 3 WLR 332 (Court of Appeal).
4   *Coin Controls v Suzo International* [1997] FSR 660 (Patents Court).
5   *Fort Dodge v Akzo* [1998] FSR 222 (Court of Appeal).
6   See fn 14 below.
7   See fn 15 below.

8 *Expandable Grafts v Boston Scientific* [1999] FSR 352 and *Boston Scientific v Cordis* [2000] ENPR 87.

9 For so long as it had application the so-called 'spider in the web' approach begged the question as to whether the 'spider' constituted the head office of the holding company, the registered office of the holding company, or some other office within the group which controlled the marketing or distribution of the allegedly infringing products. However, in further cases the lower Dutch courts assumed pan-European jurisdiction over EU- based groups of companies, where the 'spider in the web' was based outside the EU, reasoning that to do otherwise would preclude any European court ever being able to assume pan-European jurisdiction over such disputes.

10 *SKB v Connaught* (27 February 1998).

11 *Sala v LaFranchi* (10 December 1999) and *GHC v Bracco* (28 April 2000).

12 *Glaxo-Wellcome v Hoffman La Roche* (20 February 2001).

13 *BL Macheen Automatische v Windmolle* (19 December 2003).

14 Case C-4/03 *Gesellschaft fur Antriebstechnik mbH & Co. KG (GAT) v Lamellen und Kupplungsbau Beteiligungs KG (LuK)* (ECJ 13 July 2006).

15 Case C-539/03 *Roche Nederland BV v Drs Primus and Goldbenberg* (ECJ, 13 July 2006).

16 Case C-616/10 *Solvay SA v Honeywell Fluorine Products Europe BV* (CJEU 12 July 2012).

The Unified Patent Court

Background to the Unified Patent Court

4.29   The Unified Patent Court Agreement, which will provide scope to enforce most national designations of European patents on a pan-European basis in a single proceeding before a single court, and provide the mandatory court for proceedings relating to the infringement, and validity of European patents with unitary effect, may well come into force during the course of 2017. It represents the culmination of a process that has taken over 40 years to reach fruition, but the most recent phase of which can be traced back to 1999.

Recognizing the unsatisfactory state of patent litigation in Europe, and considering that it would take many years for any acceptable unitary EU patent system to come into full effect with its own special rules as to litigation, certain national governments in Europe, including those of the Netherlands and the UK, set up a working party in 1999 to see what could be done to improve matters.[1] As a result, drafting took place on a 'European Patent Litigation Agreement' (EPLA) by which signatory countries would agree to an integrated judicial system: including harmonized rules of procedure and at least a common court of appeal, for litigation concerning those patents granted by the EPO which designated their countries.[2] The draft Agreement recognized that many countries would not participate, at least to start with, but it was hoped that the most significant ones from the point of view of patent litigation in Europe would do so, were it to be agreed. The exercise proved valuable in terms of the detail in which it addressed the issues, which would also have to be dealt with by any unitary patent litigation system.

However, the European Commission challenged the competence of EU Member States to negotiate such a measure, maintaining that competence in such matters had passed to it – as a result of the passage of Brussels I Regulation, despite having assured interested parties before such passage that this would not be the case. Although it denied it, many commentators believed that the Commission sought thereby to impede progress on the EPLA, in order to try to advance its unitary patent proposals, despite the support by much of European industry for the EPLA, and the hostility of most of European industry to the Commission's proposals for a unitary patent in their then current form.[3] Late in 2005, an attempt was made to breathe new life into the EPLA when 24 leading specialist patent judges throughout Europe from ten countries agreed on a resolution in the following terms:[4]

'We:

(i) resolve that a practical way for European patents to be enforced throughout the EU and member countries of the European Patent Convention within a reasonable time and at reasonable cost would be to convene a Diplomatic Conference with a view to implementing proposals broadly along the lines of those of the Working Party for a European Patent Litigation Agreement as soon as practicable; and

(ii) urge that Member States of the EU and Turkey and Switzerland cooperate in such endeavour whether by way of Enhanced Cooperation pursuant to Art II of EC Treaty or otherwise.'

The continued failure to make progress on the unitary patent however resulted in the Commission integrating the EPLA into its thinking on European patent litigation, and proposing a single court for both the proposed unitary patent and for national designations of patents prosecuted via the EPO.[5] Although its initial proposal for such a court was held by the Court of Justice of the EU[6] to be incompatible with the EU treaties, primarily because it would have been open also to EPO Member States that were not also EU Member States, its revised proposal, for a non-EU treaty open only to EU Member States, the Agreement on the Unified Patent Court,[7] was after negotiation and amendment, signed by 25 of the then 27 EU Member States on 19 February 2013.

1 A parallel working party made progress on reducing the need for translations of European patents by establishing an Optional Protocol on Translations, the London Protocol Agreement – see **Chapter 2**, at para 2.25, fn 1.

2 See patlaw-reform.european-patent-office.org/epla/ for further details.

3 See **Chapter 2** at para 2.20, fn 6.

4 See: http://www.eplaw.org/Downloads/Venice%20Resolution.pdf.

5 Communication from the Commission to the European Parliament and the Council – *Enhancing the Patent System in Europe* (COM (2007) 29 March 2007). See **Chapter 1** at para 1.09 and at fns 3–4 for an outline of subsequent developments.

6 Opinion 1/09 (Court of Justice, 8 March 2011). See also the summary prepared by the European Commission's legal service at: http://ec.europa.eu/dgs/legal_service/arrets/09a001_en.pdf.

7   See the draft Agreement on a Unified Patent Court and draft Statute – Revised Presidency text (Document 15539/11 PI 133 COUR 59, 19 October 2011) and subsequently Council Paper 167411/11 (11 November 2011) as modified by Council Paper 17539/11 (24 November 2011).

The Unified Patent Court Agreement

4.30   This Agreement on the Unified Patent Court[1] is an international treaty, initially between 25 of the 28 EU Member States,[2] which will establish a single court, the Unified Patent Court, with mandatory jurisdiction over new European patents with unitary effect[3] and, subject to transitional provisions, over traditional European 'bundle' patents validated in individual EU Member States, and supplementary protection certificates that designate those patents as basic patents. It will have no jurisdiction over patents prosecuted through national patent offices (or supplementary protection certificates that designate those patents as basic patents) or national utility models.

The Agreement on the Unified Patent Court will come into force on the first day of the fourth month after it has been ratified by France, Germany, and the UK (being the three EU Member States with the highest number of traditional 'bundle' patents that had effect in the year before its signature) as well as by ten other EU Member States, but it will only apply to those EU Member States that ratify it, even where they participated in the 'enhanced cooperation' which provided the legal basis for the European patent with unitary effect. Thus the European patent with unitary effect will only have legal effect in those countries which have ratified the Agreement at the date when the particular European patent with unitary effect is registered as such, so for an initial period at least it can be expected that not only the Unified Patent Court itself, but also the European patent with unitary effect will have variable geographic scope. The result will be that the territorial scope of the new European patent with unitary effect will, for some time, depend on *when* it is granted. The final ratification necessary for the Agreement to come into effect will be delayed until the preparations for establishing it are completed, which is likely to be 2016 at the earliest.[4]

1   Agreement on a Unified Patent Court (2013/C 175/01) [2013] OJEU C 175/1. Also available at: http://www.unified-patent-court.org/images/documents/upc-agreement. pdf.

2   Of the now current EU Member States neither Poland nor Spain signed the Agreement when it was opened for signature on 19 February 2013, and Croatia could not as it was not an EU Member State at that date. However by Article 84(4) the Agreement is open to accession by any EU Member State so any of them, and any new EU Member State, may do so later. These three countries each have a different status with regard to the Unified Patent Court, and the European patent with unitary effect. Spain's position is consistent with its failure to participate in the 'enhanced cooperation' procedure that provides the legal basis for the European patent with unitary effect, and its objections, primarily on language grounds, to the European patent with unitary effect, as reflected in its unsuccessful challenge in Cases C-146/13 and C-147/13 *Kingdom of Spain v*

European Parliament and Council of the European Union (Court of Justice, 5 May 2015) to the legality of the implementing Regulations for this, namely Regulation (EU) No 1257/2012 of 17 December 2012 implementing enhanced cooperation in the area of the creation of unitary patent protection [2012] OJEU L361/1 and Council Regulation (EU) No 1260/2012 of 17 December 2012 implementing enhanced cooperation in the area of the creation of unitary patent protection with regard to the applicable translation arrangements [2012] OJEU L361/89. Accordingly unless Spain decides otherwise, the new European patent with unitary effect will not apply to Spain, and traditional European 'bundle' patents validated in Spain will continue to be litigated only in the Spanish courts. Italy, like Spain, again primarily on language grounds, did not participate in the 'enhanced cooperation' procedure which provides the legal basis for the European patent with unitary effect, and indeed joined Spain in Joined Cases C-274/11 *Kingdom of Spain v Council of the European Union* and C-295/11 *Italian Republic v Council of the European Union* (CJEU, 16 April 2013) in challenging unsuccessfully the measure that authorized enhanced cooperation, namely Council Decision of 10 March 2011 authorizing enhanced cooperation in the area of the creation of unitary patent protection [2011] OJEU L76/53. Despite this, Italy signed the Agreement so that if it were then to ratify this traditional European 'bundle' patents validated in Italy could be litigated, subject to transitional provisions, in the Unified Patent Court, but the European patent with unitary effect would not extend to Italy. Italy's position has changed and it has now agreed to participate in enhanced co-operation – see Commission Decision (EU) 2015/1753 of 30 September 2015 on confirming the participation of Italy in enhanced cooperation in the area of the creation of unitary patent protection [2015] OJEU L 256/19. Poland participated in the 'enhanced cooperation' procedure which provides the legal basis for the European patent with unitary effect. However, it did not sign the Agreement, and unless and until it does so, the Unified Patent Court and the European patent with unitary effect will not extend to it; but if it does so then, unlike initially Italy, and because it participated in 'enhanced cooperation' both will then do so. Poland chose not to sign the Agreement, because it came to the conclusion, after commissioning an economic review of the new system, that the discounted benefits for Poland of not participating in the new regime far outweighed those of doing so. See – Deloitte Polska, *Analysis of the potential impact from the introduction of Unitary Patent Protection in Poland* (in Polish), October 2012, available at: http://www.mg.gov.pl/files/upload/16510/Analiza%20 potencjalnych%20skutkow%20jednolitego%20patentu%20europejskiego_final.pdf. Summarized in Xenos, Dimitris, *The European Unified Patent Court: Assessment and Implications of the Federalisation of the Patent System in Europe* (31 August 2013) (2013) 10(2) SCRIPTed – *Journal of Law, Technology & Society*, 246–77 – available at: SSRN: http://ssrn.com/abstract=2324123. Since Poland, unlike Spain (or initially Italy), participated in 'enhanced cooperation', it lacks the option employed initially by Italy (and still open to Spain) of signing the Agreement – but not becoming subject to the new European patent with unitary effect. Indeed it was the forecast economic effect on Polish industry of becoming subject to the new European patent with unitary effect, when so few traditional 'bundle' patents are currently validated in Poland, that led to the adverse conclusion in the economic review as to the effect of participating in the new regime. Croatia acceded to the EU on 1 July 2013, and so could neither sign the Treaty (although it could do so now) nor participate in the 'enhanced cooperation' procedure that provided the legal basis for the two Regulations establishing the European patent with unitary effect (but it could now so participate, if it so chose).

3   As established by Regulation (EU) No 1257/2012 of 17 December 2012 implementing enhanced cooperation in the area of the creation of unitary patent protection, (OJ L 361, 31 December 2012, 1) and Council Regulation (EU) No 1260/2012 of 17 December 2012 implementing enhanced cooperation in the area of the creation of unitary patent protection with regard to the applicable translation arrangements (OJ L 361, 31 December 2012, 89). Two instruments are required because they

each have different legal bases within the EU Treaties, given the somewhat special treatment afforded language arrangements in the EU Treaties. The two Regulations are expressed only to apply as from 1 January 2014, or the date of entry into force of the Agreement on the Unified Patent Court, whichever is the latter, which now makes the establishment of the European patent with unitary effect contingent on the ratification, and entry into force of the Agreement on the Unified Patent Court the rate limiting step. See also **Chapter 1** at para 1.09 and above at para 4.29.

4   A Preparatory Committee composed of representatives from signatory states to the Agreement has been at work since its signature on the establishment of what will be an entirely new type of court system, and the preparations necessary to bring it into force: see the Unified Patent Court website at: http://www.unified-patent-court.org/. The Preparatory Committee has published an outline of the tasks that it is undertaking, which include the preparation of Rules of Procedure, the establishment of a judiciary, forming the various divisions of the Court and its Registry, providing the physical infrastructure for these, and developing financial IT systems for it, at: http://www. unified-patent-court.org/images/documents/roadmap.pdf. In parallel the EPO has been considering the changes that it needs to make to its rules to accommodate the new European patent with unitary effect, which a patentee will be able to request of it, and register at the end of the examination process as an alternative to a traditional European 'bundle' patent. However, the EPO will also have wider responsibilities for the new European patent with unitary effect, beyond administering patentees' requests for unitary effect, in that it will also be responsible for collecting, administering, and remitting renewal fees for such patents, and for keeping a register of them to include legal-status information, such as licences, transfers, limitation, revocation, or lapse – tasks which are carried out by national patent offices for traditional European 'bundle' patents. Perhaps of the greatest significance will be its decision as to the level of fees that it charges for the new European patent with unitary effect as it must compete with traditional European 'bundle patents' most of which only designate a few countries (generally no more than France, Germany, and the UK at most) as that has proven to be all that patentees in most sectors (pharmaceuticals being an exception) require in order to control trade in Europe. Good data as to this is hard to come by, as it appears that EU Member States do not adopt a consistent approach to how they treat nationally validated European patents in the data they submit to WIPO that form the basis of the statistics (as set out in 'Table P2: Patents granted by patent office and origin, and patents in force, 2011, in the 2012 World Intellectual Property Indicators' (WIPO, 2012) at 176–78). Assuming however that national patents form a relatively small proportion of patents in force, as opposed to nationally validated European patents, and taking these statistics at face value it appears that the total number of nationally validated European patents in force in each of France, Germany, and the UK is in of the order of five times the number in the EU Member State with the next largest number of validated patents, and at least ten times the number of validated patents in most EU Member States.

4.31   Although the Unified Patent Court will be a 'single court', with jurisdiction to make orders with the potential to have effect throughout all the EU Member States that have ratified it, it will consist of a number of different divisions, each with differing competences. There will be a 'central division' (itself split by subject matter, into three sections, based in Paris, Munich and London[1]) and local divisions, or multi-country 'regional' divisions.[2] It will also have a Court of Appeal, based in Luxembourg. It will have no linkage with national courts (although it may share judges with them, at least initially). Its linkage with the Court

of Justice of the EU is somewhat obscure in that although Article 20 of
the Agreement requires the Unified Patent Court to apply EU law in its
entirety, and to respect its primacy, and Article 21 requires it to cooperate
with the Court of Justice of the EU, and to be bound by its decisions,
there is no provision for appeal from its Court of Appeal to the Court
of Justice of the EU, as had been proposed in some earlier versions of
the measure. Article 21 does however envisage the Unified Patent Court
referring matters of EU law to the Court of Justice of the EU in the same
way as the national courts of EU Member States do currently. Whilst this
does not present any obvious difficulty (at least as to EU law) in relation
to a traditional European 'bundle' patents designating individual EU
Member States (as to which EU law has only limited relevance[3]) it is
unclear what more this will mean in relation to new European patents
with unitary effect, the legal basis for which lies in EU legislation.[4]

The competence of the Unified Patent Court as a whole will extend
to all of the types of patent dispute that are listed in Article 32 of the
Agreement.

'Article 32 – Competence of the Court

1. The Court shall have exclusive competence in respect of:

    (a) actions for actual or threatened infringements of patents and
         supplementary protection certificates and related defences,
         including counterclaims concerning licences;
    (b) actions for declarations of non-infringement of patents and
         supplementary protection certificates;
    (c) actions for provisional and protective measures and injunctions;
    (d) actions for revocation of patents and for declaration of invalidity of
         supplementary protection certificates;
    (e) counterclaims for revocation of patents and for declaration of
         invalidity of supplementary protection certificates;
    (f) actions for damages or compensation derived from the provisional
         protection conferred by a published European patent application;
    (g) actions relating to the use of the invention prior to the granting of
         the patent or to the right based on prior use of the invention;
    (h) actions for compensation for licences on the basis of Article 8 of
         Regulation (EU) No 1257/2012; and
    (i) actions concerning decisions of the European Patent Office in
         carrying out the tasks referred to in Article 9 of Regulation (EU)
         No 1257/2012.

2. The national courts of the Contracting Member States shall remain
competent for actions relating to patents and supplementary protection
certificates which do not come within the exclusive competence of the Court.'

Thus such competence will not extend to disputes over ownership,
which even for European patents with unitary effect will have to be dealt
with in national courts.[5]

1   The subject matter split, as between 8 sections lettered (A)–(H) is based on the International Patent Classification of the World Intellectual Property Organisation (http://www.wipo.int/classifications/ipc/en) and distributes: (A) human necessities and (C) chemistry, metallurgy to London, (B) performing operations, transporting (F) mechanical engineering, lighting, heating, weapons, blasting, (D) textiles, paper (E) fixed constructions, (G) physics and (H) electricity to Paris, and (F) mechanical engineering, lighting, heating, weapons, blasting to Munich.

2   It is thought at present that only Luxembourg and Malta will not host a local or a regional division, that most countries will host a local division, with Germany hosting the maximum of four allowed by Article 7(4) of the Agreement some countries, and that at least one regional division will be established for some countries around the Baltic Sea.

3   Namely as to matters under the Treaty on the Functioning of the European Union (TFEU), in particular Articles 34, 36, and 101–102 of this, and EU legislation affecting patents or establishing supplementary protection certificates, being primarily Regulation (EC) No 1610/96 of 23 July 1996 concerning the creation of a supplementary protection certificate for plant protection products, (see **Chapter 7** at para 7.25); Regulation (EC) No 469/2009 of 6 May 2009 concerning the supplementary protection certificate for medicinal products (see **Chapter 7** at para 7.25); Directive 98/44/EC of 6 July 1998 on the legal protection of biotechnological inventions (see **Chapter 8** at para 8.02, fn 1), and Directive 2004/48/EC of 29 April 2004 on the enforcement of intellectual property rights (see **Chapter 6** at para 6.19).

4   The Regulations that provide the legal basis for the European patent with unitary effect say very little about the substantive law that applies to it, and what these do say (in Article 5 of Regulation (EU) No 1257/2012 of 17 December 2012 implementing enhanced cooperation in the area of the creation of unitary patent protection (OJ L 361, 31 December 2012, 1) is delphic in the extreme, in a deliberate effort to avoid the Regulation having the effect of extending EU competence over all areas of substantive patent law. It is in the Agreement on the Unified Patent Court where one finds, in Articles 25–30 a complete code as to patent infringement, which however differs in certain details (notably as to certain limitations of the effects of a patent under Article 27) from that under the national laws of EU Member States. As to matters of patent validity all EU Member States are parties to the European Patent Convention.

5   See para 4.03 above.

4.32   As between the different First Instance divisions of the Unified Patent Court the split of competence, which is complicated, is set out in Article 33.

'Article 33 – Competence of the divisions of the Court of First Instance

1.   Without prejudice to paragraph 7 of this Article, actions referred to in Article 32(1)(a), (c), (f) and (g) shall be brought before:

   (a)   the local division hosted by the Contracting Member State where the actual or threatened infringement has occurred or may occur, or the regional division in which that Contracting Member State participates; or

   (b)   the local division hosted by the Contracting Member State where the defendant or, in the case of multiple defendants, one of the defendants has its residence, or principal place of business, or in the absence of residence or principal place of business, its place of business, or the regional division in which that Contracting

Member State participates. An action may be brought against multiple defendants only where the defendants have a commercial relationship and where the action relates to the same alleged infringement.

Actions referred to in Article 32(1)(h) shall be brought before the local or regional division in accordance with point (b) of the first subparagraph.

Actions against defendants having their residence, or principal place of business or, in the absence of residence or principal place of business, their place of business, outside the territory of the Contracting Member States shall be brought before the local or regional division in accordance with point (a) of the first subparagraph or before the central division.

If the Contracting Member State concerned does not host a local division and does not participate in a regional division, actions shall be brought before the central division.

2. If an action referred to in Article 32(1)(a), (c), (f), (g) or (h) is pending before a division of the Court of First Instance, any action referred to in Article 32(1)(a), (c), (f), (g) or (h) between the same parties on the same patent may not be brought before any other division.

If an action referred to in Article 32(1)(a) is pending before a regional division and the infringement has occurred in the territories of three or more regional divisions, the regional division concerned shall, at the request of the defendant, refer the case to the central division.

In case an action between the same parties on the same patent is brought before several different divisions, the division first seized shall be competent for the whole case and any division seized later shall declare the action inadmissible in accordance with the Rules of Procedure.

3. A counterclaim for revocation as referred to in Article 32(1)(e) may be brought in the case of an action for infringement as referred to in Article 32(1)(a). The local or regional division concerned shall, after having heard the parties, have the discretion either to:

   (a)   proceed with both the action for infringement and with the counterclaim for revocation and request the President of the Court of First Instance to allocate from the Pool of Judges in accordance with Article 18(3) a technically qualified judge with qualifications and experience in the field of technology concerned;

   (b)   refer the counterclaim for revocation for decision to the central division and suspend or proceed with the action for infringement; or

   (c)   with the agreement of the parties, refer the case for decision to the central division.

4. Actions referred to in Article 32(1)(b) and (d) shall be brought before the central division. If, however, an action for infringement as referred to in

Article 32(1)(a) between the same parties relating to the same patent has been brought before a local or a regional division, these actions may only be brought before the same local or regional division.

5. If an action for revocation as referred to in Article 32(1)(d) is pending before the central division, an action for infringement as referred to in Article 32(1)(a) between the same parties relating to the same patent may be brought before any division in accordance with paragraph 1 of this Article or before the central division. The local or regional division concerned shall have the discretion to proceed in accordance with paragraph 3 of this Article.

6. An action for declaration of non-infringement as referred to in Article 32(1)(b) pending before the central division shall be stayed once an infringement action as referred to in Article 32(1)(a) between the same parties or between the holder of an exclusive licence and the party requesting a declaration of non-infringement relating to the same patent is brought before a local or regional division within three months of the date on which the action was initiated before the central division.

7. Parties may agree to bring actions referred to in Article 32(1)(a) to (h) before the division of their choice, including the central division.

8. Actions referred to in Article 32(1)(d) and (e) can be brought without the applicant having to file notice of opposition with the European Patent Office.

9. Actions referred to in Article 32(1)(i) shall be brought before the central division.

10. A party shall inform the Court of any pending revocation, limitation or opposition proceedings before the European Patent Office, and of any request for accelerated processing before the European Patent Office. The Court may stay its proceedings when a rapid decision may be expected from the European Patent Office.'

Thus the competence of the local and regional divisions of the Unified Patent Court will differ from that of its central division.[1]

Broadly speaking, local and regional divisions will have competence over infringement actions (and if they so choose in a particular case, counterclaims for revocation) where the actual or threatened infringement takes place in, or where the defendant, or one of the defendants has its residence or principal place of business in the country of the local division, or one of the countries of a regional one. As to actions based on residence or principal place of business Article 33(1)(b) addresses the situation of multiple defendants, but requires that an 'action may be brought against multiple defendants only where the defendants have a commercial relationship and where the action relates to the same alleged infringement'. The third paragraph of Article 33(2) provides a limited restriction on bringing multiple proceedings by providing that where 'an action between the same parties on the same patent is brought before several different divisions, the division first seized shall be competent for the whole case and any division seized later shall declare the action inadmissible'. In practice, however, it is usually easy to so formulate another proceeding with a slightly different combination of parties.

The central division will also have infringement competence in respect of infringements taking place in those few countries which do not host a local or a regional division, or at the patentee's option, against defendants that are resident outside the EU, or in a Member State that has not ratified the Unified Patent Court Agreement. The central division will also have exclusive competence over actions seeking declarations of non-infringement and revocation other than as counterclaims to infringement actions, although such competence can in either case be sabotaged by infringement proceedings against the same party subsequently brought in a local or regional division (always assuming that such party is in fact undertaking a potentially infringing act). As a result once an infringement action is properly commenced the degree to which the central division remains, or becomes, involved will generally be in the power of the local or regional division in which the infringement action is proceeding.

The jurisdictional arrangements within the Unified Patent Court for the main types of proceeding are summarized in the following table:

Article	Subject	Division	Comment
32(1)(a)	Infringement	Local or regional if any, otherwise central, which is also an option for the patentee with a non-EU defendant or where a revocation action is on foot	Article 33(1)(a)–(b) – Where the actual or threatened infringement has occurred or may occur
32(1)(b)	Declarations of non-infringement	Central	Article 33(4) – Unless infringement action already on foot Article 33(6) – Stayed if infringement action started within three months
32(1)(c)	Provisional and protective measures and injunctions	Local or regional if any, otherwise Central	

Article	Subject	Division	Comment
32(1)(d)	Revocation	Central	Article 33(4) – Unless infringement action already on foot Article 33(5) – Infringement action may be started in a local or regional division, the powers of which are unaffected by the fact of the revocation action having been brought, or in the central division
32(1)(e)	Counterclaims for revocation	Local or regional if any, otherwise central	Article 33(3) – Local or regional division has discretion whether to hear counterclaim, refer counterclaim to central division (staying infringement action or proceeding with it) or, but only with agreement of parties, referring the whole matter to central division

Article 33(3) provides local and regional divisions with the option of bifurcating the issues of infringement and validity, leaving the latter to be determined by the central division. This has caused some concerns amongst those who note that this jurisdictional asymmetry favours patentees in the national German system where infringement actions are, absent a stay, which is rare, heard before the full challenge to validity. The current (18th) draft of the Rules of Procedure seeks to address this concern by requiring (in Rule 37) that where it orders bifurcation, but does not also stay the infringement proceedings, that the local or regional division communicate its timetable to the central division and (in Rule 40) that the judge rapporteur of the panel of the central division endeavour to set a date for the oral hearing on the revocation action prior to the date of the oral hearing of the infringement action. The control of infringement proceedings conferred on the local and regional divisions, even where the defendant has previously sought a declaration of non-infringement or to revoke the patent in issue, gives the defendant few procedural options for controlling the future course of infringement proceedings once these have been started. One limited option introduced into the Agreement at a late stage of its negotiation is the second paragraph of Article 33(2) by which a defendant, where an infringement action is pending in a regional (but not local) division has the option of requesting a transfer of the case to the central division where the alleged infringement has occurred in three or more regional divisions, but this requires that there be three regional divisions in existence, which will not necessarily be the case. The Agreement outlines the procedure to be adopted by all divisions of the Unified Patent Court in Articles 52–55, the language regime which applies in Articles 49–51,[2] and its powers in Articles 56–72.[3] The Rules of Procedure, which are still in draft,[4] elaborate on each of these.

1   See para 4.31, fn 2 as to the likely location of the local and regional divisions. The composition of local division panels depends on how many cases have been commenced before the UPC enters into force – if there have been in the past less than 50 a year on average, they have one local judge and two foreign ones; but otherwise two local judges and one foreign one (Article 8(2)–(3)). Regional divisions always have two local judges and one foreign one (Article 8(4)).

2   Local or regional divisions will, unless the parties agree otherwise, use a local official language or languages, whereas the central division will use English, French or German, depending on the language in which the patent was granted. Local or regional divisions may also designate English, French, or German, and it seems that many divisions with other official languages than these will also designate English as an option.

3   In large part these are based on the corresponding provisions of Directive 2004/48 of 29 April 2004 on the enforcement of intellectual property rights – OJEC L 195, 2 June 2004, 16.

4   The 18th Draft of the Rules of Procedure (1 July 2015) is in this respect identical to the Preliminary set of provisions for the Rules of Procedure ('Rules') of the Unified Patent Court (17th Draft) (31 October 2014) at: http://www.unified-patent-court.org/images/documents/UPC_Rules_of_Procedure_17th_Draft.pdf.

4.33 Although the Unified Patent Court will have mandatory jurisdiction over European patents with unitary effect its application to traditional 'bundle' European patents will depend on the application of transitional provisions, which envisage a period of 7 years, extendable to 14 years, during which actions on such patents can also be brought in national courts.

'Article 83 Transitional regime

1.   During a transitional period of seven years after the date of entry into force of this Agreement, an action for infringement or for revocation of a European patent or an action for infringement or for declaration of invalidity of a supplementary protection certificate issued for a product protected by a European patent may still be brought before national courts or other competent national authorities.

2.   An action pending before a national court at the end of the transitional period shall not be affected by the expiry of this period.

3.   Unless an action has already been brought before the Court, a proprietor of or an applicant for a European patent granted or applied for prior to the

end of the transitional period under paragraph 1 and, where applicable, paragraph 5, as well as a holder of a supplementary protection certificate issued for a product protected by a European patent, shall have the possibility to opt out from the exclusive competence of the Court. To this end they shall notify their opt-out to the Registry by the latest one month before expiry of the transitional period. The opt-out shall take effect upon its entry into the register.

4. Unless an action has already been brought before a national court, proprietors of or applicants for European patents or holders of supplementary protection certificates issued for a product protected by a European patent who made use of the opt-out in accordance with paragraph 3 shall be entitled to withdraw their opt-out at any moment. In this event they shall notify the Registry accordingly. The withdrawal of the opt-out shall take effect upon its entry into the register.

5. Five years after the entry into force of this Agreement, the Administrative Committee shall carry out a broad consultation with the users of the patent system and a survey on the number of European patents and supplementary protection certificates issued for products protected by European patents with respect to which actions for infringement or for revocation or declaration of invalidity are still brought before the national courts pursuant to paragraph 1, the reasons for this and the implications thereof. On the basis of this consultation and an opinion of the Court, the Administrative Committee may decide to prolong the transitional period by up to seven years.'

Thus, subject to the opt-out under Article 83(3), Article 83(1) allows the type of actions there specified[1] on traditional 'bundle' European patents to be started in either the Unified Patent Court or in the national court system for a transitional period of seven years from the entry into force of the Agreement, which period can be extended by a further seven years under Article 83(5). However if an action is started in the Unified Patent Court on a traditional 'bundle' European patent this will by the nature of the jurisdiction of the Unified Patent Court govern all designations of the patent, and so preclude bringing such litigation in a national court on that patent for so long as the action proceeds in the Unified Patent Court. Similarly, an action that is started under Article 83(1) in a national court would appear, by the nature of the jurisdiction of the Unified Patent Court, to preclude bringing such litigation in the Unified Patent Court on that patent for so long as the action continues to proceed in that or another national court, as the Unified Patent Court would be unable to make an order governing all designations of the patent.[2]

However, where no action is pending in the Unified Patent Court, Article 83(3) allows a patentee 'to opt out from the exclusive jurisdiction of the [Unified Patent] Court' in respect of a traditional 'bundle' European patent before the end of the transitional period. Article 83(4) allows a patentee to withdraw such opt out where no action is pending in a national court. Those drafting the Rules of Procedure have expressed the view 'that the provisions of Article 83 of the Agreement for opting-out are clear and provide for: (i) a complete ousting of the jurisdiction of the UPC (ii) such ouster is, subject to [Article 83(4)] for the life of the relevant patent/application and (iii) covers all designations owned by the proprietor in question.'³ To avoid a flood of applications to opt out as soon as the Agreement comes into effect, and even though the Agreement does not envisage this, the draft Rules of Procedure provide for applications for opt–outs to be registered a certain period before the Agreement comes into force.⁴ Although again not envisaged by the Agreement, the draft Rules of Procedure envisage charging a fee for each patent that is the subject of an opt-out, and a fee for each patent that is the subject of an opt-in. Whereas, absent any fee, Article 83(4) would appear to have supported the prudent course being to opt-out under Article 83(3), imposing a fee for both changes matters: depending on the level of such fees the decision faced by those with large patent portfolios as to whether or not to opt-out may be far from a foregone conclusion, and may require consideration on a case-by-case basis.

1   Which, it should be noted, are not expressed to include declarations of non-infringement, although there is controversy as to whether or not this omission was intentional.
2   This analysis is reinforced by the provisions of Regulation (EU) No 524/2014 amending Regulation (EU) No 1215/2012 as regards the rules to be applied with respect to the Unified Patent Court, and the Benelux Court of Justice (OJEU L 163, 29 May 2014, 1), and inserting Articles 71a–71d into the Brussels I Regulation, where Article 71a deems the Unified Patent Court to be a court of a Member State when, 'pursuant to the instrument establishing it, [it] exercises jurisdiction in matters falling within the scope of [the Brussels I Regulation]' and so for example Articles 29–30 of the Brussels I Regulation, and the clear risk of irreconcilable judgments (see above at paras 4.25–4.28) will apply to preclude actions proceeding on the same traditional 'bundle' European patent at the same time in the Unified Patent Court and national courts, even as between different parties, where the validity of the patent is in issue.
3   See page 11 (in the text found in the 16th draft that was deleted in the 17th draft) of the Preliminary set of provisions for the Rules of Procedure ('Rules') of the Unified Patent Court (17th Draft) (31st October 2014) at: http://www.unified-patent-court.org/images/documents/UPC_Rules_of_Procedure_17th_Draft.pdf. Although this represents the conventional view of the scope of Article 83(3) there is another interpretation that could be placed on it. This would treat it as an opt-out from 'exclusive jurisdiction' in the sense that it still leaves the Unified Patent Court with a jurisdiction to be shared with the system of national courts, as long as a patent the subject of an action started in one system stays in that system. Such an interpretation would not, despite Article 83(1), deprive Article 83(3) of purpose, as in the event that the transitional period was not extended, with the result that Article 83(1) ceased to apply, the opt-out under Article 83(3) would continue so to do. Such an interpretation would also be consistent with opting-out before the expiry of the transitional period, and would render otiose any mechanism for registering an opt-out before the entry into force of the Agreement. However, the draft Rules of Procedure purport to exclude such an interpretation, even though, as Rules made under the Agreement, they can hardly govern the interpretation of the Agreement itself.

4 See Rule 5 of the Preliminary set of provisions for the Rules of Procedure ('Rules') of the Unified Patent Court (17th Draft) (31st October 2014) at: http://www.unified-patent-court.org/images/documents/UPC_Rules_of_Procedure_17th_Draft.pdf. The 18th Draft of the Rules of Procedure (1 July 2015) is in this respect identical to the 17th draft.

4.34 The Unified Patent Court will add yet a further layer, or indeed layers, of complexity to an already complex structure of patent litigation in Europe, which already involves national patents, utility models, and traditional European patents designating one or more Member States. Given the continuing and thus parallel role envisaged, at least in the medium term, for national courts in relation to traditional European 'bundle' patents, and the uncertainty as to whether the European patent with unitary effect will ever prove sufficiently competitive in terms of price to supplant these, it remains to be seen for how much longer the criticism of the existing system as articulated by the late Mr Justice Laddie 15 years ago in the English Patents Court, when striking out patent infringement proceedings in relation to various other European jurisdictions, remains apt: 'A less sensible system could not have been dreamt up by Kafka'.[1]

1 *Sepracor v Hoechst Marion Roussel* [1999] FSR 746 (Patents Court).

Chapter 5

Patent validity – substantive law

Introduction

Grounds of invalidity

5.01   The aim of the patent examination process that takes place during most patent prosecution, as outlined in **Chapter 2**, is to ensure that the patents granted as a result of it are valid, or at least not clearly invalid. However, the process acts as a coarse sieve, primarily because of the limited time, and resources of any patent office examiner, and because of the inevitable limitations of the patent office search initially undertaken, constraints which are imposed by the level of fees which patent applicants are prepared to pay. Because of this, all patent systems provide some means for third parties to challenge the validity of patents once granted, or at least to do so in the context of attempts to enforce them. Such challenges can often succeed because commercial competitors have a greater motivation and resources than a patent office examiner. Some of the procedures involved in such challenges are outlined in **Chapter 4**. However, this chapter is concerned with the grounds on which such challenges can be mounted – namely the substantive law of patent validity.

Therefore, the principles set out in this chapter are also applied by patent office examiners during the patent prosecution process. However, because an examiner's objection can often be overcome by amending the claims in some way, in practice the most authoritative law as to validity is established in cases in which third parties attack the validity of a patent after grant, which in the UK will generally involve applications to the court and in the European Patent Office (EPO) opposition proceedings, especially once this reaches the Technical Boards of Appeal.

The provisions mandated by the Agreement on Trade Related Aspects of Intellectual Property (TRIPS) as to patent validity are set out in Articles 27(1) and 29(1). Article 27(1) requires that: 'patents shall be available for any inventions, whether products or processes, in all fields of technology, provided that they are new, involve an inventive step and are capable of industrial application'.

A footnote in the text states that for the purposes of this article, the terms 'inventive step', and 'capable of industrial application' may be deemed ... to be synonymous with the terms 'non-obvious' and 'useful' respectively. However the concepts of 'new', 'involving an inventive step', and 'capable of industrial application' are each the subject of considerable elaboration in, and indeed variation between, national laws, which also introduce other criteria with which patents must comply for them to be valid.[1] The expression 'all fields of technology' reflects a perception that some areas of innovation can properly be excluded from the scope of patentability, and indeed, as outlined below, the EPC has within it certain express exclusions that can only be justified as being consistent with TRIPS on the basis that they exclude activities which are outside 'all fields of technology'. TRIPS, Article 29(1) provides that:

'Members shall require that an applicant for a patent shall disclose the invention in a manner sufficiently clear and complete for the invention to be carried out by a person skilled in the art and may require the applicant to indicate the best mode for carrying out the invention known to the inventor at the filing date or, where priority is claimed, at the priority date of the application.'

The European Patent Convention (EPC) lacks the second, optional obligation on patentees under TRIPS, Article 29(1), namely that of disclosing the best mode.[2] Under the EPC the only grounds on which the validity of a patent can be opposed centrally after grant are those set out in EPC, Article 100:

'(a) the subject-matter of the European patent is not patentable within the terms of Articles 52 to 57

(b) the European patent does not disclose the invention in a manner sufficiently clear and complete for it to be carried out by a person skilled in the art

(c) the subject matter of the European patent extends beyond the content of the application as filed, or, if the patent was granted on a divisional application or on a new application filed in accordance with Article 61, beyond the content of the earlier application as filed.'

Of these the grounds set out in TRIPS, Article 27(1) correspond to EPC, Articles 52–57 referred to in (a). The first sentence of TRIPS, Article 29(1) corresponds to (b). The EPC, Article 138, setting out the only grounds on which a European patent may be revoked under the law of a contracting state, with effect for its territory, repeats these, but adds in two further grounds:

'(d) the protection conferred by the patent has been extended

(e) the proprietor of the European patent is not entitled under Article 60, para 1.'

In the UK all of these EPC grounds of invalidity are reflected in PA 1977, s 72.

The first of these further grounds, that of 'extended protection' (under which claims are invalid if they have been so amended as to cover material which the claims as granted did not) is not available for EPO opposition because there is no scope for the claims of a European patent which has only just been granted to have been extended by amendment. However, it is consistent with EPC, Article 123(3), by which 'the claims of the

European patent may not be amended during opposition proceedings in such a way as to extend the protection conferred'. The second of these further grounds, that of 'non-entitlement' does not feature amongst those available for EPO opposition because, as discussed in **Chapter 2**, the EPO does not consider questions of entitlement, even in relation to European patent applications.

None of these various grounds of invalidity, whether in the UK or the EPO, include two grounds of objection to the grant of patent applications that are open to patent office examiners both in the EPO, and in national patent offices such as that in the UK – unity of invention and support for the claims. Thus, by EPC, Articles 82 and 84:

'82   The European patent application shall relate to one invention only or to a group of inventions so linked as to form a single general inventive concept.

...

84   The claims shall define the matter for which the protection is sought. They shall be clear and concise and supported by the description.'

The same requirements are found in the UK in PA 1977, s 14(5). Although the 'lack of unity of invention' objection is accepted as properly being procedural, and not available as against a granted patent, there was pressure during the 1990s, particularly from the UK, to introduce a 'lack of support for the claims' objection as a substantive ground of invalidity in relation to a granted patent in the EPC (and thence into PA 1977). This was because there was a view at the time that the insufficiency ground of objection under EPC, Article 100(b) and PA 1977, s 72(c) reflecting that in EPC, Article 83 – did not provide an adequate basis for objecting to patent claims which, with a hint of nostalgia could, under UK law before PA 1977, have been attacked for 'lack of fair basis'. However, subsequent case law as to insufficiency, both in the UK[3] and the EPO, as well as that in the EPO as to lack of inventive step,[4] seems to have shown this concern to be unfounded, although the English courts still struggle with the issue of overly broad claims, particularly in the areas of pharmaceuticals and biotechnology, as instanced by the review of the case law as to this, in the context of the attack of insufficiency, in *MedImmune v Novartis Pharmaceuticals UK*.[5]

1   For example, different countries can take different views as to what is 'new'. For such purposes does one determine this by reference to material available anywhere in the world (absolute novelty, as under the EPC) or does one determine this only by reference to material available locally (relative novelty). Does one apply different such tests depending on the nature of the disclosure in issue – for example, as between a published document and a use? The trend internationally has been towards absolute novelty.
2   It used also be a feature of UK law, before PA 1977.
3   See: 'Insufficiency' at para 5.18ff below.
4   See: 'Lack of inventive step (obviousness)' at para 5.09ff below.

5   *MedImmune v Novartis Pharmaceuticals UK* [2011] EWHC 1669 at paras [458]–
    [484], also discussed at para 5.20 below. Insufficiency was not considered on appeal
    as the decision at first instance was upheld on other grounds by the Court of Appeal
    in *MedImmune v Novartis* [2012] EWCA Civ 1234.

Unpatentable subject matter

5.02   Expressing as a broad category of validity objection 'the subject
matter ... is not patentable within the terms of Articles 52–57' in the way
done in EPC, Article 100(a) (reflected in PA 1977, s 72(a)) obscures the
various real grounds of invalidity as met in practice. Thus, this particular
'ground' includes within its scope two of the most common attacks on
validity: lack of novelty (ie anticipation) (EPC, Articles 52(1) and 54)
and lack of inventive step (ie obviousness) (EPC, Articles 52(1) and 56)
that are each discussed separately below. EPC, Article 52(1) provides
that: 'European patents shall be granted for any inventions, in all fields
of technology, provided that they are new, involve an inventive step and
are susceptible of industrial application.'[1]
    The other attacks comprised within this ground, and which are all
generally met in the course of patent prosecution but are only rarely
raised after a patent has been granted are:

— the express listing in EPC, Article 52(2) (in the UK – PA 1977,
   s 1(2)) of subject matter or activities that 'in particular shall not be
   regarded as inventions';
— methods of treatment by EPC, Article 53(c)[2] (in the UK – PA 1977,
   s 4A(1)[3]);
— the other exclusions from patentability under EPC, Article 53 (in
   the UK – PA 1977, s 1(3), s 76A and Sch A2, para 3); and
— inventions which are not regarded as susceptible of industrial
   application under EPC, Article 57 (in the UK – PA 1977, ss 1(c)
   and 4).

As to the first of these various exclusions EPC, Article 52(2) sets out the
following list:

'The following in particular shall not be regarded as inventions within the
meaning of para 1:

(a)   discoveries, scientific theories and mathematical methods;
(b)   aesthetic creations;
(c)   schemes, rules and methods for performing mental acts, playing games
      or doing business, and programs for computers;
(d)   presentations of information.'

Even though, as exclusions, these ought to be, on accepted principles
of interpretation, only narrowly construed, they are yet further limited in

their application by EPC, Article 52(3): '(3) Paragraph 2 shall exclude the patentability of the subject-matter or activities referred to in therein only to the extent to which a European patent application or European patent relates to such subject-matter or activities as such.'[4]

One proposal in 2000, in the lead up to EPC 2000, had been to delete some or all of these EPC, Article 52(2) exclusions, leaving reliance to be placed instead on the 'in all fields of technology' qualification, that it was agreed had to be inserted into EPC, Article 52(1) to reflect TRIPS, Article 27(1). However, the proposal was abandoned in the light of the then ongoing controversy as to the patentability of computer programs and business methods – as to which see **Chapter 9**.

The 'mere discovery' objection under EPC, Article 52(2) is in practice rare, as it does not exclude from patentability the practical application of a discovery.[5] Thus, the English Court of Appeal in *Chiron v Murex*[6] held that applications resulting from a discovery might be patentable even if they were not inventive once the discovery had been made.

The exclusions for 'rules and methods for ... doing business, and programs for computers' are discussed in further detail in **Chapter 9**, although, as there elaborated, in the course of finding certain computer program-related inventions excluded from patentability, the English courts have had recourse on occasion to these also being 'schemes, rules and methods for performing mental acts' or 'presentations of information'. An extensive review of each of these different exclusions, pointing out that they do not constitute a logical class given their differing bases in public policy, and the effect that this has on the approach to be adopted to their interpretation, was provided by the Patents Court in *CFPH LLC's Application*.[7] A similar view as to the nature of the differences between these exclusions was expressed in *Halliburton v Smith International*:[8]

'211   The importance of the programmed computer in modern industry, and more recently the frequent attempts to push the envelope in the area of business methods, has ensured that there is a substantial body of cases in the Technical Boards of Appeal of the EPO relating to these two exclusions in particular. Discoveries and scientific theories have never given any difficulty, I suppose because it is difficult to work out how to draft a claim to either, but the scope and meaning of the other provisions is difficult.

212   It is idle to pretend that it is easy to reconcile the different cases on these questions, but part of the difficulty, I think, is caused by an unspoken belief that the various excluded matters have something in common. In my view, they do not. They are a heterogeneous collection, some of which (aesthetic creations) have their own form of protection, others of which (discoveries, mathematical methods and scientific theories) have never been accepted as suitable subjects of monopolies on obvious, but different, policy

grounds. The problems are really caused by (c) and (d), which, by reason of their exclusion 'only to the extent that the patent relates to such subject matter ... as such' are remarkably difficult to assess in cases lying near the boundary, particularly as it is difficult to discern an underlying policy. For example, do we only exclude computer programs as such because computer programs as such are protected by copyright, like aesthetic creations which can likewise be used industrially? Or is there some other reason? Whatever the reason, surely it is not the same as the reason for excluding methods of doing business?'

Likewise in *Aerotel v Telco*[9] the Court of Appeal observed:

'9.   The provisions about what are not to be "regarded as inventions" are not easy. Over the years there has been and continues to be much debate about them and about decisions on them given by national courts and the Boards of Appeal of the EPO. They form the basis of a distinct industry of conferences and are the foundation of a plethora of academic theses and publications. There has also been much political debate too: some urging removal or reduction of the categories, others their retention or enlargement. With the political debate we have no concern – it is our job to interpret them as they stand.

10.   As the decisions show this is not an easy task. There are several reasons for this:

(i)   In the first place there is no evident underlying purpose lying behind the provisions as a group – a purpose to guide the construction. The categories are there, but there is nothing to tell you one way or the other whether they should be read widely or narrowly.

(ii)   One cannot form an overall approach to the categories. They form a disparate group – no common, overarching concept, for example, links rules for playing games with computer programs or either of these with methods for doing business or aesthetic creations.

(iii)   Some categories are given protection by other intellectual property laws. Most importantly, of course, aesthetic creations and computer programs have protection under the law of copyright. So the legislator may well have formed the view that additional protection by way of patentability was unnecessary or less appropriate.

(iv)   Further, some categories are so abstract that they are unnecessary or meaningless. For instance a scientific theory as such is excluded. But how could a scientific theory ever be the subject of a patent claim in the first place? Einstein's special theory of relativity was new and non-obvious but it was inherently incapable of being patented. A patent after all is to a legal monopoly over some commercial activity carried out by human beings such as making or dealing in goods or carrying out a process. A scientific theory is not activity at all. It simply is not the sort of thing which could be made the subject of a legal monopoly. Nor can the presence of the exclusion be explained on the narrower basis that it was intended to exclude woolly and general claims such as: "Any application of E=mc^2". For such a claim would be bad for the more conventional reason that it does not disclose the invention "in a manner sufficiently clear and complete for it to be carried out by a person skilled in the art" (arts 83 and 100(b)).

(v)   There is or may be overlap between some of the exclusions themselves and between them the overall requirement that an invention be "susceptible of industrial application". The overall requirement is, perhaps surprisingly, hardly ever mentioned in the debate about the categories of "non-invention" (no one relied upon it before us) but it is clearly a factor lying behind some of the debate.'

The basis for such exclusions has also attracted a considerable body of academic commentary.[10]

A practical approach to dealing with these exclusions was advanced in *Research in Motion UK Limited v Inpro Licensing SARL*[11] as being 'taking the claims correctly construed, what does the claimed invention contribute to the art outside the excluded subject matter?' but it was also said that it was a test that had to be applied on a case-by-case basis, with 'little or no benefit ... to be gained from analogies with other cases decided on different facts in relation to different inventions'.

The exclusion for methods of treatment under EPC, Article 53(c) is discussed in **Chapter 7** as it arises in relation to pharmaceuticals.[12] The exclusion under EPC, Article 53(b), as to 'plant or animal varieties or essentially biological processes for [their] production' is discussed in **Chapter 8** as it arises in relation to biotechnology. That in EPC, Article 53(a) is to: '(a) inventions the commercial exploitation of which would be contrary to '*ordre public*' or morality; such exploitation shall not be deemed to be so contrary merely because it is prohibited by law or regulation in some or all of the Contracting States.'[13] In practice these days the *ordre public* or morality issue is also mainly met in biotechnology, and indeed Article 6(2) of Directive 98/44 on the legal protection of biotechnological inventions, as discussed in **Chapter 8**, lists a number of inventions in that field that are to be so regarded as contrary to *ordre public* or morality. However, EPC, Article 53(a) is expressed to be of general application, and so also has potential application outside biotechnology – an example sometimes given of an invention that could be objected to on this basis is one relating to letter bombs.

The 'incapable of industrial application' ground of objection, as with the 'discovery' one, is also rare in practice, no doubt because it is hard to envisage how anyone in industry could infringe a claim to something that lacked industrial application, or why they might wish to do so. It provides no basis for refusing the grant of a patent because for example it is for an intangible physical phenomenon.[14] It has traditionally been used to avoid granting patents for proposals that would contravene the established laws of nature.[15] An example of its application was *Chiron v*

Murex[16] in which, part of a claim was held invalid by the English Court of Appeal as it included within its scope a vast number of compounds which were useless for any known purpose. However, this was of little benefit to the defendants in that case, as, subject only to the scope for the patentee to amend to excise such material from the claim in issue, this left the rest of the claim, namely those compounds which were of use, valid. Another biotechnology case, this time in the EPO, in which this ground of objection was applied in invalidating all claims of a patent was T-870/04 *BDP 1 Phosphatase/MAX-PLANCK*[17] where an EPO Technical Board of Appeal observed:

> 'The case law indicates that the notion of "industry" has to be interpreted broadly so as to include all manufacturing, extracting and processing activities of enterprises that are carried out continuously, independently and for financial (commercial) gain (cf eg T 144/83 [1986] OJ EPO 301, see point 5 of the reasons).'

Despite this broad interpretation, the patent here lacked industrial application as it merely disclosed 'an interesting research result which *per se* does not yet allow a practical industrial application to be identified' since it failed to disclose any use to which the naturally occurring protein the subject of the patent could be put. More recently the UK Supreme Court reversed the English Court of Appeal, in *Eli Lilly & Company v Human Genome Sciences,*[18] which had differed on the evidence before it from an EPO Technical Board of Appeal that had rejected such an attack on the same patent. In doing so the Supreme Court disagreed with a determination in the English Courts at first instance and on appeal that claims to a protein, to the DNA sequence that coded for such protein, and to antibodies to such protein, were not susceptible of industrial application, essentially because at the time the application for the patent was filed, its teaching was too speculative to provide anything of practical value other than information upon which a research programme could be based. The Supreme Court held instead that it sufficed for this purpose, in the absence of any reason to the contrary, that a statement in the patent that the protein or any antibody to it probably had a pharmaceutical use was plausible.

1   Before EPC 2000 came into force on 13 December 2007, and under the earlier version of the EPC, this provision omitted the 'in all fields of technology' expression which has its origins in TRIPS, Article 27(1) – see **Appendix 6**. The EPO (generally in the context of computer programs and business methods) has consistently taken the view that an invention must have a 'technical character' for patent protection to be available. Quite what this means in practice is discussed further in **Chapter 9**.

2   Before EPC 2000 came into force on 13 December 2007, and under the earlier version of the EPC, this provision was found in Article 52(4), which rather than regarding such methods as an exception to patentability deemed them not be 'susceptible of industrial application' and hence not patentable by virtue of Article 52(1). Presenting this provision more logically as an exception to patentability does not change the law.

3   Before EPC 2000 came into force on 13 December 2007, and thus the relevant

provisions of PA 2004 amending PA 1977 took effect, this provision was found in PA 1977, s 4(2) and (3). Presenting this provision more logically as an exception to patentability rather than as example of something not 'susceptible of industrial application' does not change the law.

4   Before EPC 2000 came into force on 13 December 2007, and under the earlier version of the EPC, this provision was more clumsily expressed, but the rewording would not appear to be meant to alter its sense.

5   Indeed, in a sense, all patents are about protecting 'discoveries', as is reflected in the provision of the US Constitution that provides a basis for them, as quoted in **Chapter 1** at para 1.08.

6   *Chiron v Murex* [1996] RPC 535; [1996] FSR 153 (Court of Appeal). See also *Tate & Lyle Technology Ltd v Roquette Freres* [2009] EWHC 1312; [2010] EWCA Civ 1049 (Court of Appeal) in which a patent claim was held to be invalid as being both anticipated and for a mere discovery, accepting the submission that:

'... claim 10 simply informs the reader that maltotriitol, a known impurity in the manufacture of maltitol, can change the habit of maltitol crystals. This is simply a property of maltotriitol that Roquette have discovered. That is why so many known processes, if carried out, would infringe the patent. Roquette have explained why maltitol crystals take the habit that they do, but have not added anything else to the sum of human knowledge. The claim is not saved from unpatentability simply by the addition of the phrase 'the use of'. What matters is the substance of the claim, rather than its form. It would have been possible to claim particular processes or products that took advantage of the discovery, for instance, by claiming certain levels of concentration of maltotriitol within the syrup, or crystals produced with the aid of the discovery. Indeed that is what Roquette did, but all their claimed products, and processes have been declared invalid (or have been abandoned).'

The finding as to anticipation was upheld on appeal without the Court of Appeal having to consider the mere discovery ground.

7   *CFPH LLC's Application* [2005] EWHC 1589 (Pat); [2006] RPC 5. See also **Chapter 9** at paras 9.07 and 9.11 for a fuller discussion of the case in the context of later Court of Appeal authority on the computer program and business methods exclusions.

8   *Halliburton Energy Services Inc v Smith International (North Sea) Limited* [2005] EWHC 1623 (Pat).

9   *Aerotel v Telco* [2006] EWHC 997 (Pat); *Macrossan's Application* [2006] EWHC 705 (Ch); *Aerotel v Telco & Macrossan's Application* [2006] EWCA Civ 1371; [2007] 1 All ER 225 (Court of Appeal). See also **Chapter 9** at paras 9.09, 9.10, 9.11 and 9.12 for a fuller discussion of the case in the context of the computer program and business methods exclusions.

10   See for example Justine Pila – *The Requirement for an Invention in Patent Law* (Oxford University Press, 2010) and Lionel Bently (2011), 'Exclusions from Patentability and Exceptions to Patentees' Rights: Taking Exceptions Seriously', *Current Legal Problems*, pp. 1–33.

11   *Research in Motion UK Limited v Inpro Licensing SARL* [2006] EWHC 70 (Pat) at para [72].

12   See also fns 2 and 3 above.

13   Before EPC 2000 came into force on 13 December 2007, and under the earlier version of the EPC, this provision covered 'publication' as well as 'commercial exploitation' but EPC 2000 omits this as inconsistent with TRIPS, Article 27(2). In the UK, PA 1977, s 1(3)–(4) had already been amended in this way by the Patents Regulations 2000 (SI 2000/2037).

14   T-0533/09 (EPO Technical Board of Appeal 3.4.01, 11 February 2014) at [7], discussing this issue in detail and expressly rejecting at [7.2] the US approach (under 35 U.S.C. § 101 (2007)) that a patent must be for a 'new and useful process, machine, manufacture, or composition of matter, or any new and useful improvement thereof'.

15   See for example, the UK Patent Office decision *In the matter of Patent Application 8309086 by John Wilkinson* (Decision O/021/86 24 January 1986) refusing an application that contravened Newton's third law of motion.

16   *Chiron v Murex* [1996] RPC 535; [1996] FSR 153 (Court of Appeal).

17   T-870/04 *BDP 1 Phosphatase/MAX-PLANCK* (EPO Technical Board of Appeal 3.3.8, 11 May 2005) [2006] EPOR 14 at Reasons [3]. See also T-0898/05 *Hematopoietic receptor/ZYMOGENETICS* (EPO Technical Board of Appeal 3.3.8, 7 July 2006) for a case where an objection of lack of industrial applicability failed. See also **Chapter 8** at para 8.07.

18   *Eli Lilly & Company v Human Genome Sciences* [2008] EWHC 1903; [2010] EWCA Civ 33; [2011] UKSC 51 (Supreme Court). See also T-0018/09 *Neutrokine/HUMAN GENOME SCIENCES* (EPO Technical Board of Appeal 3.3.8, 21 October 2009) and **Chapter 8** at para 8.07.

Entitlement

5.03   Entitlement, as explained above, is a ground of attack on validity which can only be raised in national proceedings, and not in the EPO, which will stay any prosecution or opposition proceedings that are before it pending the outcome of such a challenge. In the UK, a challenge to entitlement of a granted patent as a ground of invalidity by PA 1977, s 72(1)(b) can by s 72(2) only be mounted by someone with a better claim to title, but may even then not be mounted more than two years after the date of grant of the patent, unless the proprietor knew at the time of grant that it was not entitled to the patent. Although such challenges can also be mounted in other EPC contracting states, the post-grant limitation period can vary.

Although entitlement disputes are relatively common in the course of patent prosecution at a national patent office level, and are sometimes also appealed to the courts in the UK, for obvious reasons they rarely feature as a defence in an infringement action as, at least under PA 1977[1] only a person having a better claim to the patent can raise entitlement as a defence.[2] The substantive law as to who is entitled to a patent is discussed in **Chapter 2** at para 2.01.

1   In contrast EPC Article 138(1)(e) is not so limited and merely sets out as one of the permitted grounds of revocation that 'the proprietor of the European patent is not entitled under Article 60, paragraph 1'.

2   One case in which such a defence was run, and in which the rights of co-owners of a patent to work the patent were also considered, was *Henry Bros v Ministry of Defence* [1997] RPC 693; [1999] RPC 442 (Court of Appeal) – see also **Chapter 6** at para 6.12.

The state of the art for novelty and inventive step

The state of the art

5.04   The concept of the 'state of the art' is critical to any determination as to both inventive step and novelty, as both are assessed in relation to it. However, it has been in the context of determinations as to novelty in which the nature of the state of the art has been most closely analysed, as it is in the nature of an objection based on inventive step that there will be some difference discernible as between the claimed invention, and the state of the art, albeit arguably one that is not great enough to deserve the grant of a patent. EPC, Article 54(2) and PA 1977, s 2(2) each define the term similarly, given the context in which it is used:

'54(2)   The state of the art shall be held to comprise everything made available to the public by means of a written or oral description, by use or in any other way, before the date of filing of the European patent application.

2(2)   The state of the art in the case of an invention shall be taken to comprise all matter (whether a product, a process, information about either, or anything else) which has at any time before the priority date of that invention been made available to the public (whether in the UK or elsewhere) by written or oral description, by use, or in any other way.'

The UK provision emphasizes that the availability to the public can arise 'whether in the UK or elsewhere', because this concept of 'absolute novelty' constituted a major departure from the 'relative novelty' which only took into account disclosures and uses in the UK, and had been a feature of UK patent law before PA 1977.

The expression 'made available to the public' does not distinguish between prior uses, prior written publications and prior oral disclosures. However, from an evidential point of view they can be rather different. Thus, in T-1212/97/*Immunoglobulin Production/GENENTECH*[1] an EPO Technical Board of Appeal observed:

'The evidence relied on to establish the information content conveyed to the public by an ephemeral disclosure, such as a lecture, must be such that the Board is certain beyond any reasonable doubt that particular information was made available to the public. The Board cannot assess novelty and inventive step in relation to an alleged prior publication whose information content remains speculative.'

By contrast, the 'information content' of a written publication should be clear on the face of the publication.

A disclosure made in confidence is not 'made available to the public'. As observed in *PLG Research v Ardon*:[2] 'Thus to form part of the state of the art, the information given by the use must have been made available to at least one member of the public who was free in law and equity to use it.'.

Indeed, if someone to whom information has been disclosed in confidence breaches that confidence, and discloses the information more widely, such disclosures, by EPC, Article 55 and PA 1977, s 2(4) do not form part of the state of the art against an application filed within six months of such disclosure by the person whose confidence was breached.[3] For an obligation of confidentiality to exist there need not be a formal agreement between the inventor, and the person to whom the disclosure is made. In *Strix v Otter*[4] the supply of samples made in accordance with the invention, despite the absence of a formal agreement between the person disclosing, and the person to whom the disclosure was made, did not make the invention available to the public, because there was an implied mutual obligation of confidence arising out of the nature of the cooperation between them.

However, to make an invention 'available to the public', it is not necessary to show that any member of the public was actually aware of it. Thus, in *Lux Traffic Controls v Pike Signals*[5] concerning traffic signal control systems, there was no dispute that the prior disclosures, and prior uses had occurred, the only issue being whether they had made the invention available to the public. The validity attack based on the prior disclosures failed, because the disclosures either failed clearly to describe a system falling within the claims or were confidential. However, the validity attack based on a prior use in the form of field trials of the system succeeded. This was so even though there was no reason to assume that the cabinet that housed the system had not been locked, and there was no evidence that anybody realized that the operation of the prototype disclosed the feature for which a patent was subsequently sought. The Patents Court held:

'There is a difference between circumstances where the public have an article in their possession to handle, measure and test and where they can only look at it. What is made available to the public will often differ in those circumstances. In the latter case it could be nothing material; whereas in the former the public would have had the opportunity of a complete examination .... In the case of a written description, what is made available to the public is the description and it is irrelevant whether it is read. In the case of a machine it is that machine which is made available and it is irrelevant whether it is operated in public.'

Here, a working system falling within the scope of the claim of interest had been made available to contractors who were free to examine its mode of operation, even though they did not actually do so. Such examination, had it been done, would have sufficed to disclose the invention the subject of a patent application subsequently filed. The details of the invention had therefore been made available to the public and formed part of the state of the art, depriving claims to the system of novelty.

Another such case was *Nestec v Dualit*[6] where the issue was whether the design of the capsule insertion and extraction mechanism of certain coffee machines had been made available to the public by field tests of such machines before what was found (because the claim to priority was successfully challenged) to be the relevant date for assessing priority. The judge held:

'[113] … The machines were supplied with so-called "tamper proof" screws. These "tamper proof" screws were screws with smooth oval heads. They were "tamper proof" in the sense that they could not be undone, in order to disassemble the machines, using an ordinary screw driver. They could be undone, however, using a screw driver with a hexagonal socket head of a kind which was widely available in hardware stores. Furthermore, a skilled person equipped with such a tool would have been able to disassemble and re-assemble a machine without damaging it. By disassembling a machine, a skilled person could discover precisely how the capsule insertion and extraction mechanism worked.

…

[117] … a skilled person in the position of one of the consumers could have ascertained how the capsule insertion and extraction mechanism worked by disassembling the machine. Nestec do not contend that the machines were provided to the consumers subject to any contractual restriction which prohibited disassembly, nor do Nestec contend that the consumers were instructed not to disassemble the machines. Nestec nevertheless rely on the fact that the machines were supplied with "tamper proof" screws as showing that the machines were not intended to be disassembled. On that basis, Nestec argue that information which would only be revealed by disassembling a machine was not made available to the public

[118] I do not accept this argument. I understood counsel for Nestec to accept that the argument would not run if the machines had been supplied with ordinary screws. In my judgment it makes no difference that the screws were "tamper proof". The screws were only "tamper proof" in the sense that slightly more specialised, but nevertheless widely available, equipment was required to undo them than ordinary screws. It follows that a skilled person in the position of the consumers could readily disassemble one of the machines. In the absence of any obligation of confidentiality, he would have been free in law and equity to disassemble the machine and to use the information gained thereby. Thus the information was made available to the public: see *Milliken Denmark A/S v Walk Off Mats Ltd* [1996] FSR 292 at 309–312.'

The EPO takes a similar approach to the English courts, although it has on occasion been tempted to do otherwise. In G-1/92 *'Availability to the Public'*[7] the Enlarged Board of Appeal reversed the decision of a Technical Board of Appeal in T-93/89 *Polyvinylester dispersion/ HOECHST*[8] that the mere fact that a new product was put on the market did not necessarily justify its analysis by competitors so as to make its composition part of the state of the art, and that there had to be some good reason, such as special properties, to justify this. The Enlarged Board held that it was irrelevant whether or not there was any motivation to analyse and further observed:

'1.2   It should be noted that Article 54(2) EPC does not make any distinction between the different means by which information is made available to the public. Thus, information deriving from a use is governed in principle by the same conditions as is information disclosed by oral or written description.

1.4   ... Where it is possible for the skilled person to discover the composition or the internal structure of the product and to reproduce it without undue burden, then both the product and its composition or internal structure become state of the art.

2   ... It is the fact that direct and unambiguous access to some particular information is possible, which makes the latter available, whether or not there is any reason for looking for it.'

The EPO has also considered the status of Internet disclosures in T-1553/06 *Public availability of documents on the World Wide Web/ PHILIPS*[9] and held:

'2.   The mere theoretical possibility of having access to a means of disclosure does not make it become available to the public within the meaning of Article 54(2) EPC 1973. What is required, rather, is a practical possibility of having access, i.e. "direct and unambiguous access" to the means of disclosure for at least one member of the public.

3.   In the case of a document stored on the World Wide Web which can only be accessed by guessing a Uniform Resource Locator (URL) not made available to the public, "direct and unambiguous access" to the document is possible in exceptional cases only, i.e. where the URL is so straightforward, or so predictable, that it can readily be guessed.

4.   The fact that a document stored on the World Wide Web could be found by entering keywords in a public web search engine before the priority or filing date of the patent or patent application is not always sufficient for reaching the conclusion that "direct and unambiguous access" to the document was possible.

Where all the conditions set out in the following test are met, it can be safely concluded that a document stored on the World Wide Web was made available to the public:

If, before the filing or priority date of the patent or patent application, a document stored on the World Wide Web and accessible via a specific URL

(1)   could be found with the help of a public web search engine by using one or more keywords all related to the essence of the content of that document and

(2)   remained accessible at that URL for a period of time long enough for a member of the public, i.e. someone under no obligation to keep the content of the document secret, to have direct and unambiguous access to the document,

then the document was made available to the public in the sense of Article 54(2) EPC 1973. If any of conditions (1) and (2) is not met, the above test does not permit to conclude whether or not the document in question was made available to the public.'

It is however self-evident that it may well be difficult, some time after the relevant date, to establish such disclosure to such a standard of proof.

To form part of the state of the art a disclosure must be 'enabling', a term first introduced into European patent law from US patent practice in the decision of an EPO Technical Board of Appeal in T-206/83 *PyridineHerbicides/ICI*[10] and into UK law in *Genentech Inc's (Human Growth Hormone) Patent*.[11] In *Asahi Kasei Kogyo KK's Application*[12] the House of Lords confirmed that UK patent law required that a disclosure be enabling if it was to be capable of forming part of the state of the art, and thus something could not be said to have been made available to the public merely by a published statement of its existence, unless the method of working the invention was such as to require no explanation to the person skilled in the art.[13] In *Synthon BV v Smithkline Beecham Plc*[14] the House of Lords held that for there to be anticipation, two requirements must be established, namely prior disclosure and enablement. Thus for there to be an 'enabling disclosure' there must be both a disclosure, and that such disclosure must be enabled, but these issues should be analysed separately. The requirement as to disclosure[15] was summarized as follows:

'22. … the matter relied upon as prior art must disclose subject-matter which, if performed, would necessarily result in an infringement of the patent. That may be because the prior art discloses the same invention. In that case there will be no question that performance of the earlier invention would infringe and usually it will be apparent to someone who is aware of both the prior art and the patent that it will do so. But patent infringement does not require that one should be aware that one is infringing: "whether or not a person is working [an] … invention is an objective fact independent of what he knows or thinks about what he is doing": *Merrell Dow Pharmaceuticals Inc v H N Norton & Co Ltd* [1996] RPC 76, 90. It follows that, whether or not it would be apparent to anyone at the time, whenever subject-matter described in the prior disclosure is capable of being performed and is such that, if performed, it must result in the patent being infringed, the disclosure condition is satisfied. The flag has been planted, even though the author or maker of the prior art was not aware that he was doing so.

Thus, in *Merrell Dow*, the ingestion of terfenadine by hay-fever sufferers, which was the subject of prior disclosure, necessarily entailed the making of the patented acid metabolite in their livers. It was therefore an anticipation of the acid metabolite, even though no one was aware that it was being made or even that it existed. But the infringement must be not merely a possible or even likely consequence of performing the invention disclosed by the prior disclosure. It must be necessarily entailed. If there is more than one possible consequence, one cannot say that performing the disclosed invention will infringe. The flag has not been planted on the patented invention, although a person performing the invention disclosed by the prior art may carry it there by accident or (if he is aware of the patented invention) by design ....'

The requirement for enablement was summarized as meaning 'that the ordinary skilled person would have been able to perform the invention which satisfies the requirement of disclosure' in considering which 'the person skilled in the art is assumed to be willing to make trial and error experiments to get it to work.' It was also emphasized that it was 'very important to keep in mind that disclosure and enablement are distinct concepts, each of which has to be satisfied and each of which has its own rules':

'63. What emerges from the authorities ... is that enabling disclosure is a compendious summary of two distinct statutory requirements, which arise (as a pair) in two different statutory contexts: explicitly in s 14 (requirements for a patent application) and implicitly (as decided by the Court of Appeal in *General Tire & Rubber Co v Firestone Tyre & Rubber Co Ltd* [1972] RPC 457 and by this House in *Asahi)* in determining the state of the art, whether for the purposes of anticipation (s 2(2) and (3)) or obviousness (s 2 as restricted by s 3). This produces a degree of symmetry in the law and avoids divergence from the practice of the European Patent Office.

64. Nevertheless the expression must be handled with some care. The practical importance of keeping the two requirements distinct will vary with the factual situation. In the case of a low-tech invention (for instance a simple agricultural machine such as the hay rake with ground-driven wheels in *Van der Lely)* the simple disclosure of the invention will probably be enough to enable the skilled person to perform it. By contrast in the case of a high-tech invention in the field of pharmaceutical science the bald assertion of the existence of the invention may have to be accompanied by detailed disclosure enabling the skilled person to perform it. But in testing the adequacy of the enablement it may be assumed that the skilled person will have to use his skill, and may have to learn by his mistakes (see Lord Reid's reference to "trial and error" in *Van der Lely* [1963] RPC 1, 71).'

Such a distinction was particularly important in *Synthon* where the enablement requirement had on the evidence been established, but the issue between the parties was one of disclosure, an incorrect characterization of the crystalline form in issue having been provided in an earlier patent application. Because, on the evidence, there was only one crystalline form and the skilled person would have been able to produce that, the earlier reference was held to anticipate the patent in suit.

The decision in *PLG Research v Ardon*[16] shows that, in relation to a patented process the products of which were themselves available to the public, one must be very careful to identify what precisely has been the subject of an enabling disclosure:

'For hundreds of years it had been the law that no monopoly may be granted to prevent the public doing that which had been done in public before the patent was applied for. The 1977 Act changed the law.

Under the 1977 Act, patents may be granted for an invention covering a product that has been put on the market provided the product does not provide an enabling disclosure of the invention claimed. In those cases, prior sale of the product will make available information as to its contents and its method of manufacture, but it is possible to imagine certain instances where that will not happen. In such cases a subsequent patent may be obtained and the only safeguard given to the public is s 64 of the Act.'[17]

Here samples of plastics netting, made in accordance with a process which was later patented, had been given to people free in law and equity to show them to anybody or to dispose of them as they wished, and so formed part of the state of the art, as did the method of production, which was apparent from inspection, and so there was an enabling disclosure of this as well. However, there was no such enabling disclosure of the nature of the starting material, which was a feature of the claimed invention. Accordingly, none of the prior uses relied on anticipated claims to such a process.

The House of Lords also analysed what was meant by 'made available to the public' in *Merrell Dow v Norton*[18] in relation to both prior publication and prior use. However, the circumstances were somewhat special, as the case concerned the extent to which publication about, or the use of, a first pharmaceutical served to make a second pharmaceutical part of the state of the art, when the first pharmaceutical metabolized in the body into the second pharmaceutical, and it is discussed in more detail in **Chapter 7**.

1   T 1212/97 *Immunoglobulin Production/GENENTECH* [2002] EPOR 27.
2   *PLG Research v Ardon* [1993] FSR 197 (Patents Court) at p. 226. This case went to appeal on other issues.
3   These provisions also apply to another type of 'non-prejudicial disclosure' in respect of inventions disclosed at certain recognized 'international exhibitions'. These are so rare as to make this exception of little practical relevance.
4   *Strix v Otter* [1995] RPC 607 (Patents Court).
5   *Lux Traffic Controls v Pike Signals* [1993] RPC 107 (Patents Court). See also *PCME Ltd v Goyen Controls Co UK Ltd* [1999] FSR 801 (Patents Court) at p. 815 for a somewhat similar situation in relation to a 'black box' whose operation could, however, be ascertained by reverse engineering, and so made such operation part of the state of the art.
6   *Nestec SA & Ors v Dualit Ltd & Ors* [2013] EWHC 923 (Patents Court) at [113] and [116].
7   G-1/92 'Availability to the Public' [1993] EPOR 241; OJ EPO 1993 at p. 277.
8   T-93/89 *Polyvinylester dispersion/HOECHST* [1992] EPOR 155; OJ EPO, 718, 1992.
9   T-1553/06 *Public availability of documents on the World Wide Web/PHILIPS* (EPO Technical Board of Appeal 3.5.04, 12 March 2012). See also T-0002/09 *Public*

availability of an e-mail transmitted via the Internet/PHILIPS (EPO Technical Board of Appeal 3.5.04, 12 March 2012) holding that 'the content of an e-mail did not become available to the public within the meaning of Article 54(2) EPC 1973 for the sole reason that the e-mail was transmitted via the Internet before the filing date ...'.

10   T-206/83 *ICI/Pyridine Herbicides* [1986] 5 EPOR 232; OJ EPO, 5, 1987.

11   *Genentech Inc's (Human Growth) Patent* [1989] RPC 613 (Patents Court) at p. 629.

12   *Asahi Kasei Kogyo KK's Application* [1991] RPC 485 (House of Lords).

13   See: 'Priority date' at para 5.05 below.

14   *Synthon BV v SmithKline Beecham Plc* [2002] EWHC 2573 (Pat); [2003] RPC 33; [2003] EWCA Civ 861; [2003] RPC 43 (Court of Appeal); [2005] UKHL 59 (House of Lords) at paras [28], and [63]–[64].

15   As set out in quotations from 'two judgments of unquestionable authority' – *Hill v Evans* (1862) 31 LJ Ch 457 at 463 and *General Tire and Rubber Co v Firestone Tyre and Rubber Co Ltd* [1972] RPC 457 at pp. 485–86, part of which is quoted below, as to lack of novelty, at para 5.07.

16   *PLG Research v Ardon* [1993] FSR 197 (Patents Court) at 225. This case went to appeal on other issues.

17   Which is why anticipation pleas often accompany a prior right defence under PA 1977, s 64 – see **Chapter 6** at para 6.16.

18   *Merrell Dow v Norton* [1994] RPC 1 (Patents Court); [1995] RPC 233 (Court of Appeal); [1996] RPC 76 (House of Lords).

Priority date

5.05   On the face of matters, the date at which the state of the art falls to be addressed is the claimed priority date of a patent. If, however, a patent claim is not entitled to the priority that has been claimed, then the state of the art will be addressed as at the filing date, which can be up to a year later. In and of itself such loss of priority does not constitute an attack on the validity of a patent. Instead it must be coupled with a prior art reference on which the party challenging validity wants to rely for the purposes of attacking novelty or inventive step, but which was made available to the public during the period between the priority date and the filing date (the priority interval[1]). Although priority can be lost where the right to priority has not properly been assigned to the person who makes the subsequent filing ('priority entitlement') and there have been several recent cases, often for inventions originating from the USA, in which such allegations have been made,[2] the most common basis for losing priority (sometimes called 'substantive priority') is that the application filed at the priority date, the convention filing, includes matter that was not found in the priority document.

Priority is governed in the UK by PA 1977, s 5 – that derives from EPC, Articles 87–88. The leading UK authority on the extent to which priority can be claimed from an earlier application is the decision of the House of Lords in *Biogen v Medeva*.[3] Here the priority document was held not to support the invention as claimed in the patent, which in view of a subsequent publication before the application was filed, proved fatal to the validity of the patent:

'In *Asahi Kasei Kogyo KK's Application* [1991] RPC 485 this House decided that for matter to be capable of supporting an invention within the meaning of s 5(2)(a) it must contain an "enabling disclosure", that is to say, it must disclose the invention in a way which will enable it to be performed by a person skilled in the art. This construction has not been challenged by the appellants before your Lordships' House. It is however important to notice the relationship between the requirement of "support" in s 5(2)(a) and certain other provisions of the Act which share the concept of an enabling disclosure.

The concept of an enabling disclosure is central to the law of patents. For present purposes, it touches the matters in issue at three different points. First, as we have seen, it forms part of the requirement of "support" in s 5(2)(a). Secondly, it is one of the requirements of a valid application in s 14 and thirdly, it is essential to one of the grounds for the revocation of a patent in s 72. I shall start with s 14. Subsection (3) says: "The specification of an application shall disclose the invention in a manner which is clear enough and complete enough for the invention to be performed by a person skilled in the art."

This is plainly a requirement of an "enabling disclosure". In addition, subsection (5)(c) says that the claim or claims shall be "supported by the description". It was by reference to subsection (3) that Lord Oliver of Aylmerton, who gave the leading speech in *Asahi*, reasoned at page 536 that a description would not "support" the claims for the purpose of subsection (5) (c) unless it contained sufficient material to enable the specification to constitute the enabling disclosure which subsection (3) required: "the Act can hardly have contemplated a complete application for a patent lacking some of the material necessary to sustain the claims made". By parity of reasoning, he said that "support" must have the same meaning in s 5(2)(a).'

In *Pharmacia v Merck*[4] the Court of Appeal noted that this approach was consistent with the then more recent decision of the EPO Enlarged Board of Appeal in G-02/98 *Entitlement to Claim Priority*[5] resolving a long-standing divergence of views in the EPO as to the meaning of the 'same invention' in EPC, Article 87(1) when deciding whether priority can be claimed from an earlier application. Under the stricter approach one could only claim for subject matter which had at least been implicitly disclosed in the priority application. The more liberal approach allowed priority to be claimed even if a technical feature was added to the application which was not derivable from the priority application, provided that the additional feature did not change the 'character and nature' of the invention. The Enlarged Board noted that because there were no clear and objective criteria for determining whether features related to the 'character or nature' of an invention, the liberal approach was likely to lead to legal uncertainty, and so supported the stricter approach.

This decision of the Enlarged Board, and some of the English case law applying it, was most recently summarized by the Court of Appeal in *HTC v Gemalto*:[6]

'[64]   The principles on which the court approaches an issue of priority have been set out in a number of cases, most recently by Kitchin LJ in *Medlmmune v Novartis Pharmaceuticals* [2012] EWCA Civ 1234:

"151. Section 5(2)(a) of the Patents Act 1977 provides that an invention is entitled to priority if it is supported by matter disclosed in the priority document. By section 130(7) of the Act, section 5 is to be interpreted as having the same effect as the corresponding provisions of Article 87(1) of the European Patent Convention. Article 87(1) says that priority may be derived from an earlier application in respect of the "same invention".

152.   The requirement that the earlier application must be in respect of the same invention was explained by the enlarged Board of Appeal of the EPO in G02/98 *Same Invention,* [2001] OJ EPO 413; [2002] EPOR 167: "The requirement for claiming priority of 'the same invention', referred to in Article 87(1) EPC, means that priority of a previous application in respect of a claim in a European patent application in accordance with Article 88 EPC is to be acknowledged only if the skilled person can derive the subject-matter of the claim directly and unambiguously, using common general knowledge, from the previous application as a whole".

153.   The approach to be adopted was elaborated by this court in *Unilin Beheer v Berry Floor* [2004] EWCA (Civ) 1021; [2005] FSR 6 at [48]: "48 The approach is not formulaic: priority is a question about technical disclosure, explicit or implicit. Is there enough in the priority document to give the skilled man essentially the same information as forms the subject of the claim and enables him to work the invention in accordance with that claim."

154.   In *Abbott Laboratories Ltd v Evysio Medical Devices plc* [2008] EWHC 800 (Pat), I added this: "228. So the important thing is not the consistory clause or the claims of the priority document but whether the disclosure as a whole is enabling and effectively gives the skilled person what is in the claim whose priority is in question. I would add that it must "give" it directly and unambiguously. It is not sufficient that it may be an obvious development of what is disclosed.

[65]   The skilled person must be able to derive the subject matter of the claim directly and unambiguously from the disclosure of the priority document. Mr Tappin stressed that the question was one of what was disclosed to the skilled person, not what was made obvious to him by the priority document, for example in the light of his common general knowledge. I agree that, as the above passage shows, that is the correct approach. That does not mean, however, that the priority document should be read in a vacuum. The question of what a document discloses to a skilled person takes account of the knowledge and background of that person. A document may mean one thing to an equity lawyer and another to a computer engineer, because each has a different background. The document still only has one meaning because it is only the relevant skilled person's understanding which is relevant. What is not permissible is to go further than eliciting the explicit or implicit disclosure and take account of what a document might lead a skilled person to do or try, or what it might prompt him to think of.'

One practical consequence of this strict approach to priority is that priority applications should be as full as possible and any important additional technical features should be made the subject of a separate filing as soon as possible rather than waiting till close to the end of the one year priority interval to include the further material in the convention filing.

Although different claims may, and often do, have different priorities these are also permitted within a single claim by EPC, Article 88(2), as to which it was observed in *Novartis AG v Johnson & Johnson Medical Ltd*:[7]

> '[122]   I discern from this passage [in G2/98] that the EPO considers it is permissible to afford different priority dates to different parts of a patent claim where those parts represent a limited number of clearly defined alternative subject-matters and those alternative subject-matters have been disclosed (and are enabled) by different priority documents. Further, this principle applies even if the claim has adopted a generic term to describe and encompass those alternatives. I do not detect anything in the decisions of the Court of Appeal in *Pharmacia* and *Unilin Beheer* which is inconsistent with this approach and in my judgment is one which this court should adopt.'

There are however some open questions as to partial priority within a single claim, notably as to, for example, in chemical claims, whether a claim enjoys partial priority to the extent that the use of a specific compound as disclosed in the priority document is encompassed by the more generic definition as used in the claim, rather than being spelt out in it, and this is now the subject of a reference to the Enlarged Board of Appeal of the EPO.[8]

<hr>

1   Where a patent application loses its claim to priority but a divisional application which properly claims such priority is published that same priority document can itself constitute prior art, but for the purposes of novelty only, as against the application which has lost priority, or the patent resulting from it by virtue of PA 1977, s 2(3), as in *Nestec SA & Ors v Dualit Ltd & Ors* [2013] EWHC 923 (Patents Court). See also T-1496/11 (EPO Technical Board of Appeal 3.2.05, 12 September 2012). See para 5.06.

2   A challenge to a claim to priority succeeded on this basis in *Edwards Life Sciences AG v Cook Biotech Inc* [2009] EWHC 1304 (Patents Court) issue not addressed at [2010] EWCA Civ 718 (Court of Appeal), but failed in *KCI Licensing v Smith & Nephew plc* [2010] EWHC 1487 (Patents Court) and *HTC Corporation v Gemalto SA* [2013] EWHC 1876 (Patents Court). The problem arises because priority cannot retroactively be assigned, and so title in the right to claim priority must pass before the filing that claims priority is made. Unlike most European applications, US ones are filed in the names of inventors as applicants, leaving more scope for error when such applicants are not employees of the company that subsequently seeks in Europe to claim priority, and where a timely assignment of the right to claim priority is needed. The issue was also addressed in *Idenix Pharmaceuticals Inc v Gilead Sciences Inc and ors* [2014] EWHC 3916 (Patents Court) where an unsuccessful attempt was made by the patentee to challenge on this basis the claim to priority of a patent application

that was cited against it on a novelty only basis under PA 1977, s 2(3) – as discussed below at para 5.06.

3   *Biogen v Medeva* [1997] RPC 1 (House of Lords) at p. 46. See 'Insufficiency and claim scope' at para 5.20 below, for further quotations from the decision.

4   *Pharmacia v Merck* [2000] RPC 709 (as *Monsanto v Merck);* [2000] IP&T 1505 (Patents Court); [2001] EWCA Civ 1610; [2002] RPC 41 (Court of Appeal).

5   G-02/98 *Entitlement to Claim Priority* [2001] OJ EPO 413.

6   *HTC Corporation v Gemalto* [2014] EWCA Civ 1335 (Court of Appeal), but see also the decision at first instance in *HTC Corporation v Gemalto* [2013] EWHC 1876 (Patents Court) at [127]–[164] for a more extensive discussion of the law. In *MedImmune v Novartis* [2011] EWHC 1669 at first instance, in which the claim to priority failed, as upheld by the Court of Appeal in *MedImmune v Novartis* [2012] EWCA Civ 1234, it was also pointed out in para [304], that the burden of establishing that the claims in issue were entitled to priority lay on the patentee, but that it was usually convenient in litigation where priority was in issue to proceed by considering the objections to the claim advanced by the opposing party. Other recent cases in which substantive priority has been in issue include *Samsung v Apple* [2013] EWHC 467 (Patents Court), *Nestec SA & Ors v Dualit Ltd & Ors* [2013] EWHC 923 (Patents Court), and *Hospira UK & Anr v Novartis AG* [2013] EWHC 516 (Patents Court); [2013] EWCA Civ 1663 (Court of Appeal).

7   *Novartis AG v Johnson & Johnson Medical Ltd* [2009] EWHC 1671 (Patents Court) at [122]; see also *Nestec SA & Ors v Dualit Ltd & Ors* [2013] EWHC 923 (Patents Court) – rejecting any claim to substantive priority, partial or otherwise.

8   Pursuant to reference in T-0557/13 *Partial Priority/INFINEUM* (EPO Technical Board of Appeal 3.3.06, 1 July 2015).

Extended state of the art for assessment of novelty in relation to conflicting applications

5.06   Patent Act 1977, s 2(3) (corresponding to EPC Article 54(3)) addresses the not uncommon situation of two patent applications X and Y, covering much the same invention, where the priority date of patent application X is earlier than that of patent application Y, but because patent application X was not published before the priority date of patent application Y, it does not, by virtue of PA 1977, s 2(2) form part of the state of the art at such priority date. This section deems the matter contained in the earlier application, X, to form part of the state of the art as against the latter one, Y, but only for the purposes of attacking novelty. Account is only taken of the earlier application if it has been subsequently published, and if it can properly claim its priority date.[1]

Where a patent application loses its claim to priority but a divisional application which properly claims such priority is published that same priority document can itself constitute prior art as against the application which has lost priority or the patent resulting from under PA 1977, s 2(3). Such a situation is variously referred as 'poisonous priority' or as a 'toxic divisional'. An attack on such basis succeeded in in *Nestec SA & Ors v Dualit Ltd & Ors,*[2] where the claims in issue were held to be broader than the disclosure in the priority document, and so lacked novelty over it, but were not entitled to claim priority from it.

Where the earlier application has only been filed in some of the countries in which the latter application has been filed, it will not benefit from this deeming provision in those countries in which it has not been filed. The situation addressed by PA 1977, s 2(3) can be readily dealt with in the course of patent prosecution in a single national patent office (eg the UK Intellectual Property Office) in which the two applications in issue are progressing together. However, the situation is rather more complicated where one application is proceeding in Europe via a national route, and the other via the EPO route. The corresponding provision of the EPC is Article 54(3). The EPO does not take into account applications of earlier date, which are prosecuted in national patent offices (which can thus only be used to mount a challenge locally to a national designation of a patent granted via the EPO route, and cannot be used in an EPO opposition). However, for EPO applications with an earlier priority date but which have not been published at the priority date of the second application, the EPO no longer distinguishes between those countries were designated in the application with the earlier priority date and other countries; an earlier EPO application is deemed for such purposes to apply in all.[3]

1   For an unsuccessful challenge to the claim to priority of a patent application cited as prior art on this basis see *Idenix Pharmaceuticals Inc v Gilead Sciences Inc and ors* [2014] EWHC 3916 (Patents Court).

2   *Nestec SA & Ors v Dualit Ltd & Ors* [2013] EWHC 923 (Patents Court) at [111]. See also T-1496/11 (EPO Technical Board of Appeal 3.2.05, 12 September 2012).

3   Before EPC 2000 came into force on 13 December 2007, and under the earlier version of the EPC when considering patents prosecuted by the EPO route, it was necessary by former Article 54(4) (which was deleted in EPC 2000) to consider the position in EPO countries separately; depending on whether or not the EPO application with the earlier priority date designated them.

Lack of novelty (anticipation)

Introduction

5.07   The concept of novelty seems at first sight straightforward. It thus might seem ironic that it should have been the subject of so much English case law under PA 1977, including three cases that got to the House of Lords,[1] but this is understandable when one appreciates that they have each primarily concerned the nature of the state of the art (as discussed above at paras 5.04–5.06) because where, for whatever reason, obviousness is not available as an attack to make up any deficiencies in the allegation of lack of novelty or anticipation, identifying the precise nature of what a disclosure places in the state of the art for the purposes of the attack of novelty becomes of critical importance. Patents Act 1977, s 2 defines what inventions are to be taken as new: '2(1) An invention shall be taken to be new if it does not form part of the state of the art'.

In addition, as observed above by virtue of PA 1977, s 2(3) a prior filed UK or EP (UK) patent application is also deemed to be part of the state of the art, but from the point of view of novelty only.

The most recent and authoritative guidance in the English case law on the law of novelty, albeit given in the context of a rather special set of facts, was that given by the House of Lords in *Synthon v SmithKline Beecham*[2] and which has been pithily summarized[3] as: 'Anticipation requires an enabling disclosure of subject – matter which, when performed, must necessarily infringe the patented invention'.

In *Dyson Appliances v Hoover*[4] the English Court of Appeal, at [23], quoted from the *EPO Guidelines for Examiners* that stated the test for novelty as follows: 'A document takes away the novelty of any claimed subject-matter derivable directly or unambiguously from that document including any features implicit to a person skilled in the art in what is expressly maintained in the document'.

The court went on to say, at [24], that the statement of the law by the Court of Appeal in *General Tire and Rubber v Firestone Tyre & Rubber*[5] (under the pre-PA 1977 law) was to similar effect. Although it quoted only the last two of the following three paragraphs from the *General Tire* case, the first is also commonly quoted, as by the Court of Appeal in *Rocky Mountain Traders v Hewlett Packard*:[6]

'The earlier publication and the patentee's claim must each be construed as they would be at the respective relevant dates by a reader skilled in the art to which they relate having regard to the state of knowledge in such art at the relevant date. The construction of these documents is a function of the court, being a matter of law, but, since documents of this nature are almost certain to contain technical material, the court must, by evidence, be put in the position of a person of the kind to whom the document is addressed, that is to say, a person skilled in the relevant art at the relevant date. If the art is one having a highly developed technology, the notional skilled reader to whom the document is addressed may not be a single person but a team, whose combined skills would normally be employed in that art in interpreting and carrying into effect instructions such as those which are contained in the document to be construed. We have already described the composite entity deemed to constitute the notional skilled addressee.

When the prior inventor's publication and the patentee's claim have respectively been construed by the court in the light of all properly admissible evidence as to technical matters, the meaning of words and expressions used in the art and so forth, the question whether the patentee's claim is new for the purposes of s 32(1)(e) [of the 1949 Act] falls to be decided as a question of fact. If the prior inventor's publication contains a clear description of, or clear instructions to do or make, something that would infringe the patentee's claim if carried out after the grant of the patentee's patent, the patentee's claim will have been shown to lack the necessary novelty, that is to say, it will have been anticipated. The prior inventor, however, and the patentee may have approached the same device from different starting points and may for this reason, or it may be for other reasons, have so described their devices that it cannot be immediately discerned from a reading of the language which they have respectively used that they have discovered in truth the same device; but if carrying out the directions contained in the prior inventor's publication will inevitably result in something being made or done which, if the patentee's patent were valid, would constitute an infringement of the patentee's claim, this circumstance demonstrates that the patentee's claim has in effect been anticipated.

If, on the other hand, the prior publication contains a direction which is capable of being carried out in a manner which would infringe the patentee's claim, but would be at least as likely to be carried out in a way which would not do so, the patentee's claim will not have been anticipated, although it may fail on the ground of obviousness. To anticipate the patentee's claim the prior publication must contain clear and unmistakeable directions to do what the patentee claims to have invented.... A signpost, however clear, upon the road to the patentee's invention will not suffice. The prior inventor must be clearly shown to have planted his flag at the precise destination before the patentee.'

The last of these paragraphs had especial application in *Dyson* in which the Patents Court, having set out that part of the evidence of the experts in relation to a prior art reference known as Campbell, concluded, in a passage which the Court of Appeal set out in their judgment and with which they did not disagree:

'135. It seems to me that there are evidently a number of ways of operating Campbell which will depend upon choice of the inlet velocity. Some may fall within a claim of the Patent, others may not. Following *General Tire,* that evidence alone is enough to dispose of the argument of "inevitable result" and thus lack of novelty. Further, a fair reading of Campbell leads Professor Allen to conclude that it was intended for a particular application wherein separation in the outer part of the separation chamber was actually to be avoided because of break-up of the working particles. That is, that it is to be operated in a manner which would not fall within any of the claims of the Patent. It must be borne in mind that the criterion in lack of novelty is that of inevitability and not "might". Furthermore, the words of Jenkins LJ in *Fomento v Mentmore* [1956] RPC 87 are particularly germane to this aspect of the case. At page 101 of that report, dealing with lack of novelty, he said:

"I do not think that the Plaintiff's patent is to be held invalid because a person working a prior specification in which, so far from being described or claimed, the relevant characteristic seems inferentially to have been excluded, might *unwittingly* produce it." (my emphasis)

There are therefore in my judgment, no "clear and unmistakable directions" in the Campbell patent, no planting of the flag "at the precise destination" and in addition, no "inevitable result" in the light of Hoover's (or Dyson's) experiment with a Campbell "re-build". The objection to the patent on the basis of lack of novelty in the light of Campbell, accordingly fails.'

The problems associated with trying to prove anticipation by seeking to show by experiments, that the inevitable result of carrying out what is described in the prior art would be a product or process falling within the scope of the claim are well illustrated by the observations in *Inhale Therapeutic Systems v Quadrant Healthcare*.[7] In contrast, if the prior art provides an enabling disclosure of something falling within the scope of the claim, then the claim is anticipated, and there should be no need to undertake experiments because the prior art describes what it achieves. Experiments ought to be relevant only in the context of anticipation in relation to the enablement aspect of the enquiry if that is in issue.

Attempts have been made in recent years to attack the novelty of apparatus claims, in particular in the context of functions which can be performed by a suitably programmed general purpose computer, which claims are either expressly or implicitly stated to be 'for' certain activities or purposes (and which is generally interpreted as meaning 'suitable for' such purpose, as discussed in **Chapter 6** at para 6.09) on the basis that the prior art discloses apparatus which is also suitable for undertaking all the activities described in the apparatus claim that is under attack. Such attempts have failed because as, for example, observed in *Koninklijke Philips Electronics N.V. v Nintendo of Europe Gmbh*:[8] '[the] fact that a general purpose computer can be programmed to become a virtual body modelling apparatus does not mean that a general purpose computer is a virtual body modelling apparatus nor is it an apparatus suitable for virtual body modelling.'

In practice, unless there is, as there was in *Synthon v SmithKline Beecham*[9] a PA 1977, s 2(3) situation which precludes attack on the ground of lack of inventive step, most prior art references which are used as the basis for an anticipation attack will also form a good basis for an obviousness attack. The rare occasions in which they do not do so tend to be those cases of 'accidental anticipation' where they can be seen to fall within the scope of a claim only with the application of hindsight. The relationship between anticipation and obviousness was summarized by the Patents Court in *Hewlett-Packard v Waters*:[10]

'... to anticipate, a document must contain a clear description of, or clear and unmistakable directions to do or make, something within the claim.... When considering obviousness, on the other hand, ambiguities in the disclosure of the document may be obviously capable of resolution in a particular way without the exercise of ingenuity: but it is not legitimate to try to resolve obscurity by an exercise in imaginative reconstruction to ascertain what it was that the [author of such document] must have been trying to describe.'

A finding that a document anticipates does however make it difficult for the court making that finding adequately to address the issue of obviousness, as was the case in *Technip France SA's Patent*.[11]

1   Namely *Asahi Kasei Kogyo KK's Application* [1991] RPC 485 (House of Lords), *Merrell Dow v Norton* [1996] RPC 76 (House of Lords), and *Synthon BV v SmithKline Beecham Plc* [2005] UKHL 59 (House of Lords).

2   *Synthon BV v SmithKline Beecham Plc* [2002] EWHC 2573 (Pat); [2003] RPC 33; [2003] EWCA Civ 861; [2003] RPC 43 (Court of Appeal), [2005] UKHL 59 (House of Lords) – see above at para 5.04.
3   *Wobben Properties GmbH v Siemens Plc & ors* [2015] EWHC 2114 (Pat).
4   *Dyson Appliances Ltd v Hoover Ltd* [2000] EWHC Patents 62; [2001] EWCA Civ 1440 (Court of Appeal) at [23]–[24].
5   *General Tire and Rubber Co v Firestone Tyre & Rubber Co Ltd* [1972] RPC 457 (Court of Appeal) at p. 485.
6   *Rocky Mountain Traders v Hewlett Packard* [2002] FSR 1 (Court of Appeal) at [26].
7   *Inhale Therapeutic Systems v Quadrant Healthcare* [2002] RPC 21 (Patents Court) correcting a statement in *Evans Medical's Patent* [1998] RPC 517; [1998] 43 BMLR 39 (Patents Court) as to the effect of such experiments.
8   *Koninklijke Philips Electronics N.V. v Nintendo of Europe Gmbh* [2014] EWHC 1959 (Pat). See also *Rovi Solutions Corporation & Anor v Virgin Media Ltd & Ors* [2014] EWHC 1559 (Pat).
9   *Synthon BV v SmithKline Beecham Plc* [2002] EWHC 2573 (Pat); [2003] RPC 33; [2003] EWCA Civ 861; [2003] RPC 43 (Court of Appeal), [2005] UKHL 59 (House of Lords) – see above at para 5.04.
10 *Hewlett-Packard GmbH v Waters Corpn* [2002] IP&T 5 (Patents Court).
11 *Technip France SA's Patent* [2003] EWHC 812 (Ch); [2004] EWCA Civ 381; [2004] RPC 46 (Court of Appeal). See also *Ferag Ag v Muller Martini Ltd* [2007] EWCA Civ 15 (Court of Appeal) where this criticism was applied to an analysis at first instance which, although correctly finding a claim novel, had omitted some differences over the prior art in so doing, and had as a result gone on incorrectly to find the claim to be obvious.

Special cases

5.08   Certain special aspects of the law of novelty, which are met most commonly in relation to inventions in the chemical field, are selection inventions, medical and other use claims, and so called 'product by process claims'. These (and in particular the first two) provide much of the case law on anticipation that is encountered in the English courts these days, and are discussed further, together with some applications of the above principles in the fields of chemistry, pharmaceuticals and agrochemicals in **Chapter 7**.

Lack of inventive step (obviousness)

Introduction

5.09   It is not that common for a claim of a granted patent that has undergone examination subsequently to be held invalid for lack of novelty, unless there is an issue as to the claim to priority, which patent examiners tend not to scrutinize too closely. Much more common is the situation where the prior disclosure is deficient, in one or two features that are found in the claim. If such differences are 'obvious' then the claim will be invalid on this ground, which is otherwise (and particularly in the EPO) called 'lack of inventive step'. This is the attack on validity which most often succeeds in UK litigation, and thus virtually every infringement proceeding involves a counterclaim against validity on the basis of obviousness, and every revocation proceeding involves an attack on the same ground, namely that the invention lacks 'inventive step' – where by PA 1977, s 3: 'An invention shall be taken to involve an inventive step if it is not obvious to a person skilled in the art, having regard to any matter which forms part of the state of the art'.

The public policy principles behind the need for an inventive step test over and above that of anticipation were set out by the Court of Appeal in *Societe Technique de Pulverisation STEP v Emson Europe*:[1]

> 'The words "obvious" and "inventive step" involve questions of fact and degree which must be answered in accordance with the general policy of the Patents Act to reward and encourage inventors without inhibiting improvements of existing technology by others. The question is therefore whether in accordance with this policy the patent discloses something sufficiently inventive to deserve the grant of a monopoly.'

The nature of what constitutes an inventive step can vary, as observed in the House of Lords in *Biogen v Medeva*:[2]

> 'Whenever anything inventive is done for the first time it is the result of the addition of a new idea to the existing stock of knowledge. Sometimes, it is the idea of using established techniques to do something which no one had previously thought of doing. In that case the inventive idea will be doing the new thing. Sometimes it is finding a way of doing something which people had wanted to do but could not think how. The inventive idea would be the way of achieving the goal. In yet other cases, many people may have a general idea of how they might achieve a goal but not know how to solve a particular problem which stands in their way. If someone devises a way of solving the problem, his inventive step will be that solution, but not the goal itself or the general method of achieving it.'

What is meant by 'the state of the art' in PA 1977, s 3 has been discussed above at paras 5.04–5.05. The extended state of the art discussed at para 5.06 applies only for the purpose of novelty, and not for those of inventive step.

However, the innocent little phrase 'not obvious to a person skilled in the art' belies the extraordinarily difficult nature of the assessment that the court or tribunal is called on to make. The nature of the assessment is made more difficult because it is also inevitably different in different technologies, although this is not always recognized. Thus, in the mechanical or electronic fields much invention takes place by combining known features in new and useful ways, the effect of so doing being to a large degree predictable once one is told of it. In contrast, the chemical pharmaceutical and biotechnological fields remain to a large degree empirical, and although much research activity may be 'obvious to try' in a sense, invention may reside in correctly identifying which particular course of many possible ones does in fact provide a beneficial result.

The English courts and the EPO each have their own, differently expressed, approaches to dealing with the issue of inventive step, but neither purport to do more than seek to put the court in the correct frame of mind to answer the question 'is it obvious?'. And neither must necessarily be applied in all cases; indeed in some cases it would be wrong so to do. The standard four-step approach of the English courts used to be termed the 'Windsurfing approach' after the case in which it was formulated[3] but has, as discussed below, been restated in the *Pozzoli* case[4] although reference is still sometimes made to the former.[5] That of the EPO is the 'problem and solution' approach. As with the issues of construction and infringement[6] commentators all participate in the futile struggle to formulate a test for inventive step which will satisfy all eventualities, but those who try to draw principles from, or analogies with, decided cases are rebuffed by the English courts with expressions such as 'the test is that set out in the statute, and none other'.[7]

The development of this aspect of the law has not been assisted by the tendency of the English courts, much more so here than in other areas of patent law, to view this issue as a 'jury question' which is largely the preserve of the trial judge, who must make an assessment having heard the totality of the evidence, making English appeal courts extremely reluctant to interfere with findings as to it by trial judges, requiring that the appellant show that they have erred in at least one point of principle.[8]

A reluctance to express anything by way of principle in relation to the issue of inventive step was notable also in the judgment of House of Lords in *Conor Medsystems v Angiotech Pharmaceuticals*[9] and in which, unlike *Biogen,* obviousness was the only issue. So striking was this reluctance that despite neither the House of Lords, nor its successor the UK Supreme Court, ever as yet revisiting this issue, all that has ever been cited from this case since is a passage that it, in turn quoted, with apparent but not express approval, from a decision at first instance in another case, *Generics (UK) v H Lundbeck.*[10]

In analysing the law on this subject it is convenient first to consider separately the four steps involved in the *Windsurfing/Pozzoli* approach of the English courts, then, briefly, the 'problem and solution' approach of the EPO, and finally the way in which both generally dispose of the so-called 'secondary indicia' of non-obviousness so beloved of patentees, such as 'long-felt want' and 'commercial success'.

1 *Societe Technique de Pulverisation STEP v Emson Europe* [1993] RPC 513 (Court of Appeal). However, shortly afterwards in *Molnlycke AB v Procter & Gamble Ltd (No 5)* [1994] RPC 49, (Court of Appeal) a member of another Court of Appeal, although not mentioning the *STEP* judgment by name, observed that 'policy considerations did not assist'.
2 *Biogen Inc v Medeva Plc* [1997] RPC 1 (House of Lords) at p. 34.
3 *Windsurfing International Inc v Tabur Marine (Great Britain) Ltd* [1985] RPC 59 (Court of Appeal).
4 *Pozzoli SpA v BDMO SA* [2007] EWCA Civ 588 (Court of Appeal).

5   See for example, *VPG Systems UK Ltd v Air-Weigh Europe Ltd* [2015] EWHC 1862 (IPEC) at [31].

6   As to which see **Chapter 6**.

7   *Unilever v Chefaro* [1994] RPC 567 (Patents Court). More recently a concurring judgment in the Court of Appeal in *MedImmune Ltd v Novartis Pharmaceuticals UK Ltd* [2012] EWCA 1234 at [177]–[181] quoted a number of similar comments from the case law and bemoaned the 'elaboration of the statutory question'.

8   *David J Instance Ltd v Denny Bros Printing Ltd* [2001] EWCA Civ 939; [2002] RPC 14 (Court of Appeal) applying *Designers Guild v Russell Williams* [2000] 1 WLR 2416; [2001] 1 All ER 700; [2001] ECDR 10; [2001] FSR 11 (House of Lords) and observing that: 'because the decision involves the application of a not altogether precise legal standard to a combination of features of varying importance ... an appellate court should not reverse the judge's decision unless he has erred in principle' – reflecting a similar observation in *Biogen Inc v Medeva Plc* [1997] RPC 1 (House of Lords) at p. 45.

9   *Conor Medsystems Inc v Angiotech Pharmaceuticals Inc* [2008] UKHL 49 in which the House of Lords reversed decisions of both the trial judge, and Court of Appeal that the patent in suit was obvious, holding that they had misdirected themselves by focusing on the contribution of the patent to the art, as opposed to directly addressing the issue by reference to what was claimed.

10 *Generics (UK) Ltd v H Lundbeck A/S* [2007] RPC 32 at [72]. The quotation is set out below at para 5.15 in the quotation from the judgment of the Court of Appeal in *MedImmune Ltd v Novartis Pharmaceuticals UK Ltd*. This case also went to the House of Lords, but on anticipation and sufficiency, and not on inventive step, and is discussed below at para 5.20, and in **Chapter 7** at para 7.17.

The 'Windsurfing/Pozzoli' approach in the English courts

5.10   The hallowed approach in the English courts to answering the question of whether an invention is obvious (at least below the level of the House of Lords, and its successor the Supreme Court, which even when discussing obviousness rarely refer to it) is that adopted by the Court of Appeal in *Windsurfing International v Tabur Marine (Great Britain)*[1] as rearranged (to reverse the order of the first two numbered questions) and adjusted in *Pozzoli SpA v BDMO SA:*[2]

'(1)(a) Identify the notional "person skilled in the art";

(1)(b) Identify the relevant common general knowledge of that person;

(2)   Identify the inventive concept of the claim in question or if that cannot readily be done, construe it;

(3)   Identify what, if any, differences exist between the matter cited as forming part of the 'state of the art' and the inventive concept of the claim or the claim as construed;

(4)   Viewed without any knowledge of the alleged invention as claimed, do those differences constitute steps which would have been obvious to the person skilled in the art or do they require any degree of invention?'

Each of these steps have had further glosses put on them over time, so if nothing else these provide a useful framework in which to analyse the case law. However, it should never be forgotten that the *Windsurfing/ Pozzoli* approach only provides a structure within which to operate, but does not ultimately provide an answer to the final and critical question

– 'is it obvious?'. This was emphasized by the Court of Appeal in its extensive (albeit, as to one of the original *Windsurfing* questions, flawed) review of the law of obviousness in *Molnlycke v Procter & Gamble (No 5)*:[3] 'The value of the analysis is not that it alters the critical question; it remains the question posed by the Act. But it is that it enables the fact finding tribunal to approach the exercise of answering that question in a structured way'.

Indeed, it is not always necessary to apply the *Windsurfing/Pozzoli* structured approach when addressing obviousness, and although the Court of Appeal did so in *Richardson-Vicks Inc's Patent*[4] it observed that in the circumstances of that case the Patents Court from which it was hearing an appeal had not been wrong not do so at first instance, and upheld its decision.

1   *Windsurfing International Inc v Tabur Marine (Great Britain) Ltd* [1985] RPC 59 (Court of Appeal).
2   *Pozzoli SpA v BDMO SA* [2007] EWCA Civ 588 at para [23].
3   *Molnlycke v Procter & Gamble (No 5)* [1994] RPC 49 (Court of Appeal) at p. 115, where the Court of Appeal reformulated one of the original *Windsurfing* questions in a way that was impliedly criticized by another Court of Appeal case – *Beloit Technologies v Valmet Paper Machinery* [1997] RPC 489 (Court of Appeal) that observed that: 'the summary set out in *Molnlycke* ... can mislead'.
4   *Richardson-Vicks Inc's Patent* [1995] RPC 568; [1997] RPC 888 (Court of Appeal). The Court of Appeal took a similar view in *Instance v Denny* [2001] EWCA Civ 939; [2002] RPC 14, as did the House of Lords in *Sabaf SpA v MFI Furniture Centres Ltd* [2002] EWCA Civ 976; [2003] RPC 14 (Court of Appeal); [2004] UKHL 45; [2005] RPC 10 (House of Lords) when criticizing the Court of Appeal for having reversed the trial judge for in effect failing to apply the *Windsurfing* approach.

First Windsurfing/Pozzoli question – addressee

5.11   The highly artificial nature of the addressee the subject of the first *Windsurfing/Pozzoli* question – the 'normally skilled but unimaginative addressee in the art' (a gloss on 'the skilled man in the art' in PA 1977, s 3) was emphasized by the Patents Court in *Lilly-ICOS v Pfizer*:[1]

'62.   The question of obviousness has to be assessed through the eyes of the skilled but non-inventive man in the art. This is not a real person. He is a legal creation. He is supposed to offer an objective test of whether a particular development can be protected by a patent. He is deemed to have looked at and read publicly available documents and to know of public uses in the prior art. He understands all languages and dialects. He never misses the obvious nor stumbles on the inventive. He has no private idiosyncratic preferences or dislikes. He never thinks laterally. He differs from all real people in one or more of these characteristics. A real worker in the field may never look at a piece of prior art – for example, he may never look at the contents of a particular public library – or he may be put off because it is in a language he does not know. But the notional addressee is taken to have done so. This is a reflection of part of the policy underlying the law of obviousness. Anything which is obvious over what is available to the public cannot subsequently be the subject of valid patent protection even if, in practice, few would have bothered looking through the prior art or would have found the particular items, relied on. Patents are not granted for the discovery and wider dissemination of public material and what is obvious over it, but only for making new inventions. A worker who finds, is given or stumbles upon any piece of public prior art must realise that that art and anything obvious over it cannot be monopolised by him and he is reassured that it cannot be monopolised by anyone else.

63.   Of particular importance in this case, in view of the way that the issue has been developed by the parties, is the difference between the plodding unerring perceptiveness of all things obvious to the notional skilled man and the personal characteristics of real workers in the field. As noted above, the notional skilled man never misses the obvious nor sees the inventive. In this respect he is quite unlike most real people ....'

The attributes of the person skilled in the art were also discussed in *Technip France SA's Patent*.[2] As also noted in *Lilly-ICOS:* 'for many years now it has been well accepted law that in some cases the addressee for the purpose of testing obviousness is considered to be a team made up of notional skilled but uninventive members from different disciplines'.

Such teams are especially common in cases in pharmaceuticals and biotechnology[3] but have been less so for mechanical and electronic inventions.[4] However, care needs to be taken in establishing whether a team is indeed the appropriate addressee, and if so in identifying the various disciplines from which its members are drawn, as by its nature this exercise by its very nature is done with hindsight, and with knowledge of the invention. An extreme example of this was provided by *Schlumberger v Electromagnetic Geoservices*[5] in which it had been held at first instance (and conceded on appeal) that the claimed invention, which was to use marine CSEM (controlled source electromagnetic) surveying on a previously identified (eg by seismic methods) layer to find out whether it contained hydrocarbon, would have been obvious to a team consisting of both an expert in marine CSEM surveying, and an exploration geophysicist, and which the court at first instance had found to be the correct addressee. The Court of Appeal held that such a team was not the correct addressee, and that the claimed invention, which lay in marrying the two arts, would not have been obvious to an individual addressee in either of these two arts on their own. One should look to real research teams, as observed in *MedImmune v Novartis* at first instance[6] in citing the following conclusion drawn in the judgment of the Court of Appeal in *Schlumberger* from the decision of the Court of Appeal in *Dyson v Hoover:*[7]

'[42] I think one can draw from this case that the Court, in considering the skills of the notional "person skilled in the art" for the purposes of obviousness will have regard to the reality of the position at the time. What the combined skills (and mind-sets) of real research teams in the art is what matters when one is constructing the notional research team to whom the invention must be obvious if the Patent is to be found invalid on this ground.'

In contrast to the Patents Court, where the issue arises rather later, the nature of the procedure in the Intellectual Property Enterprise Court requires that at an early stage, and before the CMC the parties, as part of their Statements of Case, identify what they say is the technical field of the skilled person or persons for the purposes of inventive step, and where they consider there to be a *Schlumberger* issue, to say so.[8]

1   *Lilly-ICOS v Pfizer* [2001] IP&T 190 (Patents Court).
2   *Technip France SA's Patent* [2003] EWHC 812 (Patents Court); [2004] EWCA Civ 381; [2004] RPC 46; [2005] IP&T 304 at paras [6]–[15] (Court of Appeal) quoting also from *Technograph Printed Circuits Ltd v Mills & Rockley (Electronics) Ltd* [1972] RPC 346 (House of Lords) at p. 355, although the characterization by Jacob LJ of the skilled man as a 'nerd' at para [7] but 'not a complete android' at [10] did not meet with unqualified approval from another member of the Court of Appeal at para [135]. See also *Catnic Components Ltd v Hill & Smith* [1982] RPC 183 (House of Lords) at 242–3 setting out the essential characteristics of the person skilled in the art as: 'likely to have a practical interest in the subject matter of the invention and practical knowledge and experience of the kind of work in which the invention is intended to be used.'.
3   This is also recognized in the EPO where the *Case Law of the Boards of Appeal of the European Patent Office* (7th edn, September 2013) has an entire section at I.D.8.1.3 entitled 'Definition of the person skilled in the art in the field of biotechnology' after a somewhat shorter section at I.D.8.1.2 entitled 'Competent skilled person – group of people as "skilled person"'.
4   The acceptance of a team as an addressee can be traced in English law back to *General Tire and Rubber Co v Firestone Tyre & Rubber Co Ltd* [1972] RPC 457 (Court of Appeal) at p. 485 where it was said: 'If the art is one having a highly developed technology, the notional skilled reader to whom the document is addressed may not be a single person but a team, whose combined skills would normally be employed in that art in interpreting and carrying into effect instructions such as those which are contained in the document to be construed'.
5   *Schlumberger Holdings Ltd v Electromagnetic Geoservices AS* [2010] EWCA Civ 819 (Court of Appeal). This should be distinguished from the sort of situation that arose in *Koninklijke Philips Electronics N.V. v Nintendo of Europe Gmbh* [2014] EWHC 1959 (Pat) in which it was stated at [34]: 'The case before me is different in that it is not concerned with whether it was obvious to combine skills from different fields, it is concerned with a wide claim which covers things in at least two distinct fields. Just as there were real teams of the kind described by Prof Steed, so too there were real teams of the kind described by Prof Darrell. They worked on interactive virtual environments and were not concerned with games'.
6   *Medimmune Ltd v Novartis Pharmaceuticals UK Limited* [2011] EWHC 1669 (Patents Court); [2012] EWCA 1234 (Court of Appeal).
7   *Dyson Appliances Ltd v Hoover Ltd* [2001] EWCA Civ 1440; [2002] RPC 22 (Court of Appeal).
8   *EDS v Synergy* [2014] EWHC 1306 (IPEC) at [25]–[28], following a detailed analysis of the law as to the person skilled in the art at [14]–[24].

First Windsurfing/Pozzoli question – common general knowledge

5.12 The first *Windsurfing* question also involves identifying the 'common general knowledge' of the notional skilled addressee. Its nature was important in *Beloit Technologies v Valmet Paper Machinery*[1] in which the Court of Appeal emphasized how limited such common general knowledge could in practice be:

> '[The notional addressee] lacks inventive capacity, but is deemed to have the common knowledge in the field to which the invention relates. That knowledge has come to be called the common general knowledge in the art.

It has never been easy to differentiate between common general knowledge and that which is known by some. It has become particularly difficult with the modern ability to circulate and retrieve information. Employees of some companies, with the use of libraries and patent departments, will become aware of information soon after it is published in a whole variety of documents; whereas others, without such advantages, may never do so until that information is accepted generally and put into practice. The notional skilled addressee is the ordinary man who may not have the advantages that some employees of large companies may have. The information in a patent specification is addressed to such a man and must contain sufficient details for him to understand that apply the invention. It will only lack an inventive step if it is obvious to such a man.

It follows that evidence that a fact is known or even well-known to a witness does not establish that that fact forms part of the common general knowledge. Neither does it follow that it will form part of the common general knowledge if it is recorded in a document. As stated by the Court of Appeal in the *General Tire* case [1972] RPC 452 at page 482, line 33. "The two classes of documents which call for consideration in relation to common general knowledge in the instant case were individual patent specifications and widely read publications".

As to the former, it is clear that individual patent specifications and their contents do not normally form part of the relevant *common general knowledge,* though there may be specifications which are so well known amongst those versed in the art that upon evidence of that state of affairs they form part of such knowledge, and also there may occasionally be particular industries (such as that of colour photography) in which the evidence may show that all specifications form part of the relevant knowledge.

As regards scientific papers generally, it was said by Luxmoore, J in *British Acoustic Films v Nettlefold Productions* [1935] 53 RPC 221 at 250:

> "In my judgment it is not sufficient to prove common general knowledge that a particular disclosure is made in any article, or series of articles, in a scientific journal, no matter how wide the circulation of that journal may be, in the absence of any evidence that the disclosure is accepted generally by those who are engaged in the art to which the disclosure relates. A piece of particular knowledge as disclosed in a scientific paper does not become common general knowledge merely because it is widely read, and still less because it is widely circulated. Such a piece of knowledge only becomes general knowledge when it is generally known and accepted without question by the bulk of those who are engaged in the particular art;

in other words, when it becomes part of their common stock of knowledge relating to the art."

And a little later, distinguishing between what has been written and what has been used, he said: "It is certainly difficult to appreciate how the use of something which has in fact never been used in a particular art can ever be held to be common general knowledge in the art".

Those passages have often been quoted, and there has not been cited to us any case in which they have been criticised. We accept them as correctly stating in general the law on this point, though reserving for further consideration whether the words "accepted without question" may not be putting the position rather high: for the purposes of this case we are disposed, without wishing to put forward any full definition, to substitute the words "generally regarded as a good basis for further action".'

The nature of common general knowledge has been discussed in several subsequent cases, and the observations made in these were summarized, after a quotation from the above passage in *Beloit*, in the following passage in *KCI Licensing v Smith & Nephew*:[2]

'106.   ... Another frequently-cited passage is from the judgment of Laddie J in *Raychem Corp's Patents* [1998] RPC 31 at 40:

"The court is trying to determine in a common sense way how the average skilled but non-inventive technician would have reacted to the pleaded prior art if it had been put before him in his work place or laboratory. The common general knowledge is the technical background of the notional man in the art against which the prior art must be considered. This is not limited to material he has memorised and has at the front of his mind. It includes all that material in the field he is working in which he knows exists, which he would refer to as a matter of course if he cannot remember it and which he understands is generally regarded as sufficiently reliable to use as a foundation for further work or to help understand the pleaded prior art. This does not mean that everything on the shelf which is capable of being referred to without difficulty is common general knowledge nor does it mean that every word in a common text book is either. In the case of standard textbooks, it is likely that all or most of the main text will be common general knowledge. In many cases common general knowledge will include or be reflected in readily available trade literature which a man in the art would be expected to have at his elbow and regard as basic reliable information."

107.   As Floyd J noted in *Teva UK Ltd v Merck & Co Inc* [2009] EWHC 2952 (Pat), [2010] FSR 17 at [101]–[103], there is room for argument as to whether common general knowledge has a territorial dimension. What if, for example, a particular fact was commonly known by those skilled in the art in the USA at the relevant date, but not by those skilled in the art in the UK? At one stage I thought that an issue of this kind was emerging in the present case. In the end, however, neither side argued for a territorial approach to the question of common general knowledge. Both counsel submitted that, to

be common general knowledge, information must be generally known and generally accepted by the bulk of those working in the field in question.

108. In several cases, notably *Nutrinova Nutrition Specialties & Food Ingredients GmbH v Scanchem UK Ltd* [2001] FSR 42 (Pumfrey J), *Novartis AG v Ivax Pharmaceuticals UK Ltd* [2006] EWHC 2506 (Pat) (unreported, Pumfrey J), and *Ivax Pharmaceuticals UK Ltd v Akzo Nobel NV* [2006] EWHC 1089 (Pat), [2007] RPC 3 (Lewison J), account has been taken of information that, while it was not part of the skilled addressee's common general knowledge, would have been acquired by him as a matter of routine before embarking on the problem to which the patented invention provides the solution.

109. In *Generics (UK) Ltd v Daiichi Pharmaceutical Co Ltd* [2008] EWHC 2413 (Pat), [2009] RPC 4, Kitchin J quoted passages from Pumfrey J's judgments in *Novartis v Ivax* and *Glaxo Group's Patent* [2004] RPC 43 and commented at [40]:

"It seems to me that a subtle but potentially significant point of principle emerges from these passages. I can readily accept that, faced with a disclosure which forms part of the state of the art, it may be obvious for the skilled person to seek to acquire further information before he embarks on the problem to which the patent provides a solution. But that does not make all such information part of the common general knowledge. The distinction is a fine one but it may be important. If information is part of the common general knowledge then it forms part of the stock of knowledge which will inform and guide the skilled person's approach to the problem from the outset. It may, for example, affect the steps it will be obvious for him to take, including the nature and extent of any literature search."

110. In the Court of Appeal in that case [2009] EWCA Civ 646, [2009] RPC 23, Jacob LJ quoted the passage I have cited from *Raychem* and commented at [25]:

"Of course material readily and widely to hand can be and may be part of the common general knowledge of the skilled person – stuff he is taken to know in his head and which he will bring to bear on reading or learning of a particular piece of prior art. But there will be other material readily to hand which he will not carry in his head but which he will know he can find *if he needs to do so* (my emphasis). The whole passage is about material which the skilled man would refer to 'as a matter of course.' It by no means follows that the material should be taken to be known to the skilled man if he has no particular reason for referring to it."

111. He went on to quote what Kitchin J had said at first instance in the passage I have cited and observed at [27]:

"I agree with that although I personally do not find the point of principle 'subtle'. It would be wholly subversive of patents and quite unfair to inventors if one could simply say 'piece of information A is in the standard literature, so is B (albeit in a different place or context), so an invention consisting of putting A and B together cannot be inventive.' The skilled man reads each specific piece of prior art with his common general knowledge. If that makes the invention obvious, then it does. But he does not read a specific citation with another specific citation in mind, unless the first causes him to do so or both are part of the matter taken to be in his head."

112.   It follows that, even if information is neither disclosed by a specific item of prior art nor common general knowledge, it may nevertheless be taken into account as part of a case of obviousness if it is proved that the skilled person faced with the problem to which the patent is addressed would acquire that information as a matter of routine. For example, if the problem is how to formulate a particular pharmaceutical substance for administration to patients, then it may be shown that the skilled formulator would as a matter of routine start by ascertaining certain physical and chemical properties of that substance (e.g. its aqueous solubility) from the literature or by routine testing. If so, it is legitimate to take that information into account when assessing the obviousness of a particular formulation. But that is because it is obvious for the skilled person to obtain the information, not because it is common general knowledge.'

The above formulation of the law in *KCI Licensing v Smith & Nephew* has been referred to consistently in the subsequent English case law, but a pithy summary is set out in *MedImmune Ltd v Novartis Pharmaceuticals UK Ltd*:[3]

'78.   The common general knowledge of the notional skilled addressee is all that knowledge which is generally known and generally regarded as a good basis for further action by the bulk of those engaged in a particular art: *Beloit Technologies Inc v Valmet Paper Machinery Inc* [1997] RPC 489 at 494–495. It also includes all that material in the field in which the skilled addressee is working which he knows exists, which he would refer to as a matter of course if he cannot remember it and which he understands is generally regarded as sufficiently reliable to use as a foundation for further work: *Raychem Corporation's Patent* [1998] RPC 31 at 40; [1999] RPC 497 at 503–504.'

In most cases the common general knowledge provides the technical background against which the skilled person views the cited prior art. However, there are also cases in which the claimed invention is alleged to be obvious over the common general knowledge alone. Such was the case in *Ratiopharm GmbH v Napp Pharmaceuticals Holding Ltd*[4] which situation resulted in the following observations:

'154.   The rules of pleading in patent actions require a party to identify the matter in the state of the art which is relied on to support of an attack on the ground of obviousness: see CPD Part 63 PD 11.3(1) and 11.4(1). Notwithstanding that provision, it has been the practice for allegations of obviousness to include a plea founded on nothing other than "common general knowledge". Sometimes, as here, these allegations reach trial without any further particularisation of the plea, except to the extent that the plea has been explained by the expert evidence adduced in support of it. I consider that the time has come when the matter which is said to be common general knowledge ought to receive some more formal exposition in advance of the expert evidence stage. Apart from anything else, the *Pozzoli* approach, which depends on identifying a difference between matter alleged to form part of the state of the art and the inventive concept, cannot begin to be applied without adequate particularisation of the starting point.

155 There are a number of things to note about the plea of obviousness based on common general knowledge. The first is self-evident: it is that it is essential that the starting point for the plea is indeed established to be common general knowledge. If the matter alleged to be common general knowledge is not established as such then the result is just the same as if a documentary starting point is not shown to have been published before the priority date: the attack based on it is likely to fail.'

After certain some further observations including most of the passage from *Beloit* quoted above the Patents Court went on to observe:

'158 ... allegations of obviousness in the light of common general knowledge alone need to be treated with a certain amount of care. They can be favoured by parties attacking the patent because the starting point is not obviously encumbered with inconvenient details of the kind found in documentary disclosures, such as misleading directions or distracting context. It is vitally important to make sure that the whole picture presented by the common general knowledge is considered, and not a partial one.

159 Finally, the common general knowledge does not include knowledge which does not inform the skilled person's approach from the outset. As Kitchin J said in *Generics (UK) v Daiichi Pharmaceutical* [2008] EWHC 2413 (Pat):

"I can readily accept that, faced with a disclosure which forms part of the state of the art, it may be obvious for the skilled person to seek to acquire further information before he embarks on the problem to which the patent provides a solution. But that does not make all such information part of the common general knowledge. The distinction is a fine one but it may be important. If information is part of the common general knowledge then it forms part of the stock of knowledge which will inform and guide the skilled person's approach to the problem from the outset. It may, for example, affect the steps it will be obvious for him to take, including the nature and extent of any literature search."

Whether knowledge is common and general depends on the considerations explained by Aldous LJ in *Beloit*. If information does not satisfy that criterion, it does not become common general knowledge by postulating a set of steps that the skilled team might take to find it if they had already embarked on an attempt to solve a particular problem. That is not to say that it is illegitimate, in assessing an obviousness attack, to take account of material which would inevitably be found, and treated as reliable in consequence of a step or steps which it is obvious to take. If the material so found is such as would be accepted, then it may assist in showing obviousness of a further step. But what it cannot be used for is in support of an argument that the series of steps being undertaken were obvious from the start.'

Similar comments as to the especial care needed in guarding against hindsight when assessing an obviousness argument based on common general knowledge alone, were made in *HTC v Apple*,[5] referring back to what had been said as to this danger in *Abbott v Evysio* at [180]:[6]

'It is also particularly important to be wary of hindsight when considering an obviousness attack based upon the common general knowledge. The reason is straightforward. In attacking a patent, attention is focussed upon the particular development which is said to constitute the inventive step. With this development in mind it may be possible to mount an attack which is unencumbered by any detail which might point to non obviousness: *Coflexip v Stolt Connex Seaway* (CA) [2000] IP&T 1332 at [45]. It is all too easy after the event to identify aspects of the common general knowledge which can be combined together in such a way as to lead to the claimed invention. But once again this has the potential to lead the court astray. The question is whether it would have been obvious to the skilled but uninventive person to take those features, extract them from the context in which they appear and combine them together to produce the invention.'

1   *Beloit Technologies v Valmet Paper Machinery* [1997] RPC 489 (Court of Appeal).

2   *KCI Licensing Inc v Smith & Nephew plc* [2010] EWHC 1487 (Patents Court); [2011] EWCA Civ 1260 (Court of Appeal), and in which the Court of Appeal approved the summary at first instance at para [6] and repeated para [112] of it.

3   *MedImmune Ltd v Novartis Pharmaceuticals UK Ltd* [2011] EWHC 1669 (Patents Court); [2012] EWCA 1234 (Court of Appeal), rejecting an argument that the judge at first instance had been wrong to hold that phage display at a high level formed part of the common general knowledge as an established technique, even though it was not one which was in routine use, and there had been only six published studies using the technique. The Court of Appeal observed that it had been explained in *Beloit* at p. 497 that the fact that a concept has not been used at all, does not mean that it cannot form part of the common general knowledge, though it makes it unlikely. Here, it held, one group had published three papers on the technique, and at least three other groups had also published work on it. Moreover, the judge found on the evidence that other groups were also using the technique, including in relation to subject matter of the patent, but had not yet published their work. In all these circumstances, the judge had had ample material upon which to find as a fact that the concept would have been known to the person skilled in the art.

4   *Ratiopharm GmbH v Napp Pharmaceuticals Holding Ltd* [2008] EWHC 3070 (Patents Court) concerning a patent for a slow-release pharmaceutical formulation, where the attack of obviousness based on common general knowledge alone failed, as did two other obviousness attacks based on identified items of prior art. The attack based on common general knowledge alone was abandoned on appeal, but the sole obviousness attack on appeal based on an identified item of prior art also failed. (See also Chapter 7 at para 7.05, fn 2.) See also *Koninklijke Philips Electronics N.V. v Nintendo of Europe Gmbh* [2014] EWHC 1959 (Patents Court) at paras [383]–[385] observing at [384]: 'The clear practice today is not to permit an argument developed over common general knowledge alone to be advanced unless it has been distinctly pleaded out. However it is not the case (at least in the High Court rather than the IPEC) that patentees routinely pleaded out common general knowledge which they intend to rely on as something to be added to a cited reference in an obviousness case …'.

5   *HTC v Apple* [2013] EWCA Civ 451 (Court of Appeal) at [67], cited in *HTC v Gemalto* [2013] EWHC 249.
6   *Abbott v Evysio* [2008] RPC 23 (Patents Court) at [180].

Second Windsurfing/Pozzoli question – inventive concept

5.13 The second *Windsurfing/Pozzoli* question involves the identification of the 'inventive concept', as to which the House of Lords in *Biogen v Medeva*[1] observed: 'A proper statement of the inventive concept needs to include some express or implied reference to the problem which it required invention to overcome'.

The relationship of the inventive concept to the wording of the claim was discussed in *Unilever v Chefaro*:[2]

'It is the "inventive concept" of the claim in question which must be considered, not some generalised concept to be derived from the specification as a whole. Different claims can, and generally will have, different inventive concepts. The first stage of identification of the concept is likely to be a question of construction: what does the claim mean? It might be thought that there is no second stage – the concept is what the claim covers and that is that. But that is too wooden and not what courts applying *Windsurfing* ... have done. It is too wooden because if one merely construes the claim one does not distinguish between portions which matter and portions which, although limitations on the ambit of the claim, do not. One is trying to identify the essence of the claim in this exercise.'

The Court of Appeal elaborated on this further in *Pozzoli SpA v BDMO*:[3]

'18   So what one is seeking to do is to strip out unnecessary verbiage, to do what Mummery L.J. described as make a précis.

19   In some cases the parties cannot agree on what the concept is. If one is not careful such a disagreement can develop into an unnecessary satellite debate. In the end what matters is/are the difference(s) between what is claimed and the prior art. It is those differences which form the "step" to be considered at stage (4). So if a disagreement about the inventive concept of a claim starts getting too involved, the sensible way to proceed is to forget it and simply to work on the features of the claim.

20   In other cases, however, one need not get into finer points of construction—even without them the concept is fairly apparent—in *Windsurfing*, for instance, it was the "free sail" concept. In yet other cases it is not even practical to try to identify a concept—a chemical class claim would often be a good example of this.

21   There is one other point to note. Identification of the concept is not the place where one takes into account the prior art. You are not at this point asking what was new. Of course the claim may identify that which was old (often by a pre-characterising clause) and what the patentee thinks is new (if there is characterising clause) but that does not matter at this point.'

The Court of Appeal had previously considered the relationship between the inventive concept and the wording of the claim in *Union Carbide v BP Chemicals*:[4]

'As stated by Laddie J in *Raychem Corps' Patents* [1998] RPC 31 at 37 in many cases the claim will state the inventive concept concisely. That is what a properly drafted claim should do ... *Windsurfing* does not require the court to substitute its own language for that of the patentee if the latter is clear.'

However, the Court of Appeal in *Union Carbide* omitted the sentence in *Raychem*[5] which followed its quotation, and which undermined the proposition that it was advancing: 'But where, as here, the claims are prolix and opaque [the court] should break free of the language and concern itself with what the claims really mean'.

On this basis, the Patents Court had, in *Raychem* 'broken free of the language' of the claims, and on its recasting of the 'inventive concept' found all claims of the four patents in issue obvious, having previously observed:

'One of the arguments advanced ... was that Raychem's patents were an exercise in what has become known amongst patent lawyers as parametritis. This is the practice of seeking to re-patent the prior art by limiting claims by reference to a series of parameters which were not mentioned in the prior art. Sometimes it includes reference to parameters measured on test equipment which did not exist at the time of the prior art. The attraction of this to a patentee is that it may be impossible to prove now that the prior art inevitably exhibited the parameters and therefore it is impossible for an opponent to prove anticipation. Even if that is what has happened here, it does not alter the task of the court. It must decide whether the opponent has proved anticipation or some other statutory ground of invalidity. Parametritis may make the court's task more difficult, but at the end of the day the test of invalidity must be the same, whatever the form of the claims.

There is another practice which can be used to obscure the patentee's contribution, if any, to the art. This takes the form of drafting claims in an unnecessarily complicated way so that they are difficult to work through. Since the claims in a granted patent prima facie are valid and the onus is on the party attacking validity to make out his case, this obscurity may help the patentee. This practice has been deployed extensively in this case. Many of the primary claims in the patents have been drafted in a way which is calculated, in the legal sense, to make them difficult to understand. In some of them, simply known concepts have been dressed up in an elaborate clothing of quasi-science and complicated terminology. Unnecessary obscurity is not a separate ground for invalidating a claim. Within wide limits a patentee can use what language he likes to define his invention. But the court has to guard against being impressed by the form and language of the claims rather than the substance of the patentee's alleged technical contribution.'

Thus the second *Windsurfing/Pozzoli* question involves its own element of subjectivity, although the scope for deviating from the wording of the claim is likely now to be limited given the criticism expressed by the

House of Lords in *Conor Medsystems v Angiotech Pharmaceuticals*[6] of
the lower courts for having not addressed the wording of the claim, but
having instead sought to paraphrase it.

The difficulties with, and the effectively optional nature of, the
identification of the inventive concept have been well articulated in *VPG
Systems UK Ltd v Air-Weigh Europe Ltd*:[7]

'33.   The inventive concept is not the same thing as the inventive step. The
latter can vary according to the prior art under scrutiny whereas the former
has only one identity for each claim. Identifying the essence of the claim
and thus the inventive concept comes, in both the *Windsurfing* and *Pozzoli*
analyses, before the prior art is addressed (see also *Pozzoli* at [21]). The
inventive concept is therefore what the patentee asserts to be the essence of
the invention as inferred from the words of the claim and the specification as
a whole through the eyes of the skilled person. The skilled person will make
the assessment with the common general knowledge of the relevant technical
field in mind. It may be that one way of looking at the inventive concept is
that it is the product or process claimed shorn of common general knowledge.
If so, having the inventive concept defined at an early stage makes the later
key stage of indentifying the inventive step a less cluttered assessment. This
would only apply to the *Pozzoli* analysis. The third and fourth stages of the
Windsurfing analysis require a comparison between the prior art and the
alleged invention, which is the totality of what is claimed.

34.   There have been differing judicial views as to the importance of identifying
the inventive concept. For example, Laddie J emphasised that it was important
because identifying the inventive concept can reveal the vice of a claim which
contains embodiments to which the inventive step does not apply, see *Brugger v
Medic-Aid Ltd* [1996] R.P.C. 635, at 656. By contrast in *Pozzoli* itself Jacob LJ
indicated that coming to a concluded view on the inventive concept is optional,
particularly when the parties cannot agree what it is or reaching a view on
inventive concept would serve no useful purpose (at [19]–[20]). In *Actavis UK
Ltd v Novartis AG* [2010] FSR 18, Jacob LJ said this:

"[19]   I would only add an extra word about step 2 – identifying the
inventive concept. It originally comes from Oliver L.J.'s formulation of
the approach in *Windsurfing International Inc v Tabur Marine (Great
Britain) Ltd* [1985] R.P.C. 59 at 73. Strictly, the only thing that matters
is what is claimed – as Lord Hoffmann said in *Conor Medsystems Inc v
Angiotech Pharmaceuticals Inc* [2008] UKHL 49; [2008] RPC 28 at [19]:
'The patentee is entitled to have the question of obviousness determined
by reference to his claim and not to some vague paraphrase based upon the
extent of his disclosure in the description';

[20]   The "inventive concept" can be a distraction or helpful. It is
a distraction almost as soon as there is an argument as to what it is. It
is helpful when the parties are agreed as to what it is. In this case, for
instance, although the claim has a numerical limitation defining what is
meant by "sustained release", as a practical matter both sides proceeded
on the basis that it was for a sustained release formulation of fluvastatin.

[21]   The first three steps merely orientate the tribunal properly. Step 4 is the key, statutory step."

35.   Strictly, if the court does not define the inventive concept, the third and fourth stages of the *Pozzoli* analysis cannot be done. I believe what Jacob LJ had in mind was that if identifying the inventive concept is left out, one goes back to performing the third and fourth stages of the *Windsurfing* analysis.

36.   I take from this that depending on the facts and how each side presents its case, the court has the option of either defining the inventive concept and thereby streamlining the key stage of the analysis – the statutory assessment of inventive step – or alternatively it may leave out any identification of the inventive concept, in which case the prior art will be compared with the claimed invention as a whole. I will largely do the former, but cross-check the conclusion reached by also doing the latter.'

Moreover, as discussed below in relation to the third question, in some cases, as in *Sabaf v MFI*[8] a claim may combine more than one inventive concept, and if these operate independently of each other they should each be identified, and considered separately from the point of view of obviousness.

1   *Biogen v Medeva* [1997] RPC 1 (House of Lords) at p. 45.
2   *Unilever v Chefaro* [1994] RPC 567 (Patents Court).
3   *Pozzoli SpA v BDMO SA* [2007] EWCA Civ 588 (Court of Appeal).
4   *Union Carbide v BP Chemicals* [1998] RPC 1; [1999] RPC 409 (Court of Appeal).
5   *Raychem Corps' Patents* [1998] RPC 31 (Patents Court).
6   *Conor Medsystems Incorporated v Angiotech Pharmaceuticals* [2008] UKHL 49 (House of Lords) although the House of Lords in its judgment notably did not even refer to the *Windsurfing/Pozzoli* approach.
7   *VPG Systems UK Ltd v Air-Weigh Europe Ltd* [2015] EWHC 1862 (IPEC). See also *Wobben Properties GmbH v Siemens Plc & ors* [2015] EWHC 2114 (Pat) at [117]: 'There is no need to spend time identifying an inventive concept over and above the words of the claim. The heart of the invention is the concept of running a VSVP turbine in high winds so as to reduce both speed and power in dependence on the rise in wind speed. I will identify the differences between the claim and the prior art in context below.'
8   *Sabaf SpA v MFI Furniture Centres Ltd* [2002] EWCA Civ 976; [2003] RPC 14 (Court of Appeal); [2004] UKHL 45; [2005] RPC 10 (House of Lords) – the first case since *Technograph Printed Circuits v Mills & Rockley (Electronics)* [1972] RPC 346 (House of Lords) in which the House of Lords considered obviousness in any great detail. See also para 5.14.

Third Windsurfing/Pozzoli question – the nature of the difference

5.14   The third *Windsurfing/Pozzoli* question normally poses little conceptual difficulty but it is under this head that two issues – the concepts of 'mosaicing' and of 'collocation', fall conveniently to be addressed, as both can arise when assessing inventive step over a combination of prior art references, which can complicate the analysis of the nature of the difference over the state of the art. 'Mosaicing' was explained by the Patents Court in *Tickner & Woodhouse v Honda*:[1]

'47   Since each piece of prior art is not shown to be common general knowledge, each must be approached individually. The unimaginative skilled man, having all the relevant common general knowledge, is assumed to read (or in the cases of the prior use) examine, all the art. He may "mosaic" two pieces of prior art together but only to the extent that it is obvious to do so. As Lord Reid put it in *Technograph Printed Circuits v Mills & Rockley* [1972] RPC 346 at p 355 "it must be a mosaic which can be put together by an unimaginative man with no inventive capacity".'

Thus, as observed by the Court of Appeal in *Rockwater v Technip France*:[2]

'8   The no-mosaic rule makes [the man skilled in the art] also very forgetful. He reads all the prior art, but unless it forms part of his background technical knowledge, having read (or learnt about) one piece of prior art, he forgets it before reading the next unless it can form an uninventive mosaic or there is a sufficient cross reference that it is justified to read the documents as one.'

The ability to mosaic documents, provided that it is obvious to do so, for the purposes of inventive step arguments provides an important practical difference between the attacks of lack of inventive step, and that of lack of novelty, in which no such mosaicing is ever permitted.

Mosaicing allows one to combine two references for the purposes of attacking inventive step. But what happens if the invention is said to reside in the very combination itself? The House of Lords considered this issue, sometimes called 'the law of collocation' in *Sabaf v MFI*[3] when reversing the decision of the Court of Appeal and reinstating that of the Patents Court:

'17.   On the basis of these findings, Laddie J applied what he called "the law of collocation" as formulated by Lord Tomlin in *British Celanese Ltd v Courtaulds Ltd* (1935) 52 RPC 171, 193:

"a mere placing side by side of old integers so that each performs its own proper function independently of any of the others is not a patentable combination, but that where the old integers when placed together have some working interrelation producing a new or improved result then there is patentable subject-matter in the idea of a working interrelation brought about by the collocation of the integers."

18.   Although this statement was made by reference to the pre-1977 United Kingdom law, the same principles are applied by the European Patent Office. The judge referred to the EPO Guidelines for Substantive Examination, where the following statement of principle appears in the current (Dec 2003) edition in Chapter IV:

"9.5   Combination vs. juxtaposition or aggregation 'The invention claimed must normally be considered as a whole.' When a claim consists of a 'combination of features', it is not correct to argue that the separate features of the combination taken by themselves are known or obvious and that 'therefore' the whole subject matter claimed is obvious. However, where the claim is merely an 'aggregation or juxtaposition of features' and not a true combination, it is enough to show that the individual features are obvious to prove that the aggregation of features does not involve an inventive step. A set of technical features is regarded as a combination of features if the functional interaction between the features achieves a combined technical effect which is different from, e.g. greater than, the sum of the technical effects of the individual features. In other words, the interactions of the individual features must produce a synergistic effect. If no such synergistic effect exists, there is no more than a mere aggregation of features …

Chapter IV, Annex 2.1 Obvious and consequently non inventive combination of features: The invention consists merely in the juxtaposition or association of known devices or processes functioning in their normal way and not producing any non-obvious working interrelationship.

Example: Machine for producing sausages consists of a known mincing machine and a known filling machine disposed side by side."

19.   The judge rejected a submission on behalf of SABAF that the combination would lack an inventive step only if it was obvious to combine the two obvious features. This, he said, would "turn the law of collocation on its head." It would mean that the less the technical incentive for combining the two features (and therefore the less obvious it was to do so) the more the combination was likely to be patentable.

20.   The judge remarked that it was difficult to fit the law of collocation into the well-known "structural approach" to obviousness described as follows by Oliver LJ in *Windsurfing International Inc v Tabur Marine (Great Britain) Ltd* [1985] RPC 59, 73–74 …

21.   Having referred to the *Windsurfing* case in this way, the judge said no more about it. He considered that his findings that the two individual features were obvious and the law of collocation were enough to dispose of the case.

22.   The Court of Appeal were upset by the judge's references to the "law of collocation", which they regarded as an illegitimate gloss on s 3 of the Act. On the other hand, they were equally upset by the judge's failure to apply the *Windsurfing* analysis, which they did not regard as a gloss upon s 3 of the Act. In their opinion, there was no separate law of collocation. Peter Gibson LJ said, at p 279, para 43:

"[I]t seems to us inevitable that in a case said to involve a mere collocation of two known concepts, the question is whether it will be obvious to the skilled man, using his common general knowledge, to combine those concepts."

23.   He said that the omission to apply the *Windsurfing* analysis was a dangerous short cut because application of the third step would have revealed that the matter cited as prior art consisted of two separate disclosures and that it was impermissible to combine them for the purposes of the fourth step unless it would have been obvious to do so.

24.   In my opinion the approach of the Court of Appeal is contrary to well established principles both in England and in the European Patent Office, as stated in the quotation from Lord Tomlin and the EPO Guidelines to which I have referred. I quite agree that there is no law of collocation in the sense of a qualification of, or gloss upon, or exception to, the test for obviousness stated in s 3 of the Act. But before you can apply s 3 and ask whether the invention involves an inventive step, you first have to decide what the invention is. In particular, you have to decide whether you are dealing with one invention or two or more inventions. Two inventions do not become one invention because they are included in the same hardware. A compact motor car may contain many inventions, each operating independently of each other but all designed to contribute to the overall goal of having a compact car. That does not make the car a single invention.

25.   Section 14(5)(d) of the Act provides (following article 82 of the EPC) that a claim shall "relate to one invention or to a group of inventions which are so linked as to form a single inventive concept". Although this is a procedural requirement with which an application must comply, it does suggest that the references in the Act to an "invention" (as in s 3) are to the expression of a single inventive concept and not to a collocation of separate inventions.

26.   The EPO Guidelines say that "the invention claimed must normally be considered as a whole". But equally, one must not try to consider as a whole what are in fact two separate inventions. What the Guidelines do is to state the principle upon which you decide whether you are dealing with a single invention or not. If the two integers interact upon each other, if there is synergy between them, they constitute a single invention having a combined effect and one applies s 3 to the idea of combining them. If each integer "performs its own proper function independently of any of the others", then each is for the purposes of s 3 a separate invention and it has to be applied to each one separately. That, in my opinion, is what Laddie J meant by the law of collocation.

27.   If one approaches the matter on this basis, it is clear that Laddie J correctly applied the relevant principles at each stage. He found that taking the air above the hob and having a radial Venturi had no effect upon each other and that he was therefore dealing with two alleged inventions, each of which had to pass the test laid down in s 3. He identified the inventive step in each. He asked himself what in each case were the differences between the relevant prior art and the invention. He found that there were virtually none. He concluded that it would have required no invention on the part of the skilled man armed with common general knowledge in the art to design a product in accordance with the alleged invention. In other words, he applied s 3 according to the *Windsurfing* structure to each of the features alleged to constitute the invention.'

Since many inventions, in the mechanical and electronics fields in particular, can be treated as consisting of combinations of known features the judgment is of potentially greater significance than might at first sight appear.[4]

1   *Tickner & Woodhouse v Honda* [2002] EWHC 8 (Patents Court).

2   *Rockwater v Technip France* [2004] EWCA Civ 381; [2005] IP&T 304 (Court of Appeal) at pp. 307–309.

3   *Sabaf SpA v MFI Furniture Centres Ltd* [2002] EWCA Civ 976; [2003] RPC 14 (Court of Appeal); [2004] UKHL 45; [2005] RPC 10 (House of Lords).

4   In *Degussa-Huls SA v The Comptroller General of Patents* [2004] EWHC 3213 (Patents Court); the Patents Court suggested that the sort of situation to which *Sabaf* applied was rare, exemplifying it as applying to the so-called 'sausage machine' type of claim to a combination of a known meat grinder and a known skin filler. However, in the US, there has been considerable controversy over the correct approach to adopt as to obviousness in situations similar to *Sabaf*, and the issue is considered to be one of considerable importance. Thus in *KSR International Co v Teleflex Inc* (550 US (2007)) the US Supreme Court reversed the Court of Appeals for the Federal Circuit (CAFC) the appellate court for patent matters in the US, which had found the patented combination not to be obvious on the basis that there was no teaching, suggestion or motivation in the prior art to select the teachings of separate references, and combine them to produce the claimed combination. In so doing, the US Supreme Court appears to have taken a view closer to that of the House of Lords in *Sabaf* in observing that: 'For over a half century, the Court has held that "a patent for a combination which only unites old elements with no change in their respective functions ... obviously withdraws what already is known into the field of its monopoly and diminishes the resources available to skillful men ...". *Great Atlantic & Pacific Tea Co. v Supermarket Equipment Corp* 340 US 147, 152 (1950).'

Fourth Windsurfing/Pozzoli question – is it obvious?

5.15   The fourth and critical step, having got oneself into the correct frame of mind – *is it obvious?* – has resisted much by way of analysis, although it has often attracted numerous observations over the years, some of which were summarized in 2001 in *Dyson v Hoover*[1] by the Court of Appeal, which also observed that 'the law presumes that the skilled person reads [the prior art reference] with interest':[2]

'62   The fourth step requires a decision as to whether the step from the prior art to the invention was obvious. When doing that the Court must remove from its mind the patented solution. Hindsight reasoning must be avoided. That requirement has been vividly expressed in such cases as *British Westinghouse Electric Manufacturing Co Ltd v Branish* [1910] 27 RPC 209 at 230 and *Technograph Printed Circuits Ltd v Mills & Rockley (Electronics) Ltd* [1972] RPC 346.'

The Court of Appeal in *Dyson*, a case which concerned an invention for a bag-less vacuum cleaner in a field in which all other commercially available vacuum cleaners used replaceable bags, also considered, and in the leading judgment rejected the argument that commercial, as opposed to technical, considerations could have some bearing on the question of obviousness:

'56   Mr Hobbs submitted that when considering obviousness the Court was not concerned with commercial considerations such as the perceived "mindset" in favour of the use of bags, only technical matters were relevant.

To support that submission he referred us to the judgment of Slade LJ in *Hallen & Co v Brabantia (UK) Ltd* [1991] RPC 195 at p.213 line 31:

> "If the plea of obviousness is to succeed, the court has to be satisfied that it would have appeared to the hypothetical technician, skilled in the art but lacking in inventive capacity, worthwhile to coat the helix of a self-pulling corkscrew with a friction-reducing material for purpose (a) or purpose (b) above or both of them. As cases such as *Technograph* and *Beecham* show, he is not to be expected to take steps or try processes which he would not regard as worthwhile. In using the word 'worthwhile', we mean worthwhile as a possible means of achieving or assisting in practice the objective which he has in view. This, we infer, was what the judge had in mind in saying that the word 'obvious' in s 3 is directed to whether or not an advance is 'technically or practically obvious'. We do not think that the hypothetical technician must also be taken as applying his mind to the commercial consequences which might follow if the step or process in question were found in practice to achieve or assist the objective which he had in view. As Oliver L.J. said in the *Windsurfing* case [1985] RPC 59 at 72, 'What has to be determined is whether what is now claimed as invention would have been obvious, not whether it would have appeared commercially worthwhile to exploit it'. We thus agree with the judge that the word 'obvious' in s 3 is not directed to whether an advance is 'commercially obvious'. We do not think that he misdirected himself in the relevant passage of his judgment."

Since at least the *Hallen* case, it has been recognised that the patent system is not available to protect mere commercial improvements. The observations of Slade LJ were directed at that issue which is step four of the *Windsurfing* steps.'

However, in another judgment of the Court of Appeal in *Dyson*, of Sedley LJ (whose views were also reflected in the third judgment, that of Arden LJ) one detects a view that commercial considerations cannot be wholly disregarded if they colour the 'mindset' of the skilled man:

> '84   The decided cases draw a distinction between problem-solving and commercial calculation in the mind of the skilled but unoriginal addressee against whom the obviousness or the inventiveness of a claim is to be gauged. This hypothetical person, contemplating the then current state of the art, is taken to be impelled by the former and untouched by the latter.

The distinction is not – or not obviously – present in Lord Reid's paradigmatic addressee in *Technograph Printed Circuits Ltd v Mills and Rockley (Electronics) Ltd* [1972] RPC 346, 356:

> "... what he must be supposed to have done is to try everything which would appear to him as giving any prospect of valuable results."

It is in succeeding cases in this court that "valuable" has been treated as relating to practical rather than commercial outcomes. Thus approval has been given more than once to what Aldous J, as he then was, said in *Hallen Company v Brabantia (UK) Ltd* [1989] RPC 307, 327:

"By 'obvious modifications' are meant that which technically or practically would be obvious to the unimaginative skilled addressee in the art ... He does not and should not have to look further and consider whether the step he is taking is obvious or not for commercial reasons. The prize for a good commercial decision or idea is a head start on the competition and not a monopoly for 20 years."

Accepting this unreservedly, it remains the case that the perceived limits of technical practicability are a matter of mindset, and that mindset is characteristically affected by awareness of need, of which commercial potential is both a function and an index. Just as it is highly improbable that the idea of the wheel would have occurred to anyone in a society which had no need to move loads, it is hard to believe that either the heretical idea of a heliocentric universe or the observations and calculations which eventually demonstrated its existence would have happened in a society to which chronology and marine navigation were unimportant. Historically there is always something which makes the inventive think the unthinkable and by the same token inhibits the unimaginative from doing so.

If then the intellectual horizon of practical research and innovation is in part set by the economic milieu, commercial realities cannot necessarily be divorced from the kinds of practical outcome which might occur to the law's skilled addressee as potentially worthwhile. It is one thing to accept that this technologically skilled but wholly unimaginative person is a lawyer's construct – a ventriloquist's dummy, Mr Hobbs calls him – who thinks only of how things work or could be made to work. It is another to expel him altogether from the real world, where ideas do not occur to people in (so to speak) a vacuum.

The present case, on the deputy judge's findings, is a very good illustration. The vacuum-cleaner industry was functionally deaf and blind to any technology which did not involve a replaceable bag. The fact that the handicap was entirely economically determined made it if anything more entrenched. The industrial perception of need was consequently, in the judge's happy coinage, bag ridden. It is entirely in accordance with what we know about innovation that this commercial mindset will have played a part in setting the notional skilled addressee's mental horizon, making a true inventor of the individual who was able to lift his eyes above the horizon and see a bag-free machine.

Mr Hobbs accepts that the deputy judge reminded himself of the correct principles of law. His complaint is that he failed to apply them. For reasons I have outlined it seems to me, in respectful agreement with Aldous LJ, that the complaint is unjustified. It would have been extremely odd to treat the skilled but unoriginal addressee as possessing significantly greater vision than that of the industrial and commercial milieu within which he was working, and the deputy judge was right not to do so.'

The importance of the 'mindset' of the skilled person here referred to (and the 'bagridden' mindset of real vacuum cleaner designers which had to be attributed to the person skilled in the art in *Dyson*) was reiterated much more recently in *Teva UK Ltd and anr v Leo Pharma A/s*[3] when observing that 'the law of obviousness attributes to the notional person the real prejudices and practices of persons skilled in the art.' However patentees can sometimes seek to go too far in advancing arguments based on technical prejudice, as observed in *Pozzoli SpA v BDMO*:[4]

'24 Sometimes a patentee seeks to defend his invention from a charge of obviousness by saying that there was a technical prejudice against it. Such an argument was run here. The judge said:

"[67] Mr Carr submitted that the idea of overcoming a prejudice must consist in overcoming a false prejudice; in other words a mistaken technical belief that deters the unimaginative skilled person from pursuing a particular path. Mr Carr characterised this kind of false belief as a 'lion in the path' (see Bunyan: *The Pilgrim's Progress*, The Third Stage: 'Fear not the lions, for they are chained, and are placed there for trial of faith where it is, and for discovery of those that have none: keep in the midst of the path, and no hurt shall come unto thee.'). In such a case the patent reveals that the belief was mistaken, and thus contributes to the art. If on the other hand the perceived technical problem exists in the same form both before and after the claimed invention, then the prejudice has not been overcome at all. In such circumstances overcoming the prejudice cannot be part of the inventive concept, although the technical means for dealing with the perceived problem can be. I accept this submission."

25 I would not analyse it that way myself. There is an intellectual oddity about anti-obviousness or anti-anticipation arguments based on "technical prejudice". It is this: a prejudice can only come into play once you have had the idea. You cannot reject an idea as technically unfeasible or impractical unless you have had it first. And if you have had it first, how can the idea be anything other than old or obvious? Yet when a patent demonstrates that an established prejudice is unfounded—that what was considered unfeasible does in fact work, it would be contrary to the point of the patent system to hold the disclosure unpatentable.

26 I put it this way in *Union Carbide Corp v BP Chemicals Ltd* [1998] R.P.C. 1, 13: "Invention can lie in finding out that that which those in the art thought ought not be done, ought to be done. From the point of view of the purpose of patent law it would be odd if there were no patent incentive for those who investigate the prejudices of the prior art."

27 Patentability is justified because the prior idea which was thought not to work must, as a piece of prior art, be taken as it would be understood by the person skilled in the art. He will read it with the prejudice of such a person. So that which forms part of the state of the art really consists of two things in combination, the idea and the prejudice that it would not work or be impractical. A patentee who contributes something new by showing that, contrary to the mistaken prejudice, the idea will work or is practical has shown something new. He has shown that an apparent "lion in the path" is merely a paper tiger. Then his contribution is novel and non-obvious and he deserves his patent.

28 Where, however, the patentee merely patents an old idea thought not to work or to be practical and does not explain how or why, contrary to the

prejudice, that it does work or is practical, things are different. Then his patent contributes nothing to human knowledge. The lion remains at least apparent (it may even be real) and the patent cannot be justified.

29   This analysis does not require a different way of looking at the inventive concept depending on whether or not the patentee has shown the prejudice is unjustified as the judge thought at [67]. It is simply that in the former case the patentee has disclosed something novel and non-obvious, and in the latter not. The inventive concept, as I have said, is the essence of what is in the claim and not dependent on any question about a prejudice being overcome'

The discussion of the fourth step in *Dyson* took place in the context of a mechanical invention where, for many inventions, it is possible to predict whether or not they will at some level 'work' without necessarily having to put it into practice. But in some areas, such as much of chemistry, pharmaceuticals and biotechnology, the technology is much more empirical, and one will not know whether something will work until one tries it. This was recognized in the case to which reference is now most commonly made in the case law on the fourth step, namely that of the Court of Appeal in *MedImmune Ltd v Novartis Pharmaceuticals UK Ltd*:[5]

'89.   It is step (4) which is key and requires the court to consider whether the claimed invention was obvious to the skilled but unimaginative addressee at the priority date. He is equipped with the common general knowledge; he is deemed to have read or listened to the prior disclosure properly and in that sense with interest; he has the prejudices, preferences and attitudes of those in the field; and he has no knowledge of the invention.

90.   One of the matters which it may be appropriate to take into account is whether it was obvious to try a particular route to an improved product or process. There may be no certainty of success but the skilled person might nevertheless assess the prospects of success as being sufficient to warrant a trial. In some circumstances this may be sufficient to render an invention obvious. On the other hand, there are areas of technology such as pharmaceuticals and biotechnology which are heavily dependent on research, and where workers are faced with many possible avenues to explore but have little idea if any one of them will prove fruitful. Nevertheless they do pursue them in the hope that they will find new and useful products. They plainly would not carry out this work if the prospects of success were so low as not to make them worthwhile. But denial of patent protection in all such cases would act as a significant deterrent to research.

91.   For these reasons, the judgments of the courts in England and Wales and of the Boards of Appeal of the EPO often reveal an enquiry by the tribunal into whether it was obvious to pursue a particular approach with a reasonable or fair expectation of success as opposed to a hope to succeed. Whether a route has a reasonable or fair prospect of success will depend upon all the circumstances including an ability rationally to predict a successful outcome, how long the project may take, the extent to which the field is unexplored, the complexity or otherwise of any necessary experiments, whether such

experiments can be performed by routine means and whether the skilled person will have to make a series of correct decisions along the way. Lord Hoffmann summarised the position in this way in *Conor* at [42]:

> "In the Court of Appeal, Jacob LJ dealt comprehensively with the question of when an invention could be considered obvious on the ground that it was obvious to try. He correctly summarised the authorities, starting with the judgment of Diplock LJ in *Johns-Manville Corporation's Patent* [1967] RPC 479, by saying that the notion of something being obvious to try was useful only in a case where there was a fair expectation of success. How much of an expectation would be needed depended on the particular facts of the case."

92.   Moreover, whether a route is obvious to try is only one of many considerations which it may be appropriate for the court to take into account. In *Generics (UK) Ltd v H Lundbeck*, [2008] EWCA Civ 311, [2008] RPC 19, at [24] and in *Conor* [2008] UKHL 49, [2008] RPC 28 at [42], Lord Hoffmann approved this statement of principle which I made at first instance in *Lundbeck*:

> "The question of obviousness must be considered on the facts of each case. The court must consider the weight to be attached to any particular factor in the light of all the relevant circumstances. These may include such matters as the motive to find a solution to the problem the patent addresses, the number and extent of the possible avenues of research, the effort involved in pursuing them and the expectation of success."

93.   Ultimately the court has to evaluate all the relevant circumstances in order to answer a single and relatively simple question of fact: was it obvious to the skilled but unimaginative addressee to make a product or carry out a process falling within the claim. As Aldous LJ said in *Norton Healthcare v Beecham Group Plc* (unreported, 19 June 1997):

> "Each case depends upon the invention and the surrounding facts. No formula can be substituted for the words of the statute. In every case the Court has to weigh up the evidence and decide whether the invention was obvious. This is the statutory task." '

This passage from *Generics v Lundbeck*[6] in the Patents Court quoted at [92] of *MedImmune v Novartis* in the Court of Appeal has been regularly quoted in many other cases since. This quotation touches on an argument that is often met in those technologies where one cannot be sure that a particular course of action will in fact work, which is that where there are a number of possible courses of action for the skilled man to pursue in the light of a particular prior art disclosure, no particular course is obvious. This argument does not necessarily impress the English courts, which have on occasion expressed the view that all the courses of action which present themselves without the exercise of invention are obvious.[7] They will however accept that the skilled person would not try every possible permutation or carry out extensive research.[8] The whole issue revolves around whether, and to what extent, something can be said to be 'obvious to try', as observed in *MedImmune*, and as the Court of Appeal had discussed (in the passage immediately following that quoted above in *MedImmune*) in *Norton Healthcare v Beecham*:[9]

'When deciding whether a claimed invention is obvious, it is often necessary to decide whether a particular avenue of research leading to that invention was obvious. Whether the subject matter of a claim was obvious may depend upon whether it was obvious to try in the circumstances of that particular case and in those circumstances it will be necessary to take into account the expectations of achieving a good result. But that does not mean that in every case the decision whether a claimed invention was obvious can be determined by deciding whether there was a reasonable expectation that a person might get a good result from trying a particular avenue of research.'

The year previous to the judgment in *Norton* the House of Lords had in *Biogen v Medeva*[10] observed:

'The fact that a given experimental strategy was adopted for commercial reasons, because the anticipated rewards seemed to justify the necessary expenditure, is no reason why that strategy should not involve an inventive step. An inventor need not pursue his experiments untouched by thoughts of gain. Most patents are the result of research programmes undertaken on the basis of hard-headed cost-benefit analysis. Nor do I think that the analogy of a bet is particularly helpful. In *Genentech Inc's Patent* [1989] RPC 147, 281, Mustill LJ said, in my opinion rightly, that "it cannot ... be assumed that inventiveness must have been involved somewhere, just because a wager on success could have been placed at long odds." The question is not what the odds were but whether there was an inventive step.'

These observations show how difficult it can seem to be, adopting at face value the approach of the English courts, to find an invention which emerges from organized research not to be obvious.[11] The English courts have however recognized the need to restrict the application of the 'obvious to try' approach as is apparent from the judgment of the Court of Appeal in *Saint-Gobain PAM SA v Fusion Provida Limited*:[12]

'35   ... Mere possible inclusion of something within a research programme on the basis you will find out more and something might turn up is not enough. If it were otherwise there would be few inventions that were patentable. The only research which would be worthwhile (because of the prospect of protection) would be into areas totally devoid of prospect. The "obvious to try" test really only works where it is more-or-less self-evident that what is being tested ought to work.'

This observation was seized on in subsequent cases as a response to the 'obvious to try' argument[13] and would seem to have presaged a more sympathetic view of the English courts towards inventions that can be said, at some level, to be 'obvious to try', although the 'more-or-less self-evident that ... ought to work' language of *Saint-Gobain* was replaced by a 'fair expectation of success', as can be seen from the observation at para [42] of the judgment of the House of Lords in *Conor Medsystems v Angiotech Pharmaceuticals*[14] set out in the quotation at para [92] of *Medimmune*, set out above. More recently the point was emphasized by the Court of Appeal in a rare reversal of a judgment at first instance as to obviousness, in *Teva UK v Leo Pharma*[15] when observing: 'In effect the Judge was saying that the idea of including this solvent as part of a research project amounted to obviousness. The "obvious to try" standard requires a higher expectation of success than that.' This is consistent with the approach in the EPO, as observed in *MedImmune v Novartis*[16] at first instance:

'378.   The jurisprudence of the Technical Boards of Appeal of the EPO is to similar effect: in the context of biotechnology patents, see generally Case Law of the Boards of Appeal of the European Patent Office (6th ed) at pages 177–180. Counsel for MedImmune particularly relied upon the following statement of principle by the Board in T296/93 *Biogen/Hepatitis B* [1995] OJ EPO 627 at [7.4.4], which has frequently been cited subsequently:

"... The fact that other persons (or teams) were also working on the same project might suggest that is was 'obvious to try' or that it was 'an interesting area to explore', but it does not necessarily imply that there was 'a reasonable expectation of success'. 'A reasonable expectation of success', which should not be confused with the understandable 'hope to succeed', implies the ability of the skilled person to reasonably predict, on the basis of the existing knowledge before the starting of a research project, a successful conclusion to the said project within acceptable time limits. The more unexplored a technical field of research is, the more difficult is the making of predictions about its successful conclusion and, consequently, the lower the expectation of success."

As counsel for MedImmune pointed out, this statement of the law requires not merely a reasonable expectation of success, but also an expectation of success within a reasonable time.'

As observed in *Dyson*, but not expressly recognized in the passage quoted above from *MedImmune*, hindsight reasoning must be avoided, although in a sense the very aim of the *Windsurfing/Pozzoli* approach is to do just that. The judgment at first instance in *Eugen Seitz v KHS Corpoplast*[17] conveniently quotes from a number of cases, including some which though rather old, are regularly referred to, on the dangers of hindsight reasoning:

'[69]   As regards the fourth question, the courts have repeatedly emphasised the danger of hindsight. The fact that something involved only a very simple development does not mean that it did not require invention. In *British Westinghouse Electric v. Braulik* (1910) 27 RPC 209 at 230, Fletcher-Moulton LJ said:

"I confess that I view with suspicion arguments to the effect that a new combination, bringing with it new and important consequences in the shape of practical machines, is not an invention, because, when it has once been established, it is easy to show how it might be arrived at by starting from something known, and taking a series of apparently easy steps. This ex post facto analysis of invention is unfair to the inventors, and, in my opinion, it is not countenanced by English Patent Law"

[70]   This observation was approved by Lord Russell of Killowen in *Non-Drip Measures Co., Ltd.* v. *Stranger's Lt*d (1943) 60 RPC 135 at 142; and in *Technip's Patent* Jacob LJ, at [112], described this passage as "as true today as when it was first said". He continued:

"All the "bits and pieces" of the invention were known separately for many years. The question "why was it not done before" is always a powerful consideration when considering obviousness, particularly when all the components of a combination have been long and widely known. Sometimes there is a good answer (e.g. no demand, not worth the expense, prior art only recent)".

[71]   Hence invention may lie in overcoming the prejudice or preconceptions of the skilled person in a field of technology: see *Pozzoli* at [26], where Jacob LJ quoted his earlier observation in *Union Carbide Corp v BP Chemicals*: "Invention can lie in finding out that that which those in the art thought ought not to be done, ought to be done." '

Much the same point as to the dangers of hindsight was emphasized in *Rovi Guides v Virgin Media* in which the Court of Appeal also cited *Technograph*[18] which is yet another old, but authoritative, case:[19]

'9.   The first three steps set up the necessary mental scaffolding required to approach the only statutory question, which is included in the fourth step. Also included in the fourth step is a warning against the dangers of hindsight and "reconstruction a posteriori", emphasised in many authorities: see e.g. per Moulton LJ in *British Westinghouse v Braulik* [1910] 27 RPC 209 at 230. Also very well known is Lord Diplock's warning in *Technograph Printed Circuits v Mills & Rockley (Electronics)* [1972] RPC 346, 362 about "step by step" cross-examination of the patentee's expert. The question for the court is not whether the invention looks, or can by skilful cross-examination be made to look, obvious today, given one's knowledge of what the invention is and any additional wisdom acquired since the priority date of the patent. The question is what was obvious to a person skilled in the art at the priority date of the patent.'

Another issue encountered in this context is that of so-called 'selection inventions'. As they are particularly met with pharmaceutical patents they are discussed in **Chapter 7** at para 7.16.

1   *Dyson v Hoover* [2001] EWCA Civ 1440; [2002] ENPR 5; [2002] RPC 22 (Court of Appeal).
2   A point which is emphasized by the observation by the Court of Appeal in *Asahi Medical Co Ltd v Macopharma (UK) Ltd* [2002] EWCA Civ 466 at paras [20]–[27]: 'A decision on obviousness does not require a conclusion as to whether or not the skilled person would be slightly, moderately or particularly interested in any document'.

3   *Teva UK Ltd and anr v Leo Pharma A/s* [2015] EWCA Civ 779 (Court of Appeal) at
    [29].
4   *Pozzoli SpA v BDMO SA* [2007] EWCA Civ 588 (Court of Appeal) at [24]–[29].
5   *MedImmune Ltd v Novartis Pharmaceuticals UK Ltd* [2012] EWCA 1234 (Court of
    Appeal).
6   *Generics (UK) Ltd v H Lundbeck A/S* [2007] RPC 729 (Patents Court); [2008] RPC
    437 (Court of Appeal); [2009] UKHL 12 (House of Lords).
7   *Brugger v Medic-aid* [1996] RPC 635 (Patents Court) at p. 661. The dangers of
    taking this approach too far were explained, shortly before he retired as a judge of
    the English Patents Court, by Sir Hugh Laddie, 'Patents – what's invention got to
    do with it?' in Vaver and Bently (eds) *Intellectual Property in the New Millennium,*
    (Cambridge University Press, 2004):
    > 'If the reward for finding a solution to a problem and securing a monopoly for that
    > solution is very high, then it may well be worthwhile for large players to examine
    > all potential avenues to see if one gives the right result, even though the prospects
    > of any one of them succeeding are much less than 50/50. What makes something
    > worth trying is the outcome of a simple risk to reward calculation. Yet, if the reward
    > is very large, the avenues worth trying will be expanded accordingly. So, the more
    > commercially attractive the solution and the more pressing the public clamour for
    > it, the harder it will be to avoid an obviousness attack. In those circumstances a
    > solution which is quite low down a list of alternatives, all of which are more or less
    > worth trying, will fail for obviousness; a consequence which is consistent with the
    > decision in *Brugger v Medic-Aid* ....'
    See also fn 11 below.
8   *Hallen v Brabantia* [1991] RPC 195 (Patents Court) at p. 212.
9   *Norton Healthcare Ltd v Beecham Group Plc* [1997] EWCA Civ 1905 (Court of
    Appeal).
10 *Biogen v Medeva* [1997] RPC 1 (House of Lords).
11 This was belatedly recognized, shortly before he retired as a judge of the English
    Patents Court, by Sir Hugh Laddie, in 'Patents – what's invention got to do with it?'
    in Vaver and Bently (eds) *Intellectual Property in the New Millennium,* (Cambridge
    University Press, 2004) in a passage subsequently quoted (together with that at fn 7
    above) in one of the speeches in the House of Lords in *Conor v Angiotech* [2008]
    UKHL 49. He posited a situation in which, 'every step along this path [to a successful
    vaccine] could be seen to be both technically obvious and commercially worthwhile
    – assuming, of course that patent protection can be secured. However, because each
    step is obvious, patent protection cannot be secured and, without such protection,
    the whole development process makes no commercial success', and noting that: 'If
    patents were really reserved only for developments which are unpredictable and the
    result of unconventional thought, few businessmen would pursue them.' Sir Hugh
    Laddie identified the origin of the 'obvious to try' approach as the judgment of the
    Court of Appeal in *Johns-Manville Corporation's Patent* [1967] RPC 479 in which 'it
    was said that development should be treated as obvious "if the person versed in the
    art would assess the likelihood of success as sufficient to warrant actual trial" '. The
    High Court of Australia (the second, and final, level of appeal in Australia and thus
    equivalent to the UK House of Lords) in *AB Hasssle v Alphapharm Pty Ltd* [2002]
    HCA 59 (12 December 2002) was critical of the approach that the English courts had
    come to take to the law of obviousness in such cases, observing (at para 70) that:
    > '[l]ater English decisions applying the 1977 UK Act to chemical and
    > biotechnological patents treat what was said by Diplock LJ in *Johns-Manville*
    > as synonymous with "worth a try" and "well worth trying out". On that basis, a
    > number of patents have been held invalid for obviousness. These cases include
    > *Genentech Inc's Patent* [1989] RPC 147.... The outcome may reflect the approach
    > in European law that, 'the assessment of inventive step depends upon the extent to
    > which a skilled person would have been technically motivated towards the claimed

invention. But cases such as *Genentech* mark a divergence from the treatment of obviousness in the decisions of this Court.'

See also *Lockwood Security Products Pty Ltd v Doric Products Pty Ltd* [2007] HCA 21 (23 May 2007) another decision of the High Court of Australia which agreed with this critique, having observed that (at fn 56): 'Pumfrey J in *Glaxo Group Ltd's Patent* [2004] RPC 43 has responded to those passages in *Alphapharm* thus (at 858 [41]): "Both the Scylla of considering nothing obvious except that to which the skilled man is driven and the Charybdis of considering every invention obvious that can be decomposed into a sequence of obvious steps must be avoided. The former is unfair to industry because it stifles natural development. The latter is unfair to inventors and not countenanced by English patent law".'

12 *Saint-Gobain PAM SA v Fusion Provida Limited* [2005] EWCA Civ 177 (Court of Appeal).

13 See for example the subsequent Patents Court judgments in *Norbrook Laboratories Ltd's Patent (Application for Revocation by Schering-Plough Ltd)* [2005] EWHC 2532; [2006] FSR 18 (Patents Court) noting that a wide inventive concept not limited to embodiments with technical merit was more likely to be obvious than a narrow inventive concept limited to the advantageous features, and finding certain narrow claims to a specific combination of pharmaceuticals not to be obvious because it would not have been self-evident that the claimed combination ought to retain the long acting action of one of its components given that the other component might affect the absorption rate, but finding other, broader, claims to be insufficient; *GE Healthcare Ltd v PerkinElmer Life Sciences (UK) Ltd* [2006] EWHC 214 (Patents Court) noting that the, 'obvious to try' doctrine needed to be applied with caution but finding the claims in issue, given their breadth, obvious, and *IVAX Pharmaceuticals (UK) Ltd v Chugai Seiyaku KK* [2006] EWHC 756 (Patents Court) observing that the statement in *St Gobain* 'does not mean that in every case the decision whether a claimed invention was obvious can be determined by deciding whether there was a reasonable expectation that a person might get a good result from trying a particular avenue of research: *Pfizer's Patent* [2002] EWCA Civ 1 at [57]'.

14 *Conor Medsystems Incorporated v Angiotech Pharmaceuticals Incorporated* [2008] UKHL 49 which reversed findings in both courts below that the patent in suit was obvious.

15 *Teva UK Ltd and anr v Leo Pharma A/s* [2015] EWCA Civ 779 (Court of Appeal) at [32].

16 *MedImmune Ltd v Novartis Pharmaceuticals UK Ltd & Anor* [2011] EWHC 1669 (Patents Court) at [378].

17 *Eugen Seitz Ag v KHS Corpoplast Gmbh and anr* [2014] EWHC 14 ((Patents Court) at [69]–[71].

18 *Rovi Guides, Inc v Virgin Media Ltd & Ors* [2015] EWCA Civ 781 (Court of Appeal) at [9].

19 *Technograph Printed Circuits v Mills & Rockley (Electronics)* [1972] RPC 346 (House of Lords). See *Hospira v Genentech II* [2014] EWHC 3857 (Pat) at [239]–[241] for a discussion of various distinctions between that case and *Technograph*.

Inventive step and the EPO

5.16 In contrast to the approach adopted by the UK, that generally adopted by the EPO to the issue of inventive step is termed the 'problem and solution' approach. According to the *EPO Guidelines* and the *Case Law of the Boards of Appeal* of the EPO:[1]

'In the problem and solution approach there are three main stages:

(1)   determining the 'closest prior art';

(2)   establishing the 'objective technical problem' to be solved; and
(3)   considering whether or not the claimed invention, starting from the closest prior art and the objective technical problem, would have been obvious to the skilled person.'

As with the *Windsurfing/Pozzoli* approach in the UK this provides only a framework within which to answer the question *'is it obvious?'* in its final stage, and the EPO Guidelines and the Case Law of the Boards of Appeal of the EPO elaborate on its application in a wide variety of circumstances.[2]

The background to this approach was discussed by an EPO Technical Board of Appeal in T 939/92 *Triazoles/AGREVO*[3] in the context of a finding that certain broad chemical claims were obvious under EPC, Article 56 because not everything within such claims solved the objective technical problem and so was inventive. The Board explained that this was an application of the same legal principle as governed by EPC, Articles 83–84 concerned with sufficiency, namely that 'the patent monopoly should correspond to and be justified by the technical contribution to the art':

'2.4.2   … it has for long been a generally accepted legal principle that the extent of the patent monopoly should correspond to and be justified by the technical contribution to the art (see T 409/91, OJEPO, No 3.3 and 3.4 of the Reasons, and T 435/91, OJEPO 1995, 188, Reasons No 2.2.1 and 2.2.2). Now, whereas in both the above decisions the general legal principle was applied in relation to the extent of the patent protection that was justified by reference to the requirements of Articles 83 and 84 EPC, the same legal principle also governs the decision that is required to be made under Article 56 EPC [ie inventive step], for everything falling within a valid claim has to be inventive. If this is not the case, the claim must be amended so as to exclude the obvious subject-matter in order to justify the monopoly.

Moreover, in the Board's judgement, it follows from this same legal principle that the answer to the question what a skilled person would have done in the light of the state of the art depends in large measure on the technical result he had set out to achieve. In other words, the notional "person skilled in the art" is not to be assumed to seek to perform a particular act without some concrete technical reason: he must, rather, be assumed to act not out of idle curiosity but with some specific technical purpose in mind.

2.4.3   For this reason the Boards of Appeal consistently decide the issue of obviousness on the basis of an objective assessment of the technical results achieved by the claimed subject-matter, compared with the results obtained according to the state of the art. It is then, therefore, these results are taken to be the basis for defining the technical problem (or, in other words, the objective) of the claimed invention (which problem may, as already stated above, be to provide a further or – alternative – process or physical entity, here a group of chemical compounds). The next step is then to decide whether the state of the art suggested the claimed solution of this technical problem in the way proposed by the patent in suit (see for example, T 24/81, OJEPO

1983, 133, No. 4 of the Reasons). If the state of the art consists of written disclosures, it is often convenient, for practical reasons (see T 439/92 – 3.2.4 No 6.2.1 of the Reasons), to base this examination on one document which is most closely related to the claimed subject-matter as starting point, and to consider whether the other documents suggest to obtain the technical results which distinguish the claimed subject-matter from this "closest state of the art".'

In the UK the Patents Court adopted the first of these passages in *Raychem Corpn's Patents*.[4] A further discussion of the relationship between the 'problem and solution' approach to inventive step in the EPO and that in the UK took place in *CIPLA v Glaxo*[5] in which the Patents Court, having set out the discussion of the EPO approach in the then current edition of the *Case Law of the Boards of Appeal of the EPO* and the manner in which this had been applied by a Technical Board of Appeal in T 31/84 *Test Device/MILES*[6] observed:

'[45] I am not persuaded that this is substantially different from the *Windsurfing* approach, subject to one qualification. The EPO will consider obviousness on the basis of the closest prior art only. Every pleaded starting point, however remote, needs to be considered in coming to a conclusion on obviousness in the domestic context, but I suspect that the need to concentrate on the "best" citation has a result that is not much different. When one reaches the final step (the last *Windsurfing* step seems to be the same) the factors to be taken into account in assessing obviousness are not, so far as I can see, much different. The summaries of decisions contained in the "Case Law of the Boards of Appeal", sections 6.1–2 clearly indicate the wide variety of factors that the EPO consider relevant to an assessment of obviousness. Interestingly, the question of the expectation of success seems to be considered particularly relevant where the course of action in question is long and consists of much labour, and understandably it is in the field of genetic engineering and biotechnology that the question becomes important (see s 6.2). Obviousness is a question of fact, a so-called "jury question", and I see no basis for the suggestion that UK law is out of step with the principles applied in the EPO.'

More recently the English Court of Appeal has considered in some detail the relationship between the UK and EPO approaches in *Actavis v Novartis*, and although it made some specific criticisms of certain weaknesses as it saw them in the problem and solution approach, it observed that it worked very well when there is no need to reformulate the problem.[7] However, and as with the *Windsurfing/Pozzoli* approach in the English courts, the 'problem and solution' approach is recognized by the EPO not to be appropriate in every case.[8] Irrespective however of the relationship between the EPO and UK approaches to the assessment of inventive step, and the nature of the differences, if any, as between them, the English courts rely considerably on the *Case Law of the Boards of Appeal of the EPO* as to inventive step, and try to ensure consistency with the principles set out in such case law, although this does not always mean agreeing with the decision taken by an EPO Technical Board of Appeal in any particular case.[9]

1   *Case Law of the Boards of Appeal of the European Patent Office* (7th edn, September 2013) at I.D.2 on.
2   For example in relation to the 'obvious to try' issue discussed above under English law at para 5.15, the *Case Law of the Boards of Appeal* of the European Patent Office (7th edn, September 2013) has an extensive discussion that involves the following two propositions at I.D.5 and I.D.7.1 under the respective headings, 'Could-would approach' and 'Expectation of success, especially in the field of genetic engineering and biotechnology – Reasonable expectation of success':
    'To determine whether the claimed invention, starting from the closest prior art and the objective technical problem, would have been obvious to the skilled person, the boards apply the "could-would approach" (see also Guidelines G-VII, 5.3 – June 2012 edn). This means asking not whether the skilled person could have carried out the invention, but whether he would have done so in the hope of solving the underlying technical problem or in the expectation of some improvement or advantage – the so-called "could-would approach", (T2/83 OJ 1984, 265, T90/84 [EPOR 1979–85/C 952], T7/86 OJ 1988, 381, T 200/94, T 885/97). When considering whether or not claimed subject-matter constitutes an obvious solution to an objective technical problem, the question to be answered is whether or not the skilled person, in the expectation of solving the problem, would have modified the teaching in the closest prior art document in the light of other teachings in the prior art so as to arrive at the claimed invention (T 1014/07). So the point is not whether the skilled person could have arrived at the invention by modifying the prior art, but rather whether, in expectation of the advantages actually achieved (ie in the light of the technical problem addressed), he would have done so because of promptings in the prior art (T 219/87, T455/94, T 414/98).
    … In accordance with the case law of the boards of appeal, a course of action could be considered obvious within the meaning of Art. 56 EPC if the skilled person would have carried it out in expectation of some improvement or advantage (T2/83, OJ 1984, 265). In other words, obviousness was not only at hand when the results were clearly predictable but also when there was a reasonable expectation of success (T149/93). It is not necessary to establish that the success of an envisaged solution of a technical problem was predictable with certainty. In order to render a solution obvious it is sufficient to establish that the skilled person would have followed the teaching of the prior art with a reasonable expectation of success (T 249/88, T 1053/93, T 318/02, T 1877/08).'
3   T 939/92 *Triazoles*/AGREVO OJ EPO 1996, 309; [1996] EPOR 171 cited for example, by the House of Lords in *Conor Medsystems Inc v Angiotech Pharmaceuticals Inc* [2008] UKHL 49 at paras [31]–[32] and [53].
4   *Raychem Corpn's Patents* [1998] RPC 31 (Patents Court).
5   *CIPLA v Glaxo* [2004] EWHC 477 (Patents Court).
6   T 31/84 *Test Device*/MILES [1987] EPOR 10; [1986] OJ EPO 369.
7   *Actavis v Novartis* [2010] EWCA 82 (Court of Appeal) at paras [25]–[40], also discussing the 'could/would' approach at [45]–[46]. See *Hospira v Genentech II* [2014] EWHC 3857 (Pat) at [227]–[234] for a discussion of the application of the 'could/would' approach to that case.
8   For example, where the invention lies in the discovery of a previously unknown problem, the solution to which once the problem is identified is retrospectively trivial, and is itself obvious – see *Case Law of the Boards of Appeal of the European Patent Office* (7th edn, September 2013) at I.D.9.10 under the heading 'Problem inventions'.
9   See for example, the House of Lords in *Conor Medsystems Inc v Angiotech Pharmaceuticals Inc* [2008] UKHL 49 at paras [31]–[35] quoting much more from EPO case law than from English case law.

Secondary indicia of inventive step

5.17   As will be apparent from the above discussion of the '*Windsurfing/Pozzoli*' questions, the artificial nature of the analysis which this calls for rather reduces for English courts the value of 'real life' evidence directed to the issue of inventive step. In *Raychem Corpn's Patents*[1] in which four patents were held obvious, the Patents Court observed that 'in practice the commercial performance of products or processes covered by a patent rarely is a reliable indicator of non-obviousness'. The Patents Court discussed the reason for this more fully in *Hoechst Celanese Corpn v BP Chemicals*:[2]

> 'Evidence of what are said to be contemporary events is not infrequently relied on by patentees and defendants. The former adduce evidence to show that others in the art have sought to find an answer to the same problem as faced the inventor and failed. The latter adduce evidence of others at or about the priority date who found the same or essentially the same answer. The statement from Glaverbel ... that "contemporary events can be of evidential assistance" is subject to the important qualification that its importance and weight will depend on the circumstances of the case. The primary purpose of such secondary evidence is to help the court answer the fundamental question; was it obvious to go from the pleaded prior art to the invention covered by the patent. Unless it throws a relevant light on that question, it is at best of little value and at worst potentially misleading.'

The Patents Court also explained why evidence as to what the inventor did was rarely relevant:

> 'From time to time the courts have said that the way in which the inventor reached his invention is immaterial. He may think that he has made a marvellous invention or he may have worked out his development by a process which, to him, was entirely logical. But to use what he did and thought he had achieved as evidence for or against obviousness is to put the cart before the horse. Once the court has decided whether the step was obvious it can then assess whether what the inventor did was what the notional man in the art would have done from the pleaded art or not. Evidence from the inventor that he took a long time to make the invention and thought he was very clever is no evidence that he was. Similarly, analysis after the event of the logical steps he took to arrive at the invention is no evidence that it is obvious. If he is an inventive man he will no doubt see things more clearly than his notional non-inventive colleague. It would be strange if the fact that the inventor got to the invention was used as evidence that others would also. These propositions seem to me to be supported by cases such as *Re I.G. Farbenindustrie A.G's Patent* (1930) 47 RPC 289 and *Allmanna Svenska Elektriska A/B v The Burntisland Shipbuilding Co Ltd* (1952) 69 RPC 63. In addition to this, for the same reason as are set out above, the evidence of what the inventor did or thought is even more irrelevant if he never had before him the prior art on which the defence is relying.'

The EPO is similarly sceptical as to the value of such evidence:[3]

'According to established case law of the boards of appeal, a mere investigation for indications of the presence of inventive step is no substitute for the technically skilled assessment of the invention *vis-a-vis* the state of the art pursuant to Article 56 EPC. Where such indications are present, the overall picture of the state of the art and consideration of all significant factors may show that inventive step is involved but this need not necessarily always be the case (see T24/81 OJ 1983, 133 and T55/86). Secondary indicia of this kind are only of importance in cases of doubt, ie when objective evaluation of the prior art teachings has yet to provide a clear picture (T645/94, T284/96, T 71/98, T323/99, T877/99). Indicia are merely auxiliary considerations in the assessment of inventive step (T1072/92, T 351/93).'

Despite such scepticism as to secondary evidence pleas of 'commercial success' attributable to the invention coupled with 'long felt want' are not uncommon – so much so that special provision is made in patent actions before the English courts as to what information must accompany such a plea.[4] One rare case in which such an argument was found compelling in relation to an apparently simple mechanical invention was *Haberman v Jackel*[5] which listed the matters to be addressed if a plea of commercial success was to be of value in throwing light on the question of inventive step. The place of secondary evidence has more recently been fully discussed in *Schlumberger v Electromagnetic Geoservices*[6] in which it was observed that it only generally came into play when one considered the question: 'if it was obvious, why was not it done before?' and concluded that it was wrong to read an observation in *Molnlycke v Procter & Gamble*[7] that such evidence 'must be kept firmly in its place' as saying that secondary evidence is always of minor importance, as to do so would be to jettison a vast mass of jurisprudence in which it had been applied.

1   *Raychem Corpn's Patents* [1998] RPC 31 (Patents Court).
2   *Hoechst Celanese Corpn v BP Chemicals*[1997] FSR 547 (Patents Court). The appeal on this case concerned infringement only.
3   *Case Law of the Boards of Appeal of the European Patent Office* (7th edn, September 2013) at I.D.10.1.
4   See **Chapter 4** at para 4.11.
5   *Haberman v Jackel* [1999] FSR 683 (Patents Court). A somewhat abbreviated version of the list is set out at [35] of the Patents Court judgment in *Conor Medsystems Inc v Angiotech Pharmaceuticals Inc* [2006] EWHC 260 (Pat); [2007] EWCA Civ 5 (Court of Appeal) (and approved by the Court of Appeal) in the context of a discussion of the relevance of secondary indicia to the law of obviousness. However, this concluded with the observation, as to the 'long felt want' aspect of a commercial success argument, that 'patents should not be granted for things that have been obvious for a long time'. The issue was not addressed in the subsequent successful appeal to the House of Lords.
6   *Schlumberger Holdings Ltd v Electromagnetic Geoservices AS* [2010] EWCA Civ 819 (Court of Appeal) at paras [76]–[86].
7   *Molnlycke v Procter & Gamble* [1994] RPC 49 at p. 113.

Insufficiency

Introduction

5.18   The 'insufficiency' ground of invalidity arises where, under EPC, Article 138(1)(b): 'the European patent does not disclose the invention in a manner sufficiently clear and complete for it to be carried out by a person skilled in the art.'

As such it parallels the requirement, in prosecution, under EPC, Article 83, that: 'The European patent application must disclose the invention in a manner sufficiently clear and complete for it to be carried out by a person skilled in the art.'

The corresponding provision in the UK is PA 1977, s 72(1)(c): 'the specification does not disclose the invention clearly enough and completely enough for it to be performed by a person skilled in the art'.

Although such an objection formed part of the pre-1977 law in the UK, there used also to be various other grounds of attack on validity available in the UK under the pre-PA 1977 law, namely those of lack of fair basis, in utility, ambiguity, false suggestion, and failure to disclose best method, and although these terms no longer appear in the law under PA 1977, the concept of insufficiency under the PA 1977 has been stretched to an extent by case law so as to cover all of them with the exception of the failure to disclose the best method.

The principle behind this ground of invalidity is that in order that the patent can be worked by third parties after its expiry, the patentee must disclose sufficient teaching in the specification to allow another skilled worker in the technology in question to be able to perform the invention. This is the other side of the bargain made in a patent between the inventor and the State; in exchange for a monopoly for a fixed period of time the inventor must disclose enough to enable the invention to be practiced by others at the end of that period. The principle was first established more than two centuries ago in the case of *R v Arkwright*[1] where it was said of the famous inventor of the 'Spinning Frame' that he meant his specification to be 'as obscure as the nature of the case would admit ... in order to keep it from the French' as a result of which his patent was found invalid.

As it has now developed in the English Courts insufficiency was summarized *Eli Lilly and Company v Janssen Alzheimer Immunotherapy* [2013] EWHC 1737:[2]

> '248.   In *Lilly v HGS* Sir Robin Jacob quoted with apparent approval at [11] the following summary of the relevant principles given by Kitchin J (as he then was) at first instance in the same case [2008] EWHC 1903 (Pat), [2008] RPC 29 at [239]:
>
> > "The specification must disclose the invention clearly and completely enough for it to be performed by a person skilled in the art. The key elements of this requirement which bear on the present case are these:

(i)   the first step is to identify the invention and that is to be done by reading and construing the claims;

(ii)   in the case of a product claim that means making or otherwise obtaining the product;

(iii)   in the case of a process claim, it means working the process;

(iv)   sufficiency of the disclosure must be assessed on the basis of the specification as a whole including the description and the claims;

(v)   the disclosure is aimed at the skilled person who may use his common general knowledge to supplement the information contained in the specification;

(vi)   the specification must be sufficient to allow the invention to be performed over the whole scope of the claim;

(vii)   the specification must be sufficient to allow the invention to be so performed without undue burden."

249.   Failure to enable the invention to be performed without undue burden is often referred to as "classical insufficiency" and failure to enable the invention to performed over the whole scope of the claim is often referred to as "*Biogen* insufficiency" or "excessive claim breadth", although these are aspects of the same objection and often shade into one another.'

In addition to 'classic' insufficiency and *Biogen* insufficiency,[3] one can add a third, rather more rare type of insufficiency, namely ambiguity. It is important to bear in mind, however, that all are manifestations of the same legal principle, which is that the claimed invention must be capable of being performed across its full scope without the exercise of further invention. Analysis under such separate heads can be taken too far, as is evident from *Kirin Amgen v Transkaryotic Therapies*[4] in which a finding at first instance as to there being 'classic' insufficiency was disregarded in the light of a *Biogen* insufficiency analysis, an approach which was criticized in the higher courts.

Sufficiency is determined as at the date of filing the application.[5] This represented a change from the pre-PA 1977 law, where sufficiency was assessed at the date of publication, but which, because UK patent applications used not to be published at the 18-month stage, could be some considerable time after the filing date.

1   *R v Arkwright* [1785] 1 Webster's Patent Cases 64.

2   *Eli Lilly and Company v Janssen Alzheimer Immunotherapy* [2013] EWHC 1737 (Patents Court).

3   So-called after the case in which its principles were first formulated, *Biogen v Medeva* [1995] FSR 4 (Court of Appeal); [1997] RPC 1 (House of Lords), although the degree to which they have more general application has now been put into question by the judgments of the Court of Appeal and House of Lords in *Generics (UK) Limited v H Lundbeck A/S* [2007] RPC 729 (Patents Court); [2008] RPC 437 (Court of Appeal); [2009] UKHL 12 (House of Lords) discussed below at para 5.20.

4   *Kirin Amgen v Transkaryotic Therapies* [2001] IP&T 882; [2002] RPC 1; [2002] RPC
     2 (Patents Court); [2003] RPC 3 (Court of Appeal); [2004] UKHL 46; [2005] 1 All
     ER 667; [2005] RPC 9 (House of Lords).
5   *Biogen v Medeva* [1995] FSR 4 (Court of Appeal); [1997] RPC 1 (House of Lords).

'Classic' insufficiency

5.19   The Court of Appeal in *Mentor v Hollister*[1] held that the pre-PA
1977 definition in the case law of insufficiency applied also under the
PA 1977, and thus *Valensi v British Radio Corpn*[2] was still good law. In
what has become an often quoted passage they observed:

'The question for decision in the present case is whether the specification
discloses the invention clearly enough and completely enough for it to be
performed by a person skilled in the art. This obviously involves a question
of degree. Disclosure of an invention does not have to be complete in every
detail, so that anyone, whether skilled or not, can perform it. Since the
specification is addressed to the skilled man, it is sufficient if the addressee can
understand the invention as described, and can then perform it. In performing
the invention the skilled man does not have to be told what is self-evident or
what is part of common general knowledge, that is to say, what is known to
persons versed in the art. But then comes the difficulty. How much else may
the skilled man be expected to do for himself? Is he to be able to produce what
Mr Thorley called a workable prototype of the invention at his first attempt?
Or may he be required to carry out further research or at least make some
further enquiries before achieving success? And how does one draw the line
between production of the so-called workable prototype and the subsequent
development or "optimisation" of the commercial product?'

They went on to answer the question by reference to the observations
in *Valensi*:

'If a working definition is required then one cannot do better than that
proposed by Buckley L. in giving the judgment of the Court of Appeal in
Valensi ... the hypothetical addressee is not a person of exceptional skill and
knowledge, and he is not to be expected to exercise any invention or any
prolonged research, enquiry or experiment. He must, however, be prepared
to display a reasonable degree of skill and common knowledge of the art in
making trials and to correct obvious errors in the specification if a means of
correcting them can readily be found.'

Then a little later:

'Further, we are of the opinion that it is not only inventive steps that can be
required of the addressee. While the addressee must be taken as a person
with a will to make the instructions work, he is not called upon to make
a prolonged study of matters which present some initial difficulty: and, in
particular, if there are actual errors in the specification – if the apparatus really
will not work without departing from what is described – then, unless both the
existence of the error and the way to correct it can be quickly be discovered
by an addressee of the degree of skill and knowledge which we envisage, the
description is insufficient.'

This formulation has regularly been adopted since. In *Evans Medical Ltd's Patent*[3] the Patents Court drew attention to EPO observations on the topic:

'Mr Kitchen says that the approach to be adopted is that set out by Aldous J in *Mentor v Hollister* [1991] FSR 557 at page 563 which was supported and expanded upon by the Court of Appeal, [1993] RPC 7 at page 13. Both courts emphasised that what amounted to sufficient instruction in a document depended on the facts of the case and the nature of the invention. Aldous J adopting the words of Buckley LJ in Standard Brands Incorporated's Patent (No 2) [1981] RPC 499 at page 535, said that it was still the law that an inventor is not entitled to set the reader of his specification a puzzle and call it a specification ...

If reasonable addressees can come to different conclusions there is a conundrum as to which is right. This is not enablement. This view appears to be consistent with the approach of the Technical Board of Appeal of the EPO in *Unilever/Stable Bleaches* (Decision T 226/85) [1988] OJEPO 336, which was referred to with approval both by Aldous J and the Court of Appeal in *Mentor v Hollister*:

"Even though a reasonable amount of trial and error is permissible when it comes to the sufficiency of disclosure in an unexplored field or – as it is in this case – where there are many technical difficulties, there must be available adequate instructions in the specification or on the basis of common general knowledge which would lead the skilled person *necessarily and directly* towards success through the evaluation of initial failures or through an acceptable statistical expectation rate in the case of random experiments." ' [emphasis added].

The current state of the law as to classic insufficiency was reviewed in *Sandvik Intellectual Property AB v Kennametal UK Ltd*[4] which, after discussing *Mentor* and *Evans Medical* at [109]–[113] continues:

'114 *Unilever/Stable bleaches* continues to represent the settled approach of the Boards of Appeal, although it has been elaborated in subsequent cases: *see Case Law of the Boards of Appeal of the European Patent Office* (6th ed) at 236–238. In his judgment in *Novartis AG v Johnson & Johnson Medical Ltd* [2010] EWCA Civ 1039, [2011] ECC 10 at [72]–[76] Jacob LJ cited passages from three more recent decisions of the Boards of Appeal.

115. The first is T 435/91 *Unilever/Detergents* (reported sub nom *Unilever/Hexagonal liquid crystal gel*) [1995] EPOR 314 (cited in Case Law at p. 238) at [2.2] of the reasons:

"In the Board's judgment the criteria for determining the sufficiency of the disclosure are the same for all inventions, irrespective of the way in which they are defined, be it by way of structural terms of their technical features or by their function. In both cases the requirement of sufficient disclosure can only mean that the whole subject-matter that is defined in the claims, and not only a part of it, must be capable of being carried out by the skilled person without the burden of an undue amount of experimentation or the application of inventive ingenuity.

The peculiarity of the "functional" definition of a component of a composition of matter resides in the fact that this component is not characterised in structural terms, but by means of its effect. Thus this mode of definition does not relate to a tangible component or group of components, but comprises an indefinite and abstract host of possible alternatives, which may have quite different chemical compositions, as long as they achieve the desired result. Consequently, they must all be available to the skilled person if the definition, and the claim of which it forms a part, is to meet the requirements of Article 83 or 100(b) EPC.

This approach is based on the general legal principle that the protection covered by a patent should correspond to the technical contribution to the art made by the disclosure of the invention described therein, which excludes that the patent monopoly be extended to subject-matter which, after reading the patent specification, would still not be at the disposal of the skilled person ....

There cannot, of course, be a clear-cut answer to the question of how many details in a specification are required in order to allow its reduction to practice within the comprehensive whole ambit of the claim, since this question can only be decided on the basis of the facts of each individual case. Nevertheless, it is clear that the available information must enable the skilled person to achieve the envisaged result within the whole ambit of the claim containing the respective "functional" definition without undue difficulty, and that therefore the description with or without the relevant common general knowledge must provide a fully self-sufficient technical concept as to how this result is to be achieved.

116.   The second is T 694/92 *Mycogen/Modifying plant cells* [1998] EPOR 114 (not T 494/92 *Mycogen/Plant gene expression* as stated in *Novartis v Johnson & Johnson*; not cited in Case Law in this context even though it is a decision of a five-person Board published in the *Official Journal*) at [5] of the reasons:

Article 83 EPC requires an invention to be disclosed in a manner sufficiently clear and complete for it to be carried out by a person skilled in the art. As made clear in T 409/91 (OJ EPO 1994, 653, see in particular points 3.3 to 3.5 of the Reasons), the extent to which an invention is sufficiently disclosed is highly relevant when considering the issue of support within the meaning of Article 84 EPC, because both these requirements reflect the same general principle, namely that the scope of a granted patent should correspond to its technical contribution to the state of the art.

Hence it follows that, despite being supported by the description from a purely formal point of view, claims may not be considered allowable if they encompass subject-matter which in the light of the disclosure provided by the description can be performed only with undue burden or with application of inventive skill. As for the amount of technical detail needed for a sufficient disclosure, this is a matter which depends on the correlation of the facts of each particular case with certain general parameters, such as the character of the technical field, the date on which the disclosure was presented and the corresponding common general knowledge, and the amount of reliable technical detail disclosed in a document (see decision T 158/91 of 30 July 1991).

In certain cases a description of one way of performing the claimed invention may be sufficient to support broad claims with functionally defined features, for example where the disclosure of a new technique constitutes the essence of the invention and the description of one way of carrying it out enables the skilled person to obtain without undue burden the same effect of the invention in a broad area by use of suitable variants of the component features (see T 292/85 above). In other cases, more technical details and more than one example may be necessary in order to support claims of a broad scope, for example where the achievement of a given technical effect by known techniques in different areas of application constitutes the essence of the invention and serious doubts exist as to whether the said effect can readily be obtained for the whole range of applications claimed (see T 612/92 of 28 February 1996). However, in all these cases, the guiding principle is always that the skilled person should, after reading of the description, be able to readily perform the invention over the whole area claimed without undue burden and without needing inventive skill (see T 409/91 and T 435/91 above). On the other hand, the objection of lack of sufficient disclosure presupposes that there are serious doubts, substantiated by verifiable facts, in this respect, see T 19/90 (OJ EPO 1990, 476, see point 3.3 of the Reasons).

117. The third is T 1743/06 *Ineos/Amorphous silica* (unreported; not cited in Case Law):

1.8 The appellant argued in this respect that the determination of the optimal stirring speed in the preparation of the silica claimed would be arrived at without undue burden simply by varying the stirring speed during the reaction of silicate with sulphuric acid while reworking the two examples of the patent specification.

The board can accept that such a trial and error experimentation might in the present case not be considered as undue burden as far as the silicas illustrated in the examples of the contested patent are concerned. However, this reasoning which can be accepted only for the two examples, does not hold good for the other claimed but non-exemplified amorphous silicas and in the absence of any specific recipe concerning the preparation of such silicas, the problems concerning the stirring speed still remain for silicas claimed over the whole range.

1.9 The skilled person is thus confronted with the uncontested fact that he has a lot of process variables affecting the claimed parameters, but once he has encountered failure in one parameter value, there is no clear guidance enabling him to adjust the multitude of process steps in order to arrive with certitude at silicas meeting the parameter requirements defined in claim 1 of both requests at issue. Even though a reasonable amount of trial and error is permissible when it comes to assessing sufficiency of disclosure, there must still be adequate instructions in the specification, or on the basis of common general knowledge, leading the skilled person necessarily and directly towards success, through evaluation of initial failures. This is not the case here, since the preparation of the amorphous silicas claimed is made dependent on the adjustment of different process parameters for which no guidance is given in the patent in suit, so that the broad definition of an amorphous silica as presently claimed is no more than an invitation to perform a research program in order to find a suitable way of preparing the amorphous silicas over the whole area claimed.

1.10 It follows from the above, that the principle underlying Article 83 EPC that the skilled person should be given sufficient guidance for performing the invention without undue burden over the whole range claimed is thus not fulfilled.

118. Jacob LJ summarised the position in *Novartis v Johnson & Johnson* at [74] as follows: "The heart of the test is: 'Can the skilled person readily perform the invention over the whole area claimed without undue burden and without needing inventive skill?'"

On the facts, he agreed with counsel for *Johnson & Johnson* at [77] that the patent in suit "did no more than invite the reader to perform a research program where, if he succeeded, the patent claimed the fruits of his research".'

The last case here mentioned, *Novartis v Johnson & Johnson Medical Ltd*[5] provides a good example of a patent found invalid for insufficiency and for no other reason, and of which the Court of Appeal said at [92], upholding the decision at first instance of insufficiency: 'It is no more than an "if you can find it, we claim it" patent'. *Pharmacia v Merck*[6] was another case in which there was a finding of insufficiency, and *AHP v Novartis*[7] was one in which to avoid such a finding the Court of Appeal adopted a narrow claim construction. However, both these latter two cases arose in the context of chemical prediction, by which it is easy to speculate as to analogous chemicals which might have the desired physiological activity, but where it tends also to be found that not all compounds within the claims have such activity, thereby shading into breadth of claim insufficiency. Thus, this aspect of these cases is discussed more fully in the context of chemical prediction in **Chapter 7** at paras 7.19–7.20. Another aspect of sufficiency discussed (at para 7.20) is the requirement that the specification enable the skilled person to perform the invention without undue burden in the context of a claim to the use of a product to make a medicine for a particular therapeutic purpose. In the field of biotechnology, in the context of which insufficiency is considered in **Chapter 8** at paras 8.14–8.15, particular problems of enablement used to be encountered with new micro-organisms. These have led to a system of deposit, discussed in **Chapter 8** at para 8.16.

1   *Mentor v Hollister* [1993] RPC 7 (Court of Appeal) at pp. 10 and 13.
2   *Valensi v British Radio Corpn* [1973] RPC 337 (Court of Appeal).
3   *Evans Medical Ltd's Patent* [1998] RPC 517 (Patents Court).

4   *Sandvik Intellectual Property AB v Kennametal UK Ltd* [2011] EWHC 3311 (Pat);
     [2012] RPC 23 at [109]–[124].
5   *Novartis AG & Anor v Johnson & Johnson Medical Ltd & Ors* [2009] EWHC 2029
     (Pat); [2010] EWCA Civ 10396.
6   *Pharmacia v Merck* [2000] RPC 709; [2000] IP&T 1505 (Patents Court); [2001]
     EWCA Civ 1610; [2002] RPC 41 (Court of Appeal).
7   *AHP v Novartis* [2000] IP&T 1308 (Court of Appeal).

Insufficiency and claim scope

5.20   Practitioners in the UK used to mourn the apparent loss of the ground of revocation known in the pre-PA 1977 law as 'lack of fair basis'. This was because although in the prosecution process, by EPC, Article 84, the claims as sought to be granted 'must be supported by the description',[1] when one comes to attacking the validity of a granted patent a failure of the claims to be supported by the description is no longer of itself an express ground of revocation. This is in contrast to the position on sufficiency, as to which there is an express ground of revocation which corresponds to a similarly worded requirement in the prosecution process, in EPC, Article 83. This disparity had led to the then widely-held view that issues of 'support' akin to those known under the pre-PA 1977 law as 'lack of fair basis' could not be ventilated in the context of an insufficiency attack on a granted patent, a view apparently reinforced by the decision of an EPO Technical Board of Appeal in T 292/85 *Polypeptide Expression/GENENTECH*[2] the official headnote of which states: 'An invention ... is sufficiently disclosed if at least one way is clearly indicated enabling the person skilled in the art to carry out the invention'.

However, another EPO Technical Board of Appeal in T 409/91 *Fuel Oils/EXXON*[3] made it clear that this was not a general principle, and depended on the generality at which the 'invention' was described, and whether it reflected a principle of general application:

> 'Although the requirements of Articles 83 and 84 are directed to different parts of the patent application, since Article 83 relates to disclosure of the invention, while Article 84 deals with the definition of the invention by the claims, the underlying purpose of the requirement of support by the description, insofar as its substantive aspect is concerned, and of the requirement of sufficient disclosure is the same, namely to ensure that the patent monopoly should be justified by the actual technical contribution to the art. Thus, a claim may well be supported by the description in the sense that it corresponds to it, but still encompass subject-matter which is not sufficiently disclosed within the meaning of Article 83 EPC as it cannot be performed without undue burden, or vice versa. In the present case, however, the reasons why the invention defined in the claims does not meet the requirement of Article 83 EPC are in effect the same as those that lead to their infringing Article 84 EPC as well, namely that the invention extends to technical subject-matter not made available to the person skilled in the art by the application as filed, since it was

not contested by the appellant that no information was given to perform the claimed invention successfully without using the structurally defined class of additives. Therefore, the Board does not find that the description discloses the invention defined in the present claims in the manner prescribed by Article 83 EPC.

In this respect, the Board does not accept the appellant's submission that sufficiency should be acknowledged simply because one way of performing the invention was disclosed. In the Board's judgment, the disclosure of one way of performing the invention is only sufficient within the meaning of Article 83 EPC if it allows the person skilled in the art to perform the invention in the whole range that is claimed, as was already stated in point 2 above. However, the question whether the disclosure of one way of performing the invention is sufficient to enable a person skilled in the art to carry out the invention in the whole claimed range is a question of fact that must be answered on the basis of the available evidence, and on the balance of probabilities in each individual case. In the present case, the claimed invention concerns a class of fuel oil compositions characterised by a common feature, the presence of wax crystals of a certain size under certain conditions. In the Board's judgment, this case differs from those where a class of chemical compounds is claimed and only one method of preparing them is necessary to enable a skilled person to carry out the invention, in other words, to prepare all compounds of the claimed class. Rather, the present case is comparable to cases where a group of chemical compounds is claimed, and not all of the claimed compounds can be prepared by the methods disclosed in the description or being part of the common general knowledge .... In the latter case, it was not held sufficient for the purpose of Article 83 EPC to disclose a method of obtaining *only some* members of the claimed class of chemical compositions. Thus, the Board's finding that the disclosure of the claimed invention is only sufficient if it enables the skilled person to obtain substantially *all* embodiments falling within the ambit of the claims, is consistent with the earlier jurisprudence of the Boards of Appeal of the EPO ....'

The Technical Boards of Appeal of the EPO further developed their means for dealing with broad claims, first, as in T 939/92 *Triazoles/AGREVO*[4] by finding certain broad claims to chemicals said to be effective as herbicides not insufficient, but to lack inventive step (because it was not credible that all the claimed compounds manifested the alleged technical effect that turned out be the sole reason for their alleged inventiveness) and later, in T 694/92 *Modifying plant cells/MYCOGEN*[5] by finding certain broad biotechnology claims to be insufficient, having explained the approach as follows:

'... the contribution to the state of the art by the invention disclosed in a patent or patent application resides in the actual realisation of a technical effect anticipated at a theoretical level in the prior art. In such a situation, a proper balance must be found between, on the one hand, the actual technical contribution to the state of the art by the invention disclosed in said patent or patent application, if any, and, on the other hand, the manner of claiming so that, if patent protection is granted, its scope is fair and adequate ....

The Board deems it appropriate to consider the interrelation between the requirements of Article 84, 83 and 56 EPC in order to find a fair balance in the present case.'

In the UK, the House of Lords followed T 409/91 *Fuel Oils/EXXON* in *Biogen v Medeva*.[6] Even though this decision primarily concerned priority[7] the principles there set out, are of authority both for what is meant by 'enabling disclosure' in this context, and in that of the law of insufficiency generally. As to the concept of enablement it observed (at pp. 47–49):

'The need for an enabling disclosure to satisfy the requirements of support under s 5(2)(a), valid application under s 14 and sufficiency under s 72(1)(c) has, I think, been plain and undisputed since the decision in *Asahi*. What has been less clear is what the concept of an enabling disclosure means. Part of the difficulty has been caused by a misinterpretation of what the Technical Board of Appeal of the EPO said in *Genentech I/Polypeptide expression* (T 292/85) [1989] O.J. EPO 275. This was a patent for a plasmid suitable for transforming a bacterial host which included an expression control sequence or "regulon" which could enable the expression of foreign DNA as a recoverable polypeptide. The Examining Division was willing to grant a patent only in respect of the plasmids, bacteria and polypeptides known at the date of application. The Technical Board of Appeal allowed the appeal, saying that the Examining Division had taken too narrow a view of the requirement of enabling disclosure:

"What is also important in the present case is the irrelevancy of the particular choice of a variant within the functional terms "bacteria", "regulon" or "plasmid". It is not just that some result within the range of polypeptides is obtained in each case but it is the same polypeptide which is expressed, independent of the choice of these means .... Unless variants of components are also embraced in the claims, which are, now or later on, equally suitable to achieve the same effect in a manner which could not have been envisaged without the invention, the protection provided by the patent would be ineffectual .... The character of the invention this time is one of general methodology which is fully applicable with any starting material, and is, as it was already stated, also independent from the known, trivial, or inventive character of the end-products. [paras. 3.1.3, 3.1.5, 3.3.2]"

In other words, the applicants had invented a general principle for enabling plasmids to control the expression of polypeptides in bacteria and there was no reason to believe that it would not work equally well with any plasmid, bacterium or polypeptide. The patent was therefore granted in general terms.

In *Molnlycke AB v. Procter & Gamble Ltd.* [1992] F.S.R. 549, however, Morritt J. interpreted this decision to mean that it was a general rule of European patent law that an invention was sufficiently disclosed if the skilled man could make a single embodiment. This interpretation was followed by Aldous J. in *Chiron Corporation v. Organon Teknika Ltd.* [1994] F.S.R. 202, although I think I detect in his judgment some surprise that the EPO should have adopted such a mechanistic and impoverished approach to the concept of enabling disclosure. As we shall see, he applied the same rule in the present case.

In fact the Board in *Genentech I/Polypeptide expression* was doing no more than apply a principle of patent law which has long been established in the United Kingdom, namely, that the specification must enable the invention to be performed to the full extent of the monopoly claimed. If the invention discloses a principle capable of general application, the claims may be in correspondingly general terms. The patentee need not show that he has proved its application in every individual instance. On the other hand, if the claims include a number of discrete methods or products, the patentee must enable the invention to be performed in respect of each of them.

Thus if the patentee has hit upon a new product which has a beneficial effect but cannot demonstrate that there is a common principle by which that effect will be shared by other products of the same class, he will be entitled to a patent for that product but not for the class, even though some may subsequently turn out to have the same beneficial effect: see *May & Baker Ltd. v. Boots Pure Drug Co.* Ltd. (1950) 67 RPC 23, 50. On the other hand, if he has disclosed a beneficial property which is common to the class, he will be entitled to a patent for all products of that class (assuming them to be new) even though he has not himself made more than one or two of them.

In the context of insufficiency as a ground of revocation the House of Lords had observed, earlier in its judgment (at page 47): 'The absence of an enabling disclosure is likewise one of the grounds for the revocation of a patent specified in s 72(1). Paragraph (c) says that one such ground is that – "the specification of the patent does not disclose the invention clearly enough and completely enough for it to be performed by a person skilled in the art."

This is entirely in accordance with what one would expect. The requirement of an enabling disclosure in a patent application is a matter of substance and not form. Its absence should therefore be a ground not only for refusal of the application but also for revocation of the patent after grant. Similarly, the same concept is involved in the question of whether the patent is entitled to priority from an earlier application. This is not to say that the question in each case is the same. The purposes for which the question is being asked are different. But the underlying concept is the same.

The explanation of s 14(5)(c) in *Asahi* seems to me to provide an answer to a point which puzzled the Court of Appeal in *Genentech Inc.'s Patent* [1989] RPC 147. The court noted that although s 14(5)(c) is a statutory requirement for a valid patent application, non-compliance is not a ground for revocation of a patent which has been granted. Section 72(1) states exhaustively the grounds upon which a patent may be revoked. These grounds do not, as such, include non-compliance with s 14(5). But the substantive effect of s 14(5)(c), namely that the description should, together with the rest of the specification, constitute an enabling disclosure, is given effect by s 72(1)(c). There is accordingly no gap or illogicality in the scheme of the Act.'

Relating this to EPO case law the House of Lords observed (at p. 49):

'Since *Genentech I/Polypeptide expression* the EPO has several times reasserted the well established principles for what amounts to sufficiency of disclosure. In particular, in *Exxon/Fuel Oils* (T 409/91) [1994] O.J. EPO 653, para 3.3, the Technical Board of Appeal said of the provision in the European Patent Convention equivalent to s 14(5)(c) of the Act:

"Furthermore, Article 84 EPC also requires that the claims must be supported by the description, in other words, it is the definition of the invention in the claims that needs support. In the Board's judgment, this requirement reflects the general legal principle that the extent of the patent monopoly, as defined by the claims, should correspond to the technical contribution to the art in order for it to be supported, or justified." '

In *Biogen* the House of Lords held the critical issue to be 'not whether the claimed invention could deliver the goods, [across the full width of the patent or priority document] but whether the claims covered other ways in which they might be delivered – ways which owed nothing to the teaching or to any principle which it disclosed' observing (at pp. 50–51):

'I think that in concentrating upon the question of whether Professor Murray's invention could, so to speak, deliver the goods across the full width of the patent or priority document, the courts and the EPO allowed their attention to be diverted from what seems to me in this particular case the critical issue. It is not whether the claimed invention could deliver the goods, but whether the claims cover other ways in which they might be delivered: ways which owe nothing to the teaching of the patent or any principle which it disclosed.

It will be remembered that in *Genentech I/Polypeptide expression* the Technical Board spoke of the need for the patent to give protection against other ways of achieving the same effect "in a manner which could not have been envisaged without the invention". This shows that there is more than one way in which the breadth of a claim may exceed the technical contribution to the art embodied in the invention. The patent may claim results which it does not enable, such as making a wide class of products when it enables only one of those products and discloses no principle which would enable others to be made. Or it may claim every way of achieving a result when it enables only one way and it is possible to envisage other ways of achieving that result which make no use of the invention.'

The House of Lords was conscious of the risks of excessive claims based on early exploratory research stifling further research and competition in a new technology. They likened the situation to the circumstances in the early days of electricity which led to the 1854 decision of the US Supreme Court in *O'Reilly v Morse*[8] in which claims for 'making or printing intelligible characters, signs, or letters at any distances' were rejected as too broad on the basis that the possibility of achieving communication through means of an electric current was already known but not the means of achieving that result. Here the patentee, Samuel Morse, had discovered one means of doing so, but had attempted to claim all others as well.

The House of Lords observed, in relation to the subject matter of *Biogen* (at pp. 51–52):

'I return therefore to consider the technical contribution to the art which Professor Murray made in 1978 and disclosed in Biogen 1 … it consisted in showing that despite the uncertainties which then existed over the DNA of the Dane particle – in particular, whether it included the antigen genes and whether it had introns – known recombinant techniques could nevertheless be used to make the antigens in a prokaryotic host cell. As I have said, I accept the judge's findings that the method was shown to be capable of making both antigens and I am willing to accept that it would work in any otherwise suitable host cell. Does this contribution justify a claim to a monopoly of any recombinant method of making the antigens? In my view it does not. The claimed invention is too broad. Its excessive breadth is due, not to the inability of the teaching to produce all the promised results, but to the fact that the same results could be produced by different means. Professor Murray had won a brilliant Napoleonic victory in cutting through the uncertainties which existed in his day to achieve the desired result. But his success did not in my view establish any new principle which his successors had to follow if they were to achieve the same results.

It is said that what Professor Murray showed by his invention was that it could be done. HBV antigens could be produced by expressing Dane particle DNA in a host cell. Those who followed, even by different routes, could have greater confidence by reason of his success. I do not think that this is enough to justify a monopoly of the whole field. I suppose it could be said that Samuel Morse had shown that electric telegraphy could be done. The Wright Brothers showed that heavier-than-air flight was possible, but that did not entitle them to a monopoly of heavier-than-air flying machines. It is inevitable in a young science, like electricity in the early nineteenth century or flying at the turn of the last century or recombinant DNA technology in the 1970s, that dramatically new things will be done for the first time. The technical contribution made in such cases deserves to be recognised. But care is needed not to stifle further research and healthy competition by allowing the first person who has found a way of achieving an obviously desirable goal to monopolise every other way of doing so …'

Thus, while Biogen taught how to make HBV antigens by one route, which the House of Lords was prepared to assume was inventive as at the priority date, this teaching served to do no more than give greater confidence to those who followed using other routes. This was not enough to justify a monopoly of the whole field. Thus the claims in the patent were therefore not supported by the priority document. Since Biogen had conceded that the patent was obvious as of its filing date, their Lordships did not have to consider insufficiency under PA 1977, s 72(1)(c). However, the House of Lords observed that the reasoning by which they had found the patent not entitled to its claimed priority would lead also to the conclusion that it was insufficient. The House of Lords had, in effect, reintroduced the pre-PA 1977 attack of 'fair basis' under the guise of insufficiency, observing (at p. 54):

'The disappearance of "lack of fair basis" as an express ground for revocation does not in my view mean that general principle which it expressed has been abandoned. The jurisprudence of the EPO shows that it is still in full vigour and embodied in Article 83 and 84 of the EPC, of which the equivalent in the 1977 Act are ss 14(3) and (5) and s 72(10)(c).'

In response to an attack based on an allegation of 'breadth of claim' insufficiency patentees will often assert that their invention, unlike that in issue in *Biogen,* relates to a 'principle of general application' as to which 'the claims may be in correspondingly general terms' (quoted in context above in relation to the issue of enablement). In *Kirin-Amgen v Transkaryotic Therapies*[9] Lord Hoffmann, whose was the main speech, took the opportunity to clarify what he had meant by the expression a 'principle of general application' in *Biogen* in which his had also been the main speech:

'112.   This gave rise to a good deal of argument about what amounted to a "principle of general application". In my opinion there is nothing difficult or mysterious about it. It simply means an element of the claim which is stated in general terms. Such a claim is sufficiently enabled if one can reasonably expect the invention to work with anything which falls within the general term. For example, in *Genentech I/Polypeptide expression* (T 292/85) [1989] OJ EPO 275, the patentee claimed in general terms a plasmid suitable for transforming a bacterial host which included an expression control sequence to enable the expression of exogenous DNA as a recoverable polypeptide. The patentee had obviously not tried the invention on every plasmid, every bacterial host or every sequence of exogenous DNA. But the Technical Board of Appeal found that the invention was fully enabled because it could reasonably be expected to work with any of them.

113.   This is an example of an invention of striking breadth and originality. But the notion of a "principle of general application" applies to any element of the claim, however humble, which is stated in general terms. A reference to a requirement of "connecting means" is enabled if the invention can reasonably be expected to work with any means of connection. The patentee does not have to have experimented with all of them.'

Thus, as long as an element of the claim that was stated in general terms could, given the information disclosed in the patent and the common general knowledge, reasonably be expected to work in every case, then it could not be said to be insufficient. Here, having found the claims in issue not infringed and invalid on other grounds he did not feel the need to express a concluded view on the point, but Lord Hoffmann thought, despite the 'striking breadth and originality of the invention' that on the facts the process used by the defendants was not a version of the process disclosed in the patent which, though untried, could have reasonably been expected to work just as well and hence 'the breadth of claim objection may well have been a good one'.

Although the underlying reasoning in *Biogen* has not been questioned by the English courts, the degree to which it can in practice be applied generally to address issues of claim scope has been somewhat clouded as a result of comments made by Lord Hoffmann (who had given the judgment of the House of Lords in *Biogen* but was sitting on this occasion in the Court of Appeal) in *Generics (UK) v Lundbeck*.[10] These comments were to the effect that the judgment of the House of Lords that he had delivered in *Biogen* concerned only the specific type of patent claim that was there in issue, namely a 'product by process' claim, to a class of products so defined (even though there would seem to be no logical reason why it should not also apply to any claim to a class of products, however defined, or even processes). The Court of Appeal in *Generics (UK)* reversed the trial judge to find a product claim to a single novel chemical of predictable activity sufficient where the chemical had not previously been synthesized, but the patent in which the claim appeared only disclosed, and thereby enabled, certain synthetic routes to such chemical. The practical effect of the product claim was, however, to monopolize all synthetic routes to making the single novel chemical, and not only those invented by the patentee. The House of Lords upheld the judgment of the Court of Appeal, but as observed in *MedImmune v Novartis*[11] the multiplicity of speeches in the House of Lords makes it difficult to quote particular passages from just one opinion as representing the reasoning of at least a majority. The Patents Court judgment in *MedImmune* reviewed the three House of Lords decisions in *Biogen*, *Kirin Amgen* and *Generics (UK)* along with three EPO Technical Board of Appeal decisions including T 292/85 *Polypeptide expression/GENENTECH I*.

From *Biogen*, the Patents Court judgment in *MedImmune* (at para [469]) derived the following propositions:

'(i)   A claim will be invalid for insufficiency if the breadth of the claim exceeds the technical contribution to the art made by the invention. As Lord Hoffmann confirmed elsewhere in his opinion, it follows that it is not necessarily enough to disclose one way of performing the invention in the specification.

(ii)   The breadth of the claim will exceed the technical contribution if the claim covers ways of achieving the desired result which owe nothing to the patent or any principle it discloses. Two classes of this are where the patent claims results which it does not enable, such as making a wider class of products when it enables only one and discloses no principle to enable the others to be made, and where the patent claims every way of achieving a result when it enables only one way and it is possible to envisage other ways of achieving that result which make no use of the invention.

(iii) The patent in *Biogen v Medeva* was invalid because it was an example of the second class of objectionable claim.'

From the speeches of the House of Lords in *Generics (UK)* the Patents Court judgment in *MedImmune* was able (at para [475]) to derive the following propositions:

'(i)   The House agreed with Lord Hoffmann in *Biogen v Medeva* that it was important for United Kingdom patent law to be aligned, so far as possible, with the jurisprudence of the EPO. Furthermore, the House also agreed with Lord Hoffmann that the statement of principle which he quoted from *Exxon/Fuel oils* correctly stated the law (see Lord Walker at [14], [19], [35]–[39], Lord Mance at [46]–[47], [55], Lord Neuberger at [83], [87]–[89], [96]–[98]).

(ii)   The House considered that the instant case was to be distinguished from *Biogen v Medeva* because it was concerned with claim to a single chemical compound whereas *Biogen v Medeva* concerned a product-by-process claim of broad scope (see Lord Walker at [10]–[13], [25]–[28], Lord Mance at [49]–[53], [55], Lord Neuberger at [69], [93]–[95], [98]–[99]).

(iii)   It was a mistake to equate the technical contribution of the claim with its inventive concept. In the instant case, the technical contribution made by claims 1 and 3 was the product, and not the process by which it was made, even though the inventive step lay in finding a way to make the product. It followed that the breadth of the claim did not exceed the technical contribution which the invention made to the art (see Lord Walker at [29]–[34], Lord Mance at [44], [52]–[55], Lord Neuberger at [75]–[78], [98], [101]).'

Lord Hoffmann's was not the only judgment of the Court of Appeal in *Generics (UK)*. In another such judgment, agreeing that the first instance decision be reversed, Jacob LJ discussed the problem with patent claims to desirable ends and provided an example of circumstances in which a claim to a class of products broadly defined by their properties would be regarded as insufficient:

'[61]   So, for example, if a man finds a particular way of making a new substance which is 10 times harder than diamond, he cannot just claim "a substance which is 10 times harder than diamond." He can claim his particular method and he can claim the actual new substance produced by his method, either by specifying its composition and structure or, if that cannot be done, by reference to the method (see *Kirin-Amgen* at [90]–[91]) but no more. The reason he cannot claim more is that he has not enabled more – he has claimed the entire class of products which have the known desirable properties yet he has only enabled one member of that class. Such a case is to be contrasted with the present where the desirable end is indeed fully enabled – that which makes it desirable forms no part of the claim limitation.'

A further discussion of the law on claim breadth insufficiency can be found the judgment of the Court of Appeal in *Regeneron v Genentech*:[12]

'95.   I will address these attacks in turn but must begin with the relevant legal principles. First, a patent may be revoked if the specification does not disclose the invention in a manner which is clear enough and complete enough for it to be performed by a person skilled in the art.

96. Second, it is now well established that the scope of the monopoly, as defined in the claims, must correspond to the technical contribution the patentee has made to the art. An aspect of this requirement is that the specification must enable the invention to be performed to the full extent of the monopoly claimed.

97. Third, the question whether the specification adequately discloses the invention is one of degree. I put it this way in *Novartis v Johnson & Johnson* [2009] EWHC 1671 in a passage cited by the judge in this case:

> "236. Whether the specification discloses an invention clearly and completely enough for it to be performed by a person skilled in the art involves a question of degree. It is impossible to lay down any precise rule because the degree of clarity and completeness required will vary depending on the nature of the invention and of the art in which it is made. On the one hand, the specification need not set out every detail necessary for performance. The skilled person must be prepared to display a reasonable degree of skill and use the common general knowledge of the art in making routine trials and to correct obvious errors in the specification, if a means of correcting them can readily be found. Further, he may need to carry out ordinary methods of trial and error, which involve no inventive step and generally are necessary in applying the particular discovery to produce a practical result. On the other hand, he should not be required to carry out any prolonged research, enquiry or experiment: *Mentor Corporation v Hollister Inc.* [1993] RPC 7."

98. Fourth, it is permissible to define an invention using general terms provided the patent discloses a principle of general application in the sense that it can reasonably be expected the invention will work with anything falling within the scope of these terms. As Lord Hoffmann said in *Biogen v Medeva* [1977] RPC 1 at 48–49:

> "If the invention discloses a principle capable of general application, the claims may be in correspondingly general terms. The patentee need not show that he has proved its application in every individual instance. On the other hand, if the claims include a number of discrete methods or products, the patentee must enable the invention to be performed in respect of each of them."

Thus if the patent has hit upon a new product which has a beneficial effect but cannot demonstrate that there is a common principle by which that effect will be shared by other products of the same class, he will be entitled to a patent for that product but not for the class, even though some may subsequently turn out to have the same beneficial effect: see *May & Baker Ltd v. Boots Pure Drug Co. Ltd.* (1950) 67 RPC 23, 50. On the other hand, if he has disclosed a beneficial property which is common to the class, he will be entitled to a patent for all products of that class (assuming them to be new) even though he has not himself made more than one or two of them.

99. In *Kirin Amgen v Hoechst Marion Roussel* [2004] UKHL 46; [2005] RPC 9 Lord Hoffmann further explained the concept of a principle of general application in this way:

"112. In my opinion there is nothing difficult or mysterious about [a principle of general application]. It simply means an element of the claim which is stated in general terms. Such a claim is sufficiently enabled if one can reasonably expect the invention to work with anything which falls within the general term. For example, in *Genentech I/Polypeptide expression* (T 292/85) [1989] O.J. EPO 275, the patentee claimed in general terms a plasmid suitable for transforming a bacterial host which included an expression control sequence to enable the expression of exogenous DNA as a recoverable polypeptide. The patentee had obviously not tried the invention on every plasmid, every bacterial host or every sequence of exogenous DNA. But the Technical Board of Appeal found that the invention was fully enabled because it could reasonably be expected to work with any of them."

113. This is an example of an invention of striking breadth and originality. But the notion of a 'principle of general application' applies to any element of the claim, however humble, which is stated in general terms. A reference to a requirement of 'connecting means' is enabled if the invention can reasonably be expected to work with any means of connection. The patentee does not have to have experimented with all of them."

100. It must therefore be possible to make a reasonable prediction the invention will work with substantially everything falling within the scope of the claim or, put another way, the assertion that the invention will work across the scope of the claim must be plausible or credible. The products and methods within the claim are then tied together by a unifying characteristic or a common principle. If it is possible to make such a prediction then it cannot be said the claim is insufficient simply because the patentee has not demonstrated the invention works in every case.

101. On the other hand, if it is not possible to make such a prediction or if it is shown the prediction is wrong and the invention does not work with substantially all the products or methods falling within the scope of the claim then the scope of the monopoly will exceed the technical contribution the patentee has made to the art and the claim will be insufficient. It may also be invalid for obviousness, there being no invention in simply providing a class of products or methods which have no technically useful properties or purpose.

102. Fifth, patentees not infrequently seek to avoid the possibility that a claim covers products or methods which do not work by inserting a functional limitation. Such a claim may be allowed by the EPO if the invention can only be defined in such terms or cannot otherwise be defined more precisely without unduly restricting its scope. But, it must still be possible to perform the invention across the scope of the claim without undue effort. As I said in *Novartis v Johnson & Johnson* at [244]:

"... In the case of a claim limited by function, it must still be possible to perform the invention across the scope of the scope of the claim without undue effort. That will involve a question of degree and depend upon all the circumstances including the nature of the invention and the art in which it is made. Such circumstances may include a consideration of whether the claims embrace products other than those specifically described for achieving the claimed purpose and, if they do, what those other products may be and how easily they may be found or made; whether it is possible to make a reasonable prediction as to whether any particular product satisfies the requirements of the claims; and the nature and extent of any testing which must be carried out to confirm any such prediction." '

The last point in [101], as to such a claim not only being insufficient but also obvious, is a reference to the principle established in T939/92 *Triazoles/AGREVO* (discussed above).

The principles set out in *Biogen* have also been applied in other, less esoteric fields than recombinant DNA technology that was in issue in *Biogen*, *Kirin Amgen*, *MedImmune* and *Regeneron*, albeit mainly in 'squeeze' arguments which have been run to counter a broad construction being placed on a claim. For example, in *Tickner & Woodhouse v Honda*[13] concerning engine design, the Patents Court held that had the broader claim construction as urged by the patentee applied, the claim would cover 'ways which owe nothing to the teaching of the patent or any principle which it disclosed' and thence be insufficient. Another type of 'squeeze' argument arose in *Norbrook Laboratories Patent*[14] where the Patents Court found broad claims to combinations of pharmaceuticals of two classes to lack sufficiency, consistent with the evidence that had supported the inventive step of narrower claims to a particular combination of pharmaceuticals in those two classes on the basis that pharmaceuticals of those two classes would not be expected to work together. However, it is generally in pharmaceuticals, as to which see **Chapter 7** at paras 7.19–7.20, and biotechnology, as to which see **Chapter 8** at paras 8.14–8.15, that such claim scope attacks arise. However, and despite its solid basis in EPO case law, as reflected also in the *EPO Guidelines*[15] the courts of other European jurisdictions have been reluctant expressly to follow *Biogen*.[16] Some of the observations in *Generics (UK)* cannot be expected to assist in challenging such scepticism.[17]

1   In the eyes of the particular examiner, whether at the UKIPO or the EPO, before whom a patent is prosecuted – EPC, Article 84; PA 1977, s 14(5)(c).
2   T 292/85 *GENENTECH/Polypeptide Expression* [1989] OJ EPO 275; [1989] EPOR 1.
3   T 409/91 *EXXON/Fuel Oils* [1994] EPOR 149 at pp. 155–6.
4   T 939/92 *AGREVO/Triazoles* [1996] EPOR 171.
5   T 694/92 *MYCOGEN/Modifying plant cells* [1998] EPOR 114.
6   *Biogen v Medeva* [1997] RPC 1 at p. 47ff.
7   See above at para 5.05, 'Priority date'.
8   *O'Reilly v Morse* (1854) 56 US (15 How.) 62.
9   *Kirin-Amgen v Transkaryotic Therapies* [2001] IP&T 882; [2002] RPC 1; [2002] RPC 2 (Patents Court); [2003] RPC 3 (Court of Appeal); [2004] UKHL 46; [2005] 1 All ER 667; [2005] RPC 9 (House of Lords).

10 *Generics (UK) Limited v H Lundbeck A/S* [2007] RPC 729 (Patents Court); [2008]
    RPC 437 (Court of Appeal); [2009] UKHL 12 (House of Lords).
11 *MedImmune Limited v Novartis Pharmaceuticals UK Limited* [2011] EWHC 1669
    (Patents Court).
12 *Regeneron Pharmaceuticals Inc v Bayer Pharma AG* [2013] EWCA Civ 93.
13 *Tickner & Woodhouse v Honda* [2002] EWHC 8 (Patents Court).
14 *Norbrook Laboratories Ltd's Patent (Application for Revocation by Schering-
    Plough Ltd)* [2006] FSR 18; [2005] EWHC 2532 (Patents Court).
15 See *EPO Guidelines* (September 2013) Section F-IV, entitled 'Lack of support vs.
    insufficient disclosure' observing:
      'It should be noted that, although an objection of lack of support is an objection
      under Art. 84, it can often, as in the above examples, also be considered as an
      objection of insufficient disclosure of the invention under Art. 83 (see F-III, 1 to 3),
      the objection being that the disclosure is insufficient to enable the skilled person
      to carry out the "invention" over the whole of the broad field claimed (although
      sufficient in respect of a narrow "invention"). Both requirements are designed to
      reflect the principle that the terms of a claim should be commensurate with, or be
      justified by, the invention's technical contribution to the art. Therefore, the extent
      to which an invention is sufficiently disclosed is also highly relevant to the issue of
      support. The reasons for failure to meet the requirements of Art. 83 may in effect
      be the same as those that lead to the infringement of Art. 84 as well, namely that
      the invention, over the whole range claimed, extends to technical subject-matter
      not made available to the person skilled in the art by the application as filed (see T
      409/91, Reasons 2 and 3.3 to 3.5).'
16 See for example, the BGH (German Federal Supreme Court) judgment of 24
    September 2003 in X ZR 7/00 (BPatG) published in GRUR 2004, 47, noting the
    decision of the House of Lords in *Biogen* but observing that an unreasonably broad
    claim does not in itself constitute a ground for revocation.
17 For an academic critique of *Biogen* in the light of *Generics (UK)* see Brennan,
    David, '*Biogen* sufficiency reconsidered', *Intellectual Property Law Quarterly*, Vol. 4
    (2009), pp. 476–508. See also Pila, Justine, 'Chemical Products and Proportionate
    Patents Before and After *Generics v Lundbeck*', *Kings Law Journal* (KLJ) (2009) pp.
    489–526.

Insufficiency and obscure claims

5.21   As observed by the Patents Court in *Raychem Corpn's Patents*:[1]
'Unnecessary obscurity is not a separate ground for invalidating a claim.
Within wide limits a patentee can use what language he likes to define
his invention.'

Neither do artificial problems of interpretation at the edges of a claim
render a claim insufficient, as observed in *General Tire v Firestone Tyre*:[2]
'On the basis, which we accept to be correct ... that the issue of sufficient
definition is to be decided in the light of practical considerations and not
of puzzles set at the edges of the claim, and that what the inventor is
required to do is to give the best definition that the subject matter admits
of.'

However, that is not an end of matters, as a claim may be so obscure
as to be incapable of infringement, as discussed by the Court of Appeal
in *Scanvaegt v Pelcombe*.[3] Moreover, in extreme cases a claim, despite
being conceptually clear, may be so drawn that is impossible to determine

whether or not a product or process falls within it, as in *Kirin-Amgen v Transkaryotic Therapies*[4] where such lack of clarity rendered a claim insufficient.

The Technical Boards of Appeal of the EPO have held claims to be insufficient if the skilled person cannot establish whether a product falls within the area covered by the claim, and reliably to prepare the claimed product. However, there is also case law to the effect that a failure to specify the conditions under which a claimed parameter is measured, even where there are several standardized test methods that could differ somewhat in their results does not necessarily render a claim insufficient under EPC, Article 83 but may be rather a clarity issue under EPC, Article 84 that cannot be raised (unless the claim is amended) in opposition, and so requires the value of the parameter to be interpreted broadly.[5]

The current state of the law in this area, which it terms 'ambiguity' was reviewed in *Sandvik Intellectual Property AB v Kennametal UK Ltd.*[6]

1   *Raychem Corpn's Patents* [1998] RPC 31 (Patents Court).
2   *General Tire and Rubber Co v Firestone Tyre & Rubber Co Ltd* [1972] RPC 457 at p. 511, quoted in *Wesley Jessen Corpn v Coopervision Ltd* [2003] RPC 20 at para [145].
3   *Scanvaegt v Pelcombe* [1998] FSR 786 (Court of Appeal); see also **Chapter 6** at para 6.09.
4   *Kirin-Amgen v Transkaryotic Therapies* [2004] UKHL 46; [2005] All ER 667; [2005] RPC 9 (House of Lords) at paras [121]–[131]. See also *SmithKline Beecham plc v Apotex Europe Ltd* [2004] EWCA Civ 1568; [2005] FSR 23 at [115].
5   T 1119/05 *Mitsui Chemicals* (Technical Board of Appeal 3.3.03, 8 January 2008, at para [3.4]).
6   *Sandvik Intellectual Property AB v Kennametal UK Ltd* [2011] EWHC 3311 (Pat), [2012] RPC 23 at [109]–[124].

Addition of matter and extension of protection

Introduction

5.22   The Patent Act 1977, s 72(1) concludes with two somewhat related grounds of invalidity:

'(d)   the matter disclosed in the specification for the patent extends beyond that disclosed in the application for the patent as filed ...

(e)   the protection conferred by the patent has been extended by an amendment which should not have been allowed.'

The first ground, that of added matter, arises from amendments made to the specification and claims, generally during prosecution, and over the application as filed (it is irrelevant for this purpose what differences there may be as between the priority document, and the application as filed, as that only affects the right to claim priority). It also applies to amendments made after grant, although EPC, Article 123(2) and in the

UK, PA 1997, s 76 should prevent such post-grant addition of matter, and so can also constitute a basis for objecting to a proposed amendment. It corresponds to EPC, Articles 100(c) and 138(1)(c).

The added matter objection concerns the teaching, or the disclosure of the patent, and thus does not necessarily have anything to do with claim scope, whereas the second ground concerns the protection conferred by the claims of the patent. The second ground, which corresponds to EPC, Article 138(1)(d), only arises in relation to amendments made (generally to the claims) after grant, but is rare because patent offices (mainly the EPO, in amendments made in post-grant opposition) are careful not to allow amendments after grant which extend protection (EPC, Article 123(3) and in the UK, PA 1977, s 76(3)(b) should prevent such extension of protection).[1]

1   See *Hospira UK Ltd v Genentech Inc No 2* [2014] EWHC 3857 at [105]–[124] for a
    rare example of such an objection.

Added matter

5.23   Added matter objections are an important aspect of EPO opposition practice, and also succeed from time to time in the English courts,[1] but in such circumstances as to make it hard to formulate a principle of general application, especially as they can be so dependent on issues of construction. This is well demonstrated by *AP Racing Ltd v Alcon Components Ltd,*[2] the most recent Court of Appeal decision in which the issue featured, which is devoted almost exclusively to it, and in which a finding of invalidity at first instance on this basis was reversed. It is generally accepted that the correct approach to added matter is that originally set out by the Patents Court in *Bonzel v Intervention Ltd (No* 3):[3]

> 'The decision as to whether there was extension of disclosure must be made on a comparison of the two documents [namely the application as filed and the patent as granted] read through the eyes of a skilled addressee. The task of the court is threefold:
>
> (a)   To ascertain through the eyes of a skilled addressee what is disclosed, both explicitly and implicitly in the application.
>
> (b)   To do the same in respect of the patent as granted.
>
> (c)   To compare the two disclosures and decide whether any subject matter relevant to the invention has been added whether by deletion or addition. The comparison is strict in the sense that subject matter will be added unless such matter is clearly and unambiguously disclosed in the application either explicitly or implicitly.
>
> The comparison is strict in the sense that subject matter will added unless such matter is clearly and unambiguously disclosed in the application as filed – although that disclosure may be implicit.'

This formulation was subsequently elaborated upon by the Patents Court in *European Central Bank v Document Security Systems*[4] in terms that were approved by the Court of Appeal in this, *Vector Corp v Glatt Air Techniques Ltd*[5] and *Napp Pharmaceutical Holdings Ltd v ratiopharm.*[6]

The following observations in *European Central Bank* also drew on the leading EPO authority in this area, the decision of the Enlarged Board of Appeal in G 1/93 *Limiting Feature/ADVANCED SEMICONDUCTOR PRODUCTS:*[7]

'[97]   A number of points emerge from this formulation which have a particular bearing on the present case and merit a little elaboration. First, it requires the court to construe both the original application and specification to determine what they disclose. For this purpose the claims form part of the disclosure (s. 130(3) of the Act), though clearly not everything which falls within the scope of the claims is necessarily disclosed.

[98]   Second, it is the court which must carry out the exercise and it must do so through the eyes of the skilled addressee. Such a person will approach the documents with the benefit of the common general knowledge.

[99]   Third, the two disclosures must be compared to see whether any subject matter relevant to the invention has been added. This comparison is a strict one. Subject matter will be added unless it is clearly and unambiguously disclosed in the application as filed.

[100]   Fourth, it is appropriate to consider what has been disclosed both expressly and implicitly. Thus the addition of a reference to that which the skilled person would take for granted does not matter: *DSM NV's Patent* [2001] R.P.C. 25 at [195]–[202]. On the other hand, it is to be emphasised that this is not an obviousness test. A patentee is not permitted to add matter by amendment which would have been obvious to the skilled person from the application.

[101]   Fifth, the issue is whether subject matter relevant to the invention has been added. In case G 1/93, *Advanced Semiconductor Products*, the Enlarged Board of Appeal of the EPO stated (at paragraph [9] of its reasons) that the idea underlying Art. 123(2) is that that an applicant should not be allowed to improve his position by adding subject matter not disclosed in the application as filed, which would give him an unwarranted advantage and could be damaging to the legal security of third parties relying on the content of the original application. At paragraph [16] it explained that whether an added feature which limits the scope of protection is contrary to Art 123(2) must be determined from all the circumstances. If it provides a technical contribution to the subject matter of the claimed invention then it would give an unwarranted advantage to the patentee. If, on the other hand, the feature merely excludes protection for part of the subject matter of the claimed invention as covered by the application as filed, the adding of such a feature cannot reasonably be considered to give any unwarranted advantage to the applicant. Nor does it adversely affect the interests of third parties.

[102] Sixth, it is important to avoid hindsight. Care must be taken to consider the disclosure of the application through the eyes of a skilled person who has not seen the amended specification and consequently does not know what he is looking for. This is particularly important where the subject matter is said to be implicitly disclosed in the original specification.'

Subsequent decisions have emphasized the rationale underlying EPC, Article 123(2) as stated in *European Central Bank* at [101], and so in *Vector Corp* at [6] the Court of Appeal quoted a submission on behalf of one of the parties as to how the legal security of third parties would be affected if this were not the rule:

'The applicant or patentee could gain an unwarranted advantage in two ways if subject-matter could be added: first, he could circumvent the "first-to-file" rule, namely that the first person to apply to patent an invention is entitled to the resulting patent; and secondly, he could gain a different monopoly to that which the originally filed subject-matter justified.'

As observed in *AP Racing Ltd v Alcon Components Ltd*[8] in relation to the second of these examples 'third parties should be able to look at the application and draw a conclusion as to the subject matter which is available for supporting a claimed monopoly'.

The test has also been more briefly summarized. Thus in *Richardson-Vicks Patent*[9] the Patents Court expressed the test as whether 'a skilled man would, upon looking at the amended specification, learn anything about the invention which he could not learn from the unamended specification'. In *Texas Iron Works Inc's Patent*,[10] the Court of Appeal observed that an amendment would add matter 'where a feature, which the specification has made clear is essential, has been omitted or a feature has been added which was not disclosed in the specification as filed.'

The test is not easily applied, as observed by the Patents Court in *Research in Motion v Inpro Licensing*[11] in recognizing: '... the difficulty in deciding whether particular features are disclosed as free standing aspects of the invention or only when in combination with other features'.

Where an application discloses two or more different inventions, it is not an impermissible addition of matter to claim them separately, as this is what the practice of filing divisional applications is designed to permit.[12]

Broadening a claim during the course of prosecution by the omission of a feature will not necessarily involve the addition of matter as, although it will cover the class of things claimed but without the omitted feature, it does not necessarily follow that it thereby discloses anything new. In contrast, the addition of a limiting feature in a claim during patent prosecution may well give rise to an added matter objection. As observed in *Assidoman Multipack v Mead*:[13] 'a patentee may amend his claim by the addition of limitations, but that does not mean that he can for the first time describe an invention which had not been described explicitly or implicitly in the application.'

The Patents Court made the same point in *A C Edwards v Acme Signs & Displays*[14] when it said that 'not everything within a claim is disclosed although it may fall within the ambit of the claim'. Especial care must thus be taken with narrowing amendments as to where their basis in the specification actually lies. A particularly problematic type of narrowing amendment which can give rise to an added matter objection is 'intermediate generalisation' as first described in *Palmaz's European Patents*:[15]

> 'If the specification discloses distinct sub-classes of the overall inventive concept, then it should be possible to amend down to one or other of those sub-classes, whether or not they are presented as inventively distinct in the specification before amendment. The difficulty comes when it is sought to take features which are only disclosed in a particular context and which are not disclosed as having any inventive significance and introduce them into the claim deprived of that context. This is a process sometimes called "intermediate generalisation."'

The same issue was made to look deceptively simple by the Court of Appeal (reversing the decision at first instance) in *AP Racing Ltd v Alcon Components Ltd*:[16] '[33] ... [it] is clear that the law does not prohibit the addition of claim features which state in more general terms that which is described in the specification.'

Somewhat more specific guidance on claim limitation was provided by the Court of Appeal in *Nokia OYJ (Nokia Corporation) v IPCom GmbH & Co Kg*:[17]

> '[59] ... it is not permissible to introduce into a claim a feature taken from a specific embodiment unless the skilled person would understand that the other features of the embodiment are not necessary to carry out the claimed invention. Put another way, it must be apparent to the skilled person that the selected feature is generally applicable to the claimed invention absent the other features of that embodiment.'

It has however been suggested that there may be a difference in how such principles are applied as between mechanical inventions and those in an empirical art, eg pharmaceutical formulation:[18]

> '173. *AC Edwards v Acme*, *Texas Iron Works* and *AP Racing* are each concerned with mechanical inventions in which a word or phrase has been used to identify or describe a structure in the application ("spring means" for a coil spring and cotter arrangement in *AC Edwards*, "liner hanger unit" for an arrangement of slips and cones in *Texas Iron Works*, and "asymmetric peripheral stiffening band" for a hockey stick shaped peripheral stiffening band in *AP Racing*). In each of those cases the inevitable effect of using this new descriptive language is that the claim will not be limited to the particular arrangement described in the application. The claim will have a broader scope. But in each case the court found that no other construction or thing was disclosed by the patent in which this language appeared in the claim.

174. I can see that this result follows in cases about descriptive language like this. Plainly the law cannot be that any change in descriptive language will never add matter but these cases show that some kinds of change in descriptions do not. Of course there is no reason to limit this principle to mechanical inventions, it just comes up naturally in those cases. I have more difficulty applying that principle to a case in which the skilled reader knows that the art is empirical, that the disclosure is a form of recipe, and that the point of the exercise is to produce a material which has certain properties, determined by carrying out tests on the material produced (e.g. stability).'

To add to the problem of limiting amendments those made during prosecution that impermissibly add matter can give rise to a situation which, as explained below, cannot then be put right post-grant by excising such amendment.

1   Although the sense amongst practitioners with experience of both is that the English courts are more lenient in this respect than the EPO Technical Boards of Appeal.
2   *AP Racing Ltd v Alcon Components Ltd* [2014] EWCA Civ 40 reversing *AP Racing Ltd v Alcon Components Ltd* [2013] EWPCC 3. Here, as helpfully summarized and explained in *Koninklijke Philips Electronics N.V. v Nintendo of Europe Gmbh* [2014] EWHC 1959 (Pat) at [107]:
     'The claim as granted included a feature (asymmetric peripheral stiffening band (PSB)) which was a generalisation from the disclosure of the application. The application included a clear and unambiguous disclosure of PSBs which would fall within the claim but it did not describe them in that general way. Floyd LJ held that although the claim covered asymmetric PSBs in general, it did not disclose any configuration of PSB which is not disclosed in the application ...'.
3   *Bonzel (T) v Intervention Ltd (No 3)* [1991] RPC 553 (Patents Court) at p. 574. Cited with approval in *AP Racing Ltd v Alcon Components Ltd* [2014] EWCA Civ 40 at [8].
4   *European Central Bank v Document Security Systems* [2007] EWHC 600 (Patents Court) approved on appeal at [2008] EWCA 192 (Court of Appeal) at para [12].
5   *Vector Corp v Glatt Air Techniques Ltd* [2007] EWCA 805 (Court of Appeal) at para [7].
6   *Napp Pharmaceutical Holdings Ltd v ratiopharm* [2009] EWCA 252 (Court of Appeal) at para [71].
7   G 01/93 *ADVANCED SEMICONDUCTOR PRODUCTS/Limiting feature* [1994] OJ EPO 541; [1995] EPOR 97, certain aspects of which were analysed in some detail in *Napp Pharmaceutical Holdings Ltd v ratiopharm* [2009] EWCA 252 (Court of Appeal) at paras [72]–[85].
8   *AP Racing Ltd v Alcon Components Ltd* [2014] EWCA Civ. 40.
9   *Richardson-Vicks Patent* [1995] RPC 568 (Patents Court) at p. 576. Cited with approval in *AP Racing Ltd v Alcon Components Ltd* [2014] EWCA Civ 40 at [9].
10   *Texas Iron Works Inc's Patent* [2000] RPC 207 (Court of Appeal) at pp. 244–47.
11   *Research in Motion Limited v Inpro Licensing SARL* [2006] EWHC 70 (Patents Court); [2007] EWCA 51(Court of Appeal) at [72].
12   *Virgin Atlantic Airways Ltd v Premium Aircraft Interiors UK Ltd* [2009]; EWCA 1062 (Court of Appeal) at para [68]. However, the test for divisional applications is no different, and in *Novartis AG & Ors v Focus Pharmaceuticals Ltd & Ors* [2015] EWHC 1068 (Pat) there was held to have been an impermissible addition of matter, the judge having previously observed at [104]:
     'In the present case, as counsel for *Novartis* stressed, I am concerned with a Patent which was granted as a result of a divisional application. As counsel for *Novartis* submitted, it follows that it is neither surprising, nor objectionable, that the Patent has been confined to part of the subject matter contained in the Application. The Defendants contend, however, that, at least if the claim is construed as Novartis

contend and I have accepted, the amendments made to the Application during prosecution leading to the grant of the Patent do not simply confine the Patent to part of the subject matter contained in the Application, but amount to the disclosure of a new invention altogether.'

13 *Assidoman Multipack v Mead* [1995] FSR 225 (Patents Court).

14 *A C Edwards Ltd v Acme Signs & Displays* [1990] RPC 621 (Patents Court).

15 *Palmaz's European Patents* [1999] RPC 47 (Patents Court) at p. 71.

16 *AP Racing Ltd v Alcon Components Ltd* [2014] EWCA Civ 40. As subsequently observed in *IPCOM GmbH & Co Kg v HTC Europe Co Ltd & Ors* [2015] EWHC 1034 (Pat) at [125]:

'... as the line of cases leading from *AC Edwards* to *AP Racing* paragraph 33 explains, English patent law draws a distinction between coverage and disclosure. To amount to added matter the intermediate generalisation must be a generalisation in terms of disclosure, not coverage. In other words to characterise a claim as an intermediate generalisation is not sufficient to establish the presence of added matter. Proving that a claim is an intermediate generalisation in terms of coverage does not establish added matter.'

17 *Nokia OYJ (Nokia Corporation) v IPCom GmbH & Co Kg* [2012] EWCA Civ 567. For further applications of the principle, see *Koninklijke Philips Electronics N.V. v Nintendo of Europe Gmbh* [2014] EWHC 1959 (Pat) at [106] on, and observing at [104], having summarized *AP Racing Ltd v Alcon Components Ltd*, as set out in fn 16 above: 'This does not mean that any generalising amendment is allowable but it emphasises that the fact an amendment is a generalisation does not necessarily mean it is unallowable.'

18 *Hospira UK Limited v Genentech Inc No 2* [2014] EWHC 3857. See also the discussion at paras [168]–[172].

Disclaimers

5.24   Since they will typically have no apparent basis in the application as filed, the use of disclaimers to narrow claim scope might be thought to present particular difficulties from the perspective of adding matter. A disclaimer is an amendment to a claim which incorporates a 'negative' technical feature, typically excluding from a general feature specific embodiments or areas. An appropriate use of a disclaimer would be, for example, to disclaim matter disclosed in an earlier filed application that is unpublished at the priority date of the later one (and so constitutes a novelty only referenced against the later one under PA 1977, s 2(3)). Disclaimers can be added either in the course of prosecution or post-grant.

It has been confirmed by the EPO Enlarged Board of Appeal[1] that a disclaimer need not have basis in the application as filed. However, it must comply with the other requirements there set out, and in order so as not to be regarded as adding matter must not be, or become relevant for the assessment of inventive step or insufficiency of disclosure, consistent with the following passage from the earlier decision of the Enlarged Board in G 1/93 *Limiting Feature/ADVANCED SEMICONDUCTOR PRODUCTS*:[2]

'16   Whether or not the adding of an undisclosed feature limiting the scope of protection conferred by the patent as granted would be contrary to the purpose of Article 123(2) EPC to prevent an applicant from getting an unwarranted advantage by obtaining patent protection for something he had not properly disclosed and maybe not even invented on the date of filing of the application, depends on the circumstances. If such added feature, although limiting the scope of protection conferred by the patent, has to be considered as providing a technical contribution to the subject-matter of the claimed invention, it would, in the view of the Enlarged Board, give an unwarranted advantage to the patentee contrary to the above purpose of Article 123(2) EPC. Consequently, such feature would constitute added subject-matter within the meaning of that provision. A typical example of this seems to be the case, where the limiting feature is creating an inventive selection not disclosed in the application as filed or otherwise derivable therefrom. If, on the other hand, the feature in question merely excludes protection for part of the subject-matter of the claimed invention as covered by the application as filed, the adding of such feature cannot reasonably be considered to give any unwarranted advantage to the applicant. Nor does it adversely affect the interests of third parties (cf. para 12 above). In the view of the Enlarged Board, such feature is, on a proper interpretation of Article 123(2) EPC, therefore not to be considered as *subject-matter extending beyond the content of the application as filed* within the meaning of that provision.'

The English courts have applied these principles[3] and have on occasion, as in *Sudarshan v Clariant,* rejected a proposed disclaimer on the grounds that it would add matter, having in this particular case summarized such principles as follows:

'[84]   ... In summary, and so far as relevant to this case, such a disclaimer may be allowed to restore novelty against an accidental anticipation, that is to say, an anticipation which is so unrelated to and remote from the claimed invention that the person skilled in the art would never have taken it into account when making the invention.'

The Enlarged Board has also provided further guidance in the context of disclaimers of subject matter[4] disclosed as an embodiment of the invention in the application as filed.

1   G 01/03 *Disclaimer/PPG* & G 02/03 *Disclaimer/GENETIC SYSTEMS* [2004] EPOR 33.
2   G 01/93 Limiting feature/*ADVANCED SEMICONDUCTOR PRODUCTS* [1994] OJ EPO 541; [1995] EPOR 97.
3   See for example, *LG Philips LCD Co Ltd v Tatung (UK) Ltd and others* [2006] EWCA Civ 1774; *Napp Pharmaceutical Holdings Ltd v Ratiopharm GmbH* [2009] EWCA Civ 252; [2009] RPC 18; *Sudarshan Chemical Industries Ltd v Clariant Produkte (Deutschland) GmbH* [2013] EWCA 919.
4   G 02/10 *Disclaimer/SCRIPPS* (Enlarged Board of Appeal, 30 August 2011).

Extension of protection

5.25   There is little or no case law on extension of protection because the amendment of already granted claims (or their limitation) is by its nature subject to a greater degree of administrative or judicial scrutiny than the amendment of claims, and/or description in the course of prosecution.[1] Instead the ban on extending the protection conferred by a granted claim most often arises in the context of what has come to be called the 'inescapable trap'. This arises where the addition of matter has taken place through an impermissible narrowing of a claim in prosecution, which has for example been limited by reference to a feature which has no basis in the patent, but which is not regarded as a permissible disclaimer. Such added matter cannot be excised by amendment after grant to delete the impermissible limitation from the claims, as to do so would be to extend the protection afforded by the patent after grant. Such a claim is inescapably invalid.

1   See *Hospira UK Ltd v Genentech Inc No 2* [2014] EWHC 3857 at [105]–[124] for a rare example of such an objection.

Chapter 6

Patent infringement – substantive law

Structure

Types of infringing acts

Introduction

6.01   This chapter discusses what types of act constitute infringement, as well as the special defences that can prevent a patentee whose patent is held to be valid, and within the scope of at least one claim of which the defendant is operating, from succeeding in their claim. It concludes with the remedies for infringement. It also discusses the vexed question of how one assesses whether what the defendant is doing actually falls within the scope of any claims of the patent in issue – namely the question of claim interpretation or construction, and the scope of protection.

Although it is self-evident that dealing in some way in an article that is the subject of a product claim, will infringe a patent with such a claim, as will performing a process the subject of a process claim, the law has in most countries gone rather further so that a range of other activities fall within the definition of infringement. A starting point is the current international minimum standard, setting out those acts which constitute infringement, namely that set out in the Agreement on Trade Related Aspects of Intellectual Property (TRIPS) which by Article 28(1) provides that:

'A patent shall confer on its owner the following exclusive rights:

(a)   where the subject matter of a patent is a product, to prevent third parties not having the owner's consent from the acts of: making, using, offering for sale, selling, or importing for these purposes that product;

(b)   where the subject matter of a patent is a process, to prevent third parties not having the owner's consent from the act of using the process, and from the acts of: using, offering for sale, selling, or importing for these purposes at least the product obtained directly by that process.'

Equating the 'subject matter of the patent' with the patent claims, the definition here of product claim infringement calls for no special comment, but it is to be noted that the definition of process claim infringement extends not only to using the process, but also to acts on 'at least the product obtained directly by that process'. In that one of those acts is import, this presupposes that the infringing process has been carried out in another country, where perhaps there is no corresponding patent. This reflects an earlier provision found in Article 5 quater of the Paris Convention:

'Patents: Importation of Products Manufactured by a Process Patented in the Importing Country

When a product is imported into a country of the Union where there exists a patent protecting a process of manufacture of the said product, the patentee shall have all the rights, with regard to the imported product, that are accorded to him by the legislation of the country of importation, on the basis of the process patent, with respect to products manufactured in that country.'

To infringe on these bases there is no need for the infringer to be aware that he or she is infringing, although a patentee may well not be entitled to the same remedies against an 'innocent infringer' as against one who goes into things with eyes open. Thus, in the UK, PA 1977, s 62 provides that in patent infringement proceedings 'damages shall not be awarded, and no order shall be made for an account of profits, against a defendant ... who proves that at the date of the infringement he was not aware, and had no reasonable grounds for supposing, that the patent existed ...'. Defendants have succeeded under this provision in certain cases.[1] However, this provision does not avoid liability for legal costs or preclude the grant of an injunction against future infringement, or indeed damages or an account of profits in respect of continuing acts once the defendant becomes aware of the assertion as against it.

These types of infringement are termed 'direct infringement' to distinguish them from another type of infringement, not mandated by TRIPS, but which is found in the legal systems of most countries, and which does generally require some element of knowledge – namely that of 'contributory infringement'. In the UK and most of the rest of Europe there are specific definitions of both direct and contributory infringement, based on Articles 25–26 of the Community Patent Convention (CPC) respectively. In the UK, these provide the first statutory expression of what sort of acts infringe – the law before PA 1977 as to this was entirely judge-made.

A party that does not itself directly or indirectly infringe in accordance with the statutory language (because, for example, it does nothing in the UK) may, if there is a 'common design', also be liable as a 'joint tortfeasor' with one that is a direct (or possibly indirect) infringer. The case law as to the application of this general principle of tort law to the field of patent law has primarily developed in the context of attempts to join such parties to applications for the purposes of securing disclosure from them that is not in the possession of the alleged direct infringer and so is discussed in **Chapter 4** at para 4.19.

1   See for example, *Lux Traffic v Pike Signals* [1993] RPC 107, *Texas Iron Work's Patent* [2000] RPC 207 and *Schenck Rotec v Universal Balancing* [2012] EWHC 1920.

Direct infringement

6.02   Article 25 (1989 version) of the CPC (to which PA 1977, s 60(1) is by s 130(7) 'so framed as to have, as nearly as practicable, the same effects in the United Kingdom as the corresponding [provision of the CPC has in the territories to which it applies]'), is headed 'Prohibition of direct use of the invention' and provides:

'A Community patent shall confer on its proprietor the right to prevent all third parties not having his consent:

(a)   from making, offering, putting on the market or using a product which is the subject matter of the patent, or importing or stocking the product for these purposes;

(b)   from using a process which is the subject matter of the patent or, when the third party knows, or it is obvious in the circumstances, that the use of the process is prohibited without the consent of the proprietor of the patent, from offering the process for use within the territories of the Contracting States;

(c)   from offering, putting on the market, using or importing or stocking for these purposes of the product obtained directly by a process which is the subject matter of the patent.'

The second of these provisions goes further than required by TRIPS. Its UK equivalent, PA 1977, s 60(1)(b) makes it an infringement to: '... offer [a process] for use in the United Kingdom when [one] knows, or it is obvious to a reasonable person in the circumstances, that its use there without the consent of the proprietor would be an infringement of the patent'.

The fact that the infringer in such a case is not itself using the process or dealing in its products makes this a type of indirect infringement, a categorization that is reinforced by the requirement of knowledge, although this does rather beg the question of what level of knowledge, and of what, is required to infringe on this basis. However, there is only limited English case law on this particular aspect of this ground of infringement, and such as there has been has not had cause to address such issues.[1]

Apart from this, PA 1977, s 60(1)(a)–(b) have not, in themselves provided many particular problems of interpretation. The issue of what is meant in s 60(1)(a) by the word 'make' can occasionally cause problems, particularly in the context of repair and reconditioning, as in *United Wire v Screen Repair Services (Scotland)*[2] and *Schütz v Werit.*[3] In the former case, having quoted from *Sirdar Rubber v Wallington, Weston & Co*[4] that: 'you may prolong the life of a licensed article but you must not make a new one under the cover of repair' the House of Lords found that the defendants, by reconditioning patented articles, had gone further than repair, and were making and thus infringing. In the latter case, in which the former case is also analysed, the patent claim was to a combination of a container, and a protective cage for it. The invention lay in the protective cage but the reconditioning exercise involved replacing containers in cages first placed on the market by or with the consent of the patentee. Accepting that 'the notions of making and repair may well overlap' but observing that an attempt to distinguish between the two might sometimes be useful, the Supreme Court held on the facts of this particular case that there was no 'making' of the patented article, and hence no infringement.

The application of PA 1977, s 60(1)(a) to a 'kit of parts' also arises from time to time. Thus the Patents Court in *Lacroix Duarib v Kwikform*[5] refused to strike out an assertion that a kit of parts made in the UK for export, infringed a claim of a UK patent to the assembled article, and in *Virgin Atlantic Airways v Delta Air Lines*[6] concluded, again in a summary application rather than after a full trial, that although as a matter of law it was arguable that manufacture in the UK of a complete kit of parts for assembling a patented device could infringe, it was not arguable that manufacture in the UK of an incomplete kit of parts subsequently exported could do so. On appeal in the latter case, the Court of Appeal did not address these issues but observed as to them that it did not think 'these rather abstract questions of law' should be decided on a summary judgment application as the answers could be highly fact sensitive.

It has also been held that an 'offer' to supply an infringing product after patent expiry does not itself infringe, even if the offer is made whilst the patent still subsists.[7] The same view is not necessarily taken in other European countries, where there has been controversy as to offers made whilst the patent subsists to sell pharmaceuticals after patent expiry. Also, it is no answer to a claim of infringement to argue that it is *de minimis*.[8]

The Patent Act 1977, s 60(1)(c) corresponding to the third of the CPC provisions quoted above (and also EPC, Article 64(2)), as with TRIPS, Article 28(1)(b) does however present an evident difficulty of interpretation in the word 'directly'. In *Pioneer Electronics Capital v Warner Music Manufacturing Europe*[9] the Patents Court struck out an allegation that the manufacture of compact discs infringed where the process in issue took place outside the UK, but there were three steps intervening between that process and the end product, holding that:

'[The defendants' discs] are not the immediate or direct product obtained by the claimed process. [They] differ in material to that which would be the result of using the claimed process and are the result of three further steps of production. All those steps of production are material and important steps in arriving at the end product.'

The Patents Court found assistance from the writings of Dutch and German jurists, and in commentaries on Swiss, Danish and Austrian law, in relation to the background to and intent behind the provision. The judgment was upheld by the Court of Appeal, which went behind the writings of jurists, into nine of the German cases, and identified a common principle behind these:

'The product obtained directly by means of a patented process is the product with which the process ends; it does not cease to be the product so obtained if it is subjected to further processing which does not cause it to lose its identity, there being no such loss where it retains its essential characteristics.'

The Court of Appeal also analysed the cases from the Netherlands, Switzerland, Denmark, and Austria, and found that they all supported this 'loss of identity' test, rather than a free-standing 'essential characteristics' test as had been asserted by the patentee. Applying this to the present case there was no identity between the masters and the finished discs, and so there could be no infringement.

What was meant in this context by the word 'directly' was considered in relation to a drill bit that was alleged to have been designed in accordance with a patented method in *Halliburton Energy Services v Smith International*:[10]

'93.   If I am wrong on the meaning of "axial" in the claim, there is no infringement, either of claim 3 or claim 6. Smith do not design or manufacture bits within the jurisdiction, so infringement of claim 3 is alleged by virtue of subsection 60(1)(c) of the Patents Act 1977. The invention is a process, and so the product sold in the United Kingdom must be obtained directly by means of the claimed process. "Obtained directly" has been considered in two cases cited to me, particularly *Pioneer Electronics Capital Inc v Warner Music Manufacturing Europe GmbH* [1997] RPC 757, and a decision *'Halbleiterbauelemente"* in the Landgericht Dusseldorf 6 May 1997. The Court of Appeal have held that "obtained directly" means "without intermediary" or immediately. This seems to exclude the possibility of further processing: but the *Halbleiterbauelemente* case suggests that further use or processing may take place provided that its effect is not to obscure the qualities of the product directly obtained.

94.   The result of the performance of the claimed method is, if I am right on the question of construction, a CAD file containing a design of bit balanced under design conditions. The CAD file is input to a numerically controlled milling machine to produce (separately) the cones, either milled in one piece with the teeth or with recesses to receive the inserts, which are themselves milled to the design recorded in the CAD file. The cones are then assembled with the associated bearings, seals and other ironmongery into a bit body. Is the result "directly obtained" by means of the process?

95.   Smith's approach to this question is understandably to point to the design as the endpoint of the claimed process, and to decompose the subsequent manufacturing process into as many steps as reasonably possible. Whatever is using the CAD files resulting from a session with the simulation software is not obtained directly by use of the process but (I paraphrase) by employing the design in further manufacture. They identify the following steps as producing "an independent article which is not the thing that came out of the claimed process".

96.   I do not think that it is sensible to view manufacture and design as in some way resulting in separate products. Design is no doubt interesting in the abstract, but when it is used it cannot be divorced from the article made to it. The Registered Designs Act 1949 and its predecessors encouraged lawyers to consider a design as something complete in itself and distinct from any article, but from the point of view of a bit designer the design exists only as

a depiction of a bit that is to be made and used. There is no doubt that the criterion with which the claimed method is concerned depend upon the bit shape as a whole (I shall discuss this further when I consider insufficiency) and it follows, it seems to me, that there is no intermediate between this method and the resulting bit, which is as much the direct product of the design process as it is the product of the manufacturing process of which the design is part.

97.   I should add that the EPO's great reluctance to grant "product by process" claims on the unchallengeably logical basis that novelty cannot be conferred on an old article by making it according to a new process encourages me to give s 60(1)(c) an interpretation that goes as far as a product by process claim might go, but no further.'

The decision in the German *Halbleiterbauelemente* case referred to here has not been reported, but in translation the relevant parts provide:

'2.   Contrary to the view taken by the Defendants, the semiconductor assembly elements manufactured by Defendant (2) represents direct products of the process claimed in claim 7 of the Plaintiff's patent.

Claim 7, on which the Plaintiff's current application for relief focuses, relates to a manufacturing process and not, as the Defendants claim, a simple working method. This is supported the very wording of claim 7, which speaks of a process (used) "in the *manufacture* of semiconductor assembly elements". That the process suggested by claim 7 of the Plaintiff's patent is a manufacturing process can also be seen from the general description (column 31 to 42) in which it is stated that also, according to the invention a process for the gas etching of aluminium and aluminium oxide in the manufacture of semiconductor assembly elements is suggested. It cannot therefore seriously be doubted that the so-called wafer (circuit board) created using the process described in claim 7 of the Plaintiff's patent is a direct product of a protected process in terms of § 6 clause 2 PatG (1968) – which is applicable here. Presumably even the Defendants see that this is the case when they argue that "the direct product of the claimed etching process is an etched unfinished silicon wafer, not a semiconductor assembly element" (see sheet 211 of the statement of defence).

Contrary to this view, however, the semiconductor assembly element created from the wafer also represents a direct product of a protected process in terms of § 6 clause 2 PatG (1968).

Although, as the Defendants correctly point out, the insertion of the term "direct" in the wording of the law was intended to achieve a clear limitation of the protection of the product of a protected process, this formulation makes it clear that a simple causal relationship is not in itself sufficient, that therefore it is not sufficient, in order for a product to be protected, if the protected process has only somehow come into use at some point or other in the manufacturing process. Otherwise, it does not follow, either from the letter of the law or from the purpose and history of introduction of the law, that an object would have to lose its property of being a "direct" product of the protected process simply through any further working or processing (OLG Dusseldorf), judgment of 15.9.1977

– 2 U 148/76 – cited in *Bruchhausen*, GRUR 1979, 743). Classification under patent law as a "direct product of a protected process" cannot be denied in that an object manufactured in accordance with the (protected) process subsequently undergoes a more or less trivial or obvious further treatment. As the Dusseldorf Regional Appeal Court correctly stated in its decision cited above, the protection of § 6 clause 2 PatG (1968) would be practically worthless given such an interpretation of the provision since it would be all too easy to circumvent, and the provision would not be able to fulfil its purpose of providing the inventor with the protection appropriate to their contribution. Nor, proceeding from this basis, can the Court follow the view according to which the finished product should not be regarded as a direct product of a protected process if the protected process only serves to manufacture an intermediate product (see RGSt 42, 357, 358). In such cases too, the finished product must be regarded as a "direct" product of a protected process if it is still influenced by and so strongly characterised by the important characteristics of the intermediate product that the market identifies the intermediate product with the finished product (see the Court's judgment of 21.3.1961 – 4 O 333/60 – cited by Pechmann, GRUR 1962, 7, 8; by Pechmann, GRUR 1977, 377, 378; *Klauer-Mohring, Patent Law*, 3rd edition, § 6 annotation 137; see also Beier/Ohly, GRUR int. 1966, 973 et seq.).

However, this also applies to the relationship between wafer and semiconductor assembly element, because the semiconductor assembly element does not differ, in its relevant properties resulting from the invented etching process, from the intermediate product, the wafer. The (divided) wafer is retained, in principle, in the chip. The semiconductor assembly elements created from the wafer are characterised by its functional properties and performance data. These functional properties and performance data are determined by the dimension and position of the circuit paths, the width of which is undisputedly less than 2 uM. Nothing further is changed in the circuit paths and their pattern following the manufacture of wafer. The extreme miniaturisation and conducting speed of the Defendants' finished semiconductor assembly elements is thus the direct consequence of the plasma etching process as claimed in the patent, to which the vertically straight-running walls of the conducting paths and erosion of the material are attributable.'

Both English decisions were reviewed by the Patents Court in *Medimmune v Novartis*[11] which took issue with the observation in *Halliburton* that the Court of Appeal in *Pioneer* excluded the possibility of further processing, but thought that the decision in *Halliburton* was consistent with the principle in *Pioneer* that there could be further processing provided there was no loss of identity, and that the decision in the German *Halbleiterbauelemente* case was also consistent with that. The Court in *Medimmune*, having also considered a discussion of this ground of infringement in a biotechnology context in *Monsanto v Cargill*[12] went on to reject a submission by the defendant that the loss of identity test could not be applied without qualification in the present case. Thus the English courts will not take an overly narrow view of the word 'directly' in this context.

1   See *Tamglass v Luoyang* [2006] EWHC 65 at [33]–[43].
2   *United Wire Ltd v Screen Repair Services (Scotland) Ltd* [2000] 4 All ER 353, [2001] RPC 24. See also below at para 6.13.
3   *Schütz (UK) Ltd v Werit (UK) Ltd* [2010] EWHC 660 (Pat), [2011] EWCA Civ 1337, [2013] UKSC 16. See also *Nestec SA & Ors v Dualit Ltd & Ors* [2013] EWHC 923 (Pat) at paras [183]–[205].
4   *Sirdar Rubber v Wallington, Weston & Co* (1907) 24 RPC 539 at p. 543.
5   *Lacroix Duarib v Kwikform (UK)* [1998] FSR 493.
6   *Virgin Atlantic Airways v Delta Air Lines* [2010] EWHC 3094 (Patents Court); [2011] EWCA 162 (Court of Appeal) at paras [8]–[12].
7   *Gerber Garment Technology Inc v Lectra Systems Ltd* [1995] RPC 383 (Court of Appeal) at pp. 411–12. See also **Chapter 7** at para 7.23.
8   *Monsanto v Cargill* [2007] EWHC 2257 (Patents Court) at [85]. Not addressed on appeal – see fn 12 below.
9   *Pioneer Electronics Capital v Warner Music Manufacturing Europe* [1995] RPC 487; [1997] RPC 757 (Court of Appeal).
10   *Halliburton Energy Services Inc v Smith International (North Sea) Ltd* [2005] EWHC 1623 (Pat). Appealed as to validity only.
11   *Medimmune Limited v Novartis Pharmaceuticals UK Limited* [2011] EWHC 1669 (Patents Court) at paras [529]–[549].
12   *Monsanto Technology LLC v Cargill International SA* [2006] EWHC 2864 (Patents Court – strike out application) and [2007] EWHC 2257 (Patents Court – full trial). See also **Chapter 8** at 8.18.

Indirect infringement

6.03   The TRIPS Agreement does not mandate any protection against contributory, or indirect, patent infringement, but such provisions are found in the laws of most European countries. CPC, Article 26 (1989 version) (to which PA 1977, ss 60(2)–(3) respectively correspond by s 130(7)) is headed 'Prohibition of indirect use of the invention' and paras 1–2 of this provide:

'1   A Community patent shall also confer on its proprietor the right to prevent all third parties not having his consent from supplying or offering to supply within the territories of the Contracting States a person, other than a party entitled to exploit the patented invention, with means, relating to an essential element of that invention, for putting it into effect therein, when the third party knows, or it is obvious in the circumstances, that these means are suitable and intended for putting that invention into effect.

2   Paragraph 1 shall not apply when the means are staple commercial products, except when the third party induces the person supplied to commit acts prohibited by Article 25.'

This would, for example, cover the supply of a product which is not itself the subject of a patent but which is so designed as to be used in a patented method. However, there has been remarkably little case law on these provisions in the UK, and until recently very little by way of detailed analysis. In *Lacroix Duarib SA v Kwikform (UK) Ltd*[1] it was common ground that the supply of a kit of parts in the UK would infringe a claim of a UK patent to the assembled article under PA 1977, s 60(2), and in *Virgin Atlantic Airways v Delta Air Lines*[2] the Court of Appeal accepted that the manufacture of an incomplete kit that was used in the UK to assemble the whole patented article might do so. In *Furr v Truline*[3] on an application for an interim injunction, a determination that the defendant had not intended the articles that it supplied be used in the claimed manner avoided a finding that it was a contributory infringer.[4] In contrast, in *Chapman v McAnulty*[5] although the device in issue itself fell outside the scope of the claim, it could easily be modified to fall within it, and the Patents Court, having observed that 'this must be a matter of impression' went on to hold:

'Section 60(2) does not require that the supply complained of will involve the invention being put into effect by all users of the thing supplied. It is sufficient if it is shown that the invention will be put into effect by some users. One would only disregard maverick or unlikely use of the thing.'

This decision was relied on in the extensive discussion of the section, and the background to it in *Grimme v Scott*[6] in which a submission that the 'means' for the purposes of the section must be incomplete was rejected, and the degree of knowledge required by the section was analysed in detail. Accordingly the supply of an agricultural machine for separating potatoes having a steel roller that took it outside the scope of the patent claim, but which roller could be replaced with an elastomeric one to take it within the scope of the patent claim, where this very replaceability was promoted as a selling feature, fell within the section.

The following propositions as to knowledge and intention for the purposes of PA 1977, s 60(2) were drawn from *Grimme* by the Court of Appeal in *KCI Licensing v Smith & Nephew*:[7]

'[53] ...

(i) The required intention is to put the invention into effect. The question is what the supplier knows or ought to know about the intention of the person who is in a position to put the invention into effect – the person at the end of the supply chain, [108].

(ii) It is enough if the supplier knows (or it is obvious to a reasonable person in the circumstances) that some ultimate users will intend to use or adapt the "means" so as to infringe, [107(i)] and [114].

(iii) There is no requirement that the intention of the individual ultimate user must be known to the defendant at the moment of the alleged infringement, [124].

(iv) Whilst it is the intention of the ultimate user which matters, a future intention of a future ultimate user is enough if that is what one would expect in all the circumstances, [125].

(v) The knowledge and intention requirements are satisfied if, at the time of supply or offer to supply, the supplier knows, or it is obvious to a reasonable person in the circumstances, that ultimate users will intend to put the invention into effect. This has to be proved on the usual standard of the balance of probabilities. It is not enough merely that the means are suitable for putting the invention into effect (for that is a separate requirement), but it is likely to be the case where the supplier proposes or recommends or even indicates the possibility of such use in his promotional material. [131]'

In *Agilent Technologies v Waters*[8] it was held that an instruction manual for the manual pump in issue, which recommended settings close to those required by the patent claims to an automatic pump, were not 'means' for the purposes of PA 1977, s 60(2), as the instruction manual was not a feature of the pump in issue itself. In *Menashe Business Mercantile v William Hill Organisation*[9] where the 'means' was a CD with a computer program on it that allowed a user to communicate with an offshore host computer, it was held that it was no defence to an action under PA 1977, s 60(2) in relation to a claim to a system, one component of which was a host computer, that the host computer, unlike the rest of the claimed apparatus, was not located in the UK. The assertion that the supply of a pharmaceutical which converted in the body into its active metabolite infringed a patent to the metabolite under PA 1977, s 60(2) was conceded by the defendants in *Merrell Dow v Norton*[10] so the courts had no opportunity to consider this issue.

In *Pavel v Sony*[11] the English Court of Appeal declined an opportunity to consider what was meant by 'essential element of the invention' as it found the patent invalid. The equivalent provision under German law has, however, been addressed on number of occasions by the German courts, for example, in *DIBV v HS*:[12]

'... for a means to be an "essential element of the invention" it does not have to be the means which sets the invention apart from the prior art. Individual parts which are already known in themselves, but which are used in a patented combination can be the subject of an indirect infringement of a patent, for example if the individual parts in question are an essential element in relation to the combination patent as granted. Whether this is the case, that is to say, whether a specific means is essential or inessential to the invention, can be meaningfully assessed only from the technical teaching that the patent protects. The deciding factor is whether the means in question is of essential or only secondary importance to the patented teaching, namely to the actual core of the invention.'

More recently the Patents Court has considered the issue in *Nestec v Dualit*[13] observing, at [168]–[176]:

'[168]   ... There appears to be no English authority as to the correct approach to this requirement which is directly in point, but it has been considered by the courts of a number of other countries which have implemented Article 26 CPC in their law, notably the courts of the Netherlands and Germany. Unhappily, the Supreme Court of the Netherlands and the Bundesgerichtshof (Federal Court of Justice) in Germany have adopted different approaches to this question.

[169] In *Impeller Flow Meter* [Case X ZR 48/03] the reasoning of the Federal Court of Justice in relation to section 10 of the German Patents Act, which implements Article 26 CPC, was as follows:

"The criterion of the suitability of the means to interact functionally with an essential element of the invention in the implementation of the protected inventive idea excludes such means that – such as the energy needed for the operation of a protected device – might be suitable for being used in the exploitation of the invention but which contribute nothing to the implementation of the technical teaching of the invention. If a means makes such a contribution, it will, on the other hand, generally not depend on the feature or features of the patent claim that interact with the means. For, what is an element of the patent claim is, as a rule for this reason alone, also an essential element of the invention. The patent claim defines the protected invention and limits the protection granted to the patent holder to forms of exploitation that implement all the features of the invention. As a mirror image of each individual feature's function to limit protection in this way, each individual feature is fundamentally also an appropriate point of reference for the prohibition on the supply of means within the meaning of Sec. 10 of the Patent Act. In particular, it is not possible to determine the essential element of an invention according to whether they distinguish the subject matter of the patent claim from the state of the art. It is not infrequently the case that all the features of a patent claim as such are known in the state of the art. For this reason, this does not provide a suitable criterion for differentiation."

[170] Thus the Court proceeded on the basis that the means in question must contribute to implementing the technical teaching of the invention. It rejected the contention that a feature could only be an essential element of the claim for this purpose if it served to distinguish the subject matter of the claim from the prior art i.e. was novel in its own right.

[171] This reasoning was amplified by the Court in *Pipette System* (Case X ZR 38/06) as follows:

"18. In accordance with the case law of the Senate, a means refers to an essential element of the invention if it is suitable to interact in a functional way with one or several features of the patent claim when implementing the protected thought behind the invention (BGHZ 159, 76, 85 – *Impeller Flow Meter*). Means that can be used during the application of the invention but which however contribute nothing to the implementation of the teachings of the patent are not covered by these criteria. If a means provides such a contribution, it does not in principle matter with which feature or features the means interacts. This is because what is a part of the patent claim is regularly already therefore an essential element of the invention (BGHZ 159, 76, 86). The Appeal Court has correctly assumed this.

19. The nozzles in dispute relate to an essential element of the invention. The nozzle is part of the object according to the invention, which consists of the combination of a hand pipette and nozzle, which forms the protected 'system' (feature 1). With the fastening section and nozzle piston, the

nozzle itself is designed in accordance with feature 2 and, as a result, suitable to interact with the pipette in a functional way when implementing the thought behind the invention, in that the retention device in accordance with feature 5 grips and fix in the mountings of the fastening section of the pipette housing and the piston collar of the nozzle in accordance with the features 7 and 9 grip and release again by activating the activation arms, without the nozzle itself having to be touched.

20.   This is sufficient in itself for functional interaction. In this respect, it does not matter wherein the core of the invention lies. However, a feature that has a completely subordinate importance for the technical teachings of the invention can be seen as a non-essential element of the invention; such an irrelevancy for the inventive concept cannot be explained by stating that these features are known in prior art (BGHZ 159, 76, 86). The viewpoint argued as the centrepiece of the appeal on points of law, namely that the features of the nozzle contained in the patent claim relate to conventional commercially-available nozzles, is therefore insignificant. A lack of 'essentiality' can only result in a feature not contributing anything to the performance of the product, i.e. to the solution of the technical problem on which the patent is based in a accordance with the invention, whereby a contribution that is practically meaningless can be left out of consideration. This comes into consideration if, for an invention that is concerned with the continuation of a certain function of a device known as such, features are included in the patent claim that concern another function of the device not affected by the invention. Such a situation is out of the question in the present dispute, in which the relationship of the nozzle as an essential element of the invention already results from the fact that it is precisely the nozzle, its fixing to the fastening section and nozzle pistons in a certain position that serve the design in accordance with the invention.

21.   The second appeal can therefore also not succeed with the objection that that patent claim should have been aimed at a hand pipette instead of a system consisting of pipette and nozzle. The patent applicant cannot be prescribed on how to formulate the patent claims. Instead it can basically demand the grant of the patent in each way that corresponds to the technical teachings and is patentable (BGHZ 166, 347 349 et seq. – *Microprocessor*). Since the invention deals with the problem of improving the mechanics of coupling the nozzle to the pipette and disconnecting the nozzle from the pipette, it is possible and not a breach of law to include the syringe in the definition of the patented object."

[172] Again the Court emphasised that the fact the element was known in the prior art did not prevent it being an essential element of claim, but did accept that if a feature was of completely subordinate importance for the technical teaching of the invention it could be regarded as a non-essential element.

[173] In *Sara Lee v Integro* (Case C02/227HR), on the other hand, the Dutch Supreme Court upheld the conclusion of the Court of Appeal that an essential element must be one which distinguished the invention from the prior art:

"Insofar as the part complains about the explanation that the Court of Appeal thus gave to the patent, it miscarries due to what has already been considered under 3.3.2. It also miscarries otherwise. The mere circumstance that a fitting coffee bag is needed for putting the patented mechanism into effect does not automatically mean that this bag is a means relating to an essential part of the invention. Evidently and in light of the explanation that the Court of Appeal has given to the patent, the Court of Appeal was of the opinion that the coffee bag fitting the holder does not comprise an element by which, according to the patent specifications, the doctrine of the patent distinguishes itself from the state of the art. That opinion does not show any incorrect interpretation of the law."

In addition to these cases, I was referred to decisions of French and Belgian courts which appear to be more consistent with the German approach than the Dutch one.

[174]   In my judgment the German approach is more consonant with the apparent purpose of Article 26(1), which is that third parties should not be allowed to benefit from the invention by supplying means the market for which has been created by the invention, than the Dutch one. Furthermore, I consider that the Dutch approach is difficult to reconcile with Article 26(2), which makes it clear that a staple commercial product may constitute means relating to an essential element. Accordingly, I propose to follow the German approach.'

There been little English guidance as to what is meant by the expression 'staple product' in PA 1977, s 60(3). The point arose at first instance in *Pavel v Sony*[14] in which the term was interpreted as 'a product of the kind needed every day and generally obtainable' at the time when the patent application was published, following the views of German academic writers. In *Nestec v Dualit*[15] at the Patents Court agreed, at [182] with the view expressed in the High Court of Australia in *Northern Territory of Australia v Collins* [2008] HCA 49 at [145], 'albeit in a slightly different statutory context, that in order to qualify as a staple commercial product, a product must ordinarily be one which is supplied commercially for a variety of uses.'

1   *Lacroix Duarib SA v Kwikform (UK) Ltd* [1998] FSR 493.
2   *Virgin Atlantic Airways v Delta Air Lines* [2010] EWHC 3094 (Patents Court); [2011] EWCA (Court of Appeal) at paras [8]–[12].
3   *Furr v Truline* [1985] FSR 553.
4   Other cases as to the requisite level of knowledge in the context of PA 1977, s 60(2) are *Helitune v Stewart Hughes Ltd* [1991] FSR 171, holding that to establish liability it was only necessary that the defendant know the use to which the part that it supplied would be put, and *Ward Building Systems v Hodgson Steels* (3 June 1997,unreported) (Patents Court) (British Library C/47/97) holding that it that was only necessary that the defendant know that the items supplied were essential to a product or process 'that may be patentable'.
5   *Chapman v McAnulty* (29 February 1996, unreported) Jacob J (Patents Court).
6   *Grimme Maschinenfabrik GmbH & Co KG v Derek Scott* [2009] EWHC 2691 (Patents Court), [2010] EWCA 1110 (Court of Appeal) at paras [70]–[131].
7   *KCI Licensing Inc v Smith & Nephew plc* [2010] EWCA 1260 (Court of Appeal) at para [53].

8   *Agilent Technologies Deutschland GmbH v Waters Corpn* [2004] EWHC 2992 (Patents Court).
9   *Menashe Business Mercantile v William Hill Organisation* [2002] EWHC 397 (Patents Court), [2002] EWCA 1702 (Court of Appeal).
10   *Merrell Dow v Norton* [1994] RPC 1; [1995] RPC 233 (Court of Appeal); [1996] RPC 76 (House of Lords) – discussed further in **Chapter 7** at para 7.18. See also *Idenix Pharmaceutical, Inc v Gilead Sciences, Inc & Ors* [2014] EWHC 3916 (Pat) at [615]–[619].
11   *Pavel v Sony* (21 March 1996, unreported) (Court of Appeal), partially reported in *The Times*, 22 March 1996.
12   *DIBV v HS* [2000] ENPR 194 (Dusseldorf Court of Appeal).
13   *Nestec SA & Ors v Dualit Ltd & Ors* [2013] EWHC 923 (Pat).
14   *Pavel v Sony* (13 January 1993, unreported) HHJ Ford (Patents County Court) (British Library CC/14/93). See also *DIBV v HS* [2000] ENPR 194 (Dusseldorf Court of Appeal) holding that a product cannot be a staple commercial product where it is custom made, even if of a type that is generally sold. See also several discussions of the same expression in Australian law in *Northern Territory v Collins* [2008] HCA 49 (High Court of Australia, 16 October 2008).
15   *Nestec SA & Ors v Dualit Ltd & Ors* [2013] EWHC 923 (Pat). See also *Koninklijke Philips Electronics N.V. v Nintendo of Europe Gmbh* [2014] EWHC 1959 (Pat) at [134]–[140] although as noted at [134], 'neither party explored the details of the test for infringement under s 60(2).'

Claim construction and the scope of protection

Introduction

6.04   The preceding discussion has assumed that the allegedly infringing activity in issue falls within the scope of one or more claims of the patent. However, in practice, determining whether this is so can be difficult, and much time and effort in patent infringement litigation can go into making such determinations. In the UK, the basic rule as with the construction of any document, is that one should read the claim through the eyes of, and with the mindset of its notional addressee, and simply give this the meaning which such addressee would understand the wording to bear. Given its technical nature this may not in practice be very easy, particularly as by tradition a claim, no matter how long, is always in one sentence, and it may be necessary to refer to the specification even to begin to be able to understand what the claim seems to be saying.

As the purpose of the claims is to define and to limit, one might think that the claim wording sets the absolute boundaries of what is protected. However, courts in most countries are prepared to bend the rules a little, and to hold that something which appears not literally to fall within the scope of a claim is nevertheless an infringement. The terminology for this, and the ways of so doing vary: in the UK, the terms 'pith and marrow' and 'mechanical equivalent' met in the pre-PA 1977 cases for this sort of activity have now been replaced by the term 'purposive construction', as explained in more detail below, an approach which the

English courts regard as being consistent with EPC, Article 69 and its Protocol, and which apply throughout Europe.

The USA has a more liberal approach to claim construction referred to as the 'doctrine of equivalents', as explained some time ago by the US Supreme Court in *Graver Tank & Mfg v Linde Air Product:*[1]

> 'In determining whether an accused device or composition infringes a valid patent, resort must be had in the first instance to the words of the claim. If accused matter falls clearly within the claim, infringement is made out and that is the end of it. But courts have also recognised that to permit imitation of a patented invention which does not copy every literal detail would be to convert the protection of the patent grant into a hollow and useless thing. Such a limitation would leave room for – indeed encourage – the unscrupulous copyist to make unimportant and insubstantial changes and substitutions in the patent which, though adding nothing, would be enough to take the copied matter outside the claim, and hence outside the reach of law. One who seeks to pirate an invention, like one who seeks to pirate a copyrighted book or play, may be expected to introduce minor variations to conceal and shelter the piracy. Outright and forthright duplication is a dull and very rare type of infringement. To prohibit no other would place the inventor at the mercy of verbalism and would be subordinating substance to form. It would deprive him of the benefit of his invention ...

> The essence of the doctrine is that one may not practice a fraud on a patent .... To temper unsparing logic and prevent an infringer from stealing the benefit of the invention, a patentee may invoke this doctrine to proceed against the producer of a device if it performs substantially the same function in substantially the same way to obtain the same result. The theory on which it is founded is that, if two devices do the same work in substantially the same way, and accomplish substantially the same result, they are the same, even though they differ in name, form or shape .... What constitutes equivalency must be determined against the context of the patent, the prior art, and the particular circumstances of the case.... It does not require complete identity for every purpose and in every respect .... Consideration must be given to the purpose for which an ingredient is used in a patent, the qualities it has when combined with the other ingredients, and the function which it is intended to perform. An important factor is whether persons reasonably skilled in the art would have known of the interchangeability of an ingredient not contained in the patent with one that was.'

The US Supreme Court has, more recently, twice reviewed further aspects of the doctrine of equivalents.[2] The differences between the US and UK approaches were analysed by the Supreme Court of Canada in *Free World Trust v Electro Sante*[3] and in the UK the House of Lords subsequently also reviewed these issues, and commented adversely, on the US law and the doctrine of equivalents, in its authoritative judgment in *Kirin-Amgen v Hoechst Marion Roussel*[4] as set out below (at para 6.05) explaining that its breadth has to be tempered with countervailing doctrines such as 'file wrapper estoppel' which are unnecessary when adopting the narrower approach to construction that we have in Europe.

1   *Graver Tank & Mfg v Linde Air Product* 339 US 605, 607–09 (1950).
2   In *Warner-Jenkinson v Hilton Davis Chemicals* 520 US 17 (1997) and *Festo v Shoketzu Kinzoku* KK 535 US 722 (2002); [2003] FSR 10.
3   *Free World Trust v Electro Sante* 2000 SCC 66; [2001] FSR 45 at p. 877.
4   *Kirin-Amgen v Hoechst Marion Roussel* [2001] IP&T 882; [2002] RPC 1; [2002] RPC 2 (Patents Court); [2003] RPC 3 (Court of Appeal); [2004] UKHL 46; [2005] 1 All ER 667; [2005] RPC 9 (House of Lords) at paras [36]–[44] quoted below at para 6.05.

EPC, Article 69 and its Protocol

6.05   Although EPC is not primarily concerned with matters of infringement, it establishes the principles by which the scope of protection conferred by patents in the EPC Member States falls to be determined. EPC, Article 69, entitled 'Extent of Protection', states in para 1:

'1   The extent of the protection conferred by a European patent or a European patent application shall be determined by the terms of the claims. Nevertheless, the description and drawings shall be used to interpret the claims.'

The 'Protocol on the Interpretation of Article 69 EPC' as amended by EPC 2000 provides:

'Article 1 – General Principles

Article 69 should not be interpreted as meaning that the extent of the protection conferred by a European patent is to be understood as that defined by the strict, literal meaning of the wording used in the claims, the description and drawings being employed only for the purpose of resolving an ambiguity found in the claims. Nor should it be taken to mean that the claims serve only as a guideline and that the actual protection may extend to what, from a consideration of the description and drawings by a person skilled in the art, the patent proprietor has contemplated. On the contrary, it is to be interpreted as defining a position between these extremes which combines a fair protection for the patent proprietor with a reasonable degree of legal certainty for third parties.

Article 2 – Equivalents

For the purpose of determining the extent of protection conferred by a European patent, due account shall be taken of any element which is equivalent to an element specified in the claims.'

Article 2 was introduced by EPC 2000, and so came into force on 13 December 2007. The extent to which it has in fact made any change in the law throughout Europe is unclear; it has however, as a result of comments made by the House of Lords in *Kirin-Amgen v Hoechst Marion Roussel*[1] had no effect as yet in the UK.[2]

The UK courts, as with those elsewhere in Europe, have struggled to formulate predictable and generally applicable means of determining the 'middle way' mandated by Article 1 of the Protocol. Neither, although they are applying the same legal principles, will the courts throughout Europe always agree on the application of such principles to the same set of facts, although the differences between courts in the same country can be greater than those between courts in different countries. Thus, in *Improver v Remington Consumer Products*[3] on an application for an interim injunction the English Court of Appeal took account of a first instance decision in Germany in deciding to overturn the English first instance decision. However, somewhat embarrassingly, the first instance decision in Germany was itself in due course overturned. Ironically, the first instance decision after the full hearing in the same matter in England set out a three-step approach to the issue of construction and infringement which was for 15 years, until *Kirin-Amgen* downgraded it to the status of a guideline, followed by the English courts.

For the next ten years, this three-step approach to construction made little or no appearance in the English case law, until it was applied at first instance in the decision in *Actavis v Eli Lilly*[4] in 2014 in which, interestingly, the court was also called on to consider the same issues under French, Italian and Spanish law. As observed at [100]:

'[100] Since *Kirin-Amgen*, the *Improver* questions have fallen out of fashion and have rarely been referred to in judgments of the English courts in the last 10 years. This may be regarded as unfortunate given that, although the *Improver* questions have their limitations for the reasons given by Lord Hoffmann, they do provide a structured approach to the question of equivalents and they have been influential across Europe.'

Moreover the English Patents Court in this case came to a different conclusion to that which had been reached by the German court at first instance, but this German decision was reversed on appeal to accord more closely with that of the English Patents Court.

1   *Kirin-Amgen v Hoechst Marion Roussel* [2001] IP&T 882; [2002] RPC 1; [2002] RPC 2 (Patents Court); [2003] RPC 3 (Court of Appeal); [2004] UKHL 46; [2005] 1 All ER 667; [2005] RPC 9 (House of Lords).

2   In *Kirin-Amgen* at para [49] Lord Hoffmann suggested that Article 2 ought not affect matters when he observed:

'Although Article 69 prevents equivalence from extending protection outside the claims, there is no reason why it cannot be an important part of the background of facts known to the skilled man which would affect what he understood the claims to mean. That is no more than common sense. It is also expressly provided by the new Article 2 added to the Protocol by the Munich Act revising the EPC, dated 29 November 2000 (but which has not yet come into force) …'.

3   *Improver v Remington Consumer Products* [1989] RPC 69 (Court of Appeal).

4   *Actavis UK Ltd and ors v Eli Lilly* [2014] EWHC 1511 (Pat), [2015] EWCA Civ 555 (Court of Appeal). As discussed in **Chapter 7** at para 7.21 the Court of Appeal, whilst accepting that the product in issue did not directly infringe (in any such country) disagreed with the contributory infringement analysis at first instance and remitted the case back to the Patents Court.

Purposive construction and the 'Protocol questions'

6.06   The Patents Act 1977, s 60 defining, as discussed above, those types of activity which are treated as infringing, provides that: 'a person infringes a patent for an invention if ... he does [certain defined activities] in the UK in relation to the invention without the consent of the proprietor'.

The Patents Act 1977, s 125 (corresponding to EPC, Article 69 and its Protocol) defines what is meant by the word 'invention' in this and other passages, and gives guidance as to its interpretation as follows:

'(1)   For the purposes of the Act an invention for a patent for which an application has been made or for which a patent has been granted shall, unless the context otherwise requires, be taken to be that specified in a claim of the specification of the application or patent, as the case may be, as interpreted by the description and any drawings contained in that specification, and the extent of the protection conferred by a patent or application for a patent shall be determined accordingly.

....

(3)   The Protocol on the Interpretation of Article 69 of the European Patent Convention (which Article contains a provision corresponding to subsection (1) above) shall, as for the time being in force, apply for the purposes of subsection (1) above as it applies for the purposes of that Article.'

Courts in the UK apply Article 69 and the Protocol by giving claims a 'purposive' construction, by construing them in context, as stated in *Catnic v Hill & Smith*[1] in which the word 'vertical' in a claim was held to cover a feature that was several degrees off true perpendicular, and in which Lord Diplock said in the House of Lords that:

'... a patent specification is a unilateral statement by the patentee, in words of his own choosing, addressed to those likely to have a practical interest in the subject matter of his invention (i.e. "skilled in the art"), by which he informs them what he claims to be the essential features of the new product or process for which the letters patent grant him a monopoly. It is those novel features only that he claims to be essential that constitute the so-called "pith and marrow" of the claim. A patent specification should be given a purposive construction rather than a purely literal one derived from applying to it the kind of meticulous verbal analysis in which lawyers are too often tempted by their training to indulge. The question in each case is: whether persons with practical knowledge and experience of the kind of work in which the invention was intended to be used, would understand that strict compliance with a particular descriptive word or phrase appearing in a claim was intended by the patentee to be an essential requirement of the invention so that any variant would fall outside the monopoly claimed, even though it could have no material effect upon the way the invention worked.

The question, of course, does not arise where the variant would in fact have a material effect upon the way the invention worked. Nor does it arise unless at the date of publication of the specification it would be obvious to the informed reader that this was so. Where it is not obvious, in the light of then-existing knowledge, the reader is entitled to assume that the patentee thought at the time of the specification that he had good reason for limiting his monopoly so strictly and had intended to do so, even though subsequent work by him or others in the field of the invention might show the limitation to have been unnecessary. It is to be answered in the negative only when it would be apparent to any reader skilled in the art that a particular descriptive word on phrase used in a claim cannot have been intended by a patentee, who was also skilled in the art, to exclude minor variant which, to the knowledge of both him and the readers to whom the patent was addressed, could have no material effect upon the way in which the invention worked.'

These principles were placed in the context of the general principles of construction as applied to patent claims by the Court of Appeal in *Rockwater v Technip SA.*[2] Subject to one point of difference these general principles were adopted by the House of Lords in *Kirin-Amgen v Hoechst Marion Roussel.*[3]

These principles are now quoted in the form of the following passage from the judgment of the Court of Appeal in *Virgin v Premium Aircraft*[4] approving the summary made in the Patents Court below:

'5.   One might have thought there was nothing more to say on this topic after *Kirin-Amgen v Hoechst Marion Roussel* [2005] RPC 9. The judge accurately set out the position, save that he used the old language of Art 69 EPC rather than that of the EPC 2000, a Convention now in force. The new language omits the terms of from Art. 69. No one suggested the amendment changes the meaning. We set out what the judge said, but using the language of the EPC 2000:

"[182]   The task for the court is to determine what the person skilled in the art would have understood the patentee to have been using the language of the claim to mean. The principles were summarised by Jacob LJ in *Mayne Pharma v Pharmacia Italia* [2005] EWCA Civ 137 and refined by Pumfrey J in *Halliburton v Smith International* [2005] EWHC 1623 (Pat) following their general approval by the House of Lords in *Kirin-Amgen v Hoechst Marion Roussel* [2005] RPC 9. An abbreviated version of them is as follows:

(i)   The first, overarching principle, is that contained in Article 69 of the European Patent Convention.

(ii)   Article 69 says that the extent of protection is determined by the terms of the claims. It goes on to say that the description and drawings shall be used to interpret the claims. In short the claims are to be construed in context.

(iii)   It follows that the claims are to be construed purposively – the inventor's purpose being ascertained from the description and drawings.

(iv)   It further follows that the claims must not be construed as if they stood alone – the drawings and description only being used to resolve any ambiguity. Purpose is vital to the construction of claims.

(v)   When ascertaining the inventor's purpose, it must be remembered that he may have several purposes depending on the level of generality of his invention. Typically, for instance, an inventor may have one, generally more than one, specific embodiment as well as a generalised concept. But there is no presumption that the patentee necessarily intended the widest possible meaning consistent with his purpose be given to the words that he used: purpose and meaning are different.

(vi)   Thus purpose is not the be-all and end-all. One is still at the end of the day concerned with the meaning of the language used. Hence the other extreme of the Protocol – a mere guideline – is also ruled out by Article 69 itself. It is the terms of the claims which delineate the patentee's territory.

(vii)   It follows that if the patentee has included what is obviously a deliberate limitation in his claims, it must have a meaning. One cannot disregard obviously intentional elements.

(viii) It also follows that where a patentee has used a word or phrase which, a contextually, might have a particular meaning (narrow or wide) it does not necessarily have that meaning in context.

(ix)   It further follows that there is no general "doctrine of equivalents".

[(x)]   On the other hand purposive construction can lead to the conclusion that a technically trivial or minor difference between an element of a claim and the corresponding element of the alleged infringement nonetheless falls within the meaning of the element when read purposively. This is not because there is a doctrine of equivalents: it is because that is the fair way to read the claim in context.

[(xi)] Finally purposive construction leads one to eschew the kind of meticulous verbal analysis which lawyers are too often tempted by their training to indulge. "Pedantry and patents are incompatible." '

Virtually every subsequent case in the English courts in which infringement has been in issue has quoted these principles, albeit that their application has not always produced consistent results, as issues of infringement have been more susceptible of successful appeal than other issues of patent law. By eschewing a structured approach to the issue their predictive value is also somewhat limited.

In contrast, for many years before the decision in *Kirin-Amgen*, the observations in *Catnic* were applied as reformulated by the Patents Court as three questions in *Improver v Remington Consumer Products:*[5]

'If the issue was whether a feature embodied in an alleged infringement which fell outside the primary, literal or a contextual meaning of a descriptive word or phrase in the claim ("a variant") was nevertheless within the language as properly interpreted, the court should ask itself the following three questions:

(1)   Does the variant have a material effect upon the way the invention worked? If yes, the variant is outside the claim. If no –

(2)   Would this (ie that the variant had no material effect) have been obvious at the date of publication of the patent to a reader skilled in the art? If no, the variant is outside the claim. If yes –

(3)   Would the reader skilled in the art nevertheless have understood from the language of the claim that the patentee intended that strict compliance with the primary meaning was an essential requirement of the invention? If yes, the variant is outside the claim. On the other hand, a negative answer to the last question would lead to the conclusion that the patentee was intending the word or phrase to have not a literal but a figurative meaning (the figure being a form of synecdoche or metonymy) denoting a class of things which include the variant and the literal meaning, the latter being perhaps the most perfect, best-known or striking example of the class.'

The questions, for so long known as the *Improver* questions, and then the 'Protocol questions'[6] could be related to the Protocol in the following way: the first question providing the basis for extending the protection beyond that conferred by an overly literal, and a contextual construction of the claim, to give 'fair protection' to the patentee, and the second and third questions providing a basis for cutting back such extended protection, to give 'reasonable certainty' to third parties. The Patents Court in *Improver* went on to state:

'In the end, therefore, the question is always whether the alleged infringement is covered by the language of the claim. This, I think, is what Lord Diplock meant in *Catnic* when he said that there was no dichotomy between "textual infringement" and infringement of the "pith and marrow" of the patent and why I respectfully think that Fox LJ put the question with great precision in *Anchor Building Products Ltd v Redland Roof Tiles Ltd* when he said the question was whether the absence of a feature mentioned in the claim was "an immaterial variant which a person skilled in the trade would have regarded as being within the ambit of the language". It is worth noticing that Lord Diplock's first two questions, although they cannot sensibly be answered without reference to the patent, do not primarily involve questions of construction: whether the variant would make a material difference to the way an invention worked and whether this would have been obvious to the skilled reader are questions of fact. The answers are used to provide the factual background against which the specification must be construed. It is the third question which raises the question of construction and Lord Diplock's formulation makes it clear that on this question the answers to the first two questions are not conclusive. Even a purposive construction of the language of the patent may lead to the conclusion that although the variant made no material difference and this would have been obvious at the time, the patentee for some reason was confining his claim to the primary meaning and excluding the variant. If this were not the case, there would be no point in asking the third question at all.'

Several cases leading up to *Kirin-Amgen*, the first case on the point in the House of Lords since *Catnic,* evidenced an increasing perception amongst the English judiciary that the Protocol questions had limitations. Such perceived limitations had not been apparent when the questions were applied to mechanical inventions. However, once they were applied to certain types of pharmaceutical and biotechnological inventions the courts sometimes characterized them as unsuited to the task, albeit often with little justification.[7] In *Kirin-Amgen,* itself a biotechnology case, in the House of Lords, Lord Hoffmann (who ironically, as a first instance judge, had himself formulated them in *Improver*) said that the Protocol questions were 'only guidelines, more useful in some cases than in others':

> '52. These questions, which the Court of Appeal in *Wheatley v Drillsafe Ltd* [2001] RPC 133, 142 dubbed "the Protocol questions" have been used by English courts for the past fifteen years as a framework for deciding whether equivalents fall within the scope of the claims. On the whole, the judges appear to have been comfortable with the results, although some of the cases have exposed the limitations of the method. When speaking of the "*Catnic* principle" it is important to distinguish between, on the one hand, the principle of purposive construction which I have said gives effect to the requirements of the Protocol, and on the other hand, the guidelines for applying that principle to equivalents, which are encapsulated in the Protocol questions. The former is the bedrock of patent construction, universally applicable. The latter are only guidelines, more useful in some cases than in others. I am bound to say that the cases show a tendency for counsel to treat the Protocol questions as legal rules rather than guides which will in appropriate cases help to decide what the skilled man would have understood the patentee to mean. The limits to the value of the guidelines are perhaps most clearly illustrated by the present case and therefore, instead of discussing the principles in the abstract as I have been doing so far, I shall make my comments by reference to the facts of the case.'

A framework akin to the Protocol questions had, meanwhile, been adopted the German courts, as Lord Hoffmann recognized later in *Kirin-Amgen:*

> '75. The German courts have their own guidelines for dealing with equivalents, which have some resemblance to the Protocol questions. In the "quintet" of cases before the Bundesgerichtshof (see, for example, *Kunstoffrohrteil* [2002] GRUR 511 and *Schneidemesser 1* [2003] ENPR 12 309) which concerned questions of whether figures or measurements in a claim allow some degree of approximation (and, if so, what degree), the court expressly said that its approach was similar to that adopted in *Catnic*. But there are differences from the Protocol questions which are lucidly explained by Dr Peter Meier-Beck (currently a judge of the 10th Senate) in a paper to be published in the *International Review of Intellectual Property and Competition Law* (IIC). For example, German judges do not ask whether a variant "works in the same way" but whether it solves the problem underlying the invention by means which have the same technical effect. That may be a better way of putting the question because it avoids the ambiguity illustrated by *American Home Products Corporation v Novartis Pharmaceuticals UK Ltd* [2001] RPC 159 over whether "works in the same way" involves an assumption that it works at all. On the other hand, as is illustrated by the present case, everything will depend upon what you regard as "the problem

underlying the invention." It seems to me, however, that the German courts are also approaching the question of equivalents with a view to answering the same ultimate question as that which I have suggested is raised by Article 69, namely what a person skilled in the art would have thought the patentee was using the language of the claim to mean.'

The reformulation of the Protocol questions by Dr Peter Meier-Beck and which appealed to Lord Hoffmann was:[8]

'1. Does the modified embodiment solve the problem underlying the invention with means which have objectively the same technical effect?

2. Was the person skilled in the art, using his specialist knowledge, able to find the variant at the priority date as having the same effect?

3. Are the considerations that the person skilled in the art had to apply oriented to the technical teaching of the patent claim in such a way that the person skilled in the art took the variant into account as being an equivalent solution?'

All three questions had to be answered in the affirmative for infringement to be found. Despite the complement paid to the Protocol questions by their widespread international adoption the response of the English courts has been to treat *Kirin-Amgen* as damning them with the faint praise of being 'only guidelines, more useful in some cases than in others', and to use this as an excuse to cease applying them at all for ten years. In any case, because they retain their predictive value in most cases, they have achieved a remarkable degree of international acceptance, and provide a useful framework in which to analyse the case law, and have reappeared only recently in the case law in 2014 in *Actavis v Eli Lilly*[9] it is still, therefore, worth analysing them in some detail before discussing *Kirin-Amgen* itself.

1   *Catnic v Hill & Smith* [1982] RPC 183 (House of Lords) at p. 242. In *Catnic* the rejected 'meticulous verbal analysis' was the argument that because the word 'horizontal' was qualified by 'substantially' whereas 'vertical' was not, the latter must mean 'geometrically vertical'.

2   *Rockwater v Technip SA* [2004] EWCA Civ 381; [2004] RPC 919; [2005] IP&T 304 (Court of Appeal) at para [41].

3   *Kirin-Amgen v Hoechst Marion Roussel* [2001] IP&T 882; [2002] RPC 1; [2002] RPC 2 (Patents Court); [2003] RPC 3 (Court of Appeal); [2004] UKHL 46; [2005] 1 All ER 667; [2005] RPC 9 (House of Lords) at para [33].

4   *Virgin v Premium Aircraft* [2009] EWCA 1062 at para [5].

5   *Improver v Remington Consumer Products* [1990] FSR 181 at p. 189.

6   In *Wheatley v Drillsafe* [2001] RPC 133 (Court of Appeal) at p. 141.

7   See, for example, *Pharmacia v Merck* [2001] EWCA Civ 1610 (Court of Appeal) in which the Court of Appeal, although stating that the Protocol questions 'are normally a useful tool to arrive at the middle ground required by the Protocol' went on to characterize the case, one concerning pharmaceuticals, as one 'where the difficulties in application [of the Protocol questions] outweigh the advantages', and reversed a Patents Court finding of non-infringement. The same result could, however, have been achieved by applying the Protocol questions, as indeed the Court of Appeal did in *Kirin-Amgen* to come to the same result as the House of Lords.

8   Peter Meier-Beck, 'The Scope of Patent Protection – The Test for Determining
     Equivalence' (2005) *IIC*, 339–44. In fact this article also proposed a fourth question,
     which must be answered in the negative for infringement to be found: 'Does the
     variant, having regard to the state of the art, lack novelty or is the variant obvious to a
     person skilled in the art?'. Such a question, which reflects what is known in Germany
     as the *Formstein* objection after the case in which it was first sanctioned, and which
     is rather like the so-called *Gillette* Defence in the UK (discussed later at para 6.17)
     is especially important in Germany as the courts that determine patent infringement
     cannot make determinations as to validity.
9   *Actavis UK Ltd and ors v Eli Lilly* [2014] EWHC 1511 (Pat), [2015] EWCA Civ 555
     (Court of Appeal). Here, where the issue was one of whether a claim to a particular
     pharmaceutical salt of an acid could be construed as covering the free acid or other
     pharmaceutical salts of the same acid, the first question was answered in favour of
     the patentee, but the second and third questions against it. As discussed in **Chapter
     7** at para 7.21 the Court of Appeal, whilst accepting that the product in issue did
     not directly infringe, disagreed with the contributory infringement analysis at first
     instance and remitted the case back to the Patents Court.

Applying the Protocol questions

6.07   The first and second Protocol questions both involve
determinations of fact which must be answered by reference to the
invention as described in the patent and the alleged infringement. As was
explained in *Improver v Remington Consumer Products*[1] the answers
to the first two questions: 'are used to provide the factual background
against which the specification must be construed', and it is the third
question which involves the actual question of construction. Indeed
this must be so, as the first two questions involve consideration of the
alleged infringement, and it has for long been a fundamental principle
that patent claims must be construed 'as if the defendant had never been
born'.[2]

In *Union Carbide v BP Chemicals*[3] and *Wheatley v Drillsafe*[4] the Court
of Appeal emphasized, as observed in *Improver,* that in answering the
first question the invention must be described at the level of generality
with which it is described in the claim. In *Adwest Engine Controls v
Tavismanor*[5] in holding that the first step was not fulfilled, the Patents
Court observed that even though the overall function of the claimed
device remained the same, the variant had a material effect on the way
the invention worked, and emphasized that in making that assessment
one must look to the invention, and not the claimed device as a whole.
In both *Minnesota Mining & Manufacturing Co v Plastus Kreativ*[6] and
Amersham Pharmacia Biotech v Amicon[7] the Court of Appeal answered
the first question against the patentee, even though in *Amersham* they
had held that the mechanism in issue produced an 'equivalent result' to
that which was claimed.

As formulated, the second Protocol question does not say whether the
skilled reader is told of the variant. However, in *Improver* the Patents
Court had made it clear that he had been: 'the skilled man is told of

both invention and the variant and asked whether the variant would obviously work in the same way. An affirmative answer would not be inconsistent with the variant being an inventive step'. Subsequently, in *Union Carbide v BP Chemicals*[8] the Court of Appeal accepted this when stating that: 'A skilled man told of the variant would immediately realise that it was immaterial'.

Improver concerned the use of a slit rubber rod instead of a helical spring in a ladies hair-removing device. *Union Carbide* concerned the separation of a liquid-gas mixture and the re-introduction of the separated liquid, and gas into the reactor; as opposed to the reintroduction of the liquid-gas mixture itself. In such cases, it is normally possible for the notional skilled person, when told of the variant, to predict whether or not it will work. This is not the case, however, for certain pharmaceutical inventions. In *AHP v Novartis*[9] the claim was to the second medical use of rapamycin as an immunosuppressant. The product alleged to infringe was a derivative of rapamycin – known as SDZ RAD. At first instance, the Patents Court had found that: 'There was, at the date of the patent, a strong possibility that other derivatives would work, but it was impossible to predict with certainty whether any particular one would.'

The Court of Appeal held that the claim was not infringed because it would not have been obvious to the skilled reader, when told of the SDZ RAD variant, that it would also work as an immunosuppressant. Thus the finding of non-infringement was predicated on the assumption that the skilled reader was not told whether the variant would in fact work. The issue was of importance in the lower courts in *Kirin-Amgen v Hoechst Marion Roussel*,[10] the Patents Court answering the question (as with the first one) in favour of the patentee, but the Court of Appeal answering this question (as with the first one) against it.

The third Protocol question is the one that directly addresses claim construction. On the facts of *Catnic v Hill & Smith*[11] itself (concerning whether the word 'vertical' must be so strictly construed as to exclude something several degrees off vertical) it presented the House of Lords with no difficulty, it being observed: 'No plausible reason has been advanced why any rational patentee should want to place so narrow a limitation on his invention.'

Despite this in practice it was the third Protocol question that was generally answered against a patentee arguing to disregard a limitation. Thus, in *Societe Technique de Pulverisation STEP v Emson Europe*[12] the Court of Appeal reversing a Patents County Court finding of infringement, had the third question clearly in mind when making it clear that it is not possible to simply strike out an integer, or rewrite a claim under the pretence of construing it:

'The well known principle that patent claims are to be given a purposive construction does not mean that an integer can be treated as struck out if it does not appear to make any difference to the inventive concept. It may have some purpose buried in the prior art and even if this is not discernable, the patentee may have had some reason of his own for introducing it.'

In *Optical Coating Laboratory v Pilkington Pty*[13] the Court of Appeal, again reversing a Patents County Court finding of infringement, formulated a reason why the patentee might have wished to place 'a narrow limitation on his invention': 'A plausible reason in the present case is that to make the invention as wide as is now claimed would have been to risk rendering the whole patent void for obviousness.'

Similarly, in *Johnson Electric Industrial Manufactory v Mabuchi Motor KK*[14] it was held that: 'the skilled man would have to conclude that by the very word *plurality* the patentee had, for some reason or other excluded just a single projection.'

The Court of Appeal said much the same thing in *Beloit Technologies v Valmet Paper Machinery:*[15] 'the skilled reader would believe that the patentee intended that third meant third even though he would not know why that limitation had been introduced.'

Similar reasoning to that of the third Protocol question has been applied to precise numerical limitations in claims, as discussed below at para 6.10.

1   *Improver v Remington Consumer Products* [1990] FSR 181 at p. 189.
2   *Nobel v Anderson* (1894) 11 RPC 523.
3   *Union Carbide v BP Chemicals* [1999] RPC 409 (Court of Appeal).
4   *Wheatley v Drillsafe* [2001] RPC 133 (Court of Appeal).
5   *Adwest Engine Controls v Tavismanor* (10 November 1997, unreported) Laddie J (Patents Court).
6   *Minnesota Mining & Manufacturing Co v Plastus Kreativ* [1997] RPC 737 (Court of Appeal).
7   *Amersham Pharmacia Biotech v Amicon* [2001] IP&T 1093 (Court of Appeal).
8   *Union Carbide v BP Chemicals* [1999] RPC 409 (Court of Appeal).
9   *AHP v Novartis* [2000] IP&T 1308; [2000] RPC 547 (Court of Appeal).
10 *Kirin Amgen v Hoechst Marion Roussel* [2001] IP&T 882; [2002] RPC 1; [2002] RPC 2 (Patents Court); [2003] RPC 3 (Court of Appeal); [2004] UKHL 46; [2005] 1 All ER 667; [2005] RPC 9 (House of Lords).
11 *Catnic v Hill & Smith* [1982] RPC 183 (House of Lords) at pp. 242–43.
12 *Societe Technique de Pulverisation STEP v Emson Europe* [1993] RPC 513 (Court of Appeal) at p. 522.
13 *Optical Coating Laboratory v Pilkington Pty* [1995] RPC 145 (Court of Appeal).
14 *Johnson Electric Industrial Manufactory v Mabuchi Motor KK* [1996] FSR 93 (Patents Court).
15 *Beloit Technologies v Valmet Paper Machinery* [1997] RPC 489 (Court of Appeal).

Construction according to Kirin-Amgen v Hoechst Marion Roussel

6.08   As will be apparent from the above discussion as to its effect on the degree to which the Protocol questions are now applied, the judgment of the House of Lords in *Kirin Amgen v Hoechst Marion Roussel*[1] despite upholding the decision of the Court of Appeal based on the application of such questions, and which it accepted were a useful guideline, and despite following the earlier decision of the House of Lords in *Catnic v Hill & Smith*,[2] has been treated as a watershed in the UK law of construction and infringement. Given its significance, and the breadth and authority of the comparative, and historical review that it undertakes, it is appropriate to quote at some length from the leading speech in it, that of Lord Hoffmann:

'Extent of protection: the statutory provisions

18. Until the Patents Act 1977, which gave effect to the European Patent Convention (EPC) there was nothing in any UK statute about the extent of protection conferred by a patent. It was governed by the common law, the terms of the royal grant and general principles of construction. It was these principles which Lord Diplock expounded in the leading case of *Catnic Components Ltd v Hill & Smith Ltd* [1982] RPC 183, which concerned a patent granted before 1977. But the EPC and the Act deal expressly with the matter in some detail. Article 84 specifies the role of the claims in an application to the European Patent Office for a European patent:

"The claims shall define the matter for which protection is sought. They shall be clear and concise and be supported by the description".

19. For present purposes, the most important provision is article 69 of the EPC, which applies to infringement proceedings in the domestic courts of all Contracting States:

"The extent of the protection conferred by a European patent or a European patent application shall be determined by the terms of the claims. Nevertheless, the description and drawings shall be used to interpret the claims."

20. In stating unequivocally that the extent of protection shall be "determined" (in German, "bestimm") by the "terms of the claims" (den Inhalt der Patentanspruche) the Convention followed what had long been the law in the United Kingdom. During the course of the 18th and 19th centuries, practice and common law had come to distinguish between the part of the specification in which the patentee discharged his duty to disclose the best way of performing the invention and the section which delimited the scope of the monopoly which he claimed: see Fletcher-Moulton LJ in *British United Shoe Machinery Co Ltd v A. Fussell & Sons Ltd* (1908) 25 RPC 631, 650. The best-known statement of the status of the claims in UK law is by Lord Russell of Killowen in *Electric and Musical Industries Ltd v Lissen Ltd* (1938) 56 RPC 23, 39:

"The function of the claims is to define clearly and with precision the monopoly claimed, so that others may know the exact boundary of the area within which they will be trespassers. Their primary object is to limit and not to extend the monopoly. What is not claimed is disclaimed. The claims must undoubtedly be read as part of the entire document and not as a separate document; but the forbidden field must be found in the language of the claims and not elsewhere."

21. The need to set clear limits upon the monopoly is not only, as Lord Russell emphasised, in the interests of others who need to know

the area "within which they will be trespassers" but also in the interests of the patentee, who needs to be able to make it clear that he lays no claim to prior art or insufficiently enabled products or processes which would invalidate the patent.

22.   In Germany, however, the practice before 1977 in infringement proceedings (validity is determined by a different court) was commonly to treat the claims as a point of departure *(Ausgangspunkt)* in determining the extent of protection, for which the criterion was the inventive achievement *(erfinderische Leistung)* disclosed by the specification as a whole. Likewise in the Netherlands, Professor Jan Brinkhof, former Vice-President of the Hague Court of Appeals, has written that the role of the claims before 1977 was "extremely modest": see *Is there a European Doctrine of Equivalence?* (2002) 33 IIC 911, 915. What mattered was the "essence of the invention" or what we would call the inventive concept.

The Protocol

23.   Although the EPC thus adopted the United Kingdom principle of using the claims to determine the extent of protection, the Contracting States were unwilling to accept what were understood to be the principles of construction which United Kingdom courts applied in deciding what the claims meant. These principles, which I shall explain in greater detail in a moment, were perceived as having sometimes resulted in claims being given an unduly narrow and literal construction. The Contracting Parties wanted to make it clear that legal technicalities of this kind should be rejected. On the other hand, it was accepted that countries which had previously looked to the "essence of the invention" rather than the actual terms of the claims should not carry on exactly as before under the guise of giving the claims a generous interpretation.

24.   This compromise was given effect by the "Protocol on the Interpretation of Article 69":

"Article 69 should not be interpreted in the sense that the extent of the protection conferred by a European patent is to be understood as that defined by the strict, literal meaning of the wording used in the claims, the description and drawings being employed only for the purpose of resolving an ambiguity found in the claims. Neither should it be interpreted in the sense that the claims serve only as a guideline and that the actual protection conferred may extend to what, from a consideration of the description and drawings by a person skilled in the art, the patentee has contemplated. On the contrary, it is to be interpreted as defining a position between these extremes which combines a fair protection for the patentee with a reasonable degree of certainty for third parties."

25.   It is often said, on the basis of the words "a position between these extremes", that the Protocol represents a compromise between two different approaches to the interpretation of claims. But that is not quite accurate. It is a protocol on the interpretation of article 69, not a protocol on the interpretation of claims. The first sentence does deal

with interpretation of the claims and, to understand it, one needs to know something about the rules which English courts used to apply, or impose on themselves, when construing not merely patents but documents in general. The second sentence does not deal with the interpretation of claims. Instead, it makes it clear that one cannot go beyond the claims to what, on the basis of the specification as a whole, it appears that "the patentee has contemplated". But the last sentence indicates that, in determining the extent of protection according to the content of the claims but avoiding literalism, the courts of the Contracting States should combine "a fair protection for the patentee with a reasonable degree of certainty for third parties".

26. Both article 69 and the Protocol are given effect in United Kingdom law, in relation to infringement, by ss 60 and 125 of the Act. Section 60 provides that a person infringes a patent if he does various things in the United Kingdom "in relation to the invention" without the consent of the proprietor of the patent. Section 125 defines the extent of "the invention":

"(1)   For the purpose of this Act an invention for a patent for which an application has been made or for which a patent has been granted shall, unless the context otherwise requires, be taken to be that specified in a claim of the specification of the application or patent, as the case may be, as interpreted by the description and any drawings contained in that specification, and the extent of the protection conferred by a patent or application for a patent shall be determined accordingly

....

(3)   The Protocol on the Interpretation of Article 69 of the European Patent Convention (which Article contains a provision corresponding to subsection (1) above) shall, as for the time being in force, apply for the purposes of subsection (1) above as it applies for the purposes of that Article."

The English rules of construction

27. As I indicated a moment ago, it is impossible to understand what the first sentence of the Protocol was intending to prohibit without knowing what used to be the principles applied (at any rate in theory) by an English court construing a legal document. These required the words and grammar of a sentence to be given their "natural and ordinary meaning", that is to say, the meanings assigned to the words by a dictionary and to the syntax by a grammar. This meaning was to be adopted regardless of the context or background against which the words were used, unless they were "ambiguous", that is to say, capable of having more than one meaning. As Lord Porter said in *Electric & Musical Industries Ltd v Lissen Ltd* (1938) 56 RPC 23, 57: "If the Claims have a plain meaning in themselves [emphasis supplied], then advantage cannot be taken of the language used in the body of the Specification to make them mean something different."

28. On the other hand, if the language of the claim "in itself was ambiguous, capable of having more than one meaning, the court could have regard to the context provided by the specification and drawings. If that was

insufficient to resolve the ambiguity, the court could have regard to the background, or what was called the "extrinsic evidence" of facts which an intended reader would reasonably have expected to have been within the knowledge of the author when he wrote the document.

29. These rules, if remorselessly applied, meant that unless the court could find some ambiguity in the language, it might be obliged to construe the document in a sense which a reasonable reader, aware of its context and background, would not have thought the author intended. Such a rule, adopted in the interests of certainty at an early stage in the development of English law, was capable of causing considerable injustice and occasionally did so. The fact that it did not do so more often was because judges were generally astute to find the necessary "ambiguity" which enabled them to interpret the document in its proper context. Indeed, the attempt to treat the words of the claim as having meanings "in themselves" and without regard to the context in which or the purpose for which they were used was always a highly artificial exercise.

30. It seems to me clear that the Protocol, with its reference to "resolving an ambiguity", was intended to reject these artificial English rules for the construction of patent claims. As it happens, though, by the time the Protocol was signed, the English courts had already begun to abandon them, not only for patent claims, but for commercial documents generally. The speeches of Lord Wilberforce in *Prenn v Simmonds* [1971] 1 WLR 1381 and *Rear-don Smith Line Ltd. v Yngvar Hansen-Tangen* [1976] 1 WLR 989 are milestones along this road. It came to be recognised that the author of a document such as a contract or patent specification is using language to make a communication for a practical purpose and that a rule of construction which gives his language a meaning different from the way it would have been understood by the people to whom it was actually addressed is liable to defeat his intentions. It is against that background that one must read the well known passage in the speech of Lord Diplock in *Catnic Components Ltd v Hill & Smith Ltd* [1982] RPC 183, 243 when he said that the new approach should also be applied to the construction of patent claims:

"A patent specification should be given a purposive construction rather than a purely literal one derived from applying to it the kind of meticulous verbal analysis in which lawyers are too often tempted by their training to indulge."

31. This was all of a piece with Lord Diplock's approach a few years later in The Antaios [1985] AC 191, 201 to the construction of a charter party:

"I take this opportunity of re-stating that if detailed semantic and syntactical analysis of words in a commercial contract is going to lead to a conclusion that flouts business commonsense, it must be made to yield to business commonsense."

32. Construction, whether of a patent or any other document, is of course not directly concerned with what the author meant to say. There is no window into the mind of the patentee or the author of any other

document. Construction is objective in the sense that it is concerned with what a reasonable person to whom the utterance was addressed would have understood the author to be using the words to mean. Notice, however, that it is not, as is sometimes said, "the meaning of the words the author used", but rather what the notional addressee would have understood the *author* to mean by using those words. The meaning of words is a matter of convention, governed by rules, which can be found in dictionaries and grammars. What the author would have been understood to mean by using those words is not simply a matter of rules. It is highly sensitive to the context of and background to the particular utterance. It depends not only upon the words the author has chosen but also upon the identity of the audience he is taken to have been addressing and the knowledge and assumptions which one attributes to that audience. I have discussed these questions at some length in *Mannai Investment Co Ltd v Eagle Star Life Assurance Co Ltd* [1997] AC 749 and *Investors Compensation Scheme Ltd v West Bromwich Building Society* [1998] 1 WLR896.

33. In the case of a patent specification, the notional addressee is the person skilled in the art. He (or, I say once and for all, she) comes to a reading of the specification with common general knowledge of the art. And he reads the specification on the assumption that its purpose is to both to describe and tõ demarcate an invention – a practical idea which the patentee has had for a new product or process – and not to be a textbook in mathematics or chemistry or a shopping list of chemicals or hardware. It is this insight which lies at the heart of "purposive construction". If Lord Diplock did not invent the expression, he certainly gave it wide currency in the law. But there is, I think, a tendency to regard it as a vague description of some kind of divination which mysteriously penetrates beneath the language of the specification. Lord Diplock was in my opinion being much more specific and his intention was to point out that a person may be taken to mean something different when he uses words for one purpose from what he would be taken to mean if he was using them for another. The example in the *Catnic* case was the difference between what a person would reasonably be taken to mean by using the word "vertical" in a mathematical theorem and by using it in a claimed definition of a lintel for use in the building trade. The only point on which I would question the otherwise admirable summary of the law on infringement in the judgment of Jacob LJ in *Rockwater Ltd v Technip France SA* (unreported) [2004] EWCA Civ 381, at paragraph 41, is when he says in sub-paragraph (e) that to be "fair to the patentee" one must use "the widest purpose consistent with his teaching". This, as it seems to me, is to confuse *the purpose* of the utterance with what it would be understood to *mean*. The purpose of a patent specification, as I have said, is no more nor less than to communicate the idea of an invention. An appreciation of that purpose is part of the material which one uses to ascertain the meaning. But purpose and meaning are different. If, when speaking of the widest purpose, Jacob LJ meant the widest meaning, I would respectfully disagree. There is no presumption about

the width of the claims. A patent may, for one reason or another, claim less than it teaches or enables.

34. "Purposive construction" does not mean that one is extending or going beyond the definition of the technical matter for which the patentee seeks protection in the claims. The question is always what the person skilled in the art would have understood the patentee to be using the language of the claim to mean. And for this purpose, the language he has chosen is usually of critical importance. The conventions of word meaning and syntax enable us to express our meanings with great accuracy and subtlety and the skilled man will ordinarily assume that the patentee has chosen his language accordingly. As a number of judges have pointed out, the specification is a unilateral document in words of the patentee's own choosing. Furthermore, the words will usually have been chosen upon skilled advice. The specification is not a document *inter rusticos* for which broad allowances must be made. On the other hand, it must be recognised that the patentee is trying to describe something which, at any rate in his opinion, is new; which has not existed before and of which there may be no generally accepted definition. There will be occasions upon which it will be obvious to the skilled man that the patentee must in some respect have departed from conventional use of language or included in his description of the invention some element which he did not mean to be essential. But one would not expect that to happen very often.

35. One of the reasons why it will be unusual for the notional skilled man to conclude, after construing the claim purposively in the context of the specification and drawings, that the patentee must nevertheless have meant something different from what he appears to have meant, is that there are necessarily gaps in our knowledge of the background which led him to express himself in that particular way. The courts of the United Kingdom, the Netherlands and Germany certainly discourage, if they do not actually prohibit, use of the patent office file in aid of construction. There are good reasons: the meaning of the patent should not change according to whether or not the person skilled in the art has access to the file and in any case life is too short for the limited assistance which it can provide. It is however frequently impossible to know without access, not merely to the file but to the private thoughts of the patentee and his advisors as well, what the reason was for some apparently inexplicable limitation in the extent of the monopoly claimed. One possible explanation is that it does not represent what the patentee really meant to say. But another is that he did mean it, for reasons of his own; such as wanting to avoid arguments with the examiners over enablement or prior art and have his patent granted as soon as possible. This feature of the practical life of a patent agent reduces the scope for a conclusion that the patentee could not have meant what the words appear to be saying. It has been suggested that in the absence of any explanation for a restriction in the extent of protection claimed, it should be presumed that there was some good reason between the patentee and the patent office. I do not think that it is sensible to have presumptions about what people must be taken to

have meant but a conclusion that they have departed from conventional usage obviously needs some rational basis.

The doctrine of equivalents

36.　At the time when the rules about natural and ordinary meanings were more or less rigidly applied, the United Kingdom and American courts showed understandable anxiety about applying a construction which allowed someone to avoid infringement by making an "immaterial variation" in the invention as described in the claims. In England, this led to the development of a doctrine of infringement by use of the "pith and marrow" of the invention (a phrase invented by Lord Cairns in *Clark v Adie* (1877) 2 App Cas 315, 320) as opposed to a "textual infringement". The pith and marrow doctrine was always a bit vague ("necessary to prevent sharp practice" said Lord Reid in *C Van Der Lely NV v Bamfords* Ltd [1963] RPC 61, 77) and it was unclear whether the courts regarded it as a principle of construction or an extension of protection outside the claims.

37.　In the United States, where a similar principle is called the "doctrine of equivalents", it is frankly acknowledged that it allows the patentee to extend his monopoly beyond the claims. In the leading case of *Graver Tank & Manufacturing Co Inc v Linde Air Products Company* 339 US 605, 607 (1950), Jackson J said that the American courts had recognised –

> "that to permit imitation of a patented invention which does not copy every literal detail would be to convert the protection of the patent grant into a hollow and useless thing. Such a limitation would leave room for – indeed encourage – the unscrupulous copyist to make unimportant and insubstantial changes and substitutions in the patent which, though adding nothing, would be enough to take the copied matter outside the claim, and hence outside the reach of law."

38.　In similar vein, Learned Hand J (a great patent lawyer) said that the purpose of the doctrine of equivalents was "to temper unsparing logic and prevent an infringer from stealing the benefit of the invention": *Royal Typewriter Co v Remington Rand Inc* (CA2nd Conn) 168 F2nd 691, 692. The effect of the doctrine is thus to extend protection to something outside the claims which performs substantially the same function in substantially the same way to obtain the same result.

39.　However, once the monopoly had been allowed to escape from the terms of the claims, it is not easy to know where its limits should be drawn. In *Warner-Jenkins on Co v Hilton Davis Chemical Co* 520 US 17, 28–29 (1997) the United States Supreme Court expressed some anxiety that the doctrine of equivalents had "taken on a life of its own, unbounded by the patent claims." It seems to me, however, that once the doctrine is allowed to go beyond the claims, a life of its own is exactly what it is bound to have. The American courts have restricted the scope of the doctrine by what is called prosecution history or file wrapper estoppel, by which equivalence cannot be claimed for integers restricting the monopoly which have been included by amendment during the prosecution of the application in the patent office. The patentee is estopped against the world (who need not have known of or relied upon the amendment) from denying that he intended to surrender that part of the monopoly. File wrapper estoppel means that the true scope of patent protection often cannot be established without an expensive investigation of the patent office file. Furthermore, the difficulties involved in deciding exactly what part of the claim should be taken to have been withdrawn by an amendment drove the Federal Court of Appeals in *Festo Corporation v Shoketsu Kinzoku Kogyo Kabushiki Co Ltd* 234 F3rd 558 (2000) to declare that the law was arbitrary and unworkable. Lourie J said: "The only settled expectation currently existing is the expectation that clever attorneys can argue infringement outside the scope of the claims all the way through this Court of Appeals."

40.   In order to restore some certainty, the Court of Appeals laid down a rule that any amendment for reasons of patent validity was an absolute bar to any extension of the monopoly outside the literal meaning of the amended text. But the Supreme Court reversed this retreat to literalism on the ground that the cure was worse than the disease: see *Festo Corporation v Shoketsu Kinzoku Kogyo Kabushiki Co Ltd* (28 May 2002) US Supreme Court.

41.   There is often discussion about whether we have a European doctrine of equivalents and, if not, whether we should. It seems to me that both the doctrine of equivalents in the United States and the pith and marrow doctrine in the United Kingdom were born of despair. The courts felt unable to escape from interpretations which "unsparing logic" appeared to require and which prevented them from according the patentee the full extent of the monopoly which the person skilled in the art would reasonably have thought he was claiming. The background was the tendency to literalism which then characterised the approach of the courts to the interpretation of documents generally and the fact that patents are likely to attract the skills of lawyers seeking to exploit literalism to find loopholes in the monopoly they create. (Similar skills are devoted to revenue statutes.)

42.   If literalism stands in the way of construing patent claims so as to give fair protection to the patentee, there are two things that you can do. One is to adhere to literalism in construing the claims and evolve a doctrine which supplements the claims by extending protection to equivalents. That is what the Americans have done. The other is to abandon literalism. That is what the House of Lords did in the *Catnic* case, where Lord Diplock said (at [1982] RPC 183, 242:

"... both parties to this appeal have tended to treat 'textual infringement' and infringement of the 'pith and marrow' of an invention as if they were separate causes of action, the existence of the former to be determined as a matter of construction only and of the latter upon some broader principle of colourable evasion. There is, in my view, no such dichotomy; there is but a single cause of action and to treat it otherwise ... is liable to lead to confusion."

43. The solution, said Lord Diplock, was to adopt a principle of construction which actually gave effect to what the person skilled in the art would have understood the patentee to be claiming.

44. Since the *Catnic* case we have article 69 which, as it seems to me, firmly shuts the door on any doctrine which extends protection outside the claims. I cannot say that I am sorry because the *Festo* litigation suggests, with all respect to the courts of the United States, that American patent litigants pay dearly for results which are no more just or predictable than could be achieved by simply reading the claims.

Is Catnic consistent with the Protocol?

45. In *Improver Corp v Remington Consumer Products Ltd* [1989] RPC 69 the Court of Appeal said that Lord Diplock's speech in *Catnic* advocated the same approach to construction as is required by the Protocol. (See also *Southco Inc v Dzus Fastener Europe Ltd* [1992] RPC 299.) But in *PLG Research Ltd v Ardon International Ltd* [1995] RPC 287, 309 Millett LJ said:

   "Lord Diplock was expounding the common law approach to the construction of a patent. This has been replaced by the approach laid down by the Protocol. If the two approaches are the same, reference to Lord Diplock's formulation is unnecessary, while if they are different it is dangerous."

46. This echoes, perhaps consciously, the famous justification said to have been given by the Caliph Omar for burning the library of Alexandria: "If these writings of the Greeks agree with the Book of God, they are useless and need not be preserved: if they disagree, they are pernicious and ought to be destroyed" – a story which Gibbon dismissed as Christian propaganda. But I think that the Protocol can suffer no harm from a little explanation and I entirely agree with the masterly judgment of Aldous J in *Assidoman Multipack Ltd v The Mead Corporation* [1995] RPC 321, in which he explains why the *Catnic* approach accords with the Protocol.

47. The Protocol, as I have said, is a Protocol for the construction of article 69 and does not expressly lay down any principle for the construction of claims. It does say what principle should *not* be followed, namely the old English literalism, but otherwise it says only that one should not go outside the claims. It does however say that the object is to combine a fair protection for the patentee with a reasonable degree of certainty for third parties. How is this to be achieved? The claims must be construed in a way which attempts, so far as is possible in an imperfect world, not to disappoint the reasonable expectations of either side. What principle of interpretation would give fair protection to the patentee? Surely, a principle which would give him the full extent of the monopoly which the person skilled in the art would think he was intending to claim. And what principle would provide a reasonable degree of protection for third parties? Surely again, a principle which would not give the patentee more than the full extent of the monopoly which the person skilled in the art would think that he was intending to claim. Indeed, any other principle would also be unfair to the patentee,

because it would unreasonably expose the patent to claims of invalidity on grounds of anticipation or insufficiency.

48. The *Catnic* principle of construction is therefore in my opinion precisely in accordance with the Protocol. It is intended to give the patentee the full extent, but not more than the full extent, of the monopoly which a reasonable person skilled in the art, reading the claims in context, would think he was intending to claim. Of course it is easy to say this and sometimes more difficult to apply it in practice, although the difficulty should not be exaggerated. The vast majority of patent specifications are perfectly clear about the extent of the monopoly they claim. Disputes over them never come to court. In borderline cases, however, it does happen that an interpretation which strikes one person as fair and reasonable will strike another as unfair to the patentee or unreasonable for third parties. That degree of uncertainty is inherent in any rule which involves the construction of any document. It afflicts the whole of the law of contract, to say nothing of legislation. In principle it is without remedy, although I shall consider in a moment whether uncertainty can be alleviated by guidelines or a "structured" approach to construction.'

As already observed[3] Lord Hoffmann then went on at para [49] to suggest that the revision under EPC 2000 of the Protocol to Article 69 EPC to make express reference to equivalents would not affect this analysis.

The longer-term effects of the judgment in *Kirin-Amgen* remain uncertain, although it has been suggested that in the light of it the prevailing attitude of the English courts, it has been to demonstrate an unarticulated bias towards adopting a literal interpretation of the claims.[4]

1 *Kirin-Amgen v Hoechst Marion Roussel* [2001] IP&T 882; [2002] RPC 1; [2002] RPC 2 (Patents Court); [2003] RPC 3 (Court of Appeal); [2004] UKHL 46; [2005] 1 All ER 667; [2005] RPC 9 (House of Lords).

2 *Catnic v Hill & Smith* [1982] RPC 183 (House of Lords) at p. 242.

3 See para 6.05, fn 2 above.

4 Fisher, Matthew, 'A Case-Study in Literalism? Dissecting the English Approach to Patent Claim Construction in light of *Occlutech v AGA Medical*', [2011] *Intellectual Property Quarterly*, 283, offering a critique of the reasoning of the Court of Appeal (but not the outcome) in *Occlutech v AGA Medical* [2010] EWCA 702 (Court of Appeal) which in turn, at para [27], cites Nicholas Pumfrey, Martin J Adelman, Shamnad Basheer, Raj S.Davé, Peter Meier-Beck, Yukio Nagasawa, Maximilian Rospatt and Martin Sulsky, 'The Doctrine of Equivalents in Various Patent Regimes—Does Anybody Have It Right?', 11 *Yale J L & Tech*, 261 (2009).

Applying Kirin-Amgen v Hoechst Marion Roussel

6.09 Since the judgment in *Kirin-Amgen v Hoechst Marion Roussel* eschews the structured approach of the Protocol questions, and virtually no judgments since it have adopted that structured approach, such judgments do not lend themselves to the same level of analysis as was possible under the Protocol questions. However, it is possible to identify some principles that have been developed in the course of courts seeking to apply the judgment in *Kirin-Amgen,* as well as some earlier principles which it does not affect.

As to the well-established principles, the construction of a patent claim, as with the construction of any other document, is a matter of law.[1] The patent must be construed objectively through the eyes of the notional skilled addressee, and evidence from the patentee: as to what the patentee intended it to mean, or indirect evidence said to point to the patentee's intention is inadmissible.[2]

This can limit the scope for expert evidence directed to construction, but the court will admit evidence going to the factual matrix against which the claim is construed, such as the meaning of certain technical terms, as it did in *Kirin-Amgen v Hoechst Marion Roussel.*[3] In many cases, however, where the technology is less difficult than that in *Kirin-Amgen,* technical evidence may have little place in claim construction, as the Court of Appeal observed in *Dyson Appliances v Hoover:*[4]

'13   The parties agreed that the construction of the claims was for the Court, when properly instructed. As the Court is not required to construe the specification in a vacuum, evidence as to the factual matrix can be helpful as can evidence to explain technical terms. In this case, the parties went further and adduced evidence from two distinguished professors who gave their views as to the meaning that should be attributed to certain words and phrases in the claims. I have not found their evidence helpful as they did not seek to attribute to those words and phrases the meaning required by the Protocol, namely a meaning, between the extremes of literal and patentee's contemplated interpretation, and which provides fair protection and a reasonable degree of certainty. That of course is the task required by s 125 of the 1977 Act. It is not a skill which scientists have.'

The patent should be construed as of its priority date,[5] and evidence as to what might have been understood as to it later, and in particular what patentee may subsequently have said that it meant, is not generally relevant to its construction.[6] The whole document must be read together, the body of the specification with the claims, but if the meaning of a claim is clear it cannot be extended, or cut down by reference to the rest of the specification.[7] In the event of uncertainty, recourse may be had to the specification to resolve that uncertainty although in an extreme case, as observed in *Scanvaegt v Pelcombe:*[8] 'lack of clarity … can result in the patentee being unable to establish infringement' because 'if you cannot define the invention claimed, you cannot conclude that it is being used'.

Although construction should so far as possible be undertaken without knowledge of the infringement, this is rarely entirely practicable, as recognized in *Rockwater v Technip France:*[9]

'[42]   … Although it has often been said that the question of construction does not depend on the alleged infringement ("as if we had to construe it before the defendant was born") per Lord Esher M.R. in *Nobel's Explosives Co. v Anderson* (1894) 11 R.P.C. 519 at 523), questions of construction seldom arise in the abstract. That is why most sensible discussions of the meaning of language run on the general lines "does it mean this, or that, or the other?" Rather than the open-ended "what does it mean?" '

An issue which regularly arises, albeit rather more in the context of validity than that of infringement, is how the word 'for' in a patent claim (for example, in the context of the phrase 'passenger seating system for an aircraft') is to be construed. Although as always this must depend on context, traditionally it has been construed as meaning 'suitable for' rather than, for example, the rather more specific 'intended for', as, for example, discussed in *Virgin Atlantic Airways Ltd v Delta Air Lines.*[10] As to the significance of 'suitable for' in the context of infringement this was discussed in *Qualcomm v Nokia*[11] where the issue was whether a function in a mobile telephone handset that could not be used in practice because no telephone network supported it infringed:

'[73] ... it is important not to take the meaning of "suitable for" too far. Mr Antony Watson QC, who argued the case on the 324 Patent for Qualcomm ... started from the premise that an apparatus did not cease to infringe merely because it was switched off. So an apparatus for toasting bread infringes whether connected to the mains or not. He says this is just one example, and there is a general principle that an apparatus is still suitable for performing a particular function if it can be readily modified so as to perform that function. Mr Silverleaf accepts that a claim will be infringed if all that is required is to supply power. But he contends that modifications to the apparatus are not what is contemplated by "suitable for".

[74] I think Mr Silverleaf is right. Supplying power to a toaster does not change the apparatus: it simply puts into use the apparatus which is there already. The question in each case is whether the apparatus, as it stands, is suitable for use in that way. If the apparatus has to undergo physical modification before it can be used, then prima facie it is not suitable for use and does not infringe." '

An issue which has arisen since the judgment in *Kirin Amgen* is how much of the law and practice of the patent system is the skilled reader supposed to know and thus take into account when trying to work out, by the words of the claim, what the patentee intended to mean. This was addressed by the Court of Appeal in *Virgin Atlantic Airways v Premium Aircraft Interiors,*[12] and which held that the skilled reader was taken to know some patent law, or at least could ask someone who did. Thus it held that the skilled reader would be taken to know that the numerals in parentheses in the claims of European patents that are inserted to aid intelligibility had no limiting effect.[13] It also held that the skilled reader would incline strongly to the view that the pre-characterising portion of a claim in 'two part form' described what the patentee considered to be old.[14]

1   One consequence of this is that an issue that is dependent on construction, such as infringement (as well as lack of novelty or added matter) can more readily be appealed than a mixed question of fact and law, such as obviousness.

2   *Glaverbel v British Coal* [1995] RPC 255 (Court of Appeal) at p. 268.

3   *Kirin-Amgen v Hoechst Marion Roussel* [2001] IP&T 882; [2002] RPC 1; [2002] RPC 2 (Patents Court); [2003] RPC 3 (Court of Appeal); [2004] UKHL 46; [2005] 1 All ER 667; [2005] RPC 9 (House of Lords) at paras [53]–[63].

4   *Dyson Appliances v Hoover* [2001] EWCA Civ 1440; [2002] ENPR (Court of Appeal) at p. 48. See also *Glaverbel v British Coal* [1995] RPC 255 (Court of Appeal) at p. 268; *DSM NV's Patent* [2001] RPC 35 (Patents Court) at para [55], and *Hoechst Celanese v BP Chemicals* [1999] FSR 319 (Patents Court) at pp. 325–26.

5   *Biogen v Medeva* [1997] RPC 1 (House of Lords) at pp. 53–54, and *Research in Motion UK Ltd v Inpro Licensing Sarl* [2006] EWHC 70 (Pat) at para [37].

6   *Glaverbel v British Coal* [1995] RPC 255 (Court of Appeal) at p. 268. See also the observations in *Kirin-Amgen* at para [35] and the criticism at para [39] (both quoted above) of the US approach of using the doctrine of 'file wrapper estoppel' to counteract the consequences of the 'doctrine of equivalents', although since then the Dutch Supreme Court has in *Saier* v *Dijkstra* (22 December 2006) applied similar principles to narrow the scope of a claim that it would otherwise have construed more broadly. The English Court of Appeal in *Rohm & Haas v Collag* [2001] EWCA 1589 at para [42] treated as persuasive an observation of the Dutch Supreme Court in *Ciba-Geigy v Ote Optics* (13 January 1995) that a court might in certain circumstances be 'justified in using clarifying material in the public part of the granting file when it holds that even after the average person skilled in the art has considered the description and the drawings, it is still open to question how the contents of the claim must be interpreted'. Here, however, the Court of Appeal was interested in referring to a submission which 'did contain objective information about and commentary on experiments which were conducted in response to official observations, and it could be of assistance in resolving some puzzling features of the specification', rather than any submissions by the patentee as to what terms in the claim meant. See also the discussion by the English Court of Appeal in *Occlutech v AGA Medical* [2010] EWCA 702 (Court of Appeal) at paras [30]–[33]. More recently the English law as to prosecution history as an aid to construction was reviewed in *Actavis UK Ltd and ors v Eli Lilly* [2014] EWHC 1511 (Pat) [2015] EWCA Civ 555 (Court of Appeal) at first instance at paras [108]–[112], where, applying the observations in *Rohm & Haas v Collag* the Patents Court found the prosecution history to support its interpretation of the claim, although the Court of Appeal at [54]–[60] held that the light which the prosecution history sheds on the ultimate question of construction is likely to be extremely limited. In *Idenix Pharmaceutical, Inc v Gilead Sciences, Inc & Ors* [2014] EWHC 3916 (Pat) the Patents Court also considered the prosecution history, but observed that claim limitations to avoid an objection of lack of clarity were less likely to be a useful aid to construction than those to avoid an objection of lack of support.

7   *Rosedale v Carlton* [1960] RPC 59; *Auchinloss v Agricultural & Veterinary Machinery* [1997] RPC 649; *Lubrizol v Esso* [1998] RPC 727; *Cartonneries de Thulin v CTP White Knight* [2001] RPC at 107.

8   *Scanvaegt v Pelcombe* [1998] FSR 786 (Court of Appeal). In *Kirin-Amgen* at first instance claim 19 was held not capable of being infringed, and in the House of Lords, on the basis of the same findings of fact, claim 19 was held to be insufficient. See also **Chapter 5** at para 5.21 as to 'Insufficiency and obscure claims'.

9   *Rockwater Ltd v Technip France SA* [2004] EWCA 318 at para [42].

10   *Virgin Atlantic Airways Ltd v Delta Air Lines* [2011] EWCA 162 (Court of Appeal) at paras [18]–[25]. See also *Schenck Rotec GmbH v Universal Balancing Ltd* [2012] EWHC 1920 at [76]–[86], *FH Brundle (A Private Unlimited Company) v Perry* [2014] EWHC 475 (IPEC) at paras [43]–[50], *Rovi Solutions Corporation & Anor v Virgin*

Media Ltd & Ors [2014] EWHC 1559 (Pat) at paras [128]–[132] and *Koninklijke Philips Electronics N.V. v Nintendo of Europe Gmbh* [2014] EWHC 1959 (Pat) at paras [99]–[105].

11 *Qualcomm Inc v Nokia Corp* [2008] EWHC 329 (Pat).

12 *Virgin Atlantic Airways v Premium Aircraft Interiors* [2009] EWCA 1062 (Court of Appeal) at paras [6]–[22].

13 Consistent with Rule 43(7) of the Implementing Regulations to the EPC. Indeed, in *Jarden Consumer Solutions (Europe) Ltd v SEB SA & Anor* [2014] EWCA Civ 1629 the Court of Appeal in reversing a finding of infringement by the Patents Court, inferred that such finding had been impermissibly influenced by the numerals in the claim.

14 See **Chapter 2** at para 2.08.

Numerical limits in claims

6.10 A commonly encountered controversy in patent claim construction concerns numerical limits in claims. For example, in *Auchinloss & Antec v Agricultural & Veterinary Supplies*[1] at a time when the 'Protocol Questions' were regularly applied in the Patents Court, although it did not seek to apply them in this case observed, in terms similar to the third Protocol question:

'… where the patentee has defined an integer of his claim in terms of a range with specified numerical limits at each end, his purpose must be taken to have been to claim thus far and no further. His reason for doing so may not be apparent, but it may exist all the same, for instance it may lie "buried in the prior art".'

However, care is needed as to what numerical limits do in fact mean. Thus, in *Lubrizol v Esso*[2] it was held that a claim which called for 'at least 1.3 succinic groups' was infringed by material which only had 1.27 succinct groups:

'Exxon say that this is contrary to the language of the claim. 1.27 is simply not "at least" 1.3. I do not agree. I think Lubrizol are right here. The ratio is a lower limit. There is no reason why that should be particularly precise – the effects of over succination increase with the ratio, but the exact cut-off below which a monopoly is not worth claiming need not be that precise. I think the patentee, by "1.3", means what a scientist would conventionally mean, namely "1.3 to two significant figures".

More recently both the English and the EPO case law on numerical ranges has been reviewed in *Smith & Nephew v Convatec*, both at first instance and on appeal. Although the judgment at first instance was reversed on appeal the review of the case law at first instance and of the parties' submissions remains useful:[3]

'41. The key decisions on construction in general are *Kirin Amgen* [2005] RPC 5, and the Court of Appeal's summary of the approach in *Virgin v Premium* [2009] EWCA Civ 106. As regards numerical ranges in particular, I was referred to a number of cases in the English courts and the Technical Board of Appeal in the EPO. Counsel pointed out that in *Kirin Amgen* Lord

Hoffmann referred to numerical ranges at paragraph 65, observing that the notion of strict compliance with the conventional meanings of words or phrases sits most comfortably with the use of figures, measurements, angles and the like, when the question is whether they allow for some degree of tolerance or approximation.

42.   Convatec's counsel submitted that no English court had ever adopted an interpretation of a claim containing a numerical limit in accordance with Smith & Nephew's primary construction. In most cases an approach based on significant figures has been taken. The cases were:

(i)   *Lubrizol v Esso* (13 November 1996 in a passage not reported in the report at [1997] RPC 195) in which Jacob J as he then was decided that a lower limit of 1.3 should be read as "1.3 to two significant figures" and so would include 1.27.

(ii)   *Goldschmidt v EOC Belgium* [2000] EWHC Pat 175 in which David Young QC sitting as a Deputy Judge of the High Court held that a pH of 4.6 was within the claimed pH range of 5 to 8 since "5" was stated to one significant figure and was not, for example, stated as "5.0".

(iii)   *Halliburton v Smith* [2006] RPC 8 in which Pumfrey J construed "between 31% and 35%" to include from 30.5% to 35.4% since the figures in the claimed range were stated to two significant figures.

(iv)   *FNM Corp. v Drammock* [2009] EWHC 1294 in which Arnold J held that figures up to 45.4% were embraced by a limit expressed as "45%" since that was expressed to two significant figures and was not "45.0%".

43.   I was also referred to *Auchinloss v Agricultural & Veterinary Supplies* [1997] RPC 649 (Peter Prescott QC sitting as a Deputy judge of the High Court). There the learned judge held that a product with 10 parts sulfamic acid did not infringe a claim limited to "3 to 8 parts sulfamic acid" on the basis that a numerical range admits of no variant in the *Catnic* sense or that the skilled reader would understand that strict compliance with the parameters of the range was an essential requirement of the invention. However these findings are not concerned with the issue of significant figures, rounding and numerical precision, as Mr Prescott himself recognised in the passage at p690 in 5-17.

44.   Finally I should mention *PLG v Ardon* [1993] FSR 197 as the other English case emphasised in argument. Aldous J (as he then was) held (obiter) that a thickness of 60–72% would have infringed a claim limited to a minimum thickness of 75% following an application of what were then called the *Improver* questions. I do not have to decide whether, following *Kirin-Amgen*, the court would reach a similar conclusion today. The point is that *PLG v Ardon* does not support Smith & Nephew's narrow construction of the claim.

45.   Smith & Nephew placed emphasis on a decision of the EPO Technical Board of Appeal in T74/98 (19 Oct 2000) in which the Board held that a claim limited to 5–50 mol% monomer was novel over a disclosure of 4.98 mol% monomer. The Board refused to apply the rounding up rules since they thought that would expand the scope of the claim beyond the indicated limits (paragraph 3.2, first point).

46. Convatec submitted that the settled jurisprudence of the Technical Boards of Appeal in the EPO, as reflected by the current (Sept 2013) edition of their *Case Law* textbook, did not support Smith & Nephew's primary construction. This was based on cases T1186/05 (6th Dec 2007) in which a lower limit of 0.89 was held to be satisfied by 0.885 because 0.885, when rounded appropriately, gave 0.89; T234/09 (1st June 2012) in which an upper limit of 5% was held to include 5.2%; and T871/08 (8 Dec 2011) in which 2.996 had to be rounded up to 3, the number in the claim.

47. Convatec also submitted that the Boards of Appeal clearly regard T74/98, the case relied on by Smith & Nephew, as a case which can be distinguished from these other cases (the board in T1186/05 doing exactly that). The distinction relating to a particular aspect of T74/98 in that rounding the figure for the prior art in that case would alter the true meaning of the prior disclosure. I accept Convatec's submissions about the jurisprudence of the EPO. The outcome in T74/98 may be said to favour Smith & Nephew but the reasoning in that decision is not persuasive.

48. Smith & Nephew submitted that the true principle was that the number had to be perceived to be a measured or calculated value before the skilled reader would understand that a significant figures approach was to be taken. Applied to this case, Smith & Nephew submitted that the skilled reader would see from the specification of the 510 patent that the range in the claim was one of a group of sub-ranges disclosed, none of which would be thought to have a technical basis. The skilled reader would understand that the only reason for the sub-ranges was as something drafted by a patent attorney to provide a reservoir of possible fall-back positions in case prior art was cited against the patent which required a limiting amendment to one of the more limited sub-ranges.

49. I do not accept Smith & Nephew's submission about the principle to be applied. I do not see why the significant figures approach must only be applied to values in a patent claim which can be perceived to be the result of a measurement. This case is concerned with a value which acts as the limit of a range of concentrations. The actual concentrations used in the processes which have to be compared to the claim are likely to be measured or calculated. The scope of the limit of that range should not to be treated differently depending on whether it is possible to see in the specification that it derives from an actual measurement as opposed to being the product of a choice by the patentee. When, as here, the limiting value functions as a target against which a measured or calculated value is to be compared, then in principle I can see no reason why the skilled person should not use a significant figures approach.

50. However despite all these cases it is important to remember that the true interpretation of numerical limits is a matter of the construction of the particular patent specification in its own particular context. The fact that in many earlier cases the courts in England and the EPO Boards of Appeal have held that the question of whether a value should be held to fall within a numerical limit should be decided by rounding that value to the same number of significant figures as the range is expressed in the claim, does not mean that this must always be the conclusion to be reached.

51. The common general knowledge is part of the relevant context. In T708/05 the claimed range was from 1 to 5 μm. The Board of Appeal held that in the relevant technical field (multilayer films) the values concerned would be rounded to one decimal place and so 0.9625μm would be rounded to 1.0 μm. Separately the Board accepted evidence that it was not possible to determine the layer thickness with an experimental error of less than ± 5 to 10% and so 0.9625μm would be understood as "about 1μm" and within the claim on that basis.'

Applying these principles, the Patents Court concluded on the evidence in this case that the correct construction of a claim integer to a 'concentration between 1% and 25%' was one based on a significant figures approach, which construction 'sees 1% as a number stated to one significant figure and puts the lower limit at 0.95% while 25% is a number stated to two significant figures and puts the upper limit at less than 25.5%' and thereby rejected the contending constructions, from the patentee, that the claim's lower limit was 0.5 per cent, and from the defendant, that the claim's lower limit was exactly 1 per cent. This was reversed by the Court of Appeal that, adopting a whole numbers approach, held the lower limit to be 0.5 per cent. It also discussed the correct approach to construing numerical limits at [18]–[38], and analysed the cases discussed at first instance along with a number of other English and EPO decisions, concluding at [38] that:

'38. … the approach to be adopted to the interpretation of claims containing a numerical range is no different from that to be adopted in relation to any other claim. But certain points of particular relevance to claims of this kind do emerge from the authorities to which I have referred and which are worth emphasising. First, the scope of any such claim must be exactly the same whether one is considering infringement or validity. Secondly, there can be no justification for using rounding or any other kind of approximation to change the disclosure of the prior art or to modify the alleged infringement. Thirdly, the meaning and scope of a numerical range in a patent claim must be ascertained in light of the common general knowledge and in the context of the specification as a whole. Fourthly, it may be the case that, in light of the common general knowledge and the teaching of the specification, the skilled person would understand that the patentee has chosen to express the numerals in the claim to a particular but limited degree of precision and so intends the claim to include all values which fall within the claimed range when stated with the same degree of precision. Fifthly, whether that is so or not will depend upon all the circumstances including the number of decimal places or significant figures to which the numerals in the claim appear to have been expressed.'

1 *Auchinloss & Antec v Agricultural & Veterinary Supplies* [1997] RPC 649 (Patents Court).
2 *Lubrizol v Esso* (13 November 1996 – not reported as to this aspect) Jacob J (Patents Court); otherwise reported in [1997] RPC 195.
3 *Smith & Nephew Plc v Convatec Technologies Inc & Anor* [2013] EWHC 3955 (Pat), [2015] EWCA Civ 607 (Court of Appeal).

334

Defences

Introduction

6.11   Certain types of activity, even though they fall within the scope of one or more claims of a valid patent, are deemed by statute not to infringe. In this respect UK law, and that of many other European countries reflects CPC, Article 27 (1989 version) although the list based on this in PA 1977, s 60(5) has been supplemented on a couple of occasions. Three activities on the list that have been the subject of analysis by the English courts are:

'(a)   acts "done privately and for purposes which are not commercial";

(b)   acts "done for experimental purposes relating to the subject matter of the invention;"

(c)   ...

(d)   acts consisting "of the use, exclusively for the needs of a relevant ship, of a product or process in the body of such a ship or in its machinery, tackle, apparatus or other accessories, in a case where the ship has temporarily or accidentally entered the internal or external waters of the United Kingdom."'

Cases on the defence under PA 1977, s 60(b) have been mainly in the pharmaceuticals sector (although they have also concerned herbicides, biocides and medical devices) and so this is discussed in more detail in **Chapter 7** at para 7.22, where a further important defence of specific application to pharmaceuticals, that in relation to their regulatory review, is also discussed, and which, although it has not yet been considered by the English courts, was the subject of a reference from the German courts to the Court of Justice, albeit one that was ultimately abandoned.

The scope of PA 1977, s 60(a) was canvassed in *Smith Kline & French Laboratories v Evans Medical*[1] where it was held that experiments done for legal proceedings in the court or Patent Office were undertaken privately, and not for a commercial purpose. However, the court also went on to say that if done for a dual purpose, one of which was that of obtaining commercial experience, they would not secure such exemption.

The only English decision on PA 1977, s 60(d) was *Stena Rederi v Irish Line Ferries*[2] where the defence was held to apply where the ship in issue made routine, and regular trips into UK territorial waters. By PA 1977, s 60(6) (reflecting CPC, Article 26(3) (1989 version)) the fact that someone may have a defence under PA 1977, s 60(5) does not of itself provide a defence to someone who supplies them with means relating to an essential element of the invention under PA 1977, s 60 (2).

A further statutory defence, of personal prior use, is set out in PA 1977, s 64. In addition to such statutory defences there are several other defences not set out in PA 1977 but established by case law. Some of these are based on concepts of implied licence, whereas others reflect competition law considerations. These are discussed below.

1 *Smith Kline & French Laboratories v Evans Medical* [1989] FSR 513.
2 *Stena Rederi AB v Irish Line Ferries* [2002] EWHC 7373 (Ch); [2002] RPC 50 (Patents Court); [2003] EWCA (Civ) 66; [2003] RPC 36; [2004] IP&T 301 (Court of Appeal).

Co-ownership

6.12   The respective rights of co-owners of a patent are set out in PA 1977, s 36(2):

'(2)   Where two or more persons are proprietors of a patent, then, subject to the provisions of this section and subject to any agreement to the contrary –

(a)   each of them shall be entitled, by himself or his agents, to do in respect of the invention concerned, for his own benefit and without the consent of or the need to account to the other or others, any act which would apart from this subsection and s 55 below, amount to an infringement of the patent concerned; and

(b)   any such act shall not amount to an infringement of the patent concerned.'

Thus the powers of a co-owner to practice the invention are limited. In *Henry Brothers (Magherafelt) v Ministry of Defence*[1] one issue was whether the putative co-owner was, by having products falling within the scope of the patent claims made for it, operating outside the scope of the statutory licence given to a co-owner. The Patents Court held: 'the section requires you to look at the substance of what is going on. The key words are "on his own behalf and the reference to *himself or his agents* is there essentially to take care of any argument that the patentee cannot himself exploit what is his invention through others. I do not think the word *agent* is being used in any strict sense at all. "Home use" is what is protected – and one must look to see whether that is all, in substance, the co-owner is doing.'

Although this is a broader view of the powers of a co-owner than some older cases suggest, it makes a clear distinction between 'home use', which is permitted, and a licence to a third party, which is not.

1 *Henry Brothers (Magherafelt) v The Ministry of Defence and the Northern Ireland Office* [1997] RPC 693; [1999] RPC 442 (Court of Appeal).

Implied licence, parallel imports into the UK and repair

6.13   As observed by the House of Lords in *United Wire v Screen Repair Services (Scotland)*[1] it is the concept of implied licence which explains why, notwithstanding the language of PA 1977, s 60 'a patentee cannot complain when someone to whom he has sold a patented product then, without any further consent, uses it or disposes of it to someone else'.

English law extends this principle of implied licence to patented goods put on the market outside the UK, as established long ago in *Betts v Willmott*.[2] In *Roussel Uclaf v Hockley*[3] the patentee's application for summary judgment for patent infringement against the importer into the UK of a patented product, mounted on the basis that the patentee's sales in China were labelled 'for use in PRC only, re-export forbidden' was refused, as the patentee had failed to demonstrate that such labelling was its invariable practice. However, the generally held view elsewhere in Europe is that under their national laws, and subject to EU law for imports from the rest of the EEA, as discussed below, the national patent rights in their countries can be asserted against the import from abroad of patented products first placed on the market by the patentee or with its consent. This however is presumably absent some express consent on the part of the patentee to such import.

The House of Lords held in *United Wire* that the concept of implied licence had no bearing on the question of a repair to a patented product, or to those acts which went further and amounted to making it, as discussed at para 6.02 above.

1   *United Wire v Screen Repair Services (Scotland)* [2001] FSR 365 (House of Lords).
2   *Betts v Willmott* [1871] 6 Ch App 239.
3   *Roussel Uclaf v Hockley* [1996] RPC 441.

Exhaustion of rights under EU Law

6.14   Other European countries do not follow the English concept of implied licence as discussed above. Thus as patents are national rights, the *existence* of which is not affected by the TFEU, they would have the scope elsewhere in Europe to impede the free movement of goods within the EU, had not the Court of Justice developed the concept of the 'specific subject matter' of such rights, that enables it to limit the *exercise* of such rights without challenging their *existence*. The Treaty on the Functioning of the European Union, Articles 34 and 36[1] deal with the free movement of goods within the EU:

'34   Quantitative restrictions on imports and all measures having equivalent effect shall, without prejudice to the following provisions, be prohibited between Member States.

36   The provisions of Articles 34 and 35 shall not preclude prohibition or restrictions on imports, exports or goods in transit justified on grounds of public morality, public policy or public security; the protection of health and life of humans, animals or plants; the protection of national treasures possessing artistic, historic or archaeological value; or the protection of industrial and commercial property. Such prohibitions or restrictions shall not, however, constitute a means of arbitrary discrimination or a disguised restriction on trade between Member States.'

Article 34 prohibits quantitative restrictions on imports and 'all measures having equivalent effect' between Member States. However, by Article 36 the provisions of Article 34 should not preclude prohibitions or restrictions on imports 'if the prohibitions or restrictions are justified for the protection of industrial property', such as patents. The Article 36 exception has been construed narrowly, confining the 'specific subject matter' of such right to the right to be the first to manufacture, and place the product on the market.[2] Once the rightsholder or the licensee has done so, it has exhausted all further rights over the product under the patent or other IPR, and cannot later seek to block the export of the product to other parts of the EU (or EEA) under parallel IPRs, thereby precluding the use of IPRs to partition national markets, and to restrict trade between Member States. This doctrine of 'exhaustion of rights' differs from the concept of implied licence under English law in 'that an implied licence may be excluded by express agreement or made subject to conditions while the exhaustion doctrine leaves no patent rights to be enforced'.[3]

The case law on exhaustion of rights mainly concerns pharmaceuticals because their prices in the EU are heavily regulated by Member States, and as a result there are considerable disparities in the price of the same pharmaceutical in different countries. Businesses have been established to acquire pharmaceuticals where they are cheap, and to sell them where they are expensive, thus undercutting the local owner, or licensee of patents, and other IPRs protecting that product.

In *Centrafarm v Sterling Drug*,[4] Centrafarm acquired in England an antibacterial manufactured by Sterling, and sold it in Holland for twice the English price. In both countries the drug was protected by patents held by Sterling. The Court of Justice limited what could be protected under the Dutch national patent law to the 'specific subject matter' of the right, which was the:

> 'guarantee that the patentee … has the exclusive right to use an invention with a view to manufacturing industrial products and putting them into circulation for the first time either directly or by the grant of licences to third parties, as well as the right to oppose infringements.'

In these circumstances the enforcement of patent rights was incompatible with the rules on free movement of goods. In *Merck v Stephar*[5] the Court of Justice held that Merck could not use its Dutch patent to prevent importation into the Netherlands of a pharmaceutical from Italy, placed on the market there by Merck, even though (at that time) pharmaceuticals were not patentable in Italy. However, the exhaustion doctrine will not operate to prohibit the holder of an IPR from relying on this to prevent imports where, because of the lack of such protection in the country in which the goods were first marketed, that marketing took place by someone other than the proprietor of the patent without its consent. Yet where a patentee voluntarily chooses itself to market the product in a Member State where no patent protection is available, it cannot thereafter block the import of a product first put on the market by it into another Member State where it holds such protection.

Essential to the application of the exhaustion principle, however, is the voluntary and free marketing by the holder of the IPRs, or by others with its voluntary consent. Thus the principle does not extend to compulsory licences. In *Pharmon v Hoechst*,[6] Hoechst held patents to a process for the manufacture of a drug which it marketed in the Netherlands, and the UK. A British company, DDSA, had in 1972 obtained a compulsory licence under the UK patent. DDSA sold to a Dutch company, Pharmon, a quantity of the drug shortly before the expiry of the UK patent. Pharmon sought to market the drug in the Netherlands where Hoechst secured an injunction for patent infringement stopping them from making further sales. On appeal, this matter was referred to the Court of Justice, which dismissed Pharmon's arguments and decided that:

'Articles [34] and [36] ... do not preclude the application of a law of a Member State which gives the proprietor of a patent the right to prevent the marketing in that state of a product which has been manufactured in another member state by the holder of a compulsory licence granted under a parallel patent held by the same proprietor'

A further attempt to narrow down the scope of this defence was mounted in the mid-1990s, this time in the context of pharmaceutical parallel imports from Spain and Portugal, in *Merck v Primecrown*[7] in which questions were referred to the Court of Justice as to whether the long established principle in *Merck v Stephar* should be reconsidered, or modified so as not to apply where products such as pharmaceuticals, as a result of a legal, and/or ethical obligation, were placed on a market where they could not benefit from patent protection.

When Spain and Portugal had joined the European Community (as the EU was known at the time) they did not grant product (as opposed to process) patents for pharmaceuticals. However, in their respective Accession Treaties, patentees of pharmaceuticals were permitted a period of time during which they could continue to prevent parallel importation of pharmaceuticals from Spain and Portugal until these states brought their patent laws into line with the rest of the EU. As this period was expiring Merck sued Primecrown under its UK patents to try to prevent the parallel import from Spain and Portugal of pharmaceuticals that it had placed on the market there. The Patents Court referred two sets of questions to the Court of Justice. First, what were the precise dates after which Merck could no longer oppose parallel importation from Spain and Portugal (there was a lack of clarity in the drafting of the relevant Treaty provision). Second, whether there was a justification for extending the exceptions from the exhaustion principle as patents were not available in Spain and Portugal when Merck first put its products on the market.

On the second question, Merck's case for extending exceptions to the exhaustion principle was based on a number of arguments that had not been addressed in *Merck v Stephar*:

— even though there was no patent protection available in these countries they had an ethical requirement to sell the drugs, particularly if the drugs had previously been released there and doctors were prescribing them;
— in some cases the national laws of the Member State involved imposed a legal requirement to supply the drugs;
— Community law prevented refusing to supply or to sell with an obligation not to export to those countries that did not allow patents for pharmaceuticals; and
— the time taken for a new drug to reach the market place had increased significantly.

Merck argued that on this basis they should be permitted to prevent such parallel imports, as if there was a genuine ethical or legal requirement for putting the goods into circulation, they should not be regarded as having been put on the market voluntarily. Despite support from the Advocate General for Merck's position (a right could not be exhausted if one did not have one in the first place) the Court of Justice held to the doctrine of exhaustion as formulated in *Merck v Stephar*, which struck a balance between the patentee's national patent rights on the one hand, and a central principle of free movement of goods on the other. None of the reasons advanced by Merck warranted altering this. Further, as all EU Member States now recognized pharmaceutical product patent protection, the problem encountered by Merck would disappear in time. If Merck placed the product on the market, they had to accept the consequences. However, the Court of Justice did say that if the national court decided that a patentee was legally bound under national law to sell its product, then such product would not have been sold with his consent.

A different approach to the issues addressed in *Merck v Primecrown* was adopted in more recent Accession Treaties. Thus for the eight out of the ten countries that joined the EU on 1 May 2004 which had not had longstanding product patent protection for pharmaceuticals,[8] for Bulgaria and Romania, which joined on 1 January 2007, and for Croatia which joined on 1 July 2013 these provide for a 'Specific Mechanism' as follows:[9]

'With regard to the Czech Republic, Estonia, Latvia, Lithuania, Hungary, Poland, Slovenia or Slovakia [Bulgaria, Romania or Croatia], the holder, or his beneficiary, of a patent or supplementary protection certificate for a pharmaceutical product filed in a Member State at a time when such protection could not be obtained in one of the abovementioned new Member States for that product, may rely on the rights granted by that patent or supplementary protection certificate in order to prevent the import and marketing of that product in the Member State or States where the product in question enjoys patent protection or supplementary protection, even if the product was put on the market in that new Member State for the first time by him or with his consent.

Any person intending to import or market a pharmaceutical product covered by the above paragraph in a Member State where the product enjoys patent or supplementary protection shall demonstrate to the competent authorities in the application regarding that import that one month's prior notification has been given to the holder or beneficiary of such protection.'

The principle of exhaustion of rights does not operate to exhaust all rights in a patent to prevent the general sale of infringing product following the first instance of a sample of some such product being put freely onto the market in the EU for the first time by or with the consent of the patentee. The exhaustion operates on individual items or amounts of the patented product in question. If a certain quantity of a patented product has been put freely on the market in one part of the EU by or with the consent of the patentee it can be sold on anywhere else in the EU, but this does not give *carte blanche* for all subsequent such product to be sold anywhere else in the EU.

The question of 'international exhaustion' and issues of 'deemed consent' to further dealings in articles first placed on the market outside the EEA by the holder of an IPR is one which has been under active examination in the field of trade marks. However, in contrast to trade marks, copyright and related rights, patent law has not been harmonized by any EU measure (except in the limited field of biotechnological inventions[10]) so there is as yet no scope for the Court of Justice to consider the issue in relation to patents, except in this limited field.

1   Formerly Article 28 and 30 respectively of the Treaty establishing the EC, and before that Articles 30 and 36 respectively of the Treaty establishing the European Economic Community (EEC).

2   However, this only applies where the product has first been placed on the market by or with the consent of the rights owner. Thus, for example, it cannot be used as a defence against infringement where an article is lawfully manufactured in one Community Member State but because of disparities in patent laws it cannot be marketed in another Member State, as in Case 35/87 *Thetford Corpn v Fiamma SpA* [1990] Ch 339; [1990] 2 WLR 1394; [1989] 2 All ER 801; [1988] ECR 3585; [1988] 3 CMLR 549; [1989] 1 FSR 57.

3   *United Wire v Screen Repair Services* [2001] FSR 365 (House of Lords).

4   Case 15/74 *Centrafarm v Sterling Drug* [1974] ECR 1147; [1974] ECR 1183; [1974] 2 CMLR 480; [1975] FSR 161 (Court of Justice).

5   Case 187/80 *Merck v Stephar* [1981] ECR 2063; [1981] 3 CMLR 463, [1982] FSR 57 (Court of Justice).

6   Case 19/84 *Pharmon v Hoechst* [1985] ECR 2281; [1985] 3 CMLR 775; [1986] FSR 108 (Court of Justice).

7   Cases 267/95 & 268/95 *Merck v Primecrown* [1995] FSR 909 (Patents Court); [1997] FSR 237(ECJ); [1997] 1 CMLR 83 (Court of Justice).
8   The other two countries, Cyprus and Malta, in contrast, long had such protection.
9   Paragraph 2 of Annex IV to the Act of Accession of 16 April 2003 OJ L 326, 23 September 2003, p. 797, para 1 (Company law) of Annex V to the Act of Accession of 25 April 2005 OJ L 157, 21 June 2005, 268, and para 1 of Annex IV to the Act of Accession OJ L 112, 24 April 2012, p. 60 respectively. The procedural requirements of the provision were considered by the English courts in *Merck Canada Inc v Sigma Pharmaceuticals Plc* [2012] EWPCC 18; [2013] EWCA 326, which referred questions to the Court of Justice which were answered in Case C-539/13 *Merck Canada Inc. and Merck Sharp & Dohme Ltd v Sigma Pharmaceuticals plc* (12 February 2015, Court of Justice).
10   See **Chapter 8** at para 8.02.

Competition law defences

6.15   Ever since the UK joined the European Community (as the EU was called at the time) attempts have made to use anti-trust' type arguments as a defence to a charge of patent infringement in the UK courts. These are usually based on TFEU, Article 102[1] that outlaws the abuse of 'a dominant position', although where licences are on offer TFEU, Article 101[2] that outlaws certain types of agreement, may have application. Thus, in *Philips Electronics v Ingman*[3] a defence alleging that the proceedings were intended to force the defendants into entering into a standard form licence that would itself be in breach of TFEU, Article 101 was allowed to stand, even though it was given little prospect of success. A defence under TFEU, Article 102 was, however, struck out. Indeed, TFEU, Article 102 defences, in isolation, have met with little success in practice. In *ICI v Berk Pharmaceuticals*[4] the English courts held there to be an inadequate 'nexus' between the exercise of the right, and the abuse alleged. and in *Volvo v Erik Veng*[5] it was established by the Court of Justice that a refusal to licence coupled with the mere assertion of, in this case design rights, did not in itself constitute an abuse of a dominant position, and so a breach of TFEU, Article 102. There had to be an actual abuse of that position, as was held to exist in *Magill*[6] concerning copyright in television listings. However, as copyright laws do not in general provide for compulsory licences in certain circumstances, whereas most patent laws, including that in the UK do, (as to which see para 6.18 below), there is more scope for the application of TFEU, Article 102 to copyright than to patents.

Specific non-exhaustive examples of abuses falling within the scope of TFEU, Article 102 are given in the article itself:

'102   Any abuse by one or more undertakings of a dominant position within the common market or in a substantial part of it shall be prohibited as incompatible with the common market in so far as it may affect trade between Member States. Such abuse may, in particular, consist in:

(a)   directly or indirectly imposing unfair purchase or selling prices or other unfair trading conditions;
(b)   limiting production, markets or technical development to the prejudice of consumers;
(c)   applying dissimilar conditions to equivalent transactions with other trading parties thereby placing them at a competitive disadvantage;
(d)   making the conclusion of contracts subject to acceptance by the other parties of supplementary obligations which, by their nature or according to commercial usage, have no connection with the subject of such contracts.' a

The Court of Justice has defined a dominant position as one where the enterprise in question is able to prevent effective competition being maintained in the relevant market, and to behave independently of its competitors and customers. The key issue in relation to TFEU, Article 102 in determining the presence of a monopoly situation, and anti-competitive practices is the effect on the relevant market, and this requires a determination of both the product, and geographical markets involved. In order for a company to have a dominant position it is not necessary that it should hold any particular IPRs. Indeed, most of the leading cases on TFEU, Article 102 relate purely to market power unassisted by such rights. However, in certain limited circumstances the abusive exercise of such rights could result in infringement of TFEU, Article 102, for example, the refusal by a patentee to grant a non-exclusive licence to a particular company either at all or on reasonable terms, when that patentee has granted similar licences to other parties.

The decision of the English Court of Appeal in *Chiron v Murex Diagnostics*[7] when refusing to reverse an order striking out a TFEU, Article 102 defence reinforced the view that such defences are only available in the most exceptional cases. The decision also reviews the previous cases in the area, and set out the four essentials of the defence:

- that the plaintiff should have a 'dominant position' in a 'relevant market';
- that the plaintiff should be guilty of some sort of abusive conduct;
- that there should be a sufficient connection or 'nexus' between the alleged abuse and the litigation; and
- that there should be some potential effect on trade between Member States.

Here the Court of Appeal agreed with the Patents Court that in this case the first three were not unarguable, but that the fourth one was, and could not succeed. One member of the Court of Appeal went further, finding the third point also unarguable, and then went on to observe (dealing with a view expressed in an earlier case that there were 'important points with which the courts will at some stage have to grapple'):

'For my part, I consider that the time has come when these questions should be resolved, as they must be sooner or later. The nettle should be grasped now. Otherwise this and other cases concerned with intellectual property will be encumbered at trial with a great deal of evidence and argument about market, dominant position and abuse which may be wholly unnecessary.

In the ordinary way I consider that the remedy for abuses such as are alleged in this case is not to refuse relief to the holder of the patent against an infringer. That could be altogether lacking in proportionality. It might also, as Megarry V-C points out, [in *Imperial Chemical Industries Ltd v Berk Pharmaceuticals Ltd* [1981] FSR 1] give rise to a fluctuating situation whereby a patent was sometimes enforceable and sometimes not. There are other remedies available, as the Advocate-General indicated in [*Parke, Davis & Co v Probel, Reese, Beintema – Interpharon and Centrafarm* [1968] ECR 81; [1968] CMLR 47] such as action taken under Article 3 of Regulation 17. That was the course adopted and upheld in *Hilti AG v EC Commission*. [1992] 4 CMLR 16 (CFI), [1994] ECRI-667; [1994] 4 CMLT 614 (ECJ)]

There may be extraordinary cases, where the holder of a patent should be refused relief against an infringer on the ground that he is in breach of Article [102]. But I can see nothing to indicate that this case is in that class.'

Despite this, in *Intel v Via Technologies*[8] TFEU, Articles 101 and 102 defences, having been struck out at first instance, were reinstated on appeal. However, the circumstances of this case were complex, and somewhat exceptional, and the matter never proceeded to trial.

More recently Article 102 has assumed renewed relevance to patent litigation, not in providing a defence to liability for patent infringement, but rather as potentially limiting the circumstances in which injunctive relief is available where the owner of a patent that is essential to a standard prevails on validity and infringement, and seeks to secure an excessive licence fee as a condition of granting a licence, as is discussed in **Chapter 9** at para 9.03.

Paralleling EU competition law are national such laws. UK competition law underwent radical overhaul under the Competition Act 1998 that established a system which in large part employs the same concepts as are set out in TFEU, Articles 101–102, but without their requirement for a potential effect on trade between Member States. Thus, it can be envisaged that the 'Part II Prohibition' under the Competition Act 1998 (which parallels TFEU, Article 102) could also be asserted as a defence to infringement in the same way as Article 102, but would receive equally short shrift from the English courts except in those rare occasions where there is no potential effect on trade between Member States, and where the first three points set out in *Chiron* can be made out.

---

1   Formerly Article 82 of the Treaty establishing the European Community, and before that Article 86 of the Treaty establishing the European Economic Community.
2   Formerly, Article 81 of the Treaty establishing the European Community, and before that Article 85 of the Treaty establishing the European Economic Community.

3   *Philips Electronics v Ingman* [1999] FSR 112.
4   *ICI v Berk Pharmaceuticals* [1981] 2 CMLR 91; [1981] FSR 1.
5   Case 238/87 *Volvo v Erik Veng* [1988] ECR 6211; [1989] 4 CMLR 122 (ECJ).
6   Joined Cases C-241/91 and C-242/91 *Radio Telefis Eireann and Independent Television Publications Ltd v The Commission of the European Communities (Magill Television Guide Ltd intervening)* [1995] FSR 530 (ECJ). See also Case C-418/01 *IMS Health GmbH & Co OHG v NDC Health GmbH & Co* [2004] 4 CMLR 28, and Case T-201/04 *Microsoft v Commission* [2007] 5 CMLR 11.
7   *Chiron v Murex Diagnostics* [1994] FSR 187 (Court of Appeal).
8   *Intel Corpn v Via Technologies Inc* [2002] EWHC 1159 (Ch); [2003] FSR 12 (Patents Court); [2002] EWCA Civ 1905; [2003] FSR 33 (Court of Appeal).

Personal prior use

6.16   The right to continue to do something that one had already been doing before the priority date was introduced as a defence into UK patent law by PA 1977, s 64. This (as substituted by the Copyright Designs and Patents Act 1988 for a similar but less elegant provision) provides in s 64(1):

'(1)   Where a patent is granted for an invention, a person who in the United Kingdom before the priority date of the invention,
(a)   does in good faith an act which would constitute an infringement of the patent if it were in force, or
(b)   makes in good faith effective and serious preparations to do such an act,
has the right to continue to do the act or, as the case may be, to do the act, notwithstanding the grant of the patent; but this right does not extend to granting a licence to another person to do the act.'

One major limitation in the section is that personal prior use outside the UK does not count, although within the EU this limitation could perhaps be challenged as constituting a disguised restriction on trade between Member States contrary to TFEU, Article 34.[1] There is no pre-PA 1977 guidance as to its meaning, there having been no need for it, as not only public, but also private prior use could in certain circumstances pre-PA 1977, invalidate a patent. Private, or secret, prior use can no longer do so.

It is rarely the case, particularly with a process, that an activity continues unchanged. Three English cases on this section have all addressed the application of this section to this particular issue. In *Helitune v Stewart Hughes*[2] such a defence failed, there being no 'effective and serious preparations', but it was observed, had it been available:

'Section 64 gives what can be called a statutory licence to a person who in good faith either does an infringing act or makes effective and serious preparations to do such an act. The infringing acts referred to are set out in s 60 of the Act and include, where the invention is a product, making, disposing of, offering to dispose of, using and importing the product. Where the invention is a process, infringing acts include using the process and disposing of, offering to dispose of, using or importing a product made by the process.

Section 64(2) confines the statutory licence to the right to continue to do or to do "that act", namely the act which the person had done or had made effective and serious preparations to do. Thus, the right is limited to the particular act of infringement done or for which effective and serious preparation had been made. That conclusion can be illustrated by considering a person who had in good faith imported an infringing product. The section enables him to continue to import the product but not sell it unless the importation amounted to an effective and serious preparation to sell it.

Section 64(1) relates to acts which constitute an infringement and not to any particular product or process. As I have stated the acts are those covered by a patent as set out in s 60. Thus, provided a person has carried out an infringing act before the priority date, he can continue to carry out that act even though the product or process may be different to some degree. This can be illustrated by considering a person who uses an infringing process. The fact that he alters that process after the priority date does not matter. The section states that the doing of that act, namely using an infringing process, shall not amount to an infringement.

I believe that the correct approach is to look first to see what are the acts of the defendant which are alleged to be infringements and which it wishes to continue. Thereafter I must decide whether it carried out those acts in good faith before the priority date or whether it made effective and serious preparations to do so.'

Having once determined the right to exist in the first place, this formulation of what the section would then permit the defendant to do, is broad. But in *Lubrizol Corpn v Esso Petroleum*[3] another Patents Court judge took a narrower view, observing:

'I think it is only right to say that I have some doubts, with great respect to Aldous J. as to whether *Helitune* is correct. The act which the alleged infringer is entitled to continue to conduct by virtue of s 64(2) is the act which he was committing before the priority date. It was not an infringement then. It was an act of commerce. It is that specific act of commerce which he is entitled to continue. I have difficulty in accepting that by, for example, manufacturing product A before the priority date, he was thereby given a right to manufacture any product after the priority date. In my view, s 64 is intended to safeguard the existing commercial activity of a person in the United Kingdom which is overtaken by the subsequent grant of a patent. It is not meant to be a charter allowing him to expand into other products and other processes.'

Further observations on PA 1977, s 64 were made in the final hearing at first instance on the same case, by yet another Patents Court judge, in *Lubrizol Corpn v Esso Petroleum*:[4]

'I agree with Laddie J for all the reasons he gave in his decision, and because I do not think the actual language of s 64 is appropriate were Aldous J correct.

It is *"the doing of that act"* which is protected, not *"any act which would otherwise be an infringement"*.

However there was a slight gloss. I think Laddie J's reference to "existing commercial activity" – the protected act of the section – means an activity which is substantially the same as the prior act or act for which serious and effective preparations were made. In deciding whether the activity is substantially the same all the circumstances must be considered. Both technical and commercial matters must be taken into account. That is important in a case such as the present where there are inherent minor variations in starting materials or the like. If the protected act has to be *exactly* the same (whatever that may mean) as the prior act then the protection given by the section would be illusory. The section is intended to give a practical protection to enable a man to continue doing what he was doing before'

Again no 'effective and serious preparations' were found to have been made in *Lubrizol,* so such observations, as with all those above, have limited value as precedents. The Court of Appeal agreed with the views of the Patents Court, in that the preparations in issue had not been 'effective' as at the priority date they were only in preliminary, planning, stages. However, one of the Court of Appeal judges, Aldous LJ, who had when in the Patents Court given judgment in *Helitune,* noted that his own observations in that case as to the scope of the section 'had been read in a way not intended', and agreed with the observations made by the judge at first instance in this case that limiting the protected act to exactly what had been done before would render the protection illusory, and that the intent was to give a practical protection to continue doing in substance what had been done before. A more recent analysis of the provision took place in *Forticrete v Lafarge Roofing*[5] where the defendants were allowed to introduce such a plea on amendment as they were able to show an arguable case that they had made 'effective and serious preparations' as to one of the articles in issue, but not as to another article said to have been derived from the first, because it was not the same article of commerce as or in substance the same, as the first.

1   Most other EU Member States also have such a provision, but as with the UK one, these are expressed only to relate to local prior use. For a decision of the Federal Supreme Court under the corresponding German provision see: *JB GmbH v CML ('Bending Apparatus')* [2003] ENPR 6.
2   *Helitune v Stewart Hughes* [1991] RPC 78; [1991] FSR 171. The Judge observed:
    'At the priority date of the patent, the defendant had not sold an active tracker. It had, however, produced a prototype of an active tracker using a laser with a view to its further development. The position had not been reached where the defendant had decided to sell active trackers, and by the priority date its efforts were concentrated on producing a passive tracker. I do not believe the defendant had reached the state of making effective and serious preparations to sell an active tracker, and, therefore, s 64 does not give it a defence to the action.'
3   *Lubrizol Corpn v Esso Petroleum* [1992] RPC 281 (Patents Court). This issue was not considered on appeal – [1992] RPC 467 (Court of Appeal).

4   *Lubrizol Corpn v Esso Petroleum* [1997] RPC 195 (Patents Court); [1998] RPC 727 (Court of Appeal).

5   *Forticrete Ltd v Lafarge Roofing Ltd* [2005] EWHC 3024 (Ch) (Patents Court). See also *H Lundbeck v Norpharma SpA* [2011] EWHC 907 (Patents Court) at paras [163]–[172] holding a process not to be 'substantially the same' as that undertaken before the priority date of the patent in suit and *Schenck Rotec GmbH v Universal Balancing Limited* [2012] EWHC 1920 (Pat) holding making or selling a certain product not to be in substance the same act as that making or selling another product before the priority date.

'Gillette' Defence

6.17   The assertion that one cannot be infringing a patent because one is practicing no more than something that formed part of the state of the art at the priority date of that patent is termed a 'Gillette' Defence, after *Gillette Safety Razor v Anglo-American Trading.*[1] Even though it is not really a defence, because it usually means that a patent is invalid for lack of novelty, or that the patentee is seeking to construe the claims too widely, the term is still met, as in the Patents Court judgment in *Merrell Dow v Norton*[2] quoting 'the well-known words of Lord Moulton' in *Gillette,* which were considered to be 'still correct in law':

> 'It is impossible for an ordinary member of the public to keep watch on all the numerous patents which are taken out and to ascertain the validity and scope of their claims. But he is entitled to feel secure if he knows that that which he is doing differs from that which has been done of old only in non-patentable variations, such as the substitution of mechanical equivalents or changes of material, shape or size. The defence that "the alleged infringement was not novel at the date of the Plaintiff's letters patent" is a good defence in law, and it would sometimes obviate the great length and expense of patent cases if the defendant could and would put forth his case in this form, and thus spare himself the trouble of demonstrating on which horn of the well-known dilemma the plaintiff had impaled himself, invalidity or non-infringement.'

The Patents Court also emphasized: 'I am of course only considering the question of invalidity, but I believe it still to be the law that any person is entitled to do that which is old, namely that which has been described in a prior published document and be confident that he will not infringe the patent of another.'

However, in *Merrell Dow* the patent was held to have been anticipated (contributory infringement having been conceded) although in a parallel action in Germany, in which only infringement was in issue, the patent was so construed as to find it not infringed.[3]

1   *Gillette Safety Razor v Anglo-American Trading* (1913) 30 RPC 465 at p. 480.

2   *Merrell Dow v Norton* [1994] RPC 1; [1995] RPC 233 (Court of Appeal); [1996] RPC 76 (House of Lords) (discussed further in **Chapter 7** at para 7.18).

3   *Terfenadin* [1998] FSR 145.

'**Article 3 – General obligation**
1.   Member States shall provide for the measures, procedures and remedies necessary to ensure the enforcement of the intellectual property rights covered by this Directive. Those measures, procedures and remedies shall be fair and equitable and shall not be unnecessarily complicated or costly, or entail unreasonable time-limits or unwarranted delays.
2.   Those measures, procedures and remedies shall also be effective, proportionate and dissuasive and shall be applied in such a manner as to avoid the creation of barriers to legitimate trade and to provide for safeguards against their abuse.'

As observed below, Article 3 has also started to inform the approach that the English courts are taking to the issue of remedies.

1   Directive 2004/48/EC of 29 April 2004 on the enforcement of intellectual property rights OJ L 157, 30 April 2004, Corrigendum OJ L 195 2 June 2004, 16.
2   One exception of a sort is Article 15, implemented in England and Wales by changes made to the Civil Procedure Rules by SI 2005/3515 and by which a court may order an infringer, at its expense, to publicise the decision finding it to infringe, although English courts may already have had that power under their inherent jurisdiction.

Injunctions

6.20   The standard form of final injunction in a patent action in England and Wales is an injunction not to infringe the patent the subject of the infringement action. In *Coflexip v Stolt Comex Seaway*[1] a narrower form of injunction, directed to the articles that had been found to infringe, was granted by the Patents Court, but this approach was criticized by the Court of Appeal, despite such narrower injunctions being the usual form in certain other jurisdictions such as Germany.

Although the standard form of injunction will cease to have effect when the underlying patent expires, in certain circumstances the court will express an injunction so as to extend beyond expiry of the subject patent. The aim of such relief is to prevent the infringer from relying on the 'springboard' that it secured by infringing close to patent expiry, and as a result of which it might otherwise be able to get onto market earlier after patent expiry than would otherwise have been the case. Such an injunction was first granted in Germany in *Ethofumesat*[2] in which the defendant had undertaken infringing field trials whilst the patent was in force. The practice spread to the Netherlands, and its consistency with EU law was confirmed by the Court of Justice in Case C-316/95 *Smith Kline & French Laboratories v Generics*[3] in which samples of an infringing pharmaceutical had been submitted to the regulatory authority before patent expiry in order to secure an authorization effective immediately on patent expiry and which as to this aspect of the reference to it held:

'(3)   Where a person other than the patentee has infringed the patent laws of a Member State by submitting samples of a medicinal product manufactured in accordance with a patented process to [such an authority] and has thus obtained the authorisation sought, an order of a national court prohibiting the infringer from marketing such a product for a specified period after the expiry of the patent in order to prevent him from deriving any unfair profit from his infringement constitutes a measure having equivalent effect under [TFEU] Article [34] capable of being justified under [TFEU] Article [36]].

(4)   Where the submission of samples of a medicinal product to the competent authority with a view to obtaining a marketing authorisations has given rise to a patent infringement, [EU] law, and in particular [TFEU] Article [34], does not preclude a national court from prohibiting the infringer from marketing that product for 14 months after the expiry of the patent in question, when that period, although exceeding the maximum period authorised by [Community code on medicinal products for human use] corresponds to the actual average duration of such a procedure in the Member State concerned.'

Although English courts had taken 'springboard' considerations into account in determining awards of damages, as in *Gerber Garment Technology v Lectra Systems*[4] discussed later, it was not until *Dyson Appliances v Hoover*[5] that the Patents Court granted a post-patent expiry injunction. The court found that the defendant had established a significant 'springboard' into the relevant market through an accelerated development programme, and costly advertising campaign. The infringing product had taken 12 months to develop, and without a post-patent expiry injunction its sales could recommence shortly after expiry of the patent. The court also found that other competitors had chosen not to 'jump the gun', and so the time to market for the infringing product following patent expiry would be significantly less than theirs. The court held that PA 1977, ss 60–61 did not set out an exhaustive list of remedies precluding the grant of other remedies, referring in particular to the phrase 'without prejudice to any other jurisdiction of the court' in PA 1977, s 61(1). The court had the power to grant final injunctions on such terms as it thought fit where it appeared that such is 'just and convenient', as to which the court followed the Case C-316/95 *SmithKline & French*. Thus the Patents Court awarded a final injunction to restrain the defendant from selling the infringing product for a period of 12 months following expiry of the patent, which injunction effectively put the patentee 'in the position it would, in principle, have been had its rights been respected'. More recently, such an injunction was refused in *Smith & Nephew Plc v Convatec Technologies*[6] as the Patents Court, that held the current product in issue not to infringe, found that any springboard gained by virtue of past infringement by certain samples of the product that had infringed had expired by the time that judgment was given.

The Patents Court in *Dyson* refused to grant two other injunctions which had been sought. One was to restrain the defendant from selling other products made in accordance with the claimed invention, and designed whilst the patent was still in force, again for a period of 12 months following expiry of the patent. There was no evidence that any such products were being developed, so it was held that such an injunction was neither convenient nor necessary. The other was to restrain use of a trade mark which had previously been used on infringing products for six months from the date of the order. The court held that such an injunction would be unjust and disproportionate. The trade mark, although previously used on infringing products, was now being used on non-infringing products, and any misrepresentation was unlikely. There was no sufficient nexus between the act of patent infringement, and ongoing competitive benefit to the defendant arising out of such use.

Other more extensive types of injunction than those provided for in PA 1977, s 61 have also been sought on occasion. In *Union Carbide v BP Chemicals*[7] the patentee sought, but was not allowed in the circumstances to add, a new cause of action, namely: 'An injunction to restrain the Defendant, whether acting by its directors, officers, servants, agents or otherwise howsoever from unjustly enriching itself by licensing to any third parties any process or information the development or generation of which was enabled wholly or in part by the infringement of either or both of the said patents'. The Patents Court did, however, observe that: 'there may be cases where the strict rights as set out in section 61 of the Patents Act do not limit what the court can do in furtherance of the policy of the Patents Act'.

In *Kirin-Amgen v Hoechst Marion Roussel*[8] the patentees, having obtained at first instance a decision that a valid claim of their patent was infringed, sought to claim injunctive relief of a 'long-arm' or extraterritorial, nature (such as prohibiting activities abroad based on manufacture in, and export from, the UK not only of the protein the subject of such claim but also of master cells from which such protein could be made; and also use of data generated by alleged infringing activities in the UK to obtain marketing authorizations in other countries) as well as orders for delivery up, and destruction of such protein and cells. The Patents Court[9] found this not to be within the scope of the 'further and other relief' sought in the original particulars of claim, and refused an application to amend such particulars as the request should have been formulated before trial. In any event, the court doubted the availability of such extra-territorial relief as going beyond the ambit of a patent which relates only to activities within the UK in the absence of any special facts. 'Domestic relief' was also sought in respect of use of the data obtained from the alleged infringing clinical trials, but was likewise rejected as not having been pleaded pre-trial. However, the patentee was allowed to claim 'springboard relief', as in *Dyson,* in relation to pre-patent expiry infringing activities. The issue of relief was never resolved as the patent was subsequently found not to be infringed.

An issue that has become of especial interest in recent years is whether a final injunction must always be awarded where a defendant is found to have infringed a valid patent, especially as it has now been established that the law in the USA (especially in the context of actions brought by 'non-practising entities') provides otherwise.[10] This was discussed in *Virgin Atlantic v Premium Aircraft*[11] where it was held that although under English law the grant of a final injunction was a discretionary remedy (as indeed is consistent with Article 11 of Directive 2004/48/EC on the enforcement of IPRs) the case for withholding it must be strong, the test for doing so being whether granting it would be 'grossly disproportionate'. The issue was revisited more recently in *HTC Corporation v Nokia Corporation*[12] where, after an extensive review of the authorities, the Patents Court held at [32] that:

> '[32]   ... Article 3(2) of the Enforcement Directive permits and requires the court to refuse to grant an injunction where it would be disproportionate to grant one even having regard to the requirements of efficacy and dissuasiveness. Where the right sought to be enforced by the injunction is a patent, however, the court must be very cautious before making an order which is tantamount to a compulsory licence in circumstances where no compulsory licence would be available. It follows that, where no other countervailing right is in play, the burden on the party seeking to show that the injunction would be disproportionate is a heavy one'

However, as discussed in **Chapter 9** at para 9.03 TFEU, Article 102 has been deployed to limit the circumstances in which injunctive relief is available where the owner of a patent that is essential to a standard prevails on validity and infringement, and seeks to secure an excessive licence fee as a condition of granting a licence.

1   *Coflexip v Stolt Comex Seaway* [2001] RPC 182; [2001] 1 All ER 952.
2   *Ethofumesat* (Berlin District Court – 1985 GRUR 375, Federal Supreme Court – 1990 GRUR 997, 22 IIC 541).
3   Case C-316/95 *Smith Kline & French Laboratories v Generics* [1997] ECR I-3929; [1998] 1 CMLR 1; [1997] RPC 801; (1998) 41 BMLR 116.
4   *Gerber Garment Technology v Lectra Systems* [1995] RPC 383, see later at para 6.22.
5   *Dyson Appliances v Hoover* [2001] RPC 27. The matter was not in issue on the appeal. However, in *Mayne Pharma Pty Ltd and Another v Pharmacia Italia sPA* [2005] EWCA 294 (Court of Appeal) at para [6] the Court questioned, but without deciding matters, whether English courts had jurisdiction to grant such an order.
6   *Smith & Nephew Plc v Convatec Technologies Inc & Anor* [2013] EWHC 3955 (Pat) at [114]–[170]. See also *Smith & Nephew Plc v Convatec Technologies Inc & Ors* [2015] EWCA Civ 803, when, after a successful appeal by the patentee on the issue of liability as to the current product in issue, the Court of Appeal stayed the grant of any injunction pending the decision of the Supreme Court in relation to an application for permission to appeal or, if later, a decision of the EPO Technical Board of Appeal in relation to a pending opposition.
7   *Union Carbide v BP Chemicals* [1998] FSR 1.
8   *Kirin-Amgen v Hoechst Marion Roussel* [2001] IP&T 882; [2002] RPC 1; [2002] RPC 2 (Patents Court); [2003] RPC 3 (Court of Appeal); [2004] UKHL 46; [2005] 1 All ER 667; [2005] RPC 9 (House of Lords).
9   *Kirin-Amgen v Hoechst Marion Roussel* [2002] RPC 3 (Patents Court).
10 *eBay Inc v MercExchange LLC* 547 US 388 (2006) (US Supreme Court).

11   *Virgin Atlantic v Premium Aircraft* [2009] EWCA 1513 (Court of Appeal) at paras [23]–[27].
12   *HTC Corporation v Nokia Corporation* [2013] EWHC 3778 (Pat).

Financial remedies – damages and accounts of profits contrasted

6.21   A successful patentee in an infringement action has a choice of seeking, in a subsequent stage of proceedings, an enquiry as to the damages it has suffered, or an account of the defendant's profits. Historically, successful patentees presented with this choice have nearly always opted for the relative certainty of a damages inquiry, because even if the patentee cannot show that he has lost profits as a result of the infringer's activities, it will nevertheless be able to recover a reasonable royalty on the sales of the infringing product, or the use of the infringing process. By contrast, an account of profits has been regarded in most cases as much too uncertain to warrant the risk of recovering a smaller sum than that awarded on a damages enquiry or even nothing at all. However, since *Island Records v Tring International*[1] it has been possible to secure a degree of pre-election disclosure to provide the successful patentee with the financial, and commercial information about the infringer's activities to enable it to make a more informed choice. However, the information so disclosed cannot be as accurate or complete as the account itself.

These two approaches to securing a financial remedy for infringement are also provided for, and are subject to, Article 13 of Directive 2004/48/EC on the enforcement of IPRs:[2]

'1.   Member States shall ensure that the competent judicial authorities, on application of the injured party, order the infringer who knowingly, or with reasonable grounds to know, engaged in an infringing activity, to pay the rightholder damages appropriate to the actual prejudice suffered by him/her as a result of the infringement.

When the judicial authorities set the damages:

(a)   they shall take into account all appropriate aspects, such as the negative economic consequences, including lost profits, which the injured party has suffered, any unfair profits made by the infringer and, in appropriate cases, elements other than economic factors, such as the moral prejudice caused to the rightholder by the infringement; or

(b)   as an alternative to (a), they may, in appropriate cases, set the damages as a lump sum on the basis of elements such as at least the amount of royalties or fees which would have been due if the infringer had requested authorisation to use the intellectual property right in question.

2.   Where the infringer did not knowingly, or with reasonable grounds know, engage in infringing activity, Member States may lay down

that the judicial authorities may order the recovery of profits or the payment of damages, which may be pre-established.'

This somewhat confusingly appears to treat 'unfair profits made by the infringer' as a type of 'negative economic consequence' suffered by the rightholder, but it is not on its face inconsistent with English law as to damages and accounts of profits.[3]

In *Celanese International v BP Chemicals,*[4] concerning an account of profits, the general legal principles applicable to the two alternative approaches to securing a financial remedy for infringement were contrasted as follows:

Damages	Account
The purpose is to determine what loss the patentee has suffered.	The purpose is to determine what profits have been made by the infringer.
The loss to the patentee may exceed the gain to the infringer.	The maximum payment, being the total profit made by the infringer, may far exceed the loss to the patentee.
If the same activity infringes multiple patent rights, the defendant has to compensate each rightholder for the damage each of them has suffered.	If the same activity infringes multiple patent rights, the totality of the profits ordered to be paid should not exceed the total profits made by the defendant in the relevant business.

Although, in the UK, actions for infringement can only be brought after grant of a patent, by PA 1977, s 69 a patentee can claim damages (and an account of profits[5]) from publication of a patent application, provided that the activity complained of would have fallen within a claim of the application as published, and provided that the application was in English or a translation into English was filed at the appropriate time. Damages cannot usually be sought in respect of infringements more than six years in the past, although in *Morton-Norwich v Intercen & United Chemicals*[6] such damages were awarded where there had been concealed fraud on the part of the defendants. Where the patent has been or is amended in the proceedings, or the patent is found in the proceedings to be only partially valid, the court must take into account in determining damages, and accounts of profits the factors set out in PA 1977, s 62(3) and s 63(2) respectively. No account is taken of the behaviour of the defendant, unless it can bring itself within s 62(1) as not being aware, and as having no reasonable grounds for supposing, that the patent existed.[7]

1   *Island Records v Tring International* [1995] FSR 560. This was a copyright case.
2   Directive 2004/48/EC of 29 April 2004 on the enforcement of IPRs OJ L 157, 30 April 2004, Corrigendum OJ L 195, 2 June 2004 p. 16. See Trevor Cook – 'Making sense of

Article 13 of the Enforcement Directive: Monetary compensation for the infringement of intellectual property rights', in Paul Torremans, ed – *Research Handbook on Cross Border Enforcement of Intellectual Property*, Edward Elgar (2014).

3   See The Intellectual Property (Enforcement, etc.) Regulations 2006 (SI 2006 No 1028), Regulations 3(1)–(2) of which effectively restate Article 13 of Directive 2004/48/EC but Regulation 3(3) of which states: 'This regulation does not affect the operation of any enactment or rule of law relating to remedies for the infringement of intellectual property rights except to the extent that it is inconsistent with the provisions of this regulation', suggesting that it was not apparent to the Parliamentary draughtsman that there was any such inconsistency, and no subsequent cases have given cause to doubt this view.

4   *Celanese International v BP Chemicals* [1999] RPC 203.

5   *Spring Form v Toy Brokers* [2002] FSR 17.

6   *Morton-Norwich v Intercen & United Chemicals* [1981] FSR 337.

7   This is a high threshold in practice to overcome, so is rarely advanced in practice, and can have no further relevance once a defendant is on actual notice. It was successfully asserted as to certain past activities in *Lux Traffic v Pike Signals* [1993] RPC 107, *Texas Iron Works' Patent* [2000] RPC 207 and *Schenck Rotec GmbH v Universal Balancing Limited* [2012] EWHC 1920 (Pat) but failed in *Collingwood Lighting Limited v Aurora Limited* [2014] EWHC 228.

Damages

6.22   Although very much more common than cases on accounts of profits those on damages are also relatively rare, because it is quite common once liability for infringement has been established for the parties to be able to agree a figure for damages. Where the patentee does not itself manufacture, damages are usually determined by application of a notional royalty as between a willing licensor, and a willing licensee. If any licences have already been granted under the patent this will provide the best evidence under this head of damage, a factor which should always be taken into account in granting licences, particularly in settlement of litigation, at a low royalty rate, as doing so can, as in *General Tire and Rubber Co v Firestone Tyre and Rubber Co Ltd*[1] have the effect of setting a ceiling on the level of recovery in subsequent litigation concerning the same patents.[2] In addition to a royalty a patentee (or its exclusive licensee under PA 1977, s 67 if registered at the UK Patent Office under s 33 and also a claimant in the action) may, if it has been exploiting the patent itself, be able to recover its lost profits attributable to the infringement.

The principles to be applied to the assessment of damages in patent matters were summarized in *Ultraframe (UK) Ltd v Eurocell Building Products Ltd* at [47]:[3]

'(i)   Damages are compensatory. The general rule is that the measure of damages is to be, as far as possible, that sum of money that will put the claimant in the same position as he would have been in if he had not sustained the wrong.

(ii)   The claimant can recover loss which was (i) foreseeable, (ii) caused by the wrong, and (iii) not excluded from recovery by public or social policy. It is not enough that the loss would not have occurred but for the tort. The tort must be, as a matter of common sense, a cause of the loss.

(iii) The burden of proof rests on the claimant. Damages are to be assessed liberally. But the object is to compensate the claimant and not to punish the defendant.

(iv) It is irrelevant that the defendant could have competed lawfully.

(v) Where a claimant has exploited his patent by manufacture and sale he can claim (a) lost profit on sales by the defendant that he would have made otherwise; (b) lost profit on his own sales to the extent that he was forced by the infringement to reduce his own price; and (c) a reasonable royalty on sales by the defendant which he would not have made.

(vi) As to lost sales, the court should form a general view as to what proportion of the defendant's sales the claimant would have made.

(vii) The assessment of damages for lost profits should take into account the fact that the lost sales are of "extra production" (and that only certain specific extra costs marginal costs) have been incurred in making the additional sales. Nevertheless, in practice costs go up and so it may be appropriate to temper the approach somewhat in making the assessment.

(viii) The reasonable royalty is to be assessed as the royalty that a willing licensor and a willing licensee would have agreed. Where there are truly comparable licences in the relevant field these are the most useful guidance for the court as to the reasonable royalty. Another approach is the profits available approach. This involves an assessment of the profits that would be available to the licensee, absent a licence, and apportioning them between the licensor and the licensee.

(ix) Where damages are difficult to assess with precision, the court should make the best estimate it can, having regard to all the circumstances of the case and dealing with the matter broadly, with common sense and fairness.'

The patentee sought damages for loss of profits, the issues in dispute being how many infringing products were sold, whether the claimant would have sold even more of its own product but for the infringement, and the profit margin on each lost sale, the patentee contending that it had had to reduce its prices to maintain market share in the face of the infringement. The court awarded damages for lost profit on lost sales of its product, a royalty of 8 per cent on sales of the defendants product that did not represent lost sales (the patentee sought 17.5 per cent and the defendant 5 per cent), damages for price depression, damages for losses post-infringement caused by price depression, and disruption of the market and interest.

Many of the principles set out in *Ultraframe* for assessing lost profits had previously been considered in *Gerber v Lectra*[4] in which the Court of Appeal largely upheld the Patents Court, which had addressed a number of heads of damage for patent infringement, including those for lost sales, and had awarded damages, which on the facts of that case, far exceeded the defendant's turnover in the infringing articles. The Court of Appeal accepted the Patents Court approach in all except one respect (which could be cured in future cases) but as a consequence of which on the facts of this case the award was substantially reduced. The patentee had succeeded in an action for infringement of two of its patents for a process for the automatic cutting of fabric. On the subsequent inquiry into damages that it had suffered it was awarded in the Patents Court:

'(i)   loss of profit on the lost sales of the cutting machines that the patentee would have otherwise made (plus a reasonable royalty on the rest of the sales);

(ii)   loss of profit on spare parts, associated machinery and servicing contracts even though these were not claimed in any of the patents (so called 'parasitic' or 'ancillary' damages);

(iii)   loss occasioned to the patentee by having to lower its prices to compete with the defendant ('price depression');

(iv)   loss of profits for machines sold after the expiry of the patent but due to the defendants activities before the expiry of the patents ('springboard damages'); and

(v)   loss occasioned to the patentee and to its subsidiaries via its shareholding in its subsidiaries in the United Kingdom and Belgium.'

The defendant's main challenge was to the last four heads of loss. As to head (ii), the Patents Court first considered whether damages in a patent action were limited to the scope of the monopoly claimed in the patent. The purpose of damages in tort was to place the injured party in the position it would have been in if the tort had not occurred. The defendant argued that this did not apply to damages in patent actions, which should be limited to the scope of the claimed monopoly. In addition to its patented cutting machines the patentee also sold other items such as spare parts, computers to guide the cutter, training for the customers' employees, and servicing contracts as part of a package deal. They argued that a purchaser of one of their patented cutting machines would usually buy all these other items. The defendant argued that damages could only be awarded in respect of the loss of profits for the patented article itself, but it was held that there was no such limitation. If the patentee could establish that the loss it suffered was foreseeable, was caused by the wrong, and was not excluded by public or social policy, then it could recover its losses even if these related to matters that were not within the scope of the patent claims. As per (iv) the defendant had entered into 'serious negotiations' with a number of parties for sales of its infringing machines before patent expiry, although the sales themselves had not been concluded until after patent expiry. The Patents Court also rejected the defendant's arguments against such 'springboard damages' for the same reason as given for the sales of non-patented matters. If there was causation, and such sales were foreseeable, and not too remote, then a patentee could recover for them. The Patents

Court had also awarded substantial damages as per (v) (the patentee's subsidiaries were non-exclusive licensees and had no independent cause of action against the defendant under the PA 1977) but this part of the award was, on the facts of this case, struck out by the Court of Appeal.

Despite the comprehensive nature of the principles set out in *Ultraframe* it does not appear, in the rare examples subsequently of decisions involving the assessment of damages, that the courts have felt it necessary to refer to them even though it does not appear that there has been any departure from them. In one of these cases, *Fabio Perini v LPC*[5] it was observed that:

'[68]   As Aldous LJ observed in *Coflexip*[6] (at p.735) many reported cases in this field are useful illustrations of judicial reasoning, but are apt to mislead if decisions on particular sets of facts (or observations in judgments leading up to such decisions) are later relied on as establishing rules of the law. I would hold only:-

i)   that the legal burden of establishing that the loss claimed was caused by the infringement proved lies on [the patentee];

ii)   that in general, since the object of a patent is to confer a monopoly of profit and advantage, any infringement of that monopoly is likely to cause some loss or damage by the loss of actual sales or the chance of sales or through the appropriation of something of value;

iii)   that in general, where the patent belongs to a manufacturer who exploits the invention by selling products at a profit (whether the products embody a patented invention, or in their operation employ a patented process, or are themselves produced by a patented process) the legal burden will be discharged (and the nexus between infringement and loss established) by the inference which the court is prepared to draw that the effect of the infringement is to divert sales from the owner of the patent to the infringer;

iv)   that the infringer may adduce evidence which demonstrates that the usual inference does not hold good in a particular case, so that whether the claimed loss is caused by the proven infringement must simply be decided on the proved facts and the inferences properly drawn from those facts;

v)   that is to be done using commercial common-sense, avoiding over-refined analysis, but taking account of all factors which may reasonably bear on the issue and (in particular) giving full weight to the consideration that the patent owner has a right to a monopoly in respect of the invention and that the infringer's putting into the marketplace the infringing product or process has destroyed that monopoly;

vi)   that the focus of any such inquiry is not why the infringer or infringers actually entered the real contract, but whether (on the assumption that the infringing product or service was not available) the owner of the patent would or might have secured the infringer's contract for himself.'

Fabio Perini also involved an initial analysis of the scope of the enquiry as to damages as the patentee sought also to recover damages

in respect of contributory infringement and joint tortfeasance, which
however, it was held had already been determined against the patentee
in the liability phase of the proceedings.

1   *General Tire and Rubber Co v Firestone Tyre and Rubber Co Ltd* [1975] 1 WLR 819;
    [1975] 2 All ER 173; [1975] FSR 273; [1976] RPC 197 (House of Lords). This was
    despite the observation of Lord Wilberforce in the House of Lords (at p. 212) that:
    'The defendants being wrongdoers, damages should be liberally assessed but … the
    object is to compensate the plaintiffs and not to punish the defendants.'
2   The position in Germany is different. There, where an arm's length commercial
    licence that was negotiated before a determination that the licensed patent is valid and
    infringed is used as a comparable, the courts will typically apply an uplift of up to
    100 per cent to take account of the fact that the notional licensee of a patent which has
    been determined to be valid and infringed is in rather a different position to one who
    takes a licence before such determination, although the compatibility of this practice
    with Article 13 of Directive 2004/48/EC has been questioned in a reference to the
    Court of Justice from a German court in a plant variety rights case, Case C-481/14
    Jorn Hansson.
3   *Ultraframe (UK) Ltd v Eurocell Building Products Ltd* [2006] EWHC 1344 (Pat).
4   *Gerber v Lectra* [1995] RPC 383 (Patents Court); [1997] RPC 443 (Court of Appeal).
5   *Fabio Perini v LPC* [2012] EWHC 911 (Ch); [2012] EWHC 1393 (Pat); and *Xena
    Systems v Cantideck and anr* [2013] EWPCC 1.
6   *Coflexip v Stolt Comex* [2003] EWCA Civ 296.

Account of profits

6.23   Although claims for accounts of the profits made by the defendant
from its infringement are rare, the principles are well established by case
law – namely *Celanese International v BP Chemicals*[1] the first judgment
on an account in a patent infringement action since 1892 in *Siddell v
Vickers*[2] and in which the Court of Appeal said:

> 'The Plaintiff was perfectly within his right in electing as he did in this case
> to have an account of profits; but I do not know of any form of account which
> is more difficult to work out, or may be more difficult to work out than an
> account of profit…. The litigation is enormous, the expense is great, and the
> time consumed is out of all proportion to the advantage ultimately attained; ….
> Therefore, although the law is that a Patentee has a right to elect which course
> he will take, as a matter of business he would generally be inclined to take an
> inquiry as to damages rather than launch upon an inquiry as to profits.'

The Patents Court in *Celanese* held that both an enquiry as to
damages, and an account of profits proceeded on the basis of a common
principle of legal causation, as had been held in *Imperial Oil v Lubrizol*[3]
in Canada:

> 'Just as in a reference on a claim for damages issues of fact relating to
> causality and remoteness may properly be explored, so may they likewise
> on an accounting of profits…. It may be possible for Imperial to show that
> some part of the profits made on the infringing sales are not profits "arising
> from" the infringement in that they are not caused by but simply made on the
> occasion of such infringement.'

The court in *Celanese* thus held:

— If a defendant carries on multiple businesses or sells multiple products and only one infringes, the defendant only has to compensate the patentee for the damage caused by the infringements or the defendant only has to account to the patentee for the profits by the infringements.

— It is no answer to a claim for damages or an account that the defendant could have caused the same damage or made the same profits by using a non-infringing alternative.

As to considerations specific to an account of profits the court held:

— 'Profits' means the profits of the business in which the infringement is used and not the benefits derived by the defendant from the use of the infringement in that business.

— Just as the defendant cannot say that it could have made the same profits by using a non-infringing alternative, the patentee must take the defendant as he finds him and cannot argue that the defendant should have generated higher profits than it actually did.

— Just as a defendant with multiple businesses has only to account for the profits from the infringing business, a defendant who sells a product or uses a process only part of which infringes, should only have to account for the part of the profits attributable to the use of the invention and thus an apportionment may be relevant. There might be some cases where apportionment would not be appropriate, such as where the court concluded that the infringement was an essential ingredient to the creation of the defendant's product. Whilst the onus was on the defendant to show that there should be an apportionment in principle, there was no onus on it to show what the level of apportionment should be over and above the obligation to give full and proper disclosure, and provide relevant evidence so as to allow the court to make a fair adjudication.

— Thus the court should start by determining the total profits 'pot' of the business activity in question, spreading the profits evenly over the infringing and non-infringing parts of such business activity. Then, if appropriate, it should apportion the total profits 'pot' to determine the 'base allocated profit'. If supported by credible evidence, it should then weight the base allocated profits to reflect any general arguments on the relative value of the infringement, and also any differential profits attributable to the infringement. Then it should deduct any tax paid on those profits.

In *Celanese*, the claims of the patent were to a method for removing iodides from acetic acid by contacting the acid with a particular form of ion exchange resin loaded with silver, iodides being a catalyst poison in at least one major use of acetic acid. Although two of the defendants' plants had used the infringing process two other plants had not, but instead produced iodide free acetic acid to start with. The existence of the two non-infringing plants at the same site and the acceptance by the Patents Court of the defendants' evidence that it could have met the low iodide acetic acid requirements of its iodide-sensitive customers by using non-infringing acetic acid during the period of the account had a significant impact on the final award. Initially, the patentee had claimed £180 million in respect of the acetic acid made on the infringing plants based on the fact that the acetic acid itself was an infringing product, and therefore that they were entitled to the profits on its sales, and that apportionment, even if appropriate in principle, was not appropriate in this case. In closing, the patentee conceded that an apportionment was appropriate, and suggested a level of between 20 per cent and 50 per cent of the total profits. The defendants put forward a figure of about £1.7m in respect to one of the infringing plants, and nothing in respect to the other based in each case on an 'incremental profits approach', ie a comparison of the revenues and costs of the business before the use of the infringing process, and during the period of use of the infringing process. However, the incremental or differential profits approach was rejected as the *sole* determinant of the profits derived from the infringement, comparing as it did the actual profits made using the infringement with the notional profits which would have been made using a non-infringing alternative. On the particular facts of *Celanese,* the court found that:

— one infringing plant had made a profit of £94m and the other a loss of £89m, but that the use of the infringing process on the two plants should be treated separately and therefore that the loss on one plant could not be set off against the profit of the other;

— apportionment was appropriate in the circumstances of the case, the appropriate starting point for this being the relative capital cost of the infringing part of the plant which on the profitable infringing plant was 0.6 per cent, but there was no reason to weight the resultant figure; and

— the Defendants were therefore liable in the sum of £0.5m less the corporation tax of 33 per cent that had been paid during the period of the account.

This was a smaller award than the patentee would have been likely to have received had it elected for damages calculated on the basis of a notional royalty. One can however envisage cases (such as a successful and high margin pharmaceutical) where an account of the infringer's profits will in certain circumstances be an attractive option. In most cases, however, the limitations inherent in the pre-election disclosure procedure, and the application of the general legal, and accounting principles laid down in *Celanese* will mean that successful patentees in the future will do well to heed the warning in *Siddell*, and choose the relative certainty of a damages inquiry, before opting for an account of profits.

1   *Celanese International v BP Chemicals* [1999] RPC 203.
2   *Siddell v Vickers* [1892] RPC 152 at pp. 162–63.
3   *Imperial Oil v Lubrizol* [1996] 71 CPR (3d) 26.

Part II
Patents in specific areas of technology

Part II

Patents in specific areas of technology

Chapter 7

Patents for chemicals, pharmaceuticals and agrochemicals

Structure

Introduction

Special aspects of chemical and pharmaceutical patents

7.01 This chapter is concerned with a number of issues that are specific to patents for chemicals, and in particular for pharmaceuticals and agrochemicals. Although patents in these areas are subject to much the same legal regime as other patents, these areas have given rise to a number of patent law issues which are not met in other sectors. Such issues are met less in connection with new synthetic routes than in connection with the protection of new chemical entities (NCEs) and the pharmaceutical uses (or 'indications') to which these are put.

One reason for the differences between patents for NCEs, and other types of patent is that unlike other commonly patented areas (eg engineering or electronics) chemistry has a very clear and precise terminology for defining chemicals. This enables one to define a particular chemical with precision, and at the same time to define, with a greater degree of precision (and thus in a more limiting way than in many other areas) a whole set of currently 'unknown' chemicals without actually having made or tested them. Such chemicals, while all being different, are closely related in significant respects, and thus have a real prospect of having similar efficacy, for example, as a pharmaceutical, even though medicinal chemistry remains far from a predictive science. Pharmaceuticals, even when produced by biotechnology, are nothing more than chemicals having a certain physiological effect. Therefore, many pharmaceutical patent issues are a special case of those relating to chemical patents. Moreover, since the products of biotechnology, eg DNA and proteins, are also chemicals (even though, because many have been isolated from nature, or are not readily described by conventional chemical nomenclature, are better described, along with NCEs as new active substances (NASs)), this chapter also discusses some examples from biotechnology, although the patent issues unique to that particular sector are discussed in **Chapter 8**.

One consequence of the use of such precise terminology as that available in chemistry is that some traditional areas of dispute normally met in patent litigation in other sectors, such as infringement, are less open to question than say, when met in mechanical engineering or electronics. As a result, other routes are adopted by disputing parties to challenge each others' patent position, which is why issues such as insufficiency (related in particular to excessive claim breadth and the vagaries of prediction) are more common with chemical patents. Priority disputes are also common with such patents, reflecting what might be termed the 'herd instinct' where differing teams of researchers will all rush to undertake research in the same area once an indication of some useful, typically biological, activity has been found in a particular type of molecule. They will commonly file overlapping patent applications in ignorance of the specifics of each other's parallel research activities, and often within a short period of each other.

Some aspects of patent law are specific to pharmaceuticals, and not to other chemicals. One reflects policy issues that accompany the desire not to interfere with the freedom of medical practitioners to use whatever treatment they consider best for their patients. This imposes limitations on the sort of claims that can be granted to the use of pharmaceuticals. Medical device and diagnostics patents are also caught by such considerations. Other issues met with pharmaceuticals involve attempts to compensate for the delays arising from the need to secure regulatory approval before a pharmaceutical can be marketed, and the extent to which certain activities undertaken by generic companies during patent term, such as certain types of trial so that they can secure regulatory approval allowing them to come onto the market immediately on patent expiry, might infringe. Such issues are also met in relation to agrochemicals. Both pharmaceuticals and agrochemicals are also high-value products that are easily transported, and price differences between different countries render them particularly susceptible to the phenomenon of parallel importation, by which a product placed on the market in one country by the owner of a patent protecting that product, or with its consent, is purchased in that country, and imported without its express consent into a second country where it also has rights. This is an especial problem for pharmaceuticals, whose prices are in Europe controlled by national governments. Can rights in that second country be used to prevent the import or sale of such product in that country? Although virtually all of the case law in this area of parallel imports has concerned pharmaceuticals, it provides a defence to a patent infringement action that is of general application, and so is discussed in **Chapter 6** at para 6.13.

Claims in chemical patents

Product and process claims and exclusions from patentability

7.02   Patent claims can be to articles or to activities. The primary examples in chemistry of these two categories of claim are those to compounds ('a compound of the formula') and to processes ('a process for the production of a compound of the formula ... which'). However, other types of claim within these two broad categories are also important. The ideal chemical claim is one to specific NCEs of proven utility, and to a broad, novel, class of compounds similar to such NCEs and likely to have similar utility, but claims to intermediates, compositions, and processes for their production, and to methods of using them are also common.

The TRIPS Agreement requires, and most major patent jurisdictions now grant, product patent protection for NCEs. Such protection will be per se protection, meaning protection for the compound itself, however made or used, and not just for the compound synthesized in a particular way, or put to a particular use. Thus, even where the patent to an NCE discloses only one use for the NCE, such per se protection will allow the patent to be asserted against any use of that NCE. Such protection has not always been available from the patent system. Indeed, there remain some countries, particularly in the developing world, in which no matter how novel the chemical, patent protection is only available on processes for making such chemicals, and not on the chemicals themselves. Certain countries that are members of the WTO, and must thus adhere to TRIPS have been able to defer extending product patent protection for chemicals under TRIPS, Articles 65.2 and 65.4.[1] However, in the interim they must provide 'pipeline' protection, and a measure of marketing exclusivity for pharmaceuticals, and agrochemicals patented elsewhere by means of the so-called 'black box' provisions of TRIPS, Articles 70.8 and 70.9.

Between 1919 and 1949, the UK did not allow claims to novel chemical substances, and it was only in the latter half of the twentieth century that it, and many other leading economies introduced such protection. The situation was recognized in Article 167 of the European Patent Convention (EPC) which permits EPC Member States to make reservations for a limited time precluding claims to chemicals (and to pharmaceuticals and food products) as opposed to claims to processes for manufacturing these. Thus, for example Austria, long a member of the EPC, retained process protection only for chemicals and pharmaceuticals until 1987. European patents for NCEs designating, inter alia, Austria, thus used to issue with a different set of claims directed to process protection for such NCEs, drafted to meet the specific requirements of Austrian law.

Process patent protection is generally regarded as less satisfactory than product protection, although in many cases it may be all that can be secured. First, there will be several different processes for making a given chemical, and even if one exhaustively (and expensively) patents all of these, the imitator will often be able to devise, and patent a new synthetic route. The imitator may seek such a patent itself even if it has no intention of using it, as it can be put forward as an example of the route it is using, in order to make it hard to infer that it is using another patented route. This reflects the second problem with claims to processes: that of proving their infringement when one does not have access to details of the process. This is a problem that is addressed in the UK by disclosure of documents, in some other European jurisdictions such as France by the *saisi contrefacon* procedure, and to some extent in other countries by reversing the burden of proof. By way of contrast, a patent with a product claim to a chemical can be asserted against any third party from making selling or using that chemical, no matter how it was made, and even though made by a process different to that taught in the original patent. Later filed patents to improved methods of making such chemical could only have claims to the particular new process (and any new intermediate) that they disclosed. However, as a patent confers no positive right to use the patented invention, the product of such subsequent processes (which processes could differ considerably from, and be much better than the one described by the original inventor) could not be used without the licence of the owner of the original patent because of its per se claim to such chemical.

1   This is now subject to the *Decision of the Council for TRIPS of 27 June 2002* and by virtue of which, 'the least-developed country members will not be obliged, with respect to pharmaceutical products, to implement or apply Sections 5 and 7 of Pt II of the TRIPS Agreement or to enforce rights provided for under these Sections until 1 January 2016'. This was followed in August 2003 by a waiver from TRIPS, Article 31 to make it easier for countries lacking local pharmaceutical manufacturing capacity, and which were therefore unable locally to avail themselves of the compulsory licensing provisions of Article 31 for local health emergencies, to obtain generic versions of patented medicines from countries having such capacity, but which could not otherwise, by virtue of Article 31, grant compulsory licences for export. This waiver was formalized in December 2005 by an amendment to the TRIPS Agreement to insert a new Annex 31 bis, pursuant to which, for example, the EU has established a mechanism to provide for compulsory licences for medicines for export – see **Chapter 6** at para 6.18, fn 1. A request has been made to extend the 2002 waiver beyond 2016, but since its 2002 decision the TRIPS Council has granted more generally expressed waivers, not limited to pharmaceutical products, the most recent of which is the *Decision of the Council for TRIPS of 11 June 2013* that allows: 'Least developed country Members ... not ... to apply the provisions of the Agreement, other than Articles 3, 4 and 5, until 1 July 2021, or until such a date on which they cease to be a least developed country Member, whichever date is earlier'.

Claims to chemicals

7.03 It is usual to characterize a chemical compound by its chemical formula. Whilst it is clearly preferable to characterize and to claim an NCE in this way, this is not obligatory, and if its formula is not known (which, however, is increasingly uncommon with current analytical techniques) an NCE may also be characterized by the process by which it is produced, or by its parameters, such as an infra-red spectrum, an approach which is common when claiming a particular physical form of NCE, where, for example, it exists in different crystalline forms. In the case of some large, and difficult to analyse molecules, such physical parameters, before modern techniques of analysis became available, used to provide the only way of defining them. Alternatively, where such a hard to analyse molecule was secreted by a micro-organism, a claim based on the process of production might similarly have provided the only way of defining it.

As observed above, the first person to make a useful NCE will seek a product claim to that compound. However, such person would be likely to try also to obtain product claims to structurally similar compounds having the potential for similar utility, by for example, defining in a single claim a range of alternative substituents at various positions in the compound.[1] The possible permutations that such a 'generic claim' permits has the consequence that the number of compounds so claimed can rapidly run into incalculably large numbers, although the consequences of this may provide the basis for attacks on validity as outlined below (on grounds of obviousness) at para 7.15 and (on grounds of insufficiency) at paras 7.19–7.20. For example, as observed in *Idenix Pharmaceutical, Inc v Gilead Sciences, Inc & Ors*:[2]

> '444. … the claims of the Application were stupendously broad. They could well have covered as many as a trillion compounds. Furthermore, it was common ground … that it was not plausible that all the compounds claimed would be effective against … Counsel for Gilead characterised the Application as a "land grab", and in my view that is a fair description. It does not necessarily follow that the Patent is invalid, however.'

A further element of prediction can usually be 'built into' a product claim for an NCE. If the biologically active compound is a base or acid, it may often be administered more conveniently as a salt or ester. In such a case it has become common, where the NCE is a pharmaceutical, to claim 'a physiologically acceptable base or ester' rather than try to list every imaginable such base or ester, and inevitably omit one which might enable a competitor to escape literal infringement. It is also now usual to undertake 'salt screens', where the compound will form a salt, to identify the salt with the best combination of physical properties for processing, thus rendering it difficult to patent novel and inventive salts of compounds where the compound already forms part of the state of the art.[3]

When dealing with certain entirely new classes of material, claims to chemicals defined in novel ways may well be appropriate. One example is provided by the type of nanotechnology material known as dendrimers, which, in their earliest days, could have claims granted which were expressed in terms of the overall shape, and structure of the molecule, rather than in terms of conventional chemical nomenclature – see claim 1 of EP 0,115,771 B to The Dow Chemical Company:

'1 A dense star polymer having at least three symmetrical core branches emanating from a core, each core branch having at least one terminal group, wherein (1) the ratio of terminal groups to the core branches is greater than 2:1, (2) the density of terminal groups per unit volume in the polymer is at least 1.5 times that of a conventional star polymer having the same core, monomeric components, molecular weight and number of core branches, said monomeric components being such that each of the branches bears only one terminal group, and (3) the molecular volume is not more than 60 percent of the molecular volume of said conventional star polymer.'

More conventionally drawn chemical claims can still permit of an infinite number of compounds within their scope. Claim 1 of UK Patent GB 1,399,086 to Glaxo Laboratories, granted in 1975 (under the Patents Act 1949), was to:

'1 7ß-Acylamidoceph-3-em-4-carboxylic acid antibiotics and their non-toxic salts and esters and the corresponding sulphoxides wherein the acyl amido group has the structure R.C(=N-OR^a).CO.NH- (where R is a hydrogen atom or an organic group and R^a is an etherifying monovalent organic group linked to the oxygen atom through a carbon atom), the said compounds being the *syn* and *anti* isomers containing at least 75% of the *syn* isomers.'

It is the 'R is ... an organic group ' language which confers on this claim its real breadth, at least in comparison with a detailed and exhaustive, but finite, listing of potential chemical substituents that is the common stuff of generically drawn chemical claims. Such claims are now rare, but other techniques for defining a wide range of molecules exist. One is that of functional claiming, as exemplified by claims to antibodies to identified proteins (as in **Chapter 8** at para 8.03). Another potential such approach, that of 'Reach through claims', as discussed below, generally founders on issues of sufficiency of description.

Many biologically active chemicals exhibit optical and other types of isomerism, and these are discussed separately below. Many chemicals can also be produced in a number of different physical forms, such as different hydration states or different crystalline states (the phenomenon of polymorphism). Certain of these physical forms may have benefits over other forms of the same chemical in terms of ease of formulation, or stability, which provides a utility which enables such new forms also to be protected by means of product claims.[4] Patents with claims to such refinements are a common feature of pharmaceuticals patenting, especially as such issues tend only to be explored some time after the initial discovery of the NCE of interest, and thus patents on them can offer some scope to provide protection that outlives that on the NCE itself. Thus they may then be used to try to delay the entry of generic versions of a pharmaceutical on expiry of the NCE patent, although the validity of such other patents has in practice proved generally rather easier to challenge than patents to NCEs.

Claims to an already known chemical compound but of a particular purity that is alleged not previously to have been disclosed will in general lack novelty, as observed in T-0990/96 *Eythro-compounds/NOVARTIS*:[5]

'7 Conventional methods for the purification of low molecular organic reaction products such as recrystallisation, distillation, chromatography, etc., which normally can be successfully applied in purification steps, are within the common general knowledge of those skilled in the art. It follows that, in general, a document disclosing a low molecular chemical compound and its manufacture makes available this compound to the public in the sense of Article 54 EPC in all grades of purity as desired by a person skilled in the art.'

This is an application of the principle that parameters which are not attributable to the chemical compound itself, in the sense of not being inherent in it, cannot be taken into account when assessing novelty since they do not belong to the compound's chemical structure. However, such principle does not necessarily apply to high molecular weight molecules such as the proteins produced by biotechnology, although in such cases terms, such as 'substantially pure' will not be allowed in claims as they lack clarity.

1   Such claims are called 'Markush' claims, named after Eugene Markush, the named inventor of US patent 1,506,316, granted in 1924, which was one of the earliest patents to include such claims.
2   *Idenix Pharmaceutical, Inc v Gilead Sciences, Inc & Ors* [2014] EWHC 3916 (Patents Court) at [444].
3   *Ranbaxy (UK) v Warner Lambert Co* [2005] EWHC 2142 (Patents Court) at paras [53]–[74]; inventive step was not addressed on appeal at [2006] EWCA 876 (Court of Appeal).
4   See, for example, *SKF Laboratories v Evans Medical* [1989] FSR 561. Another decided dispute that involved claims to different crystalline forms concerned the medicinal product paroxetine hydrochloride, and culminated in *Smithkline Beecham v Apotex Europe* [2004] EWCA 1568; [2005] FSR 23 (Court of Appeal). Claims to an allegedly new form of perindopril were held to lack novelty in *Servier v Apotex* [2008] EWCA 445 (Court of Appeal) but claims to a new form of calcipitriol were held to be both novel, and inventive in *Leo Pharma A/S v Sandoz Limited* [2009] EWCA 1188 (Court of Appeal) the finding on inventive step reflecting certain specificities of Vitamin D, and its analogues of which this was one, namely that no-one in that field did full polymorph screening at the priority date. However, as to inventive step, an EPO Technical Board of Appeal has, in T-777/08 *Atorvastatin* (24 May 2011), recognized the desirability of screening for polymorphic, hydrated or amorphous forms of a medicinal product and observed that, 'in the absence of any technical prejudice ... the mere provision of a crystalline form of a known pharmaceutically active compound cannot be regarded as involving an inventive step'. In contrast in

T-1422/12 *Tigecycline crystalline forms/TEVA* (Technical Board of Appeal 3.3.10, 11 April 2013) a specific crystalline form of tigecycline was held not to be obvious over the amorphous form in view of the unexpected improvement in stability with respect to epimerisation specific to this type of tetracycline antibiotic.

5   T-0990/96 *Eythro-compounds/NOVARTIS* [1998] EPOR 441, also applied in T-0728/98 *Pure Terfenadine/ALBANY* and T-996/02 *Melamine/DSM* [2006] EPOR 21.

Product-by-process claims

7.04   Claims are on occasion granted for 'product X obtained by process Y'. This is a type of product claim known as a 'product by process' claim, and so for infringement purposes only covers the product in question when produced by the claimed route; it is thus much more limited than a per se claim to the product itself. In the UK and other European countries that have modelled their infringement law on the Community Patent Convention (CPC) (as well as most other countries by virtue of TRIPS, Article 28(1)) this would provide little or no benefit over a process claim given that the direct product of a patented process would infringe a process claim.[1] In some jurisdictions such a claim can be used to shift the burden of proof so that if the end product in issue is identical to that made by the process of the patent it is for the defendant to demonstrate that it was made by a non-infringing process.

In the EPO, such claims will only be allowed if the products themselves are new and inventive, and therefore patentable. A product is not to be regarded as novel merely because it is produced by a new process and if it is novel it should just be claimed as a novel product. Thus the *EPO Guidelines* suggest that 'product by process' claims should take the form 'product X obtainable by process Y', making it clear that the product is covered by the claim even when not in fact produced by the process described in the claim. Practice in the UK used to differ by allowing claims to 'product X obtained by process Y' where product X was not itself novel but process Y for its preparation was. However in *Kirin Amgen v Transkaryotic Therapies*[2] the House of Lords held that the UK should follow the EPO practice, and that a claim in such form to a protein made by recombinant DNA engineering lacked novelty over the identical protein from natural sources, and which formed part of the state-of-the-art.

Product by process claims were the subject of an extensive analysis in *Hospira v Genentech No 2*[3] which started with the observation (at [125]) that: 'product by process claims are tricky', and concluded (at [147]) with the following principles derived from this analysis:

'i)   A new process which produces a product identical to an old product cannot confer novelty on that product. To be novel a product obtained or obtainable by a process has to have some novel attribute conferred on it by the process as compared to the known product.

ii)   This rule is a rule of the law of novelty. It is not a principle of claim construction. Although in effect the rule treats "obtained by" language as "obtainable by" language, nevertheless as a matter of claim construction a claim to a product "obtained by" a process means what it says. That will be the relevant scope of the claim as far as infringement and sufficiency are concerned.

iii)   Although normally a patent is drafted by the inventor "in words of his own choosing", the EPO will not permit overt product by process language unless there is no other alternative available. By no other alternative, they mean no other way of defining a particular characteristic of the product in question.'

1   As explained in **Chapter 6** at para 6.02.
2   *Kirin Amgen v Transkaryotic Therapies* [2001] IP&T 882; [2002] RPC 1; [2002] RPC 2 (Patents Court); [2003] RPC 3 (Court of Appeal); [2004] UKHL 46; [2005] 1 All ER 667; [2005] RPC 9 (House of Lords).
3   *Hospira UK Ltd v Genentech Inc* [2014] EWHC 3857 at [125]–[147].

Method of use, composition, and formulation claims

7.05   In addition to claims for NCEs (or in substitution for them if the compound is already known) chemical patents commonly have claims to compositions of a compound for the disclosed utility, and to the method of use of such compound. As explained below, there are restrictions on public policy grounds on claims for the method of use of a pharmaceutical ('method of treatment' claims) but the underlying principle behind use claims can be seen from the patent (granted under the Patents Act 1949, although such claims would also be permissible under the 1977 Act) to an agrochemical that was the subject of *Monsanto v Stauffer*[1] UK 1,366,379. Claim 1 was to: '1. A herbicidal composition comprising an adjuvant and (A) a compound of the formula ... or (B) a salt of the compound of the above formula'.

Claims 2–29 were for more narrowly defined compositions, and claims 39–60 were to novel compounds. Claim 30 however was to: '30. A method for killing of undesired plants, which comprises applying to the undesired plants a herbicidal amount of (A) a compound of the formula ... or (B) a salt of the compound of the above formula.'

There were other claims to various 'methods of crop cultivation', and 'methods of killing undesired plants' in the patent. The reasons for having different types of claim protecting much the same inventive concept lies in the question of who infringes, and how one proves infringement, and the benefits of maintaining flexibility as to how one deals with such matters. With a method of use claim, on the face of it, only the person using it will directly infringe, and the supplier of the composition may not infringe, unless it knows of such use, when it may be a contributory infringer. Moreover, the patentee must show that the use is taking place. However, a composition claim can be asserted against those supplying the compositions for use by others. It may be undesirable to sue an actual or potential customer for use of the competitor's product.

Claims in such form are unlikely to be inventive if the chemical, and its utility already forms part of the state of the art, and so are generally only found in the same patent application as claims the new chemical itself. However, invention may lie in so formulating a known chemical as to overcome a technical problem in prior art formulations of that chemical, or to produce improved formulations such as slow release ones. As with patents to new physical forms of known chemicals, such patents may be used as part of a strategy to impede the entry of generic competition on expiry of a patent to the NCE, and thereby attract a disproportionate share of litigation from those seeking to 'clear the path' for generic entry. They have in practice, however, proved to be at greater risk than NCE patents of being found obvious.[2]

1   *Monsanto v Stauffer* [1984] FSR 574 (Court of Appeal).
2   It has in practice proved difficult to sustain the validity of medicinal product formulation claims against obviousness attacks in the English courts, as for example, in *Cairnstores v AB Hassle* [2002] EWCA Civ 1504; [2003] FSR 23; [2003] IP&T 266 (Court of Appeal), *Actavis UK Ltd v Novartis AG* [2010] EWCA 82 (Court of Appeal), *AstraZeneca AB v Hexal AG & Ors* [2012] EWHC 655 (Patents Court) [2013] EWCA Civ 454 (Court of Appeal) *Hospira UK Ltd v Genentech Inc* [2014] EWHC 3857 (Patents Court) (discussing several arguments encountered in such cases at [227]–[242], including at [227]–[234] the difficulties implicit in the 'could/would' argument often met in EPO practice – see *Case Law of the EPO*, 7th edn, 203 at I.D.5 – and at [239]–[242] the dangers of a hindsight approach) and *Novartis AG & Ors v Focus Pharmaceuticals Ltd & Ors* [2015] EWHC 1068 (Patents Court). For examples of formulation claims to already known pharmaceuticals being found valid see *Novartis v Ivax Pharmaceuticals* [2007] EWCA 971 (Court of Appeal) (although this was found not to be infringed) and *Napp Pharmaceutical Holdings Ltd v Ratiopharm GmbH* [2008] EWHC 3070 (Pat) [2009] EWCA 252 (Court of Appeal) (and which was also found to be infringed, and where the judge at first instance expressed the view that he had been sceptical as to patent's validity before he heard the evidence). See also *Teva UK Ltd and anr v Leo Pharma A/s* [2014] EWHC 3096 (Patents Court) [2015] EWCA Civ 779 (Court of Appeal) in which a finding at first instance that a patent to a formulation for a new combination of active pharmaceutical ingredients was obvious, was reversed on appeal.

Mixture or combination claims

7.06   Composition claims may also be to mixtures, and such claims frequently contain the words 'consisting' and 'comprising'. A claim to a composition *consisting* of A, B, and C will generally mean that one must have A, B, and C in order to infringe, but that the addition of D (not mentioned in the claim) will (subject to questions of purposive construction) probably not infringe. On the other hand, if the claim is to a composition *comprising* A, B, and C, then one still must have A, B, and C in order to infringe but the addition of D will not have any effect on the question of infringement. This is likely to be so even if the combination of A, B, C, and D is much better than the original, reflecting the principle that 'adding ingenuity to robbery will not avoid infringement'. If, however, there is wording in the claim to the effect that the composition comprises A, B, and C but contains no E, then on the face of it a composition containing E as well, will not infringe.

Claims to mixtures having no more than the additive utility of the components of the mixture are unlikely to be inventive unless there is some real technical prejudice against such a combination, or at least one component does not form part of the state of the art. However, invention may lie in making a selection of components which provide an overall effect greater than merely additive, although such 'synergy' should be disclosed in the patent, and can be hard to show, as in *Richardson-Vicks Patent*[1] and *CIPLA v Glaxo*[2] in each of which patents to a mixture of two medicinal products which had proved commercially successful were held obvious.[3] Alternatively, the evidence may show a concern about the efficacy of one of the components being compromised in the combination, as in *Schering-Plough v Norbrook Laboratories*[4] where claims to a combination of two specific medicinal products were held not to be obvious, but broader claims to a combination of classes of such medicinal products were held to be insufficient, as there it was to be expected that the self-same concern was well founded for many other combinations also within the scope of such broader claims.

1   *Richardson-Vicks Patent* [1995] RPC 568 (Patents Court); [1997] RPC 888 (Court of Appeal).
2   *CIPLA v Glaxo Group* [2004] EWHC 477 (Ch); [2004] RPC 43 (Patents Court).
3   For other cases concerning patents to combinations of known active pharmaceutical ingredients, see *Glenmark Generics (Europe) Ltd & Anor (t/a Mylan) v The Wellcome Foundation Ltd & Anor* [2013] EWHC 148 (Patents Court) (patent held obvious), and *Teva UK Ltd and anr v Leo Pharma A/s* [2014] EWHC 3096 (Patents Court) [2015] EWCA Civ 779 (Court of Appeal) (first instance finding that a patent to a formulation for a combination of active pharmaceutical ingredients was obvious reversed on appeal as although the combination would have been known to be desirable formulating it presented a technical problem the solution to which required invention).
4   *Schering-Plough v Norbrook Laboratories* [2005] EWHC 2532; [2006] FSR 16 (Patents Court).

Second use claims

7.07   In G2/88 *Friction Reducing Additive/MOBIL OIL III*[1] the Enlarged Board of Appeal of the EPO established that product claims directed to a known substance, but intended for a new use were allowable where they reflected the recognition or discovery of a previously unknown property of a known compound, and such property provided a new technical effect. Here the claim was to the use of a known compound as a friction-reducing additive in lubricants, even though such use would have been inherent, but unappreciated, in the state of the art, which was the use of the same compound, also in lubricants, and in the same amounts, but instead as a rust inhibitor. Such 'use' claims are product claims, although as they are 'use bound' they can be contrasted with the per se protection available for a useful new compound. Suitable process claims will also be available for such inventions.

On the assumption that this approach is adopted by the English Courts (which follow the Enlarged Board, for the sake of comity, even if they do not agree with it) it would represent a change in UK law as set out in *Adhesive Dry Mounting v Trapp.*[2] There a claim to an article 'suitable for use' in a specified method was treated as a claim to the article per se, no matter for what purpose the article was used, and was accordingly anticipated by a prior disclosure of that article. As discussed below, the English courts do, however, allow claims for novel uses for a known product, but the case law has only been in respect of patents for pharmaceutical uses.

1   G2/88 *Friction Reducing Additive/MOBIL OIL III* [1990] OJ EPO 93.
2   *Adhesive Dry Mounting v Trapp* [1910] 27 RPC 341.

Claims in pharmaceutical patents

Exclusions from patentability in certain jurisdictions

7.08   As noted above, TRIPS requires, and most major patent jurisdictions now grant, product claim protection for NCEs, but a few jurisdictions still do not confer protection on chemicals themselves. Naturally, this also precludes protecting pharmaceuticals by product claims in those jurisdictions. However, some jurisdictions also have their own special restrictions on pharmaceutical patents. Subject to the transitional provisions in TRIPS this is also contrary to TRIPS, except insofar as directed to claims to medical treatment. The special situation of medical treatment claims is discussed below.

Restrictions directed to product claim protection for pharmaceuticals were, until recently, not uncommon, even in Europe. For example, until 1978 neither product, nor even process, claim protection was available in Italy for pharmaceuticals, when a court decision, conveniently coinciding with the accession of Italy to the EPC, held that there was no constitutional basis for the exclusion. EPC, Article 167, permitting reservations for a limited period in respect of claims to chemicals, pharmaceuticals, and foodstuffs, was relied on by certain countries, eg Spain, that had availed themselves of the reservation in relation to claims to chemicals (and thereby pharmaceuticals). In contrast Greece had availed itself of the reservation for pharmaceutical products but not for chemical products.[1]

1   See Case C-414/11 *Daiichi Sankyo et Sanofi-Aventis Deutschland* (Court of Justice, 18 July 2013) and Case C-372/13 *Warner-Lambert Company LLC and Pfizer Ellas AE v SiegerPharma Anonymi Farmakeftiki Etaireia* (Court of Justice, 30 January 2014) for cases that have considered the relationship between EPC, Article 167 and TRIPS, Article 27.

Medical use exclusions from patentability

7.09   'Public policy' type arguments, ostensibly based on a desire not to impede the freedom of medical practitioners to provide the treatment they judge appropriate, are a common feature of many jurisdictions, including the EPC jurisdictions such as the UK, and render unpatentable claims for methods of medical treatment. Such exclusions are permitted by TRIPS, Article 27(3)(a). The EPC jurisdictions have, however, responded with special types of 'medical use' claim which achieve the same end as a claim to a method of medical treatment, and are discussed below under 'First medical use', and 'Second and subsequent medical uses'. The USA has no restrictions of this sort on patentability, and hence no need for such 'workarounds'.

EPC 2000, Article 53(c)[1] (reflected in the UK by PA 1977, s 4A as amended[2]) provides:

'53   European patents shall not be granted in respect of: ...

(c)   methods for treatment of the human or animal body by surgery or therapy and diagnostic methods practised on the human or animal body; this provision shall not apply to products, in particular substances or compositions, for use in any of these methods.'

This exclusion from patentability prevents a patent being granted for the process of treating a patient with a pharmaceutical, even though an NCE which has therapeutic utility can be patented as an NCE as discussed above. This is confirmed by the final sentence of Article 53(c) that provides that patent protection can be obtained for products which are used in such treatment even though such methods of treatment are not themselves patentable.

Not all operations on or manipulations of the human or animal body are excluded by Article 53(c) from patentability. The exclusion for surgery would clearly include plastic surgery even for purely cosmetic reasons. However, methods for harming the human body, or cosmetic operations (of no curative value whatsoever) provided they are not 'surgery' could probably be patented, and on this basis, for example, novel tattooing and ear piercing techniques might be patentable. The EPO Enlarged Board of Appeal has considered the scope of the exclusion for surgery, albeit only in the context of diagnostic procedures, in G-1/07 *Treatment by Surgery/ MEDI-PHYSICS*[3] a Technical Board of Appeal having previously found, that by virtue of the decision of the EPO Enlarged Board of Appeal in G-1/04 *Diagnostic Methods*[4] discussed below, the method claims in issue did not relate to excluded diagnostic methods. The Enlarged Board held that:

'1.   A claimed imaging method, in which, when carried out, maintaining the life and health of the subject is important and which comprises or encompasses an invasive step representing a substantial physical intervention on the body which requires professional medical expertise to be carried out and which entails a substantial health risk even when carried out with the required professional care and expertise, is excluded from patentability as a method for treatment of the human or animal body by surgery pursuant to Article 53 (c) EPC.

2a.   A claim which comprises a step encompassing an embodiment which is a "method for treatment of the human or animal body by surgery" within the meaning of Article 53(c) EPC cannot be left to encompass that embodiment.

2b.   The exclusion from patentability under Article 53(c) EPC can be avoided by disclaiming the embodiment, it being understood that in order to be patentable the claim including the disclaimer must fulfil all the requirements of the EPC and, where applicable, the requirements for a disclaimer to be allowable as defined in decisions G 1/03 and G 2/03 of the Enlarged Board of Appeal.

2c.   Whether or not the wording of the claim can be amended so as to omit the surgical step without offending against the EPC must be assessed on the basis of the overall circumstances of the individual case under consideration.

3.   A claimed imaging method is not to be considered as being a 'treatment of the human or animal body by surgery' within the meaning of Article 53(c) EPC merely because during a surgical intervention the data obtained by the use of the method immediately allow a surgeon to decide on the course of action to be taken during a surgical intervention.'

Thus it should be possible, by careful claim drafting, to sidestep this exclusion, certainly in the context of diagnostic procedures where surgery is only one aspect of the overall process. However, and given the relatively narrow construction placed on this exclusion, this may not always be necessary, and thus in T-663/02[5] a Technical Board of Appeal, applying G-1/07, held that the exclusion did not apply to the intravenous injection of a magnetic resonance contrast agent, which could be delegated by a physician to a qualified paramedical professional, as this indicated that such an injection may be considered as representing a minor routine intervention which does not imply a substantial health risk when carried out with the required care and skill.

As for the exclusion for therapy, a treatment is no less a therapy for the purposes of Article 53 because it only relieves symptoms and not the underlying causes: thus in T-81/84 *Dysmenorrhea/RORER*[6] a treatment for relieving discomfort associated with menstruation was held to be therapy. Both prophylactic and curative treatments are within the term 'therapy' as was established in T-19/86 *Pigs II/DUPHAR*[7] since both have the same aim; the maintenance or restoration of health. Therapy also includes treatment applied on a large scale by farmers, such as the treatment of external parasites on pigs discussed in T-116/85 *Pigs/ DUPHAR*.[8] Treatment by therapy with medical devices is, however, narrowly construed, and for example, in T-245/87 *Flow Measurement/ SIEMENS*[9] it was held that a method for measuring liquid flow used in an implanted device for controlled drug administration was not excluded from patentability as a therapy, as there was no functional link between the claimed method, and the dosage of the drug administered by the implanted device.

The artificiality of a distinction based on the concept of therapy is apparent when applied to conditions, such as snoring or obesity, the treatment of which can be regarded either as therapeutic or cosmetic, depending on the circumstances, or the opinion of the practitioner giving the treatment. To the extent that the treatment is regarded as therapeutic it is restricted by the first and second medical use format (discussed subsequently) but to the extent that it is not, there are no such restrictions. The nature of the borderline between therapy and cosmetic treatment was discussed in relation to obesity treatments in T-144/83 *Appetite Suppressant/DUPONT*[10] that held such a treatment to be cosmetic, and not therapeutic and in relation to treatment for dental plaque in T-290/86 *Cleaning Plaque/ICI*[11] which was held to be a therapy even though it had a cosmetic effect. An alternative approach, where there is a continuum of therapeutic and non-therapeutic treatments, is to have two different sorts of claims such as those eventually allowed in T-584/88 *Anti snoring means/REICHERT*[12] when another medical use of the substance was already known and which were to:

'Use of a substance ... to manufacture an agent for the therapeutic treatment of snoring which might be harmful to health

Use of a substance ... to combat troublesome snoring'

The first claim was to a second medical use (as discussed below) and the second to a cosmetic use. The important limitation introduced into the first claim on the successful appeal by the patentee was the wording 'which might be harmful to health'.

The scope of the exclusion when applied to diagnostic treatment has given rise to especial difficulty as so much of the activity associated with the process of diagnosis has in recent years moved away from the realm of the patient, and this issue was considered by the EPO Enlarged Board of Appeal in G-1/04 *Diagnostic Methods*[13] which took a narrow view of the exclusion, deciding that:

'(1)   In order that the subject-matter of a claim relating to a diagnostic method practised on the human or animal body falls under the prohibition of Article [53(c)] EPC, the claim is to include the features relating to:

(i)   the diagnosis for curative purposes *stricto sensu* representing the deductive medical or veterinary decision phase as a purely intellectual exercise,

(ii)   the preceding steps which are constitutive for making that diagnosis, and

(iii)   the specific interactions with the human or animal body which occur when carrying those out among these preceding steps which are of a technical nature.

(2)   Whether or not a method is a diagnostic method within the meaning of Article [53(c)] EPC may neither depend on the participation of a medical or veterinary practitioner, by being present or by bearing the responsibility, nor on the fact that all method steps can also, or only, be practised by medical or technical support staff, the patient himself or herself or an automated system. Moreover, no distinction is to be made in this context between essential method steps having diagnostic character and non-essential method steps lacking it.

(3)   In a diagnostic method under Article [53(c)] EPC, the method steps of a technical nature belonging to the preceding steps which are constitutive for making the diagnosis for curative purposes *stricto sensu* must satisfy the criterion "practised on the human or animal body".

(4)   Article [53(c)] EPC does not require a specific type and intensity of interaction with the human or animal body; a preceding step of a technical nature thus satisfies the criterion "practised on the human or animal body" if its performance implies any interaction with the human or animal body, necessitating the presence of the latter.'

Thus, diagnostic methods in which at least one of the essential technical steps is performed away from the human or animal body, such as where blood samples are first taken from the patient, and only then analysed in vitro in a new way, are not excluded from patentability on the basis of this exclusion.

1   Before EPC 2000 came into force on 13 December 2007, this provision was found in EPC 1973, Article 52(4) which rather than regarding such methods as an exclusion from patentability deemed them not be 'susceptible of industrial application', and hence not patentable by virtue of EPC, Article 52(1). Presenting this provision more logically as an exclusion from patentability does not change the law.

2   Before EPC 2000 came into force on 13 December 2007, and thus the relevant provisions of PA 2004 amending PA 1977 took effect, this provision was found in 4(2)–(3). Presenting this provision more logically as an exception to patentability rather than as example of something not 'susceptible of industrial application' does not change the law.

3   G 1/07 *Treatment by Surgery/MEDI-PHYSICS* (15 February 2010).

4   G 1/04 *Diagnostic Methods* [2006] OJ EPO 334; [2006] EPOR 15.

5   T 663/02 (17 March 2011).

6   T 81/84 *Dysmenorrhea RORER* [1988] OJ EPO 207.

7   T 19/86 *Pigs II/DUPHAR* [1988] OJ EPO 24; [1988] EPOR 10.

8   T 116/85 *Pigs/DUPHAR* [1988] OJ EPO 13; [1988] EPOR 1.

9   T 245/87 *Flow Measurement/SIEMENS* [1989] OJ EPO 171; [1989] EPOR 241.

10   T 144/83 *Appetite Suppressant/DUPONT* [1987] EPOR 6.

11   T 290/86 *Cleaning Plaque/ICI* [1991] EPOR 157.

12   T 584/88 *Anti snoring means/REICHERT* [1989] EPOR 449.

13   G 1/04 *Diagnostic Methods* [2006] OJ EPO 334; [2006] EPOR 15.

First medical use

7.10   If one discovers that a known chemical has value as a pharmaceutical how can this be patented if one cannot patent the method of treatment with that chemical? Because the chemical already forms part of the state of the art it cannot be patented as an NCE. The effect of EPC 2000, Article 53(c)[1] (reflected in the UK by PA 1977, s 4A(1) as amended[2]) which would otherwise be to invalidate any claim to the method of using a known substance for the treatment of disease is in such cases tempered by EPC 2000, Article 54(4)[3] that states:

'(4)   Paragraphs 2 and 3 [which concern novelty] shall not exclude the patentability of any substance or composition, comprised in the state of the art, for use in a method referred to in Article 53(c), provided that its use for any such method is not comprised in the state of the art.'

Thus 'use bound' product claims are allowed for inventions that consist of the first medical use of an already known chemical entity. A typical first medical use claim was allowed in T 128/82 *Pyrrolidine-derivatives/HOFFMAN-LA ROCHE*:[4] 'Pyrrolidine derivatives having [a certain general formula] for use as an active therapeutic substance', even though the only therapeutic utility disclosed was for 'combating cerebral insufficiency and improving intellectual ability', as to which specific utility there was also a claim. Composition claims were also allowed in the following forms: 'A medical preparation containing a pyrrolidine derivative having [a certain general formula] and a pharmaceutically inert excipient', and: 'A substance combating cerebral insufficiency and improving intellectual ability containing a pyrrolidine derivative having [a certain general formula] and a pharmaceutically inert excipient'.

Claims to first medical uses have featured little in litigation, because in practice most novel pharmaceutical uses that are not also associated with a new chemical entity are for second, and subsequent uses, various aspects of which are discussed below.

1   Before EPC 2000 came into force on 13 December 2007, and under the earlier version of the EPC this provision was found in EPC 1973, Article 52(4) which rather than regarding such methods as an exclusion from patentability deemed them not be 'susceptible of industrial application', and hence not patentable by virtue of EPC 1973, Article 52(1). Presenting this provision more logically as an exclusion from patentability does not change the law.

2   Before EPC 2000 came into force on 13 December 2007, and thus the relevant provisions of PA 2004 amending PA 1977 took effect, this provision was found in s 4(2)–(3). Presenting this provision more logically as an exception to patentability rather than as example of something not 'susceptible of industrial application' does not change the law.

3   Before EPC 2000 came into force on 13 December 2007, and under the earlier version of EPC, this provision was at EPC 1973, Article 54(5). In the UK, it is now reflected in PA 1977, s 4A(3).

4   T 128/82 *Pyrrolidine-derivatives/HOFFMAN-LA ROCHE* [1984] OJ EPO 164; [1979–85] EPOR B 591.

Second and subsequent medical uses

7.11   Many pharmacologically active compounds have an additional, and different, pharmacological effect to that for which they were originally known. A need has accordingly arisen to protect such second (and third and so on) medical uses. Since the toxicological and metabolic profile of known pharmaceuticals is already well established, it is often quicker, and easier to obtain regulatory approval for a new medical use of a known pharmaceutical. How does one claim such a second medical use, again recognizing that EPC 2000, Article 53(c) precludes claiming this as a method? The issue is now addressed by EPC 2000, Article 54(5)[1] that states:

'(5)   Paragraphs 2 and 3 [which concern novelty] shall also not exclude the patentability of any substance or composition referred to in paragraph 4 for any specific use in a method referred to in Article 53(c), provided that its use for any such method is not comprised in the state of the art.'

The critical distinction over EPC 2000, Article 54(4) lies in the reference to 'specific use'. However, EPC 1973 lacked any such provision, and did not permit product claims for the second medical use. However, creative patent practitioners, aided by sympathetic tribunals, enabled broadly equivalent protection to be secured, although now that this creative approach is no longer required it is, since the middle of 2010 by virtue of the decision of the EPO Enlarged Board of Appeal in G-2/08 *Dosage Regime/ABBOTT*[2] no longer permitted, although this decision does not have retroactive effect on the validity of such claims that had already been secured.

The 'legal fiction' that enabled second medical uses to be claimed under EPC 1973 was established, in G-05/83 *Second medical indication/EISAI*[3] where the EPO Enlarged Board of Appeal allowed in principle a claim to: 'The use of [a certain substance or composition] for the manufacture of a medicament for a specified new and inventive therapeutic application', even where such process of manufacture did not differ from known processes of manufacture for the same substance or composition. The Enlarged Board had, however, refused to allow a claim directed to: 'The use of a [certain substance or composition] for the treatment of the human or animal body by therapy', holding this to be equivalent to a claim directed to: 'A method of treatment of the human or animal body by therapy with [a certain substance or composition]', which was excluded from patentability by as a method of medical treatment.

The form of claim acceptable to the Enlarged Board followed a precedent set in Switzerland. Thus such claims, which speak of the 'manufacture of a medicament' are accordingly said to be in the 'Swiss form'. The Enlarged Board's decision was followed, albeit with misgivings, in the UK by the Patents Court in *John Wyeth's and Scherings Applications.*[4] In one of these applications the second use was the discovery that certain guanidines were useful for treating or preventing diarrhoea in mammals and poultry where the known uses of such compounds were the treatment of high blood pressure, hypoglycaemia, and ulcers.

In the other application the second use was the treatment of prostatic hyperplasia when the known use was the treatment of breast cancer, and the claim allowed in this case provides an early example of a type of second medical use claim that has come to be known as a 'field of use' claim as it is to a particular use of a type of compound described in pharmacological rather than chemical terms: 'The use of an aromatise-inhibitor for the manufacture of a medicament for the therapeutic and/or prophylactic treatment of hyperplasia'.

Such a 'field of use' claim was at issue in *Lilly ICOS v Pfizer*:[5]

'10. The use of a cGMP PDE inhibitor, or a pharmaceutically acceptable salt thereof, or a pharmaceutical composition containing either entity, for the manufacture of a medicament for the curative or prophylactic oral treatment of erectile dysfunction in man.'

However, this claim together with more conventionally drawn second use claims to the same new use for certain compounds, identified instead by means of chemical structures, was found to lack inventive step.

Second medical use claims in the Swiss form, being based on a 'legal fiction', can present especial difficulties of construction in the context of infringement proceedings.[6] These can in particular arise where there are both infringing and non-infringing medical uses, and where the medicinal product in issue is neither authorized nor ostensibly supplied for the infringing use but it is inevitable that some infringing use, the degree of which will depend on the nature of the market and the respective significance of the indications in issue, will take place. Given their artificial focus on manufacture such difficulties are greater for Swiss form claims (when literally construed) than for use bound product claims, and will only cease once the last patent granted with such Swiss form claims expires. A recent example of these difficulties is provided by the various decisions in the ongoing dispute in *Warner-Lambert Company, LLC v Actavis Group Ptc EHF & Ors,* and in the course of which judgments in which decisions from other European jurisdictions on the same issue (but in some cases on different products) have also been reviewed.[7]

1   Before EPC 2000 came into force on 13 December 2007, there was no equivalent provision in EPC 1973, similar protection having been obtained by 'second medical use' type claims as explained in the text. Likewise, until the relevant provisions of PA 2004 amending PA 1977 to introduce s 4A(4) then took effect, there was no equivalent provision in UK law.
2   G-2/08 *Dosage Regime/ABBOTT* [2010] OJ EPO 456.
3   G-05/83 *Second medical indication/EISAI* [1985] OJ EPO 64; [1979–85] EPOR B 241.
4   *John Wyeth's and Schering's Applications* [1986] OJ EPO 175; RPC [1985] 545.
5   *Lilly ICOS v Pfizer.* [2001] 59 BMLR 123; [2001] FSR 16; [2001] IP&T 190 (Patents Court); [2002] EWCA Civ 1 (Court of Appeal).

6   See *Ranbaxy (UK) v AstraZeneca* [2011] EWHC 1831 (Patents Court), and *Monsanto Co v Merck & Co Inc* [1999] EWCA 1946 (Court of Appeal). In the latter case the Court of Appeal reversed summary judgment at first instance rejecting a construction of a Swiss form claim advanced by the patentee. That particular construction does not, however, appear to have been advanced in the subsequent full hearing, reported as *Monsanto Co v Merck & Co Inc* [2000] EWHC 154 (Patents Court); *Pharmacia v Merck & Co Inc* [2001] EWCA 1610 (Court of Appeal).

7   *Warner-Lambert Company, LLC v Actavis Group Ptc EHF & Ors* [2015] EWHC 72 (Pat); [2015] EWHC 223 (Pat); [2015] EWHC 249 (Pat); [2015] EWCA Civ 556, [2015] EWHC 2548 (Pat), where, after expiry of product patent protection, marketing authorizations had been secured for the use of a medicinal product only in unpatented indications but the medicinal product could also be used in patented indications (ie 'cross-label', as opposed to 'off-label' use). Various attempts at formulating interim injunctions of appropriate scope pending full trial of the action failed until NHS England submitted to an interim injunction made against it to provide appropriate prescribing guidance to doctors. Summary judgment at first instance in favour of the defendants in relation to an infringement argument based on PA 1977, s 60(2) and rejecting a construction of the Swiss form claims advanced by the patentee was reversed on appeal, leaving the matter to be resolved at full trial, where such construction was also rejected, so that there was held to be no infringement under PA 1977, s 60(1)(c) or s 60(2), even had the relevant claims of the patent in suit (which were held to be invalid for insufficiency) been valid. It is however to be expected that this decision will be appealed.

What constitutes a patentable second and subsequent medical use?

7.12   The principles established in G-05/83 *Second Medical Indication/ EISAI*[1] for second medical use claims were subsequently extended in various ways. Thus, patents have been obtained for a method of treatment known in respect of a certain condition in a certain class of animal where its use for the same condition was already known in another class of the same animal, as in T-19/86 *Pigs II/DUPHAR*[2] where the known class of animals was seronegative pigs (lacking maternal antibodies) and the class claimed in the patent was seropositive pigs (possessing maternal immunity). Claims could also be secured protecting use in new patient populations, to reflect discoveries in pharmacogenomics, as in T-893/90 *Controlling Bleeding/QUEEN'S UNIVERSITY KINGSTON*.[3] Second use claims have also been granted for new pharmaceutical forms, and new modes of administration.[4]

However, second use claims have been refused where the invention consists of no more than the recognition of a known effect present to a hitherto unknown extent.[5] Second use claims have been refused to surgical methods involving the use of known medical devices in a new way, as in T-775/97 *Surgical Device/EXPANDABLE GRAFTS*.[6] Such claims were also refused to an adsorbent which was not administered to a patient's body to treat a disease, and so was not 'medicament' within the meaning of established case law, as in T-138/02 *Second Medical Use/KANEGAFUCHI*[7] which meant that an earlier disclosure of a first medical use for such adsorbent was novelty destroying. Claims have also been refused where the condition to be treated is defined in functional terms but there is no teaching as to which conditions fall within the functional definition, and thus within the scope of the claims, as in T-241/95 *Serotonin receptor/ELI LILLY.*[8]

The English courts (along with those in the Netherlands) were for many years reluctant to apply EPO Technical Board of Appeal case law to uphold second medical use claims other than to entirely new indications, and were thus reluctant to uphold claims where the novelty lay only in a new dosing schedule.[9]

These national decisions, along with some EPO ones, were the subject of an extensive and critical review by an EPO Technical Board of Appeal in T-1020/03 *Method of Administration of IGF-1/GENENTECH*[10] and which urged taking a permissive view of second medical use claiming, as reflected in its headnote:

'Any use to which [Article 52(4) EPC 1973] first sentence applies in circumstances where the composition has already been suggested for some therapeutic use, allows a second medical use claim to the preparation of the composition for that second medical use, irrespective of in what detail that use was specified, subject to the use being novel and inventive. For the purposes of novelty also under [Article 54(5) EPC 1973] this depends on whether use for therapy is novel, irrespective of the detail with which the therapy is stated in the claim.'

In the UK the Court of Appeal, in *Actavis UK v Merck*[11] that concerned a Swiss form second medical use claim to a new dosing schedule, and after a thorough review of earlier English case law, held that, when properly analysed, this did not compel it to differ from the Technical Board of Appeal in T-1020/03, and so upheld the validity of the claim.

The same approach as in T-1020/03 applies equally to second medical use bound product claims under EPC 2000, Article 54(5) as confirmed authoritatively by the EPO Enlarged Board of Appeal in G-2/08 *Dosage Regime/ABBOTT RESPIRATORY*[12] which held:

'1) Where it is already known to use a medicament to treat an illness, Article 54(5) EPC does not exclude that this medicament be patented for use in a different treatment by therapy of the same illness.

2) Such patenting is also not excluded where a dosage regime is the only feature claimed which is not comprised in the state of the art.'

The Enlarged Board also, as observed above at para 7.11, held that as there was no longer any need for Swiss form second medical use claims under EPC 2000 they should no longer be granted.

1   G-05/83 *Second medical indication/EISAI* [1985] OJ EPO 64; [1979–85] EPOR B 241.
2   T-19/86 *Pigs II/DUPHAR* [1988] EPOR 10.
3   T-893/90 *Controlling Bleeding/QUEEN'S UNIVERSITY KINGSTON* (22 July 1993).
4   T-143/94 *Trigonelltine/MAI* (6 October 1995); T-51/93 *HCG/SERONO* [1996] OJ EPO 430; [1996] EPOR 65.

5   T-958/90 *Sequestering Agent/DOW* [1994] EPOR 1 and T-279/93 *Melamine Derivatives/AMERICAN CYANAMID* [1999] EPOR 88.
6   T-775/97 *Surgical Device/EXPANDABLE GRAFTS* [2002] EPOR 24.
7   T-138/02 *Second Medical Use/KANEGAFUCHI* [2007] EPOR 3.
8   T-241/95 *Serotonin receptor/ELI LILLY* [2001] EPOR 38.
9   See *Bristol Myers Squibb v Baker Norton Pharmaceuticals* [1999] RPC 253 (Patents Court); [2001] 58 BMLR 121; [2000] ENPR 230; [2000] IP&T 908; [2001] RPC 1 (Court of Appeal), and *Teva Pharmaceutical Industries v Instituto Gentili (Merck & Co's Patents)* [2003] EWHC 5 (Patents Court); [2003] EWCA 1545 (Court of Appeal).
10   T-1020/03 *Method of Administration of IGF-1/GENENTECH* [2007] OJ EPO 204.
11   *Actavis UK v Merck* [2008] EWCA 444 (Court of Appeal).
12   G-2/08 *Dosage Regime/ABBOTT REPIRATORY* [2010] OJ EPO 456.

Reach through claims

7.13 Applications for patents for certain types of 'research tool' may have claims to screening methods, to compounds identified using these screening methods, and claims to use of these compounds in human therapy. The first such claim is unlikely to be infringed by dealings in the end product of the screening, as such end product is unlikely to be regarded as the direct product of such a screening process. It is also relatively easy to ensure that any screening only takes place in a country where there is no patent that covers it. There would be no such scope for avoidance with the latter two such claim types, and which, where expressed to be to compounds not yet identified, are examples of so-called 'reach through' claims.

Such claims have only rarely been granted but an early example of such a claim can be found in a patent granted in 1998 to Harvard College and Xenometrix, EP 0680 517 B, claims 1–27 of which as granted were to methods of characterizing the toxicity of a compound by determining the level of transcription of various stress genes present in a eukaryotic cell. Claim 28 as granted was to an iterative method of identifying an antitoxin to a new toxic compound by the repeated application of such methods. However, claims 29–31 as granted read:

'29   A method of decreasing the toxicity of a drug, comprising the steps of
      (a)   determining the type of stresses caused by said drug using the methods according to any one of claim 5 to 27 and
      (b)   modifying said drug to alter or eliminate the portion thereof suspected of causing said determined stresses
30   The method according to claim 29, further comprising, after step (b), the additional step of:
      (c)   repeating the method used to determine the types of stresses caused by said drug according to step (a) using the modified drug according to step (b)
31   A modified drug produced by the method according to claim 29 or 30.'

Claim 31 was a classic reach through claim, purporting to dominate any drug, of any structure, and of any utility, discovered by means of the patented technology, although it was later abandoned by the patentee in the course of subsequent opposition proceedings. Such claims are, however, generally likely to be regarded as insufficient as not being commensurate with the technical contribution made by the invention.[1] This was demonstrated in T-1063/06 *Reach-through claim/BAYER SCHERING PHARMA AG.*[2] An EPO Technical Board of Appeal held a reach through claim to be insufficiently disclosed. The headnote states:

> 'A formulation of a claim whereby functionally defined chemical compounds are to be found by means of a new kind of research tool using a screening method set out in the description constitutes a reach-through claim which is also directed to future inventions based on the one now being disclosed. As the applicant is entitled to claim patent protection only for his actual contribution to the art, it is therefore both reasonable and imperative to limit the claim's subject-matter accordingly. Patent protection under the EPC is not designed for the purpose of reserving an unexplored field of research for a particular applicant, as reach through claims do, but to protect factual results of successful research as a reward for making concrete technical results available to the public.
>
> A functional definition of a chemical compound (in this case in a reach through claim) covers all compounds possessing the capability according to the claim. In the absence of any selection rule in the application in suit, the skilled person, without the possibility of having recourse to his common general knowledge, must resort to trial-and-error experimentation on arbitrarily selected chemical compounds to establish whether they possess the capability according to the claim; this represents for the skilled person an invitation to perform a research programme and thus an undue burden (following T 435/91).'

This formulation of the law would seem to shut the door firmly on reach through claims in the absence of any disclosure of a selection rule. However, care needs to be taken in applying the decision outside that specific area, and so an attempt to use it as a basis for arguing that any clam which covered embodiments the making of which required invention must necessarily be invalid for insufficiency, failed before the English Patents Court in *MedImmune v Novartis*[3] as being counter to the well-established jurisprudence of the EPO.

1 See the comparative study on biotechnology patent practices – *Reports on 'Comparative study on reach-through claims'*, at: www.trilateral.net/projects/biotechnology/B3b.pdf.
2 T-1063/06 *Reach-through claim/BAYER SCHERING PHARMA AG.*
3 *MedImmune v Novartis* [2011] EWHC 1669 at paras [480]–[482] and [491]. Insufficiency was not in issue on appeal in *MedImmune v Novartis* [2012] EWCA Civ 1234 (Court of Appeal).

Validity issues

Construction

7.14 Pharmaceutical patents often raise certain specific issues of construction that bear on the assessment of validity. The main one, that is encountered with claims to compounds, has the effect of incorporating a functional limitation into such claims, and was first articulated in *Pharmacia v Merck*[1] but was put into its wider context in *Idenix Pharmaceutical, Inc v Gilead Sciences, Inc & Ors*:[2]

'304. Claims 1, 2 and 5 of the Patent are, on their face, pure compound claims. The general rule is that the validity of such claims must be assessed by reference to what is claimed and not by reference to what is said about the claimed invention in the specification: see *Conor Medsystems Inc v Angiotech Pharmaceuticals Inc* [2008] UKHL 49, [2008] RPC 28 at [17]–[19] (Lord Hoffmann) and *Eli Lilly & Co v Human Genome Sciences Inc* [2012] EWCA Civ 1185. [2013] RPC 22 at [18] (Sir Robin Jacob). In principle, it is possible for a patentee to claim a chemical compound, or a class of chemical compounds, that is novel and non-obvious and which the specification teaches the skilled person how to make. This is true even if the compound was per se one which was obvious to make, but there was no known way to make it and the inventor has devised a non-obvious way in which to do so: see *Generics (UK) Ltd v H. Lundbeck A/S* [2009] UKHL 12, [2009] RPC 13. Such a claim covers the compound even when made in other ways and regardless of the use to which the compound may be put (which may be quite different to that envisaged by the inventor).

305. Nevertheless, there are some cases in which the specification makes it clear to the skilled reader that, even though the claims are expressed as pure compound claims, it was not the inventor's intention to claim the compounds in the abstract and without reference to their intended use. In *Pharmacia Corp v Merck & Co Inc* [2001] EWCA Civ 1610, [2002] RPC 41 the patent in suit contained broad compound claims in Markush form (see claim 1 set out at [11]). The specification said that such compounds were anti-inflammatory, and in particular were gastric sparing by reason of their being COX II selective. Aldous LJ rejected the argument that functional limitations should not be read into the invention:

17. Mr Kitchin QC, who appeared for the patentees, drew attention to section 125 of the 1977 Act which provides that an invention 'shall, unless the context otherwise requires be that specified in a claim.' He then drew to our attention claims 1–12 which claim chemical compounds. He submitted that they could be used for any purpose because they were claimed without limitation as to use. That was emphasised by the terms of claims 13 to 26 which claimed compounds which were therapeutically-effective as an anti-inflammatory and claims 21–30 which had to be effective for the particular complaints set out. It followed that the invention of claim 1 was the compounds themselves.

18. Mr Kitchin is correct that claims 1 to 12 do not include any limitation as to use. Thus when construed without recourse to the rest of the specification, the invention claimed is to the chemical compounds set out. But that construction makes the invention inconsistent with, amongst other passages, the description

of the invention in the specification. It states that 'A class of compounds useful in treating inflammation-related disorders is defined by Formula 1'. I will deal with this submission and the other submissions on construction later in this judgment in the context in which they arise. But I will first decide whether the judge was right to accept Merck's submission which is set out in paragraph 42 of his judgment as to what was the 'invention' or 'technical contribution' in the specification:

> 42. On the other hand the defendants contended that the invention of the specification was a class of compounds substantially all of which were both anti-inflammatory and had significantly less harmful side effects than the existing NSAIDs. They further said that the specification taught only two mechanisms for reducing harmful side effects: to provide Cox II selectivity, and further to provide Cox I inactivity. They submitted that while gastric-sparing qualities might arise from other causes, so far as the specification was concerned the teaching was such that the addressee would understand that the inventor's contribution lay in a class of compounds which possessed Cox II/Cox I selectivity at least when assayed in the manner described in the specification. However, apart from a specific teaching in respect of the thiophenes at page 3 line 29 (see paragraph 27 above) the patent neither identifies the members of the claimed class which possess Cox II selectivity nor those which do not inhibit Cox I. The defendants contend that accordingly the teaching of the patent is that all the claimed classes, or at least all the thiophenes, possess Cox II selectivity, and moreover produce a reduced amount of side effects. This question as to the teaching of the specification is fundamental to the dispute between the parties....

> 20.   I agree with the judge. Nobody reading the specification could believe that the 'invention' was the compounds claimed in claim 1. The specification makes clear that the patentees had found a class of compounds that could be made which at least had anti-inflammatory action. It was that contribution that merited a 20 year monopoly. In my view the only question capable of argument is whether the compounds in the class were chosen merely for their anti-inflammatory action or because in addition they had reduced side-effects due to them being Cox II selective.'

Another issue of construction encountered with pharmaceutical and biotechnology patents arises where their claims, especially in those cases of claims to new medical uses, incorporate reference to the treatment of a disease as a "functional technical feature". Such claims are generally interpreted as being to something which is indeed an effective treatment for the disease.[3]

The effect of such implied functional limitations on validity is twofold: they make it easier to resist attacks of anticipation based on speculative references in the prior art, but also make it harder to resist attacks based on insufficiency by reason of excessive claim breadth or for lack on inventive step on *Agrevo* type grounds.[4]

1   *Pharmacia v Merck* [2000] IP&T 1505; [2001] EWCA Civ 1610 (Court of Appeal).
2   *Idenix Pharmaceutical, Inc v Gilead Sciences, Inc & Ors* [2014] EWHC 3916 (Patents Court).
3   *Regeneron Pharmaceuticals Inc v Bayer Pharma AG* [2013] EWCA Civ 93 (Court of Appeal) at [56]. See also *Eli Lilly v Janssen Alzheimer Immunotherapy* [2013] EWHC 1737 (Patents Court) at [190]–[194]; *Hospira v Genentech* [2014] EWHC 1094 (Patents Court) at [57]–[84], and *Hospira v Genentech (No 2)* (Patents Court) [2014] EWHC 3857 at [88]–[102] but see the warning as to such construction depending on context in *Generics (UK) Ltd (t/a Mylan) v Richter Gedeon Vegyeszeti Gyar RT* [2014] EWHC 1666 (Patents Court).
4   See para 7.16.

Anticipation and obviousness

7.15 Anticipation, and especially obviousness, often constitute grounds of attack on chemical and pharmaceutical patents and the general principles as to these that are set out in **Chapter 5** apply in such cases. A number of examples as applied to various different types of invention as encountered in this area of technology are provided elsewhere in this chapter.[1] However, certain types of issue as to anticipation and obviousness tend to be specific to patents with compound claims to pharmaceuticals or other chemicals.

One such issue encountered with such patents is a consequence of the precision with which NCEs can be defined, and the relative ease with which analogous NCEs with real prospects of similar activity can be predicted. This ease of definition makes it simple to illustrate the difference between anticipation, and obviousness in the context of NCE patents. Consider an invention relating to a particular organic compound, say a heterocyclic compound substituted at a certain position on the heterocyclic ring with a propyl group. If the prior art discloses exactly that same compound then the claim will lack novelty. If however, the closest disclosure in the prior art is otherwise the same heterocyclic compound but substituted at the same position with, say a methyl rather than a propyl group, then such prior art does not anticipate the later claim to the propyl substituted heterocyclic compound. However, such a claim may still lack inventive step given that the similarities between the two groups are such that little change in properties would be expected to result from such substitution. Such an obviousness attack would be difficult to answer if the propyl compound had much the same properties as the methyl one. On the other hand, if it can be shown that the propyl compound has exceptional properties then it may well be easier to meet such an attack. However, for special properties to be relied on in support of inventive step they must be set out in application, or at least implied by or related to an effect disclosed in it.[2]

The position both before the EPO, and the English courts as to new chemical compounds having a particular therapeutic activity that are structurally similar to known compounds having the same therapeutic activity turns: First, on whether the skilled person would reasonably expect the new compounds to have the same therapeutic activity as the prior art compounds. Second, if that is the case, on whether the claimed compounds exhibit a new or improved therapeutic, or other property. The EPO Technical Board of Appeal decisions in T-939/92 *Triazoles/AGREVO*[3] T-852/91 *Leukotriene Antagonist/ICI AMERICAS*[4] T-643/96 *Bioisosterism/BEECHAM*[5] and T-309/91 *Benzopyrans/BEECHAM*[6] each reflect something of the EPO approach to such claims. In all of these cases except in the special circumstances of T-939/92 *Triazoles/AGREVO* (in which certain broad chemical claims were held to be obvious under EPC, Article 56, because it was not plausible that everything within such claims solved the technical problem) the Technical Board of Appeal set aside decisions denying inventive step for novel chemical compounds because of their structural similarity to known chemical compounds, observing in T-643/96 *Bioisosterism/BEECHAM* that: 'In the field of drug design any structural modification of a pharmacologically active compound is, in the absence of an established correlation between structural features and activity, *a priori* expected to disturb the pharmacological activity profile of that initial structure'.

The issue subsequently arose in the UK in *Pharmacia v Merck*[7] where, on the evidence, the step from the 2,3-substitution pattern on a 5-membered heterocyclic ring in the prior art to a 3,4-substitution on such a ring of the novel compounds claimed in the patent was held to be obvious, although the patent was also held to be invalid for other reasons, notably that of insufficiency, as discussed below at para 7.19. This, however, is an isolated case as attacks on validity based on structural similarity are only ever rarely made in practice in the UK and the EPO, and succeed even more rarely.

A related objection as to lack of inventive step that can be encountered in the context of pharmaceutical, and biotechnological inventions arises where the data in the patent application does not render it plausible that the teaching of the application solves the technical problem that it purports to solve across the breadth of the claims, and thus makes no contribution to the art. This approach was first developed by an EPO Technical Board of Appeal in T-939/92 *Triazoles/AGREVO* and is accordingly termed '*Agrevo* obviousness'. This case, and the subsequent English case law that has considered it was analysed by the Court of Appeal in *Generics (UK) v Yeda Research & Development*:[8]

'39   As with any consideration of obviousness, the technical results or effects must be shared by everything falling within the claim under attack. This follows from the fundamental principle of patent law, which underpins many of the grounds of objection to validity, that the extent of the monopoly conferred by a patent must be justified by the technical contribution to the art. If some of the products covered by a claim demonstrate a particular property, but others do not, then the technical problem cannot be formulated by reference to that property. Either the products which do not exhibit the property must be excised from the claim by amendment, or the problem must be formulated by reference to some other, perhaps more mundane, technical contribution common to the whole claim.

...

49   I would summarise the position thus far in the following way:

(i)   Article 56 of the EPC is in part based on the underlying principle that the scope of the patent monopoly must be justified by the patentee's contribution to the art.

(ii)   If the alleged contribution is a technical effect which is not common to substantially everything covered by a claim, it cannot be used to formulate the question for the purposes of judging obviousness.

(iii)   In such circumstances the claim must either be restricted to the subject matter which makes good the technical contribution, or a different technical solution common to the whole claim must be found.

(iv)   A selection from the prior art which is purely arbitrary and cannot be justified by some useful technical property is likely to be held to be obvious because it does not make a real technical advance.

(v)   A technical effect which is not rendered plausible by the patent specification may not be taken into account in assessing inventive step.

(vi)   Later evidence may be adduced to support a technical effect made plausible by the specification.

(vii)   Provided the technical effect is made plausible, no further proof of the existence of the effect is to be demanded of the specification before judging obviousness by reference to the technical effect propounded.'

It has often been the case when pharmaceutical and biotechnology patents have been held to be insufficient for excessive claim breadth[9] they have also been found to be invalid for '*Agrevo*' obviousness where this argument has also been run, but the case law has not sought to analyse in any depth the relationship as between the two attacks on validity.[10]

1   See the observations on patents with claims to salts and crystalline forms at para 7.03, formulations at para 7.05, mixtures or combinations at para 7.06, selections at para 7.16, optical isomers at para 7.17, and metabolites at para 7.18.

2   See *EPO Guidelines for Examination*, November 2014, Part G – Chapter VII, para 11 observing that: 'Care must be taken, however, whenever new effects in support of inventive step are referred to. Such new effects can only be taken into account if they are implied by or at least related to the technical problem initially suggested in the originally filed application (see also G-VII, 5.2, T 386/89 and T 184/82)'.

3   T-939/92 *Triazoles/AGREVO* [1996] EPOR 171. Although this was a case concerning plant protection products, the principles that it established have been applied mostly in the areas of pharmaceuticals and biotechnology.

4   T-852/91 *Leukotriene Antagonist/ICI AMERICAS* [1998] EPOR 31.

5   T- 643/96 *Bioisosterism/BEECHAM* [1998] EPOR 18.

6   T-309/91 *Benzopyrans/ BEECHAM* [1998] EPOR 11.

7   *Pharmacia v Merck* [2000] IP&T 1505; [2001] EWCA Civ 1610 (Court of Appeal).

8   *Generics (UK) Ltd v Yeda Research & Development Co Ltd* [2013] EWCA Civ 925, [2014] RPC 4 (Court of Appeal) at [36]–[65] where such attack failed. See also *Idenix Pharmaceutical, Inc v Gilead Sciences, Inc & Ors* [2014] EWHC 3916 (Patents Court) at paras [426]–[443] where such an attack succeeded.

9   As to which, see below, at para 7.19. See also **Chapter 5**, at para 5.20, and in the specific context of biotechnology **Chapter 8** at paras 8.14–8.15.

10   T- 694/92 *Modifying plant cells/MYCOGEN* (quoted from more fully in **Chapter 8** at para 8.14) notes, but does not analyse such overlap, stating at [8]: 'how closely interrelated and how critical the issues of support of the claims, sufficiency of disclosure and inventive step are in such cases'. In *Eli Lilly & Company v Janssen Alzheimer Immunotherapy* [2013] EWHC 1737 (Patents Court) the Court declined to address the argument based on *Agrevo* obviousness, simply observing that 'the real objection is not one of obviousness, but of insufficiency' which attack it then found to have been made out. In *Idenix Pharmaceutical, Inc v Gilead Sciences, Inc & Ors* [2014] EWHC 3916 (Patents Court) attacks on each basis were found independently to be made out, but the relationship as between them was not discussed.

Selection inventions

7.16   The selection of one particular compound out of a broad disclosure of a class of such compounds, particularly where this compound provides advantages over and above those previously known to be shared by the members of the class the subject of the broad disclosure, may provide the basis for a patent on that one compound. Although at one time such an end was achieved in the English courts by applying principles specific to so-called 'selection inventions' that seemed to elide issues of novelty, and obviousness,[1] this can now be achieved by careful application of the usual principles of novelty, and inventive step, consistent with the practice and case law of the EPO, and as held by the Court of Appeal in *Dr Reddy's Laboratories v Eli Lilly*.[2]

If the claimed subject matter of the selection is novel, in that it has not been the subject of an enabling disclosure that specifically identifies it,[3] then the next issue to address is that of inventive step. Inventive selections have been assimilated into EPO thinking, and the *EPO Guidelines* provide[4] a number of contrasting examples of selections that are inventive, and those which are not. The headings as to obvious, and consequently non-inventive, selections are:

'(i)   The invention consists merely in choosing from a number of equally likely alternatives.

(ii)   The invention resides in the choice of particular ... parameters from a limited range of possibilities, and it is clear that these parameters could be arrived at by routine trial and error or by the application of normal design procedures.

(iii)   The invention can be arrived at merely by a simple extrapolation in a straightforward way from the known art.

(iv)   The invention consists merely in selecting particular chemical compounds or compositions ... from a broad field ..., [where for example] ... the resulting compounds are neither described as having nor shown to possess any advantageous properties not possessed by the prior art examples; or ... are described as possessing advantageous properties compared with the compounds specifically referred to in the prior art but these properties are ones which the person skilled in the art would expect such compounds to possess, so that he is likely to be led to make this selection.'

These are contrasted with the following headings for selections that are not obvious and are consequently inventive:

'(i)   The invention involves special selection in a process of particular operating conditions ... within a known range, such selection producing unexpected results in the operation of the process or the properties of the resulting product.

(ii)   The invention consists in selecting particular chemical compounds or compositions ... from a broad field, such compounds or compositions having unexpected advantages.'

It can be easy to fall into error when analysing selection inventions by failing to keep issues of novelty, and inventive step separate, as observed in T-0230/07 *Colloidal Binder/PAROC*[5] the headnote for which states:

'Novelty and inventive step are two distinct requirements for the patentability of an invention and therefore different criteria should apply for their assessment. So, when assessing novelty of an invention, the presence or absence of a technical effect within a sub-range of numerical values is not to be taken into account in the assessment of novelty.

For establishing novelty of a sub-range of numerical values from a broader range, the selected sub-range should be narrow and sufficiently far removed from the known broader range illustrated by means of examples. A sub-range is not rendered novel by virtue of a newly discovered effect occurring within it.'

Most of the reported selection patent cases in the EPO have tended to involve attempts to patent selections from a numerical range of a particular parameter, rather than the selection of certain compounds from a broad field. An often-quoted decision of an EPO Technical Board of Appeal on the issue of compound selection is T-12/81 *Diastereoisomers/BAYER*[6] although the principles there set out are somewhat hard to reconcile with the decision actually reached. A more easily reconciled decision, in the pharmaceutical field, in which such principles were applied, was T-7/86 *Xanthines/DRACO*.[7] Claim 1 was for:

'(1)   A pharmaceutical preparation for use in the treatment of chronic obstructive airway disease or cardiac disease comprising as active ingredient an effective amount of a compound of the formula [3-propylxanthine] or a therapeutically acceptable salt thereof, in association with a pharmaceutically acceptable carrier.'

and claim 2 was in corresponding, first medical use, form: '(2) A compound of the formula [3-propylxanthine] or a therapeutically acceptable salt thereof, for use in the treatment of chronic obstructive airway disease or cardiac disease'.

The compound 3-propylxanthine had previously been specifically disclosed in a certain document (and therefore no simple product claim protection for it was available) but no pharmacological activity for it had been taught in this. Another document disclosed a variety of di-substituted xanthines in which the substituent radicals were chosen from two different lists (comprising at the 8-position H, and lower alkyl, and at the 3-position methyl, ethyl, propyl, butyl, and lower alkyl) and a physiological effect, albeit as diuretics. Thus, 3-propylxanthine was within its scope. The Technical Board of Appeal found, however, that there was no specific disclosure of each of the individual compounds which would result from the combination of all the possible variants, and that the document could therefore not be regarded as being detrimental to the novelty of the pharmaceutical use of 3-propylxanthine. From the point of view of inventive step 1,3-dimethylxanthine and its metabolite 3-methylxanthine were of known physiological activity which was similar, but inferior, to that which had been discovered for 3-propylxanthine. However, there was nothing in any of the prior art that would have allowed the inference to be drawn that choosing the 3-propyl substituted xanthine out of the great number of possible xanthine derivatives would provide a medicine which was superior to the 3-methyl substituted compound. This case concerned the selection of a single compound, but when selecting a group of compounds from a wider generic disclosure not only must the selection not be arbitrary but it must be justified by a hitherto unknown technical effect which is caused by those structural features which distinguish the claimed compounds from the numerous other compounds within the scope of the wider generic disclosure.[8]

1   The principle was first established in the English courts in *IG Farbenindustrie's Patents* [1930] 47 RPC 289 although this was in the context of obviousness. The high point in selection cases in the English Courts was *DuPont (Witsiepe's) Application* [1981] FSR 377; [1982] FSR 303 in which a claim 'to the use of glycol having four carbon atoms' was allowed, despite an earlier patent teaching the use in the same process of glycol having from one to ten carbon atoms, and which specifically disclosed the use of a four carbon glycol, although not as an example of the claimed invention itself. It is hard to explain this latter case, in which the disclosed compound would on current principles appear to lack novelty, by reference to such principles, but fortunately, as explained in *Dr Reddy's Laboratories v Eli Lilly* (see fn 2 below) it should no longer be necessary to attempt so to do.

2   *Dr Reddy's Laboratories v Eli Lilly* [2008] EWHC 2345 (Patents Court); [2009] EWCA 1362 (Court of Appeal).
3   An instructive example of how specific the disclosure in the prior art document must be to be novelty destroying is provided by optical isomers, as discussed below at para 7.17.
4   *EPO Guidelines for Substantive Examination*, November 2014, Part G – Chapter VII, para 12 – Annex paras 3.1–3.2.
5   T-0230/07 *Colloidal Binder/PAROC* (Technical Board of Appeal 3.3.05, 5 May 2007).
6   T-12/81 *Diastereoisomers/BAYER* [1982] OJ EPO 296.
7   T-7/86 *Xanthines/DRACO* [1988] OJ EPO 381.
8   T-939/92 *Triazoles/AGREVO* [1996] OJEPO 309.

Optical isomers

7.17   Most complex organic molecules are likely to contain in their structure at least one asymmetric carbon atom, a carbon atom which is joined to four different types of substituents. The presence in a molecule of such a 'chiral centre' results in the molecule being capable of existence in two different forms, each of which is a mirror image of each other. Such forms (the R form and the S form) are termed 'enantiomers'. An equal mixture of these forms (which is what most ordinary chemical processes produce) is termed a 'racemic' mixture. Separating them is termed 'resolving' them, and is not necessarily easy, at least on a commercial scale, and to high levels of purity, as they have virtually identical physical properties – for commercialization it will generally be necessary to devise a stereospecific synthesis that favours the production of one enantiomer over the other. A molecule containing more than one asymmetric carbon atom may exist in a variety of forms, and those that are not mirror images of each other (because not all the chiral centres are inverted) are called 'diastereoisomers'. Enantiomers and diastereoisomers are together referred to as 'optical isomers'. Many pharmaceuticals exhibit chirality, and it is an important issue for other biologically active molecules such as herbicides.

Biological processes generally involve only one enantiomer of a chiral molecule, and so often only one optical isomer has a therapeutic effect. Indeed, in some cases the optical isomers may have different physiological effects; one beneficial and one adverse. Despite the difficulties of synthesizing them, optical isomers, having effectively up to twice the activity of the racemic mixture but an equivalent impurity profile enable lower dosages of purer compounds to be administered, and in the case of some pharmaceuticals their use would prevent the harmful form of the compound being administered. This has been recognized in the case law, and the identities of the useful optical isomer have on occasion been held to constitute a selection even if only between two alternatives. Much of this case law relates, however, to products that were developed in the 1980s when, in response to regulatory pressures, the significance of optical activity was only just starting to be explored as part of the drug discovery process, and when there were no reliable physical means of separating enantiomers. Thus they reflect situations that would be much less likely to apply to products developed after that time frame or today.

The attitude of the EPO to inventions claiming optical isomers of known compounds is summarized in T-296/87 *Enantiomers/HOECHST*[1] in which a Technical Board of Appeal held, as to the novelty of optical isomers of certain known herbicides:

> 'Given the asymmetrical carbon atoms in the formula, the substances in question can indeed occur in many conceivable configurations (D- and L-enantiomers); that alone does not mean, however, that these configurations are disclosed in individualised form. The novelty of the D- and L- enantiomers is not therefore destroyed by the description of the racemates. The situation is different if the state of the art includes enantiomers – howsoever designated (D, d, L, l or + or –) which are specifically named and can be produced. The Board's present view accords with its established case law on the novelty of chemical substances whereby the only technical teachings which are prejudicial to novelty are those which disclose a substance as the inevitable result of a prescribed method or in specific, ie individualised, form (cf T 12/81, *Diastereoisomers*[2]; T 181/82, *Spiro Compounds*[3]; T 7/86 *Xanthines*.'[4]

The Board went on to explain that it was irrelevant for the purposes of novelty that the optical isomers claimed already existed, in unseparated form, in the racemate, and that there were well-known techniques that often succeeded for separating such enantiomers by reacting them with other optically active compounds to obtain diastereoisomers that having unlike the original enantiomers different physical properties could then be separated enabling the original enantiomers to be recovered in an isolated (resolved) form.

However, inventive step is a different issue, and in T-296/87 *Enantiomers/HOECHST* the Board found claims to optical isomers obvious where the racemates already formed part of the state of the art:

> 'Long before the contested patents priority date, it was generally known to specialists that, in physiologically active substances (eg herbicides, fungicides, insecticides and growth regulators, but also in pharmaceuticals and foodstuffs) with an asymmetrical carbon atom enabling them to occur in the form of a racemate or one or two enantiomers, one of the latter frequently has a quantitatively greater effect than the other or than the racemate. If – as here – the aim is therefore to develop agents with increased physiological activity from a physiologically active racemate the obvious first step – before any thought is given say to synthesising structurally modified products – is to produce the two enantiomers in isolation and test whether one or the other is more active than the racemate. Such tests are routine. Under established Board case law, an enhanced effect cannot be adduced as evidence of inventive step if it emerges from obvious tests.'

However, the Board did not shut the door on inventive step in relation to known optically active molecules as they went on to give possible examples of situations where there might be invention:

'Thus the outcome might well differ with compounds having more than one asymmetrical carbon atom, the number of possible isomers multiplying exponentially. Moreover if the basic racemate were indeed known but not in line with the general technical trend, the proposal that enantiomers be produced by splitting the racemate could be inventive. Other cases are also conceivable in which a different result would be achieved – eg the isolation of active enantiomers, or ones with a qualitatively different activity, from essentially inactive racemates or ones acting differently.'

One early pharmaceutical case where a substantial body of evidence directed to the unexpected nature of the advantage obtained by resolution (exceptional oral absorption characteristics for a semi-synthetic penicillin) succeeded in overcoming an obviousness objection was *Beecham Group's (Amoxycillin) Application.*[5] Claims to 'pharmaceutical compositions adapted for oral administration to human beings', containing a particular stereoisomer were secured. However, here the selection was not just between two stereoisomers but was also between three geometrical isomers, making a total class of six.

Alternatively, in some cases it may, as at the relevant date, have been very hard to separate (resolve) the enantiomers. Thus, in *Generics v Lundbeck*[6] the patentees had made numerous attempts that failed to separate the enantiomers, and they only succeeded in preparing isolated enantiomers not by resolving the racemate, but by resolving an intermediate, which synthetic route to the enantiomer was found to be inventive.

1 T-296/87 *Enantiomers/HOECHST* OJ EPO 1990 at p. 195, followed in *Generics (UK) Ltd v H Lundbeck A/S* (see fn 6 below).
2 T-12/81 *Diastereoisomers* OJ EPO 1982 at p. 296.
3 T-181/82 *Spiro Compounds* OJ EPO 1984 at p. 401.
4 T-7/86 *Xanthines* OJ EPO 1988 at p. 381.
5 *Beecham Group's (Amoxycillin) Application* [1980] RPC 261.
6 *Generics (UK) Ltd v H Lundbeck A/S* [2007] EWHC 1040 (Patents Court) [2008] EWCA 311 (Court of Appeal); [2009] UKHL 12 (House of Lords). The Court of Appeal and House of Lords upheld the validity of all claims, reversing the decision at first instance that found the claims to such process valid but had found product claims to the active enantiomer not to be, because although they were not obvious in that they could not be made without the exercise of invention, they were insufficient as the patentees had only provided one way of achieving an obviously desirable goal, and so should not be permitted to monopolize every other way of doing so. For another case in which claims to an enantiomer of a known compound were not held to be obvious, essentially because the evidence showed that with an antibiotic such as this there would not have been thought to be any especial benefit in proceeding with it, see *Generics (UK) Ltd v Daiichi* [2009] EWCA Civ 646 (Court of Appeal). A more recent case in which claims to an enantiomer of a known compound were found to be obvious was *Generics (UK) Ltd v Novartis AG* [2011] EWHC 2403 (Patents Court) [2012] EWCA Civ 1623 (Court of Appeal).

Metabolites

7.18 Active metabolites of known pharmaceuticals are potentially patentable by those who are the first to identify such metabolite and its utility. The metabolite may itself be commercialized but attempts have also been made to use patents to such metabolites against generic market entrants on the expiry of the patent to the precursor pharmaceutical as in *Merrell Dow v Norton*.[1] Here, one claim of the patent was to a pharmaceutical that was later discovered to be the active metabolite of terfenadine, and was responsible for the physiological effect of terfenadine as an antihistamine. On expiry of the patent to terfenadine, the defendants were sued for contributory infringement of the patent to the metabolite by supplying the precursor drug terfenadine, knowing that it would convert in the body into the patented metabolite. The defendants conceded infringement but argued that the terfenadine patent, and clinical trials of terfenadine in humans, had destroyed the novelty of the metabolite patent.

The Patents Court, though accepting that no one knew of the existence of the metabolite before the priority date of the metabolite patent, and that the terfenadine patent was silent as to the metabolism of terfenadine, went on to observe that this did not prevent the metabolite forming part of the 'state of the art', being 'matter which has been made available to the public by written or oral description by use or in any other way' as this was: 'the result of clear and unmistakable directions which enable the public to produce the claimed product. The fact that the public does not know how the process works or what is the product produced is irrelevant.'

On appeal the Court of Appeal upheld this decision, as did the House of Lords on a further appeal. All held that the terfenadine patent, but not the clinical trials of terfenadine, deprived the metabolite patent of novelty, although only as to the metabolite as produced in the body. The House of Lords sought to distinguish between the two situations by saying that: 'It is therefore part of the state of the art if the information which has been disclosed enables the public to know the product under a description sufficient to work the invention'. Despite this, it is hard to understand how there can be such a difference between being told to do something (as in the terfenadine patent) and actually doing something (administering terfenadine) a point which was later addressed in *Chiron v Evans Medical*:[2]

> 'Lord Hoffmann went on to point out that where the invention is a new product, in most cases knowledge of the product's chemical composition will be necessary to enable the public to work the invention. But that is not always so ... It is not necessary to describe the product or process in the same terms as used in the subsequent patent. Indeed it is not even necessary for the reader to realise that the process was being used or product was being made. This is

because whether or not the prior art enables the reader to work the claimed invention: "is an objective fact independent of what he knows or thinks about what he is doing".

...

But is this understanding of the law of anticipation affected by what was said in *Merrell Dow* about prior use? It will be remembered that terfenadine had been ingested by a number of patients who did not know that they were as a consequence producing the metabolites.

This was held not to invalidate the second patent ... the prior use relied solely on the fact that the pills of terfenadine, which did not in themselves contain the metabolite, were ingested. In no real sense were the persons carrying out the alleged prior use, ie the patients, in possession of any information which would allow them to make the metabolite ... not only were the users, the patients, ignorant of the creation of the metabolite but the case was not put forward on the basis that they had been told to take the pills for the antihistamine effect.'

Accordingly, the 'not an invalidating prior use' aspect of the *Merrell Dow* judgment is narrow. Perhaps, the House of Lords would not have been driven into such a corner had not the defendants conceded infringement, which was not the case in corresponding cases in Germany and the USA.[3] In both cases, the defendants succeeded on non-infringement arguments, and validity was not in issue. In the UK, the metabolite patent was subsequently amended to disclaim the metabolite when formed by the metabolism of terfenadine in the body.

1   *Merrell Dow v Norton* [1994] RPC 1; [1995] RPC 253 (Court of Appeal); [1996] RPC 76 (House of Lords).
2   *Chiron v Evans Medical* [1997] FSR 268.
3   *Terfenadin* [1998] FSR 145 and *Marion Merrell Dow v Baker Norton Pharmaceuticals* [1998] FSR 158.

Sufficiency – enablement and plausibility

7.19   Issues of sufficiency under EPC, Article 83 are more commonly encountered in the context of pharmaceuticals and biotechnology than in most other technical areas, although those specific to the latter, are discussed in **Chapter 8** at paras 8.14–8.15. The issue of reach through claims has been discussed above at para 7.13, and that of appropriate claim scope, a particular issue for pharmaceutical and agrochemical patents, is discussed separately below at para 7.20 as it can often overlap with EPC, Article 56 as to inventive step, and Article 84 as to support. There are, however, two specific aspects of insufficiency that are often encountered in isolation with pharmaceutical and agrochemical patents – those of enablement and plausibility.

As to enablement the House of Lords held in *Asahi*[1] (a biotechnology case, although the principle applies equally to pharmaceuticals) that for a prior disclosure of a chemical compound to form part of the state of the art such disclosure must be enabling. The case concerned two conflicting applications for a certain physiologically active polypeptide, effective as a Human Tumour Necrosis Factor. For the purpose of the decision it was assumed that the application with an earlier priority date than the *Asahi* one, and which accordingly conflicted with it, claimed the relevant substance but did not provide, until the subsequent convention filing of the other application (after the *Asahi* priority date) a method of synthesizing it. It was also assumed that it would not have been self-evident to the 'skilled man' from the formula of the polypeptide how the substance could be produced, and that to practice the invention he would need also to be provided with such a method. The earlier filed application was held not be effective to deprive the *Asahi* one of novelty. Assistance was derived from some EPO Technical Board of Appeal decisions[2] as well as the *EPO Guidelines for Examination*[3] that state:

'4 ... it should be noted that a chemical compound, the name or formula of which was mentioned in a prior-art document, is not considered as known, unless the information in the document, together, where appropriate, with knowledge generally available on the relevant date of the document, enables it to be prepared and separated or, for instance in the case of a product of nature, only to be separated.'

The question of whether or not a defect in the description, or an omission from the description, renders such description non-enabling, and thus a priority document containing it an ineffective reference for that purpose or a resulting patent possibly invalid on the ground of insufficiency depends on whether the skilled man could rectify matters from the 'common general knowledge'. Thus in T-171/84 *Redox Catalysts/AIR PRODUCTS*[4] it was stated that 'an error in the description ... is immaterial to the sufficiency of the disclosure if the skilled person would ... rectify it using its common general knowledge'.

The requirement for plausibility relates to the potential therapeutic utility of a claimed product, and is an issue that has been encountered in particular with second medical use claims as to which it was stated in T-609/02 *AP-1 complex/SALK INSTITUTE*:[5]

'9) ... under Article 83 EPC, unless this is already known to the skilled person at the priority date, the application must disclose the suitability of the product to be manufactured for the claimed therapeutic application. It is a well-known fact that proving the suitability of a given compound as an active ingredient in a pharmaceutical composition might require years and very high developmental costs which will only be borne by the industry if it has some form of protective rights. Nonetheless, variously formulated claims to pharmaceutical products have been granted under the EPC, all through the years. The patent system takes account of the intrinsic difficulties for a compound to be officially certified as a drug by not requiring an absolute proof that the compound is approved as a drug before it may be claimed as such. The boards of appeal have accepted that for a sufficient disclosure of a therapeutic application, it is not always necessary that results of applying the claimed composition in clinical trials, or at least to animals are reported. Yet, this does not mean that a simple verbal statement in a patent specification that compound X may be used to treat disease Y is enough to ensure sufficiency of disclosure in relation to a claim to a pharmaceutical. It is required that the patent provides some information in the form of, for example, experimental tests, to the avail that the claimed compound has a direct effect on a metabolic mechanism specifically involved in the disease, this mechanism being either known from the prior art or demonstrated in the patent per se. Showing a pharmaceutical effect in vitro may be sufficient if for the skilled person this observed effect directly and unambiguously reflects such a therapeutic application (T 241/95, OJ EPO 2001, 103, point 4.1.2 of the reasons, see also T 158/96 of 28 October 1998, point 3.5.2 of the reasons) or, as decision T 158/96 also put it, if there is a "clear and accepted established relationship" between the shown physiological activities and the disease (loc. cit.). Once this evidence is available from the patent application, then post-published (so-called) expert evidence (if any) may be taken into account, but only to back-up the findings in the patent application in relation to the use of the ingredient as a pharmaceutical, and not to establish sufficiency of disclosure on their own'

The rejected claim was in effect a type of 'reach through' claim as discussed above at para 7.13:

'6   The use of a steroid hormone or steroid hormone analogue as identified by the method of claims 1 to 5, which fails to promote transcriptional activation of glucocorticoid receptor or retinoic acid receptor genes, for the preparation of a pharmaceutical for the treatment of AP-1 stimulated tumour formation, arthritis, asthma, allergies and rashes.'

The patent did not exemplify any such steroid hormone, but the applicants later presented evidence that some years after the filing date of the patent, some steroid hormone analogues were indeed shown to interfere with AP-1 stimulated transcription as required by this claim. However, the Technical Board of Appeal observed:

'13   In summary, sufficiency of description must, in principle, be shown to exist at the effective date of a patent. If the description of the patent specification, like in the present case, provides no more than a vague indication of a possible medical use for a chemical compound yet to be identified, later more detailed evidence cannot be used to remedy the fundamental insufficiency of disclosure of such subject matter.'

Thus sufficiency of disclosure must be satisfied at the effective date of the patent, on the basis of the information in the patent application together with the common general knowledge available to the skilled person.

1   *Re Asahi Kasei Kogyo Kabushiki Kaisha* [1991] RPC 485 (House of Lords).
2   T-206/83 *Pyridine Herbicides/ICI* OJ EPO 1987 at 5; and T-81/87 *Preprorennin/ COLLABORATIVE* [1990] EPOR 361. In T-206/83 *Pyridine Herbicides/ICI* it was

held that in the chemical field a synthesis set out in a patent example that could only be located by reference to 'Chemical Abstracts' did not provide an enabling disclosure of the product of that synthesis as 'Chemical Abstracts' was not part of the common general knowledge as evidenced by basic handbooks and textbooks.

3   *EPO Guidelines for Examination*, November 2014 Part G – Chapter VI, para 4.
4   T-171/84 *Redox Catalysts/AIR PRODUCTS* [1986] OJ EPO 95.
5   T-609/02 *AP-1 complex/SALK INSTITUTE* (TBA 3.3.8, 27 October 2004) quoted in *Regeneron Pharmaceuticals Inc v Bayer Pharma AG* [2013] EWCA Civ 93 (Court of Appeal) at [103] which summarized this as:
> 'the Boards of Appeal of the EPO have recognised that in the case of a claim to the use of a product to make a medicine for a particular therapeutic purpose it would impose too great a burden on the patentee to require him to provide absolute proof that the compound has approval as a medicine. Further, it is not always necessary to report the results of clinical trials or even animal testing. Nevertheless, he must show, for example by appropriate experiments, that the product has an effect on a disease process so as to make the claimed therapeutic effect plausible'.

Sufficiency and claim scope

7.20   Enablement and plausibility (as discussed above) are not the only aspects of the sufficiency requirements of EPC, Article 83. Pharmaceutical and biotechnology patents frequently run into issues of claim scope that as explained in **Chapter 5** at para 5.20, if not addressed in the course of prosecution under EPC, Article 84 as an issue of support can also post-grant provide the basis for challenge under EPC, Article 83. The approach adopted by the EPO in prosecution is set out in the *EPO Guidelines for Examination* that in commenting on EPC, Article 84 state:[1]

> '6.2   Most claims are generalisations from one or more particular examples. The extent of generalization permissible is a matter which the examiner must judge in each particular case in the light of the relevant prior art. Thus an invention which opens up a whole new field is entitled to more generality in the claims than one which is concerned with advances in a known technology. A fair statement of claims is one which is not so broad as it goes beyond the invention nor yet so narrow as to deprive the applicant of a just reward for the disclosure of his invention. The applicant should be allowed to cover all obvious modifications of, equivalents to and uses of that which he has described. In particular, if it is reasonable to predict that all the variants covered by the claims have the properties or uses the applicant ascribes to them in the description, he should be allowed to draw his claim accordingly. After the date of filing, however, he should be allowed to do so only if this does not contravene Art. 123(2).'

The last sentence is a reminder that after the application has been filed the invention cannot be redefined in such a way as to add matter, as discussed in **Chapter 5** at para 5.23.

Issues of claim scope are common in chemical patents because most patents protecting NCEs (unless to enantiomers of known compounds) are rarely expressed only to protect the one compound. Instead their claims usually extend to a wide range of similar compounds that can be expected to have similar activity. Thus, it is common in pharmaceutical patenting for claims to cover millions of compounds but be based on exemplification and testing of only a few of these. But some element of prediction is an essential part of drafting a patent specification, especially in these sectors. Otherwise competitors could reap the benefits of another's invention by a minor modification, for example, in the case of NCEs replacing a methyl group by a propyl group, just because the patentee had not got round to synthesizing all the homologues of a new compound before it filed its patent application. Such predictive claiming is facilitated by the clear, and precise terminology which chemistry employs to characterize structures. Even so, 'generic' claims of broad scope drawn by the techniques of chemical nomenclature have still left scope for new, previously unclaimed compounds of similar efficacy, and similar structure to those that have already been patented to be developed.

Assuming that a claim does not cover what is old, or specific compounds that are not themselves obvious, to what extent can it validly cover a whole range of compounds predicted on the basis of a single isolated discovery, especially when there may well be (unless the claims contain some functional limitation) materials within the scope of a claim that do not work, or cannot be made, without the exercise of further invention?[2] After grant, when EPC, Article 84 has no application, EPC, Article 56 (inventive step) and EPC, Article 83 (sufficiency) may both have application, although the English courts have tended to favour the latter approach, taking the view that the breadth of claim must be commensurate with the inventive contribution. This is not a new problem, and was for example, addressed nearly 50 years ago, under the pre-PA 1977 law, in *Olin Mathieson v Biorex*[3] which introduced the principle of 'sound prediction':

> 'If it is possible for the patentee to make a sound prediction and to frame a claim which does not go beyond the limits within which the prediction remains sound, then he is entitled to do so. Of course, in so doing he takes the risk that a defendant may be able to show that his prediction is unsound or that some bodies falling within the words he has used have no utility or that all are obvious or that some promise that he has made in his specification is false in a material respect; but if, when attacked, he survives this risk successfully, then his claim does not go beyond the consideration given by his disclosure, his claim is fairly based on such disclosures in these respects, and is valid.'

This was a UK case decided under the pre-PA 1977 law, and under which claims had to be 'fairly based' on the disclosure of the patent, and when 'inutility' also constituted a separate ground of invalidity. Neither of these applies to patents granted under PA 1977, implementing the EPC but the principle of 'sound prediction' remains, even though in *Pharmacia v Merck*[4] the English Court of Appeal observed that it was not helpful to assume that the test of sufficiency under PA 1977 was that applied in *Olin Mathieson*. However, it then observed:

> '56   Where the claimed invention is to a class of compounds, the same principle applies and, as was made clear by the House of Lords in *Biogen,* is that the disclosure in the specification must enable the invention to be performed to the full extent of the monopoly claimed. Thus if the invention is a selection of certain compounds, in order to secure an advantage or avoid some disadvantage, not only must the specification contain sufficient information on how to make the compounds, it must also describe the advantage or how to avoid the disadvantage. Further the compounds monopolised by the claim must all have that advantage or avoid the disadvantage. The same principle applies where the claim is to a class of compounds. To be sufficient, the specification must identify the characteristics of the class and a method of manufacture. Further all the claimed compounds must in substance have the characteristics of the class.'

Having quoted from *Biogen v Medeva*[5] and T-939/92 *Triazoles/ AGREVO*[6] the Court then went on to consider the present case that concerned claims to a class of compounds that were alleged to be selective Cox II inhibitors:

> '61.   The patent in this case claims a class of compounds. There is no technical contribution in a list of compounds which a skilled person would know how to make at the priority date. The 20 year monopoly was granted because of the disclosure in the specification that the class of compounds claimed had the quality disclosed in the specification. The invention or technical contribution justifying the monopoly claimed can only be that quality. I have already decided that the judge was right when he held that the specification would be read by the skilled person as disclosing that the claimed class of compounds had anti-inflammatory and/or analgesic effect with fewer and less drastic side-effects, the reduction in side-effects being due to Cox II selectivity. It is that disclosure which is the technical contribution and invention.
>
> ...
>
> 71.   The task of this Court is to ascertain whether the technical contribution in the specification applies to the class of compounds claimed. It was Merck's case that certain subclasses of the claimed class did not have the attributes asserted for the claimed class. That being so, the extent of the monopoly claimed exceeded the technical contribution. Thus the Court had to consider the subclasses relied on by Merck and to decide whether, on the balance of probabilities, they met the technical contribution. I do not accept that it necessarily follows from the evidence that if one compound in a subclass showed some activity, the conclusion sought to be drawn by Merck should be rejected. The evidence must be considered as a whole. Any evidence of activity must be weighed against the rest of the evidence.'

As it had been found that it had been shown that a substantial number of compounds falling within claim 1 were inactive as anti-inflammatory compounds, and were not selective Cox II inhibitors, the Court of Appeal held that claim 1, as well as the other claims for which independent validity had been asserted, were insufficient both as granted, and as proposed to be amended, and thus the patent as a whole was invalid. The legal basis may be different, but the effect would seem much the same as in *Olin Mathieson.*

One cannot avoid the need for 'sound prediction' by including a functional limitation to, in effect, those compounds which 'work' without providing some means of predicting this or by simply claiming 'derivatives' of a compound known to have useful activity rather than predicting (potentially unsoundly) such compounds. In *American Home Products v Novartis*[7] the patentees argued that, by virtue of certain wording in the specification, on a purposive construction 'derivatives' of the compound identified in a second use claim (rapamycin) would infringe such claim. As noted in **Chapter 6** at para 6.07, the English Court of Appeal held there to be no infringement on a purposive basis, but went further to say that had there been infringement on such basis the claims in issue would have been insufficient as there was no disclosure in the specification of how to make or select suitable such derivatives.

The Court of Appeal in *Pharmacia v Merck* took care to explain how its views were consistent with those of the EPO Technical Boards of Appeal. Thus it referred to T-939/92 *Triazoles/AGREVO* in which claims were held to lack inventive step as, given their breadth and such evidence as was before it, a Technical Board of Appeal was not satisfied that substantially all the compounds claimed were likely to be herbicidally active, and thus the technical problem of providing such compounds could not be said to be solved across the full breadth of the claims. The Technical Board of Appeal had also explained that the principle that the extent of the patent monopoly should correspond to, and be justified by the technical contribution applied no less to the issue of inventive step under EPC, Article 56 than it did to support, and sufficiency under EPC, Articles 83–84 an issue which was further explored by a Technical Board of Appeal in T-694/92 *Modifying Plant Cells/MYCOGEN.*[8]

The issue of what has come to be known as "claim breadth insufficiency" has featured in much recent   pharmaceuticals and biotechnology litigation, and the law as to this has most recently summarized in *Idenix Pharmaceuticals v Gilead Sciences*, and which explains how the issue of plausibility, discussed above, also factors into such assessment:[9]

'466. *Excessive claim breadth.* I reviewed the law with regard to excessive claim breadth at some length in *MedImmune Ltd v Novartis Pharmaceuticals UK Ltd* [2011] EWHC 1699 (Pat) at [458]–[484] and summarised that analysis in *Sandvik v Kennametal* at [121]–[124]. As Kitchin LJ stated in *Regeneron v Genentech*:

"100.   It must therefore be possible to make a reasonable prediction the invention will work with substantially everything falling within the scope of the claim or, put another way, the assertion that the invention will work across the scope of the claim must be plausible or credible. The products and methods within the claim are then tied together by a unifying characteristic or a common principle. If it is possible to make such a prediction then it cannot be said the claim is insufficient simply because the patentee has not demonstrated the invention works in every case.

101.   On the other hand, if it is not possible to make such a prediction or if it is shown the prediction is wrong and the invention does not work with substantially all the products or methods falling within the scope of the claim then the scope of the monopoly will exceed the technical contribution the patentee has made to the art and the claim will be insufficient. It may also be invalid for obviousness, there being no invention in simply providing a class of products or methods which have no technically useful properties or purpose."

467.   For the reasons set out above, the court must undertake a two-stage enquiry. The first stage is to determine whether the disclosure of the Patent, read in the light of the common general knowledge of the skilled team, makes it plausible that the invention will work across the scope of the claim. If the disclosure does make it plausible, the second stage is to consider whether the later evidence establishes that in fact the invention cannot be performed across the scope of the claim without undue burden. In some cases, it is convenient to divide the second stage into two, first considering whether the invention can be performed without undue burden at all and then whether the claim is of excessive breadth.

468.   It has been held in a number of cases that a patent will be insufficient if the specification requires the skilled person to undertake a substantial research project in order to perform the invention (either at all or across the breadth of the claim) and claims the results: see e.g. *Halliburton Energy Services Inc v Smith International (North Sea) Ltd* [2006] EWCA Civ 1715 at [18] (Jacob LJ), *American Home Products Corp v Novartis Pharmaceuticals UK Ltd* [2001] RPC 8 at [41]–[47] (Aldous LJ) and *Novartis AG v Johnson & Johnson Medical Ltd* [2010] EWCA Civ 1039, [2011] ECC 10 at [50]–[92] (Jacob LJ).'

As made clear in this final passage, the test is really no different whether the question is one as to whether the invention could be performed at all on the basis of the teaching in the patent (in the light of the common general knowledge), ie the more conventional type of insufficiency question, or across the breadth of the claims, the question which encountered more commonly in the context of pharmaceuticals and biotechnology patents.

1   *EPO Guidelines for Examination*, November 2014, Part F – Chapter IV, para 6.2.
2   For example, *May & Baker v Boots* [1950] 67 RPC 23.
3   *Olin Mathieson v Biorex* [1970] RPC 157 at p. 193.

4   *Pharmacia v Merck* [2000] RPC 709 (Patents Court); [2001] EWCA Civ 1610; [2002] RPC 775; [2002] IP&T 328 (Court of Appeal).

5   *Biogen v Medeva* [1997] RPC 1 (House of Lords) – see **Chapter 5** in connection with priority at para 5.05 and insufficiency and claim scope at para 5.20 and **Chapter 8** at para 8.15 for a discussion of, and passages from, the judgment in this case.

6   T-939/92 *Triazoles/AGREVO* [1996] OJ EPO 309.

7   *American Home Products v Novartis* [2000] RPC 547 (Patents Court); [2001] RPC 159 (Court of Appeal).

8   T-694/92 *Modifying Plant Cells/MYCOGEN* [1998] EPOR 114; [1997] OJ EPO 408 – see **Chapter 8** at para 8.14 for some passages from the decision in this case.

9   *Idenix Pharmaceuticals Inc, v Gilead Sciences, Inc.* [2014] EWHC 3916 (Patents Court) at [466]–[468] repeating the observations made in *Eli Lilly and Company v Janssen Alzheimer Immunotherapy* [2013] EWHC 1737 (Patents Court) at [251]–[258] and which had held that plausibility could be challenged by post-dated evidence at paragraphs [252]–[257]. In both cases the patent was found to be insufficient, in *Eli Lilly* because: 'the patent does no more than invite the skilled person to perform ... a very significant research project with a high prospect of failure and if they succeed, claim the fruits of their research', and in *Idenix* not only because it did not enable the skilled team to perform the invention across the breadth of the claim without undue burden: 'because it sets the skilled team a research project and claims the results', but also on the basis of the more traditional type of insufficiency in that the patent did not enable the skilled person to make the claimed compounds without undue burden.

Infringement issues

Introduction

7.21   Claims to chemical processes present the same problems of construction and scope for the application of 'purposive construction', as outlined in **Chapter 6**; if the process claims specify a temperature range of 180–200°C for the reaction, does the otherwise identical reaction running at 205°C infringe? Claims to chemical processes raise a further infringement issue. It is normally best to try to enforce a process patent in the country where the allegedly infringing process is being carried out, to stop this at source. However, where manufacture takes place in a country with a weak patent or court system, or in which no application for such process patent was ever filed, one is either reluctant, or without a local patent unable, to embark on such litigation. However, TRIPS mandates national patent laws to permit patent infringement actions to be brought on a process patent in a country other than that in which the process is conducted, in respect of the import into a country where there is such process patent of 'the directly infringing product of a patented process'. It would seem to have been accepted that a formulated pharmaceutical is the 'direct' product of the process for the manufacture of the active for that pharmaceutical, notwithstanding that the active must be formulated to produce the final pharmaceutical product, an approach that is consistent with the 'loss of identity' test adopted by the English courts.[1]

It will sometimes be the case that only a trace of the infringing chemical is found in the material in issue, as an impurity, but in general this does not affect the issue of whether the material infringes a claim to such product, unless this is qualified in some way, as observed in *Monsanto v Cargill*:[2]

'[89]   I should also deal with a *de minimis* point. The DNA present in the meal, such as it is, is entirely irrelevant to the meal as an animal feedstuff, is present in small, variable, quantities and may not be present at all if processing conditions are changed. It is not in any serious sense genetic material. It is just the remains of the material which was in the soybeans from which the meal was extracted. This, it seems to me, is irrelevant. It may raise a question on damages, that there is no causative relationship between acts of infringement, as opposed to acts which are not infringing by English law, and the loss suffered by Monsanto, but this was not argued. There is, generally, no authority in favour of trace quantities of infringing material being held not to infringe, and some authority against it....'

It might be thought by way of contrast with chemical processes that the precision of chemical nomenclature claims to NCEs should present few difficulties of construction, and thus of determining whether or not a claim is infringed. One early instance of such an approach in relation to chemical patent is provided by *Beecham Group v Bristol Laboratories*[3] (the *Hetacillin* case) (under pre-PA 1977 law) concerning a pharmaceutical which metabolized in the body into a patented pharmaceutical. The patent related to a class of semisynthetic penicillins, one of which was ampicillin. The defendants imported hetacillin (an acetone derivative of ampicillin) into the UK. This hydrolysed in the body to ampicillin, and as a result the defendants were held to have infringed the patents under the prevailing infringement theory at the time, and called the doctrine of 'pith and marrow'. Under the law as it now stands under the PA 1977 it would be easier for a patentee in such a situation to assert contributory, or indirect infringement under PA 1977 s 60(2) as was done in the metabolite case *Merrell Dow v Norton*.[4]

Decisions in *American Home Products v Novartis*[5] and the genetic engineering case of *Kirin Amgen v Transkaryotic Therapies*[6] have addressed the application of EPC, Article 69, and the Protocol to this[7], and *Pharmacia v Merck*[8] addressed the issue of keto-enol tautomerism where the claim was to one tautomer but the product in issue was largely in the form of the other tautomer. More recently, in *Actavis UK Limited and ors v Eli Lilly & Company*[9] the Court at first instance, in the context of an application for a declaration of non-infringement, held that certain salts of pharmaceutical, which it was accepted were not within the scope of the claims on a literal interpretation, as the claims identified a different (sodium) salt, did not infringe under EPC, Article 69, and the Protocol to this, either under UK or under French, Italian or Spanish law (having heard expert evidence as to such other laws). However, the

Court of Appeal, whilst accepting that such salts did not directly infringe such claims (in any such country) disagreed with the contributory infringement analysis at first instance, that had rejected the argument that the claimed invention would be put into effect when the non-sodium salt product was reconstituted in saline (ie sodium containing) solution, as a result of which sodium ions would be present.

As discussed above at para 7.11 a current subject of controversy is the degree to which second medical use claims, especially those in the Swiss form, can be asserted against the supply of a medicinal product in situations in which there are also other authorized medical uses for such medicinal product, and the medicinal product in issue is not authorized, nor ostensibly supplied, for the infringing use but it is inevitable that some such infringing use, its degree depending on the nature of the market, will take place.

As discussed below, much litigation in the pharmaceutical and agrochemical sectors concerns those activities, short of actual sale, which generic companies seek to undertake shortly before expiry of a patent, so as to position themselves to secure a marketing authorization, and enter the market immediately on such patent expiry – for example, by undertaking trials or submitting samples to regulatory authorities. By such activities, shortly prior to patent expiry a generic applicant obtains the benefit of a 'springboard', and how, if such activities infringe, should that benefit be penalized, or the damage to the patentee compensated, and if it should be, how does one go about doing so? One approach which has developed in Europe is that of the 'post-patent expiry' injunction, discussed in **Chapter 6** at para 6.20.

1   See **Chapter 6** at para 6.02. The only pharmaceuticals case before the English courts in which the issue of what constitutes the direct product of a patented process has been addressed is *Medimmune Limited v Novartis Pharmaceuticals UK Ltd* [2012] EWHC 181 (Patents Court) in a challenge to the validity of a Supplementary Protection Certificate for which the patent in issue had been nominated as the 'basic patent'. In this, the issue was specific to the claim structure of the patent in suit, and also to an argument specific to the Biotechnology Directive, discussed in **Chapter 8** at para 8.18.

2   *Monsanto Technology LLC v Cargill International SA* [2007] EWHC 2257(Patents Court).

3   *Beecham Group v Bristol Laboratories* [1978] RPC 153; [1977] FSR 215.

4   *Merrell Dow v Norton* [1994] RPC 1; [1995] RPC 253 (Court of Appeal); [1996] RPC 76 (House of Lords) – discussed above at para 7.18. In *Idenix Pharmaceuticals Inc, v Gilead Sciences, Inc.* [2014] EWHC 3916 (Patents Court) the Court at [615]–[617] found the supply of a compound indirectly to infringe on this basis because it would metabolize to a compound within the scope of the claim.

5   *American Home Products v Novartis* [2000] RPC 547; [2001] RPC 159 (Court of Appeal).

6   *Kirin Amgen v Transkaryotic Therapies* [2001] IP&T 882; [2002] RPC 1; [2002] RPC 2 (Patents Court); [2003] RPC 3 (Court of Appeal); [2004] UKHL 46; [2005] 1 All ER 667; [2005] RPC 9 (House of Lords).

7   See **Chapter 6** at para 6.05ff.

8   *Pharmacia v Merck* [2000] RPC 709 (Patents Court); [2001] EWCA Civ 1610; [2002] RPC 775; [2002] IP&T 828 (Court of Appeal).
9   *Actavis UK Limited and ors v Eli Lilly & Company* [2014] EWHC 1511(Patents Court); [2015] EWCA Civ 555 (Court of Appeal). The Court of Appeal also criticized the reasoning of the Court at first instance insofar as it had relied in construing the claims on the prosecution history of the patent.

Clinical trials and experimentation as an exception to patent infringement

7.22   The scope of the defence to infringement set out in PA 1977, s 60(5)(b) and reflecting that in the CPC (and thus also found in most other countries in Europe) for 'use for experimental purposes relating to the subject matter of the invention' has proved to be of considerable importance to those sectors; such as pharmaceuticals and agrochemicals where 'trials' must be undertaken to satisfy the requirements of regulatory authorities before a new pharmaceutical or plant protection product can be placed on the market.[1] However, the defence is of much more general application, although it is generally in the context of agrochemical and pharmaceutical patents that it arises.

It provides a defence for preliminary work, which may be commercial in nature, directed to issues such as whether one can actually perform the patented invention. A useful indication is provided by the English Court of Appeal in *Monsanto v Stauffer*[2] in which it was observed:

'The distinction between the wording of sub-head (a) and the wording of sub-head (b) in section 60(5) indicates that experimental purposes in sub-head (b) may yet have a commercial end in view.... I would regard the sort of experimental activity which was considered by the Supreme Court of Canada in *Microchemicals Ltd v Smith Kline and French* ..., viz, a limited experiment to establish whether the experimenter could manufacture a quality product commercially in accordance with the specification of a patent, as being covered by the words "for experimental purposes relating to the subject matter of the invention"'

To fall within the defence, the experimental use must relate to the 'subject matter of the invention', which distinguishes between work done on the invention, and work done using it. Thus, experimentation in relation to something else but using an established patented process (often referred to in biotechnology as use of a 'research tool') would be unlikely to fall within its scope, as such experimentation would not be 'in relation to the subject matter of the invention'. In contrast, the defence would be likely to apply to work undertaken on the patented process in an attempt to improve on it.

On the application of the defence to pre-clinical, and clinical trials in medicine, and field trials on agrochemicals, which must be undertaken to satisfy the requirements of regulatory authorities before a marketing authorization can be granted, *Monsanto v Stauffer,* concerning herbicides, remains the leading UK case, and in this it was held that:

'Trials carried out in order to discover something unknown or to test a hypothesis or even in order to find out whether something which is known to work in a specific conditions ... will work in different conditions can fairly ... be regarded as experiments. But trials carried out in order to demonstrate to a third party that a product works or, in order to amass information to satisfy a third party, whether a customer or a [regulatory] body ... that the product works as its maker claims are not ... to be regarded as acts done for experimental purposes.'

This judgment, as to the scope of the 'experimental purposes' limb of the defence, was subsequently reviewed by the German Federal Supreme Court in two cases concerning trials of therapeutic proteins produced by biotechnology. In *Clinical Trials I*[3] in 1995, concerning therapeutic applications of the protein gamma-interferon, the court found that certain clinical trials were covered by the defence. The court accepted, but was also able to distinguish, *Monsanto* as the English case had proceeded on the basis that the only purpose of the trials had been to generate data for the regulatory authority, whereas in the present case the trials had a dual purpose, of discovering if, and in what form the active was effective in treating certain previously unapproved indications, as well as submitting such data to the regulatory authorities. The court noted: 'it is therefore appropriate to exempt clinical tests and investigations with active substances on humans as experimental actions ... as long as these experiments are directly aimed at obtaining information', and also that: ' it is not contrary to the permissibility of clinical tests that the defendants are carrying out or supporting these with the further aim of licensing under the laws relating to pharmaceuticals.'

The expression 'further aim' in this second extract is important, as it emphasizes that a collateral non-experimental purpose does not prevent true experimentation from falling within the defence.

In 1997 in *Clinical Trials II*[4] the German Federal Supreme Court held that the defence applied also to clinical trials on another therapeutic protein, erythropoeitin, produced by a different expression system from that used to produce the patentee's version of erythropoeitin, notwithstanding that such trials concerned indications for which erythropoeitin was already authorized. The court held that the intention that is associated with an activity begun, and carried out for research purposes cannot render such activity infringing merely because the results of the research will not solely serve research purposes but above all will serve commercial purposes as well. It held that an activity is covered by the defence if it is: 'oriented towards clearing up insecurities with regards to the patented invention or bringing out new discoveries about said object, provided these activities ... relate to the object of the patented invention'.

In contrast, most who seek to introduce a generic small molecule pharmaceutical will be doing no more than undertaking limited bio-equivalence or stability testing. In such cases the alleged infringer can less easily be said to be investigating an unknown in the same way as in the *Clinical Trials* cases, which both concerned proteins, and where there can be small differences in amino acid sequences or glycosylation patterns between different commercial products, even though they may both well be dominated by the same patent, and so the results of the trials can truly be said to be unknown. However, in a series of judgments culminating in *Wellcome v Parexel*[5] French courts were prepared to treat clinical trials of a reformulated version of the antiviral aciclovir, where the reformulation and different dosing means would permit higher dosages to be administered, as experimental use that was covered by the defence.

Continuing uncertainty as to the degree to which the experimental use defence could be relied on by applicants for generic authorizations led to the introduction of new 'regulatory review' defences by Article 10(6) of the 'Community code relating to medicinal products for human use', and Article 13(6) of the 'Community code relating to veterinary medicinal products' as introduced by the Future Medicines Legislation 2004:[6]

'10(6) Conducting the necessary studies and trials with a view to the application of paragraphs 1, 2, 3 and 4 and the consequential practical requirements shall not be regarded as contrary to patent rights or to supplementary protection certificates for medicinal products.

...

13(6) Conducting the necessary studies, tests and trials with a view to the application of paragraphs 1 to 5 and the consequential practical requirements shall not be regarded as contrary to patent-related *[sic]* rights or to supplementary-protection certificates for medicinal products.'

These were introduced into UK law as a new subsection, PA 1977, s 60(5)(i) in the following terms, providing a defence to infringement for an otherwise infringing act where:

'(i)   it consists of –
...
    (i)   an act done in conducting a study, test or trial which is necessary for and is conducted with a view to the application of paragraphs 1 to 5 of article 13 of Directive 2001/82/EC or paragraphs 1 to 4 of article 10 of Directive 2001/83/EC, or (ii) any other act which is required for the purpose of the application of those paragraphs'

So implemented, closely following the Directive, the UK implementation of the regulatory review defence was, by virtue of the reference to certain specific paragraphs in these Directives, limited in application to trials done for the purpose of generic applications (as well as those as to biosimilars) and so did not cover clinical trials undertaken by innovators, who had to continue to rely on the experimental use defence despite its application to such activities in the UK never having been established in the caselaw.

However, a number of other European countries, including France and Germany, implemented the provision in rather broader terms, with the result that it did also cover such trials. As a result the UK law has now been further amended[7] by inserting subsections 6D–6G into PA 1977, s 60 to provide that such trials are deemed to be a type of experimental use relating to the subject matter of the invention:

'(6D) For the purposes of subsection (5)(b), anything done in or for the purposes of a medicinal product assessment which would otherwise constitute an infringement of a patent for an invention is to be regarded as done for experimental purposes relating to the subject matter of the invention.

(6E) In subsection (6D), "medicinal product assessment" means any testing, course of testing or other activity undertaken with a view to providing data for any of the following purposes—

(a) obtaining or varying an authorisation to sell or supply, or offer to sell or supply, a medicinal product (whether in the United Kingdom or elsewhere);

(b) complying with any regulatory requirement imposed (whether in the United Kingdom or elsewhere) in relation to such an authorisation;

(c) enabling a government or public authority (whether in the United Kingdom or elsewhere), or a person (whether in the United Kingdom or elsewhere) with functions of—

(i) providing health care on behalf of such a government or public authority, or

(ii) providing advice to, or on behalf of, such a government or public authority about the provision of health care,

to carry out an assessment of suitability of a medicinal product for human use for the purpose of determining whether to use it, or recommend its use, in the provision of health care.

(6F) In subsection (6E) and this subsection—
"medicinal product" means a medicinal product for human use or a veterinary medicinal product;
"medicinal product for human use" has the meaning given by article 1 of Directive 2001/83/EC;
"veterinary medicinal product" has the meaning given by article 1 of Directive 2001/82/EC(b).

(6G) Nothing in subsections (6D) to (6F) is to be read as affecting the application of subsection (5)(b) in relation to any act of a kind not falling within subsection (6D).'

What is notable about this new formulation of the regulatory review defence is its potential breadth given that the definition of "medicinal product assessment" provided by new Section 60(6E) is much wider than simply undertaking clinical trials in order to secure a marketing authorization for a new product.

The introduction of the regulatory review defence, even in its original form, has limited the extent to which future case law on the scope for the experimental use defence will be developed for pharmaceuticals. One area where such development has however taken place is that of medical devices, for which, in *Corevalve v Edwards*[8] the regulatory requirement of a 'CE' mark had already been secured. Although referring at paras [74]–[75] to the German *Clinical Trials I* case, which the Court observed did not address the issue that it had to consider, it failed to discuss the more relevant German *Clinical Trials II* case. The Court held (at para [77]) that the purposes of the trials which had been undertaken were threefold: '(1) to establish confidence in the product within the relevant market; (2) to generate immediate revenue of a substantial character; and (3) to gain information about clinical indications and, possibly, future modifications to be made to the physical structure of the device in the light of experience'. As purpose (3) was not found to be the preponderant purpose, it was held that the defence did not apply. The same result could, however, have been achieved by application of *Clinical Trials II* in which it was observed that the defence would not apply to experiments: (a) directed to clarification of commercial facts such as the needs of the market, acceptance of prices, and possibilities of distribution; (b) undertaken in such proportions as to no longer allow for justification on research ground; or (c) carried out with the purpose of hindering the inventor's product distribution.

1   For a more detailed discussion of this defence, directed in particular to its application to early stage research, and also that under PA 1977, s 60(5)(i) see Cook, Trevor, *A European Perspective as to the Extent to which Experimental Use, and Certain Other, Defences to Patent Infringement, Apply to Differing Types of Research* (Intellectual Property Institute, 2006).
2   *Monsanto v Stauffer* (Court of Appeal) [1985] RPC 515 at p. 542.
3   *Clinical Trials I* (German Federal Supreme Court) [1997] RPC 623.
4   *Clinical Trials II* (German Federal Supreme Court) [1998] RPC 423.
5   *Wellcome v Parexel* (High Court of Paris, 20 February 2001).
6   Namely Directive 2001/83 on the Community Code relating to medicinal products for human use, as amended by Directive 2004/27 of 31 March 2004, (OJ L 136, 34, 30 April 2004) and Directive 2001/82 on the Community Code relating to veterinary medicinal products, as amended by Directive 2004/28 of 31 March 2004, (OJ L 136, 58, 30 April 2004).
7   See the Legislative Reform (Patents) Order 2014 (SI 2014 No 1997).
8   *Corevalve v Edwards* [2009] EWHC 6 (Patents Court) – not in issue on appeal.

Applications for marketing authorizations

7.23   Although herbicides must in general be tested locally because of local climate and soil conditions, those seeking to introduce generic versions of pharmaceuticals in Europe were able, even before the introduction of defences specifically directed towards such trials, to apply for a marketing authorization before patent expiry, on the basis of test data generated in a non-patent jurisdiction. Typically, after the appropriate period of regulatory data exclusivity protection has expired,[1] they may seek a marketing authorization by means of a so-called 'generic' application relying on the originator's own approval, supported, for small molecule pharmaceuticals, by limited clinical trials to show bioequivalence with the originator's product. In England in *Upjohn v Kerfoot*[2] it was held that seeking a marketing authorization, where this involves neither any trial activity in the UK (the status of which at the time was uncertain), nor the submission of a sample (which is not in general needed by the regulatory authorities in the UK) was not of itself an infringing act. In contrast, in those cases elsewhere in Europe in which it has been held that the applicant for a marketing authorization, before patent expiry, infringed, these have been so decided on the basis that in applying for marketing authorization in some countries it used to be necessary to submit to the regulatory authorities, prior to such grant, a physical sample of the infringing material, this being regarded as a non-experimental and infringing use. This can be seen from the decision of the Dutch courts in *Wellcome v Centrafarm*[3] in which the application for a marketing authorization was filed before patent expiry, but the sample required by the regulatory authorities was submitted after. This was found not to infringe, a distinction being drawn between the timing of the two acts, despite the linkage between them.

It was thus the submission of the sample in those cases, which concerned applications for marketing authorization that was the critical factor in establishing infringement. This view was reinforced, when the legitimacy of this approach of the Dutch courts under the 'free movement of goods' provisions of European law was reviewed, and upheld by the Court of Justice, in Case C-316/95 *Generics v Smith Kline & French.*[4] However, and largely as a result of such litigation, the Dutch regulatory authorities changed their practice of requiring prior sample submission as a prerequisite for the grant of a marketing authorization, and few if any other such authorities now require this.

However, as it is possible in the UK to launch a medicinal product as soon as one has a marketing authorization, the grant of a generic marketing authorization has, in certain special circumstances, such as the past behaviour of such applicant, and absent suitable undertakings on the part of such applicant, been treated as a threat to infringe, providing a basis for seeking an interim injunction.[5] In certain other European jurisdictions, which require the price for the medicinal product to be negotiated with the local health service provider before launch the consequential listing of such price before actual launch may itself be regarded as an infringing act, as has advertising before patent expiry offering to launch on patent expiry.[6]

1   This is now throughout the EU, eight years after the first marketing authorization for the active moiety in the medicinal product in the EU, although the generic marketing authorization cannot take effect until ten (or in some cases eleven) years

after such first marketing authorization. See Articles 6 and 10 of Directive 2001/83 on the Community Code relating to medicinal products for human use, as amended by Directive 2004/27 of 31 March 2004, amending Directive 2001/83 on the Community Code relating to medicinal products for human use (OJ L 136, 34, 30 April 2004).

2   *Upjohn v Kerfoot* [1988] FSR 1 (Patents Court).

3   *Wellcome v Centrafarm* (Hague Court of Appeals, 1997).

4   Case C-316/95 *Generics v Smith Kline & French* [1997] RPC 801 (Court of Justice). See **Chapter 6** at para 6.20.

5   *Merck Sharp Dohme Corp & Anor v Teva Pharma BV & Anor* [2012] EWHC 627 (Patents Court).

6   *Simvastatin* (BGH XZR 76/05 of 5 December 2006, German Federal Supreme Court) GRUR 2007, p. 221 et seq. However, as to the UK, it would seem from *Gerber Garment Technology Inc v Lectra Sytems Ltd and anr* [1995] RPC 383 that such pre-expiry advertising may not infringe.

De facto extension of patent protection for pharmaceuticals and agrochemicals in the EU by the SPC Regulations

Background to the SPC Regulations

7.24   Since the 1980s there has been a recognition, in many countries of the world, that is appropriate to extend the term of patent protection afforded pharmaceuticals, on the basis that the delay in getting to market attributable to the regulation to which these are subject has reduced the effective patent term.

In the UK, under the pre-PA 1977 law, patents subsisted for 16 years from filing but could be extended by up to a further ten years on the grounds of 'inadequate remuneration'. This provided a self-regulating mechanism for extending the term of pharmaceutical patents where the costs of research had not been fully recouped. Demonstrating this involved approaching remuneration from the point of view that one successful pharmaceutical represented the outcome of research on thousands of unsuccessful pharmaceuticals, and had to support the costs of such research. Regulatory delays in the usually understood sense of the time taken to undertake clinical trials, and to secure regulatory approval were not the only cause of delayed exploitation resulting in inadequate remuneration; for example in one case, that of a highly effective antibiotic, the regulatory authorities wished to keep it in reserve pending the inevitable development of bacteria resistant to then existing antibiotics, and deliberately delayed its wider use.

With the accession of the UK to the EPC, and the passage of PA 1977 that provided for patent terms of 20 years not subject to extension, the extension provisions of the pre-PA 1977 law were repealed for all except the oldest patents. The more recent patents already in existence on the entry into force of PA 1977 (those with five years or more still to run on 1 June 1978 and called 'new existing patents') had their terms automatically extended from 16 years to 20 years. In exchange for this extension, such patents were, during the four-year period of that extension deemed endorsed 'licences available as of right' that provided a form of automatic compulsory licensing. Some saw in this a business opportunity, and a number of applications for licences of right were made in respect of pharmaceuticals then protected by new existing patents approaching their 'licence of right' period, particularly the 'blockbuster' drugs. This was resisted by the various patentees, and initiated several years of intensive litigation, which reached the higher courts on several occasions.[1] Although the last 'new existing patent' expired long ago (and indeed the provisions were repealed early for pharmaceutical and agrochemical patents) the accounting approaches adopted for assessing royalties on a 'willing licensor – willing licensee basis', where there were no willing licensors, may well continue however to have application.

However, a 20-year patent term is generally recognized to be inadequate in the pharmaceutical and agrochemical sectors as the effective patent term is greatly reduced by the delays attendant on getting a product to market, such as those involved in securing regulatory approval. This has resulted in pharmaceutical patent term extension measures in the USA under the Drug Price Competition and Patent Term Restoration Act (the Waxman-Hatch Act) 1984, in Japan under its 1987 legislation, and in Europe under the Supplementary Protection Certificate (SPC) Regulations for medicinal products since 1993[2], and for plant protection products since 1997.[3] Unlike the old UK patent term extension regime, which required a determination as to inadequate remuneration, all of these systems provide for an extra effective patent term, the duration of which is linked mechanistically to certain types of regulatory delay. The US system applies also to medical devices. Those in Europe and Japan apply also to agrochemicals.

1   *Allen & Hanbury's v Generics* [1986] RPC 203 (House of Lords) and *Smith Kline and French's (Cimetidine) Patent* [1990] RPC 203 (Court of Appeal).
2   Regulation (EEC) No 459/2006 of 6 May 2009 concerning the supplementary protection certificate for medicinal products (OJ L 152, 1, 16 June 2009) replacing on codification Regulation (EEC) No 1768/92 of 18 June 1992 concerning the creation of a supplementary protection certificate for medicinal products (OJ L 182, 1, 2 July 1992) as amended – see **Appendix 6**.
3   Regulation (EC) No. 1610/96 of 23 July 1996 concerning the creation of a supplementary protection certificate for plant protection products (OJ L 198, 30, 8 August 1996) as amended – see **Appendix 6**.

The SPC Regulations

7.25 In Europe (for this purpose the EU, together with, by virtue of the EEA Agreement, as explained below, Iceland and Norway) the effect of patent term extension is achieved by means of a Supplementary Protection Certificate (SPC) that although not itself a patent, comes into effect on expiry of the 'basic patent' chosen for such purpose and confers, for a limited period, the same rights on its holder as are conferred by the basic patent, except that it protects only the pharmaceutical or agrochemical in respect of which a marketing authorization has been granted and which is protected by the basic patent.

To seek SPC protection for a medicinal or plant protection product that has received a marketing authorization, the patentee must choose in each Member State in which such authorization has been received, or in respect of which an authorization applies, a suitable patent effective in such Member State protecting the 'product' (ie the active substance or combination of active substances in such medicinal product or plant protection product) which becomes the 'basic patent'. The SPC can only be granted in respect of a product contained in such medicinal product or plant protection product the subject of a marketing authorization under the relevant Directive or Regulation.[1] The product cannot already have been the subject of an SPC in that Member State. A single patentee can have no more than one SPC protecting the product in each Member State, irrespective of how many different presentations or formulations of it have received a marketing authorization. The SPC must be applied for, at the relevant national patent office, within six months of the first marketing authorization for the product effective in that Member State, unless such authorization is received before the basic patent is granted, in which case it must be applied for within six months of such grant. Some national patent offices, such as those of the UK and Germany, examine the application in an effort to check that an SPC meets the requirements of the appropriate SPC Regulation, but the SPC Regulations do not require such examination, and so whereas in the UK and Germany much litigation over SPCs concerns challenges to national patent office decisions refusing to grant SPCs, in others most litigation over SPCs concerns those that have already been granted.

The SPC comes into force when the basic patent expires. It cannot last for more than five years from the date on which it takes effect, and expires 15 years (or potentially, for medicinal product SPCs, 15 years and six months[2]) after the first marketing authorization in the EEA if that is earlier. Thus, irrespective of whichever basic patent is chosen in each Member State, all SPCs must expire no later than a single date for a particular product. The SPC attaches only to the product for which the marketing authorization had been given, and for any other use of such product authorized before the expiry of the basic patent. Member States may specify the renewal fees payable. The SPC can be invalidated on the same grounds as would be effective against the basic patent, and additionally on the grounds that the SPC should not have been granted, for example, because the product had been the subject of an earlier marketing authorization than that identified by the applicant for an SPC, or because the basic patent does not in fact 'protect' the product.

It is not, strictly speaking, correct to speak of the SPC as conferring 'patent extension' even though it is convenient so to do – instead the SPC is a separate right which comes into force immediately on patent expiry, but confers, in relation to the relevant product, the 'same rights as conferred by the basic patent and [is] subject to the same limitations and the same obligations'. This approach was adopted because EPC 1973 could not readily, or sufficiently rapidly, be amended to permit extensions of the standard 20-year patent term provided for by EPC 1973, Article 63 – only in 1996 were sufficient ratifications secured to permit a corresponding amendment.

The original medicinal products SPC Regulation 1768/92 (it has since been replaced on codification by Regulation 469/2009) came into force throughout most of the EU on 2 January 1993, and since 1 July 1994 has applied also throughout most of the rest of the then European Economic Area (EEA) but most of the non-EU countries formerly within the EEA have now joined the EU as from 1 January 1995. Now the only country in the EEA to which it does not apply is Liechtenstein, as that has a patent union with Switzerland, and is subject to a comparable SPC regime but under Swiss law, that is based on the first marketing authorization in Switzerland, rather than that in the EU or the rest of the EEA.[3] The plant protection products SPC Regulation 1610/96 is in similar terms, and came into force on 8 February 1997. Despite one relating to medicinal products and the other to plant protection products, the former has to be read in association with the latter as, although the plant protection products SPC Regulation does not actually amend the medicinal products SPC Regulation, it is expressed to have the effect of clarifying certain problems of interpretation that had arisen with the earlier measure since by Recital 17 the plant protection products SPC Regulation provides: '17 Whereas the detailed rules in recitals 12,13 and 14 and in Articles 3(2), 4, 8(1)(c) and 17(2) of this Regulation are also valid, *mutatis mutandis,* for the interpretation in particular of recital 9 and Articles 3, 4, 8(1)(c) and 17 of Council Regulation (EEC) No 1768/92'. The Spanish government sought unsuccessfully to challenge the original medicinal products of SPC Regulation under EU law.[4]

The original medicinal products SPC Regulation was, on its entry into force, subject to a wide variety of transitional provisions, differing as between differing Member States, in particular for products already on the market, which resulted in SPCs being available to extend protection in some countries but not others, occasioning significant scope for differences in the effective term of protection for pharmaceuticals as between Member States.[5] This approach, which was in any event relatively short-term in its effects, was to a large extent avoided in the plant protection products SPC.

Added to these differences implicit in the transitional provisions of the original medicinal products SPC Regulation itself there were those consequential upon the pre-existing national SPC type regimes in France and Italy, introduced before 1993. These provided for different, longer terms than the EU regime, had different starting points for calculating the term of protection, and different approaches to the nature of what was protected.[6] The subsequent accession of new Member States to the EU has also involved introducing a range of differing transitional provisions applying to such Member States so that medicinal products that were already authorized, and were the subject of granted patents on accession could under certain circumstances allow SPCs to be secured in such Member States, despite applications for these not complying with the usual time limits set by the SPC Regulations.

1   For the medicinal products SPC Regulation 469/2009/EC this is Directive 2001/83/EC of 6 November 2001 (as amended) on the Community Code relating to medicinal products for human use, Directive 2001/82/EC of 6 November 2001 (as amended) on the Community Code relating to veterinary medicinal products, or Regulation No 726/2004/EC of 31 March 2004 laying down procedures for the authorization and supervision of medicinal products for human and veterinary use and establishing a European Medicines Agency. For the plant protection products SPC Regulation 1610/96/EC this was formerly Directive 91/414/EEC of 15 July 1991 concerning the placing of plant protection products on the market (OJ L 230, 1, 19 August 1991) but this was replaced as from June 2011 by Regulation (EC) No 1107/2009 of 21 October 2009 concerning the placing of plant protection products on the market and repealing Council Directives 79/117/EEC and 91/414/EEC.

2   The scope to secure a six-month extension to an SPC for medicinal products in certain cases as an incentive for complying with a paediatric investigation plan arises under Article 36 of Regulation (EC) No. 1901/2006 of 12 December 2006 on medicinal products for paediatric use and amending Regulation (EEC) No. 1768/92, Directive 2001/20, Directive 2001/83, and Regulation (EC) No. 726/2004 (OJ L 378, 1, 27 December 2006) as amended by Regulation (EC) No. 1902/2006 of 20 December 2006 amending Regulation 1901/2006 on medicinal products for paediatric use (OJ L 378, 20, 27 December 2006). An SPC having a 'negative term' of less than six months can be secured in order to preserve the scope for a paediatric extension – see Case C-125/10 *Merck Sharpe & Dohm v Deutsches Patentamt* (Court of Justice, 8 December 2011).

3   Although the first marketing authorization in the EU or the rest of the EEA does not affect the term of a Swiss SPC, as noted below at para 7.26, by reason of the special status of Liechtenstein, a first marketing authorization in Switzerland has the potential to affect the term of an SPC in an EU Member State, Iceland or Norway.

4   Case C-350/92 *Kingdom of Spain v Council of the European Union* [1996] FSR 73; [1996] 1 CMLR 415.

5   One aspect of the transitional provisions was addressed by the Court of Justice in a reference from the UK in Case C-110/09 *Yamanouchi Pharmaceuticals v Comptroller General* [1997] RPC 844. It is under the transitional provisions that much interpretation has taken place which is of continued importance as it concerns what constitutes the first marketing authorization for a product.

6   See for example, the Judgments of the Tribunal de Grande Instance in Paris on 30 January 1988, and 18 February 1998 in various *Allen & Hanburys* cases, and on 28 March 2000, and 9 May 2000 in various *Glaxo* cases.

Issues that have arisen under the SPC Regulations

7.26 The SPC Regulations combine aspects of two wholly differing systems with different aims, and approaches – patents and regulation, and this has resulted in several problems of definition, most of which have been reflected in litigation, but some of which, as observed above, the plant protection products SPC Regulation legislation attempted to address. Moreover, by reason of the Regulations being EU legislation, the Court of Justice of the EU has the ultimate say as to their interpretation, and it has taken the view that because patent law is not in general harmonized at an EU level most of the expressions used in the Regulations are to be given an autonomous meaning, uninformed by national legislation. This is nowhere more counterintuitive for patent practitioners than in the question of what can constitute a basic patent, which is defined by Article 4 of the medicinal products SPC Regulation as 'a patent which protects a product as such, a process to obtain a product or an application of a product, and which is designated by its holder for the purpose of the procedure for grant of a certificate'.

It has now been established by the Court of Justice that although for a basic patent to 'protect' a product it is necessary that such product infringe such basic patent[1] this is not sufficient as it must also be 'specified' or 'identified' in the wording of the claims.[2] Quite what this means remains unclear, although the Court of Justice has also held that to be treated as 'protected' it is not necessary for the product to be identified in the claims of the patent by a structural formula, but that where it was not it had to be possible 'to reach the conclusion on the basis of those claims, interpreted inter alia in the light of the description of the invention ... that the claims relate, implicitly but necessarily and specifically, to the active ingredient in question'[3]. What is clear, however, from this is that a patent with claims that identify only one component of a 'product' which consists of a fixed dose combination of active ingredients cannot constitute a basic patent for such product, even though such product would infringe it.

The approach adopted by the Court of Justice to what constitutes a 'product' is also counterintuitive for regulatory lawyers familiar with treating a fixed dose combination of active ingredients as a wholly different 'product' for regulatory purposes to each active ingredient alone, or to each active ingredient in combination with other active ingredients. Thus it has held that an SPC may be granted:

(1) For an active ingredient specified in the wording of the claims of the basic patent relied on, where the medicinal product for which the marketing authorization submitted in support of the SPC application contains not only that active ingredient but also other active ingredients.[4]

(2) For a combination of two active ingredients, corresponding to that specified in the wording of the claims of the basic patent relied on,

where the medicinal product for which the marketing authorization is submitted in support of the SPC application contains not only that combination of the two active ingredients but also other active ingredients.[5]

In practice it is uncommon for a medicinal product containing a fixed dose combination of active ingredients to receive a marketing authorization before marketing authorizations have been secured for medicinal products containing such active ingredients separately, the main exception to this being in the area of vaccines, where some of this case law was developed.

There are two corollaries of this unique concept of what might be described as a notional 'product' for the purposes of the SPC Regulations, but which is unknown to medicinal product regulation. The first is that an SPC for a product consisting of a single active ingredient can be asserted against a medicinal product containing that active ingredient in combination with other active ingredients, always assuming that the basic patent permits of this.[6] The second is that one cannot validly secure, even where the claim wording of the nominated basic patent would permit of this, an SPC for a product consisting of a combination of active ingredients where one of those active ingredients has already been the subject of an SPC on the same basic patent that could be asserted against such combination.[7] This thus reduces the scope in practice for securing an SPC in respect of a combination of active ingredients that would endure beyond an SPC in respect of one of such active ingredients, unless one has a wholly separate patent that protects the combination.

One practical issue that can arise is how, when applying for an SPC, one goes about defining what actually is protected by an SPC. Article 4 of the medicinal products SPC Regulation states:

'4   Within the limits of protection conferred by the basic patent, the protection conferred by a certificate shall extend only to the product covered by the authorization to place the corresponding medicinal product on the market'

The difference between what is meant by the terms 'product' and 'medicinal product' is critical, and it is this article which attempts to link the two. By Article 1(b) of the medicinal products SPC Regulation, 'product' means 'the active ingredient or combination of active ingredients of a medicinal product'. By Article 1(a), 'medicinal product' means any substance or combination of substances presented for treating or preventing disease …'. However, patent claims are drafted as broadly as possible. Although the SPC Regulations provide no legal basis for specifying an SPC 'claim', practice in the UK requires one so to do and thus, in a similar way to patent claims, there has been a tendency to try to 'claim' SPCs broadly, with SPC 'claims' typically to: '[chemical formula of active ingredient], optionally in the form of a pharmaceutically acceptable salt.'

Other applicants have been quite content to seek apparently narrower protection to: '[chemical formula of active ingredient]'.

Many claims in patents for NCEs refer generally to 'pharmaceutically acceptable salts and esters' of a particular NCE, recognising that to specifically claim only certain of these would invite potential infringers to produce a different salt or ester to that specifically claimed, even though such salt or ester would metabolize to the same NCE and so have the same biological effect, even though its physical properties might differ. However the published extracts from the Council Minutes for the passage of the medicinal products SPC Regulation somewhat cryptically observe that: 'The definition of "product" does not mean that salts and esters are excluded from protection and does not rule out the possibility of obtaining a new certificate for a salt or ester regarded as a new active ingredient.'

This suggests that apparently narrow SPC 'claims' (always assuming, despite their lacking any basis in the SPC Regulations, that these have any relevance to the interpretation of the protective scope of an SPC) should not to be treated as limiting, and yet such broad interpretation should not prevent one from obtaining a new SPC for a different salt or ester of the same active. One good reason for a narrow SPC 'claim' is to leave scope for later seeking a new SPC for a different salt or ester. If instead one starts with a broad SPC 'claim', it would seem unlikely that one could seek another SPC for a compound within the scope of that broad SPC 'claim', and thus one is limited to the date of the marketing authorization for the first salt or ester of a particular active on the market as determining the authorization date for the entire group of salts or esters. The plant protection product SPC Regulation, in the light of which the medicinal product SPC Regulation is to be read, addresses the issue in a slightly different way, by means of the following recitals:

'13   Whereas the certificate confers the same rights as those conferred by the basic patent; whereas, consequently, where the basic patent covers an active substance and its various derivatives (salts and esters), the certificate confers the same protection.

14   Whereas the issue of a certificate for a product consisting of an active substance does not prejudice the issue of other certificates for derivatives (salts and esters) of the substance, provided that the derivatives are the subject of patents specifically covering them.'

These provisions were explored to an extent in a referral from the German courts to the Court of Justice under the medicinal products SPC Regulation in Case C-392/97 *Farmitalia Carlo Erba's SPC Application*[8] in which the Court held:

'21   ... where an active ingredient in the form of a salt is referred to in the ... authorization concerned and is protected by a basic patent in force, the [SPC] is capable of covering the active ingredient as such and also its various derived forms such as salts and esters, as medicinal products, in so far as they are covered by the protection of the basic patent.

22   ... where a product in the form referred to in the marketing authorization is protected by a basic patent in force, the [SPC] is capable of covering that product, as a medicinal product, in any of the forms enjoying the protection of the basic patent.'

The German Federal Supreme Court subsequently applied this to rule that where, as here, the medicinal product was the salt idarubicin hydrochloride and the basic patent disclosed this, but only claimed the free base idarubicin, the patentee could secure an SPC, but not to idarubicin and all its salts, but only to idarubicin hydrochloride.

Many issues have arisen in relation to SPCs in the context of attempts to establish what constitutes the 'first authorization' to place a product on the market. This is important not only as to SPC duration (if any) (under Article 13) but also to its availability at all (under Article 3), and was also relevant under the transitional provisions for products already on the market when the SPC Regulations originally came into force. Under Articles 13 and the transitional provisions what matters is: what is the 'first authorization' to place a product on the market in the EU. Thus, where a pharmaceutical has been authorized for veterinary use as well as for human use, it is the earlier of those two authorizations in the EU that has been regarded as the first marketing authorization in the EU for both purposes.[9] The Court of Justice has also held that a French marketing authorization, which was in practice ineffective because it did not of itself allow the product to be marketed, as before doing so a price had to be agreed with the authorities, had still to be treated as the first in the EU.[10] It has also held that even though Switzerland is not a member of the EEA, a Swiss marketing authorization also counts as one in the EU for the purposes of the medicinal products SPC Regulation because Swiss marketing authorizations had at the time immediate automatic effect in Liechtenstein, which is a member of the EEA.[11] Plant protection products, for which one can also secure a 'provisional' authorization, cause problems of their own in this respect[12] as do veterinary medicinal products.[13]

Medicinal products which were previously on the market in the EU, not necessarily by reason of receipt of a marketing authorization under EU law, but by application of transitional provisions which allowed them to remain on the market once regulation of medicinal products at an EU level commenced, have been held by the Court of Justice to be outside the scope of the medicinal products SPC Regulation by virtue of Article 2.[14]

The question of what can constitute a first authorization is one that has also arisen when the same active substance has received different authorizations at different times, in relation to what may be very different formulations or indications. In an attempt to avoid the consequences of the earliest authorization for a particular active substance, the applicant in such cases has sought to define 'the product' in such a way as to enable it to try to rely on the later authorization as being that for 'the product'. Such an attempt was rejected by the English Patents Court in *AB Draco's SPC Application*[15] where the first delivery means to receive an authorization, which was held to be the relevant one for the purposes of the SPC Regulation, was for the active substance in aerosol form, suspended in propellants. The later delivery means avoided propellants and carrier liquids, and involved the use, in a different delivery system, of agglomerated micronized particles of the active ingredient. Despite being the product of research, and rendering the active substance twice as effective, the authorization for the later delivery means was held to not provide a basis for an SPC, it being observed that there is 'nothing indicating that formulation research ... is to be protected by the SPC scheme'.

The Court of Justice has come to similar conclusions. Thus in Case C-431/04 *Massachusetts Institute of Technology v Deutsches Patentamt*[16] it held that an attempt to avoid the consequences of an earlier authorization for a particular formulation of the active ingredient by arguing that its reformulated version was a new product which was instead a 'combination of active ingredients of a medicinal product' in which the other element of the combination was an excipient failed, observing:

'Article 1(b) of [the SPC Regulation] must be interpreted so as not to include in the concept of "combination of active ingredients of a medicinal product" a combination of two substances, only one of which has therapeutic effects of its own for a specific indication, the other rendering possible a pharmaceutical form of the medicinal product, which is necessary for the first substance for that indication.'

This was so even though the reformulation had so improved the toxicology profile of the product that it could for the first time be authorized for an indication for which authorization had not previously been possible.

The Court has also taken a rigid approach to the definition of product in subsequent cases but there are signs that this is now starting to change. Thus in Case C-202/05 *Yissum v Comptroller General*[17] the Court of Justice held that 'where a basic patent protects a second medical use of an active, that use does not form an integral part of the definition of the product'. Also in Case C-210/13 *GlaxoSmithKline Biologicals*[18] it held that: 'just as an adjuvant does not fall within the definition of "active ingredient" within the meaning of that provision, so a combination of two substances, namely an active ingredient having therapeutic effects on its own, and an adjuvant which, while enhancing those therapeutic effects, has no therapeutic effect on its own, does not fall within the definition of "combination of active ingredients"'.

However, in Case C-11/13, *Bayer CropScience AG v Deutsches Patent-und Markenamt*[19] a plant protection product SPC case, it held that the terms 'product' and 'active substances' could 'cover a substance intended to be used as a safener, where that substance has a toxic, phytotoxic or plant protection action of its own', and in Case C-631/13, *Arne Forsgren v Österreichisches Patentamt*[20] it held that an active ingredient could be the subject of an SPC 'where it is covalently bound to other active ingredients which are part of a medicinal product', but that 'a carrier protein conjugated with a polysaccharide antigen by means of a covalent binding may be categorized as an "active ingredient" only if it is established that it produces a pharmacological, immunological or metabolic action of its own which is covered by the therapeutic indications of the marketing authorization.'

An earlier authorization for an impure version of an active substance will also preclude an attempt to secure an SPC in respect of a subsequent authorization for a pure version of that active substance, as in Case C-258/99 *BASF v Bureau voor de Industriële Eigendom*[21] another plant protection product SPC case, in which one finding was that:

> '2   Two products which differ only in the proportion of the active chemical compound to the impurity they contain, one having a greater percentage of the impurity than the other, must be regarded as the same product within the meaning of Article 3 of [the SPC Regulation].'

However, attempts to apply this in the context of medicinal products as a basis for arguing that an earlier marketing authorization for the racemate precludes securing a valid SPC based on a marketing authorization for the active enantiomer, arguing that the racemate is merely impure enantiomer, have generally failed.[22]

The holder of a potential basic patent and the person holding the marketing authorization will not always be the same, and their interests may not coincide. Such problems can arise where a licensee is responsible for getting the pharmaceutical to market, and so has the authorization, and yet the patentee, lacking access to the authorization, has difficulty applying for an SPC. If the licensee has its own 'follow on' patent coverage, perhaps of a formulation or selection nature, it can enhance its own rights to the product by choosing its own patent as the 'basic' patent, and securing an SPC in relation to that. Then the licensor has no benefit of any royalties during the extension, and indeed may itself, subject to the terms of the licence, even be prevented from commercializing the product after expiry of its own patent. An example of a similar problem occasioned a referral to the Court of Justice in Case 181/95 *Biogen Inc v SmithKline Beecham Biologicals.*[23] The situation was one not uncommon with biotechnology patents, where the party with the marketing authorisation (in this case SmithKline Beecham) had licences from two separate companies (here Biogen and Institut Pasteur) under two separate patents. As the medicinal products SPC Regulation appeared at first sight only to permit one SPC to be granted in relation to one product, it was thought the first licensor to secure an SPC 'scooped the pool' of extended protection after the expiry of its own patent. Biogen sought a declaration that SmithKline Beecham, by discriminating against Biogen, in refusing to provide them with a copy of their Belgian marketing authorization so that they could obtain an SPC in Belgium (whereas it had provided such a copy to Institut Pasteur) had committed an act of unfair competition contrary to honest commercial practices, and sought an order compelling them to provide the authorization. The Court of Justice found broadly in favour of Biogen, holding that multiple SPCs could be granted to the holders of different basic patents in respect of the same medicinal product, and also that where the basic patent, and the marketing authorization were in different hands, and the patent holder was unable to provide a copy of the marketing authorization in accordance with Article 8(1)(b) of the medicinal products SPC Regulation, an SPC could not be refused on that ground alone. By simple cooperation, the national authority responsible for granting the SPC could itself obtain a copy of the authorization from the national authority that issued it.

Article 8.1(c) of the plant protection products SPC Regulation, and which also applies to the medicinal products SPC Regulation, complements this by relieving the applicant for an SPC from the need to provide the first marketing authorization itself if it can provide the necessary details of it. However, the issue addressed in Case 181/95 *Biogen* as to whether multiple SPCs can exist for the one product must now be read in the light of the amendments made by the plant protection products SPC Regulation:

> '3.2   The holder of more than one patent for the same product shall not be granted more than one certificate for that product. However, where two or more applications concerning the same product and emanating from two or more holders of different patents are pending, one certificate for this product may be issued to each of these holders.'

Apart from apparently allowing SPCs to be granted on multiple basic patents held by different companies, even if those companies are in common ownership, this does not address the situation that arises under Article 3(c) of the medicinal products SPC Regulation where, one SPC having been granted on one basic patent held by one party, another SPC is only later sought by the different holder of a patent but which has taken much longer to proceed to grant. On the face of matters Article 3(c), which prevents the grant of an SPC where the product has already been the subject of an SPC, would appear to cause the second patentee to lose out as a result of the delays of patent offices for which it was not responsible. However, the Court of Justice has rejected such an unfair interpretation of Article 3(c).[24]

A consequence of the decision of the decision of the Court of Justice in Case 181/95 *Biogen*, and the amendment effected by the plant protection products SPC Regulation has been to remove any formal impediment to the holder of a potential basic patent from seeking an SPC on the basis of a marketing authorization for a product that has been brought to market by an unrelated third party where the holder of such potential basic patent is able to assert that it protects such product. Although this has been touched on in the case law[25] it does not as yet appear to have proved necessary to come to a conclusion as to whether this practice is permitted under the SPC Regulations, although the Court of Justice did make the following observation as to it in Case C-493/12 *Eli Lilly v Human Genome Sciences*:[26]

'[43]   In the light of the objective of Regulation No 469/2009, the refusal of an SPC application for an active ingredient which is not specifically referred to by a patent issued by the EPO relied on in support of such an application may be justified – in circumstances such as those in the main proceedings and as observed by Eli Lilly – where the holder of the patent in question has failed to take any steps to carry out more in-depth research and identify his invention specifically, making it possible to ascertain clearly the active ingredient which may be commercially exploited in a medicinal product corresponding to the needs of certain patients. In such a situation, if an SPC were granted to the patent holder, even though – since he was not the holder of the MA granted for the medicinal product developed from the specifications of the source patent – that patent holder had not made any investment in research relating to that aspect of his original invention, that would undermine the objective of Regulation No 469/2009, as referred to in recital 4 in the preamble thereto.'

Pending any definitive answer however to this, the approach of those who seek to bring such a product to market and who cannot achieve a settlement with such patentee, or are unwilling to defer launch until after the expiry of such potential basic patent, must be either to challenge the validity of such potential basic patent or to seek a declaration of non-infringement as to it.[27]

1   Thus, a patent for a combination of active ingredients cannot be a basic patent for one component only of the combination, even where the medicinal product was a formulated version of such component, and might commonly be co-administered along with the other component of the patented combination: *Centocor's SPC Application* [1996] RPC 118.
2   Cases C-322/10 *Medeva* and C-422/10 *Georgetown University* (Court of Justice 24 November 2011). See also Cases C-518/10 *Yeda Research and Development*,

C-630/10 University of Queensland, and C-6/11 *Daiichi Sankyo* (Court of Justice, 25 November 2011).

3   Case C-493/12 *Eli Lilly v Human Genome Sciences* (Court of Justice, 12 December 2013).

4   Cases C-422/10 *Georgetown University* (Court of Justice, 24 November 2011) and C-630/10 *University of Queensland* (Court of Justice, 25 November 2011).

5   Case C-322/10 *Medeva* (Court of Justice, 24 November 2011).

6   Cases C-442/11 *Novartis v Actavis* and C-574/11 *Novartis Deutschland v Actavis* (Court of Justice, 9 February 2012).

7   Case C-443/12 *Actavis v Sanofi* (Court of Justice, 12 December 2013). See also Case C-577/13 *Actavis v Boehringer Ingelheim Pharma GmbH & Co. KG* (Court of Justice, 24 March 2015).

8   Case C-392/97 *Farmitalia Carlo Erba's SPC Application* (Court of Justice, 16 September 1999); [2000] RPC 580; [2000] 2 CMLR 253. Paragraph 23 of this decision, observing that, 'in order to determine, in connection with the [SPC Regulation] whether a product is protected by a basic patent', reference must be made to the rules which govern that patent', would appear to have been superseded by the case law described above as to what is meant by 'protects' in the SPC Regulations.

9   Case C-31/03 *Pharmacia Italia v Deutsches Patentamt* (Court of Justice, 19 October 2004); [2005] RPC 27. See also the earlier UK decision *Farmitalia Carlo Erba's SPC Application* [1996] RPC 111. It has been possible, however, to distinguish these decisions in the case of a basic patent (here to an indication for human use) that would not have protected the product the subject of the earlier marketing authorization (here to an indication for veterinary use) – see Case C-130/11 *Neurim Pharmaceuticals* (1991) Ltd (Court of Justice, 19 July 2012), although the wider ramifications of this decision have not been explored.

10 Case C-127/00 *AB Hassle v Ratiopharm* (Court of Justice, 26 February 2002).

11 Case C-207/03 *Novartis v Comptroller General* and Case C-252/03 *Ministere de l'Economie v Millenium Pharmaceuticals* (Court of Justice, 21 April 2005); [2005] RPC 33. See also Case C-617/12 *AstraZeneca* (Court of Justice, 14 November 2013).

12 See Case C-229/09 *Hogan Lovells International LLP v Bayer CropScience AG* (Court of Justice, 11 November 2010).

13 See Case E-16/14 *Pharmaq AS v Intervet International BV* (EFTA Advisory Court, 9 April 2015).

14 Cases C-195/09 *Synthon BV v Merz Pharma GmbH & Co KgaA* and C-427/09 *Generics (UK) Ltd v Synaptech Inc* (Court of Justice, 28 July 2011).

15 *AB Draco's SPC Application* [1996] RPC 417.

16 Case C-431/04 *Massachussets Institute of Technology v Deutsches Patentamt* (Court of Justice, 4 May 2006).

17 *Case C-202/05 Yissum Research and Development Company of the Hebrew University of Jerusalem v Comptroller-General* (Court of Justice, 17 April 2007).

18 Case C-210/13 *GlaxoSmithKline Biologicals* (Court of Justice, 14 November 2013).

19 Case C-11/13 *Bayer CropScience AG v Deutsches Patent-und Markenamt* (Court of Justice, 19 June 2014).

20 Case C-631/13 *Arne Forsgren v Osterreichisches Patentamt* (Court of Justice, 19 January 2015).

21 Case C-258/99 *BASF v Bureau voor de Industrielle Eigendom* (Court of Justice, 10 May 2001) [2002] RPC 9.

22 *Generics v Daiichi* [2009] EWCA 646. See also *Escitalopram* (German Federal Supreme Court, 10 September 2009).

23 Case 181/95 *Biogen Inc v SmithKline Beecham Biologicals* [1997] RPC 833; [1987] 1 ECR 386; [1997] 1 CMLR 704.

24 Case C-482/07 *AHP Manufacturing BV v Bureau voor de Industriële Eigendom* (Court of Justice, 3 September 2009). See also *In the matter of, Chiron Corporation's and Novo Nordisk A/S's SPC Application* [2005] RPC 24.

25   See for example, *Novartis Pharmaceuticals UK Ltd v Medimmune Ltd & Anor* [2012] EWHC 181 (Patents Court) at [61].

26   Case C-493/12 *Eli Lilly v Human Genome Sciences* (Court of Justice, 12 December 2013).

27   See *Lilly & Company v Human Genome Sciences Inc* [2012] EWHC 2290 (Patents Court), and *Eli Lilly And Co v Human Genome Sciences Inc* [2014] EWHC 2404 (Patents Court).

Chapter 8

Biotechnology patents

Introduction

Patent concerns of the biotechnology sector

8.01 Although the term 'biotechnology' has come in much commercial usage to mean virtually any life sciences activity, it is used here in the relatively narrow sense of genetic engineering. Viewed from one perspective, genetic engineering is no more than an aspect of chemistry in that its raw material, and its products – most commonly DNA and proteins – are merely chemicals, generally having use as pharmaceuticals, albeit that some of them occur in nature. Thus, much of **Chapter 7** also applies to its products, and indeed much litigation in the English courts in the area of biotechnology, which these days has come primarily to concern monoclonal antibodies, given their commercial importance as medicinal products, now concerns second medical use or formulation patents, as discussed in **Chapter 7**, as any patents that more directly protect the monoclonal antibodies in issue are likely to have expired by the time that a marketing authorization can be sought for any 'biosimilar' of such monoclonal antibody.[1]

However, biotechnology has become a controversial area of patent law in its own right. Much of such controversy ignores the fact that the patent system has been protecting inventions of this sort for many years, for example, in relation to antibiotics produced by fermentation techniques from micro-organisms. Yet genetic engineering techniques such as recombinant DNA technology have posed problems for a patent system that was not designed with the specific needs of the biotechnology sector in mind, and it is these with which this chapter is concerned.

Limits on patentable subject matter present the clearest problem for biotechnology patenting. Limits on what, as a matter of principle, can and what cannot be, patented may be inherent in the patent system given that some of the products that the biotechnology sector has sought to protect, at least originally, exist in nature, but other limits are arbitrary, and are a consequence of certain express provisions in the European Patent Convention (EPC). These different limits can be categorized, as follows:

— The *Product of Nature* issue, concerning the extent to which the requirements as to novelty and inventive step and as to not being a mere discovery can be met with patents to materials that already exist in nature.

— The *Variety* issue, concerning the express exclusion from patentability for 'plant and animal varieties'.

— The *Public Policy* issue, primarily concerning the express exclusion from patentability for inventions which are contrary to *ordre public* but also now concerning the issues of prior informed consent and disclosure of origin.

The first of these issues is not unique to European patent law, and is inherent in patent law in general. The second and third are, however, an especial feature of European patent law, and result from certain express exclusions included in the EPC when it was finalized back in 1973, long before biotechnology was developed. The second and third categories of exclusion, although often met together, as in T-19/90 *Oncomouse/HARVARD* and T-0315/03 *Method for producing transgenic animals/HARVARD* discussed later, and only ever met in relation to biotechnology, have different origins. In the second category, the area of potential overlap relevant to biotechnology, and which the exclusion sought originally to address is that of plant varieties, although there is no longer any reason for this with the current version of the UPOV Convention allowing their overlap with patents. The third category is the most problematic of all, and involves not only the vexed moral, and ethical questions of whether one should, as a matter of principle, be permitted to patent living entities, and if so to what extent, but also attempts to use the patent system to challenge, and control the underlying technology that it seeks to protect and various of its practices.

Further, and assuming that the above exceptions do not arise or can be overcome, patents for biotechnological inventions have in practice presented particular problems in terms of the breadth of protection that is regarded as appropriate. For granted patents this is usually manifested as attacks on validity on grounds of insufficiency, also discussed later. Another insufficiency issue met with such inventions concerns their reproducibility by third parties, which has resulted in systems for the deposit of biological material. Many of these issues are addressed to some extent in Directive 98/44/EC of 6 July 1998 on the legal protection of biotechnological inventions, although by and large this is little more than declaratory of the law as it has been established in the cases.

1   See for example, *Hospira UK Limited v Genentech Inc* [2014] EWHC 1094 (Pat) and *Hospira UK Limited v Genentech Inc* [2014] EWHC 3857 (Pat).

Directive 98/44/EC on the legal protection of biotechnological inventions

8.02   Directive 98/44/EC of 6 July 1998 on the legal protection of biotechnological inventions ('the Directive') first started life as a proposal in 1988[1] but the first product of the long drawn out EU legislative process was rejected by the European Parliament in 1995. It was resuscitated in amended form, overcame its legislative hurdles, and a challenge to its legality[2] came into force,[3] and ought to have been implemented in national patent legislation by Member States by July 2000.[4] Article 16(c) of the Directive requires the Commission to provide reports on the development, and implications of patent law in the field of biotechnology and genetic engineering. There have been two such reports to date.[5]

The Directive was meant to establish 'harmonised, clear and improved standards for protecting biotechnological inventions' within the framework of the existing patent law. It is thus ironic that differences in its national implementation have resulted in a decrease in harmonization in some areas, such as how gene sequences are claimed. Moreover, many of the benefits, in terms of harmonization, that the Directive was meant to deliver when it was first introduced had been achieved by the time it became law through a succession of decisions of the European Patent Office (EPO), a fact recognized by the EPO in amending the EPC Implementing Regulations to accord with the Directive using a quasi-administrative procedure that is only open to it on the basis that it is declaratory of the EPC. The amendments introduced a new chapter to the EPC Implementing Regulations on Biotechnological Inventions[6] grouping definitions, and rules of interpretation to be applied to European patents, and patent applications that concern biotechnological inventions. The new Rules provide that the Directive 'shall be used as supplementary means of interpretation' (which allows its recitals to be taken into account) and reflect the provisions of Chapter I of the Directive, as to which the EPO notes that:

'Although the principles set forth there regarding the patentability of biotechnological inventions are based on the relevant provisions of the EPC and essentially reflect current practice as developed by the Office and its boards of appeal in applying the Convention, some extensions and clarifications are required in this area to ensure that the patentability provisions of the EPC also continue to be interpreted in keeping with the Directive.'

How the Directive deals with the three types of issue identified above is discussed below in relation to each of them, along with certain other aspects of biotechnology patenting that the Directive also addresses.

1   See [1989] OJ C10/3 for Original Commission Proposal of October 1988 – COM (88) 496 final.
2   C-377/98 *Netherlands v European Parliament* [2002] *IP&T* 121.
3   Directive 98/44 on the legal protection of biotechnological inventions ([1998] OJ L213/13).
4   Implemented in the UK as to Articles 1–11 by the Patents Regulations 2000 (SI 2000/2037). Articles 12–14 were implemented in the UK by other provisions, as set out later. The Directive was implemented late by most Member States.
5   *Report from the Commission to the Council and the European Parliament – Development and implications of patent law in the field of biotechnology and genetic engineering* – COM (2002) 545 final, 7 October 2002, and COM (2005) 312 final, SEC (2005) 943, 14 July 2005.
6   Now Chapter V, Rules 26–34 of the Implementing Regulation to Part II EPC (as last amended 15 October 2014).

Patent claims in biotechnology

8.03   As biotechnology is a collection of techniques, many important inventions in this sector are processes (for example, the polymerase chain reaction (PCR) for amplifying small amounts of DNA) and are claimed in corresponding terms. Many product claims are not to end products but to intermediates or 'research tools', which from the point of view of enforcement against third parties offer little or no advantage over process claims, which are infringed not only by conducting the process, offering (with knowledge) such process, or dealing in the direct product of such process. Claims to products of genetic engineering techniques have been obtained for novel:

— micro-organisms, whether or not naturally occurring;
— cell lines (including hybridoma cells);
— natural products artificially obtained such as bacterial mutants, attenuated viruses and protozoa;
— natural products such as enzymes and other proteins isolated from micro-organisms;
— the products of recombinant DNA technology such as DNA itself, and the polypeptides produced from it, including various therapeutic proteins such as monoclonal antibodies; and
— materials useful in recombinant DNA technology (eg vectors, promoters and transferable micro-organisms).

Notably, claims to various sorts of living organisms have been allowed. For example, GB 2 093 017 B to Queen Elizabeth College, granted in 1985, concerned a novel species of *Streptomyces* bacterium isolated from soil samples in London, which produced a novel polyene antibiotic with a unique antifungal spectrum of activity. Claims were obtained to the polyene characterized in different ways such as the process of its production, an antibiotic agent produced by any such process, and as well as to the micro-organism itself: '12. Streptomyces elizabethii NCIB 11545 or an artificially produced mutant or variant strain thereof capable of producing a polyene as defined in claim 1 or 2'.

Claims were also obtained to the use of such micro-organisms for producing a polyene as claimed, and for an antibiotic composition containing the polyene. In the quoted claim, the letters 'NCIB' identify the culture collection where a sample of the micro-organism has been deposited.[1]

Claims to proteins produced by recombinant DNA technology, together with associated processes, and tools, have been the main subject of UK biotechnology patent litigation. An early example of such claims is provided by GB 2 119 804 B, the patent that was held invalid in *Genentech's Patent*[2] claims 1–5 of which as granted were all independent product claims, each essentially seeking to claim the naturally occurring protein human tissue plasminogen activator (t-PA) by identifying it in a variety of ways in which it was asserted that it was not found in nature:

'1.   Recombinant human tissue plasminogen activator essentially free of other proteins of human origin.

2.   Human tissue plasminogen activator unaccompanied by associated native glycosylation.
3.   Human tissue plasminogen activator as produced by recombinant DNA technology.
4.   Biologically active human tissue plasminogen activator in essentially pure form, unaccompanied by protein with which it is ordinarily associated.
5.   Human tissue plasminogen activator per se, of the kind produced by expression of a recombinant DNA sequence coding therefor in a mammalian cell line.'

No such claims were allowed in the corresponding patent prosecuted via the EPO[3] but a 'product by process' claim[4] was initially allowed in such patent as claim 18, although this did not however survive opposition: '18. A protein as prepared by the process of claim 3 or claim 4 which is unaccompanied by glycosilation native to human tissue plasminogen activator'.

This effectively corresponded to the limitation in product claim 2 of the GB patent applied to the 'product by process' claim 20 in the GB patent: '20 Human tissue plasminogen activator produced by a process according to any one of claims 16 to 19'. The GB patent also had product claims to vectors containing DNA sequences for coding t-PA, that functioned as intermediates in the process for its production.

'7.   A recombinant cloning vector comprising a DNA sequence encoding human tissue plasminogen activator.
8.   A replicable expression vector capable, in a transformant microorganism or cell culture, of expressing a DNA sequence according to claim 7.
9.   The plasmid ...'

Claim 9 was characterized by the court as a product claim 'for two of the tools made and used by Genentech in their process' but would in practice have been of limited of any value as against third parties. Claim 10 was also a product claim, but for cells transformed with the vectors or plasmids containing the DNA sequence coding for t-PA: '10. A micro-organism or cell culture transformed with the vehicle according to claim 8 or 9'.

Finally, there were process claims, the independent ones of which were to:

'15.   A process involving the use of human tissue plasminogen activator according to claims 1–6 in preparing pharmaceutical compositions useful for treatment of vascular diseases or conditions.
16.   A process which comprises expressing DNA encoding human tissue plasminogen activator in a recombinant host cell.
17.   A process for producing human t-PA, which process comprises:
        a.   preparing a replicable expression vector capable of expressing the DNA sequence encoding human t-PA in a host cell;

> b.   transforming a host cell culture to obtain a recombinant host cell;
>
> c.   culturing said recombinant host cells under conditions permitting expression of said t-PA encoding DNA sequence to produce human t-PA;
>
> d.   recovering said human t-PA.
>
> 19.   A process for producing human tissue plasminogen activator, substantially as described herein.'

The claims of EP (UK) 0 148 605 B2 the patent at issue in *Kirin-Amgen v Hoechst Marion Roussel*[5] and which has a slightly later priority date, 1983, than that in *Genentech,* are more typical of the sort met in relation to patents based on sequencing the DNA which codes for a therapeutic protein – such claims are for DNA sequences, proteins and processes for expressing proteins, as well as pharmaceutical compositions. Tables VI and VII referred to in these claims set out DNA sequences, and the corresponding proteins coded by them as discovered by the patentee. The sequence claims are limited not only to these two sequences, but also to other (albeit in (b) and (c) undisclosed) sequences which could be expected to code for the same or similar proteins having similar desired activity. The only independent such claim is to:

> '1.   A DNA sequence for use in securing expression in a procaryotic or eucaryotic host cell of a polypeptide product having at least part of the primary structural conformation of that of erythropoietin to allow possession of the biological property of causing bone marrow cells to increase production of reticulocytes and red blood cells and to increase hemoglobin synthesis or iron uptake, said DNA sequence selected from the group consisting of:
>
> a.   the DNA sequences set out in Tables V and VI or their complementary strands;
>
> b.   DNA sequences which hybridise under stringent conditions to the protein coding regions of the DNA sequences defined in (a) or fragments thereof; and
>
> c.   DNA sequences which, but for the degeneracy of the genetic coded would hybridise to the DNA sequences defined in (a) and (b).'

There were two independent protein claims, both based on the assumption that the protein expressed by cells containing the sequences of claim 1 was in some way different to that found in nature (which resulted in their ultimately both being found invalid):[6]

> '19.   A recombinant polypeptide having part or all of the primary structural conformation of human or monkey erythropoietin as set forth in Table VI or Table V or any allelic variant or derivative thereof possessing the biological property of causing bone marrow cells to increase production of reticulocytes and red blood cells to increase hemoglobin synthesis or iron uptake and characterized by being the product of eukaryotic expression of an exogenous

DNA sequence and which has higher molecular weight by SDS-PAGE from erythropoietin isolated from urinary sources.

26.   A polypeptide product of the expression in a eukaryotic host cell of a DNA sequence according to any of Claims 1, 2, 3, 5, 6 and 7.'

In addition, there was one independent process claim, although this was not asserted in such litigation against Hoechst Marion Roussel, but only against its co-defendant at first instance Roche:

'27.   A process for production of a polypeptide having at least part of the primary structural conformation of erythropoietin to allow possession of the biological property of causing bone marrow cells to increase production of reticulocytes and red blood cells and to increase hemoglobin synthesis or iron uptake, which process is characterized by culturing under suitable nutrient conditions a prokaryotic or eukaryotic host cell transformed or transfected with a DNA sequence according to any of Claims 1, 2, 3, 5, 6 and 7 in a manner allowing the host cell to express said polypeptide; and optionally isolating the desired polypeptide product of the expression of the DNA sequence.'

In each of the above two cases there were also conventional pharmaceutical composition claims. Claim 1 of EP (UK) 0 939 804 B1, the main independent claim of the patent in issue in *Eli Lilly v Human Genome Sciences*[7] provides an example of a DNA sequence claim based on early work done in sequencing the human genome, this time with a 1995 priority date. Its commercial importance lay in therapeutics, and the impediment that Lilly perceived that it presented to it in developing a monoclonal antibody to the protein neutrokine-α. Unlike the early patents in issue in the *Genentech* and the *Kirin-Amgen* cases the claims of which are set out above, in each of which the natural protein, and its utility had been identified before its sequence was determined, and so compromised the novelty of claims to such proteins, even where produced artificially, in this case the identification of the gene sequence preceded the identification of the utility of the protein for which it coded. As amended on appeal in the EPO, the independent claims read:

'1.   An isolated nucleic acid molecule comprising a polynucleotide sequence encoding a Neutrokine-α polypeptide wherein said polynucleotide sequence is selected from the group consisting of:

(a)   a polynucleotide sequence encoding the full length Neutrokine-α polypeptide having the amino acid sequence of residues 1 to 285 of SEQ ID NO:2; and

(b)   a polynucleotide sequence encoding the extracellular domain of the Neutrokine-α polypeptide having the amino acid sequence of residues 73 to 285 of SEQ ID NO:2;

6.   A recombinant vector containing an isolated nucleic acid molecule consisting of a polynucleotide sequence encoding a Neutrokine-α polypeptide wherein said polynucleotide sequence is selected from the group consisting of:

(a) a polynucleotide sequence encoding the full length Neutrokine-α polypeptide having the amino acid sequence of residues 1 to 285 of SEQ ID NO:2; and

(b) a polynucleotide sequence encoding the extracellular domain of the Neutrokine-α polypeptide having the amino acid sequence of residues 73 to 285 of SEQ ID NO:2;

13. An isolated antibody or portion thereof that binds specifically to:

(a) the full length Neutrokine-α polypeptide (amino acid sequence of residues 1 to 285 of SEQ ID NO:2); or

(b) the extracellular domain of the Neutrokine-α polypeptide (amino acid sequence of residues 73 to 285 of SEQ ID NO:2);'

The word 'isolated' had not been in the claims as originally granted. Although claims to the naturally occurring protein itself might also have been novel in such a case, as the protein in issue had not previously been isolated, the important claim here from a commercial point of view was claim 13, as it was this claim which would cover a therapeutic monoclonal antibody used in treatment which relied on modulating the effect of such protein.

The claims at issue in the two *Monsanto* cases which are set out, and discussed below in the context of infringement[8] provide further examples of claims to DNA sequences, with priority dates in 1990 but for genetically modified plants that are undeniably artificial in their resistance to certain herbicides, and so should have presented no especial problems of claiming.

1 See below at para 8.16.
2 *Genentech's Patent* [1987] RPC 553 (Patents Court); [1989] RPC 147 (Court of Appeal) discussed further below at paras 8.04–8.05.
3 EP 0 093 619, the subject of T 923/92 *t-PA/GENENTECH* [1996] EPOR 275.
4 Such 'product-by-process' claims, as discussed below, and in **Chapter 7** at para 7.04 should only be allowed where the process of production confers on the product some new property which differentiates it from the prior art, and where the product cannot otherwise be defined.
5 *Kirin-Amgen v Hoechst Marion Roussel* [2001] IP&T 882; [2002] RPC 1; [2002] RPC 2 (Patents Court); [2003] IP&T 694; [2003] RPC 3 (Court of Appeal); [2004] UKHL 46; [2005] 1 All ER 667; [2005] IP&T 352; [2005] RPC 9 (House of Lords) discussed further below at paras 8.04, 8.15 and 8.18.
6 See below at paras 8.04 and 8.15.
7 *Eli Lilly v Human Genome Sciences* [2008] EWHC 1903 (Patents Court); [2010] EWCA 33 (Court of Appeal); [2011] UKSC 51 (Supreme Court). See also T-18/09 *Neutrokine/HUMAN GENOME SCIENCES* (Technical Board of Appeal 3.3.08, 21 October 2009) also upholding the validity of such claim.
8 See below at paras 8.17 and 8.18.

The 'product of nature' issue

Novelty

8.04 The 'product of nature' issue is not limited to biotechnology and has equal application to pharmaceuticals, and indeed to chemistry. It is primarily an anticipation objection, which may also give rise to an obviousness objection (discussed in para 8.05) although it can also be encountered in the context of the exclusions from patentability of 'mere discoveries' (also discussed in para 8.04) or inventions that lack industrial application (discussed in para 8.07). It is an objection that is only effective as against attempts to secure *per se* product protection, and has no relevance to process protection, or to protection for medical uses, be that as 'Swiss form' process claims or use bound product protection.

There is no absolute ban in Europe on patenting products of nature as otherwise bacteria newly isolated from some sewage outfall, useful for example, in the production of antibiotics, could never be patentable, which is not the case, and no one has ever been troubled by or has criticized the availability of such patents in Europe.[1] Instead, the issue arises with such products that have previously been isolated and identified. The effect of the product of nature issue has been felt particularly in biotechnology, in that many of the substances for which product protection was sought in the early days of biotechnology patenting, typically proteins with evident therapeutic potential, were not 'new' in the absolute sense of having no previously recognized existence. Moreover, where such products were already known, and had a known utility it was arguably obvious to try to make them by the processes of biotechnology, given their previous, and published, identification and known utility, taken together with the availability of biotechnological techniques enabling one to do so.

In the UK, the pre-PA 1977 law specifically provided[2] that claims to new substances were to be construed as not extending to that substance when found in nature. European (and UK) patent law instead takes the approach that a product as found in nature is not patentable, either because it is a mere discovery or because it is not new. Thus, EPC, Article 52(1) provides that: 'European patents shall be granted for any inventions which are susceptible of industrial application, which are new and which involve an inventive step.'

Moreover, by EPC, Article 52(2) certain specified types of subject matter, one of which is 'discoveries', are not to be regarded as inventions within the meaning of Article 52(1). The four attacks implicit in this formulation of patentability – namely: (i) lack of novelty; (ii) inventive step; (iii) industrial applicability (or utility); or (iv) being a mere discovery – can all arise when one deals with materials which can be said to exist already to some extent in nature. The *EPO Guidelines* express the extent to which a product of nature can be patented in the following way:[3]

> 'To find a previously unrecognised substance occurring in nature is also mere discovery and therefore unpatentable. However, if a substance found in nature can be shown to produce a technical effect, it may be patentable. An example of such a case is that of a substance occurring in nature which is found to have an antibiotic effect. In addition, if a micro-organism is discovered to exist in nature and to produce an antibiotic, the microorganism may itself be patentable as one aspect of the invention. Similarly, a gene which is discovered to exist in nature may be patentable if a technical effect is revealed, eg its use in making a certain polypeptide or in gene therapy.'

The grounds of attack as to lack of novelty and being a discovery in the biotechnology field were both addressed by an EPO Opposition Division in *Relaxin/HOWARD FLOREY INSTITUTE*[4] where claims to DNA fragments encoding for a certain form of a protein, the human hormone relaxin, were upheld. These claims were novel, despite the hormone, and the gene that coded for it, always having been present in the human body, as it is an established principle of European patent law to recognize novelty for a natural substance which has been isolated for the first time, and which has had no previously recognized existence, as here.[5] Moreover, the isolation and characterization of such a DNA fragment did not represent a mere discovery, such as finding something freely available in nature. In *Genentech's Patent*[6] a similarly narrow view was taken in the UK by the Patents Court of the 'mere discovery' ground of attack, as not applying to the practical application of a discovery, even though such practical application might be obvious once the discovery was made.

A claim to a previously identified and isolated naturally occurring product would lack novelty. However, claims 1–5 of the patent the subject of *Genentech's Patent* show various types of claim from the early days of biotechnology which were drawn so as to attempt to exclude from their scope the naturally occurring material whilst at the same time covering the same product made artificially. Irrespective of issues of inventive step (which was the main, and successful, attack in *Genentech's Patent*) such claims would be unlikely to be allowed nowadays as they would lack clarity, and novelty unless they could identify a specific measurable parameter or parameters which consistently differentiated the natural from the synthetic product. The invention in such a case, and hence the protection, is likely to reside in the manner of extraction, purification, or synthesis rather than for the material itself, as proved to be the case in *Kirin-Amgen v Hoechst Marion Roussel*.[7] This concerned a patent for the naturally occurring protein erythropoietin, which is used to treat anaemia in patients with kidney failure. The two independent product claims (19 and 26) and those claims dependant on them, were ultimately found invalid on the grounds of insufficiency, and lack of novelty respectively. The House of Lords found that the variability of erythropoietin (EPO) (a consequence of its variable glycosylation) was such that there was no difference between 'recombinant erythropoietin' as a class and erythropoietin 'isolated from urinary sources' (uEPO), which latter feature had been added to claim 19 in opposition proceedings in an attempt to differentiate the two. This rendered claim 19 not only incapable of infringement but also insufficient. No such feature had been added to claim 26 which was found by the House of Lords to be anticipated by erythropoietin isolated from urinary sources, because there was no difference in properties between such erythropoietin as a class, and that isolated from urinary sources, and the process of producing such erythropoietin could not, in accordance with the established practice, be treated as a limitation in the claim which conferred novelty.[8] Lord Hoffmann's judgment summarized the situation on the two product claims as follows:

> '132. ... Standing back from the detail, it is clear that Amgen have got themselves into difficulties because, having invented a perfectly good and ground-breaking process for making EPO and its analogues, they were determined to try to patent the protein itself, notwithstanding that, even when isolated, it was not new. Hence the patenting of the two product-by-process claims which have failed, one because the last-minute amendment to distinguish the product from the natural EPO turned out to based upon the false premise that all uEPO had the same molecular weight and the other because the factual basis on which the European Patent Office allowed it turned out to be wrong.'

Such attacks had no bearing on the validity of the process claims such as claim 27, that had at first instance been successfully asserted against the co-defendant Roche, but these had not been asserted against Hoechst Marion Roussel, whose was the only product in issue in the House of Lords.

The 'product of nature' concern should be seen in perspective as for therapeutics it is really only a 'first generation' problem in biotechnology. The sector has already started to develop and there are already on the market the biotechnological equivalents of new chemical entities such as modified naturally occurring proteins with superior, artificially tailored properties[9] with which such concerns fall away, and the fruits of such research will be protected just as novel chemical entities would be. As biotechnology comes more and more to seek to improve on nature, rather than simply to replicate it, such issues will become less significant.

1   The position would appear now to be different in the USA, as a result of the decision of the US Supreme Court in *Association for Molecular Pathology et al. v Myriad Genetics, Inc., et al.* 133 S. Ct. 2107 (2013), holding that a 'naturally occurring DNA segment is a product of nature and not patent eligible merely because it has been isolated, but cDNA is patent eligible because it is not naturally occurring'.
2   Patents Act 1949, s 4(7).

3   *EPO Guidelines for Examination*, November 2014, Part G, Ch II, 3.1.

4   *Relaxin/HOWARD FLOREY INSTITUTE* [1995] OJ EPO 388. Although not a decision of a Technical Board of Appeal, its importance and authority is reflected in its publication in the *Official Journal* of the EPO, which publishes very few Technical Board of Appeal decisions.

5   'It was common ground amongst the parties that until a cDNA encoding human H2-relaxin and its precursors was isolated by the proprietor, the existence of this form of relaxin was unknown' – para 4.3.1 of Decision.

6   *Genentech's Patent* [1987] RPC 553 (Patents Court); [1989] RPC 147 (Court of Appeal) – see representative claims set out above at para 8.03.

7   *Kirin-Amgen v Hoechst Marion Roussel* [2001] IP&T 882; [2002] RPC 1; [2002] RPC 2 (Patents Court); [2003] IP&T 694; [2003] RPC 3 (Court of Appeal); [2004] UKHL 46; [2005] 1 All ER 667; [2005] IP&T 352; [2005] RPC 9 (House of Lords).

8   The EPO considers such 'product-by-process' claims (whether expressed as 'produced by' or 'producible by') to be allowable, and novel only where the process of production confers on the product some new property which differentiates it from the prior art, and where the product cannot otherwise be defined. See **Chapter 7** at para 7.04.

9   Such as longer lasting or more rapidly acting forms of insulin, or longer lasting forms of erythropoietin, the latter achieved either by modifying the amino acid sequence of the natural product to add more glycosylation sites, or by pegylation. Neither, in contrast to polyclonal antibodies, do monoclonal antibodies, which as a class constitute most new biotechnology products, exist naturally.

Inventive step

8.05   Assuming product claims for proteins such as those discussed above to be novel, they may still be at risk of challenge for lack of inventive step on the basis that if one knows that something which is naturally occurring is useful it is then obvious to try to produce the same material artificially. Patents based on the discovery of gene sequences of speculative utility have also been held to be obvious on the basis that the invention provides no technical contribution, as discussed in **Chapter 7**, although in such cases they tend also to be open to attack on other grounds, such as insufficiency.[1]

In *Genentech's Patent*[2] a claim to an already known, isolated and characterized protein, when produced by means of recombinant DNA technology, was held by the English Court of Appeal to lack inventive step as no more than a statement of what was an obvious research goal. Being the first to achieve that goal through the use of conventional techniques did not therefore merit a patent. The patent was to human tissue plasminogen activator (t-PA) a protein that was known to occur, albeit in very small amounts, in the human body, and was believed to have potential in the treatment of blood clots because it activates the conversion of the already existing enzyme precursor, plasminogen into plasmin, an enzyme which dissolves fibrin in blood clots. Genentech was the first of several teams working in this area to successfully discover by the use of laborious, costly, and time consuming, but essentially known, techniques, the nucleotide sequence of the complementary DNA corresponding to t-PA, and accordingly the amino acid sequence of t-PA itself. Such complementary DNA could be inserted into plasmids that could in turn transform other suitable micro-organisms that could produce the t-PA in pure form, and in relatively large quantities. Genentech's achievements in reaching this stage were characterized by one member of the Court of Appeal as follows:

'What was it that Genentech achieved? The answer seems to me as follows.

First, they won the race. The goal was known, and others were trying to reach it. Genentech got there first.

Second, the goal was to find a means of making, and having found it actually to make, the desired protein – a substance identical to that which already existed in nature.

Third, they reached the goal by a route the general nature of which was already practised.

Fourth, the success was due to the fact that they were the first to create by recombinant means a full-length insert.

Fifth, on the way to the goal they constructed a number of organisms, of which the two expression vectors referred to in claim 9 were examples, which had never existed before. Some of them contained the full length insert. These constructs were of no value except as a means to an end.

Sixth, on the way to the goal they discovered the nucleotide and amino acid sequences of "natural t-PA". This discovery was not in itself a goal, and it is a fair inference that Genentech would not have set out to achieve it simply as a matter of pure research. Seventh, the publication of Genentech's work was of value to subsequent workers in two respects. It demonstrated that the desired protein could be made by recombinant methods within the existing technologies; and (by communicating the sequences and the restriction map) enabled the subsequent workers to reach the goal by a more direct route, at less expense and in a shorter time, and with a lesser risk of failure.

Eighth, the publication of Genentech's work also enabled other workers to know what route Genentech had taken. But nobody would ever wish to take the first part of the route again, or to traverse any of the later parts in precisely the way described.'

The majority in the Court of Appeal found all the claims of the patent to be invalid by reason of obviousness. They considered that the patentee was not operating in an entirely empirical field. The patentee's aim was known, as was sufficient of the theory and practice for it to know how, eventually, and with enough hard work, to get there. It was obvious to the patentee (and also to several rival teams working on the same problem and aiming for the same goal, itself a strong indication of obviousness) that it was desirable to produce human t-PA by recombinant DNA technology and that obvious aim was all that claim 3 stated. The fact that the patentee achieved this aim before anybody else, did not by itself entitle it to a patent, as patents were only granted for getting there first if the goal was not an obvious one. All the steps taken by the patentee to find out the composition of the sequences, and their use of that knowledge to produce t-PA were therefore, despite the effort which had gone into it, no more than an obvious application of known technology. In addition, the majority in the Court of Appeal considered that most of the claims (excluding only claims 9 and 19) were also insufficient. They did indicate that some limited claims to the described process (eg claim 9) could have been salvaged, but there would have been no purpose served in so doing, as these had no value as against third parties. However, a Technical Board of the EPO, admittedly considering different claims of the equivalent patent prosecuted by the EPO, held the patent valid on amended claims (that omitted 'product by process' protection for the protein itself) listing a number of factors that would have influenced the degree of confidence of the skilled person in the successful conclusion of cloning, and expressing human t-PA, and accordingly rejecting an attack based on lack of inventive step, noting that: 'In 1982 the synthesis and cloning of cDNA was not yet routinely established because genetic engineering had not made all the technical and theoretical advances which nowadays (13 years later) are available to a competent laboratory.'

By contrast, in *Genentech Inc's (Human Growth Hormone) Patent*[3] claims to cloning vectors comprising the cDNA of Human Growth Hormone were held by the English Patents Court not to lack inventive step, as the work of a competing team showed that the patentee had taken non-obvious cloning steps. Other claims were, however, held to have been anticipated.

A later case concerning cloning and expression in which a patent with a much later priority date was also held by the English Patents Court to lack inventive step is *DSM's Patent*.[4] The patent was for the DNA sequence of a particular phytase enzyme from a particular fungus in which it was known to be present. As to the common general knowledge at the priority date, the Patents Court held that, once a pure sample of a protein or protein fragment had become available, 'working out the identity and order of the amino acids in the chain was a well-known exercise', with various purification techniques also being well known to protein biochemists. Also, the ordinary skilled molecular biologist would know that 'in order to isolate a gene of interest, it would be necessary first to construct a DNA library, which would have to be screened with an appropriate oligonucleotide probe', the success of which would depend upon the quality of the available probes and there would have to be 'a degree of trial and error in varying the stringency conditions in which the hybridization and post-hybridization washing was carried out'. The patentee argued that it had been able to make the invention only by using a particular apparatus (flat bed IFF) in the purification step, when other similar techniques had failed.

However, the flat bed IFF technique was well known, simple, commercially available, not time-consuming and, while it might not have been the first choice, would have been an obvious technique to invoke for separating proteins for further use. Therefore, its use did not confer inventive step. The cited prior art paper had stated that phytase had been purified, but the patentee argued that this statement was wrong. However, it was held that the skilled worker would not have disbelieved this statement, and indeed one of the inventors had accepted (in evidence to the EPO) that his view on first reading this paper was that success had been achieved. The Patents Court also held that the skilled worker would not be dissuaded from trying to repeat the work described there, and that success would have probably followed from so doing, at least from one aspect of such work, as in fact had later independently been done after the priority date. The claims were also found obvious over this document. However, arguments that because the enzymatic activity of the natural fungus was known there could be no invention in purifying this, and determining the gene sequence of that enzyme, or that such was a mere discovery, or no more than mere obvious *desiderata*, were each rejected.

Although the House of Lords briefly discussed the question of obviousness in *Biogen v Medeva*[5] it did not analyse whether what the inventor had done would have been obvious at the priority date, being content in that case to assume, without having to decide, that it was not. Thus, although the patent was found invalid for obviousness, this was a consequence of a concession as to the consequence of losing priority, without which the patent would have been found invalid for insufficiency in view of its claim breadth.

In contrast, in *Chiron v Organon Teknika*[6] an obviousness attack failed, both in the English Patents Court and Court of Appeal, against a patent that was based on the work of the first to identify, isolate, and characterize, after many years of failed attempts, the virus responsible for most cases of non-A non-B Hepatitis – namely Hepatitis C. The critical difference between this and cases such as *Genentech's Patent* and *Biogen v Medeva* was that in these latter two cases the naturally occurring material being sequenced had already been isolated and characterized, and its significance and thus its potential utility, already established. In *Chiron,* the patentee was also the first to isolate and characterize Hepatitis C, as a consequence of the molecular biology it undertook. The utility of that discovery lay in the use of the relevant sequence in diagnostic kits for HCV infection. However, claims in the patent to HCV vaccine were held invalid as insufficient as the teaching in the patent did not enable the production of such vaccines.

1   See T-1329/04 *Factor-9/JOHN HOPKINS* (Board 3.3.08, 28 June 2005) finding a patent based on the identification of a gene sequence to lack inventive step, where the data in the patent application as filed did not render it plausible that the teaching of the application solved the technical problem that it purported to solve. This was

cited in *Conor Medsystems Inc v Angiotech Pharmaceuticals Inc* [2008] UKHL 49 at paras [33]–[35] and applied in *Eli Lilly v Human Genome Sciences* [2008] EWHC 1903 (Patents Court) at paras [316]–[317] to find the patent invalid, although other attacks on the grounds of lack of inventive step failed). The patent was also found to be invalid as insufficient, and lacking industrial applicability, though only the finding on the latter ground was analysed, and upheld in [2010] EWCA Civ 33 (Court of Appeal) although this industrial applicability finding was reversed, along with the first instance finding of insufficiency, on further appeal to the Supreme Court at [2011] UKSC 51. When the action was remitted to the Court of Appeal [2012] EWCA Civ 1185 it was conceded that this ground of lack of inventive step stood or fell with the issue of industrial applicability, and the Court of Appeal held the claims in issue to be sufficient.

2   *Genentech's Patent* [1987] RPC 553 (Patents Court); [1989] RPC 147 (Court of Appeal) – see representative claims set out above at para 8.03.

3   *Genentech Inc's (Human Growth Hormone) Patent* [1989] RPC 613.

4   *DSM's Patent* [2001] RPC 675. The patent in issue in this case was also the subject of successful opposition at the EPO, an appeal against which decision failed in T-0875/02 *BASF/Microbial Phytase* (Technical Board of Appeal 3.3.08, 7 December 2004).

5   *Biogen v Medeva* [1997] RPC 1 (House of Lords) – see below at para 8.15, and **Chapter 5** in connection with priority at para 5.05, and insufficiency and claim scope at para 5.20.

6   *Chiron Corpn v Organon Teknika* [1994] FSR 202 (Patents Court); [1996] RPC 535 (Court of Appeal) – see also T-0188/97 *NANBV/Chiron* (Technical Board of Appeal 3.3.04, 8 February 2001) where the equivalent claims were to a large extent successfully challenged in the EPO on grounds other than inventive step, namely insufficiency.

Impact of Directive 98/44/EC

8.06   Articles 3 and 5 of the Directive address the 'product of nature' issue. Article 3 (and corresponding Recitals 20–21) explains how, in general terms, the principles in Article 52 EPC are to be applied in the case of 'biological material', which is itself, by Article 2.1(a) of the Directive a narrowly defined concept extending to cell lines and genes but not, for example, to proteins:

'3.1   For the purposes of this Directive, inventions which are new, which involve an inventive step, and which are susceptible of industrial application shall be patentable even if they concern a product consisting of or containing biological material or a process by means of which biological material is produced, processed or used.

3.2   Biological material which is isolated from its natural environment or produced by means of a technical process may be the subject of an invention even if it previously occurred in nature.

2.1(a) "Biological material" means any material containing genetic information and capable of reproducing itself or being reproduced in a biological system;'

These principles, which are effectively declaratory of what were the existing interpretations of EPC, Article 52 by the time the Directive came into effect, are further refined in relation to biological material found in the human body, by Article 5 of the Directive (and the corresponding Recitals 22–25):

'5.1   The human body, at the various stages of its formation and development, and the simple discovery of one of its elements, including the sequence or partial sequence of a gene, cannot constitute patentable inventions

5.2   An element isolated from the human body or otherwise produced by means of a technical process, including the sequence or partial sequence of a gene, may constitute a patentable invention, even if the structure of that element is identical to that of a natural element

5.3   The industrial application of a sequence or a partial sequence of a gene must be disclosed in the patent application.'

As with Article 3 of the Directive these principles can effectively be seen as no more than declaratory of existing European law. They address the novelty, 'mere discovery', and industrial applicability issues, but are silent on the question of inventive step. EPC, Article 57, defining industrial applicability, which by EPC, Article 52(1) is one of the requirements for patentability, and as to which Article 5.3 provides exemplification, has become increasingly important for biotechnology patents, as discussed below at para 8.07. Moreover, Article 5.3 has been used as basis in France and Germany for so implementing the Directive as to require that the industrial application of a gene sequence is included as a limiting feature of any claim to such sequence. Thus, claims in patents prosecuted nationally for gene sequences must be 'use bound' or 'purpose bound' (ie limited as to use or purpose) for inventions concerning material isolated from the human body (in France) and human or primate gene sequences (in Germany). In contrast, the EPO takes the same approach in claims to novel gene sequences as it would with claims to any novel chemical, and requires no such limitation. The same position also applies for patents prosecuted nationally in the UK. The European Commission has, in relation to the position in France and Germany, indicated that it 'does not at present intend to take a position on the validity of transposition according to the choice between classical and limited scope of protection for gene sequences' so these divergences will continue.[1]

1   See *Report from the Commission to the Council and the European Parliament – Development and implications of patent law in the field of biotechnology and genetic engineering*, 14 July 2005 – COM (2005) 312 final, SEC (2005) 943.

Industrial applicability

8.07   In biotechnology, the objection of lack of industrial applicability to much 'product of nature' patenting has become of greater importance in recent years in Europe, reflecting in part the increased importance in the USA of the corresponding objection there, that of lack of utility.[1] As observed in **Chapter 5** at para 5.02, a new chemical cannot be patented unless it has some use – say as a pharmaceutical, as a lubricant, or as an intermediate – even though such utility does not form part of the claim. The application of the principle in biotechnology can most clearly be seen in relation to the attempts made to patent gene sequences of unknown or speculative utility, namely gene fragments, or expressed sequence tags (ESTs) or variations in differing gene sequences as between individuals at single locations in their genomes, namely single nucleotide polymorphisms (SNPs). Such sequences can be contrasted with those in issue in the reported decision of the Opposition Division in *Relaxin/HOWARD FLOREY INSTITUTE*[2] where the utility of the gene sequence, as coding for a specific hormone, the function of which was known, was taught.

Whether the legal basis is lack of inventive step or insufficiency,[3] or lack of industrial applicability, it is generally accepted that, as with anything else, one cannot patent gene sequences of wholly unknown utility or variations in such sequences, the technical significance of which is not known. Thus, in T-870/04 *BDP1 Phosphatase/MAX-PLANCK*[4] a Technical Board of Appeal rejected an appeal against an Examining Division determination that an application relating to a brain derived phosphatase lacked industrial applicability, observing:

'5.   Biotechnological inventions are quite often concerned with substances found in nature (eg a protein, a DNA sequence, etc). In cases where the structure and function of the substance is elucidated and means are provided for extracting it or producing it in large amounts, industrial applicability exists in relation to the possibility to exploit the information and technical means disclosed in order to manufacture the substance and use it for some function related to its natural one or for some other previously unknown (now disclosed) function or as a starting material for making useful analogs or derivatives with some improved features. If a function is well known to be essential for human health, then the identification of the substance having this function will immediately suggest a practical application in the case of a disease or condition caused by a deficiency, as was the case, for example, for insulin, human growth hormone or erythropoietin. In such cases, an adequate description will ensure in accordance with the requirements of Article 57 EPC that *"the invention* can be made or used in industry" [*emphasis added*]

6.   In cases where a substance, naturally occurring in the human body, is identified, and possibly also structurally characterised and made available through some method, but either its function is not known or it is complex and incompletely understood, and no disease or condition has yet been identified as being attributable to an excess or deficiency of the substance, and no other practical use is suggested for the substance, then industrial applicability cannot be acknowledged. While the jurisprudence has tended to be generous to applicants, there must be a borderline between what can be accepted, and what can only be categorized as an interesting research result which per se does not yet allow a practical industrial application to be identified. Even

though research results may be a scientific achievement of considerable merit, they are not necessarily an invention which can be applied industrially.

7. In the present application, while the claimed BDP1 polypeptide is described as a substance found in the human body and as having unique properties, the question arises whether any disclosure or suggestion has been made as to how these properties of BDP1 might be exploited.'

The Technical Board of Appeal then went on to answer this question in the negative:

'21. In the board's judgment, although the present application describes a product (a polypeptide), means and methods for making it, and its prospective use thereof for basic science activities, it identifies no practical way of exploiting it in at least one field of industrial activity. In this respect, it is considered that a vague and speculative indication of possible objectives that might or might not be achievable by carrying out further research with the tool as described is not sufficient for fulfilment of the requirement of industrial applicability. The purpose of granting a patent is not to reserve an unexplored field of research for an applicant.'

It went on to explain why this particular objection succeeded in this case but had not done so in the earlier Case T-338/00 *Multimeric Receptors/SALK INSTITUTE*[5]:

'22. ... This suggested exploitation of the properties of what was claimed in that case [T-338/00] was applicable to a variety of expression systems, and so could be recognized as an industrial application for the purposes of Article 57 EPC. This contrasts with the present case where the only practicable use suggested is to use what is claimed to find out more about the natural functions of what is claimed itself. This is not in itself an industrial application, but rather research undertaken either for its own sake or with the mere hope that some useful application will be identified.'

In subsequent decisions in T-0604/04 *F4A receptors/GENENTECH*[6] and T-0895/05/*Hematopoietic cytokine receptor/ZYMOGENETICS*[7] two Technical Boards of Appeal found the respective inventions for gene sequences, and the polypeptides for which these coded to have industrial application. In the latter case, which concerned a receptor invention defined in terms of a gene sequence, and the polypeptide for which such gene sequence codes, the Technical Board of Appeal was prepared to accept industrial applicability for an invention based on computer-assisted sequence homology, and tissue distribution studies already on file because these formed a proper basis for a reasonably credible educated guess (that was confirmed by subsequent experimental evidence) as to a suggested role for the receptor that was not so vaguely defined as not to suggest any therapeutic or diagnostic use.

These EPO Technical Board of Appeal cases, together with a decision of the EPO Opposition Division that had also been reported in the

Official Journal, and was thus regarded as being of some authority[8] were reviewed, and applied in *Eli Lilly v Human Genome Sciences*[9] in which claims based on the identification of a gene sequence (some of which would read onto a monoclonal antibody to Neutrokine-α that was in development for the treatment of rheumatoid arthritis amongst other conditions) were held by the Supreme Court, reversing the lower courts, not to lack industrial application. The Supreme Court considered that the lower courts had incorrectly applied EPO case law by in effect requiring that a particular use for the product must actually have been demonstrated rather than that it had plausibly been shown to be 'useful'. In so finding, the Supreme Court agreed with an EPO Technical Board of Appeal[10] that had upheld the validity of the patent in the face of the same objections.

1   Historically, the lack of utility objection became much more important under US law because it was for a while extremely difficult to argue in the USA that a novel gene sequence was obvious, a consequence of the decisions of the Court of Appeal for the Federal Circuit in *In re Bell* 991 F.2d 781, 785 (Fed. Cir. 1993) and *In re Deuel*. 51 F.3d 1552, 1559 (Fed. Cir. 1995), and which remained the law until *In re Kubin* 561 F.3d 1351, 1352 (Fed. Cir. 2009). It was in the context of developing guidelines for the application of the lack of utility objection in the USA that the principle was formulated that the application must disclose a 'specific, substantial and credible utility', a concept that was then fed into European patent law, despite it lacking the same underlying driver for this that the USA used to have – see Thambisetty, Sivaramjani, *Legal Transplants in Patent Law: Why Utility is the New Industrial Applicability*, LSE Law, Society and Economy Working Papers, 6/2008. However, much more recently the US Supreme Court, in *Association for Molecular Pathology et al. v Myriad Genetics, Inc., et al.* 133 S. Ct. 2107, (2013) has held that a 'naturally occurring DNA segment is a product of nature and not patent eligible merely because it has been isolated, but cDNA is patent eligible because it is not naturally occurring'.
2   *Relaxin/HOWARD FLOREY INSTITUTE* [1995] OJ EPO 388.
3   See **Chapter 7** at para 7.20 and above at para 8.05 at fn 1 as to speculative assertions of therapeutic utility. Neither is utility that is merely described as 'use as a probe' likely to confer inventive step on a gene sequence the significance of which is unknown, as such utility is itself obvious. Similarly a gene sequence whose likely utility, as to the protein for which it is thought that it might code, is assigned by known computer programmes comparing its degree of similarity, or homology, with sequences of known function, is also likely to lack inventive step. See the *Mutual Understanding in Search and Examination: Nucleic Acid Molecule-related inventions whose functions are inferred based on sequence homology search*. Available at: http://www.trilateral.net/projects/biotechnology.html.
4   *BDP1 Phosphatase/MAX-PLANCK* [2006] EPOR 14.
5   T-338/00 *Multimeric Receptors/SALK INSTITUTE* (Board 3.3.08, 6 November 2002). Although the patent was held not to lack industrial applicability, the broadest claim was held to lack inventive step.
6   T-0604/04 *F4A receptors/GENENTECH* (Board 3.3.08, 16 March 2006). Although the attack on the opposed patent of lack of industrial applicability was rejected in this case, one as to insufficiency of claims to antibodies to the disclosed proteins was upheld, as discussed below at para 8.14.
7   T-0895/05 *Hematopoietic cytokine receptor/ZYMOGENETICS* [2007] EPOR 2. Inventive step and sufficiency were not under consideration in this decision.
8   *ICOS Corporation* [2002] OJ EPO 293.

9   *Eli Lilly v Human Genome Sciences* [2008] EWHC 1903 (Patents Court); [2010] EWCA 33 (Court of Appeal); [2011] UKSC 51 (Supreme Court).
10 T-18/09 *Neutrokine/HUMAN GENOME SCIENCES* (Technical Board of Appeal 3.3.08, 21 October 2009).

The 'variety' issue

Introduction

8.08   EPC, Article 53(b) prevents patents being granted for: 'plant or animal varieties or essentially biological processes for the production of plants or animals; this provision shall not apply to microbiological processes or the products thereof'.

This provision has no equivalent in US patent law[1] but is permitted under Article 27(3)(b) of the TRIPS Agreement, and was originally intended to exclude the results of conventional plant breeding activities, on the basis that they can also be protected by another IPR: the plant variety right. However, the exclusion goes wider than is necessary to achieve the mere avoidance of overlap, by excluding conventionally developed animal breeds.

There is no particular logic behind the proviso to this exclusion that brings microbiological processes, and their products back into patentability under EPC, Article 53(b) except the fact that for many years previously they had been patentable, as micro-organisms were the main source of antibiotics. The term 'microbiological processes' is construed widely, so as to include not only traditional processes using micro-organisms but also techniques of genetic engineering. However, the reference to 'microbiological processes' is not taken to override the earlier part of Article 53(b) so as to render the products of such processes patentable if they are plant or animal varieties.

1   In *JEM AG Supply v Pioneer Hi-Bred International, Inc* 534 US 124 (2001) the US Supreme Court held that despite Congress having passed other statutes – namely the Plant Patent Act 1930, and the Plant Variety Protection Act 1970 providing protection for plants, plants could still be the subject of ordinary (utility) patents.

Development of the law in the EPO

8.09   At first sight, EPC, Article 53(b) would appear to exclude from patentability genetically altered crops or transgenic animals. However, in T-49/83 *Propagating Material/CIBA GEIGY*[1] it was held that no 'general exclusion of inventions in the sphere of animate nature could be inferred from the EPC'. The case related to an invention consisting of the treatment of propagating material in order to make it resistant to certain herbicides. The decision in T-320/87 *Hybrid plants/LUBRIZOL*[2] manifested a similarly sympathetic approach to patentability, and addressed both the question of what constitutes an 'essentially biological' process and what is a 'plant variety', issues which have also been addressed, sometimes separately, in several subsequent cases. The patent related to the genetic modification of plant cells by means of T-plasmids, and had claims to certain DNA, vectors and methods for genetically modifying plant cells, together with modified cells, and whole plants produced from these.

The Technical Board of Appeal held that the question of whether or not a non-microbiological process could be considered to be 'essentially biological' had to be judged 'on the basis of the essence of the invention taking into account the totality of human intervention and its impact on the result achieved', holding that the 'claimed processes for the preparation of hybrid plants represent an essential modification of known biological and classical breeders processes, and the efficiency and high yield associated with the product ... show important technological character', and so be patented. The Enlarged Board of Appeal of the EPO has considered what is meant by an 'essentially biological process' in the context of plant breeding in a number of recent cases, the first pair of which was G2/07 and G1/08:[3]

'1.   A non-microbiological process for the production of plants which contains or consists of the steps of sexually crossing the whole genomes of plants and of subsequently selecting plants is in principle excluded from patentability as being "essentially biological" within the meaning of Article 53(b) EPC.

2.   Such a process does not escape the exclusion of Article 53(b) EPC merely because it contains, as a further step or as part of any of the steps of crossing and selection, a step of a technical nature which serves to enable or assist the performance of the steps of sexually crossing the whole genomes of plants or of subsequently selecting plants.

3.   If, however, such a process contains within the steps of sexually crossing and selecting an additional step of a technical nature, which step by itself introduces a trait into the genome or modifies a trait in the genome of the plant produced, so that the introduction or modification of that trait is not the result of the mixing of the genes of the plants chosen for sexual crossing, then the process is not excluded from patentability under Article 53(b) EPC.

4.   In the context of examining whether such a process is excluded from patentability as being "essentially biological" within the meaning of Article 53(b) EPC, it is not relevant whether a step of a technical nature is a new or known measure, whether it is trivial or a fundamental alteration of a known process, whether it does or could occur in nature or whether the essence of the invention lies in it.'

Whereas the decision in these cases concerned the status of the exclusion for an 'essentially biological process' in the context of process claims, the second pair of cases: G-2/12 *Tomatoes II* and G3/12 *Broccoli II*[4] in which similar but slightly differently worded decisions were given, concerned the exclusion in the context of claims to the products of such processes. Thus in G-2/12 *Tomatoes II* the Board held:

'1. The exclusion of essentially biological processes for the production of plants in Article 53(b) EPC does not have a negative effect on the allowability of a product claim directed to plants or plant material such as a fruit.

2. In particular, the fact that the only method available at the filing date for generating the claimed subject-matter is an essentially biological process for the production of plants disclosed in the patent application does not render a claim directed to plants or plant material other than a plant variety unallowable.

3. In the circumstances, it is of no relevance that the protection conferred by the product claim encompasses the generation of the claimed product by means of an essentially biological process for the production of plants excluded as such under Article 53(b) EPC.'

And in G-3/12 *Broccoli II:* the Board held:

'1. The exclusion of essentially biological processes for the production of plants in Article 53(b) EPC does not have a negative effect on the allowability of a product claim directed to plants or plant material such as plant parts.

2.(a) The fact that the process features of a product-by-process claim directed to plants or plant material other than a plant variety define an essentially biological process for the production of plants does not render the claim unallowable.

2.(b) The fact that the only method available at the filing date for generating the claimed subject-matter is an essentially biological process for the production of plants disclosed in the patent application does not render a claim directed to plants or plant material other than a plant variety unallowable.

3. In the circumstances, it is of no relevance that the protection conferred by the product claim encompasses the generation of the claimed product by means of an essentially biological process for the production of plants excluded as such under Article 53(b) EPC.'

Thus, the exclusion, as to product claims, only affects the patentability of claims to products that are expressed as plant or animal varieties.

As to what constitutes a plant variety, the Technical Board of Appeal in T-320/87 *Hybrid plants/LUBRIZOL* followed the approach in T-49/83 *Propagating Material/CIBA GEIGY* and held that 'homogeneity' and 'stability' (both of which are required for protection by means of a plant variety right) were essential elements of this. Here the hybrid seed 'lacked stability in some trait of the whole generation population', and so did not constitute a plant variety excluded from patentability. Thus, both the process claims (to a particular process for rapidly developing hybrids and producing hybrid seeds) and product claims (to hybrid seed that yields plants that are phenotypically uniform, said seed having been produced by a certain process) were allowed.

The effect of these decisions as to what constitutes a plant variety was to place a narrow construction on the exception under EPC, Article 53(b) as applied to plants. This was followed in T-19/90 *Oncomouse/HARVARD*[5] in relation to animals (mice with a genetic predisposition to cancer, useful for research into the disease) where the subject of the main claims was not a single variety, but rather an entire species. In 1995 however, the decision in T-356/93 *Glutamine synthesase inhibitors/PLANT GENETIC SYSTEMS*[6] cast doubt on this approach by rejecting claims to plants on the basis that such claims embraced plant varieties. Five years later, during which time the continued prosecution of European patent applications with claims to plants and animals had been suspended, this decision was held to have been wrong, and the law was put back on its previous track by the decision of the EPO Enlarged Board of Appeal in G-1/98 *Transgenic plant/NOVARTIS II*.[7]

In T-19/90 *Oncomouse/HARVARD* claims to a method for producing a transgenic mouse, and the transgenic mouse itself were initially refused, it being held that the exception from patentability in the case of animals was not aimed at avoiding (as in the case of plants) overlap with other IPRs, but rather for the reason that animal varieties were not an appropriate subject matter for patent protection. The relevant claims in issue read at the time:

'1.   A method for producing a transgenic non-human mammalian animal having an increased probability of developing neoplasms, said method comprising introducing an activated oncogene sequence into a non-human mammalian animal at a stage no later than the 8-cell stage.

...

17.   A transgenic non-human mammalian animal whose germ cells and somatic cells contain an activated oncogene sequence introduced into said animal or an ancestor of said animal, at a stage no later than the 8-cell stage, said oncogene optionally being further defined accordingly to any one of claims 3 to 10.

18.   An animal as claimed in claim 17 which is a rodent.'

On appeal, a Technical Board of Appeal held that the insertion of the oncogene did not occur by an 'essentially biological process', and that the exception from patentability under EPC, Article 53(b) for animal varieties had to be construed narrowly in relation to animals, just as with plants, and that it applied only to animal varieties, and not animals generally. Accordingly, it remitted the case to the Examining Division to consider whether under EPC, Article 53(b) the 'oncomouse' was an 'animal variety', and thereby excepted from patentability and to review the position under EPC, Article 53(a) from a public policy point of view, given the suffering that was inevitable on the part of an animal, as in this case, which had been genetically predisposed to develop cancer, and the risk in other cases of genetically engineered animals being introduced into the environment.[8] Opposition proceedings were suspended pending the passage of Directive 98/44/EC, after which a Technical Board of Appeal in T-0315/03 *Transgenic animals/HARVARD*[9] upheld the patent but restricted the scope of its claims to mice:

'1. A method for producing a transgenic mouse having an increased probability of developing neoplasms, said method comprising chromosomally incorporating an activated oncogene sequence into the genome of a mouse.

...

19. A transgenic mouse whose germ cells and somatic cells contain an activated oncogene sequence as a result of chromosomal incorporation into the animal genome, or into the genome of an ancestor of said animal, said oncogene optionally being further defined according to any one of claims 3 to 10.'

The equivalent US patent (US 4736866) to that the subject of the controversy in the EPO was granted in 1988, before even the first instance EPO decision. Its broadest granted claim corresponded in scope to claim 17 of the EP application in relating to 'a transgenic non-human mammalian animal'.

The exception from patentability for 'essentially biological processes' had also initially been thought to make it difficult to secure claims of adequate scope as discussed in T-19/90 *Oncomouse/HARVARD* in relation to the product claims to a genetically altered mouse into which (or into whose ancestor) the gene had been introduced. It was initially held that a claim was not allowable to the extent that it covered a descendant of a genetically altered animal as such an animal would be derived from its ancestor by the 'essentially biological processes' of sexual reproduction. Some suggested that this did not matter as this did not of itself prevent such a descendant infringing a claim to the genetically-altered ancestor. On appeal, however, this aspect of the decision was reversed, a claim to the descendants of the animal into which the gene had been introduced being regarded as a 'product by process' claim that defined the product, irrespective of the process used for so doing.

1   T-49/83 *Propagating Material/CIBA GEIGY* [1984] OJ EP0 112; EPOR Vol. C 758.
2   T-320/87 *Hybrid plants/LUBRIZOL* [1990] OJ EPO 71; [1990] 3 EPOR 173.
3   G-2/07 *Essentially Biological Processes* and G-1/08 *Essentially Biological Processes* (Enlarged Board of Appeal, 9 December 2010).
4   G-2/12 *Tomatoes II* and G3/12 *Broccoli II* (Enlarged Board Appeal, 25 March 2015).
5   T-19/90 *Oncomouse/HARVARD* [1989] OJ EPO 451; [1990] OJ EPO 476; [1990] 1 EPOR 4; [1990] EPOR 501.
6   T-356/93 *Glutamine synthesase inhibitors/PLANT GENETIC SYSTEMS* [1995] EPOR 357.
7   G-1/98 *Transgenic plant/NOVARTIS II* [2000] EPOR 303. See below at para 8.10 for the principles that this set out.

The 'variety' issue   8.10

8   Discussed below at paras 8.11–8.12.
9   T-0315/03 *Transgenic animals/HARVARD* [2005] OJ EPO 246; [2006] OJ EPO 15.

Impact of Directive 98/44/EC

8.10   Even before the decision of the Enlarged Board of Appeal in
G-1/98 *Transgenic plant/NOVARTIS II* discussed above in para 8.09,
Directive 98/44/EC mandated a position contrary to that in T-356/93
Glutamine synthesase inhibitors/PLANT GENETIC SYSTEMS.
Uncontroversially, Articles 2 and 4 of the Directive (and corresponding
Recitals 29–33) provide:

'2.2   A process for the production of plants or animals is essentially biological
if it consists entirely of natural phenomena such as crossing or selection.'

4.1   The following shall not be patentable:

(a)   plant and animal varieties;
(b)   essentially biological procedures for the breeding of plants or animals.'

Apart from the useful definition in Article 2.2, this does little more
than rearrange the words of EPC, Article 53(b). However, Article 4 of
the Directive continued, in contrast to the now discredited decision in
T-356/93 *Glutamine synthesase inhibitors/PLANT GENETIC SYSTEMS*:
'4.2 Inventions which concern plants or animals shall be patentable if
the technical feasibility of the invention is not confined to a particular
plant or animal variety'.
Article 2(3) of the Directive defined 'plant variety' by reference to
Article 5 of the Community Plant Variety Rights Regulation[1] that states:
'5.2 ... "variety" shall be taken to mean a plant grouping within a single
botanical taxon of the lowest known rank ...'.
A position consistent with Article 4 of the Directive was subsequently
taken by the Enlarged Board of Appeal in G-1/98 *Transgenic plant/
NOVARTIS II*:

'(1)   A claim wherein specific plant varieties are not individually claimed is
not excluded from patentability under Article 53(b) EPC, even though
it may embrace plant varieties.
(2)   When a claim to a process for the production of a plant variety is
examined, Article 64(2) EPC, is not to be taken into consideration.
(3)   The exception to patentability applies to plant varieties irrespective
of the way in which they were produced. Therefore, plant varieties
containing genes introduced into an ancestral plant by recombinant
gene technology are themselves excluded from patentability.'

In G-1/98 *Transgenic plant/NOVARTIS II* the Enlarged Board of
Appeal noted that 'in the absence of the identification of specific
varieties in the product claims, the subject matter of the claimed
invention is neither limited nor even directed to a variety or varieties',
and that 'the exclusion in Article 53(b) EPC was made to serve the

purpose of excluding from patentability subject matter which is eligible for protection under the plant breeders' rights system'. By EPC, Article 64(2) the protection conferred by a patent on a process extends to the products directly obtained by that process.[2] Thus, the second finding confirms that, despite this, Article 53(b) has no relevance to process claims, where these are not to an essentially biological process. As to these, as noted above in para 8.09, the most recent clarification as what is meant by an 'essentially biological process' has been that provided by the Enlarged Board of Appeal of the EPO in G-2/07 *Essentially Biological Processes* and G-1/08 *Essentially Biological Processes*[3] and in G-2/12 *Tomatoes II* and G-3/12 *Broccoli II*.[4]

1   Council Regulation (EC) No. 2100/94 of 27 July 1994 on Community plant variety rights.
2   See **Chapter 6** at para 6.02.
3   G-2/07 and 1/08 (Enlarged Board of Appeal, 9 December 2010).
4   G-2/12 *Tomatoes II* and G3/12 *Broccoli II* (Enlarged Board Appeal 25 March 2015).

Public policy issues

Introduction

8.11   EPC, Article 53(a) prevents the grant of patents for: 'inventions the commercial exploitation of which would be contrary to "ordre public" or morality; exploitation shall not be deemed to be so contrary merely because it is prohibited by law or regulation in some or all of the Contracting States'.

To show how standards of 'morality' change, a similar principle was implied by common law in the UK, and was once the basis for rejecting patents for contraceptives. But times change, and Article 53(a) has been pressed into service by various pressure groups as a basis for attacking biotechnology itself. It is not the basis for one single attack. Instead, the arguments advanced in support of such an attack are many and varied, such as:

— in relation to the human body, it confers rights of 'ownership' over the body;
— in relation to transgenic animals, it might involve cruelty to such animals; and
— it risks damaging the environment.

The latter two objections concern less the principle of patenting than the underlying research the results of which it is sought to patent. Indeed, they each relate to areas where such underlying work is already to a large extent the subject of regulation. But each of these objections is based on a fundamental misconception as to what patents are about. Thus, in relation to each of these three objections it should be emphasized that the owner of a patent is not thereby granted a positive right to do something – instead a patent provides a limited right, for 20 years to stop others doing certain things commercially, and other than for experimental purposes relating to the subject matter of the patented invention. To prevent, as such critics seek, the grant of a patent because one disagrees with the underlying work it protects is not to deal with the root of the problem that such critics have with biotechnology. Why therefore should such considerations have any place in patent law, as opposed to regulatory law? Surely, patent offices are not the correct forum in which to discuss such matters? Moreover, when such critics advance their objections, who is there to speak for, and to represent the wider public interest that exists in many cases – that of the patients, and especially those with genetically-based diseases? However, in cases such as T-19/90 *Oncomouse/HARVARD*[1] the EPO Technical Boards of Appeal were forced to consider the question, and established guidelines that involve weighing possible suffering of animals, and risks to the Environment on the one hand against the invention's usefulness to mankind on the other. Here, such objections failed, as they also did before the Opposition Division in *Relaxin/HOWARD FLOREY INSTITUTE*[2] and before a Technical Board of Appeal in T-356/93 *Glutamine synthesase inhibitors/PLANT GENETIC SYSTEMS*.[3] In the latter case, the objections were mainly of an environmental nature. In the former the objection was a generalized one as to 'the alleged intrinsic immorality of patenting human genes', as to which the Opposition Division observed:

> 'It cannot be overemphasised that patents covering DNA encoding human H2 relaxin, or any other human gene, do not confer on their proprietors any rights whatever to individual human beings .... No woman is affected in any way by the present patent – she is free to live her life as she wishes and has exactly the same rights to self determination as she had before the patent was granted.'

Another more recent attempt to suggest that EPC, Article 53(a) should be used to address the 'socio-economic consequences of the patenting of the claimed subject matter', here in the context of genetic testing for increased risk of breast cancer, failed in T-1213/05 *Breast & Ovarian Cancer/UNIVERSITY OF UTAH*.[4]

It is ironic that the procedures of the patent system have in this way provided an accessible, and low cost mechanism by which such public policy issues, that should be the preserve of legislatures, together with objections to the underlying practices associated with biotechnology, have been ventilated. Indeed, the patent system has had the misfortune to provide, by proxy, one of the few accessible, and public forums in which such objections can readily be advanced.

1   T-19/90 *Oncomouse/HARVARD* [1989] OJ EPO 451; [1990] OJ EPO 476; [1990] 1
     EPOR 4; [1990] EPOR 501.
2   *Relaxin/HOWARD FLOREY INSTITUTE* [1995] OJEPO 388.

3   T-356/93 *Glutamine synthesase inhibitors/PLANT GENETIC SYSTEMS* [1995] EPOR 357.
4   T-1213/05 *Breast & Ovarian Cancer/UNIVERSITY OF UTAH* (Technical Board of Appeal 3.3.04, 23 September 2007) at paras [47]–[51].

Impact of Directive 98/44/EC

8.12   Many had hoped that Directive 98/44/EC, by giving specific examples of activities regarded as contrary to EPC, Article 53(a) would take the controversies consequential on objections to the use of biotechnology out of the EPO. Article 6.1 of the Directive (to which Recitals 36–39, and 43–44 correspond) starts by restating Article 53(a) with the omission of the 'publication' wording which it had before EPC 2000, and was deleted as being inconsistent with TRIPS:

'6.1   Inventions shall be considered unpatentable where their commercial exploitation would be contrary to ordre public or morality; however, exploitation shall not be deemed to be so contrary merely because it is prohibited by law or regulation.'

Article 6.2 of the Directive (to which Recitals 40–42 and 45 correspond) goes on to provide a non-exhaustive list of examples of uses and processes that are unpatentable on this public policy or morality grounds. The non-exhaustive nature of the list is also emphasised by Recital 38, which also gives as an example of a process: 'the use of which offends against human dignity ... processes to produce chimeras from germ cells or totipotent cells of humans and animals', which process is not one of those specifically listed in Article 6.2:

'6.2   On the basis of paragraph 1, the following, in particular, shall be considered unpatentable:
(a)   processes for cloning human beings;
(b)   processes for modifying the germ line genetic identity of human beings;
(c)   use of human embryos for industrial or commercial purposes;
(d)   processes for modifying the genetic identity of animals which are likely to cause them suffering without any substantial medical benefit to man or animal, and also animals resulting from such processes;'

The expression 'cloning human beings' in (a) (Recitals 40–41) replaced the term 'human reproductive cloning' in an earlier draft, which latter term is generally taken to mean the production of genetically identical human beings[1] but can be distinguished, for example, from what the Human Genetics Advisory Commission (HGAC) in the UK called 'therapeutic cloning', and which term the HGAC used to describe 'other applications of nuclear replacement technology, which do not involve the creation of genetically identical individuals'.[2] Presumably, the wording in the final version of the Directive is meant more clearly to make this differentiation. By (b) (Recital 40) somatic gene therapy is (at least from this point of view[3]) regarded as patentable. Paragraph (c) (Recital 42) replaced that in an earlier draft which excluded 'methods in which human embryos are used'.

Paragraph (d) (Recital 45) would at first sight seem to be declaratory of the law as established by an EPO Technical Board of Appeal in T-19/90 *Oncomouse/HARVARD*[4] in which a mouse with a genetic predisposition to cancer, but which was useful as a research tool in cancer research, was held to be patentable under EPC, Article 53(a). In *Modified animal/LELAND STANFORD*[5], one of the first EPO decisions applying the Directive, an Opposition Division considered this, and other issues and upheld a patent to a modified animal, exemplified by an immuno-compromised mouse implanted with human hemotopoietic tissue (an animal-human chimera) which provided the only available animal model for HIV-I infection, and also the promise of providing human cells and organs for transplant in the future. Subsequently, in T-0315/03 *Method for producing transgenic animals/HARVARD*[6] a Technical Board of Appeal held that even if an invention complied with the EPC Rule corresponding to Article 6.2(d) of the Directive it had still to comply with EPC, Article 53(a), that in applying the EPC Rule in issue it was necessary to consider only three matters: (i) animal suffering; (ii) medical benefit; and (iii) the necessary correspondence between the two in terms of the animals in question, but that in subsequently applying EPC, Article 53(a) in animal manipulation cases the approach adopted in T-19/90 *Oncomouse/HARVARD* remained appropriate, which differed from that under the EPC Rule corresponding to Article 6.2(d) of the Directive in several respects, most importantly by allowing matters other than animal suffering, and medical benefit to be taken into account.

In recent years, the public policy controversy has shifted to stem cells, and both of the Commission Reports[7] discussed the issue, which Article 6.2 of the Directive does not directly address except insofar as products derived from human embryonic stem cells may be regarded as unpatentable by virtue of Article 6.2(c). Separately, the European Group of Ethics[8] concluded that there was no ethical reason for a complete ban on the patenting of inventions relating to stem cells or stem cell lines.

The second Commission Report took the view that totipotent stem cells, having the potential to develop into an entire human body, should not be patentable, but for pluripotent embryonic stem cells, that arise from the further division of totipotent cells, and lack such potential, noted that the situation was more complex, given the 'clear divergences which currently exist between Member States as regards the acceptability of research relating to embryonic stem cells', and considered it premature for the Commission to give further definition, or provide for further harmonization. Such understandable restraint in the face of different ethical positions in different Member States was not, however, an option for the EPO, the Enlarged Board of Appeal of which had to deal with a reference to it by a Technical Board of Appeal on the subject of stem cells. In G2/06 *Use of embryos/WARF*[9] it held that those provisions of the EPC Implementing Regulations that had been amended to conform to Directive 98/44/EC forbad: 'the patenting of claims directed to products which – as described in the application – at the filing date could be prepared exclusively by a method which necessarily involved the destruction of the human embryos from which the said products are derived, even if the said method is not part of the claims'. In the light of this, the UKIPO revised its earlier practice note on the subject to issue one[10] which, as to human embryonic pluripotent stem cells, observed (footnotes omitted):

> 'Although there is some opposition in the United Kingdom to research involving embryonic stem cells, a number of reports from influential UK political, medical and scientific bodies in recent years have emphasised the enormous potential of stem cell research, including embryonic stem cell research, to deliver new treatments for a wide range of serious diseases. This indicates that on balance the commercial exploitation of inventions concerning human embryonic pluripotent stem cells would not be contrary to public policy or morality in the United Kingdom. Thus, the IPO is ready to grant patents for inventions involving such cells provided they satisfy the normal requirements for patentability and provided that, at the filing or priority date, the invention could be obtained by means other than the destruction of human embryos.'

This was not, however, the last word on such matters, as the UK does not have a free hand in them, especially where, as here, these are also matters of EU competence, and as a result the IPO has had to revise its policy further. Thus the controversy over human embryonic stem cells and patents has taken on an EU dimension and so, in Case C-34/10 *Brüstle v Greenpeace eV*[11] the Court of Justice held that an invention cannot be patentable where the technical teaching of the patent necessitates the prior destruction of human embryos or their use as base material, even if the description of that teaching does not contain any reference to the use of human embryo:

> '1.   Article 6(2)(c) of Directive 98/44/EC ... must be interpreted as meaning that:
>   – any human ovum after fertilisation, any non-fertilised human ovum into which the cell nucleus from a mature human cell has been transplanted, and any non-fertilised human ovum whose division and further development have been stimulated by parthenogenesis constitute a 'human embryo';
>   – it is for the referring court to ascertain, in the light of scientific developments, whether a stem cell obtained from a human embryo at the blastocyst stage constitutes a 'human embryo' within the meaning of Article 6(2)(c) of Directive 98/44.
> 2.   The exclusion from patentability concerning the use of human embryos for industrial or commercial purposes set out in Article 6(2)(c) of Directive 98/44 also covers the use of human embryos for purposes

of scientific research, only use for therapeutic or diagnostic purposes which are applied to the human embryo and are useful to it being patentable.

3.   Article 6(2)(c) of Directive 98/44 excludes an invention from patentability where the technical teaching which is the subject-matter of the patent application requires the prior destruction of human embryos or their use as base material, whatever the stage at which that takes place and even if the description of the technical teaching claimed does not refer to the use of human embryos.'

This decision was widely criticized[12] but one specific criticism was that it was scientifically inaccurate insofar as there were certain types of non-fertilised human ovum whose division, and further development have been stimulated by parthenogenesis that were incapable of developing into a human being, and so ought not be defined as a 'human embryo', which criticism the Court of Justice was able to address in Case C-364/13 *International Stem Cell Corporation v Comptroller General of Patents, Designs and Trade Marks*[13] in which it held:

'Article 6(2)(c) of Directive 98/44/EC ... must be interpreted as meaning that an unfertilised human ovum whose division and further development have been stimulated by parthenogenesis does not constitute a 'human embryo', within the meaning of that provision, if, in the light of current scientific knowledge, it does not, in itself, have the inherent capacity of developing into a human being, this being a matter for the national court to determine.'

Decisions of the Court of Justice are not binding on the EPO, or its Boards of Appeal but the latter consider them to be persuasive, and a Technical Board of Appeal considered its decision in Case T 2221/10 *Culturing stem cells/TECHNION*[14] to be in line with that in Case C-34/10 *Brüstle* when it concluded, as noted in the headnote, that:

'Inventions which make use of publicly available human embryonic stem cell lines which were initially derived by a process resulting in the destruction of the human embryos are excluded from patentability under the provisions of Article 53(a) EPC in combination with Rule 28(c) EPC'

It was irrelevant that the destruction of human embryos might have taken place at a stage long before the implementation of the invention, as in the case of the production of embryonic stem cells from a lineage of stem cells the mere production of which implied the destruction of human embryos. Meanwhile, the German national patent that had been the subject of the reference to the Court of Justice in Case C-34/10 *Brüstle* was, in the light of the Court of Justice decision, maintained in amended form which referred only to methods of obtaining human embryonic stem cells that do not require the destruction of embryos.[15]

The degree to which these various decisions ought adversely affect the patent incentive to conduct research in this area now or in the future[16] should however be limited as these decisions have no application to other forms of stem cell, such as induced pluripotent stem cells, or, it would appear, those human embryonic stem cells, the production of which does not necessitate the prior destruction of human embryos as so defined, wherein lies the importance of the clarification provided by the Court of Justice in Case C-364/13 *International Stem Cell Corporation.*

1   Banned in the UK under the Human Fertilisation and Embryology Act 1990 as most recently amended by the Human Fertilisation and Embryology Act 2008.
2   See the HGAC covering letter of 29 January 1998 to the HGAC and Human Fertilisation and Embryology Authority Consultation Document: 'Cloning Issues in Reproduction, Science and Medicine', January 1998.
3   Thus claims to gene therapy as such would not be patentable in Europe as methods of medical treatment, although this would not prevent materials for use in gene therapy, such as vectors, being patented.
4   T-19/90 *Oncomouse/HARVARD* [1989] OJ EPO 451; [1990] OJ EPO 476; [1990] 1 EPOR 4; [1990] EPOR 501.
5   *Modified animal/LELAND STANFORD* [2002] EPOR at p. 16.
6   T-0315/03 *Method for producing transgenic animals/HARVARD* (Technical Board of Appeal, 3 March 2008).
7   Report from the Commission to the Council and the European Parliament – Development and implications of patent law in the field of biotechnology and genetic engineering – COM (2002) 545 final, 07 October 2002, and COM (2005) 312 final, SEC (2005) 943, 14 July 2005.
8   *Opinion on ethical aspects of patenting inventions involving human stem cells* – The European Group of Ethics in Science and New Technologies to the European Commission (Opinion No 16 of 7 May 2002).
9   G2/06 *Use of embryos/WARF* [2009], OJEPO, pp. 306–32. See T-522/04 *Stem Cells/CALIFORNIA* [2009] EPOR 450A applying this, and finding that a disclaimer 'not derived from or by destruction of an embryo' did not save a claim that was otherwise invalid for this reason as this constituted an addition of matter. See also Sterckx, Sigrid & Cockbain, Julian, *Assessing the Morality of the Commercial Exploitation of Inventions Concerning Uses of Human Embryos and the Relevance of Moral Complicity: Comments on the EPO's WARF Decision* (2010) 7:1 *SCRIPTed*, 83–103.
10 *IPO Practice Notice*, 3 February 2009 – '*Inventions involving human embryonic stem cells*'. This *Notice* was updated by subsequent *Notices* on 17 May 2012 and 27 June 2014, and has now been superseded by a new *Notice* dated 25 March 2015.
11 Case C-34/10 *Brüstle v Greenpeace eV* (Court of Justice, 18 October 2011).
12 See Plomer, Aurora, *After Brüstle: EU accession to the ECHR and the future of European patent law* – Queen Mary Journal of Intellectual Property, Vol 2 No 2, 110–35, suggesting 'that the CJEU ruling represents a disproportionate interference with the autonomy of Member States and is inconsistent with the degree of autonomy vested in Member States by the European Convention [on Human Rights] legal order'.
13 Case C-364/13 *International Stem Cell Corporation v Comptroller General of Patents, Designs and Trade Marks* (Court of Justice 18 December 2014). For a commentary on this see Plomer, Aurora, Case C-364/13 *Patentability of embryonic stem cells and parthenotes: Inherently Uncertain?* At: http://eutopialaw.com/2014/12/19/case-c-36413-patentability-of-embryonicstem-cells-and-parthenotes-inherently-uncertain/ – observing that the judgment refrains from providing a more extensive legal definition of the 'commencement' test as contemplated in the Advocate General's opinion, and considers that the issues at stake are essentially questions of fact which national courts should answer by reference to the state of scientific knowledge at the time, but potentially opens new areas of uncertainty by arguably introducing a new test relating to the 'inherent capacities' of an organism for which there is no legal definition in Directive 98/44/EC or in the national laws of Member States.

14 Case T 2221/10 *Culturing stem cells/TECHNION* (Board 3.3.08, 4 February 2014).
15 Case X ZR 58/07 (German Federal Supreme Court, 27 November 2012). An *EPO Opposition Division* subsequently, on 11 April 2013, revoked EP 1040185 B1, the European patent corresponding to the German national patent the subject of the reference to the Court of Justice in Case C-34/10 *Brüstle,* but on the ground of added matter.
16 In contrast to research undertaken in the past and that had been conducted on human embryonic stem cell lines derived from tissue which did have the inherent capacity of developing into a human being.

Prior informed consent and disclosure of origin

8.13 Recital 26 to Directive 98/44/EC observes that where a patent application is filed for an invention that is based on biological material of human origin or which uses such material, the person from whose body such material was taken must have had an opportunity of expressing free and informed consent to this, in accordance with national law. The Directive, however, makes no provision for any consequences for the patent if that obligation is not complied with. An attempt to oppose a granted patent under EPC, Article 53(a) based on a failure to demonstrate such consent failed in T-1213/05 *Breast & Ovarian Cancer/ UNIVERSITY OF UTAH.*[1]

Recital 27 to Directive 98/44/EC observes that where a patent application is filed for an invention that is based on biological material of plant or animal origin or which uses such material, the patent application, where appropriate, should include information on the geographical origin of such material, if known. However, it also states that 'this is without prejudice to the processing of patent applications or the validity of rights arising from granted patents'. Although not expressly so stated, this recital reflects discussions as to mandating the disclosure of the origin of genetic resources in patent applications, and which took place in the context of the Convention on Biological Diversity of 5 June 1992, which Convention is referred to in Recitals 55–56 to the Directive, and which discussions have continued.[2]

The obligations under the Convention were somewhat vaguely expressed, but it has now been supplemented by the Nagoya Protocol on Access to Genetic Resources, and the Fair and Equitable Sharing of Benefits Arising from their Utilization to the Convention on Biological Diversity ('the Nagoya Protocol') of 29 October 2010, and this is now the subject of Regulation (EU) No 511/2014 of 16 April 2014 on compliance measures for users from the Nagoya Protocol on Access to Genetic Resources, and the Fair and Equitable Sharing of Benefits Arising from their Utilization in the Union[3] and which, as Recital (2) to the Regulation observes: 'further elaborates upon the general rules of the Convention on access to genetic resources and sharing of monetary and non-monetary benefits arising from the utilisation of genetic resources and traditional knowledge associated with genetic resources ('access and benefit-sharing').' The Regulation sets out a number of specific obligations on the part of those who 'utilise' 'genetic resources', and 'traditional knowledge associated with genetic resources' where 'genetic resources' are defined as 'genetic material of actual or potential value', and 'genetic material' is defined as 'any material of plant, animal, microbial or other origin containing functional units of heredity'. Although none of these obligations are expressed to have any impact on patent prosecution or validity, the 'utilisation of genetic resources', which is defined as 'to conduct research and development on the genetic and/or biochemical composition of genetic resources, including through the application of biotechnology as defined in Article 2 of the Convention' could certainly be evidenced by a disclosure made in a patent application. Moreover, the proposal to impose a disclosure of source obligation in patent applications has not been forgotten, and indeed the European Parliament had sought, ultimately unsuccessfully, to include such an obligation in the text of the Regulation in the course of its legislative passage.[4]

1   T-1213/05 *Breast & Ovarian Cancer/UNIVERSITY OF UTAH* (Technical Board of Appeal 3.3.04, 23 September 2007) at paras [47]–[51]. See Odell-West, Amanda, *The Absence of Informed Consent to Commercial Exploitation for Inventions Derived from Human Biological Material: A Bar to Patentability?* [2009] IPQ, 373–90.

2   See for example: *Disclosure of origin and prior informed consent for applications of intellectual property rights based on genetic resources: a technical study of implementation issues*, (Final Report July 2003 UNEP/CBD/WG-ABS/2/INF/2). For a comparative review of the laws of different laws as to the degree to which disclosure of origin is required in patent applications, and the sanctions for failure so to do see: *Technical Study on Disclosure Requirements in Patent Systems related to Genetic Resources and Traditional Knowledge* – WIPO, 2004.

3   Regulation (EU) No 511/2014 of 16 April 2014 on compliance measures for users from the Nagoya Protocol on Access to Genetic Resources and the Fair and Equitable Sharing of Benefits Arising from their Utilization in the Union, OJ L 150, 20 May 2014, 59–71.

4   See Comments on the Proposal for a Regulation of the European Parliament and of the Council on Access to Genetic Resources and the Fair and Equitable Sharing of Benefits from their Utilization in the Union (as amended by the European Parliament) – International Chamber of Commerce (Document No 450/1082, 29 October 2013).

Adequacy of description and deposit requirements

EPO case law on sufficiency and claim scope

8.14   As explained in **Chapter 5** at para 5.18ff, and in **Chapter 7** in relation to chemical and pharmaceutical patents at para 7.19, patents and their claims must to be valid be 'sufficient', one aspect of which involves the provision of an enabling disclosure, and another is that of plausibility.

The rigid requirements for enablement established at the EPO in the case of chemical patents, and discussed at para 7.19 as for example established in T-206/83 *Pyridine Herbicides/ICI*[1] in relation to what it is permissible to regard as 'common general knowledge' for the purposes of enablement have, however, been relaxed somewhat in the case of biotechnology. Thus, in T-51/87 *Starting Compounds/MERCK*[2] a Technical Board of Appeal reversed an Opposition Division (that had followed T-206/83 *Pyridine Herbicides/ICI*) to hold that where the starting compounds are highly elaborate microbial metabolites, opening a field of research so new that technical knowledge is not yet available from textbooks, it was permissible for the man skilled in the art also to look at patent specifications. However, enablement remains important for biotechnology. Thus, in T-60/89 *Fusion Proteins/HARVARD*[3] a Technical Board of Appeal held that a method of making a selected protein by culturing bacteria to express it had been insufficiently disclosed when it was established that it could only be made to work by the use of expedients (eg restriction enzymes and exonucleases) the use of which had not been disclosed in the specification. Here there was no enabling disclosure at all.

It is, however, less in relation to enablement, and plausibility specifically than as to permissible claim scope (a topic also discussed in **Chapter 5** at paras 5.19–5.20, and in **Chapter 7** in relation to pharmaceutical patents, at para 7.13 as to reach through claims, and para 7.20 more generally) that the law of sufficiency has featured strongly in biotechnology. Early EPO practice appears to have been permissive, with in the particular circumstances of T-292/85 *Polypeptide Expression/GENENTECH I*[4] an invention being held to be sufficiently disclosed if at least one way is clearly indicated enabling the skilled man to carry out the invention. Another such instance is provided by T-301/87 *Alpha-interferons/BIOGEN*[5] concerning claims to certain recombinant DNA molecules. Here it was recognized that individual variation was inevitable in processes starting from natural sources aimed at genes coding for polypeptides, and it was held that:

'… variations in the construction within a class of genetic precursors, such as recombinant DNA molecules claimed by a combination of structural limitations and functional tests, are immaterial to the sufficiency of the disclosure provided the skilled person could reliably obtain some members of the class without necessarily knowing in advance which member would thereby be made available.'

Protection was sought for 'an open definition which relates to an unknown but probably finite number of human and animal interferons of the alpha type'. Successfully maintaining claims that provided such broad protection was only frustrated in that case by certain problems of novelty and inventive step, rather than questions of sufficiency.

Questions of scope of claim and sufficiency were also reviewed in T-19/90 *Oncomouse/HARVARD*.[6] The Examining Division had held that the disclosure that only related to one oncogene, and to a mouse was not sufficient to support the granted claims to the use of any oncogene in any non-human mammal, but regarded it a reasonable extrapolation to limit the claim to rodents. On appeal, a Technical Board of Appeal rejected this approach, saying there was no evidence that the claims were too broad, and the invention could not be performed on other animals, and that it could be assumed that the skilled person was aware of other suitable mammals on which the invention could be successfully performed. However, on renewed prosecution after the passage of Directive 98/44/EC, such an objection was renewed, and upheld in T-315/03 *Method for producing transgenic animals/HARVARD*[7] so that the claims allowed were limited to mice.

The inter-relationship as between sufficiency, obviousness, and support in the context of biotechnology was summarized in T-694/92 *Modifying Plant Cells/MYCOGEN*:[8]

'3.   The present case is a typical example of a not uncommon situation – especially in the context of inventions in the field of biotechnology – in which the contribution to the state of the art by the invention disclosed in a patent or patent application resides in the actual realisation of a technical effect anticipated at a theoretical level in the prior art. In such a situation, a proper balance must be found between, on the one hand, the *actual* technical contribution to the state of the art by the invention disclosed in said patent or patent application, if any, and, on the other hand, the *manner of claiming* so that, if patent protection is granted, the scope is fair and adequate ...

4.   *Article 84 EPO* requires that the matter for which protection is sought be defined in the claims in a clear and concise manner and that the claims be supported by the description. This means not only that a claim must be non-ambiguous and comprehensible, but also that all the essential features of the claimed invention have to be indicated in the claim, these being the features which are necessary in order to obtain the desired effect .... The essential technical features may also be expressed in general functional terms, if, from an objective point of view, such features cannot otherwise be defined more precisely without restricting the scope of the claim, and if these features provide instructions which are sufficiently clear for the skilled person to reduce them to practice without undue burden, ie with no more than a reasonable amount of experimentation, and without applying inventive skills ...

5.   Article 83 EPC requires an invention to be disclosed in a manner sufficiently clear and complete for it to be carried out by a person skilled in the art ... the extent to which an invention is sufficiently disclosed is highly relevant when considering the issue of support within the meaning of Article 84 EPC, because both these requirements reflect the same general principle, namely that the scope of a granted patent should correspond to its technical contribution to the state of the art.

Hence it follows that, despite being supported by the description from a purely formal point of view, claims may not be considered allowable if they encompass subject-matter which in the light of the disclosure provided by the description can be performed only with undue burden or with application of inventive skill. As for the amount of technical detail needed for a sufficient disclosure, this is a matter which depends on the correlation of the facts of each particular case with certain general parameters, such as the character of the technical field, the date on which the disclosure was presented and the corresponding common general knowledge, and the amount of reliable technical detail disclosed in a document ...

In certain cases a description of one way of performing the claimed invention may be sufficient to support broad claims with functionally defined features, for example where the disclosure of a new technique constitutes the essence of the invention and the description of *one way* of carrying it out enables the skilled person to obtain without undue burden the same effect of the invention in a broad area by use of suitable variants of the component features .... In other cases, more technical details and *more than one example* may be necessary in order to support claims of a broad scope, for example where the achievement of a given technical effect by known techniques in different areas of application constitutes the essence of the invention and serious doubts exist as to whether the said effect can readily be obtained for the whole range of applications claimed.... However, in all these cases, the guiding principle is always that the skilled person should, after reading of the description, be able to readily perform the invention over the whole area claimed without undue burden and without needed inventive skill.... On the other hand, the objection of lack of sufficient disclosure presupposes that there are serious doubts, substantiated by verifiable facts ...

6. *Article 56 EPC* requires the claimed invention, ie the proposed technical solution for a given technical problem, not to be obvious to a person skilled in the art. If the non-obviousness of a claimed invention is based on a given technical effect, the latter should, in principle, be achievable over the whole area claimed ...

7. For the purposes of Articles 56 and 83 EPC the same level of skill is required from the *person skilled in the art* ... in two different technical situations: whereas for the purpose of evaluating inventive step the skilled person has knowledge of the prior art only, for the purpose of evaluating sufficiency of disclosure (and, hence, support) he or she has knowledge of the prior art *and* of the invention as disclosed.

8. The above considerations show how closely interrelated and how critical the issues of support of the claims, sufficiency of disclosure and inventive step are in cases – such as the present one – where it is particularly difficult to find a proper balance between the breadth of the claims and the actual contribution to the state of the art by the disclosure of the patent in suit.'

The decision related to a patent claiming broadly certain genetically modified plants, but is of general application, and identifies the importance of the actual technical contribution in determining what claim scope is fair and adequate.

Subsequently, with the phase of biotechnology patent practice which saw the increased importance of the lack of industrial applicability objection to claims of speculative utility for gene sequences, and the proteins for which they code, cases which might have been found insufficient in the past have instead been disposed of as lacking industrial applicability, as discussed above at para 8.07. There is, however, a distinction between the two, as was explained in T-0604/04 *F4A receptors/GENENTECH*[9] Technical Board of Appeal which having found the claims in issue to have industrial application went on to draw the distinction between this and sufficiency:

'26.   At oral proceedings, the appellant remarked that it would somehow be odd if industrial applicability was to be acknowledged to the polypeptides of Figures 4 and 5 on the basis of them being receptors of members of a family of proteins involved in the inflammatory response while sufficiency of disclosure would be denied in respect of monoclonal antibodies against these polypeptides for use in therapy.

27.   However, the board's decision to accept industrial applicability was not made on the above mentioned basis but on the basis that, at the priority date, the person skilled in the art perceived chemokines and any molecules capable of interfering with their activity as of great interest to the pharmaceutical industry if only to investigate their potential as targets for drug development, irrespective of what the end result might be …. The conclusion cannot be drawn from this reasoning that monoclonal antibodies to the polypeptides of Figures 4 or 5 could necessarily be of use in therapy or as a pharmaceutical composition.'

Thus the Technical Board of Appeal held the claims to monoclonal antibodies that were capable of specifically binding the PF4AR polypeptides were insufficient, but allowed ones to the specific isolated PF4AR polypeptides that the patentee had discovered. Thus, whereas an insufficiency objection is often directed to particular claims of scope that are not enabled across their breadth, that as to industrial applicability is directed more fundamentally to the underlying alleged invention, and tends to preclude the grant of any claim.

1   T-206/83 *Pyridine Herbicides/ICI* [1987] OJ EPO 5.
2   T-51/87 *Starting Compounds/MERCK* [1991] OJ EPO 177.
3   T-60/89 *Fusion Proteins/HARVARD* [1992] EPOR 320.
4   T-292/85 *Polypeptide Expression/GENENTECH I* [1989] OJ EPO 275.
5   T-301/87 *Alpha-interferons/BIOGEN* [1990] OJ EPO 335; [1990] EPOR 190.
6   T-19/90 *Oncomouse/HARVARD* [1989] OJ EPO 451; [1990] OJ EPO 476; [1990] 1 EPOR 4; [1990] EPOR 501.
7   T-315/03 *Transgenic animals/HARVARD* (Board 3.3.08, 6 July 2004).
8   T-694/92 *Modifying Plant Cells/MYCOGEN* [1997] OJ EPO 408; [1998] EPOR 114.
9   T-0604/04 *F4A receptors/GENENTECH* (Board 3.3.08, 16 March 2006.)

UK case law on sufficiency

8.15   The first UK biotechnology case in which insufficiency featured was *Chiron v Organon Teknika*[1] in which the patentee was the first to isolate, characterize, and sequence the naturally occurring virus, Hepatitis C (HCV). The utility of that discovery lay in the use of the relevant sequence in diagnostic kits for HCV infection, but claims to an HCV vaccine were held insufficient as there was no teaching as to how such vaccines might be produced, and the skilled person could not produce them without the exercise of invention.

In another virus case, concerning genetically engineered vaccines to the Hepatitis B virus, and shortly before the EPO Technical Board of Appeal decision in T-694/92 *Modifying Plant Cells/MYCOGEN* quoted from above in para 8.14, the House of Lords in the UK used sufficiency considerations to take a restricted view of legitimate claim breadth in *Biogen v Medeva*.[2] It held the patent invalid because the priority document did not support the claims in the patent, finding these too broad, not because of the inability of the teaching to produce all the promised results (the teaching was held to be enabling), but because the same results could be produced by different means, and the invention did not establish any new principle which successors had to follow if they were to achieve the same results. The House of Lords decided that the specification must enable the invention to be performed to the full extent of the monopoly claimed.

One of Biogen's first projects when established in 1978 was to try to make antigens to the Hepatitis B virus (HBV) which could be used to test for and immunize against HBV. Work for Biogen produced two of the known HBV antigens in colonies of *E. coli,* and Biogen filed a patent application describing what had been done, applying for a European patent a year later claiming priority from the earlier application. The resultant patent claimed an artificially constructed molecule of DNA carrying a genetic code which, when introduced into a suitable host cell, would cause that cell to make antigens of HBV. At the claimed priority date, the skilled man seeking to make HBV antigens by recombinant DNA technology had the choice of two strategies. The first was to sequence the HBV genome in order to provide the information needed to express the relevant genes, enabling him to choose restriction enzymes that digested the sites closest to the relevant gene or to the part of the gene that expressed an antigenic fragment. The alternative strategy, adopted by Biogen, was to try to express genomic DNA in a suitable host. Not knowing the genomic sequence, Biogen guessed that large DNA fragments had the best chance of expression, and chose restriction enzymes that would cleave the DNA accordingly. This technique, with expression in bacterial host cells, happened to work against the then current expectations. However, shortly after this was done, the HBV genome was sequenced at the University of California. Thus the first strategy could then be used, and no one needed to adopt the Biogen approach. Biogen conceded that if the patent could not maintain its claim to priority it was rendered obvious by the University of California's work. The House of Lords found that the skilled man following the teaching of the priority document (the embodiment in which described how to make core antigen for HBV in bacterial cells) would have been able to make both surface, and core antigens for HBV in any cells. That was, however, not determinative of sufficiency. The critical issue was:

> 'not whether the invention could deliver the goods [across the full width of the patent or priority document] but whether the claims cover other ways in which they might be delivered: methods which owed nothing to the teaching or to any principle which was disclosed.'

While Biogen taught how to make HBV antigens by one route which might be inventive, this served only to give greater confidence to those who followed using other routes. Thus the House of Lords found that Biogen's contribution was not sufficient to justify a claim to the whole field – namely a monopoly of *any* recombinant method of making HBV antigens. Its excessive breadth was not because the teaching could not produce all the promised results, but because the same results could be produced by different means. Therefore, the claims in the patent were not supported by the priority document. Since Biogen had conceded that the patent was obvious as of its filing date, the question of insufficiency did not arise, but the House of Lords indicated that as the test for insufficiency was the same as that for claiming priority, had they not held the patent obvious they would have held it insufficient.

Sufficiency has continued to feature in litigation in the UK over biotechnology patents. Thus, in *DSM's Patent*[3] claim 1 of the patent was directed to:

> 'A DNA sequence ... selected from the group consisting of (a) [a sequence depicted in part of Figure 8]; (b) [a sequence depicted in Figure 6 or Figure 8] and (c) DNA sequences hybridizing at low stringency conditions (...) with a DNA fragment corresponding to the cDNA of the nucleotide sequence depicted in Figure 6 from position 210 to 1129.'

The patentees contended that any DNA sequence which hybridized under the conditions described in claim 1(c) was within the scope of that claim, even if such DNA sequence was unrelated to the phytase gene in issue. The Patents Court accepted this, but saw no reason for excluding from the claim 'unrelated DNA', and limiting the claim to 'related phytases', whatever that term might mean. Thus, claim 1 was held to be of wide scope, and to cover 'the great majority of phytase DNA', with most of the DNA binding under the low stringency conditions specified in claim: 1(c) not being the phytase gene in issue. Thus: 'the exercise involved [to construct DNA sequences across the entire scope of claim 1(c)] would require the skilled worker to depart from the express teaching of the patent, to experiment over what may be a long passage of time, and even after that, he may not achieve the desired result'. This was admitted to be unworkable; and, if, as the patentee contended, a narrower functional imitation (to fungal enzymes) were to be impliedly read into the claim, the patent provided no teaching as to what stringency conditions were appropriate. Thus, interpretation of the claim depended on the conditions selected by the person carrying out the work, and was accordingly insufficient. The problem was one of claim drafting in identifying the 'relation' with the fungal phytase in issue 'so as to be clear and sufficient on the one hand, while, on the other hand, putting forward a formula which has commercial efficacy'.

In *Kirin-Amgen v Hoechst Marion Roussel*[4] the House of Lords considered several separate attacks on sufficiency on the two product claims. It found claim 19 insufficient because the 'and which has a higher molecular weight by SDS-PAGE from erythropoietin [EPO] isolated from urinary sources' [uEPO] limitation introduced in the course of the EPO opposition at TBA level had introduced what proved to be a meaningless test:

'124.   The claim appeared to assume that all uEPOs had effectively the same molecular weight, irrespective of source and method of isolation. This had been shown not to be the case. So which uEPO did the claim require to be used for the test? Simply to use the first uEPO which came to hand would turn the claim into a lottery. On the other hand, it would be burdensome to have to work one's way through several specimens of uEPO (which were, as I mentioned at the beginning of my speech, extremely hard to come by) and even then the result would be inconclusive because *non constat* that some untried specimen did not have a different molecular weight.

125.   The judge decided that the lack of clarity made the specification insufficient. It did not merely throw up the possibility of doubtful cases but made it impossible to determine in *any* case whether the product fell within the claim. The invention was not disclosed "clearly enough and completely enough for it to be performed by a person skilled in the art": s 72(1)(c)'

As claim 26 was held to lack novelty, no finding on sufficiency was necessary, but Lord Hoffmann expressed sympathy with an attack based on the argument that the patent did not enable the process that was still in issue, and which had been found in any event not to infringe, developed by the co-defendant TKT:

'114.   ... Assuming the claims can be read, as the judge thought, to include any way of making EPO by recombinant DNA technology, the specification does not disclose a way of making it in sufficiently general terms to include the TKT process. It discloses only how to make EPO by introducing exogenous DNA coding for EPO into a host cell. The TKT method is not a version of this process which, although untried, could reasonably be expected to work just as well. It is different.'

In contrast, another insufficiency attack on both claims based on the assertion that the patent only taught how to get adequate levels of expression of erythropoeitin from one type of cell-line (CHO cells), was rejected:

'118. ... I entirely agree with the Court of Appeal that the specification enabled the use of any cell for the expression of exogenous DNA. It is true that Amgen were only able to secure high-level expression in CHO cells. But the invention did not promise high-level expression and the discovery of another cell which enabled high-level expression would have been exactly the kind of improvement which the Court of Appeal said did not have to be enabled by the specification. The use of such a cell is a way of making EPO disclosed by the invention.'

Finally, it was not necessary to express any concluded view on an attack based on the assertion that the patent did not enable the production of erythropoietin analogues that were also claimed, although Lord Hoffmann observed that he could see the force of the reasoning that led a US court to such a conclusion in earlier litigation on a corresponding patent.

In *Eli Lilly v Human Genome Sciences*[5] per se claims to, inter alia, certain types of monoclonal antibody based on the identification of a gene sequence were held at first instance, because of the speculative nature of the suggested utilities, the specifics of which it would take a research programme to pin down, to be insufficient. The claims were also, effectively on the same basis, held to lack industrial application, and to be obvious. Only the finding as to lack of industrial application was addressed on appeal, and upheld, although on appeal to the Supreme Court the finding as to lack of industrial applicability was reversed, and subsequently the challenge on grounds of insufficiency was also rejected by the Court of Appeal.

Other insufficiency challenges to monoclonal antibody patents have concerned those with medical use claims and raise the same issues, for example as to plausibility, as claims to the medical use of small molecules, and so are discussed in **Chapter 7** at paras 7.19–7.20. For a recent example of such a case see *Eli Lilly and Company v Janssen Alzheimer Immunotherapy.*[6] The claims in issue were:

'1. A pharmaceutical composition comprising an antibody to Aß and a pharmaceutically acceptable non-toxic carrier or diluent, for use in preventing or treating a disease characterised by amyloid deposit in a patient, wherein the isotype of the antibody is human IgG1.

...

4. The pharmaceutical composition for use in preventing or treating a disease characterised by amyloid deposit in a patient of any preceding claim wherein the antibody binds specifically to the aggregated form of Aß peptide without binding to the dissociated form.

5. The pharmaceutical composition for use in preventing or treating a disease characterised by amyloid deposit in a patient of any of claims 1–3 where the antibody binds specifically to the dissociated form of Aß peptide without binding to the aggregated form.

6. The pharmaceutical composition for use in preventing or treating a disease characterised by amyloid deposit in a patient of any of claims

1–3 where the antibody binds specifically to both aggregated and dissociated forms of Aß peptide.'

The court held at [271] that the teaching of the patent did not render it plausible that *any* antibody to Aß (provided it is of IgG1 isotype), other than an N-terminal antibody, would be effective to prevent and/or treat a disease characterised by amyloid deposit. Neither, it held, could the claimed invention be performed without undue burden, accepting at [296] a submission that:

'... despite the best efforts of the patentee and its collaborators, despite the application of a very great deal of effort for over a decade (and many person years) and despite huge expenditure, the patentee had not succeeded in making an antibody to Aß which was "for use in preventing or treating a disease characterised by amyloid deposit".'

Thus having concluded at [312] that, 'the Patent does no more than invite the skilled team to perform what Prof Wisniewski rightly described as a "very significant research project with a high prospect of failure" and, if they succeed, claims the fruits of their research' – held the patent to be insufficient.

1   *Chiron Corpn v Organon Teknika* [1994] FSR 202 (Pat Ct); [1996] RPC 535 (Court of Appeal) – see also T-0188/97 *Chiron/NANBV* (Technical Board of Appeal 3.4.04, 8 February 2001) where other claims that had survived attack in the UK were to a large extent successfully challenged in the EPO on grounds of insufficiency.

2   *Biogen v Medeva* [1997] RPC 1, several passages from which are quoted in **Chapter 5** in connection with priority at para 5.05 and enablement at para 5.21.

3   *DSM's Patent* [2001] RPC at 675 – see above at para 8.05.

4   *Kirin-Amgen v Hoechst Marion Roussel* [2001] IP&T 882; [2002] IP& T 22; [2002] RPC 1; [2002] RPC 2 (Patents Court); [2003] IP&T 694; [2003] RPC 3 (Court of Appeal); [2004] UKHL 46; [2005] 1 All ER 667; [2005] IP&T 352; [2005] RPC 9 (House of Lords) – see above at para 8.03 for the claims in issue.

5   *Eli Lilly v Human Genome Sciences* [2008] EWHC 1903 (Patents Court); [2010] EWCA 33 (Court of Appeal); [2011] UKSC 51 (Supreme Court). When the action was remitted to the Court of Appeal [2012] EWCA Civ 1185 the Court of Appeal held the claims in issue to be sufficient, although this to a degree reflects the procedural posture of the case as the finding in isolation as to industrial applicability in the Court of Appeal and thus the Supreme Court may have compromised the argument challenging the patent's sufficiency. See above at para 8.07 for a discussion of this case in the context of industrial applicability.

6   *Eli Lilly and Company v Janssen Alzheimer Immunotherapy* [2013] EWHC 1737.

Deposit requirements

8.16   A further issue with many biotechnological inventions is that whereas in more traditional areas a written description of the invention suffices fully to disclose the invention to third parties, it can however be very difficult to describe micro-organisms adequately; but even if that can be done, mere description will not thereby permit the reader to obtain the micro-organism. For example, a particular antibiotic-producing micro-organism may be found only after very extensive screening of soil samples from some obscure part of the world. Making them available may be the only way, at least initially, to enable one to manufacture the antibiotic of interest.

In recognition of this, certain special provisions were introduced that required the deposit of samples of new or inaccessible micro-organisms in recognized culture collections. The Treaty on the International Recognition of the Deposit of Micro-Organisms for the Purposes of Patent Procedure 1977 (the Budapest Treaty) set up a system of internationally recognized depositories where inventors can deposit their samples. A single such deposit can then be referred to in patent applications filed in all the countries which adhere to this Treaty, for the purposes of ensuring that the description is, from this point of view, sufficient. There are also various housekeeping provisions in the Treaty dealing with matters such as what happens if the original sample ceases to be viable, and how this is to be replaced. The effect of such deposit was considered in *Chinoin's Application*[1] in which the applicant was unsuccessful in his attempt to claim as a new species all strains of a newly discovered micro-organism *Micromonospora*. Only one strain had been deposited. It was held that the deposit of a single strain was sufficient to support claims relating to strains of *Micromonospora* derived from the deposited strain, but not sufficient to support claims relating to the species as a whole.

1   *Chinoin's Application* [1986] RPC 39.

Impact of Directive 98/44/EC

8.17   The Directive has nothing to say about the wider issues of sufficiency, but it does address the question of the deposit of biological material. Thus, Articles 13–14 of the Directive[1] direct national patent offices to allow applicants to adopt the 'expert solution' approach to access deposited biological material. This limits access to the deposited material to an independent expert until the patent is granted. Undertakings must be given, whilst the patent is in force, not to make the sample supplied in response to a request, or any material derived from it, available to third parties, nor to use it or such derived material except for experimental purposes.

1   Implemented in the UK by The Patents (Amendment) Rules 2001 (SI 2001/1412).

Infringement issues

Introduction

8.18   Given the breadth of many biotechnology claims, and the manner in which they are often functionally defined, there has been less scope for non-infringement arguments in the decided cases in this than in other areas of patent law. One notable exception was *Kirin-Amgen v Hoechst Marion Roussel*[1] in which the process used by the co-defendant Roche to produce its erythropoietin product, that involved producing by conventional recombinant DNA technology the cell line that expressed such product, was found literally to infringe product claim 26 (that at first instance was held valid) and process claim 27. The process used by another co-defendant, Hoechst Marion Roussel, for producing the cell line from which it manufactured its erythropoietin product involved use of a differing type of DNA technology which did not involve splicing the gene of interest into the host cell (to which it was thus exogenous) but instead splicing a construct that 'switched on' the gene of interest that was already in the cell (and thus was not exogenous to it). It was not alleged to infringe claim 27, and its product was found not literally to infringe claim 26. However, such product was found at first instance to infringe claim 26 on what was said to be the application of the principle of 'purposive construction', despite evidence going to the second 'protocol question' that the skilled man when told of it would not have believed that the process would work. The finding of infringement was reversed on appeal by Hoechst Marion Roussel (Roche having settled) the Court of Appeal finding both claims 19 and 26 valid, but answering the first two 'protocol questions' in relation to both claims in favour of Hoechst Marion Roussel's product, and the third one against it. On appeal the House of Lords held both claims 19 and 26 to be invalid, as explained above, and upheld the Court of Appeal finding of non-infringement, having observed that in construing claim 26 so as to find that such erythropoietin (EPO) product did not 'literally' infringe the trial judge had already undertaken an exercise in purposive construction of claim 26:

'67.   The judge thought that the invention was the discovery of the sequence of the EPO gene and the associated information. It followed that any method of making EPO which used that information, whether by the expression of exogenous or endogenous DNA, would operate in the same way and that this would be obvious to the person skilled in the art. Furthermore, there was no reason why the patentee should have wished to insist upon any particular method of using the information to obtain the expression of EPO.

68.   The Court of Appeal, on the other hand, thought that the invention was a way of making EPO. The information about the sequence of the gene was necessary to enable the invention to be performed but was not and could not be the invention itself. It followed that a different way of making EPO worked in a different way from that described in the invention and that this would have been obvious to a person skilled in the art.

...

76.   I agree with the Court of Appeal on construction for a number of reasons. First, I think that the judge's construction pays no attention to the claims. It does not even use them as "guidelines" but goes straight to Table VI [setting

out the sequence of the EPO gene] and declares that to be the invention. Secondly, I think that the Court of Appeal was right in saying that Table VI could not have been the invention. Standing alone, it was a "discovery ... as such" within the meaning of s 1(2) of the Act: see *Genentech Inc's Patent* [1989] RPC 147, per Purchas LJ at p 204 and per Dillon LJ at p 237. On the other hand, as Whitford J said in the *Genentech* case ([1987] RPC 553, 566):

> "It is trite law that you cannot patent a discovery, but if on the basis of that discovery you can tell people how it can be usefully employed, then a patentable invention may result. This in my view would be the case, even though once you have made the discovery, the way in which it can be usefully employed is obvious enough."

77. In such a case, while it may be true to say, as the Court of Appeal did ([2003] RPC 31, 62) that Table VI lay "at the heart of the invention", it was not the invention. An invention is a practical product or process, not information about the natural world. That seems to me to accord with the social contract between the state and the inventor which underlies patent law. The state gives the inventor a monopoly in return for an immediate disclosure of all the information necessary to enable performance of the invention. That disclosure is not only to enable other people to perform the invention after the patent has expired. If that were all, the inventor might as well be allowed to keep it secret during the life of the patent. It is also to enable anyone to make immediate use of the information for any purpose which does not infringe the claims. The specifications of valid and subsisting patents are an important source of information for further research, as is abundantly shown by a reading of the sources cited in the specification for the patent in suit. Of course a patentee may in some cases be able to frame his claim to a product or process so broadly that in practice it will be impossible to use the information he has disclosed, even to develop important improvements, in a way which does not infringe. But it cannot be right to give him a monopoly of the use of the information as such.'

However, as discussed in **Chapter 6**, the House of Lords went further and discussed, for the first time in any technical field in a generation, the correct approach to use in seeking purposively to construe patent claims.

A subsequent biotechnology case in which the claims in issue were found to be valid but not infringed, essentially on the basis of particular claim construction, including that as to the meaning of the term 'isolated', was *Monsanto v Cargill*.[2] This also, as with some other biotechnology patent litigation, concerned issues as to what constitutes the 'direct product of a patented process', which, in the context of Directive 98/44/EC are discussed below at para 8.19. However, because most biotechnology patent litigation is concerned with proteins, which are what is normally commercially important, but which are not 'biological materials', Directive 98/44/EC has no bearing on claims to processes for the production of proteins, and it is irrelevant that the processes for such production involve biological materials. In *Medimmune Limited v Novartis Pharmaceuticals UK Limited*[3] (in which an argument based on Directive 98/44/EC was rejected for that reason) the Patents Court applied the 'loss of identity' test established in other technical areas[4] to reject a non-infringement argument to the effect that one should focus upon the inventive concept, or inventive part of the claim, and ask whether the allegedly infringing product is obtained directly from that process. Thus it held that a claim to a method of manufacturing a monoclonal antibody that had been identified by another claimed process would have been infringed by dealings in such monoclonal antibody, even though it was not a product obtained directly by the identification process, and in which the invention was alleged to reside, and where the subsequent manufacturing process that was part of the claim was conventional, and non-inventive.

1   *Kirin-Amgen v Hoechst Marion Roussel* [2001] IP&T 882; [2002] IP& T 22; [2002] RPC 1; [2002] RPC 2 (Patents Court); [2003] IP&T 694; [2003] RPC 3 (Court of Appeal); [2004] UKHL 46; [2005] 1 All ER 667; [2005] IP&T 352; [2005] RPC 9 (House of Lords) – see above at para 8.03 for the claims in issue.
2   *Monsanto Technology LLC v Cargill International SA* [2007] EWHC 2257 – see above at para 8.03 for the claims in issue. See **Chapter 7** at para 7.21 where it rejected 'de minimis' considerations as relevant to infringement. See below at para 8.19 for a discussion of the parallel Dutch litigation, where the claim in issue was slightly differently worded, and that concerned a different issue on infringement.
3   *Medimmune Limited v Novartis Pharmaceuticals UK Limited* [2011] EWHC 1669 (infringement not addressed on appeal).
4   See **Chapter 6** at para 6.03.

Impact of Directive 98/44/EC

8.19   Articles 8–11 of the Directive establish special instances of infringement (and certain exceptions) thought to be appropriate to 'biological material' as defined, for example, extending protection automatically to a subsequent generation as if it were the first, and to other products than those claimed which incorporate genetic material where that is an essential characteristic of the invention. It might be argued that such provisions should hardly be necessary, especially for well drafted patents, as for example seen in relation to the protection for descendants specifically claimed in the application in T-19/90 *Oncomouse/HARVARD,* discussed above at para 8.09.

Article 8.1 relates to product protection for 'biological material', and Article 8.2 the issue of the protection afforded to such material as the direct product of a patented processes, along the lines already afforded under the laws of EPO Member States to the direct product of a patented processes:[1]

'8.1   The protection conferred by a patent on a biological material possessing specific characteristics as a result of the invention shall extend to any biological material derived from that biological material through propagation or multiplication in an identical or divergent form and possessing those same characteristics.

8.2   The protection conferred by a patent on a process that enables a biological material to be produced possessing specific characteristics as a result of the invention shall extend to biological material directly obtained through that process and to any other biological material derived from the directly obtained biological material through propagation or multiplication in an identical or divergent form and possessing those same characteristics. Article 9 adds a qualification to such protection:

9   The protection conferred by a patent on a product containing or consisting of genetic information shall extend to all material, save as provided in Article 5(1) in which the product is incorporated and in which the genetic information is contained and performs its function.'

The interpretation of the 'performs its function' aspect of this qualifying provision was in issue in Case C-428/08 *Monsanto v Cefetra*[2] concerning an allegation that traces of DNA (ie 'genetic information') from genetically modified soy plants that remained in soy meal that had been imported, infringed a patent that claimed such DNA. The Court, having held that TRIPS, Articles 27 and 30 had no bearing on the interpretation of Article 9, and that, because the Directive lacked transitional provisions it applied to patents granted before it came into force on 30 July 2000, held that:

'Article 9 of the Directive must be interpreted as not conferring patent right protection in circumstances such as those of the case in the main proceedings, in which the patented product is contained in the soy meal, where it does not perform the function for which it was patented, but did perform that function previously in the soy plant, of which the meal is a processed product, or would possibly again be able to perform that function after it had been extracted from the soy meal and inserted into the cell of a living organism.'

Both Articles 8 and 9 are subject to Article 10 on exhaustion of rights:[3]

'10   The protection referred to in Articles 8 and 9 shall not extend to biological material obtained from the multiplication or propagation of biological material placed on the market in the territory of a Member State by the holder of the patent or with his consent, where the multiplication or propagation necessarily results from the application for which the biological material was marketed, provided that the obtained material is not subsequently used for other multiplication or propagation.'

Article 11 goes on to provide an exception from infringement as to both plants and animals (the so-called 'farmer's privilege') and Article 12[4] provides for compulsory licensing to the extent that patent precludes exploitation of a plant variety right, on condition that there be a licence back of such right, and vice versa. Article 14 provides for licences of right in favour of holders of plant variety rights dominated by a patent, in recognition of the scope for overlap between the two systems.

1   See **Chapter 6** at para 6.02.
2   Case C-428/08 *Monsanto v Cefetra* (EU Court of Justice, 6 July 2010). See also *Medimmune Limited v Novartis Pharmaceuticals UK Limited* [2011] EWHC 1669 for a discussion of this decision, and that also considered the scope of Article 8.2. See also the Opinion of the Advocate General in Case C-377/98 *Kingdom of the Netherlands v European Parliament and Council of the European Union* [2001] ECR I-7079 at [121]–[123] rejecting an argument that there was an inconsistency between Article 4(1)(a), and Articles 8–9.
3   See **Chapter 6** at para 6.14.
4   Implemented in the UK by the Patents and Plant Variety Rights (Compulsory Licensing) Regulations 2002 (SI 2002/247).

Chapter 9

Patents in electronics, communications, and computing

Introduction

Importance of patents in these sectors

9.01 Statistics of patent applications filed regularly feature companies in the electronics communications, and computing sectors (often referred to as: information and computing technologies (ICT)) at the top of the list, and far ahead of even the largest companies in the pharmaceuticals and biotechnology sectors, despite the evident importance of patents to those sectors.[1] Until relatively recently patents have been little used in the ICT sectors as exclusionary rights to keep out competitors (as for example, they tend to be in the pharmaceutical sector) but instead as a way to secure royalties, or by cross-licensing to reduce net liability for royalties, and still much patent litigation in the ICT sector consists of attempts to secure royalties from those unwilling to pay the going rate for a licence. Naturally, this has particularly been the case in the area of patents for systems or standards, which also raise particular issues of competition law for 'standards essential' patents that must inevitably be infringed by a product that adheres to a particular standard. Here the threat of an injunction under a single standards essential patent in one country as against a product, eg smartphone, that incorporates many thousands of patented inventions, can be used in an attempt to secure a more favourable royalty rate for the much larger, international, portfolio of patents held by that patentee than would be secured in a normal arms-length negotiation.[2]

The field of computing has also seen especially strong growth in patenting activity, much of which is a result of the manner in which microprocessors controlled by computer programs have become a fundamental, and pervasive aspect of so much technology, from smartphones to cars. However, patents in the computer sector in Europe have been bedevilled by the issue of computer programs. This is a consequence of certain express exclusions in the European Patent Convention (EPC) including one for computer programs 'as such'. This has meant that European law has tended to concern itself with the scope of the exception, rather than with other issues that typically arise with most patents, such as inventive step. Associated with the issue of computer program patents has been that of business methods, often implemented by means of a computer system, and again in Europe the subject of an express exclusion in the EPC, for business methods 'as such'.

Although patents of relevance to the electronics sector can also take a variety of other forms, many do not raise issues which are unique to these sectors, and so these are not addressed further in this chapter.[3]

1 Comparisons between numbers of patents can mislead, and especially so as between different industry sectors, given the different nature of the technologies that are protected. They certainly do not in this case meaningfully reflect any difference in research and development activity as between different sectors. Thus the major pharmaceutical company, Eli Lilly and Company, in its Amicus Curiae Brief to the Supreme Court in *Microsoft Corpn v AT&T Corpn*, discussing 'overprotection' in the information technology (IT) industry sector, observed that: 'Microsoft has expended $6 billion on R&D in its fiscal year 2005 ending on June 30. During 2005, the USPTO issued a total of 750 patents to Microsoft. By comparison, Amicus Eli Lilly and Company expended $3 billion on R&D during 2005 and was issued 48 patents – one-half of Microsoft's R&D expenses, but one-fifteenth as many issued US patents'.

2 For an idea of the number of different technologies used in a smartphone, and the level of royalties demanded for licences of the patents that protect such technologies, see Armstrong, Mueller and Syrett – *The Smartphone Royalty Stack: Surveying Royalty Demands for the Components Within Modern Smartphones* (29 May 2014).

Available at SSRN: http://ssrn.com/abstract=2443848 or http://dx.doi.org/10.2139/ssrn.2443848.

3   Thus for example, although patents to particular semiconductor fabrication techniques, or structures, are important to the sector, the issues met with these tend to be more those of physics, and surface chemistry than electronics. There are also certain circuit techniques which touch more on matters of pure electronics. Both, for example, are involved in the protection of microprocessor and memory technology, as to which the *sui generis* right in specific integrated circuit layouts, namely semiconductor chip topography protection as mandated by Articles 35–38 of the TRIPS Agreement, and in Europe by Directive 87/54/EEC of 16 December 1986 on the Legal Protection of Topographies of Semiconductor Products [1987] OJ L 24/36, has proved to be of little practical significance as a result of developments in technology, and has resulted in no reported European litigation. For economic studies as to the significance of patents in relation to the semiconductor sector: see Bessen and Maskin, 'Sequential Innovation, Patents and Imitation', MIT Working Paper (Department of Economics No. 00–01) January 2000; and Hall & Ziedonis, 'The Patent Paradox Revisited: an Empirical Study of Patenting in the US Semiconductor Industry, 1979–1995', *Rand Journal of Economics*, Spring, 2002.

Standards

Introduction

9.02 Patents can be used to establish and ensure compliance with various standards, to secure remuneration for work in researching and developing such standards, and to provide a basis for a framework of cooperation between those working on developing a standard.[1] Standards are pervasive in networked sectors such as electronics, communications and computing because of the need for some element of interoperability in all of these. Such standards can take many forms. In consumer electronics one has the examples of the compact audio cassette from Philips, the VHS video cassette from JVC, the compact disc from Philips and Sony, and the DVD digital versatile disc from the DVD consortium. More recently, attention has focused on various telecommunications standards, and on the 'codec' standards used to compress electronic files that represent speech, music, photographs, and video. Each standard can be backed up by one or more (and quite often a very large number) of patents, detailing a certain aspect of the standard (those which detail a purely physical aspect of a standard are sometimes referred to as 'form factor' patents). Standards are nowadays most commonly established by industry bodies, such as ETSI or IEEE, but many standards in the past, such as those for compact audio cassettes, videocassettes and compact discs were 'de facto' standards, established by sometimes only one company, and sometimes (as in the case of videocassettes) in competition with other companies also with their own potential standards.

The patentee's aim as to a 'de facto' standard may be to secure income from its own exploitation of that standard by manufacturing activity, but it will also want to secure income by licensing patents protecting the standard to third parties; which activity a patentee will wish to encourage as widely as possible because it brings about even wider use of the standard. Philips and Sony were able to do this with the compact disc (CD) although some objected to the licence terms offered (and already accepted by the rest of the industry) as in *Philips Electronics v Ingman*.[2] Here the defendants sought to argue that Philips was using the proceedings as part of an abuse of a dominant position, in breach of TFEU, Article 102.[3] The defendants also argued that the proceedings were intended to force them into entering into a standard form licence which would itself be in breach of TFEU, Article 101.[4] The Article 102 defence was struck out, as well as most of that based on Article 101, as unarguable. In striking out the Article 102 defence, the Patents Court held that mere ownership of an IPR such as a patent did not, in and of itself, confer a dominant position in the relevant market on its owner. It also held that even if a patentee had such a dominant position, it was not in itself an abuse of it either to refuse to licence the patent on reasonable terms, or only to do so on grounds that were objectively unreasonable, and had the effect of destroying the competitiveness of the defendant. In so doing, it followed the decisions of the EU Court of Justice in *CICRA v Renault* and *Volvo v Veng*[5] and treated the Court of Justice decision in *Magill*[6] mandating the grant of a compulsory licence of certain copyrights, as a special case. Although the Patents Court expressed 'grave doubts' as to the Article 101 defence, it held that an assertion that the royalty rate was too high could arguably be said to be contrary to Article 101, unlike the other criticized features of the standard form agreement.

Patents have also been used to retain control of standards in terms of preventing unauthorized modifications to and enhancements of the standard by third parties. Although at first sight, such an activity may seem to hamper technical progress, once a standard has been set, uncontrolled modifications may be undesirable for reasons such as retaining backward compatibility, or to prevent others in effect 'hijacking' a standard, and operating outside the wider industry involvement in standards setting which almost inevitably develops once a standard has been set. Thus, JVC found itself the subject of complaint in the early 1990s by third parties over the manner in which it had used its patents over VHS video cassette technology to restrict certain third-party developments of the technology.

Another area in which standards have been set and maintained, at least in part by patents, but in which certain patent licensing arrangements have included a wide range of restrictions on licensees, including even 'tying' provisions, and which the patentees have also sought to justify to competition law authorities, has been that of video games, where the patentees have used such patents in an effort, for example, to retain an element of exclusivity for certain games on their particular system.

If the development of a *de facto* standard involves collaboration between a number of parties, each of who are likely to own patents relevant to the standard which it hoped to establish, competition law issues may become potentially problematic. One approach is for the companies involved to cross-license each other in a patent pool, as discussed below. Such arrangements tend to be more common in the consumer electronics sector, where *de facto* standards are established, initially by a few companies, as opposed to those established during a formal standard-setting process open to all but generally managed by an already existing body, often operating under public sector authority. The latter approach is more common in the communications sector, and where the standards setting activity proceeds under a set of rules established by such Standards Setting Organization (SSO) (also called a Standards Development Organization (SDO)) and to which all participants in the process must adhere. There is a continuum of arrangements between what have been presented here as two extremes, and they both present similar issues of competition law.

Even without specific obligations assumed in the course of a formal standard setting process, standards may attract special treatment under national patent laws in Europe. Thus the judgment of the German Federal Supreme Court in *Standard Tight-Head Drum (Standard Spundfass[7])* shows how competition law considerations can, in the context of attempts to assert patents for industry standards, impose obligations on patentees to grant licences irrespective of whether or not a licence might be available under the statutory patent compulsory licensing mechanisms that exist in national European patent laws.

1   There is a large body of primarily US literature on the subject of patents and standards, including the free monthly electronic journal, *Standards Today* – available at: www.consortiuminfo.org/. However, for discussions of it from a European perspective see Verbruggen and Lorincz, 'Patents and Technical Standards' (2002) 33, IIC 125, and Ohana, Hanson and Shah, *'Disclosure and Negotiation of Licensing Terms Prior to Adoption of Industry Standards: Preventing Another Patent Ambush'* (2003) 24(12) ECLR, 644–56. For more recent European studies, see the *Final Report on the Study on the Interplay between Standards and Intellectual Property Rights (IPRs)*, published by the European Commission in April 2011, and *Patents and Standards – A modern framework for IPR-based standardization*, published by the European Commission in March 2014 (Ref. Ares (2014)917720 – 25/03/2014). In 2014 the European Commission also launched: *Public Consultation on Patents and Standards* – responses to which can be found at: http://ec.europa.eu/growth/tools-databases/newsroom/cf/itemdetail.cfm?item_id=7833&lang=en&title=Patents-and-Standards%3A-A-modern-framework-for-standardization-involving-intellectual-property-rights.
2   *Philips Electronics v Ingman* [1999] FSR 112.
3   Formerly (and at the time) EEC, Article 86 and then EC, Article 82. See also **Chapter 6** at para 6.15.
4   Formerly (and at the time) EEC, Article 85 and then EC, Article 81.
5   Case C-53/87 *CICRA v Renault* [1988] ECR 6039; [1990] 4 CMLR 265 and Case C-238/87 *Volvo v Veng* [1988] ECR 6211; [1989] 4 CMLR 122. Both cases concerned rights in designs, rather than patents, and both concerned a refusal on the part of car manufacturers to license their designs for spare body parts, where the designs were not ancillary, parts remained available from the manufacturer, and the spare parts supplier was not putting out a new product.

6 Cases C-241/91P and C-242/91P *Radio Telefís Eireann and Independent Television Publications Ltd v EC Commission (Magill Television Guide Ltd intervening)* [1995] ECRI–473; [1995] 4 CMLR; [1995] FSR 530, in which Irish and UK television broadcasters were held to be in breach of what is now TFEU, Article 102 in having abused their dominant position by refusing to license their copyrights in television listing information to the publishers of a television listings magazine that provided such information, a week ahead, for all channels. However, and in contrast to patents, there are not in general any compulsory licensing provisions for copyright. Since then the nature of the special circumstances which were found to apply in *Magill* have been further clarified in the decision in Case C-418/01 *IMS Health GmbH & Co OHG v NDC Health GmbH & Co* [2004] 4 CMLR 28, also in the field of copyright, and in Case T-201/04 *Microsoft* [2007] 5 CMLR 11 which although primarily concerning copyright, related also to patents, and to trade secrets.

7 *Standard Tight-Head Drum (Standard-Spundfass)* 9 (Case KZR 40/02, German Federal Supreme Court, 13 July 2004); reported at [2005] IIC (36) 741.

Standard setting organizations, essentiality, and FRAND licensing terms

9.03 Some SSOs, such as the World Wide Web Consortium, seek only to issue recommendations as to standards that can be implemented on a royalty free basis, and so, subject to the conditions of its policy will not approve a recommendation if it is aware that patent claims essential to such recommendation exist which are not available on royalty free terms.[1] It has been more common however for standards to be set on terms that only mandate the participants in the standard setting process to offer licences, albeit generally on terms that are 'FRAND' (fair reasonable and non-discriminatory), of those of their patents that are 'essential' to a standard, albeit that most provide no guidance as to what this expression means.[2] Such is the case in telecommunications, as to which mobile telephony[3] also provides an example of an international collaboration between different SSOs, be these national[4] or regional. The best-known example of the latter is the European Telecommunications Standards Institute (ETSI).[5] The significance of patents in standards setting is such that much European activity in relation to patents, and standards in the telecommunications and broadcasting sectors was subsumed into a broad review of harmonization of new standards in these sectors, one result of which was as the European Commission's *Communication on Intellectual Property Rights and Standardization*[6] in 1992, in response to the licensing policies then being developed by ETSI.

The nature of the obligations associated with ETSI membership was summarized in *Nokia v Interdigital*[7] where the English Court of Appeal quoted the following from the judgment at first instance:

'4. Turning to the formal statement of the ETSI IPR Policy, which is Annex A to the [November 2004 edition of the ETSI Guide on Intellectual Property Rights], the obligation of disclosure is stated in para 4 as follows:

"Each MEMBER shall use its reasonable endeavours to timely inform ETSI of Essential IPRs it becomes aware of. In particular, a MEMBER submitting a technical proposal for a STANDARD or TECHNICAL SPECIFICATION shall, on a bona fide basis, draw the attention of ETSI to any of that MEMBER'S IPR which might be essential if that proposal is adopted."

5.   Paragraph 6 of the Policy requires that:

"When an ESSENTIAL IPR relating to a particular STANDARD or TECHNICAL SPECIFICATION is brought to the attention of ETSI, the Director-General of ETSI shall immediately request the owner to give within three months an undertaking in writing that it is prepared to grant irrevocable licences on fair, reasonable and non-discriminatory terms and conditions under such IPR ..."

6.   The nature of an essential right is clearly defined. By the sixth definition of para 15 of the Policy:

"'ESSENTIAL' as applied to IPR means that it is not possible on technical (but not commercial) grounds, taking into account normal technical practice and the state of the art generally available at the time of standardisation, to make, sell, lease, otherwise dispose of, repair, use or operate EQUIPMENT or METHODS which comply with a STANDARD without infringing that IPR. For the avoidance of doubt in exceptional cases where a STANDARD can only be implemented by technical solutions, all of which are infringement of IPRs, all such IPRs shall be considered ESSENTIAL."'

The issue in this particular case was whether a declaration within the ETSI scheme that a patent was essential to a standard, and that licences were available on FRAND terms under it, was, without more, an adequate basis under the inherent jurisdiction of the court for a manufacturer affected by such declaration to seek a declaration from the court that the declared patents were not essential to the standard to which they had been declared. The Court of Appeal, upholding the judgment of the Patents Court, found that it was.

The consequences of the offer of a licence on FRAND terms for a standards essential patent on the remedies that are available, as against someone who has refused a licence on the terms offered (for example, because it does not regard the terms as FRAND[8] or the patent to be valid or essential) to the holder of a patent that is then successfully enforced, and is essential to that standard have yet to be addressed by the English courts, although those in Germany and the Netherlands have done so to some degree, and come to rather different conclusions.[9] The issue is particularly important because the nature of a standard will usually preclude there being a non-infringing alternative, and although the courts in the EU Member States have in theory a discretion under the Enforcement Directive as to whether or not to grant a final injunction where a valid patent has been found to be infringed, the practice has been almost invariably to do so. This is in stark contrast to the USA where, since the decision of the Supreme Court in *eBay v MercExchange*[10] courts do not do so in a substantial number of cases. Instead, the courts in Europe have analysed the issue of injunctive relief on standards essential patents in the context of Article 102 TFEU, an approach that has been encouraged by the actions of the European Commission in the proceedings that it has brought against certain holders of standards essential patents alleging that manner in which these sought to enforce their stands essential patents constituted an abuse of their dominant position.[11] The Court of Justice, in Case C-170/13 *Huawei v ZTE*[12] has now clarified the approach to be taken in such cases:

'1)   Article 102 TFEU must be interpreted as meaning that the proprietor of a patent essential to a standard established by a standardisation body, which has given an irrevocable undertaking to that body to grant a licence to third parties on fair, reasonable and non-discriminatory ('FRAND') terms, does not abuse its dominant position, within the meaning of that article, by bringing an action for infringement seeking an injunction prohibiting the infringement of its patent or seeking the recall of products for the manufacture of which that patent has been used, as long as:
   –   prior to bringing that action, the proprietor has, first, alerted the alleged infringer of the infringement complained about by designating that patent and specifying the way in which it has been infringed, and, secondly, after the alleged infringer has expressed its willingness to conclude a licensing agreement on FRAND terms, presented to that infringer a specific, written offer for a licence on such terms, specifying, in particular, the royalty and the way in which it is to be calculated, and
   –   where the alleged infringer continues to use the patent in question, the alleged infringer has not diligently responded to that offer, in accordance with recognised commercial practices in the field and in good faith, this being a matter which must be established on the basis of objective factors and which implies, in particular, that there are no delaying tactics..

2)   Article 102 TFEU must be interpreted as not prohibiting, in circumstances such as those in the main proceedings, an undertaking in a dominant position and holding a patent essential to a standard established by a standardisation body, which has given an undertaking to the standardisation body to grant licences for that patent on FRAND terms, from bringing an action for infringement against the alleged infringer of its patent and seeking the rendering of accounts in relation to past acts of use of that patent or an award of damages in respect of those acts of use.'

Also in contrast to the USA no English court (or, at least to the author's knowledge, any other European court), has as yet made any determination as to what constitutes a FRAND royalty, reflecting in large part the practice in the UK and the rest of Europe for courts to consider issues of quantum only after liability has been determined in favour of the patentee. English courts, as with others in Europe, have resisted attempts to get them to determine what constitutes a FRAND royalty for global licence of a portfolio of patents before dealing with the infringement and validity of the patents that have been asserted.[13] Neither have the English courts as yet been prepared to grant an injunction on a single standards essential patent that had been found to be valid and infringed where the defendant had refused a global licence of a portfolio of patents but had not been offered the opportunity to take a licence on FRAND terms of that single patent.[14]

Much patent litigation in the UK (and in Germany) in recent years has been directed at manufacturers of mobile telephone handsets, and has primarily concerned patents that have been declared essential to various ETSI telecommunications standards. Given the large number of such patents it is common in such cases for the patentee to assert in proceedings only a small proportion of the patents that it has declared to be essential,[15] although even then the outcome of such cases, where these were fought through to trial, has been that only a very small percentage of the standards essential patents actually asserted have been held to be valid and essential.[16]

1   See the *W3C patent policy* at: www.w3.org/Consortium/Patent-Policy-20040205.
2   More recently however the IEEE, in March 2015, in its SSO role, which for example has involved the development of WiFi standards amended the IEEE-SA Standards Board Bylaws which require a: 'statement that the Submitter will make available a license for Essential Patent Claims to an unrestricted number of Applicants on a worldwide basis without compensation or under Reasonable Rates, with other reasonable terms and conditions that are demonstrably free of any unfair discrimination to make, have made, use, sell, offer to sell, or import any Compliant Implementation that practices the Essential Patent Claims for use in conforming with the IEEE Standard', defines such, 'Reasonable Rate' as 'appropriate compensation to the patent holder for the practice of an Essential Patent Claim excluding the value, if any, resulting from the inclusion of that Essential Patent Claim's technology in the IEEE Standard', and has provided that in addition, determination of such Reasonable Rates should include, but need not be limited to, the consideration of various parameters that it also sets out at: https://standards.ieee.org/develop/policies/bylaws/sb_bylaws.pdf.
3   See the Third Generation Partnership Project website at: www.3gpp.org.
4   Such as ARIB for Japan and for the USA the American National Standards Institution (ANSI) at: web.ansi.org. ANSI for example has an online database of 'patent letters' which contain patent holder statements that have been provided to ANSI, and claim patents or patent applications as being essential, or potentially essential, to the implementation of an American National Standard.
5   See: www.etsi.org/legal/home.htm.
6   COM (92) 445 final (27 October 1992).
7   *Nokia Corpn v Interdigital Corpn* [2006] EWHC 802 (Patents Court); [2006] EWCA (Civ) 1618 (Court of Appeal), in which it was established that the English courts had a discretion under their inherent jurisdiction to make a declaration that a patent was not essential to a standard. See also *Nokia Corpn v Interdigital Corpn* [2004] EWHC 2920 (Patents Court); [2005] EWCA (Civ) 614 (Court of Appeal) for an earlier decision in other litigation between the same parties on a similar point.
8   As to which there is a substantial literature, one contribution to which is Mariniello, Mario, *'Fair, Reasonable and Non-Discriminatory (FRAND) Terms: A Challenge for Competition Authorities'*, *Journal of Competition Law & Economics* [2011] 7(3),

523–41, discussing the role of competition law in such assessment. Much of the literature on the subject originates from the USA, but for a recent European review of such matters see Meniere, Yann: *JRC Science and Policy Report – Fair Reasonable and Non-Discriminatory (FRAND) Licensing Terms* (EU, 2015). Moreover the European Commission in its *Public Consultation on Patents and Standards* (see fn 1 to para 9.02 above) asked what principles and methods the respondents found useful in order to apply such terms in practice,

9   See *Orange Book Standard* (Case KZR 39/06 German Federal Supreme Court, 6 May 2009); *Philips v SK Kassetten* (The Hague District Court, 17 March 2010). Decisions of lower German infringement courts subsequent to *Orange Book Standard* have applied it in a variety of different ways, but this disparity should be resolved by the decision of the Court of Justice in Case C-170/13 *Huawei Technologies Co. Ltd v ZTE Corp. and anr* referred to in fn 12 below.

10 *eBay Inc v MercExchange LLC* 547 US 338 (2006).

11 See the full European Commission decision in Case AT.39985 – *Motorola – Enforcement Of GPRS Standard Essential Patents* (EC, 29 April 2014) and associated Press Release Antitrust: Commission finds that Motorola Mobility infringed EU competition rules by misusing standard essential patents (IP/14/489, 29 April 2014) and the full Commission Decision accepting undertakings in Case AT.39939 – Samsung – Enforcement Of UMTS Standard Essential Patents, the associated Press Release Antitrust: Commission accepts legally binding commitments by Samsung Electronics on standard essential patent injunctions (IP/14/490, 29 April 2014) and the commitments as given, at: http://ec.europa.eu/competition/antitrust/cases/dec_docs/39939/39939_1502_5.pdf. See also Antitrust decisions on standard essential patents (SEPs) – *Motorola Mobility and Samsung Electronics – Frequently asked questions MEMO/14/322*, 29 April 2014) and the more recent comments on these decisions, and on current European Commission policy in this area by the new Director-General for Competition Law in the Commission: Italianer, Alexander, *Shaken, not stirred. Competition Law Enforcement and Standard Essential Patents*, 21 April 2015, at: http://ec.europa.eu/competition/speeches/text/sp2015_03_en.pdf. For an approach to such matters which does not depend on competition law from Professor Sir Robin Jacob, a former English Patents Court, and subsequently Court of Appeal Judge, see Jacob, Robin, *FRAND: A Legal Analysis*, October 2014, at: http://is.jrc.ec.europa.eu/pages/ISG/EURIPIDIS/documents/RobinJacob.pdf and for a critique of the use of competition law in such cases from the same source see Jacob, Robin, 'Competition Authorities Support Grasshoppers: Competition Law as a Threat to Innovation', *Competition Policy International*, Vol 9, No 2, Autumn 2013, 15–29) at: https://www.competitionpolicyinternational.com/file/view/7056.

12 Case C-170/13 *Huawei Technologies Co. Ltd v ZTE Corp. and anr* (Court of Justice, 16 July 2015).

13 *Vringo v ZTE* [2013] EWHC 1591 (Pat).

14 *Vringo v ZTE* [2015] EWHC 214 (Pat) and *Unwired Planet v Huawei Technologies and ors* [2015] EWHC 1029 (Pat).

15 Although even then more patents may be in issue than can be the subject of a single trial. From a case management point of view the practice has developed in the English courts when, say for example a dozen patents are asserted, of splitting these into trials of two or three related cases at a time, separated by three or four months, and allowing the patentee to choose the first set of patents to be tried, the defendant the second set of patents to be tried, and so on. As the patentee will tend to choose the cases on which it thinks it is most likely to prevail, and the defendant those on which it thinks the patentee least likely to prevail, it has never yet proved necessary to have trials as to all the patents that were initially asserted, and it has been possible to resolve disputes after no more than two such trials.

16 Indeed *Nokia v IPCom* [2011] EWHC 1470 (Pat), [2012] EWCA Civ 567 and *Vringo v ZTE* [2014] EWHC 3924 (Pat) [2015] EWHC 214 are the only such English cases

to date in which standards essential patents that have been asserted have been held to be valid and essential, although the patent in the first of these cases (in which declarations of non-infringement as to certain other designs of handset were also given) was amended in EPO opposition proceedings as a result of which it was held in *IPCom v HTC* [2015] EWHC 1034 no longer to be essential to the relevant standard, and not to be infringed by the handsets in issue.

Patent pools

9.04 Underlying many standards are 'patent pools'. In their broadest sense, these arise in the following way. When two or more companies each have patent rights that overlap, they can find themselves in a 'standoff' which can only be resolved in one of two ways if they each want to commercialize their own technology. One option is for each to attack the validity and scope of the other's patent in long drawn out proceedings. An easier solution, although one which may only be achieved after litigation has been started or threatened, is to reach a negotiated settlement. If both sides are to commercialize the patented technology, such a settlement will involve a cross-licence, by which each party grants to the other a licence under its own patent. Sometimes no money will pass hands, but if one party's patent rights are more valuable than those of the other, then a balancing royalty payment may be agreed. Such arrangements, whilst satisfactory for the parties involved, can serve to raise the barriers to market entry against third parties, which have then to face, and to overcome or to avoid, two sets of patents held by parties which had formerly used such rights against each other but now co-operate in their exploitation. Although there is no generally accepted definition of the term, a 'patent pool' is no more than a cross-licensing arrangement taken a stage further. Thus, it will typically involve more than two parties licensing their patents to each other, or to some commonly owned vehicle, in a particular technical field. As such an arrangement has the potential to raise the barrier to market entry even further as against third parties, such pools have been the subject of especial scrutiny from competition law authorities over the years. Such pools, however, also have the potential to confer benefits on third parties, by serving to reduce barriers to entry where they also make licences under all the pooled patents available on a non-discriminatory basis to third parties. Then, instead of having to approach all patentees separately, a prospective licensee can seek a 'one stop shop' for the licence that it needs.

The approach of the US competition law authorities to patent pools was established in 1931 in *Standard Oil Company (Indiana) v United States*[1] concerning such agreements between four oil companies and which had brought to an end a decade of hard fought patent litigation over patented methods of increasing gasoline yields from crude oil. The Supreme Court recognized that without such an agreement technical progress had been impeded, and noted that: 'An interchange of patent rights and a division of royalties … is frequently necessary if technical advancement is not to be blocked by threatened litigation … such interchange may promote rather than restrain competition'.

Despite this however, patent pools were commonly the subject of antitrust actions in the US until the 1980s, when the US Department of Justice (DOJ) started taking a more tolerant view and recognized that patent pools could provide benefits, very much as articulated in *Standard Oil,* which could be set against the risk of reducing competition between companies that might otherwise have competed in the relevant market. Now the DOJ adopts a two-part test in examining a patent pool before challenging it: First, does the pool damage competition that already existed or is likely otherwise to have come into existence. Second, is such damage reasonably necessary in order to achieve an even greater procompetitive benefit? Such procompetitive benefit is normally manifested by making licences under the pooled patents available to third parties on non-discriminatory terms, as should be the case with patents for standards, and as to which patent pools can provide in large part a method by which new standards can be set, maintained, and policed so that users adhere to the standard and interoperability is enhanced. An example of the application of this principle was the DOJ's approval in 1997 of the MPEG-2 digital compression patent pool, established by eight companies and a university, under 27 patents. The pool made a package licence of patents that control the MPEG-2 standard available not only to other members of the pool but to third parties, with each of the members of the pool sharing in the royalty income.

Competition law has the potential to apply to such activities in the EU under TFEU, Articles 101–102 the former being directed towards arrangements between parties that affect competition, and the latter towards the abuse of a dominant position. Both provide means to control patent pools, and have indeed been so used, as for example in *IGR Stereo Television*[2] in 1980 when an attempt by the German television industry, which had pooled patents in relation to stereo television reception, not to grant equivalent licences under the pooled patents to a manufacturer based in Finland, which was not at the time a member of the EU, was blocked by the European Commission. Moreover, the general 'safe harbour' provided for patent and know how licences under Article 101 by virtue of the Technology Transfer Block Exemption[3] does not, by Recital 7, apply to agreements between members of a patent or know-how pool which relate to the pooled technologies.

However, in the EU, TFEU, Article 101 also permits an otherwise potentially anticompetitive arrangement such as a patent pool, to proceed where this confers a public benefit. Agreements on standards, however, need not necessarily involve patents, and the European Commission's thinking on such agreements is set out in the Commission

Notice, *Guidelines on the applicability of [TFEU, Article 101] to horizontal cooperation agreements*, under the section on standardization agreements.[4] The Commission's approach to 'technology pools' (which term includes patent pools, is set out in the Communication from the Commission, *Guidelines on the application of Article 101 of the Treaty on the Functioning of the European Union to technology transfer agreements*[5]).

As an example of the European Commission approach in Europe, the major consumer electronics companies Hitachi, Matsushita Electrical, Mitsubishi Electrical, Time Warner, and Toshiba notified their DVD (Digital Versatile Disc) technology agreement to the Commission in May 1999. Under the agreement, the parties pooled their respective patents covering applications of DVD technology. Certain holders of essential patents had agreed to licence their patents through a single nonexclusive, and non-discriminatory licence programme to be administered by Toshiba. The Commission's investigation concluded that this patent pool would help promote technical and economic progress by allowing quick and efficient introduction of the DVD technology. The Commission also found that the agreement did not contain any unnecessary or excessive restrictions on competition, and on that basis provided an administrative 'comfort' letter.[6] Another example, is provided by the Commission's provision of a 'comfort letter' in relation to a number of patent licensing agreements relating to certain patents held by the notifying parties that were asserted to be essential to third generation (3G) mobile telephony.[7]

1   *Standard Oil Company (Indiana) v United States* 51 S Ct 421; 51 S Ct 429.
2   IGR Stereo Television – see European Commission, *Eleventh Report on Competition Policy*, p. 63.
3   As to which see **Chapter 3** at paras 3.13ff.
4   [2011] OJ C11/1, paras 257–335.
5   [2014] OJ C89/031, paras 244–273.
6   *Commission Press Release, IP/00/1135* of 9 October 2000, referring to the notification of the programme published at [1999] OJ C242/05. Such notification was necessary at the time in order to secure the application of what is now TFEU, Article 101(3) to an agreement that was potentially in breach of Article 101(1), but it is no longer necessary, or possible, as national courts can now make their own assessments under Article 101(3) as well as under Article 101(1), and so there is no longer any basis for 'comfort letters' either.
7   *Commission Press Release, IP/02/1651* of 12 November 2002. Again there is no longer any need for the Commission to review proposed such arrangements in advance, or any scope for them so to do, so there is no longer any basis for 'comfort letters'.

Patent ambush and patent overdeclaration

9.05   'Patent ambush' is a somewhat unspecific term for the situation that occurs when a participant in an SSO fails during the standards development process to disclose that it has rights that are essential to the standard. In its most extreme form it involves that party also actively promoting the incorporation of such technology in the standard. But irrespective of how the situation comes about, it can mean that the possibility of considering alternative technologies in full knowledge of their IP consequences is foreclosed, and the competitive process distorted. An early example in the USA concerned Dell Computer.[1]

Another example concerned Rambus Inc, that develops technologies used in computer memory devices. Rambus participated in the work of an SSO, the Joint Electron Device Engineering Council (JEDEC) without revealing to JEDEC or its members that it possessed a patent, and pending patent applications that involved technologies ultimately adopted in JEDEC standards. Rambus subsequently sued memory device manufacturers for infringement of certain such patents, and although a complaint against Rambus under US antitrust laws was initially upheld by the US Federal Trade Commission in August 2006, an appeal against this succeeded, in part because of uncertainty as what the SSO rules at the time mandated by way of disclosure.[2]

In Europe, an investigation initiated by the European Commission against Rambus, alleging 'patent ambush', was dropped in December 2009 after Rambus agreed to a worldwide royalty cap on the patents in issue, including a zero royalty rate for those standards adopted when it was a JEDEC member.[3]

A concern as to 'patent ambush' also featured in an investigation of the ETSI rules by the European Commission which was closed in December 2005 when ETSI changed its rules to strengthen yet further its already existing requirement for early disclosure of patents, and other IP that is essential for the implementation of a standard.[4] Ensuring that such rules are sufficiently rigorous is especially important for the Commission given the need in challenging patent ambush under TFEU, Article 102 to show that the abuse is by a company that is dominant in the relevant market in the first place.

In practice however there is a greater tendency to over-declare patents as essential to a standard, in an effort to boost licensing income from a portfolio, rather than to undeclare, so allegations of patent ambush are now rare.[5]

1   *In re Dell Computer* (1996) 121 FTC 616, at p. 626.
2   *In the matter of Rambus Inc* (Federal Trade Commission, 2 August 2006). A remedy was subsequently ordered by the FTC involving a compulsory licence remedy at a rate fixed by the FTC, and dropping over time to zero, but was suspended by the FTC pending the successful appeal in *Rambus Inc v Federal Trade Commission* (CADC, 22 April 2008).
3   *Commission Press Release*, IP/09/1897, 9 December 2009.
4   *Commission Press Release*, IP/05/1565, 12 December 2005.
5   See eg Goodman, David and Myers, Robert, '3G Cellular Standards and Patents' (*IEEE Wireless Communications*, 13 June 2005) and other papers published by these authors, some as Fairfield Resources International.

Patents and computer programs

Introduction

9.06 Most people are used to the idea that the law of copyright protects computer programs. Many struggle, however, with the concept that patents can also protect them. This is especially so for the uninitiated, who reading the express exclusions for computer programs from patentability in the UK under PA 1977, and EPC on which it is based, might be forgiven for thinking that computer programs were not patentable. Thus, in Europe computer programs appear at first sight to be excluded from patentability by the express language of EPC, Article 52(2) (reflected in the UK by PA 1977, s 1(2)) which not only appears to exclude: 'programs for computers' but also, amongst others, 'mathematical methods', 'methods for performing mental acts ... or doing business', or 'presentations of information'. However, by EPC, Article 52(3) (also reflected in the UK by PA 1977, s 1(2)) these exceptions only apply to the extent that a patent or applications 'relates to that thing as such'.

The EPO has adopted a narrow interpretation of the Article 52(2) exclusion for computer programs which has resulted in its granting tens of thousands of patents for computer-implemented inventions. Many of these patents are held by large non-European companies, which may well reflect the perceived value of patents as means for protecting such inventions in the USA and the Far East, as against the (evidently incorrect, at least for computer programs, although entirely understandable) perception prevalent amongst many in Europe that the Article 52(2) exclusion means what it appears at first sight to say. The EPO has felt able to grant patents for many computer-implemented inventions by focusing increasingly on the need for the invention to have 'technical character', and instancing some of the other Article 52(2) exclusions, such as that for business methods, as examples of cases which lack technical character. The pressure to secure such protection has been recognized by the English courts, and thus in *Aerotel/Macrossan*[1] the Court of Appeal observed:

'18 Th[e] pressure [on the European patent regimes to permit patents to business methods and computer programs] in part stems from the fact that, following *State Street* (business methods) and *Alappat* (computer programs) people have been getting patents for these subject-matters in the USA. Since they can get them there, they must as a commercial necessity apply for them everywhere. If your competitors are getting or trying to get the weapons of business method or computer program patents you must too. An arms race in which the weapons are patents has set in. The race has naturally spread worldwide'

The US cases here referred to were decisions of the Court of Appeals for the Federal Circuit in 1998, and 1994 respectively, but which are now no longer treated as authoritative in the light of more recent US Supreme Court decisions culminating in that in *Alice Corporation v CLS Bank*[2] and which have had the result of making patents for computer implemented inventions harder to obtain, and harder to defend in the USA. None the less, the effects of such cases were felt at the time.

The pressure to try to use patents to protect computer programs initially arose as a consequence in part of many technical processes being now computer controlled, and indeed many types of electronic device which would once have consisted of discrete components and the patent eligibility of which no-one would have questioned are now implemented by programmed microprocessors. However, more generally it has arisen because copyright, the IPR most generally understood as protecting computer programs, protects only expression and not ideas and principles,[3] namely procedures, methods of operation, and mathematical concepts.[4] Thus, although copyright is a perfectly adequate right to prevent piracy of computer programs (in the context 'bit for bit' copying[5]) its efficacy has been limited, and rightly so, in protecting what has come to be called the 'look and feel' of computer programs, the very term recognizing that what is really being copied is the idea, and that such 'look and feel' provides the only link between the two. Much computer program copyright litigation over the years has been concerned with the question of where one draws the line along the continuum between mere ideas (not protected by copyright) and their expression (protected by copyright) – the 'idea-expression dichotomy'.[6] In contrast, patents provide inappropriate protection against piracy, for which copyright, with its relatively relaxed requirements as to originality, has proved its worth and remains unchallenged for such purpose. But patents provide an ideal, readymade solution to demands for protection of broader scope, protecting the ideas and principles behind, or 'look and feel' in programmes.

Although Europe is not alone in excluding computer programs from patentability[7] their apparent exclusion has had two major adverse effects from the perspective of European interests. The first is that many people and organizations based in Europe have been misled into thinking that the novel, and inventive principles underlying computer programs could not be patented, either in Europe or elsewhere. Thus, European companies may have lost out elsewhere, whilst US and Far Eastern companies have persevered and secured protection in Europe. The second is that the sterile discussion as to exclusions, and the almost philosophical issues involved in the analysis, when undertaken in isolation, of the 'technical effect' required under the EPC for patentability of computer program-related inventions has distracted attention in this field from analysing, and developing the law as to the real core issues in patentability, and which are met daily in other fields of industry – namely what is obvious over the prior art, and what is the legitimate scope of claim given the underlying contribution to the art.

Thus, many in the computer programming community object to many applications for computer program-related patents on the basis that they are obvious, or seek claims of over-broad scope given the inventive contribution. Such objections, which are often well founded, would be better addressed directly, rather than by seeking to use them to justify a broad interpretation of the exclusion for computer programs. EPO practice has however in effect come to take account of this point of view by conflating the analysis of the applicability of the 'computer program as such' exclusion with that of inventive step, rather than dealing with the exclusion separately at the outset, although the English courts still deal with them separately.

1   *Aerotel v Telco* [2006] EWHC 997 (Pat); *Macrossan's Application* [2006] EWHC 705 (Ch) (Patents Court); *Aerotel v Telco Holdings Ltd & Macrossan's Application* [2006] EWCA Civ 1371; [2007] 1 All ER 225 (Court of Appeal).
2   *Alice Corporation Pty. Ltd. v. CLS Bank International, et al* 134 S. Ct. 2347, 2359 (2014).
3   Article 1.2 of Council Directive 91/250 on the Legal Protection of Computer Programs, [1991] OJ L122/42.
4   Although where the name of the computer program is registered as a trade mark this provides a more convenient means of enforcement in such cases where, as will usually be the case for computer programs which are widely commercialized, such pirated computer programs are sold by reference to such trade mark.
5   TRIPS, Article 9.2.
6   In the UK one can instance the computer program copyright litigation in *John Richardson Computers v Flanders* [1993] FSR 497; *Ibcos Computers v Barclays Mercantile Finance* [1994] FSR 275; *Cantor Fitzgerald International v Tradition (UK)* [2000] RPC 95; *Navitaire v Easyjet* [2004] EWHC 1725 (Ch); and *Nova Productions v Mazooma Games* [2006] EWHC 24 (Ch); [2006] EWCA Civ 1044 (Court of Appeal). See also the decision of the EU Court of Justice in Case C-406/10 *SAS Institute Inc v World Programming Ltd*, on a reference from the English courts, whose judgments are at [2010] EWHC 1829. [2013] EWHC 69 (Ch) and [2013] EWCA Civ 1482. Although the USA had a considerable body of such 'look and feel' computer software copyright litigation in the 1980s and early 1990s, there has been much less since, presumably reflecting the increasing importance of patents as a way of protecting the principles behind computer programmes and a recognition of this.
7   See Lionel Bently, et al, *Exclusions from Patentability and Exceptions and Limitations to Patentees' Rights*, WIPO Standing Committee on Patents, 2 September 2010) (SCP/15/3 Annex I) and Brad Sherman, *Computer Programs As Excluded Patentable Subject Matter* (WIPO Standing Committee on Patents, 2 September 2010) (SCP/15/3 Annex II).

Patenting of computer programs – development of the law in the EPO

9.07   The express statutory exclusion of computer programs from patentability in Europe was established back in the early 1970s when computer programs were often provided at no charge to those who had purchased the large expensive computers of the time and no one could have predicted how all pervasive computer programs were to

become, or how for example they would come to control the operation
of most items of electronic and electrical apparatus. Much of the case
law has been concerned with establishing quite what these exclusions,
and in particular that for computer programs, mean in practice. Thus,
EPC, Article 52(2)(c) declares that: 'schemes, rules and methods for
performing mental acts, playing games or doing business, and programs
for computers' (along with, in other sub-paragraphs, amongst other
things, mathematical methods and presentations of information) 'shall
not be regarded as inventions'. This is qualified in Article 52(3) by which
such exclusion applies: 'only to the extent that a ... patent relates to such
subject matter or activities as such'.

The public policy background to the computer program exclusion
was discussed in 2005 by the English Patents Court, when holding two
applications for patents on computerised business methods so excepted
as methods of doing business in *CFPH's Applications*[1] in which an
extensive analysis of the different exclusions was undertaken in an
effort to demonstrate that they had no unifying theme, and so should
not be approached consistently. In the course of this discussion it was
observed:[2]

'35 ... Although it is hotly disputed now by some special interest groups,
the truth is, or ought to be, well known. It is because at the time the EPC was
under consideration it was felt in the computer industry that such patents
were not really needed,[3] were too cumbersome (it was felt that searching the
prior art would be a big problem[4]) and would do more harm than good.[5] I
shall not go into details here but it is worth noting that the software industry
in America developed at an astonishing pace when no patent protection was
available.[6] Copyright law protects computer programs against copying. A
patent on a computer program would stop others from using it even though
there had been no copying at all. So there would have to be infringement
searches. Furthermore you cannot have a sensible patent system unless there
exists a proper body of prior art that can be searched. Not only are most
computer programs supplied in binary form – unintelligible to humans – but
most of the time it is actually illegal to convert them into human-readable
form.[7] A patent system where it is illegal to search most of the prior art is
something of an absurdity.'

However, the alleged problem to which one of the last sentences in
this passage this alludes, as to establishing a prior art base, is one that is
faced with all new technologies, and it is the patent literature itself that
is generated in those early days of a new technology which provides, as
time goes on, by far the most useful prior art base, and response to such
problem. Neither, as to the final sentence, would searching against such
patents, the scope of which is defined by their claims, infringe copyright
in the computer programs that such patents protect, and as for searching
the non-patent literature the most relevant such material in this field
consists of manuals, and documentation rather than the programs with

which they are associated. Indeed such old manuals and documentation are now hard to come by, which has made the patent literature all the more important.

It should also be recalled that the exclusion in the EPC of computer programs from patentability is only one of the hurdles on the road to a granted patent. Thus, to obtain a patent it is also necessary that the invention be novel and inventive. However, the emphasis on trying to analyse the scope of the computer program exclusion in isolation from these other issues, as used to be the case in the EPO, and remains to some degree the case in the UK, has diverted attention from the proper analysis of these other more traditional patent issues in relation to such inventions. This is unfortunate as much of the criticism of the patent applications that have been the subject of the reported cases in this area has been that they are obvious or of over-broad scope and seems, wrongly, to proceed on the basis that the exclusion is the only barrier to the grant of such patents. In those cases where this criticism is indeed well founded these other hurdles, were they ever to reach the stage where they came to be applied, would prevent patents being granted.

Notwithstanding the exclusion, patents in Europe, both at the EPO and in national patent offices, have long been granted on inventions involving computer programs, and by mid-2005, ten years ago, in *CFPH's Applications* it was said that more than 40,000 such patents had been granted. This had happened by granting patents for inventions involving computer programs which are novel and inventive provided, under the approach which the EPO has applied, ever since the decision of a Technical Board of Appeal in T-1173/97 *Computer Program Product/IBM*[8] in 1998, that the invention brings about a technical effect which goes beyond the normal physical interactions between the computer programme, and the computer hardware on which it is run – ie it confers a 'further technical effect'. The manner in which this approach is applied is discussed in further detail below at para 9.08.

The EPO had previously adopted a 'technical contribution' approach although it appears to have been somewhat inconsistently applied. Such earlier EPO cases do however provide useful examples of inventions which would be found to confer a 'further technical effect' today. Thus an invention that prolongs the useful life of X-ray tubes by connecting an X-ray device to a programmed computer that controls the X-ray tube to achieve optimum exposure while avoiding overload can readily be seen to do so.[9] In another early case[10] an EPO Technical Board of Appeal had found a software-related invention for a new, and substantially faster, method of and apparatus for manipulating images to make the requisite 'technical contribution' (in the approach of the time), observing:

'16. Generally speaking, an invention which would be patentable in accordance with conventional patentability criteria should not be excluded from protection by the mere fact that, for its implementation, modern technical means in the form of a computer program are used. Decisive is what technical contribution the invention as defined in the claim when considered as a whole makes to the known art.'

This final sentence of this quotation makes clear the distinction between the current 'further technical effect' approach, and the former 'technical contribution' approach; thus the former assessment is applied independently of the state of the art, whereas the latter is dependent on it. It was explained in T-1173/97 *Computer Program Product/IBM* why the 'further technical effect' approach was an improvement on the 'contribution' approach:

'(8) Determining the technical contribution an invention achieves with respect to the prior art is therefore more appropriate for the purpose of examining novelty and inventive step than for deciding on possible exclusion under Article 52(2) and (3),'

The technical contribution for such purpose cannot lie in excluded subject matter, so the result of adopting the 'further technical effect' approach in the case of a programmed computer is to defer the analysis of such technical contribution to the assessment of novelty and inventive step. The common basis for the requirement for 'technical contribution' under the old approach and for 'technical effect' under the new in analysing whether or not the exclusion applies comes not from the EPC itself but instead from the EPC Implementing Rules, which implicitly recognize that an invention must have technical character, and state:

'Rule 27(11) The description shall: (a) specify the technical field to which the invention relates ...

Rule 29(1) The claims shall define the matter for which protection is sought in terms of the technical features of the invention.'

As to what actually is meant by the word 'technical' in T-0931/95/ *Controlling Pension Benefits System/PBS PARTNERSHIP*[11] an EPO Technical Board of Appeal did recognize the difficulty but observed that:

'It may very well be that, as put forward by the applicant, the meaning of the term "technical" or "technical character" is not particularly clear. However this also applies to the term "invention". In the Board's view the fact that the exact meaning of a term may be disputed does in itself not necessarily constitute a good reason for not using that term as a criterion, certainly not in the absence of a better term; case law may clarify the issue.'

A further significant development took place in 2006 with the decision of a Technical Board of Appeal in T-154/04 *Estimating Sales Activity/DUNS LICENSING ASSOCIATES*.[12] This analysed the EPO case law and practice to date, including that of some national courts, explained why the EPO approach had a sound legal basis in the EPC, and refused the applicant's request to refer matters to the Enlarged

Board of Appeal. It observed that non-technical features, to the extent that they do not interact with the technical subject matter of the claim for solving a technical problem, ie non-technical features 'as such', do not provide a technical contribution over the prior art, and are thus ignored in assessing novelty and inventive step. In other words, the improvement provided by the invention must be in a field that is not excluded, and thus contributions in the business method field, as here, not being technical, cannot contribute towards novelty and inventive step.[13]

While the statutory provisions governing patentability are the same throughout Europe, there have long been differences in relation to software related patents between the case law, and practice of the Technical Boards of Appeal of the EPO, and the patent offices and courts of Member States. This is well instanced by the UK, in which the exclusion from patentability for computer programs was only one of the exclusions in practice to present an applicant with problems, because the courts, on appeal, often held patent applications for software also to fall within other of the exclusions. As explained below, although there may be fewer rejections in the UK on other excluded grounds in the future, the English Court of Appeal in *Aerotel/Macrossan*[14] made it clear that the UK was, in view of its own precedents, not following the current EPO approach, and case law on computer programs, especially as in its view it could not identify an entirely consistent approach in the EPO case law.

The Court of Appeal decision was itself criticized in T-154/04 *Estimating Sales Activity/DUNS LICENSING ASSOCIATES* but in the light of its perception as to inconsistencies in the EPO approach the Court of Appeal in *Aerotel/Macrossan* had suggested various questions directed to resolving these that might be referred to the EPO Enlarged Board of Appeal, since as a national court it lacks any power to do so directly. These particular questions were not referred by the then President of the EPO, but eventually the subsequent President of the EPO referred other questions to the Enlarged Board of Appeal. Numerous *amicus* briefs were filed but the Enlarged Board of Appeal, in its opinion G-3/08 *Programs for Computers*[15] held the four questions referred to it to be inadmissible as it could not, and contrary to the arguments advanced in the reference to it, identify any divergence in the case law of the EPO Technical Boards of Appeal, subject to one point only, that on analysis reflected a legitimate development of the case law rather than a divergence, as only the one approach had subsequently been followed by the Technical Boards of Appeal. In explaining its reasons for rejecting the reference, the Enlarged Board Decision provided a useful analysis of the development of EPO law and practice in this area, although the opinion, both in holding the reference to be inadmissible, and in its support for the approach of the Technical Boards of Appeal, has not escaped criticism.[16]

1   *CFPH LLC v Comptroller General of Patents Designs and Trade Marks* [2005] EWHC 1589 (Pat); [2006] IP&T; [2006] RPC 259 (Patents Court).
2   See also **Chapter 5** at para 5.02 for observations to similar effect by the English Court of Appeal in *Aerotel v Telco Holdings Ltd & Macrossan's Application* [2006] EWCA Civ 1371; [2007] 1 All ER 225 (Court of Appeal).
3   [Footnote in Original] As late as 1971 the industry declared that it was content to be protected by the law of contract and trade secrets alone: Dworkin, 'The Nature of Computer Programs', *Information Technology: The Challenge to Copyright*, Sweet & Maxwell, 1984, p. 89.
4   [Footnote in Original] Rule 39(1) of the Patent Cooperation Treaty recognized that an International Searching Authority might not be suitably equipped.
5   [Footnote in Original] The fact that computer programmes (or, what comes to much the same thing, computers when programmed) could be patented in the UK under the 1949 Act adds force to my observations, because it goes to show that the exclusion in the EPC must have been a deliberate act of policy.
6   [Footnote in Original] See Rossi, Maria Alessandra, 'Software Patents: A Closer Look at the European Commission's Proposal' (2005) *Siena Memos and Papers in Law and Economics*, No 30, Universita di Siena.
7   [Footnote in Original] See, for example, the Software Directive (91/250/EEC), arts 4 and 6; Rossi, *op cit* p. 38. On the policy problems in general see Rossi, 31–45.
8   T-1173/97 *Computer Program Product/IBM* (Board 3.5.01, 1 July 1998), [2000] EPOR 219.
9   T-0026/86 *X-ray apparatus/KOCH AND STERZEL* [1988] OJ EPO 19; [1988] EPOR 72.
10 T-0208/84 *Computer-related invention/VICOM* [1987] OJ EPO 14; [1987] 2 EPOR 74.
11 T-0931/95 *Controlling Pension Benefits System/PBS PARTNERSHIP* (Board 3.5.01, 8 September 2000), [2002] EPOR 52.
12 T-154/04 *Estimating Sales Activity/DUNS LICENSING ASSOCIATES* (Board 3.5.01, 15 November 2006) [2008] OJEPO, 46–79.
13 See below at para 9.11 for further discussion of the EPO approach to attempts to patent business methods.
14 *Aerotel v Telco* [2006] EWHC 997 (Pat); *Macrossan's Application* [2006] EWHC 705 (Ch) (Patents Court); *Aerotel v Telco & Macrossan 's Application* [2006] EWCA Civ 1371 (Court of Appeal).
15 G3/08 *Programs for Computers* (Enlarged Board of Appeal, 12 May 2010).
16 Such as Pila, Justine, 'Software Patents, Separation of Powers, and Failed Syllogisms: A Cornucopia from the Enlarged Board of Appeal of the European Patent Office', *University of Oxford Legal Research Paper*, No 48/2010, May 2010.

Unsuccessful attempts to amend the law in the EU

9.08   As already observed, the exclusions from patentability in the EPC, when considered in isolation, have limited the extent to which the EPO, in performing its role in the patent prosecution process, has had an opportunity to analyse one of the main, and most valid, complaints about many applications for computer program (and business method) patents – that they are for inventions that are trivial, or that they seek protection which is of too broad scope given their contribution to the art. Both of these are issues – obviousness and insufficiency – that get tested by the EPO before granting patent applications in other technologies, but in the cases of applications for computer program patents, matters used rarely to get that far as discussion instead was limited to the rather sterile, and philosophical issue of whether or not the alleged invention fell within one of the exclusions. This left a confused and unsatisfactory situation in Europe, with many granted software-related patents (often for applicants from outside Europe) likely to be enforceable in some courts but probably not in others, whilst many Europeans either fail to try to protect their own software-related inventions (either in Europe or in the USA) or remain oblivious to the fact that their activities (either in Europe or in the USA) may fall within the scope of such a granted patent belonging to a third party.

The mismatch between appearance and reality in the protection of computer-implemented inventions in Europe has long been recognized. Thus, in July 1997 the European Commission, in its 'Green Paper on the Community Patent and the patent system in Europe – Promoting innovation through patents'[1] also addressed the patentability of computer programs and software-related inventions. In its 'Follow-up to the Green Paper on the Community patent and the patent system in Europe'[2] it discussed the difficulties caused by the then current situation, identified an urgent need to remove apparent ambiguities, and the lack of legal certainty arising from the different ways in which Member States were implementing laws governing patents for software-related inventions, and noted, in relation to the action that it planned:

'The European Parliament supported the patentability of computer programs, on condition that the product in question meets the conditions of novelty and industrial application of a technical invention, as is the case of our economic partners at international level. The Commission shares this analysis and suggests action on two fronts. On the one hand, to fully ensure the achievement and operation of the internal market in this field, the Commission will present, as soon as possible, a draft Directive based on Article 100A of the EC Treaty aimed at harmonising Member States' legislation on the patentability of computer programs. This Directive should ensure uniform application and interpretation of the new rules on the patentability of computer programs throughout the whole Community. In this context, the parallel application of copyright and patent rights in the area of computer programs does not pose any particular difficulties, owing to the specific material covered by the two types of rights. The draft Directive will have to closely examine the question of possible exceptions to the general system covering the patentability of computer programs. In parallel with this legal action, the contracting states to the Munich Convention will need to take steps to modify Article 52(2) (c) of the European Patent Convention, in particular to abolish computer programs from the list of non-patentable inventions. This is necessary to ensure harmony between the work carried out a Community level and that undertaken in the framework of the Munich Convention.'

Meanwhile, the EPO had circulated a paper[3] in preparation for Intergovernmental Conferences in 1999 and 2000 aimed at revising the EPC. The EPO paper proposed that EPC 1973, Article 52(1)–(3) should be replaced with wording in line with TRIPS, Article 27(1) as follows: 'European patents shall be granted for any inventions in all fields of technology which are susceptible of industrial application which are new and which involve an inventive step'.

The EPO paper noted, however, that:

> 'Deletion of Article 52(2) and (3) EPC would get round the problems associated with the application and interpretation of any exception to patentability (what is a computer program as such?), but would not mean that the subject-matter and activities currently listed in Article 52(2) would then suddenly become patentable. Discoveries, scientific theories, mathematical methods, aesthetic creations, and purely mental or business acts, in particular, will continue not be eligible for patent protection as long as they do not involve a technical teaching. Thus any fundamental change in current granting practice and case law is unlikely to occur.
>
> Patentability would continue to depend solely on whether the claimed subject-matter, considered as a whole, had a technical character or not. The task of determining this can be left to the departments of the EPO, its boards of appeal and the national courts, who are best equipped to do it. They are better able than the legislator to take the right decision in each individual case, as well as to take account of technical advances and thus to promote the pragmatic development and harmonisation of European patent practice. If necessary, special interpretative provisions could be incorporated into the EPC's implementing Regulations.'

Deleting EPC, Article 52(2), as suggested by the EPO paper, would not only have addressed the exclusion for computer programs as such but would also have removed that for methods of doing business. However, matters in the end did not go so far, and it was not suggested, as one of the revisions to the EPC to be discussed in London at the Diplomatic Conference in November 2000 (the first since the EPC was first negotiated to undertake a wholesale revision) that the exclusion for computer programs be deleted.

The issue of protecting the ideas behind a computer program was also addressed tangentially by the European Commission in its *Report from the Commission on the implementation and effects of Directive 91/250/EEC*[4] in the context of a brief discussion of patent protection for software related inventions in which it was observed: 'One aim of patent protection would be to cover the underlying ideas and principles of a computer program, which according to recital 14 of Directive 91/250/EEC can never be protected by copyright.'

Shortly before the November 2000 Diplomatic Conference on the EPC, the European Commission, in October 2000, launched consultations on the topic of computer-implemented inventions. Comments were invited on the basis of a Consultation Paper whose aim was stated to be to help the Commission to identify the best approach to the issue so as to strike the right balance between promoting innovation, and ensuring adequate competition in the market place. The immediate result of launching the consultation was that the proposal to delete the relevant Article 52(2) exclusion at the Diplomatic Conference in November 2000 to amend the EPC was dropped. Answers to the Commission consultation were summarized in a report dated July 2001.[5]

At the end of this consultation process, the European Commission presented its 'Proposal for a Directive on the Patentability of Computer-implemented Inventions'[6] on 20 February 2002. The outcome of its consultations was a proposal aimed at harmonizing protection for computer-related inventions while avoiding any sudden change in the legal position. The proposal was a subtly drafted document that sought to tread a path between extending the scope of patent protection for computer programs, and resisting the call to exclude patent protection for them entirely. It would have preserved the principle that a 'technical contribution' is an essential requirement for any invention to be patentable. However, it would have defined this term in Article 2 as 'a contribution to the state of the art in a technical field that would not be obvious to a person skilled in the art', which expressly brings the issue of inventive step into the assessment, consistent with the approach that was by then being adopted by the EPO in the light of T-1173/97 *Computer Program Product/IBM*.[7] The other definition in Article 2 would have been as to those inventions to which the Proposal applied:

'"computer-implemented invention" means any invention the performance of which involves the use of a computer, computer network or other programmable apparatus and having one or more prima facie novel features which are realised wholly or partly by means of a computer program or computer programs.'

The accompanying explanatory memorandum noted that this definition excluded algorithms defined without reference to a physical environment, and that as a consequence of this definition 'the novelty' of such invention 'does not necessarily need to reside in a technical feature'. This is consistent with the technical contribution being assessed by reference to inventive step. Such inventions would, by Article 3 of the proposal, have been considered 'to belong to a field of technology' for which, under TRIPS, patents are to be available for inventions that are new, involve an inventive step, and are susceptible of industrial application, as was also declared in Article 4(1).

Article 4(2) of the proposal would have made it 'a condition of involving an inventive step that a computer-implemented invention must make a technical contribution' which by Article 4(3): 'shall be assessed by consideration of the difference between the scope of the patent claim considered as a whole, elements of which may comprise both technical and non-technical features, and the state of the art'.

Thus, as the explanatory memorandum stated, an invention, aspects of which are within the accompanying EPC, Article 52(2) exclusions, such as a method of doing business, might still be patentable if a non-obvious technical contribution were present. However, if there is no technical contribution, so that the contribution to the state of the art lay wholly in non-technical aspects, such as any excluded matter, there would be no patentable subject matter. Although the explanatory memorandum did not say this, expressly integrating the assessment of exclusions into that of inventive step might have heralded a significant difference in approach to software patents in the longer term, both by patent offices and those opposed to software patents, by addressing one of the real objections to many applications for such patents, which lies in the belief that they relate to contributions that are obvious, an issue that has been overshadowed in European patent law, and practice by the sterile focus on exclusions.

The balance struck by the regime for copyright protection for computer software in Europe would have been expressly preserved by Article 6, by which:

> 'Acts permitted under Directive 91/250 EC on the legal protection of computer programs by copyright, in particular provisions thereof relating to decompilation and interoperability ... shall not be affected through the protection granted by patents for inventions within the scope of this Directive.'[8]

Articles 7–8 of the proposal would have provided for monitoring as to the impact of computer-implemented inventions on innovation and competition, both within Europe and internationally, and on European business including e-commerce, with a view to producing a report on whether or not the rules governing patentability were adequate.

The proposal would thus seem to have been almost the minimum that the European Commission could do to try to deal with the issue without running into irreconcilable conflict with the established practice of the EPO. However, by focussing the investigation in prosecution onto issues of inventive step, instead of the sterile one of exclusions, the proposal would have had real value. However, the proposal elicited a furore of debate, and when it was ultimately rejected by the European Parliament in July 2005 the European Commission made it clear that, unlike the Biotechnology Directive, which had initially met, and then had overcome, such a fate, they would not introduce a further such proposal. Thus the law has continued to be developed in national courts and the EPO, which, as in the case of the English courts and the EPO, can sometimes diverge. However, as matters have transpired the EPO has come to adopt in its own case law a similar approach to that suggested by the proposal.

1   COM (97) 314.
2   COM (1999) 42 final – OJ EPO 1999, 197.
3   SACEPO 6/99.
4   COM(2000) 199 final, 10 April 2000.
5   The consultation paper, its replies and the analysis of the responses no longer appear to be available on the European Commission website. The European Commission also

commissioned a study specifically to look at the implications for small- and medium-sized enterprises (SMEs) involved in the development of software investigating how they managed their IP. This revealed that many smaller software, and IT companies were uncomfortable with, or uncertain about the protection offered by the patent system. This was not just due to uncertainties over infringement and patentability, but also because of the cost and the time taken in trying to secure protection.

6   COM (2002) 92 final: www.europa.eu.int/comm/internalmarket/en/indprop/com02–92en.pdf. For the full legislative history see: http://eur-lex.europa.eu/procedure/EN/172020.

7   T-1173/97 *Computer Program Product/IBM* (Board 3.5.01, 1 July 1998), [2000] EPOR 219.

8   Although this defence has not been introduced into any national patent laws in Europe, it will apply to litigation in the proposed Unified Patent Court as both European patents with unitary effect and non-opted out traditional European patents by virtue of Article 27(k) of the Agreement on a Unified Patent Court, which provides that, '[the rights conferred by a patent shall not extend to] the acts and the use of the obtained information as allowed under Articles 5 and 6 of Directive 2009/24/EC, in particular, by its provisions on decompilation and interoperability'. Directive 2009/24/EC has replaced, on codification, Directive 91/250 EC on the legal protection of computer programs. This is likely to lead in due course to the introduction of the defence in national patent laws. As to the Unified Patent Court see **Chapter 4** at para 4.29 et seq.

Current situation in EPO

9.09   As outlined above at para 9.07, the approach of the EPO to examining patent applications for computer implemented inventions changed as a result of the 1998 decision of a Technical Board of Appeal in T-1173/97 *Computer Program Product/IBM*.[1] The approach adopted as a result of this change remains the basis for the current approach to such examination, as explained in the *EPO Examination Guidelines*.[2]

At about the same time as the European Commission was launching the consultation which eventually led to its own proposal as to computer implemented inventions, as discussed above in para 9.08, the EPO was applying this approach to computer implementations of other excluded subject matter, in this case business methods, in a Technical Board of Appeal decision in T-0931/95 *Controlling pension benefits system/PBS PARTNERSHIP*[3] an appeal against a finding that the invention lacked patentability as excluded matter as a method of doing business. It concluded that: '[3] ... Methods only involving economic concepts and practices of doing business are not inventions within the meaning of Article 52(1) EPC'.

The Board thus rejected the appeal as to the method claims, which it considered, even though implemented on computer, to be excluded subject matter as claims only to a method of doing business, and considered that the fact that they used technical means for a purely nontechnical purpose and/or for processing nontechnical information did not necessarily confer the required technical character. However, the Board held in contrast that as the apparatus claims were not to a method, whether of doing business or anything else, the exclusion did not apply to them, concluding that: '[5] ... An apparatus constituting a physical entity or concrete product suitable for performing or supporting an economic activity, is an invention within the meaning of Article 52(1) EPC'.

However, the Board then addressed the business method exclusion in the context of examining inventive step of the apparatus claims over the prior art identified in the application itself and found this to be lacking, stating: ' the improvement envisaged by the invention according to the application is an essentially economic one ... which there cannot contribute to inventive step'.

The approach of moving the assessment of the exclusion into the assessment of novelty and inventive step, is reflected in the last paragraph of the section in the current *EPO Guidelines* dealing with computer programs (in Part G, Chapter II) and with the separate section (Part G, Chapter VII) discussing the assessment of inventive step in such cases:

'**3.6 Programs for computers**

Inventions involving programs for computers can be protected in different forms of "computer-implemented invention", an expression intended to cover claims which involve computers, computer networks or other programmable apparatus whereby prima facie one or more of the features of the claimed invention are realised by means of a program or programs. Such claims directed at computer-implemented inventions may e.g. take the form of a method of operating said apparatus, the apparatus set up to execute the method, or, following T 1173/97, the computer program itself as well as the physical media carrying the program (see T 424/03), i.e. computer program product claims, such as "data carrier", "storage medium" computer readable medium" or "signal". Insofar as the scheme for examination is concerned, no distinctions are made on the basis of the overall purpose of the invention, i.e. whether it is intended to fill a business niche, to provide some new entertainment, etc.

The category of a claim directed to a computer-implemented method is distinguished from that of a claim directed to a computer program corresponding to that method (T 424/03 and G 3/08). Such claims therefore have to be examined separately.

Technical character should be assessed without regard to the prior art (see T 1173/97, confirmed by G 3/08). Features of the computer program itself (see T 1173/97) as well as the presence of a device defined in the claim (see T 424/03 and T 258/03) may potentially lend technical character to the claimed subject-matter as explained below. In particular in embedded systems, a data processing operation implemented by means of a computer program can equally be implemented by means of special circuits (e.g. by field-programmable gate arrays).

The basic patentability considerations in respect of claims for computer programs are in principle the same as for other subject-matter. While "programs for computers" are included among the items listed in Art. 52(2), if the claimed subject-matter has a technical character it is not excluded from patentability by the provisions of Art. 52(2) and (3).

A computer program claimed by itself is not excluded from patentability if it is capable of bringing about, when running on or loaded into a computer, a further technical effect going beyond the "normal" physical interactions between the program (software) and the computer (hardware) on which it is run (T 1173/97 and G 3/08). The normal physical effects of the execution of a program, e.g. electrical currents, are not in themselves sufficient to lend a computer program technical character, and a further technical effect is needed. The further technical effect may be known in the prior art.

Likewise, although it may be said that all computer programming involves technical considerations since it is concerned with defining a method which can be carried out by a machine, that in itself is not enough to demonstrate that the program which results from the programming has technical character; the programmer must have had technical considerations beyond "merely" finding a computer algorithm to carry out some procedure (G 3/08).

A further technical effect which lends technical character to a computer program may be found e.g. in the control of an industrial process or in the internal functioning of the computer itself or its interfaces under the influence of the program and could, for example, affect the efficiency or security of a process, the management of computer resources required or the rate of data transfer in a communication link. A computer program implementing a mathematical method that itself makes a technical contribution (see G-II, 3.3) would also be considered to be capable of bringing about a further technical effect when it is run on a computer.

A patent may be granted on one of the different forms of a computer program product claim if all the requirements of the EPC are met; see in particular Art. 84, 83, 54 and 56, and G-III,3 below. Such claims should not contain program listings (see II, 4.15), but should define all the features which assure patentability of the process which the program is intended to carry out when it is run (see F-IV, 4.5.2, last sentence). Short excerpts from programs might be accepted in the description (see F-II, 4.12).

Whether a computer program can contribute to the technical character of the claimed subject-matter is frequently an issue separate and distinct from the technical character of the hardware components which may be defined in order to execute the computer program. When a computer program produces a further technical effect (T 1173/97), it is by itself considered technical and not excluded. In contrast, any claimed subject-matter defining or using technical means is an invention within the meaning of Art. 52(1) (see T 424/03 and T 258/03, and confirmed in G 3/08). This applies even if the technical means are commonly known; for example, the inclusion of a computer, a computer network, a readable medium carrying a program, etc. in a claim lends technical character to the claimed subject-matter ....

If claimed subject-matter does not have a technical character, it should be rejected under Art. 52(2) and (3). If the subject matter passes this prima facie test for technicality, the examiner should then proceed to the questions of novelty and inventive step (see G-VI and VII).'

As to questions of novelty the *Guidelines* in Part G, Chapter VI provide no specific discussion of such claims but as to inventive step the relevant passages of the *Guidelines* in Part G, Chapter VII provide:

'5.4 Claims comprising technical and non-technical aspects

It is legitimate to have a mix of technical and "non-technical" features appearing in a claim, and the non-technical features may even form a major part of the claimed subject-matter.

Inventive step, however, can be based only on technical features, which thus have to be clearly defined in the claim. Non-technical features, to the extent that they do not interact with the technical subject-matter of the claim for solving a technical problem, i.e. non-technical features "as such", do not provide a technical contribution to the prior art and are thus ignored in assessing inventive step.

The problem-solution approach is in principle applied as follows to this type of claim, in particular for computer-implemented inventions:

(i)   The non-technical aspects of the claim(s) are identified; a requirements specification (see G-VII, 5.4.1) is derived from the non-technical aspect(s) set out in the claims and the description so that the person skilled in the art of a technical field (e.g. an expert in computer science) is informed of the non-technical concept.

(ii)   The closest prior art is selected on the basis of the technical aspects of the claimed subject-matter and the related description, also taking into account the considerations defined in G-VII, 5.1.

(iii)   The differences from the closest prior art are identified.

(a)   If there are none (not even non-technical differences), an objection under Art. 54 is raised.

(b)   If the differences are not technical, an objection under Art. 56 is raised. The reasoning for the objection should be that the subject-matter of a claim cannot be inventive if there is no technical contribution to the art, i.e. if there is no technical problem solved by the claimed subject-matter vis-à-vis the closest prior art.

(c)   If the differences include technical aspects, the following applies: firstly, the objective technical problem is formulated, taking into account the requirements specification as under point (i) above; the solution of the objective technical problem must comprise the technical aspects of the identified differences; secondly, if the solution of the technical problem is obvious to the person skilled in the art, an objection under Art. 56 is raised.

Care should be taken to avoid missing any features that might contribute to the technical character of the claimed subject-matter, in particular when the wording of the claim is paraphrased for the purpose of analysis (T 756/06).'

The 'requirements specification' called for at (i) in formulating the objective technical problem for the application of the EPO 'problem and solution' approach to analyse inventive step (as discussed in **Chapter 5** at para 5.16) is further discussed in that part of the Examination Guidelines that deals with inventive step, and which refer to the Technical Board of Appeal decision in T-641/00 *Two identities/COMVIK*[4] in which the EPO approach to assessing the inventive step of inventions having a mix of technical and non-technical features was developed:

'5.4.1 "Requirements specification" in the formulation of the objective technical problem

Features which do not contribute to the technical character or do not make any contribution, either independently or in combination with other features, to the technical solution of a technical problem are not relevant for assessing inventive step (see T 641/00). Such a situation may arise, for instance, if a feature contributes only to the solution of a non-technical problem, e.g. a problem in a field excluded from patentability.

Where aspects of a claim define an aim to be achieved in a non-technical field and thus do not contribute to the technical character of the invention, this aim may legitimately appear in the formulation of the objective technical problem in the form of a "requirements specification" (i.e. a complete description of the behaviour of the system to be developed) provided to the person skilled in a technical field as part of the framework of the technical problem that is to be solved, in particular as a constraint that has to be met. If no such objective technical problem is found, the claimed subject-matter does not satisfy at least the requirement for an inventive step because there can be no technical contribution to the art, and the claim is to be rejected on this ground.

The objective technical problem must be so formulated as not to contain pointers to the technical solution, since including part of a technical solution offered by an invention in the statement of the problem must, when the state of the art is assessed in terms of that problem, necessarily result in an ex post facto view being taken of inventive activity. The requirements specification is not deemed to belong to the prior art; it is merely used in the formulation of the technical problem.'

The Enlarged Board, in its decision holding the reference to it to be inadmissible in G3/08 *Programs for Computers*[5] faced up to certain criticisms of this approach as set out in an earlier, though not in this respect materially different, version of the *Guidelines* when it observed:

'10.13 … While the Enlarged Board is aware that this rejection for lack of an inventive step rather than exclusion under Article 52(2) EPC is in some way distasteful to many people, it is the approach which has been consistently developed since T 1173/97 and since no divergences from that development have been identified in the referral we consider it not to be the function of the Enlarged Board in this Opinion to overturn it.'

This is likely to continue to be the case despite criticisms of it, such as the somewhat intemperate attack, on the part of the English Court of Appeal in 2006 on the EPO approach, which it suggested was internally inconsistent, in *Aerotel/Macrossan*.[6] In so doing, the English Court sought to trace in detail in a lengthy appendix to its decision and, from its own perspective, the history of UK and EPO law in this area. However, by downplaying the continuing need under EPO Technical Board of Appeal case law for an invention to have a technical effect, albeit no longer addressed in isolation at the outset in the context of excluded subject matter, but rather in the context of determining the issue of inventive step, its criticism did a disservice to such case law. It did however set in train the sequence of events by which the EPO Enlarged Board of Appeal reviewed, explained, and stood by, such case law in G-3/08 *Programs for Computers.*

In summary, the effect of the current EPO approach is that the settled practice is for many rejections for computer-implemented inventions now to take place under Article 56, as lacking inventive step, rather than under Article 52, for excluded subject matter, and in analysing such issues under Article 56 the focus is on technical character and technical effect, rather than on definitional issues such as whether or not an invention is for particular types of excluded subject matter such as a 'computer program' as such.[7]

1 T-1173/97 *Computer Program Product/IBM* (Board 3.5.01, 1 July 1998), [2000] EPOR 219.
2 *Guidelines for Examination in the European Patent Office*, Part G, Chapter II-3, 3.6 (last updated 26 September 2014).
3 T 0931/95 *Controlling pension benefits system/PBS PARTNERSHIP* (Board 3.5.01, 8 September 2000) [2002] EPOR 52.
4 T-641/00 *Two identities/COMVIK* (Board 3.5.01, 26 September 2002).
5 G-3/08 *Programs for Computers* (Enlarged Board of Appeal, 12 May 2010).
6 *Aerotel v Telco* [2006] EWHC 997 (Pat); *Macrossan's Application* [2006] EWHC 705 (Ch) (Patents Court); *Aerotel v Telco & Macrossan's Application* [2006] EWCA Civ 1371 (Court of Appeal).
7 For examples of relatively recent Technical Board of Appeal decisions in which the claims were rejected under Article 56 see T 1741/08 *GUI layout/SAP* (Board 3.5.06, 2 August 2012), T 1954/08 *Marketing Simulation/SAP* (Board 3.5.01, 6 March 2013) and T-1670/07 *Shopping with mobile device/NOKIA* (Board 3.5.01, 11 July 2013).

Current situation in the UK

9.10 UK law implements the EPC and so by PA 1977, s 1(2), declares that inter alia, 'a program for a computer' is not an invention for the purposes of the Act, but this 'shall prevent anything being treated as an invention for the purposes of this Act only to the extent that a patent or application relates to that thing as such'. As observed in the Patents Court in *Fujitsu Ltd's Application*[1] with masterly understatement 'the application of this exclusion, and the proviso to it, have proved difficult'. In practice, however, the UK courts have only rarely allowed appeals against rejections of such applications by the UK Intellectual Property

Office (UKIPO). Analysis of the underlying principles has been complicated by the fact that such rejections have usually taken place in situations in which the subject matter is also excluded for some other reason than being a computer program 'as such', namely for 'business methods',[2] a 'mental act', or a 'mathematical method'.

An early example was *Merrill Lynch's Application*,[3] concerning an application to patent a data processing-based system for making a market in securities. The UKIPO and, on appeal, the Patents Court, rejected the application because it held, applying the 'technical contribution' that this lay only in the computer program involved. On appeal the Court of Appeal disagreed with the approach adopted by the Patents Court, but upheld the decision on a different basis. The Court of Appeal held that to be patentable the application had to provide some technical advance on the prior art in the form of a new technical result, but with the qualification that matter excluded by PA 1977, s 1(2) could not count as a technical contribution. In so holding, the Court of Appeal said it was following the decision of an EPO Technical Board of Appeal in T-0208/84 *Computer-related invention/VICOM*.[4] Applying this test, the Court of Appeal held that the new result in *Merrill Lynch* was simply a method of doing business, and excluded subject matter and thus the application failed.[5]

Any analysis of the scope under UK law of the exclusions for computer programs (and also for other excluded matter, although business methods are also discussed separately below) must now start with the decisions of the English Court of Appeal in *Aerotel/Macrossan*[6] and *Symbian*.[7] The *Aerotel/Macrossan* decision concerned two parallel appeals. In the first one Aerotel sought the restoration of its patent, that had been granted but had been summarily revoked in the course of infringement proceedings, for a telephone system whereby the caller had a prepaid account with the telephone company. To place a call, the caller dialled the telephone company's exchange, input an account code and then dialled the callee's number. The patent was invalidated as a method of doing business. The second case involved a patent application by an Australian inventor, Neal Macrossan, for an automated method of producing the documents necessary to incorporate a limited company. This involved asking the user a series of questions with subsequent questions taken from a database depending on the answers to previous questions. The application had been rejected by the UKIPO as a computer program, a method of performing a mental act, and of doing business, but the Patents Court had held it not to be a business method.

The Court of Appeal in *Aerotel/Macrossan* chose to work from the wording of EPC, Articles 52(2)–(3) rather than PA 1977, s 1(2) to obviate any risk of an erroneous construction arising from the literally different wording of the latter. It chose, in relation to the Article 52 exclusions, to adopt a neutral, rather than a narrow, construction (as is usual when dealing with exclusions), as it saw the exclusions as a 'positive' list of disparate things that are not to be regarded as inventions. Having sought to summarize the various approaches employed to date, and criticized the current EPO 'technical character' approach, the Court of Appeal also rejected the former EPO 'technical contribution' approach because it was bound by its prior rejection by the Court of Appeal in *Merrill Lynch's Application*. Had it been otherwise, the Court of Appeal in *Aerotel/Macrossan* might have adopted this earlier EPO approach, which it considered had 'a lot to be said for it'. In the event, it held it was bound by its own precedent, and therefore, was constrained to adopt the approach adopted in *Merrill Lynch's Application*, including the rider applied in that case that novel, or inventive purely excluded matter does not count as a 'technical contribution'. It agreed that this was reflected in the following four-step approach:

(1) properly construe the claim;
(2) identify the actual contribution;
(3) ask whether it falls solely within the excluded subject matter; and
(4) check whether the contribution is actually technical in nature.

The Court of Appeal in *Aerotel/Macrossan* acknowledged that the step 2 assessment in particular could in some cases be difficult, and would require an investigation into what the invention involved, how it worked and the problems that it solved, looking at the substance of the claim, and not its form. It also noted that step 4 might well not be necessary because step 3 should already have covered it. It had however to form part of the approach for consistency with *Merrill Lynch's Application*. In applying the four-step test to Aerotel's patent the system as a whole was found to be new in itself, not merely because it was to be used in the business of selling phone calls. The contribution for the purposes of step 2 was therefore a new system. While it was possible to implement it using conventional computers it was a new combination of hardware, and therefore did not fall at step 3 because it amounted to more than just a method of doing business as such. The system was clearly technical in nature, and therefore did not fail step 4. The equivalent reasoning applied to the method claims. The validity of Aerotel's patent was therefore upheld. As for Macrossan's application, from the perspective of the business method exclusion the contribution under step 2 was the provision of an interactive system that did a job that might otherwise have been done by a solicitor or company formation agent. This was a business method and thus excluded subject matter under step 3. Although the application failed at this point for the purposes of step 4 there was nothing technical about the contribution beyond the mere fact of running the computer program. From the perspective of the computer program exclusion the contribution in Macrossan's application under step 2 was the provision of a computer program (in practice probably an interactive website) which could be used to carry out the method. This was thus excluded subject matter under step 3. Although the application again failed at this point for the purposes of step 4 there was nothing technical about the contribution.

Shortly after the judgment in *Aerotel/Macrossan,* the UKIPO issued on 2 November 2006 a notice setting out its approach to assessing patentable subject matter, paragraphs 1–12 and 15–18 of which are set out below:[8]

'Patents Act 1977: Patentable subject matter

1.   This notice announces an immediate change in the way patent examiners will assess whether inventions are for patentable subject matter. The change results from the recent judgment of the Court of Appeal in the matters of *Aerotel Ltd v Telco Holdings Ltd (and others)* and *Macrossan's Application* [2006] EWCA Civ 1371 ("*Aerotel/Macrossan*").

Background

2.   *Aerotel/Macrossan* is a single judgment covering two cases which both concerned the interpretation of s 1(2) of the Patents Act 1977 and its equivalent in the European Patent Convention (EPC), Article 52. The judgment was handed down on 27 October 2006.

3.   The Court was clearly mindful of the desirability of consistency of practice across Europe, and took due account of the way that the courts of other EPC Contracting States and the Boards of Appeal of the European Patent Office (EPO) interpret these provisions. However, the Court decided not to follow EPO practice, which they did not consider to have stabilised sufficiently. Instead, the Court approved a 4 step test that had been proposed by the Office.

4.   In reaching its judgment, the Court also fully considered all the precedent UK case law in this area. Following the principles discussed in, for example, *Colchester Estates (Cardiff) v Carlton Industries* [1986] 1 Ch 80, [1984] 2 All ER 601 and [1984] 3 WLR 693, the Office takes the view that *Aerotel/Macrossan* must be treated as a definitive statement of how the law on patentable subject matter is now to be applied in the United Kingdom (UK). It should therefore rarely be necessary to refer back to previous UK or EPO case law.

The New Test

5.   The test approved by the Court comprises the following steps:

(1)   properly construe the claim
(2)   identify the actual contribution
(3)   ask whether it falls solely within the excluded subject matter
(4)   check whether the actual or alleged contribution is actually technical in nature.

The Court decided that the new approach provided a structured and more helpful way of applying the statutory test for assessing patentability which was consistent with previous decisions of the Court. This test will be applied by examiners with immediate effect.

Details of the new approach

6.   The Court saw the first step, properly construing the claim, as something that always has to be done and involves deciding what the monopoly is before going on to the question of whether it is excluded. If, as can happen when dealing with applications from unrepresented applicants, examiners are faced with no meaningful statement of the monopoly sought, they will do their best to assess what it might be.

7.   The Court equated the second step to identifying what the inventor has really added to the stock of human knowledge. The Court reaffirmed that in identifying the contribution, it is the substance of the invention that is important rather than the form of the claim adopted. Thus in the Macrossan case it held that the presence of conventional hardware elements in the claim did not change the contribution.

8.   What the applicant alleges he/she has contributed is not conclusive and ultimately it is the actual contribution that counts. However, the Court acknowledged that at the application stage, it is quite in order to consider the third and fourth steps on the basis of the alleged contribution. Thus it will not always be necessary to conduct a search to identify the actual contribution before any objection can be raised. Accordingly, examiners will continue the existing practice of issuing a report under s 17(5)(b) that a search would not serve any useful purpose if the application seems to have little prospect of maturing into a valid patent and a search is not necessary for the purposes of the second step. The Office does not consider that informing decisions on filing abroad constitutes a "useful purpose" within the meaning of s 17(5).

9.   The third step comprises deciding whether the contribution is solely unpatentable subject matter, ie matter listed in Article 52(2). The Court saw "solely" as merely an expression of the "as such" qualification of Article 52(3). Thus if the contribution falls wholly within one or more of the listed categories, it is not a patentable invention. If it falls partly within one or more of the listed categories and partly outside, it passes the third step.

10.   If the invention passes the third step, one must then check whether the contribution is technical in nature. Of course it is not necessary to apply this fourth step if the invention has failed at the third, and the Court effectively acknowledged this, although it chose to apply it anyway in Macrossan.

Construing the list of excluded matter

11.   In para 12 of its judgment, the Court said that Article 52(2) is not a list of exceptions. Rather, it sets out positive categories of things which are not to be regarded as inventions. Accordingly, the general UK and European principle of statutory interpretation that exceptions should be construed narrowly does not apply to them.

12.   Adopting this approach, the Court of Appeal rejected the narrow interpretation afforded to the business method category by Mann J in the court below in Macrossan [2006] EWHC 705 Ch. At para 30 of his judgment, Mann J concluded that this category "is aimed more at the underlying abstraction of business method" rather than a tool or activity which might be used in a business activity. In rejecting that, the Court of Appeal decided that the categories in Article 52(2) are not limited to abstract things and that business methods are not limited to completed transactions. "Methods for doing business" will be interpreted by examiners accordingly in future.

13.   ...

14.   ...

Benefit of the doubt

15.   In para 5 of its judgment, the Court makes it clear that whether an invention covers patentable subject matter is a question of law which should be decided during prosecution of the patent application. It is not a question on which applicants are entitled to the benefit of the doubt. Consequently examiners will assess the position fully and not simply drop objections merely because the applicant has managed to put up what at first sight may be a plausible argument that the invention relates to patentable subject matter.

16.   As the judgment says, giving benefit of reasonable doubt at the application stage may still be appropriate if debatable questions of pure fact, not law, arise – for example, determining the date of a particular disclosure or the correct amount of common general knowledge to impute to the person skilled in the art. However, this is more likely to occur when considering novelty or obviousness, not patentable subject matter.

Effect of the new approach

17.   It is the Office's view that the change in approach does not fundamentally change the boundary between what is and is not patentable in the UK although we recognise that there will inevitably be the odd case right on the boundary that may be decided differently under different tests. To illustrate this, the Office is issuing separately an assessment of how a sample of applications that were refused by hearing officers earlier this year would have fared under the Aerotel/Macrossan approach.

18.   Furthermore, whilst that approach is different from the one currently adopted in the EPO (as exemplified by the Board of Appeal decision in Hitachi T 0258/03 we consider that the end result will be the same in nearly every case irrespective of whether the approach followed is the Court of Appeal's or that of the EPO. The Court suggested that the issue was one which might benefit from a reference to the Enlarged Board of Appeal.'

The four-step approach of *Aerotel/Macrossan* was applied by the Court of Appeal in *Symbian* to find an application to be patentable even though it was implemented entirely on a computer and even though the way it worked was entirely as a result of a computer program operating on that computer. This was because the invention made a contribution to the art that was technical in nature – ie a 'better computer' since the program in issue made a computer operate on other programs faster than prior art operating programs enabled it to do by virtue of the claimed features. It is notable that in this case no other exclusion than that for computer programs was engaged. In the light of this decision, the UKIPO issued on 8 November 2008 a further notice on patentable subject matter in which it observed, inter alia:[9]

'Identifying whether a contribution is solely a computer program

4.   The Symbian judgment (especially paragraphs 54–56) provides an insight into what constitutes a technical contribution; in other words, a contribution that is more than solely a computer program. An important factor is what the program does as a matter of practical reality.

5.   The Intellectual Property Office has previously recognised that an invention which either solves a technical problem external to the computer or solves "a technical problem within the computer" is not excluded. What Symbian has now shown is that improving the operation of a computer by solving a problem arising from the way the computer was programmed – for example, a tendency to crash due to conflicting library program calls – can also be regarded as solving "a technical problem within the computer" if it leads to a more reliable computer. Thus, a program that results in a computer running faster or more reliably may be considered to provide a technical contribution even if the invention solely addresses a problem in the programming.'

A subsequent Patents Court decision that also provides a useful review of *Aerotel/Macrossan, Symbian* and some other English case law was *Halliburton Energy Services Inc's Application*.[10] The particular issue addressed in this case was the scope of the 'mental act' exclusion which had been applied here by the UKIPO to reject claims to a computer simulation method for designing drill bits. The computer program exclusion had been held also by the UKIPO to apply, although the main focus of the reasoning in the UKIPO had been on the mental act exclusion, which had been broadly interpreted. The Patents Court, applying the four-step *Aerotel/Macrossan* test, held the computer program exclusion not to apply, having observed:

'32.   … when confronted by an invention which is implemented in computer software, the mere fact that it works that way does not normally answer the question of patentability. The question is decided by considering what task it is that the program (or the programmed computer) actually performs. A computer programmed to perform a task which makes a contribution to the art which is technical in nature, is a patentable invention and may be claimed as such. Indeed (see *Astron Clinica* [2008] RPC 14) in those circumstances the patentee is perfectly entitled to claim the computer program itself.'

The scope of the mental act exclusion had not been in issue in *Aerotel/Macrossan* but an observation had been made by the Court of Appeal in its judgment in this to the effect that this exclusion should be given a narrow interpretation. There was however also earlier English case law which had adopted a wider interpretation of this particular exclusion. Having analysed the English case law, and also an EPO Technical Board of Appeal decision in T-1227/05 *Circuit simulation I/Infineon Technologies*[11] the Patents Court in *Halliburton* reversed the rejection by the UKIPO Hearing Officer, holding the narrow construction, rather than the wide one applied by the UKIPO, to be the correct one. It held that its purpose is: 'to make sure that patent claims cannot be performed by purely mental means and that is all [– the] exclusion will not apply if there are appropriate non-mental limitations in the claim'. It also observed that the English case law in which patents had been refused as being for computer programs as such had almost always involved the interplay of the computer program exclusion with another exclusion, generally that as to business methods, but here, and incorrectly, given the narrow construction that ought apply to it, to mental acts. The Patents Court went on to observe, commenting on an invitation (which it rejected) to depart from the approach of *Aerotel/Macrossan* and *Symbian* and to embrace the EPO approach as reinforced by the subsequently expressed views of the EPO Enlarged Board of Appeal in G-3/08 *Programs for Computers* that it was far from clear that the EPO approach when applied as a whole, and correctly is any more favourable to patentees than the UK one, a view which echoes the opinion of the UKIPO at para 18 of its November 2006 *Notice*.

Since its decisions in *Aerotel/Macrossan* and *Symbian* the Court of Appeal has revisited the issue of computer implemented inventions twice[12] and although it has retained the four-step test as set out in *Aerotel/Macrossan* it has clarified certain aspects of its application, notably as to whether there is any technical contribution. Thus it observed in *Lantana*:

'10.   The courts have worked out "signposts" to assist in determining whether there was any technical contribution. These signposts will not assist in every case. These signposts originated in the judgment of Lewison J in *AT&T Knowledge Ventures' Application* [2009] EWHC 343 but were refined on appeal in *HTC v Apple*. It is sufficient to repeat the judge's summary of the signposts from *HTC v Apple*:

"13   The signposts to a relevant technical effect (as modified in *HTC v Apple*) are:
   i)   whether the claimed technical effect has a technical effect on a process which is carried on outside the computer;"
   ii)   whether the claimed technical effect operates at the level of the architecture of the computer, that is to say whether the effect is produced irrespective of the data being processed or the applications being run;

iii)   whether the claimed technical effect results in the
        computer being made to operate in a new way;
iv)   whether the program makes the computer a better
        computer in the sense of running more efficiently and
        effectively as a computer;
v)   whether the perceived problem is overcome by the
        invention as opposed to merely being circumvented." '

It also observed in *Lantana*:

'26.   There is no comprehensive test for determining technical contribution,
        but paragraphs [45] to [49] of the judgment of this court in *HTC v
        Apple* provide a helpful starting point:

    "[45]   How then is it to be determined whether an invention has
            made a technical contribution to the art? A number of points
            emerge from the decision in *Symbian* and the earlier authorities
            to which it refers. First, it is not possible to define a clear rule
            to determine whether or not a program is excluded, and each
            case must be determined on its own facts bearing in mind the
            guidance given by the Court of Appeal in *Merrill Lynch* and
            Gale and by the Boards of Appeal in Case T 0208/84 *Vicom
            Systems Inc* [1987] 2 EPOR 74, [1987] OJ EPO 14, Case T
            06/83 *IBM Corporation/Data processing network* [1990] OJ
            EPO 5, [1990] EPOR 91 and Case T 115/85 *IBM Corporation/
            Computer-related invention* [1990] EPOR 107.

    [46]   Second, the fact that improvements are made to the software
            programmed into the computer rather than hardware forming
            part of the computer does not make a difference. As I have said,
            the analysis must be carried out as a matter of substance not
            form.

    [47]   Third, the exclusions operate cumulatively. So, for example, the
            invention in *Gale* related to a new way of calculating a square
            root of a number with the aid of a computer and Mr Gale sought
            to claim it as a ROM in which his program was stored. This
            was not permissible. The incorporation of the program in a
            ROM did not alter its nature: it was still a computer program
            (excluded matter) incorporating a mathematical method (also
            excluded matter). So also the invention in *Macrossan [Aerotel]*
            related to a way of making company formation documents
            and Mr Macrossan sought to claim it as a method using a data
            processing system. This was not permissible either: it was a
            computer program (excluded matter) for carrying out a method
            for doing business (also excluded matter).

    [48]   Fourth, it follows that it is helpful to ask: what does the invention
            contribute to the art as a matter of practical reality over and above
            the fact that it relates to a program for a computer? If the only
            contribution lies in excluded matter then it is not patentable.

    [49]   Fifth, and conversely, it is also helpful to consider whether
            the invention may be regarded as solving a problem which is
            essentially technical, and that is so whether that problem lies

inside or outside the computer. An invention which solves a technical problem within the computer will have a relevant technical effect in that it will make the computer, as a computer, an improved device, for example by increasing its speed. An invention which solves a technical problem outside the computer will also have a relevant technical effect, for example by controlling an improved technical process. In either case it will not be excluded by Art 52 as relating to a computer program as such."'

Thus, despite their differences in approach, the focus of the English courts is, like the EPO, increasingly on the technical nature of the invention, and less on attempting to define specific exclusions from patentability. There is probably little between them as to this, and it may be that the main practical difficulty for the English courts in adopting the EPO approach would be in adopting the 'problem and solution' approach to inventive step that forms an integral part of the EPO approach.

1 *Fujitsu Ltd's Application* [1997] RPC 608 (Court of Appeal).
2 See also below at para 9.11 as to the business method exclusion.
3 *Merrill Lynch's Application* [1988] RPC 1 (Patents Court); [1989] RPC 561 (Court of Appeal).
4 T-0208/84 *Computer-related invention/VICOM* [1987] OJ EPO 14; [1987] 2 EPOR 74. See above at para 9.07.
5 Despite this decision, Merrill Lynch did in fact succeed in prosecuting the disputed patent application to grant as GB 2 180 380 B. They dispensed with claims to a data processing 'system', 'combination' and 'method'. The amended claims focused instead on the arrangement of hardware 'apparatus' needed to implement the software. They described the configuration of CPU, two-way communications links, trader terminal positions, display screens, database and customer accounts processor. While these individual items of hardware were conventional the program itself was unchanged from that which had been the subject of the rejected patent application.
6 *Aerotel v Telco* [2006] EWHC 997 (Patents Court); *Macrossan's Application* [2006] EWHC 705 (Ch) (Patents Court); *Aerotel v Telco & Macrossan's* [2006] EWCA Civ 1371 (Court of Appeal).
7 *Symbian v Comptroller* [2008] EWCA 1066 (Court of Appeal).
8 http://webarchive.nationalarchives.gov.uk/tna/20140603093547/http://www.ipo.gov. uk/pro-types/pro-patent/p-law/p-pn/p-pn-subjectmatter.htm. Further practice notices reflecting Patents Court or Court of Appeal decisions were issued on 7 February 2008, at: http://webarchive.nationalarchives.gov.uk/tna/20140603093547/http:// www.ipo.gov.uk/pro-types/pro-patent/p-law/p-pn/p-pn-subjectmatter-20080207. htm, 8 December 2008 (see fn 9 below) and 17 October 2011, on the patentability of mental acts, at: http://webarchive.nationalarchives.gov.uk/tna/20140603093547/ http://www.ipo.gov.uk/pro-types/pro-patent/p-law/p-pn/p-pn-patentability.htm. Paragraphs 13–14 are omitted from the quotation as these refer to what were expressed to be then open questions. The former, as to the breadth of the exclusion for 'mental acts' is clarified by the 17 October 2011 *Notice* (made in consequence of the decision in *Halliburton Energy Services Inc's Application* [2011] EWHC 2508 (Patents Court) and the latter, as to permissible types of claim, by the 7 February 2008 one. The current approach of the UKIPO is set out in its *Manual of Patent Practice* at: https:// www.gov.uk/government/uploads/system/uploads/attachment_data/file/416890/ manual_of_patent_practice.pdf (April 2015) at paras [1.07]–[1.40.4] where the English case law is also extensively discussed.

9   http://webarchive.nationalarchives.gov.uk/tna/20140603093547/http://www.ipo.gov.
    uk/pro-types/pro-patent/p-law/p-pn/p-pn-computer.htm
10 *Halliburton Energy Services Inc's Application* [2011] EWHC 2508 (Patents Court).
    See also *AT&T Knowledge Ventures' Application* [2009] EWHC 343 (Patents Court)
    and *Protecting Kids the World Over (PKTWO) Ltd's Application* [2011] EWHC 2720
    (Patents Court).
11 T-1227/05 *Circuit simulation I/Infineon Technologies* (Board 3.5.01, 13 December
    2006).
12 *HTC Europe Co. Ltd v Apple Inc* [2012] EWHC 1789 (Patents Court); [2013]
    EWCA Civ 451 (Court of Appeal) (reversing Patents Court to find that an invention
    that addresses the problem of how to deal with multiple simultaneous touches on a
    multi-touch device makes a technical contribution and its contribution does not lie
    in excluded subject matter) and *Lantana Limited v Comptroller* [2013] EWHC 2673
    (Patents Court); [2014] EWCA Civ 463 (Court of Appeal) (upholding a finding by
    UKIPO Hearing Officer and Patents Court that an invention that addresses, by the
    use of email, the problem of how to retrieve data from a remote computer without
    the usual problems associated with trying to maintain a continuous connection with
    it, circumvents but does not provide a technical solution to the problem, and so its
    contribution lies in excluded subject matter).

Patents and business methods

Computer program implemented methods of doing business in the EPO

9.11   As with programs for computers, methods of doing business
'as such' are excluded by EPC, Article 52(2)(c). The public policy
background to this exclusion, and its relationship with that for computer
programs was discussed by the English Patents Court, when holding two
applications for patents on computerised business methods so excluded
as methods of doing business in *CFPH's Applications:*[1]

'41   Now let us consider business methods. What is the policy reason
that lies behind the exclusion of those? It is because, historically, patents
for business methods were never granted yet business innovation went on
very well without the benefit of that protection and without the red tape.
Businessmen have been every bit as inventive as engineers. It was probably
business administrators (and not poets or priests) who made the greatest
"invention" of all time: phonetic writing. Consider as further examples:
the invention of money; of double-entry bookkeeping; of negotiable bills
of exchange; of joint-stock companies; of insurance policies; of clearance
banking; of business name franchising; of the supermarket; and so on. None
of these needed patent protection to get started. A patent system is always a
burden on trade, commerce and industry: if only because of the "red tape"
effect. The only question is whether the benefits outweigh the burdens.
That has to be demonstrated by those who assert it is so, and in any case the
decision is for the legislature. In this country and in Europe the legislature has
not yet been persuaded.

42   The point often comes up when the alleged invention has to do with
carrying out a business using a computer system. Is the applicant trying to
patent a method of doing business? That is not allowed. Or is he trying to

patent computer technology? That may be allowed (it depends). But how do you tell the difference? In one sense, a computer that is programmed so as to implement a novel business technique *is* a new technological artefact. It is a machine with millions of switches arranged as never before. If you say, "Yes, but it is not the sort of switch-arrangement that ought to be allowed to count", you must explain why. It is not always as easy as it might sound.'

However, the EPO requirement for an invention to be technical means that the EPO, in applying this exclusion, takes a harder line than it does to computer-implemented inventions that do not involve business methods. The section of the current EPO *Guidelines* that addresses business methods[2] has little specifically to say about them, merely instancing them as examples of the principle that purely abstract or intellectual methods are not patentable:

'**3.5 Schemes, rules and methods for performing mental acts, playing games or doing business**

These are further examples of items of an abstract or intellectual character. In particular, a scheme for learning a language, a method of solving crossword puzzles, a game (as an abstract entity defined by its rules), modelling information or a scheme for organising a commercial operation would not be patentable. A method of doing business is excluded from patentability even where it implies the possibility of making use of unspecified technical means or has practical utility (see T-388/04). Another example is that of a method for designing a nuclear core loading arrangement, which neither specifies the use of means or measures of a technical nature nor includes the provision of a physical entity as the resulting product (e.g. a reactor core loaded according to the given design). This method may exclusively be carried out mentally and thus lacks technical character, regardless of the complexity of the method or any technical considerations involved (see T 914/02).

However, if the claimed subject-matter specifies an apparatus or technical process for carrying out at least some part of the scheme, that scheme and the apparatus or process have to be examined as a whole. In particular, if the claim specifies computers, computer networks or other conventional programmable apparatus, or a program therefor, or a storage medium carrying the program, for executing at least some steps of a scheme, it may comprise a mix of technical and non-technical features, with the technical features directed to a computer or a comparable programmed device. In these cases the claim is to be examined as a "computer implemented invention"''

This last paragraph recognizes that many of the computer-implemented invention cases that have been considered by the EPO Technical Boards of Appeal and by national courts have, in fact been for computer-implemented business methods.[3]

More details of the approach of the EPO to business method patents were set out in the EPO Paper on 'Examination of "business method" applications' at Appendix 6 of the Trilateral Study undertaken by the European, Japanese, and US Patent Offices (dated November 2001) that followed up on the Comparative Trilateral Study on the subject of business method patents in June 2000.[4] The EPO Paper, which would appear to reflect what remains the current approach, divides business methods into three types which it treats as follows:

'(1)   Claims to abstract business methods should be rejected on the grounds that they are excluded by Articles 52(2) and (3) EPC, since they are methods of doing business "as such".

(2)   Claims for computer-implemented business methods should be treated in exactly the same way as any other computer-implemented invention.

(3)   Claims for other implementations of business methods should be treated using the same scheme for examination as for computer implementations.'

The Paper further notes:

'The expression "computer-implemented inventions" is intended to cover claims which specify computers, computer networks or other conventional programmable digital apparatus whereby prima facie the novel features of the claimed invention are realised by means of a new program or programs. Such claims may take the form of a method of operating said conventional apparatus, the apparatus set up to execute the method (loaded with the program), or, following T 1173/97 *IBM/Computer programs,* the program itself. Insofar as the scheme for examination is concerned no distinction is made on the basis of the overall purpose of the invention, i.e. whether it is intended to fill a business niche or to provide some new entertainment etc.'

It then outlines the EPO approach to examining computer-implemented business method inventions:

'(1)   The claimed subject-matter, which by definition includes elements such as a computer or code which is intended to run on a computer, is presumed, prima facie, not to be excluded from patentability by Articles 52(2) and (3) EPC.

(2)   The subject-matter of the claim is therefore to be examined for novelty and inventive step. This is done according to the Guidelines for Examination as currently specified. In particular, in the examination for inventive step the objective technical problem solved by the invention as claimed considered as a whole when compared with the closest prior art is to be determined. If no such objective technical problem can be determined, the claim is to be rejected on the ground that its subject-matter lacks an inventive step.'

Consistent with this, in T-931/95 *Controlling Pension Benefits System/ PBS PARTNERSHIP*[5] a Technical Board of Appeal found a computerised pension benefits system not to be excluded from patentability under EPC, Article 52, observing that: 'a computer system suitably programmed for use in a particular field, even if that is the field of business and economy, has the character of a concrete apparatus in the sense of physical entity, man-made for a utilitarian purpose and is thus an invention within the meaning of Article 52(1) of the EPC'.

However, the Board then went on to address the exclusion in the context of examining the inventive step of the apparatus claims over the prior art identified in the application itself, and found this to be lacking, stating: 'the improvement envisaged by the invention according to the application is an essentially economic one ... which there cannot contribute to inventive step'. Subsequently in another business method case, T-258/03 *Auction method/HITACHI*[6] a Technical Board of Appeal took matters further by holding that not just the apparatus claims but also the method claims were not excluded by EPC, Article 52(2). However, as in T-931/05 *Controlling pension benefits system/PBS PARTNERSHIP* it went on to consider the question of technical character when assessing inventive step, which it found to be lacking, observing that: 'method steps consisting of modifications to a business scheme and aimed at circumventing a technical problem rather than solving it by technical means cannot contribute to the technical character of the subject-matter claimed'.

In summary therefore, there is a high chance of rejection in the EPO of business method applications on the grounds of lack of inventive step unless it can be shown that these relate other than to an obvious implementation of non-technical ideas in a notorious technical system such as a programmed computer.[7]

1   *CFPH LLC v Comptroller General of Patents Designs and Trade Marks* [2005] EWHC 1589 (Pat); [2006] IP&T; [2006] RPC 259 (Patents Court).

2   *Guidelines for Examination in the European Patent Office* (April 2010) Part G, Chapter II-3, 3.5 (last updated 26 September 2014).

3   For example, in the UK *Merrell Lynch's Application* [1988] RPC 1 (Patents Court); [1989] RPC 561 (Court of Appeal) and *Macrossan's Application* [2006] EWHC 705 (Ch) (Patents Court); *Aerotel v Telco & Macrossan's Application* [2006] EWCA Civ 1371 (Court of Appeal), both of which were to computer implemented business methods that were found unpatentable as lacking any technical contribution. See section above at para 9.09. See also the EPO cases discussed later in para 9.12.

4   www.trilateral.net/projects/Comparative/business/Main.pdf.

5   T-0931/95 *Controlling Pension Benefits System/PBS PARTNERSHIP* [2002] EPOR 52.

6   T-0258/03 *Auction method/HITACHI* [2004] EPOR 55.

7   See for example EP 0 927 945 B and EP 1 134 680 A, two related cases in the same family as those the subject of controversy in the USA as the Amazon 'one-click' patent in *Amazon.com, Inc v Barnesandnoble.com, Inc and Barnesandnoble.com, LLC* 239 F 3d 1343; (2001) 57 USPQ 2D 1747 (Fed Cir). EP 0 927 945 B was initially successfully opposed on grounds of added matter and lack of inventive step but was then the subject of a successful appeal, in T-1616/08 *Gift Order/AMAZON* (Technical Board of Appeal 3.5.01, 11 November 2009) which found the main claim and two auxiliary requests to lack inventive step but remitted a third auxiliary request to the Opposition Division which held this to lack inventive step and revoked the patent accordingly, which decision was not appealed. In so doing the Opposition Division expressly rejected the argument advanced by one opponent that the patent should instead be revoked as being excluded from patentability under Articles 52(2) and (3) EPC. Meanwhile the rejection by the Examining Division of EP 1 134 680 A was the subject of an unsuccessful appeal in T-1244/07 *1-Click/AMAZON* (Technical

Board of Appeal 3.5.01, 27 January 2011), the prior art in which was then applied by the Opposition Division in the proceedings concerning EP 0 927 945 B to revoke the patent on ground of lack of inventive step, which decision was not appealed.

Situation in the UK

9.12 As with computer programs, any analysis in the UK of the exclusion from patentability for business methods as such must now start with the decision of the English Court of Appeal in *Aerotel/Macrossan*.[1] In this, a finding at first instance in one of the two cases (*Aerotel*) that the patent was for a method of doing business, and so excluded from patentability was reversed on appeal as the claimed telephone call handling system as a whole, although consisting of known components, was a novel apparatus. A finding at first instance in the other (*Macrossan*) that a patent application for a computer-implemented method of company formation was not an excluded business method since it was a tool to facilitate business transactions, or procedural steps having administrative or financial character, rather than to a way of conducting an entire business, was reversed because there was no reason to limit the exclusions to abstract matters or completed transactions. Most significant, however, was the rejection in *Aerotel/Macrossan* of the approach to examination of such issues in the EPO as reflected in the decision in T-0931/95 *Controlling Pension Benefits System/PBS PARTNERSHIP*[2] – namely that of examining computer-implemented business method inventions in the context of the assessment of inventive step rather than as an isolated initial enquiry.

The rejection by the UK courts of the EPO approach was emphasized in the Patents Court in *Cappellini's Application and Bloomberg's Application*:[3]

'9. … It is only necessary to emphasise that I consider that Case T-0931/95 *Pension Benefits,* while correct in the result, is incorrectly reasoned. The case is summarised in *Aerotel* at [100] to [106]. This was a case of a computer program to perform a particular business method, the business method itself being held to be excluded subject matter, but the computer so programmed held to be patentable subject matter but to be obvious. The basic reasoning appears to have been that the Technical Board of Appeal considered that contributions to inventive step lying in excluded matter should not be *taken into account* in considering the obviousness of the claim. I really cannot see how this is permissible reasoning, if only because a vast class of inventions depend for their non-obviousness on a new discovery of some property of nature – such a discovery being excluded subject matter. I prefer to approach this problem from the direction indicated by the Court of Appeal in *Aerotel:* what is the claimed invention *as a matter of substance?* A claim to a programmed computer as a matter of substance is just a claim to the program on a kind of carrier. A program on a kind of carrier which, if run, performs a business method adds nothing to the art that does not lie in excluded subject matter.'

It should, however, be observed that the 'discovery' analogy that is drawn here is the one that led to the decision of the Court of Appeal in *Merrill Lynch's Application*[4] as explained in *Aerotel/Macrossan* at paras [78]–[83] but as to which the Court of Appeal itself expressed doubts at paras [34]–[35].

Returning to *Aerotel/Macrossan* it is ironic that the parallel case in Australia to the application rejected by the English Court of Appeal as a business method (*Macrossan*) had in fact been granted in Australia,[5] where the applicant lived, especially when one considers that Australian patent law follows much more closely than does modern UK patent law, the tradition established under the pre-PA 1977 law of the UK, stretching back to the English Statute of Monopolies in 1623.

1   *Aerotel v Telco* [2006] EWHC 997 (Pat); *Macrossan's Application* [2006] EWHC 705 (Ch) (Patents Court); *Aerotel v Telco & Macrossan's Application* [2006] EWCA Civ 1371 (Court of Appeal). See above at para 9.10.
2   T-0931/95 *Controlling Pension Benefits System/PBS PARTNERSHIP* [2002] EPOR 52.
3   *Cappellini's Application and Bloomberg LP's Application* [2007] EWHC 476 (Patents Court). Only one of the applications in issue (Capellini's) had been rejected as, inter alia, a business method, and this rejection was upheld.
4   *Merrell Lynch's Application* [1988] RPC 1 (Patents Court); [1989] RPC 561 (Court of Appeal). See above at para 9.10.
5   See para [18] of *Aerotel v Telco*. This also refers to the Australian case of *Grant v Commissioner of Patents* [2006] FCAFC 120; [2006] 221 IPR 221 where the Full Federal Court refused a patent for a method of protecting assets from bankruptcy involving the setting up of a trust, a gift to the trust and a loan back with the trustee taking a charge on the loan. However, the reason for this was that the alleged invention: 'is a mere scheme, an abstract idea, mere intellectual information, which has never been held to be patentable.... There is no physical consequence at all', when a 'physical effect in the sense of a concrete effect or phenomenon or manifestation or transformation is required'. In so ruling it drew parallels with US law, and confirmed that there had been the requisite physical effect in an earlier business methods case, *Welcome Real-Time v Catuity* [2001] FCA 445; (2001) 51 IPR 327, concerning a 'smartcard' system for use in loyalty programmes and which the court in that case was prepared to enforce. The Australian Patent Office subsequently allowed in part, on grounds of lack of novelty, and obviousness, but also rejected in part, an opposition to AU 762175, the Amazon '1-Click' patent corresponding to those in the USA, and the EPO identified at para 9.10, fn 7, in *Amazon.com, Inc* [2011] APO 28 (Australian Patent Office, 9 May 2011). Despite this, it appears that the resulting patent would have the broadest surviving claim of any of the '1-Click' family members. More recently however, in *Research Affiliates LLC v Commissioner of Patents* [2014] FCAFC 150 the Full Federal Court has held that describing a scheme that is not itself eligible for patenting, and merely giving directions to implement it on a standard computer, is not sufficiently transformative to be patent eligible.

Part III
Appendices

Appendix I

Adherence to International Patent Treaties (including latest version acceded to, or the accession date)

Adherence to International Patent Treaties

Country	Code[1]	Paris Convention	Patent Cooperation Treaty	TRIPs
Afghanistan	AF	—	—	—
Albania	AL	1995	1995	8.9.2000
Algeria	DZ	1966	2000	—
Andorra	AD	2004	—	—
Angola	AO	2007	2007	23.11.1996
Anguilla	AI	—	—	—
Antigua & Barbuda	AG	2000	2000	1.1.1995
Argentina	AR	1967	—	1.1.1995
Armenia	AM	1991	1991	5.2.2003
Aruba	AW	—	—	—
Australia	AU	1925	1980	1.1.1995
Austria	AT	1909	1979	1.1.1995
Azerbaijan	AZ	1995	1995	—
Bahamas	BS	1973	—	—
Bahrain	BH	1997	2007	1.1.1995
Bangladesh	BD	1991	—	1.1.1995
Barbados	BB	1985	1985	1.1.1995
Belarus	BY	1991	1991	—

1   Standards – ST.3 WIPO Handbook on Industrial Property Information and Documentation, March 2011.

Country	Code	Paris Convention	Patent Cooperation Treaty	TRIPs
Belgium	BE	1884	1981	1.1.1995
Belize	BZ	2000	2000	1.1.1995
Benin	BJ	1967	1987	22.2.1996
Bermuda	BM	—	—	—
Bhutan	BT	2000	—	—
Bolivia	BO	1993	—	12.9.1995
Bosnia & Herzegovina	BA	1992	1996	—
Botswana	BW	1998	2003	31.5.1995
Brazil	BR	1884	1978	1.1.1995
British Virgin Islands	VG	—	—	—
Brunei Darussalam	BN	2012	2012	1.1.1995
Bulgaria	BG	1921	1984	1.12.1996
Burkina Faso	BF	1963	1989	3.6.1995
Burundi	BI	1977	—	22.7.1995
Cambodia	KH	1998	—	13.10.2004
Cameroon	CM	1964	1978	13.12.1995
Canada	CA	1923	1990	1.1.1995
Cape Verde	CV	—	—	23.7.2008
Cayman Islands	KY	—	—	—
Central African Republic	CF	1963	1978	31.5.1995
Chad	TD	1963	1978	19.10.1996
Chile	CL	1991	—	1.1.1995
China	CN	1985[1]	1994[2]	11.12.2001
Colombia	CO	1996	2001	30.4.1995
Comoros	KM	2005	2005	—
Congo, Democratic Republic of	CD	1975	—	1.1.1997
Congo, Republic of	CG	1963	1978	27.3.1997
Costa Rica	CR	1995	1999	1.1.1995
Cote d'Ivoire	CI	1963	1991	1.1.1995

1   Paris Convention also applies to the Hong Kong Special Administrative Region and the Macau Special Administrative Region.

2   PCT also applies to the Hong Kong Special Administrative Region with effect from 1 July 1997, but not to the Macau Special Administrative Region.

Country	Code	Paris Convention	Patent Cooperation Treaty	TRIPs
Croatia	HR	1991	1998	30.11.2000
Cuba	CU	1904	1996	20.4.1995
Cyprus	CY	1966	1998	30.7.1995
Czech Republic	CZ	1993	1993	1.1.1995
Denmark	DK	1894	1978	1.1.1995
Djibouti	DJ	2002	—	31.5.1995
Dominica	DM	1999	1999	1.1.1995
Dominican Republic	DO	1890	2007	9.3.1995
Ecuador	EC	1999	2001	21.1.1996
Egypt	EG	1951	2003	30.6.1995
El Salvador	SV	1994	2006	7.5.1995
Equatorial Guinea	GQ	1997	2001	—
Eritrea	ER	—	—	—
Estonia	EE	1994	1994	13.11.1999
Ethiopia	ET	—	—	—
European Union	EU	—	—	1.1.1995
Falkland Islands	FK	—	—	—
Fiji	FJ	—	—	14.1.1996
Finland	FI	1921	1980	1.1.1995
France	FR	1884	1978	1.1.1995
Gabon	GA	1964	1978	1.1.1995
Gambia	GM	1992	1997	23.10.1996
Georgia	GE	1991	1991	14.6.2000
Germany	DE	1903	1978	1.1.1995
Ghana	GH	1976	1997	1.1.1995
Gibraltar	GI	—	—	—
Greece	GR	1924	1990	1.1.1995
Grenada	GD	1998	1998	22.2.1996
Guatemala	GT	1998	2006	21.7.1995
Guernsey	GG	—	—	—
Guinea	GN	1982	1991	25.10.1995
Guinea-Bissau	GW	1988	1997	31.5.1995

Country	Code	Paris Convention	Patent Cooperation Treaty	TRIPs
Guyana	GY	1994	—	1.1.1995
Haiti	HT	1958	—	30.1.1996
Holy See	VA	1960	—	—
Honduras	HN	1994	2006	1.1.1995
Hong Kong, China	HK	[see China]	[see China]	1.1.1995
Hungary	HU	1909	1980	1.1.1995
Iceland	IS	1962	1995	1.1.1995
India	IN	1998	1998	1.1.1995
Indonesia	ID	1950	1997	1.1.1995
Iran	IR	1959	2013	—
Iraq	IQ	1976	—	—
Ireland	IE	1925	1992	1.1.1995
Isle of Man	IM	—	—	—
Israel	IL	1950	1996	21.4.1995
Italy	IT	1884	1985	1.1.1995
Jamaica	JM	1999	—	9.3.1995
Japan	JP	1899	1978	1.1.1995
Jersey	JE	—	—	—
Jordan	JO	1972	—	11.4.2000
Kazakhstan	KZ	1991	1991	—
Kenya	KE	1965	1994	1.1.1995
Kiribati	KI	—	—	—
Korea, Democratic People's Republic of	KP	1980	1980	—
Korea, Republic of	KR	1980	1984	1.1.1995
Kuwait	KW	2014	—	1.1.1995
Kyrgyzstan	KG	1991	1991	20.12.1998
Laos	LA	1998	2006	2.2.2013
Latvia	LV	1993	1993	10.2.1999
Lebanon	LB	1924	—	—
Lesotho	LS	1989	1995	31.5.1995
Liberia	LR	1994	1994	—

Country	Code	Paris Convention	Patent Cooperation Treaty	TRIPs
Libya	LY	1976	2005	—
Liechtenstein	LI	1933	1980	1.9.1995
Lithuania	LT	1994	1994	31.5.2001
Luxembourg	LU	1922	1978	1.1.1995
Macao, China	MO	[see China]	—	1.1.1995
Macedonia, The former Yugoslav Republic of	MK	1991	1995	4.4.2003
Madagascar	MG	1963	1978	17.11.1995
Malawi	MW	1964	1978	31.5.1995
Malaysia	MY	1989	2006	1.1.1995
Maldives	MV	—	—	31.5.1995
Mali	ML	1983	1984	31.5.1995
Malta	MT	1967	2007	1.1.1995
Mauritania	MR	1965	1983	31.5.1995
Mauritius	MU	1976	—	1.1.1995
Mexico	MX	1903	1995	1.1.1995
Moldova	MD	1991	1991	26.7.2001
Monaco	MC	1956	1979	—
Mongolia	MN	1985	1991	29.1.1997
Montenegro	ME	2006	2006	—
Montserrat	MS	—	—	—
Morocco	MA	1917	1999	1.1.1995
Mozambique	MX	1998	2000	26.8.1995
Myanmar	MY	—	—	1.1.1995
Namibia	NA	2004	2004	1.1.1995
Nauru	NR	—	—	—
Nepal	NP	2001	—	23.4.2004
Netherlands	NL	1884	1979	1.1.1995
New Zealand	NZ	1931	1992	1.1.1995
Nicaragua	NI	1996	2003	3.9.1995
Niger	NE	1964	1993	13.12.1996
Nigeria	NG	1963	2005	1.1.1995

Appendix 1

Country	Code	Paris Convention	Patent Cooperation Treaty	TRIPs
Norway	NO	1885	1980	1.1.1995
Oman	OM	1999	2001	9.11.2000
Pakistan	PK	2004	—	1.1.1995
Panama	PA	1996	2012	6.9.1997
Papua New Guinea	PG	1999	2003	9.6.1996
Paraguay	PY	1994	—	1.1.1995
Peru	PE	1995	2009	1.1.1995
Philippines	PH	1965	2001	1.1.1995
Poland	PL	1919	1990	1.7.1995
Portugal	PT	1884	1992	1.1.1995
Qatar	QA	2000	2011	13.1.1996
Romania	RO	1920	1979	1.1.1995
Russian Federation	RU	1965	1978	—
Rwanda	RW	1984	2011	22.5.1996
St Helena	SH	—	—	—
St Kitts and Nevis	KN	1995	2005	21.2.1996
St Lucia	LC	1995	1996	1.1.1995
St Vincent & Grenadines	VC	1995	2002	1.1.1995
Samoa	WS	2013	—	20.5.2012
San Marino	MS	1960	2004	—
Sao Tome and Principe	ST	1998	2008	—
Saudi Arabia	SA	2004	2013	11.12.2005
Senegal	SN	1963	1978	1.1.1995
Serbia	RS	1992	1997	—
Seychelles	SC	2002	2002	26.4.2015
Sierra Leone	SL	1997	1997	23.7.1995
Singapore	SG	1995	1995	1.1.1995
Slovakia	SK	1993	1993	1.1.1995
Slovenia	SI	1991	1994	30.7.1995
Solomon Islands	SB	—	—	26.7.1996
Somalia	SO	—	—	—
South Africa	ZA	1947	1999	1.1.1995

Country	Code	Paris Convention	Patent Cooperation Treaty	TRIPs
South Sudan	SS	—	—	—
Spain	ES	1884	1989	1.1.1995
Sri Lanka	LK	1952	1982	1.1.1995
Sudan	SD	1984	1984	—
Suriname	SR	1975	—	1.1.1995
Swaziland	SZ	1991	1994	1.1.1995
Sweden	SE	1885	1978	1.1.1995
Switzerland	CH	1884	1978	1.7.1995
Syria	SY	1924	2003	—
Taiwan	TW	—	—	1.1.2002[1]
Tajikistan	TJ	1991	1991	2.3.2013
Tanzania, United Republic of	TZ	1963	1999	1.1.1995
Thailand	TH	2008	2009	1.1.1995
Timor-Leste	TL	—	—	—
Togo	TG	1967	1978	31.5.1995
Tonga	TO	2001	—	27.7.2007
Trinidad & Tobago	TT	1964	1994	1.3.1995
Tunisia	TN	1884	2001	29.3.1995
Turkey	TR	1925	1996	26.3.1995
Turkmenistan	TM	1991	1991	—
Turks & Caicos Islands	TC	—	—	—
Tuvalu	TV	—	—	—
Uganda	UG	1965	1995	1.1.1995
Ukraine	UA	1991	1991	16.5.2008
United Arab Emirates	AE	1996	1999	10.4.1996
United Kingdom	GB	1884	1978	1.1.1995
United States of America	US	1887	1978	1.1.1995
Uruguay	UY	1967	—	1.1.1995
Uzbekistan	UZ	1991	1991	—

1 As Chinese Taipei or Separate Customs Territory of Taiwan, Penghu, Kinmen, and Matsu.

Country	Code	Paris Convention	Patent Cooperation Treaty	TRIPs
Vanuatu	VU	—	—	24.8.2012
Venezuela	VE	1995	—	1.1.1995
Viet Nam	VN	1949	1993	11.1.2007
Western Sahara	EH	—	—	—
Yemen	YM	2007	—	26.6.2014
Zambia	ZM	1965	2001	1.1.1995
Zimbabwe	ZW	1980	1997	5.3.1995

Intergovernmental Patent Organizations	
African Intellectual Property Organization (OAPI)	OA
African Regional Intellectual Property Organization (ARIPO)	AP
Eurasian Patent Convention	EA
European Patent Office	EP
World Intellectual Property Organization (WIPO)	WO

Appendix 2

Patents Court and Court of Appeal workload

Numbers of patent and registered design actions commenced in England and Wales

The following table summarizes trends in patent (and registered design, as this is not separated out in the figures) litigation in England and Wales in each calendar year since 1981 by reference to numbers of such actions started, as against all actions started by Writ, or latterly Claim Form, in London in the Chancery Division of the High Court (of which the Patents Court is a part) over that period. It also includes figures for the Patents County Court since its inception in the autumn of 1990 through to 1997, after which such figures were no longer published. Neither are such figures published for the Intellectual Property Enterprise Court that replaced the Patent County Court as from the autumn of 2013.[1]

Numbers of patent and registered design actions started 1981–2013[2]

Year	Total claims (formerly writs) and other originating proceedings (Chancery Division) – London	Patents and registered designs	Percentage of Chancery proceedings concerning patents and registered designs
1981	8,224	304	3.7%
1982	7,607	313	4.1%
1983	5,410	184	3.4%
1984	5,714	273	4.8%
1985	6,412	271	4.2%
1986	7,225	258	3.6%
1987	8,019	333	4.1%
1988	9,101	238	2.6%
1989	10,656	201	1.9%

Year	Total claims (formerly writs) and other originating proceedings (Chancery Division) – London	Patents and registered designs	Percentage of Chancery proceedings concerning patents and registered designs
1990	13,215	87 [+18 PCC]	0.7% [0.8% inc PCC]
1991	12,732	181 [+78 PCC]	1.4% [2.0% inc PCC]
1992	10,101	133 [+84 PCC]	1.3% [2.2% inc PCC]
1993	8,296	102 [+81 PCC]	1.2% [2.2% inc PCC]
1994	7,169	96 [+53 PCC]	1.3% [2.1% inc PCC]
1995	8,193	185 [+27 PCC]	2.3% [2.6% inc PCC]
1996	7,990	132 [+37 PCC]	1.7% [2.1% inc PCC]
1997	7,065	177 [+30 PCC]	2.5% [2.9% inc PCC]
1998	6,878	172 [+22 PCC]	2.5% [2.8% inc PCC]
1999	5,406	86	1.6%
2000	5,787	105	1.8%
2001	5,458	61	1.1%
2002	3,924	187	4.7%
2003	4,533	238	5.2%
2004	4,049	153	3.8%
2005	4,219	54	1.2%
2006	4,528	57	1.3%
2007	3,534	111	3.1%
2008	3,779	111	2.9%
2009	4,887	130	2.6%
2010	4,810	65	1.4%
2011	4,568	183	4.0%
2012	4,999	183	3.7%
2013	5,546	356	6.4%

It can be seen from this table that the number of patent actions (and registered design actions, although there are considerably fewer of these than there are patent actions) started over the years in the English courts since the 1990s has been relatively steady, but at nearly always less than 200 represents a tiny fraction of the hundreds of thousands of patents in force in the UK, as tens of thousands of patents having effect in the UK are granted each year. The figure remains highly variable, but oscillates around a mean of about 100.[3] The high figure for 2013 seems anomalous, especially as it is not reflected in a corresponding rise in the number of patent actions heard in 2014, as can be seen from the tabulation below of such actions.

1   Sources: Judicial Statistics 1981–2011; and Court Statistics (Quarterly) January to March 2014 (Lord Chancellor's Department, Ministry of Justice); and Patents County Court Cause List 1990–1995 (no Patents County Court figures were published after 1995).

2   Helmers et al, in Examining Patent Cases at the Patents Court and Intellectual Property Enterprise Court 2007–2013 (UKIPO, March 2015) and Evaluation of the Reforms of the Intellectual Property Enterprise Court 2010–2013 (UKIPO, 22 June 2015) have derived case counts from a number of sources for the period 2007–2013 that show those for patent cases in the Patents County Court and Intellectual Property Enterprise Court over that seven-year period as 6, 4, 8, 8, 27, 26, and 17 respectively, noting that the increase in 2010 coincides with the imposition of a cap on recoverable costs in the Patents County Court.

3   Helmers et al, in Examining Patent Cases at the Patents Court and Intellectual Property Enterprise Court, 2007–2013, UKIPO, March 2015, and Evaluation of the Reforms of the Intellectual Property Enterprise Court, 2010–2013 (UKIPO, 22 June 2015) have derived case counts from a number of sources for the period 2007–2013 that show those for patent cases in the Patents Court over that seven-year period as 33, 71, 49, 50, 92, 89, and 61 respectively. They also provide separate figures for registered design cases in each of those years that are, unsurprisingly, lower, and which do not total up to the figures shown in the Court Statistics, suggesting that the latter over-report.

Intellectual property litigation in the High Court in England and Wales

The following table compares patent (and registered design) litigation with other IP litigation since 1993 by reference to the numbers of actions started.

Intellectual property litigation in the High Court in England and Wales 1993–2013[1]

Year	Total Chancery claims (formerly writs) and other originating proceedings issued in London	Confidential information		Passing off and trade mark		Patent and registered design		Copyright and design right	
1993	8,296	20	(0.2%)	236	(2.8%)	102	(1.2%)	1095	(13.2%)
1994	7,169	36	(0.5%)	244	(3.4%)	96	(1.3%)	1068	(14.9%)
1995	8,195	78	(1.0%)	387	(1.9%)	185	(2.3%)	779	(9.5%)
1996	7,990	28	(0.4%)	288	(3.6%)	132	(1.7%)	796	(10.0%)
1997	7,065	85	(1.2%)	405	(5.7%)	177	(2.5%)	565	(8.0%)

Appendix 2

Year	Total Chancery claims (formerly writs) and other originating proceedings issued in London	Confidential information		Passing off and trade mark		Patent and registered design		Copyright and design right	
1998	6,878	44	(0.6%)	324	(4.7%)	172	(2.5%)	743	(10.8%)
1999	5,406	29	(0.5%)	304	(5.6%)	86	(1.6%)	463	(8.6%)
2000	5,787	39	(0.7%)	335	(5.8%)	105	(1.8%)	564	(9.7%)
2001	5,458	30	(0.5%)	247	(4.5%)	61	(1.1%)	289	(5.2%)
2002	3,924	93	(2.3%)	181	(4.6%)	187	(4.7%)	207	(5.3%)
2003	4,533	81	(1.8%)	212	(4.6%)	238	(5.2%)	306	(6.7%)
2004	4,049	5	(0.1%)	66	(1.6%)	153	(3.8%)	195	(4.8%)
2005	4,219	11	(0.2%)	105	(2.4%)	54	(1.2%)	148	(3.5%)
2006	4528	3	(0.1%)	50	(1.1%)	57	(1.3%)	120	(2.7%)
2007	3534	21	(0.6%)	118	(2.0%)	111	(3.1%)	172	(4.9%)
2008	3779	23	(0.6%)	142	(3.8%)	111	(2.9%)	286	(7.6%)
2009	4887	95	(1.9%)	171	(3.5%)	130	(2.6%)	374	(7.7%)
2010	4810	45	(0.9%)	146	(3.0%)	65	(1.4%)	306	(6.4%)
2011	4568	106	(2.0%)	88	(1.9%)	183	(4.0%)	290	(4.5%)
2012	4999	167	(3.3%)	114	(2.3%)	183	(3.7%)	315	(6.3%)
2013	5546	166	(3.0%)	107	(1.9%)	356	(6.4%)	320	(5.8%)

1   Sources: Judicial Statistics 1993–2011 and Court Statistics (Quarterly) January to March 2014 (Lord Chancellor's Department, Ministry of Justice).

Despite fewer patent and registered design actions being started than, for example, those in trade marks, passing off, copyright, and (unregistered) design right there is a tendency for more patent actions to get a final hearing than these other types of action.

Patent Court Decisions as to validity and infringement

The above tables tell us nothing about what happened in those cases which got as far as a full hearing on the merits. The situation since the beginning of 1997 can be summarized in the following table, that is based on the outcomes of full trials as to validity, and infringement heard in the Patents Court since 1997, and fuller details of which are set out in **Appendix 3**. There is an inevitable degree of subjectivity about the manner in which these figures are presented, given that this table aggregates infringement actions, declarations of non-infringement, and revocation petitions together, and that sometimes even in an infringement action either validity or infringement was not seriously in issue, or at least was not so by the end of the hearing, in which case such facts are not always clear from the judgment. Moreover, the table takes no account of those cases that were reversed in the Court of Appeal, although as demonstrated below most such appeals as are heard are dismissed.

Patent Court Decisions as to validity and infringement 1997–2014[1]

Year	Hearings as to validity and infringement in which judgment was delivered	Patents in issue	Patents found valid (at least in part)	Patents with valid claims found or admitted infringed (by at least some activities in issue)[2]	Patents found either invalid or not infringed
1997	15	21	7 (+3 not in issue)	3	14
1998	17	24	9	4	19
1999	14	18	8	6	12
2000	14	19	5 (+2 not in issue)	4	13
2001	11	13	6 (+1 not in issue)	2	11
2002	11	13	4	1	11
2003	10	11	6 (+1 not in issue)	4	5
2004	12	13	5 (+3 not in issue)	1	9
2005	6	8	2 (+1 not in issue)	1	6
2006	12	14	3	1	12
2007	14	21	4 (+4 not in issue)	1	18
2008	16	22	11	4	15
2009	27	34	12	7	24
2010	10	15	7 (+1 not in issue)	3	12
2011	15	21	6 (+1 not yet in issue)	2	16
2012	16	22	12	5	15
2013	23	27	11 (+5 not in issue)	7	16
2014	23	30	9 (+4 not in issue)	10	20

1   Source: **Appendix 3**.
2   This understates effective successes on the part of patentees as this omits those cases in which either validity or infringement was never put in issue, as opposed to being conceded in the course of the proceedings.

Appendix 2

Patent appeals to the Court of Appeal

The Patents Court and Court of Appeal workload: the following two tables summarize the activities of the English Court of Appeal in relation to patent matters. The first sets out figures to 1997 showing the number of cases appealed, and the number actually dealt with by the Court of Appeal, as not all appeals that are filed are pursued. The second is based on the rather more detailed data available as to the activities of the Court of Appeal since 1998, and shows the relatively poor success rate of such appeals.

Patent appeals to the Court of Appeal 1989–1997[1]

Year	Type	Outstanding at start of year	Set down	Disposed of	Outstanding at end of year
1989	All	9	10	11	8
1990	All	8	9	8	9
1991	All	9	13	7	15
1992	All	15	5	15	5
1993	Final	5	5	4	6
	Interlocutory	2	4	4	2
1994	Final	6	7	4	9
	Interlocutory	2	6	4	4
1995	Final	9	7	7	9
	Interlocutory	4	6	8	2
1996	Final	9	11	3	17
	Interlocutory	2	1	3	0
1997	Final	17	19	16	20
	Interlocutory	0	2	0	2

1   Sources: Judicial Statistics 1989–1997 (Lord Chancellor's Department).

Patent appeals to the Court of Appeal 1998–2013[1]

Year	Type	Filed	Allowed	Dismissed	Dismissed by consent	Struck out for failure to provide documents	Otherwise disposed of
1998	Final	19	4	3	11	1	2
	Interlocutory	12	1	2	2	0	1
1999	Final	17	1	3	10	0	3
	Interlocutory	19	5	12	3	0	0
2000	Final	18	4	9	6	0	1
	Interlocutory	2	0	2	0	0	0
2001	Final	15	1	8	4	0	3
	Interlocutory	0	1	0	0	0	0
2002	Final	17	8	7	4	1	2
	Interlocutory	6	0	2	2	0	0
2003	Final	8	3	10	2	0	0
	Interlocutory	1	1	2	0	0	0
2004	Final	11	2	3	1	0	0
	Interlocutory	2	0	0	2	0	0
2005	Final	26	5	16	4	0	0
	Interlocutory	2	0	0	0	0	0
2006	Final	23	3	18	7	0	0
	Interlocutory	0	1	1	0	0	0

Year	Type	Filed	Allowed	Dismissed	Dismissed by consent	Struck out for failure to provide documents	Otherwise disposed of
2007	Final	23	4	9	6	0	2
	Interlocutory	0	0	0	0	0	0
2008	Final	20	7	8	8	2	1
	Interlocutory	0	0	0	0	0	0
2009	Final	27	7	10	1	0	1
	Interlocutory	0	0	0	0	0	0
2010	Final	14	7	13	2	0	0
	Interlocutory	1	0	0	0	0	0
2011	Final	18	4	6	3	0	0
	Interlocutory	0	0	0	0	0	0
2012	Final	33	6	11	5	0	0
	Interlocutory	0	0	0	0	0	0
2013	Final	14	5	22	7	0	0
	Interlocutory	0	0	0	0	0	0

1   Sources: Judicial Statistics 1998–2011 and Court Statistics (Quarterly) January to March 2014 (Lord Chancellor's Department, Ministry of Justice).

In the last table, the drop in figures for interlocutory appeals in 2000 will represent the consequences of changes effected by the Civil Procedure Rules (CPR) that were intended to discourage appeals in interlocutory (ie mainly procedural) matters.

Appendix 3

Patents Court and Court of Appeal judgments on validity and infringement since 1997

The following tables list final hearings on matters of validity and/or infringement in the English courts over nearly two decades, and appeals from these. They include applications for summary judgment and, from 2001, hearings in the Patents County Court and now the Intellectual Property Enterprise Court but as the latter used not to be consistently reported will record these less reliably. They exclude appeals from the few hearings in the UK Patent Office on such matters, procedural applications, and applications for interim injunctions or brought to determine preliminary points of substantive law. First instance hearings are tabulated by year, and appeal hearings in two tables, the first for the period 1997–2001, and the other the period 2002–2014. In the following tables the following conventions have been used:

— 'Case': is in general the reported name of the case, but only listing the first named claimant and defendant, and for individuals omitting first names, and for corporations omitting any generic corporate identifiers such as 'company', 'corporation' or 'limited' or their equivalents in other languages. Cases in **bold italics** in the listings were the subject of further appeals to the House of Lords (now the Supreme Court).

— 'Citation': only lists citations in Fleet Street Reports (FSR), Reports of Patent Cases (RPC), and All England Reports (All ER), and since 2000 the 'neutral citations' provided by the courts themselves – namely 'EWHC' for Patents Court, and other High Court decisions and Intellectual Property Enterprise Court decisions, and 'EWCA' for Court of Appeal decisions. Since the Intellectual Property Enterprise Court took the place of the Patents County Court its decisions have had the suffix 'IPEC' to distinguish them from Patents Court decisions which have the suffix 'Pat'. Patents County Court decisions were not in general given neutral citations. Except where necessary to distinguish between Intellectual Property Enterprise Court, and Patents Court decisions the suffixes '(Pat)' or sometimes '(Ch)' to EWHC numbers, and the prefix '(Civ)' to EWCA numbers have been omitted, and thus [2000] EWHC 49 (Pat) is shown as [2000] EWHC 49, and [2000] EWCA Civ 169 is shown as [2000] EWCA 169. FSR and RPC citations were originally to page numbers in sets of law reports, but since 2001 the number instead identifies where in the sequential numbering in each year in each set of law reports these appear. However, these have generally been omitted since 2000 as the neutral citations EWHC and EWCA suffice, and the judgments can be accessed free of charge on BAILII at: www.bailii.org.

Patents Court judgments on validity and infringement for 1997

Date	Case	Citation	Judge	Infringed?	Valid?	Appealed?
14.01.97	Scanvaegt v Pelcombe		Young QC	[Yes]	Yes	Reversed as to infringement – [1998] FSR 786
21.01.97	Buhler v Satake	[1997] RPC 232	Jacob J	No	No in part – obvious (1949)	No
06.02.97	Hoechst Celanese v BP Chemicals	[1997] FSR 547	Laddie J	Yes	Yes	Upheld – [1999] FSR 319
24.04.97	Auchincloss v Agricultural & Veterinary Supplies	[1997] RPC 649	Prescott QC	Yes (some old) [No (new)]	NA	Reversed as to infringement – [1999] RPC 397
28.04.97	Norling v Eez-Away		Laddie J	No	NA	No
07.05.97	LB Europe v David Smith Packaging		Pumfrey QC	No	Yes	No
23.05.97	Ward Building Systems v Hodgson Steels		Robert Walker J	Yes (issue as to innocence)	No – obvious	No
05.06.97	Henry Brothers (Magherafelt) v Ministry of Defence	[1997] RPC 693	Jacob J	NA	No – not entitled	Upheld – [1999] RPC 442
12.06.97	Raychem Corp's Patents	[1998] RPC 31	Laddie J	NA	No × 4 – obvious	Upheld – [1999] RPC 497

Date	Case	Citation	Judge	Infringed?	Valid?	Appealed?
25.06.97	Riker Laboratories v Norton Healthcare		Jacob J	NA	No × 3 – obvious	No
31.07.97	Union Carbide v BP Chemicals		Jacob J	Yes × 2 (old process – admitted) [No × 2 (new processes)]	Yes × 2	Reversed as to infringement – [1999] RPC 409
29.07.97	*United Wire v Screen Repair*		Robert Walker J	[No (only issue as to repair)]	Yes	Reversed as to infringement – [2000] FSR 204
18.12.97	Parlok v Jonesco (Preston)		Pumfrey J	No	No – obvious	No
09.12.97	Lacroix Duarib v Kwikform (UK)	[1998] FSR 493	Laddie J	Possibly (striking out motion)	NA	No
10.12.97	Adwest v Tavismanor		Laddie J	No	Yes	No

Patents Court judgments on validity and infringement for 1998

Date	Case	Citation	Judge	Infringed?	Valid?	Appealed?
16.01.98	Chiron v Evans Medical	[1998] RPC 517	Laddie J	NA	No – anticipated, obvious	No
27.01.98	Dorricott v Glennan		Laddie J	No	Yes	No
02.02.98	Uni-Continental Holdings v Eurobond Adhesives	[1999] FSR 263	Pumfrey J	Yes	No – anticipated by prior use, obvious	No
20.03.98	Hoechst Celanese v BP Chemicals	[1998] FSR 586	Jacob J	No	Yes	No
23.03.98	Compaq v Ma		Laddie J	NA	No – obvious	No
29.04.98	Demel v Jefferson	[1999] FSR 204	Laddie J	Yes	Yes	No
07.05.98	Oneac v Raychem		Laddie J	Yes	Yes	No
26.06.98	Palmaz's European Patents (UK)	[1999] RPC 47	Pumfrey J	No × 2	No × 1 – obvious No × 1 – not novel	Upheld – [2000] RPC 631
28.07.98	Minnesota Mining & Manufacturing's (Suspension Aerosol Formulation) Patent	[1999] RPC 135	Pumfrey J	No – but invalid	No – anticipated (main claims)	No

Date	Case	Citation	Judge	Infringed?	Valid?	Appealed?
29.07.98	Discovision v Pioneer	[1999] FSR 196	Pumfrey J	Yes × 2 – but invalid No × 4	No × 5 – obvious Yes × 1 – but not infringed	No
20.08.98	Bristol Myers Squibb v Norton	[1999] RPC 253	Jacob J	NA	No – anticipated, obvious	Upheld – [2001] RPC 1
08.09.98	Consafe v Emtunga	[1999] RPC 154	Pumfrey J	No	No – obvious over prior use	No
19.10.98	Visx v Nidek	[1999] FSR 405	Neuberger J	Yes × 1 – but invalid No × 1	No × 1 – obvious Yes × 1 – but not infringed	No
13.11.98	Hadley v Metal Sections		Neuberger J	Yes	Yes – on amendment	No
27.11.98	Quadrant Holdings (Cambridge) v Quadrant Research Foundation		Pumfrey J	Yes	Yes	No
16.12.98	Pifco v Philips		Pumfrey J	Yes but invalid	No – obvious	No
21.12.98	Cartonneries de Thulin v White Knight		Neuberger J	[No]	[Yes]	Reversed – [2001] RPC 6

Patents Court judgments on validity and infringement for 1999

Date	Case	Citation	Judge	Infringed?	Valid?	Appealed?
05.01.99	Bayer v Octapharma		Fysh QC	No	Yes	No
15.01.99	Haberman v Jackel	[1999] FSR 683	Laddie J	Yes	Yes	No
22.01.99	PCME v Goyen Controls	[1999] FSR 801	Laddie J	Yes × 2	No × 1 – anticipated by prior use No × 1 – obvious	No
29.01.99	Coflexip v Stolt Comex Seaway	[1999] 2 All ER 593, [1999] FSR 473	Laddie J	Yes	Yes	Upheld, other than as to injunction scope – [2001] 1 All ER 952, [2001] RPC 9
23.02.99	Wheatley v Drillsafe		Ferris J	No	[No] – anticipated, obvious	Reversed – [2001] RPC 7
21.05.99	Lighting Electronics v Thorn		Pumfrey J	No	No – obvious	No
10.06.99	Horne v Reliance	[2000] FSR 90	Pumfrey J	No	No – obvious, insufficient	No

Date	Case	Citation	Judge	Infringed?	Valid?	Appealed?
20.07.99	Charlesworth v Relay Roads	[1999] 4 All ER 397	Neuberger J	Yes × 3	No × 2 – obvious Yes × 1	No
30.07.99	Taylor v Ishida		Pumfrey J	Yes	Yes	Upheld – [2001] EWCA 1042
30.07.99	Texas Instruments v Hyundai		Pumfrey J	NA (settled)	No – obvious	No
08.10.99	Spring Form v Playhut	[2000] FSR 327	Laddie J	Yes	Yes	No
11.10.99	Rocky Mountain Traders v Hewlett Packard	[2000] FSR 411	Pumfrey J	Yes × 2 except for one device	No × 2 – obvious	Upheld – [2002] FSR 1
06.12.99	American Home Products v Novartis Pharmaceuticals UK	[2000] RPC 547	Laddie J	[Yes]	Yes as to sufficiency. Issues of anticipation and obviousness held over	Reversed – [2001] RPC 8
20.12.99	Sara Lee Household Products v Johnson Wax	[2001] FSR 17	Young QC	No	Yes	Upheld – [2001] EWCA 1609

Patents Court judgments on validity and infringement for 2000

Date	Case	Citation	Judge	Infringed?	Valid?	Appealed?
25.01.00	TH Goldschmidt v EOC Belgium	[2000] EWHC 175	Young QC	Yes × 3	No × 2 Yes × 1	No
04.02.00	Monsanto v Merck	[2000] RPC 709	Pumfrey J	[No]	No	Reversed as to infringement – [2001] EWCA 1610, [2002] RPC 41
17.03.00	Nutrinova v Scanchem	[2000] EWHC 124, [2001] FSR 42	Pumfrey J	Yes	Yes	No
14.04.00	David John Instance v Denny Bros Printing	[2000] EWHC 112	Laddie J	NA	No × 3 – obvious	Upheld – [2002] RPC 14
21.07.00	Kimberly-Clark v Procter & Gamble	[2000] EWHC 74, [2001] FSR 22	Pumfrey J	No	No – obvious, insufficient	No
28.07.00	Stoves v Baumatic		Pumfrey J	Yes	No – obvious	No
28.07.00	Rohm & Haas v Collag	[2000] EWHC 72, [2001] FSR 28	Neuberger J	No	Held over	Upheld – [2001] EWCA 1589, [2002] FSR 28
03.10.00	Dyson Appliances v Hoover	[2000] EWHC 62, [2001] RPC 26	Fysh QC	Yes	Yes	Upheld – [2001] EWCA 1440, [2002] RPC 22

Date	Case	Citation	Judge	Infringed?	Valid?	Appealed?
25.10.00	City Technology v Alphasense	[2000] EWHC 56	Young QC	Yes	Yes	Upheld – [2002] EWCA 347
26.10.00	Amersham Pharmacia Biotech AB v Amicon		Laddie J	No × 2 (except as admitted on one claim of one patent)	No 1 – obvious (except on one unchallenged claim). Other patent not in issue	Upheld – [2001] EWCA 1042
31.10.00	Minnesota Mining & Manufacturing v Atlas ATI	[2001] FSR 31	Pumfrey J	Yes	No – obvious	No
08.11.00	Pfizer's Patent	[2000] EWHC 49, [2001] FSR 16	Laddie J	NA	No – obvious	Upheld – [2002] EWCA 1
05.12.00	Asahi Medical v Macopharma		Laddie J	Admitted as to one claim, not addressed as to the other in issue	No – obvious	Upheld – [2002] EWCA 466
21.12.00	DSM's Patent	[2000] EWHC 34, [2001] RPC 35	Neuberger J	NA	No – obvious and insufficient	No

Patents Court and Patents County Court judgments on validity and infringement for 2001

Date	Case	Citation	Judge	Infringed?	Valid?	Appealed?
28.02.01	McGhan v Nagor and Biosil	[2001] EWHC 452, [2002] FSR 9	Fysh QC	No	Yes	No
11.04.01	*Kirin-Amgen v Hoechst Marion Roussel*	[2002] RPC 1	Neuberger J	(1) [Yes] (2) NA	(1) Yes [(partially – 1 claim insufficient)] (2) No – anticipated, obvious	Reversed on (1) against Hoechst Marion Roussel as to both infringement and as to the 1 claim found invalid – [2002] EWCA 1096, [2003] RPC 3
25.04.01	Agilent v Waters		Pumfrey J	[No]	Yes	Reversed as to infringement – [2002] EWCA 612
09.05.01	Micromatic v DSI		Neuberger J	Yes	No – anticipated, obvious	No

564

Date	Case	Citation	Judge	Infringed?	Valid?	Appealed?
20.06.01	Inhale Therapeutic v Quadrant Healthcare	[2002] RPC 21	Laddie J	No	No – anticipated, obvious	No
20.06.01	Icon Health v Precise Exercise Equipment		Laddie J	No	NA	No
31.07.01	Sapey v Trianco Redfyre Ltd		Pumfrey J	Not as to valid claim	Not as to infringed claim – obvious	No
31.07.01	*Sabaf v MFI Furniture Centres*		Laddie J	Yes	[No – obvious]	Reversed as to validity – [2002] EWCA 976
07.09.01	Warheit v Olympia Tools		Thorley QC (PCC)	No	Yes	Reversed as to infringement – [2002] EWCA 1161
08.11.01	Arjo & Impro v Liko		Laddie J	No	No – anticipated, obvious	No

Patents Court and Patents County Court judgments on validity and infringement for 2002

Date	Parties	Citation	Subject matter	Judge	Infringed?	Valid?	Appealed?
24.01.02	Tickner v Honda	[2002] EWHC 8	Engine	Jacob J	No	Yes	No
25.04.02	Stena v Irish Ferries	[2002] EWHC 737, [2002] RPC 50	Multi-hull vessel	Laddie J	No	Yes	Upheld – [2003] EWCA 66, [2003] RPC 36
06.03.02	Cairnstores v Hassle	[2002] EWHC 309	Pharmaceutical – Omeprazole	Laddie J	NA	No × 2 – obvious	Upheld – [2002] EWCA 1504, [2003] FSR 23
04.07.02	Stannah v Freelift		Lifting apparatus	Fysh HHJ (PCC)	Yes	No – obvious	No
12.07.02	BASF v SmithKline Beecham	[2002] EWHC 1373	Pharmaceutical – Paroxetine hydrochloride	Pumfrey J	NA	Yes (partially)	Upheld – [2003] EWCA 872, RPC 49
24.07.02	Ash v Fixing Point		Bracket	Fysh HHJ (PCC)	Yes	Yes	No

Date	Parties	Citation	Subject matter	Judge	Infringed?	Valid?	Appealed?
26.07.02	SEB v De'Longhi	[2002] EWHC 1556	Fryers	Pumfrey J	Yes	No – obvious	Upheld – [2003] EWCA 952
21.08.02	Storage Computer v Hitachi Data Systems	[2002] EWHC 1776	Data Storage	Pumfrey J	(1) No (2) No	(1) No – obvious (2) No – added matter	Upheld – [2003] EWCA 1155
02.10.02	Wesley Jessen v Coopervision	[2003] RPC 20	Contact lenses	FyshHHJ (PCC)	No	No – anticipated, obvious	No
03.12.02	Synthon v SmithKline Beecham	[2002] EWHC 2573, [2003] RPC 33	Pharmaceutical – paroxetine mesylate	Jacob J	NA	[No – anticipated]	Reversed – [2003] EWCA 861, RPC 43
20.12.02	Memcor Australia v Norit Membran Technology	[2003] FSR 43	Water filter Membrane testing method	FyshHH (PCC)	Yes	No – anticipated, obvious	No

Patents Court and Patents County Court judgments on validity and infringement for 2003

Date	Parties	Citation	Subject matter	Judge	Infringed?	Valid?	Appealed?
21.01.03	Teva Pharmaceutical Industries v Institute Gentili	[2003] EWHC 5, [2003] FSR 29	Pharmaceutical – alendronate	Jacob J	NA	(1) No – anticipated, obvious (2) No – anticipated	Upheld – [2003] EWCA 1545, [2004] FSR 16
11.02.03	NMI v Unwin		Tracker device	Fysh HHJ (PCC)	Yes	Yes	No
31.03.03	Kavanagh Balloons v Cameron Balloons	[2004] RPC 5	Balloons	Fysh HHJ (PCC)	Yes	Yes (partial)	No
15.04.03	Rockwater v Coflexip	[2003] EWHC 812	Pipe laying device	Laddie J	[No]	[No – anticipated, obvious]	Reversed as to both validity and infringement – [2004] EWCA 381, [2004] RPC 46

Date	Parties	Citation	Subject matter	Judge	Infringed?	Valid?	Appealed?
07.05.03	Daesang v Ajinomoto	[2003] EWHC 973	Process for purification of aspartame	Laddie J	NA	Yes	No
07.07.03	Koninkijke Philips Electronics v Princo Digital Disc	[2003] EWHC 1598	CD boxes	Pumfrey J	NA	Yes	No
26.09.03	Unilin Beheer v Berry Floor	[2004] FSR 14	Laminated floors	Fysh HHJ (PCC)	Yes	Yes (partially)	Upheld – [2004] EWCA 1021
28.10.03	Building Products v Sandtoft		Roofs	FyshHHJ (PCC)	Yes	Yes	No
27.11.03	Merck v Generics (UK)	[2003] EWHC 2842, [2004] RPC 31	Pharmaceutical – alendronate	Laddie J	No	NA	No
05.12.03	Apotex Europe v SmithKline Beecham	[2003] EWHC 2939, [2004] FSR 26	Pharmaceutical – paroxetine hydrochloride	Pumfrey J	No	[No – anticipated, obvious]	Reversed as to validity – [2004] EWCA 1568

Patents Court and Patents County Court judgments on validity and infringement for 2004

Date	Parties	Citation	Subject matter	Judge	Infringed?	Valid?	Appealed?
17.03.04	Russell Finex v Telesonic	[2004] EWHC 474, [2004] RPC 38	Sieving process	Laddie J	No	NA	No
19.03.04	CIPLA v Glaxo	[2004] EWHC 477	Pharmaceutical – salmeterol/ fluticasone mixture	Pumfrey J	NA	No – obvious	No
12.05.04	Machinery Developments v St Merryn Meat		Packaging system	Fysh HHJ (PCC)	Yes	Yes	No
17.06.04	Secretary of State for Education and Skills v Frontline Technology	[2004] EWHC 1487	Attendance system	D Young QC	NA	Yes (partially)	No
22.07.04	Ultraframe (UK) v Eurocell Building Plastics	[2004] EWHC 1785, [2005] RPC 7	Conservatories	Lewison J	[No]	Yes	Reversed as to infringement – [2005] EWCA 761, [2006] RPC 36
28.07.04	Sandoz v Roche Diagnostics	[2004] EWHC 1313	Pharmaceutical – erythropoeitin formulation	Patten J	NA	Yes	No

Date	Parties	Citation	Subject matter	Judge	Infringed?	Valid?	Appealed?
16.09.04	Burnden Group v Ultraframe (UK)		Conservatories	Fysh HHJ (PCC)	Held over in part	(1) No – anticipated, obvious (2) No – obvious	Upheld – [2005] EWCA 867
08.10.04	Nikken Kosakusho Works v Pioneer Trading	[2004] EWHC 2246, [2005] FSR 2458	Milling chuck	Mann J	NA	No – anticipated, obvious	No
01.11.04	Mayne Pharma v Pharmacia Italia	[2004] EWHC 2458	Pharmaceutical – epirubicin formulation	Wyand QC	[No]	NA	Reversed as to infringement – [2005] EWCA 137
03.11.04	St Gobain PAM v Fusion Provida	[2004] EWHC 2469	Iron pipes	Pumfrey J	NA	Yes	Upheld – [2005] EWCA 177
19.11.04	Abbott Laboratories v Ranbaxy Europe	[2004] EWHC 2723	Pharmaceutical clarithromycin	Pumfrey J	NA	No – anticipated, added matter	No
21.12.04	Agilent Technologies Deutschland v Waters	[2004] EWHC 2992	HPLC pump	Pumfrey J	No	NA	Upheld – [2005] EWCA 987

Patents Court and Patents County Court judgments on validity and infringement for 2005

Date	Parties	Citation	Subject matter	Judge	Infringed?	Valid?	Appealed?
08.06.05	E Data v Getty Images	[2005] EWHC 1527	Internet sales	Arnold QC (PCC)	No	Yes	No
21.07.05	Halliburton Energy Services v Smith International (North Sea)	[2005] EWHC 1623, [2006] RPC 2	Drill bits	Pumfrey J	(1) Yes (2) No	(1) No – insufficient (2) No – insufficient	Upheld – [2006] EWCA 1715
12.10.05	Mayne Pharma (US) v Teva UK	[2005] EWHC 2141	Pharmaceutical – paclitaxel formulation	Pumfrey J	Yes	No – obvious	No
12.10.05	Ranbaxy UK v Warner-Lambert	[2005] EWHC 2142, [2006] FSR 14	Pharmaceutical – Atorvastatin	Pumfrey J	(1) Yes (2) NA	(1) Yes (2) No – anticipated, obvious	Upheld – [2006] EWCA 876, [2007] RPC 4
18.11.05	Schering-Plough v Norbrook Laboratories	[2005] EWHC 2532, [2006] FSR 18	Pharmaceutical – mixture	Floyd QC	NA	Yes (partially)	No
28.11.05	LG Philips LCD v Tatung (UK)		Mountings for flat panel display devices	Fysh HHJ (PCC)	No	No – obvious	Upheld – [2006] EWCA 1774
21.12.05	Canady v Erbe Elektromedezin	[2005] EWHC 2946	Surgical tissue coagulator	Pumfrey J	No	NA	No

Patents Court and Patents County Court judgments on validity and infringement for 2006

Date	Parties	Citation	Subject matter	Judge	Infringed?	Valid?	Appealed?
27.01.06	Tamglass v Luoyang North Glass Technology	[2006] EWHC65	Glass bending and tempering	Mann J	Yes	Yes	No
02.02.06	Research In Motion UK v Inpro Licensing	[2006] EWHC 70, [2006] RPC 20	Mobile telephony	Pumfrey J	Yes (but invalid)	No – anticipated, obvious	Upheld – [2007] EWCA 51
17.02.06	GE Healthcare v PerkinElmer Life Sciences (UK)	[2006] EWHC 214	Scintillation proximity test	Kitchin J	NA	No – obvious	No
22.02.06	Ferag v Müller Martini	[2006] EWHC 225	Cutting/trimming print materials	Lewison J	[No]	[No – obvious]	Reversed as to both validity and infringement – [2007] EWCA 15
24.02.06	*Conor Medsystems v Angiotech Pharmaceuticals*	[2006] EWHC 260, [2006] RPC 28	Medical device – drug impregnated stent	Pumfrey J	NA	No – obvious	Upheld – [2007] EWCA 5
10.04.06	Ivax Pharmaceuticals (UK) v Chugai Seiyaku	[2006] EWHC 756	Pharmaceutical – nicorandil	Kitchin J	NA	No – obvious	No
19.05.06	Mayne Pharma v Debiopharm	[2006] EWHC 1123	Pharmaceutical – oxaliplatin	Pumfrey J	(1) No (2) NA	No × 2 – obvious	No

Date	Parties	Citation	Subject matter	Judge	Infringed?	Valid?	Appealed'?
22.05.06	Ivax Pharmaceuticals UK v Akzo Nobel UK	[2006] EWHC 1089, [2007] RPC 3	Pharmaceutical – tibolone	Lewison J	NA	No – obvious	No
21.06.06	Pozzoli v BDMO	[2006] EWHC 1398	CD & DVD Packaging	Lewison J	No	No – obvious	Upheld – [2007] EWCA 588
07.07.06	Vector v Glatt Air Technologies	[2006] EWHC 1638, [2007] RPC 12	Fluid bed	Lewison J	NA	Yes, as amended	Reversed in part as to one claim as proposed amended – [2007] EWCA 805
16.10.06	Novartis v Ivax Pharmaceuticals (UK)	[2006] EWHC 2506	Pharmaceutical – cyclosporine formulation	Pumfrey J	No × 2	(1) Yes (2) No – obvious	Upheld – [2007] EWCA 971
30.10.06	Merz Pharma v Allergan	[2006] EWHC 2686	Pharmaceutical – botulinum toxin	Kitchin J	NA	No – anticipated, added matter, obvious	No

Patents Court and Patents County Court judgments on validity and infringement for 2007

Date	Parties	Citation	Subject matter	Judge	Infringed?	Valid?	Appealed?
02.03.07	Baxter v Abbott	[2007] EWHC 348	Pharmaceutical – sevoflurane	Pumfrey J	No	No – anticipated, added matter and insufficient	No
15.03.07	LB Europe v Smurfit Bag in Box	[2007] EWHC 510	Tap for wine box	Wyand QC	No	Yes	Upheld – [2007] EWCA 933
26.03.07	European Central Bank v Document Security System	[2007] EWHC 600	Method of making a document incapable of replication by a scanning type copying device	Kitchin J	N/A	No – added matter	Upheld – [2008] EWCA 192
04.05.07	*Generics v H Lundbeck A/S*	[2007] EWHC 1040	Pharmaceutical – escitalopram	Kitchin J	N/A	C6: Yes [C1&3: No – insufficient]	Reversed – [2008] EWCA 311
06.06.07	Actavis v Merck	[2007] EWHC 1311	Pharmaceutical – finasteride	Warren J	N/A	[No – anticipated]	Reversed – [2008] EWCA 444
15.06.07	Triumph Actuation Systems v Aeroquip-Vickers	[2007] EWHC 1367	Power transfer unit	Pumfrey J	Yes	No – added matter	No

Date	Parties	Citation	Subject matter	Judge	Infringed?	Valid?	Appealed?
11.07.07	Servier v Apotex	[2007] EWHC 1538	Pharmaceutical – perindropil	Pumfrey J	Yes	No – anticipated and obvious	Upheld – [2008] EWCA 445
06.09.07	Handi-Craft v B Free World	[2007] EWHC B10	Baby bottles	Fysh HHJ	Yes	No – obvious	Upheld – [2008] EWCA 868
04.10.07	Siemens Schweiz v Thorn Security	[2007] EWHC 2242	Coating for printed circuit board	Mann J	Yes	Yes	Reversed as to infringement – [2008] EWCA 1161
10.10.07	Monsanto Technology v Cargill International	[2007] EWHC 2257	GM crops	Pumfrey J	No	Yes	No
10.10.07	University of Queensland v Siemens Magnet Technology	[2007] EWHC 2258	MRI Magnets	Pumfrey J	Yes [in part]	No – added matter and obvious	No
12.10.07	Teva Pharmaceutical Industries v Merrell Pharmaceuticals	[2007] EWHC 2276	Pharmaceutical – fexofenadine	Warren J	NA	No as to the 9 claims in issue of the 3 patents in issue – 8 anticipated, 9 obvious	No

Date	Parties	Citation	Subject matter	Judge	Infringed?	Valid?	Appealed?
14.11.07	Wobben v Vestas-Celtic Wind Technology	[2007] EWHC 2636	Wind turbine technology	Kitchin J	No × 2 Abandoned × 1	No × 3 – (1) added matter, obvious and insufficient; (2) conceded claim 1 invalid but amendment refused for added matter and either obvious or insufficient; (3) conceded all except 2 claims invalid, one proposed amendment refused as obvious but other allowed.	No

Date	Parties	Citation	Subject matter	Judge	Infringed?	Valid?	Appealed?
21.12.07	Nokia v Interdigital Technology	[2007] EWHC 3077	3G mobile phone technology	Pumfrey LJ	No × 3 Yes × 1 [as to essentiality]	NA	No

Patents Court and Patents County Court judgments on validity and infringement for 2008

Date	Parties	Citation	Subject matter and patents	Judge	Infringed?	Valid?	Appealed?
07.02.08	Qual-Chem Ltd v Corus UK Ltd	[2008] EWPCC 1	Steel-making process GB 2 363 635 C	HHJ Fysh	Yes	Yes	Upheld [2008] EWCA 1177
28.02.08	Research in Motion UK Ltd v Visto Corporation	[2008] EWHC 335	Telecoms EP 0 996 905 B	Floyd J	Yes	No – obvious, and computer program as such	No
03.03.08	Qualcomm Incorporated v Nokia Corporation	[2008] EWHC 329	Telecoms EP 0 629 324 B EP 0 695 482 B	Floyd J	Yes × 2	No × 2 – '324 anticipated and obvious, claims 1, 2, 9 and 11 of '482 obvious and claims 9 and 11 insufficient	No

Date	Parties	Citation	Subject matter and patents	Judge	Infringed?	Valid?	Appealed?
21.04.08	Abbott Laboratories Ltd v Eyvisio Medical Devices ULC	[2008] EWHC 800	Medical devices – coronary stents EP 0 888 093 B EP 0 888 094 B EP 1 066 804 B	Kitchin J	Yes as to '093 and '084 No as to '094	No × 2 – '093 and '804 obvious Yes as to '094	No
21.04.08	Buhler AG v FP Spomax SA	[2008] EWHC 823	Milling process EP 0 336 939 B	Mann J	Admitted	No – obvious	No
14.05.08	Aerotel Ltd v Wavecrest Group Enterprises Ltd	[2008] EWHC B4	Telecoms GB 2 171 877 B	Fysh HHJ	Yes	No – obvious, and business method, and computer programme as such	Upheld as obvious – [2009] EWCA 408
12.06.08	Alan Nuttall Ltd v Fri-Jado UK Ltd	[2008] EWHC 1311	Hot food display cabinet GB 2 348 697 B	Prescott QC	Yes	Yes	No
25.06.08	Zipher Ltd v Markem Systems Ltd	[2008] EWHC 1379	Tape drives GB 2 369 602 B EP 1 767 375 B	Floyd J	Yes × 2	No × 2 – '602 and '375 insufficient	No

Date	Parties	Citation	Subject matter and patents	Judge	Infringed?	Valid?	Appealed?
30.06.08	Actavis UK Ltd v Janssen Pharmaceutica NV	[2008] EWHC 1422	Pharmaceutical – nebivolol EP 0 334 429 B	Floyd J	NA	Partially – all claims except claim 5 anticipated & obvious	No
31.07.08	*Eli Lilly & Company v Human Genome Sciences, Inc*	[2008] EWHC 1903	Neutrokine-α polypeptide EP 0 939 804 B	Kitchin J	NA	No – obvious, insufficient, and lacks industrial applicability	Upheld as to lack of industrial applicability – [2010] EWCA 1903[1]
07.10.08	WL Gore & Associates GmbH v Geoxx SpA	[2008] EWHC 2311	Shoes EP 0 858 270 B EP 1 185 183 B	Floyd J	Yes as to '270 No as to '183	Yes × 2	Upheld as to both infringement holdings – [2009] EWCA 794
13.10.08	Dr Reddy's Laboratories (UK) Limited v Eli Lilly & Company	[2008] EWHC 2345	Pharmaceutical – olanzapine EP 0 454 436 B	Floyd J	NA	Yes	Upheld – [2010] EWCA 1362

1 Reversed by UK Supreme Court [2011] UKSC 51.

Date	Parties	Citation	Subject matter and patents	Judge	Infringed?	Valid?	Appealed?
15.10.08	Generics (UK) Ltd v Daiichi Pharmaceutical Company	[2008] EWHC 2413	Pharmaceutical – levofloxacin EP 0206283 & SPC	Kitchin J	NA	Yes	Upheld [2009] EWCA646
21.10.08	Ancon v ACS Stainless Steel Fixings	[2008] EWHC 2489	Steel channel assembly EP 0 882 164 B	Patten J	No	Yes	Reversed on infringement [2009] EWCA 498
14.11.08	Armour Group plc v Leisuretech Electronics Pty Ltd	[2008] EWHC 2797	Distributed audio system EP 1 004 221 B	Arnold J	Admitted	No – obvious	No
16.12.08	Ratiopharm GmbH v Napp Pharmaceutical Holdings Ltd Sandoz Ltd v Napp Pharmaceutical Holdings Ltd	[2008] EWHC 3070	Pharmaceutical formulation – oxycodone EP 0722730 B EP 1258246 B	Floyd J	No × 2	Yes × 2	Reversed on infringement × 2 – [2009] EWCA 252

Patents Court and Patents County Court judgments on validity, and infringement for 2009

Date	Parties	Citation	Subject matter and patents	Judge	Infringed?	Valid?	Appealed?
09.01.09	Corevalve Inc v Edwards Lifesciences AG	[2009] EWHC 0006	Artificial heart valve EP 0 592 410	Prescott QC	No	Yes	Upheld – [2010] EWCA 704
16.01.09	Actavis UK Ltd v Novartis AG	[2009] EWHC 0041	Sustained release fluvastatin formulation EP 0 948 320	Warren J	NA	No – all claims obvious	Upheld – [2010] EWCA 82
19.01.09	Schlumberger Holdings Ltd v Electromagnetic Geoservices AS	[2009] EWHC 0058	Oil exploration using controlled source electromagnetism EP 1 256 019 EP 1 309 887 GB 2 399 640	Mann J	NA	No × 3 – all claims obvious	Reversed as to obviousness – [2010] EWCA 819
21.01.09	Virgin Atlantic Airways Ltd v Premium Aircraft Interiors Group Ltd	[2009] EWHC 0026	Aircraft seats EP 1 495 908	Lewison J	No	Yes	Reversed as to infringement – [2009] EWCA 1062

Date	Parties	Citation	Subject matter and patents	Judge	Infringed?	Valid?	Appealed?
22.01.09	Dyson Technology Ltd v Samsung Gwangju Electronics Co Ltd	[2009] EWHC 0055	Vacuum cleaners GB 2 424 603 GB 2 424 606	Arnold J	NA	No × 2 as to all claims in issue, all of which obvious, with some anticipated	No
23.01.09	Laboratoires Almirall SA v Boehringer Ingelheim International GmbH	[2009] EWHC 0102	Combination aclidinium and B2 agonists EP 1 651 270 GB 2 419 819	HHJ Fysh	NA	No × 2 – all claims obvious, claim 20 of 819 invalid as method of medical treatment	No
12.02.09	Ratiopharm (UK) Ltd v Alza Corp: Alza Corp v Sandoz Ltd	[2009] EWHC 0123	Transdermal patches for administering fentanyl EP 1 381 352	Kitchin J	Yes	No – all claims anticipated (which could have been overcome by amendment) and obvious	No

Date	Parties	Citation	Subject matter and patents	Judge	Infringed?	Valid?	Appealed?
26.02.09	Belvac Production Machinery Inc v Carnaudmetalbox Engineering Ltd	[2009] EWHC 0292	Can processing machinery EP 0 767 713	Baldwin QC	No	No – all claims obvious	No
03.03.09	Novartis AG v Dexcel-Pharma	[2009] EWHC 0336	Cyclosporin formulation GB 2 222 770[1]	Arnold J	Yes	NA	No
11.03.09	MMI Research Ltd v Cellxion Ltd	[2009] EWHC 0418 [2009] EWHC 1938	Method for breaking through GSM network security EP 1 051 053	Floyd J	Yes, but no as to redesign	Yes	Yes – remitted to trial judge in view of new evidence[2]
27.03.09	Scinopharm Taiwan Ltd v Eli Lilly & Co	[2009] EWHC 631	Gemcitabine process EP 0 577 303	Kitchin J	NA	Yes	No
01.05.09	Wake Forest University v Smith & Nephew plc	[2009] EWHC 908	Apparatus for promoting wound healing EP 0 620 720	Wyand QC	Yes – claims 1, 2, 4, 9, 13, 15, 16, 17, 19	Partially, and subject to amendment – claims 1, 2 and 15 anticipated, claims 8, 9, 13 and 17 obvious	Reversed as to obviousness – [2010] EWCA 848

1   Same patent as previously in issue in *Novartis AG v Ivax Pharmaceuticals UK Ltd* [2006] EWHC 2506; [2007] EWCA 971.
2   See *MMI Research Ltd v Cellxion Ltd* [2011] EWHC 426 and [2013] EWCA 7. [AQ] fn2 marker?

Date	Parties	Citation	Subject matter and patents	Judge	Infringed?	Valid?	Appealed?
15.05.09	Leo Pharma A/S v Sandoz Limited	[2009] EWHC 996	Crystalline hydrate of calcipotriol EP 0 679 154	Floyd J	Conceded	Yes	Upheld [2009] EWCA 1188
09.06.09	Folding Attic Stairs Ltd v The Loft Stairs Company Ltd	[2009] EWHC 1221	Folding attic stairs GB 2 319 051	Prescott QC	Yes	Yes	No
12.06.09	Edwards Lifesciences AG v Cook Biotech Inc	[2009] EWHC 1304	Artificial heart valve EP 1 255 510	Kitchin J	No	No – all claims obvious	Upheld [2010] EWCA 718
15.06.09	FNM Corporation Ltd v Drammock International Ltd	[2009] EWHC 1294	Cooling spray aerosol EP 0 673 403	Arnold J	NA	No – all claims for which independent validity asserted anticipated and obvious	No

Date	Parties	Citation	Subject matter and patents	Judge	Infringed?	Valid?	Appealed?
16.06.09	Tate & Lyle Technology Ltd v Roquette Freres	[2009] EWHC 1312	Use of maltotritol to control the crystal structure of maltitol EP 0 905 138	Lewison J	NA	No – only claim to have survived EPO opposition anticipated and to mere discovery	Upheld [2010] EWCA 1049
07.07.09	Cranway Ltd v Playtech Ltd	[2009] EWHC 1588	Online gambling EP 0 625 760	Lewison J	Yes – claim 1	No – claim 1 anticipated, and obvious, claim 3 & 5 obvious, all claims to excluded subject matter	No
10.07.09	Novartis AG v Johnson & Johnson Medical Limited	[2009] EWHC 1671	Contact lens EP 0 819 258	Kitchin J	Yes – claims 8 & 11	No – all claims insufficient	Upheld – [2010] EWCA 1039

Date	Parties	Citation	Subject matter and patents	Judge	Infringed?	Valid?	Appealed?
29.07.09	Zeno Corporation v BSM-Bionic Solutions Management GmBH	[2009] EWHC 1829	Medical device EP 1 231 875	Lewison J	No	Yes	No
31.07.09	Fabio Perini SPA v LPC Group PLC	[2009] EWHC 1929	Paper machinery EP 0 481 929 EP 0 699 168	Floyd J	Yes × 2 – claims 16 & 17 of '929, claims 1 & 7 of '168	Yes as to '929 No as to '168 – obvious	Upheld [2010] EWCA 525
31.07.09	Occlutech GmbH v AGA Medical Corp	[2009] EWHC 2013	Stent EP 0 808 138	Mann J	No	Yes	Upheld – [2010] EWCA 702
28.08.09	Mölnlycke Health Care AB v Wake Forest University	[2009] EWHC 2204	Apparatus for promoting wound healing EP 0 620 720[1]	Kitchin J	NA	No – obvious, and protection extended	No
29.10.09	Boegli-Gravures SA v Darsail-ASP Ltd	[2009] EWHC 2690	Apparatus for satinising and embossing metal packaging foils EP 1 324 877	Arnold J	Yes	Yes	No

1 Same patent as previously in issue in *Wake Forest University v Smith & Nephew plc* [2009] EWHC 908; [2009] EWCA 84.

Date	Parties	Citation	Subject matter and patents	Judge	Infringed?	Valid?	Appealed?
03.11.09	Grimme Land-maschinenfabrik Gmbh & Co. KG v Derek Scott	[2009] EWHC 2691	Machinery for separating potatoes from weeds, earth, clods, stones and haulm EP 0 730 399	Floyd J	Yes – as to claim 17	Partially – claim 1 obvious, claims 17 & 24 valid	Reversed as to obviousness of claim 1 – [2010] EWCA 1110
20.11.09	Teva v Merck	[2009] EWHC 2952	Ophthalmic formulations of timolol and dorzolamide for the treatment of glaucoma EP 0 509 752	Floyd J	NA	No – obvious	Upheld [2011] EWCA 382

Date	Parties	Citation	Subject matter and patents	Judge	Infringed?	Valid?	Appealed?
26.11.09	Gemstar-TV Guide International Inc v Virgin Media Limited	[2009] EWHC 3068	Electronic programming guide EP 0 969 662 EP 1 337 049 EP1 613 066	Mann J	Yes as to '662 Yes as to '049 Yes as to '066	No as to '662 – obvious and excluded subject matter No as to '049 – anticipated and excluded subject matter No as to '066 – anticipated	Upheld [2011] EWCA 302

Patents Court and Patents County Court judgments on validity, and infringement for 2010

Date	Parties	Citation	Subject matter and patents	Judge	Infringed?	Valid?	Appealed?
18.01.10	Nokia GmbH v IPCom GmbH & Co, KG	[2009] EWHC 3482	Mobile telephony EP 0 540 808 EP 1 186 189	Floyd	Yes × 2	No × 2 – '808 obvious, '189 anticipated and obvious	Upheld – [2011] EWCA 6
20.01.10	Red Spider Technology v Omega Completions Technology	[2010] EWHC 59	Water injection valve UK 2424438	Mann	No	No – all claims obvious, and some anticipated	
03.02.10	Research in Motion UK Ltd v Motorola Inc	[2010] EWHC 118	Mobile telephony EP 0 818 009	Arnold	No	No – obvious	
23.02.10	Intervet UK Ltd v Merial	[2010] EWHC 294	Animal vaccines EP 1 386 617	Arnold	No	No – obvious, and anticipated on loss of priority	

Date	Parties	Citation	Subject matter and patents	Judge	Infringed?	Valid?	Appealed?
31.03.10	*Shutz (UK) Ltd v Werit UK Ltd*	[2010] EWHC 660	Intermediate bulk containers EP 0 370 307 EP 0 734 947	Floyd	No × 2	Yes × 2	Only on '947 – reversed as to infringement – [2011] EWCA 303
20.04.10	HTC Corporation v Yozmot 33 Limited	[2010] EWHC 786	Telephone identification calling apparatus EP 0 909 499	Arnold	Yes	No as to claims asserted infringed – anticipated and obvious	
23.06.10	KCI Licensing Inc v Smith & Nephew plc	[2010] EWHC 1487	Wound drainage equipment EP 0 777 504 EP 0 853 950	Arnold	Yes × 2	Yes × 2	Reversed to hold Claim 5 of 504 not infringed but claim 8 of 950 infringed – [2010] EWCA 1487

Date	Parties	Citation	Subject matter and patents	Judge	Infringed?	Valid?	Appealed?
12.07.10	Fosroc International Ltd v WR Grace & Co	[2010] EWHC 1702	Cement EP 0 415 799	Floyd	NA	Yes, as amended	
12.11.10	Abbott Laboratories Ltd v Medinol Ltd	[2010] EWHC 2865	Stents EP 0 846 449 EP 1 181 901 EP 1 181 902	Arnold	No × 3	Yes as to '449 and '902. No as to '901 – anticipated	
30.11.10	Virgin Atlantic Airways Ltd v Delta Airways, Inc	[2010] EWHC 3094	Aircraft seating EP 1 495 908[1]	Arnold	No, on summary judgment application	NA	Reversed only as to being suitable for summary judgment

1 Previously in issue in *Virgin v Premier* [2009] EWHC 26; [2009] EWCA 1062; [2009] EWCA 1513.

Patents Court and Patents County Court Judgments on validity, and infringement for 2011

Date	Parties	Citation	Subject Matter and Patents	Judge	Infringed?	Valid?	Appealed?
14.01.11	Apimed Medical Honey Limited v Brightwake Limited	[2012] EWCA 5	Medical dressings comprising gelled honey EP 1237561	HHJ Fysh QC	No	No – obvious	Reversed on validity [2012] EWCA 5
14.02.11	Datacard Corporation v Eagle Technologies Limited	[2011] EWHC 244	Card printers EP 1458572 EP 1534530	Arnold J	Yes – 2	No × 2 as to claims in issue – '572 obvious and AM '530 obvious	
25.02.11	Mölnlycke Health Care AB v Brightwake Limited	[2011] EWHC 376	Wound dressing EP 0633757	HHJ Birss QC	No	No as to claims in issue - obvious	Reversed on validity [2012] EWCA 602
07.03.11	MMI Research Ltd v Cellxion Ltd & ors[1]	[2011] EWHC 426	Method for breaking through GSM network security EP 1051053	Floyd J	NA	Yes	Reversed on validity [2012] EWCA 7

1 Same case as *MMI Research Ltd v Cellxion Ltd & ors* [2009] EWHC 0418 and [2009] EWHC 1938, having been remitted to try new issues in [2009] EWCA 1120.

Date	Parties	Citation	Subject Matter and Patents	Judge	Infringed?	Valid?	Appealed?
17.03.11	Gedeon Richter plc v Bayer Schering Pharma AG	[2011] EWHC 583	Pharmaceutical combination of ethinylestradiol and drospirenone for use as a contraceptive EP 1380301 EP 1598069	Floyd J	NA	Yes as to '301 when amended Yes as to claim 6 of '069 but claims 1 & 19 obvious	Upheld [2012] EWCA 235
14.04.11	H. Lundbeck A/S v Norpharma and anr	[2011] EWHC 907	Chemical process for manufacture of a pharmaceutical intermediate EP 1118614	Floyd J	Yes	No as to claims in issue – obvious	
16.06.11	Nokia OYJ v IPCom GmbH & Co, KG	[2011] EWHC 1470	Mobile telephony EP 1841268	Floyd J	Yes as to A1 & A2 devices, no as to B-G devices	Yes	Upheld [2012] EWCA 567

Date	Parties	Citation	Subject Matter and Patents	Judge	Infringed?	Valid?	Appealed?
24.09.11	Cephalon, Inc v Orchid Europe Ltd	[2011] EWHC 1591	Pharmaceutical – modafinil formulation EP 0731698 EP 0966962 EP 1088549	Floyd J	No × 3	No × 3 – obvious	
05.07.11	Medimmune Limited v Novartis Pharmaceuticals UK Limited & anr	[2011] EWHC 1669	Antibody production EP 0774511 EP 2055777	Arnold J	No × 2	No × 2 as to claims in issue – obvious in view of loss of priority	Only on 777 – upheld [2012] EWCA 1234
15.07.11	Select Healthcare (UK) Limited v Cromptons Healthcare Limited and anr	[2011] EWHC 1830	Patient slide sheets GB 2 433 244 B.	Kitchin J	No	No – obvious	
15.07.11	Ranbaxy (UK) Limited v AstraZeneca AB	[2011] EWHC 1831	Pharmaceutical – magnesium esomeprazole with a high optical purity EP 1 020 461	Kitchin J	No	NA – Infringement heard as a preliminary issue	

Date	Parties	Citation	Subject Matter and Patents	Judge	Infringed?	Valid?	Appealed?
27.07.11	Convatec Limited & ors v Smith & Nephew Healthcare Limited & amr	[2011] EWHC 2039	Wound dressing EP 0927013	HHJ Birss QC	No	Yes, in part	Upheld [2012] EWCA 520
30.09.11	Generics (UK) Ltd v Novartis AG	[2011] EWHC 2403	Pharmaceutical – rivastigmine UK 2203040	Floyd J	Conceded	No – obvious	Upheld [2012] EWCA 1623
15.12.11	Sandvik Intellectual Property AB v Kennametal Uk Limited & amr	[2011] EWHC 3311	Oxide coated cutting tool EP 0603144	Arnold J	Yes, as to some articles only	No – insufficient, and as to some claims only, obvious	
21.12.11	Omnipharm Ltd v Merial	[2011] EWHC 3393	Flea treatments EP 0881881 UK 2317564	Floyd J	Conceded that some did not	Yes as to 881 as amended No as to 564 – insufficient	Upheld [2013] EWCA 3393

Patents Court and Patents County Court judgments on validity, and infringement for 2012

Date	Parties	Citation	Subject Matter and Patents	Judge	Infringed?	Valid?	Appealed?
20.02.12	Nokia GmbH v IPCom GmbH & Co, KG	[2012] EWHC 225	Mobile telephony EP 1 018 849	Floyd J	Claims as amended not essential to standards in issue	Yes as amended	
22.03.12	Teva UK Ltd and ors v AstraZeneca AB	[2012] EWHC 655	Sustained release formulation of quetiapine EP 0 907 364	Arnold J	NA	No – obvious	Upheld [2013] EWCA 454
22.03.12	Regeneron Pharmaceuticals and Bayer Pharma AG v Genentech Inc	[2012] EWHC 657	Use of VEGF antagonists EP 1 506 986	Floyd J	Yes	Yes	Upheld [2013] EWCA 93
18.04.12	Wagner International AG and ors v Earlex Ltd	[2012] EWHC 984	Paint spray guns EP 0 596 939	Floyd J	No	No – obvious, and added matter	

Date	Parties	Citation	Subject Matter and Patents	Judge	Infringed?	Valid?	Appealed?
25.05.12	Unilever plc v S.C. Johnson & Sons Inc.	[2012] EWPCC 19	Automated cleansing sprayer GB 2 389 547 GB 2 403 169	HHJ Birss QC	NA	No as to 169 – one claim anticipated and other obvious Yes in part as to 547	
13.06.12	Sudarshan v Clariant	[2012] EWHC 1569	Pigment manufacturing process EP 1 170 338	John Baldwin QC	Yes	No – anticipated as to product claims, obvious as to use claims	Upheld [2013] EWCA 919
13.06.12	Smith & Nephew Plc v Convatec Technologies Inc	[2012] EWHC 1602	Wound dressing EP 1 343 510	HHJ Birss QC	NA	Conceded not as granted, but held yes as amended	Upheld [2012] EWCA 520

Date	Parties	Citation	Subject Matter and Patents	Judge	Infringed?	Valid?	Appealed?
04.07.12	HTC Europe Co. Ltd v Apple Inc.	[2012] EWHC 1789	User Interfaces EP 1 168 859 EP 2 098 948 EP 2 964 022 EP 2 059 868	Floyd J	Yes as to 859. No as to 948. Yes as to 022. No as to 868.	No as to 859 – obvious No as to 948 as to claims in issue – obvious and excluded subject matter No as to 022 – obvious, some claims anticipated Yes as to 868.	Only on 948 and 022 – reversed on claim 2 of 948 as excluded subject matter
11.07.12	Generics (UK) Limited t/a Mylan v Yeda Research and Development Co. Ltd & anr	[2012] EWHC 1848	Glatirimer acetate EP 0 762 888	Arnold J	No DNI	Yes	Upheld [2013] EWCA 925
12.07.12	Schenck Rotec Gmbh v Universal Balancing Ltd	[2012] EWHC 1920	Balancing weights for rotors EP 1 520 161	HHJ Birss QC	Yes	Yes	

Date	Parties	Citation	Subject Matter and Patents	Judge	Infringed?	Valid?	Appealed?
19.07.12	Vernacare Ltd v Environmental Pulp Product Ltd	[2012] EWPCC 41	Disposable washing bowls GB 2 446 793	HHJ Birss QC	Yes, by two versions, but not by another.	Yes	
26.07.12	Barry Liversidge v Owen Munford Limited & anr	[2012] EWPCC 33	Medical injector EP 2 067 496	HHJ Birss QC	No	No – added matter and anticipation.	
27.07.12	Virgin Atlantic Airways Ltd v Jet Airways (India) [& anr & other actions]	[2012] EWHC 2153	Aircraft Seating EP 1 495 908[1] EP 2 272 711 EP 2 289 734	Floyd J	Yes as to '734 for some designs. No as to 711. No as to 908.	Yes × 3	

1 Same patent as previously in issue in *Virgin v Premier* [2009] EWHC 26, [2009] EWCA 1062, [2009] EWCA 1513, [2011] EWCA 163, but amended.

Date	Parties	Citation	Subject Matter and Patents	Judge	Infringed?	Valid?	Appealed?
27.07.12	Bos Gmbh & Co KG v Cobra Automotive Products Division Limited	[2012] EWPCC 38	Security net installation EP 0 649 778	HHJ Birss QC	No	No – obvious	
09.11.12	Molnlycke Health Care v BSN Medical	[2012] EWHC 3157	Wound dressings EP 0 855 921	Floyd J	No	Yes	
21.12.12	Microsoft Corporation v Motorola Mobility	[2012] EWHC 3677	Communications software EP 0 847 654	Arnold J	No (and in part licenced anyway)	No – obvious, some claims anticipated	

Patents Court and Patents County Court / Intellectual Property Enterprise Court judgments on validity and infringement for 2013

Date	Parties	Citation	Subject Matter and Patents	Judge	Infringed?	Valid?	Appealed?
16.01.13	Mastermailer Stationery v Everseal and anr	[2013] EWPCC 6	Business forms GB 2340073	HHJ Birss QC	No	N/A	
05.02.13	AP Racing Ltd v Alcon Components Ltd	[2013] EWPCC 3	Disc brake UK 2451690	HHJ Birss QC	Yes, as to 4 out of 5 articles in issue	No – added matter	Reversed [2014] EWCA 40
05.02.13	Environmental Recycling Technologies plc v Upcycle Holdings Ltd	[2013] EWPCC 4	Plastics moulding process UK 2460838	HHJ Birss QC	NA	Yes, as amended	
07.02.13	Glenmark Generics (Europe) Ltd and anr v The Wellcome Foundation Limited and anr	[2013] EWHC 148	Combination anti-malarial composition EP(UK) 0670719	Arnold J	NA	No – obvious	

603

Date	Parties	Citation	Subject Matter and Patents	Judge	Infringed?	Valid?	Appealed?
07.03.13	Samsung Electronics Co. Ltd v Apple Retail UK Ltd and anr	[2013] EWHC 467	Channel coding in mobile telephones EP (UK) 1005726 EP (UK) 1357675	Floyd J	NA as to 675. Yes as to 726.	No × 2 – anticipated on loss of priority and obvious	
07.03.13	Samsung Electronics Co. Ltd v Apple Retail UK Ltd and anr	[2013] EWHC 468	Methods of transmitting packet data in mobile phones EP (UK) 1714404	Floyd J	Yes	No – anticipated on loss of priority and obvious	
15.03.13	Hospira UK Ltd and anr v Novartis AG	[2013] EWHC 516	Dosing regime for administration of zoledronate for the treatment of osteoporosis EP (UK) 1296689 EP (UK) 1591122	Arnold J	NA	No – anticipated on loss of priority, some claims otherwise obvious or insufficient.	Only on 689 – upheld [2013] EWCA 1633

Date	Parties	Citation	Subject Matter and Patents	Judge	Infringed?	Valid?	Appealed?
11.04.13	Lizzanno Partitions (UK) Ltd v Interiors Manufacturing Ltd	[2013] EWPCC 12	Gasket for sealing between glass partitions GB 2432617	HHJ Birss QC	Yes	Yes	
19.04.13	Brigade (BBS-Tek) Ltd v Amber Valley Ltd	[2013] EWPCC 16	Vehicle reversing alarm GB 2318662	HHJ Birss QC	Yes	Yes, as amended	
22.04.13	Nestec SA and ors v Dualit Ltd and ors	[2013] EWHC 923	Capsule extraction device EP (UK) 2103236	Arnold J	Yes, as certain systems only	No – anticipated	
08.05.13	Phil & Ted's Most Excellent Buggy Company Ltd v TFK Trends For Kids Gmbh and anr	[2013] EWPCC 21	Baby buggy EP (UK) 1795424	HHJ Birss QC	Yes	No – obvious	Upheld [2014] EWCA 469
10.05.13	Swarovski-Optik KG v Leica Camera AG & anr	[2013] EWHC 1227	Riflescopes EP (UK) 1746451	Vos J	Yes	Yes	Upheld [2014] EWCA 637

Date	Parties	Citation	Subject Matter and Patents	Judge	Infringed?	Valid?	Appealed?
30.05.13	OOO Abbott and anr v Design & Display Ltd and anr	[2013] EWPCC 27	Shop display panel EP (UK) 1816931	Birss J	Yes	Yes	
14.06.13	Master Distributor v SDL Hair Ltd & ors	[2013] EWPCC 31	Heating units for hair rollers GB 2472483	Meade QC	No	NA	
25.06.13	Eli Lilly and Company v Janssen Alzheimer Immunotherapy	[2013] EWHC 1737	Monoclonal antibodies EP (UK) 1994937	Arnold J	Yes	No – insufficient	
09.07.13	Merck Sharp Dohme Corp & anr v Teva Pharma BV & anr	[2013] EWHC 1958	Efavirenz EP (UK) 0582455	Birss J	Yes, as to basis for bringing the action	NA	

Date	Parties	Citation	Subject Matter and Patents	Judge	Infringed?	Valid?	Appealed?
10.07.13	HTC Corporation v Gemalto SA HTC Corporation v Gemalto NV	[2013] EWHC 1876	Using a high level programming language with a microcontroller EP (UK) 0932865 Smart card reader EP (UK) 0829062	Birss J	No as to 865. Yes as to 062.	Yes as to claim 3 of 865 – others anticipated or obvious on loss of priority No as to 062 – anticipated and obvious.	Only on 865 – upheld [2014] EWCA 1335
16.07.13	Scopema Sarl v Scot Seat Direct Ltd	[2013] EWPCC 32	Tilting device for a seat back EP (UK) 2121377	Wilson QC	No	NA	
31.10.13	HTC Corporation v Nokia Corporation	[2013] EWHC 3247	Modulator structure for a transmitter and a mobile station EP (UK) 0998024	Arnold J	Yes	Yes	

Date	Parties	Citation	Subject Matter and Patents	Judge	Infringed?	Valid?	Appealed?
07.11.13	Manvers Engineering Limited & anr v Lubetech Industries Limited & ors	[2013] EWHC 3393 (IPEC)	Equipment for catching oil leakages from equipment GB 2428032	Mann J	No	Yes	
3.12.13	Adaptive Spectrum and Signal Alignment Inc v British Telecommunications PLC	[2013] EWHC 3768 (Pat)	DSL control EP (UK) 2259495 EP (UK) 1869790	Birss J	No as to 495. Yes as to 790.	Yes *2	Reversed on infringement of 495 but upheld as to 790 – [2014] EWCA 1462
12.12.13	Smith & Nephew plc v Convatec Technologies Inc[1]	[2013] EWHC 3955 (Pat)	Light stabilised antimicrobial materials EP (UK) 1343510[1]	Birss J	No, except some preliminary work.	NA	Reversed [2015] EWCA 607
20.12.13	Blue Gentian LLC & anr v Tristar Products (UK) Ltd & anr	[2013] EWHC 4098 (Pat)	Expandable hose assembly GB 2490276	Birss J	NA	Yes	

1 Same patent and parties as in *Smith & Nephew plc v Convatec Technologies Inc* [2012] EWHC 1602; [2012] EWCA 1638.

Patents Court and Intellectual Property Enterprise Court judgments on validity and infringement for 2014

Date	Parties	Citation	Subject Matter and Patents	Judge	Infringed?	Valid?	Appealed?
15.01.14	Eugen Seitz AG v KHS Corpoplast Gmbh and anr	[2014] EWHC 14 (Pat)	Rotary stretch blow moulding machines used to make plastic bottles EP (UK) 1271029	Roth J	Yes	Yes	
10.02.14	Collingwood Lighting Limited v Aurora Limited	[2014] EWHC 228 (Pat)	Fire resistant LED downlight GB 2475649	Roth J	Yes	Yes	
28.02.14	Jarden Consumer Solutions (Europe) Limited v SEB SA	[2014] EWHC 445 (Pat)	Fryer with automatic fat coating EP (UK) 2085003	Arnold J	Yes, as to claims 1, 3, 10, 11, 13	Yes as to claims 10, 11, 13 Claims 1, 3 & 8 obvious	Reversed on infringement [2014] EWCA 1629
05.03.14	Kennametal Inc v Pramet Tools SRO and anr	[2014] EWHC 565 (Pat)	Milling cutter tool for high feed face milling EP (UK) 01897643	Carr QC	No	All claims in issue obvious	

Date	Parties	Citation	Subject Matter and Patents	Judge	Infringed?	Valid?	Appealed?
06.03.14	F H Brundle v Richard Perry	[2014] EWHC 475 (IPEC)	Fence bracket GB 2390104	HHJ Hacon	No (only argued as a defence to action for groundless threats)	NA	
26.03.14	Starsight Telecast Inc and amr v Virgin Media Limited and ors	[2014] EWHC 828 (Pat)	Improved electronic television programme schedule guide system and method EP (UK) 1763234 Merging multi-source information in a television system EP (UK) 0821 856	Arnold J	'234 – Yes as to some devices on granted claims, not on claims accepted by EPO OD '856 – No	'234 – granted claims obvious and invalid also for added matter, claims accepted by EPO OD obvious. '856 – all claims anticipated and obvious	

Date	Parties	Citation	Subject Matter and Patents	Judge	Infringed?	Valid?	Appealed?
10.04.14	Hospira UK Ltd v Genentech Inc	[2014] EWHC 1094 (Pat)	Dosages for treatment with anti-ErbB2 antibodies (trastuzumab) EP (UK) 1210115 Composition comprising anti-HER2 antibodies. (trastuzumab) EP (UK) 1308455	Birss J	'115 – NA '455 – No	'115 – claim 1 obvious '455 – claims 1, 2, 4 anticipated and, together with claim 3, obvious	Only on 115 – Upheld [2015] EWCA 57
01.05.14	Environmental Defence Systems Ltd v Synergy Health Plc	[2014] EWHC 1306 (IPEC)	Method of manufacturing barrage units used for flood defences EP (UK) 2393989	HHJ Hacon	NA	Claims 1, 6 and 9 obvious	

Date	Parties	Citation	Subject Matter and Patents	Judge	Infringed?	Valid?	Appealed?
15.05.14	Actavis UK Ltd v Eli Lilly & Co	[2014] EWHC 1511 (Pat)	Use of pemetrexed disodium in combination with vitamin B12 or a pharmaceutical derivative thereof and optionally a folic protein binding agent EP (UK) 0432677 (& ES, FR, IT Designations)	Arnold J	Declaration of non-infringement granted	NA	Reversed as to contributory infringement and remitted [2015] EWCA 555

Date	Parties	Citation	Subject Matter and Patents	Judge	Infringed?	Valid?	Appealed?
15.05.14	Rovi Solutions Corporation v Virgin Media Limited	[2014] EWHC 1559 (Pat)	A system interactively controlled by a TV viewer remote for superimposing identification and information characters over normal programming on a viewer's display screen EP (UK) XXXX833	Mann J	Conceded	All claims in issue obvious	
22.05.14	Generics (UK) Ltd v Richter Gedeon Vegyeszeti Gyar RT	[2014] EWHC 1666 (Pat)	Dosage regimen for use of levonorgestrel as a method of emergency contraception EP (UK) 1 448 207	Sales J	NA	All claims in issue obvious	

Date	Parties	Citation	Subject Matter and Patents	Judge	Infringed?	Valid?	Appealed?
20.06.14	Koninklijke Philips Electronics N.V. v Nintendo of Europe Gmbh	[2014] EWHC 1959 (Pat)	Method and apparatus for controlling the movement of a virtual body EP (UK) 0 808 484 User interface system based on a pointing device. EP (UK) 1 573 498 EP (UK) 2 093 650	Birss J	'484 – Yes '498 – Yes '650 – Yes	'484 – All claims in issue anticipated and/or obvious '498 – Yes on amendment '650 – Yes on amendment	
03.07.14	Nampak Plastics Europe Limited v Alpla UK Limited	[2014] EWHC 2196 (Pat)	Plastic container GB 2 494 349	Birss J	No (on summary judgment)	NA	Upheld [2014] EWCA 1293
14.07.14	Rovi Solutions and anr v Virgin Media Ltd & ors	[2014] EWHC 2301 (Pat)	Set top boxes EP (UK) 1 327 209	Baldwin QC	Conceded	All claims in issue obvious	Upheld [2015] EWCA 781

Date	Parties	Citation	Subject Matter and Patents	Judge	Infringed?	Valid?	Appealed?
22.07.14	Aga Medical Corporation v Occlutech (UK) Limited	[2014] EWHC 2506 (Pat)	Medical device for occluding defects in the atrial septum of the heart EP (UK) 0 957 773	Roth J	Yes as one device No as to other device	All claims in issue anticipated and obvious	
22.08.14	William Mark Corporation and anr v Gift House International Limited	[2014] EWHC 2845 (IPEC)	Flying fish toys GB 2 482 275 GB 2 483 597	HHJ Hacon	275 – Yes 597 – Yes	275 – Yes. 597 – Claims 1, 3 and 4 obvious but claim 2 not and infringed	
02.09.14	Teva UK Limited and anr v AstraZeneca AB	[2014] EWHC 2873 (Pat)	Use of a composition comprising formoterol and budesonide for the prevention or treatment of an acute condition of asthma EP (UK) 1 085 877	Sales J	NA at this stage.	All claims in issue obvious, proposed amendments would add matter and are obvious	

Date	Parties	Citation	Subject Matter and Patents	Judge	Infringed?	Valid?	Appealed?
22.09.14	CompactGTL Limited v Velocys Plc	[2014] EWHC 2951 (Pat)	Catalysts for use in the Fischer-Tropsch process EP (UK) 1 206 508 EP (UK) 1 206 509	Arnold J	Yes × 2	Yes × 2, after amendment	
06.10.14	Teva v Leo	[2014] EWHC 3096 (Pat)	Pharmaceutical composition comprising a vitamin and a corticosteroid for treatment of psoriasis EP (UK) 1 178 808 EP (UK) 2 455 083	Birss J	NA	2 × All claims in issue as proposed to be amended obvious.	Reversed [2015] EWCA 779

Date	Parties	Citation	Subject Matter and Patents	Judge	Infringed?	Valid?	Appealed?
21.11.14	Hospira UK Ltd v Genentech Inc.	[2014] EWHC 3857 (Pat)	Stable Isotonic lyophilized protein formulation (trastuzumab) EP (UK) 1 516 628 EP (UK) 2 275 119	Birss J	NA	'628 – claims in issue obvious. '119 – all claims obvious Proposed amendments to both patents would add matter, certain lack clarity and certain constitute impermissible product by process claims.	
28.11.14	Vringo Infrastructure Inc v ZTE (UK) Ltd	[2014] EWHC 3924 (Pat)	Relocation in a communication system EP (UK) 1 212 919	Birss J	Yes, indirectly	Yes	

Date	Parties	Citation	Subject Matter and Patents	Judge	Infringed?	Valid?	Appealed?
01.12.14	Idenix Pharmaceutical, Inc v Gilead Sciences, Inc & Ors	[2014] EWHC 3916 (Pat)	Modified 2' and 3' –Nucleoside Prodrugs for Treating Flaviridae Infections (sofusbuvir) EP (UK) 1 523 489	Arnold J	Yes, indirectly as to claims 1, 5–7, 21 and 24	No – All but claims 20 and 37 lack novelty, all claims in which independent validity asserted lack inventive step and are insufficient, claim 4 adds matter, proposed amendments to all claims would add matter	
18.12.14	Adaptive Spectrum And Signal Alignment Inc v British Telecommunications Plc[1]	[2014] EWHC 4194 (Pat)	DSL state and line profile control EP (UK) 1869790	Birss J	Yes	NA	

1 One of the same patents and the same parties as in *Adaptive Spectrum And Signal Alignment Inc v British Telecommunications Plc* [2013] EWHC 3768 (Pat) and [2014] EWCA 1462.

Patents Court and Intellectual Property Enterprise Court judgments on validity and infringement for 2015 *(to summer vacation)*

Date	Parties	Citation	Subject Matter and Patents	Judge	Infringed?	Valid?	Appealed?
01.04.15	Everseal Stationery Products Ltd v Document Management Solutions Ltd & anr	[2015] EWHC 842 (IPEC)	Business form with an adhesive closure UK 2 340 073[1]	HHJ Hacon	1 product yes, 2 products not.	No – anticipated and obvious.	
24.04.15	IPCom Gmbh & Co KG v HTC Europe Co. Ltd & ors	[2015] EWHC 1034 (Pat)	Access of a mobile station to a random access channel in dependence of its user class. EP (UK) 1 841 268[2]	Birss J	No	Yes, as amended.	
27.04.15	Novartis AG & ors v Focus Pharmaceuticals Ltd & ors	[2015] EWHC 1068 (Pat)	Transdermal therapeutic system for the administration of rivastigmine EP (UK) 2 292 219	Arnold J	Yes	No – obvious and added matter.	

1 Also considered in *Mastermailer Stationery v Everseal and anr* [2013] EWPCC 6.
2 Also considered in *Nokia and IPCom* [2011] EWHC 1470 (Pat); [2011] EWHC 1871 (Pat); [2012] EWCA Civ 567.

Date	Parties	Citation	Subject Matter and Patents	Judge	Infringed?	Valid?	Appealed?
21.05.15	Synthon BV v Teva Pharmaceutical Industries Ltd	[2015] EWHC 1395 (Pat)	Process for the preparation of mixtures of trifluoroacetyl GA using purified hydrobromic acid EP (UK) 2 177 528 EP (UK) 2 361 924	Birss J	NA	Yes × 2, as amended	
24.06.15	Hospira UK Ltd v Genentech Inc	[2015] EWHC 1796 (Pat)	Use of trastuzumab in combination with a taxane for the treatment of HER-2 positive breast cancer EP (UK) 1 037 926	Arnold J	NA	No – obvious	

Date	Parties	Citation	Subject Matter and Patents	Judge	Infringed?	Valid?	Appealed?
01.07.15	VPG Systems UK Limited v Air-Weigh Europe Ltd	[2015] EWHC 1862 (IPEC)	System for indicating the state of loading of a vehicle EP (UK) 2 099 626	HHJ Hacon	NA	No – claims in issue obvious	
20.07.15	Wobben Properties GmbH v Siemens Plc & ors	[2015] EWHC 2114 (Pat)	Method of operating a wind power station EP (UK) 0 847 496	Birss J	No	No – obvious	

Appeals to Court of Appeal from Patents Court (except where otherwise stated) and Patents County Court judgments on validity and infringement 1997–2001

Date	Case	Citation	Judge upheld	Infringed?	Valid?
12.02.97	Beloit v Valmet	[1997] RPC 489	Yes	Yes (old) No (new)	No – obvious
23.04.97	Richardson-Vicks' Patent	[1997] RPC 888	Yes	NA	No – obvious
01.05.97	3M v Plastus Kreativ	[1997] RPC 737	Yes	No	NA
19.06.97	Norton Healthcare v Beecham Group	Unreported	Yes	NA	No – obvious
20.06.97	Novamedix v NDM	Unreported	In part (PCC)	Yes × 2	No × 2 – anticipated, obvious (reversing 1)
11.03.98	Scanvaegt v Pelcombe	[1998] FSR 786	No	No (reversing)	Yes
30.04.98	Lubrizol v Esso	[1998] RPC 727	In part	Yes (reversing)	No – obvious
24.06.98	Hoechst Celanese v BP Chemicals	[1999] FSR 319	Yes	Yes	NA
29.10.98	Auchinloss v Agricultural & Veterinary Supplies	[1999] RPC 397	In part	Yes (as to new) (reversing). No (as to another)	NA
06.11.98	Henry Brothers (Magherafelt) v Ministry of Defence	[1999] RPC 442	Yes	NA	No – not entitled

622

Date	Case	Citation	Judge upheld	Infringed?	Valid?
26.11.98	Union Carbide v BP Chemicals	[1999] RPC 409	In part	Yes (as to one) (reversing) No (as to another)	Yes
17.12.98	Raychem's Patents	[1999] RPC 497	Yes	NA	No × 4 – obvious
19.05.99	Texas Iron Works' Patent	[2000] RPC 207	In part (one ground of invalidity reversed) (PCC).	Yes	No – obvious
27.07.99	*United Wire v Screen Repair*[1]	[2000] FSR 204	In part	Yes × 2 (reversing as to law on repair)	Yes
20.03.00	Palmaz's European Patents (UK)	[2000] EWCA 83, [2000] RPC 631	Yes	No × 2	No × 2
23.05.00	Bristol Myers Squibb v Baker Norton	[2000] EWCA 169, [2001] RPC 1	Yes	NA	No – anticipated, obvious
25.05.00	Cartonneries de Thulin v CTP White Knight	[2000] EWCA 174, [2001] RPC 6	No	Yes (reversing)	No (reversing) – added matter
05.07.00	Wheatley v Drillsafe	[2000] EWCA 209, [2001] RPC 7	No	No	Yes (reversing)
27.07.00	American Home Products v Novartis Pharmaceuticals UK	[2000] EWCA 231, [2001] RPC 8	No	No (reversing)	Yes on sufficiency – anticipation and obviousness held over

1 Upheld by House of Lords – see [2000] UKHL 42.

Date	Case	Citation	Judge upheld	Infringed?	Valid?
31.07.00	Coflexip v Stolt Comex Seaway MS	[2000] EWCA 242, [2001] 1 All ER 952, [2001] RPC 9	Yes	Yes	Yes
20.12.00	Rocky Mountain Traders v Hewlett Packard	[2000] EWCA 347, [2002] FSR 1	Yes	Yes	No × 2 – obvious
20.06.01	David John Instance v Denny Bros Printing	[2001] EWCA 939, [2002] RPC 14	Yes	NA	No × 3 – obvious
05.07.01	Amersham Pharmacia Biotech v Amicon	[2001] EWCA 1042	Yes	No	Yes – not addressed by judge
12.07.01	Taylor v Ishida (Europe)	[2001] EWCA 1092	Yes	Yes	Yes
04.10.01	Dyson Appliances v Hoover	[2001] EWCA 1440, [2002] RPC 22	Yes	Yes	Yes
29.10.01	Rohm & Haas v Collag	[2001] EWCA 1589, [2002] FSR 28	Yes	No	NA
20.11.01	Sara Lee v Johnson Wax	[2001] EWCA 1609	Yes	No	NA
14.12.01	Pharmacia v Merck	[2001] EWCA 1610, [2002] RPC 41	Only as to validity.	Yes	No – anticipated, obvious, insufficient

Court of Appeal judgments on validity and infringement for period January 2002–July 2015

Date	Case	Citation	Subject matter	Judge upheld	Infringed?	Valid?
23.01.02	Lilly Icos v Pfizer	[2002] EWCA 1	Pharmaceutical – sildenafil	Yes	NA	No – obvious
07.03.02	Maccaferri v Hesco Bastion	[2002] EWCA 264	Gabions	Yes (PCC)	Yes	Yes
16.04.02	Asahi Medical v Macopharma (UK)	[2002] EWCA 466	Blood separation	Yes	NA	No – obvious
25.04.02	Panduit v Band-it	[2002] EWCA 465, [2003] FSR 8	Cable ties	No (PCC)	Yes	Yes (reversing)
26.03.02	City Technology v Alphasense	[2002] EWCA 347	Gas sensor	Yes	Yes	Yes
10.05.02	Hewlett Packard v Waters	[2002] EWCA 612	HPLC pump	No	Yes (reversing)	Yes
11.07.02	*Sabaf v MFI Furniture Centres*	[2002] EWCA 976	Gas burners	Yes (for different reasons).	No (reversing) (no importation)	Yes (reversing)[1]
31.07.02	*Kirin Amgen v Hoechst Marion Roussel*	[2002] EWCA 1096, [2003] RPC 3	Pharmaceutical – erythropoietin	No	No (reversing)[2]	Yes[3]
31.07.02	Warheit v Olympia Tools	[2002] EWCA 1161	Pliers	Yes (although Mark II also held to infringe)	Yes (reversing on Mark II)	Yes

1 Reversed by House of Lords – see [2004] UKHL 45.
2 Upheld by House of Lords – see [2004] UKHL 46.
3 Reversed by House of Lords – see [2004] UKHL 46.

Date	Case	Citation	Subject matter	Judge upheld	Infringed?	Valid?
22.10.02	Cairnstores v Hassle	[2002] EWCA 1504, [2003] FSR 23	Pharmaceutical – omeprazole	Yes	NA	No – obvious
06.02.03	Stena Rederi v Irish Ferries	[2003] EWCA 66, [2003] RPC 36	Multi-hull vessel	Yes	No	NA
25.06.03	*Synthon v SmithKline Beecham*	[2003] EWCA 861, [2003] RPC 43	Pharmaceutical – paroxetine mesylate	No	NA	Yes (reversing)[1]
25.06.03	BASF v SmithKline Beecham	[2003] EWCA 872, [2003] RPC 49	Pharmaceutical – paroxetine hydrochloride	Yes (albeit on a different construction)	NA	Yes
04.07.03	SEB v De'Longhi	[2003] EWCA 952	Fryer	Yes	Yes	No – obvious
30.07.03	Storage Computer v Hitachi Data Systems	[2003] EWCA 1155	Data storage	Yes	Not decided	No – obvious
06.11.03	Teva Pharmaceutical v Institute Gentili	[2003] EWCA 1545, [2004] FSR 16	Pharmaceutical – alendronate	Yes	NA	(1) No –anticipated and obvious. (2) No – anticipated
01.04.04	Rockwater v Technip France (formerly Coflexip)	[2004] EWCA 381, [2004] RPC 46	Flexible pipes	No	Yes (reversing)	Yes (reversing)
30.07.04	Unilin Beheer v Berry Floor	[2004] EWCA 1021	Laminated flooring	Yes (on a wider construction)	Yes	Yes

1 Reversed by House of Lords – see [2005] UKHL 59.

Date	Case	Citation	Subject matter	Judge upheld	Infringed?	Valid?
29.11.04	SmithKline Beecham v Apotex Europe	[2004] EWCA 1568	Pharmaceutical – paroxetine hydrochloride	No	No	Yes (reversing).
17.02.05	Mayne Pharma v Pharmacia Italia	[2005] EWCA 137	Pharmaceutical – epirubicin	No	Yes (reversing)	NA
25.02.05	St-Gobain PAM v Fusion Provida	[2005] EWCA 177	Steel pipes	Yes	NA	Yes
24.06.05	Ultraframe (UK) v Eurocell Building Plastics	[2005] EWCA 761 [2005] RPC 36	Conservatories	No	Yes (reversing)	Yes
20.07.05	The Burnden Group v Ultraframe (UK)	[2005] EWCA 867	Conservatories	Yes (from PCC)	NA	No – anticipated and obvious
29.07.05	Agilent Technologies Deutschland v Waters	[2005] EWCA 987	HPLC pump	Yes	No	NA
28.06.06	Ranbaxy UK v Warner-Lambert	[2006] EWCA 876, [2007] RPC 4	Pharmaceutical – atorvastatin	Yes	Yes NA	NA No – anticipated
15.12.06	Halliburton Energy Services v Smith International (North Sea)	[2006] EWCA 1715	Oil drilling bits	Yes	NA	No – insufficient

Date	Case	Citation	Subject matter	Judge upheld	Infringed?	Valid?
20.12.06	LG Philips LCD v Tatung (UK)	[2006] EWCA 1774	Mountings for flat panel display devices	Yes (from PCC)	No	No – obvious
16.01.07	*Conor Medsystems v Angiotech*	[2007] EWCA 5	Drug coated stents	Yes	NA	No – obvious[1]
23.01.07	Ferag v Müller Martini	[2007] EWCA 15	Cutting/trimming print materials	No	Yes, (reversing)	Yes (reversing)
07.02.07	Research In Motion UK v Inpro Licensing	[2007] EWCA 51	Mobile telephony	Yes	NA	No – obvious
22.06.07	Pozzoli v BDMO	[2007] EWCA 588	CD & DVD packaging	Yes	No	No – obvious
02.08.07	LB Europe v Smurfit Bag in Box	[2007] EWCA 933	Tap for wine box	Yes	No	NA
18.10.07	Novartis v Ivax	[2007] EWCA 971	Cyclosporin formulation	Yes	No	NA
19.10.07	Vector v Glatt Air Technologies	[2007] EWCA 805	Fluid bed	Lewison J	NA	Yes – but reversing as to one claim of proposed amendment which was held to add matter

1   Reversed by House of Lords – see [2008] UKHL 45.

Date	Case	Citation	Subject matter	Judge upheld	Infringed?	Valid?
19.03.08	European Central Bank v Document Security System	[2008] EWCA 192	Method of making a document incapable of replication by a scanning type copying device	Yes	NA	No – added matter
14.04.08	*Generics v H Lundbeck A/S*	[2008] EWCA 311	Pharmaceutical – escitalopram	No	NA	Yes[1]
21.05.08	Actavis v Merck	[2008] EWCA 444	Pharmaceutical use – finasteride	No	NA	Yes
09.05.08	Servier v Apotex	[2008] EWCA 445	Pharmaceutical form – perindropil	Yes	NA	No – anticipated
30.07.08	Handicraft Company v B Free World Ltd	[2008] EWCA 868	Baby bottle	Yes	NA	No – obvious
22.10.08	Thorn Security v Siemens Schweiz	[2008] EWCA 1161	Coating for printed circuit board	No	No, reversing judge	Yes but no longer in issue on appeal
29.10.08	Qual-Chem Ltd v Corus UK Ltd	[2008] EWCA 1177	Steel-making process GB 2 363 635 C	Yes	Yes	Yes

1 Upheld by House of Lords – see [2009] UKHL 12.

Date	Case	Citation	Subject matter	Judge upheld	Infringed?	Valid?
01.04.09	Napp Pharmaceutical Holdings Ltd v Ratiopharm GmbH Napp Pharmaceutical Holdings Ltd v Sandoz Ltd	[2009] EWCA 252	Pharmaceutical formulation – oxycodone EP 0722730 B EP 1258246 B	No	Yes × 2, reversing judge	Yes × 2
20.05.09	Aerotel Ltd v Wavecrest Group Enterprises Ltd	[2009] EWCA 408	Telecoms GB 2 171 877 B	Yes, as obvious	NA	Yes
16.06.09	Ancon v ACS Stainless Steel Fixings	[2009] EWCA 498	Steel channel assembly EP 0 882 164 B	No	Yes, reversing judge	Yes – not in issue on appeal
02.07.09	Generics (UK) Ltd v Daiichi Pharmaceutical Company	[2009] EWCA 646	Pharmaceutical – levofloxacin EP 0206283 & SPC	Yes	NA	Yes
29.07.09	WL Gore & Associates GmbH v Geoxx SpA	[2009] EWCA 794	Shoes EP 0 858 270 B EP 1 185 183 B	Yes	Yes as to '270. No as to '183	Yes × 2 – not in issue on appeal

Date	Case	Citation	Subject matter	Judge upheld	Infringed?	Valid?
31.07.09	Wake Forest University v Smith & Nephew plc	[2009] EWCA 848	Apparatus for promoting wound healing EP 0 620 720	Yes as to anticipation of claim 1, no as to obviousness of claims 4, 16 & 19	NA	No, reversing judge on obviousness
22.10.09	Virgin Atlantic Airways Ltd v Premium Aircraft Interiors Group Ltd	[2009] EWCA 1062	Aircraft seats EP 1 495 908	Yes as to validity, no as to infringement	Yes, reversing judge	Yes[1]
17.11.09	Leo Pharma A/S v Sandoz Limited	[2009] EWCA 1188	Crystalline hydrate of calcipotriol EP 0 679 154	Yes	NA	Yes

1   Subsequent order for assessment of damages reversed by the Supreme Court in the light of a subsequent amendment and a determination that the amended claims were not infringed – see [2013] UKSC 46.

Date	Case	Citation	Subject matter	Judge upheld	Infringed?	Valid?
18.12.09	Dr Reddy's Laboratories (UK) Limited v Eli Lilly & Company	[2009] EWCA 1362	Pharmaceutical – olanzapine EP 0 454 436 B	Yes	NA	Yes
09.02.10	*Eli Lilly & Company v Human Genome Sciences Inc*	[2010] EWCA 1903	Neutrokine-α polypeptide EP 0 939 804 B	Yes	NA	No – lack of industrial applicability[1]
17.02.10	Actavis UK Ltd v Novartis AG	[2010] EWCA 82	Sustained release fluvastatin formulation EP 0 948 320	Yes	NA	No – obvious
14.05.10	Fabio Perini v LPC & PCMC	[2010] EWCA 525	Paper machinery EP 0 481 929 EP 0 699 168	Yes	Yes × 1 – claims 16 & 17 of '929	Yes as to '929. No as to '168 – obvious
22.06.10	Occlutech v Aga Medical	[2010] EWCA 702	Stent EP 0 808 138	Yes	No	NA
28.06.10	Cook Biotech Inc v Edwards Lifesciences AG	[2010] EWCA 718	Artificial heart valve EP 1 255 510	Yes	NA	No – all claims obvious

1   Reversed by Supreme Court – see [2011] UKSC 51.

Date	Case	Citation	Subject matter	Judge upheld	Infringed	Valid?
30.06.10	Medtronic CoreValve LLC v Edwards Lifesciences AG	[2010] EWCA 704	Artificial heart valve EP 0 592 410	Yes	No	NA
23.07.10	Schlumberger Holdings Ltd v Electromagnetic Geoservices AS	[2010] EWCA 819	Oil exploration using controlled source electromagnetism EP 1 256 019 EP 1 309 887	No	NA	Yes × 2
29.09.10	Novartis AG v Johnson & Johnson Medical	[2010] EWCA 1039	Contact lens EP 0 819 258	Yes	Conceded	No – all claims insufficient
15.10.10	Grimme Landmaschinenfabrik Gmbh & Co. KG v Derek Scott	[2010] EWCA 1110	Machinery for separating potatoes from weeds, earth, clods, stones and haulm EP 0 730 399	Yes, although holding that claim 1 obvious reversed	Yes	Yes
11.10.10	Tate & Lyle Technology Ltd v Roquette Freres	[2010] EWCA 1049	Use of maltotritol to control the crystal structure of maltitol EP 0 905 138	Yes	NA	No

Date	Case	Citation	Subject matter	Judge upheld	Infringed	Valid?
18.11.10	KCI Licensing Inc and ors v Smith & Nephew plc and ors	[2010] EWCA 1290	Wound drainage equipment EP 0 777 504 EP 0 853 950	In part	No as to '504 as to GO pumps and canisters, reversing. Yes as to '950 as to GO canisters, reversing	24.04.12
20.01.11	Nokia GmbH v IPCom GmbH & Co, KG	[2011] EWCA 6	Mobile telephony EP 0 540 808 EP 1 186 189	Yes	Yes × 2	No × 2 – '808 obvious, '189 anticipated and obvious, amendment to latter refused
23.02.11	Virgin Atlantic Airways Ltd v Delta Airways, Inc	[2011] EWCA 163	Aircraft seating EP 1 495 908[1]	Not as to summary judgment	Possibly, to be determined at full trial	NA
29.03.11	Gemstar-TV Guide International Inc and ors v Virgin Media Limited and anr	[2011] EWCA 302	Electronic programming guide EP 1 337 049 EP1 613 066	Yes	NA	No × 2 – anticipated

1   Same patent as previously in issue in *Virgin v Premier* [2009] EWHC 26; [2009] EWCA 1062; [2009] EWCA 1513.

Date	Case	Citation	Subject matter	Judge upheld	Infringed	Valid?
29.03.11	**Shutz (UK) Ltd v Werit (UK) Ltd**	[2011] EWCA 303	Intermediate bulk containers EP 0 734 947	Yes as to validity, not as to infringement	Yes	Yes[1]
08.04.11	Merck Sharp & Dohme Corp v Teva UK Ltd	[2011] EWCA 382	Ophthalmic formulations of timolol and dorzolamide for the treatment of glaucoma EP 0 509 752	Yes	NA	No – obvious
20.01.12	Apimed Medical Honey Limited v Brightwake Limited	[2012] EWCA 5	Medical dressings comprising gelled honey EP 1237561	No	NA (Parties having settled)	Yes
24.01.12	MMI Research Ltd v Cellxion Ltd & ors	[2012] EWCA 7	Method for breaking through GSM network security EP 1051053	No	NA	No – obvious

1 Reversed by Supreme Court – see [2013] UKSC 16.

Date	Case	Citation	Subject matter	Judge upheld	Infringed	Valid?
07.03.12	Gedeon Richter plc v Bayer Schering Pharma AG	[2012] EWCA 235	Pharmaceutical combination of ethinylestradiol and drospirenone for use as a contraceptive EP 1380301 EP 1598069	Yes	NA	Yes as to '301 when amended Claims 1 and 19 of '069 obvious but claim 6 valid
24.04.12	Mölnlycke Health Care AB v Brightwake Limited	[2011] EWCA 602	Wound dressing EP 0633757	No	NA (parties having settled).	Yes
02.05.12	ConvaTec Ltd & ors v Smith & Nephew Healthcare Ltd & ors	[2012] EWCA 520	Wound dressing EP 0927013	Yes	No	Yes, in part
10.05.12	Nokia OYJ v IPCom GmbH & Co, KG	[2012] EWCA 567	Mobile telephony EP 1841268	Yes	Yes as to A2 device	Yes
05.09.12	Eli Lilly v Human Genome Sciences Inc	[2012] EWCA 1185	Neutrokine-α polypeptide and mAbs EP 0939804[1]	No	NA	Yes, as to all claims
10.10.12	Medimmune v Novartis	[2012] EWCA 1234	Antibody production EP 2055777	Yes	N/A	No – obvious
10.12.12	Novartis v Generics	[2012] EWCA 1623	Rivastigmine	Yes	NA	No – obvious

1 Consideration of issues not addressed in *Eli Lilly v Human Genome Sciences Inc* [2010] EWCA 1903 but opened for consideration in the view of the reversal of that judgment in *Eli Lilly v Human Genome Sciences Inc* [2011] UKSC 51.

Date	Case	Citation	Subject matter	Judge upheld	Infringed	Valid?
14.12.12	Smith & Nephew Plc v Convatec Technologies Inc	[2012] EWCA 1638	Wound dressing EP 1343510	Yes	NA	Conceded not as granted, but held yes as amended
23.01.13	Omnipharm Ltd v Merial	[2013] EWCA 2	Flea treatments EP (UK) 0881881 UK 2317564	Yes (only '564 in issue)	NA	No as to '564 – insufficient
21.02.13	Regeneron Pharmaceuticals and Bayer Pharma AG v Genentech Inc	[2013] EWCA 67	Use of VEGF antagonists EP (UK) 1506986	Yes	Yes	Yes
30.04.13	AstraZeneca AB v Hexal AG	[2013] EWCA 454	Sustained release formulation of quetiapine EP (UK) 0090364	Yes	NA	No – obvious
03.05.13	HTC Europe Co. Ltd v Apple Inc.	[2013] EWCA 451	User Interfaces EP (UK) 2 098 948 EP (UK) 2 964 022	Yes, except as to one claim of '848 on excluded subject matter	NA	No, except as to one claim of '948 – all others obvious
29.07.13	Generics UK Ltd v Yeda and Teva	[2013] EWCA 925	Copolymer-1 EP (UK) 0762888	Yes	DNI refused	Yes

Date	Case	Citation	Subject matter	Judge upheld	Infringed	Valid?
30.07.13	Sudarshan Chemical Industries v Clariant Produtke	[2013] EWCA 919	Polymorph of pigment known as PY 191 EP (UK) 1170338	Yes	NA	No – amended claims both obvious and added matter
11.12.13	Microsoft Corporation v Motorola Mobility	[2013] EWCA 1613	Communications software EP (UK) 0 847 654	Yes	NA	No – obvious
15.12.13	Hospira UK Ltd and anr v Novartis AG	[2013] EWCA 1633	Dosing regime for administration of zoledronate for the treatment of osteoporosis EP (UK) 1296689	Yes	NA	No – anticipated on loss of priority
20.12.13	Virgin Atlantic Airways Ltd v Jet Airways (India) [& anr & other actions]	[2013] EWCA 1713	Aircraft Seating EP (UK) 1 495 908[1] EP (UK) 2 272 711 EP (UK) 2 289 734	Yes	No as to 908 No as to 711 NA as to 734	Yes × 3

1 Same patent as previously in issue in *Virgin v Premier* [2009] EWHC 26; [2009] EWCA 1062; [2009] EWCA 1513; [2011] EWCA 163; [2013] UKSC 46 but amended.

Date	Case	Citation	Subject matter	Judge upheld	Infringed	Valid?
28.01.14	AP Racing Ltd v Alcon Components Ltd	[2014] EWCA 40	Disc brake GB 2451690	No	NA	Yes
16.04.14	Phil & Ted's Most Excellent Buggy Company Ltd v TFK Trends For Kids Gmbh and anr	[2014] EWCA 469	Baby buggy EP (UK) 1795424	Yes	NA	No – obvious
15.05.14	Swarovski-Optik KG v Leica Camera AG & anr	[2014] EWCA 637	Riflescopes EP (UK) 1746451	Yes	Yes	Yes
09.10.14	Nampak Plastics Europe Limited v Alpla UK Limited	[2014] EWCA 1293	Plastic Container GB 2 494 349	Yes	No[1]	NA
22.10.14	HTC Corporation v Gemalto SA HTC Corporation v Gemalto NV	[2014] EWCA 1335	Using a high level programming language with a microcontroller EP (UK) 0932865	Yes	No	Yes as to claim 3
11.11.14	Adaptive Spectrum and Signal Alignment Inc v British Telecommunications PLC	[2014] EWCA 1462	DSL control EP (UK) 2259495 EP (UK) 1869790	Yes as to 790 No as to 495	Yes *2	Yes *2

1   Upholding summary judgment.

Date	Case	Citation	Subject matter	Judge upheld	Infringed	Valid?
17.12.14	Jarden Consumer Solutions (Europe) Limited v SEB SA	[2014] EWCA 1629	Fryer with automatic fat coating EP (UK) 2085003	Not on Infringement	No	Yes as to claims in issue
06.02.15	Hospira UK Ltd v Genentech Inc.	[2015] EWCA 57	Dosages for treatment with Anti-ErbB2 antibodies (trastuzumab) EP (UK) 1210115	Yes	NA	No – claim 1 obvious
24.06.15	Smith & Nephew plc v ConvaTec Technologies Inc[1]	[2015] EWCA 607	Light stabilised antimicrobial materials EP (UK) 1343510[1]	No	Yes	NA

1 Same patent and parties as in *Smith & Nephew plc v Convatec Technologies Inc.* [2012] EWHC 1602; [2012] EWCA 1638.

Date	Case	Citation	Subject matter	Judge upheld	Infringed	Valid?
25.06.15	Actavis UK Ltd v Eli Lilly & Co	[2015] EWCA 555	Use of pemetrexed disodium in combination with vitamin B12 or a pharmaceutical derivative thereof and optionally a folic protein binding agent EP (UK) 0432677 (& ES, FR, IT Designations)	Not as to contributory infringement	Declaration of non-infringement refused and remitted for further consideration	NA
23.07.15	Rovi Solutions and anr v Virgin Media Ltd & ors	[2015] EWCA 781	Set top boxes EP (UK) 1 327 209	Yes	NA	No – all claims in issue obvious
28.07.15	Teva UK Ltd v Leo Pharma A/S and anr	[2015] EWCA 779	Pharmaceutical composition comprising a vitamin and a corticosteroid for treatment of psoriasis EP (UK) 1 178 808 EP (UK) 2 455 083	No	NA	Yes

Appendix 4

Further reading

**Suggestions as to books for further reading
(in addition to books and articles listed in the text)**

Generally

Cole et al, *CIPA Guide to the Patents Act* (7th edn, Sweet & Maxwell, 2011).

EPO – *European National Patent Decisions Report* (EPO 2004) supplemented by *Case Law from the Contracting States to the EPC 2004–2011* (EPO 2011, available as a PDF on the EPO website), and *Case Law from the Contracting States to the EPC 2011–2014* (EPO 2015, available as a PDF on the EPO website).

de Carvalho, *The TRIPS Regime of Patent Rights* (3rd edn, Kluwer, 2010).

Kuhnen, *Patent Litigation Proceedings in Germany* (7th edn, Carl Heymanns Verlag 2013).

Miller et al, *Terrell on the Law of Patents* (17th edn, Sweet & Maxwell, 2011).

Roberts et al, *CIPA European Patent Handbook* (Sweet & Maxwell, to date).

Roughton, Johnson & Cook, *The Modern Law of Patents* (3rd edn, LexisNexis Butterworths, 2014).

Chapter 2

Cole, *Fundamentals of Patent Drafting* (CIPA, 2006).

Roberts, *A Practical Guide to Drafting Patents* (Sweet & Maxwell, 2006).

Appendix 4

Chapter 3

Anderson, *Technology Transfer – Law and Practice* (3rd edn, Bloomsbury Professional, 2010).

Cook & Horton, *Practical Intellectual Property Precedents* (Sweet & Maxwell, 1997 to date).

Korah, *Intellectual Property Rights and the EC Competition Rules* (Hart Publishing, 2006).

Chapter 5

EPO, *Case Law of the Boards of Appeal of the European Patent Office* (7th edn, EPO, 2013). (Available as a PDF on the EPO website.)

Pila, *The Requirement for an Invention in Patent Law* (Oxford University Press, 2010).

Chapter 6

Cotter, *Comparative Patent Remedies – A Legal and Economic Analysis* (Oxford University Press, 2013).

Fisher, *Fundamentals of Patent Law – Interpretation and Scope of Protection* (Hart Publishing, 2007).

Chapters 7 & 8

Bruckner & Czettritz, *Supplementary Protection Certificates with Paediatric Extension of Duration* (Carl Heymanns Verlag, 2012)

Cook, *Pharmaceuticals Biotechnology and the Law* (3rd edn, LexisNexis Butterworths, 2016).

Grubb & Thomsen, *Patents for Chemicals, Pharmaceuticals and Biotechnology* (5th edn, Oxford University Press, 2010).

Appendix 5

Patent resources on the Internet

There is a vast amount of patent resources on the Internet. Although websites come and go, and change name, the following small selection of websites (arranged alphabetically within groupings, and chosen primarily for the range of links that they provide, or for some unique content) were all active as at August 2015.

Site	Operator and description
Official organizations	
International	
http://www.wipo.int/ patentscope/en/ http://www.wipo.int/wipolex/en/	World Intellectual Property Organization (WIPO) with access to PCT information and reference material, and also the Collection of Laws for Electronic Access (CLEA) with the IP laws of many countries.
http://www.wto.org/english/ tratop_e/trips_e/trips_e. htm#issues	World Trade Organization (WTO) gateway to materials about TRIPs – that it administers.
UK	
http://www.justice.gov.uk/ courts/court-lists/list-patents-court-diary	Patents Court Diary, setting out hearings scheduled for the future, and the outcomes of past hearings.
http://www.justice.gov.uk/ downloads/courts/patents-court/ patent-court-guide.pdf	*Patents Court Guide.*
http://www.justice.gov.uk/ courts/rcj-rolls-building/ intellectual-property-enterprise-court	Intellectual Property Enterprise Court website, with links to its *Guides.*
www.legislation.gov.uk	UK Public Acts and Statutory Instruments.
www.publications.parliament. uk/pa/ld/ldjudgmt.htm	House of Lords judgments to 2009 – when the UK Supreme Court took over its jurisdiction.

Appendix 5

Site	Operator and description
https://www.supremecourt.uk/decided-cases/index.html	Supreme Court judgments since it took over the jurisdiction of the House of Lords in 2009.
https://www.ipo.gov.uk/pro-types/pro-patent/pro-p-os/p-challenge-decision-results.htm	UK Intellectual Property Office (UKIPO) (formerly UK Patent Office) Patent Decisions since 1988.
https://www.gov.uk/search-for-patent	UK Intellectual Property Office (UKIPO) (formerly UK Patent Office) online patent services (including search).
https://www.gov.uk/topic/intellectual-property/patents	UK Intellectual Property Office (UKIPO) (formerly UK Patent Office) general patent information, and in its professional section, reference material on patent law, and practice such as the *Manual of Patent Practice*.
Other European	
www.epo.org	European Patent Office (EPO) with user information, links, reference material, including case law of the EPO Boards of Appeal, and for searching the files of EPO patents and applications.
worldwide.espacenet.com	Free access to a database of over 90 million patents.
http://curia.europa.eu/jcms/jcms/j_6/	Website of the Court of Justice of the EU.
http://www.unified-patent-court.org/	Website of the Preparatory Committee for the Unified Patent Court.
USA	
www.cafc.uscourts.gov	US Court of Appeals for the Federal Circuit – that hears all US patent appeals.
www.supremecourt.gov	US Supreme Court – that hears appeals from the Court of Appeals for the Federal Circuit (that hears all US patent appeals).
www.uspto.gov/patents/index.jsp	US Patent and Trade Mark Office, with information as to US patent practice, links, and with a facility (via the Public PAIR system) for searching the files of US patents and applications.

Site	Operator and description
IP organizations, etc	
www.aippi.org	The International Association for the Protection of Intellectual Property, whose objective is 'to improve and promote the protection of intellectual property on both an international and national basis'. It 'operates by conducting studies of existing national laws and proposes measures to achieve harmonisation of these laws on an international basis'. The site provides useful comparative law summaries of the various issues (named 'questions') that it has studied.
www.cipa.org.uk	Chartered Institute of Patent Attorneys, the professional body for UK patent attorneys. The site has a comprehensive set of useful links, including to various national patent offices.
www.eplaw.org	Association of experienced patent lawyers in the EU who aim to promote the equitable, and efficacious handling of patent disputes across Europe.
Other organizations providing case law	
http://www.bailii.org	British and Irish Legal Information Institute, with comprehensive access to freely available British and Irish public legal information (and that from many other jurisdictions) eg statutes, statutory instruments, and case law (not just as to IP). Of greatest importance to patent practitioners it includes most decisions of the Patents Court, the Intellectual Property Enterprise Court, and the Court of Appeal since 2000, and some from before then.
http://www.veron.com/ FPCL.aspx	Important patent decisions of French courts with English translations.

Appendix 5

Site	Operator and description
Blogs	
http://www.eplawpatentblog.com	EPLAW Patent Blog – A European blog on patent law, providing access to patent judgments, and patent information from various European jurisdictions.
http://www.ipkat.com	IPKat – Probably the leading European general IP blog. It looks at matters from a mainly UK and European perspective, and has a fair proportion of patent material.
http://kluwerpatentblog.com/	Kluwer patent blog – A blog on European patent law, providing access to patent judgments, and patent information from various European jurisdictions.
http://patlit.blogspot.com/	Pat Lit – A blog that focuses on patent litigation law, practice and strategy, primarily from a UK perspective.
http://thespcblog.blogspot.com/	SPC Blog – A niche blog dedicated to the issues that arise when supplementary protection certificates (SPCs) extend patents beyond their normal life.

Appendix 6

Legislative materials

Paris Convention for the Protection of Industrial Property (20 March 1883)

Appendix 6 – as revised at Brussels on 14 December 1900; at Washington on 2 June 2 1911; at The Hague on 6 November 1925; at London on 2 June 1934; at Lisbon on 31 October 1958; and at Stockholm on 14 July 1967, and as amended on 28 September 1979.

NOTES
The original source for this Convention is the World Intellectual Property Organization (WIPO). Articles have been given titles to facilitate their identification. There are no titles in the signed (French) text.

Article I
[Establishment of the Union; Scope of Industrial Property][1]
(1) The countries to which this Convention applies constitute a Union for the protection of industrial property.
(2) The protection of industrial property has as its object patents, utility models, industrial designs, trademarks, service marks, trade names, indications of source or appellations of origin, and the repression of unfair competition.
(3) Industrial property shall be understood in the broadest sense and shall apply not only to industry and commerce proper, but likewise to agricultural and extractive industries and to all manufactured or natural products, for example, wines, grain, tobacco leaf, fruit, cattle, minerals, mineral waters, beer, flowers, and flour.
(4) Patents shall include the various kinds of industrial patents recognized by the laws of the countries of the Union, such as patents of importation, patents of improvement, patents and certificates of addition, etc.

1   Articles have been given titles to facilitate their identification. There are no titles in the signed (French) text.

Article 2
[National Treatment for Nationals of Countries of the Union]

(1) Nationals of any country of the Union shall, as regards the protection of industrial property, enjoy in all the other countries of the Union the advantages that their respective laws now grant, or may hereafter grant, to nationals; all without prejudice to the rights specially provided for by this Convention. Consequently, they shall have the same protection as the latter, and the same legal remedy against any infringement of their rights, provided that the conditions and formalities imposed upon nationals are complied with.

(2) However, no requirement as to domicile or establishment in the country where protection is claimed may be imposed upon nationals of countries of the Union for the enjoyment of any industrial property rights.

(3) The provisions of the laws of each of the countries of the Union relating to judicial and administrative procedure and to jurisdiction, and to the designation of an address for service or the appointment of an agent, which may be required by the laws on industrial property are expressly reserved.

Article 3
[Same Treatment for Certain Categories of Persons as for Nationals of Countries of the Union]

Nationals of countries outside the Union who are domiciled or who have real and effective industrial or commercial establishments in the territory of one of the countries of the Union shall be treated in the same manner as nationals of the countries of the Union.

Article 4
[A to I. Patents, Utility Models, Industrial Designs, Marks, Inventors' Certificates: Right of Priority. – G. Patents: Division of the Application]

A. (1) Any person who has duly filed an application for a patent, or for the registration of a utility model, or of an industrial design, or of a trademark, in one of the countries of the Union, or his successor in title, shall enjoy, for the purpose of filing in the other countries, a right of priority during the periods hereinafter fixed.

   (2) Any filing that is equivalent to a regular national filing under the domestic legislation of any country of the Union or under bilateral or multilateral treaties concluded between countries of the Union shall be recognized as giving rise to the right of priority.

   (3) By a regular national filing is meant any filing that is adequate to establish the date on which the application was filed in the country concerned, whatever may be the subsequent fate of the application.

B. Consequently, any subsequent filing in any of the other countries of the Union before the expiration of the periods referred to above shall not be invalidated by reason of any acts accomplished in the interval, in particular, another filing, the publication or exploitation of the invention, the putting on sale of copies of the design, or the use of the mark, and such acts cannot give rise to any third-party right or any right of personal possession. Rights acquired by third parties before the date of the first application that serves as the basis for the right of priority are reserved in accordance with the domestic legislation of each country of the Union.

C. (1) The periods of priority referred to above shall be twelve months for patents and utility models, and six months for industrial designs and trademarks.

(2) These periods shall start from the date of filing of the first application; the day of filing shall not be included in the period.

(3) If the last day of the period is an official holiday, or a day when the Office is not open for the filing of applications in the country where protection is claimed, the period shall be extended until the first following working day.

(4) A subsequent application concerning the same subject as a previous first application within the meaning of paragraph (2), above, filed in the same country of the Union shall be considered as the first application, of which the filing date shall be the starting point of the period of priority, if, at the time of filing the subsequent application, the said previous application has been withdrawn, abandoned, or refused, without having been laid open to public inspection and without leaving any rights outstanding, and if it has not yet served as a basis for claiming a right of priority. The previous application may not thereafter serve as a basis for claiming a right of priority.

D. (1) Any person desiring to take advantage of the priority of a previous filing shall be required to make a declaration indicating the date of such filing and the country in which it was made. Each country shall determine the latest date on which such declaration must be made.

(2) These particulars shall be mentioned in the publications issued by the competent authority, and in particular in the patents and the specifications relating thereto.

(3) The countries of the Union may require any person making a declaration of priority to produce a copy of the application (description, drawings, etc) previously filed. The copy, certified as correct by the authority which received such application, shall not require any authentication, and may in any case be filed, without fee, at any time within three months of the filing of the subsequent application. They may require it to be accompanied by a certificate from the same authority showing the date of filing, and by a translation.

(4) No other formalities may be required for the declaration of priority at the time of filing the application. Each country of the Union shall determine the consequences of failure to comply with the formalities prescribed by this Article, but such consequences shall in no case go beyond the loss of the right of priority.

(5) Subsequently, further proof may be required.

Any person who avails himself of the priority of a previous application shall be required to specify the number of that application; this number shall be published as provided for by paragraph (2), above.

E. (1) Where an industrial design is filed in a country by virtue of a right of priority based on the filing of a utility model, the period of priority shall be the same as that fixed for industrial designs.

    (2) Furthermore, it is permissible to file a utility model in a country by virtue of a right of priority based on the filing of a patent application, and vice versa.

F.   No country of the Union may refuse a priority or a patent application on the ground that the applicant claims multiple priorities, even if they originate in different countries, or on the ground that an application claiming one or more priorities contains one or more elements that were not included in the application or applications whose priority is claimed, provided that, in both cases, there is unity of invention within the meaning of the law of the country.

With respect to the elements not included in the application or applications whose priority is claimed, the filing of the subsequent application shall give rise to a right of priority under ordinary conditions.

G. (1) If the examination reveals that an application for a patent contains more than one invention, the applicant may divide the application into a certain number of divisional applications and preserve as the date of each the date of the initial application and the benefit of the right of priority, if any.

    (2) The applicant may also, on his own initiative, divide a patent application and preserve as the date of each divisional application the date of the initial application and the benefit of the right of priority, if any. Each country of the Union shall have the right to determine the conditions under which such division shall be authorized.

H.   Priority may not be refused on the ground that certain elements of the invention for which priority is claimed do not appear among the claims formulated in the application in the country of origin, provided that the application documents as a whole specifically disclose such elements.

I.   (1) Applications for inventors' certificates filed in a country in which applicants have the right to apply at their own option either for a patent or for an inventor's certificate shall give rise to the right of priority provided for by this Article, under the same conditions and with the same effects as applications for patents.

    (2) In a country in which applicants have the right to apply at their own option either for a patent or for an inventor's certificate, an applicant for an inventor's certificate shall, in accordance with the provisions of this Article relating to patent applications, enjoy a right of priority based on an application for a patent, a utility model, or an inventor's certificate.

Article 4bis
[Patents: Independence of Patents Obtained for the Same Invention in Different Countries]

(1) Patents applied for in the various countries of the Union by nationals of countries of the Union shall be independent of patents obtained for the same invention in other countries, whether members of the Union or not.

(2) The foregoing provision is to be understood in an unrestricted sense, in particular, in the sense that patents applied for during the period of priority are independent, both as regards the grounds for nullity and forfeiture, and as regards their normal duration.

(3) The provision shall apply to all patents existing at the time when it comes into effect.

(4) Similarly, it shall apply, in the case of the accession of new countries, to patents in existence on either side at the time of accession.

(5) Patents obtained with the benefit of priority shall, in the various countries of the Union, have a duration equal to that which they would have, had they been applied for or granted without the benefit of priority.

Article 4ter
[Patents: Mention of the Inventor in the Patent]
The inventor shall have the right to be mentioned as such in the patent.

Article 4quater
[Patents: Patentability in Case of Restrictions of Sale by Law]
The grant of a patent shall not be refused and a patent shall not be invalidated on the ground that the sale of the patented product or of a product obtained by means of a patented process is subject to restrictions or limitations resulting from the domestic law.

Article 5
[A. Patents: Importation of Articles; Failure to Work or Insufficient Working; Compulsory Licenses. – B. Industrial Designs: Failure to Work; Importation of Articles. – C. Marks: Failure to Use; Different Forms; Use by Co-proprietors. – D. Patents, Utility Models, Marks, Industrial Designs: Marking]

A. (1) Importation by the patentee into the country where the patent has been granted of articles manufactured in any of the countries of the Union shall not entail forfeiture of the patent.

(2) Each country of the Union shall have the right to take legislative measures providing for the grant of compulsory licenses to prevent the abuses which might result from the exercise of the exclusive rights conferred by the patent, for example, failure to work.

(3) Forfeiture of the patent shall not be provided for except in cases where the grant of compulsory licenses would not have been sufficient to prevent the said abuses. No proceedings for the forfeiture or revocation of a patent may be instituted before the expiration of two years from the grant of the first compulsory license.

(4) A compulsory license may not be applied for on the ground of failure to work or insufficient working before the expiration of a period of four years from the date of filing of the patent application or three years from the date of the grant of the patent, whichever period expires last; it shall be refused if the patentee justifies his inaction by legitimate reasons. Such a compulsory license shall be non-exclusive and shall not be transferable, even in the form of the grant of a sub-license, except with that part of the enterprise or goodwill which exploits such license.

(5) The foregoing provisions shall be applicable, *mutatis mutandis*, to utility models.

Appendix 6

B. The protection of industrial designs shall not, under any circumstance, be subject to any forfeiture, either by reason of failure to work or by reason of the importation of articles corresponding to those which are protected.

C. (1) If, in any country, use of the registered mark is compulsory, the registration may be cancelled only after a reasonable period, and then only if the person concerned does not justify his inaction.

(2) Use of a trademark by the proprietor in a form differing in elements which do not alter the distinctive character of the mark in the form in which it was registered in one of the countries of the Union shall not entail invalidation of the registration and shall not diminish the protection granted to the mark.

(3) Concurrent use of the same mark on identical or similar goods by industrial or commercial establishments considered as co-proprietors of the mark according to the provisions of the domestic law of the country where protection is claimed shall not prevent registration or diminish in any way the protection granted to the said mark in any country of the Union, provided that such use does not result in misleading the public and is not contrary to the public interest.

D. No indication or mention of the patent, of the utility model, of the registration of the trademark, or of the deposit of the industrial design, shall be required upon the goods as a condition of recognition of the right to protection.

Article 5bis
[All Industrial Property Rights: Period of Grace for the Payment of Fees for the Maintenance of Rights; Patents: Restoration]

(1) A period of grace of not less than six months shall be allowed for the payment of the fees prescribed for the maintenance of industrial property rights, subject, if the domestic legislation so provides, to the payment of a surcharge.

(2) The countries of the Union shall have the right to provide for the restoration of patents which have lapsed by reason of non-payment of fees.

Article 5ter
[Patents: Patented Devices Forming Part of Vessels, Aircraft, or Land Vehicles]

In any country of the Union the following shall not be considered as infringements of the rights of a patentee:

(1) the use on board vessels of other countries of the Union of devices forming the subject of his patent in the body of the vessel, in the machinery, tackle, gear and other accessories, when such vessels temporarily or accidentally enter the waters of the said country, provided that such devices are used there exclusively for the needs of the vessel;

(2) the use of devices forming the subject of the patent in the construction or operation of aircraft or land vehicles of other countries of the Union, or of accessories of such aircraft or land vehicles, when those aircraft or land vehicles temporarily or accidentally enter the said country.

Article 5^{quater}
[Patents: Importation of Products Manufactured by a Process Patented in the Importing Country]

When a product is imported into a country of the Union where there exists a patent protecting a process of manufacture of the said product, the patentee shall have all the rights, with regard to the imported product, that are accorded to him by the legislation of the country of importation, on the basis of the process patent, with respect to products manufactured in that country.

Article 5^{quinquies}
[Industrial Designs]

Industrial designs shall be protected in all the countries of the Union.

Articles 6–10ter
[...]

Article 11
[Inventions, Utility Models, Industrial Designs, Marks: Temporary Protection at Certain International Exhibitions]

(1) The countries of the Union shall, in conformity with their domestic legislation, grant temporary protection to patentable inventions, utility models, industrial designs, and trademarks, in respect of goods exhibited at official or officially recognized international exhibitions held in the territory of any of them.

(2) Such temporary protection shall not extend the periods provided by Article 4. If, later, the right of priority is invoked, the authorities of any country may provide that the period shall start from the date of introduction of the goods into the exhibition.

(3) Each country may require, as proof of the identity of the article exhibited and of the date of its introduction, such documentary evidence as it considers necessary.

Article 12
[Special National Industrial Property Services]

(1) Each country of the Union undertakes to establish a special industrial property service and a central office for the communication to the public of patents, utility models, industrial designs, and trademarks.

(2) This service shall publish an official periodical journal. It shall publish regularly:
 (a) the names of the proprietors of patents granted, with a brief designation of the inventions patented;
 (b) the reproductions of registered trademarks.

Articles 13–30
[...]

Appendix 6

Agreement on Trade-related Aspects of Intellectual Property Rights (TRIPS)

NOTES
The original source for this agreement is the World Trade Organisation (WTO).

Members,

Agreement on TRIPS *Desiring* to reduce distortions and impediments to international trade, and taking into account the need to promote effective and adequate protection of intellectual property rights, and to ensure that measures and procedures to enforce intellectual property rights do not themselves become barriers to legitimate trade;

Recognizing, to this end, the need for new rules and disciplines concerning:

(a) the applicability of the basic principles of GATT 1994 and of relevant international intellectual property agreements or conventions;
(b) the provision of adequate standards and principles concerning the availability, scope and use of trade-related intellectual property rights;
(c) the provision of effective and appropriate means for the enforcement of trade-related intellectual property rights, taking into account differences in national legal systems;
(d) the provision of effective and expeditious procedures for the multilateral prevention and settlement of disputes between governments; and
(e) transitional arrangements aiming at the fullest participation in the results of the negotiations;

Recognizing the need for a multilateral framework of principles, rules and disciplines dealing with international trade in counterfeit goods;

Recognizing that intellectual property rights are private rights;

Recognizing the underlying public policy objectives of national systems for the protection of intellectual property, including developmental and technological objectives;

Recognizing also the special needs of the least-developed country Members in respect of maximum flexibility in the domestic implementation of laws and regulations in order to enable them to create a sound and viable technological base;

Emphasizing the importance of reducing tensions by reaching strengthened commitments to resolve disputes on trade-related intellectual property issues through multilateral procedures;

Desiring to establish a mutually supportive relationship between the WTO and the World Intellectual Property Organization (referred to in this Agreement as "WIPO") as well as other relevant international organizations;

Hereby agree as follows:

PART I
GENERAL PROVISIONS AND BASIC PRINCIPLES

Article I
Nature and Scope of Obligations

1. Members shall give effect to the provisions of this Agreement. Members may, but shall not be obliged to, implement in their law more extensive protection than is required by this Agreement, provided that such protection does not contravene the provisions of this Agreement. Members shall be free to determine the appropriate method of implementing the provisions of this Agreement within their own legal system and practice.

2. For the purposes of this Agreement, the term "intellectual property" refers to all categories of intellectual property that are the subject of Sections 1 through 7 of Part II.

3. Members shall accord the treatment provided for in this Agreement to the nationals of other Members.[1] In respect of the relevant intellectual property right, the nationals of other Members shall be understood as those natural or legal persons that would meet the criteria for eligibility for protection provided for in the Paris Convention (1967), the Berne Convention (1971), the Rome Convention and the Treaty on Intellectual Property in Respect of Integrated Circuits, were all Members of the WTO members of those conventions.[2] Any Member availing itself of the possibilities provided in paragraph 3 of Article 5 or paragraph 2 of Article 6 of the Rome Convention shall make a notification as foreseen in those provisions to the Council for Trade-Related Aspects of Intellectual Property Rights (the "Council for TRIPS").

1   When "nationals" are referred to in this Agreement, they shall be deemed, in the case of a separate customs territory Member of the WTO, to mean persons, natural or legal, who are domiciled or who have a real and effective industrial or commercial establishment in that customs territory.

2   In this Agreement, "Paris Convention" refers to the Paris Convention for the Protection of Industrial Property; "Paris Convention (1967)' refers to the Stockholm Act of this Convention of 14 July 1967. "Berne Convention" refers to the Berne Convention for the Protection of Literary and Artistic Works; "Berne Convention (1971)' refers to the Paris Act of this Convention of 24 July 1971. "Rome Convention" refers to the International Convention for the Protection of Performers, Producers of Phonograms and Broadcasting Organizations, adopted at Rome on 26 October 1961. "Treaty on Intellectual Property in Respect of Integrated Circuits" (IPIC Treaty) refers to the Treaty on Intellectual Property in Respect of Integrated Circuits, adopted at Washington on 26 May 1989. "WTO Agreement" refers to the Agreement Establishing the WTO.

Article 2
Intellectual Property Conventions

1. In respect of Parts II, III and IV of this Agreement, Members shall comply with Articles 1 through 12, and Article 19, of the Paris Convention (1967).

2. Nothing in Parts I to IV of this Agreement shall derogate from existing obligations that Members may have to each other under the Paris Convention, the Berne Convention, the Rome Convention and the Treaty on Intellectual Property in Respect of Integrated Circuits.

Appendix 6

Article 3
National Treatment

1. Each Member shall accord to the nationals of other Members treatment no less favourable than that it accords to its own nationals with regard to the protection[1] of intellectual property, subject to the exceptions already provided in, respectively, the Paris Convention (1967), the Berne Convention (1971), the Rome Convention or the Treaty on Intellectual Property in Respect of Integrated Circuits. In respect of performers, producers of phonograms and broadcasting organizations, this obligation only applies in respect of the rights provided under this Agreement. Any Member availing itself of the possibilities provided in Article 6 of the Berne Convention (1971) or paragraph 1(b) of Article 16 of the Rome Convention shall make a notification as foreseen in those provisions to the Council for TRIPS.

2. Members may avail themselves of the exceptions permitted under paragraph 1 in relation to judicial and administrative procedures, including the designation of an address for service or the appointment of an agent within the jurisdiction of a Member, only where such exceptions are necessary to secure compliance with laws and regulations which are not inconsistent with the provisions of this Agreement and where such practices are not applied in a manner which would constitute a disguised restriction on trade.

[1]   For the purposes of Articles 3 and 4, "protection" shall include matters affecting the availability, acquisition, scope, maintenance and enforcement of intellectual property rights as well as those matters affecting the use of intellectual property rights specifically addressed in this Agreement.

Article 4
Most-Favoured-Nation Treatment

With regard to the protection of intellectual property, any advantage, favour, privilege or immunity granted by a Member to the nationals of any other country shall be accorded immediately and unconditionally to the nationals of all other Members. Exempted from this obligation are any advantage, favour, privilege or immunity accorded by a Member:

(a)   deriving from international agreements on judicial assistance or law enforcement of a general nature and not particularly confined to the protection of intellectual property;

(b)   granted in accordance with the provisions of the Berne Convention (1971) or the Rome Convention authorizing that the treatment accorded be a function not of national treatment but of the treatment accorded in another country;

(c)   in respect of the rights of performers, producers of phonograms and broadcasting organizations not provided under this Agreement;

(d)   deriving from international agreements related to the protection of intellectual property which entered into force prior to the entry into force of the WTO Agreement, provided that such agreements are notified to the Council for TRIPS and do not constitute an arbitrary or unjustifiable discrimination against nationals of other Members.

Article 5
Multilateral Agreements on Acquisition or Maintenance of Protection

The obligations under Articles 3 and 4 do not apply to procedures provided in multilateral agreements concluded under the auspices of WIPO relating to the acquisition or maintenance of intellectual property rights.

Article 6
Exhaustion

For the purposes of dispute settlement under this Agreement, subject to the provisions of Articles 3 and 4 nothing in this Agreement shall be used to address the issue of the exhaustion of intellectual property rights.

Article 7
Objectives

The protection and enforcement of intellectual property rights should contribute to the promotion of technological innovation and to the transfer and dissemination of technology, to the mutual advantage of producers and users of technological knowledge and in a manner conducive to social and economic welfare, and to a balance of rights and obligations.

Article 8
Principles

1. Members may, in formulating or amending their laws and regulations, adopt measures necessary to protect public health and nutrition, and to promote the public interest in sectors of vital importance to their socio-economic and technological development, provided that such measures are consistent with the provisions of this Agreement.
2. Appropriate measures, provided that they are consistent with the provisions of this Agreement, may be needed to prevent the abuse of intellectual property rights by right holders or the resort to practices which unreasonably restrain trade or adversely affect the international transfer of technology.

PART II
STANDARDS CONCERNING THE AVAILABILITY, SCOPE AND USE OF
INTELLECTUAL PROPERTY RIGHTS SECTION 1: [...]
SECTION 2: [...]
SECTION 3: [...]
SECTION 4: [...]
SECTION 5:
PATENTS

Article 27
Patentable Subject Matter

1. Subject to the provisions of paragraphs 2 and 3, patents shall be available for any inventions, whether products or processes, in all fields of technology, provided that they are new, involve an inventive step and are capable of industrial application.1 Subject to paragraph 4 of Article 65, paragraph 8 of Article 70 and paragraph 3 of this Article, patents shall be available and patent rights enjoyable without discrimination as to the place of invention, the field of technology and whether products are imported or locally produced.

2. Members may exclude from patentability inventions, the prevention within their territory of the commercial exploitation of which is necessary to protect *ordre public* or morality, including to protect human, animal or plant life or health or to avoid serious prejudice to the environment, provided that such exclusion is not made merely because the exploitation is prohibited by their law.

3. Members may also exclude from patentability:

    (a) diagnostic, therapeutic and surgical methods for the treatment of humans or animals;

    (b) plants and animals other than micro-organisms, and essentially biological processes for the production of plants or animals other than non-biological and microbiological processes. However, Members shall provide for the protection of plant varieties either by patents or by an effective *sui generis* system or by any combination thereof. The provisions of this subparagraph shall be reviewed four years after the date of entry into force of the WTO Agreement.

1   For the purposes of this Article, the terms "inventive step" and "capable of industrial application" may be deemed by a Member to be synonymous with the terms "non-obvious" and "useful" respectively.

Article 28
Rights Conferred

1. A patent shall confer on its owner the following exclusive rights:

    (a) where the subject matter of a patent is a product, to prevent third parties not having the owner's consent from the acts of: making, using, offering for sale, selling, or importing[1] for these purposes that product;

    (b) where the subject matter of a patent is a process, to prevent third parties not having the owner's consent from the act of using the process, and from the acts of: using, offering for sale, selling, or importing for these purposes at least the product obtained directly by that process.

2. Patent owners shall also have the right to assign, or transfer by succession, the patent and to conclude licensing contracts.

1 This right, like all other rights conferred under this Agreement in respect of the use, sale, importation or other distribution of goods, is subject to the provisions of Article 6.

Article 29
Conditions on Patent Applicants

1. Members shall require that an applicant for a patent shall disclose the invention in a manner sufficiently clear and complete for the invention to be carried out by a person skilled in the art and may require the applicant to indicate the best mode for carrying out the invention known to the inventor at the filing date or, where priority is claimed, at the priority date of the application.
2. Members may require an applicant for a patent to provide information concerning the applicant's corresponding foreign applications and grants.

Article 30
Exceptions to Rights Conferred

Members may provide limited exceptions to the exclusive rights conferred by a patent, provided that such exceptions do not unreasonably conflict with a normal exploitation of the patent and do not unreasonably prejudice the legitimate interests of the patent owner, taking account of the legitimate interests of third parties.

Article 31
Other Use Without Authorization of the Right Holder

Where the law of a Member allows for other use[1] of the subject matter of a patent without the authorization of the right holder, including use by the government or third parties authorized by the government, the following provisions shall be respected:

(a) authorization of such use shall be considered on its individual merits;

(b) such use may only be permitted if, prior to such use, the proposed user has made efforts to obtain authorization from the right holder on reasonable commercial terms and conditions and that such efforts have not been successful within a reasonable period of time. This requirement may be waived by a Member in the case of a national emergency or other circumstances of extreme urgency or in cases of public non-commercial use. In situations of national emergency or other circumstances of extreme urgency, the right holder shall, nevertheless, be notified as soon as reasonably practicable. In the case of public non-commercial use, where the government or contractor, without making a patent search, knows or has demonstrable grounds to know that a valid patent is or will be used by or for the government, the right holder shall be informed promptly;

(c) the scope and duration of such use shall be limited to the purpose for which it was authorized, and in the case of semi-conductor technology shall only be for public non-commercial use or to remedy a practice determined after judicial or administrative process to be anti-competitive;

(d)   such use shall be non-exclusive;

(e)   such use shall be non-assignable, except with that part of the enterprise or goodwill which enjoys such use;

(f)   any such use shall be authorized predominantly for the supply of the domestic market of the Member authorizing such use;

(g)   authorization for such use shall be liable, subject to adequate protection of the legitimate interests of the persons so authorized, to be terminated if and when the circumstances which led to it cease to exist and are unlikely to recur. The competent authority shall have the authority to review, upon motivated request, the continued existence of these circumstances;

(h)   the right holder shall be paid adequate remuneration in the circumstances of each case, taking into account the economic value of the authorization;

(i)   the legal validity of any decision relating to the authorization of such use shall be subject to judicial review or other independent review by a distinct higher authority in that Member;

(j)   any decision relating to the remuneration provided in respect of such use shall be subject to judicial review or other independent review by a distinct higher authority in that Member;

(k)   Members are not obliged to apply the conditions set forth in subparagraphs (b) and (f) where such use is permitted to remedy a practice determined after judicial or administrative process to be anti-competitive. The need to correct anti-competitive practices may be taken into account in determining the amount of remuneration in such cases. Competent authorities shall have the authority to refuse termination of authorization if and when the conditions which led to such authorization are likely to recur;

(l)   where such use is authorized to permit the exploitation of a patent ('the second patent") which cannot be exploited without infringing another patent ("the first patent"), the following additional conditions shall apply:

   (i)   the invention claimed in the second patent shall involve an important technical advance of considerable economic significance in relation to the invention claimed in the first patent;

   (ii)   the owner of the first patent shall be entitled to a cross-licence on reasonable terms to use the invention claimed in the second patent; and

   (iii)   the use authorized in respect of the first patent shall be non-assignable except with the assignment of the second patent.

1   "Other use" refers to use other than that allowed under Article 30.

Article 32
Revocation/Forfeiture

An opportunity for judicial review of any decision to revoke or forfeit a patent shall be available.

Article 33
Term of Protection

The term of protection available shall not end before the expiration of a period of twenty years counted from the filing date.[1]

1 It is understood that those Members which do not have a system of original grant may provide that the term of protection shall be computed from the filing date in the system of original grant.

Article 34
Process Patents: Burden of Proof

1. For the purposes of civil proceedings in respect of the infringement of the rights of the owner referred to in paragraph 1(b) of Article 28, if the subject matter of a patent is a process for obtaining a product, the judicial authorities shall have the authority to order the defendant to prove that the process to obtain an identical product is different from the patented process. Therefore, Members shall provide, in at least one of the following circumstances, that any identical product when produced without the consent of the patent owner shall, in the absence of proof to the contrary, be deemed to have been obtained by the patented process:

   (a) if the product obtained by the patented process is new;
   (b) if there is a substantial likelihood that the identical product was made by the process and the owner of the patent has been unable through reasonable efforts to determine the process actually used.

2. Any Member shall be free to provide that the burden of proof indicated in paragraph 1 shall be on the alleged infringer only if the condition referred to in subparagraph (a) is fulfilled or only if the condition referred to in subparagraph (b) is fulfilled.

3. In the adduction of proof to the contrary, the legitimate interests of defendants in protecting their manufacturing and business secrets shall be taken into account.

SECTION 6: [...]
SECTION 7: [...]
SECTION 8
CONTROL OF ANTI-COMPETITIVE PRACTICES IN
CONTRACTUAL LICENCES

Article 40

1. Members agree that some licensing practices or conditions pertaining to intellectual property rights which restrain competition may have adverse effects on trade and may impede the transfer and dissemination of technology.

2. Nothing in this Agreement shall prevent Members from specifying in their legislation licensing practices or conditions that may in particular cases constitute an abuse of intellectual property rights having an adverse effect on competition in the relevant market. As provided above, a Member may adopt, consistently with the other provisions of this Agreement, appropriate measures to prevent or control such practices, which may include for example exclusive grant back conditions, conditions preventing challenges to validity and coercive package licensing, in the light of the relevant laws and regulations of that Member.

3. Each Member shall enter, upon request, into consultations with any other Member which has cause to believe that an intellectual property right

owner that is a national or domiciliary of the Member to which the request for consultations has been addressed is undertaking practices in violation of the requesting Member's laws and regulations on the subject matter of this Section, and which wishes to secure compliance with such legislation, without prejudice to any action under the law and to the full freedom of an ultimate decision of either Member. The Member addressed shall accord full and sympathetic consideration to, and shall afford adequate opportunity for, consultations with the requesting Member, and shall cooperate through supply of publicly available non-confidential information of relevance to the matter in question and of other information available to the Member, subject to domestic law and to the conclusion of mutually satisfactory agreements concerning the safeguarding of its confidentiality by the requesting Member.

4. A Member whose nationals or domiciliaries are subject to proceedings in another Member concerning alleged violation of that other Member's laws and regulations on the subject matter of this Section shall, upon request, be granted an opportunity for consultations by the other Member under the same conditions as those foreseen in paragraph 3.

PART III
ENFORCEMENT OF INTELLECTUAL PROPERTY RIGHTS
SECTION 1
GENERAL OBLIGATIONS

Article 41

1. Members shall ensure that enforcement procedures as specified in this Part are available under their law so as to permit effective action against any act of infringement of intellectual property rights covered by this Agreement, including expeditious remedies to prevent infringements and remedies which constitute a deterrent to further infringements. These procedures shall be applied in such a manner as to avoid the creation of barriers to legitimate trade and to provide for safeguards against their abuse.

2. Procedures concerning the enforcement of intellectual property rights shall be fair and equitable. They shall not be unnecessarily complicated or costly, or entail unreasonable time-limits or unwarranted delays.

3. Decisions on the merits of a case shall preferably be in writing and reasoned. They shall be made available at least to the parties to the proceeding without undue delay. Decisions on the merits of a case shall be based only on evidence in respect of which parties were offered the opportunity to be heard.

4. Parties to a proceeding shall have an opportunity for review by a judicial authority of final administrative decisions and, subject to jurisdictional provisions in a Member's law concerning the importance of a case, of at least the legal aspects of initial judicial decisions on the merits of a case. However, there shall be no obligation to provide an opportunity for review of acquittals in criminal cases.

5. It is understood that this Part does not create any obligation to put in place a judicial system for the enforcement of intellectual property rights distinct from that for the enforcement of law in general, nor does it affect

the capacity of Members to enforce their law in general. Nothing in this Part creates any obligation with respect to the distribution of resources as between enforcement of intellectual property rights and the enforcement of law in general.

SECTION 2
CIVIL AND ADMINISTRATIVE PROCEDURES AND REMEDIES

Article 42
Fair and Equitable Procedures
Members shall make available to right holders[1] civil judicial procedures concerning the enforcement of any intellectual property right covered by this Agreement. Defendants shall have the right to written notice which is timely and contains sufficient detail, including the basis of the claims. Parties shall be allowed to be represented by independent legal counsel, and procedures shall not impose overly burdensome requirements concerning mandatory personal appearances. All parties to such procedures shall be duly entitled to substantiate their claims and to present all relevant evidence. The procedure shall provide a means to identify and protect confidential information, unless this would be contrary to existing constitutional requirements.

1   For the purpose of this Part, the term "right holder" includes federations and associations having legal standing to assert such rights.

Article 43
Evidence
1.   The judicial authorities shall have the authority, where a party has presented reasonably available evidence sufficient to support its claims and has specified evidence relevant to substantiation of its claims which lies in the control of the opposing party, to order that this evidence be produced by the opposing party, subject in appropriate cases to conditions which ensure the protection of confidential information.
2.   In cases in which a party to a proceeding voluntarily and without good reason refuses access to, or otherwise does not provide necessary information within a reasonable period, or significantly impedes a procedure relating to an enforcement action, a Member may accord judicial authorities the authority to make preliminary and final determinations, affirmative or negative, on the basis of the information presented to them, including the complaint or the allegation presented by the party adversely affected by the denial of access to information, subject to providing the parties an opportunity to be heard on the allegations or evidence.

Article 44
Injunctions
1.   The judicial authorities shall have the authority to order a party to desist from an infringement, inter alia to prevent the entry into the channels of commerce in their jurisdiction of imported goods that involve the infringement of an intellectual property right, immediately after customs clearance of such goods. Members are not obliged to accord such authority in respect of protected subject matter acquired or ordered by a person prior

to knowing or having reasonable grounds to know that dealing in such subject matter would entail the infringement of an intellectual property right.

2. Notwithstanding the other provisions of this Part and provided that the provisions of Part II specifically addressing use by governments, or by third parties authorized by a government, without the authorization of the right holder are complied with, Members may limit the remedies available against such use to payment of remuneration in accordance with subparagraph (h) of Article 31. In other cases, the remedies under this Part shall apply or, where these remedies are inconsistent with a Member's law, declaratory judgments and adequate compensation shall be available.

Article 45
Damages

1. The judicial authorities shall have the authority to order the infringer to pay the right holder damages adequate to compensate for the injury the right holder has suffered because of an infringement of that person's intellectual property right by an infringer who knowingly, or with reasonable grounds to know, engaged in infringing activity.

2. The judicial authorities shall also have the authority to order the infringer to pay the right holder expenses, which may include appropriate attorney's fees. In appropriate cases, Members may authorize the judicial authorities to order recovery of profits and/or payment of pre-established damages even where the infringer did not knowingly, or with reasonable grounds to know, engage in infringing activity.

Article 46
Other Remedies

In order to create an effective deterrent to infringement, the judicial authorities shall have the authority to order that goods that they have found to be infringing be, without compensation of any sort, disposed of outside the channels of commerce in such a manner as to avoid any harm caused to the right holder, or, unless this would be contrary to existing constitutional requirements, destroyed. The judicial authorities shall also have the authority to order that materials and implements the predominant use of which has been in the creation of the infringing goods be, without compensation of any sort, disposed of outside the channels of commerce in such a manner as to minimize the risks of further infringements. In considering such requests, the need for proportionality between the seriousness of the infringement and the remedies ordered as well as the interests of third parties shall be taken into account. In regard to counterfeit trademark goods, the simple removal of the trademark unlawfully affixed shall not be sufficient, other than in exceptional cases, to permit release of the goods into the channels of commerce.

Article 47
Right of Information

Members may provide that the judicial authorities shall have the authority, unless this would be out of proportion to the seriousness of the infringement, to order the infringer to inform the right holder of the identity of third persons involved in the production and distribution of the infringing goods or services and of their channels of distribution.

Article 48
Indemnification of the Defendant

1. The judicial authorities shall have the authority to order a party at whose request measures were taken and who has abused enforcement procedures to provide to a party wrongfully enjoined or restrained adequate compensation for the injury suffered because of such abuse. The judicial authorities shall also have the authority to order the applicant to pay the defendant expenses, which may include appropriate attorney's fees.
2. In respect of the administration of any law pertaining to the protection or enforcement of intellectual property rights, Members shall only exempt both public authorities and officials from liability to appropriate remedial measures where actions are taken or intended in good faith in the course of the administration of that law.

Article 49
Administrative Procedures

To the extent that any civil remedy can be ordered as a result of administrative procedures on the merits of a case, such procedures shall conform to principles equivalent in substance to those set forth in this Section.

SECTION 3
PROVISIONAL MEASURES

Article 50

1. The judicial authorities shall have the authority to order prompt and effective provisional measures:
    (a) to prevent an infringement of any intellectual property right from occurring, and in particular to prevent the entry into the channels of commerce in their jurisdiction of goods, including imported goods immediately after customs clearance;
    (b) to preserve relevant evidence in regard to the alleged infringement.
2. The judicial authorities shall have the authority to adopt provisional measures *in audita alter a parte* where appropriate, in particular where any delay is likely to cause irreparable harm to the right holder, or where there is a demonstrable risk of evidence being destroyed.
3. The judicial authorities shall have the authority to require the applicant to provide any reasonably available evidence in order to satisfy themselves with a sufficient degree of certainty that the applicant is the right holder and that the applicant's right is being infringed or that such infringement is imminent, and to order the applicant to provide a security or equivalent assurance sufficient to protect the defendant and to prevent abuse.
4. Where provisional measures have been adopted *in audita alter a parte*, the parties affected shall be given notice, without delay after the execution of the measures at the latest. A review, including a right to be heard, shall

take place upon request of the defendant with a view to deciding, within a reasonable period after the notification of the measures, whether these measures shall be modified, revoked or confirmed.

5. The applicant may be required to supply other information necessary for the identification of the goods concerned by the authority that will execute the provisional measures.

6. Without prejudice to paragraph 4, provisional measures taken on the basis of paragraphs 1 and 2 shall, upon request by the defendant, be revoked or otherwise cease to have effect, if proceedings leading to a decision on the merits of the case are not initiated within a reasonable period, to be determined by the judicial authority ordering the measures where a Member's law so permits or, in the absence of such a determination, not to exceed 20 working days or 31 calendar days, whichever is the longer.

7. Where the provisional measures are revoked or where they lapse due to any act or omission by the applicant, or where it is subsequently found that there has been no infringement or threat of infringement of an intellectual property right, the judicial authorities shall have the authority to order the applicant, upon request of the defendant, to provide the defendant appropriate compensation for any injury caused by these measures.

8. To the extent that any provisional measure can be ordered as a result of administrative procedures, such procedures shall conform to principles equivalent in substance to those set forth in this Section.

SECTION 4
SPECIAL REQUIREMENTS RELATED TO BORDER MEASURES[1]

Article 51
Suspension of Release by Customs Authorities

Members shall, in conformity with the provisions set out below, adopt procedures[2] to enable a right holder, who has valid grounds for suspecting that the importation of counterfeit trademark or pirated copyright goods[3] may take place, to lodge an application in writing with competent authorities, administrative or judicial, for the suspension by the customs authorities of the release into free circulation of such goods. Members may enable such an application to be made in respect of goods which involve other infringements of intellectual property rights, provided that the requirements of this Section are met. Members may also provide for corresponding procedures concerning the suspension by the customs authorities of the release of infringing goods destined for exportation from their territories.

1 Where a Member has dismantled substantially all controls over movement of goods across its border with another Member with which it forms part of a customs union, it shall not be required to apply the provisions of this Section at that border.

2 It is understood that there shall be no obligation to apply such procedures to imports of goods put on the market in another country by or with the consent of the right holder, or to goods in transit.

3 For the purposes of this Agreement:

   (a) "counterfeit trademark goods" shall mean any goods, including packaging, bearing without authorization a trademark which is identical to the trademark validly registered in respect of such goods, or which cannot be distinguished in its essential aspects from such a trademark, and which thereby infringes the rights of the owner of the trademark in question under the law of the country of importation;

(b) "pirated copyright goods" shall mean any goods which are copies made without the consent of the right holder or person duly authorized by the right holder in the country of production and which are made directly or indirectly from an article where the making of that copy would have constituted an infringement of a copyright or a related right under the law of the country of importation.

Article 52
Application

Any right holder initiating the procedures under Article 51 shall be required to provide adequate evidence to satisfy the competent authorities that, under the laws of the country of importation, there is *prima facie* an infringement of the right holder's intellectual property right and to supply a sufficiently detailed description of the goods to make them readily recognizable by the customs authorities. The competent authorities shall inform the applicant within a reasonable period whether they have accepted the application and, where determined by the competent authorities, the period for which the customs authorities will take action.

Article 53
Security or Equivalent Assurance

1. The competent authorities shall have the authority to require an applicant to provide a security or equivalent assurance sufficient to protect the defendant and the competent authorities and to prevent abuse. Such security or equivalent assurance shall not unreasonably deter recourse to these procedures.

2. Where pursuant to an application under this Section the release of goods involving industrial designs, patents, layout-designs or undisclosed information into free circulation has been suspended by customs authorities on the basis of a decision other than by a judicial or other independent authority, and the period provided for in Article 55 has expired without the granting of provisional relief by the duly empowered authority, and provided that all other conditions for importation have been complied with, the owner, importer, or consignee of such goods shall be entitled to their release on the posting of a security in an amount sufficient to protect the right holder for any infringement. Payment of such security shall not prejudice any other remedy available to the right holder, it being understood that the security shall be released if the right holder fails to pursue the right of action within a reasonable period of time.

Article 54
Notice of Suspension

The importer and the applicant shall be promptly notified of the suspension of the release of goods according to Article 51.

Article 55
Duration of Suspension

If, within a period not exceeding 10 working days after the applicant has been served notice of the suspension, the customs authorities have not been informed that proceedings leading to a decision on the merits of the case have been initiated by a party other than the defendant, or that the duly empowered authority has taken provisional measures prolonging the suspension of the release of the goods, the goods shall be released, provided that all other conditions for importation or exportation have been complied with; in appropriate cases, this time-limit may be extended by another 10 working days. If proceedings leading to a decision on the merits of the case have been initiated, a review, including a right to be heard, shall take place upon request of the defendant with a view to deciding, within a reasonable period, whether these measures shall be modified, revoked or confirmed. Notwithstanding the above, where the suspension of the release of goods is carried out or continued in accordance with a provisional judicial measure, the provisions of paragraph 6 of Article 50 shall apply.

Article 56
Indemnification of the Importer and of the Owner of the Goods
Relevant authorities shall have the authority to order the applicant to pay the importer, the consignee and the owner of the goods appropriate compensation for any injury caused to them through the wrongful detention of goods or through the detention of goods released pursuant to Article 55.

Article 57
Right of Inspection and Information
Without prejudice to the protection of confidential information, Members shall provide the competent authorities the authority to give the right holder sufficient opportunity to have any goods detained by the customs authorities inspected in order to substantiate the right holder's claims. The competent authorities shall also have authority to give the importer an equivalent opportunity to have any such goods inspected. Where a positive determination has been made on the merits of a case, Members may provide the competent authorities the authority to inform the right holder of the names and addresses of the consignor, the importer and the consignee and of the quantity of the goods in question.

Article 58
Ex Officio Action
Where Members require competent authorities to act upon their own initiative and to suspend the release of goods in respect of which they have acquired *prima facie* evidence that an intellectual property right is being infringed:

(a) the competent authorities may at any time seek from the right holder any information that may assist them to exercise these powers;
(b) the importer and the right holder shall be promptly notified of the suspension. Where the importer has lodged an appeal against the suspension with the competent authorities, the suspension shall be subject to the conditions, *mutatis mutandis,* set out at Article 55;
(c) Members shall only exempt both public authorities and officials from liability to appropriate remedial measures where actions are taken or intended in good faith.

Article 59
Remedies
Without prejudice to other rights of action open to the right holder and subject to the right of the defendant to seek review by a judicial authority, competent authorities shall have the authority to order the destruction or disposal of infringing goods in accordance with the principles set out in Article 46. In regard to counterfeit trademark goods, the authorities shall not allow the re-exportation of the infringing goods in an unaltered state or subject them to a different customs procedure, other than in exceptional circumstances.

Article 60
De Minimis Imports
Members may exclude from the application of the above provisions small quantities of goods of a non-commercial nature contained in travellers' personal luggage or sent in small consignments.

SECTION 5
CRIMINAL PROCEDURES

Article 61
Members shall provide for criminal procedures and penalties to be applied at least in cases of wilful trademark counterfeiting or copyright piracy on a commercial scale. Remedies available shall include imprisonment and/or monetary fines sufficient to provide a deterrent, consistently with the level of penalties applied for crimes of a corresponding gravity. In appropriate cases, remedies available shall also include the seizure, forfeiture and destruction of the infringing goods and of any materials and implements the predominant use of which has been in the commission of the offence. Members may provide for criminal procedures and penalties to be applied in other cases of infringement of intellectual property rights, in particular where they are committed wilfully and on a commercial scale.

PART IV
ACQUISITION AND MAINTENANCE OF INTELLECTUAL PROPERTY
RIGHTS AND RELATED INTER-PARTES PROCEDURES

Article 62
1.   Members may require, as a condition of the acquisition or maintenance of the intellectual property rights provided for under Sections 2 through 6 of Part II, compliance with reasonable procedures and formalities. Such procedures and formalities shall be consistent with the provisions of this Agreement.
2.   Where the acquisition of an intellectual property right is subject to the right being granted or registered, Members shall ensure that the procedures for grant or registration, subject to compliance with the substantive conditions for acquisition of the right, permit the granting or registration of the right within a reasonable period of time so as to avoid unwarranted curtailment of the period of protection.

Appendix 6

3. Article 4 of the Paris Convention (1967) shall apply *mutatis mutandis* to service marks.

4. Procedures concerning the acquisition or maintenance of intellectual property rights and, where a Member's law provides for such procedures, administrative revocation and *inter partes* procedures such as opposition, revocation and cancellation, shall be governed by the general principles set out in paragraphs 2 and 3 of Article 41.

5. Final administrative decisions in any of the procedures referred to under paragraph 4 shall be subject to review by a judicial or quasi-judicial authority. However, there shall be no obligation to provide an opportunity for such review of decisions in cases of unsuccessful opposition or administrative revocation, provided that the grounds for such procedures can be the subject of invalidation procedures.

PART V
DISPUTE PREVENTION AND SETTLEMENT

Article 63
Transparency

1. Laws and regulations, and final judicial decisions and administrative rulings of general application, made effective by a Member pertaining to the subject matter of this Agreement (the availability, scope, acquisition, enforcement and prevention of the abuse of intellectual property rights) shall be published, or where such publication is not practicable made publicly available, in a national language, in such a manner as to enable governments and right holders to become acquainted with them. Agreements concerning the subject matter of this Agreement which are in force between the government or a governmental agency of a Member and the government or a governmental agency of another Member shall also be published.

2. Members shall notify the laws and regulations referred to in paragraph 1 to the Council for TRIPS in order to assist that Council in its review of the operation of this Agreement. The Council shall attempt to minimize the burden on Members in carrying out this obligation and may decide to waive the obligation to notify such laws and regulations directly to the Council if consultations with WIPO on the establishment of a common register containing these laws and regulations are successful. The Council shall also consider in this connection any action required regarding notifications pursuant to the obligations under this Agreement stemming from the provisions of Article *6ter* of the Paris Convention (1967).

3. Each Member shall be prepared to supply, in response to a written request from another Member, information of the sort referred to in paragraph 1. A Member, having reason to believe that a specific judicial decision or administrative ruling or bilateral agreement in the area of intellectual property rights affects its rights under this Agreement, may also request in writing to be given access to or be informed in sufficient detail of such specific judicial decisions or administrative rulings or bilateral agreements.

4. Nothing in paragraphs 1, 2 and 3 shall require Members to disclose confidential information which would impede law enforcement or

otherwise be contrary to the public interest or would prejudice the legitimate commercial interests of particular enterprises, public or private.

Article 64
Dispute Settlement

1. The provisions of Articles XXII and XXIII of GATT 1994 as elaborated and applied by the Dispute Settlement Understanding shall apply to consultations and the settlement of disputes under this Agreement except as otherwise specifically provided herein.
2. Subparagraphs 1(b) and 1(c) of Article XXIII of GATT 1994 shall not apply to the settlement of disputes under this Agreement for a period of five years from the date of entry into force of the WTO Agreement.
3. During the time period referred to in paragraph 2, the Council for TRIPS shall examine the scope and modalities for complaints of the type provided for under subparagraphs 1(b) and 1(c) of Article XXIII of GATT 1994 made pursuant to this Agreement, and submit its recommendations to the Ministerial Conference for approval. Any decision of the Ministerial Conference to approve such recommendations or to extend the period in paragraph 2 shall be made only by consensus, and approved recommendations shall be effective for all Members without further formal acceptance process.

PART VI

TRANSITIONAL ARRANGEMENTS

Article 65
Transitional Arrangements

1. Subject to the provisions of paragraphs 2, 3 and 4, no Member shall be obliged to apply the provisions of this Agreement before the expiry of a general period of one year following the date of entry into force of the WTO Agreement.
2. A developing country Member is entitled to delay for a further period of four years the date of application, as defined in paragraph 1, of the provisions of this Agreement other than Articles 3, 4 and 5.
3. Any other Member which is in the process of transformation from a centrally-planned into a market, free-enterprise economy and which is undertaking structural reform of its intellectual property system and facing special problems in the preparation and implementation of intellectual property laws and regulations, may also benefit from a period of delay as foreseen in paragraph 2.
4. To the extent that a developing country Member is obliged by this Agreement to extend product patent protection to areas of technology not so protectable in its territory on the general date of application of this Agreement for that Member, as defined in paragraph 2, it may delay the application of the provisions on product patents of Section 5 of Part n to such areas of technology for an additional period of five years.
5. A Member availing itself of a transitional period under paragraphs 1, 2, 3 or 4 shall ensure that any changes in its laws, regulations and practice made during that period do not result in a lesser degree of consistency with the provisions of this Agreement.

Appendix 6

Article 66
Least-Developed Country Members
1. In view of the special needs and requirements of least-developed country Members, their economic, financial and administrative constraints, and their need for flexibility to create a viable technological base, such Members shall not be required to apply the provisions of this Agreement, other than Articles 3, 4 and 5, for a period of 10 years from the date of application as defined under paragraph 1 of Article 65. The Council for TRIPS shall, upon duly motivated request by a least-developed country Member, accord extensions of this period.
2. Developed country Members shall provide incentives to enterprises and institutions in their territories for the purpose of promoting and encouraging technology transfer to least-developed country Members in order to enable them to create a sound and viable technological base.

Article 67
Technical Cooperation
In order to facilitate the implementation of this Agreement, developed country Members shall provide, on request and on mutually agreed terms and conditions, technical and financial cooperation in favour of developing and least-developed country Members. Such cooperation shall include assistance in the preparation of laws and regulations on the protection and enforcement of intellectual property rights as well as on the prevention of their abuse, and shall include support regarding the establishment or reinforcement of domestic offices and agencies relevant to these matters, including the training of personnel.

PART VII
INSTITUTIONAL ARRANGEMENTS; FINAL PROVISIONS

Article 68
Council for Trade-Related Aspects of Intellectual Property Rights
The Council for TRIPS shall monitor the operation of this Agreement and, in particular, Members' compliance with their obligations hereunder, and shall afford Members the opportunity of consulting on matters relating to the trade-related aspects of intellectual property rights. It shall carry out such other responsibilities as assigned to it by the Members, and it shall, in particular, provide any assistance requested by them in the context of dispute settlement procedures. In carrying out its functions, the Council for TRIPS may consult with and seek information from any source it deems appropriate. In consultation with WIPO, the Council shall seek to establish, within one year of its first meeting, appropriate arrangements for cooperation with bodies of that Organization.

Article 69
International Cooperation
Members agree to cooperate with each other with a view to eliminating international trade in goods infringing intellectual property rights. For this purpose, they shall establish and notify contact points in their administrations and be ready to exchange information on trade in infringing goods. They shall, in particular, promote the exchange of information and cooperation between

customs authorities with regard to trade in counterfeit trademark goods and pirated copyright goods.

Article 70
Protection of Existing Subject Matter

1. This Agreement does not give rise to obligations in respect of acts which occurred before the date of application of the Agreement for the Member in question.

2. Except as otherwise provided for in this Agreement, this Agreement gives rise to obligations in respect of all subject matter existing at the date of application of this Agreement for the Member in question, and which is protected in that Member on the said date, or which meets or comes subsequently to meet the criteria for protection under the terms of this Agreement. In respect of this paragraph and paragraphs 3 and 4, copyright obligations with respect to existing works shall be solely determined under Article 18 of the Berne Convention (1971), and obligations with respect to the rights of producers of phonograms and performers in existing phonograms shall be determined solely under Article 18 of the Berne Convention (1971) as made applicable under paragraph 6 of Article 14 of this Agreement.

3. There shall be no obligation to restore protection to subject matter which on the date of application of this Agreement for the Member in question has fallen into the public domain.

4. In respect of any acts in respect of specific objects embodying protected subject matter which become infringing under the terms of legislation in conformity with this Agreement, and which were commenced, or in respect of which a significant investment was made, before the date of acceptance of the WTO Agreement by that Member, any Member may provide for a limitation of the remedies available to the right holder as to the continued performance of such acts after the date of application of this Agreement for that Member. In such cases the Member shall, however, at least provide for the payment of equitable remuneration.

5. A Member is not obliged to apply the provisions of Article 11 and of paragraph 4 of Article 14 with respect to originals or copies purchased prior to the date of application of this Agreement for that Member.

6. Members shall not be required to apply Article 31, or the requirement in paragraph 1 of Article 27 that patent rights shall be enjoyable without discrimination as to the field of technology, to use without the authorization of the right holder where authorization for such use was granted by the government before the date this Agreement became known.

7. In the case of intellectual property rights for which protection is conditional upon registration, applications for protection which are pending on the date of application of this Agreement for the Member in question shall be permitted to be amended to claim any enhanced protection provided under the provisions of this Agreement. Such amendments shall not include new matter.

8. Where a Member does not make available as of the date of entry into force of the WTO Agreement patent protection for pharmaceutical and agricultural chemical products commensurate with its obligations under Article 27, that Member shall:

(a)   notwithstanding the provisions of Part VI, provide as from the date of entry into force of the WTO Agreement a means by which applications for patents for such inventions can be filed;

(b)   apply to these applications, as of the date of application of this Agreement, the criteria for patentability as laid down in this Agreement as if those criteria were being applied on the date of filing in that Member or, where priority is available and claimed, the priority date of the application; and

(c)   provide patent protection in accordance with this Agreement as from the grant of the patent and for the remainder of the patent term, counted from the filing date in accordance with Article 33 of this Agreement, for those of these applications that meet the criteria for protection referred to in subparagraph (b).

9.   Where a product is the subject of a patent application in a Member in accordance with paragraph 8(a), exclusive marketing rights shall be granted, notwithstanding the provisions of Part VI, for a period of five years after obtaining marketing approval in that Member or until a product patent is granted or rejected in that Member, whichever period is shorter, provided that, subsequent to the entry into force of the WTO Agreement, a patent application has been filed and a patent granted for that product in another Member and marketing approval obtained in such other Member.

Article 71
Review and Amendment

1.   The Council for TRIPS shall review the implementation of this Agreement after the expiration of the transitional period referred to in paragraph 2 of Article 65. The Council shall, having regard to the experience gained in its implementation, review it two years after that date, and at identical intervals thereafter. The Council may also undertake reviews in the light of any relevant new developments which might warrant modification or amendment of this Agreement.

2.   Amendments merely serving the purpose of adjusting to higher levels of protection of intellectual property rights achieved, and in force, in other multilateral agreements and accepted under those agreements by all Members of the WTO may be referred to the Ministerial Conference for action in accordance with paragraph 6 of Article X of the WTO Agreement on the basis of a consensus proposal from the Council for TRIPS.

Article 72
Reservations

Reservations may not be entered in respect of any of the provisions of this Agreement without the consent of the other Members.

Article 73
Security Exceptions

Nothing in this Agreement shall be construed:

(a)   to require a Member to furnish any information the disclosure of which it considers contrary to its essential security interests; or

(b) to prevent a Member from taking any action which it considers necessary for the protection of its essential security interests;

    (i) relating to fissionable materials or the materials from which they are derived;

    (ii) relating to the traffic in arms, ammunition and implements of war and to such traffic in other goods and materials as is carried on directly or indirectly for the purpose of supplying a military establishment;

    (iii) taken in time of war or other emergency in international relations; or

(c) to prevent a Member from taking any action in pursuance of its obligations under the United Nations Charter for the maintenance of international peace and security.

Appendix 6

Convention on the Grant of European Patents
(EUROPEAN PATENT CONVENTION 2000)
as adopted by decision of the Administrative Council of
European Patent Convention 2000 28 June 2001 (extracts)

PART I
GENERAL AND INSTITUTIONAL PROVISIONS
CHAPTER I
GENERAL PROVISIONS

Article 1
European law for the grant of patents
A system of law, common to the Contracting States, for the grant of patents for invention is established by this Convention.

Article 2 European patent
(1) Patents granted under this Convention shall be called European patents.
(2) The European patent shall, in each of the Contracting States for which it is granted, have the effect of and be subject to the same conditions as a national patent granted by that State, unless this Convention provides otherwise.

Article 3
Territorial effect
The grant of a European patent may be requested for one or more of the Contracting States.

Article 4
European Patent Organisation
(1) A European Patent Organisation, hereinafter referred to as the Organisation, is established by this Convention. It shall have administrative and financial autonomy.
(2) The organs of the Organisation shall be:

   (a)   the European Patent Office;
   (b)   the Administrative Council.

(3) The task of the Organisation shall be to grant European patents. This shall be carried out by the European Patent Office supervised by the Administrative Council.

Article 4a
Conference of ministers of the Contracting States
A conference of ministers of the Contracting States responsible for patent matters shall meet at least every five years to discuss issues pertaining to the Organisation and to the European patent system.

PART II
SUBSTANTIVE PATENT LAW
CHAPTER I
PATENTABILITY

Article 52
Patentable inventions

(1) European patents shall be granted for any inventions, in all fields of technology, provided that they are new, involve an inventive step and are susceptible of industrial application.

(2) The following in particular shall not be regarded as inventions within the meaning of paragraph 1:

    (a) discoveries, scientific theories and mathematical methods;

    (b) aesthetic creations;

    (c) schemes, rules and methods for performing mental acts, playing games or doing business, and programs for computers;

    (d) presentations of information.

(3) Paragraph 2 shall exclude the patentability of the subject-matter or activities referred to therein only to the extent to which a European patent application or European patent relates to such subject-matter or activities as such.

Article 53
Exceptions to patentability

European patents shall not be granted in respect of:

(a) inventions the commercial exploitation of which would be contrary to "ordre public" or morality; such exploitation shall not be deemed to be so contrary merely because it is prohibited by law or regulation in some or all of the Contracting States;

(b) plant or animal varieties or essentially biological processes for the production of plants or animals; this provision shall not apply to microbiological processes or the products thereof;

(c) methods for treatment of the human or animal body by surgery or therapy and diagnostic methods practised on the human or animal body; this provision shall not apply to products, in particular substances or compositions, for use in any of these methods.

Article 54
Novelty

(1) An invention shall be considered to be new if it does not form part of the state of the art.

(2) The state of the art shall be held to comprise everything made available to the public by means of a written or oral description, by use, or in any other way, before the date of filing of the European patent application.

(3) Additionally, the content of European patent applications as filed, the dates of filing of which are prior to the date referred to in paragraph 2 and which were published on or after that date, shall be considered as comprised in the state of the art.

Appendix 6

(4) Paragraphs 2 and 3 shall not exclude the patentability of any substance or composition, comprised in the state of the art, for use in a method referred to in Article 53(c), provided that its use for any such method is not comprised in the state of the art.

(5) Paragraphs 2 and 3 shall also not exclude the patentability of any substance or composition referred to in paragraph 4 for any specific use in a method referred to in Article 53(c), provided that such use is not comprised in the state of the art.

Article 55
Non-prejudicial disclosures

(1) For the application of Article 54, a disclosure of the invention shall not be taken into consideration if it occurred no earlier than six months preceding the filing of the European patent application and if it was due to, or in consequence of:

   (a) an evident abuse in relation to the applicant or his legal predecessor, or
   (b) the fact that the applicant or his legal predecessor has displayed the invention at an official, or officially recognised, international exhibition falling within the terms of the Convention on international exhibitions signed at Paris on 22 November 1928 and last revised on 30 November 1972.

(2) In the case of paragraph 1(b), paragraph 1 shall apply only if the applicant states, when filing the European patent application, that the invention has been so displayed and files a supporting certificate within the time limit and under the conditions laid down in the Implementing Regulations.

Article 56
Inventive step

An invention shall be considered as involving an inventive step if, having regard to the state of the art, it is not obvious to a person skilled in the art. If the state of the art also includes documents within the meaning of Article 54, paragraph 3, these documents shall not be considered in deciding whether there has been an inventive step.

Article 57
Industrial application

An invention shall be considered as susceptible of industrial application if it can be made or used in any kind of industry, including agriculture.

CHAPTER II
PERSONS ENTITLED TO APPLY FOR AND OBTAIN A EUROPEAN
PATENT — MENTION OF THE INVENTOR

Article 58
Entitlement to file a European patent application
A European patent application may be filed by any natural or legal person, or any body equivalent to a legal person by virtue of the law governing it.

Article 59
Multiple applicants
A European patent application may also be filed either by joint applicants or by two or more applicants designating different Contracting States.

Article 60
Right to a European patent
(1) The right to a European patent shall belong to the inventor or his successor in title. If the inventor is an employee, the right to a European patent shall be determined in accordance with the law of the State in which the employee is mainly employed; if the State in which the employee is mainly employed cannot be determined, the law to be applied shall be that of the State in which the employer has the place of business to which the employee is attached.
(2) If two or more persons have made an invention independently of each other, the right to a European patent therefore shall belong to the person whose European patent application has the earliest date of filing, provided that this first application has been published.
(3) In proceedings before the European Patent Office, the applicant shall be deemed to be entitled to exercise the right to a European patent.

Article 61
European patent applications filed by non-entitled persons
(1) If by a final decision it is adjudged that a person other than the applicant is entitled to the grant of the European patent, that person may, in accordance with the Implementing Regulations:

   (a) prosecute the European patent application as his own application in place of the applicant;
   (b) file a new European patent application in respect of the same invention; or
   (c) request that the European patent application be refused.

(2) Article 76, paragraph 1, shall apply *mutatis mutandis* to a new European patent application filed under paragraph 1(b).

Article 62
Right of the inventor to be mentioned
The inventor shall have the right, *vis-à-vis* the applicant for or proprietor of a European patent, to be mentioned as such before the European Patent Office.

Appendix 6

CHAPTER III

EFFECTS OF THE EUROPEAN PATENT AND THE EUROPEAN
PATENT APPLICATION

Article 63
Term of the European patent

(1) The term of the European patent shall be 20 years from the date of filing of the application.

(2) Nothing in the preceding paragraph shall limit the right of a Contracting State to extend the term of a European patent, or to grant corresponding protection which follows immediately on expiry of the term of the patent, under the same conditions as those applying to national patents:

(a) in order to take account of a state of war or similar emergency conditions affecting that State;

(b) if the subject-matter of the European patent is a product or a process for manufacturing a product or a use of a product which has to undergo an administrative authorisation procedure required by law before it can be put on the market in that State.

(3) Paragraph 2 shall apply *mutatis mutandis* to European patents granted jointly for a group of Contracting States in accordance with Article 142.

(4) A Contracting State which makes provision for extension of the term or corresponding protection under paragraph 2(b) may, in accordance with an agreement concluded with the Organisation, entrust to the European Patent Office tasks associated with implementation of the relevant provisions.

Article 64
Rights conferred by a European patent

(1) A European patent shall, subject to the provisions of paragraph 2, confer on its proprietor from the date on which the mention of its grant is published in the European Patent Bulletin, in each Contracting State in respect of which it is granted, the same rights as would be conferred by a national patent granted in that State.

(2) If the subject-matter of the European patent is a process, the protection conferred by the patent shall extend to the products directly obtained by such process.

(3) Any infringement of a European patent shall be dealt with by national law.

Article 65
Translation of the European patent

(1) Any Contracting State may, if the European patent as granted, amended or limited by the European Patent Office is not drawn up in one of its official languages, prescribe that the proprietor of the patent shall supply to its central industrial property office a translation of the patent as granted, amended or limited in one of its official languages at his option or, where that State has prescribed the use of one specific official language, in that language. The period for supplying the translation shall end three months after the date on which the mention of the grant, maintenance in amended form or limitation of the European patent is published in the European Patent Bulletin, unless the State concerned prescribes a longer period.

(2) Any Contracting State which has adopted provisions pursuant to paragraph 1 may prescribe that the proprietor of the patent must pay all or part of the costs of publication of such translation within a period laid down by that State.

(3) Any Contracting State may prescribe that in the event of failure to observe the provisions adopted in accordance with paragraphs 1 and 2, the European patent shall be deemed to be void ab initio in that State.

Article 66
Equivalence of European filing with national filing
A European patent application which has been accorded a date of filing shall, in the designated Contracting States, be equivalent to a regular national filing, where appropriate with the priority claimed for the European patent application.

Article 67
Rights conferred by a European patent application after publication
(1) A European patent application shall, from the date of its publication, provisionally confer upon the applicant the protection provided for by Article 64, in the Contracting States designated in the application.

(2) Any Contracting State may prescribe that a European patent application shall not confer such protection as is conferred by Article 64. However, the protection attached to the publication of the European patent application may not be less than that which the laws of the State concerned attach to the compulsory publication of unexamined national patent applications. In any event, each State shall ensure at least that, from the date of publication of a European patent application, the applicant can claim compensation reasonable in the circumstances from any person who has used the invention in that State in circumstances where that person would be liable under national law for infringement of a national patent.

(3) Any Contracting State which does not have as an official language the language of the proceedings may prescribe that provisional protection in accordance with paragraphs 1 and 2 above shall not be effective until such time as a translation of the claims in one of its official languages at the option of the applicant or, where that State has prescribed the use of one specific official language, in that language:

(a) has been made available to the public in the manner prescribed by national law, or

(b) has been communicated to the person using the invention in the said State.

(4) The European patent application shall be deemed never to have had the effects set out in paragraphs 1 and 2 when it has been withdrawn, deemed to be withdrawn or finally refused. The same shall apply in respect of the effects of the European patent application in a Contracting State the designation of which is withdrawn or deemed to be withdrawn.

Article 68
Effect of revocation or limitation of the European patent
The European patent application and the resulting European patent shall be deemed not to have had, from the outset, the effects specified in Articles 64

and 67, to the extent that the patent has been revoked or limited in opposition, limitation or revocation proceedings.

Article 69
Extent of protection

(1) The extent of the protection conferred by a European patent or a European patent application shall be determined by the claims. Nevertheless, the description and drawings shall be used to interpret the claims.

(2) For the period up to grant of the European patent, the extent of the protection conferred by the European patent application shall be determined by the claims contained in the application as published. However, the European patent as granted or as amended in opposition, limitation or revocation proceedings shall determine retroactively the protection conferred by the application, in so far as such protection is not thereby extended.

Article 70
Authentic text of a European patent application or European patent

(1) The text of a European patent application or a European patent in the language of the proceedings shall be the authentic text in any proceedings before the European Patent Office and in any Contracting State.

(2) If, however, the European patent application has been filed in a language which is not an official language of the European Patent Office, that text shall be the application as filed within the meaning of this Convention.

(3) Any Contracting State may provide that a translation into one of its official languages, as prescribed by it according to this Convention, shall in that State be regarded as authentic, except for revocation proceedings, in the event of the European patent application or European patent in the language of the translation conferring protection which is narrower than that conferred by it in the language of the proceedings.

(4) Any Contracting State which adopts a provision under paragraph 3:

(a) shall allow the applicant for or proprietor of the patent to file a corrected translation of the European patent application or European patent. Such corrected translation shall not have any legal effect until any conditions established by the Contracting State under Article 65, paragraph 2, or Article 67, paragraph 3, have been complied with;

(b) may prescribe that any person who, in that State, in good faith has used or has made effective and serious preparations for using an invention the use of which would not constitute infringement of the application or patent in the original translation, may, after the corrected translation takes effect, continue such use in the course of his business or for the needs thereof without payment.

CHAPTER IV

THE EUROPEAN PATENT APPLICATION AS AN OBJECT OF PROPERTY

Article 71
Transfer and constitution of rights

A European patent application may be transferred or give rise to rights for one or more of the designated Contracting States.

Article 72
Assignment
An assignment of a European patent application shall be made in writing and shall require the signature of the parties to the contract.

Article 73
Contractual licensing
A European patent application may be licensed in whole or in part for the whole or part of the territories of the designated Contracting States.

Article 74
Law applicable
Unless this Convention provides otherwise, the European patent application as an object of property shall, in each designated Contracting State and with effect for such State, be subject to the law applicable in that State to national patent applications.

PART III
THE EUROPEAN PATENT APPLICATION
CHAPTER I FILING AND REQUIREMENTS OF THE EUROPEAN
PATENT APPLICATION

Article 75
Filing of a European patent application
(1) A European patent application may be filed:

    (a) with the European Patent Office, or

    (b) if the law of a Contracting State so permits, and subject to Article 76, paragraph 1, with the central industrial property office or other competent authority of that State. Any application filed in this way shall have the same effect as if it had been filed on the same date with the European Patent Office.

(2) Paragraph 1 shall not preclude the application of legislative or regulatory provisions which, in any Contracting State:

    (a) govern inventions which, owing to the nature of their subject-matter, may not be communicated abroad without the prior authorisation of the competent authorities of that State, or

    (b) prescribe that any application is to be filed initially with a national authority, or make direct filing with another authority subject to prior authorisation.

Article 76
European divisional applications
(1) A European divisional application shall be filed directly with the European Patent Office in accordance with the Implementing Regulations. It may be filed only in respect of subject-matter which does not extend beyond the content of the earlier application as filed; in so far as this requirement is complied with, the divisional application shall be deemed to have been filed

on the date of filing of the earlier application and shall enjoy any right of priority.

(2) All the Contracting States designated in the earlier application at the time of filing of a European divisional application shall be deemed to be designated in the divisional application.

Article 77
Forwarding of European patent applications

(1) The central industrial property office of a Contracting State shall forward to the European Patent Office any European patent application filed with it or any other competent authority in that State, in accordance with the Implementing Regulations.

(2) A European patent application the subject of which has been made secret shall not be forwarded to the European Patent Office.

(3) A European patent application not forwarded to the European Patent Office in due time shall be deemed to be withdrawn.

Article 78
Requirements of a European patent application

(1) A European patent application shall contain:

    (a) a request for the grant of a European patent;
    (b) a description of the invention;
    (c) one or more claims;
    (d) any drawings referred to in the description or the claims;
    (e) an abstract,

and satisfy the requirements laid down in the Implementing Regulations.

(2) A European patent application shall be subject to the payment of the filing fee and the search fee. If the filing fee or the search fee is not paid in due time, the application shall be deemed to be withdrawn.

Article 79
Designation of Contracting States

(1) All the Contracting States party to this Convention at the time of filing of the European patent application shall be deemed to be designated in the request for grant of a European patent.

(2) The designation of a Contracting State may be subject to the payment of a designation fee.

(3) The designation of a Contracting State may be withdrawn at any time up to the grant of the European patent.

Article 80
Date of filing

The date of filing of a European patent application shall be the date on which the requirements laid down in the Implementing Regulations are fulfilled.

Article 81
Designation of the inventor

The European patent application shall designate the inventor. If the applicant is not the inventor or is not the sole inventor, the designation shall contain a statement indicating the origin of the right to the European patent.

Article 82
Unity of invention
The European patent application shall relate to one invention only or to a group of inventions so linked as to form a single general inventive concept.

Article 83
Disclosure of the invention
The European patent application shall disclose the invention in a manner sufficiently clear and complete for it to be carried out by a person skilled in the art.

Article 84
Claims
The claims shall define the matter for which protection is sought. They shall be clear and concise and be supported by the description.

Article 85
Abstract
The abstract shall serve the purpose of technical information only; it may not be taken into account for any other purpose, in particular for interpreting the scope of the protection sought or applying Article 54, paragraph 3.

Article 86
Renewal fees for the European patent application
(1) Renewal fees for the European patent application shall be paid to the European Patent Office in accordance with the Implementing Regulations. These fees shall be due in respect of the third year and each subsequent year, calculated from the date of filing of the application. If a renewal fee is not paid in due time, the application shall be deemed to be withdrawn.
(2) The obligation to pay renewal fees shall terminate with the payment of the renewal fee due in respect of the year in which the mention of the grant of the European patent is published in the European Patent Bulletin.

CHAPTER II
PRIORITY

Article 87
Priority right
(1) Any person who has duly filed, in or for

    (a) any State party to the Paris Convention for the Protection of Industrial Property or
    (b) any Member of the World Trade Organization,

an application for a patent, a utility model or a utility certificate, or his successor in title, shall enjoy, for the purpose of filing a European patent application in respect of the same invention, a right of priority during a period of twelve months from the date of filing of the first application.

(2) Every filing that is equivalent to a regular national filing under the national law of the State where it was made or under bilateral or multilateral agreements, including this Convention, shall be recognised as giving rise to a right of priority.

(3) A regular national filing shall mean any filing that is sufficient to establish the date on which the application was filed, whatever the outcome of the application may be.

(4) A subsequent application in respect of the same subject-matter as a previous first application and filed in or for the same State shall be considered as the first application for the purposes of determining priority, provided that, at the date of filing the subsequent application, the previous application has been withdrawn, abandoned or refused, without being open to public inspection and without leaving any rights outstanding, and has not served as a basis for claiming a right of priority. The previous application may not thereafter serve as a basis for claiming a right of priority.

(5) If the first filing has been made with an industrial property authority which is not subject to the Paris Convention for the Protection of Industrial Property or the Agreement Establishing the World Trade Organization, paragraphs 1 to 4 shall apply if that authority, according to a communication issued by the President of the European Patent Office, recognises that a first filing made with the European Patent Office gives rise to a right of priority under conditions and with effects equivalent to those laid down in the Paris Convention.

Article 88
Claiming priority

(1) An applicant desiring to take advantage of the priority of a previous application shall file a declaration of priority and any other document required, in accordance with the Implementing Regulations.

(2) Multiple priorities may be claimed in respect of a European patent application, notwithstanding the fact that they originated in different countries. Where appropriate, multiple priorities may be claimed for any one claim. Where multiple priorities are claimed, time limits which run from the date of priority shall run from the earliest date of priority.

(3) If one or more priorities are claimed in respect of a European patent application, the right of priority shall cover only those elements of the European patent application which are included in the application or applications whose priority is claimed.

(5) If certain elements of the invention for which priority is claimed do not appear among the claims formulated in the previous application, priority may nonetheless be granted, provided that the documents of the previous application as a whole specifically disclose such elements.

Article 89
Effect of priority right

The right of priority shall have the effect that the date of priority shall count as the date of filing of the European patent application for the purposes of Article 54, paragraphs 2 and 3, and Article 60, paragraph 2.

PART IV
PROCEDURE UP TO GRANT

Article 90
Examination on filing and examination as to formal requirements

(1) The European Patent Office shall examine, in accordance with the Implementing Regulations, whether the application satisfies the requirements for the accordance of a date of filing.

(2) If a date of filing cannot be accorded following the examination under paragraph 1, the application shall not be dealt with as a European patent application.

(3) If the European patent application has been accorded a date of filing, the European Patent Office shall examine, in accordance with the Implementing Regulations, whether the requirements in Articles 14, 78 and 81, and, where applicable, Article 88, paragraph 1, and Article 133, paragraph 2, as well as any other requirement laid down in the Implementing Regulations, have been satisfied.

(4) Where the European Patent Office in carrying out the examination under paragraphs 1 or 3 notes that there are deficiencies which may be corrected, it shall give the applicant an opportunity to correct them.

(5) If any deficiency noted in the examination under paragraph 3 is not corrected, the European patent application shall be refused unless a different legal consequence is provided for by this Convention. Where the deficiency concerns the right of priority, this right shall be lost for the application.

Article 91
Examination as to formal requirements (deleted)

Article 92
Drawing up of the European search report

The European Patent Office shall, in accordance with the Implementing Regulations, draw up and publish a European search report in respect of the European patent application on the basis of the claims, with due regard to the description and any drawings.

Article 93
Publication of the European patent application

(1) The European Patent Office shall publish the European patent application as soon as possible

    (a) after the expiry of a period of eighteen months from the date of filing or, if priority has been claimed, from the date of priority, or

    (b) at the request of the applicant, before the expiry of that period.

(2) The European patent application shall be published at the same time as the specification of the European patent when the decision to grant the patent becomes effective before the expiry of the period referred to in paragraph

Appendix 6

Article 94
Examination of the European patent application

(1) The European Patent Office shall, in accordance with the Implementing Regulations, examine on request whether the European patent application and the invention to which it relates meet the requirements of this Convention. The request shall not be deemed to be filed until the examination fee has been paid.

(2) If no request for examination has been made in due time, the application shall be deemed to be withdrawn.

(3) If the examination reveals that the application or the invention to which it relates does not meet the requirements of this Convention, the Examining Division shall invite the applicant, as often as necessary, to file his observations and, subject to Article 123, paragraph 1, to amend the application.

(4) If the applicant fails to reply in due time to any communication from the Examining Division, the application shall be deemed to be withdrawn.

Article 95
Extension of the period within which requests for examination may be filed (deleted)

Article 96
Examination of the European patent application (deleted)

Article 97
Grant or refusal

(1) If the Examining Division is of the opinion that the European patent application and the invention to which it relates meet the requirements of this Convention, it shall decide to grant a European patent, provided that the conditions laid down in the Implementing Regulations are fulfilled.

(2) If the Examining Division is of the opinion that the European patent application or the invention to which it relates does not meet the requirements of this Convention, it shall refuse the application unless this Convention provides for a different legal consequence.

(3) The decision to grant a European patent shall take effect on the date on which the mention of the grant is published in the European Patent Bulletin.

Article 98
Publication of the specification of the European patent

The European Patent Office shall publish the specification of the European patent as soon as possible after the mention of the grant of the European patent has been published in the European Patent Bulletin.

PART V
OPPOSITION AND LIMITATION PROCEDURE

Article 99
Opposition

(1) Within nine months of the publication of the mention of the grant of the European patent in the European Patent Bulletin, any person may give notice to the European Patent Office of opposition to that patent, in accordance with the Implementing Regulations. Notice of opposition shall not be deemed to have been filed until the opposition fee has been paid.

(2) The opposition shall apply to the European patent in all the Contracting States in which that patent has effect.

(3) Opponents shall be parties to the opposition proceedings as well as the proprietor of the patent.

(4) Where a person provides evidence that in a Contracting State, following a final decision, he has been entered in the patent register of such State instead of the previous proprietor, such person shall, at his request, replace the previous proprietor in respect of such State. Notwithstanding Article 118, the previous proprietor and the person making the request shall not be regarded as joint proprietors unless both so request.

Article 100
Grounds for opposition

Opposition may only be filed on the grounds that:

(a) the subject-matter of the European patent is not patentable under Articles 52 to 57;

(b) the European patent does not disclose the invention in a manner sufficiently clear and complete for it to be carried out by a person skilled in the art;

(c) the subject-matter of the European patent extends beyond the content of the application as filed, or, if the patent was granted on a divisional application or on a new application filed under Article 61, beyond the content of the earlier application as filed.

Article 101
Examination of the opposition — Revocation or maintenance of the European patent

(1) If the opposition is admissible, the Opposition Division shall examine, in accordance with the Implementing Regulations, whether at least one ground for opposition under Article 100 prejudices the maintenance of the European patent. During this examination, the Opposition Division shall invite the parties, as often as necessary, to file observations on communications from another party or issued by itself.

(2) If the Opposition Division is of the opinion that at least one ground for opposition prejudices the maintenance of the European patent, it shall revoke the patent. Otherwise, it shall reject the opposition.

(3) If the Opposition Division is of the opinion that, taking into consideration the amendments made by the proprietor of the European patent during the opposition proceedings, the patent and the invention to which it relates

(a) meet the requirements of this Convention, it shall decide to maintain
the patent as amended, provided that the conditions laid down in the
Implementing Regulations are fulfilled;

(b) do not meet the requirements of this Convention, it shall revoke the
patent.

Article 102
Revocation or maintenance of the European patent (deleted)

Article 103
Publication of a new specification of the European patent
If the European patent is maintained as amended under Article 101,
paragraph 3(a), the European Patent Office shall publish a new specification
of the European patent as soon as possible after the mention of the opposition
decision has been published in the European Patent Bulletin.

Article 104
Costs
(1) Each party to the opposition proceedings shall bear the costs it has incurred,
unless the Opposition Division, for reasons of equity, orders, in accordance
with the Implementing Regulations, a different apportionment of costs.

(2) The procedure for fixing costs shall be laid down in the Implementing
Regulations.

(3) Any final decision of the European Patent Office fixing the amount of
costs shall be dealt with, for the purpose of enforcement in the Contracting
States, in the same way as a final decision given by a civil court of the State
in which enforcement is to take place. Verification of such decision shall be
limited to its authenticity.

Article 105
Intervention of the assumed infringer
(1) Any third party may, in accordance with the Implementing Regulations,
intervene in opposition proceedings after the opposition period has expired,
if the third party proves that

(a) proceedings for infringement of the same patent have been instituted
against him, or

(b) following a request of the proprietor of the patent to cease alleged
infringement, the third party has instituted proceedings for a ruling
that he is not infringing the patent.

(2) An admissible intervention shall be treated as an opposition.

Article 105a
Request for limitation or revocation
(1) At the request of the proprietor, the European patent may be revoked or be
limited by an amendment of the claims. The request shall be filed with the
European Patent Office in accordance with the Implementing Regulations.
It shall not be deemed to have been filed until the limitation or revocation
fee has been paid.

(2) The request may not be filed while opposition proceedings in respect of the European patent are pending.

Article 105b
Limitation or revocation of the European patent

(1) The European Patent Office shall examine whether the requirements laid down in the Implementing Regulations for limiting or revoking the European patent have been met.

(2) If the European Patent Office considers that the request for limitation or revocation of the European patent meets these requirements, it shall decide to limit or revoke the European patent in accordance with the Implementing Regulations. Otherwise, it shall reject the request.

(3) The decision to limit or revoke the European patent shall apply to the European patent in all the Contracting States in respect of which it has been granted. It shall take effect on the date on which the mention of the decision is published in the European Patent Bulletin.

Article 105c
Publication of the amended specification of the European patent

If the European patent is limited under Article 105b, paragraph 2, the European Patent Office shall publish the amended specification of the European patent as soon as possible after the mention of the limitation has been published in the European Patent Bulletin.

PART VI
APPEALS PROCEDURE

Article 106
Decisions subject to appeal

(1) An appeal shall lie from decisions of the Receiving Section, Examining Divisions, Opposition Divisions and the Legal Division. It shall have suspensive effect.

(2) A decision which does not terminate proceedings as regards one of the parties can only be appealed together with the final decision, unless the decision allows a separate appeal.

(3) The right to file an appeal against decisions relating to the apportionment or fixing of costs in opposition proceedings may be restricted in the Implementing Regulations.

Article 107
Persons entitled to appeal and to be parties to appeal proceedings

Any party to proceedings adversely affected by a decision may appeal. Any other parties to the proceedings shall be parties to the appeal proceedings as of right.

Article 108
Time limit and form

Notice of appeal shall be filed, in accordance with the Implementing Regulations, at the European Patent Office within two months of notification of the decision. Notice of appeal shall not be deemed to have been filed until the fee for appeal has been paid. Within four months of notification of the decision, a statement setting out the grounds of appeal shall be filed in accordance with the Implementing Regulations.

Article 109
Interlocutory revision

(1) If the department whose decision is contested considers the appeal to be admissible and well founded, it shall rectify its decision. This shall not apply where the appellant is opposed by another party to the proceedings.

(2) If the appeal is not allowed within three months of receipt of the statement of grounds, it shall be remitted to the Board of Appeal without delay, and without comment as to its merit.

Article 110
Examination of appeals

If the appeal is admissible, the Board of Appeal shall examine whether the appeal is allowable. The examination of the appeal shall be conducted in accordance with the Implementing Regulations.

Article 111
Decision in respect of appeals

(1) Following the examination as to the allowability of the appeal, the Board of Appeal shall decide on the appeal. The Board of Appeal may either exercise any power within the competence of the department which was responsible for the decision appealed or remit the case to that department for further prosecution.

(2) If the Board of Appeal remits the case for further prosecution to the department whose decision was appealed, that department shall be bound by the ratio decidendi of the Board of Appeal, in so far as the facts are the same. If the decision under appeal was taken by the Receiving Section, the Examining Division shall also be bound by the ratio decidendi of the Board of Appeal.

Article 112
Decision or opinion of the Enlarged Board of Appeal

(1) In order to ensure uniform application of the law, or if a point of law of fundamental importance arises:

(a) the Board of Appeal shall, during proceedings on a case and either of its own motion or following a request from a party to the appeal, refer any question to the Enlarged Board of Appeal if it considers that a decision is required for the above purposes. If the Board of Appeal rejects the request, it shall give the reasons in its final decision;

(b) the President of the European Patent Office may refer a point of law to the Enlarged Board of Appeal where two Boards of Appeal have given different decisions on that question.

(2) In the cases referred to in paragraph 1(a) the parties to the appeal proceedings shall be parties to the proceedings before the Enlarged Board of Appeal.

(3)   The decision of the Enlarged Board of Appeal referred to in paragraph 1(a) shall be binding on the Board of Appeal in respect of the appeal in question.

Article 112a
Petition for review by the Enlarged Board of Appeal

(1)   Any party to appeal proceedings adversely affected by the decision of the Board of Appeal may file a petition for review of the decision by the Enlarged Board of Appeal.

(2)   The petition may only be filed on the grounds that:

(a)   a member of the Board of Appeal took part in the decision in breach of Article 24, paragraph 1, or despite being excluded pursuant to a decision under Article 24, paragraph 4;

(b)   the Board of Appeal included a person not appointed as a member of the Boards of Appeal;

(c)   a fundamental violation of Article 113 occurred;

(d)   any other fundamental procedural defect defined in the Implementing Regulations occurred in the appeal proceedings; or

(e)   a criminal act established under the conditions laid down in the Implementing Regulations may have had an impact on the decision.

(3)   The petition for review shall not have suspensive effect.

(4)   The petition for review shall be filed in a reasoned statement, in accordance with the Implementing Regulations. If based on paragraph 2(a) to (d), the petition shall be filed within two months of notification of the decision of the Board of Appeal. If based on paragraph 2(e), the petition shall be filed within two months of the date on which the criminal act has been established and in any event no later than five years from notification of the decision of the Board of Appeal. The petition shall not be deemed to have been filed until after the prescribed fee has been paid.

(5)   The Enlarged Board of Appeal shall examine the petition for review in accordance with the Implementing Regulations. If the petition is allowable, the Enlarged Board of Appeal shall set aside the decision and shall re-open proceedings before the Boards of Appeal in accordance with the Implementing Regulations.

(6)   Any person who, in a designated Contracting State, has in good faith used or made effective and serious preparations for using an invention which is the subject of a published European patent application or a European patent in the period between the decision of the Board of Appeal and publication in the European Patent Bulletin of the mention of the decision of the Enlarged Board of Appeal on the petition, may without payment continue such use in the course of his business or for the needs thereof.

PART VII
COMMON PROVISIONS
CHAPTER I
COMMON PROVISIONS GOVERNING
PROCEDURE

Article 113
Right to be heard and basis of decisions

(1) The decisions of the European Patent Office may only be based on grounds or evidence on which the parties concerned have had an opportunity to present their comments.

(2) The European Patent Office shall examine, and decide upon, the European patent application or the European patent only in the text submitted to it, or agreed, by the applicant or the proprietor of the patent.

Article 114
Examination by the European Patent Office of its own motion

(1) In proceedings before it, the European Patent Office shall examine the facts of its own motion; it shall not be restricted in this examination to the facts, evidence and arguments provided by the parties and the relief sought.

(2) The European Patent Office may disregard facts or evidence which are not submitted in due time by the parties concerned.

Article 115
Observations by third parties

In proceedings before the European Patent Office, following the publication of the European patent application, any third party may, in accordance with the Implementing Regulations, present observations concerning the patentability of the invention to which the application or patent relates. That person shall not be a party to the proceedings.

Article 116
Oral proceedings

(1) Oral proceedings shall take place either at the instance of the European Patent Office if it considers this to be expedient or at the request of any party to the proceedings. However, the European Patent Office may reject a request for further oral proceedings before the same department where the parties and the subject of the proceedings are the same.

(2) Nevertheless, oral proceedings shall take place before the Receiving Section at the request of the applicant only where the Receiving Section considers this to be expedient or where it intends to refuse the European patent application.

(3) Oral proceedings before the Receiving Section, the Examining Divisions and the Legal Division shall not be public.

(4) Oral proceedings, including delivery of the decision, shall be public, as regards the Boards of Appeal and the Enlarged Board of Appeal,

after publication of the European patent application, and also before the Opposition Divisions, in so far as the department before which the proceedings are taking place does not decide otherwise in cases where admission of the public could have serious and unjustified disadvantages, in particular for a party to the proceedings.

Article 117
Means and taking of evidence

(1) In proceedings before the European Patent Office the means of giving or obtaining evidence shall include the following:

    (a) hearing the parties;

    (b) requests for information;

    (c) production of documents;

    (d) hearing witnesses;

    (e) opinions by experts;

    (f) inspection;

    (g) sworn statements in writing.

(2) The procedure for taking such evidence shall be laid down in the Implementing Regulations.

Article 118
Unity of the European patent application or European patent

Where the applicants for or proprietors of a European patent are not the same in respect of different designated Contracting States, they shall be regarded as joint applicants or proprietors for the purposes of proceedings before the European Patent Office. The unity of the application or patent in these proceedings shall not be affected; in particular the text of the application or patent shall be uniform for all designated Contracting States, unless this Convention provides otherwise.

Article 119
Notification

Decisions, summonses, notices and communications shall be notified by the European Patent Office of its own motion in accordance with the Implementing Regulations. Notification may, where exceptional circumstances so require, be effected through the intermediary of the central industrial property offices of the Contracting States.

Article 120
Time limits

The Implementing Regulations shall specify:

    (a) the time limits which are to be observed in proceedings before the European Patent Office and are not fixed by this Convention;

    (b) the manner of computation of time limits and the conditions under which time limits may be extended;

(c)   the minima and maxima for time limits to be determined by the European Patent Office.

Article 121
Further processing of the European patent application
(1)   If an applicant fails to observe a time limit vis-à-vis the European Patent Office, he may request further processing of the European patent application.
(2)   The European Patent Office shall grant the request, provided that the requirements laid down in the Implementing Regulations are met. Otherwise, it shall reject the request.
(3)   If the request is granted, the legal consequences of the failure to observe the time limit shall be deemed not to have ensued.
(4)   Further processing shall be ruled out in respect of the time limits in Article 87, paragraph 1, Article 108 and Article 112a, paragraph 4, as well as the time limits for requesting further processing or re-establishment of rights. The Implementing Regulations may rule out further processing for other time limits.

Article 122
Re-establishment of rights
(1)   An applicant for or proprietor of a European patent who, in spite of all due care required by the circumstances having been taken, was unable to observe a time limit vis-a-vis the European Patent Office shall have his rights re-established upon request if the non-observance of this time limit has the direct consequence of causing the refusal of the European patent application or of a request, or the deeming of the application to have been withdrawn, or the revocation of the European patent, or the loss of any other right or means of redress.
(2)   The European Patent Office shall grant the request, provided that the conditions of paragraph 1 and any other requirements laid down in the Implementing Regulations are met. Otherwise, it shall reject the request.
(3)   If the request is granted, the legal consequences of the failure to observe the time limit shall be deemed not to have ensued.
(4)   Re-establishment of rights shall be ruled out in respect of the time limit for requesting re-establishment of rights. The Implementing Regulations may rule out re-establishment for other time limits.
(5)   Any person who, in a designated Contracting State, has in good faith used or made effective and serious preparations for using an invention which is the subject of a published European patent application or a European patent in the period between the loss of rights referred to in paragraph 1 and publication in the European Patent Bulletin of the mention of re-establishment of those rights, may without payment continue such use in the course of his business or for the needs thereof.
(6)   Nothing in this Article shall limit the right of a Contracting State to grant re-establishment of rights in respect of time limits provided for in this Convention and to be observed vis-à-vis the authorities of such State.

Article 123
Amendments
(1) The European patent application or European patent may be amended in proceedings before the European Patent Office, in accordance with the Implementing Regulations. In any event, the applicant shall be given at least one opportunity to amend the application of his own volition.
(2) The European patent application or European patent may not be amended in such a way that it contains subject-matter which extends beyond the content of the application as filed.
(3) The European patent may not be amended in such a way as to extend the protection it confers.

Article 124
Information on prior art
(1) The European Patent Office may, in accordance with the Implementing Regulations, invite the applicant to provide information on prior art taken into consideration in national or regional patent proceedings and concerning an invention to which the European patent application relates.
(2) If the applicant fails to reply in due time to an invitation under paragraph 1, the European patent application shall be deemed to be withdrawn.

Article 125
Reference to general principles
In the absence of procedural provisions in this Convention, the European Patent Office shall take into account the principles of procedural law generally recognised in the Contracting States.

Article 126
Termination of financial obligations (deleted)

CHAPTER II
INFORMATION TO THE PUBLIC OR TO OFFICIAL AUTHORITIES

Article 127
European Patent Register
The European Patent Office shall keep a European Patent Register, in which the particulars specified in the Implementing Regulations shall be recorded. No entry shall be made in the European Patent Register before the publication of the European patent application. The European Patent Register shall be open to public inspection.

Article 128
Inspection of files
(1) Files relating to European patent applications which have not yet been published shall not be made available for inspection without the consent of the applicant.
(2) Any person who can prove that the applicant has invoked the rights under the European patent application against him may obtain inspection of the files before the publication of that application and without the consent of the applicant.

(3) Where a European divisional application or a new European patent application filed under Article 61, paragraph 1, is published, any person may obtain inspection of the files of the earlier application before the publication of that application and without the consent of the applicant.

(4) After the publication of the European patent application, the files relating to the application and the resulting European patent may be inspected on request, subject to the restrictions laid down in the Implementing Regulations.

(5) Even before the publication of the European patent application, the European Patent Office may communicate to third parties or publish the particulars specified in the Implementing Regulations.

Article 129
Periodical publications
The European Patent Office shall periodically publish:

(a) a European Patent Bulletin containing the particulars the publication of which is prescribed by this Convention, the Implementing Regulations or the President of the European Patent Office;

(b) an Official Journal containing notices and information of a general character issued by the President of the European Patent Office, as well as any other information relevant to this Convention or its implementation.

Article 130
Exchange of information
(1) Unless this Convention or national laws provide otherwise, the European Patent Office and the central industrial property office of any Contracting State shall, on request, communicate to each other any useful information regarding European or national patent applications and patents and any proceedings concerning them.

(2) Paragraph 1 shall apply to the communication of information by virtue of working agreements between the European Patent Office and

(a) the central industrial property offices of other States;

(b) any intergovernmental organisation entrusted with the task of granting patents;

(c) any other organisation.

(3) Communications under paragraphs 1 and 2(a) and (b) shall not be subject to the restrictions laid down in Article 128. The Administrative Council may decide that communications under paragraph 2(c) shall not be subject to such restrictions, provided that the organisation concerned treats the information communicated as confidential until the European patent application has been published.

Article 131
Administrative and legal co-operation
(1) Unless this Convention or national laws provide otherwise, the European Patent Office and the courts or authorities of Contracting States shall on request give assistance to each other by communicating information or opening files for inspection. Where the European Patent Office makes

files available for inspection by courts, Public Prosecutors' Offices or central industrial property offices, the inspection shall not be subject to the restrictions laid down in Article 128.

(2) At the request of the European Patent Office, the courts or other competent authorities of Contracting States shall undertake, on behalf of the Office and within the limits of their jurisdiction, any necessary enquiries or other legal measures.

Article 132
Exchange of publications
(1) The European Patent Office and the central industrial property offices of the Contracting States shall despatch to each other on request and for their own use one or more copies of their respective publications free of charge.
(2) The European Patent Office may conclude agreements relating to the exchange or supply of publications.

CHAPTER III
REPRESENTATION

Article 133
General principles of representation
(1) Subject to paragraph 2, no person shall be compelled to be represented by a professional representative in proceedings established by this Convention.
(2) Natural or legal persons not having their residence or principal place of business in a Contracting State shall be represented by a professional representative and act through him in all proceedings established by this Convention, other than in filing a European patent application; the Implementing Regulations may permit other exceptions.
(3) Natural or legal persons having their residence or principal place of business in a Contracting State may be represented in proceedings established by this Convention by an employee, who need not be a professional representative but who shall be authorised in accordance with the Implementing Regulations. The Implementing Regulations may provide whether and under what conditions an employee of a legal person may also represent other legal persons which have their principal place of business in a Contracting State and which have economic connections with the first legal person.
(4) The Implementing Regulations may lay down special provisions concerning the common representation of parties acting in common.

Article 134
Representation before the European Patent Office
(1) Representation of natural or legal persons in proceedings established by this Convention may only be undertaken by professional representatives whose names appear on a list maintained for this purpose by the European Patent Office.
(2) Any natural person who
   (a) is a national of a Contracting State,
   (b) has his place of business or employment in a Contracting State and

(c)   has passed the European qualifying examination

may be entered on the list of professional representatives.

(3)   During a period of one year from the date on which the accession of a State to this Convention takes effect, entry on that list may also be requested by any natural person who

(a)   is a national of a Contracting State,

(b)   has his place of business or employment in the State having acceded to the Convention and

(c)   is entitled to represent natural or legal persons in patent matters before the central industrial property office of that State. Where such entitlement is not conditional upon the requirement of special professional qualifications, the person shall have regularly so acted in that State for at least five years.

(4)   Entry shall be effected upon request, accompanied by certificates indicating that the conditions laid down in paragraph 2 or 3 are fulfilled.

(5)   Persons whose names appear on the list of professional representatives shall be entitled to act in all proceedings established by this Convention.

(6)   For the purpose of acting as a professional representative, any person whose name appears on the list of professional representatives shall be entitled to establish a place of business in any Contracting State in which proceedings established by this Convention may be conducted, having regard to the Protocol on Centralisation annexed to this Convention. The authorities of such State may remove that entitlement in individual cases only in application of legal provisions adopted for the purpose of protecting public security and law and order. Before such action is taken, the President of the European Patent Office shall be consulted.

(7)   The President of the European Patent Office may grant exemption from:

(a)   the requirement of paragraphs 2(a) or 3(a) in special circumstances;

(b)   the requirement of paragraph 3(c), second sentence, if the applicant furnishes proof that he has acquired the requisite qualification in another way.

(8)   Representation in proceedings established by this Convention may also be undertaken, in the same way as by a professional representative, by any legal practitioner qualified in a Contracting State and having his place of business in that State, to the extent that he is entitled in that State to act as a professional representative in patent matters. Paragraph 6 shall apply *mutatis mutandis*.

Article 134a
Institute of Professional Representatives before the European Patent Office

(1)   The Administrative Council shall be competent to adopt and amend provisions governing:

(a)   the Institute of Professional Representatives before the European Patent Office, hereinafter referred to as the Institute;

(b)   the qualifications and training required of a person for admission to the European qualifying examination and the conduct of such examination;

(c)   the disciplinary power exercised by the Institute or the European Patent Office in respect of professional representatives;

(d)   the obligation of confidentiality on the professional representative and the privilege from disclosure in proceedings before the European Patent Office in respect of communications between a professional representative and his client or any other person.

(2)   Any person entered on the list of professional representatives referred to in Article 134, paragraph 1, shall be a member of the Institute.

PART VIII
IMPACT ON NATIONAL LAW
CHAPTER I
CONVERSION INTO A NATIONAL PATENT APPLICATION

Article 135
Request for conversion

(1)   The central industrial property office of a designated Contracting State shall, at the request of the applicant for or proprietor of a European patent, apply the procedure for the grant of a national patent in the following circumstances:

(a)   where the European patent application is deemed to be withdrawn under Article 77, paragraph 3;

(b)   in such other cases as are provided for by the national law, in which the European patent application is refused or withdrawn or deemed to be withdrawn, or the European patent is revoked under this Convention.

(2)   In the case referred to in paragraph 1(a), the request for conversion shall be filed with the central industrial property office with which the European patent application has been filed. That office shall, subject to the provisions governing national security, transmit the request directly to the central industrial property offices of the Contracting States specified therein.

(3)   In the cases referred to in paragraph 1(b), the request for conversion shall be submitted to the European Patent Office in accordance with the Implementing Regulations. It shall not be deemed to be filed until the conversion fee has been paid. The European Patent Office shall transmit the request to the central industrial property offices of the Contracting States specified therein.

(4)   The effect of the European patent application referred to in Article 66 shall lapse if the request for conversion is not submitted in due time.

Article 136
Submission and transmission of the request (deleted)

Article 137
Formal requirements for conversion

(1)   A European patent application transmitted in accordance with Article 135, paragraph 2 or 3, shall not be subjected to formal requirements of national

law which are different from or additional to those provided for in this Convention.

(2) Any central industrial property office to which the European patent application is transmitted may require that the applicant shall, within a period of not less than two months:

(a) pay the national application fee; and

(b) file a translation of the original text of the European patent application in an official language of the State in question and, where appropriate, of the text as amended during proceedings before the European Patent Office which the applicant wishes to use as the basis for the national procedure.

CHAPTER II
REVOCATION AND PRIOR RIGHTS

Article 138
Revocation of European patents

(1) Subject to Article 139, a European patent may be revoked with effect for a Contracting State only on the grounds that:

(a) the subject-matter of the European patent is not patentable under Articles 52 to 57;

(b) the European patent does not disclose the invention in a manner sufficiently clear and complete for it to be carried out by a person skilled in the art;

(c) the subject-matter of the European patent extends beyond the content of the application as filed or, if the patent was granted on a divisional application or on a new application filed under Article 61, beyond the content of the earlier application as filed;

(d) the protection conferred by the European patent has been extended; or

(e) the proprietor of the European patent is not entitled under Article 60, paragraph 1.

(2) If the grounds for revocation affect the European patent only in part, the patent shall be limited by a corresponding amendment of the claims and revoked in part.

(3) In proceedings before the competent court or authority relating to the validity of the European patent, the proprietor of the patent shall have the right to limit the patent by amending the claims. The patent as thus limited shall form the basis for the proceedings.

Article 139
Prior rights and rights arising on the same date

(1) In any designated Contracting State a European patent application and a European patent shall have with regard to a national patent application and a national patent the same prior right effect as a national patent application and a national patent.

(2) A national patent application and a national patent in a Contracting State shall have with regard to a European patent designating that Contracting

State the same prior right effect as if the European patent were a national patent.

(3) Any Contracting State may prescribe whether and on what terms an invention disclosed in both a European patent application or patent and a national application or patent having the same date of filing or, where priority is claimed, the same date of priority, may be protected simultaneously by both applications or patents.

CHAPTER III
MISCELLANEOUS EFFECTS

Article 140
National utility models and utility certificates

Articles 66, 124, 135, 137 and 139 shall apply to utility models and utility certificates and to applications for utility models and utility certificates registered or deposited in the Contracting States whose laws make provision for such models or certificates.

Article 141
Renewal fees for European patents

(1) Renewal fees for a European patent may only be imposed for the years which follow that referred to in Article 86, paragraph 2.

(2) Any renewal fees falling due within two months of the publication in the European Patent Bulletin of the mention of the grant of the European patent shall be deemed to have been validly paid if they are paid within that period. Any additional fee provided for under national law shall not be charged.

PART IX
SPECIAL AGREEMENTS

Article 142
Unitary patents

(1) Any group of Contracting States, which has provided by a special agreement that a European patent granted for those States has a unitary character throughout their territories, may provide that a European patent may only be granted jointly in respect of all those States.

(2) Where any group of Contracting States has availed itself of the authorisation given in paragraph 1, the provisions of this Part shall apply.

Article 143
Special departments of the European Patent Office

(1) The group of Contracting States may give additional tasks to the European Patent Office.

(2) Special departments common to the Contracting States in the group may be set up within the European Patent Office in order to carry out the additional tasks. The President of the European Patent Office shall direct such special departments; Article 10, paragraphs 2 and 3, shall apply *mutatis mutandis*.

Appendix 6

Article 144
Representation before special departments
The group of Contracting States may lay down special provisions to govern representation of parties before the departments referred to in Article 143, paragraph 2.

Article 145
Select committee of the Administrative Council
(1) The group of Contracting States may set up a select committee of the Administrative Council for the purpose of supervising the activities of the special departments set up under Article 143, paragraph 2; the European Patent Office shall place at its disposal such staff, premises and equipment as may be necessary for the performance of its duties. The President of the European Patent Office shall be responsible for the activities of the special departments to the select committee of the Administrative Council.
(2) The composition, powers and functions of the select committee shall be determined by the group of Contracting States.

Article 146
Cover for expenditure for carrying out special tasks
Where additional tasks have been given to the European Patent Office under Article 143, the group of Contracting States shall bear the expenses incurred by the Organisation in carrying out these tasks. Where special departments have been set up in the European Patent Office to carry out these additional tasks, the group shall bear the expenditure on staff, premises and equipment chargeable in respect of these departments. Article 39, paragraphs 3 and 4, Article 41 and Article 47 shall apply *mutatis mutandis*.

Article 147
Payments in respect of renewal fees for unitary patents
If the group of Contracting States has fixed a common scale of renewal fees in respect of European patents, the proportion referred to in Article 39, paragraph 1, shall be calculated on the basis of the common scale; the minimum amount referred to in Article 39, paragraph 1, shall apply to the unitary patent. Article 39, paragraphs 3 and 4, shall apply *mutatis mutandis*.

Article 148
The European patent application as an object of property
(1) Article 74 shall apply unless the group of Contracting States has specified otherwise.
(2) The group of Contracting States may provide that a European patent application for which these Contracting States are designated may only be transferred, mortgaged or subjected to any legal means of execution in respect of all the Contracting States of the group and in accordance with the provisions of the special agreement.

Article 149
Joint designation
(1) The group of Contracting States may provide that these States may only be designated jointly, and that the designation of one or some only of such States shall be deemed to constitute the designation of all the States of the group.

(2) Where the European Patent Office acts as a designated Office under Article 153, paragraph 1, paragraph 1 shall apply if the applicant has indicated in the international application that he wishes to obtain a European patent for one or more of the designated States of the group. The same shall apply if the applicant designates in the international application one of the Contracting States in the group, whose national law provides that the designation of that State shall have the effect of the application being for a European patent.

Article 149a
Other agreements between the Contracting States
(1) Nothing in this Convention shall be construed as limiting the right of some or all of the Contracting States to conclude special agreements on any matters concerning European patent applications or European patents which under this Convention are subject to and governed by national law, such as, in particular

(a) an agreement establishing a European patent court common to the Contracting States party to it;

(b) an agreement establishing an entity common to the Contracting States party to it to deliver, at the request of national courts or quasi-judicial authorities, opinions on issues of European or harmonised national patent law;

(c) an agreement under which the Contracting States party to it dispense fully or in part with translations of European patents under Article 65;

(d) an agreement under which the Contracting States party to it provide that translations of European patents as required under Article 65 may be filed with, and published by, the European Patent Office.

(2) The Administrative Council shall be competent to decide that:

(a) the members of the Boards of Appeal or the Enlarged Board of Appeal may serve on a European patent court or a common entity and take part in proceedings before that court or entity in accordance with any such agreement;

(b) the European Patent Office shall provide a common entity with such support staff, premises and equipment as may be necessary for the performance of its duties, and the expenses incurred by that entity shall be borne fully or in part by the Organisation.

Appendix 6

PART X

INTERNATIONAL APPLICATIONS UNDER THE PATENT
COOPERATION TREATY – EURO-PCT APPLICATIONS

Article 150
Application of the Patent Cooperation Treaty
(1) The Patent Cooperation Treaty of 19 June 1970, hereinafter referred to as the PCT, shall be applied in accordance with the provisions of this Part.
(2) International applications filed under the PCT may be the subject of proceedings before the European Patent Office. In such proceedings, the provisions of the PCT and its Regulations shall be applied, supplemented by the provisions of this Convention. In case of conflict, the provisions of the PCT or its Regulations shall prevail.

Article 151
The European Patent Office as a receiving Office
The European Patent Office shall act as a receiving Office within the meaning of the PCT, in accordance with the Implementing Regulations. Article 75, paragraph 2, shall apply.

Article 152
The European Patent Office as an International Searching Authority or International Preliminary Examining Authority
The European Patent Office shall act as an International Searching Authority and International Preliminary Examining Authority within the meaning of the PCT, in accordance with an agreement between the Organisation and the International Bureau of the World Intellectual Property Organization, for applicants who are residents or nationals of a State party to this Convention. This agreement may provide that the European Patent Office shall also act for other applicants.

Article 153
The European Patent Office as designated Office or elected Office
(1) The European Patent Office shall be

(a) a designated Office for any State party to this Convention in respect of which the PCT is in force, which is designated in the international application and for which the applicant wishes to obtain a European patent, and

(b) an elected Office, if the applicant has elected a State designated pursuant to letter (a).

(2) An international application for which the European Patent Office is a designated or elected Office, and which has been accorded an international date of filing, shall be equivalent to a regular European application (Euro-PCT application).

(3) The international publication of a Euro-PCT application in an official language of the European Patent Office shall take the place of the publication of the European patent application and shall be mentioned in the European Patent Bulletin.

(4) If the Euro-PCT application is published in another language, a translation into one of the official languages shall be filed with the European Patent Office, which shall publish it. Subject to Article 67, paragraph 3, the provisional protection under Article 67, paragraphs 1 and 2, shall be effective from the date of that publication.

(5) The Euro-PCT application shall be treated as a European patent application and shall be considered as comprised in the state of the art under Article 54, paragraph 3, if the conditions laid down in paragraph 3 or 4 and in the Implementing Regulations are fulfilled.

(6) The international search report drawn up in respect of a Euro-PCT application or the declaration replacing it, and their international publication, shall take the place of the European search report and the mention of its publication in the European Patent Bulletin.

(7) A supplementary European search report shall be drawn up in respect of any Euro-PCT application under paragraph 5. The Administrative Council may decide that the supplementary search report is to be dispensed with or that the search fee is to be reduced.

Article 154
The European Patent Office as an International Searching Authority (deleted)

Article 155
The European Patent Office as an International Preliminary Examining Authority (deleted)

Article 156
The European Patent Office as an elected Office (deleted)

Article 157
International search report (deleted)

Article 158
Publication of the international application and its supply to the European Patent Office (deleted)

PART XI
TRANSITIONAL PROVISIONS (deleted)
PART XII
FINAL PROVISIONS

Article 164
Implementing Regulations and Protocols

(1) The Implementing Regulations, the Protocol on Recognition, the Protocol on Privileges and Immunities, the Protocol on Centralisation, the Protocol on the Interpretation of Article 69 and the Protocol on Staff Complement shall be integral parts of this Convention.

(2) In case of conflict between the provisions of this Convention and those of the Implementing Regulations, the provisions of this Convention shall prevail.

Appendix 6

Article 165
Signature – Ratification
(1) This Convention shall be open for signature until 5 April 1974 by the States which took part in the Inter-Governmental Conference for the setting up of a European System for the Grant of Patents or were informed of the holding of that conference and offered the option of taking part therein.
(2) This Convention shall be subject to ratification; instruments of ratification shall be deposited with the Government of the Federal Republic of Germany.

Article 166
Accession
(1) This Convention shall be open to accession by:

    (a) the States referred to in Article 165, paragraph 1;
    (b) any other European State at the invitation of the Administrative Council.

(2) Any State which has been a party to the Convention and has ceased to be so as a result of the application of Article 172, paragraph 4, may again become a party to the Convention by acceding to it.
(3) Instruments of accession shall be deposited with the Government of the Federal Republic of Germany.

Article 167
Reservations (deleted)

Article 168
Territorial field of application
(1) Any Contracting State may declare in its instrument of ratification or accession, or may inform the Government of the Federal Republic of Germany by written notification at any time thereafter, that this Convention shall be applicable to one or more of the territories for the external relations of which it is responsible. European patents granted for that Contracting State shall also have effect in the territories for which such a declaration has taken effect.
(2) If the declaration referred to in paragraph 1 is contained in the instrument of ratification or accession, it shall take effect on the same date as the ratification or accession; if the declaration is notified after the deposit of the instrument of ratification or accession, such notification shall take effect six months after the date of its receipt by the Government of the Federal Republic of Germany.
(3) Any Contracting State may at any time declare that the Convention shall cease to apply to some or to all of the territories in respect of which it has given notification pursuant to paragraph 1. Such declaration shall take effect one year after the date on which the Government of the Federal Republic of Germany received notification thereof.

Article 169
Entry into force
(1) This Convention shall enter into force three months after the deposit of the last instrument of ratification or accession by six States on whose territory

the total number of patent applications filed in 1970 amounted to at least 180 000 for all the said States.

(2) Any ratification or accession after the entry into force of this Convention shall take effect on the first day of the third month after the deposit of the instrument of ratification or accession.

Article 170
Initial contribution

(1) Any State which ratifies or accedes to this Convention after its entry into force shall pay to the Organisation an initial contribution, which shall not be refunded.

(2) The initial contribution shall be 5% of an amount calculated by applying the percentage obtained for the State in question, on the date on which ratification or accession takes effect, in accordance with the scale provided for in Article 40, paragraphs 3 and 4, to the sum of the special financial contributions due from the other Contracting States in respect of the accounting periods preceding the date referred to above.

(3) In the event that special financial contributions were not required in respect of the accounting period immediately preceding the date referred to in paragraph 2, the scale of contributions referred to in that paragraph shall be the scale that would have been applicable to the State concerned in respect of the last year for which financial contributions were required.

Article 171
Duration of the Convention

The present Convention shall be of unlimited duration.

Article 172 Revision

(1) This Convention may be revised by a Conference of the Contracting States.

(2) The Conference shall be prepared and convened by the Administrative Council. The Conference shall not be validly constituted unless at least three-quarters of the Contracting States are represented at it. Adoption of the revise text shall require a majority of three-quarters of the Contracting States represented and voting at the Conference. Abstentions shall not be considered as votes.

(3) The revised text shall enter into force when it has been ratified or acceded to by the number of Contracting States specified by the Conference, and at the time specified by that Conference.

(4) Such States as have not ratified or acceded to the revised text of the Convention at the time of its entry into force shall cease to be parties to this Convention as from that time.

Article 173
Disputes between Contracting States

(1) Any dispute between Contracting States concerning the interpretation or application of the present Convention which is not settled by negotiation shall be submitted, at the request of one of the States concerned, to the Administrative Council, which shall endeavour to bring about agreement between the States concerned.

(2) If such agreement is not reached within six months from the date when the dispute was referred to the Administrative Council, any one of the States concerned may submit the dispute to the International Court of Justice for a binding decision.

Article 174
Denunciation

Any Contracting State may at any time denounce this Convention. Denunciation shall be notified to the Government of the Federal Republic of Germany. It shall take effect one year after the date of receipt of such notification.

Article 175
Preservation of acquired rights

(1) In the event of a State ceasing to be party to this Convention in accordance with Article 172, paragraph 4, or Article 174, rights already acquired pursuant to this Convention shall not be impaired.

(2) A European patent application which is pending when a designated State ceases to be party to the Convention shall be processed by the European Patent Office, as far as that State is concerned, as if the Convention in force thereafter were applicable to that State.

(3) Paragraph 2 shall apply to European patents in respect of which, on the date mentioned in that paragraph, an opposition is pending or the opposition period has not expired.

(4) Nothing in this Article shall affect the right of any State that has ceased to be a party to this Convention to treat any European patent in accordance with the text to which it was a party.

Article 176
Financial rights and obligations of former Contracting States

(1) Any State which has ceased to be a party to this Convention in accordance with Article 172, paragraph 4, or Article 174 shall have the special financial contributions which it has paid pursuant to Article 40, paragraph 2, refunded to it by the Organisation only at the time when and under the conditions whereby the Organisation refunds special financial contributions paid by other States during the same accounting period.

(2) The State referred to in paragraph 1 shall, even after ceasing to be a party to this Convention, continue to pay the proportion pursuant to Article 39 of renewal fees in respect of European patents remaining in force in that State, at the rate current on the date on which it ceased to be a party.

Article 177
Languages of the Convention

(1) This Convention, drawn up in a single original, in the English, French and German languages, shall be deposited in the archives of the Government of the Federal Republic of Germany, the three texts being equally authentic.

(2) The texts of this Convention drawn up in official languages of Contracting States other than those specified in paragraph 1 shall, if they have been approved by the Administrative Council, be considered as official texts. In the event of disagreement on the interpretation of the various texts, the texts referred to in paragraph 1 shall be authentic.

Article 178
Transmission and notifications

(1) The Government of the Federal Republic of Germany shall draw up certified true copies of this Convention and shall transmit them to the Governments of all signatory or acceding States.

(2) The Government of the Federal Republic of Germany shall notify to the Governments of the States referred to in paragraph 1:

   (a) the deposit of any instrument of ratification or accession;

   (b) any declaration or notification received pursuant to Article 168;

   (c) any denunciation received pursuant to Article 174 and the date on which such denunciation comes into force.

(3) The Government of the Federal Republic of Germany shall register this Convention with the Secretariat of the United Nations.

IN WITNESS WHEREOF, the Plenipotentiaries authorised thereto, having presented their Full Powers, found to be in good and due form, have signed this Convention.

   Done at Munich this fifth day of October one thousand nine hundred and seventy-three.

Protocol on Jurisdiction and the Recognition of Decisions in Respect of the Right to the Grant of a European Patent
(PROTOCOL ON RECOGNITION)
of 5 October 1973

SECTION I
JURISDICTION

Article 1[1]

(1) Protocol on Jurisdiction and Recognition The courts of the Contracting States shall, in accordance with Articles 2 to 6, have jurisdiction to decide claims, against the applicant, to the right to the grant of a European patent in respect of one or more of the Contracting States designated in the European patent application.

(2) For the purposes of this Protocol, the term "courts" shall include authorities which, under the national law of a Contracting State, have jurisdiction to decide the claims referred to in paragraph 1. Any Contracting State shall notify the European Patent Office of the identity of any authority on which such a jurisdiction is conferred, and the European Patent Office shall inform the other Contracting States accordingly.

(3) For the purposes of this Protocol, the term "Contracting State" refers to a Contracting State which has not excluded application of this Protocol pursuant to Article 167 of the Convention.

1   See decision of the Enlarged Board of Appeal G 3/92 (Annex I).

Article 2

Subject to Articles 4 and 5, if an applicant for a European patent has his residence or principal place of business within one of the Contracting States, proceedings shall be brought against him in the courts of that Contracting State.

Article 3

Subject to Articles 4 and 5, if an applicant for a European patent has his residence or principal place of business outside the Contracting States, and if the party claiming the right to the grant of the European patent has his residence or principal place of business within one of the Contracting States, the courts of the latter State shall have exclusive jurisdiction.

Article 4

Subject to Article 5, if the subject-matter of a European patent application is the invention of an employee, the courts of the Contracting State, if any, whose law determines the right to the European patent pursuant to Article 60, paragraph 1, second sentence, of the Convention, shall have exclusive jurisdiction over proceedings between the employee and the employer.

Article 5

(1) If the parties to a dispute concerning the right to the grant of a European patent have concluded an agreement, either in writing or verbally with

written confirmation, to the effect that a court or the courts of a particular
Contracting State shall decide on such a dispute, the court or courts of that
State shall have exclusive jurisdiction.

(2) However, if the parties are an employee and his employer, paragraph 1
shall only apply in so far as the national law governing the contract of
employment allows the agreement in question.

Article 6
In cases where neither Articles 2 to 4 nor Article 5, paragraph 1, apply, the courts
of the Federal Republic of Germany shall have exclusive jurisdiction.

Article 7
The courts of Contracting States before which claims referred to in Article 1 are
brought shall of their own motion decide whether or not they have jurisdiction
pursuant to Articles 2 to 6.

Article 8
(1) In the event of proceedings based on the same claim and between the same
parties being brought before courts of different Contracting States, the
court to which a later application is made shall of its own motion decline
jurisdiction in favour of the court to which an earlier application was made.
(2) In the event of the jurisdiction of the court to which an earlier application is
made being challenged, the court to which a later application is made shall
stay the proceedings until the other court takes a final decision.

SECTION II
RECOGNITION

Article 9[1]
(1) Subject to the provisions of Article 11, paragraph 2, final decisions given
in any Contracting State on the right to the grant of a European patent in
respect of one or more of the Contracting States designated in the European
patent application shall be recognised without requiring a special procedure
in the other Contracting States.
(2) The jurisdiction of the court whose decision is to be recognised and the
validity of such decision may not be reviewed.

1 See decision of the Enlarged Board of Appeal G 3/92 (Annex I).

Article 10
Article 9, paragraph 1, shall not be applicable where:

(a) an applicant for a European patent who has not contested a claim proves that
the document initiating the proceedings was not notified to him regularly
and sufficiently early for him to defend himself; or
(b) an applicant proves that the decision is incompatible with another decision
given in a Contracting State in proceedings between the same parties
which were started before those in which the decision to be recognised
was given.

Appendix 6

Article 11
(1) In relations between any Contracting States the provisions of this Protocol shall prevail over any conflicting provisions of other agreements on jurisdiction or the recognition of judgments.
(2) This Protocol shall not affect the implementation of any agreement between a Contracting State and a State which is not bound by the Protocol.

Protocol on the Interpretation of Article 69 EPC

Article 1
General principles
Article 69 should not be interpreted as meaning that the extent of the protection conferred by a European patent is to be understood as that defined by the strict, literal meaning of the wording used in the claims, the description and drawings being employed only for the purpose of resolving an ambiguity found in the claims. Nor should it be taken to mean that the claims serve only as a guideline and that the actual protection conferred may extend to what, from a consideration of the description and drawings by a person skilled in the art, the patent proprietor has contemplated. On the contrary, it is to be interpreted as defining a position between these extremes which combines a fair protection for the patent proprietor with a reasonable degree of legal certainty for third parties.

Article 2
Equivalents
For the purpose of determining the extent of protection conferred by a European patent, due account shall be taken of any element which is equivalent to an element specified in the claims.

REGULATION (EC) No 1610/96 OF THE EUROPEAN PARLIAMENT AND OF THE COUNCIL

of 23 July 1996
concerning the creation of a supplementary protection certificate for plant protection products

THE EUROPEAN PARLIAMENT AND THE COUNCIL OF THE EUROPEAN UNION,

Having regard to the Treaty establishing the European Community, and in particular Article 1001 thereof,

Having regard to the proposal from the Commission ([1]),

Having regard to the opinion of the Economic and Social Committee ([2]),

Acting in accordance with the procedure referred to in Article 189b of the Treaty ([3]),

(1) Whereas research into plant protection products contributes to the continuing improvement in the production and procurement of plentiful food of good quality at affordable prices;

(2) Whereas plant protection research contributes to the continuing improvement in crop production;

(3) Whereas plant protection products, especially those that are the result of long, costly research, will continue to be developed in the Community and in Europe if they are covered by favourable rules that provide for sufficient protection to encourage such research;

(4) Whereas the competitiveness of the plant protection sector, by the very nature of the industry, requires a level of protection for innovation which is equivalent to that granted to medicinal products by Council Regulation (EEC) No 1768/92 of 18 June 1992 concerning the creation of a supplementary protection certificate for medicinal products ([4]);

(5) Whereas, at the moment, the period that elapses between the filing of an application for a patent for a new plant protection product and authorization to place the said plant protection product on the market makes the period of effective protection under the patent insufficient to cover the investment put into the research and to generate the resources needed to maintain a high level of research;

(6) Whereas this situation leads to a lack of protection which penalizes plant protection research and the competitiveness of the sector;

(7) Whereas one of the main objectives of the supplementary protection certificate is to place European industry on the same competitive footing as its North American and Japanese counterparts;

(8) Whereas, in its Resolution of 1 February 1993 ([5]) on a Community programme of policy and action in relation to the environment and sustainable development, the Council adopted the general approach and strategy of the programme presented by the Commission, which stressed the interdependence of economic growth and environmental quality; whereas improving protection of the environment means maintaining the economic competitiveness of industry; whereas, accordingly, the issue of a

supplementary protection certificate can be regarded as a positive measure in favour of environmental protection;

(9) Whereas a uniform solution at Community level should be provided for, thereby preventing the heterogeneous development of national laws leading to further disparities which would be likely to hinder the free movement of plant protection products within the Community and thus directly affect the functioning of the internal market; whereas this is in accordance with the principle of subsidiarity as defined by Article 3b of the Treaty;

(10) Whereas, therefore, there is a need to create a supplementary protection certificate granted, under the same conditions, by each of the Member States at the request of the holder of a national or European patent relating to a plant protection product for which marketing authorization has been granted is necessary; whereas a Regulation is therefore the most appropriate legal instrument;

(11) Whereas the duration of the protection granted by the certificate should be such as to provide adequate, effective protection; whereas, for this purpose, the holder of both a patent and a certificate should be able to enjoy an overall maximum of fifteen years of exclusivity from the time the plant protection product in question first obtains authorization to be placed on the market in the Community;

(12) Whereas all the interests at stake in a sector as complex and sensitive as plant protection must nevertheless be taken into account; whereas, for this purpose, the certificate cannot be granted for a period exceeding five years;

(13) Whereas the certificate confers the same rights as those conferred by the basic patent; whereas, consequently, where the basic patent covers an active substance and its various derivatives (salts and esters), the certificate confers the same protection;

(14) Whereas the issue of a certificate for a product consisting of an active substance does not prejudice the issue of other certificates for derivatives (salts and esters) of the substance, provided that the derivatives are the subject of patents specifically covering them;

(15) Whereas a fair balance should also be stuck with regard to the determination of the transitional arrangements; whereas such arrangements should enable the Community plant protection industry to catch up to some extent with its main competitors, while making sure that the arrangements do not compromise the achievement of other legitimate objectives concerning the agricultural policy and environment protection policy pursued at both national and Community level;

(16) Whereas only action at Community level will enable the objective, which consists in ensuring adequate protection for innovation in the field of plant protection, while guaranteeing the proper functioning of the internal market for plant protection products, to be attained effectively;

(17) Whereas the detailed rules in recitals 12, 13 and 14 and in Articles 3 (2), 4, 8 (1) (c) and 17 (2) of this Regulation are also valid, *mutatis mutandis*, for the interpretation in particular of recital 9 and Articles 3, 4, 8 (1) (c) and 17 of Council Regulation (EEC) No 1768/92.

1   OJ C 390, 31. 12. 1994, p. 21 and OJ C 335, 13. 12. 1995, p. 15.
2   OJ No C 155, 21. 6. 1995, p. 14.

3   Opinion of the European Parliament of 15 June 1995 (OJ C 166, 3. 7. 1995, p. 89), common position of the Council of 27 November 1995 (OJ C 353, 30. 12. 1995, p. 36) and decision of the European Parliament of 12 March 1996 (OJ C 96, 1. 4. 1996, p. 30).
4   OJ No L 182, 2. 7. 1992, p. 1.
5   OJ No C 138, 17. 5. 1993, p. 1.

HAVE ADOPTED THIS REGULATION:

Article I
Definitions

For the purposes of this Regulation, the following definitions shall apply:

1.   'plant protection products': active substances and preparations containing one or more active substances, put up in the form in which they are supplied to the user, intended to:

   (a)   protect plants or plant products against all harmful organisms or prevent the action of such organisms, in so far as such substances or preparations are not otherwise defined below;
   (b)   influence the life processes of plants, other than as a nutrient (e.g. plant growth regulators);
   (c)   preserve plant products, in so far as such substances or products are not subject to special Council or Commission provisions on preservatives;
   (d)   destroy undesirable plants; or
   (e)   destroy parts of plants, check or prevent undesirable growth of plants;

2.   'substances': chemical elements and their compounds, as they occur naturally or by manufacture, including any impurity inevitably resulting from the manufacturing process;

3.   'active substances': substances or micro-organisms including viruses, having general or specific action:

   (a)   against harmful organisms; or
   (b)   on plants, parts of plants or plant products;

4.   'preparations': mixtures or solutions composed of two or more substances, of which at least one is an active substance, intended for use as plant protection products;

5.   'plants': live plants and live parts of plants, including fresh fruit and seeds;

6.   'plant products': products in the unprocessed state or having undergone only simple preparation such as milling, drying or pressing, derived from plants, but excluding plants themselves as defined in point 5;

7.   'harmful organisms': pests of plants or plant products belonging to the animal or plant kingdom, and also viruses, bacteria and mycoplasmas and other pathogens;

8.   'product': the active substance as defined in point 3 or combination of active substances of a plant protection product;

9.   'basic patent': a patent which protects a product as defined in point 8 as such, a preparation as defined in point 4, a process to obtain a product or

an application of a product, and which is designated by its holder for the purpose of the procedure for grant of a certificate;
10. 'certificate': the supplementary protection certificate.

Article 2
Scope
Any product protected by a patent in the territory of a Member State and subject, prior to being placed on the market as a plant protection product, to an administrative authorization procedure as laid down in Article 4 of Directive 91/414/EEC (^{1}), or pursuant to an equivalent provision of national law if it is a plant protection product in respect of which the application for authorization was lodged before Directive 91/414/EEC was implemented by the Member State concerned, may, under the terms and conditions provided for in this Regulation, be the subject of a certificate.

1   OJ L 230, 19. 8. 1991, p. 1. Directive as last amended by Directive 95/36/EC (OJ L 172, 22. 7. 1995, p. 8).

Article 3
Conditions for obtaining a certificate
1.   A certificate shall be granted if, in the Member State in which the application referred to in Article 7 is submitted, at the date of that application:

   (a)   the product is protected by a basic patent in force;
   (b)   a valid authorization to place the product on the market as a plant protection product has been granted in accordance with Article 4 of Directive 91/414/EEC or an equivalent provision of national law;
   (c)   the product has not already been the subject of a certificate;
   (d)   the authorization referred to in (b) is the first authorization to place the product on the market as a plant protection product.

2.   The holder of more than one patent for the same product shall not be granted more than one certificate for that product. However, where two or more applications concerning the same product and emanating from two or more holders of different patents are pending, one certificate for this product may be issued to each of these holders.

Article 4
Subject-matter of protection
Within the limits of the protection conferred by the basic patent, the protection conferred by a certificate shall extend only to the product covered by the authorizations to place the corresponding plant protection product on the market and for any use of the product as a plant protection product that has been authorized before the expiry of the certificate.

Article 5
Effects of the certificate
Subject to Article 4, the certificate shall confer the same rights as conferred by the basic patent and shall be subject to the same limitations and the same obligations.

Appendix 6

Article 6
Entitlement to the certificate
The certificate shall be granted to the holder of the basic patent or his successor in title.

Article 7
Application for a certificate
1. The application for a certificate shall be lodged within six months of the date on which the authorization referred to in Article 3 (1) (b) to place the product on the market as a plant protection product was granted.
2. Notwithstanding paragraph 1, where the authorization to place the product on the market is granted before the basic patent is granted, the application for a certificate shall be lodged within six months of the date on which the patent is granted.

Article 8
Content of the application for a certificate
1. The application for a certificate shall contain:

   (a) a request for the grant of a certificate, stating in particular:

       (i) the name and address of the applicant;
       (ii) the name and address of the representative, if any;
       (iii) the number of the basic patent and the title of the invention;
       (iv) the number and date of the first authorization to place the product on the market, as referred to in Article 3 (1) (b) and, if this authorization is not the first authorization to place the product on the market in the Community, the number and date of that authorization;

   (b) a copy of the authorization to place the product on the market, as referred to in Article 3 (1) (b), in which the product is identified, containing in particular the number and date of the authorization and the summary of the product characteristics listed in Part A.I (points 1-7) or B.I (points 1-7) of Annex II to Directive 91/414/EEC or in equivalent national laws of the Member State in which the application was lodged;

   (c) if the authorization referred to in (b) is not the first authorization to place the product on the market as a plant protection product in the Community, information regarding the identity of the product thus authorized and the legal provision under which the authorization procedure took place, together with a copy of the notice publishing the authorization in the appropriate official publication or, failing such a notice, any other document proving that the authorization has been issued, the date on which it was issued and the identity of the product authorized.

2. Member States may require a fee to be payable upon application for a certificate.

Article 9
Lodging of an application for a certificate
1. The application for a certificate shall be lodged with the competent industrial property office of the Member State which granted the basic patent or on whose behalf it was granted and in which the authorization referred to in Article 3 (1) (b) to place the product on the market was obtained, unless the member State designates another authority for the purpose.
2. Notification of the application for a certificate shall be published by the authority referred to in paragraph 1. The notification shall contain at least the following information:

   (a) the name and address of the applicant;
   (b) the number of the basic patent;
   (c) the title of the invention;
   (d) the number and date of the authorization to place the product on the market, referred to in Article 3 (1) (b), and the product identified in that authorization;
   (e) where relevant, the number and date of the first authorization to place the product on the market in the Community.

Article 10
Grant of the certificate or rejection of the application
1. Where the application for a certificate and the product to which it relates meet the conditions laid down in this Regulation, the authority referred to in Article 9 (1) shall grant the certificate.
2. The authority referred to in Article 9 (1) shall, subject to paragraph 3, reject the application for a certificate if the application or the product to which it relates does not meet the conditions laid down in this Regulation.
3. Where the application for a certificate does not meet the conditions laid down in Article 8, the authority referred to in Article 9 (1) shall ask the applicant to rectify the irregularity, or to settle the fee, within a stated time.
4. If the irregularity is not rectified or the fee is not settled under paragraph 3 within the stated time, application shall be rejected.
5. Member States may provide that the authority referred to in Article 9 (1) is to grant certificates without verifying that the conditions laid down in Article 3 (1) (c) and (d) are met.

Article 11
Publication
1. Notification of the fact that a certificate has been granted shall be published by the authority referred to in Article 9 (1). The notification shall contain at least the following information:

   (a) the name and address of the holder of the certificate;
   (b) the number of the basic patent;
   (c) the title of the invention;
   (d) the number and date of the authorization to place the product on the market referred to in Article 3 (1) (b) and the product identified in that authorization;

> (e) where relevant, the number and date of the first authorization to place the product on the market in the Community;
>
> (f) the duration of the certificate.

2. Notification of the fact that the application for a certificate has been rejected shall be published by the authority referred to in Article 9 (1). The notification shall contain at least the information listed in Article 9 (2).

Article 12
Annual fees

Member States may require the certificate to be subject to the payment of annual fees.

Article 13
Duration of the certificate

1. The certificate shall take effect at the end of the lawful term of the basic patent for a period equal to the period which elapsed between the date on which the application for a basic patent was lodged and the date of the first authorization to place the product on the market in the Community, reduced by a period of five years.
2. Notwithstanding paragraph 1, the duration of the certificate may not exceed five years from the date on which it takes effect.
3. For the purposes of calculating the duration of the certificate, account shall be taken of a provisional first marketing authorization only if it is directly followed by a definitive authorization concerning the same product.

Article 14
Expiry of the certificate

The certificate shall lapse:

(a) at the end of the period provided for in Article 13;
(b) if the certificate-holder surrenders it;
(c) if the annual fee laid down in accordance with Article 12 is not paid in time;
(d) if and as long as the product covered by the certificate may no longer be placed on the market following the withdrawal of the appropriate authorization or authorizations to place it on the market in accordance with Article 4 of Directive 91/414/EEC or equivalent provisions of national law. The authority referred to in Article 9 (1) may decide on the lapse of the certificate either on its own initiative or at the request of a third party.

Article 15
Invalidity of the certificate

1. The certificate shall be invalid if:

(a) it was granted contrary to the provisions of Article 3;
(b) the basic patent has lapsed before its lawful term expires;
(c) the basic patent is revoked or limited to the extent that the product for which the certificate was granted would no longer be protected by the claims of the basic patent or, after the basic patent has expired, grounds for revocation exist which would have justified such revocation or limitation.

2. Any person may submit an application or bring an action for a declaration of invalidity of the certificate before the body responsible under national law for the revocation of the corresponding basic patent.

Article 16
Notification of lapse or invalidity
If the certificate lapses in accordance with Article 14 (b), (c) or (d) or is invalid in accordance with Article 15, notification thereof shall be published by the authority referred to in Article 9 (1).

Article 17
Appeals
1. The decisions of the authority referred to in Article 9 (1) or of the body referred to in Article 15 (2) taken under this Regulation shall be open to the same appeals as those provided for in national law against similar decisions taken in respect of national patents.
2. The decision to grant the certificate shall be open to an appeal aimed at rectifying the duration of the certificate where the date of the first authorization to place the product on the market in the Community, contained in the application for a certificate as provided for in Article 8, is incorrect.

Article 18
Procedure
1. In the absence of procedural provisions in this Regulation, the procedural provisions applicable under national law to the corresponding basic patent and, where appropriate, the procedural provisions applicable to the certificates referred to in Regulation (EEC) No 1768/92, shall apply to the certificate, unless national law lays down special procedural provisions for certificates as referred to in this Regulation.
2. Notwithstanding paragraph 1, the procedure for opposition to the granting of a certificate shall be excluded.

TRANSITIONAL PROVISIONS

Article 19
1. Any product which, on the date on which this Regulation enters into force, is protected by a valid basic patent and for which the first authorization to place it on the market as a plant protection product in the Community was obtained after 1 January 1985 under Article 4 of Directive 91/414/EEC or an equivalent national provision may be granted a certificate.
2. An application made under paragraph 1 for a certificate shall be submitted within six months of the date on which this Regulation enters into force.

Article 19a
Provisions relating to the enlargement of the Community
Without prejudice to the other provisions of this Regulation, the following shall apply:

Appendix 6

(a) (i) any plant protection product protected by a valid basic patent in the Czech Republic and for which the first authorisation to place it on the market as a plant protection product was obtained in the Czech Republic after 10 November 1999 may be granted a certificate, provided that the application for a certificate was lodged within six months of the date on which the first market authorisation was obtained,

    (ii) any plant protection product protected by a valid basic patent in the Czech Republic and for which the first authorisation to place it on the market as a plant protection product was obtained in the Community not earlier than six months prior to the date of accession may be granted a certificate, provided that the application for a certificate was lodged within six months of the date on which the first market authorisation was obtained;

(b) any plant protection product protected by a valid basic patent and for which the first authorisation to place it on the market as a plant protection product was obtained in Estonia prior to the date of accession may be granted a certificate, provided that the application for a certificate was lodged within six months of the date on which the first market authorisation was obtained or, in the case of those patents granted prior to 1 January 2000, within the six month period provided for in the Patents Act of October 1999;

(c) any plant protection product protected by a valid basic patent and for which the first authorisation to place it on the market as a plant protection product was obtained in Cyprus prior to the date of accession may be granted a certificate, provided that the application for a certificate was lodged within six months of the date on which the first market authorisation was obtained; notwithstanding the above, where the market authorisation was obtained before the grant of the basic patent, the application for a certificate must be lodged within six months of the date on which the patent was granted;

(d) any plant protection product protected by a valid basic patent and for which the first authorisation to place it on the market as a plant protection product was obtained in Latvia prior to the date of accession may be granted a certificate. In cases where the period provided for in Article 7(1) has expired, the possibility of applying for a certificate shall be open for a period of six months starting no later than the date of accession;

(e) any plant protection product protected by a valid basic patent applied for after 1 February 1994 and for which the first authorisation to place it on the market as a plant protection product was obtained in Lithuania prior to the date of accession may be granted a certificate, provided that the application for a certificate is lodged within six months of the date of accession;

(f) any plant protection product protected by a valid basic patent and for which the first authorisation to place it on the market as a plant protection product was obtained after 1 January 2000 may be granted a certificate in Hungary, provided that the application for a certificate is lodged within six months of the date of accession;

(g) any plant protection product protected by a valid basic patent and for which the first authorisation to place it on the market as a plant protection product was obtained in Malta prior to the date of accession may be granted a certificate. In cases where the period provided for in Article 7(1) has expired, the possibility of applying for a certificate shall be open for a period of six months starting no later than the date of accession;

(h) any plant protection product protected by a valid basic patent and for which the first authorisation to place it on the market as a plant protection product was obtained after 1 January 2000 may be granted a certificate in Poland, provided that the application for a certificate is lodged within six months starting no later than the date of accession;

(i) any plant protection product protected by a valid basic patent and for which the first authorisation to place it on the market as a plant protection product was obtained in Slovenia prior to the date of accession may be granted a certificate, provided that the application for a certificate is lodged within six months of the date of accession, including in cases where the period provided for in Article 7(1) has expired;

(j) any plant protection product protected by a valid basic patent and for which the first authorisation to place it on the market as a plant protection product was obtained in Slovakia after 1 January 2000 may be granted a certificate, provided that the application for a certificate was lodged within six months of the date on which the first market authorisation was obtained or within six months of 1 July 2002 if the market authorisation was obtained before that date;

(k) any plant protection product protected by a valid basic patent and for which the first authorisation to place it on the market as a plant protection product was obtained after 1 January 2000 may be granted a certificate in Bulgaria, provided that the application for a certificate is lodged within six months of the date of accession;

(l) any plant protection product protected by a valid basic patent and for which the first authorisation to place it on the market as a plant protection product was obtained after 1 January 2000 may be granted a certificate in Romania. In cases where the period provided for in Article 7(1) has expired, the possibility of applying for a certificate shall be open for a period of six months starting no later than the date of accession;

(m) any plant protection product protected by a valid basic patent and for which the first authorisation to place it on the market as a plant protection product was obtained after 1 January 2003 may be granted a certificate in Croatia, provided that the application for a certificate is lodged within six months from the date of accession.

Article 20

1. In those Member States whose national law did not, on 1 January 1990, provide for the patentability of plant protection products, this Regulation shall apply from 2 January 1998.

   Article 19 shall not apply in those Member States.

2. This Regulation shall apply to supplementary protection certificates granted in accordance with the national legislation of the Czech Republic, Estonia, Croatia, Cyprus, Latvia, Lithuania, Malta, Poland, Romania, Slovenia and Slovakia prior to their respective date of accession.

Appendix 6

FINAL PROVISION

Article 21
Entry into force
This Regulation shall enter into force six months after its publication in the *Official Journal of the European Communities*.

This Regulation shall be binding in its entirety and directly applicable in all Member States.

REGULATION (EC) No 469/2009 OF THE EUROPEAN PARLIAMENT AND OF THE COUNCIL
of 6 May 2009
concerning the supplementary protection certificate for medicinal products
(Codified version)

THE EUROPEAN PARLIAMENT AND THE COUNCIL OF THE EUROPEAN UNION,

Having regard to the Treaty establishing the European Community, and in particular Article 95 thereof,

Having regard to the proposal from the Commission,

Having regard to the opinion of the European Economic and Social Committee (^{1}),

Acting in accordance with the procedure laid down in Article 251 of the Treaty (^{2}),

Whereas:

(1) Council Regulation (EEC) No 1768/92 of 18 June 1992 concerning the creation of a supplementary protection certificate for medicinal products (^{3}) has been substantially amended several times (^{4}). In the interests of clarity and rationality the said Regulation should be codified.

(2) Pharmaceutical research plays a decisive role in the continuing improvement in public health.

(3) Medicinal products, especially those that are the result of long, costly research will not continue to be developed in the Community and in Europe unless they are covered by favourable rules that provide for sufficient protection to encourage such research.

(4) At the moment, the period that elapses between the filing of an application for a patent for a new medicinal product and authorisation to place the medicinal product on the market makes the period of effective protection under the patent insufficient to cover the investment put into the research.

(5) This situation leads to a lack of protection which penalises pharmaceutical research.

(6) There exists a risk of research centres situated in the Member States relocating to countries that offer greater protection.

(7) A uniform solution at Community level should be provided for, thereby preventing the heterogeneous development of national laws leading to further disparities which would be likely to create obstacles to the free movement of medicinal products within the Community and thus directly affect the functioning of the internal market.

---

1 OJ C 77, 31.3.2009, p. 42.
2 Opinion of the European Parliament of 21 October 2008 (not yet published in the Official Journal) and Council Decision of 6 April 2009.
3 OJ L 182, 2.7.1992, p. 1.
4 See Annex I.

Appendix 6

(8) Therefore, the provision of a supplementary protection certificate granted, under the same conditions, by each of the Member States at the request of the holder of a national or European patent relating to a medicinal product for which marketing authorisation has been granted is necessary. A regulation is therefore the most appropriate legal instrument.

(9) The duration of the protection granted by the certificate should be such as to provide adequate effective protection. For this purpose, the holder of both a patent and a certificate should be able to enjoy an overall maximum of 15 years of exclusivity from the time the medicinal product in question first obtains authorisation to be placed on the market in the Community.

(10) All the interests at stake, including those of public health, in a sector as complex and sensitive as the pharmaceutical sector should nevertheless be taken into account. For this purpose, the certificate cannot be granted for a period exceeding five years. The protection granted should furthermore be strictly confined to the product which obtained authorisation to be placed on the market as a medicinal product.

(11) Provision should be made for appropriate limitation of the duration of the certificate in the special case where a patent term has already been extended under a specific national law,

HAVE ADOPTED THIS REGULATION:

Article I
Definitions

For the purposes of this Regulation, the following definitions shall apply:

(a) 'medicinal product' means any substance or combination of substances presented for treating or preventing disease in human beings or animals and any substance or combination of substances which may be administered to human beings or animals with a view to making a medical diagnosis or to restoring, correcting or modifying physiological functions in humans or in animals;

(b) 'product' means the active ingredient or combination of active ingredients of a medicinal product;

(c) 'basic patent' means a patent which protects a product as such, a process to obtain a product or an application of a product, and which is designated by its holder for the purpose of the procedure for grant of a certificate;

(d) 'certificate' means the supplementary protection certificate;

(e) 'application for an extension of the duration' means an application for an extension of the duration of the certificate pursuant to Article 13(3) of this Regulation and Article 36 of Regulation (EC) No 1901/2006 of the European Parliament and of the Council of 12 December 2006 on medicinal products for paediatric use ([1]).

1 OJ L 378, 27.12.2006, p. 1.

Article 2
Scope

Any product protected by a patent in the territory of a Member State and subject, prior to being placed on the market as a medicinal product, to an administrative authorisation procedure as laid down in Directive 2001/83/EC of the European Parliament and of the Council of 6 November 2001 on the Community code relating to medicinal products for human use (^{2}) or Directive 2001/82/EC of the European Parliament and of the Council of 6 November 2001 on the Community code relating to veterinary medicinal products (^{3}) may, under the terms and conditions provided for in this Regulation, be the subject of a certificate.

2   OJ L 311, 28.11.2001, p. 67.
3   OJ L 311, 28.11.2001, p. 1.

Article 3
Conditions for obtaining a certificate
A certificate shall be granted if, in the Member State in which the application referred to in Article 7 is submitted and at the date of that application:

(a)   the product is protected by a basic patent in force;
(b)   a valid authorisation to place the product on the market as a medicinal product has been granted in accordance with Directive 2001/83/EC or Directive 2001/82/EC, as appropriate;
(c)   the product has not already been the subject of a certificate;
(d)   the authorisation referred to in point (b) is the first authorisation to place the product on the market as a medicinal product.

Article 4
Subject matter of protection
Within the limits of the protection conferred by the basic patent, the protection conferred by a certificate shall extend only to the product covered by the authorisation to place the corresponding medicinal product on the market and for any use of the product as a medicinal product that has been authorised before the expiry of the certificate.

Article 5
Effects of the certificate
Subject to the provisions of Article 4, the certificate shall confer the same rights as conferred by the basic patent and shall be subject to the same limitations and the same obligations.

Article 6
Entitlement to the certificate
The certificate shall be granted to the holder of the basic patent or his successor in title.

Appendix 6

Article 7
Application for a certificate

1. The application for a certificate shall be lodged within six months of the date on which the authorisation referred to in Article 3(b) to place the product on the market as a medicinal product was granted.

2. Notwithstanding paragraph 1, where the authorisation to place the product on the market is granted before the basic patent is granted, the application for a certificate shall be lodged within six months of the date on which the patent is granted.

3. The application for an extension of the duration may be made when lodging the application for a certificate or when the application for the certificate is pending and the appropriate requirements of Article 8(1)(d) or Article 8(2), respectively, are fulfilled.

4. The application for an extension of the duration of a certificate already granted shall be lodged not later than two years before the expiry of the certificate.

5. Notwithstanding paragraph 4, for five years following the entry into force of Regulation (EC) No 1901/2006, the application for an extension of the duration of a certificate already granted shall be lodged not later than six months before the expiry of the certificate.

Article 8
Content of the application for a certificate

1. The application for a certificate shall contain:

   (a) a request for the grant of a certificate, stating in particular:

       (i)   the name and address of the applicant;
       (ii) if he has appointed a representative, the name and address of the representative;
       (iii) the number of the basic patent and the title of the invention;
       (iv) the number and date of the first authorisation to place the product on the market, as referred to in Article 3(b) and, if this authorisation is not the first authorisation for placing the product on the market in the Community, the number and date of that authorisation;

   (b) a copy of the authorisation to place the product on the market, as referred to in Article 3(b), in which the product is identified, containing in particular the number and date of the authorisation and the summary of the product characteristics listed in Article 11 of Directive 2001/83/EC or Article 14 of Directive 2001/82/EC;

   (c) if the authorisation referred to in point (b) is not the first authorisation for placing the product on the market as a medicinal product in the Community, information regarding the identity of the product thus authorised and the legal provision under which the authorisation procedure took place, together with a copy of the notice publishing the authorisation in the appropriate official publication;

   (d) where the application for a certificate includes a request for an extension of the duration:

    (i)   a copy of the statement indicating compliance with an agreed completed paediatric investigation plan as referred to in Article 36(1) of Regulation (EC) No 1901/2006;

    (ii) where necessary, in addition to the copy of the authorisation to place the product on the market as referred to in point (b), proof of possession of authorisations to place the product on the market of all other Member States, as referred to in Article 36(3) of Regulation (EC) No 1901/2006.

2. Where an application for a certificate is pending, an application for an extended duration in accordance with Article 7(3) shall include the particulars referred to in paragraph 1(d) of this Article and a reference to the application for a certificate already filed.

3. The application for an extension of the duration of a certificate already granted shall contain the particulars referred to in paragraph 1(d) and a copy of the certificate already granted.

4. Member States may provide that a fee is to be payable upon application for a certificate and upon application for the extension of the duration of a certificate.

Article 9
Lodging of an application for a certificate

1. The application for a certificate shall be lodged with the competent industrial property office of the Member State which granted the basic patent or on whose behalf it was granted and in which the authorisation referred to in Article 3(b) to place the product on the market was obtained, unless the Member State designates another authority for the purpose.

The application for an extension of the duration of a certificate shall be lodged with the competent authority of the Member State concerned.

2. Notification of the application for a certificate shall be published by the authority referred to in paragraph 1. The notification shall contain at least the following information:

    (a) the name and address of the applicant;

    (b) the number of the basic patent;

    (c) the title of the invention;

    (d) the number and date of the authorisation to place the product on the market, referred to in Article 3(b), and the product identified in that authorisation;

    (e) where relevant, the number and date of the first authorisation to place the product on the market in the Community;

    (f) where applicable, an indication that the application includes an application for an extension of the duration.

3. Paragraph 2 shall apply to the notification of the application for an extension of the duration of a certificate already granted or where an application for a certificate is pending. The notification shall additionally contain an indication of the application for an extended duration of the certificate.

Appendix 6

Article 10
Grant of the certificate or rejection of the application for a certificate

1. Where the application for a certificate and the product to which it relates meet the conditions laid down in this Regulation, the authority referred to in Article 9(1) shall grant the certificate.
2. The authority referred to in Article 9(1) shall, subject to paragraph 3, reject the application for a certificate if the application or the product to which it relates does not meet the conditions laid down in this Regulation.
3. Where the application for a certificate does not meet the conditions laid down in Article 8, the authority referred to in Article 9(1) shall ask the applicant to rectify the irregularity, or to settle the fee, within a stated time.
4. If the irregularity is not rectified or the fee is not settled under paragraph 3 within the stated time, the authority shall reject the application.
5. Member States may provide that the authority referred to in Article 9(1) is to grant certificates without verifying that the conditions laid down in Article 3(c) and (d) are met.
6. Paragraphs 1 to 4 shall apply *mutatis mutandis* to the application for an extension of the duration.

Article 11
Publication

1. Notification of the fact that a certificate has been granted shall be published by the authority referred to in Article 9(1). The notification shall contain at least the following information:

   (a) the name and address of the holder of the certificate;
   (b) the number of the basic patent;
   (c) the title of the invention;
   (d) the number and date of the authorisation to place the product on the market referred to in Article 3(b) and the product identified in that authorisation;
   (e) where relevant, the number and date of the first authorisation to place the product on the market in the Community;
   (f) the duration of the certificate.

2. Notification of the fact that the application for a certificate has been rejected shall be published by the authority referred to in Article 9(1). The notification shall contain at least the information listed in Article 9(2).
3. Paragraphs 1 and 2 shall apply to the notification of the fact that an extension of the duration of a certificate has been granted or of the fact that the application for an extension has been rejected.

Article 12
Annual fees

Member States may require that the certificate be subject to the payment of annual fees.

Article 13
Duration of the certificate

1. The certificate shall take effect at the end of the lawful term of the basic patent for a period equal to the period which elapsed between the date on which the application for a basic patent was lodged and the date of the first authorisation to place the product on the market in the Community, reduced by a period of five years.
2. Notwithstanding paragraph 1, the duration of the certificate may not exceed five years from the date on which it takes effect.
3. The periods laid down in paragraphs 1 and 2 shall be extended by six months in the case where Article 36 of Regulation (EC) No 1901/2006 applies. In that case, the duration of the period laid down in paragraph 1 of this Article may be extended only once.
4. Where a certificate is granted for a product protected by a patent which, before 2 January 1993, had its term extended or for which such extension was applied for, under national law, the term of protection to be afforded under this certificate shall be reduced by the number of years by which the term of the patent exceeds 20 years.

Article 14
Expiry of the certificate
The certificate shall lapse:

(a) at the end of the period provided for in Article 13;
(b) if the certificate holder surrenders it;
(c) if the annual fee laid down in accordance with Article 12 is not paid in time;
(d) if and as long as the product covered by the certificate may no longer be placed on the market following the withdrawal of the appropriate authorisation or authorisations to place on the market in accordance with Directive 2001/83/EC or Directive 2001/82/EC. The authority referred to in Article 9(1) of this Regulation may decide on the lapse of the certificate either of its own motion or at the request of a third party.

Article 15
Invalidity of the certificate

1. The certificate shall be invalid if:

(a) it was granted contrary to the provisions of Article 3;
(b) the basic patent has lapsed before its lawful term expires;
(c) the basic patent is revoked or limited to the extent that the product for which the certificate was granted would no longer be protected by the claims of the basic patent or, after the basic patent has expired, grounds for revocation exist which would have justified such revocation or limitation.

2. Any person may submit an application or bring an action for a declaration of invalidity of the certificate before the body responsible under national law for the revocation of the corresponding basic patent.

Appendix 6

Article 16
Revocation of an extension of the duration
1. The extension of the duration may be revoked if it was granted contrary to the provisions of Article 36 of Regulation (EC) No 1901/2006.
2. Any person may submit an application for revocation of the extension of the duration to the body responsible under national law for the revocation of the corresponding basic patent.

Article 17
Notification of lapse or invalidity
1. If the certificate lapses in accordance with point (b), (c) or (d) of Article 14, or is invalid in accordance with Article 15, notification thereof shall be published by the authority referred to in Article 9(1).
2. If the extension of the duration is revoked in accordance with Article 16, notification thereof shall be published by the authority referred to in Article 9(1).

Article 18
Appeals
The decisions of the authority referred to in Article 9(1) or of the bodies referred to in Articles 15(2) and 16(2) taken under this Regulation shall be open to the same appeals as those provided for in national law against similar decisions taken in respect of national patents.

Article 19
Procedure
1. In the absence of procedural provisions in this Regulation, the procedural provisions applicable under national law to the corresponding basic patent shall apply to the certificate, unless the national law lays down special procedural provisions for certificates.
2. Notwithstanding paragraph 1, the procedure for opposition to the granting of a certificate shall be excluded.

Article 20
Additional provisions relating to the enlargement of the Community
Without prejudice to the other provisions of this Regulation, the following provisions shall apply:

(a) any medicinal product protected by a valid basic patent and for which the first authorisation to place it on the market as a medicinal product was obtained after 1 January 2000 may be granted a certificate in Bulgaria, provided that the application for a certificate was lodged within six months from 1 January 2007;

(b) any medicinal product protected by a valid basic patent in the Czech Republic and for which the first authorisation to place it on the market as a medicinal product was obtained:

   (i) in the Czech Republic after 10 November 1999 may be granted a certificate, provided that the application for a certificate was lodged within six months of the date on which the first market authorisation was obtained;

(ii) in the Community not earlier than six months prior to 1 May 2004 may be granted a certificate, provided that the application for a certificate was lodged within six months of the date on which the first market authorisation was obtained;

(c) any medicinal product protected by a valid basic patent and for which the first authorisation to place it on the market as a medicinal product was obtained in Estonia prior to 1 May 2004 may be granted a certificate, provided that the application for a certificate was lodged within six months of the date on which the first market authorisation was obtained or, in the case of those patents granted prior to 1 January 2000, within the six months provided for in the Patents Act of October 1999;

(d) any medicinal product protected by a valid basic patent and for which the first authorisation to place it on the market as a medicinal product was obtained in Cyprus prior to 1 May 2004 may be granted a certificate, provided that the application for a certificate was lodged within six months of the date on which the first market authorisation was obtained; notwithstanding the above, where the market authorisation was obtained before the grant of the basic patent, the application for a certificate must be lodged within six months of the date on which the patent was granted;

(e) any medicinal product protected by a valid basic patent and for which the first authorisation to place it on the market as a medicinal product was obtained in Latvia prior to 1 May 2004 may be granted a certificate. In cases where the period provided for in Article 7(1) has expired, the possibility of applying for a certificate shall be open for a period of six months starting no later than 1 May 2004;

(f) any medicinal product protected by a valid basic patent applied for after 1 February 1994 and for which the first authorisation to place it on the market as a medicinal product was obtained in Lithuania prior to 1 May 2004 may be granted a certificate, provided that the application for a certificate was lodged within six months from 1 May 2004;

(g) any medicinal product protected by a valid basic patent and for which the first authorisation to place it on the market as a medicinal product was obtained after 1 January 2000 may be granted a certificate in Hungary, provided that the application for a certificate was lodged within six months from 1 May 2004;

(h) any medicinal product protected by a valid basic patent and for which the first authorisation to place it on the market as a medicinal product was obtained in Malta prior to 1 May 2004 may be granted a certificate. In cases where the period provided for in Article 7(1) has expired, the possibility of applying for a certificate shall be open for a period of six months starting no later than 1 May 2004;

(i) any medicinal product protected by a valid basic patent and for which the first authorisation to place it on the market as a medicinal product was obtained after 1 January 2000 may be granted a certificate in Poland, provided that the application for a certificate was lodged within six months starting no later than 1 May 2004;

Appendix 6

(j) any medicinal product protected by a valid basic patent and for which the first authorisation to place it on the market as a medicinal product was obtained after 1 January 2000 may be granted a certificate in Romania. In cases where the period provided for in Article 7(1) has expired, the possibility of applying for a certificate shall be open for a period of six months starting no later than 1 January 2007;

(k) any medicinal product protected by a valid basic patent and for which the first authorisation to place it on the market as a medicinal product was obtained in Slovenia prior to 1 May 2004 may be granted a certificate, provided that the application for a certificate was lodged within six months from 1 May 2004, including in cases where the period provided for in Article 7(1) has expired;

(l) any medicinal product protected by a valid basic patent and for which the first authorisation to place it on the market as a medicinal product was obtained in Slovakia after 1 January 2000 may be granted a certificate, provided that the application for a certificate was lodged within six months of the date on which the first market authorisation was obtained or within six months of 1 July 2002 if the market authorisation was obtained before that date;

(m) any medicinal product protected by a valid basic patent and for which the first authorisation to place it on the market as a medicinal product was obtained after 1 January 2003 may be granted a certificate in Croatia, provided that the application for a certificate is lodged within six months from the date of accession.

Article 21
Transitional provisions

1. This Regulation shall not apply to certificates granted in accordance with the national legislation of a Member State before 2 January 1993 or to applications for a certificate filed in accordance with that legislation before 2 July 1992.

   With regard to Austria, Finland and Sweden, this Regulation shall not apply to certificates granted in accordance with their national legislation before 1 January 1995.

2. This Regulation shall apply to supplementary protection certificates granted in accordance with the national legislation of the Czech Republic, Estonia, Croatia, Cyprus, Latvia, Lithuania, Malta, Poland, Romania, Slovenia and Slovakia prior to their respective date of accession.

Article 22
Repeal

Regulation (EEC) No 1768/92, as amended by the acts listed in Annex I, is repealed.

References to the repealed Regulation shall be construed as references to this Regulation and shall be read in accordance with the correlation table in Annex II.

Article 23
Entry into force
This Regulation shall enter into force on the 20th day following its publication in the *Official Journal of the European Union.*

This Regulation shall be binding in its entirety and directly applicable in all Member States.

ANNEX I
REPEALED REGULATION WITH LIST OF ITS
SUCCESSIVE AMENDMENTS
(**referred to in Article 22**)

Council Regulation (EEC) No 1768/92 (OJ L 182, 2.7.1992, p. 1)

Annex I, point XI.F.I, of the 1994 Act of Accession
(OJ C 241, 29.8.1994, p. 233)

Annex II, point 4.C.II, of the 2003 Act of Accession
(OJ L 236, 23.9.2003, p. 342)

Annex III, point 1.II, of the 2005 Act of Accession
(OJ L 157, 21.6.2005, p. 56)

Regulation (EC) No 1901/2006 of the European Parliament and of the Council
(OJ L 378, 27.12.2006, p. 1)   Only Article 52

Appendix 6

ANNEX II

CORRELATION TABLE
Regulation (EEC) No 1768/92

This Regulation

Regulation (EEC) No 1768/92	This Regulation
—	Recital 1
Recital 1	Recital 2
Recital 2	Recital 3
Recital 3	Recital 4
Recital 4	Recital 5
Recital 5	Recital 6
Recital 6	Recital 7
Recital 7	Recital 8
Recital 8	Recital 9
Recital 9	Recital 10
Recital 10	—
Recital 11	—
Recital 12	—
Recital 13	Recital 11
Article 1	Article 1
Article 2	Article 2
Article 3, introductory wording	Article 3, introductory wording
Article 3, point (a)	Article 3, point (a)
Article 3, point (b), first sentence	Article 3, point (b)
Article 3, point (b), second sentence	—
Article 3, points (c) and (d)	Article 3, points (c) and (d)
Articles 4 to 7	Articles 4 to 7
Article 8(1)	Article 8(1)
Article 8(1a)	Article 8(2)
Article 8(1b)	Article 8(3)
Article 8(2)	Article 8(4)
Articles 9 to 12	Articles 9 to 12
Article 13(1), (2) and (3)	Article 13(1), (2) and (3)
Articles 14 and 15	Articles 14 and 15
Article 15a	Article 16

Regulation (EEC) No 1768/92	This Regulation
Articles 16, 17 and 18	Articles 17, 18 and 19
Article 19	—
Article 19a, introductory wording	Article 20, introductory wording
Article 19a, point (a), points (i) and (ii)	Article 20, point (b), introductory wording, points (i) and (ii)
Article 19a, point (b)	Article 20, point (c)
Article 19a, point (c)	Article 20, point (d)
Article 19a, point (d)	Article 20, point (e)
Article 19a, point (e)	Article 20, point (f)
Article 19a, point (f)	Article 20, point (g)
Article 19a, point (g)	Article 20, point (h)
Article 19a, point (h)	Article 20, point (i)
Article 19a, point (i)	Article 20, point (k)
Article 19a, point (j)	Article 20, point (l)
Article 19a, point (k)	Article 20, point (a)
Article 19a, point (l)	Article 20, point (j)
Article 20	Article 21
Article 21	—
Article 22	Article 13(4)
—	Article 22
Article 23	Article 23
—	Annex I
—	Annex II

DIRECTIVE 98/44/EC OF THE EUROPEAN PARLIAMENT AND OF THE COUNCIL
of 6 July 1998 on the legal protection of biotechnological inventions

THE EUROPEAN PARLIAMENT AND THE COUNCIL OF THE EUROPEAN UNION,

Having regard to the Treaty establishing the European Community, and in particular Article 100a thereof,

Directive 98/44/EC of the European Parliament Having regard to the proposal from the Commission,[1]

Having regard to the opinion of the Economic and Social Committee,[2]

Acting in accordance with the procedure laid down in Article 189b of the Treaty,[3]

(1) Whereas biotechnology and genetic engineering are playing an increasingly important role in a broad range of industries and the protection of biotechnological inventions will certainly be of fundamental importance for the Community's industrial development.

(2) Whereas, in particular in the field of genetic engineering, research and development require a considerable amount of high-risk investment and therefore only adequate legal protection can make them profitable.

(3) Whereas effective and harmonised protection throughout the Member States is essential in order to maintain and encourage investment in the field of biotechnology.

(4) Whereas following the European Parliament's rejection of the joint text, approved by the Conciliation Committee, for a European Parliament and Council Directive on the legal protection of biotechnological inventions[4], the European Parliament and the Council have determined that the legal protection of biotechnological inventions requires clarification.

(5) Whereas differences exist in the legal protection of biotechnological inventions offered by the laws and practices of the different Member States whereas such differences could create barriers to trade and hence impede the proper functioning of the internal market.

(6) Whereas such differences could well become greater as Member States adopt new and different legislation and administrative practices, or whereas national case-law interpreting such legislation develops differently.

(7) Whereas uncoordinated development of national laws on the legal protection of biotechnological inventions in the Community could lead to further disincentives to trade, to the detriment of the industrial development of such inventions and of the smooth operation of the internal market.

(8) Whereas legal protection of biotechnological inventions does not necessitate the creation of a separate body of law in place of the rules of national patent law whereas the rules of national patent law remain the essential basis for the legal protection of biotechnological inventions given that they must be adapted or added to in certain specific respects in order to take adequate account of technological developments involving biological material which also fulfil the requirements for patentability.

(9) Whereas in certain cases, such as the exclusion from patentability of plant and animal varieties and of essentially biological processes for the production of plants and animals, certain concepts in national laws based

upon international patent and plant variety conventions have created uncertainty regarding the protection of biotechnological and certain microbiological inventions whereas harmonisation is necessary to clarify the said uncertainty.

(10) Whereas regard should be had to the potential of the development of biotechnology for the environment and in particular the utility of this technology for the development of methods of cultivation which are less polluting and more economical in their use of ground whereas the patent system should be used to encourage research into, and the application of, such processes.

(11) Whereas the development of biotechnology is important to developing countries, both in the field of health and combating major epidemics and endemic diseases and in that of combating hunger in the world whereas the patent system should likewise be used to encourage research in these fields whereas international procedures for the dissemination of such technology in the Third World and to the benefit of the population groups concerned should be promoted.

(12) Whereas the Agreement on Trade-Related Aspects of Intellectual Property Rights (TRIPs)[5] signed by the European Community and the Member States, has entered into force and provides that patent protection must be guaranteed for products and processes in all areas of technology.

(13) Whereas the Community's legal framework for the protection of biotechnological inventions can be limited to laying down certain principles as they apply to the patentability of biological material as such, such principles being intended in particular to determine the difference between inventions and discoveries with regard to the patentability of certain elements of human origin, to the scope of protection conferred by a patent on a biotechnological invention, to the right to use a deposit mechanism in addition to written descriptions and lastly to the option of obtaining non-exclusive compulsory licences in respect of interdependence between plant varieties and inventions, and conversely.

(14) Whereas a patent for invention does not authorise the holder to implement that invention, but merely entitles him to prohibit third parties from exploiting it for industrial and commercial purposes whereas, consequently, substantive patent law cannot serve to replace or render superfluous national, European or international law which may impose restrictions or prohibitions or which concerns the monitoring of research and of the use or commercialisation of its results, notably from the point of view of the requirements of public health, safety, environmental protection, animal welfare, the preservation of genetic diversity and compliance with certain ethical standards.

(15) Whereas no prohibition or exclusion exists in national or European patent law (Munich Convention) which precludes a priori the patentability of biological matter.

(16) Whereas patent law must be applied so as to respect the fundamental principles safeguarding the dignity and integrity of the person whereas it is important to assert the principle that the human body, at any stage in its formation or development, including germ cells, and the simple discovery of one of its elements or one of its products, including the sequence or

partial sequence of a human gene, cannot be patented whereas these principles are in line with the criteria of patentability proper to patent law, whereby a mere discovery cannot be patented.

(17) Whereas significant progress in the treatment of diseases has already been made thanks to the existence of medicinal products derived from elements isolated from the human body and/or otherwise produced, such medicinal products resulting from technical processes aimed at obtaining elements similar in structure to those existing naturally in the human body and whereas, consequently, research aimed at obtaining and isolating such elements valuable to medicinal production should be encouraged by means of the patent system.

(18) Whereas, since the patent system provides insufficient incentive for encouraging research into and production of biotechnological medicines which are needed to combat rare or 'orphan' diseases, the Community and the Member States have a duty to respond adequately to this problem.

(19) Whereas account has been taken of Opinion No 8 of the Group of Advisers on the Ethical Implications of Biotechnology to the European Commission.

(20) Whereas, therefore, it should be made clear that an invention based on an element isolated from the human body or otherwise produced by means of a technical process, which is susceptible of industrial application, is not excluded from patentability, even where the structure of that element is identical to that of a natural element, given that the rights conferred by the patent do not extend to the human body and its elements in their natural environment.

(21) Whereas such an element isolated from the human body or otherwise produced is not excluded from patentability since it is, for example, the result of technical processes used to identify, purify and classify it and to reproduce it outside the human body, techniques which human beings alone are capable of putting into practice and which nature is incapable of accomplishing by itself.

(22) Whereas the discussion on the patentability of sequences or partial sequences of genes is controversial whereas, according to this Directive, the granting of a patent for inventions which concern such sequences or partial sequences should be subject to the same criteria of patentability as in all other areas of technology: novelty, inventive step and industrial application whereas the industrial application of a sequence or partial sequence must be disclosed in the patent application as filed.

(23) Whereas a mere DNA sequence without indication of a function does not contain any technical information and is therefore not a patentable invention.

(24) Whereas, in order to comply with the industrial application criterion it is necessary in cases where a sequence or partial sequence of a gene is used to produce a protein or part of a protein, to specify which protein or part of a protein is produced or what function it performs.

(25) Whereas, for the purposes of interpreting rights conferred by a patent, when sequences overlap only in parts which are not essential to the invention, each sequence will be considered as an independent sequence in patent law terms.

(26) Whereas if an invention is based on biological material of human origin or if it uses such material, where a patent application is filed, the person from whose body the material is taken must have had an opportunity of expressing free and informed consent thereto, in accordance with national law.

(27) Whereas if an invention is based on biological material of plant or animal origin or if it uses such material, the patent application should, where appropriate, include information on the geographical origin of such material, if known whereas this is without prejudice to the processing of patent applications or the validity of rights arising from granted patents.

(28) Whereas this Directive does not in any way affect the basis of current patent law, according to which a patent may be granted for any new application of a patented product.

(29) Whereas this Directive is without prejudice to the exclusion of plant and animal varieties from patentability whereas on the other hand inventions which concern plants or animals are patentable provided that the application of the invention is not technically confined to a single plant or animal variety.

(30) Whereas the concept 'plant variety' is defined by the legislation protecting new varieties, pursuant to which a variety is defined by its whole genome and therefore possesses individuality and is clearly distinguishable from other varieties.

(31) Whereas a plant grouping which is characterised by a particular gene (and not its whole genome) is not covered by the protection of new varieties and is therefore not excluded from patentability even if it comprises new varieties of plants.

(32) Whereas, however, if an invention consists only in genetically modifying a particular plant variety, and if a new plant variety is bred, it will still be excluded from patentability even if the genetic modification is the result not of an essentially biological process but of a biotechnological process.

(33) Whereas it is necessary to define for the purposes of this Directive when a process for the breeding of plants and animals is essentially biological.

(34) Whereas this Directive shall be without prejudice to concepts of invention and discovery, as developed by national, European or international patent law.

(35) Whereas this Directive shall be without prejudice to the provisions of national patent law whereby processes for treatment of the human or animal body by surgery or therapy and diagnostic methods practised on the human or animal body are excluded from patentability.

(36) Whereas the TRIPs Agreement provides for the possibility that members of the World Trade Organisation may exclude from patentability inventions, the prevention within their territory of the commercial exploitation of which is necessary to protect *ordre public* or morality, including to protect human, animal or plant life or health or to avoid serious prejudice to the environment, provided that such exclusion is not made merely because the exploitation is prohibited by their law.

(37) Whereas the principle whereby inventions must be excluded from patentability where their commercial exploitation offends against order public or morality must also be stressed in this Directive.

(38) Whereas the operative part of this Directive should also include an illustrative list of inventions excluded from patentability so as to provide national courts and patent offices with a general guide to interpreting the reference to *ordre public* and morality whereas this list obviously cannot presume to be exhaustive whereas processes, the use of which offend against human dignity, such as processes to produce chimeras from germ cells or totipotent cells of humans and animals, are obviously also excluded from patentability.

(39) Whereas *ordre public* and morality correspond in particular to ethical or moral principles recognised in a Member State, respect for which is particularly important in the field of biotechnology in view of the potential scope of inventions in this field and their inherent relationship to living matter whereas such ethical or moral principles supplement the standard legal examinations under patent law regardless of the technical field of the invention.

(40) Whereas there is a consensus within the Community that interventions in the human germ line and the cloning of human beings offends against *ordre public* and morality whereas it is therefore important to exclude unequivocally from patentability processes for modifying the germ line genetic identity of human beings and processes for cloning human beings.

(41) Whereas a process for cloning human beings may be defined as any process, including techniques of embryo splitting, designed to create a human being with the same nuclear genetic information as another living or deceased human being.

(42) Whereas, moreover, uses of human embryos for industrial or commercial purposes must also be excluded from patentability whereas in any case such exclusion does not affect inventions for therapeutic or diagnostic purposes which are applied to the human embryo and are useful to it.

(43) Whereas pursuant to Article F(2) of the Treaty on European Union, the Union is to respect fundamental rights, as guaranteed by the European Convention for the Protection of Human Rights and Fundamental Freedoms signed in Rome on 4 November 1950 and as they result from the constitutional traditions common to the Member States, as general principles of Community law.

(44) Whereas the Commission's European Group on Ethics in Science and New Technologies evaluates all ethical aspects of biotechnology whereas it should be pointed out in this connection that that Group may be consulted only where biotechnology is to be evaluated at the level of basic ethical principles, including where it is consulted on patent law.

(45) Whereas processes for modifying the genetic identity of animals which are likely to cause them suffering without any substantial medical benefit in terms of research, prevention, diagnosis or therapy to man or animal, and also animals resulting from such processes, must be excluded from patentability.

(46) Whereas, in view of the fact that the function of a patent is to reward the inventor for his creative efforts by granting an exclusive but time-bound right, and thereby encourage inventive activities, the holder of the patent should be entitled to prohibit the use of patented self-reproducing material in situations analogous to those where it would be permitted to prohibit the

use of patented, non-self-reproducing products, that is to say the production of the patented product itself.

(47) Whereas it is necessary to provide for a first derogation from the rights of the holder of the patent when the propagating material incorporating the protected invention is sold to a farmer for farming purposes by the holder of the patent or with his consent whereas that initial derogation must authorise the farmer to use the product of his harvest for further multiplication or propagation on his own farm whereas the extent and the conditions of that derogation must be limited in accordance with the extent and conditions set out in Council Regulation (EC) No 2100/94 of 27 July 1994 on Community plant variety rights;[6]

(48) Whereas only the fee envisaged under Community law relating to plant variety rights as a condition for applying the derogation from Community plant variety rights can be required of the farmer.

(49) Whereas, however, the holder of the patent may defend his rights against a farmer abusing the derogation or against a breeder who has developed a plant variety incorporating the protected invention if the latter fails to adhere to his commitments.

(50) Whereas a second derogation from the rights of the holder of the patent must authorise the farmer to use protected livestock for agricultural purposes.

(51) Whereas the extent and the conditions of that second derogation must be determined by national laws, regulations and practices, since there is no Community legislation on animal variety rights.

(52) Whereas, in the field of exploitation of new plant characteristics resulting from genetic engineering, guaranteed access must, on payment of a fee, be granted in the form of a compulsory licence where, in relation to the genus or species concerned, the plant variety represents significant technical progress of considerable economic interest compared to the invention claimed in the patent.

(53) Whereas, in the field of the use of new plant characteristics resulting from new plant varieties in genetic engineering, guaranteed access must, on payment of a fee, be granted in the form of a compulsory licence where the invention represents significant technical progress of considerable economic interest.

(54) Whereas Article 34 of the TRIPs Agreement contains detailed provisions on the burden of proof which is binding on all Member States whereas, therefore, a provision in this Directive is not necessary.

(55) Whereas following Decision 93/626/EEC[7] the Community is party to the Convention on Biological Diversity of 5 June 1992 whereas, in this regard, Member States must give particular weight to Article 3 and Article 8(j), the second sentence of Article 16(2) and Article 16(5) of the Convention when bringing into force the laws, regulations and administrative provisions necessary to comply with this Directive.

(56) Whereas the Third Conference of the Parties to the Biodiversity Convention, which took place in November 1996, noted in Decision III/17 that 'further work is required to help develop a common appreciation of the relationship between intellectual property rights and the relevant provisions of the TRIPs Agreement and the Convention on Biological Diversity, in particular on issues relating to technology transfer and conservation and sustainable use

of biological diversity and the fair and equitable sharing of benefits arising out of the use of genetic resources, including the protection of knowledge, innovations and practices of indigenous and local communities embodying traditional lifestyles relevant for the conservation and sustainable use of biological diversity'.

1   OJ C 296, 8.10.1996, p. 4 and OJ C 311, 11.10.1997, p. 12.
2   OJC295, 7.10.1996, p. 11.
3   Opinion of the European Parliament of 16 July 1997 (OJ C 286, 22.9.1997, p. 87). Council Common Position of 26 February 1998 (OJ C 110, 8.4.1998, p. 17) and Decision of the European Parliament of 12 May 1998 (OJ C 167, 1.6.1998). Council Decision of 16 June 1998.
4   OJ C 68, 20.3.1995, p. 26.
5   OJ L 336, 23.12.1994, p. 213.
6   OJ L 227, 1.9.1994, p. 1. Regulation as amended by Regulation (EC) No 2506/95 (OJ L 258, 28.10.1995, p. 3).
7   OJ L 309, 31.12.1993, p. 1.

HAVE ADOPTED THIS DIRECTIVE:

CHAPTER I
PATENTABILITY

Article 1
1.   Member States shall protect biotechnological inventions under national patent law. They shall, if necessary, adjust their national patent law to take account of the provisions of this Directive.
2.   This Directive shall be without prejudice to the obligations of the Member States pursuant to international agreements, and in particular the TRIPs Agreement and the Convention on Biological Diversity.

Article 2
1.   For the purposes of this Directive,

   (a) 'biological material' means any material containing genetic information and capable of reproducing itself or being reproduced in a biological system
   (b) 'microbiological process' means any process involving or performed upon or resulting in microbiological material.

2.   A process for the production of plants or animals is essentially biological if it consists entirely of natural phenomena such as crossing or selection.
3.   The concept of 'plant variety' is defined by Article 5 of Regulation (EC) No 2100/94.

Article 3
1.   For the purposes of this Directive, inventions which are new, which involve an inventive step and which are susceptible of industrial application shall be patentable even if they concern a product consisting of or containing biological material or a process by means of which biological material is produced, processed or used.

2. Biological material which is isolated from its natural environment or produced by means of a technical process may be the subject of an invention even if it previously occurred in nature.

Article 4

1. The following shall not be patentable:

   (a) plant and animal varieties;
   (b) essentially biological processes for the production of plants or animals.

2. Inventions which concern plants or animals shall be patentable if the technical feasibility of the invention is not confined to a particular plant or animal variety.

3. Paragraph 1(b) shall be without prejudice to the patentability of inventions which concern a microbiological or other technical process or a product obtained by means of such a process.

Article 5

1. The human body, at the various stages of its formation and development, and the simple discovery of one of its elements, including the sequence or partial sequence of a gene, cannot constitute patentable inventions.

2. An element isolated from the human body or otherwise produced by means of a technical process, including the sequence or partial sequence of a gene, may constitute a patentable invention, even if the structure of that element is identical to that of a natural element.

3. The industrial application of a sequence or a partial sequence of a gene must be disclosed in the patent application.

Article 6

1. Inventions shall be considered unpatentable where their commercial exploitation would be contrary to *ordre public* or morality however, exploitation shall not be deemed to be so contrary merely because it is prohibited by law or regulation.

2. On the basis of paragraph 1, the following, in particular, shall be considered unpatentable:

   (a) processes for cloning human beings;
   (b) processes for modifying the germ line genetic identity of human beings;
   (c) uses of human embryos for industrial or commercial purposes;
   (d) processes for modifying the genetic identity of animals which are likely to cause them suffering without any substantial medical benefit to man or animal, and also animals resulting from such processes.

Article 7

The Commission's European Group on Ethics in Science and New Technologies evaluates all ethical aspects of biotechnology.

CHAPTER II
SCOPE OF PROTECTION

Article 8

1. The protection conferred by a patent on a biological material possessing specific characteristics as a result of the invention shall extend to any biological material derived from that biological material through propagation or multiplication in an identical or divergent form and possessing those same characteristics.

2. The protection conferred by a patent on a process that enables a biological material to be produced possessing specific characteristics as a result of the invention shall extend to biological material directly obtained through that process and to any other biological material derived from the directly obtained biological material through propagation or multiplication in an identical or divergent form and possessing those same characteristics.

Article 9

The protection conferred by a patent on a product containing or consisting of genetic information shall extend to all material, save as provided in Article 5(1), in which the product in incorporated and in which the genetic information is contained and performs its function.

Article 10

The protection referred to in Articles 8 and 9 shall not extend to biological material obtained from the propagation or multiplication of biological material placed on the market in the territory of a Member State by the holder of the patent or with his consent, where the multiplication or propagation necessarily results from the application for which the biological material was marketed, provided that the material obtained is not subsequently used for other propagation or multiplication.

Article 11

1. By way of derogation from Articles 8 and 9, the sale or other form of commercialisation of plant propagating material to a farmer by the holder of the patent or with his consent for agricultural use implies authorisation for the farmer to use the product of his harvest for propagation or multiplication by him on his own farm, the extent and conditions of this derogation corresponding to those under Article 14 of Regulation (EC) No 2100/94.

2. By way of derogation from Articles 8 and 9, the sale or any other form of commercialisation of breeding stock or other animal reproductive material to a farmer by the holder of the patent or with his consent implies authorisation for the farmer to use the protected livestock for an agricultural purpose. This includes making the animal or other animal reproductive material available for the purposes of pursuing his agricultural activity but not sale within the framework or for the purpose of a commercial reproduction activity.

3. The extent and the conditions of the derogation provided for in paragraph 2 shall be determined by national laws, regulations and practices.

CHAPTER III
COMPULSORY CROSS-LICENSING

Article 12

1. Where a breeder cannot acquire or exploit a plant variety right without infringing a prior patent, he may apply for a compulsory licence for non-exclusive use of the invention protected by the patent inasmuch as the licence is necessary for the exploitation of the plant variety to be protected, subject to payment of an appropriate royalty. Member States shall provide that, where such a licence is granted, the holder of the patent will be entitled to a cross-licence on reasonable terms to use the protected variety.

2. Where the holder of a patent concerning a biotechnological invention cannot exploit it without infringing a prior plant variety right, he may apply for a compulsory licence for non-exclusive use of the plant variety protected by that right, subject to payment of an appropriate royalty. Member States shall provide that, where such a licence is granted, the holder of the variety right will be entitled to a cross-licence on reasonable terms to use the protected invention.

3. Applicants for the licences referred to in paragraphs 1 and 2 must demonstrate that:

    (a) they have applied unsuccessfully to the holder of the patent or of the plant variety right to obtain a contractual licence;

    (b) the plant variety or the invention constitutes significant technical progress of considerable economic interest compared with the invention claimed in the patent or the protected plant variety.

4. Each Member State shall designate the authority or authorities responsible for granting the licence. Where a licence for a plant variety can be granted only by the Community Plant Variety Office, Article 29 of Regulation (EC) No 2100/94 shall apply.

CHAPTER IV
DEPOSIT, ACCESS AND RE-DEPOSIT OF A BIOLOGICAL MATERIAL

Article 13

1. Where an invention involves the use of or concerns biological material which is not available to the public and which cannot be described in a patent application in such a manner as to enable the invention to be reproduced by a person skilled in the art, the description shall be considered inadequate for the purposes of patent law unless:

    (a) the biological material has been deposited no later than the date on which the patent application was filed with a recognised depositary institution. At least the international depositary authorities which acquired this status by virtue of Article 7 of the Budapest Treaty of 28 April 1977 on the international recognition of the deposit of micro-organisms for the purposes of patent procedure, hereinafter referred to as the 'Budapest Treaty' shall be recognised;

    (b) the application as filed contains such relevant information as is available to the applicant on the characteristics of the biological material deposited;

(c) the patent application states the name of the depository institution and the accession number.

2. Access to the deposited biological material shall be provided through the supply of a sample:

(a) up to the first publication of the patent application, only to those persons who are authorised under national patent law;

(b) between the first publication of the application and the granting of the patent, to anyone requesting it or, if the applicant so requests, only to an independent expert;

(c) after the patent has been granted, and notwithstanding revocation or cancellation of the patent, to anyone requesting it.

3. The sample shall be supplied only if the person requesting it undertakes, for the term during which the patent is in force:

(a) not to make it or any material derived from it available to third parties; and

(b) not to use it or any material derived from it except for experimental purposes, unless the applicant for or proprietor of the patent, as applicable, expressly waives such an undertaking.

4. At the applicant's request, where an application is refused or withdrawn, access to the deposited material shall be limited to an independent expert for 20 years from the date on which the patent application was filed. In that case, paragraph 3 shall apply.

5. The applicant's requests referred to in point (b) of paragraph 2 and in paragraph 4 may only be made up to the date on which the technical preparations for publishing the patent application are deemed to have been completed.

Article 14

1. If the biological material deposited in accordance with Article 13 ceases to be available from the recognised depositary institution, a new deposit of the material shall be permitted on the same terms as those laid down in the Budapest Treaty.

2. Any new deposit shall be accompanied by a statement signed by the depositor certifying that the newly deposited biological material is the same as that originally deposited.

CHAPTER V
FINAL PROVISIONS

Article 15

1. Member States shall bring into force the laws, regulations and administrative provisions necessary to comply with this Directive not later than 30 July 2000. They shall forthwith inform the Commission thereof.

When Member States adopt these measures, they shall contain a reference to this Directive or shall be accompanied by such reference on the occasion of their official publication. The methods of making such reference shall be laid down by Member States.

2. Member States shall communicate to the Commission the text of the provisions of national law which they adopt in the field covered by this Directive.

Article 16
The Commission shall send the European Parliament and the Council:

(a) every five years as from the date specified in Article 15(1) a report on any problems encountered with regard to the relationship between this Directive and international agreements on the protection of human rights to which the Member States have acceded;
(b) within two years of entry into force of this Directive, a report assessing the implications for basic genetic engineering research of failure to publish, or late publication of, papers on subjects which could be patentable;
(c) annually as from the date specified in Article 15(1), a report on the development and implications of patent law in the field of biotechnology and genetic engineering.

Article 17
This Directive shall enter into force on the day of its publication in the Official Journal of the European Communities.

Article 18
This Directive is addressed to the Member States. Done at Brussels, 6 July 1998.

Appendix 6

COMMISSION REGULATION (EU) No 316/2014
of 21 March 2014
on the application of Article 101(3) of the Treaty on the Functioning of the European Union to categories of technology transfer agreements
(Text with EEA relevance)

THE EUROPEAN COMMISSION,

Having regard to the Treaty on the Functioning of the European Union,

Having regard to Regulation No 19/65/EEC of the Council of 2 March 1965 on application of Article 85(3) of the Treaty to certain categories of agreements and concerted practices (¹), and in particular Article 1 thereof,

Having published a draft of this Regulation,

After consulting the Advisory Committee on Restrictive Practices and Dominant Positions,

Whereas:

(1) Regulation No 19/65/EEC empowers the Commission to apply Article 101(3) of the Treaty by regulation to certain categories of technology transfer agreements and corresponding concerted practices to which only two undertakings are party which fall within Article 101(1) of the Treaty.

(2) Pursuant to Regulation No 19/65/EEC, the Commission has, in particular, adopted Commission Regulation (EC) No 772/2004 (²). Regulation (EC) No 772/2004 defines categories of technology transfer agreements which the Commission regarded as normally satisfying the conditions laid down in Article 101(³) of the Treaty. In view of the overall positive experience with the application of that Regulation, which expires on 30 April 2014, and taking into account further experience acquired since its adoption, it is appropriate to adopt a new block exemption regulation.

(3) This Regulation should meet the two requirements of ensuring effective protection of competition and providing adequate legal security for undertakings. The pursuit of those objectives should take account of the need to simplify administrative supervision and the legislative framework to as great an extent as possible.

(4) Technology transfer agreements concern the licensing of technology rights. Such agreements will usually improve economic efficiency and be pro-competitive as they can reduce duplication of research and development, strengthen the incentive for the initial research and development, spur incremental innovation, facilitate diffusion and generate product market competition.

(5) The likelihood that such efficiency-enhancing and pro- competitive effects will outweigh any anti-competitive effects due to restrictions contained in technology transfer agreements depends on the degree of market power of the undertakings concerned and, therefore, on the extent to which those undertakings face competition from undertakings owning substitute technologies or undertakings producing substitute products.

(6) This Regulation should cover only technology transfer agreements between a licensor and a licensee. It should cover such agreements even if the agreement contains conditions relating to more than one level of trade, for instance requiring the licensee to set up a particular distribution system and

specifying the obligations the licensee must or may impose on resellers of the products produced under the licence. However, such conditions and obligations should comply with the competition rules applicable to supply and distribution agreements set out in Commission Regulation (EU) No 330/2010 (³). Supply and distribution agreements concluded between a licensee and buyers of its contract products should not be exempted by this Regulation.

(7) This Regulation should only apply to agreements where the licensor permits the licensee and/or one or more of its sub-contractors to exploit the licensed technology rights, possibly after further research and development by the licensee and/or its sub-contractors, for the purpose of producing goods or services. It should not apply to licensing in the context of research and development agreements which are covered by Commission Regulation (EU) No 1217/2010 (⁴) or to licensing in the context of specialisation agreements which are covered by Commission Regulation (EU) No 1218/2010 (⁵). It should also not apply to agreements, the purpose of which is the mere reproduction and distribution of software copyright protected products as such agreements do not concern the licensing of a technology to produce but are more akin to distribution agreements. Nor should it apply to agreements to set up technology pools, that is to say, agreements for the pooling of technologies with the purpose of licensing them to third parties, or to agreements whereby the pooled technology is licensed out to those third parties.

(8) For the application of Article 101(3) of the Treaty by regulation, it is not necessary to define those technology transfer agreements that are capable of falling within Article 101(1) of the Treaty. In the individual assessment of agreements pursuant to Article 101(1), account has to be taken of several factors, and in particular the structure and the dynamics of the relevant technology and product markets.

(9) The benefit of the block exemption established by this Regulation should be limited to those agreements which can be assumed with sufficient certainty to satisfy the conditions of Article 101(3) of the Treaty. In order to attain the benefits and objectives of technology transfer, this Regulation should not only cover the transfer of technology as such but also other provisions contained in technology transfer agreements if, and to the extent that, those provisions are directly related to the production or sale of the contract products.

(10) For technology transfer agreements between competitors it can be presumed that, where the combined share of the relevant markets accounted for by the parties does not exceed 20 % and the agreements do not contain certain severely anti-competitive restrictions, they generally lead to an improvement in production or distribution and allow consumers a fair share of the resulting benefits.

(11) For technology transfer agreements between non-competitors it can be presumed that, where the individual share of the relevant markets accounted for by each of the parties does not exceed 30% and the agreements do not contain certain severely anti-competitive restrictions, they generally lead to an improvement in production or distribution and allow consumers a fair share of the resulting benefits.

(12) If the applicable market-share threshold is exceeded on one or more product or technology markets, the block exemption should not apply to the agreement for the relevant markets concerned.

(13) There can be no presumption that, above those market-share thresholds, technology transfer agreements fall within the scope of Article 101(1) of the Treaty. For instance, exclusive licensing agreements between non- competing undertakings often fall outside the scope of Article 101(1). There can also be no presumption that, above those market-share thresholds, technology transfer agreements falling within the scope of Article 101(1) will not satisfy the conditions for exemption. However, it can also not be presumed that they will usually give rise to objective advantages of such a character and size as to compensate for the disadvantages which they create for competition.

(14) This Regulation should not exempt technology transfer agreements containing restrictions which are not indispensable to the improvement of production or distribution. In particular, technology transfer agreements containing certain severely anti-competitive restrictions, such as the fixing of prices charged to third parties, should be excluded from the benefit of the block exemption established by this Regulation irrespective of the market shares of the undertakings concerned. In the case of such hardcore restrictions the whole agreement should be excluded from the benefit of the block exemption.

(15) In order to protect incentives to innovate and the appropriate application of intellectual property rights, certain restrictions should be excluded from the benefit of the block exemption. In particular certain grant back obligations and non-challenge clauses should be excluded. Where such a restriction is included in a licence agreement only the restriction in question should be excluded from the benefit of the block exemption.

(16) The market-share thresholds and the non-exemption of technology transfer agreements containing the severely anti-competitive restrictions and the excluded restrictions provided for in this Regulation will normally ensure that the agreements to which the block exemption applies do not enable the participating undertakings to eliminate competition in respect of a substantial part of the products in question.

(17) The Commission may withdraw the benefit of this Regulation, pursuant to Article 29(1) of Council Regulation (EC) No 1/2003 (⁶), where it finds in a particular case that an agreement to which the exemption provided for in this Regulation applies nevertheless has effects which are incompatible with Article 101(3) of the Treaty. This may occur in particular where the incentives to innovate are reduced or where access to markets is hindered.

(18) The competition authority of a Member State may withdraw the benefit of this Regulation pursuant to Article 29(2) of Regulation (EC) No 1/2003 in respect of the territory of that Member State, or a part thereof where, in a particular case, an agreement to which the exemption provided for in this Regulation applies nevertheless has effects which are incompatible with Article 101(3) of the Treaty in the territory of that Member State, or in a part thereof, and where such territory has all the characteristics of a distinct geographic market.

(19) In order to strengthen supervision of parallel networks of technology transfer agreements which have similar restrictive effects and which cover more than 50% of a given market, the Commission may by regulation declare this Regulation inapplicable to technology transfer agreements containing specific restrictions relating to the market concerned, thereby restoring the full application of Article 101 of the Treaty to such agreements,

1   OJ 36, 6.3.1965, p. 533/65.
2   Commission Regulation (EC) No 772/2004 of 7 April 2004 on the application of Article 81(3) of the Treaty to categories of technology transfer agreements (OJ L 123, 27.4.2004, p. 11).
3   Commission Regulation (EU) No 330/2010 of 20 April 2010 on the application of Article 101(3) of the Treaty on the Functioning of the European Union to categories of vertical agreements and concerted practices (OJ L 102, 23.4.2010, p. 1).
4   Commission Regulation (EU) No 1217/2010 of 14 December 2010 on the application of Article 101(3) of the Treaty on the Functioning of the European Union to certain categories of research and development agreements (OJ L 335, 18.12.2010, p. 36).
5   Commission Regulation (EU) No 1218/2010 of 14 December 2010 on the application of Article 101(3) of the Treaty on the Functioning of the European Union to certain categories of specialisation agreements (OJ L 335, 18.12.2010, p. 43).
6   Council Regulation (EC) No 1/2003 of 16 December 2002 on the implementation of the rules on competition laid down in Articles 81 and 82 of the Treaty (OJ L 1, 4.1.2003, p. 1).

HAS ADOPTED THIS REGULATION:

Article 1
Definitions
1. For the purposes of this Regulation, the following definitions shall apply:

(a) 'agreement' means an agreement, a decision of an association of undertakings or a concerted practice;

(b) 'technology rights' means know-how and the following rights, or a combination thereof, including applications for or applications for registration of those rights:

(i)   patents,
(ii) utility models,
(iii) design rights,
(iv) topographies of semiconductor products,
(v)   supplementary protection certificates for medicinal products or other products for which such supplementary protection certificates may be obtained,
(vi) plant breeder's certificates and
(vii) software copyrights;

(c) 'technology transfer agreement' means:

(i) a technology rights licensing agreement entered into between two undertakings for the purpose of the production of contract products by the licensee and/or its sub-contractor(s),

(ii) an assignment of technology rights between two undertakings for the purpose of the production of contract products where part of the risk associated with the exploitation of the technology remains with the assignor;

(d) 'reciprocal agreement' means a technology transfer agreement where two undertakings grant each other, in the same or separate contracts, a technology rights licence, and where those licences concern competing technologies or can be used for the production of competing products;

(e) 'non-reciprocal agreement' means a technology transfer agreement where one undertaking grants another undertaking a technology rights licence, or where two undertakings grant each other such a licence but where those licences do not concern competing technologies and cannot be used for the production of competing products;

(f) 'product' means goods or a service, including both intermediary goods and services and final goods and services;

(g) 'contract product' means a product produced, directly or indirectly, on the basis of the licensed technology rights;

(h) 'intellectual property rights' includes industrial property rights, in particular patents and trademarks, copyright and neighbouring rights;

(i) 'know-how' means a package of practical information, resulting from experience and testing, which is:

(i) secret, that is to say, not generally known or easily accessible,

(ii) substantial, that is to say, significant and useful for the production of the contract products, and

(iii) identified, that is to say, described in a sufficiently comprehensive manner so as to make it possible to verify that it fulfils the criteria of secrecy and substantiality;

(j) 'relevant product market' means the market for the contract products and their substitutes, that is to say all those products which are regarded as interchangeable or substitutable by the buyer, by reason of the products' characteristics, their prices and their intended use;

(k) 'relevant technology market' means the market for the licensed technology rights and their substitutes, that is to say all those technology rights which are regarded as interchangeable or substitutable by the licensee, by reason of the technology rights' characteristics, the royalties payable in respect of those rights and their intended use;

(l) 'relevant geographic market' means the area in which the undertakings concerned are involved in the supply of and demand for products or the licensing of technology rights, in which the conditions of competition are sufficiently homogeneous and which can be distinguished from neighbouring areas because the conditions of competition are appreciably different in those areas;

(m) 'relevant market' means the combination of the relevant product or technology market with the relevant geographic market;

(n) 'competing undertakings' means undertakings which compete on the relevant market, that is to say:

      (i)   competing undertakings on the relevant market where the technology rights are licensed, that is to say, undertakings which license out competing technology rights (actual competitors on the relevant market),

      (ii) competing undertakings on the relevant market where the contract products are sold, that is to say, undertakings which, in the absence of the technology transfer agreement, would both be active on the relevant market(s) on which the contract products are sold (actual competitors on the relevant market) or which, in the absence of the technology transfer agreement, would, on realistic grounds and not just as a mere theroetical possibility, in response to a small and permanent increase in relative prices, be likely to undertake, within a short period of time, the necessary additional investments or other necessary switching costs to enter the relevant market(s) (potential competitors on the relevant market);

(o) 'selective distribution system' means a distribution system where the licensor undertakes to license the production of the contract products, either directly or indirectly, only to licensees selected on the basis of specified criteria and where those licensees undertake not to sell the contract products to unauthorised distributors within the territory reserved by the licensor to operate that system;

(p) 'exclusive licence' means a licence under which the licensor itself is not permitted to produce on the basis of the licensed technology rights and is not permitted to license the licensed technology rights to third parties, in general or for a particular use or in a particular territory;

(q) 'exclusive territory' means a given territory within which only one undertaking is allowed to produce the contract products, but where it is nevertheless possible to allow another licensee to produce the contract products within that territory only for a particular customer where the second licence was granted in order to create an alternative source of supply for that customer;

(r) 'exclusive customer group' means a group of customers to which only one party to the technology transfer agreement is allowed to actively sell the contract products produced with the licensed technology.

2.   For the purposes of this Regulation, the terms 'undertaking', 'licensor' and 'licensee' shall include their respective connected undertakings.

'Connected undertakings' means:

(a) undertakings in which a party to the technology transfer agreement, directly or indirectly:

      (i)   has the power to exercise more than half the voting rights, or

      (ii) has the power to appoint more than half the members of the supervisory board, board of management or bodies legally representing the undertaking, or

      (iii) has the right to manage the undertaking's affairs;

(b) undertakings which directly or indirectly have, over a party to the technology transfer agreement, the rights or powers listed in point (a);

759

    (c)   undertakings in which an undertaking referred to in point (b) has, directly or indirectly, the rights or powers listed in point (a);

    (d)   undertakings in which a party to the technology transfer agreement together with one or more of the undertakings referred to in points (a), (b) or (c), or in which two or more of the latter undertakings, jointly have the rights or powers listed in point (a);

    (e)   undertakings in which the rights or the powers listed in point (a) are jointly held by:

        (i)   parties to the technology transfer agreement or their respective connected undertakings referred to in points (a) to (d), or

        (ii)   one or more of the parties to the technology transfer agreement or one or more of their connected undertakings referred to in points (a) to (d) and one or more third parties.

Article 2
Exemption

1.   Pursuant to Article 101(3) of the Treaty and subject to the provisions of this Regulation, Article 101(1) of the Treaty shall not apply to technology transfer agreements.

2.   The exemption provided for in paragraph 1 shall apply to the extent that technology transfer agreements contain restrictions of competition falling within the scope of Article 101(1) of the Treaty. The exemption shall apply for as long as the licensed technology rights have not expired, lapsed or been declared invalid or, in the case of know-how, for as long as the know-how remains secret. However, where know-how becomes publicly known as a result of action by the licensee, the exemption shall apply for the duration of the agreement.

3.   The exemption provided for in paragraph 1 shall also apply to provisions, in technology transfer agreements, which relate to the purchase of products by the licensee or which relate to the licensing or assignment of other intellectual property rights or know-how to the licensee, if, and to the extent that, those provisions are directly related to the production or sale of the contract products.

Article 3
Market-share thresholds

1.   Where the undertakings party to the agreement are competing undertakings, the exemption provided for in Article 2 shall apply on condition that the combined market share of the parties does not exceed 20% on the relevant market(s).

2.   Where the undertakings party to the agreement are not competing undertakings, the exemption provided for in Article 2 shall apply on condition that the market share of each of the parties does not exceed 30% on the relevant market(s).

Article 4
Hardcore restrictions

1.   Where the undertakings party to the agreement are competing undertakings, the exemption provided for in Article 2 shall not apply to agreements which,

directly or indirectly, in isolation or in combination with other factors under the control of the parties, have as their object any of the following:

(a) the restriction of a party's ability to determine its prices when selling products to third parties;

(b) the limitation of output, except limitations on the output of contract products imposed on the licensee in a non- reciprocal agreement or imposed on only one of the licensees in a reciprocal agreement;

(c) the allocation of markets or customers except:

(i) the obligation on the licensor and/or the licensee, in a non-reciprocal agreement, not to produce with the licensed technology rights within the exclusive territory reserved for the other party and/or not to sell actively and/or passively into the exclusive territory or to the exclusive customer group reserved for the other party,

(ii) the restriction, in a non-reciprocal agreement, of active sales by the licensee into the exclusive territory or to the exclusive customer group allocated by the licensor to another licensee provided the latter was not a competing undertaking of the licensor at the time of the conclusion of its own licence,

(iii) the obligation on the licensee to produce the contract products only for its own use provided that the licensee is not restricted in selling the contract products actively and passively as spare parts for its own products,

(iv) the obligation on the licensee, in a non-reciprocal agreement, to produce the contract products only for a particular customer, where the licence was granted in order to create an alternative source of supply for that customer;

(d) the restriction of the licensee's ability to exploit its own technology rights or the restriction of the ability of any of the parties to the agreement to carry out research and development, unless such latter restriction is indispensable to prevent the disclosure of the licensed know-how to third parties.

2. Where the undertakings party to the agreement are not competing undertakings, the exemption provided for in Article 2 shall not apply to agreements which, directly or indirectly, in isolation or in combination with other factors under the control of the parties, have as their object any of the following:

(a) the restriction of a party's ability to determine its prices when selling products to third parties, without prejudice to the possibility of imposing a maximum sale price or recommending a sale price, provided that it does not amount to a fixed or minimum sale price as a result of pressure from, or incentives offered by, any of the parties;

(b) the restriction of the territory into which, or of the customers to whom, the licensee may passively sell the contract products, except:

(i) the restriction of passive sales into an exclusive territory or to an exclusive customer group reserved for the licensor,

(ii) the obligation to produce the contract products only for its own use provided that the licensee is not restricted in selling the contract products actively and passively as spare parts for its own products,

(iii) the obligation to produce the contract products only for a particular customer, where the licence was granted in order to create an alternative source of supply for that customer,

(iv) the restriction of sales to end-users by a licensee operating at the wholesale level of trade,

(v) the restriction of sales to unauthorised distributors by the members of a selective distribution system;

(c) the restriction of active or passive sales to end-users by a licensee which is a member of a selective distribution system and which operates at the retail level, without prejudice to the possibility of prohibiting a member of the system from operating out of an unauthorised place of establishment.

3. Where the undertakings party to the agreement are not competing undertakings at the time of the conclusion of the agreement but become competing undertakings afterwards, paragraph 2 and not paragraph 1 shall apply for the full life of the agreement unless the agreement is subsequently amended in any material respect. Such an amendment includes the conclusion of a new technology transfer agreement between the parties concerning competing technology rights.

Article 5
Excluded restrictions

1. The exemption provided for in Article 2 shall not apply to any of the following obligations contained in technology transfer agreements:

(a) any direct or indirect obligation on the licensee to grant an exclusive licence or to assign rights, in whole or in part, to the licensor or to a third party designated by the licensor in respect of its own improvements to, or its own new applications of, the licensed technology;

(b) any direct or indirect obligation on a party not to challenge the validity of intellectual property rights which the other party holds in the Union, without prejudice to the possibility, in the case of an exclusive licence, of providing for termination of the technology transfer agreement in the event that the licensee challenges the validity of any of the licensed technology rights.

2. Where the undertakings party to the agreement are not competing undertakings, the exemption provided for in Article 2 shall not apply to any direct or indirect obligation limiting the licensee's ability to exploit its own technology rights or limiting the ability of any of the parties to the agreement to carry out research and development, unless such latter restriction is indispensable to prevent the disclosure of the licensed know-how to third parties.

Article 6
Withdrawal in individual cases

1. The Commission may withdraw the benefit of this Regulation, pursuant to Article 29(1) of Regulation (EC) No 1/2003, where it finds in any particular case that a technology transfer agreement to which the exemption provided for in Article 2 of this Regulation applies nevertheless has effects which are incompatible with Article 101(3) of the Treaty, and in particular where:

   (a) access of third parties' technologies to the market is restricted, for instance by the cumulative effect of parallel networks of similar restrictive agreements prohibiting licensees from using third parties' technologies;

   (b) access of potential licensees to the market is restricted, for instance by the cumulative effect of parallel networks of similar restrictive agreements prohibiting licensors from licensing to other licensees or because the only technology owner licensing out relevant technology rights concludes an exclusive license with a licensee who is already active on the product market on the basis of substitutable technology rights.

2. Where, in any particular case, a technology transfer agreement to which the exemption provided for in Article 2 of this Regulation applies has effects which are incompatible with Article 101(3) of the Treaty in the territory of a Member State, or in a part thereof, which has all the characteristics of a distinct geographic market, the competition authority of that Member State may withdraw the benefit of this Regulation, pursuant to Article 29(2) of Regulation (EC) No 1/2003, in respect of that territory, under the same circumstances as those set out in paragraph 1 of this Article.

Article 7
Non-application of this Regulation

1. Pursuant to Article 1a of Regulation (EC) No 19/65/EEC, the Commission may by regulation declare that, where parallel networks of similar technology transfer agreements cover more than 50% of a relevant market, this Regulation is not to apply to technology transfer agreements containing specific restrictions relating to that market.

2. A regulation pursuant to paragraph 1 shall not become applicable earlier than six months following its adoption.

Article 8
Application of the market-share thresholds

For the purposes of applying the market-share thresholds laid down in Article 3 the following rules shall apply:

   (a) the market share shall be calculated on the basis of market sales value data; if market sales value data are not available, estimates based on other reliable market information, including market sales volumes, may be used to establish the market share of the undertaking concerned;

   (b) the market share shall be calculated on the basis of data relating to the preceding calendar year;

Appendix 6

(c) the market share held by the undertakings referred to in point (e) of the second subparagraph of Article 1(2) shall be apportioned equally to each undertaking having the rights or the powers listed in point (a) of the second subparagraph of Article 1(2);

(d) the market share of a licensor on a relevant market for the licensed technology rights shall be calculated on the basis of the presence of the licensed technology rights on the relevant market(s) (that is the product market(s) and the geographic market(s)) where the contract products are sold, that is on the basis of the sales data relating to the contract products produced by the licensor and its licensees combined;

(e) if the market share referred to in Article 3(1) or (2) is initially not more than 20 % or 30 % respectively, but subsequently rises above those levels, the exemption provided for in Article 2 shall continue to apply for a period of two consecutive calendar years following the year in which the 20% threshold or 30 % threshold was first exceeded.

Article 9
Relationship with other block exemption regulations
This Regulation shall not apply to licensing arrangements in research and development agreements which fall within the scope of Regulation (EU) No 1217/2010 or in specialisation agreements which fall within the scope of Regulation (EU) No 1218/2010.

Article 10
Transitional period
The prohibition laid down in Article 101(1) of the Treaty shall not apply from 1 May 2014 until 30 April 2015 to agreements already in force on 30 April 2014 which do not satisfy the conditions for exemption provided for in this Regulation but which, on 30 April 2014, satisfied the conditions for exemption provided for in Regulation (EC) No 772/2004.

Article 11
Period of validity
This Regulation shall enter into force on 1 May 2014.

It shall expire on 30 April 2026.

This Regulation shall be binding in its entirety and directly applicable in all Member States.

Done at Brussels, 21 March 2014.

For the Commission, On behalf of the President,
Joaquín ALMUNIA
Vice-President

Patents Act 1977 (as amended)
Intellectual Property Office
Intellectual Property Office is an operating name of the Patent Office
An unofficial consolidation produced by
Patents Legal Section
1 October 2014

Note to users

This is an unofficial consolidation of the Patents Act 1977, as amended up to and including 1 October 2014. This consolidation therefore includes (amongst other changes) the amendments to the 1977 Act made by:

the Copyright, Designs and Patents Act 1988
the Patents and Trade Marks (World Trade Organisation) Regulations 1999
the Patents Regulations 2000
the Enterprise Act 2002
the Regulatory Reform (Patents) Order 2004
the Patents Act 2004
the Medicines (Marketing Authorisations etc.) Amendment Regulations 2005
the Intellectual Property (Enforcement, etc.) Regulations 2006
the Patents (Compulsory Licensing and Supplementary Protection Certificates) Regulations 2007
the Legal Services Act 2007
the Crime and Courts Act 2013
the Enterprise and Regulatory Reform Act 2013 (Competition) (Consequential, Transitional and Saving Provisions) Order 2014
the Copyright (Public Administration) Regulations 2014
the Intellectual Property Act 2014
the Legislative Reform (Patents) Order 2014, and
the Patents (Supplementary Protection Certificates) Regulations 2014

In some cases, the amending legislation applies transitional provisions to the changes made to the 1977 Act. A number of the repealed provisions of the 1977 Act have been re-enacted or replaced by provisions in other legislation, and are therefore not reproduced in this document. Some wording of the 1977 Act has been 'modified in effect' by other pieces of legislation, although not actually amended, and footnotes show where this is the case. The *Manual of Patent Practice* should be consulted for more guidance on these matters.

…

While the greatest care has been taken in this unofficial consolidation, the Office does not accept any responsibility for errors or omissions, nor for any consequences of such errors or omissions.

Patents Legal Section

1 October 2014

PATENTS ACT 1977

Chapter 37

ARRANGEMENT OF SECTIONS

PART I NEW DOMESTIC LAW

Appendix 6

PATENTS ACT 1977

An Act to establish a new law of patents applicable to future patents and
applications for patents; to amend the law of patents applicable to existing patents
and applications for patents; to give effect to certain international conventions on
patents; and for connected purposes.

Be it enacted by the Queen's most Excellent Majesty, by and with the advice
and consent of the Lords Spiritual and Temporal, and Commons, in this present
Parliament assembled, and by authority of the same, as follows:–

PART I
NEW DOMESTIC LAW
PATENTABILITY

Patentable inventions

1.(1) A patent may be granted only for an invention in respect of which the
       following conditions are satisfied, that is to say –

   (a) the invention is new;
   (b) it involves an inventive step;
   (c) it is capable of industrial application;
   (d) the grant of a patent for it is not excluded by subsections (2) and (3) or
        section 4A below;

   and references in this Act to a patentable invention shall be construed
   accordingly.

(2) It is hereby declared that the following (among other things) are not
     inventions for the purposes of this Act, that is to say, anything which
     consists of –

   (a) a discovery, scientific theory or mathematical method;

Appendix 6

(b) a literary, dramatic, musical or artistic work or any other aesthetic creation whatsoever;

(c) a scheme, rule or method for performing a mental act, playing a game or doing business, or a program for a computer;

(d) the presentation of information;

but the foregoing provision shall prevent anything from being treated as an invention for the purposes of this Act only to the extent that a patent or application for a patent relates to that thing as such.

(3) A patent shall not be granted for an invention the commercial exploitation of which would be contrary to public policy or morality.

(4) For the purposes of subsection (3) above exploitation shall not be regarded as contrary to public policy or morality only because it is prohibited by any law in force in the United Kingdom or any part of it.

(5) The Secretary of State may by order vary the provisions of subsection (2) above for the purpose of maintaining them in conformity with developments in science and technology; and no such order shall be made unless a draft of the order has been laid before, and approved by resolution of, each House of Parliament.

Novelty

2.(1) An invention shall be taken to be new if it does not form part of the state of the art.

(2) The state of the art in the case of an invention shall be taken to comprise all matter (whether a product, a process, information about either, or anything else) which has at any time before the priority date of that invention been made available to the public (whether in the United Kingdom or elsewhere) by written or oral description, by use or in any other way.

(3) The state of the art in the case of an invention to which an application for a patent or a patent relates shall be taken also to comprise matter contained in an application for another patent which was published on or after the priority date of that invention, if the following conditions are satisfied, that is to say –

(a) that matter was contained in the application for that other patent both as filed and as published; and

(b) the priority date of that matter is earlier than that of the invention.

(4) For the purposes of this section the disclosure of matter constituting an invention shall be disregarded in the case of a patent or an application for a patent if occurring later than the beginning of the period of six months immediately preceding the date of filing the application for the patent and either –

(a) the disclosure was due to, or made in consequence of, the matter having been obtained unlawfully or in breach of confidence by any person –

(i) from the inventor or from any other person to whom the matter was made available in confidence by the inventor or who obtained it from the inventor because he or the inventor believed that he was entitled to obtain it; or

      (ii)   from any other person to whom the matter was made available in confidence by any person mentioned in sub-paragraph (i) above or in this sub-paragraph or who obtained it from any person so mentioned because he or the person from whom he obtained it believed that he was entitled to obtain it;

  (b) the disclosure was made in breach of confidence by any person who obtained the matter in confidence from the inventor or from any other person to whom it was made available, or who obtained it, from the inventor; or

  (c) the disclosure was due to, or made in consequence of the inventor displaying the invention at an international exhibition and the applicant states, on filing the application, that the invention has been so displayed and also, within the prescribed period, files written evidence in support of the statement complying with any prescribed conditions.

(5)   In this section references to the inventor include references to any proprietor of the invention for the time being.

(6)   [repealed]

Inventive step

3.   An invention shall be taken to involve an inventive step if it is not obvious to a person skilled in the art, having regard to any matter which forms part of the state of the art by virtue only of section 2(2) above (and disregarding section 2(3) above).

Industrial application

4.(1)An invention shall be taken to be capable of industrial application if it can be made or used in any kind of industry, including agriculture.

(2)   [repealed]

(3)   [repealed]

Methods of treatment or diagnosis

4A.(1) A patent shall not be granted for the invention of –

  (a) a method of treatment of the human or animal body by surgery or therapy, or

  (b) a method of diagnosis practised on the human or animal body.

(2)   Subsection (1) above does not apply to an invention consisting of a substance or composition for use in any such method.

(3)   In the case of an invention consisting of a substance or composition for use in any such method, the fact that the substance or composition forms part of the state of the art shall not prevent the invention from being taken to be new if the use of the substance or composition in any such method does not form part of the state of the art.

(4)   In the case of an invention consisting of a substance or composition for a specific use in any such method, the fact that the substance or composition forms part of the state of the art shall not prevent the invention from being taken to be new if that specific use does not form part of the state of the art.

Appendix 6

Priority date

5.(1) For the purposes of this Act the priority date of an invention to which an application for a patent relates and also of any matter (whether or not the same as the invention) contained in any such application is, except as provided by the following provisions of this Act, the date of filing the application.

(2) If in or in connection with an application for a patent (the application in suit) a declaration is made, whether by the applicant or any predecessor in title of his, complying with the relevant requirements of rules and specifying one or more earlier relevant applications for the purposes of this section made by the applicant or a predecessor in title of his and the application in suit has a date of filing during the period allowed under subsection (2A)(a) or (b) below, then –

    (a) if an invention to which the application in suit relates is supported by matter disclosed in the earlier relevant application or applications, the priority date of that invention shall instead of being the date of filing the application in suit be the date of filing the relevant application in which that matter was disclosed, or, if it was disclosed in more than one relevant application, the earliest of them;

    (b) the priority date of any matter contained in the application in suit which was also disclosed in the earlier relevant application or applications shall be the date of filing the relevant application in which that matter was disclosed or, if it was disclosed in more than one relevant application, the earliest of them.

(2A) The periods are –

    (a) the period of twelve months immediately following the date of filing of the earlier specified relevant application, or if there is more than one, of the earliest of them; and

    (b) where the comptroller has given permission under subsection (2B) below for a late declaration to be made under subsection (2) above, the period commencing immediately after the end of the period allowed under paragraph (a) above and ending at the end of the prescribed period.

(2B) The applicant may make a request to the comptroller for permission to make a late declaration under subsection (2) above.

(2C) The comptroller shall grant a request made under subsection (2B) above if, and only if –

    (a) the request complies with the relevant requirements of rules; and

    (b) the comptroller is satisfied that the applicant's failure to file the application in suit within the period allowed under subsection (2A)(a) above was unintentional.

(3) Where an invention or other matter contained in the application in suit was also disclosed in two earlier relevant applications filed by the same applicant as in the case of the application in suit or a predecessor in title of his and the second of those relevant applications was specified in or in connection with the application in suit, the second of those relevant applications shall, so far as concerns that invention or matter, be disregarded unless –

(a) it was filed in or in respect of the same country as the first; and

(b) not later than the date of filing the second, the first (whether or not so specified) was unconditionally withdrawn, or was abandoned or refused, without –

    (i) having been made available to the public (whether in the United Kingdom or elsewhere);

    (ii) leaving any rights outstanding; and

    (iii) having served to establish a priority date in relation to another application, wherever made.

(4) The foregoing provisions of this section shall apply for determining the priority date of an invention for which a patent has been granted as they apply for determining the priority date of an invention to which an application for that patent relates.

(5) In this section "relevant application" means any of the following applications which has a date of filing, namely –

(a) an application for a patent under this Act;

    (aa) an application in or for a country (other than the United Kingdom) which is a member of the World Trade Organisation for protection in respect of an invention which, in accordance with the law of that country or a treaty or international obligation to which it is a party, is equivalent to an application for a patent under this Act;

(b) an application in or for a convention country (specified under section 90 below) for protection in respect of an invention or an application which, in accordance with the law of a convention country or a treaty or international convention to which a convention country is a party, is equivalent to an application for a patent under this Act.

(6) [repealed]

Disclosure of matter, etc., between earlier and later application

6.(1) It is hereby declared for the avoidance of doubt that where an application (the application in suit) is made for a patent and a declaration is made in accordance with section 5(2) above in or in connection with that application specifying an earlier relevant application, the application in suit and any patent granted in pursuance of it shall not be invalidated by reason only of relevant intervening acts.

(2) In this section –

"relevant application" has the same meaning as in section 5 above; and

"relevant intervening acts" means acts done in relation to matter disclosed in an earlier relevant application between the dates of the earlier relevant application and the application in suit, as for example, filing another application for the invention for which the earlier relevant application was made, making information available to the public about that invention or that matter or working that invention, but disregarding any application, or the disclosure to the public of matter contained in any application, which is itself to be disregarded for the purposes of section 5(3) above.

Appendix 6

Right to apply for and obtain a patent and be mentioned as inventor

Right to apply for and obtain a patent

7.(1)Any person may make an application for a patent either alone or jointly with another.

(2)   A patent for an invention may be granted –

    (a)   primarily to the inventor or joint inventors;

    (b)   in preference to the foregoing, to any person or persons who, by virtue of any enactment or rule of law, or any foreign law or treaty or international convention, or by virtue of an enforceable term of any agreement entered into with the inventor before the making of the invention, was or were at the time of the making of the invention entitled to the whole of the property in it (other than equitable interests) in the United Kingdom;

    (c)   in any event, to the successor or successors in title of any person or persons mentioned in paragraph (a) or (b) above or any person so mentioned and the successor or successors in title of another person so mentioned; and to no other person.

(3)   In this Act "inventor" in relation to an invention means the actual deviser of the invention and "joint inventor" shall be construed accordingly.

(4)   Except so far as the contrary is established, a person who makes an application for a patent shall be taken to be the person who is entitled under subsection (2) above to be granted a patent and two or more persons who make such an application jointly shall be taken to be the persons so entitled.

Determination before grant of questions about entitlement to patents, etc.

8.(1)At any time before a patent has been granted for an invention (whether or not an application has been made for it) –

    (a)   any person may refer to the comptroller the question whether he is entitled to be granted (alone or with any other persons) a patent for that invention or has or would have any right in or under any patent so granted or any application for such a patent; or

    (b)   any of two or more co-proprietors of an application for a patent for that invention may so refer the question whether any right in or under the application should be transferred or granted to any other person;

and the comptroller shall determine the question and may make such order as he thinks fit to give effect to the determination.

(2)   Where a person refers a question relating to an invention under subsection (1)(a) above to the comptroller after an application for a patent for the invention has been filed and before a patent is granted in pursuance of the application, then, unless the application is refused or withdrawn before the reference is disposed of by the comptroller, the comptroller may, without prejudice to the generality of subsection (1) above and subject to subsection (6) below –

(a) order that the application shall proceed in the name of that person, either solely or jointly with that of any other applicant, instead of in the name of the applicant or any specified applicant;

(b) where the reference was made by two or more persons, order that the application shall proceed in all their names jointly;

(c) refuse to grant a patent in pursuance of the application or order the application to be amended so as to exclude any of the matter in respect of which the question was referred;

(d) make an order transferring or granting any licence or other right in or under the application and give directions to any person for carrying out the provisions of any such order.

(3) Where a question is referred to the comptroller under subsection (1)(a) above and –

(a) the comptroller orders an application for a patent for the invention to which the question relates to be so amended;

(b) any such application is refused under subsection 2(c) above before the comptroller has disposed of the reference (whether the reference was made before or after the publication of the application); or

(c) any such application is refused under any other provision of this Act or is withdrawn before the comptroller has disposed of the reference, (whether the application is refused or withdrawn before or after its publication) the comptroller may order that any person by whom the reference was made may within the prescribed period make a new application for a patent for the whole or part of any matter comprised in the earlier application or, as the case may be, for all or any of the matter excluded from the earlier application, subject in either case to section 76 below, and in either case that, if such a new application is made, it shall be treated as having been filed on the date of filing the earlier application.

(4) Where a person refers a question under subsection (1)(b) above relating to an application, any order under subsection (1) above may contain directions to any person for transferring or granting any right in or under the application.

(5) If any person to whom directions have been given under subsection (2) (d) or (4) above fails to do anything necessary for carrying out any such directions within 14 days after the date of the directions, the comptroller may, on application made to him by any person in whose favour or on whose reference the directions were given, authorise him to do that thing on behalf of the person to whom the directions were given.

(6) Where on a reference under this section it is alleged that, by virtue of any transaction, instrument or event relating to an invention or an application for a patent, any person other than the inventor or the applicant for the patent has become entitled to be granted (whether alone or with any other persons) a patent for the invention or has or would have any right in or under any patent so granted or any application for any such patent, an order shall not be made under subsection (2)(a), (b) or (d) above on the reference unless notice of the reference is given to the applicant and any such person, except any of them who is a party to the reference.

(7) If it appears to the comptroller on a reference of a question under this section that the question involves matters which would more properly be determined by the court, he may decline to deal with it and, without prejudice to the court's jurisdiction to determine any such question and make a declaration, or any declaratory jurisdiction of the court in Scotland, the court shall have jurisdiction to do so.

(8) No directions shall be given under this section so as to affect the mutual rights or obligations of trustees or of the personal representatives of deceased persons, or their rights or obligations as such.

Determination after grant of questions referred to before grant

9. If a question with respect to a patent or application is referred by any person to the comptroller under section 8 above, whether before or after the making of an application for the patent, and is not determined before the time when the application is first in order for a grant of a patent in pursuance of the application, that fact shall not prevent the grant of a patent, but on its grant that person shall be treated as having referred to the comptroller under section 37 below any question mentioned in that section which the comptroller thinks appropriate.

Handling of application by joint applicants

10. If any dispute arises between joint applicants for a patent whether or in what manner the application should be proceeded with, the comptroller may, on a request made by any of the parties, give such directions as he thinks fit for enabling the application to proceed in the name of one or more of the parties alone or for regulating the manner in which it shall be proceeded with, or for both those purposes, according as the case may require.

Effect of transfer of application under section 8 or 10

11.(1) Where an order is made or directions are given under section 8 or 10 above that an application for a patent shall proceed in the name of one or some of the original applicants (whether or not it is also to proceed in the name of some other person), any licences or other rights in or under the application shall, subject to the provisions of the order and any directions under either of those sections, continue in force and be treated as granted by the persons in whose name the application is to proceed.

(2) Where an order is made or directions are given under section 8 above that an application for a patent shall proceed in the name of one or more persons none of whom was an original applicant (on the ground that the original applicant or applicants was or were not entitled to be granted the patent), any licences or other rights in or under the application shall, subject to the provisions of the order and any directions under that section and subject to subsection (3) below, lapse on the registration of that person or those persons as the applicant or applicants or, where the application has not been published, on the making of the order.

(3) If before registration of a reference under section 8 above resulting in the making of any order mentioned in subsection (2) above –

(a) the original applicant or any of the applicants, acting in good faith, worked the invention in question in the United Kingdom or made effective and serious preparations to do so; or

(b) a licensee of the applicant, acting in good faith, worked the invention in the United Kingdom or made effective and serious preparations to do so;

that or those original applicant or applicants or the licensee shall, on making a request within the prescribed period to the person in whose name the application is to proceed, be entitled to be granted a licence (but not an exclusive licence) to continue working or, as the case may be, to work the invention.

(3A) If, before registration of a reference under section 8 above resulting in the making of an order under subsection (3) of that section, the condition in subsection (3)(a) or (b) above is met, the original applicant or any of the applicants or the licensee shall, on making a request within the prescribed period to the new applicant, be entitled to be granted a licence (but not an exclusive licence) to continue working or, as the case may be, to work the invention so far as it is the subject of the new application.

(4) A licence under subsection (3) or (3A) above shall be granted for a reasonable period and on reasonable terms.

(5) Where an order is made as mentioned in subsection (2) or (3A) above, the person in whose name the application is to proceed or, as the case may be, who makes the new application or any person claiming that he is entitled to be granted any such licence may refer to the comptroller the question whether the latter is so entitled and whether any such period is or terms are reasonable, and the comptroller shall determine the question and may, if he considers it appropriate, order the grant of such a licence.

Determination of questions about entitlement to foreign and convention patents, etc.

12.(1) At any time before a patent is granted for an invention in pursuance of an application made under the law of any country other than the United Kingdom or under any treaty or international convention (whether or not that application has been made) –

(a) any person may refer to the comptroller the question whether he is entitled to be granted (alone or with any other persons) any such patent for that invention or has or would have any right in or under any such patent or an application for such a patent; or

(b) any of two or more co-proprietors of an application for such a patent for that invention may so refer the question whether any right in or under the application should be transferred or granted to any other person;

and the comptroller shall determine the question so far as he is able to and may make such order as he thinks fit to give effect to the determination.

(2) If it appears to the comptroller on a reference of a question under this section that the question involves matters which would more properly be determined by the court, he may decline to deal with it and, without

prejudice to the court's jurisdiction to determine any such question and make a declaration, or any declaratory jurisdiction of the court in Scotland, the court shall have jurisdiction to do so.

(3) Subsection (1) above, in its application to a European patent and an application for any such patent, shall have effect subject to section 82 below.

(4) Section 10 above, except so much of it as enables the comptroller to regulate the manner in which an application is to proceed, shall apply to disputes between joint applicants for any such patent as is mentioned in subsection (1) above as it applies to joint applicants for a patent under this Act.

(5) Section 11 above shall apply in relation to –

(a) any orders made under subsection (1) above and any directions given under section 10 above by virtue of subsection (4) above; and

(b) any orders made and directions given by the relevant convention court with respect to a question corresponding to any question which may be determined under subsection (1) above;

as it applies to orders made and directions given apart from this section under section 8 or 10 above.

(6) In the following cases, that is to say –

(a) where an application for a European patent (UK) is refused or withdrawn, or the designation of the United Kingdom in the application is withdrawn whether before or after publication of the application but before a question relating to the right to the patent has been referred to the comptroller under subsection (1) above or before proceedings relating to that right have begun before the relevant convention court;

(b) where an application has been made for a European patent (UK) and on a reference under subsection (1) above or any such proceedings as are mentioned in paragraph (a) above the comptroller, the court or the relevant convention court determines by a final decision (whether before or after publication of the application) that a person other than the applicant has the right to the patent, but that person requests the European Patent Office that the application for the patent should be refused; or

(c) where an international application for a patent (UK) is withdrawn, or the designation of the United Kingdom in the application is withdrawn, whether before or after the making of any reference under subsection (1) above or the publication of the application;

the comptroller may order that any person (other than the applicant) appearing to him to be entitled to be granted a patent under this Act may within the prescribed period make an application for such a patent for the whole or part of any matter comprised in the earlier application (subject, however, to section 76 below) and that if the application for a patent under this Act is filed, it shall be treated as having been filed on the date of filing the earlier application.

(7) In this section –

(a) references to a patent and an application for a patent include respectively references to protection in respect of an invention and an application which, in accordance with the law of any country other than the United Kingdom or any treaty or international convention, is equivalent to an application for a patent or for such protection; and

(b) a decision shall be taken to be final for the purposes of this section when the time for appealing from it has expired without an appeal being brought or, where an appeal is brought, when it is finally disposed of.

Mention of inventor

13.(1) The inventor or joint inventors of an invention shall have a right to be mentioned as such in any patent granted for the invention and shall also have a right to be so mentioned if possible in any published application for a patent for the invention and, if not so mentioned, a right to be so mentioned in accordance with rules in a prescribed document.

(2) Unless he has already given the Patent Office the information hereinafter mentioned, an applicant for a patent shall within the prescribed period file with the Patent Office a statement –

(a) identifying the person or persons whom he believes to be the inventor or inventors; and

(b) where the applicant is not the sole inventor or the applicants are not the joint inventors, indicating the derivation of his or their right to be granted the patent;

and, if he fails to do so, the application shall be taken to be withdrawn.

(3) Where a person has been mentioned as sole or joint inventor in pursuance of this section, any other person who alleges that the former ought not to have been so mentioned may at any time apply to the comptroller for a certificate to that effect, and the comptroller may issue such a certificate; and if he does so, he shall accordingly rectify any undistributed copies of the patent and of any documents prescribed for the purposes of subsection (1) above.

Applications

Making of application

14.(1) Every application for a patent –

(a) shall be made in the prescribed form and shall be filed at the Patent Office in the prescribed manner;

(b) [repealed]

(1A) Where an application for a patent is made, the fee prescribed for the purposes of this subsection ("the application fee") shall be paid not later than the end of the period prescribed for the purposes of section 15(10)(c) below.

(2) Every application for a patent shall contain –

(a) a request for the grant of a patent;

(b) a specification containing a description of the invention, a claim or claims and any drawing referred to in the description or any claim; and

(c) an abstract;

but the foregoing provision shall not prevent an application being initiated by documents complying with section 15(1) below.

(3) The specification of an application shall disclose the invention in a manner which is clear enough and complete enough for the invention to be performed by a person skilled in the art.

(4) [repealed]

(5) The claim or claims shall –

(a) define the matter for which the applicant seeks protection;
(b) be clear and concise;
(c) be supported by the description; and
(d) relate to one invention or to a group of inventions which are so linked as to form a single inventive concept.

(6) Without prejudice to the generality of subsection (5)(d) above, rules may provide for treating two or more inventions as being so linked as to form a single inventive concept for the purposes of this Act.

(7) The purpose of the abstract is to give technical information and on publication it shall not form part of the state of the art by virtue of section 2(3) above, and the comptroller may determine whether the abstract adequately fulfils its purpose and, if it does not, may reframe it so that it does.

(8) [repealed]

(9) An application for a patent may be withdrawn at any time before the patent is granted and any withdrawal of such an application may not be revoked.

(10) Subsection (9) above does not affect the power of the comptroller under section 117(1) below to correct an error or mistake in a withdrawal of an application for a patent.

Date of filing application

15.(1) Subject to the following provisions of this Act, the date of filing an application for a patent shall be taken to be the earliest date on which documents filed at the Patent Office to initiate the application satisfy the following conditions –

(a) the documents indicate that a patent is sought;
(b) the documents identify the person applying for a patent or contain information sufficient to enable that person to be contacted by the Patent Office; and
(c) the documents contain either –

(i) something which is or appears to be a description of the invention for which a patent is sought; or
(ii) a reference, complying with the relevant requirements of rules, to an earlier relevant application made by the applicant or a predecessor in title of his.

(2) It is immaterial for the purposes of subsection (1)(c)(i) above –

(a) whether the thing is in, or is accompanied by a translation into, a language accepted by the Patent Office in accordance with rules;
(b) whether the thing otherwise complies with the other provisions of this Act and with any relevant rules.

(3) Where documents filed at the Patent Office to initiate an application for a patent satisfy one or more of the conditions specified in subsection (1) above, but do not satisfy all those conditions, the comptroller shall as soon as practicable after the filing of those documents notify the applicant of what else must be filed in order for the application to have a date of filing.

(4) Where documents filed at the Patent Office to initiate an application for a patent satisfy all the conditions specified in subsection (1) above, the comptroller shall as soon as practicable after the filing of the last of those documents notify the applicant of –

    (a) the date of filing the application, and

    (b) the requirements that must be complied with, and the periods within which they are required by this Act or rules to be complied with, if the application is not to be treated as having been withdrawn.

(5) Subsection (6) below applies where –

    (a) an application has a date of filing by virtue of subsection (1) above;

    (b) within the prescribed period the applicant files at the Patent Office –

        (i) a drawing, or

        (ii) part of the description of the invention for which a patent is sought, and

    (c) that drawing or that part of the description was missing from the application at the date of filing.

(6) Unless the applicant withdraws the drawing or the part of the description filed under subsection (5)(b) above ("the missing part") before the end of the prescribed period –

    (a) the missing part shall be treated as included in the application; and

    (b) the date of filing the application shall be the date on which the missing part is filed at the Patent Office.

(7) Subsection (6)(b) above does not apply if –

    (a) on or before the date which is the date of filing the application by virtue of subsection (1) above a declaration is made under section 5(2) above in or in connection with the application;

    (b) the applicant makes a request for subsection (6)(b) above not to apply; and

    (c) the request complies with the relevant requirements of rules and is made within the prescribed period.

(8) Subsections (6) and (7) above do not affect the power of the comptroller under section 117(1) below to correct an error or mistake.

(9) Where, after an application for a patent has been filed and before the patent is granted –

    (a) a new application is filed by the original applicant or his successor in title in accordance with rules in respect of any part of the matter contained in the earlier application, and

    (b) the conditions mentioned in subsection (1) above are satisfied in relation to the new application (without the new application contravening section 76 below), the new application shall be treated as having, as its date of filing, the date of filing the earlier application.

(10) Where an application has a date of filing by virtue of this section, the application shall be treated as having been withdrawn if any of the following applies –

    (a) the applicant fails to file at the Patent Office, before the end of the prescribed period, one or more claims and the abstract;

    (b) where a reference to an earlier relevant application has been filed as mentioned in subsection (1)(c)(ii) above –

        (i) the applicant fails to file at the Patent Office, before the end of the prescribed period, a description of the invention for which the patent is sought;

        (ii) the applicant fails to file at the Patent Office, before the end of the prescribed period, a copy of the application referred to, complying with the relevant requirements of rules;

    (c) the applicant fails to pay the application fee before the end of the prescribed period;

    (d) the applicant fails, before the end of the prescribed period, to make a request for a search under section 17 below and pay the search fee.

(11) In this section "relevant application" has the meaning given by section 5(5) above.

Preliminary examination

15A.(1) The comptroller shall refer an application for a patent to an examiner for a preliminary examination if –

    (a) the application has a date of filing;

    (b) the application has not been withdrawn or treated as withdrawn; and

    (c) the application fee has been paid.

(2) On a preliminary examination of an application the examiner shall –

    (a) determine whether the application complies with those requirements of this Act and the rules which are designated by the rules as formal requirements for the purposes of this Act; and

    (b) determine whether any requirements under section 13(2) or 15(10) above remain to be complied with.

(3) The examiner shall report to the comptroller his determinations under subsection (2) above.

(4) If on the preliminary examination of an application it is found that –

    (a) any drawing referred to in the application, or

    (b) part of the description of the invention for which the patent is sought,

is missing from the application, then the examiner shall include this finding in his report under subsection (3) above.

(5) Subsections (6) to (8) below apply if a report is made to the comptroller under subsection (3) above that not all the formal requirements have been complied with.

(6) The comptroller shall specify a period during which the applicant shall have the opportunity –

(a) to make observations on the report, and
(b) to amend the application so as to comply with those requirements (subject to section 76 below).

(7) The comptroller may refuse the application if the applicant fails to amend the application as mentioned in subsection (6)(b) above before the end of the period specified by the comptroller under that subsection.

(8) Subsection (7) above does not apply if –

(a) the applicant makes observations as mentioned in subsection (6)(a) above before the end of the period specified by the comptroller under that subsection, and
(b) as a result of the observations, the comptroller is satisfied that the formal requirements have been complied with.

(9) If a report is made to the comptroller under subsection (3) above –

(a) that any requirement of section 13(2) or 15(10) above has not been complied with; or
(b) that a drawing or part of the description of the invention has been found to be missing, then the comptroller shall notify the applicant accordingly.

Publication of application

16.(1) Subject to section 22 below and to any prescribed restrictions, where an application has a date of filing, then, as soon as possible after the end of the prescribed period, the comptroller shall, unless the application is withdrawn or refused before preparations for its publication have been completed by the Patent Office, publish it as filed (including not only the original claims but also any amendments of those claims and new claims subsisting immediately before the completion of those preparations) and he may, if so requested by the applicant, publish it as aforesaid during that period, and in either event shall advertise the fact and date of its publication in the journal.

(2) The comptroller may omit from the specification of a published application for a patent any matter –

(a) which in his opinion disparages any person in a way likely to damage him, or
(b) the publication or exploitation of which would in his opinion be generally expected to encourage offensive, immoral or anti-social behaviour.

Examination and search

Search

17.(1) The comptroller shall refer an application for a patent to an examiner for a search if, and only if –

(a) the comptroller has referred the application to an examiner for a preliminary examination under section 15A(1) above;

(b) the application has not been withdrawn or treated as withdrawn;

(c) before the end of the prescribed period –

   (i) the applicant makes a request to the Patent Office in the prescribed form for a search; and

   (ii) the fee prescribed for the search ("the search fee") is paid;

(d) the application includes –

   (i) a description of the invention for which a patent is sought; and

   (ii) one or more claims; and

(e) the description and each of the claims comply with the requirements of rules as to language.

(2) [repealed]

(3) [repealed]

(4) Subject to subsections (5) and (6) below, on a search requested under this section, the examiner shall make such investigation as in his opinion is reasonably practicable and necessary for him to identify the documents which he thinks will be needed to decide, on a substantive examination under section 18 below, whether the invention for which a patent is sought is new and involves an inventive step.

(5) On any such search the examiner shall determine whether or not the search would serve any useful purpose on the application as for the time being constituted and –

(a) if he determines that it would serve such a purpose in relation to the whole or part of the application, he shall proceed to conduct the search so far as it would serve such a purpose and shall report on the results of the search to the comptroller; and

(b) if he determines that the search would not serve such a purpose in relation to the whole or part of the application, he shall report accordingly to the comptroller;

and in either event the applicant shall be informed of the examiner's report.

(6) If it appears to the examiner, either before or on conducting a search under this section, that an application relates to two or more inventions, but that they are not so linked as to form a single inventive concept, he shall initially only conduct a search in relation to the first invention specified in the claims of the application, but may proceed to conduct a search in relation to another invention so specified if the applicant pays the search fee in respect of the application so far as it relates to that other invention.

(7) After a search has been requested under this section for an application the comptroller may at any time refer the application to an examiner for a supplementary search, and subsections (4) and (5) above shall apply in relation to a supplementary search as they apply in relation to any other search under this section.

(8) A reference for a supplementary search in consequence of –

(a) an amendment of the application made by the applicant under section 18(3) or 19(1) below, or

(b) a correction of the application, or of a document filed in connection with the application, under section 117 below,

shall be made only on payment of the prescribed fee, unless the comptroller directs otherwise.

Substantive examination and grant or refusal of patent

18.(1) Where the conditions imposed by section 17(1) above for the comptroller to refer an application to an examiner for a search are satisfied and at the time of the request under that subsection or within the prescribed period –

(a) a request is made by the applicant to the Patent Office in the prescribed form for a substantive examination; and

(b) the prescribed fee is paid for the examination;

the comptroller shall refer the application to an examiner for a substantive examination; and if no such request is made or the prescribed fee is not paid within that period, the application shall be treated as having been withdrawn at the end of that period.

(1A) If the examiner forms the view that a supplementary search under section 17 above is required for which a fee is payable, he shall inform the comptroller, who may decide that the substantive examination should not proceed until the fee is paid; and if he so decides, then unless within such period as he may allow –

(a) the fee is paid, or

(b) the application is amended so as to render the supplementary search unnecessary, he may refuse the application.

(2) On a substantive examination of an application the examiner shall investigate, to such extent as he considers necessary in view of any examination carried out under section 15A above and search carried out under section 17 above, whether the application complies with the requirements of this Act and the rules and shall determine that question and report his determination to the comptroller.

(3) If the examiner reports that any of those requirements are not complied with, the comptroller shall give the applicant an opportunity within a specified period to make observations on the report and to amend the application so as to comply with those requirements (subject, however, to section 76 below), and if the applicant fails to satisfy the comptroller that those requirements are complied with, or to amend the application so as to comply with them, the comptroller may refuse the application.

(4) If the examiner reports that the application, whether as originally filed or as amended in pursuance of section 15A above, this section or section 19 below, complies with those requirements at any time before the end of the prescribed period, the comptroller shall notify the applicant of that fact and, subject to subsection (5) and sections 19 and 22 below and on payment within the prescribed period of any fee prescribed for the grant, grant him a patent.

(5) Where two or more applications for a patent for the same invention having the same priority date are filed by the same applicant or his successor in title, the comptroller may on that ground refuse to grant a patent in pursuance of more than one of the applications.

Appendix 6

General power to amend application before grant

19.(1) At any time before a patent is granted in pursuance of an application the applicant may, in accordance with the prescribed conditions and subject to section 76 below, amend the application of his own volition.

(2) The comptroller may, without an application being made to him for the purpose, amend the specification and abstract contained in an application for a patent so as to acknowledge a registered trade mark.

Failure of application

20.(1) If it is not determined that an application for a patent complies before the end of the prescribed period with all the requirements of this Act and the rules, the application shall be treated as having been refused by the comptroller at the end of that period, and section 97 below shall apply accordingly.

(2) If at the end of that period an appeal to the court is pending in respect of the application or the time within which such an appeal could be brought has not expired, that period –

    (a) where such an appeal is pending, or is brought within the said time or before the expiration of any extension of that time granted (in the case of a first extension) on an application made within that time or (in the case of a subsequent extension) on an application made before the expiration of the last previous extension, shall be extended until such date as the court may determine;

    (b) where no such appeal is pending or is so brought, shall continue until the end of the same time or, if any extension of that time is so granted, until the expiration of the extension or last extension so granted.

Reinstatement of applications

20A.(1) Subsection (2) below applies where an application for a patent is refused, or is treated as having been refused or withdrawn, as a direct consequence of a failure by the applicant to comply with a requirement of this Act or rules within a period which is –

    (a) set out in this Act or rules, or

    (b) specified by the comptroller.

(2) Subject to subsection (3) below, the comptroller shall reinstate the application if, and only if –

    (a) the applicant requests him to do so;

    (b) the request complies with the relevant requirements of rules; and

    (c) he is satisfied that the failure to comply referred to in subsection (1) above was unintentional.

(3) The comptroller shall not reinstate the application if –

    (a) an extension remains available under this Act or rules for the period referred to in subsection (1) above; or

    (b) the period referred to in subsection (1) above is set out or specified –

        (i)   in relation to any proceedings before the comptroller;

        (ii) for the purposes of section 5(2A)(b) above; or

        (iii) for the purposes of a request under this section or section 117B below.

(4) Where the application was made by two or more persons jointly, a request under subsection (2) above may, with the leave of the comptroller, be made by one or more of those persons without joining the others.

(5) If the application has been published under section 16 above, then the comptroller shall publish notice of a request under subsection (2) above in the prescribed manner.

(6) The reinstatement of an application under this section shall be by order.

(7) If an application is reinstated under this section the applicant shall comply with the requirement referred to in subsection (1) above within the further period specified by the comptroller in the order reinstating the application.

(8) The further period specified under subsection (7) above shall not be less than two months.

(9) If the applicant fails to comply with subsection (7) above the application shall be treated as having been withdrawn on the expiry of the period specified under that subsection.

Effect of reinstatement under section 20A

20B.(1) The effect of reinstatement under section 20A of an application for a patent is as follows.

(2) Anything done under or in relation to the application during the period between termination and reinstatement shall be treated as valid.

(3) If the application has been published under section 16 above before its termination anything done during that period which would have constituted an infringement of the rights conferred by publication of the application if the termination had not occurred shall be treated as an infringement of those rights –

(a) if done at a time when it was possible for the period referred to in section 20A(1) above to be extended, or

(b) if it was a continuation or repetition of an earlier act infringing those rights.

(4) If the application has been published under section 16 above before its termination and, after the termination and before publication of notice of the request for its reinstatement, a person –

(a) began in good faith to do an act which would have constituted an infringement of the rights conferred by publication of the application if the termination had not taken place, or

(b) made in good faith effective and serious preparations to do such an act,

he has the right to continue to do the act or, as the case may be, to do the act, notwithstanding the reinstatement of the application and the grant of the patent; but this right does not extend to granting a licence to another person to do the act.

(4A) The right conferred by subsection (4) does not become exercisable until the end of the period during which a request may be made under this Act, or under the rules, for an extension of the period referred to in section 20A(1).

(5) If the act was done, or the preparations were made, in the course of a business, the person entitled to the right conferred by subsection (4) above may –

(a) authorise the doing of that act by any partners of his for the time being in that business, and

(b) assign that right, or transmit it on death (or in the case of a body corporate on its dissolution), to any person who acquires that part of the business in the course of which the act was done or the preparations were made.

(6) Where a product is disposed of to another in exercise of a right conferred by subsection (4) or (5) above, that other and any person claiming through him may deal with the product in the same way as if it had been disposed of by the applicant.

(6A) The above provisions apply in relation to the use of a patented invention for the services of the Crown as they apply in relation to infringement of the rights conferred by publication of the application for a patent (or, as the case may be, infringement of the patent).

"Patented invention" has the same meaning as in section 55 below.

(7) In this section "termination", in relation to an application, means –

(a) the refusal of the application, or

(b) the application being treated as having been refused or withdrawn.

Observations by third party on patentability

21.(1) Where an application for a patent has been published but a patent has not been granted to the applicant, any other person may make observations in writing to the comptroller on the question whether the invention is a patentable invention, stating reasons for the observations, and the comptroller shall consider the observations in accordance with rules.

(2) It is hereby declared that a person does not become a party to any proceedings under this Act before the comptroller by reason only that he makes observations under this section.

Security and safety

Information prejudicial to national security or safety of public

22.(1) Where an application for a patent is filed in the Patent Office (whether under this Act or any treaty or international convention to which the United Kingdom is a party and whether before or after the appointed day) and it appears to the comptroller that the application contains information of a description notified to him by the Secretary of State as being information the publication of which might be prejudicial to national security, the comptroller may give directions prohibiting or restricting the publication of that information or its communication to any specified person or description of persons.

(2) If it appears to the comptroller that any application so filed contains information the publication of which might be prejudicial to the safety of the public, he may give directions prohibiting or restricting the publication of that information or its communication to any specified person or description of persons until the end of a period not exceeding three months from the end of the period prescribed for the purposes of section 16 above.

(3) While directions are in force under this section with respect to an application –

    (a) if the application is made under this Act, it may proceed to the stage where it is in order for the grant of a patent, but it shall not be published and that information shall not be so communicated and no patent shall be granted in pursuance of the application;

    (b) if it is an application for a European patent, it shall not be sent to the European Patent Office; and

    (c) if it is an international application for a patent, a copy of it shall not be sent to the International Bureau or any international searching authority appointed under the Patent Co-operation Treaty.

(4) Subsection (3)(b) above shall not prevent the comptroller from sending the European Patent Office any information which it is his duty to send that office under the European Patent Convention.

(5) Where the comptroller gives directions under this section with respect to any application, he shall give notice of the application and of the directions to the Secretary of State, and the following provisions shall then have effect –

    (a) the Secretary of State shall, on receipt of the notice, consider whether the publication of the application or the publication or communication of the information in question would be prejudicial to national security or the safety of the public;

    (b) if the Secretary of State determines under paragraph (a) above that the publication of the application or the publication or communication of that information would be prejudicial to the safety of the public, he shall notify the comptroller who shall continue his directions under subsection (2) above until they are revoked under paragraph (e) below;

    (c) if the Secretary of State determines under paragraph (a) above that the publication of the application or the publication or communication of that information would be prejudicial to national security or the safety of the public, he shall (unless a notice under (d) below has previously been given by the Secretary of State to the comptroller) reconsider that question during the period of nine months from the date of filing the application and at least once in every subsequent period of twelve months;

    (d) if on consideration of an application at any time it appears to the Secretary of State that the publication of the application or the publication or communication of the information contained in it would not, or would no longer, be prejudicial to national security or the safety of the public, he shall give notice to the comptroller to that effect; and

    (e) on receipt of such a notice the comptroller shall revoke the directions and may, subject to such conditions (if any) as he thinks fit, extend the time for doing anything required or authorised to be done by or under this Act in connection with the application, whether or not that time has previously expired.

Appendix 6

(6) The Secretary of State may do the following for the purpose of enabling him to decide the question referred to in subsection (5)(c) above –

  (a) where the application contains information relating to the production or use of atomic energy or research into matters connected with such production or use, he may at any time do one or both of the following, that is to say,

   (i) inspect the application and any documents sent to the comptroller in connection with it;

   (ii) authorise a government body with responsibility for the production of atomic energy or for research into matters connected with its production or use, or a person appointed by such a government body, to inspect the application and any documents sent to the comptroller in connection with it; and

  (b) in any other case, he may at any time after (or, with the applicant's consent, before) the end of the period prescribed for the purposes of section 16 above inspect the application and any such documents;

  and where a government body or a person appointed by a government body carries out an inspection which the body or person is authorised to carry out under paragraph (a) above, the body or (as the case may be) the person shall report on the inspection to the Secretary of State as soon as practicable.

(7) Where directions have been given under this section in respect of an application for a patent for an invention and, before the directions are revoked, that prescribed period expires and the application is brought in order for the grant of a patent, then –

  (a) if while the directions are in force the invention is worked by (or with the written authorisation of or to the order of) a government department, the provisions of sections 55 to 59 below shall apply as if –

   (i) the working were use made by section 55;

   (ii) the application had been published at the end of that period; and

   (iii) a patent had been granted for the invention at the time the application is brought in order for the grant of a patent (taking the terms of the patent to be those of the application as it stood at the time it was so brought in order); and

  (b) if it appears to the Secretary of State that the applicant for the patent has suffered hardship by reason of the continuance in force of the directions, the Secretary of State may, with the consent of the Treasury, make such payment (if any) by way of compensation to the applicant as appears to the Secretary of State and the Treasury to be reasonable having regard to the inventive merit and utility of the invention, the purpose for which it is designed and any other relevant circumstances.

(8) Where a patent is granted in pursuance of an application in respect of which directions have been given under this section, no renewal fees shall be payable in respect of any period during which those directions were in force.

(9) A person who fails to comply with any direction under this section shall be liable

    (a) on summary conviction, to a fine not exceeding £1,0001; or

    (b) on conviction on indictment, to imprisonment for a term not exceeding two years or a fine, or both.

Restrictions on applications abroad by United Kingdom residents

23.(1) Subject to the following provisions of this section, no person resident in the United Kingdom shall, without written authority granted by the comptroller, file or cause to be filed outside the United Kingdom an application for a patent for an invention if subsection (1A) below applies to that application, unless –

    (a) an application for a patent for the same invention has been filed in the Patent Office (whether before, on or after the appointed day) not less than six weeks before the application outside the United Kingdom; and

    (b) either no directions have been given under section 22 above in relation to the application in the United Kingdom or all such directions have been revoked.

(1A) This subsection applies to an application if –

    (a) the application contains information which relates to military technology or for any other reason publication of the information might be prejudicial to national security; or

    (b) the application contains information the publication of which might be prejudicial to the safety of the public.

(2) Subsection (1) above does not apply to an application for a patent for an invention for which an application for a patent has first been filed (whether before or after the appointed day) in a country outside the United Kingdom by a person resident outside the United Kingdom.

(3) A person who files or causes to be filed an application for the grant of a patent in contravention of this section shall be liable –

    (a) on summary conviction, to a fine not exceeding £1,0002; or

    (b) on conviction on indictment, to imprisonment for a term not exceeding two years or a fine, or both.

(3A) A person is liable under subsection (3) above only if –

    (a) he knows that filing the application, or causing it to be filed, would contravene this section; or

    (b) he is reckless as to whether filing this application, or causing it to be filed, would contravene this section.

(4) In this section –

    (a) any reference to an application for a patent includes a reference to an application for other protection for an invention;

    (b) any reference to either kind of application is a reference to an application under this Act, under the law of any country other than the United Kingdom or under any treaty or international convention to which the United Kingdom is a party.

Appendix 6

Provisions as to patents after grant

Publication and certificate of grant

24.(1) As soon as practicable after a patent has been granted under this Act the comptroller shall publish in the journal a notice that it has been granted.

(2) The comptroller shall, as soon as practicable after he publishes a notice under subsection (1) above, send the proprietor of the patent a certificate in the prescribed form that the patent has been granted to the proprietor.

(3) The comptroller shall, at the same time as he publishes a notice under subsection (1) above in relation to a patent publish the specification of the patent, the names of the proprietor and (if different) the inventor and any other matters constituting or relating to the patent which in the comptroller's opinion it is desirable to publish.

(4) Subsection (3) above shall not require the comptroller to identify as inventor a person who has waived his right to be mentioned as inventor in any patent granted for the invention.

Term of patent

25.(1) A patent granted under this Act shall be treated for the purposes of the following provisions of this Act as having been granted, and shall take effect, on the date on which notice of its grant is published in the journal and, subject to subsection (3) below, shall continue in force until the end of the period of 20 years beginning with the date of filing the application for the patent or with such other date as may be prescribed.

(2) A rule prescribing any such other date under this section shall not be made unless a draft of the rule has been laid before, and approved by resolution of, each House of Parliament.

(3) Where any renewal fee in respect of a patent is not paid by the end of the period prescribed for payment (the "prescribed period") the patent shall cease to have effect at the end of such day, in the final month of that period, as may be prescribed.

(4) If during the period ending with the sixth month after the month in which the prescribed period ends the renewal fee and any prescribed additional fee are paid, the patent shall be treated for the purposes of this Act as if it had never expired, and accordingly –

(a) anything done under or in relation to it during that further period shall be valid;

(b) an act which would constitute an infringement of it if it had not expired shall constitute such an infringement; and

(c) an act which would constitute the use of the patented invention for the services of the Crown if the patent had not expired shall constitute that use.

(5) Rules shall include provision requiring the comptroller to notify the registered proprietor of a patent that a renewal fee has not been received from him in the Patent Office before the end of the prescribed period and before the framing of the notification.

Patent not to be impugned for lack of unity

26. No person may in any proceeding object to a patent or to an amendment of a specification of a patent on the ground that the claims contained in the specification of the patent, as they stand or, as the case may be, as proposed to be amended, relate –

(a) to more than one invention, or

(b) to a group of inventions which are not so linked as to form a single inventive concept.

General power to amend specification after grant

27.(1) Subject to the following provisions of this section and to section 76 below, the comptroller may, on an application made by the proprietor of a patent, allow the specification of the patent to be amended subject to such conditions, if any, as he thinks fit.

(2) No such amendment shall be allowed under this section where there are pending before the court or the comptroller proceedings in which the validity of the patent may be put in issue.

(3) An amendment of a specification of a patent under this section shall have effect and be deemed always to have had effect from the grant of the patent.

(4) The comptroller may, without an application being made to him for the purpose, amend the specification of a patent so as to acknowledge a registered trade-mark.

(5) A person may give notice to the comptroller of his opposition to an application under this section by the proprietor of a patent, and if he does so the comptroller shall notify the proprietor and consider the opposition in deciding whether to grant the application.

(6) In considering whether or not to allow an application under this section, the comptroller shall have regard to any relevant principles under the European Patent Convention.

Restoration of lapsed patents

28.(1) Where a patent has ceased to have effect by reason of a failure to pay any renewal fee, an application for the restoration of the patent may be made to the comptroller within the prescribed period.

(1A) Rules prescribing that period may contain such transitional provisions and savings as appear to the Secretary of State to be necessary or expedient.

(2) An application under this section may be made by the person who was the proprietor of the patent or by any other person who would have been entitled to the patent if it had not ceased to have effect; and where the patent was held by two or more persons jointly, the application may, with the leave of the comptroller, be made by one or more of them without joining the others.

(2A) Notice of the application shall be published by the comptroller in the prescribed manner.

(3) If the comptroller is satisfied that the failure of the proprietor of the patent –

(a) to pay the renewal fee within the prescribed period; or

(b) to pay that fee and any prescribed additional fee within the period ending with the sixth month after the month in which the prescribed period ended, was unintentional, the comptroller shall by order restore the patent on payment of any unpaid renewal fee and any prescribed additional fee.

(4) An order under this section may be made subject to such conditions as the comptroller thinks fit (including a condition requiring compliance with any provisions of the rules relating to registration which have not been complied with), and if the proprietor of the patent does not comply with any condition of such an order the comptroller may revoke the order and give such directions consequential on the revocation as he thinks fit.

(5) to (9) [repealed]

Effect of order for restoration of patent

28A.(1) The effect of an order for the restoration of a patent is as follows.

(2) Anything done under or in relation to the patent during the period between expiry and restoration shall be treated as valid.

(3) Anything done during that period which would have constituted an infringement if the patent had not expired shall be treated as an infringement –

   (a) if done at a time when it was possible for the patent to be renewed under section 25(4), or
   (b) if it was a continuation or repetition of an earlier infringing act.

(4) If after it was no longer possible for the patent to be so renewed, and before publication of notice of the application for restoration, a person –

   (a) began in good faith to do an act which would have constituted an infringement of the patent if it had not expired, or
   (b) made in good faith effective and serious preparations to do such an act,

   he has the right to continue to do the act or, as the case may be, to do the act, notwithstanding the restoration of the patent; but this right does not extend to granting a licence to another person to do the act.

(5) If the act was done, or the preparations were made, in the course of a business, the person entitled to the right conferred by subsection (4) may –

   (a) authorise the doing of that act by any partners of his for the time being in that business, and
   (b) assign that right, or transmit it on death (or in the case of a body corporate on its dissolution), to any person who acquires that part of the business in the course of which the act was done or the preparations were made.

(6) Where a product is disposed of to another in exercise of the rights conferred by subsection (4) or (5), that other and any person claiming through him may deal with the product in the same way as if it had been disposed of by the registered proprietor of the patent.

(7) The above provisions apply in relation to the use of a patent for the services of the Crown as they apply in relation to infringement of the patent.

Surrender of patents

29.(1) The proprietor of a patent may at any time by notice given to the comptroller offer to surrender his patent.

(2) A person may give notice to the comptroller of his opposition to the surrender of a patent under this section, and if he does so the comptroller shall notify the proprietor of the patent and determine the question.

(3) If the comptroller is satisfied that the patent may properly be surrendered, he may accept the offer and, as from the date when notice of his acceptance is published in the journal, the patent shall cease to have effect, but no action for infringement shall lie in respect of any act done before that date and no right to compensation shall accrue for any use of the patented invention before that date for the services of the Crown.

Property in patents and applications, and registration

Nature of, and transactions in, patents and applications for patents

30.(1) Any patent or application for a patent is personal property (without being a thing in action), and any patent or any such application and rights in or under it may be transferred, created or granted in accordance with subsections (2) to (7) below.

(2) Subject to section 36(3) below, any patent or any such application, or any right in it, may be assigned or mortgaged.

(3) Any patent or any such application or right shall vest by operation of law in the same way as any other personal property and may be vested by an assent of personal representatives.

(4) Subject to section 36(3) below, a licence may be granted under any patent or any such application for working the invention which is the subject of the patent or the application; and –

(a) to the extent that the licence so provides, a sub-licence may be granted under any such licence and any such licence or sub-licence may be assigned or mortgaged; and

(b) any such licence or sub-licence shall vest by operation of law in the same way as any other personal property and may be vested by an assent of personal representatives.

(5) Subsections (2) to (4) above shall have effect subject to the following provisions of this Act.

(6) Any of the following transactions, that is to say –

(a) any assignment or mortgage of a patent or any such application, or any right in a patent or any such application;

(b) any assent relating to any patent or any such application or right;

shall be void unless it is in writing and is signed by or on behalf of the assignor or mortgagor (or, in the case of an assent or other transaction by a personal representative, by or on behalf of the personal representative).

(6A) If a transaction mentioned in subsection (6) above is by a body corporate, references in that subsection to such a transaction being signed by or on behalf of the assignor or mortgagor shall be taken to include references to its being under the seal of the body corporate.

(7) An assignment of a patent or any such application or a share in it, and an exclusive licence granted under any patent or any such application, may confer on the assignee or licensee the right of the assignor or licensor to bring proceedings by virtue of section 61 or 69 below for a previous infringement or to bring proceedings under section 58 below for a previous act.

Nature of, and transactions in, patents and applications for patents in Scotland

31.(1) Section 30 above shall not extend to Scotland, but instead the following provisions of this section shall apply there.

(2) Any patent or application for a patent, and any right in or under any patent or any such application, is incorporeal moveable property, and the provisions of the following sub-sections and of section 36(3) below shall apply to any grant of licences, assignations and securities in relation to such property.

(3) Any patent or any such application, or any right in it, may be assigned and security may be granted over a patent or any such application or right.

(4) A licence may be granted, under any patent or any application for a patent, for working the invention which is the subject of the patent or the application.

(5) To the extent that any licence granted under subsection (4) above so provides, a sub-licence may be granted under any such licence and any such licence or sub-licence may be assigned and security may be granted over it.

(6) Any assignation or grant of security under this section may be carried out only by writing subscribed in accordance with the Requirements of Writing (Scotland) Act 1995.

(7) An assignation of a patent or application for a patent or a share in it, and an exclusive licence granted under any patent or any such application, may confer on the assignee or licensee the right of the assignor or licensor to bring proceedings by virtue of section 61 or 69 below for a previous infringement or to bring proceedings under section 58 below for a previous act.

Register of patents, etc.

32(1) The comptroller shall maintain the register of patents, which shall comply with rules made by virtue of this section and shall be kept in accordance with such rules.

(2) Without prejudice to any other provision of this Act or rules, rules may make provision with respect to the following matters, including provision imposing requirements as to any of those matters –

    (a) the registration of patents and of published applications for patents;

    (b) the registration of transactions, instruments or events affecting rights in or under patents and applications;

        (ba) the entering on the register of notices concerning opinions issued, or to be issued, under section 74A below;

    (c) the furnishing to the comptroller of any prescribed documents or description of documents in connection with any matter which is required to be registered;

(d)   the correction of errors in the register and in any documents filed at the Patent Office in connection with registration;

(e)   the publication and advertisement of anything done under this Act or rules in relation to the register.

(3)   Notwithstanding anything in subsection (2)(b) above, no notice of any trust, whether express, implied or constructive, shall be entered in the register and the comptroller shall not be affected by any such notice.

(4)   The register need not be kept in documentary form.

(5)   Subject to rules, the public shall have a right to inspect the register at the Patent Office at all convenient times.

(6)   Any person who applies for a certified copy of an entry in the register or a certified extract from the register shall be entitled to obtain such a copy or extract on payment of a fee prescribed in relation to certified copies and extracts; and rules may provide that any person who applies for an uncertified copy or extract shall be entitled to such a copy or extract on payment of a fee prescribed in relation to uncertified copies and extracts.

(7)   Applications under subsection (6) above or rules made by virtue of that subsection shall be made in such manner as may be prescribed.

(8)   In relation to any portion of the register kept otherwise than in documentary form –

(a)   the right of inspection conferred by subsection (5) above is a right to inspect the material on the register; and

(b)   the right to a copy or extract conferred by subsection (6) above or rules is a right to a copy or extract in a form in which it can be taken away and in which it is visible and legible.

(9)   Subject to subsection (12) below, the register shall be prima facie evidence of anything required or authorised by this Act or rules to be registered and in Scotland shall be sufficient evidence of any such thing.

(10) A certificate purporting to be signed by the comptroller and certifying that any entry which he is authorised by this Act or rules to make has or has not been made, or that any other thing which he is so authorised to do has or has not been done, shall be prima facie evidence, and in Scotland shall be sufficient evidence, of the matters so certified.

(11) Each of the following, that is to say –

(a)   a copy of an entry in the register or an extract from the register which is supplied under subsection (6) above;

(b)   a copy of any document kept in the Patent Office or an extract from any such document, any specification of a patent or any application for a patent which has been published,

which purports to be a certified copy or a certified extract shall, subject to subsection (12) below, be admitted in evidence without further proof and without production of any original; and in Scotland such evidence shall be sufficient evidence.

(12) [repealed]

(13) In this section "certified copy" and "certified extract" mean a copy and extract certified by the comptroller and sealed with the seal of the Patent Office.

(14) In this Act, except so far as the context otherwise requires –

"register", as a noun, means the register of patents;

"register", as a verb, means, in relation to any thing, to register or register particulars, or enter notice, of that thing in the register and, in relation to a person, means to enter his name in the register;

and cognate expressions shall be construed accordingly.

Effect of registration, etc., on rights in patents

33.(1) Any person who claims to have acquired the property in a patent or application for a patent by virtue of any transaction, instrument or event to which this section applies shall be entitled as against any other person who claims to have acquired that property by virtue of an earlier transaction, instrument or event to which this section applies if, at the time of the later transaction, instrument or event –

(a) the earlier transaction, instrument or event was not registered, or

(b) in the case of any application which has not been published, notice of the earlier transaction, instrument or event had not been given to the comptroller, and

(c) in any case, the person claiming under the later transaction, instrument or event, did not know of the earlier transaction, instrument or event.

(2) Subsection (1) above shall apply equally to the case where any person claims to have acquired any right in or under a patent or application for a patent, by virtue of a transaction, instrument or event to which this section applies, and that right is incompatible with any such right acquired by virtue of an earlier transaction, instrument or event to which this section applies.

(3) This section applies to the following transactions, instruments and events –

(a) the assignment or assignation of a patent or application for a patent, or a right in it;

(b) the mortgage of a patent or application or the granting of security over it;

(c) the grant, assignment or assignation of a licence or sub-licence, or mortgage of a licence or sub-licence, under a patent or application;

(d) the death of the proprietor or one of the proprietors of any such patent or application or any person having a right in or under a patent or application and the vesting by an assent of personal representatives of a patent, application or any such right; and

(e) any order or directions of a court or other competent authority –

(i) transferring a patent or application or any right in or under it to any person; or

(ii) that an application should proceed in the name of any person;

and in either case the event by virtue of which the court or authority had power to make any such order or give any such directions.

(4) Where an application for the registration of a transaction, instrument or event has been made, but the transaction, instrument or event has not been

registered, then, for the purposes of subsection (1)(a) above, registration of the application shall be treated as registration of the transaction, instrument or event.

Rectification of register

34.(1) The court may, on the application of any person aggrieved, order the register to be rectified by the making, or the variation or deletion, of any entry in it.

(2) In proceedings under this section the court may determine any question which it may be necessary or expedient to decide in connection with the rectification of the register.

(3) Rules of court may provide for the notification of any application under this section to the comptroller and for his appearance on the application and for giving effect to any order of the court on the application.

Evidence of register, documents, etc.

35. [repealed]

Co-ownership of patents and applications for patents

36.(1) Where a patent is granted to two or more persons, each of them shall, subject to any agreement to the contrary, be entitled to an equal undivided share in the patent.

(2) Where two or more persons are proprietors of a patent, then, subject to the provisions of this section and subject to any agreement to the contrary –

(a) each of them shall be entitled, by himself or his agents, to do in respect of the invention concerned, for his own benefit and without the consent of or the need to account to the other or others, any act which would apart from this subsection and section 55 below, amount to an infringement of the patent concerned; and

(b) any such act shall not amount to an infringement of the patent concerned.

(3) Subject to the provisions of sections 8 and 12 above and section 37 below and to any agreement for the time being in force, where two or more persons are proprietors of a patent one of them shall not without the consent of the other or others –

(a) amend the specification of the patent or apply for such an amendment to be allowed or for the patent to be revoked, or

(b) grant a licence under the patent or assign or mortgage a share in the patent or in Scotland cause or permit security to be granted over it.

(4) Subject to the provisions of those sections, where two or more persons are proprietors of a patent, anyone else may supply one of those persons with the means, relating to an essential element of the invention, for putting the invention into effect, and the supply of those means by virtue of this subsection shall not amount to an infringement of the patent.

(5) Where a patented product is disposed of by any of two or more proprietors to any person, that person and any other person claiming through him shall be entitled to deal with the product in the same way as if it had been disposed of by a sole registered proprietor.

(6) Nothing in subsection (1) or (2) above shall affect the mutual rights or obligations of trustees or of the personal representatives of a deceased person, or their rights or obligations as such.

(7) The foregoing provisions of this section shall have effect in relation to an application for a patent which is filed as they have effect in relation to a patent and –

    (a) references to a patent and a patent being granted shall accordingly include references respectively to any such application and to the application being filed; and

    (b) the reference in subsection (5) above to a patented product shall be construed accordingly.

Determination of right to patent after grant

37.(1) After a patent has been granted for an invention any person having or claiming a proprietary interest in or under the patent may refer to the comptroller the question –

    (a) who is or are the true proprietor or proprietors of the patent,

    (b) whether the patent should have been granted to the person or persons to whom it was granted, or

    (c) whether any right in or under the patent should be transferred or granted to any other person or persons;

and the comptroller shall determine the question and make such order as he thinks fit to give effect to the determination.

(2) Without prejudice to the generality of subsection (1) above, an order under that subsection may contain provision –

    (a) directing that the person by whom the reference is made under that subsection shall be included (whether or not to the exclusion of any other person) among the persons registered as proprietors of the patent;

    (b) directing the registration of a transaction, instrument or event by virtue of which that person has acquired any right in or under the patent;

    (c) granting any licence or other right in or under the patent;

    (d) directing the proprietor of the patent or any person having any right in or under the patent to do anything specified in the order as necessary to carry out the other provisions of the order.

(3) If any person to whom directions have been given under subsection (2)(d) above fails to do anything necessary for carrying out any such directions within 14 days after the date of the order containing the directions, the comptroller may, on application made to him by any person in whose favour or on whose reference the order containing the directions was made, authorise him to do that thing on behalf of the person to whom the directions were given.

(4) Where the comptroller finds on a reference under this section that the patent was granted to a person not entitled to be granted that patent (whether alone or with other persons) and on application made under section 72 below makes an order on that ground for the conditional or unconditional

revocation of the patent, the comptroller may order that the person by whom the application was made or his successor in title may, subject to section 76 below, make a new application for a patent –

(a) in the case of unconditional revocation, for the whole of the matter comprised in the specification of that patent; and

(b) in the case of conditional revocation, for the matter which in the opinion of the comptroller should be excluded from that specification by amendment under section 75 below;

and where such new application is made, it shall be treated as having been filed on the date of filing the application for the patent to which the reference relates.

(5) On any such reference no order shall be made under this section transferring the patent to which the reference relates on the ground that the patent was granted to a person not so entitled, and no order shall be made under subsection (4) above on that ground, if the reference was made after the second anniversary of the date of the grant, unless it is shown that any person registered as a proprietor of the patent knew at the time of the grant or, as the case may be, of the transfer of the patent to him that he was not entitled to the patent.

(6) An order under this section shall not be so made as to affect the mutual rights or obligations of trustees or of the personal representatives of a deceased person, or their rights or obligations as such.

(7) Where a question is referred to the comptroller under this section an order shall not be made by virtue of subsection (2) or under subsection (4) above on the reference unless notice of the reference is given to all persons registered as proprietor of the patent or as having a right in or under the patent, except those who are parties to the reference.

(8) If it appears to the comptroller on a reference under this section that the question referred to him would more properly be determined by the court, he may decline to deal with it and, without prejudice to the court's jurisdiction to determine any such question and make a declaration, or any declaratory jurisdiction of the court in Scotland, the court shall have jurisdiction to do so.

(9) The court shall not in the exercise of any such declaratory jurisdiction determine a question whether a patent was granted to a person not entitled to be granted the patent if the proceedings in which the jurisdiction is invoked were commenced after the second anniversary of the date of the grant of the patent, unless it is shown that any person registered as a proprietor of the patent knew at the time of the grant or, as the case may be, of the transfer of the patent to him that he was not entitled to the patent.

Effect of transfer of patent under section 37

38.(1) Where an order is made under section 37 above that a patent shall be transferred from any person or persons (the old proprietor or proprietors) to one or more persons (whether or not including an old proprietor), then, except in a case falling within subsection (2) below, any licences or other rights granted or created by the old proprietor or proprietors shall, subject to section 33 above and to the provisions of the order, continue in force and be treated as granted by the person or persons to whom the patent is ordered to be transferred (the new proprietor or proprietors).

(2) Where an order is so made that a patent shall be transferred from the old proprietor or proprietors to one or more persons none of whom was an old proprietor (on the ground that the patent was granted to a person not entitled to be granted the patent), any licences or other rights in or under the patent shall, subject to the provisions of the order and subsection (3) below, lapse on the registration of that person or those persons as the new proprietor or proprietors of the patent.

(3) Where an order is so made that a patent shall be transferred as mentioned in subsection (2) above or that a person other than an old proprietor may make a new application for a patent and before the reference of the question under that section resulting in the making of any such order is registered, the old proprietor or proprietors or a licensee of the patent, acting in good faith, worked the invention in question in the United Kingdom or made effective and serious preparations to do so, the old proprietor or proprietors or the licensee shall, on making a request to the new proprietor or proprietors or, as the case may be, the new applicant within the prescribed period, be entitled to be granted a licence (but not an exclusive licence) to continue working or, as the case may be, to work the invention, so far as it is the subject of the new application.

(4) Any such licence shall be granted for a reasonable period and on reasonable terms.

(5) The new proprietor or proprietors of the patent or, as the case may be, the new applicant or any person claiming that he is entitled to be granted any such licence may refer to the comptroller the question whether that person is so entitled and whether any such period is or terms are reasonable, and the comptroller shall determine the question and may, if he considers it appropriate, order the grant of such a licence.

Employees' inventions

Right to employees' inventions

39.(1) Notwithstanding anything in any rule of law, an invention made by an employee shall, as between him and his employer, be taken to belong to his employer for the purposes of this Act and all other purposes if –

(a) it was made in the course of the normal duties of the employee or in the course of duties falling outside his normal duties, but specifically assigned to him, and the circumstances in either case were such that an invention might reasonably be expected to result from the carrying out of his duties; or

(b) the invention was made in the course of the duties of the employee and, at the time of making the invention, because of the nature of his duties and the particular responsibilities arising from the nature of his duties he had a special obligation to further the interests of the employer's undertaking.

(2) Any other invention made by an employee shall, as between him and his employer, be taken for those purposes to belong to the employee.

(3) Where by virtue of this section an invention belongs, as between him and his employer, to an employee, nothing done –

(a) by or on behalf of the employee or any person claiming under him for the purposes of pursuing an application for a patent, or
(b) by any person for the purpose of performing or working the invention,

shall be taken to infringe any copyright or design right to which, as between him and his employer, his employer is entitled in any model or document relating to the invention.

Compensation of employees for certain inventions

40.(1) Where it appears to the court or the comptroller on an application made by an employee within the prescribed period that –

(a) the employee has made an invention belonging to the employer for which a patent has been granted,
(b) having regard among other things to the size and nature of the employer's undertaking, the invention or the patent for it (or the combination of both) is of outstanding benefit to the employer, and
(c) by reason of those facts it is just that the employee should be awarded compensation to be paid by the employer,

the court or the comptroller may award him such compensation of an amount determined under section 41 below.

(2) Where it appears to the court or the comptroller on an application made by an employee within the prescribed period that –

(a) a patent has been granted for an invention made by and belonging to the employee;
(b) his rights in the invention, or in any patent or application for a patent for the invention, have since the appointed day been assigned to the employer or an exclusive licence under the patent or application has since the appointed day been granted to the employer;
(c) the benefit derived by the employee from the contract of assignment, assignation or grant or any ancillary contract ("the relevant contract") is inadequate in relation to the benefit derived by the employer from the invention or the patent for it (or both); and
(d) by reason of those facts it is just that the employee should be awarded compensation to be paid by the employer in addition to the benefit derived from the relevant contract;

the court or the comptroller may award him such compensation of an amount determined under section 41 below.

(3) Subsections (1) and (2) above shall not apply to the invention of an employee where a relevant collective agreement provides for the payment of compensation in respect of inventions of the same description as that invention to employees of the same description as that employee.

(4) Subsection (2) above shall have effect notwithstanding anything in the relevant contract or any agreement applicable to the invention (other than any such collective agreement).

(5) If it appears to the comptroller on an application under this section that the application involves matters which would more properly be determined by the court, he may decline to deal with it.

(6) In this section –

"the prescribed period", in relation to proceedings before the court, means the period prescribed by rules of court, and

"relevant collective agreement" means a collective agreement within the meaning of the Trade Union and Labour Relations (Consolidation) Act 1992, made by or on behalf of a trade union to which the employee belongs, and by the employer or an employers' association to which the employer belongs which is in force at the time of the making of the invention.

(7) References in this section to an invention belonging to an employer or employee are references to it belonging as between the employer and the employee.

Amount of compensation

41.(1) An award of compensation to an employee under section 40(1) or (2) above shall be such as will secure for the employee a fair share (having regard to all the circumstances) of the benefit which the employer has derived, or may reasonably be expected to derive, from any of the following –

    (a) the invention in question;

    (b) the patent for the invention;

    (c) the assignment, assignation or grant of –

        (i) the property or any right in the invention, or

        (ii) the property in, or any right in or under, an application for the patent,

    to a person connected with the employer.

(2) For the purposes of subsection (1) above the amount of any benefit derived or expected to be derived by an employer from the assignment, assignation or grant of –

    (a) the property in, or any right in or under, a patent for the invention or an application for such a patent; or

    (b) the property or any right in the invention;

to a person connected with him shall be taken to be the amount which could reasonably be expected to be so derived by the employer if that person had not been connected with him.

(3) Where the Crown or a Research Council in its capacity as employer assigns or grants the property in, or any right in or under, an invention, patent or application for a patent to a body having among its functions that of developing or exploiting inventions resulting from public research and does so for no consideration or only a nominal consideration, any benefit derived from the invention, patent or application by that body shall be treated for the purposes of the foregoing provisions of this section as so derived by the Crown or, as the case may be, Research Council.

In this subsection "Research Council" means a body which is a Research Council for the purposes of the Science and Technology Act 1965.

(4) In determining the fair share of the benefit to be secured for an employee in respect of an invention which has always belonged to an employer, the court or the comptroller shall, among other things, take the following matters into account, that is to say –

   (a) the nature of the employee's duties, his remuneration and the other advantages he derives or has derived from his employment or has derived in relation to the invention under this Act;

   (b) the effort and skill which the employee has devoted to making the invention;

   (c) the effort and skill which any other person has devoted to making the invention jointly with the employee concerned, and the advice and other assistance contributed by any other who is not a joint inventor of the invention; and

   (d) the contribution made by the employer to the making, developing and working of the invention by the provision of advice, facilities and other assistance, by the provision of opportunities and by his managerial and commercial skill and activities.

(5) In determining the fair share of the benefit to be secured for an employee in respect of an invention which originally belonged to him, the court or the comptroller shall, among other things, take the following matters into account, that is to say –

   (a) any conditions in a licence or licences granted under this Act or otherwise in respect of the invention or the patent for it;

   (b) the extent to which the invention was made jointly by the employee with any other person; and

   (c) the contribution made by the employer to the making, developing and working of the invention as mentioned in subsection (4)(d) above.

(6) Any order for the payment of compensation under section 40 above may be an order for the payment of a lump sum or for periodical payment, or both.

(7) Without prejudice to section 32 of the Interpretation Act 18893 (which provides that a statutory power may in general be exercised from time to time), the refusal of the court or the comptroller to make any such order on an application made by an employee under section 40 above shall not prevent a further application being made under that section by him or any successor in title of his.

(8) Where the court or the comptroller has made any such order, the court or he may on the application of either the employer or the employee vary or discharge it or suspend any provision of the order and revive any provision so suspended, and section 40(5) above shall apply to the application as it applies to an application under that section.

(9) In England and Wales any sums awarded by the comptroller under section 40 above shall, if the county court so orders, be recoverable by execution issued from the county court or otherwise as if they were payable under an order of that court.

(10) In Scotland an order made under section 40 above by the comptroller for the payment of any sums may be enforced in like manner as an extract registered decree arbitral bearing a warrant for execution issued by the sheriff court of any sheriffdom in Scotland.

(11) In Northern Ireland an order made under section 40 above by the comptroller for the payment of any sums may be enforced as if it were a money judgment.

(12) In the Isle of Man an order made under section 40 above by the comptroller for the payment of any sums may be enforced in like manner as an execution issued out of the court.

Enforceability of contracts relating to employees' inventions

42.(1) This section applies to any contract (whenever made) relating to inventions made by an employee, being a contract entered into by him –

(a) with the employer (alone or with another); or

(b) with some other person at the request of the employer or in pursuance of the employee's contract of employment.

(2) Any term in a contract to which this section applies which diminishes the employee's rights in inventions of any description made by him after the appointed day and the date of the contract, or in or under patents for those inventions or applications for such patents, shall be unenforceable against him to the extent that it diminishes his rights in an invention of that description so made, or in or under a patent for such an invention or an application for any such patent.

(3) Subsection (2) above shall not be construed as derogating from any duty of confidentiality owed to his employer by an employee by virtue of any rule of law or otherwise.

(4) This section applies to any arrangements made with a Crown employee by or on behalf of the Crown as his employer as it applies to any contract made between an employee and an employer other than the Crown, and for the purposes of his section "Crown employee" means a person employed under or for the purposes of a government department or any officer or body exercising on behalf of the Crown functions conferred by any enactment or a person serving in the naval, military or air forces of the Crown.

Supplementary

43.(1) Sections 39 to 42 above shall not apply to an invention made before the appointed day.

(2) Sections 39 to 42 above shall not apply to an invention made by an employee unless at the time he made the invention one of the following conditions was satisfied in his case, that is to say –

(a) he was mainly employed in the United Kingdom; or

(b) he was not mainly employed anywhere or his place of employment could not be determined, but his employer had a place of business in the United Kingdom to which the employee was attached, whether or not he was also attached elsewhere.

(3) In sections 39 to 42 above and this section, except so far as the context otherwise requires, references to the making of an invention by an employee are references to his making it alone or jointly with any other person, but do not include references to his merely contributing advice or other assistance in the making of an invention by another employee.

(4) Any references in sections 39 to 42 above to a patent and to a patent being granted are respectively references to a patent or other protection and to its being granted whether under the law of the United Kingdom or the law in force in any other country or under any treaty or international convention.

(5) For the purposes of sections 40 and 41 above the benefit derived or expected to be derived by an employer from an invention or patent shall, where he dies before any award is made under section 40 above in respect of it, include any benefit derived or expected to be derived from it by his personal representatives or by any person in whom it was vested by their assent.

(5A) For the purposes of sections 40 and 41 above the benefit derived or expected to be derived by an employer from an invention shall not include any benefit derived or expected to be derived from the invention after the patent for it has expired or has been surrendered or revoked.

(6) Where an employee dies before an award is made under section 40 above in respect of a patented invention made by him, his personal representatives or their successors in title may exercise his right to make or proceed with an application for compensation under subsection (1) or (2) of that section.

(7) In sections 40 and 41 above and this section "benefit" means benefit in money or money's worth.

(8) Section 533 of the Income and Corporation Taxes Act 19704 (definition of connected persons) shall apply for determining for the purposes of section 41(2) above whether one person is connected with another as it applies for determining that question for the purposes of the Tax Acts.

Contracts as to patented products, etc.

Avoidance of certain restrictive conditions
44. [repealed]

Determination of parts of certain contracts
45. [repealed]

Licences of right and compulsory licences

Patentee's application for entry in register that licences are available as of right
46.(1) At any time after the grant of a patent its proprietor may apply to the comptroller for an entry to be made in the register to the effect that licences under the patent are to be available as of right.

(2) Where such an application is made, the comptroller shall give notice of the application to any person registered as having a right in or under the patent and, if satisfied that the proprietor of the patent is not precluded by contract from granting licences under the patent, shall make that entry.

(3) Where such an entry is made in respect of a patent –

(a) any person shall, at any time after the entry is made, be entitled as of right to a licence under the patent on such terms as may be settled by agreement or, in default of agreement, by the comptroller on the application of the proprietor of the patent or the person requiring the licence;

(b) the comptroller may, on the application of the holder of any licence granted under the patent before the entry was made, order the licence to be exchanged for a licence of right on terms so settled.

(c) if in proceedings for infringement of the patent (otherwise than by the importation of any article from a country which is not a member State of the European Economic Community5) the defendant or defender undertakes to take a licence on such terms, no injunction or interdict shall be granted against him and the amount (if any) recoverable against him by way of damages shall not exceed double the amount which would have been payable by him as licensee if such a licence on those terms had been granted before the earliest infringement;

(d) if the expiry date in relation to a renewal fee falls after the date of the entry, that fee shall be half the fee which would be payable had the entry not been made.

(3A) An undertaking under subsection (3)(c) above may be given at any time before final order in the proceedings, without any admission of liability.

(3B) For the purposes of subsection (3)(d) above the expiry date in relation to a renewal fee is the day at the end of which, by virtue of section 25(3) above, the patent in question ceases to have effect if that fee is not paid.

(4) The licensee under a licence of right may (unless, in the case of a licence the terms of which are settled by agreement, the licence otherwise expressly provides) request the proprietor of the patent to take proceedings to prevent any infringement of the patent; and if the proprietor refuses or neglects to do so within two months after being so requested, the licensee may institute proceedings for the infringement in his own name as if he were proprietor, making the proprietor a defendant or defender.

(5) A proprietor so added as defendant or defender shall not be liable for any costs or expenses unless he enters an appearance and takes part in the proceedings.

Cancellation of entry made under s.46

47.(1) At any time after an entry has been made under section 46 above in respect of a patent, the proprietor of the patent may apply to the comptroller for cancellation of the entry.

(2) Where such an application is made and the balance paid of all renewal fees which would have been payable if the entry had not been made, the comptroller may cancel the entry, if satisfied that there is no existing licence under the patent or that all licensees under the patent consent to the application.

(3) Within the prescribed period after an entry has been made under section 46 above in respect of a patent, any person who claims that the proprietor of the patent is, and was at the time of the entry, precluded by a contract in which the claimant is interested from granting licences under the patent may apply to the comptroller for cancellation of the entry.

(4) Where the comptroller is satisfied, on an application under subsection (3) above, that the proprietor of the patent is and was so precluded, he shall cancel the entry; and the proprietor shall then be liable to pay, within a period specified by the comptroller, a sum equal to the balance of all renewal fees which would have been payable if the entry had not been

made, and the patent shall cease to have effect at the expiration of that period if that sum is not so paid.

(5) Where an entry is cancelled under this section, the rights and liabilities of the proprietor of the patent shall afterwards be the same as if the entry had not been made.

(6) Where an application has been made under this section, then –

(a) in the case of an application under subsection (1) above, any person, and

(b) in the case of an application under subsection (3) above, the proprietor of the patent,

may within the prescribed period give notice to the comptroller of opposition to the cancellation; and the comptroller shall, in considering the application, determine whether the opposition is justified.

Compulsory licences: general

48.(1) At any time after the expiration of three years, or of such other period as may be prescribed, from the date of the grant of a patent, any person may apply to the comptroller on one or more of the relevant grounds –

(a) for a licence under the patent;

(b) for an entry to be made in the register to the effect that licences under the patent are to be available as of right; or

(c) where the applicant is a government department, for the grant to any person specified in the application of a licence under the patent.

(2) Subject to sections 48A and 48B below, if he is satisfied that any of the relevant grounds are established, the comptroller may –

(a) where the application is under subsection (1)(a) above, order the grant of a licence to the applicant on such terms as the comptroller thinks fit;

(b) where the application is under subsection (1)(b) above, make such an entry as is there mentioned;

(c) where the application is under subsection (1)(c) above, order the grant of a licence to the person specified in the application on such terms as the comptroller thinks fit.

(3) An application may be made under this section in respect of a patent even though the applicant is already the holder of a licence under the patent; and no person shall be estopped or barred from alleging any of the matters specified in the relevant grounds by reason of any admission made by him, whether in such a licence or otherwise, or by reason of his having accepted a licence.

(4) In this section "the relevant grounds" means –

(a) in the case of an application made in respect of a patent whose proprietor is a WTO proprietor, the grounds set out in section 48A(1) below;

(b) in any other case, the grounds set out in section 48B(1) below.

(5) A proprietor is a WTO proprietor for the purposes of this section and sections 48A, 48B, 50 and 52 below if –

(a) he is a national of, or is domiciled in, a country which is a member of the World Trade Organisation; or

(b) he has a real and effective industrial or commercial establishment in such a country.

(6) A rule prescribing any such other period under subsection (1) above shall not be made unless a draft of the rule has been laid before, and approved by resolution of, each House of Parliament.

Compulsory licences: WTO proprietors

48A.(1) In the case of an application made under section 48 above in respect of a patent whose proprietor is a WTO proprietor, the relevant grounds are –

(a) where the patented invention is a product, that a demand in the United Kingdom for that product is not being met on reasonable terms;

(b) that by reason of the refusal of the proprietor of the patent concerned to grant a licence or licences on reasonable terms –

    (i) the exploitation in the United Kingdom of any other patented invention which involves an important technical advance of considerable economic significance in relation to the invention for which the patent concerned was granted is prevented or hindered, or

    (ii) the establishment or development of commercial or industrial activities in the United Kingdom is unfairly prejudiced;

(c) that by reason of conditions imposed by the proprietor of the patent concerned on the grant of licences under the patent, or on the disposal or use of the patented product or on the use of the patented process, the manufacture, use or disposal of materials not protected by the patent, or the establishment or development of commercial or industrial activities in the United Kingdom, is unfairly prejudiced.

(2) No order or entry shall be made under section 48 above in respect of a patent whose proprietor is a WTO proprietor unless –

(a) the applicant has made efforts to obtain a licence from the proprietor on reasonable commercial terms and conditions; and

(b) his efforts have not been successful within a reasonable period.

(3) No order or entry shall be so made if the patented invention is in the field of semi-conductor technology.

(4) No order or entry shall be made under section 48 above in respect of a patent on the ground mentioned in subsection (1)(b)(i) above unless the comptroller is satisfied that the proprietor of the patent for the other invention is able and willing to grant the proprietor of the patent concerned and his licensees a licence under the patent for the other invention on reasonable terms.

(5) A licence granted in pursuance of an order or entry so made shall not be assigned except to a person to whom the patent for the other invention is also assigned.

(6) A licence granted in pursuance of an order or entry made under section 48 above in respect of a patent whose proprietor is a WTO proprietor –

(a) shall not be exclusive;
(b) shall not be assigned except to a person to whom there is also assigned the part of the enterprise that enjoys the use of the patented invention, or the part of the goodwill that belongs to that part;
(c) shall be predominantly for the supply of the market in the United Kingdom;
(d) shall include conditions entitling the proprietor of the patent concerned to remuneration adequate in the circumstances of the case, taking into account the economic value of the licence; and
(e) shall be limited in scope and in duration to the purpose for which the licence was granted.

Compulsory licences: other cases

48B.(1) In the case of an application made under section 48 above in respect of a patent whose proprietor is not a WTO proprietor, the relevant grounds are –

(a) where the patented invention is capable of being commercially worked in the United Kingdom, that it is not being so worked or is not being so worked to the fullest extent that is reasonably practicable;
(b) where the patented invention is a product, that a demand for the product in the United Kingdom –

(i) is not being met on reasonable terms, or
(ii) is being met to a substantial extent by importation from a country which is not a member State;

(c) where the patented invention is capable of being commercially worked in the United Kingdom, that it is being prevented or hindered from being so worked –

(i) where the invention is a product, by the importation of the product from a country which is not a member State,
(ii) where the invention is a process, by the importation from such a country of a product obtained directly by means of the process or to which the process has been applied;

(d) that by reason of the refusal of the proprietor of the patent to grant a licence or licences on reasonable terms –

(i) a market for the export of any patented product made in the United Kingdom is not being supplied, or
(ii) the working or efficient working in the United Kingdom of any other patented invention which makes a substantial contribution to the art is prevented or hindered, or
(iii) the establishment or development of commercial or industrial activities in the United Kingdom is unfairly prejudiced;

(e) that by reason of conditions imposed by the proprietor of the patent on the grant of licences under the patent, or on the disposal or use of the patented product or on the use of the patented process, the manufacture, use or disposal of materials not protected by the patent, or the establishment or development of commercial or industrial activities in the United Kingdom, is unfairly prejudiced.

(2) Where –

    (a) an application is made on the ground that the patented invention is not being commercially worked in the United Kingdom or is not being so worked to the fullest extent that is reasonably practicable; and

    (b) it appears to the comptroller that the time which has elapsed since the publication in the journal of a notice of the grant of the patent has for any reason been insufficient to enable the invention to be so worked,

he may by order adjourn the application for such period as will in his opinion give sufficient time for the invention to be so worked.

(3) No order or entry shall be made under section 48 above in respect of a patent on the ground mentioned in subsection (1)(a) above if –

    (a) the patented invention is being commercially worked in a country which is a member State; and

    (b) demand in the United Kingdom is being met by importation from that country.

(4) No entry shall be made in the register under section 48 above on the ground mentioned in subsection (1)(d)(i) above, and any licence granted under section 48 above on that ground shall contain such provisions as appear to the comptroller to be expedient for restricting the countries in which any product concerned may be disposed of or used by the licensee.

(5) No order or entry shall be made under section 48 above in respect of a patent on the ground mentioned in subsection (1)(d)(ii) above unless the comptroller is satisfied that the proprietor of the patent for the other invention is able and willing to grant to the proprietor of the patent concerned and his licensees a licence under the patent for the other invention on reasonable terms.

Provisions about licences under section 48

49.(1) Where the comptroller is satisfied, on an application made under section 48 above in respect of a patent, that the manufacture, use or disposal of materials not protected by the patent is unfairly prejudiced by reason of conditions imposed by the proprietor of the patent on the grant of licences under the patent, or on the disposal or use of the patented product or the use of the patented process, he may (subject to the provisions of that section) order the grant of licences under the patent to such customers of the applicant as he thinks fit as well as to the applicant.

(2) Where an application under section 48 above is made in respect of a patent by a person who holds a licence under the patent, the comptroller –

    (a) may, if he orders the grant of a licence to the applicant, order the existing licence to be cancelled, or

    (b) may, instead of ordering the grant of a licence to the applicant, order the existing licence to be amended.

(3) [repealed]

(4) Section 46(4) and (5) above shall apply to a licence granted in pursuance of an order under section 48 above and to a licence granted by virtue of an entry under that section as it applies to a licence granted by virtue of an entry under section 46 above.

Exercise of powers on application under section 48

50.(1) The powers of the comptroller on an application under section 48 above in respect of a patent whose proprietor is not a WTO proprietor shall be exercised with a view to securing the following general purposes –

(a) that inventions which can be worked on a commercial scale in the United Kingdom and which should in the public interest be so worked shall be worked there without undue delay and to the fullest extent that is reasonably practicable;

(b) that the inventor or other person beneficially entitled to a patent shall receive reasonable remuneration having regard to the nature of the invention;

(c) that the interests of any person for the time being working or developing an invention in the United Kingdom under the protection of a patent shall not be unfairly prejudiced.

(2) Subject to subsection (1) above, the comptroller shall, in determining whether to make an order or entry in pursuance of any application under section 48 above, take account of the following matters, that is to say –

(a) the nature of the invention, the time which has elapsed since the publication in the journal of a notice of the grant of the patent and the measures already taken by the proprietor of the patent or any licensee to make full use of the invention;

(b) the ability of any person to whom a licence would be granted under the order concerned to work the invention to the public advantage; and

(c) the risks to be undertaken by that person in providing capital and working the invention if the application for an order is granted,

but shall not be required to take account of matters subsequent to the making of the application.

Powers exercisable following merger and market investigations

50A.(1) Subsection (2) below applies where –

(a) section 41(2), 55(2), 66(6), 75(2), 83(2), 138(2), 147(2), 147A(2) or 160(2) of, or paragraph 5(2) or 10(2) of Schedule 7 to, the Enterprise Act 2002 (powers to take remedial action following merger or market investigations) applies6;

(b) the Competition and Markets Authority or (as the case may be) the Secretary of State considers that it would be appropriate to make an application under this section for the purpose of remedying, mitigating or preventing a matter which cannot be dealt with under the enactment concerned; and

(c) the matter concerned involves –

(i) conditions in licences granted under a patent by its proprietor restricting the use of the invention by the licensee or the right of the proprietor to grant other licences; or

> (ii) a refusal by the proprietor of a patent to grant licences on reasonable terms.

(2) The Competition and Markets Authority or (as the case may be) the Secretary of State may apply to the comptroller to take action under this section.

(3) Before making an application the Competition Markets Authority or (as the case may be) the Secretary of State shall publish, in such manner as it or he thinks appropriate, a notice describing the nature of the proposed application and shall consider any representations which may be made within 30 days of such publication by persons whose interests appear to it or him to be affected.

(4) The comptroller may, if it appears to him on an application under this section that the application is made in accordance with this section, by order cancel or modify any condition concerned of the kind mentioned in subsection (1)(c)(i) above or may, instead or in addition, make an entry in the register to the effect that licences under the patent are to be available as of right.

(5) References in this section to the Competition and Markets Authority are references to a CMA group except where –

   (a) section 75(2) of the Enterprise Act 2002 applies; or
   (b) any other enactment mentioned in subsection (1)(a) above applies and the functions of the Competition and Markets Authority under that enactment are being performed by the CMA Board by virtue of section 34C(3) or 133A(2) of the Enterprise Act 2002.

(6) References in section 35, 36, 47, 63, 134 or 141 or 141A of the Enterprise Act 2002 (questions to be decided by the Competition and Markets Authority in its reports) to taking action under section 41(2), 55, 66, 138 or 147 or 147A shall include references to taking action under subsection (2) above7.

(7) Action taken by virtue of subsection (4) above in consequence of an application under subsection (2) above where an enactment mentioned in subsection (1)(a) above applies shall be treated, for the purposes of sections 91(3), 92(1)(a), 162(1) and 166(3) of the Enterprise Act 2002 (duties to register and keep under review enforcement orders etc.), as if it were the making of an enforcement order (within the meaning of the Part concerned) under the relevant power in Part 3 or (as the case may be) 4 of that Act8.

(8) In subsection (5) "CMA Board" and "CMA group" have the same meaning as in Schedule 4 to the Enterprise and Regulatory Reform Act 2013.

Powers exercisable in consequence of report of Competition and Markets Authority

51.(1) Where a report of the Competition and Markets Authority has been laid before Parliament containing conclusions to the effect –

   (a) [repealed]
   (b) [repealed]
   (c) on a competition reference, that a person was engaged in an anti-competitive practice which operated or may be expected to operate against the public interest, or

(d) on a reference under section 11 of the Competition Act 1980 (reference of public bodies and certain other persons), that a person is pursuing a course of conduct which operates against the public interest,

the appropriate Minister or Ministers may apply to the comptroller to take action under this section.

(2) Before making an application the appropriate Minister or Ministers shall publish, in such manner as he or they think appropriate, a notice describing the nature of the proposed application and shall consider any representations which may be made within 30 days of such publication by persons whose interests appear to him or them to be affected.

(3) If on an application under this section it appears to the comptroller that the matters specified in the Competition and Markets Authority's report as being those which in the opinion of the Competition and Markets Authority operate, or operated or may be expected to operate, against the public interest include –

(a) conditions in licences granted under a patent by its proprietor restricting the use of the invention by the licensee or the right of the proprietor to grant other licences, or

(b) a refusal by the proprietor of a patent to grant licences on reasonable terms

he may by order cancel or modify any such condition or may, instead or in addition, make an entry in the register to the effect that licences under the patent are to be available as of right.

(4) In this section "the appropriate Minister or Ministers" means the Minister or Ministers to whom the report of the Competition and Markets Authority was made.

Opposition, appeal and arbitration

52.(1) The proprietor of the patent concerned or any other person wishing to oppose an application under sections 48 to 51 above may, in accordance with rules, give to the comptroller notice of opposition; and the comptroller shall consider any opposition in deciding whether to grant the application.

(2) Where an order or entry has been made under section 48 above in respect of a patent whose proprietor is a WTO proprietor –

(a) the proprietor or any other person may, in accordance with rules, apply to the comptroller to have the order revoked or the entry cancelled on the grounds that the circumstances which led to the making of the order or entry have ceased to exist and are unlikely to recur;

(b) any person wishing to oppose an application under paragraph (a) above may, in accordance with rules, give to the comptroller notice of opposition; and

(c) the comptroller shall consider any opposition in deciding whether to grant the application.

(3) If it appears to the comptroller on an application under subsection (2)(a) above that the circumstances which led to the making of the order or entry have ceased to exist and are unlikely to recur, he may –

(a) revoke the order or cancel the entry; and

(b) terminate any licence granted to a person in pursuance of the order or entry subject to such terms and conditions as he thinks necessary for the protection of the legitimate interests of that person.

(4) Where an appeal is brought –

(a) from an order made by the comptroller in pursuance of an application under sections 48 to 51 above;

(b) from a decision of his to make an entry in the register in pursuance of such an application;

(c) from a revocation or cancellation made by him under subsection (3) above; or

(d) from a refusal of his to make such an order, entry, revocation or cancellation,

the Attorney General, the appropriate Law Officer within the meaning of section 4A of the Crown Suits (Scotland) Act 1857 or the Attorney General for Northern Ireland, or such other person who has a right of audience as any of them may appoint, shall be entitled to appear and be heard.

(5) Where an application under sections 48 to 51 above or subsection (2) above is opposed, and either –

(a) the parties consent, or

(b) the proceedings require a prolonged examination of documents or any scientific or local investigation which cannot in the opinion of the comptroller conveniently be made before him,

the comptroller may at any time order the whole proceedings, or any question or issue of fact arising in them, to be referred to an arbitrator or arbiter agreed on by the parties or, in default of agreement, appointed by the comptroller.

(6) Where the whole proceedings are so referred, unless the parties otherwise agree before the award of the arbitrator or arbiter is made, an appeal shall lie from the award to the court.

(7) Where a question or issue of fact is so referred, the arbitrator shall report his findings to the comptroller.

Compulsory licences: supplementary provisions

53.(1) [repealed]

(2) In any proceedings on an application made under section 48 above in respect of a patent, any statement with respect to any activity in relation to the patented invention, or with respect to the grant or refusal of licences under the patent, contained in a report of the Competition and Markets Authority laid before Parliament under Part VII of the Fair Trading Act 1973 or section 17 of the Competition Act 1980 or published under Part 3 or 4 of the Enterprise Act 2002 shall be prima facie evidence of the matters stated, and in Scotland shall be sufficient evidence of those matters9.

(3) The comptroller may make an entry in the register under sections 48 to 51 above notwithstanding any contract which would have precluded the entry on the application of the proprietor of the patent under section 46 above.

(4) An entry made in the register under sections 48 to 51 above shall for all purposes have the same effect as an entry made under section 46 above.

(5) No order or entry shall be made in pursuance of an application under sections 48 to 51 above which would be at variance with any treaty or international convention to which the United Kingdom is a party.

Special provisions where patented invention is being worked abroad

54.(1) Her Majesty may by Order in Council provide that the comptroller may not (otherwise than for purposes of the public interest) make an order or entry in respect of a patent in pursuance of an application under sections 48 to 51 above if the invention concerned is being commercially worked in any relevant country specified in the Order and demand in the United Kingdom for any patented product resulting from that working is being met by importation from that country.

(2) In subsection (1) above "relevant country" means a country other than a member state or a member of the World Trade Organisation whose law in the opinion of Her Majesty in Council incorporates or will incorporate provisions treating the working of an invention in, and importation from, the United Kingdom in a similar way to that in which the Order in Council would (if made) treat the working of an invention in, and importation from, that country.

Use of patented inventions for services of the Crown

Use of patented inventions for services of the Crown

55.(1) Notwithstanding anything in this Act, any government department and any person authorised in writing by a government department may, for the services of the Crown and in accordance with this section, do any of the following acts in the United Kingdom in relation to a patented invention without the consent of the proprietor of the patent, that is to say –

(a) where the invention is a product, may –

    (i) make, use, import or keep the product, or sell or offer to sell it where to do so would be incidental or ancillary to making, using, importing or keeping it; or

    (ii) in any event, sell or offer to sell it for foreign defence purposes or for the production or supply of specified drugs and medicines, or dispose or offer to dispose of it (otherwise than by selling it) for any purpose whatever;

(b) where the invention is a process, may use it or do in relation to any product obtained directly by means of the process anything mentioned in paragraph (a) above;

(c) without prejudice to the foregoing, where the invention or any product obtained directly by means of the invention is a specified drug or medicine, may sell or offer to sell the drug or medicine;

(d) may supply or offer to supply to any person any of the means, relating to an essential element of the invention, for putting the invention into effect;

(e)   may dispose or offer to dispose of anything which was made, used, imported or kept in the exercise of the powers conferred by this section and which is no longer required for the purpose for which it was made, used, imported or kept (as the case may be),

and anything done by virtue of this subsection shall not amount to an infringement of the patent concerned.

(2)   Any act done in relation to an invention by virtue of this section is in the following provisions of this section referred to as use of the invention; and "use", in relation to an invention, in sections 56 to 58 below shall be construed accordingly.

(3)   So far as the invention has before its priority date been duly recorded by or tried by or on behalf of a government department or the United Kingdom Atomic Energy Authority otherwise than in consequence of a relevant communication made in confidence, any use of the invention by virtue of this section may be made free of any royalty or other payment to the proprietor.

(4)   So far as the invention has not been so recorded or tried, any use of it made by virtue of this section at any time either –

(a)   after the publication of the application for the patent for the invention; or

(b)   without prejudice to paragraph (a) above, in consequence of a relevant communication made after the priority date of the invention otherwise than in confidence;

shall be made on such terms as may be agreed either before or after the use by the government department and the proprietor of the patent with the approval of the Treasury or as may in default of agreement be determined by the court on a reference under section 58 below.

(5)   Where an invention is used by virtue of this section at any time after publication of an application for a patent for the invention but before such a patent is granted, and the terms for its use agreed or determined as mentioned in subsection (4) above include terms as to payment for the use, then (notwithstanding anything in those terms) any such payment shall be recoverable only –

(a)   after such a patent is granted; and

(b)   if (apart from this section) the use would, if the patent had been granted on the date of the publication of the application, have infringed not only the patent but also the claims (as interpreted by the description and any drawings referred to in the description or claims) in the form in which they were contained in the application immediately before the preparations for its publication were completed by the Patent Office.

(6)   The authority of a government department in respect of an invention may be given under this section either before or after the patent is granted and either before or after the use in respect of which the authority is given is made, and may be given to any person whether or not he is authorised directly or indirectly by the proprietor of the patent to do anything in relation to the invention.

(7) Where any use of an invention is made by or with the authority of a government department under this section, then, unless it appears to the department that it would be contrary to the public interest to do so, the department shall notify the proprietor of the patent as soon as practicable after the second of the following events, that is to say, the use is begun and the patent is granted, and furnish him with such information as to the extent of the use as he may from time to time require.

(8) A person acquiring anything disposed of in the exercise of powers conferred by this section, and any person claiming through him, may deal with it in the same manner as if the patent were held on behalf of the Crown.

(9) In this section "relevant communication", in relation to an invention, means a communication of the invention directly or indirectly by the proprietor of the patent or any person from whom he derives title.

(10) Subsection (4) above is without prejudice to any rule of law relating to the confidentiality of information.

(11) In the application of this section to Northern Ireland, the reference in subsection (4) above to the Treasury shall, where the government department referred to in that subsection is a department of the Government of Northern Ireland, be construed as a reference to the Department of Finance for Northern Ireland.

Interpretation, etc., of provisions about Crown use

56.(1) Any reference in section 55 above to a patented invention, in relation to any time, is a reference to an invention for which a patent has before that time been, or is subsequently, granted.

(2) In this Act, except so far as the context otherwise requires, "the services of the Crown" includes –

(a) the supply of anything for foreign defence purposes;

(b) the production or supply of specified drugs and medicines; and

(c) such purposes relating to the production or use of atomic energy or research into matters connected therewith as the Secretary of State thinks necessary or expedient;

and "use for the services of the Crown" shall be construed accordingly.

(3) In section 55(1)(a) above and subsection (2)(a) above, references to a sale or supply of anything for foreign defence purposes are references to a sale or supply of the thing –

(a) to the government of any country outside the United Kingdom, in pursuance of an agreement or arrangement between Her Majesty's Government in the United Kingdom and the government of that country, where the thing is required for the defence of that country or of any other country whose government is party to any agreement or arrangement with Her Majesty's Government in respect of defence matters; or

(b) to the United Nations, or to the government of any country belonging to that organisation, in pursuance of an agreement or arrangement between Her Majesty's Government and that organisation or government, where the thing is required for any armed forces operating in pursuance of a resolution of that organisation or any organ of that organisation.

(4) For the purposes of section 55(1)(a) and (c) above and subsection (2)(b) above, specified drugs and medicines are drugs and medicines which are both –

(a) required for the provision of –

(ai) primary medical services under the National Health Service Act 2006, the National Health Service (Wales) Act 2006, part I of the National Health Service (Scotland) Act 1978 or any corresponding provisions of the law in force in Northern Ireland or the Isle of Man or primary dental services under the National Health Service Act 2006, the National Health Service (Wales) Act 2006, or any corresponding provisions of the law in force in Northern Ireland or the Isle of Man, or

(i) pharmaceutical services, general medical services or general dental services under Chapter 1 of Part 7 of the National Health Service Act 2006 or Chapter 1 of Part 7 of the National Health Service (Wales) Act 2006 (in the case of pharmaceutical services), Part II of the National Health Service (Scotland) Act 1978 (in the case of pharmaceutical services or general dental services), or the corresponding provisions of the law in force in Northern Ireland or the Isle of Man, or

(ii) personal medical services or personal dental services provided in accordance with arrangements made under section 17C of the 1978 Act (in the case of personal dental services), or the corresponding provisions of the law in force in Northern Ireland or the Isle of Man, or

(iii) local pharmaceutical services provided under a pilot scheme established under section 134 of the National Health Service Act 2006, or section 92 of the National Health Service (Wales) Act 2006, or an LPS scheme established under Schedule 12 to the National Health Service Act 2006, or Schedule 7 to the National Health Service (Wales) Act 2006, or under any corresponding provision of the law in force in the Isle of Man, and

(b) specified for the purposes of this subsection in regulations made by the Secretary of State.

Rights of third parties in respect of Crown use
57.(1) In relation to –

(a) any use made for the services of the Crown of an invention by a government department, or a person authorised by a government department, by virtue of section 55 above, or

(b) anything done for the services of the Crown to the order of a government department by the proprietor of a patent in respect of a patented invention or by the proprietor of an application in respect of an invention for which an application for a patent has been filed and is still pending,

the provisions of any licence, assignment, assignation or agreement to which this subsection applies shall be of no effect so far as those provisions restrict or regulate the working of the invention, or the use of any model, document or information relating to it, or provide for the making of payments in respect of, or calculated by reference to, such working or use; and the reproduction or publication of any model or document in connection with the said working or use shall not be deemed to be an infringement of any copyright or design right subsisting in the model or document.

(2) Subsection (1) above applies to a licence, assignment, assignation or agreement which is made, whether before or after the appointed day, between (on the one hand) any person who is a proprietor of or an applicant for the patent, or anyone who derives title from any such person or from whom such person derives title, and (on the other hand) any person whatever other than a government department.

(3) Where an exclusive licence granted otherwise than for royalties or other benefits determined by reference to the working of the invention is in force under the patent or application concerned, then –

    (a) in relation to anything done in respect of the invention which, but for the provisions of this section and section 55 above, would constitute an infringement of the rights of the licensee, subsection (4) of that section shall have effect as if for the reference to the proprietor of the patent there were substituted a reference to the licensee; and

    (b) in relation to anything done in respect of the invention by virtue of an authority given under that section, that section shall have effect as if the said subsection (4) were omitted.

(4) Subject to the provisions of subsection (3) above, where the patent, or the right to the grant of the patent, has been assigned to the proprietor of the patent or application in consideration of royalties or other benefits determined by reference to the working of the invention, then –

    (a) in relation to any use of the invention by virtue of section 55 above, subsection (4) of that section shall have effect as if the reference to the proprietor of the patent included a reference to the assignor, and any sum payable by virtue of that subsection shall be divided between the proprietor of the patent or application and the assignor in such proportion as may be agreed on by them or as may in default of agreement be determined by the court on a reference under section 58 below; and

    (b) in relation to any act done in respect of the invention for the services of the Crown by the proprietor of the patent or application to the order of a government department, section 55(4) above shall have effect as if that act were use made by virtue of an authority given under that section.

(5) Where section 55(4) above applies to any use of an invention and a person holds an exclusive licence under the patent or application concerned (other than such a licence as is mentioned in subsection (3) above) authorising him to work the invention, then subsections (7) and (8) below shall apply.

(6) In those subsections "the section 55(4)" payment means such payment (if any) as the proprietor of the patent or application and the department agree under section 55 above, or the court determines under section 58 below, should be made by the department to the proprietor in respect of the use of the invention.

(7) The licensee shall be entitled to recover from the proprietor of the patent or application such part (if any) of the section 55(4) payment as may be agreed on by them or as may in default of agreement be determined by the court under section 58 below to be just having regard to any expenditure incurred by the licensee –

(a) in developing the invention, or
(b) in making payments to the proprietor in consideration of the licence, other than royalties or other payments determined by reference to the use of the invention.

(8) Any agreement by the proprietor of the patent or application and the department under section 55(4) above as to the amount of the section 55(4) payment shall be of no effect unless the licensee consents to the agreement; and any determination by the court under section 55(4) above as to the amount of that payment shall be of no effect unless the licensee has been informed of the reference to the court and is given an opportunity to be heard.

(9) Where any models, documents or information relating to an invention are used in connection with any use of the invention which falls within subsection (1)(a) above, or with anything done in respect of the invention which falls within subsection (1)(b) above, subsection (4) of section 55 above shall (whether or not it applies to any such use of the invention) apply to the use of the models, documents or information as if for the reference in it to the proprietor of the patent there were substituted a reference to the person entitled to the benefit of any provision of an agreement which is rendered inoperative by this section in relation to that use; and in section 58 below the references to terms for the use of an invention shall be construed accordingly.

(10) Nothing in this section shall be construed as authorising the disclosure to a government department or any other person of any model, document or information to the use of which this section applies in contravention of any such licence, assignment, assignation or agreement as is mentioned in this section.

Compensation for loss of profit

57A.(1) Where use is made of an invention for the services of the Crown, the government department concerned shall pay –

(a) to the proprietor of the patent, or
(b) if there is an exclusive licence in force in respect of the patent, to the exclusive licensee, compensation for any loss resulting from his not

being awarded a contract to supply the patented product or, as the case may be, to perform the patented process or supply a thing made by means of the patented process.

(2) Compensation is payable only to the extent that such a contract could have been fulfilled from his existing manufacturing or other capacity; but is payable notwithstanding the existence of circumstances rendering him ineligible for the award of such a contract.

(3) In determining the loss, regard shall be had to the profit which would have been made on such a contract and to the extent to which any manufacturing or other capacity was under-used.

(4) No compensation is payable in respect of any failure to secure contracts to supply the patented product or, as the case may be, to perform the patented process or supply a thing made by means of the patented process, otherwise than for the services of the Crown.

(5) The amount payable shall, if not agreed between the proprietor or licensee and the government department concerned with the approval of the Treasury, be determined by the court on a reference under section 58, and is in addition to any amount payable under section 55 or 57.

(6) In this section "the government department concerned", in relation to any use of an invention for the services of the Crown, means the government department by whom or on whose authority the use was made.

(7) In the application of this section to Northern Ireland, the reference in subsection (5) above to the Treasury shall, where the government department concerned is a department of the Government of Northern Ireland, be construed as a reference to the Department of Finance and Personnel.

References of disputes as to Crown use

58.(1) Any dispute as to –

(a) the exercise by a government department, or a person authorised by a government department, of the powers conferred by section 55 above,

(b) terms for the use of an invention for the services of the Crown under that section,

(c) the right of any person to receive any part of a payment made in pursuance of subsection (4) of that section, or

(d) the right of any person to receive a payment under section 57A,

may be referred to the court by either party to the dispute after a patent has been granted for the invention.

(2) If in such proceedings any question arises whether an invention has been recorded or tried as mentioned in section 55 above, and the disclosure of any document recording the invention, or of any evidence of the trial thereof, would in the opinion of the department be prejudicial to the public interest, the disclosure may be made confidentially to the other party's legal representative or to an independent expert mutually agreed upon.

(3) In determining under this section any dispute between a government department and any person as to the terms for the use of an invention for the services of the Crown, the court shall have regard –

(a) to any benefit or compensation which that person or any person from whom he derives title may have received or may be entitled to receive directly or indirectly from any government department in respect of the invention in question;

(b) to whether that person or any person from whom he derives title has in the court's opinion without reasonable cause failed to comply with a request of the department to use the invention for the services of the Crown on reasonable terms.

(4) In determining whether or not to grant any relief under subsection (1) (a), (b) or (c) above and the nature and extent of the relief granted the court shall, subject to the following provisions of this section, apply the principles applied by the court immediately before the appointed day to the granting of relief under section 48 of the 1949 Act.

(5) On a reference under this section the court may refuse to grant relief by way of compensation in respect of the use of an invention for the services of the Crown during any further period specified under section 25(4) above, but before the payment of the renewal fee and any additional fee prescribed for the purposes of that section.

(6) Where an amendment of the specification of a patent has been allowed under any of the provisions of this Act, the court shall not grant relief by way of compensation under this section in respect of any such use before the decision to allow the amendment unless the court is satisfied that –

(a) the specification of the patent as published was framed in good faith and with reasonable skill and knowledge and

(b) the relief is sought in good faith.

(7) If the validity of a patent is put in issue in proceedings under this section and it is found that the patent is only partially valid, the court may, subject to subsection (8) below, grant relief to the proprietor of the patent in respect of that part of the patent which is found to be valid and to have been used for the services of the Crown.

(8) Where in any such proceedings it is found that a patent is only partially valid the Court shall not grant relief by way of compensation, costs or expenses except where the proprietor of the patent proves that –

(a) the specification of the patent was framed in good faith and with reasonable skill and knowledge, and

(b) the relief is sought in good faith,

and in that event the court may grant relief in respect of the part of the patent which is valid and has been so used, subject to the discretion of the court as to costs and expenses and as to the date from which compensation should be awarded.

(9) As a condition of any such relief the court may direct that the specification of the patent shall be amended to its satisfaction upon an application made for that purpose under section 75 below, and an application may be so made accordingly, whether or not all other issues in the proceedings have been determined.

(9A) The court may also grant such relief in the case of a European patent (UK) on condition that the claims of the patent are limited to its satisfaction by the European Patent Office at the request of the proprietor.

(10) In considering the amount of any compensation for the use of an invention for the services of the Crown after publication of an application for a patent for the invention and before such a patent is granted, the court shall consider whether or not it would have been reasonable to expect, from a consideration of the application as published under section 16 above, that a patent would be granted conferring on the proprietor of the patent protection for an act of the same description as that found to constitute that use, and if the court finds that it would not have been reasonable, it shall reduce the compensation to such amount as it thinks just.

(11) Where by virtue of a transaction, instrument or event to which section 33 above applies a person becomes the proprietor or one of the proprietors or an exclusive licensee of a patent (the new proprietor or licensee) and a government department or a person authorised by a government department subsequently makes use under section 55 above of the patented invention, the new proprietor or licensee shall not be entitled to any compensation under section 55(4) above (as it stands or as modified by section 57(3) above), or to any compensation under section 57A above, in respect of a subsequent use of the invention before the transaction, instrument or event is registered unless –

    (a)   the transaction, instrument or event is registered within the period of six months beginning with its date; or

    (b)   the court is satisfied that it was not practicable to register the transaction, instrument or event before the end of that period and that it was registered as soon as practicable thereafter.

(12) In any proceedings under this section the court may at any time order the whole proceedings or any question or issue of fact arising in them to be referred, on such terms as the court may direct, to a Circuit judge discharging the functions of an official referee or an arbitrator in England and Wales, the Isle of Man or Northern Ireland, or to an arbiter in Scotland; and references to the court in the foregoing provisions of this section shall be construed accordingly.

(13) One of two or more joint proprietors of a patent or application for a patent may without the concurrence of the others refer a dispute to the court under this section, but shall not do so unless the others are made parties to the proceedings; but any of the others made a defendant or defender shall not be liable for any costs or expenses unless he enters an appearance and takes part in the proceedings.

Special provisions as to Crown use during emergency

59.(1) During any period of emergency within the meaning of this section the powers exercisable in relation to an invention by a government department or a person authorised by a government department under section 55 above shall include power to use the invention for any purpose which appears to the department necessary or expedient –

(a) for the efficient prosecution of any war in which Her Majesty may be engaged;

(b) for the maintenance of supplies and services essential to the life of the community;

(c) for securing a sufficiency of supplies and services essential to the well-being of the community;

(d) for promoting the productivity of industry, commerce and agriculture;

(e) for fostering and directing exports and reducing imports, or imports of any classes, from all or any countries and for redressing the balance of trade;

(f) generally for ensuring that the whole resources of the community are available for use, and are used, in a manner best calculated to serve the interests of the community; or

(g) for assisting the relief of suffering and the restoration and distribution of essential supplies and services in any country or territory outside the United Kingdom which is in grave distress as the result of war;

and any reference in this Act to the services of the Crown shall, as respects any period of emergency, include a reference to those purposes.

(2) In this section the use of an invention includes, in addition to any act constituting such use by virtue of section 55 above, any act which would, apart from that section and this section, amount to an infringement of the patent concerned or, as the case may be, give rise to a right under section 69 below to bring proceedings in respect of the application concerned, and any reference in this Act to "use for the services of the Crown" shall, as respects any period of emergency, be construed accordingly.

(3) In this section "period of emergency" means any period beginning with such date as may be declared by Order in Council to be the commencement, and ending with such date as may be so declared to be the termination, of a period of emergency for the purposes of this section.

(4) A draft of an Order under this section shall not be submitted to Her Majesty unless it has been laid before, and approved by resolution of, each House of Parliament.

Infringement

Meaning of infringement

60.(1) Subject to the provisions of this section, a person infringes a patent for an invention if, but only if, while the patent is in force, he does any of the following things in the United Kingdom in relation to the invention without the consent of the proprietor of the patent, that is to say –

(a) where the invention is a product, he makes, disposes of, offers to dispose of, uses or imports the product or keeps it whether for disposal or otherwise;

(b) where the invention is a process, he uses the process or he offers it for use in the United Kingdom when he knows, or it is obvious to a reasonable person in the circumstances, that its use there without the consent of the proprietor would be an infringement of the patent;

(c)   where the invention is a process, he disposes of, offers to dispose of, uses or imports any product obtained directly by means of that process or keeps any such product whether for disposal or otherwise.

(2)   Subject to the following provisions of this section, a person (other than the proprietor of the patent) also infringes a patent for an invention if, while the patent is in force and without the consent of the proprietor, he supplies or offers to supply in the United Kingdom a person other than a licensee or other person entitled to work the invention with any of the means, relating to an essential element of the invention, for putting the invention into effect when he knows, or it is obvious to a reasonable person in the circumstances, that those means are suitable for putting, and are intended to put, the invention into effect in the United Kingdom.

(3)   Subsection (2) above shall not apply to the supply or offer of a staple commercial product unless the supply or the offer is made for the purpose of inducing the person supplied or, as the case may be, the person to whom the offer is made to do an act which constitutes an infringement of the patent by virtue of subsection (1) above.

(4)   [repealed]

(5)   An act which, apart from this subsection, would constitute an infringement of a patent for an invention shall not do so if –

(a)   it is done privately and for purposes which are not commercial;

(b)   it is done for experimental purposes relating to the subject-matter of the invention;

(c)   it consists of the extemporaneous preparation in a pharmacy of a medicine for an individual in accordance with a prescription given by a registered medical or dental practitioner or consists of dealing with a medicine so prepared;

(d)   it consists of the use, exclusively for the needs of a relevant ship, of a product or process in the body of such a ship or in its machinery, tackle, apparatus or other accessories, in a case where the ship has temporarily or accidentally entered the internal or territorial waters of the United Kingdom;

(e)   it consists of the use of a product or process in the body or operation of a relevant aircraft, hovercraft or vehicle which has temporarily or accidentally entered or is crossing the United Kingdom (including the air space above it and its territorial waters) or the use of accessories for such a relevant aircraft, hovercraft or vehicle;

(f)   it consists of the use of an exempted aircraft which has lawfully entered or is lawfully crossing the United Kingdom as aforesaid or of the importation into the United Kingdom, or the use or storage there, of any part or accessory for such an aircraft.

(g)   it consists of the use by a farmer of the product of his harvest for propagation or multiplication by him on his own holding, where there has been a sale of plant propagating material to the farmer by the proprietor of the patent or with his consent for agricultural use;

(h)   it consists of the use of an animal or animal reproductive material by a farmer for an agricultural purpose following a sale to the farmer, by the proprietor of the patent or with his consent, of breeding stock or other animal reproductive material which constitutes or contains the patented invention

(i)   it consists of –

(i)   an act done in conducting a study, test or trial which is necessary for and is conducted with a view to the application of paragraphs 1 to 5 of article 13 of Directive 2001/82/EC or paragraphs 1 to 4 of article 10 of Directive 2001/83/EC, or

(ii)   any other act which is required for the purpose of the application of those paragraphs.

(6) For the purposes of subsection (2) above a person who does an act in relation to an invention which is prevented only by virtue of paragraph (a), (b) or (c) of subsection (5) above from constituting an infringement of a patent for the invention shall not be treated as a person entitled to work the invention, but –

(a)   the reference in that subsection to a person entitled to work an invention includes a reference to a person so entitled by virtue of section 55 above, and

(b)   a person who by virtue of section 20B(4) or (5) above or section 28A(4) or (5) above or section 64 below or section 117A(4) or (5) below is entitled to do an act in relation to the invention without it constituting such an infringement shall, so far as concerns that act, be treated as a person entitled to work the invention.

(6A) Schedule A1 contains –

(a)   provisions restricting the circumstances in which subsection (5)(g) applies; and

(b)   provisions which apply where an act would constitute an infringement of a patent but for subsection (5)(g).

(6B) For the purposes of subsection (5)(h), use for an agricultural purpose –

(a)   includes making an animal or animal reproductive material available for the purposes of pursuing the farmer's agricultural activity; but

(b)   does not include sale within the framework, or for the purposes, of a commercial reproduction activity.

(6C) In paragraphs (g) and (h) of subsection (5) "sale" includes any other form of commercialisation.

(6D) For the purposes of subsection (5)(b), anything done in or for the purposes of a medicinal product assessment which would otherwise constitute an infringement of a patent for an invention is to be regarded as done for experimental purposes relating to the subject-matter of the invention.

(6E) In subsection (6D), "medicinal product assessment" means any testing, course of testing or other activity undertaken with a view to providing data for any of the following purposes –

(a)   obtaining or varying an authorisation to sell or supply, or offer to sell or supply, a medicinal product (whether in the United Kingdom or elsewhere);

(b)   complying with any regulatory requirement imposed (whether in the United Kingdom or elsewhere) in relation to such an authorisation;

(c)   enabling a government or public authority (whether in the United Kingdom or elsewhere), or a person (whether in the United Kingdom or elsewhere) with functions of –

   (i)   providing health care on behalf of such a government or public authority, or

   (ii) providing advice to, or on behalf of, such a government or public authority about the provision of health care,

to carry out an assessment of suitability of a medicinal product for human use for the purpose of determining whether to use it, or recommend its use, in the provision of health care.

(6F) In subsection (6E) and this subsection –

"medicinal product" means a medicinal product for human use or a veterinary medicinal product;

"medicinal product for human use" has the meaning given by article 1 of Directive 2001/83/EC(**2**);

"veterinary medicinal product" has the meaning given by article 1 of Directive 2001/82/EC(**3**).

(6G) Nothing in subsections (6D) to (6F) is to be read as affecting the application of subsection (5)(b) in relation to any act of a kind not falling within subsection (6D).

(7)   In this section –

"relevant ship" and "relevant aircraft, hovercraft or vehicle" mean respectively a ship and an aircraft, hovercraft or vehicle registered in, or belonging to, any country, other than the United Kingdom, which is a party to the Convention for the Protection of Industrial Property signed at Paris on 20th March 1883 or which is a member of the World Trade Organisation; and

"exempted aircraft" means an aircraft to which section 89 of the Civil Aviation Act 1982 (aircraft exempted from seizure in respect of patent claims) applies

"Directive 2001/82/EC" means Directive 2001/82/EC of the European Parliament and of the Council on the Community code relating to veterinary medicinal products as amended by Directive 2004/28/EC of the European Parliament and of the Council;

"Directive 2001/83/EC" means Directive 2001/83/EC of the European Parliament and of the Council on the Community code relating to medicinal products for human use, as amended by Directive 2002/98/EC of the European Parliament and of the Council, by Commission Directive 2003/63/EC, and by Directives 2004/24/EC and 2004/27/EC of the European Parliament and of the Council.

Appendix 6

Proceedings for infringement of patent

61.(1) Subject to the following provisions of this Part of this Act, civil proceedings may be brought in the court by the proprietor of a patent in respect of any act alleged to infringe the patent and (without prejudice to any other jurisdiction of the court) in those proceedings a claim may be made –

(a) for an injunction or interdict restraining the defendant or defender from any apprehended act of infringement;

(b) for an order for him to deliver up or destroy any patented product in relation to which the patent is infringed or any article in which that product is inextricably comprised;

(c) for damages in respect of the infringement;

(d) for an account of the profits derived by him from the infringement;

(e) for a declaration or declarator that the patent is valid and has been infringed by him.

(2) The court shall not, in respect of the same infringement, both award the proprietor of a patent damages and order that he shall be given an account of the profits.

(3) The proprietor of a patent and any other person may by agreement with each other refer to the comptroller the question whether that other person has infringed the patent and on the reference the proprietor of the patent may make any claim mentioned in subsection (1)(c) or (e) above.

(4) Except so far as the context requires, in the following provisions of this Act –

(a) any reference to proceedings for infringement and the bringing of such proceedings includes a reference to a reference under subsection (3) above and the making of such a reference;

(b) any reference to a claimant or pursuer includes a reference to the proprietor of the patent; and

(c) any reference to a defendant or defender includes a reference to any other party to the reference.

(5) If it appears to the comptroller on a reference under subsection (3) above that the question referred to him would more properly be determined by the court, he may decline to deal with it and the court shall have jurisdiction to determine the question as if the reference were proceedings brought in the court.

(6) Subject to the following provisions of this Part of this Act, in determining whether or not to grant any kind of relief claimed under this section and the extent of the relief granted the court or the comptroller shall apply the principles applied by the court in relation to that kind of relief immediately before the appointed day.

(7) If the comptroller awards any sum by way of damages on a reference under subsection (3) above, then –

(a) in England and Wales, the sum shall be recoverable, if the county court so orders, by execution issued from the county court or otherwise as if it were payable under an order of that court;

(b) in Scotland, payment of the sum may be enforced in like manner as an extract registered decree arbitral bearing a warrant for execution issued by the sheriff court of any sheriffdom in Scotland;

(c) in Northern Ireland, payment of the sum may be enforced as if it were a money judgment.

Restrictions on recovery of damages for infringement

62.(1) In proceedings for infringement of a patent damages shall not be awarded, and no order shall be made for an account of profits, against a defendant or defender who proves that at the date of the infringement he was not aware, and had no reasonable grounds for supposing, that the patent existed; and a person shall not be taken to have been so aware or to have had reasonable grounds for so supposing by reason only of the application to a product of the word "patent" or "patented", or any word or words expressing or implying that a patent has been obtained for the product, unless the number of the patent or a relevant internet link accompanied the word or words in question.

(1A) The reference in subsection (1) to a relevant internet link is a reference to an address of a posting on the internet –

(a) which is accessible to the public free of charge, and

(b) which clearly associates the product with the number of the patent.

(2) In proceedings for infringement of a patent the court or the comptroller may, if it or he thinks fit, refuse to award any damages or make any such order in respect of an infringement committed during the further period specified in section 25(4) above, but before the payment of the renewal fee and any additional fee prescribed for the purposes of that subsection.

(3) Where an amendment of the specification of a patent has been allowed under any of the provisions of this Act, the court or comptroller shall, when awarding damages or making an order for an account of profits in proceedings for an infringement of the patent committed before the decision to allow the amendment, take into account the following –

(a) whether at the date of infringement the defendant or defender knew, or had reasonable grounds to know, that he was infringing the patent;

(b) whether the specification of the patent as published was framed in good faith and with reasonable skill and knowledge;

(c) whether the proceedings are brought in good faith.

Relief for infringement of partially valid patent

63.(1) If the validity of a patent is put in issue in proceedings for infringement of the patent and it is found that the patent is only partially valid, the court or the comptroller may, subject to subsection (2) below, grant relief in respect of that part of the patent which is found to be valid and infringed.

(2) Where in any such proceedings it is found that a patent is only partially valid, the court or the comptroller shall, when awarding damages, costs or expenses or making an order for an account of profits, take into account the following –

(a) whether at the date of the infringement the defendant or defender knew, or had reasonable grounds to know, that he was infringing the patent;

(b)   whether the specification of the patent was framed in good faith and with reasonable skill and knowledge;

(c)   whether the proceedings are brought in good faith;

and any relief granted shall be subject to the discretion of the court or comptroller as to costs or expenses and as to the date from which damages or an account should be reckoned.

(3)   As a condition of relief under this section the court or the comptroller may direct that the specification of the patent shall be amended to its or his satisfaction upon an application made for that purpose under section 75 below, and an application may be so made accordingly, whether or not all other issues in the proceedings have been determined.

(4)   The court or the comptroller may also grant relief under this section in the case of a European patent (UK) on condition that the claims of the patent are limited to its or his satisfaction by the European Patent Office at the request of the proprietor.

Right to continue use begun before priority date

64.(1) Where a patent is granted for an invention, a person who in the United Kingdom before the priority date of the invention –

(a)   does in good faith an act which would constitute an infringement of the patent if it were in force, or

(b)   makes in good faith effective and serious preparations to do such an act,

has the right to continue to do the act or, as the case may be, to do the act, notwithstanding the grant of the patent; but this right does not extend to granting a licence to another person to do the act.

(2)   If the act was done, or the preparations were made, in the course of a business, the person entitled to the right conferred by subsection (1) may –

(a)   authorise the doing of that act by any partners of his for the time being in that business, and

(b)   assign that right, or transmit it on death (or in the case of a body corporate on its dissolution), to any person who acquires that part of the business in the course of which the act was done or the preparations were made.

(3)   Where a product is disposed of to another in exercise of the rights conferred by subsection (1) or (2), that other and any person claiming through him may deal with the product in the same way as if it had been disposed of by the registered proprietor of the patent.

Certificate of contested validity

65.(1) If in any proceedings before the court or the comptroller the validity of a patent to any extent is contested and that patent is found by the court or the comptroller to be wholly or partially valid, the court or the comptroller may certify the finding and the fact that the validity of the patent was so contested.

(2) Where a certificate is granted under this section, then, if in any subsequent proceedings before the court or the comptroller for infringement of the patent concerned or for revocation of the patent a final order or judgment or interlocutor is made or given in favour of the party relying on the validity of the patent as found in the earlier proceedings, that party shall, unless the court or the comptroller otherwise directs, be entitled to his costs or expenses as between solicitor and own client (other than the costs or expenses of any appeal in the subsequent proceedings).

Proceedings for infringement by a co-owner

66.(1) In the application of section 60 above to a patent of which there are two or more joint proprietors the reference to the proprietor shall be construed –

   (a) in relation to any act, as a reference to that proprietor or those proprietors who, by virtue of section 36 above or any agreement referred to in that section, is or are entitled to do that act without its amounting to an infringement; and

   (b) in relation to any consent, as a reference to that proprietor or those proprietors who, by virtue of section 36 above or any such agreement, is or are the proper person or persons to give the requisite consent.

(2) One of two or more joint proprietors of a patent may without the concurrence of the others bring proceedings in respect of an act alleged to infringe the patent, but shall not do so unless the others are made parties to the proceedings; but any of the others made a defendant or defender shall not be liable for any costs or expenses unless he enters an appearance and takes part in the proceedings.

Proceedings for infringement by exclusive licensee

67.(1) Subject to the provisions of this section, the holder of an exclusive licence under a patent shall have the same right as the proprietor of the patent to bring proceedings in respect of any infringement of the patent committed after the date of the licence; and references to the proprietor of the patent in the provisions of this Act relating to infringement shall be construed accordingly.

(2) In awarding damages or granting any other relief in any such proceedings the court or the comptroller shall take into consideration any loss suffered or likely to be suffered by the exclusive licensee as such as a result of the infringement, or, as the case may be, the profits derived from the infringement, so far as it constitutes an infringement of the rights of the exclusive licensee as such.

(3) In any proceedings taken by an exclusive licensee by virtue of this section the proprietor of the patent shall be made a party to the proceedings, but if made a defendant or defender shall not be liable for any costs or expenses unless he enters an appearance and takes part in the proceedings.

Effect on non-registration on infringement proceedings

68. Where by virtue of a transaction, instrument or event to which section 33 above applies a person becomes the proprietor or one of the proprietors or an exclusive licensee of a patent and the patent is subsequently infringed,

before the transaction, instrument or event is registered, in proceedings for such an infringement, the court or comptroller shall not award him costs or expenses unless –

(a) the transaction, instrument or event is registered within the period of six months beginning with its date; or
(b) the court or the comptroller is satisfied that it was not practicable to register the transaction, instrument or event before the end of that period and that it was registered as soon as practicable thereafter.

Infringement of rights conferred by publication of application

69.(1) Where an application for a patent for an invention is published, then, subject to subsections (2) and (3) below, the applicant shall have, as from the publication and until the grant of the patent, the same right as he would have had, if the patent had been granted on the date of the publication of the application, to bring proceedings in the court or before the comptroller for damages in respect of any act which would have infringed the patent; and (subject to subsections (2) and (3) below) references in sections 60 to 62 and 66 to 68 above to a patent and the proprietor of a patent shall be respectively construed as including references to any such application and the applicant, and references to a patent being in force, being granted, being valid or existing shall be construed accordingly.

(2) The applicant shall be entitled to bring proceedings by virtue of this section in respect of any act only –

(a) after the patent has been granted; and
(b) if the act would, if the patent had been granted on the date of the publication of the application, have infringed not only the patent, but also the claims (as interpreted by the description and any drawings referred to in the description or claims) in the form in which they were contained in the application immediately before the preparations for its publication were completed by the Patent Office.

(3) Section 62(2) and (3) above shall not apply to an infringement of the rights conferred by this section, but in considering the amount of any damages for such an infringement the court or the comptroller shall consider whether or not it would have been reasonable to expect from a consideration of the application as published under section 16 above, that a patent would be granted conferring on the proprietor of the patent protection from an act of the same description as that found to infringe those rights, and if the court or the comptroller finds that it would not have been reasonable, it or he shall reduce the damages to such an amount as it or he thinks just.

Remedy for groundless threats of infringement proceedings

70.(1) Where a person (whether or not the proprietor of, or entitled to any right in, a patent) by circulars, advertisements or otherwise threatens another person with proceedings for any infringement of a patent, a person aggrieved by the threats (whether or not he is the person to whom the threats are made) may, subject to subsection (4) below, bring proceedings in the court against the person making the threats, claiming any relief mentioned in subsection (3) below.

(2)   In any such proceedings the claimant or pursuer shall, subject to subsection (2A) below, be entitled to the relief claimed if he proves that the threats were so made and satisfies the court that he is a person aggrieved by them.

(2A) If the defendant or defender proves that the acts in respect of which proceedings were threatened constitute or, if done, would constitute an infringement of a patent –

   (a)   the claimant or pursuer shall be entitled to the relief claimed only if he shows that the patent alleged to be infringed is invalid in a relevant respect;

   (b)   even if the claimant or pursuer does show that the patent is invalid in a relevant respect, he shall not be entitled to the relief claimed if the defendant or defender proves that at the time of making the threats he did not know, and had no reason to suspect, that the patent was invalid in that respect.

(3)   The said relief is –

   (a)   a declaration or declarator to the effect that the threats are unjustifiable;

   (b)   an injunction or interdict against the continuance of the threats; and

   (c)   damages in respect of any loss which the claimant or pursuer has sustained by the threats.

(4)   Proceedings may not be brought under this section for –

   (a)   a threat to bring proceedings for an infringement alleged to consist of making or importing a product for disposal or of using a process, or

   (b)   a threat, made to a person who has made or imported a product for disposal or used a process, to bring proceedings for an infringement alleged to consist of doing anything else in relation to that product or process.

(5)   For the purposes of this section a person does not threaten another person with proceedings for infringement of a patent if he merely –

   (a)   provides factual information about the patent,

   (b)   makes enquiries of the other person for the sole purpose of discovering whether, or by whom, the patent has been infringed as mentioned in subsection (4)(a) above, or

   (c)   makes an assertion about the patent for the purpose of any enquiries so made.

(6)   In proceedings under this section for threats made by one person (A) to another (B) in respect of an alleged infringement of a patent for an invention, it shall be a defence for A to prove that he used his best endeavours, without success, to discover –

   (a)   where the invention is a product, the identity of the person (if any) who made or (in the case of an imported product) imported it for disposal;

   (b)   where the invention is a process and the alleged infringement consists of offering it for use, the identity of a person who used the process;

   (c)   where the invention is a process and the alleged infringement is an act falling within section 60(1)(c) above, the identity of the person who used the process to produce the product in question;

and that he notified B accordingly, before or at the time of making the threats, identifying the endeavours used.

Declaration or declarator as to non-infringement

71.(1) Without prejudice to the court's jurisdiction to make a declaration or declarator apart from this section, a declaration or declarator that an act does not, or a proposed act would not, constitute an infringement of a patent may be made by the court or the comptroller in proceedings between the person doing or proposing to do the act and the proprietor of the patent, notwithstanding that no assertion to the contrary has been made by the proprietor, if it is shown –

(a) that that person has applied in writing to the proprietor for a written acknowledgment to the effect of the declaration or declarator claimed, and has furnished him with full particulars in writing of the act in question; and

(b) that the proprietor has refused or failed to give any such acknowledgment.

(2) Subject to section 72(5) below, a declaration made by the comptroller under this section shall have the same effect as a declaration or declarator by the court.

Revocation of patents

Power to revoke patents on application

72.(1) Subject to the following provisions of this Act, the court or the comptroller may by order revoke a patent for an invention on the application of any person (including the proprietor of the patent) on (but only on) any of the following grounds, that is to say –

(a) the invention is not a patentable invention;

(b) that the patent was granted to a person who was not entitled to be granted that patent;

(c) the specification of the patent does not disclose the invention clearly enough and completely enough for it to be performed by a person skilled in the art;

(d) the matter disclosed in the specification of the patent extends beyond that disclosed in the application for the patent, as filed, or, if the patent was granted on a new application filed under section 8(3), 12 or 37(4) above or as mentioned in section 15(9) above, in the earlier application, as filed;

(e) the protection conferred by the patent has been extended by an amendment which should not have been allowed.

(2) An application for the revocation of a patent on the ground mentioned in subsection (1)(b) above –

(a) may only be made by a person found by the court in an action for a declaration or declarator, or found by the court or the comptroller on a reference under section 37 above, to be entitled to be granted that patent or to be granted a patent for part of the matter comprised in the specification of the patent sought to be revoked; and

(b) may not be made if that action was commenced or that reference was made after the second anniversary of the date of the grant of the patent sought to be revoked, unless it is shown that any person registered as a proprietor of the patent knew at the time of the grant or of the transfer of the patent to him that he was not entitled to the patent.

(3) [repealed]

(4) An order under this section may be an order for the unconditional revocation of the patent or, where the court or the comptroller determines that one of the grounds mentioned in subsection (1) above has been established, but only so as to invalidate the patent to a limited extent, an order that the patent should be revoked unless within a specified time the specification is amended to the satisfaction of the court or the comptroller, as the case may be.

(4A) The reference in subsection (4) above to the specification being amended is to its being amended under section 75 below and also, in the case of a European Patent (UK), to its being amended under any provision of the European Patent Convention under which the claims of the patent may be limited by amendment at the request of the proprietor.

(5) A decision of the comptroller or on appeal from the comptroller shall not estop any party to civil proceedings in which infringement of a patent is in issue from alleging invalidity of the patent on any of the grounds referred to in subsection (1) above, whether or not any of the issues involved were decided in the said decision.

(6) Where the comptroller refuses to grant an application made to him by any person under this section, no application (otherwise than by way of appeal or by way of putting validity in issue in proceedings for infringement) may be made to the court by that person under this section in relation to the patent concerned, without the leave of the court.

(7) Where the comptroller has not disposed of an application made to him under this section, the applicant may not apply to the court under this section in respect of the patent concerned unless either –

(a) the proprietor of the patent agrees that the applicant may so apply, or

(b) the comptroller certifies in writing that it appears to him that the question whether the patent should be revoked is one which would more properly be determined by the court.

Comptroller's power to revoke patents on his own initiative

73.(1) If it appears to the comptroller that an invention for which a patent has been granted formed part of the state of the art by virtue only of section 2(3) above, he may on his own initiative by order revoke the patent, but shall not do so without giving the proprietor of the patent an opportunity of making any observations and of amending the specification of the patent so as to exclude any matter which formed part of the state of the art as aforesaid without contravening section 76 below.

(1A) Where the comptroller issues an opinion under section 74A that section 1(1)(a) or (b) is not satisfied in relation to an invention for which there is a patent, the comptroller may revoke the patent.

(1B) The power under subsection (1A) may not be exercised before –

    (a)   the end of the period in which the proprietor of the patent may apply under the rules (by virtue of section 74B) for a review of the opinion, or

    (b)   if the proprietor applies for a review, the decision on the review is made (or, if there is an appeal against that decision, the appeal is determined).

(1C) The comptroller shall not exercise the power under subsection (1A) without giving the proprietor of the patent an opportunity to make any observations and to amend the specification of the patent without contravening section 76.

(2)   If it appears to the comptroller that a patent under this Act and a European patent (UK) have been granted for the same invention having the same priority date, and that the applications for the patents were filed by the same applicant or his successor in title, he shall give the proprietor of the patent under this Act an opportunity of making observations and of amending the specification of the patent, and if the proprietor fails to satisfy the comptroller that there are not two patents in respect of the same invention, or to amend the specification so as to prevent there being two patents in respect of the same invention, the comptroller shall revoke the patent.

(3)   The comptroller shall not take action under subsection (2) above before –

    (a)   the end of the period for filing an opposition to the European patent (UK) under the European Patent Convention, or

    (b)   if later, the date on which opposition proceedings are finally disposed of;

and he shall not then take any action if the decision is not to maintain the European patent or if it is amended so that there are not two patents in respect of the same invention.

(4)   The comptroller shall not take action under subsection (2) above if the European patent (UK) has been surrendered under section 29(1) above before the date on which by virtue of section 25(1) above the patent under this Act is to be treated as having been granted or, if proceedings for the surrender of the European patent (UK) have been begun before that date, until those proceedings are finally disposed of; and he shall not then take any action if the decision is to accept the surrender of the European patent.

Putting validity in issue

Proceedings in which validity of patent may be put in issue

74.(1) Subject to the following provisions of this section, the validity of a patent may be put in issue –

    (a)   by way of defence, in proceedings for infringement of the patent under section 61 above or proceedings under section 69 above for infringement of rights conferred by the publication of an application;

    (b)   in proceedings under section 70 above;

    (c)   in proceedings in which a declaration in relation to the patent is sought under section 71 above;

(d) in proceedings before the court or the comptroller under section 72 above for the revocation of the patent;

(e) in proceedings under section 58 above.

(2) The validity of a patent may not be put in issue in any other proceedings and, in particular, no proceedings may be instituted (whether under this Act or otherwise) seeking only a declaration as to the validity or invalidity of a patent.

(3) The only grounds on which the validity of a patent may be put in issue (whether in proceedings for revocation under section 72 above or otherwise) are the grounds on which the patent may be revoked under that section.

(4) No determination shall be made in any proceedings mentioned in subsection (1) above on the validity of a patent which any person puts in issue on the ground mentioned in section 72(1)(b) above unless –

(a) it has been determined in entitlement proceedings commenced by that person or in the proceedings in which the validity of the patent is in issue that the patent should have been granted to him and not some other person; and

(b) except where it has been so determined in entitlement proceedings, the proceedings in which the validity of the patent is in issue are commenced on or before the second anniversary of the date of the grant of the patent or it is shown that any person registered as a proprietor of the patent knew at the time of the grant or of the transfer of the patent to him that he was not entitled to the patent.

(5) Where the validity of a patent is put in issue by way of defence or counterclaim the court or the comptroller shall, if it or he thinks it just to do so, give the defendant an opportunity to comply with the condition in subsection (4)(a) above.

(6) In subsection (4) above "entitlement proceedings", in relation to a patent, means a reference under section 37(1) above on the ground that the patent was granted to a person not entitled to it or proceedings for a declaration or declarator that it was so granted.

(7) Where proceedings with respect to a patent are pending in the court under any provision of this Act mentioned in sub-section (1) above, no proceedings may be instituted without the leave of the court before the comptroller with respect to that patent under section 61(3), 69, 71 or 72 above.

(8) It is hereby declared that for the purposes of this Act the validity of a patent is not put in issue merely because –

(a) the comptroller is considering its validity in order to decide whether to revoke it under section 73 above, or

(b) its validity is being considered in connection with an opinion under section 74A below or a review of such an opinion.

Opinions by Patent Office

Opinions on matters prescribed in the rules

74A.(1) The proprietor of a patent or any other person may request the comptroller to issue an opinion on a prescribed matter in relation to the patent.

(2) Subsection (1) above applies even if the patent has expired or has been surrendered.

(3) The comptroller shall issue an opinion if requested to do so under subsection (1) above, but shall not do so –

   (a) in such circumstances as may be prescribed, or

   (b) if for any reason he considers it inappropriate in all the circumstances to do so.

(4) An opinion under this section shall not be binding for any purposes.

(5) An opinion under this section shall be prepared by an examiner.

(6) In relation to a decision of the comptroller whether to issue an opinion under this section –

   (a) for the purposes of section 101 below, only the person making the request under subsection (1) above shall be regarded as a party to a proceeding before the comptroller; and

   (b) no appeal shall lie at the instance of any other person.

Reviews of opinions under section 74A

74B.(1) Rules may make provision for a review before the comptroller, on an application by the proprietor or an exclusive licensee of the patent in question, of an opinion under section 74A above.

(2) The rules may, in particular –

   (a) prescribe the circumstances in which, and the period within which, an application may be made;

   (b) provide that, in prescribed circumstances, proceedings for a review may not be brought or continued where other proceedings have been brought;

   (c) [repealed]

   (d) provide for there to be a right of appeal against a decision made on a review only in prescribed cases.

General provisions as to amendment of patents and applications

Amendment of patent in infringement or revocation proceedings

75.(1) In any proceedings before the court or the comptroller in which the validity of a patent may be put in issue the court or, as the case may be, the comptroller may, subject to section 76 below, allow the proprietor of the patent to amend the specification of the patent in such manner, and subject to such terms as to advertising the proposed amendment and as to costs, expenses or otherwise, as the court or comptroller thinks fit.

(2) A person may give notice to the court or the comptroller of his opposition to an amendment proposed by the proprietor of the patent under this section, and if he does so the court or the comptroller shall notify the proprietor and consider the opposition in deciding whether the amendment or any amendment should be allowed.

(3) An amendment of a specification of a patent under this section shall have effect and be deemed always to have had effect from the grant of the patent.

(4) Where an application for an order under this section is made to the court, the applicant shall notify the comptroller, who shall be entitled to appear and be heard and shall appear if so directed by the court.

(5) In considering whether or not to allow an amendment proposed under this section, the court or the comptroller shall have regard to any relevant principles applicable under the European Patent Convention.

Amendment of applications and patents not to include added matter

76.(1) An application for a patent which –

(a) is made in respect of matter disclosed in an earlier application, or in the specification of a patent which has been granted, and

(b) discloses additional matter, that is, matter extending beyond that disclosed in the earlier application, as filed, or the application for the patent, as filed,

may be filed under section 8(3), 12 or 37(4) above, or as mentioned in section 15(9) above, but shall not be allowed to proceed unless it is amended so as to exclude the additional matter.

(1A) Where, in relation to an application for a patent –

(a) a reference to an earlier relevant application has been filed as mentioned in section 15(1)(c)(ii) above; and

(b) the description filed under section 15(10)(b)(i) above discloses additional matter, that is, matter extending beyond that disclosed in the earlier relevant application,

the application shall not be allowed to proceed unless it is amended so as to exclude the additional matter.

(2) No amendment of an application for a patent shall be allowed under section 15A(6), 18(3) or 19(1) if it results in the application disclosing matter extending beyond that disclosed in the application as filed.

(3) No amendment of the specification of a patent shall be allowed under section 27(1), 73 or 75 if it –

(a) results in the specification disclosing additional matter, or

(b) extends the protection conferred by the patent.

(4) In subsection (1A) above "relevant application" has the meaning given by section 5(5) above.

Biotechnological inventions

76A.(1) Any provision of, or made under, this Act is to have effect in relation to a patent or an application for a patent which concerns a biotechnological invention, subject to the provisions of Schedule A2.

(2) Nothing in this section or Schedule A2 is to be read as affecting the application of any provision in relation to any other kind of patent or application for a patent.

PART II
PROVISIONS ABOUT INTERNATIONAL CONVENTIONS

European patents and patent applications

Effect of European patent (UK)

77.(1) Subject to the provisions of this Act, a European patent (UK) shall, as from the publication of the mention of its grant in the European Patent Bulletin, be treated for the purposes of Parts I and III of this Act as if it were a patent under this Act granted in pursuance of an application made under this Act and as if notice of the grant of the patent had, on the date of that publication, been published under section 24 above in the journal; and –

(a) the proprietor of a European patent (UK) shall accordingly as respects the United Kingdom have the same rights and remedies, subject to the same conditions, as the proprietor of a patent under this Act;

(b) references in Parts I and III of this Act to a patent shall be construed accordingly; and

(c) any statement made and any certificate filed for the purposes of the provision of the convention corresponding to section 2(4)(c) above shall be respectively treated as a statement made and written evidence filed for the purposes of the said paragraph (c).

(2) Subsection (1) above shall not affect the operation in relation to a European patent (UK) of any provisions of the European Patent Convention relating to the amendment or revocation of such a patent in proceedings before the European Patent Office.

(3) Where in the case of a European patent (UK) –

(a) proceedings for infringement, or proceedings under section 58 above, have been commenced before the court or the comptroller and have not been finally disposed of, and

(b) it is established in proceedings before the European Patent Office that the patent is only partially valid,

the provisions of section 63 or, as the case may be, of subsections (7) to (9) of section 58 apply as they apply to proceedings in which the validity of a patent is put in issue and in which it is found that the patent is only partially valid.

(4) Where a European patent (UK) is amended in accordance with the European Patent Convention, the amendment shall have effect for the purposes of Parts I and III of this Act as if the specification of the patent had been amended under this Act; but subject to subsection (6)(b) below.

(4A) Where a European patent (UK) is revoked in accordance with the European Patent Convention, the patent shall be treated for the purposes of Parts I and III of this Act as having been revoked under this Act.

(5) Where –

(a) under the European Patent Convention a European patent (UK) is revoked for failure to observe a time limit and is subsequently restored or is revoked by the Board of Appeal and is subsequently restored by the Enlarged Board of Appeal; and

(b)   between the revocation and publication of the fact that it has been restored a person begins in good faith to do an act which would, apart from section 55 above, constitute an infringement of the patent or makes in good faith effective and serious preparations to do such an act;

he shall have the rights conferred by section 28A(4) and (5) above, and subsections (6) and (7) of that section shall apply accordingly.

(5A) Where, under the European Patent Convention, a European patent (UK) is revoked and subsequently restored (including where it is revoked by the Board of Appeal and subsequently restored by the Enlarged Board of Appeal), any fee that would have been imposed in relation to the patent after the revocation but before the restoration is payable within the prescribed period following the restoration.

(6)   While this subsection is in force –

    (a)   subsection (1) above shall not apply to a European patent (UK) the specification of which was published in French or German, unless a translation of the specification into English is filed at the Patent Office and the prescribed fee is paid before the end of the prescribed period;

    (b)   subsection (4) above shall not apply to an amendment made in French or German unless a translation into English of the specification as amended is filed at the Patent Office and the prescribed fee is paid before the end of the prescribed period.

(7)   Where such a translation is not filed, the patent shall be treated as always having been void.

(8)   The comptroller shall publish any translation filed at the Patent Office under subsection (6) above.

(9)   Subsection (6) above shall come into force on a day appointed for the purpose by rules and shall cease to have effect on a day so appointed, without prejudice, however, to the power to bring it into force again.

Effect of filing an application for a European patent (UK)

78.(1) Subject to the provisions of this Act, an application for a European patent (UK) having a date of filing under the European Patent Convention shall be treated for the purposes of the provisions of this Act to which this section applies as an application for a patent under this Act having that date as its date of filing and having the other incidents listed in subsection (3) below, but subject to the modifications mentioned in the following provisions of this section.

(2)   This section applies to the following provisions of this Act:–

section 2(3) and so much of section 14(7) as relates to section 2(3);

section 5;

section 6;

so much of section 13(3) as relates to an application for and issue of a certificate under that subsection;

sections 30 to 33;

section 36;

sections 55 to 69;

section 74, so far as relevant to any of the provisions mentioned above;
section 111; and
section 125.

(3) The incidents referred to in subsection (1) above in relation to an application for a European patent (UK) are as follows:–

    (a) any declaration of priority made in connection with the application under the European Patent Convention shall be treated for the purposes of this Act as a declaration made under section 5(2) above;

    (b) where a period of time relevant to priority is extended under that convention, the period of twelve months allowed under section 5(2A) (a) above shall be so treated as altered correspondingly;

    (c) where the date of filing an application is re-dated under that convention to a later date, that date shall be so treated as the date of filing the application;

    (d) the application, if published in accordance with that convention, shall, subject to subsection (7) and section 79 below, be so treated as published under section 16 above;

    (e) any designation of the inventor under that convention or any statement under it indicating the origin of the right to a European patent shall be treated for the purposes of section 13(3) above as a statement filed under section 13(2) above;

    (f) registration of the application in the register of European patents shall be treated as registration under this Act.

(4) Rules under section 32 above may not impose any requirements as to the registration of applications for European patents (UK) but may provide for the registration of copies of entries relating to such applications in the European register of patents.

(5) Subsections (1) to (3) above shall cease to apply to an application for a European patent (UK), except as mentioned in subsection (5A) below, if –

    (a) the application is refused or withdrawn or deemed to be withdrawn, or

    (b) the designation of the United Kingdom in the application is withdrawn or deemed to be withdrawn, but shall apply again if the rights of the applicant are re-established under the European Patent Convention, as from their reestablishment.

(5A) The occurrence of any of the events mentioned in subsection (5)(a) or (b) shall not affect the continued operation of section 2(3) above in relation to matter contained in an application for a European patent (UK) which by virtue of that provision has become part of the state of the art as regards other inventions; and the occurrence of any event mentioned in subsection (5)(b) shall not prevent matter contained in an application for a European patent (UK) becoming part of the state of the art by virtue of section 2(3) above as regards other inventions where the event occurs before the publication of that application.

(6) Where, between subsections (1) to (3) above ceasing to apply to an application for a European patent (UK) and the re-establishment of the rights of the applicant, a person –

(a) begins in good faith to do an act which would constitute an infringement of the rights conferred by publication of the application if those subsections then applied, or

(b) makes in good faith effective and serious preparations to do such an act,

he shall have the right to continue to do the act, or as the case may be, to do the act, notwithstanding subsections (1) to (3) applying again and notwithstanding the grant of the patent.

(6A) Subsections (5) and (6) of section 20B above have effect for the purposes of subsection (6) above as they have effect for the purposes of that section and as if the references to subsection (4) of that section were references to subsection 6 above.

(6B) Subject to subsection (6A) above, the right conferred by subsection (6) above does not extend to granting a licence to another person to do the act in question.

(6C) Subsections (6) to (6B) above apply in relation to the use of a patented invention for the services of the Crown as they apply in relation to an infringement of the rights conferred by publication of the application (or, as the case may be, infringement of the patent). "Patented invention" has the same meaning as in section 55 above.

(7) While this subsection is in force, an application for a European patent (UK) published by the European Patent Office under the European Patent Convention in French or German shall be treated for the purposes of sections 55 and 69 above as published under section 16 above when a translation into English of the claims of the specification of the application has been filed at and published by the Patent Office and the prescribed fee has been paid, but an applicant –

(a) may recover a payment by virtue of section 55(5) above in respect of the use of the invention in question before publication of that translation; or

(b) may bring proceedings by virtue of section 69 above in respect of an act mentioned in that section which is done before publication of that translation;

if before that use or the doing of that act he has sent by post or delivered to the government department who made use or authorised the use of the invention, or, as the case may be, to the person alleged to have done the act, a translation into English of those claims.

(8) Subsection (7) above shall come into force on a day appointed for the purpose by rules and shall cease to have effect on a day so appointed, without prejudice, however, to the power to bring it into force again.

Operation of section 78 in relation to certain European patent applications

79.(1) Subject to the following provisions of this section, section 78 above, in its operation in relation to an international application for a patent (UK) which is treated by virtue of the European Patent Convention as an application for a European patent (UK), shall have effect as if any reference in that section to anything done in relation to the application under the European Patent Convention included a reference to the corresponding thing done under the Patent Co-operation Treaty.

(2) Any such international application which is published under that treaty shall be treated for the purposes of section 2(3) above as published only when a copy of the application has been supplied to the European Patent Office in English, French or German and the relevant fee has been paid under that convention.

(3) Any such international application which is published under that treaty in a language other than English, French or German shall, subject to section 78(7) above, be treated for the purposes of sections 55 and 69 above as published only when it is re-published in English, French or German by the European Patent Office under that convention.

Authentic text of European patents and patent applications

80.(1) Subject to subsection (2) below, the text of a European patent or application for such a patent in the language of the proceedings, that is to say, the language in which proceedings relating to the patent or the application are to be conducted before the European Patent Office, shall be the authentic text for the purposes of any domestic proceedings, that is to say, any proceedings relating to the patent or application before the comptroller or the court.

(2) Where the language of the proceedings is French or German, a translation into English of the specification of the patent under section 77 above or of the claims of the application under section 78 above shall be treated as the authentic text for the purpose of any domestic proceedings, other than proceedings for the revocation of the patent, if the patent or application as translated into English confers protection which is narrower than that conferred by it in French or German.

(3) If any such translation results in a European patent or application conferring the narrower protection, the proprietor of or applicant for the patent may file a corrected translation with the Patent Office and, if he pays the prescribed fee within the prescribed period, the Patent Office shall publish it, but –

(a) any payment for any use of the invention which (apart from section 55 above) would have infringed the patent as correctly translated, but not as originally translated, or in the case of an application would have infringed it as aforesaid if the patent had been granted, shall not be recoverable under that section,

(b) the proprietor or applicant shall not be entitled to bring proceedings in respect of an act which infringed the patent as correctly translated, but not as originally translated, or in the case of an application would have infringed it as aforesaid if the patent had been granted,

unless before that use or the doing of the act the corrected translation has been published by the Patent Office or the proprietor or applicant has sent the corrected translation by post or delivered it to the government department who made use or authorised the use of the invention or, as the case may be, to the person alleged to have done that act.

(4) Where a correction of a translation is published under subsection (3) above and before it is so published a person –

   (a) begins in good faith to do an act which would not constitute an infringement of the patent as originally translated, or of the rights conferred by publication of the application as originally translated, but would do so under the amended translation, or

   (b) makes in good faith effective and serious preparations to do such an act,

he shall have the right to continue to do the act or, as the case may be, to do the act, notwithstanding the publication of the corrected translation and notwithstanding the grant of the patent.

(5) Subsections (5) and (6) of section 28A above have effect for the purposes of subsection (4) above as they have effect for the purposes of that section and as if –

   (a) the references to subsection (4) of that section were references to subsection (4) above;

   (b) the reference to the registered proprietor of the patent included a reference to the applicant.

(6) Subject to subsection (5) above, the right conferred by subsection (4) above does not extend to granting a licence to another person to do the act in question.

(7) Subsections (4) to (6) above apply in relation to the use of a patented invention for the services of the Crown as they apply in relation to an infringement of the patent or of the rights conferred by the publication of the application. "Patented invention" has the same meaning as in section 55 above.

Conversion of European patent applications

81.(1) The comptroller may direct that on compliance with the relevant conditions mentioned in subsection (2) below an application for a European patent (UK) shall be treated as an application for a patent under this Act where the application is deemed to be withdrawn under the provisions of the European Patent Convention relating to the time for forwarding applications to the European Patent Office.

(2) The relevant conditions referred to above are –

   (a) [repealed]

   (b) that –

      (i) the applicant requests the comptroller within the relevant prescribed period (where the application was filed with the Patent Office) to give a direction under this section, or

      (ii) the central industrial property office of a country which is party to the convention, other than the United Kingdom, with which the application was filed transmits within the relevant prescribed period a request that the application should be converted into an application under this Act, together with a copy of the application; and

    (c) that the applicant within the relevant prescribed period pays the application fee and if the application is in a language other than English, files a translation into English of the application and of any amendments previously made in accordance with the convention.

(3) Where an application for a European patent falls to be treated as an application for a patent under this Act by virtue of a direction under this section –

    (a) the date which is the date of filing the application under the European Patent Convention shall be treated as its date of filing for the purposes of this Act, but if that date is re-dated under the convention to a later date, that later date shall be treated for those purposes as the date of filing the application;

    (b) if the application satisfies a requirement of the convention corresponding to any of the requirements of this Act or rules designated as formal requirements, it shall be treated as satisfying that formal requirement;

    (c) any document filed with the European Patent Office under any provision of the convention corresponding to any of the following provisions of this Act, that is to say, sections 2(4)(c), 5, 13(2) and 14, or any rule made for the purposes of any of those provisions, shall be treated as filed with the Patent Office under that provision or rule; and

    (d) the comptroller shall refer the application for only so much of the examination and search required by sections 15A, 17 and 18 above as he considers appropriate in view of any examination and search carried out under the convention, and those sections shall apply with any necessary modifications accordingly.

Jurisdiction to determine questions as to right to a patent

82.(1) The court shall not have jurisdiction to determine a question to which this section applies except in accordance with the following provisions of this section.

(2) Section 12 above shall not confer jurisdiction on the comptroller to determine a question to which this section applies except in accordance with the following provisions of this section.

(3) This section applies to a question arising before the grant of a European patent whether a person has a right to be granted a European patent, or a share in any such patent, and in this section "employer-employee question" means any such question between an employer and an employee, or their successors in title, arising out of an application for a European patent for an invention made by the employee.

(4) The court and the comptroller shall have jurisdiction to determine any question to which this section applies, other than an employer-employee question, if either of the following conditions is satisfied, that is to say –

    (a) the applicant has his residence or principal place of business in the United Kingdom; or

    (b) the other party claims that the patent should be granted to him and he has his residence or principal place of business in the United Kingdom and the applicant does not have his residence or principal place of business in any of the relevant contracting states;

and also if in either of those cases there is no written evidence that the parties have agreed to submit to the jurisdiction of the competent authority of a relevant contracting state other than the United Kingdom.

(5) The court and the comptroller shall have jurisdiction to determine an employer-employee question if either of the following conditions is satisfied, that is to say –

    (a) the employee is mainly employed in the United Kingdom; or

    (b) the employee is not mainly employed anywhere or his place of main employment cannot be determined, but the employer has a place of business in the United Kingdom to which the employee is attached (whether or not he is also attached elsewhere);

and also if in either of those cases there is no written evidence that the parties have agreed to submit to the jurisdiction of the competent authority of a relevant contracting state other than the United Kingdom or, where there is such evidence of such an agreement, if the law applicable to the contract of employment does not recognise the validity of the agreement.

(6) Without prejudice to subsections (2) to (5) above, the court and the comptroller shall have jurisdiction to determine any question to which this section applies if there is written evidence that the parties have agreed to submit to the jurisdiction of the court or the comptroller, as the case may be, and, in the case of an employer-employee question, the law applicable to the contract of employment recognises the validity of the agreement.

(7) If, after proceedings to determine a question to which this section applies have been brought before the competent authority of a relevant contracting state other than the United Kingdom, proceedings are begun before the court or a reference is made to the comptroller under section 12 above to determine that question, the court or the comptroller, as the case may be, shall stay or sist the proceedings before the court or the comptroller unless or until the competent authority of that other state either –

    (a) determines to decline jurisdiction and no appeal lies from the determination or the time for appealing expires, or

    (b) makes a determination which the court or the comptroller refuses to recognise under section 83 below.

(8) References in this section to the determination of a question include respectively references to –

    (a) the making of a declaration or the grant of a declarator with respect to that question (in the case of the court); and

    (b) the making of an order under section 12 above in relation to that question (in the case of the court or the comptroller).

(9) In this section and section 83 below "relevant contracting state" means a country which is a party to the European Patent Convention and has not exercised its right under the convention to exclude the application of the protocol to the convention known as the Protocol on Recognition.

Appendix 6

Effect of patent decisions of competent authorities of other states

83.(1) A determination of a question to which section 82 above applies by the competent authority of a relevant contracting state other than the United Kingdom shall, if no appeal lies from the determination or the time for appealing has expired, be recognised in the United Kingdom as if it had been made by the court or the comptroller unless the court or he refuses to recognise it under subsection (2) below.

(2) The court or the comptroller may refuse to recognise any such determination that the applicant for a European patent had no right to be granted the patent, or any share in it, if either –

   (a) the applicant did not contest the proceedings in question because he was not notified of them at all or in the proper manner or was not notified of them in time for him to contest the proceedings; or

   (b) the determination in the proceedings in question conflicts with the determination of the competent authority of any relevant contracting state in proceedings instituted earlier between the same parties as in the proceedings in question.

Patent agents and other representatives

84. [repealed]

European patent attorneys

85. [repealed]

Community patents

Implementation of Community Patent Convention

86. [repealed]

Decisions on Community Patent Convention

87. [repealed]

Jurisdiction in legal proceedings in connection with Community Patent Convention

88. [repealed]

Unified Patent Court

Implementation of Agreement on a Unified Patent Court

88A.(1) The Secretary of State may by order make provision for giving effect in the United Kingdom to the provisions of the Agreement on a Unified Patent Court made in Brussels on 19 February 2013.

(2) An order under this section may, in particular, make provision –

   (a) to confer jurisdiction on a court, remove jurisdiction from a court or vary the jurisdiction of a court;

   (b) to require the payment of fees.

(3)   An order under this section may also make provision for varying the application of specified provisions of this Act so that they correspond to provision made by the Agreement.

(4)   An order under this section may –

(a)   make provision which applies generally or in relation only to specified cases;

(b)   make different provision for different cases.

(5)   An order under this section may amend this Act or any other enactment.

(6)   An order under this section may not be made unless a draft of the order has been laid before, and approved by resolution of, each House of Parliament.

(7)   The meaning of "court" in this section is not limited by the definition of that expression in section 130(1).

Designation as international organisation of which UK is member
88B. The Unified Patent Court is to be treated for the purposes of section 1 of the International Organisations Act 1968 (organisations of which the United Kingdom is a member) as an organisation to which that section applies.

International applications for patents

Effect of international application for patent
89.(1) An international application for a patent (UK) for which a date of filing has been accorded under the Patent Co-operation Treaty shall, subject to –

section 89A (international and national phases of application), and

section 89B (adaptation of provisions in relation to international application),

be treated for the purposes of Parts I and III of this Act as an application for a patent under this Act.

(2)   If the application, or the designation of the United Kingdom in it, is withdrawn or (except as mentioned in subsection (3)) deemed to be withdrawn under the Treaty, it shall be treated as withdrawn under this Act.

(3)   An application shall not be treated as withdrawn under this Act if it, or the designation of the United Kingdom in it, is deemed to be withdrawn under the Treaty –

(a)   because of an error or omission in an institution having functions under the Treaty, or

(b)   because, owing to circumstances outside the applicant's control, a copy of the application was not received by the International Bureau before the end of the time limited for that purpose under the Treaty,

or in such other circumstances as may be prescribed.

(4)   [repealed]

(5)   If an international application for a patent which designates the United Kingdom is refused a filing date under the Treaty and the comptroller determines that the refusal was caused by an error or omission in an

institution having functions under the Treaty, he may direct that the application shall be treated as an application under this Act, having such date of filing as he may direct.

International and national phases of application

89A.(1) The provisions of the Patent Co-operation Treaty relating to publication, search, examination and amendment, and not those of this Act, apply to an international application for a patent (UK) during the international phase of the application.

(2) The international phase of the application means the period from the filing of the application in accordance with the Treaty until the national phase of the application begins.

(3) The national phase of the application begins –

    (a) when the prescribed period expires, provided any necessary translation of the application into English has been filed at the Patent Office and the prescribed fee has been paid by the applicant; or

    (b) on the applicant expressly requesting the comptroller to proceed earlier with the national phase of the application, filing at the Patent Office –

        (i) a copy of the application, if none has yet been sent to the Patent Office in accordance with the Treaty, and

        (ii) any necessary translation of the application into English,

and paying the prescribed fee.

For this purpose a "copy of the application" includes a copy published in accordance with the Treaty in a language other than that in which it was originally filed.

(4) If the prescribed period expires without the conditions mentioned in subsection (3)(a) being satisfied, the application shall be taken to be withdrawn.

(5) Where during the international phase the application is amended in accordance with the Treaty, the amendment shall be treated as made under this Act if –

    (a) when the prescribed period expires, any necessary translation of the amendment into English has been filed at the Patent Office, or

    (b) where the applicant expressly requests the comptroller to proceed earlier with the national phase of the application, there is then filed at the Patent Office –

        (i) a copy of the amendment, if none has yet been sent to the Patent Office in accordance with the Treaty, and

        (ii) any necessary translation of the amendment into English;

otherwise the amendment shall be disregarded.

(6) The comptroller shall on payment of the prescribed fee publish any translation filed at the Patent Office under subsection (3) or (5) above.

Adaptation of provisions in relation to international application

89B.(1) Where an international application for a patent (UK) is accorded a filing date under the Patent Co-operation Treaty –

(a) that date, or if the application is re-dated under the Treaty to a later date that later date, shall be treated as the date of filing the application under this Act,

(b) any declaration of priority made under the Treaty shall be treated as made under section 5(2) above, and where in accordance with the Treaty any extra days are allowed, the period of 12 months allowed under section 5(2A)(a) above shall be treated as altered accordingly, and

(c) any statement of the name of the inventor under the Treaty shall be treated as a statement filed under section 13(2) above.

(2) If the application, not having been published under this Act, is published in accordance with the Treaty it shall be treated, for purposes other than those mentioned in subsection (3), as published under section 16 above when the national phase of the application begins or, if later, when published in accordance with the Treaty.

(3) For the purposes of section 55 (use of invention for service of the Crown) and section 69 (infringement of rights conferred by publication) the application, not having been published under this Act, shall be treated as published under section 16 above –

(a) if it is published in accordance with the Treaty in English, on its being so published; and

(b) if it is so published in a language other than English –

(i) on the publication of a translation of the application in accordance with section 89A(6) above, or

(ii) on the service by the applicant of a translation into English of the specification of the application of the government department concerned or, as the case may be, on the person committing the infringing act.

The reference in paragraph (b)(ii) to the service of a translation on a government department or other person is to its being sent by post or delivered to that department or person.

(4) During the international phase of the application, section 8 above does not apply (determination of questions of entitlement in relation to application under this Act) and section 12 above (determination of entitlement in relation to foreign and convention patents) applies notwithstanding the application; but after the end of the international phase, section 8 applies and section 12 does not.

(5) When the national phase begins the comptroller shall refer the application for so much of the examination and search under sections 15A, 17 and 18 above as he considers appropriate in view of any examination or search carried out under the Treaty.

Appendix 6

Convention countries

Orders in Council as to convention countries

90.(1) Her Majesty may with a view to the fulfilment of a treaty or international convention, arrangement or engagement, by Order in Council declare that any country specified in the Order is a convention country for the purposes of section 5 above.

(2) Her Majesty may by Order in Council direct that any of the Channel Islands, any colony shall be taken to be a convention country for those purposes.

(3) For the purposes of subsection (1) above every colony, protectorate, and territory subject to the authority or under the suzerainty of another country, and every territory administered by another country under the trusteeship system of the United Nations shall be taken to be a country in the case of which a declaration may be made under that subsection.

Miscellaneous

Evidence of conventions and instruments under conventions

91.(1) Judicial notice shall be taken of the following, that is to say –

(a) the European Patent Convention, the Community Patent Convention and the Patent Co-operation Treaty (each of which is hereafter in this section referred to as the relevant convention);

(b) any bulletin, journal or gazette published under the relevant convention and the register of European patents kept under the European Patent Convention; and

(c) any decision of, or expression of opinion by, the relevant convention court on any question arising under or in connection with the relevant convention.

(2) Any document mentioned in subsection (1)(b) above shall be admissible as evidence of any instrument or other act thereby communicated of any convention institution.

(3) Evidence of any instrument issued under the relevant convention by any such institution, including any judgment or order of the relevant convention court, or of any document in the custody of any such institution or reproducing in legible form any information in such custody otherwise than in legible form, or any entry in or extract from such a document, may be given in any legal proceedings by production of a copy certified as a true copy by an official of that institution; and any document purporting to be such a copy shall be received in evidence without proof of the official position or handwriting of the person signing the certificate.

(4) Evidence of any such instrument may also be given in any legal proceedings –

(a) by production of a copy purporting to be printed by the Queen's Printer;

(b) where the instrument is in the custody of a government department, by production of a copy certified on behalf of the department to be a true copy by an officer of the department generally or specially authorised to do so;

and any document purporting to be such a copy as is mentioned in paragraph (b) above of an instrument in the custody of a department shall be received in evidence without proof of the official position or handwriting of the person signing the certificate, or of his authority to do so, or of the document being in the custody of the department.

(5) In any legal proceedings in Scotland evidence of any matter given in a manner authorised by this section shall be sufficient evidence of it.

(6) In this section –

"convention institution" means an institution established by or having functions under the relevant convention;

"relevant convention court" does not include a court of the United Kingdom or of any other country which is a party to the relevant convention; and

"legal proceedings", in relation to the United Kingdom, includes proceedings before the comptroller.

Obtaining evidence for proceedings under the European Patent Convention

92.(1) Sections 1 to 3 of the Evidence (Proceedings in Other Jurisdictions) Act 1975 (provisions enabling United Kingdom courts to assist in obtaining evidence for foreign courts) shall apply for the purpose of proceedings before a relevant convention court under the European Patent Convention as they apply for the purpose of civil proceedings in a court exercising jurisdiction in a country outside the United Kingdom.

(2) In the application of those sections by virtue of this section any reference to the High Court, the Court of Session or the High Court of Justice in Northern Ireland shall include a reference to the comptroller.

(3) Rules under this Act may include provision –

(a) as to the manner in which an application under section 1 of the said Act of 1975 is to be made to the comptroller for the purpose of proceedings before a relevant convention court under the European Patent Convention; and

(b) subject to the provisions of that Act, as to the circumstances in which an order can be made under section 2 of that Act on any such application.

(4) Rules of the court and rules under this Act may provide for an officer of the European Patent Office to attend the hearing of an application under section 1 of that Act before the court or the comptroller, as the case may be, and examine the witnesses or request the court or comptroller to put specified questions to the witnesses.

(5) Section 1(4) of the Perjury Act 1911 and article 3(4) of the Perjury (Northern Ireland) Order 1979 (statements made for the purposes, among others, of judicial proceedings in a tribunal of a foreign state) shall apply in relation to proceedings before a relevant convention court under the European Patent Convention as they apply to a judicial proceeding in a tribunal of a foreign state.

Appendix 6

Enforcement of orders for costs

93. If the European Patent Office orders the payment of costs in any proceedings before it –

(a) in England and Wales the costs shall, if the county court so orders, be recoverable by execution issued from the county court or otherwise as if they were payable under an order of that court;

(b) in Scotland the order may be enforced in like manner as an extract registered decree arbitral bearing a warrant for execution issued by the sheriff court of any sheriffdom in Scotland;

(c) in Northern Ireland the order may be enforced as if it were a money judgment;

(d) in the Isle of Man the order may be enforced in like manner as an execution issued out of the court.

Communication of information to the European Patent Office, etc.

94. It shall not be unlawful by virtue of any enactment to communicate the following information in pursuance of the European Patent Convention to the European Patent Office or the competent authority of any country which is party to the Convention, that is to say –

(a) information in the files of the court which, in accordance with the rules of court, the court authorises to be so communicated;

(b) information in the files of the Patent Office which, in accordance with rules under this Act, the comptroller authorises to be so communicated.

Financial provisions

95.(1) There shall be paid out of moneys provided by Parliament any sums required by any Minister of the Crown or government department to meet any financial obligation of the United Kingdom under the European Patent Convention or the Patent Co-operation Treaty.

(2) Any sums received by any Minister of the Crown or government department in pursuance of that convention or that treaty shall be paid into the Consolidated Fund.

PART III
MISCELLANEOUS AND GENERAL

Legal Proceedings

The Patents Court

96. [repealed]

Appeals from the comptroller

97.(1) Except as provided by subsection (4) below, an appeal shall lie to the Patents Court from any decision of the comptroller under this Act or rules except any of the following decisions, that is to say –

(a) a decision falling within section 14(7) above;

(b) a decision under section 16(2) above to omit matter from a specification;

(c) a decision to give directions under subsection (1) or (2) of section 22 above;

(d) a decision under rules which is excepted by rules from the right of appeal conferred by this section.

(2) For the purpose of hearing appeals under this section the Patents Court may consist of one or more judges of that court in accordance with directions given by the Lord Chief Justice of England and Wales after consulting the Lord Chancellor.

(3) An appeal shall not lie to the Court of Appeal from a decision of the Patents Court on appeal from a decision of the comptroller under this Act or rules –

(a) except where the comptroller's decision was given under section 8, 12, 18, 20, 27, 37, 40, 61, 72, 73 or 75 above; or

(b) except where the ground of appeal is that the decision of the Patents Court is wrong in law;

but an appeal shall only lie to the Court of Appeal under this section if leave to appeal is given by the Patents Court or the Court of Appeal.

(4) The Lord Chief Justice may nominate a judicial office holder (as defined in section 109(4) of the 69 Constitutional Reform Act 2005) to exercise his functions under subsection (2)10.

(5) An appeal shall lie to the Court of Session from any decision of the comptroller in proceedings which under rules are held in Scotland, except any decision mentioned in paragraphs (a) to (d) of subsection (1) above.

(6) An appeal shall not lie to the Inner House of the Court of Session from a decision of an Outer House judge on appeal from a decision of the comptroller under this Act or rules –

(a) except where the comptroller's decision was given under section 8, 12, 18, 20, 27, 37, 40, 61, 72, 73 or 75 above; or

(b) except where the ground of appeal is that the decision of the Outer House judge is wrong in law.

Proceedings in Scotland

98.(1) In Scotland proceedings relating primarily to patents (other than proceedings before the comptroller) shall be competent in the Court of Session only, and any jurisdiction of the sheriff court relating to patents is hereby abolished except in relation to questions which are incidental to the issue in proceedings which are otherwise competent there.

(2) The remuneration of any assessor appointed to assist the court in proceedings under this Act in the Court of Session shall be determined by the Lord President of the Court of Session with the consent of the Treasury and shall be defrayed out of moneys provided by Parliament.

General powers of the court

99. The court may, for the purpose of determining any question in the exercise of its original or appellate jurisdiction under this Act or any treaty or international convention to which the United Kingdom is a party, make any order or exercise any other power which the comptroller could have made or exercised for the purpose of determining that question.

Appendix 6

Power of Patents Court to order report

99A.(1) Rules of court shall make provision empowering the Patents Court in any proceedings before it under this Act, on or without the application of any party, to order the Patent Office to inquire into and report on any question of fact or opinion.

(2) Where the court makes such an order on the application of a party, the fee payable to the Patent Office shall be at such rate as may be determined in accordance with rules of court and shall be costs of the proceedings unless otherwise ordered by the court.

(3) Where the court makes such an order of its own motion, the fee payable to the Patent Office shall be at such rate as may be determined by the Lord Chancellor with the approval of the Treasury and shall be paid out of money provided by Parliament.

Power of Court of Session to order report

99B.(1) In any proceedings before the Court of Session under this Act the court may, either of its own volition or on the application of any party, order the Patent Office to inquire into and report on any question of fact or opinion.

(2) Where the court makes an order under subsection (1) above of its own volition the fee payable to the Patent Office shall be at such rate as may be determined by the Lord President of the Court of Session with the consent of the Treasury and shall be defrayed out of moneys provided by Parliament.

(3) Where the court makes an order under subsection (1) above on the application of a party, the fee payable to the Patent Office shall be at such rate as may be provided for in rules of court and shall be treated as expenses in the cause.

Burden of proof in certain cases

100.(1) If the invention for which a patent is granted is a process for obtaining a new product, the same product produced by a person other than the proprietor of the patent or a licensee of his shall, unless the contrary is proved, be taken in any proceedings to have been obtained by that process.

(2) In considering whether a party has discharged the burden imposed upon him by this section, the court shall not require him to disclose any manufacturing or commercial secrets if it appears to the court that it would be unreasonable to do so.

Exercise of comptroller's discretionary powers

101. Without prejudice to any rule of law, the comptroller shall give any party to a proceeding before him an opportunity of being heard before exercising adversely to that party any discretion vested in the comptroller by this Act or rules.

Right of audience, etc., in proceedings before the comptroller

102.(1) A party to proceedings before the comptroller under this Act, or under any treaty or international convention to which the United Kingdom is a party, may appear before the comptroller in person or be represented by any person whom he desires to represent him.

(2) No offence is committed under the enactments relating to the preparation of documents by persons not legally qualified by reason only of the preparation by any person of a document, other than a deed, for use in such proceedings.

(2A) For the purposes of subsection (2), as it has effect in relation to England and Wales, "the enactment relating to the preparation of documents by persons not qualified" means section 14 of the Legal Services Act 2007 (offence to carry on a reserved legal activity if not entitled) as it applies in relation to an activity which amounts to the carrying on of reserved instrument activities within the meaning of that Act.

(3) Subsection (1) has effect subject to rules made under section 281 of the Copyright, Designs and Patents Act 1988 (power of comptroller to refuse to recognise certain agents).

(4) In its application to proceedings in relation to application for, or otherwise in connection with, European patents, this section has effect subject to any restrictions imposed by or under the European Patent Convention.

(5) Nothing in this section is to be taken to limit any entitlement to prepare deeds conferred on a registered patent attorney by virtue of the Legal Services Act 2007.

Right of audience, etc., in proceedings on appeal from the comptroller
102A [repealed]

Extension of privilege for communications with solicitors relating to patent proceedings
103.(1) It is hereby declared that the rule of law which confers privilege from disclosure in legal proceedings in respect of communications made with a solicitor11 or a person acting on his behalf, or in relation to information obtained or supplied for submission to a solicitor or a person acting on his behalf, for the purpose of any pending or contemplated proceedings before a court in the United Kingdom extends to such communications so made for the purpose of any pending or contemplated –

(a) proceedings before the comptroller under this Act or any of the relevant conventions, or

(b) proceedings before the relevant convention court under any of those conventions.

(2) In this section –

"legal proceedings" includes proceedings before the comptroller;

the references to legal proceedings and pending or contemplated proceedings include references to applications for a patent or a European patent and to international applications for a patent; and

"the relevant conventions" means the European Patent Convention and the Patent Co-operation Treaty.

(3) This section shall not extend to Scotland.

Appendix 6

Privilege for communication with patent agents relating to patent proceedings
104. [repealed]

Extension of privilege in Scotland for communications relating to patent proceedings
105.(1) It is hereby declared that in Scotland the rules of law which confer privilege from disclosure in legal proceedings in respect of communications, reports or other documents (by whomsoever made) made for the purpose of any pending or contemplated proceedings in a court in the United Kingdom extend to communications, reports or other documents made for the purpose of patent proceedings.

(2) In this section –

"patent proceedings" means proceedings under this Act or any of the relevant conventions, before the court, the comptroller or the relevant convention court, whether contested or uncontested and including an application for a patent; and

"the relevant conventions" means the European Patent Convention and the Patent Co-operation Treaty.

Costs and expenses in proceedings before the Court
106.(1) In proceedings to which this section applies, the court, in determining whether to award costs or expenses to any party and what costs or expenses to award, shall have regard to all the relevant circumstances, including the financial position of the parties.

(1A) This section applies to proceedings before the court (including proceedings on an appeal to the court) which are –

(a) proceedings under section 40;
(b) proceedings for infringement;
(c) proceedings under section 70; or
(d) proceedings on an application for a declaration or declarator under section 71.

(2) If in any such proceedings the Patents Court directs that any costs of one party shall be paid by another party, the court may settle the amount of the costs by fixing a lump sum or may direct that the costs shall be taxed on a scale specified by the court, being a scale of costs prescribed by the Rules of the Supreme Court or by the County Court Rules.

Costs and expenses in proceedings before the comptroller
107.(1) The comptroller may, in proceedings before him under this Act, by order award to any party such costs or, in Scotland, such expenses as he may consider reasonable and direct how and by what parties they are to be paid.

(2) In England and Wales any costs awarded under this section shall, if the county court so orders, be recoverable by execution issued from the county court or otherwise as if they were payable under an order of that court.

(3) In Scotland any order under this section for the payment of expenses may be enforced in like manner as an extract registered decree arbitral bearing

a warrant for execution issued by the sheriff court of any sheriffdom in Scotland.

(4) The comptroller may make an order for security for costs or expenses against any party to proceedings before him under this Act if –

    (a) the prescribed conditions are met, and

    (b) he is satisfied that it is just to make the order, having regard to all the circumstances of the case;

and in default of the required security being given the comptroller may treat the reference, application or notice in question as abandoned.

(5) In Northern Ireland any order under this section for the payment of costs may be enforced as if it were a money judgment.

(6) In the Isle of Man any order under this section for the payment of costs may be enforced in like manner to an execution issued out of the court.

Licences granted by order of comptroller

108. Any order for the grant of a licence under section 11, 38, 48 or 49 above shall, without prejudice to any other method of enforcement, have effect as if it were a deed, executed by the proprietor of the patent and all other necessary parties, granting a licence in accordance with the order.

Offences

Falsification of register etc.

109. If a person makes or causes to be made a false entry in any register kept under this Act, or a writing falsely purporting to be a copy or reproduction of an entry in any such register, or produces or tenders or causes to be produced or tendered in evidence any such writing, knowing the entry or writing to be false, he shall be liable –

    (a) on summary conviction, to a fine not exceeding the prescribed sum,

    (b) conviction on indictment, to imprisonment for a term not exceeding two years or a fine, or both.

Unauthorised claim of patent rights

110.(1) If a person falsely represents that anything disposed of by him for value is a patented product he shall, subject to the following provisions of this section, be liable on summary conviction to a fine not exceeding level 3 on the standard scale.

(2) For the purposes of subsection (1) above a person who for value disposes of an article having stamped, engraved or impressed on it or otherwise applied to it the word "patent" or "patented" or anything expressing or implying that the article is a patented product, shall be taken to represent that the article is a patented product.

(3) Subsection (1) above does not apply where the representation is made in respect of a product after the patent for that product or, as the case may be, the process in question has expired or been revoked and before the end of a period which is reasonably sufficient to enable the accused to take steps to ensure that the representation is not made (or does not continue to be made).

Appendix 6

(4)   In proceedings for an offence under this section it shall be a defence for the accused to prove that he used due diligence to prevent the commission of the offence.

Unauthorised claim that patent has been applied for

111.(1) If a person represents that a patent has been applied for in respect of any article disposed of for value by him and –

(a)   no such application has been made, or
(b)   any such application has been refused or withdrawn,

he shall, subject to the following provisions of this section, be liable on summary conviction to a fine not exceeding level 3 on the standard scale.

(2)   Subsection (1)(b) above does not apply where the representation is made (or continues to be made) before the expiry of a period which commences with the refusal or withdrawal and which is reasonably sufficient to enable the accused to take steps to ensure that the representation is not made (or does not continue to be made).

(3)   For the purposes of subsection (1) above a person who for value disposes of an article having stamped, engraved or impressed on it or otherwise applied to it the words "patent applied for" or "patent pending", or anything expressing or implying that a patent has been applied for in respect of the article, shall be taken to represent that a patent has been applied for in respect of it.

(4)   In any proceedings for an offence under this section it shall be a defence for the accused to prove that he used due diligence to prevent the commission of such an offence.

Misuse of title "Patent Office"

112.   If any person uses on his place of business, or on any document issued by him, or otherwise, the words "Patent Office" or any other words suggesting that his place of business is, or is officially connected with, the Patent Office, he shall be liable on summary conviction to a fine not exceeding level 4 on the standard scale.

Offences by corporations

113.(1) Where an offence under this Act which has been committed by a body corporate is proved to have been committed with the consent or connivance of, or to be attributable to any neglect on the part of, a director, manager, secretary or other similar officer of the body corporate, or any person who was purporting to act in any such capacity, he, as well as the body corporate, shall be guilty of that offence and shall be liable to be proceeded against and punished accordingly.

(2)   Where the affairs of a body corporate are managed by its members, subsection (1) above shall apply in relation to acts and defaults of a member in connection with his functions of management as if he were a director of the body corporate.

Patent agents

Restrictions on practice as patent agent
114. [repealed]

Power of comptroller to refuse to deal with certain agents
115. [repealed]

Immunity of department

Immunity of department as regards official acts
116. Neither the Secretary of State nor any officer of his –

(a) shall be taken to warrant the validity of any patent granted under this Act or any treaty or international convention to which the United Kingdom is a party; or

(b) shall incur any liability by reason of or in connection with any examination or investigation required or authorised by this Act or any such treaty or convention, or any report or other proceedings consequent on any such examination or investigation.

Administrative provisions

Correction of errors in patents and applications
117.(1) The comptroller may, subject to any provision of rules, correct any error of translation or transcription, clerical error or mistake in any specification of a patent or application for a patent or any document filed in connection with a patent or such an application.

(2) Where the comptroller is requested to correct such an error or mistake, any person may in accordance with rules give the comptroller notice of opposition to the request and the comptroller shall determine the matter.

(3) Where the comptroller is requested to correct an error or mistake in a withdrawal of an application for a patent, and –

(a) the application was published under section 16 above; and

(b) details of the withdrawal were published by the comptroller;

the comptroller shall publish notice of such a request in the prescribed manner.

(4) Where the comptroller publishes a notice under subsection (3) above, the comptroller may only correct an error or mistake under subsection (1) above by order.

Effect of resuscitation of a withdrawn application under section 117
117A.(1) Where –

(a) the comptroller is requested to correct an error or mistake in a withdrawal of an application for a patent; and

(b) an application has been resuscitated in accordance with that request,

the effect of that resuscitation is as follows.

(2) Anything done under or in relation to the application during the period between the application being withdrawn and its resuscitation shall be treated as valid.

Appendix 6

(3) If the comptroller has published notice of the request as mentioned in section 117(3) above, anything done during that period which would have constituted an infringement of the rights conferred by publication of the application if the application had not been withdrawn shall be treated as an infringement of those rights if it was a continuation or repetition of an earlier act infringing those rights.

(4) If the comptroller has published notice of the request as mentioned in section 117(3) above and, after the withdrawal of the application and before publication of the notice, a person –

    (a) began in good faith to do an act which would have constituted an infringement of the rights conferred by publication of the application if the withdrawal had not taken place, or

    (b) made in good faith effective and serious preparations to do such an act,

he has the right to continue to do the act or, as the case may be, to do the act, notwithstanding the resuscitation of the application and the grant of the patent; but this right does not extend to granting a licence to another person to do the act.

(5) If the act was done, or the preparations were made, in the course of a business, the person entitled to the right conferred by subsection (4) above may –

    (a) authorise the doing of that act by any partners of his for the time being in that business, and

    (b) assign that right, or transmit it on death (or in the case of a body corporate on its dissolution), to any person who acquires that part of the business in the course of which the act was done or the preparations were made.

(6) Where a product is disposed of to another in exercise of a right conferred by subsection (4) or (5) above, that other and any person claiming through him may deal with the product in the same way as if it had been disposed of by the applicant.

(7) The above provisions apply in relation to the use of a patented invention for the services of the Crown as they apply in relation to infringement of the rights conferred by publication of the application for a patent (or, as the case may be, infringement of the patent).

"Patented invention" has the same meaning as in section 55 above.

Extension of time limits specified by comptroller
117B.(1) Subsection (2) below applies in relation to a period if it is specified by the comptroller in connection with an application for a patent, or a patent.

(2) Subject to subsections (4) and (5) below, the comptroller shall extend a period to which this subsection applies if –

    (a) the applicant or the proprietor of the patent requests him to do so; and

    (b) the request complies with the relevant requirements of rules.

(3) An extension of a period under subsection (2) above expires –

    (a) at the end of the period prescribed for the purposes of this subsection, or

(b) if sooner, at the end of the period prescribed for the purposes of section 20 above.

(4) If a period has already been extended under subsection (2) above –

(a) that subsection does not apply in relation to it again;

(b) the comptroller may further extend the period subject to such conditions as he thinks fit.

(5) Subsection (2) above does not apply to a period specified in relation to proceedings before the comptroller.

Information about patent applications and patents, and inspection of documents

118.(1) After publication of an application for a patent in accordance with section 16 above the comptroller shall on a request being made to him in the prescribed manner and on payment of the prescribed fee (if any) give the person making the request such information, and permit him to inspect such documents, relating to the application or to any patent granted in pursuance of the application as may be specified in the request, subject, however, to any prescribed restrictions.

(2) Subject to the following provisions of this section, until an application for a patent is so published documents or information constituting or relating to the application shall not, without the consent of the applicant, be published or communicated to any person by the comptroller.

(3) Subsection (2) above shall not prevent the comptroller from –

(a) sending the European Patent Office information which it is his duty to send that office in accordance with any provision of the European Patent Convention;

(aa) sending any patent office outside the United Kingdom such information about unpublished applications for patents as that office requests; or

(b) publishing or communicating to others any prescribed bibliographic information about an unpublished application for a patent;

nor shall that subsection prevent the Secretary of State from inspecting or authorising the inspection of an application for a patent or any connected documents under section 22(6) above.

(3A) Information may not be sent to a patent office in reliance on subsection (3) (aa) otherwise than in accordance with the working arrangements that the comptroller has made for that purpose with that office.

(3B) Those arrangements must include provision for ensuring that the confidentiality of information of the kind referred to in subsection (3)(aa) sent by the comptroller to the patent office in question is protected.

(3C) The reference in subsection (3)(aa) to a patent office is to an organisation which carries out, in relation to patents, functions of the kind carried out at the Patent Office.

(4) Where a person is notified that an application for a patent has been made, but not published in accordance with section 16 above, and that the applicant will, if the patent is granted, bring proceedings against that person in the

event of his doing an act specified in the notification after the application is so published, that person may make a request under subsection (1) above, notwithstanding that the application has not been published, and that subsection shall apply accordingly.

(5) Where an application for a patent is filed, but not published, and a new application is filed in respect of any part of the subject-matter of the earlier application (either in accordance with rules or in pursuance of an order under section 8 above) and is published, any person may make a request under subsection (1) above relating to the earlier application and on payment of the prescribed fee the comptroller shall give him such information and permit him to inspect such documents as could have been given or inspected if the earlier application had been published.

Copyright in documents made available electronically for inspection under section 118(1)

118A. [repealed]

Service by post

119. Any notice required or authorised to be given by this Act or rules, and any application or other document so authorised or required to be made or filed, may be given, made or filed by post.

Hours of business and excluded days

120.(1) The comptroller may give directions specifying the hour at which the Patent Office shall be taken to be closed on any day for purposes of the transaction by the public of business under this Act or of any class of such business, and the directions may specify days as excluded days for any such purposes.

(2) Any business done under this Act on any day after the hour so specified in relation to business of that class, or on a day which is an excluded day in relation to business of that class, shall be taken to have been done on the next following day not being an excluded day; and where the time for doing anything under this Act expires on an excluded day that time shall be extended to the next following day not being an excluded day.

(3) Directions under this section shall be published in the prescribed manner.

Comptroller's annual report

121. Before 1st December in every financial year the comptroller shall cause to be laid before both Houses of Parliament a report with respect to the execution of this Act and the discharge of his functions under the European Patent Convention and the Patent Co-operation Treaty, and every such report shall include an account of all fees, salaries and allowances, and other money received and paid by him under this Act, that convention and that treaty during the previous financial year.

Supplemental

Crown's right to sell forfeited articles

122. Nothing in this Act affects the right of the Crown or any person deriving title directly or indirectly from the Crown to dispose of or use articles forfeited under the laws relating to customs or excise.

Rules

123.(1) The Secretary of State may make such rules as he thinks expedient for regulating the business of the Patent Office in relation to patents and applications for patents (including European patents, applications for European patents and international applications for patents) and for regulating all matters placed by this Act under the direction or control of the comptroller; and in this Act, except so far as the context otherwise requires, "prescribed" means prescribed by rules and "rules" means rules made under this section.

(2) Without prejudice to the generality of subsection (1) above, rules may make provision –

(a) prescribing the form and contents of applications for patents and other documents which may be filed at the Patent Office and requiring copies to be furnished of any such documents;

(b) regulating the procedure to be followed in connection with any proceeding or other matter before the comptroller or the Patent Office and authorising the rectification of irregularities of procedure;

(c) requiring fees to be paid in connection with any such proceeding or matter or in connection with the provision of any service by the Patent Office and providing for the remission of fees in the prescribed circumstances;

(d) regulating the mode of giving evidence in any such proceeding and empowering the comptroller to compel the attendance of witnesses and the discovery of and production of documents;

(e) requiring the comptroller to advertise any proposed amendments of patents and any other prescribed matters, including any prescribed steps in any such proceeding

(f) requiring the comptroller to hold proceedings in Scotland in such circumstances as may be specified in the rules where there is more than one party to proceedings under section 8, 12, 37, 40(1) or (2), 41(8), 61(3), 71 or 72 above;

(g) providing for the appointment of advisers to assist the comptroller in any proceeding before him;

(h) prescribing time limits for doing anything required to be done in connection with any such proceeding by this Act or the rules and providing for the alteration of any period of time specified in this Act or the rules;

(i) giving effect to an inventor's rights to be mentioned conferred by section 13, and providing for an inventor's waiver of any such right to be subject to acceptance by the comptroller;

(j) without prejudice to any other provision of this Act, requiring and regulating the translation of documents in connection with an application for a patent or a European patent or an international application for a patent and the filing and authentication of any such translations;

(k) [repealed]

(l) providing for the publication and sale of documents in the Patent Office and of information about such documents.

Appendix 6

(2A) The comptroller may set out in directions any forms the use of which is required by rules; and any such directions shall be published in the prescribed manner.

(3) Rules may make different provision for different cases.

(3A) It is hereby declared that rules –

(a) authorising the rectification of irregularities of procedure, or
(b) providing for the alteration of any period of time, may authorise the comptroller to extend or further extend any period notwithstanding that the period has already expired.

(4) [repealed]

(5) [repealed]

(6) Rules shall provide for the publication by the comptroller of a journal (in this Act referred to as "the journal") containing particulars of applications for and grants of patents, and of other proceedings under this Act.

(7) Rules shall require or authorise the comptroller to make arrangements for the publication of reports of cases relating to patents, trade marks, registered designs or design right decided by him and of cases relating to patents (whether under this Act or otherwise) trade marks, registered designs, copyright and design right decided by any court or body (whether in the United Kingdom or elsewhere).

Rules, regulations and orders; supplementary

124.(1) Any power conferred on the Secretary of State by this Act to make rules, regulations or orders shall be exercisable by statutory instrument.

(2) Any Order in Council and any statutory instrument containing an order, rules or regulations under this Act, other than an order or rule required to be laid before Parliament in draft or an order under section 132(5) below, shall be subject to annulment in pursuance of a resolution of either House of Parliament.

(3) Any Order in Council or order under any provision of this Act may be varied or revoked by a subsequent order.

Use of electronic communications

124A.(1) The comptroller may give directions as to the form and manner in which documents to be delivered t to the comptroller

(a) in electronic form; or
(b) using electronic communications,

are to be delivered to him.

(2) A direction under subsection (1) may provide that in order for a document to be delivered in compliance with the direction it shall be accompanied by one or more additional documents specified in the direction.

(3) Subject to subsections (14) and (15), if a document to which a direction under subsection (1) or (2) applies is delivered to the comptroller in a form or manner which does not comply with the direction the comptroller may treat the document as not having been delivered.

(4) Subsection (5) applies in relation to a case where –

(a) a document is delivered using electronic communications, and

    (b)   there is a requirement for a fee to accompany the document.

(5)   The comptroller may give directions specifying

    (a)   how the fee shall be paid; and
    (b)   when the fee shall be deemed to have been paid.

(6)   The comptroller may give directions specifying that a person who delivers a document to the comptroller in electronic form or using electronic communications cannot treat the document as having been delivered unless its delivery has been acknowledged.

(7)   The comptroller may give directions specifying how a time of delivery is to be accorded to a document delivered to him in electronic form or using electronic communications.

(8)   A direction under this section may be given

    (a)   generally
    (b)   in relation to a description of cases specified in the direction;
    (c)   in relation to a particular person or persons.

(9)   [repealed]

(10) [repealed]

(11) A direction under this section may be varied or revoked by a subsequent direction under this section.

(12) [repealed]

(13) The delivery using electronic communications to any person by the comptroller of any document is deemed to be effected, unless the comptroller has otherwise specified, by transmitting an electronic communication containing the document to an address provided or made available to the comptroller by that person as an address of his for the receipt of electronic communications; and unless the contrary is proved such delivery is deemed to be effected immediately upon the transmission of the communication.

(14) A requirement of this Act that something must be done in the prescribed manner is satisfied in the case of something that is done –

    (a)   using a document in electronic form, or
    (b)   using electronic communications,

only if the directions under this section that apply to the manner in which it is done are complied with.

(15) In the case of an application made as mentioned in subsection (14)(a) or (b) above, a reference in this Act to the application not having been made in compliance with rules or requirements of this Act includes a reference to its not having been made in compliance with any applicable directions under this section.

(16) This section applies –

    (a)   to delivery at, in, with or to the Patent Office as it applies to delivery to the comptroller; and
    (b)   to delivery by the Patent Office as it applies to delivery by the comptroller.

Appendix 6

Extent of invention

125.(1) For the purposes of this Act an invention for a patent for which an application has been made or for which a patent has been granted shall, unless the context otherwise requires, be taken to be that specified in a claim of the specification of the application or patent, as the case may be, as interpreted by the description and any drawings contained in that specification, and the extent of the protection conferred by a patent or application for a patent shall be determined accordingly.

(2) It is hereby declared for the avoidance of doubt that where more than one invention is specified in any such claim, each invention may have a different priority date under section 5 above.

(3) The Protocol on the Interpretation of Article 69 of the European Patent Convention (which Article contains a provision corresponding to subsection (1) above) shall, as for the time being in force, apply for the purposes of subsection (1) above as it applies for the purposes of that Article.

Disclosure of invention by specification: availability of samples of biological material

125A.(1) Provision may be made by rules prescribing the circumstances in which the specification of an application for a patent, or of a patent, for an invention which involves the use of or concerns biological material is to be treated as disclosing the invention in a manner which is clear enough and complete enough for the invention to be performed by a person skilled in the art.

(2) The rules may in particular require the applicant or patentee –

(a) to take such steps as may be prescribed for the purposes of making available to the public samples of the biological material, and

(b) not to impose or maintain restrictions on the uses to which such samples may be put, except as may be prescribed.

(3) The rules may provide that, in such cases as may be prescribed, samples need only be made available to such persons or descriptions of persons as may be prescribed; and the rules may identify a description of persons by reference to whether the comptroller has given his certificate as to any matter.

(4) An application for revocation of the patent under section 72(1)(c) above may be made if any of the requirements of the rules cease to be complied with.

Stamp duty

126. [repealed]

Existing patents and applications

127.(1) No application for a patent may be made under the 1949 Act on or after the appointed day.

(2) Schedule 1 to this Act shall have effect for securing that certain provisions of the 1949 Act shall continue to apply on and after the appointed day to –

(a) a patent granted before that day:

(b) an application for a patent which is filed before that day, and which is accompanied by a complete specification or in respect of which a complete specification is filed before that day;

(c) a patent granted in pursuance of such an application.

(3) Schedule 2 to this Act shall have effect for securing that (subject to the provisions of that Schedule) certain provisions of this Act shall apply on and after the appointed day to any patent and application to which subsection (2) above relates, but, except as provided by the following provisions of this Act, this Act shall not apply to any such patent or application.

(4) An application for a patent which is made before the appointed day, but which does not comply with subsection (2)(b) above, shall be taken to have been abandoned immediately before that day, but, notwithstanding anything in section 5(3) above, the application may nevertheless serve to establish a priority date in relation to a later application for a patent under this Act if the date of filing the abandoned application falls within the period of fifteen months immediately preceding the filing of the later application.

(5) Schedule 3 to this Act shall have effect for repealing certain provisions of the 1949 Act.

(6) The transitional provisions and savings in Schedule 4 to this Act shall have effect.

(7) In Schedules 1 to 4 to this Act "existing patent" means a patent mentioned in subsection (2)(a) and (c) above, "existing application" means an application mentioned in subsection (2)(b) above, and expressions used in the 1949 Act and those Schedules have the same meanings in those Schedules as in that Act.

Priorities between patents and applications under the 1949 Act and this Act

128.(1) The following provisions of this section shall have effect for the purpose of resolving questions of priority arising between patents and applications for patents under the 1949 Act and patents and applications for patents under this Act.

(2) A complete specification under the 1949 Act shall be treated for the purposes of sections 2(3) and 5(2) above –

(a) if published under that Act, as a published application for a patent under this Act;

(b) if it has a date of filing under that Act, as an application for a patent under this Act which has a date of filing under this Act;

and in the said section 2(3), as it applies by virtue of this sub-section in relation to any such specification, the words "both as filed and" shall be omitted.

(3) In section 8(1), (2) and (4) of the 1949 Act (search for anticipation by prior claim) the references to any claim of a complete specification, other than the applicant's, published and filed as mentioned in section 8(1) shall include references to any claim contained in an application made and published under this Act or in the specification of a patent granted under this Act, being a claim in respect of an invention having a priority date earlier than the date of filing the complete specification under the 1949 Act.

(4) In section 32(1)(a) of the 1949 Act (which specifies, as one of the grounds of revoking a patent, that the invention was claimed in a valid claim of earlier priority date contained in the complete specification of another patent), the reference to such a claim shall include a reference to a claim contained in the specification of a patent granted under this Act (a new claim) which satisfies the following conditions –

    (a) the new claim must be in respect of an invention having an earlier priority date than that of the relevant claim of the complete specification of the patent sought to be revoked; and

    (b) the patent containing the new claim must be wholly valid or be valid in those respects which have a bearing on that relevant claim.

(5) For the purposes of this section and the provisions of the 1949 Act mentioned in this section the date of filing an application for a patent under that Act and the priority date of a claim of a complete specification under that Act shall be determined in accordance with the provisions of that Act, and the priority date of an invention which is the subject of a patent or application for a patent under this Act shall be determined in accordance with the provisions of this Act.

EU compulsory licences

128A.(1) In this Act an "EU compulsory licence" means a compulsory licence granted under Regulation (EC) No 816/2006 of the European Parliament and of the Council of 17 May 2006 on compulsory licensing of patents relating to the manufacture of pharmaceutical products for export to countries with public health problems12 (referred to in this Act as "the Compulsory Licensing Regulation").

 (2) In the application to EU compulsory licences of the provisions of this Act listed in subsection (3) –

    (a) references to a licence under a patent,

    (b) references to a right under a patent, and

    (c) references to a proprietary interest under a patent,

include an EU compulsory licence.

(3) The provisions referred to in subsection (2) are –

sections 32 and 33 (registration of patents etc);
section 37 (determination of right to patent after grant);
section 38 (effect of transfer etc of patent under section 37), apart from subsection (2) and subsections (3) to (5) so far as relating to subsection (2);
section 41 (amount of compensation);
section 46(2) (notice of application for entry that licences are available as of right);
section 57(1) and (2) (rights of third parties in respect of Crown use).

(4) In the following provisions references to this Act include the Compulsory Licensing Regulation –

sections 97 to 99B, 101 to 103, 105 and 107 (legal proceedings);
section 119 (service by post);
section 120 (hours of business and excluded days);

section 121 (comptroller's annual report);

section 123 (rules);

section 124A (use of electronic communications);

section 130(8) (disapplication of Part 1 of Arbitration Act 1996).

(5) In section 108 (licences granted by order of comptroller) the reference to a licence under section 11, 38, 48 or 49 includes an EU compulsory licence.

(6) References in this Act to the Compulsory Licensing Regulation are to that Regulation as amended from time to time.

Supplementary protection certificates

128B.(1) Schedule 4A contains provision about the application of this Act in relation to supplementary protection certificates and other provision about such certificates.

(2) In this Act a "supplementary protection certificate" means a certificate issued under –

(a) Regulation (EC) No 469/2009 of the European Parliament and of the Council of 6th May 2009 concerning the supplementary protection certificate for medicinal products, or

(b) Regulation (EC) No 1610/96 of the European Parliament and of the Council of 23 July 1996 concerning the creation of a supplementary protection certificate for plant protection products 13.

Application of Act to Crown

129. This Act does not affect Her Majesty in her private capacity, but subject to that, it binds the Crown.

Interpretation

130.(1) In this Act, except so far as the context otherwise requires –

"application fee" means the fee prescribed for the purposes of section 14(1A) above;

"application for a European patent (UK)" and (subject to subsection (4A) below) "international application for a patent (UK)" each mean an application of the relevant description which, on its date of filing, designates the United Kingdom;

"appointed day", in any provision of this Act, means the day appointed under section 132 below for the coming into operation of that provision;

"biological material" means any material containing genetic information and capable of reproducing itself or being reproduced in a biological system;

"biotechnological invention" means an invention which concerns a product consisting of or containing biological material or a process by means of which biological material is produced, processed or used;

"Community Patent Convention" means the Convention for the European Patent for the Common Market;

"comptroller" means the Comptroller-General of Patents, Designs and Trade Marks;

"Convention on International Exhibitions" means the Convention relating to International Exhibitions signed in Paris on 22 November 1928, as amended or

supplemented by any protocol to that convention which is for the time being in force;

"court" means

(a) as respects England and Wales, the High Court;
(b) as respects Scotland, the Court of Session;
(c) as respects Northern Ireland, the High Court in Northern Ireland;
(d) as respects the Isle of Man, Her Majesty's High Court of Justice of the Isle of Man;

"date of filing" means –

(a) in relation to an application for a patent made under this Act, the date which is the date of filing that application by virtue of section 15 above; and
(b) in relation to any other application, the date which, under the law of the country where the application was made or in accordance with the terms of a treaty or convention to which that country is a party, is to be treated as the date of filing that application or is equivalent to the date of filing an application in that country (whatever the outcome of the application);

"designate" in relation to an application or a patent, means designate the country or countries (in pursuance of the European Patent Convention or the Patent Co-operation Treaty) in which protection is sought for the invention which is the subject of the application or patent and includes a reference to a country being treated as designated in pursuance of the convention or treaty.

"electronic communication" has the same meaning as in the Electronic Communications Act 2000;

"employee" means a person who works or (where the employment has ceased) worked under a contract of employment or in employment under or for the purposes of a government department or a person who serves (or served) in the naval, military or air forces of the Crown;

"employer" in relation to an employee, means the person by whom the employee is or was employed;

"enactment" includes an Act of Tynwald;

"European Patent Convention" means the Convention on the Grant of European Patents, "European patent" means a patent granted under that convention, "European patent (UK)" means a European patent designating the United Kingdom, "European Patent Bulletin" means the bulletin of that name published under the convention, and "European Patent Office" means the office of that name established by that convention;

"exclusive licence" means a licence from the proprietor of or applicant for a patent conferring on the licensee, or on him and persons authorised by him, to the exclusion of all other persons (including the proprietor or applicant), any right in respect of the invention to which the patent or application relates, and "exclusive licensee" and "non-exclusive licence" shall be construed accordingly;

"formal requirements" means those requirements designated as such by rules made for the purposes of section 15A above;

"international application for a patent" means an application made under the Patent Co-operation Treaty;

"International Bureau" means the secretariat of the World Intellectual Property Organization established by a convention signed at Stockholm on 14 July 1967;

"international exhibition" means an official or officially recognised international exhibition falling within the terms of the Convention on International Exhibitions or falling within the terms of any subsequent treaty or convention replacing that convention;

"inventor" has the meaning assigned to it by section 7 above;

"journal" has the meaning assigned to it by section 123(6) above;

"mortgage", when used as a noun, includes a charge for securing money or money's worth and, when used as a verb, shall be construed accordingly;

"1949 Act" means the Patents Act 1949;

"patent" means a patent under this Act;

"Patent Co-operation Treaty" means the treaty of that name signed at Washington on 19 June 1970;

"patented invention" means an invention for which a patent is granted and "patented process" shall be construed accordingly;

"patented product" means a product which is a patented invention or, in relation to a patented process, a product obtained directly by means of the process or to which the process has been applied;

"prescribed" and "rules" have the meanings assigned to them by section 123 above;

"priority date" means the date determined as such under section 5 above;

"published" means made available to the public (whether in the United Kingdom or elsewhere) and a document shall be taken to be published under any provision of this Act if it can be inspected as of right at any place in the United Kingdom by members of the public, whether on payment of a fee or not; and "republished" shall be construed accordingly;

"register" and cognate expressions have the meanings assigned to them by section 32 above;

"relevant convention court", in relation to any proceedings under the European Patent Convention or the Patent Co-operation Treaty, means that court or other body which under that convention or treaty has jurisdiction over those proceedings, including (where it has such jurisdiction) any department of the European Patent Office;

"right", in relation to any patent or application, includes an interest in the patent or application and, without prejudice to the foregoing, any reference to a right in a patent includes a reference to a share in the patent;

"search fee" means the fee prescribed for the purposes of section 17(1) above;

"services of the Crown" and "use for the services of the Crown" have the meanings assigned to them by section 56(2) above,

including, as respects any period of emergency within the meaning of section 59 above, the meanings assigned to them by the said section 59.

(2) Rules may provide for stating in the journal that an exhibition falls within the definition of international exhibition in subsection (1) above and any such statement shall be conclusive evidence that the exhibition falls within that definition.

(3) For the purposes of this Act matter shall be taken to have been disclosed in any relevant application within the meaning of section 5 above or in the specification of a patent if it was either claimed or disclosed (otherwise than by way of disclaimer or acknowledgment of prior art) in that application or specification.

(4) References in this Act to an application for a patent, as filed, are references to such an application in the state it was on the date of filing.

(4A) An international application for a patent is not, by reason of being treated by virtue of the European Patent Convention as an application for a European patent (UK), to be treated also as an international application for a patent (UK).

(5) References in this Act to an application for a patent being published are references to its being published under section 16 above.

(5A) References in this Act to the amendment of a patent or its specification (whether under this Act or by the European Patent Office) include, in particular, limitation of the claims (as interpreted by the description and any drawings referred to in the description or claims).

(6) References in this Act to any of the following conventions, that is to say –

    (a) The European Patent Convention;
    (b) The Community Patent Convention;
    (c) The Patent Co-operation Treaty;

are references to that convention or any other international convention or agreement replacing it, as amended or supplemented by any convention or international agreement (including in either case any protocol or annex), or in accordance with the terms of any such convention or agreement, and include references to any instrument made under any such convention or agreement.

(7) Whereas by a resolution made on the signature of the Community Patent Convention the governments of the member states of the European Economic Community resolved to adjust their laws relating to patents so as (among other things) to bring those laws into conformity with the corresponding

provisions of the European Patent Convention, the Community Patent Convention and the Patent Co-operation Treaty, it is hereby declared that the following provisions of this Act, that is to say, sections 1(1) to (4), 2 to 6, 14(3), (5) and (6), 37(5), 54, 60, 69, 72(1) and (2), 74(4), 82, 83, 100 and 125, are so framed as to have, as nearly as practicable, the same effects in the United Kingdom as the corresponding provisions of the European Patent Convention, the Community Patent Convention and the Patent Co-operation Treaty have in the territories to which those Conventions apply.

(8) Part I of the Arbitration Act 1996 shall not apply to any proceedings before the comptroller under this Act.

(9) Except so far as the context otherwise requires, any reference in this Act to any enactment shall be construed as a reference to that enactment as amended or extended by or under any other enactment, including this Act.

Northern Ireland

131. In the application of this Act to Northern Ireland –

(a) "enactment" includes an enactment of the Parliament of Northern Ireland and a Measure of the Northern Ireland Assembly;

(b) any reference to a government department includes a reference to a Department of the Government of Northern Ireland;

(c) any reference to the Crown includes a reference to the Crown in right of Her Majesty's Government in Northern Ireland;

(d) any reference to the Companies Act 1985 includes a reference to the corresponding enactments in force in Northern Ireland; and

(e) [repealed]

(f) any reference to a claimant includes a reference to a plaintiff.

Scotland

131A. In the application of this Act to Scotland –

(a) "enactment" includes an enactment comprised in, or in an instrument made under, an Act of the Scottish Parliament;

(b) any reference to a government department includes a reference to any part of the Scottish Administration; and

(c) any reference to the Crown includes a reference to the Crown in right of the Scottish Administration.

Short title, extent, commencement, consequential amendments and repeals

132.(1) This Act may be cited as the Patents Act 1977.

(2) This Act shall extend to the Isle of Man, subject to any modifications contained in an Order made by Her Majesty in Council, and accordingly, subject to any such order, references in this Act to the United Kingdom shall be construed as including references to the Isle of Man.

(3) For the purposes of this Act the territorial waters of the United Kingdom shall be treated as part of the United Kingdom.

(4) This Act applies to acts done in an area designated by order under section 1(7) of the Continental Shelf Act 1964, or specified by Order under section 10(8) of the Petroleum Act 1998 in connection with any activity falling

within section 11(2) of that Act, as it applies to acts done in the United Kingdom.

(5) This Act (except sections 77(6), (7) and (9), 78(7) and (8), this subsection and the repeal of section 41 of the 1949 Act) shall come into operation on such day as may be appointed by the Secretary of State by order, and different days may be appointed under this subsection for different purposes.

(6) The consequential amendments in Schedule 5 shall have effect.

(7) Subject to the provisions of Schedule 4 to this Act, the enactments specified in Schedule 6 to this Act (which include certain enactments which were spent before the passing of this Act) are hereby repealed to the extent specified in column 3 of that Schedule.

SCHEDULES

SCHEDULE I (section 127)

APPLICATION OF 1949 ACT TO EXISTING PATENTS AND APPLICATIONS

1.(1) The provisions of the 1949 Act referred to in sub-paragraph (2) below shall continue to apply on and after the appointed day in relation to existing patents and applications (but not in relation to patents and applications for patents under this Act).

(2) The provisions are sections 1 to 10, 11(1) and (2), 12, 13, 15 to 17, 19 to 21, 22(1) to (3), 23 to 26, 28 to 33, 46 to 53, 55, 56, 59 to 67, 69, 76, 80, 87(2), 92(1), 96, 101, 102(1) and 103 to 107.

(3) Sub-paragraph (1) above shall have effect subject to the following provisions of this Schedule, paragraph 2(b) of Schedule 3 below and the provisions of Schedule 4 below.

2.(1) In section 6 of the 1949 Act, at the end of the proviso to subsection (3) (post-dating of application) there shall be inserted "and –

(c) no application shall, on or after the appointed day, be post-dated under this section to a date which is that of the appointed day or which falls after it",

and there shall be inserted at the end of subsection (4) "; but no application shall on or after the appointed day be post-dated under this subsection to a date which is that of the appointed day or falls after it".

(2) At the end of subsection (5) of that section (ante-dating) there shall be inserted "; but a fresh application or specification may not be filed on or after the appointed day in accordance with this subsection and those rules unless the comptroller agrees that he will direct that the application or specification shall be ante-dated to a date which falls before the appointed day.".

3.(1) This paragraph and paragraph 4 below shall have effect with respect to the duration of existing patents after the appointed day, and in those paragraphs –

(a) "old existing patent" means an existing patent the date of which fell eleven years or more before the appointed day and also any patent of addition where the patent for the main invention is, or was at any time, an old existing patent by virtue of the foregoing provision;

(b) "new existing patent" means any existing patent not falling within paragraph (a) above; and

(c) any reference to the date of a patent shall, in relation to a patent of addition, be construed as a reference to the date of the patent for the main invention.

(2) Sections 23 to 25 of the 1949 Act (extension of patents on grounds of inadequate remuneration and war loss) shall not apply to a new existing patent.

(3) The period for which the term of an old existing patent may be extended under section 23 or 24 of that Act shall not exceed in the aggregate four years, except where an application for an order under the relevant section has been made before the appointed day and has not been disposed of before that day.

4.(1) The term of every new existing patent under section 22(3) of the 1949 Act shall be twenty instead of sixteen years from the date of the patent, but –

(a) the foregoing provision shall have effect subject to section 25(3) to (5) above; and

(b) on and after the end of the sixteenth year from that date a patent shall not be renewed under section 25(3) to (5) above except by or with the consent of the proprietor of the patent.

(2) Where the term of a new existing patent is extended by this paragraph, –

(a) any licence in force under the patent from immediately before the appointed day until the end of the sixteenth year from the date of the patent shall, together with any contract relating to the licence, continue in force so long as the patent remains in force (unless determined otherwise than in accordance with this sub-paragraph), but, if it is an exclusive licence, it shall after the end of that year be treated as a non-exclusive licence;

(b) notwithstanding the terms of the licence, the licensee shall not be required to make any payment to the proprietor for working the invention in question after the end of that year;

(c) every such patent shall after the end of that year be treated as endorsed under section 35 of the 1949 Act (licences of right), but subject to paragraph 4A below.

(3) Where the term of a new existing patent is extended by this paragraph and any government department or any person authorised by a government department –

(a) has before the appointed day, used the invention in question for the services of the Crown; and

(b) continues to so use it until the end of the sixteenth year from the date of the patent, any such use of the invention by any government department or person so authorised, after the end of that year, may be made free of any payment to the proprietor of the patent.

(4) Without prejudice to any rule of law about the frustration of contracts, where any person suffers loss or is subjected to liability by reason of the extension of the term of a patent by this paragraph, the court may on the application of that person determine how and by whom the loss or liability is to be borne and make such order as it thinks fit to give effect to the determination.

(5) No order shall be made on an application under sub-paragraph (4) above which has the effect of imposing a liability on any person other than the applicant unless notification of the application is given to that person.

4A.(1) If the proprietor of a patent for an invention which is a product files a declaration with the Patent Office in accordance with this paragraph, the licences to which persons are entitled by virtue of paragraph 4(2)(c) above shall not extend to a use of the product which is excepted by or under this paragraph.

(2) Pharmaceutical use is excepted, that is –

   (a) use as a medicinal product within the meaning of the Medicines Act 1968, and

   (b) the doing of any other act mentioned in section 60(1)(a) above with a view to such use.

(3) The Secretary of State may by order except such other uses as he thinks fit; and an order may –

   (a) specify as an excepted use any act mentioned in section 60(1)(a) above, and

   (b) make different provision with respect to acts done in different circumstances or for different purposes.

(4) For the purposes of this paragraph the question what uses are excepted, so far as that depends on –

   (a) orders under section 130 of the Medicines Act 1968 (meaning of "medicinal product"), or

   (b) orders under sub-paragraph (3) above,

shall be determined in relation to a patent at the beginning of the sixteenth year of the patent.

(5) A declaration under this paragraph shall be in the prescribed form and shall be filed in the prescribed manner and within the prescribed time limits.

(6) A declaration may not be filed –

   (a) in respect of a patent which has at the commencement of section 293 of the Copyright, Designs and Patents Act 1988 passed the end of its fifteenth year; or

   (b) if at the date of filing there is –

       (i) an existing licence for any description of excepted use of the product, or

       (ii) an outstanding application under section 46(3)(a) or (b) above for the settlement by the comptroller of the terms of a licence for any description of excepted use of the product,

and, in either case, the licence took or is to take effect at or after the end of the sixteenth year of the patent.

(7) Where a declaration has been filed under this paragraph in respect of a patent –

    (a) section 46(3)(c) above (restriction of remedies for infringement where licences available as of right) does not apply to an infringement of the patent in so far as it consists of the excepted use of the product after the filing of the declaration; and

    (b) section 46(3)(d) above (abatement of renewal fee if licences available as of right) does not apply to the patent.

4B.(1) An application under section 46(3)(a) or (b) above for the settlement by the comptroller of the terms on which a person is entitled to a licence by virtue of paragraph 4(2)(c) above is ineffective if made before the beginning of the sixteenth year of the patent.

(2) This paragraph applies to applications made after the commencement of section 294 of the Copyright, Designs and Patents Act 1988 and to any application made before the commencement of that section in respect of a patent which has not at the commencement of that section passed the end of its fifteenth year.

5.   In section 26(3) of the 1949 Act (no patent of addition unless date of filing of complete specification was the same as or later than the date of filing of complete specification in respect of main invention) after "main invention" there shall be inserted "and was earlier than the date of the appointed day".

6.   Notwithstanding anything in section 32(1)(j) of the 1949 Act (ground for revocation that patent was obtained on a false suggestion or representation), it shall not be a ground of revoking a patent under that subsection that the patent was obtained on a false suggestion or representation that a claim of the complete specification of the patent had a priority date earlier than the date of filing the application for the patent, but if it is shown –

    (a) on a petition under that section or an application under section 33 of that Act; or

    (b) by way of defence or on a counterclaim on an action for infringement;

that such a suggestion or representation was falsely made, the priority date of the claim shall be taken to be the date of filing the application for that patent.

7.(1) In section 33 of the 1949 Act (revocation of patent by comptroller), in subsection (1) for the words preceding the proviso there shall be substituted –

"(1) Subject to the provisions of this Act, a patent may, on the application of any person interested, be revoked by the comptroller on any of the grounds set out in section 32(1) of this Act:".

(2) At the end of the said section 33 there shall be added the following subsection:–

"(5) A decision of the comptroller or on appeal from the comptroller shall not estop any party to civil proceedings in which infringement of the patent is in issue from alleging that any claim of the specification is invalid on any of the grounds set out in section 32(1) of this Act, whether or not any of the issues were decided in that decision.".

8. In Section 101(1) of the 1949 Act (interpretation) there shall be inserted in the appropriate place –

    "appointed day" means the day appointed under section 132 of the Patents Act 1977 for the coming into operation of Schedule 1 to that Act;".

SCHEDULE 2 (section 127)

APPLICATION OF THIS ACT TO EXISTING PATENTS AND APPLICATIONS

1.(1) Without prejudice to those provisions of Schedule 4 below which apply (in certain circumstances) provisions of this Act in relation to existing patents and applications, the provisions of this Act referred to in sub-paragraph (2) below shall apply in relation to existing patents and applications on and after the appointed day subject to the following provisions of this Schedule and the provisions of Schedule 4 below.

(2) The provisions are sections 22, 23, 25(3) to (5), 28 to 36, 44 to 54, 86, 98, 99, 101 to 105, 107 to 111, 113 to 116, 118(1) to (3), 119 to 124, 130 and 132(2), (3) and (4).

2. In those provisions as they apply by virtue of this Schedule –

    (a) a reference to this Act includes a reference to the 1949 Act;
    (b) a reference to a specified provision of this Act other than one of those provisions shall be construed as a reference to the corresponding provision of the 1949 Act (any provision of that Act being treated as corresponding to a provision of this Act if it was enacted for purposes which are the same as or similar to that provision of this Act);
    (c) a reference to rules includes a reference to rules under the 1949 Act;
    (d) references to a patent under this Act and to an application for such a patent include respectively a reference to an existing patent and application;
    (e) references to the grant of a patent under this Act includes a reference to the sealing and grant of an existing patent;
    (f) a reference to a patented product and to a patented invention include respectively a reference to a product and invention patented under an existing patent;
    (g) references to a published application for a patent under this Act, and to publication of such an application, include respectively references to a complete specification which has been published under the 1949 Act and to publication of such a specification (and a reference to an application for a patent under this Act which has not been published shall be construed accordingly);
    (h) a reference to the publication in the journal of a notice of the grant of a patent includes a reference to the date of an existing patent;
    (i) a reference to the priority date of an invention includes a reference to the priority date of the relevant claim of the complete specification.

SCHEDULE 3 (section 127)

REPEALS OF PROVISIONS OF 1949 ACT

1. Subject to the provisions of Schedule 4 below, the provisions of the 1949 Act referred to in paragraph 2 below (which have no counterpart in the new law of patents established by this Act in relation to future patents and applications) shall cease to have effect.

2. The provisions are:–

    (a) section 14 (opposition to grant of patent);

    (b) section 32(3) (revocation for refusal to comply with Crown request to use invention);

    (c) section 41 (inventions relating to food or medicine, etc.);

    (d) section 42 (controller's power to revoke patent after expiry of two years from grant of compulsory licence);

    (e) section 71 (extension of time for certain convention applications);

    (f) section 72 (protection of inventions communicated under international agreements).

SCHEDULE 4 (section 127)

TRANSITIONAL PROVISIONS

General

1. In so far as any instrument made or other thing done under any provision of the 1949 Act which is repealed by virtue of this Act could have been made or done under a corresponding provision of this Act, it shall not be invalidated by the repeals made by virtue of this Act but shall have effect as if made or done under that corresponding provision.

Use of patented invention for services of the Crown

2.(1) Any question whether –

    (a) an act done before the appointed day by a government department or a person authorised in writing by a government department amounts to the use of an invention for the services of the Crown; or

    (b) any payment falls to be made in respect of any such use (whether to a person entitled to apply for a patent for the invention, to the patentee or to an exclusive licensee);

shall be determined under sections 46 to 49 of that Act and those sections shall apply accordingly.

(2) Sections 55 to 59 above shall apply to an act so done on or after the appointed day in relation to an invention –

    (a) for which an existing patent has been granted or an existing application for a patent has been made; or

    (b) which was communicated before that day to a government department or any person authorised in writing by a government department by the proprietor of the patent or any person from whom he derives title;

and shall so apply subject to sub-paragraph (3) below, the modifications contained in paragraph 2 of Schedule 2 above and the further modification that section 55(5)(b) and 58(10) above shall not apply in relation to an existing application.

(3) Where an act is commenced before the appointed day and continues to be done on or after that day, then, if it would not amount to the use of an invention for the services of the Crown under the 1949 Act, its continuance on or after that day shall not amount to such use under this Act.

Infringement

3.(1) Any question whether an act done before the appointed day infringes an existing patent or the privileges or rights arising under a complete specification which has been published shall be determined in accordance with the law relating to infringement in force immediately before that day and, in addition to those provisions of the 1949 Act which continue to apply by virtue of Schedule 1 above, section 70 of that Act shall apply accordingly.

(2) Sections 60 to 71 above shall apply to an act done on or after the appointed day which infringes an existing patent or the privileges or rights arising under a complete specification which has been published (whether before, on or after the appointed day) as they apply to infringements of a patent under this Act or the rights conferred by an application for such a patent, and shall so apply subject to sub-paragraph (3) below, the modifications contained in paragraph 2 of Schedule 2 above and the further modification that section 69(2) and (3) above shall not apply in relation to an existing application.

(3) Where an act is commenced before the appointed day and continues to be done on or after that day, then, if it would not, under the law in force immediately before that day, amount to an infringement of an existing patent or the privileges or rights arising under a complete specification, its continuance on or after that day shall not amount to the infringement of that patent or those privileges or rights.

Notice of opposition

4.(1) Where notice of opposition to the grant of a patent has been given under section 14 of the 1949 Act before the appointed day, the following provisions shall apply:–

(a) if issue has been joined on the notice before the appointed day, the opposition, any appeal from the comptroller's decision on it and any further appeal shall be prosecuted under the old law, but as if references in the 1949 Act and rules made under it to the Appeal Tribunal were references to the Patents Court;

(b) in any other case, the notice shall be taken to have abated immediately before the appointed day.

(2) Sub-paragraph (1)(a) above shall have effect subject to paragraph 12(2) below.

Secrecy

5.(1) Where directions given under section 18 of the 1949 Act in respect of an existing application (directions restricting publication of information about inventions) are in force immediately before the appointed day, they shall continue in force on and after that day and that section shall continue to apply accordingly.

(2) Where sub-paragraph (1) above does not apply in the case of an existing application section 18 of the 1949 Act shall not apply to the application but section 22 of this Act shall.

(3) Where the comptroller has before the appointed day served a notice under section 12 of the Atomic Energy Act 1946 (restrictions on publication of information about atomic energy etc.) in respect of an existing application that section shall continue to apply to the application on and after that day; but where no such notice has been so served that section shall not apply to the application on and after that day.

Revocation

6.(1) Where before the appointed day an application has been made under section 33 of the 1949 Act for the revocation of a patent (the original application), the following provisions shall apply:–

(a) if issue has been joined on the application before the appointed day, the application, any appeal from the comptroller's decision on it and any further appeal shall be prosecuted under the old law, but as if references in the 1949 Act and rules made under it to the Appeal Tribunal were references to the Patents Court;

(b) if issue has not been so joined, the original application shall be taken to be an application under section 33 of the 1949 Act for the revocation of the patent on whichever of the grounds referred to in section 32(1) of that Act corresponds (in the comptroller's opinion) to the ground on which the original application was made, or, if there is no ground which so corresponds, shall be taken to have abated immediately before the appointed day.

(2) Sub-paragraph (1)(a) above shall have effect subject to paragraph 11(3) below.

7.(1) This paragraph applies where an application has been made before the appointed day under section 42 of the 1949 Act for the revocation of a patent.

(2) Where the comptroller has made no order before that day for the revocation of the patent under that section, the application shall be taken to have abated immediately before that day.

(3) Where the comptroller has made such an order before that day, then, without prejudice to section 38 of the Interpretation Act 1889, section 42 shall continue to apply to the patent concerned on and after that day as if this Act had not been enacted.

Licences of right and compulsory licences

8.(1) Sections 35 to 41 and 43 to 45 of the 1949 Act shall continue to apply on and after the relevant day –

(a) to any endorsement or order made or licence granted under sections 35 to 41 which is in force immediately before that day; and

(b) to any application made before that day under sections 35 to 41.

(2) Any appeal from a decision or order of the comptroller instituted under sections 35 to 41 or 43 to 45 on or after the relevant day (and any further appeal) shall be prosecuted under the old law, but as if references in the 1949 Act and rules made under it to the Appeal Tribunal were references to the Patents Court.

(3) In this paragraph "the relevant day" means, in relation to section 41, the date of the passing of this Act and, in relation to sections 35 to 40 and 43 to 45, the appointed day.

Convention countries

9.(1) Without prejudice to paragraph 1 above, an Order in Council declaring any country to be a convention country for all purposes of the 1949 Act or for the purposes of section 1(2) of that Act and in force immediately before the appointed day shall be treated as an Order in Council under section 90 above declaring that country to be a convention country for the purposes of section 5 above.

(2) Where an Order in Council declaring any country to be a convention country for all purposes of the 1949 Act or for the purposes of section 70 of that Act is in force immediately before the appointed day, a vessel registered in that country (whether before, on or after that day) shall be treated for the purposes of section 60 above, as it applies by virtue of paragraph 3(2) above to an existing patent or existing application, as a relevant ship and an aircraft so registered and a land vehicle owned by a person ordinarily resident in that country shall be so treated respectively as a relevant aircraft and a relevant vehicle.

Appeal from court on certain petitions for revocation

10. Where the court has given judgment on a petition under section 32(1)(j) of the 1949 Act before the appointed day, any appeal from the judgment (whether instituted before, on or after that day) shall be continued or instituted and be disposed of under the old law.

Appeals from comptroller under continuing provisions of 1949 Act

11.(1) In this paragraph "the continuing 1949 Act provisions" means the provisions of the 1949 Act which continue to apply on and after the appointed day as mentioned in paragraph 1 of Schedule 1 above.

(2) This paragraph applies where –

(a) the comptroller gives a decision or direction (whether before or on or after the appointed day) under any of the continuing 1949 Act provisions, and

(b) an appeal lies under those provisions from the decision or direction;

but this paragraph applies subject to the foregoing provisions of this Schedule.

(3) Where such an appeal has been instituted before the Appeal Tribunal before the appointed day, and the hearing of the appeal has begun but has not

been completed before that day, the appeal (and any further appeal) shall be continued and disposed of under the old law.

(4) Where such an appeal has been so instituted, but the hearing of it has not begun before the appointed day, it shall be transferred by virtue of this sub-paragraph to the Patents Court on that day and the appeal (and any further appeal) shall be prosecuted under the old law, but as if references in the 1949 Act and rules made under it to the Appeal Tribunal were references to the Patents Court.

(5) Any such appeal instituted on or after the appointed day shall lie to the Patents Court or, where the proceedings appealed against were held in Scotland, the Court of Session; and accordingly, the reference to the Appeal Tribunal in section 31(2) of the 1949 Act shall be taken to include a reference to the Patents Court or (as the case may be) the Court of Session.

(6) Section 97(3) of this Act shall apply to any decision of the Patents Court on an appeal instituted on or after the appointed day from a decision or direction of the comptroller under any of the continuing 1949 Act provisions as it applies to a decision of that Court referred to in that subsection, except that for references to the sections mentioned in paragraph (a) of that subsection there shall be substituted references to sections 33, 55 and 56 of the 1949 Act.

Appeals from comptroller under repealed provisions of 1949 Act

12.(1) This paragraph applies where an appeal to the Appeal Tribunal has been instituted before the appointed day under any provision of the 1949 Act repealed by this Act.

(2) Where the hearing of such an appeal has begun but has not been completed before that day, the appeal (and any further appeal) shall be continued and disposed of under the old law.

(3) Where the hearing of such an appeal has not begun before that day, it shall be transferred by virtue of this sub-paragraph to the Patents Court on that day and the appeal (and any further appeal) shall be prosecuted under the old law, but as if references in the 1949 Act and rules made under it to the Appeal Tribunal were references to the Patents Court.

Appeals from Appeal Tribunal to Court of Appeal

13. Section 87(1) of the 1949 Act shall continue to apply on and after the appointed day to any decision of the Appeal Tribunal given before that day, and any appeal by virtue of this paragraph (and any further appeal) shall be prosecuted under the old law.

Rules

14. The power to make rules under section 123 of this Act shall include power to make rules for any purpose mentioned in section 94 of the 1949 Act.

Supplementary

15. Section 97(2) of this Act applies to –

(a) any appeal to the Patents Court by virtue of paragraph 4(1)(a), 6(1)(a), 8(2) or 11(5) above, and

(b) any appeal which is transferred to that Court by virtue of paragraph 11(4) or 12(3) above,

as it applies to an appeal under that section; and section 97 of this Act shall apply for the purposes of any such appeal instead of section 85 of the 1949 Act.

16. In this Schedule "the old law" means the 1949 Act, any rules made under it and any relevant rule of law as it was or they were immediately before the appointed day.

17. For the purposes of this Schedule –

(a) issue is joined on a notice of opposition to the grant of a patent under section 14 of the 1949 Act when the applicant for the patent files a counterstatement fully setting out the grounds on which the opposition is contested;

(b) issue is joined on an application for the revocation of a patent under section 33 of that Act when the patentee files a counter-statement fully setting out the grounds on which the application is contested.

18.(1) Nothing in the repeals made by this Act in section 23 and 24 of the 1949 Act shall have effect as respects any such application as is mentioned in paragraph 3(3) of Schedule 1 above.

(2) Nothing in the repeal by this Act of the Patents Act 1957 shall have effect as respects existing applications.

(3) Section 69 of the 1949 Act (which is not repealed by this Act) and section 70 of that Act (which continues to have effect for certain purposes by virtue of paragraph 3 above) shall apply as if section 68 of that Act has not been repealed by this Act and as if paragraph 9 above had not been enacted.

SCHEDULE 4A (section 128B)

SUPPLEMENTARY PROTECTION CERTIFICATES

References to patents etc

1.(1) In the application to supplementary protection certificates of the provisions of this Act listed in sub-paragraph (2) –

(a) references to a patent are to a supplementary protection certificate;

(b) references to an application or the applicant for a patent are to an application or the applicant –

(i) for a supplementary protection certificate, or

(ii) for an extension of the duration of a supplementary protection certificate;

(c) references to the proprietor of a patent are to the holder of a supplementary protection certificate;

(d) references to the specification of a patent are to the text of a supplementary protection certificate;

(e) references to a patented product or an invention (including a patented invention) are to a product for which a supplementary protection certificate has effect;

(f) references to a patent having expired or having been revoked are to a supplementary protection certificate having lapsed or having been declared invalid;

(g) references to proceedings for the revocation of a patent are to proceedings –

(i) for a decision that a supplementary protection certificate has lapsed, or

(ii) for a declaration that a supplementary protection certificate is invalid;

(h) references to the issue of the validity of a patent include the issue of whether a supplementary protection certificate has lapsed or is invalid.

(2) The provisions referred to in sub-paragraph (1) are –

section 14(1), (9) and (10) (making of application);
section 19(1) (general power to amend application before grant);
sections 20A and 20B (reinstatement of applications);
section 21 (observations by third party on patentability);
section 27 (general power to amend specification after grant);
section 29 (surrender of patents);
sections 30 to 36, 37(1) to (3) and (5) to (9) and 38 (property in patents and applications, and registration);
sections 39 to 59 (employees' inventions, licences of right and compulsory licences and use of patented inventions for services of the Crown);
sections 60 to 71 (infringement);
section 74(1) and (7) (proceedings in which validity of patent may be put in issue);
sections 74A and 74B (opinions by the Patent Office);
section 75 (amendment of patent in infringement or revocation proceedings);
sections 103 and 105 (privilege for communications relating to patent proceedings);
section 108 (licences granted by order of comptroller);
sections 110 and 111 (unauthorised claim of patent rights or that patent has been applied for);
section 116 (immunity of department as regards official acts);
sections 117 to 118 (administrative provisions);
section 123 (rules);
section 130 (interpretation).

2.(1) In the case of the provisions of this Act listed in sub-paragraph (2), paragraph 1 applies in relation to an application for a supplementary protection certificate only if the basic patent expires before the certificate is granted.

(2) The provisions referred to in sub-paragraph (1) are –

section 20B(3) to (6A) (effect of reinstatement under section 20A);
section 55(5) and (7) (use of patented inventions for services of the Crown);
section 58(10) (disputes as to Crown use);
section 69 (infringement of rights conferred by publication of application);
section 117A(3) to (7) (effect of resuscitating a withdrawn application under section 117).

Appendix 6

References to this Act etc

3.(1) In the provisions of this Act listed in sub-paragraph (2) –

    (a) references to this Act include the Medicinal Products Regulation and the Plant Protection Products Regulation, and

    (b) references to a provision of this Act include any equivalent provision of the Medicinal Products Regulation and the Plant Protection Products Regulation.

(2) The provisions referred to in sub-paragraph (1) are –

sections 20A and 20B (reinstatement of applications);
section 21 (observations by third party on patentability);
section 69 (infringement of rights conferred by publication of application);
section 74(1) and (7) (proceedings in which validity of patent may be put in issue);
sections 97 to 99B, 101 to 103, 105 and 107 (legal proceedings);
section 116 (immunity of department as regards official acts);
sections 117 and 118 to 121 (administrative provisions);
section 122 (Crown's right to sell forfeited articles);
section 123 (rules);
section 124A (use of electronic communications);
section 130 (interpretation).

Other references

4.(1) In the application of section 21(1) (observations by third party on patentability) to supplementary protection certificates, the reference to the question whether the invention is a patentable invention is to the question whether the product is one for which a supplementary protection certificate may have effect.

(2) In the application of section 69(2) (conditions for infringement of rights conferred by publication of application) to supplementary protection certificates, the condition in paragraph (b) is that the act would, if the certificate had been granted on the date of the publication of the application, have infringed not only the certificate as granted but also the certificate for which the application was made.

Fees

5. A supplementary protection certificate does not take effect unless –

    (a) the prescribed fee is paid before the end of the prescribed period, or

    (b) the prescribed fee and any prescribed additional fee are paid before the end of the period of six months beginning immediately after the prescribed period.

Interpretation

6.(1) Expressions used in this Act that are defined in the Medicinal Products Regulation or the Plant Protection Products Regulation have the same meaning as in that Regulation.

(2) References in this Act to, or to a provision of, the Medicinal Products Regulation or the Plant Protection Products Regulation are to that Regulation or that provision as amended from time to time.

7.   In this Act –

(a)   "the Medicinal Products Regulation" means Regulation (EC) No 469/2009 of the European Parliament and of the Council of 6th May 2009 concerning the supplementary protection certificate for medicinal products, and

(b)   "the Plant Protection Products Regulation" means Regulation (EC) No 1610/96 of the European Parliament and of the Council of 23 July 1996 concerning the creation of a supplementary protection certificate for plant protection products.

Transitional provision

8.(1) A reference (express or implied) in this Act to the Medicinal Products Regulation, or a provision of it, is to be read as being or (subject to context) including a reference to the old Regulation, or the corresponding provision of the old Regulation, in relation to times, circumstances or purposes in relation to which the old Regulation, or that provision, had effect.

(2)   Other than in relation to times, circumstances or purposes referred to in subparagraph (1), anything done, or having effect as if done, under (or for the purposes of or in reliance on) the old Regulation or a provision of the old Regulation and in force or effective immediately before 1st October 2014 (the day on which the Patents (Supplementary Protection Certificates) Regulations 2014 came into force) has effect on or after that date for the purposes of this Act as if done under (or for the purpose of or in reliance on) the Medicinal Products Regulation or the corresponding provision of it.

(3)   In this paragraph "the old Regulation" means Council Regulation (EEC) No 1768/92 of 18th June 1992 concerning the creation of a supplementary protection certificate for medicinal products.

SCHEDULE 5 (section 132)

CONSEQUENTIAL AMENDMENTS

Crown Proceedings Act 1947 (c.44)

1.   [repealed]

Registered Designs Act 1949 (c.88)

2.   [repealed]
3.   [repealed]

Defence Contracts Act 1958 (c.38)

4.   In subsection (4) of section 4 of the Defence Contracts Act 1958, for the words from "Patents Act 1949" to the end there shall be substituted "Patents Act 1977".

Administration of Justice Act 1970 (c.31)

5.(1) In subsections (2) and (3) of section 10 of the Administration of Justice Act 1970 for "either" there shall be substituted, in each case, "the".

(2)   In subsection (4) of the said section 10, for "(as so amended)" there shall be substituted "(as amended by section 24 of the Administration of Justice Act 1969)".

(3) For subsection (5) of the said section 10, there shall be substituted:–

"(5) In subsection (8) of the said section 28 (which confers power on the Tribunal to make rules about procedure etc.), there shall be inserted at the end of the subsection the words "including right of audience".

Atomic Energy Authority (Weapons Group) Act 1973 (c.4)

6. In section 5(2) of the Atomic Weapons Authority (Weapons Group) Act 1973 –

(a) after the first "Patents Act 1949" there shall be inserted ", the Patents Act 1977"; and

(b) after the second "Patents Act 1949" there shall be inserted "section 55(4) of the Patents Act 1977".

Fair Trading Act 1973 (c.41)

7. [repealed]

Restrictive Trade Practices Act 1976 (c.34)

8. [repealed]

SCHEDULE 6 (section 132)

ENACTMENTS REPEALED		
Chapter	*Short Title*	*Extent of Repeal*
7 Edw. 7. c.29	The Patents and Designs Act 1907.	Section 47(2).
9 & 10 Geo. 6. c.80	The Atomic Energy Act 1946.	In section 12, subsections (1) to (7).
12, 13 & 14 Geo. 6. c.87.	The Patents Act 1949.	Section 11(3). Section 14. Section 16(6). Section 18. Section 22(4) and (5). In section 23(1), the words from "(not exceeding" to "ten years)". In Section 24, in subsection (1) the words "(not exceeding ten years)" and, in subsection (7) the words from "but" to the end. Section 27. In Section 32, subsection (3). In section 33(3), the proviso. Sections 34 to 45. Sections 54, 57 and 58. Section 68. Sections 70 to 75. Sections 77 to 79. Sections 81 to 86. Section 87(1) and (3). Sections 88 to 91. Sections 93 to 95. Sections 97 to 100. Section 102(2). Schedule 1. Schedule 3, except paragraphs 1 and 26.
5 & 6 Eliz. 2. c.13.	The Patents Act 1957.	The whole Act, except in relation to existing applications. 9 & 10 Eliz. 2. c.25.

Appendix 6

ENACTMENTS REPEALED		
Chapter	*Short Title*	*Extent of Repeal*
9 & 10 Eliz. 2. c.25.	The Patents and Designs (Renewals, Extensions and Fees) Act 1961.	In Section 1(1), the words from "subsection (5)" to "and in".
10 & 11 Eliz. 2. c.30.	The Northern Ireland Act 1962.	In Schedule 1, the entry relating to section 84 of the Patents Act 1949.
1967 c.80.	The Criminal Justice Act 1967.	In Schedule 3, in Parts I and IV, the entries relating to the Patents Act 1949.
1968. c.64.	The Civil Evidence Act 1968.	Section 15.
1969 c.58.	The Administration of Justice Act 1969.	In Section 24, in subsection (1), the words "85 of the Patents Act 1949 and section" and "each of", in subsections (2), (3) and (4) the words "of each of those sections" and in subsection (4) the words from "as subsection (11)" to "and" and the words "in the case of the said section 28".

[SCHEDULE A1
DEROGATION FROM PATENT PROTECTION IN RESPECT OF BIOTECHNOLOGICAL INVENTIONS][1]
Section 60(5)(g)

[1.– Interpretation
In this Schedule –

"Council Regulation" means Council Regulation (EC) No.2100/94 of 27th July 1994 on Community plant variety rights;

"farmer's own holding" means any land which a farmer actually exploits for plant growing, whether as his property or otherwise managed under his own responsibility and on his own account;

"the gazette" means the gazette published under section 34 of the Plant Variety and Seeds Act 1964;

"protected material" means plant propagating material which incorporates material subject to a patent;

"relevant activity" means the use by a farmer of the product of his harvest for propagation or multiplication by him on his own holding, where the product of the harvest constitutes or contains protected material;

"relevant rights holder" means the proprietor of a patent to which protected material is subject;

"seed" includes seed potatoes;

"seed year" means the period from 1st July in one year to 30th June in the following year, both dates inclusive.][2]

1   Added by Patents Regulations 2000, SI 2000/2037 Sch. 1 para. 1.
2   Added by Patents Regulations 2000, SI 2000/2037 Sch. 1 para. 1.

[2.– Specified species
Section 60(5)(g) applies only to varieties of the following plant species and groups:

Name	Common Name
Fodder plants	
Cicer arietinum L.	Chickpea milk vetch
Lupinus luteus L.	Yellow lupin
Medicago sativa L.	Lucerne
Pisum sativum L.(partim)	Field pea
Trifolium alexandrinum L.	Berseem/Egyptian clover
Trifolium resupinatum L.	Persian clover
Viciafaba	Field bean
Vicia sativa L.	Common vetch
Cereals	
Avena sativa	Oats

Appendix 6

Name	Common Name
Hordeum vulgare L.	Barley
Oryza sativa L.	Rice
Phalaris canariensis L.	Canary grass
Secale cereale L.	Rye
X *Triticosecale* Wittm.	Triticale
Triticum aestivum L. emend. Fiori et Paol.	Wheat
Triticum durum Desf.	Durum wheat
Triticum spelta L.	Spelt wheat
Potatoes	
Solarium tuberosum	Potatoes
Oil and fibre plants	
Brassica napus L. (partim)	Swede rape
Brassica rapa L. (partim)	Turnip rape
Linum usitatissimum	Linseed with the exclusion of flax

[3. – Liability to pay equitable remuneration

(1) If a farmer's use of protected material is authorised by section 60(5)(g), he shall, at the time of the use, become liable to pay the relevant rights holder equitable remuneration.

(2) That remuneration must be sensibly lower than the amount charged for the production of protected material of the same variety in the same area with the holder's authority.

(3) Remuneration is to be taken to be sensibly lower if it would be taken to be sensibly lower within the meaning of Article 14(3) fourth indent of the Council Regulation.][1]

1 Added by Patents Regulations 2000, SI 2000/2037 Sch. 1 para. 1.

[4. – Exemption for small farmers

(1) Paragraph 3 does not apply to a farmer who is considered to be a small farmer for the purposes of Article 14(3) third indent of the Regulation.

(2) It is for a farmer who claims to be a small farmer to prove that he is such a farmer.][1]

1 Added by Patents Regulations 2000, SI 2000/2037 Sch. 1 para. 1.

[5. – Information to be supplied by farmer

(1) At the request of a relevant rights holder ("H"), a farmer must tell H –

    (a) his name and address;

    (b) whether he has performed a relevant activity; and

(c) if he has performed such an activity, the address of the holding on which he performed it.

(2) If the farmer has performed such an activity, he must tell H whether he is –
    (a) liable to pay remuneration as a result of paragraph 3; or
    (b) not liable because he is a small farmer.

(3) If the farmer has told H that he is liable to pay remuneration as a result of paragraph 3, he must tell H –
    (a) the amount of the protected material used;
    (b) whether the protected material has been processed for planting; and
    (c) if it has, the name and address of the person who processed it.

(4) The farmer must comply with sub-paragraph (2) and (3) when complying with sub-paragraph (1).

(5) If the farmer has told H that he is liable to pay remuneration as a result of paragraph 3, he must (if H asks him to do so) tell H –
    (a) whether he used any protected material with the authority of H within the same seed year; and
    (b) if he did, the amount used and the name and address of the person who supplied it.[1]

1   Added by Patents Regulations 2000, SI 2000/2037 Sch. 1 para. 1.

[6. – Information to be supplied by seed processor
(1) On the request of a relevant rights holder, a seed processor shall supply the following information –
    (a) the name and address of the seed processor;
    (b) the address of the seed processor's principal place of business; and
    (c) whether the seed processor has processed seed of a species specified in paragraph 2 above.

(2) If the seed processor has processed seed of a species specified in paragraph 2 above he shall also supply the following information with the information referred to in sub-paragraph (1) –
    (a) the name and address of the person for whom the processing was carried out;
    (b) the amount of seed resulting from the processing;
    (c) the date processing commenced;
    (d) the date processing was completed;
    (e) the place where processing was carried out.][1]

1   Added by Patents Regulations 2000, SI 2000/2037 Sch. 1 para. 1.

[7. – Information to be supplied by relevant rights holder
On the request of a farmer or a seed processor a relevant rights holder shall supply the following information –

(a) his name and address; and
(b) the amount of royalty charged for certified seed of the lowest certification category for seed containing that protected material.][1]

1   Added by Patents Regulations 2000, SI 2000/2037 Sch. 1 para. 1.

Appendix 6

[8. – Period in respect of which inquiry may be made
A request may be made under paragraphs 5, 6 and 7 in respect of the current seed year and the three preceding seed years.]¹

1   Added by Patents Regulations 2000, SI 2000/2037 Sch. 1 para. 1.

[9. – Restriction on movement for processing from the holding
No person shall remove or cause to be removed from a holding protected material in order to process it unless –

(a)   he has the permission of the relevant rights holder in respect of that protected material; he has taken measures to ensure that the same protected material is returned from processing as is sent for processing and the processor has undertaken to him that the processor has taken measures to ensure that the same protected material is returned from processing as is sent for processing; or

(b)   he has the protected material processed by a seed processor on the list of processors referred to in the gazette as being permitted to process seed away from a holding.]¹

1   Added by Patents Regulations 2000, SI 2000/2037 Sch. 1 para. 1.

[10. – Confidentiality
(1)   A person who obtains information pursuant to this Schedule shall owe an obligation of confidence in respect of the information to the person who supplied it.
(2)   Sub-paragraph (1) shall not have effect to restrict disclosure of information –
    (a)   for the purposes of, or in connection with, establishing the amount to be paid to the holder of rights pursuant to paragraph 3 and obtaining payment of that amount,
    (b)   for the purposes of, or in connection with, establishing whether a patent has been infringed, or
    (c)   for the purposes of, or in connection with, any proceedings for the infringement of a patent.]¹

1   Added by Patents Regulations 2000, SI 2000/2037 Sch. 1 para. 1.

[11. – Formalities
(1)   A request for information under this Schedule, and any information given in response to such a request, must be in writing.
(2)   Information requested under this Schedule must be given –
    (a)   within 28 days; or
    (b)   if the request specifies a longer period, within the specified period.]¹

1   Added by Patents Regulations 2000, SI 2000/2037 Sch. 1 para. 1.

[12. – Remedies
(1)   If, in response to a request under this Schedule, a person –
    (a)   knowingly fails to provide information which he is required by this Schedule to give, or

(b) refuses to provide any such information, the court may order him to provide it.

(2) Sub-paragraph (1) does not effect any of the court's other powers to make orders.

(3) A person who knowingly provides false information in response to a request under this Schedule is liable in damages to the person who made the request.

(4) In any action for damages under sub-paragraph (3) the court must have regard, in particular to –

(a) how flagrant the defendant was in providing the false information, and

(b) any benefit which accrued to him as a result of his providing false information, and shall award such additional damages as the justice of the case may require.][1]

1   Added by Patents Regulations 2000, SI 2000/2037 Sch. 1 para. 1.

[SCHEDULE A2
BIOTECHNOLOGICAL INVENTIONS][1]

Section 76A

[1.–
An invention shall not be considered unpatentable solely on the ground that it concerns –

(a) a product consisting of or containing biological material; or

(b) a process by which biological material is produced, processed or used.][2]

1   Added by Patents Regulations 2000, SI 2000/2037 Sch. 2 para. 1.
2   Added by Patents Regulations 2000, SI 2000/2037 Sch. 2 para. 1.

[2.–
Biological material which is isolated from its natural environment or produced by means of a technical process may be the subject of an invention even if it previously occurred in nature.][1]

1   Added by Patents Regulations 2000, SI 2000/2037 Sch. 2 para. 1.

[3.–
The following are not patentable inventions –

(a) the human body, at the various stages of its formation and development, and the simple discovery of one of its elements, including the sequence or partial sequence of a gene;

(b) processes for cloning human beings;

(c) processes for modifying the germ line genetic identity of human beings;

(d) uses of human embryos for industrial or commercial purposes;

(e) processes for modifying the genetic identity of animals which are likely to cause them suffering without any substantial medical benefit to man or animal, and also animals resulting from such processes;

Appendix 6

(f) any variety of animal or plant or any essentially biological process for the production of animals or plants, not being a micro-biological or other technical process or the product of such a process.]¹

1   Added by Patents Regulations 2000, SI 2000/2037 Sch. 2 para. 1.

[4. –
Inventions which concern plants or animals may be patentable if the technical feasibility of the invention is not confined to a particular plant or animal variety.]¹

1   Added by Patents Regulations 2000, SI 2000/2037 Sch. 2 para. 1.

[5. –
An element isolated from the human body or otherwise produced by means of a technical process, including the sequence or partial sequence of a gene, may constitute a patentable invention, even if the structure of that element is identical to that of a natural element.]¹

1   Added by Patents Regulations 2000, SI 2000/2037 Sch. 2 para. 1.

[6. –
The industrial application of a sequence or partial sequence of a gene must be disclosed in the patent application as filed.]¹

1   Added by Patents Regulations 2000, SI 2000/2037 Sch. 2 para. 1.

[7. –
The protection conferred by a patent on a biological material possessing specific characteristics as a result of the invention shall extend to any biological material derived from that biological material through propagation or multiplication in an identical or divergent form and possessing those same characteristics.]¹

1   Added by Patents Regulations 2000, SI 2000/2037 Sch. 2 para. 1.

[8. –
The protection conferred by a patent on a process that enables a biological material to be produced possessing specific characteristics as a result of the invention shall extend to biological material directly obtained through that process and to any other biological material derived from the directly obtained biological material through propagation or multiplication in an identical or divergent form and possessing those same characteristics.]¹

1   Added by Patents Regulations 2000, SI 2000/2037 Sch. 2 para. 1.

[9. –
The protection conferred by a patent on a product containing or consisting of genetic information shall extend to all material, save as provided for in paragraph 3 (a) above, in which the product is incorporated and in which the genetic information is contained and performs its function.]¹

1   Added by Patents Regulations 2000, SI 2000/2037 Sch. 2 para. 1.

[10. –

The protection referred to in paragraphs 7, 8 and 9 above shall not extend to biological material obtained from the propagation or multiplication of biological material placed on the market by the proprietor of the patent or with his consent, where the multiplication or propagation necessarily results from the application for which the biological material was marketed, provided that the material obtained is not subsequently used for other propagation or multiplication.]¹

1   Added by Patents Regulations 2000, SI 2000/2037 Sch. 2 para. 1.

[11. –

In this Schedule:

"essentially biological process" means a process for the production of animals and plants which consists entirely of natural phenomena such as crossing and selection; "microbiological process" means any process involving or performed upon or resulting in microbiological material; "plant variety" means a plant grouping within a single botanical taxon of the lowest known rank, which grouping can be:

(a) defined by the expression of the characteristics that results from a given genotype or combination of genotypes; and

(b) distinguished from any other plant grouping by the expression of at least one of the said characteristics; and

(c) considered as a unit with regard to its suitability for being propagated unchanged.]¹

1   Added by Patents Regulations 2000, SI 2000/2037 Sch. 2 para. 1.

Index

All references are to paragraph number.

Index

Index

B

Biotechnology patents
adequacy of description
claim scope, 8.14
deposit requirements, 8.16
effect of EC Directive, 8.17
EPO case law, 8.14
UK case law, 8.15
cell lines, 8.03
claims, 8.03
cloning, 8.12
deposit requirement, 8.16
Directive 98/44/EC, 8.02
'ethical' issues
effect of EC Directive, 8.12
introduction, 8.11
prior informed consent, 8.13
examples, 8.03
general concerns, 8.01
importance of patent system, and,
1.11
industrial application, 8.07
infringement
effect of EC Directive, 8.19
introduction, 8.18
introduction, 8.01
inventive step, 8.05
limits, 8.01
living organisms, 8.03
micro-organisms, 8.03
morality
effect of EC Directive, 8.12
introduction, 8.11
prior informed consent, 8.13
natural products, 8.03
novelty, 8.04
prior informed consent, 8.13
product claims, 8.03
'product of nature' issue
effect of EC Directive, 8.06
industrial application, 8.07
inventive step, 8.05
novelty, 8.04
overview, 8.01
proteins, 8.03
public policy
effect of EC Directive, 8.12
introduction, 8.11
prior informed consent, 8.13
recombinant DNA products and
materials, 8.03
sufficiency of description
claim scope, 8.14
deposit requirements, 8.16
effect of EC Directive, 8.17

Biotechnology patents – *contd*
sufficiency of description – *contd*
EPO case law, 8.14
UK case law, 8.15
'variety' issue
development of law, 8.09
effect of EC Directive, 8.10
introduction, 8.08
overview, 8.01
Boilerplate clauses
patent licences, and, 3.42
Brussels I Regulation
application to pan-European relief, 4.28
introduction, 4.24
jurisdiction, 4.26
related actions, 4.27
relevant provisions, 4.25

C

Capable of industrial application
patentable subject matter, and, 5.02
Cascading claims
patent applications, and, 2.06
Case law
sources of patent law, and, 1.13
Cell lines
biotechnology patents, and, 8.03
Characterized
two-part claims, and, 2.08
Chemical patents
anticipation, 7.15
chemicals, 7.03
claim construction, 7.21
claims
chemicals, 7.03
combination claims, 7.06
composition claims, 7.05
compounds, 7.02
formulation claims, 7.05
generic claims, 7.03
method of use claims, 7.05
mixture claims, 7.06
New Chemical Entities, 7.01
process claims, 7.02
product by process claims, 7.04
product claims, 7.02
production of compounds, 7.02
second use claims, 7.07
clinical trials, 7.22
combination claims, 7.06
composition claims, 7.05
compounds, 7.02
DNA, 7.01
enablement, 7.19
exclusions from patentability, 7.02

Index

Index

Index

Index

Invalidity of patents – *contd*
state of the art – *contd*
generally, 5.04
priority date, 5.05
sufficiency
chemical patents, and, 7.19–7.20
'classic' approach, 5.19
introduction, 5.18
scope of claim, 5.20
TRIPs, and, 5.01
unpatentable subject matter, 5.02
Invalidity proceedings
and see Civil proceedings
EPO, in, 4.08
introduction, 4.06
purpose, 4.06
UK, in, 4.07
Inventions
development of 1.10
Inventive step
addressee's skills, 5.11
biotechnology patents, and, 8.05
common general knowledge, 5.12
differences between matters cited and
invention, 5.14
EPO approach, 5.16
introduction, 5.09
inventive concept, 5.13
nature of the difference, 5.14
obvious to skilled man, 5.15
pharmaceutical patents, and, 7.15
Pozzoli decision, 5.10–5.15
secondary indicia, 5.17
skilled man in the art, 5.11
state of the art, and, 5.04–5.06
Windsurfing International decision,
5.10–5.15
Inventors
applicants, as, 2.01
Inventor's certificates
relationship with patents, and, 1.05

J
Joinder of defendants
infringement actions, and, 4.19
Joint ventures
and see Transactions
generally, 3.04
Judgment
infringement actions, and, 4.14

L
Lack of entitlement
validity of patents, and, 5.03

Lack of inventive step
see also Validity of patents
addressee's skills, 5.11
common general knowledge, 5.12
differences between matters cited and
invention, 5.14
EPO approach, 5.16
introduction, 5.09
inventive concept, 5.13
nature of the difference, 5.14
obvious to skilled man, 5.15
pharmaceutical patents, and, 7.15
secondary indicia, 5.17
skilled man in the art, 5.11
Windsurfing International decision,
5.10
Lack of novelty
see also Validity of patents
introduction, 5.07
pharmaceutical patents, and, 7.15
special cases, 5.08
Law reports
sources of patent law, and, 1.13
Licences
and see Transactions
anti-competitive agreements, 3.11
approach, 3.10
assignment, 3.37
boilerplate clauses, 3.42
competition law
block exemptions, 3.12
national laws, 3.14
notification, 3.12
relevance, 3.11
technology transfer block exemption,
3.13
confidentiality, 3.36
customer limitations, 3.20
dispute resolution, 3.41
early termination, 3.39
exclusive licences, 3.10
field of use limitations, 3.19
generally, 3.08–3.10
grant and scope
customer limitations, 3.20
field of use limitations, 3.19
identification of licensed patents,
3.16
identification of licensed product,
3.17
introduction, 3.15
product market, 3.19
right to sublicense, 3.21
territorial limitations, 3.18
identification of licensed patents, 3.16

Index

Index

Index

Index

Index

Index